2020

Sixties Shockers

Sixties Shockers

A Critical Filmography of Horror Cinema, 1960–1969

MARK CLARK *and*
BRYAN SENN

Foreword by Robert Tinnell

McFarland & Company, Inc., Publishers
Jefferson, North Carolina, and London

Also of Interest

Smirk, Sneer and Scream: Great Acting in Horror Cinema, by Mark Clark (McFarland, 2004; paperback 2011)

Fantastic Cinema Subject Guide: A Topical Index to 2,500 Horror, Science Fiction, and Fantasy Films, by Bryan Senn and John Johnson (McFarland, 1992; paperback 2008)

A Year of Fear: A Day-by-Day Guide to 366 Horror Films, by Bryan Senn (McFarland, 2007)

Golden Horrors: An Illustrated Critical Filmography of Terror Cinema, 1931–1939, by Bryan Senn (McFarland, 1996; paperback 2006)

Library of Congress Cataloguing-in-Publication Data

Clark, Mark, 1966–
Sixties shockers : a critical filmography of horror cinema, 1960–1969 /
Mark Clark and Bryan Senn ; foreword by Robert Tinnell.
p. cm.
Includes bibliographical references and index.

ISBN 978-0-7864-3381-0
illustrated case binding : 50# alkaline paper 

1. Horror films—Catalogs. 2. Horror films—History and criticism.
3. Motion pictures—History—20th century. I. Senn, Bryan, 1962– II. Title.
PN1995.9.H6C513 2011 791.43'6164—dc22 2011015002

British Library cataloguing data are available

On the cover: Germán Robles in the 1958 Mexican horror film *El ataúd del vampiro (The Vampire's Coffin),* not released in the U.S. until 1965

Manufactured in the United States of America

McFarland & Company, Inc., Publishers
Box 611, Jefferson, North Carolina 28640
www.mcfarlandpub.co

For my long-suffering wife and children,
The book is finally over, Daddy's back
(at least until the next one begins).—*Mark*

For Lesley Hallick,
Who introduced me to giant throw pillows,
tie-dyed t-shirts, and Berkeley back in the day;
and who, through her intelligence, tolerance, good humor
and generosity, always leads by example.
And for Chuck.—*Bryan*

Acknowledgments

A work like this is shaped by many hands, and we extend ours in hearty thanks to the following:

Ron Adams, John Gibbon, Holger Haase, Bruce Holecheck, Mark Miller, Bryan "Buzz" Russell, Bob Sargent (of the Eurotrashparadise group), and David Zuzelo for their amazing film-finding abilities.

Anthony Ambrogio, Cindy Collins-Smith, Bruce Dettman, Jonathan Malcolm Lampley, Arthur Lundquist, Brian Smith, Midnight Marquee's Gary Svehla, Steve Thornton, Bob Tinnell and Neil Vokes for their insights, suggestions, and vast store of cinematic knowledge.

Ron Borst, Jim Clatterbaugh, Kip Doto, Tim Lucas, and Lynn Naron for their photo-finding expertise.

Ted Okuda for providing his insightful and amusing assessment of the obscure cinematic artifact that is *The Maltese Bippy* (as well securing a number of wonderful photos and ads).

Gina Beretta for her editorial efforts and unswerving — and loving — support.

And the following interviewees for their participation: Rosalie Crutchley, Robert Day, Freddie Francis, Jack Hill, Robert Horton, Richard Gordon, Joseph Green, Richard Matheson, German Robles, Barbara Shelley, Sam Sherman, Nicholas Webster, and Robert Wise.

Table of Contents

Foreword

by Robert Tinnell

If you think about it, the concept of focusing on one decade instead of another when compiling a survey of horror films— or any film genre, for that matter — runs the risk of seeming gimmicky or even arbitrary. Properly researched and executed, however, the results of such an approach can prove quite insightful, specifically when the author or authors examines the subject matter within the context of the larger events of the era under study. For instance, one might choose the twenties, situating the films in question against such relevant backdrops as the German Expressionist movement or the horrors of World War I. In fact, one could (and in the case of David Skal, one has) quite effectively pursue that approach well into the Thirties and the Golden Age of Classic Horror. Then again, one could approach the Thirties as the birthplace of most of horror's visual iconography, which nearly the entire world has come to embrace (Count Chocula, anyone?). Want to tackle the fifties? It proved a watershed decade for genre cinema, with the rise of atomic terrors, the birth of Hammer Film's gothic/sexual/visceral cinema, and of course, the Corman-AIP school of teen-angst thrillers— each of which clearly parallels events and concerns in the popular zeitgeist during the Eisenhower era. Decade after decade, the collision of genre cinema and human events can lead us to thoughtful analysis and discussion.

Fortunately for us, Mark Clark and Bryan Senn have chosen quite possibly the single most eventful decade in cinema's short history — the 1960s. For it is in the Sixties that the classic horror film ran head-on into the modern horror film, against a background of tremendous social turmoil. Even a casual overview of that ten-year-period illustrates the point, culminating most evidently, I think (and I'm happy to report the authors agree), in George A. Romero's *Night of the Living Dead*. Visually (and God knows, musically), the classic horror approach may have dominated *NOLD*, but the story and characterization and graphic depiction of heretofore forbidden activities enabled the film to usher in a new era. Romero's mix of the classic and modern approaches to horror represents an interesting metaphor for the evolution of horror cinema as a whole during the Sixties. In many ways that volatile decade emerged quite literally as a black-and-white, cut-and-dried Mason-Dixon Line separating classic and modern horror. What makes this all so interesting is the fact that beyond the horror genre, beyond cinema, across the wider spectrum of the culture, many new ideas and approaches, good and bad, were born, experimented with, sometimes adopted, sometimes discarded. Historians and anthropologists, critics and clerics, grandfathers and granddaughters all can discuss the era and disagree on much of what occurred or what it means—but it would be a rare thing indeed to find any one of those who would dispute the impact of that ten-year period.

I'm glad that Mark and Bryan are the guys writing this book. They're thoughtful, obsessive-compulsive types who are interested in doing more than stringing together plot recaps. It helps that they were alive during the sixties and as such can bring some personal context to their research. I'm anxious to gain insight from their conclusions about a decade that gave us *The Innocents*, *The Haunting*, *Brides of Dracula*, *Spider Baby*, *Repulsion*, *Night of the Living Dead*, *Rosemary's Baby*, *Frankenstein Must Be Destroyed*, *Black Sunday*, *Peeping Tom*, *Blood and Black Lace*, *Masque of the Red Death*, *The Conqueror Worm*, *Carnival of Souls*, *Psycho* and *The Birds*. I hope you just read that list and are saying to yourself, "Hey, the jerk left out (fill in your favorite non-mentioned Sixties' horror film), because if you're that passionate you're going to love this book as much as I do.

Robert Tinnell is the writer (and sometimes director) of movies including The Living and the Dead *(2012),* Romeo Must Hang *(2010), and* Frankenstein and Me *(1996), as well as comic books such as* The Wicked West *and* The Black Forest, *both of which won Rondo Awards.*

Preface: The Why and the How

Why the 1960s?

We have been asked that question many times over the years, as we researched and wrote *Sixties Shockers*. Why devote a book to horror films made during the 1960s? The simple answer: Because during those tumultuous years horror cinema flourished, proving as innovative and unpredictable as the decade itself. It was a time of transition for the genre, when stately gothics coexisted with edgy gore-fests, when color features played alongside black-and-white ones (sometimes on the same twin bill), and when the genre's original stars (actors such as Boris Karloff and Vincent Price) worked alongside its new luminaries (actors Peter Cushing and Christopher Lee). It was also an era of envelope-pushing and taboo-breaking, when a more worldly audience demanded more realistic and daring product, inspiring filmmakers to brave previously unexplored terrain, smashing through traditional boundaries governing screen violence, nudity and sexuality. While a few bold-spirited established directors, such as Alfred Hitchcock, made key films, this charge was led primarily by new talents such as Mario Bava, Roman Polanski, George Romero and Michael Reeves. Trend-setting pictures emerged from the major Hollywood studios and from gutsy independent filmmakers alike, from the U.S. and from the booming movie industries of Italy, Japan, Mexico, Spain, West Germany, the Philippines and of course England. They were made on budgets large and small, with major stars and with unknowns. There was no common formula, but one key element linked these films: a creative wanderlust, an unwillingness to stay penned into the tried-and-true formulas of the past.

Yet, this fascinating and formative period in horror cinema history remains little studied, especially in comparison to the much-written-about 1930s. The Thirties have long reigned as the Golden Age of horror cinema, and justifiably so. Following a lengthy gestation during the silent era, the Thirties birthed the fledgling genre and cradled its early masterworks. These Golden Age chillers introduced an eternally endearing rogues' gallery of monsters, headlined by Bela Lugosi's Dracula, Karloff's Frankenstein Monster and animator Willis O'Brien's King Kong. The decade's beloved horror classics boast amazing consistency, both in terms of quality (with a staggering number of great films per capita, considering that comparatively few horror pictures were produced during the Thirties) and style (with a distinct and unifying look and feel, highly imitative of the German Expressionist masterpieces of Robert Weine, F.W. Murnau and Fritz Lang).

Nevertheless, if any decade can rival the golden Thirties, it is the explosive Sixties, which introduced breathtaking diversity to the genre. If the horror films of the 1960s have, as a class, received less critical attention than those of the 1930s, this is in part because it's nearly impossible to speak in sweeping generalities about the wildly divergent and sometimes highly idiosyncratic pictures of the Sixties. Any classic Universal chiller—for instance, *The Mummy* (1932)—serves as a ready example of the Golden Age fright film. There is no such simple, emblematic representative for the horror movies of the Sixties. What *is* a Sixties shocker? Is it a gothic thriller like *Masque of the Red Death* (1962)? A groundbreaking thriller like *Peeping Tom* (1960/62)? A haunting mood piece like *Kill, Baby... Kill!* (1966/68)? A rubber-suit monster romp like *Godzilla vs. the Thing* (1964)? The correct answer is all of the above, and more. No other decade in the history of the genre can claim a richer tapestry of styles and themes.

Perhaps the best argument to be mounted in defense of the horror films of the 1960s is simply to rattle off a partial list of the decade's best chillers, which include *The Birds* (1963) *Black Sunday* (1960/61), *Brides of Dracula* (1960), *Carnival of Souls* (1962), *The Conqueror Worm* (1968), *The Haunting* (1963), *The Innocents* (1961), *Mania* (1960), *Night of the Living Dead* (1968), *Peeping Tom* (1960), *Psycho* (1960), *Rosemary's Baby* (1968), *Targets* (1968), *Village of the Damned* (1960), *What Ever Happened to Baby Jane?* (1962), and many more. Grant bonus points for fantasy and science fiction films—including such visionary works as *Planet of the Apes* and *2001: A Space Odyssey* (both 1968)—the Sixties can match or better any decade for its contributions to the cinema of the fantastic. For an examination of why and how the 1960s emerged as such a watershed era for horror cinema in particular and film fantasy in general, turn to section one, The Decade.

How to Read This Book

Sixties Shockers is designed to serve, primarily, as a reference guide. We have endeavored to make this volume as close to comprehensive as possible. We include reviews of more than 600 movies, as well as a narrative history of the decade in horror cinema, including economic, technological and political developments that changed the course of the genre. This content is divided into three sections: (1) The Decade, which features the historical narrative; (2) The Movies, which contains detailed analysis and often production history or other background information for every horror film released theatrically in the United States from 1960 through 1969; and (3) More Movies, which offers shorter entries for horror films made during the 1960s but not released theatrically in the U.S. during the decade (for instance, pictures that premiered in the early 1970s, or foreign films that were sold directly to American television). To place these works in context with the wider canvas of the fantastic cinema, the More Movies section also includes summaries of most science fiction and fantasy films of the 1960s.

We expect readers to dip in and out of this material according to their whims. It is not necessary to read *Sixties Shockers* front to back. However, those who elect to read The Decade section first may find the individual entries more illuminating. Also, some of the entries have been written so that, if read in a certain order, they link to form mini-histories of influential studios, trends or directors. For instance, fans of England's Hammer Films will notice that entries beginning with *Brides of Dracula* and continuing in chronological order with *House of Fright* (1960/61), *Scream of Fear* (1961) and so on (as well as More Movies entries for *Stranglers of Bombay* [1960], *Terror of the Hatchet Men* [1961], etc.) form a critical overview of the studio's output. Similar arcs link entries devoted to Toho's *kaiju eiga* pictures, *Psycho* and its many imitators, and the careers of directors such as Mario Bava, William Castle, Roger Corman and Herschel Gordon Lewis, among other topics.

However you choose to read it, we hope that *Sixties Shockers* provides an enjoyable and illuminating chronicle of the evolution of horror cinema during this dynamic period, and reflects how these films were shaped by the anxious, joyous, revolutionary times in which they were made.

1

The Decade

It's no coincidence that the two most trying decades of the Twentieth Century provided the richest soil for the cultivation of horror cinema. Screen terror is distilled from the fears and anxieties of the moment, although this isn't always discernable until that moment has passed. Even when moviemakers do not consciously set out to make any sort of social commentary, motion pictures—especially horror films—inevitably reflect the times in which they are made. The despair of the Great Depression and growing menaces of Nazi Germany and Imperialist Japan made the 1930s an unusually powerful crucible for fright pictures. Growing tensions created by changing roles for women, African Americans' struggle for civil rights, the looming threat of nuclear conflict between the U.S. and the Soviet Union, and the bloody escalation of the Vietnam War provided rich subtext for the cinematic nightmares of the 1960s.

Just as importantly, both the 1930s and the 1960s were times of economic struggle, technological innovation and stylistic maturation for the American film industry. Although hit hard by the depression, Hollywood in the Thirties introduced Technicolor, made dramatic advances in sound recording and editing and introduced optical printing (and with it modern special visual effects). A new generation of stars and directors moved away from the theatricality of the silent era and toward a more naturalistic narrative style. Major new genres were codified, including the gangster movie, the musical, and—with *Dracula* and *Frankenstein* (both 1931)—the horror film. It was the dawn of the movies' Golden Age.

Several factors, including competition from television, greatly reduced Hollywood revenues in the 1960s, yet during this era the industry developed light-weight hand-held cameras, lower-cost color film stocks and sophisticated anamorphic lenses; these advances provided greater flexibility for cinematographers, and standardized color and the 1.85:1 aspect ratio (a boon to exhibitors). A new generation of stars, many schooled in the Stanislavski Method popularized by the Actors Studio in New York, and of directors, many influenced by the French Nouvelle Vague, moved beyond Hollywood's classic style toward a more frank and adventurous brand of storytelling. Major genres were revitalized, including the Western, the crime drama and—with movies like *Psycho* (1960) and *Night of the Living Dead* (1968)—the horror film. It was the dawn of the movies' Modern Age.

These innovations arrived with particular immediacy and impact in the realm of film fantasy, which was hardly surprising considering that as far back as *A Trip to the Moon* (1902) and *The Cabinet of Dr. Caligari* (1918) such movies had served as laboratories for stylistic experimentation. Throughout the Sixties, horror and science fiction films remained on the leading edge of formal and artistic development, and, as a result, were ahead of the growth curve for American cinema in general. Acclaimed directors such as Alfred Hitchcock,

Roman Polanski, Francis Ford Coppola, John Frankenheimer and Peter Bogdanovich made horror movies during the decade, while Stanley Kubrick, Jean-Luc Godard and François Truffaut made sci-fi pictures. In 1968 the science fiction and horror genres produced five classics (*2001: A Space Odyssey*, *Night of the Living Dead*, *Planet of the Apes*, *Rosemary's Baby* and *Targets*), all of which were arguably superior to the Academy of Motion Picture Arts and Sciences' five nominees for Best Picture: *Funny Girl*, *The Lion in Winter*, *Oliver!* (the year's Oscar winner), *Romeo and Juliet* and *Rachel, Rachel*.

Of course, history never breaks neatly into ten-year chunks. In many respects, the horror cinema of the 1960s arose from economic, political, technological and artistic forces set in motion as far back as the late 1940s. Our story begins there.

Before the Beginning

As the Second World War drew to a close, Hollywood was at the zenith of its powers, both financial and artistic. The industry had thrived during the war years. Since tickets were still cheap (admission cost as little as 25 cents), a night at the movies was one of few luxuries Americans could afford during an era of privation and rationing. Hollywood enjoyed the enthusiastic support of President Franklin D. Roosevelt, who understood the vital role the industry played in shaping opinion and boosting morale on the home front. Legendary actors, directors and producers churned out great pictures with apparent ease, including beloved classics such as *Citizen Kane* (1941), *Casablanca* (1942) and *Yankee Doodle Dandy* (1943). But just when Hollywood seemed invincible, the major studios received two crushing blows, one creative and one economic, that would dramatically alter the course of American moviemaking.

The Italian neorealist movement, spearheaded by director Roberto Rossellini's *Rome: Open City* (1945) and *Paisan* (1946), landed a sucker punch to the classic Hollywood narrative style. The movement was short-lived and produced few films (depending on how stringently one defines the term, as few as 21 neorealist pictures were made between 1945 and 1952), most of which were unpopular with Italian audiences. Nevertheless, these gritty, politically-charged pictures, shot predominantly on location with mostly non-professional actors, earned prizes at major film festivals and rave reviews from critics around the world. Director Vittorio de Sica's neorealist touchstones *Shoeshine* and *The Bicycle Thief* won special Oscars in 1947 and 1949, respectively. Andre Bazin, editor of the influential French film journal *Cahiers du Cinema*, was an enthusiastic supporter of neorealism. When Bazin's staff, including Truffaut, Godard, Claude Chabrol and Eric Rohmer, began making movies in the late 1950s, they were profoundly influenced by neorealism. (Truffaut briefly worked as assistant to Rossellini.) Neorealism also exerted a guiding influence on the emerging Third World cinema and on Direct Cinema documentaries. The movement spread quickly, in part because American tax incentives, aimed at helping war-devastated European and Asian economies, encouraged Hollywood to invest in overseas productions and to distribute foreign-made films in the U.S. This, combined with the emergence of visionary filmmakers such as Sweden's Ingmar Bergman, Japan's Akira Kurosawa, Italy's Federico Fellini and Michelangelo Antonioni, and India's Satyajit Ray, helped foster a halcyon era of international art cinema. Foreign films reached American audiences in numbers unparalleled since the outbreak of World War I. To reflect the growing significance of imported pictures, the Academy introduced the Best Foreign Language Film category at its 1956 Oscar ceremony; the first winner was Fellini's *La Strada*. In both content and approach, these movies represented a radical departure from, and direct challenge to, the typical Hollywood product.

The U.S. Supreme Court delivered a haymaker with its 1948 decision *United States v. Paramount Pictures, Inc., et al.*, which found the eight major film companies in violation of federal anti-trust laws. Since the late silent era, the major studios had been "vertically integrated"— not only producing films but, as owners of all the major theater chains, distributing and exhibiting them as well. Money poured in from all three links in the cinematic food chain. Individually owned theaters were forced to book entire blocks of films, including not only prestige productions with major stars but also B-budget programmers with less box office appeal. Through the auspices of the Motion Pictures Producers and Distributors of America (MPPDA), the eight major studios (Paramount, MGM, 20th Century–Fox, Warner Brothers, RKO, Universal, Columbia and United Artists) not only enforced their Production Code (which regulated the content of films) but colluded to prevent any significant new competitor from entering the marketplace. The court ordered the companies to sell their theater chains and end block-booking and other monopolistic practices, but allowed the studios to remain in the film distribution businesses. With a major revenue source eliminated, however, studio coffers dwindled. Movie moguls lost not only cash, but clout. Independent producers found it much easier to distribute their films. Many stars opted to freelance rather than renew their exclusive studio contracts. Agents gained greater power and began packaging scripts with freelance talent (directors and actors) and selling packaged projects to the highest bidder. Although it would take nearly a decade for all of its provisions to be carried out, the Paramount decision sounded the death knell for the Hollywood studio system.

Still reeling from these hardships, Hollywood soon faced a major new threat — television. As stations opened across the country and the sale of TV sets proliferated, the new medium rapidly siphoned viewers away from movie theaters. For instance, the popularity of television Westerns decimated the audience for low-budget "oaters," which had been a bread-and-butter Hollywood staple since the early silent era. Even though hundreds were produced during the 1950s, by the early 1960s the breed was virtually extinct. Hollywood responded by introducing Cinerama and various other widescreen processes, shooting more features in color, trying gimmicks like 3-D and reviving "road show" exhibition spectacles (prestige productions offered at escalated ticket prices, with floor shows, live music or other added attractions) — anything to differentiate its product from its black-and-white, small-screen rival. Another response was the rise of art house and drive-in theaters, both of which offered more exotic viewing experiences than those available on TV.

One unintended consequence of the Paramount decision was that, with the MPPDA weakened, enforcement of the studios' Production Code became more difficult. Simultaneously, the success of foreign films suggested that audiences were interested in edgier, less sanitized stories. *Rome: Open City*, for instance, featured lesbianism, narcotics abuse and a downbeat ending with evil triumphant, all of which was forbidden under the Code. Racy Hollywood productions like *A Streetcar Named Desire* (1951) pushed the Code to its limits. Then, in 1952, the U.S. Supreme Court ruled, in *Joseph Burstyn, Inc. v. Wilson*, that motion pictures were entitled to First Amendment protection, eliminating the threat of government censorship that had inspired the creation of the Code in the first place. (The case was filed by a New York exhibitor who wanted to show Rossellini's 1948 short film *The Miracle*, about a pregnant nun who believes she carries an immaculately conceived child, which had been banned by the state's Board of Regents.) In 1959, Billy Wilder's independently produced cross-dressing farce *Some Like It Hot* was released without Code approval, yet became a major hit. As the Sixties dawned, the Code was fading into irrelevancy.

As Hollywood's fortunes turned for the worse in the late Forties, the old-fashioned, gothic horror film also fell into decline. Numerous theories have been posited for the genre's waning box office appeal to postwar audiences. The best explanation, however, may be that most of these pictures simply weren't very good. In the mid–1940s, studios seemed to lose faith in the genre, relegating monster movies to low-budget filler assigned to inferior talent both in front of and behind the camera. By 1948, when the Paramount decision was handed down, Universal had turned Dracula and the Frankenstein Monster into straight men for comedians Bud Abbott and Lou Costello. Although fright pictures continued to be made during this era, they were mostly sad sack productions like *The Black Castle* (1952). As gothic chillers receded, science fiction moved to the forefront. *The Day the Earth Stood Still* and *The Thing (from Another World)* (both 1951), twin pillars equivalent to Universal's *Dracula* and *Frankenstein*, ushered in the heyday of screen sci-fi, during which audiences thrilled to alien invasions, giant irradiated insects, unfrozen dinosaurs and other Atom Age terrors.

But traditional horror refused to stay dead. Its resurrection began in 1957 when Universal packaged 52 of its fright classics (under the title *Shock!*) for sale to television. Across the U.S., local stations launched weekly, late-night broadcasts devoted to vintage horror movies. Many featured costumed hosts such as Vampira (Maila Nurmi) of KABC in Los Angeles and Zacherley (John Zacherle) of WABC in New York City. *Shock!* proved so successful that a year later Universal assembled a second bundle, *Son of Shock*, featuring 20 more classic chillers. These films caused a sensation among the Baby Boom generation, adolescents not yet born when movies like *The Mummy* (1932) and *The Wolf Man* (1941) were originally released. Thanks to the American economy's robust postwar recovery, most of these youngsters had money to spend. An array of products soon appeared that catered to their newfound interest: monster-themed toys, games, fright masks, figure models, 8 mm film "digests" for home viewing, and more. In 1958, publisher James Warren and editor Forrest J Ackerman launched *Famous Monsters of Filmland* magazine, which quickly found a sizable readership. Horror mania continued unabated into the early Sixties, reaching a cultural crescendo when Bobby "Boris" Pickett's novelty song "The Monster Mash" topped the *Billboard* Hot 100 Chart on October 20, 1962. The classic monsters also re-emerged on movie screens. At first producers hedged their bets, offering science fictional variations of the classic monsters. In movies such as *The Werewolf* (1956), *The Vampire* and *I Was a Teenage Werewolf* (both 1957), the creatures are the result of unscrupulous medical experiments rather than of supernatural origin. But the success of Hammer Films' *Curse of Frankenstein* (1957) and *Horror of Dracula* (1958) proved that audiences would readily embrace classicist, supernatural chillers if done well. Hammer, founded in 1934 as a humble producer of "quota quickies" from various genres, scored its greatest previous success with a series of black-and-white sci-fi chillers. But *Curse* and *Horror* were something thrillingly new — were shot in full color, with bloodletting and sensuality far more graphic than anything found in the Golden Age horror shows playing on late night TV.

All these trends positioned the horror genre for explosive growth during the 1960s. The genre claimed a young, expanding and relatively affluent fan base. Horror films offered the kind of hard-hitting content that lured viewers away from their television sets, material that would grow increasingly daring as the Production Code finally disintegrated. The popularity of imported movies helped audiences embrace chillers not only from the U.S. and England, but also from countries like Italy, Mexico, Japan, West Germany, Spain and the Philippines, all of which emerged as major horror movie-producing nations as the decade progressed. Such open-mindedness, along with the fact that most horror films of the era were produced independently, rather than by the major studios, enabled the genre to more quickly assimilate new stylistic approaches. Simultaneously, ever-rising tension created by America's escalating Cold War with the Soviet Union and a host of worsening domestic issues created a fertile subtext for celluloid terrors. The cinematic soil had been tilled, and the seeds planted, watered and fertilized. And, as the new decade began, the first green shoots began to appear.

1960

From the very beginning, the Sixties were rocked by controversial, life-altering and sometimes frightening events. On February 1, 1960, four African American students from North Carolina A & T staged a sit-in at a segregated

Woolworth's lunch counter in Greensboro, N.C. The protests continued for six months until the students were finally served. For the next several years this form of non-violent civil disobedience would be widely imitated by black activists in restaurants, theaters and other businesses throughout the Southern U.S. On May 1 the Soviets shot down an American U-2 spy plane on a secret mission over Russian airspace. Friction between the two rival nations ratcheted up to new heights, as Eisenhower at first denied the incident and was forced to recant when the Soviets produced the captured pilot. Later in May, the Food and Drug Administration approved the sale of Enovid, a female oral contraceptive that quickly became known as the Pill. Initially, the Pill was sold only to married women. Thirty states had laws forbidding birth control (the last of these would be abolished in 1965). Yet by 1980 the average number of children born to American women had dropped from 3.6 to below 2. Meanwhile, the number of women working outside the home skyrocketed, increasing by 10 percent in 1966 alone. Finally, in November, a charismatic young senator from Massachusetts defeated the sitting vice president in one of the narrowest victories in U.S. electoral history. A decisive factor in the race was that the cool, confident John F. Kennedy had trounced the fidgety, flop sweat-soaked Richard M. Nixon in the first televised presidential debates. (Tellingly, those who listened to the debates on the radio believed Nixon had won.) Henceforth, campaigns would be waged not only in speeches and on whistle-stop train tours but on TV—through debates and tit-for-tat sound bites on the evening news.

The Academy's 1960 Best Picture winner was Billy Wilder's *The Apartment*, a wry, seriocomic indictment of both infidelity and cunning corporate ladder-climbing, while the Best Foreign Language Film Oscar went to Ingmar Bergman's *The Virgin Spring*, a poetic yet gruesome revenge parable later remade by Wes Craven as *Last House on the Left* (1972). But the French Nouvelle Vague remained the buzz of the film world. François Truffaut's *The 400 Blows*, Claude Chabrol's *Les Cousins* and Louis Malle's *The Lovers* had reached the U.S. in late 1959. Alain Resnais' *Hiroshima Mon Amour* arrived in May 1960, and Jean-Luc Godard's *Breathless*, Chabrol's *The Good Girls* and Malle's *Elevator to the Gallows* would reach the States in early 1961. Although not a unified movement like neorealism, these films—which combined unflinching realism with unorthodox editing techniques and featured distinctive authorial voices—inspired an entire generation of filmmakers as they made the rounds at art houses, cinema clubs and college campuses across the country and around the world. The Nouvelle Vague spawned the Italian, Russian and Polish Young Cinema, Czech and Japanese New Wave, Yugoslavian New Film, Hungarian New Cinema, Brazilian Cinema Novo and British Kitchen Sink Cinema movements. It also inspired future New Hollywood filmmakers such as Martin Scorsese, Francis Ford Coppola, George Lucas, Steven Spielberg, Terrence Malick, Bob Refelson and Dennis Hopper, who would launch their careers in the late Sixties.

But no single film released in 1960 proved more influential than Alfred Hitchcock's *Psycho*. Made on a thrifty $800,000 budget personally funded by its producer-director (unsure about the project, Paramount agreed to distribute but refused to produce the film), *Psycho* became one of the decade's greatest box office sensations (Hitch, individually, cleared over $15 million). Although initially panned by critics, many of whom were miffed that they were forced to watch the film (from the beginning) with a theatrical audience rather than at their usual private screenings, *Psycho* would eventually be recognized as the masterpiece it is. The American Film Institute placed it at number 18 on its Top 100 movies list in 1998 and number 1 on its Top 100 thrillers survey in 2001. The movie pushed the envelope of the Production Code not only with its jolting murder sequences, but with its lingering shots of Janet Leigh in her brassiere, and by including Hollywood's first onscreen toilet flush. *Psycho* even changed exhibition practices. Previously, movies (along with cartoons, short subjects and trailers) ran continuously all day. Patrons paid admission and entered the theater at will; if the movie was half over, they would stick around until the picture began again to see the first part. In a brilliant combination of artistic integrity and promotional ballyhoo, Hitchcock refused to allow viewers to enter the theater after *Psycho* began (thus preserving the integrity of the story's shocking plot twists). As film fans lined up around the block, theater owners realized the money-making possibilities of turning over audiences between showings.

Beyond all this, however, *Psycho* signaled a new epoch in the horror genre. Immediately it spawned a legion of black-and-white psychological thrillers that swarmed movie theaters throughout the early 1960s, some of which—like Robert Aldrich's *What Ever Happened to Baby Jane?* (1962) and Roman Polanski's *Repulsion* (1963)—became classics themselves. England's Hammer Films launched a long-running series of pseudo *Psychos*, beginning with the excellent *Scream of Fear* (1961). *Psycho* seemed to fascinate European horror filmmakers in particular, becoming—along with Henri-Georges Clouzot's mystery-thriller *Diabolique* (1955) and Georges Franju's Nouvelle Vague shocker *The Horror Chamber of Dr. Faustus* (1959)—one of the most-imitated pictures of the 1960s, or ever. More significantly, *Psycho* led a turning away from the Old School gothic horror formula. After *Psycho,* fright films increasingly would be set in cozy suburban homes rather than spooky Carpathian castles, and the serial killer would supplant the vampire as the screen's chief bogeyman. Before *Psycho*, horror was something that came from outside to attack our communities; after *Psycho*, it was something that could arise from within them. In this respect, *Psycho* arguably represents the first modern horror movie.

According to screenwriter Joseph Stefano, Hitchcock was inspired to make *Psycho* by the success of other low-budget, black-and-white chillers. "He mentioned another company that was making very low budget movies which were not terribly good and were doing very well at the box office," Stefano said. "His feeling was, 'How would it be if somebody good did one of these low budget movies?'" Although not mentioned by name, Hitch was likely referring to the early works of Roger Corman and William Castle. Coincidentally, 1960 proved to be a banner year for both of those filmmakers as well.

With *House of Usher*, Corman launched his wildly successful series of Edgar Allan Poe adaptations, which not only fattened the producer-director's wallet but burnished his reputation with critics. Made in color and on a (somewhat) higher budget than previous Corman pictures (about $200,000), *Usher* proved that the director was capable of more sophisticated and polished work, with greater thematic and psychological depth. Corman would shoot seven more Poe adaptations before halting the series with *Tomb of Ligeia* (1964/65). Because Corman used a core group of key collaborators for most of these films—including star Vincent Price, screenwriter Richard Matheson, production designer Daniel Haller and cinematographer Floyd Crosby—the series had a uniform visual identity. Yet its entries generally improved as the cycle progressed, reaching an artistic peak with *The Masque of the Red Death* in 1964. Corman's horror films sometimes obliquely touched on social and political themes. But the Poe series' success enabled Corman to undertake more ambitious exploitation projects dealing directly with counter-culture phenomena like motorcycle gangs (*The Wild Angels*, 1966) and LSD (*The Trip*, 1967). Also in 1960, Corman released what would become a cult classic—*Little Shop of Horrors*, about a nebbish young florist who grows a giant man-eating plant. Famously shot in just two and a half days, the picture added nothing to Corman's critical reputation and very little to his bank account (during its original release, *Little Shop* was a minor box office disappointment). But over the years, through late-night TV reruns, this darkly hilarious film gained a devoted following and eventually inspired a successful off-Broadway musical, which was adapted for the screen in 1986. During his career, Corman directed 56 features and produced nearly 400 (so far), but his personal favorite among his own films remains one of his few flops—*The Intruder* (1962), which starred William Shatner as a demagogue who incites white residents of a racially divided community to violence against their black neighbors. As a producer, Corman helped advance the careers of many promising young filmmakers, including future Oscar-winning directors Martin Scorsese, Francis Ford Coppola, James Cameron, Jonathan Demme and Ron Howard. In 2010 the Academy honored Corman with its Lifetime Achievement Award

For Castle, 1960 was the year of *13 Ghosts*, the last of the producer-director's elaborate gimmick movies. The film, about a little boy whose family movies into a house haunted by a baker's-dozen spooks, was presented in "Illusion-O," a simple but clever process utilizing tinted film and a cardboard "Ghost Viewer" containing strips of red and blue cellophane. During selected scenes the picture would suddenly shift from standard black-and-white to tinted blue, and red-hued poltergeists would appear. Audience members could look through the blue cellophane of their Ghost Viewers to see the ghosts more clearly, or (if they became too scared) look through the red lens to make the ghosts disappear. "Illusion-O" followed "Emergo" (a plastic skeleton which flew over audiences' heads during the climax of *House on Haunted Hill*, 1959) and "Percepto" (wired theater seats which delivered an electrical shock during a key sequence from *The Tingler*, also 1959). His next picture, a *Psycho* rip-off called *Homicidal* (1961), included a "Fright Break" in which viewers were supposed to gather their wits before the picture's (allegedly) nerve-shattering finale. *Mr. Sardonicus* (also 1961) featured its "Punishment Poll," which pretended to let audiences vote on whether or not the villain deserved a gruesome fate (in reality, the answer was always yes; only one ending was shot). Some later Castle pictures would include giveaways (souvenir coins for *Zotz!* [1962], cardboard axes for *Strait-Jacket* [1964]), but never again would a Castle production require costly customization of theaters or specialized printing processes for the film itself. Instead, Castle — who had carefully nurtured his personal image and, like Hitchcock, presented himself as a good-humored impresario of the macabre — used his own celebrity to promote his pictures, appearing in their trailers and sometimes in the movies themselves. His shameless huckstering obscured the fact that at least some of Castle's efforts (especially *House on Haunted Hill*, *Mr. Sardonicus*, *Zotz!* and *Straight-Jacket*) were solidly crafted entertainments. The filmmaker's career reached an apex in 1968 when he produced director Roman Polanski's watershed chiller *Rosemary's Baby*. Yet, he is still remembered primarily as the purveyor of tricked-out camp fests like *13 Ghosts*.

Still a year removed from its entry into the suddenly booming psychological thriller business, Hammer Films continued to concentrate on making handsome Technicolor gothics, and in 1960 the studio delivered one of its best — the brilliant *Brides of Dracula*. It was the latest in a series of triumphs, following the sensational *Curse of Frankenstein* (1957), *Horror of Dracula*, *Revenge of Frankenstein* (both 1958), and *The Mummy* (1959). Although critics (especially in Britain) disdained these pictures, which brought a new level of gore and sexuality to horror cinema, audiences loved them — and rightly so. Hammer's early chillers featured impeccable production values, engrossing and sometimes thought-provoking stories, and superb acting. Much of the credit for the studio's success belonged to three men, two of whom collaborated on *Brides*— director Terence Fisher and star Peter Cushing.

Fisher belongs in the company of James Whale, Mario Bava, George Romero and John Carpenter as the most gifted filmmakers ever to specialize in the horror genre. A former editor, Fisher never included a meaningless shot. His meticulous attention to detail, keen eye for dynamic compositions and rapport with actors gave his pictures palpable vitality and even though the director seldom resorted to showy camera moves or other attention-grabbing tricks. And while Fisher took on assignments as a director-for-hire (and never rejected a single script he was offered), he was able, through his deft handling of the material, to create unifying thematic threads that run throughout his filmography. The most significant of these was Fisher's vision of life as a struggle between Christian good and Satanic evil. Other than *The Devil's Bride* (1968), *Brides of Dracula* represents the most overt expression of this theme. (Van Helsing states the case openly when he describes vampirism as "a strange sickness ... partly physical, partly spiritual" and "a survivor of one of the ancient pagan religions in its struggle against Christianity.") Fisher sees Van Helsing—a "doctor of philosophy and doctor of theology," according to his calling card—as not merely a swashbuckling vampire hunter but a super-powered evangelist whose learned use of Christian iconography (a crucifix and a flask of holy water, alongside his handy hammer and stake) enable him to defeat the demonic vampire and release his victims from Satan's grip, restoring them to a righteous relationship with God. As the Sixties progressed, racked by spasms of violence and unrest, surely many viewers found comfort in Fisher's pictures, which insisted that the forces of chaos would not, could not, win in the end. "If my films reflect my own personal view of the world, it is in their showing the ultimate victory of good over evil, in which I do believe," Fisher said.

In Cushing, also a devout Christian, Fisher found a sympathetic collaborator in this thematic endeavor. More importantly, he also had one of horror cinema's most talented actors. Cushing brought unflagging energy, focus and creativity to every role, pairing his earnest, often clipped, delivery with ingenious physical bits of business, usually in his handling of various props, which provided visual interest while revealing his character's state of mind. Tireless dedication to these details of his craft enabled Cushing to deliver high-quality work with uncanny consistency. The actor's ardent fans often boast that he "never gave a bad performance," an outlandish claim that is very nearly true. Certainly *Brides* contains one of the actor's best portrayals. Returning to his role as Van Helsing from *Horror of Dracula*, Cushing shines in moments large (confronting Baron Meinster [David Peel] in the film's breathless finale) and small (bringing life and veritas to a potentially dry, expository sequence by delivering it while packing a suitcase). Cushing, who worked mostly for Hammer during the Sixties, was one of the studio's most valuable assets. His mere presence guaranteed the picture would contain something worth watching. Since he so often performed on such a high level, it's challenging to name Cushing's best efforts, but he is remembered first and foremost for his appearances as the imperious, implacable Victor Frankenstein in Hammer's *Curse of Frankenstein* (1957), *Revenge of Frankenstein* (1958), *Evil of Frankenstein* (1964), *Frankenstein Created Woman* (1967), *Frankenstein Must Be Destroyed* (1969/70) and *Frankenstein and the Monster from Hell* (1974). Although the material wasn't always ideal, Cushing's performances were never less than scintillating. In the independently produced *Mania* (1960/61), Cushing delivered one of his most subtle and finely nuanced performances as the kindly, well-intentioned Dr. Knox, who becomes entangled in the crimes of grave robbers-turned-murderers Burke and Hare. Later, Cushing channeled his grief over the recent death of his wife, Helen, into his role as the meek Arthur Grimsdyke and came up with perhaps his most emotionally powerful portrayal in the "Poetic Justice" segment of the Amicus anthology film *Tales from the Crypt* (1972). Late in life he would achieve a new level of fame by playing Grand Moff Tarkin in George Lucas' *Star Wars* (1977). Even if the role was not among his richest, it was fitting that Cushing finally became a household name, considering that his contributions to the genre were unsurpassed by any actor except Boris Karloff, Bela Lugosi and Lon Chaney.

Frequently (though not, due to a salary dispute, in *Brides*), Hammer teamed Cushing with Christopher Lee (they co-starred in three of the studio's first four color gothics—*Curse of Frankenstein*, *Horror of Dracula* and *The Mummy*). Despite bowing out of *Bride*, Lee made three feature films and a TV appearance in 1960, including the exceptional *Horror Hotel*, an atmospheric chiller about a coven of devil-worshipers, in which he made an extended cameo. His delightful supporting performances in Hammer's *House of Fright* as the caddish Paul Allen and in *Hands of Orlac* as the sadistic Nero the Magician are the highlight of those two otherwise lackluster pictures. Few stars command viewers' attention as readily as the charismatic 6-foot-4 Lee, who projects an aura of power and mystery seemingly without effort. On the other hand, Lee appears to have to work hard (and commendably so) to tone down his screen presence for roles such as the weak-kneed Sir Henry in Hammer's *Hound of the Baskervilles* (1959). Even though he has appeared in more than 260 films (and counting), Lee remains most identified as Dracula from his appearances in Hammer's *Horror of Dracula* (1957), *Dracula: Prince of Darkness* (1966), *Dracula Has Risen from the Grave* (1968), *Taste the Blood of Dracula* (1970), *Scars of Dracula* (1970/71), *Dracula A.D. 1972* (1972) and *Count Dracula and His Vampire Brides* (1973). This is not only because Lee played the role so often but because he played it so well, bringing an almost animalistic menace and sensuality to the part that differentiated his characterization from prior screen Draculas like Bela Lugosi and John Carradine. Clearly, however, Lee's abilities go far beyond a single character. He delivered one of his most rousing performances as the cult-busting Duc de Richleau in Fisher's *The Devil's Bride* (1968) and has contributed memorable turns in scores of other films both within and outside the horror genre. A dedicated craftsman and tireless worker, Lee has enjoyed one of the longest and most prolific careers in movie history, working steadily for more than 50 years, appearing in movies great and small made all over the world. A new generation of fans met Lee through director Peter Jackson's *Lord of the Rings* trilogy (2001–2003) and George Lucas' *Star Wars* sequels *Attack of the Clones* (2002) and *Revenge of the Sith* (2005). Director Tim Burton has worked with Lee on four occasions so far, for *Sleepy Hollow* (1999), *Charlie and the Chocolate Factory* (2005), *Corpse Bride* (2005) and *Alice in Wonderland* (2010). During the Sixties, Lee's name on a marquee might not have offered the same sort of guarantee as Cushing's, but it remained attractive enough to draw many moviegoers.

Cushing and Lee appeared together in 22 films and were originally slated to co-star in *Brides*. Instead, they would team next in Hammer's *The Gorgon* (1964/65). Following *Brides*, Hammer's string of hits came to an abrupt end. Fisher's *House of Fright* (1960/61), an ambitious attempt to reimagine the Jekyll and Hyde story (with Lee in a supporting role) became the first of the studio's gothic chillers to fail commercially. The company's fortunes, and the quality of its productions, would wax and wane throughout the decade. Still, Hammer produced many outstanding pictures, including *The Curse of the Werewolf* (1961), *The Nanny* (1965), *The Plague of the Zombies* (1966), *Five Million Years to Earth* (1967), *The Devil's Bride* (1968) and *Frankenstein Must Be Destroyed* (1969/70). Despite some misfires along the way, the studio's place of honor in the history of horror cinema was well earned.

1961–1962

Throughout 1961 and 1962 the Cold War escalated and, in an obscure, civil war-torn Southeast Asian country called Vietnam, began to heat up. African Americans' struggle for civil rights faced renewed and sometimes violent opposition. But revolutionary events were not confined to the realm of politics.

On April 12, 1961, the Cold War went extraterrestrial when cosmonaut Yuri Gagarin became the first man into space, orbiting the earth in his Volstak 1 capsule and dealing a blow to the rival American space program. Three days later the U.S. suffered a far more grievous defeat when an ill-conceived Cuban invasion plot went awry on the beaches of the Bay of Pigs, and became a debacle when President Kennedy failed to provide promised air support to the invaders. In August events took a more threatening turn when communist East Germany erected the Berlin Wall. Simmering tensions threatened to boil over in October 1962 during the Cuban Missile Crisis. The world breathed a sigh of relief when, after moving within an eyelash of nuclear war with the U.S., the Soviets backed down and removed atomic missiles from Cuba (after Kennedy secretly agreed to remove similar weapons from Turkey). But few Americans had yet noticed the buildup of military advisors and support personnel (now numbering more than 3,000) Kennedy had sent to embattled South Vietnam. Over the spring and summer of 1961, student activists (black and white) known as "Freedom Riders" began taking bus tours through the South to test the strength of a recent Supreme Court decision (*Boynton v. Virginia*) that declared segregated bus and railway stations illegal.

Freedom Riders were attacked and viciously beaten by angry mobs (including members of the Ku Klux Klan) in Anniston and Montgomery, Alabama, and many were illegally arrested in Jackson, Mississippi. Much of the violence was caught on film and broadcast on the evening news, polarizing public opinion on both the institution of segregation and the tactics of the Civil Rights movement.

In July 1962, at New York's Stable Gallery, Andy Warhol premiered his *Campbell's Soup Cans*— minimalist, un-painterly reproductions of banal household items that were part of the burgeoning Pop Art movement, which forced audiences to ponder the meaning, role and significance of art itself. (Dennis Hopper, who had recently starred in the arty chiller *Night Tide* [1961] and would later direct the landmark *Easy Rider* [1969], was one of a half-dozen patrons who paid $100 for an original Warhol soup can painting at the premiere.) Warhol later adorned canvasses with reproductions of Coca Cola bottles, Brillo pad boxes and the likenesses of celebrities such as Marilyn Monroe and Elvis Presley. In September, Houghton-Mifflin published scientist Rachel Carson's *Silent Spring*, which called for an end to the indiscriminate use of pesticides such as DDT. The book helped galvanize the growing ecological movement in the U.S. Robert Wise's *West Side Story* and David Lean's *Lawrence of Arabia* won the Oscar for Best Picture in 1961 and '62, respectively, but the highest profile movie news was the tragic demise of the 36-year-old Monroe, found dead in her Los Angeles home in the wee hours of August 5, 1962. An autopsy revealed an overdose of sedatives and barbiturates in the actress' system, and the coroner ruled the death a suicide. Nevertheless, conspiracy theories— some involving organized crime, others implicating President Kennedy — swirled around the event.

Horror cinema also witnessed groundbreaking developments throughout 1961 and '62. For the past few years, a trickle of foreign-made chillers had dripped into U.S. theaters. Following director Mario Bava's international smash *Black Sunday* (1961), however, the faucets opened wide, with shockers pouring in from all over the globe. Initially, British, Mexican and Japanese features had been the most common genre imports. But Italy, which had produced only two fright films since 1920, suddenly emerged as a major exporter of horror fare. The Fascist government of Benito Mussolini prohibited Italian studios from making horror movies during its rule, from 1922 to 1943. After World War II, such films were repressed by powerful, conservative Catholic censors at both the national and local levels in Italy. As the censors' grip finally began to loosen, director Riccardo Freda made two attempts to reboot the horror genre in Italy, first with the tepid *I Vampiri* (1957, released in the U.S. in bastardized form as *The Devil's Commandment* in 1963), and the sci-fi shocker *Caltiki, the Immortal Monster* (1959/60). In both instances, but for different reasons, Freda abandoned those projects in mid-production, leaving his gifted cinematographer, Mario Bava, to finish the films. *Black Sunday* marked Bava's credited directorial debut, and it remains one of the genre's most auspicious. This gorgeously photographed yarn, about a vampire (Barbara Steele) who is brutally executed for witchcraft, then returns from the dead to wreak vengeance on the ancestors of her persecutors, would be widely imitated but seldom matched for pictorial beauty or spine-tingling power. The Italian movie industry of the 1960s (like most movie industries of any era) was extremely reactionary and imitative, as the tremendous numbers of sword-and-sandal "peplum" pictures and Spaghetti Westerns made there during the Sixties attests. So naturally the box office returns raked in by Bava's film inspired a wave of Italian gothic chillers. Over the next few years, Italy produced several noteworthy gothics, including Freda's *The Horrible Dr. Hichcock* (1962/64) and *The Ghost* (1963/65), Antonio Margheriti's *Castle of Blood* (1964), Mario Ciano's *Nightmare Castle* (1965/66) and Massimo Pupillo's *Terror Creatures from the Grave* (1965/67)— all of which starred Barbara Steele — not to mention Bava's subsequent work. These Italian gothics were eerily atmospheric, featuring moments of hair-raising frisson, but placed greater value on striking visuals than coherent plots. Like the Spaghetti Westerns, these pictures maintained a distinct identity from their stateside counterparts, even though American movies later integrated elements of the Italian style.

For Bava, *Black Sunday* was only the first in a series of masterpieces. Although the director worked in a number of genres (he made Spaghetti Westerns, pepla, sex farces and crime dramas, plus unclassifiable one-offs like the campy fumetti adaptation *Danger: Diabolik*, 1967), horror movies were Bava's forte. Whether working in the gothic register with *What* (aka *The Whip and the Body*, 1963/65) and *Kill, Baby ... Kill!* (1966/68), in contemporary settings with *Blood and Black Lace* (1964/65), or both, as in the superior horror anthology *Black Sabbath* (1963/64), his mastery of *mise en scène*, composition, symbolic imagery and special visual effects made practically every frame Bava directed a feast for the eyes. *Black Sunday* demonstrated Bava's extraordinary acumen for black-and-white moviemaking, yet he soon abandoned the format and distinguished himself with his daring use of expressionist color. Most of Bava's later films are awash with eerie blue, yellow, green or purple light, usually combined with thickly draped shadows. In addition to this immediately recognizable visual signature, many of the filmmaker's pictures are linked by a common theme — the folly of greed. In movie after movie, characters that put personal gain ahead of compassion for other people are consumed and ultimately undone by their own selfishness, often in spectacularly gruesome ways. One of the director's most impressive works was the atmospheric *Kill, Baby ... Kill!*, a compelling thriller conjured up almost entirely from Bava's visual magic and some carefully selected library music. During the Sixties, Bava also made one of the most enjoyable horror-peplum hybrids in *Hercules in the Haunted World* (1961/64) and an influential horror-sci-fi blend, *Planet of the Vampires* (1965). Apart from *Black Sunday*, however, Bava's most significant contribution to the genre was *Blood and Black Lace*, which we will consider later.

With her showy dual role in *Black Sunday* (playing both the reanimated witch and her own great-great-great granddaughter), Barbara Steele broke into the boys' club of horror superstardom. Although women such as Fay Wray had gained fame in the genre before, they had done so in one-dimensional "shrieking violet" parts. Steele was the first actress to earn recognition for playing the villain, placing her on even footing with contemporaries such as Christopher Lee. Steele's exotic looks— raven hair, angular cheek bones and large, expressive eyes— enabled her to portray monsters and heroines alike and never look less than radiant. Born in Cheshire, England, she came to Hollywood in the late 1950s, where producers struggled to handle the talented but temperamental ingénue. Assigned to co-star in the Elvis Presley Western *Flaming Star* (1960), Steele became frustrated with director Don Siegel, walked off the set and left the country. For the balance of the Sixties she worked almost exclusively in Italy, alternating between starring roles in gothic chillers and supporting roles in art films such as Federico Fellini's *8½* (1963) and Volker Schlondorff's *Young Torless* (1966/68), although Roger Corman brought Steele back to the States for an extended cameo in his *Pit and the Pendulum* (1961). As the quality of her roles declined, Steele became disenchanted with horror movies. After the disappointing *Crimson Cult* (1968/70), which relegated her to a speechless cameo covered in blue body paint and a rams-horn headdress, the actress left Italy and swore off horror roles. In the 1970s, Steele worked primarily for American television, but eventually returned to the horror genre at the behest of fans-turned-filmmakers like Joe Dante, who gave her a small role in *Piranha* (1978). She also appeared in the short-lived revival of the horror soap opera *Dark Shadows* in 1990. Steele remains active; her most recent screen appearance as of this writing was in *The Butterfly Room* (2010).

Steele's ascendance was part of a wider trend in horror cinema that mirrored events in the real world. As the feminist movement surged forward and women aggressively pursued leadership roles outside the home, the genre began to develop better and more prominent parts for actresses. Two prime examples of this are *The Innocents* (1961) with Deborah Kerr and *The Haunting* (1963) with Julie Harris. Both movies unfold from the perspective of a complex, multi-faceted female protagonist. Kerr, as an English governess who comes to suspect the children in her care may be possessed by evil spirits, and Harris, playing a psychic medium on the verge of a nervous breakdown, handle their challenging roles with dexterity, subtlety and conviction. Although both pictures are superbly written, directed and photographed—indeed, they rank among the most satisfying horror shows of the Sixties—neither would succeed without the outstanding work of its stars. These female-centric horrors would reach a creative high water mark with *Rosemary's Baby* (1968), starring Mia Farrow as an expectant mother trapped in a Satanic conspiracy.

Robert Aldrich's psychological thriller *What Ever Happened to Baby Jane* (1962) went those films one better by featuring *two* female leads—aging screen legends Bette Davis and Joan Crawford. In the title role, as a geriatric former child star, Davis delivered one of the greatest and most courageous performances of her career. Davis, always sensitive about her lack of classic movie star beauty, nevertheless appeared under harsh white light, either bare-faced or in grotesque makeup, playing a character who's both utterly sadistic and bizarrely infantile, with childlike speech patterns and immature gestures, such as covering her ears to avoid hearing something unpleasant. (Davis was rewarded with a Best Actress nomination from the Academy.) Crawford, in a more sympathetic but less flashy role as Jane's tormented sister, also performed admirably. Although conceived as a *Psycho* variant, the robust box office returns for *Baby Jane* helped the picture spawn its own legion of imitators, inaugurating the so-called "horror hag" sub-genre. Aldrich followed *Baby Jane* with the similar *Hush, Hush Sweet Charlotte* (1965), co-starring Davis and Olivia De Havilland. Crawford returned to the oeuvre for William Castle's *Straight-Jacket* (1964). Tallulah Bankhead headlined Hammer's *Die, Die, My Darling* (1965), Geraldine Page appeared in *What Ever Happened to Aunt Alice?* (1969), Debbie Reynolds and Shelley Winters co-starred in *What's the Matter with Helen?* (1971) and Agnes Moorehead made *Dear Dead Delilah* (1972). *Baby Jane* and its imitators addressed feminist themes (demonstrating how women are objectified in their youth and marginalized in old age) but also dealt with the universal problem of aging itself, bringing viewers face to face with the inescapability of human mortality. These films also offered plum roles that helped extend the careers of many talented performers. In Hollywood, actresses' careers usually begin to falter once they reach age 40 (if not sooner), whereas their male co-stars can work into their 60s and beyond. Typical Hollywood movies simply aren't written for older women, a problem that has, if anything, only worsened since *Baby Jane*.

The Innocents and *What Ever Happened to Baby Jane* were prestige pictures that earned Oscar nominations. On the other end of the spectrum, horror fans of the early Sixties could revel in the outré delights offered by Mexican fright flicks, many of the best of which were produced at this time—*The Curse of the Crying Woman, The Black Pit of Dr. M.* (both 1961), *The Brainiac, World of the Vampires* and *The Witch's Mirror* (all 1962). Filmgoers have two men to thank (or curse, depending upon one's perspective) for bringing Mexi-monster madness north of the border: Actor-producer Abel Salazar, whose Cinematografica A.B.S.A. company basically *created* the Gothic-style Mexican horror movie in the late 1950s and early Sixties, and theater owner K. Gordon Murray, who purchased the American rights to Salazar's (and numerous other) movies, dubbed them into English and exhibited them in a series of Saturday matinees before sending them off to television (via American International Pictures' television arm). Actor-turned-producer Salazar started the Mexican horror revival in 1957 when he both produced and starred in the watershed *The Vampire* (featuring Germán Robles in the title role and Salazar as a substitute Van Helsing) and its sequel, *The Vampire's Coffin* (also 1958). Salazar's films were classicist black-and-white gothics made in the style popularized by Universal in the 1930s. Produced just before Hammer Films' *Horror of Dracula*, *The Vampire* provided further evidence that audiences were ready for the return to traditional horror stories. Salazar continued the cycle with *The Curse of the Crying Woman* and *The Living Head*, (also 1961), as well as the aforementioned

The Brainiac, *World of the Vampires* and *The Witch's Mirror*. Salazar's success, predictably, inspired many imitators, some of which reached the U.S. (either in theatrical releases or via television), and many of which did not. As the Mexican horror boom continued, aging Hollywood stars ventured south to extend their careers. Lon Chaney, Jr., starred in a slapdash Wolf Man clone, *Face of the Screaming Werewolf* (1964), and the great Boris Karloff ended his career in a quartet of cheaply made Mexi-chillers (*The Fear Chamber*, *Isle of the Snake People*, *The Incredible Invasion* and *Macabre Serenade*), some of which weren't released until the early 1970s. While many of these productions were cut-rate, addle-brained dreck, the best of them — pictures like *Curse of the Crying Woman* and *World of the Vampires*— proved very effective, imbued with an otherworldly ambiance and macabre, sometimes startling, imagery. Others, like *The Brainiac*, may not be "good" in any meaningful sense of the word but remain very entertaining — action-packed and wildly imaginative (where else can viewers watch the monster eat chilled brains with a spoon, like a bowl of corn flakes?). While only a handful of these south-of-the-border oddities made it to U.S. theaters in English language versions, many later became available on home video. They now claim an ardent cult following.

In addition to "straight" horror films such as these, Mexico also produced a long-running series of wrestling movies, many of which crossed over into the horror genre by having real-life grapplers battle menaces like Dracula and the Frankenstein Monster. This unique sub-genre began in the 1950s and continued through the Seventies, but saw its heyday in the Sixties, when famous wrestlers Blue Demon (real name: Alejandro Cruz), Neutron (Wolf Rubinskis), Mil Mascaras, the Bat, the Blue Angel and the one-and-only El Santo dove off the top turnbuckle and into the hearts of movie audiences. In Mexico, professional wrestling was not considered a tongue-in-cheek guilty pleasure like in America. One of the country's top sporting events, wrestling was taken very seriously, and the stars of the ring were elevated to near-superhero status. So it was only natural that these masked marauders throw their hats (or masks) into the celluloid ring. Literally hundreds of Mexican wrestling pictures were produced in the 1960s, many of them featuring supernatural villains as well as the more standard criminal masterminds and dastardly wrasslin' opponents. Unfortunately (or fortunately, again depending on one's perspective), few made it north of the border. By far the most popular of the wrestling heroes was El Santo, the silver mask and cape-wearing Rodolfo Guzman Huerta (at least to begin with — since no one ever saw Santo without his mask, others are believed to have donned it later on, including Eric del Castillo). A national hero in his homeland, Santo made his film debut in 1952 with *El Enmascarado de Plata* (The Silver Maskman). In less than three decades, El Santo appeared in over 50 films. Sometimes renamed Samson or even Superman in other countries, the valiant Santo (often teamed with his rival/ companion Blue Demon) battled (sometimes in the wrestling ring!) vampires, werewolves, witches, mummies, zombies, a Frankenstein Monster, mad scientists, a robot and even a Cyclops. Although only three Santo adventures reached English-speaking U.S. theaters during the Sixties—*Invasion of the Zombies*, *Samson vs. the Vampire Women* and *Samson in the Wax Museum*— many more subsequently became available on DVD. Some of the best of these include: *The Diabolical Axe* (1965), *Santo vs. the Martian Invasion* (1966), *Santo in the Treasure of Dracula* (1968) and *Santo and Blue Demon vs. the Monsters* (1969. These offbeat epics certainly are not for everyone, but may appeal to those with a taste for the eccentric. If you like *The Brainiac*, you'll probably go for *Santo in the Treasure of Dracula*, too.

1963–1964

These were years of dreams and nightmares, when leaders from all points on the political and cultural map provided visions for the future. Inevitably, conflict arose between the adherents of these widely divergent ideologies. In February 1963, Betty Friedan published her best-selling book *The Feminine Mystique*, which described the frustration many middle-class housewives felt with their lives; it served as a rallying cry for American feminists. In the midst of ongoing racial violence (including the June murder of NAACP field secretary Medgar Evers and the September deaths of four young girls when an African American church was bombed in Birmingham), Martin Luther King, Jr., delivered his hope-filled "I Have a Dream" speech to a crowd of 200,000 civil rights activists gathered around the Lincoln Memorial. An entire generation of Americans was stunned and horrified when on November 22, 1963, assassin Lee Harvey Oswald gunned down President Kennedy in Dallas. Even though a congressional investigation completed the following year would determine that Oswald acted alone, numerous conspiracy theories clung to the assassination (and still do). In June 1964 President Lyndon B. Johnson signed the landmark Civil Rights Act, which prohibited discrimination of all kinds based on race, religion and national origin, and empowered the government to enforce desegregation. A month later, at the Republican National Convention, conservatives overthrew the ruling party moderates, nominating arch right-winger Barry Goldwater for president and publicly challenging the constitutionality of the recently passed Civil Rights Act. Although Johnson defeated Goldwater in a landslide, these events shifted the formerly centrist G.O.P. further right and won the party robust new support in the traditionally Democratic South and burgeoning conservative enclaves such as Orange County, California.

While conservatives were changing the face of the Republican Party, the Beatles were changing the face of popular music. On February 7, 1964, the Fab Four touched down in New York City and took America by storm, altering the course of music, fashion and pop culture over the course of the next six years. Later in February, poetry-spouting heavyweight Cassius Clay knocked out Sonny Liston to claim his first world championship. Clay, who shortly after defeating Liston converted to Islam and changed his name to Muhammad Ali, would emerge as one of the most controversial public figures of the era, especially when he declared himself a conscientious objector to the rapidly escalating Vietnam War. At the movies, the Production Code continued to weaken. Director Sidney Lumet's *The Pawnbroker* (1964) was granted a "special exception" and became the first Code-approved film to feature bare breasts. The studios' financial problems—stemming in part from stratospheric overhead costs associated with maintaining huge soundstages and back lots—approached crisis levels. In 1964, MGM lost nearly $20 million and Fox lost over $40 million. The Academy's stodgy choices for Best Picture—*Tom Jones* in 1963 and *My Fair Lady* in 1964—demonstrated how resistant Hollywood seemed to new ideas. Influential, forward-looking pictures like *Hud*, *The Birds* (both 1963), *Goldfinger* and *A Hard Day's Night* (both 1964)—not to mention watershed foreign movies like *8½*, *The Leopard* (both 1963) and *Woman in the Dunes* (1964)—weren't considered Best Picture material, but bloated, self-important road show fodder like *Cleopatra* and *How the West Was Won* (both nominated in 1963) were. *Goldfinger*, the third entry in the James Bond movie series, was a watershed hit that helped spur a craze for super-spies, which in this film's wake became ubiquitous both on the big screen (with Bond imitators such as Matt Helm, Derek Flint and Jerry Cotton, etc.) and TV (*The Man from U.N.C.L.E.*, *The Wild Wild West*, a revival of *Secret Agent*, etc.), as well as in pulp novels, magazines and comic books. Super-villains such as Fu Manchu and Dr. Mabuse enjoyed a revival during the same era, with several foreign-produced pictures starring those characters finally earning a U.S. release during the mid- to late-1960s. Occasionally, some of these films brushed the borders of the horror genre.

Fear of progress was not a problem that vexed horror cinema, which continued to push boldly into previously uncharted terrain. Easily the best genre entry of this period was director Alfred Hitchcock's *The Birds* (1963), although it was little appreciated at the time. In fact, the film was widely considered a disappointment, although almost anything Hitch had issued as a successor to the cultural phenomenon that was *Psycho* (1960) would have seemed like a letdown. In the years since, *The Birds*' reputation has deservedly soared; it stands as one of the last great Hitchcock pictures and, arguably, the most terrifying entry in the legendary director's filmography. This offbeat tale about a series of unexplained bird attacks certainly ranks among his most uncompromising and artistically sophisticated works. *The Birds* features some of the most hair-raising moments of any Sixties shocker (for instance, a scene in which terrorized grade-schoolers are attacked by demonic-looking crows). Federico Fellini, who admired the film, called it "an apocalyptic poem." On a less ethereal level, *The Birds* can be seen as the grand-daddy of all animal-attack thrillers, inspiring a subgenre that runs from the sublime (*Jaws*, 1975) to the ridiculous (*Night of the Lepus*, 1972). It's also worth noting the many similarities in dramatic structure between this film and George Romero's *Night of the Living Dead* (1968): Both feature protagonists confined to a remote, boarded-up farmhouse fighting off inhuman attackers. Neither picture spends much time explaining why these attacks occur, and neither one has a happy ending. Both, however, are masterpieces. If *The Birds* failed to earn all due critical respect, however, it remained infinitely more prestigious than most of the other historically significant chillers from 1963 and '64.

Consider director Herschell Gordon Lewis' notorious *Blood Feast* (1963), which pushed far beyond all accepted boundaries for screen violence (or good taste). Lewis, an exploitation filmmaker who previously had specialized in no-budget softcore porn, keenly observed the box office receipts reaped by Hammer's blood-spattered gothics and decided to shoot a picture that would trade one prurient interest for another — with gratuitous gore replacing gratuitous nudity as the film's *raison d'etre*. While *Blood Feast*'s murders are mostly suggested rather than shown (usually filmed through subjective shots from the victim's perspective, followed by a quick cutaway), Lewis' camera lingers on scenes of dismemberment and cannibalism, showing the killer chopping off legs, tearing out his victim's tongue, slicing out an eyeball, and, later, baking severed limbs in an oven and stirring a pot of grue stew. All of this was far more graphic than anything unleashed on movie audiences before, and many viewers were left stunned and astonished. Lewis' film craft (especially his special gore effects) remained inept — on par with his earlier grade Z nudie cuties. As a result, nowadays *Blood Feast* is far more likely to inspire gales of derisive laughter than wholesale vomiting (even though, as a promotional gimmick, barf bags were distributed to moviegoers at some cinemas during the film's initial theatrical run).

Nevertheless, the movie proved astoundingly profitable, leading Lewis to make another scandalous gore-fest, *Two Thousand Maniacs!* (1964). By far the most ambitious and best realized entry in the director's filmography, *Two Thousand Maniacs!* remains a semi-professional production riddled with fundamental flaws and clumsy mistakes, but Lewis' tongue-in-cheek approach softens the impact of those problems. The story's basic premise (Confederate townsfolk wiped out by Union soldiers during the Civil War return from the dead to take revenge on Yankee interlopers) is intriguing, and its gruesome set pieces display a sort of demented creativity sure to satisfy gore fans. The ghost-rebels chop off a woman's arm and then barbecue her; tie a man's arms and legs to four horses and set them bolting away in different directions; play a game that results in a giant boulder falling on another victim; and send a fourth victim rolling down a hill in a barrel full of spikes. Lewis made a handful of subsequent gore features— including *Color Me Blood Red* (1965), *The Gruesome Twosome* (1967), *The Wizard of Gore* (1970), *The Gore-Gore Girls* (1972) and the belated *Blood Feast 2: All U Can Eat* (2002)— and explored other exploitation genres, as well. Although it took years for graphic bloodletting to become a mainstay of horror cinema, its emergence was inevitable after the success of *Blood Feast* and its kin. "Think of what this picture spawned," said David Friedman, producer of *Blood Feast*. "We basically invented the slasher film, the blood-and-guts film." The horror genre had taken a decisive turn — whether for better or worse may be debated.

By the mid–1960s, another exploitation craze was winding down — the fad for Italian sword-and-sandal pictures, commonly referred to as peplum (derived from the Greek word for "tunic") films. These low-budget, lowbrow action epics, set in the ancient past and starring former body builders such as Steve Reeves, Reg Park and Gordon Scott as muscle-bound mythological heroes like Hercules, Samson and Goliath, were produced by the scores each year from 1958 through 1965, when the Italian film industry abruptly abandoned the cycle in favor of Spaghetti Westerns. The pepla were popularized by director Pietro Francisci's *Hercules* (1958/59), starring Steve Reeves and photographed by cinematographer Mario Bava. Following the international triumph of Bava's directorial debut, the gothic chiller *Black Sunday* (1960), Italian producers not only rushed similar gothics into production, but began to integrate prominent horror elements into their sword-and-sandal pictures. By 1963 and '64, some of the best of these peplum-horror hybrids reached U.S. audiences. Not surprisingly, the best of these was Bava's *Hercules in the Haunted World* (1961/63), in which the titular strongman (played here by Reg Park) journeys to the underworld to defeat a vampiric villain (Christopher Lee). Imaginative, atmospheric and action-packed, with a sly, tongue-in-cheek performance by Lee, *Haunted World* is one of the few pepla that may appeal to viewers not already enamored with the sword-and-sandal oeuvre. Other noteworthy peplum-horror blends include director Riccardo Freda's dark *The Witch's Curse* (1962), starring Kirk Morris as Goliath ("Maciste" in the original Italian); Duccio Tessari's mildly comedic *My Son, the Hero* (1962/63), starring Giuliano Gemma as the heroic Krios; Sergio Corbuccci and Giacomo Gentilomo's brutal *Goliath and the Vampires* (1961/64), featuring Gordon Scott in the title role (again, "Maciste" in Italy); and Alberto De Martino's finely-crafted *Medusa Against the Son of Hercules* (1963, issued directly to TV in America), starring Richard Harrison as Perseus.

If anything was less respected than the brawny, sandal-clad peplum heroes, it was the rubber suit-encased creatures of the Japanese *kaiju eiga* (monster movies). Still, in 1964 Toho Studios released a pair of films that changed the course of this popular, albeit critically reviled (at least in the U.S.), sub-genre. The company, which had scored a surprising box-office triumph with *King Kong vs. Godzilla* in 1962, naturally wanted to pair Godzilla with another high-profile beastie. Mothra, which had jump-started the studio's moribund *kaiju* cycle in 1961, seemed like the logical choice — at least to Toho. AIP may have disagreed, since it removed all images of Mothra from movie posters and retitled the film known in Japan as *Mothra vs. Godzilla* (*Mosura tai Gojira*) to *Godzilla vs. The Thing* for the picture's American release. Perhaps AIP hid Mothra's identity because executives feared fans wouldn't pay to see Godzilla fight an oversized butterfly. Yet, it's just this oddball pairing that makes the film's monster battles work so well. Unlike *King Kong vs. Godzilla*, in which the creatures throw rocks at each other and grapple like professional wrestlers, in this film the monsters use their unique abilities to combat their opponent: Mothra waylays Godzilla by releasing a cloud of dusty yellow poison; Godzilla fires back with a burst of atomic breath. In short, these scenes play out like a contest between two animals, not between two guys in rubber suits. *Godzilla vs. the Thing* is a lively adventure with likeable human characters as well as first-rate monster sequences, and boasts some of the most impressive work in the history of Toho's visual effects department — far superior to *King Kong vs. Godzilla* in every aspect. American audiences were fortunate that, unlike many *kaiju eiga, Godzilla vs. The Thing* reached U.S. audiences without extensive re-editing. *Godzilla vs. The Thing* also remains memorable as the final film in which Godzilla would appear as a villain — until Toho re-launched the series in 1984.

The success of *Godzilla vs. the Thing* (1964) validated the appeal of the monster-versus-monster format and proved that this gambit could work with international audiences even when both contestants were Japanese creatures (rather than American imports like Kong). Toho immediately rushed a new *kaiju* battle royale into production. Taking a cue from vintage Universal horror shows like *House of Frankenstein* (1944) and *House of Dracula* (1945), producers decided to throw together a whole gang of monsters — Godzilla, Mothra, Rodan and the newly created title menace — for *Ghidrah, the Three-Headed Monster* (1964), about alien invaders who control a giant, three-headed space dragon. Unfortunately, the haste with which *Ghidrah* was made is all too apparent in the final product. Its visual effects are wildly inconsistent, its production values are below par and its screenplay is a disorganized mess, full of subplots left dangling and plot points that are never explained. The U.S. release version places some scenes out of sequence, only worsening the helter-skelter feel of the production. This film completes Godzilla's transformation from walking metaphor for nuclear holocaust (as in *Godzilla, King of the Monsters* [1954/56]) to Japanese national superhero. He's the good guy here, teaming with his monster mates to defeat the evil three-headed space dragon Ghidrah and his extraterrestrial cronies. Although not as successful commercially or artistically as either of its immediate predecessors, *Ghidrah* set the template for the remainder of the long-running Godzilla series, with a heroic Godzilla fighting alongside other monsters, often to defeat malevolent extraterrestrials.

Upon its arrival in the U.S. in 1964, Jesus Franco's *The Awful Dr. Orlof* seemed like just another sleazy European import. But in retrospect, it can only be viewed as a *landmark* sleazy European import. Not only did this movie announce the arrival of a significant new horror filmmaker, but it gave Spanish horror a toehold in the American market. Franco would go on to write and direct nearly 200 features, many of those horror movies. In the 1970s he gained notoriety for pictures such as *Vampiros Lesbos* (1971) and *A Virgin Among the Living Dead* (1973) that combined eroticism and horror. Franco's self-consciously stylized approach to this material (full of heavy-handed symbolism, often with flash forwards, slow motion, tinted and distorted images, a hyperactive zoom lens and other flashy devices) blurred the line between exploitation and art house fare. Although offbeat, even downright weird, the director's early films are more stylistically restrained than his Seventies work. *The Awful Dr. Orlof* is one of the earliest imitators of Georges Franju's Nouvelle Vague shocker *Horror Chamber of Dr. Faustus* (1959/62; aka *Eyes Without a Face*). Orlof (Howard Vernon) stalks and kills young women, with the aid of his blind homicidal servant Morpho (Ricardo Valle), to obtain the skin needed to restore his comatose daughter's disfigured face. The picture boasts some evocative photography (silhouetted shots of the two villains carrying a coffin towards a forbidding castle; a murder taking place in front of an upstairs window viewed solely from the street below) and takes atmospheric advantage of authentic castle settings to add some much-needed gothic mood and verisimilitude. Despite glaring flaws including a glacial pace, the picture was a hit and led Franco to shoot several Orlof sequels, as well as the similarly titled *The Sadistic Baron Von Klaus* (1962, unreleased in America until the DVD age) and *The Diabolical Dr. Z* (1966/67). Of these early efforts, *Dr. Z* remains the most satisfying. It centers on the daughter of one Dr. Zimmer, who has developed a strange machine that combines acupuncture and hypnosis to transform people into obedient slaves. When her father is killed, the daughter uses the machine to exact vengeance, turning a gorgeous exotic dancer with two-inch fingernails that goes by the stage name of "Miss Death" into a remorseless assassin. This outré outing features some of the most bizarre imagery of the entire, extensive Franco filmography, as well as an undercurrent of Sadean sensuality.

The success of Franco's films paved the way for Spain's emergence as a major producer of horror films. However, the genre was slower to develop in Spain than in neighboring Italy, in part due to stringent censorship by the government of Geralisimo Francisco Franco (no relation to the director), who seized power in Spain in 1939 and held it until his death in 1975. In the final years of the dictator's life, censorship began to loosen and important horror moviemakers began to emerge, including actor-writer-sometimes-director Paul Naschy (real name: Jacinto Molina), best known for his long-running series of "Waldemar Daninsky" werewolf movies. The first entry in the Daninsky cycle, *Frankenstein's Bloody Terror*, was produced in 1968, although it didn't reach the U.S. until 1971. Other notable Spanish horror film specialists who followed in Franco's footsteps include Amando De Ossorio, best remembered for his *Blind Dead* series (featuring the mummified Knights Templar) and Leon Klimovsky, who helmed many of Naschy's best films as well as the racy *Dracula Saga* (1973). Indeed, although some of the best Spanish chillers, like Jorge Grau's *Let Sleeping Corpses Lie* (1974/75) and Carlos Aured's *Horror Rises from the Tomb* (1973/75, starring Naschy) played it straight, many such as Vicente Aranda's *The Blood-Spattered Bride* (1972) and Jose Ramon Larraz's *Vampyres* (1974) followed Franco's lead and incorporated lesbianism or other erotic elements. Eventually, of course, Spain produced acclaimed genre filmmakers such as Guillermo del Toro (the Oscar-nominated *Pan's Labyrinth*, 2006), Nacho Vigalondo (*Timecrimes*, 2007) and Juan Antonios Bayona (*The Orphanage*, 2007/08), whose pictures helped Spanish horror scale new heights of popularity and critical esteem. While the merits of Franco's own works may be debatable, he remains a formative influence on the development of horror cinema in his homeland and, given the impact of those who followed him, a key figure in the history of the genre as a whole.

Just next door to the horror genre, in the world of apocalyptic science fiction, Cold War paranoia crested with a pair of 1964 classics, Stanley Kubrick's *Dr. Strangelove, or How I Learned to Stop Worrying and Love the Bomb* and Sidney Lumet's *Fail-Safe*, released just months apart by the same studio (Columbia). Possibly the funniest political satire ever committed to celluloid, and assuredly one of the signature films of the 1960s, *Dr. Strangelove* is also the best realized, most plausible movie apocalypse. A paranoid general (Sterling Hayden) launches an unauthorized air attack on the Soviet Union. The planes are successfully recalled or shot down — except for one, plunging the U.S. and U.S.S.R. into a nuclear conflagration. Kubrick's impeccably written and performed film comically underscores the lunacy inherent in the doctrine of Mutual Assured Destruction, which held the Eastern and Western superpowers at bay during the hottest days of the Cold War. The sheer audacity it took to make *Dr. Strangelove* and send it to movie theaters less than 15 months after the Cuban Missile Crisis remains inspiring. *Fail-Safe* features a scenario very similar to *Dr. Strangelove*'s — a computer malfunction accidentally triggers a U.S. air strike on Moscow; technical problems and procedural snafus prevent the planes from being recalled. But instead of comedy, *Fail-Safe* delivers white-knuckle suspense, as Lumet slowly, inexorably ratchets up the dramatic tension, climbing toward a shocking climax. While not as daring or historic as *Dr. Strangelove, Fail-Safe* remains a gripping experience. Taken together, these films vividly demonstrate the level of popular anxiety stemming from the looming specter of nuclear Armageddon. Tensions were high in the U.S.S.R., too, where Nikita Khrushchev was sent to his dacha in 1964 because Leonid Brezhnev and other hardliners thought he had become too friendly with the West. Party bosses' suspicions may have began in 1959, when Khrushchev became the first Soviet premier to tour the U.S., including a stopover in Hollywood, where he was feted by movie stars including Marilyn Monroe.

1965–1967

Political and cultural upheavals continued with quickening pace during these years. On August 6, 1965, President Johnson signed the Voting Rights Act into law, yet five days later African Americans rioted in the Watts neighborhood of Los Angeles. As black Americans began to lose faith in legislation as a means of improving their lives, more radical approaches were taken, as evidenced by subsequent race riots in other major cities and the formation of the Black Panther Party in October 1966. Also in 1965, the first American combat troops arrived in Vietnam, and "Operation Rolling Thunder" — the first in a series of extensive bombing campaigns — was undertaken. The war escalated quickly, with troop levels rising from about 185,000 at the end of 1965 to approximately 486,000 by the close of 1967. During this period, China was seized by Communist Party Chairman Mao Zedong's Cultural Revolution, which called for young people to overthrow the elderly ruling elite as part of a "permanent revolution." Political, cultural and economic instability ensued, yet Mao became a leftist icon around the world, and his "Little Red Book" (seldom referred to by its actual title, *Quotations from Chairman Mao Tse-tung*) sold briskly to college students in the West. In Greece right-wing elements of the Greek military seized power on April 21, 1967. This brutal junta, which tortured political opponents in various sadistic ways (shoving high-pressure water hoses into victims' anuses, ripping out fingernails and toenails, shoving urine-soaked rags down victims' throats, etc.), held power until the generals that led the takeover were, in turn, deposed in a second *coup d'état* by their subordinates in July 1974. In the Middle East from June 5 through 10, 1967 Israel defeated Syria, Jordan and Egypt in the Six Day War. As the Muslim nations massed forces, the Israelis launched a preemptive strike and gained control of the Sinai Peninsula, the Golan Heights, the Gaza Strip, the West Bank and East Jerusalem, tripling the size of their tiny nation. The brief but decisive conflict dramatically altered the balance of power in the region and continues to influence global geopolitics.

Popular culture proved nearly as incendiary. In 1965, Bob Dylan began recording with electric instruments and played a controversial, plugged-in set at the prestigious Newport Folk Festival. It was a severe blow to the American folk music revival, of which Dylan had been a leading light. Meanwhile, new rock bands including the Jimi Hendrix Experience, Cream, the Doors and the Byrds formed. In 1967, the Beatles released their watershed album *Sgt. Pepper's Lonely Hearts Club Band*, and hundreds of thousands of young people descended on San Francisco's Haight-Ashbury neighborhood, a counter-culture Mecca, during the so-called "Summer of Love." On television in 1965, *I-Spy* became the first series to star an African American (Bill Cosby). Gene Roddenberry's *Star Trek*, which depicted a future in which people of all ethnic and national backgrounds lived together in peace, premiered in 1966. It honored a pair of usual suspects in 1965 (the family-friendly musical *The Sound of Music*) and 1966 (the historical epic A *Man for All Seasons*), in 1967 the Academy begrudgingly began to reflect the changing face of the wider culture, if not advances in cinematic technique, with its 1967 Best Picture winner, *In the Heat of the Night*, about a black detective from the North investigating a murder in the deep South. These years also saw the final collapse of the Production Code. The MPPDA reluctantly passed Mike Nichols' controversial, profanity-filled *Who's Afraid of Virginia Woolf* (1966), adapted from Edward Albee's acclaimed Broadway play and co-starring Elizabeth Taylor and Richard Burton, after some of Albee's dialogue was altered ("Screw you!" became "God damn you!"). The film version earned 13 Oscar nominations, and won Taylor a Best Actress statuette. When the MPPDA refused to pass Michelangelo Antonioni's British-produced but American-financed *Blow-Up* in 1966, MGM simply released it anyway, becoming the first MPPDA member to ignore the Code. For the next two years, Code enforcement was abandoned entirely. Films featuring nudity, graphic violence or other objectionable content were simply labeled as "Suggested for Mature Audiences." This free-wheeling policy was clearly inadequate, however, and was replaced by the MPPDA's film rating system in 1968.

At this time multinational corporate conglomerates began gobbling up the enfeebled American movie studios. In 1966 Gulf + Western purchased Paramount; the following year Seven Arts bought Warner Brothers and Transamerica acquired United Artists. The executives who authorized these deals knew nothing about moviemaking (Transamerica, for example, was a life insurance company whose other investment properties included Budget Rent-a-Car), but they recognized that the studios were underperforming assets that might regain value over time. For that to occur, however, Hollywood would have to recapture its knack for giving audiences the kind of entertainment they wanted. The major studios had become overly reliant on prestigious historical dramas and glossy musicals, which audiences were rapidly abandoning. The disastrous performance of pictures like *Doctor Doolittle* and *Thoroughly Modern Millie* (both 1967) signaled the end of the road for "road show" spectacles. But that same year a pair of scrappy, modestly-budgeted pictures aimed at younger audiences pointed the way toward a solution. Director Arthur Penn's Nouvelle

Vague-inflected gangster film *Bonnie and Clyde*, starring Warren Beatty and Faye Dunaway, grossed more than $24 million against a production cost of $3 million. (François Truffaut was briefly attached to the project but decided to make the futuristic *Fahrenheit 451* instead.) Director Mike Nichols' *The Graduate*, a dark comedy starring Dustin Hoffman as a disaffected college grad trapped in a romantic triangle with his girlfriend and her mother, returned over $49 million on its $3 million budget. In the wake of these successes, the studios turned to young filmmakers—most of whom were deeply influenced by European films, and many of whom had understudied with producer-director Roger Corman—because the likes of Francis Ford Coppola, Peter Bogdanovich and Dennis Hopper seemed to have a better grasp on the kind of stories that would appeal to young viewers. The New Hollywood era was dawning.

Within the realm of horror cinema, Mario Bava continued to break new ground with *Blood and Black Lace* (1965). It's first and foremost a terrific movie—an engrossing, well-plotted whodunit, briskly paced, beautifully composed and lovingly photographed, with some stunning murder scenes. But today *Blood and Black Lace* is best remembered as the first "giallo" thriller, the starting point for a particularly bloodthirsty brand of murder mysteries originating in Italy, with singular stylistic and thematic conventions, most of which originate with this film. In developing the giallo style, Bava was profoundly influenced by Alfred Hitchcock (especially *Psycho*) and a series of lurid, pulpy Italian mystery novels with yellow covers ("giallo" is Italian for yellow). Bava had introduced elements of the giallo style in earlier films, such as *The Evil Eye* (aka *The Girl Who Knew Too Much* [1963/64]) and "The Telephone" segment in *Black Sabbath* (1963/64), but he assembles all the form's signature components for the first time in *Blood and Black Lace*: a masked, knife-wielding killer; a "target-rich" setting (like a girls' school, a dance studio or, here, a fashion salon); a high body count; and, most importantly, brutal murders filmed with bravura (often sexualized) visual style. Bava's approach would be widely imitated, especially after the breakthrough international success of director Dario Argento's *The Bird with the Crystal Plumage* (1970). In the early 1970s the gialli were nearly as plentiful as Italy's earlier torrents of peplum sword-and-sandal adventures and Spaghetti Westerns. Bava made a few more giallo thrillers himself, including *Bay of Blood* (aka *Twitch of the Death Nerve*, 1971/72), which served as a pivotal influence on *Friday the 13th* (1980). *Friday*, in turn, precipitated the rise of the slasher sub-genre—slasher films being, essentially, dumbed-down, Americanized gialli lacking the artistic stylization of their progenitors. Given this extensive family tree, *Blood and Black Lace* stands as one of the most important horror pictures of the decade. Bava's career extended well into the 1970s but as the Sixties drew to a close his star began to fade, at least in terms of commercial success. Two of the director's best pictures never saw release in his lifetime. *Lisa and the Devil* (1972) enjoyed successful screenings at European film festivals yet couldn't find a theatrical distributor. Finally, a butchered version of the film (with new, non–Bava footage inserted) was issued in 1976 as *House of Exorcism*. Bava's nail-biting neo-noir thriller *Rabid Dogs*, shot in 1974, was never completed, kicking around until 1998, when it was finally assembled and exhibited. To the very end, however, Bava's work remained compelling and handsomely crafted.

In authoring the giallo sub-genre, Bava was influenced also by the "krimi" ("crime") thrillers then originating from West Germany's Rialto studio. Like the gialli, these blood-soaked mysteries were devoid of supernatural content, but featured deformed criminal masterminds, knife-wielding lunatics, sinister cabals and other macabre elements that pushed them to the borders of the horror genre. Shot in a rough-hewn but energetic style, and pulsing with jazzy scores provided by such composers as Martin Bottcher and Peter Thomas, these pictures had a unique visual and aural sensibility and shared a common literary origin in the stories of the prolific Edgar Wallace. During his lengthy career, the London-born Richard Horatio Edgar Wallace wrote 175 novels, 24 plays and numerous short stories, mostly gaudy mysteries and pulpy police procedurals. Although most famous today as the co-creator of *King Kong* (1933), more than 160 movies have been drawn from his work, and countless others misleadingly promoted as Wallace adaptations. After his death, his son Bryan Edgar Wallace took over the family business, penning wild and woolly crime novels that were quickly adapted for the screen. Director Alfred Vohrer, a reclusive Stuttgart native who lost an arm in World War II, made 14 krimis for Rialto, including many of the best — such as *The Hunchback of Soho* (1966), *The College Girl Murders*, *The Creature with the Blue Hand* (both 1967) and *The Gorilla of Soho* (1968). Harald Reinl directed only five Rialto krimis but helmed key entries, including *The Fellowship of the Frog* (1959), which launched the cycle. In all, Rialto issued 35 krimis from 1959 to 1972, and rival studios released numerous copycat thrillers, such as Central Cinema's *The Phantom of Soho* (1964/67). Many of these films took circuitous routes to the U.S. Early entries in the series, such as Vohrer's *Dead Eyes of London* (1961/66), finally saw U.S. release in the mid–1960s, but later Rialto krimis, including *Creature with Blue Hand*, wouldn't reach American theaters until the Seventies. Many more were issued directed to television in America or failed to earn any release at all in the States. Nevertheless, these pictures exerted a gravitational pull on the development of the horror genre, especially in Europe. As the krimi cycle began to wind down in the early 1970s, due in part to competition from the more stylishly crafted and sexually charged gialli, Rialto began co-producing with Italian studios. A few hybrid features emerged, with Spanish and Italian filmmakers, including Jesus Franco, Riccardo Freda, Massimo Dallamano and Umberto Lenzi, providing a Latin spin on this uniquely Teutonic subgenre. Although not as popular today as the gialli, the krimis retain a loyal cult fan base.

The Nouvelle Vague had inspired New Cinema movements across Eastern Europe, but as the Cold War escalated, the Soviets began exerting pressure on their vassal states to reign in "subversive" Western influences. Rather than knuckle under to governmental authorities, young filmmakers, such as Czechoslovakia's Milos Forman and Ivan Passer, departed for the West. One such director was Polish auteur Roman Polanski. His debut feature *Knife in the Water* (1962) had earned an Oscar nomination for Best Foreign Film and enthusiastic reviews from critics around the world, yet Polanski's work remained unpopular within the communist film bureau, which Polish moviemakers relied upon for funding. When exploitation producer Gene Gutowski asked the stymied director to travel to England and helm a *Psycho* clone, Polanski leapt at the chance. Rather than the simple Hitchcock rip-off Gutowski envisaged, however, Polanski made *Repulsion*, a deeply disturbing rumination on the corrosive power of loneliness that stands as not merely the finest of the many black-and-white *Psycho* imitators, but as a truly great film in its own right. In its unflinching examination of isolation and urban paranoia, *Repulsion* seems ahead of its time, prefiguring pictures such as Martin Scorsese's harrowing *Taxi Driver* (1976). Thanks to Polanski's masterful handling of its simplistic story — a neurotic, sexually repressed young woman (Catherine Deneuve) suffers a homicidal mental breakdown when her sister and her married boyfriend leave for an Italian vacation —*Repulsion* proved just as suspenseful as *Psycho*, but more naturalistic (Polanski eschews bravura camera moves and flashy set pieces, such as the murders of Marion Crane and Arbogast) and less playful (Polanski replaces Hitchcock's dark humor with a sense of existential despair). The picture clearly signaled the arrival of a major new talent, although Polanski's next couple of films—*Cul de Sac* (1966) and the Hammer-esque horror spoof *The Fearless Vampire Killers* (1967), both also made in England — were projects beneath the director's gifts. In 1968, with his first American picture, Polanski would discover a suitable vehicle and deliver his first masterpiece.

Around this same time, a rival emerged to challenge Hammer Films' commanding position as England's foremost producer of horror films— Amicus Productions, operating out of Shepperton Studios in Surrey. The studio was founded by expatriate New Yorkers Milton Subotsky, who had worked in American TV as a writer and director, and Max Rosenberg, who had distributed foreign films in the U.S. In October 1959 the duo teamed (under the banner "Vulcan Productions") to produce the witchcraft yarn *Horror Hotel* (1960), one of the most atmospheric chillers of the decade. After their next project, the trendy musical comedy *Ring-a-Ding Rhythm* (1962), Rosenberg and Subotsky launched the Amicus brand. The freshly minted studio found its métier with *Dr. Terror's House of Horrors* (1964/65), a chilling anthology of short horror stories featuring Hammer regulars Christopher Lee, Peter Cushing and Michael Gough. (In the picture's most effective episode, the disembodied hand of a dead artist [Gough] takes revenge on a pompous art critic [Lee].) *Dr. Terror's* was the first of seven Amicus horror anthologies, a series that concluded with *The Monster Club* (1980/81). While the quality of these entries varied, not only from film to film but often from segment to segment within each movie, Amicus remains best remembered for these portmanteau pictures, the best of which—including *The House That Dripped Blood* (1970) and *Tales from the Crypt* (1972)—rank among the finest examples of their type. The studio's other, non-anthology chillers were a mixed bag, including both minor gems (like *Horror Hotel* and *The Skull* [1965]) and major disappointments (like *The Deadly Bees* [1967] and *I, Monster* [1971/73]). Amicus also dabbled in science fiction, making two delightful features based on the BBC TV serial *Dr. Who* in the 1960s and a series of Edgar Rice Burroughs adaptations in the Seventies. Despite the ambitions of Rosenberg and Subotsky, however, Amicus never approached Hammer in terms of either quantity or (at least on a consistent basis) quality. The disparity in production values was glaring, with Hammer's glossy, polished gothics far outshining Amicus' scruffy horrors, which were usually set in (cheaper) modern settings. Throughout its history, Amicus struggled with funding, a problem that vexed its sci-fi films in particular. Subotsky and Rosenberg "were never able to raise the proper amount of money for their films," director Freddie Francis told the authors, adding with a laugh, "but they were good guys and I liked the films we made anyway."

Francis helmed most of Amicus' best movies, including *Dr. Terror's* and *The Skull.* He was one of cinema's great cinematographers, an Oscar winner for *Sons and Lovers* (1960) whose directorial career began with the romantic comedy *Two and Two Make Six* (1962). He wanted to continue to make comedies and explore other genres but quickly earned a reputation as an outstanding director of low-budget horror pictures—and soon found himself pigeon-holed. For the rest of his career Francis led something of a double life—as the director of disreputable genre films and the cinematographer of prestigious mainstream movies, winning a second Academy Award for *Glory* in 1989. "The sort of people I've been mixed up with as a cameraman, that sort of circle of my friends, they obviously never see my horror films," Francis told author Paul Jensen in 1975. "I don't even discuss my films with them, we don't talk about it." Francis' technique as a director, influenced by Michael Powell and John Huston (for whom he worked as a camera operator), involved a great deal of on-set improvisation. "I do plan out shots ahead of time, but that's usually just to have something I can deviate from on the set," Francis explained. This nimble approach enabled Francis to overcome numerous obstacles created by his films' tight-fisted budgets. He made six features for Amicus (including the anthologies *Dr. Terror's*, *Torture Garden* [1967/68] and *Tales from the Crypt*) and five for Hammer. His finest directorial efforts include *The Skull* (1965), an eerie yarn about a collector (Peter Cushing) of macabre artifacts whose personality changes when he comes into possession of the skull of the Marquis de Sade; Hammer's *Dracula Has Risen from the Grave* (1968), the most visually sumptuous entry in the studio's long-running Dracula series; and *The Creeping Flesh* (1973), a pseudo-remake of *The Skull* about a well-meaning scientist (Cushing again) who thinks he's made an archeological breakthrough with a rare skeleton, only to discover the bones contain an ancient evil. Together, Francis and Hammer's Terence Fisher directed most of the best horror films made in England in the 1960s.

The middle and later Sixties were also a sort of Golden Age (or perhaps "Pyrite Age" would be the more appropriate term) for trash cinema, as schlock purveyors like Jerry Warren, Ted V. Mikels, Ray Dennis Steckler, Andy Milligan and Al Adamson served up Grade-Z exploitation fare for shock-hungry grindhouse customers. Although their films were never distributed through the MPPDA, the collapse of the Production Code seemed to embolden these filmmakers, who specialized in salacious, blood-splattered, ultra-low-budget features. Producer-director Warren was the first to enter the fray with *The Incredible Petrified World* and *Teenage Zombies* in 1959, wretched productions that nevertheless earned wide distribution and turned tidy profits. As the 1960s wore on, Warren directed fewer films, finding it easier and cheaper to simply purchase foreign movies, including Mexican cheapies like *Face of the Screaming Werewolf* and *Attack of the Mayan Mummy* (both 1964), which he dubbed into English, usually adding newly shot footage to further Americanize the product. Steckler, a former protégé of producer-director Arch Hall, Sr. (maker of the immortal caveman epic *Eegah!* [1962]), released a handful of low-rent horror and juvenile delinquency flicks before sinking into softcore, and later hardcore, pornography. Milligan *began* with softcore sex films, often with horror undertones— pictures like the now-lost *Naked Witch* (1967) and *The Ghastly Ones* (1968). Mikels and Adamson began their careers in the late Sixties— when Mikels created *The Astro-Zombies* (1968) and Adamson made *Blood of Dracula's Castle* (1969)— but left a greater impression on the 1970s, with notorious productions such as Adamson's *Horror of the Blood Monsters* (1970) and *Dracula vs. Frankenstein* (1971), and Mikels' *The Corpse Grinders* (1971). Both men's personal lives (and deaths) were more entertaining than their movies. Mikels, an eccentric Croatian-American bodybuilding enthusiast, built a castle-shaped home in Glendale, California, complete with secret passageways and live-in strippers. Adamson, who co-founded Independent-International Pictures with producer Sam Sherman, was remodeling his bathroom when he was murdered by his contractor in 1995, his body hidden beneath a newly installed whirlpool bath.

Most of these super-cheap, semi-pro shockers were abysmal, but a few display a kind of feverish creativity that makes them curiously endearing. Steckler's *The Incredibly Strange Creatures Who Stopped Living and Became Mixed-Up Zombies?!!?* (1964), for instance, set in a seedy burlesque club and a fleabag carnival sideshow, features not only an evil fortune teller and rampaging zombies but standup comedy, go-go music, a strip-tease and ballroom dancing interludes. Steckler seems bent on making sure there's something entertaining happening onscreen every second of the film's 82 minutes— even if any given scene has nothing to do with the preceding one, or with anything else.

Steckler and the other young schlock meisters weren't the only ones churning out grindhouse filler, however. Veteran William "One-Shot" Beaudine gave these upstarts a run for their money with such notorious productions as *Jesse James Meets Frankenstein's Daughter* and *Billy the Kid vs. Dracula* (both 1966), a loopy but strangely appealing bargain basement horror-Western double feature. These outrageous, genre-bending films may leave viewers shaking their heads like a cowpoke trying to clear his rattled brain after a barroom brawl, but they remain as irresistibly fascinating as a steam-engine train wreck. In one of its title roles (care to guess which?), *Billy the Kid vs. Dracula* starred John Carradine, who appeared in several of these awful, no-budget chillers and was a particular favorite of Adamson. Once, in 1940s when he ranked among the most respected actors in Hollywood, Carradine had accepted Poverty Row horror parts to fund his ambitious theatrical productions. Now, in the 1960s thanks to his boundless appetite for wine, women and whatever, Carradine was reduced to accepting such roles simply to pay the bills. Although his reputation would later be rehabilitated — especially once his sons, David, Keith and Robert, followed in their father's footsteps to movie stardom — John Carradine's film career never recovered. From the Sixties onward he was a giant talent laboring in Lilluputian pictures.

1968–1969

As the 1960s drew to a close, the U.S. moved closer to self-destruction than at any time since the 1860s. The nation seemed ready to tear itself apart in 1968, rocked by a grinding war, tragic assassinations, race riots, student protests and other spasms of violence. On January 31 North Vietnamese guerrillas launched a frontal assault that caught U.S. forces flat-footed, killing more than 100,000 American, South Vietnamese and allied forces. (For the Americans, 1968 was the bloodiest year of the war, with approximately 11,000 killed and another 45,000 wounded.) While the Tet Offensive failed to topple the South Vietnamese government as the Vietcong had hoped, the high number of casualties (and gory news footage shown on U.S. television) damaged public support for the war. Nevertheless, President Johnson stayed the course, raising troop levels to 587,000 by the end of the year. On April 4 escaped convict and avowed racist James Earl Ray shot and killed civil rights icon Martin Luther King, Jr., in Memphis, Tennessee, triggering riots in Baltimore, Louisville, Kansas City, Chicago and Washington, D.C. Just two months later, in Los Angeles, presidential candidate Robert F. Kennedy (brother of the slain John F. Kennedy) was murdered by Sirhan Sirhan, a Palestinian immigrant and radical anti–Zionist. (Kennedy was killed on June 5, a year to the day after the start of the Six Day War.) In August thousands of anti-war protestors descended on the Democratic National Convention in Chicago. On August 28 violence broke out when a protestor at a demonstration in Grant Park lowered a U.S. flag. Police attacked the young man with billy clubs, and the protestors responded by pelting the police with rocks, bricks and bags of urine. The melee spilled out of the park and into the streets surrounding the convention, where it was filmed and broadcast on network TV. With the Democrats in disarray, Republican Richard Nixon, who promised "law and order," narrowly defeated Democratic nominee Hubert Humphrey and segregationist third party candidate George Wallace for the presidency.

The following year brought reasons to hope and to despair. On July 20 astronauts Neil Armstrong and Buzz Aldrin set foot on the moon, completing one of the greatest achievements in human history. The ARPANET, precursor to the internet, was created, opening the door to new scientific and cultural innovations undreamed of at the time. The Sixties counterculture enjoyed its finest hours August 15 through 18 when upwards of half a million young people gathered for "three days of peace and music" at the Woodstock Music and Art Fair in White Lake, New York. This utopian moment proved short-lived, however, when members of the Hells Angels motorcycle gang murdered a concertgoer at a similar music festival in Altamont, California, in December. Also in December, cult leader Charles Manson and his followers were arrested for a series of gruesome killings and mutilations, including the murder of actress Sharon Tate, the pregnant wife of director Roman Polanski. Beginning in March and continuing throughout the balance of 1969, the American public learned the details of an atrocity that occurred the year before, on March 16, 1968, when U.S. troops murdered nearly 500 Vietnamese civilians in the My Lai region. For many people, this was the final straw; public sentiment turned decisively against the war in Vietnam.

At the movies, the MPPDA's new film rating system went into effect on November 1, 1968, with four ratings: G, M, R and X (the M rating was renamed GP in 1970 and PG in 1972). Yet controversy over film content continued when Swedish director Vilgot Sjoman's sexually explicit drama *I Am Curious (Yellow)* was declared obscene by authorities in Massachusetts, a ruling later overturned by the U.S. Supreme Court. The nascent New Hollywood movement began to gather momentum. *Easy Rider* (1969), a scruffy road picture about a pair of amiable, drug-dealing, hippie bikers (Peter Fonda and actor-director Dennis Hopper), became a surprising box office hit. The picture was innovative not only for its subject matter but for its style, which employed flash forwards, Nouvelle Vague–type editing and a pulsing rock music soundtrack. John Schlesinger's *Midnight Cowboy* (1969), an even more unlikely buddy film about a naïve Texan (Jon Voight) who comes to New York with aspirations of becoming a gigolo and is taken in by a sickly petty thief (Dustin Hoffman), earned an X rating for its sexual content yet won the Oscar for Best Picture. Meanwhile,

Sam Peckinpah's *The Wild Bunch* (1969), with its slow-motion shoot-outs, brought a new brand of stylized violence to the screen; while Sergio Leone's *Once Upon a Time in the West* (1968/69) introduced new lyricism to the Western genre.

A year earlier there had been fewer signs of progress. Nineteen sixty-eight was a dismal year for Hollywood movies, as evidenced by a lackluster Oscar champion (*Oliver!*). The year's best films came from overseas (Ingmar Bergman's disturbing *Shame*, Luis Bunuel's saucy *Belle du Jour* and Jean-Luc Godard's unclassifiable *Week End*); from young auteurs like Mel Brooks (*The Producers*), Paul Mazursky (*Bob & Carol & Ted & Alice*) and John Cassavetes (*Faces*) working outside or on the margins of Hollywood; or from "unimportant" genres like crime drama (Peter Yates' high-octane *Bullitt*), animation (the DayGlo Beatles fantasia *Yellow Submarine*) and, of course, horror. Even as mainstream cinema bottomed out, horror and science fiction cinema reached a new peak.

Of the many great horror and sci-fi films released in 1968, however, none were more significant than director George Romero's *Night of the Living Dead*, which remains relevant, influential and utterly terrifying, even while it serves as a celluloid time capsule, vividly reflecting the tensions and anxieties of its moment. It's one of the great directorial debuts in horror cinema history, the best low-budget monster movie of all time (indeed, one of the finest chillers ever made at any cost), and arguably the most culturally significant horror film since *Dracula* (1931). *Night*'s apocalyptic scenario—in which the unburied dead suddenly reanimate and begin attacking and feeding on the living—remains one of the most imitated in cinema history. And yet the scariest part of *Night* isn't its monsters; it's the way people treat one another. Unable to overcome selfishness, fear and prejudice, humankind—represented by middle-aged, white Harry (Karl Hardman) and young, black Ben (Duane Jones)—chooses self-destruction rather than cooperation. With the zombie apocalypse standing in for the Vietnam war, *Night of the Living Dead* almost inadvertently begins to play like a fun house mirror reflection of the boiling political, racial and generational tensions that threatened to rip America apart in 1968.

Night seems to encapsulate all the innovations that swept through the horror genre during the Sixties. The screenplay, by Romero and John Russo, is a fascinating combination of the traditional and the revolutionary. The eerie, shadow-draped farmhouse creates an Old School gothic backdrop for the story, which concludes with a bitterly ironic twist that E.C. Comics publisher William Gaines would have loved. Yet in most respects, *Night of the Living Dead* rejects genre conventions. The picture offers no romantic subplots, no all-knowing scientists or heroic military leaders, and no happy ending. In lieu of comedy relief and other distractions, *Night* offers horror and more horror, with ever-escalating dramatic tension punctuated by moments of (then) shocking violence and gore. But *Night of the Living Dead* didn't succeed on shock value alone. It's an extraordinarily well-crafted picture. Although made inexpensively (the total budget ran to $114,000), *Night* never looks cheap, mostly due to Romero's polished technique. The director also elicited convincing performances from key cast members, especially Jones, whose haunting, unaffected, multifaceted performance galvanizes the entire production.

Romero returned to the zombie oeuvre for a series' worth of sequels, beginning with the masterful *Dawn of the Dead* (1978)—which proved even more violent and gory than its predecessor and was widely copied, especially by European filmmakers—and continuing with diminishing artistry through *Day of the Dead* (1985), *Land of the Dead* (2005), *Diary of the Dead* (2007) and *Survival of the Dead* (2010). Consistently, Romero has used the apocalyptic zombie setting as a mechanism for satire and social commentary. ("If there's something I'd like to criticize," Romero told *Time* magazine in 2010, "I can bring the zombies out.") Eventually, however, Romero's living dead yarns were eclipsed by those of his disciples. Danny Boyle's *28 Days Later* (2002), Edgar Wright's comedic *Shaun of the Dead* (2004) and even Zack Snyder's *Dawn of the Dead* remake (2004), for instance, all overshadowed Romero's *Diary*, which did not receive a major theatrical release in the U.S. Although the director made other excellent chillers, including *The Crazies* (1973), *Martin* (1977) and *Creepshow* (1982), Romero's name will forever remain synonymous with zombie movies—an occupational hazard of making one of the greatest horror films of all time.

With *Rosemary's Baby*, Roman Polanski delivered *another* of the greatest horror films of all time. Filmmaker William Castle purchased the rights to Ira Levin's not-yet-published novel *Rosemary's Baby*—about an Everywoman housewife caught up in a web of paranoid intrigue involving her husband, her unborn child and a Satanic cult—and brought it to Paramount Pictures. Robert Evans, the studio's head of production, recognizing that the project was potentially "very important," agreed to make the film and retain Castle (still best known for gimmicky thrillers such as *House on Haunted Hill* and *The Tingler*, both 1959) as producer. But Evans lured Polanski (a Polish director then working in England) to Hollywood to helm the project. Like *Night of the Living Dead*, *Rosemary's Baby* tapped into the zeitgeist. The frustration and loneliness experienced by Rosemary (played by Mia Farrow) are an amplified expression of the same dissatisfaction described by authors like Betty Friedan (*The Feminist Mystique*), turned up to 11. The story also takes expectant mothers' natural fears and carries them to their logical endpoint: Rosemary endures a torturous pregnancy and gives birth to a hideously deformed, evil child—and in the process her marriage collapses. *Rosemary's Baby* was one of the first films (along with Polanski's earlier *Repulsion*) to address urban paranoia, suggesting that even your kindly elderly neighbors could literally be in league with the Devil. What's more, *Rosemary's Baby* popularized Satan as a horror movie villain. Movie audiences in previous decades may not have accepted this, but within the increasingly secularized culture of the late 1960s (*Time*'s famous *Is God Dead?* cover appears in the film), making the devil himself an essential character in the drama became fair game. Simultaneously, however, enough residual faith (or at least distant memories of Sunday school) lingered in the popular imagination for Lucifer to carry a great deal more emotional power than worn-out monsters such as vampires or werewolves. Dozens of movies followed *Rosemary's Baby* down this path, most notably *The Exorcist* (1973) and *The Omen* (1976). *Rosemary's Baby*'s downbeat ending, with evil triumphant, which would not have been possible during the era of the Production Code, soon became a cliché as well.

A year later Polanski's personal life turned as horrifying as his movies. On August 9, 1969, while Polanski was in London discussing a new project (the ill-fated *Day of the Dolphin* [1973], later turned over to Mike Nichols), Charles Manson and his followers broke into Polanski's home and murdered and mutilated the director's pregnant wife, Sharon Tate, and four family friends. Although clearly shaken by the crimes, Polanski continued to work, making a macabre version of *Macbeth* in 1971, the neo-noir masterpiece *Chinatown* in 1974 and his final horror film, *The Tenant*, in 1976. Then, in 1977, Polanski was arrested and charged with statutory rape after he allegedly had sexual contact with a 13-year-old girl at the home of actor Jack Nicholson (who was away at the time). Polanski agreed to a plea bargain, but when the judge appeared ready to renege on the sentencing agreement, Polanski fled to France, where he lived as a fugitive from justice until he was arrested again in 2009 and ordered to return to the U.S. for sentencing. While in France, Polanski made some extraordinary films, including the holocaust drama *The Pianist* (2002), which earned him an Oscar as Best Director.

Saturation coverage of Manson's crimes capped a decade dominated by news stories about war, riots, assassinations and other terrors. Not surprisingly, movies had grown more violent during the same era—a topic tackled by two other 1968 classics, Peter Bogdanovich's *Targets* and Michael Reeves' *The Conqueror Worm*. The Bogdanovich film—which tells two parallel stories, one about a fading horror star (Boris Karloff) and the other about a mentally unstable young man (Tim O'Kelly) who goes on a killing spree—overtly addresses both onscreen and real-world violence. The Karloff character, Byron Orlok, bemoans the passing of a gentler, more naïve era in which fright films were scarier than newspaper headlines. "I'm an anachronism," he laments, and so is his style of horror. Writer-director Bogdanovich drew inspiration for the parallel story from the 1966 sniper killings of Charles J. Whitman, who murdered his wife and mother and then barricaded himself in a tower at the University of Texas, killing 14 and wounding 31 with a high-powered rifle before being shot by police. The O'Kelly character in *Targets* kills his wife and mother and then snipes several victims, first from the top of a refinery tower and then through a hole in the screen of a drive-in theater hosting the premiere of a new Orlok picture. Although Bogdanovich avoids pointed political statements, his matter-of-fact depiction of the ease with which the killer acquires weapons and ammunition clearly is intended to raise questions about America's gun culture. The film's converging storylines also suggest a relationship between audiences' thirst for *reel* violence and the rise of *real* violence. Ironically, a true-life crime — namely, the murder of Robert Kennedy — dashed the film's chances of commercial success. Released in the wake of the assassination, *Targets* sank like a stone at the box office, but was rediscovered during the home video era.

Targets was a film of beginnings and endings. It marked the ascendance of Bogdanovich from Roger Corman's stable of young protégés (previously, working for Corman under the pseudonym Derek Thomas, Bogdanovich had cobbled together *Voyage to the Planet of Prehistoric Women* out of footage from a Soviet space opera and new scenes featuring bikini-clad beach babes). Following *Targets*, Bogdanovich, a former film critic, ranked among the most promising young directors in the business, a filmmaker who brought a classic Hollywood stylistic sensibility to emotionally raw New Hollywood subject matter in *The Last Picture Show* (1971), which earned eight Oscar nominations, including Best Picture and Best Director. The director went on to make the well-received *What's Up, Doc?* (1972) and *Paper Moon* (1973), but as the New Hollywood movement came unglued in the mid–1970s, so did Bogdanovich's career, which never fully recovered from the disappointing *Daisy Miller* (1974) and the disastrous *At Long Last Love* (1975). *Targets* also served as a valedictory address from the horror genre's elder statesman, Boris Karloff. Although not his final film — he would still appear in *The Crimson Cult* (1968/70) and a quartet of bargain basement Mexican chillers — *Targets* gave the star a final great role, something to help remind audiences (and himself) why he had become such an icon. Although it's often written that Karloff "played himself" in this film, that's not entirely true; his portrayal is actually more complex. Orlok is a burned-out, irascible, salty-tongued curmudgeon — nothing like the warm-and-fuzzy off-screen Karloff, even at this stage in his career. But the actor agreed with Orlok's assessment of the horror film genre, and some of the true Karloff shines through in Orlok's prickly yet warm-hearted verbal jousts with his young director, Sammy Michaels (played by Bogdanovich). Karloff, who battled emphysema, arthritis and chronic back pain, and was confined to a wheelchair toward the end of his life, succumbed to pneumonia on February 2, 1969, leaving behind an unparalleled legacy of great performances and beloved characters.

Director Michael Reeves' harrowing *The Conqueror Worm*, known in England as *Witchfinder General*, delivered a subversive indictment of the use of violence for any purpose — whether in capital punishment, for personal revenge or even as popular entertainment. The story, set during the English Civil War, involves a government witch-hunter, Matthew Hopkins (Vincent Price), who offers to spare the life of a denounced warlock in exchange for a night of passion with the man's daughter, Sara (Hilary Dwyer). When the night is over and Hopkins' appetites are sated, however, he executes the accused man anyway. When Sara's husband Richard (Ian Ogilvy), a soldier away at battle, returns and learns all this, he pursues Hopkins across England and exacts brutal vengeance. Hopkins' torturous "examinations," witch burnings and other gruesome activities — all presented in graphic detail — underscore the dangers inherent in empowering the state to take the lives of its citizens. But Reeves' most daring choice is to play bait-and-switch with audience expectations by presenting Richard's savage revenge (crazed with rage, he hacks Hopkins to bits with an exe, as the witchfinder writhes and moans in agony) with the same unflinching realism as Hopkins' killings. This shocking climax makes two points at once: It demonstrates vividly that revenge destroys the soul, because when a victim of violence resorts to violence, the former victim becomes just another perpetrator. Simultaneously, this sickening sequence not only robs viewers of the anticipated vicarious thrill of watching the Good Guy bump off the Bad Guy, it makes them feel guilty about looking forward to it in the first place. All this makes *The Conqueror Worm* a gut-wrenching but undeniably powerful experience.

This grim masterwork cemented Reeves' position as one of the screen's foremost horror specialists, and should have propelled the young British director toward a long and fruitful career, perhaps as the successor to the likes of Terence Fisher and Freddie Francis. Tragically, however, Reeves, just 25 years old, died from an overdose of barbiturates and alcohol on February 11, 1969, less than six months after the American premiere of *The Conqueror Worm*. Beset by pre-production problems on his latest project, *The Oblong Box* (1969, completed by director Gordon Hessler), Reeves had been struggling with depression and insomnia, but the coroner ruled his death an accident. The director left behind a small but impressive legacy that includes the stylish and thought-provoking *The Sorcerers* (1967), featuring Boris Karloff, and an uneven but intermittently clever debut, *The She-Beast* (1966), starring Barbara Steele. His senseless, premature death was one of the greatest wastes in the history of the genre.

Reeves helped wring a career-best performance out of star Vincent Price as Hopkins. The director browbeat Price mercilessly, forcing the star to abandon his trademark mannerisms and play with greater subtlety and intensity. "[Reeves] said, 'I didn't want you and I still don't want you, but I'm stuck with you,'" Price recalled in 1990. "[He] made me so self-conscious I was poker-faced — and, as it turned out, he was right! He wanted it that concentrated, so it would be that much more menacing." Simply put, Price was never scarier than in *The Conqueror Worm*. This towering performance capped a decade full of superb portrayals by Price. The years 1963 and '64 were particularly strong for the actor. During this period, Price appeared in an incredible nine films, including half of director Roger Corman's Edgar Allan Poe adaptations (*The Raven* [1963], *The Haunted Palace* [1963], *The Masque of the Red Death* [1964] and *The Tomb of Ligeia* [1964]). The actor's work during this period is remarkable not only for both its quantity and quality, but for its splendid diversity, which ranged from light comedy in *The Raven*, *The Comedy of Terrors* and *Beach Party* (all 1963), to demonic villainy in *Masque* to fatalistic tragedy in *Diary of a Madman* (1963) and *Ligeia*. The best of this splendid lot, however, remains his debauched Prince Prospero from *Masque of the Red Death*, which ranks alongside Matthew Hopkins as the most memorable characterization in the actor's legendary career. Price would continue delighting movie audiences for more than 20 years after *The Conqueror Worm*, although his output slowed considerably in the late 1970s due to age, health problems and changing audience tastes. Traditional, gothic horror — Price's specialty — nearly vanished from movie screens during the 1980s. Nevertheless, Price achieved a new level of pop stardom when singer Michael Jackson engaged him to provide a spoken word interlude for the horror-themed title track of *Thriller*, which became the biggest-selling album of all time. Nine years later, on October 25, 1993, Price, a heavy smoker, died of lung cancer.

Another aging horror star, Lon Chaney, Jr.,, contributed one of his best performances to director Jack Hill's oddball black comedy *Spider Baby or, The Maddest Story Ever Told* (also released in 1968). Chaney plays Bruno, the loving, devoted caretaker of the Merrye family — two teenage sisters, an older brother and some aunts and uncles kept locked away in the basement, all of whom suffer from a rare genetic disorder that causes the Merryes to regress to uncivilized behavior and cannibalism. Filmed on an anemic budget in 1964 under the title

Cannibal Orgy, it took four years this bizarre but brilliant picture, which plays like an episode of *Father Knows Best* directed by Tod Browning, to find a distributor. Chaney gave his all to the production, delivering a warm, sympathetic portrayal that ranks among the richest of his career. The film's final scenes, in which Bruno is pushed to desperate measures to protect the world from the Merrye children (and vice-versa) is heartbreaking. Chaney even sings the picture's theme song! By turns hilarious, unnerving and curiously affecting, *Spider Baby* is a complete original. Despite his outstanding work in this film, Chaney's career, hampered by throat problems, ground nearly to a halt in the late 1960s. He would make just five more movie appearances, mostly cameos, after *Spider Baby*. Al Adamson's dreadful *Dracula vs. Frankenstein* (1971) proved to be his swan song. Chaney died of heart failure in 1973 and donated his body for medical research.

No discussion of late Sixties film history can be complete without at least a brief mention of two landmark science fiction movies released in 1968—*Planet of the Apes* and *2001: A Space Odyssey*. Revered by legions of fans and critics, *Planet of the Apes* lives up to its lofty reputation; it's one of the most durable genre films of the 1960s and remains fascinating even if you've seen it a dozen times (or more). Screenwriters Michael Wilson and Rod Serling retained the basic premise of Pierre Boulle's novel (astronaut George Taylor crash-lands on an unidentified planet where humans live like animals, lorded over by intelligent gorillas, chimpanzees and orangutans) but jettisoned nearly everything else. Instead, they recast the story as a thinly veiled commentary on contemporary politics, with various species of ape standing in for the pro- and anti-war points of view. These parallels became even clearer in the first sequel, *Beneath the Planet of the Apes* (1970), in which a group of young chimpanzees stage a sit-in! In all, *Planet of the Apes* spawned four sequels, a prime-time television show, a Saturday morning cartoon and an unfortunate remake. The original movie's opening half-hour, in which astronaut Taylor (Charlton Heston) and his companions fight for survival in a strange, desolate world, remains one of the finest pure sci-fi sequences ever filmed. Director Franklin J. Schaffner frequently employed unorthodox (ultra-high, ultra-low or tilted) camera angles to heighten the tension. But the real keys to the film's success were John Chambers' groundbreaking ape makeup designs, Jerry Goldsmith's eerie, dissonant score, and Charlton Heston's commanding performance as Taylor.

Director Stanley Kubrick's *2001: A Space Odyssey* stands among the defining motion pictures of the 1960s, and not just because of its acid trip finale. Epic in length and scope, yet reflectively paced, intellectually challenging and philosophically brooding, *2001* couldn't have been made in any prior era and probably wouldn't be green-lighted today. Its revolutionary special effects set a new standard for sci-fi cinema, and Kubrick's brilliant melding of visuals and music (for instance, pairing Strauss' stately "Blue Danube" waltz with images of a slowly rotating space station) remains unsurpassed. But it's neither the film's technical innovations nor Kubrick's directorial genius that make it so emblematic of its era. Rather, it's the picture's underlying theme. By comparing the behavior of ape men during the film's prehistoric "dawn of man" sequence with that of scientists and astronauts in its futuristic scenes (in both cases, people eat, care for their children, and attend to other basic tasks), *2001* suggests that, although technology has advanced spectacularly from the days of bone clubs to the era of the HAL-9000 super-computer, man himself hasn't changed much. Technology can carry humankind only so far (even a creation as "perfect" as HAL can break down, since he must be programmed by people); to evolve as a species, to discover our "star child" within, we must look beyond technology to contact with a higher power or toward expanded consciousness, possibly both. The picture's famously enigmatic resolution doesn't spell out everything clearly, but the general idea flows directly from the American counter-culture of the era. While it led to only one belated and inferior sequel by director Peter Hyams, *2010* (1984), *2001* nevertheless overshadowed every science fiction film that followed it until 1977, when director George Lucas reinvented the genre with *Star Wars*.

A fabulous decade of horror cinema wound down uneventfully in 1969, as if the genre had burned itself out in a supernova of creativity the preceding year. In truth, however, even though no watershed horror films reached U.S. theaters that year, the genre remained vital. After harvesting a bumper crop in 1968 the field lay fallow for a season, but planting began anew the following year. While not as fertile as the preceding decade, the 1970s would bear some remarkable fruit.

After the End

History never breaks neatly into ten-year chunks, and many of the political and cultural themes of the 1960s spilled over into the early Seventies, their storylines unresolved for years, even decades.

War protests turned deadly at Ohio's Kent State University on May 4, 1970, when national guardsmen opened fire on unarmed student demonstrators, killing four and wounding nine (one of whom was permanently paralyzed). Over the next few years, in the face of growing anti-war sentiment, President Nixon gradually stepped down troop levels in Vietnam. A cease-fire agreement between the U.S. and North Vietnam was signed in Paris on January 27, 1973, and on March 29 the last American combat troops left the country. By then, however, Nixon's presidency was crumbling. The politician who had run on a law-and-order platform in 1968 became embroiled in a scandal related to a break-in at the Democratic National Headquarters at the Watergate Hotel in Washington, D.C., during Nixon's 1972 re-election campaign. An FBI investigation revealed that the five Watergate burglars had received funds from the Committee to Re-Elect the President, and it was discovered that Nixon had surreptitiously taped conversations about covering up the crime. Facing near-certain impeachment, Nixon resigned the presidency on August 4, 1974. Even though the war and the Watergate scandal were finished by the mid–1970s, these divisive events continued to shape American politics for a generation. Vietnam-era stereotypes became calcified, with Democrats ridiculed by Republicans as dope-smoking, morally bankrupt peaceniks, and Republicans lambasted by Democrats as greedy, racist warmongerers. Historical facts contradicted the clichés (the "dovish" Democrats, for instance, led the U.S. during all the major conflicts of the Twentieth Century, including both World Wars, the Korean and Vietnamese conflicts, and the hottest days of the Cold War). Yet the persistence of these stereotypes polarized public perception and made it increasingly difficult for leaders of the two major parties to cooperate for the common good.

The Cold War continued for another 20 years but never again approached the near-apocalyptic intensity of the Cuban Missile Crisis. Relations between the U.S. and the U.S.S.R. began to thaw in the mid–1980s under the administrations of reform-minded Soviet leader Mikhail Gorbachev and American president Ronald Reagan. With the Soviets buckling under financial pressure from a decades-long arms race, the two nations forged a series of agreements that reduced their stockpiles of nuclear weapons and moved toward "normalized" relations. As the Soviets relinquished control, Democratic reforms swept through Soviet vassal states in Eastern Europe. Finally, on December 31, 1991, the financially bankrupt Soviet Union officially dissolved, becoming 14 separate nations.

As the Sixties ended, so did the Beatles. The decade's most popular musical group, and one of its most dominant cultural forces, disintegrated amid a collection of professional and interpersonal disagreements. Paul McCartney filed papers to dissolve the band's business partnership on December 31, 1970. By then, two other rock and roll icons had also vanished. The drug-related deaths of guitarist Jimi Hendrix in September 1970 and singer Janis Joplin less than a month later, followed by the demise of Doors vocalist Jim Morrison in July 1971, wrote a grim coda to the era in popular music. The Seventies would witness the rise of more extreme musical genres like heavy metal, disco and punk. Meanwhile, the edgy, topical style of the New Hollywood films began seeping into network TV with shows like the controversial situation comedies *All in the Family*, which debuted in the fall of 1971 and became the top-rated program for the next five seasons, and *M*A*S*H*, based on Robert Altman's satirical 1970 film of the same title, which premiered in the fall of 1972.

Hollywood received a crucial economic boost from generous new tax laws passed in 1971, which allowed the studios to claim tax credits on production costs for films made in the U.S., including projects dating back to the 1960s. The new regulations also created a tax shelter for private investors in American film productions, making such investments tax deductible. These laws were repealed in the early 1980s, but in the meantime, the major studios recouped hundreds of millions of dollars, while the tax shelter helped fund movies like Milos Forman's *One Flew Over the Cuckoo's Nest* (1975) and Martin Scorsese's *Taxi Driver* (1976). The early 1970s were the heyday of the New Hollywood, as up-and-coming filmmakers such as Scorsese, Francis Ford Coppola, George Lucas, Hal Ashby, Robert Altman, William Friedkin, John Boorman and Bob Rafelson released a raft of now-classic pictures including *M*A*S*H*, *Five Easy Pieces* (both 1970), *McCabe & Mrs. Miller*, *Harold and Maude*, *The French Connection* (all 1971), *The Godfather*, *Deliverance* (both 1972), *American Graffiti* and *Mean Streets* (both 1973). Few (if any) of these films would have been produced during any other period in cinema history. But the New Hollywood wave crested in the mid–1970s. The movement's upstart auteurs demanded greater creative control than Hollywood executives were comfortable ceding, and when these wunderkind directors began to falter — like Altman with *Buffalo Bill and the Indians* (1976), Scorsese with *New York, New York*, and Friedkin with *Sorcerer* (both 1977)—the studios began to reassert their authority. In 1974 the spectacular success of Steven Spielberg's *Jaws*, which raked in a record-setting $260 million in the U.S. alone against a $12 million production cost, demonstrated the profit potential of a major summer hit that inspired repeat viewings. But the landscape changed forever in 1977 when four colossal hits—George Lucas' *Star Wars*, Spielberg's *Close Encounters of the Third Kind*, Hal Needham's *Smokey and the Bandit* and John Badham's *Saturday Night Fever*—permanently altered Hollywood's business model. These four blockbusters leveraged exploitable phenomena (fanning the flames of popular crazes for UFO conspiracy theories, citizen's band radios and disco) to open new streams of ancillary revenue through targeted merchandising. *Star Wars* was a cultural phenomenon unto itself, grossing a staggering $461 in the U.S., but even more from the sale of tie-ins such as t-shirts, posters, toys and soundtrack albums. Instantly, Hollywood lost interest in small, personal movies by talented but difficult filmmakers. Like a new California Gold Rush, the studios raced to find the next special effects-laden cultural bonanza. The New Hollywood era was over, and the Age of the Blockbuster had arrived.

Fortunately, the horror genre had already proven that it could be part of the blockbuster equation. Friedkin's *The Exorcist* had earned a whopping $232 million in 1973, setting a box office record soon shattered by *Jaws*, a picture which also can be placed within the boundaries of the horror genre. Both films owed debts to earlier chillers—*The Exorcist* to *Rosemary's Baby* (1968), *Jaws* to *The Birds* (1963)—and both were widely imitated during the remainder of the decade and beyond. Both *The Exorcist*, featuring a devil-possessed child spewing profanity and projectile vomit, and *Jaws*, with its brutal shark attacks, were part of a wider trend toward more graphic content in horror movies. ("Director William Friedkin has revolutionized the movie business by going further than anyone had dared," Steven Farber wrote in a 1973 *New York Times* think piece devoted to *The Exorcist*.) Other early Seventies chillers like Wes Craven's *Last House on the Left* (1972) and Tobe Hooper's *The Texas Chainsaw Massacre* (1974) were predicated on gruesome violence. Graphic bloodletting, usually combined with nudity, were also signature elements of the European horror films that reached America in the 1970s. The international breakthrough of Dario Argento's *Bird with the Crystal Plumage* (1970), for instance, popularized the giallo subgenre with viewers around the world.

With the rising popularity of gritty, modern-era horror shows, Euro shockers, and special effects-driven sci-fi spectaculars, the horror factories of the 1950s and Sixties fell on hard times. Hammer Films, which had built its reputation on glossy gothics that were now out of fashion, suffered a series of damaging flops. The studio spicing up its familiar gothics with topless starlets in pictures such as *The Vampire Lovers* (1970), *Lust for a Vampire* (1971) and *Countess Dracula* (1971/72), with little box office impact. Hammer tried moving its popular Dracula franchise into present day, with disastrous results (*Dracula A.D. 1972* [1972], *Count Dracula and his Vampire Brides* [1973]), then attempted to combine vampires with kung-fu in *The Seven Brothers Meet Draula* (1974), a debacle co-produced with Hong Kong's Shaw Brothers. When a remake of Hitchcock's *The Lady Vanishes*, starring Americans Elliott Gould and Cybill Shepherd, tanked in 1979, the studio ceased feature film production entirely. Rival Amicus Productions scored minor hits with a series of Edgar Rice Burroughs adaptations (*The Land That Time Forgot* [1974], *At the Earth's Core* [1976] and *The People That Time Forgot* [1977]). But Subotsky and Rosenberg realized they could not compete in the big-budget, post–*Star Wars* marketplace with such films and disbanded the company after one more feature, *The Monster Club* (1980/81), a poorly received parody of its trademark horror anthologies. American International, which was a glorified distribution company rather than a full-fledged studio like Hammer or Amicus, proved more nimble, picking up hit shockers like *Count Yorga, Vampire* (1970) and *The Abominable Dr. Phibes* (1971) early in the decade, and *Mad Max* and *The Amityville Horror* (both 1979) later on, all the while dabbling in numerous other genres such as blaxploitation, sexploitation and biker films. Nevertheless, AIP bowed to financial reality and exited the theatrical market in 1980, although it continued to sell movies to TV and on home video.

With the demise of Hammer and Amicus, the careers of Terence Fisher and Freddie Francis also wound down. Fisher made just one film in the 1970s, *Frankenstein and the Monster from Hell* (1974), before passing away in 1980. Francis continued to work steadily as a cinematographer in the mid–1970s and beyond, but only intermittently as a director (usually in television). He died in 2007. Mario Bava's career also ground to a halt. He released a pair of films in 1972, the sex farce *Four Times That Night* and the supernatural thriller *Baron Blood*, but only completed one more film (*Shock* [1977]) before his death in 1980. Only the much younger George Romero and Jesus Franco remained prolific.

However, a new generation of horror film specialist arose, including Wes Craven, who followed *Last House* with the nerve-jangling *The Hills Have Eyes* in 1977 and later launched the *Nightmare on Elm Street* and *Scream* franchises; Dario Argento, who after *Bird* made several more thrilling gialli, including *Deep Red* (1975), as well as the unnerving witchcraft yarn *Suspiria* (1977) and other gems; prolific gore purveyor Lucio Fulci, whose work included stylish gialli (such as *Lizard in a Woman's Skin* [1971]) and gruesome zombie pictures (including *Zombie* [1979] and *City of the Living Dead* [1972]); and David Cronenberg, who specialized in tales of bodily infection, insanity and medical malfeasance with pictures such as *Shivers* (1975), *Rabid* (1977) and *The Brood* (1979), and who would go on to make latter-day classics like *Videodrome* (1983) and *The Fly* (1986). But the new filmmaker who left the most significant impression on the genre during the 1970s and Eighties was John Carpenter, whose *Halloween* (1978) represented the next major turning point for the screen terror, ushering in the slasher subgenre, an Americanization of the giallo form. Carpenter, who had already made a fascinating seriocomic sci-fi picture, *Dark Star* (1974), would go on to make several outstanding horror and science fiction films, including movies like *The Thing* (1982) that effortlessly blended elements from both genres.

The Seventies produced many serious-minded horror shows— including Robert Mulligan's *The Other* (1972), Robin Hardy's *The Wicker Man* (1973), Bob Clark's *Deathdream* (1974), and Romero's *Dawn of the Dead* (1978)— mounted with obvious artistic aspirations and intended to address topical concerns of the era. But, paradoxically, the era also produced a high number of horror parodies, including *Young Frankenstein* (1974), *The Rocky*

Horror Picture Show (1975) and *Attack of the Killer Tomatoes* (1979). The decade closed with Ridley Scott's forward-looking *Alien* (1979), a seamless hybrid of horror and science fiction that pointed the way toward later genre-bending blockbusters like the *Terminator*, *Predator*, *Species* and *Matrix* series, as well the several *Alien* sequels—action films with settings and concepts derived from the horror and sci-fi genres. While other long-running, bankable genres (most notably the Western and musical) collapsed, unable to compete with the visual effects-laden sci-fi action blockbusters that came to dominate the American movie marketplace in the Eighties and beyond, horror films evolved and survived. They continue to rank among the most popular box office attractions. Along with the rest of the industry, horror cinema became dominated by sequels in the 1980s and Nineties, and by remakes (and sequels to remakes) after the turn of the millennium. Nevertheless, inventive, skillfully made chillers continued to be made—even if many of these pictures found only a cult audience.

As long as people have been making movies they have made horror movies; as long as movies are made, horror movies will be made. From the very beginning (or at least as far back as Georges Melies' *The House of the Devil* in 1898) filmmakers have been drawn to horror tales. Such films stem from the same primal urge that inspired prehistoric storytellers who spun tales of wonder and terror around the fire pit—and who reveled in making their audience shriek with fear. Eventually, perhaps, history will present another decade as volatile and anxiety-filled as the 1960s. If so, we can only hope that the world survives to appreciate the great horror stories that will arise from it.

2

The Movies

This section includes critical analysis and, where available, production information for every horror film (as well as fantasy and science fiction films with prominent horror elements) released theatrically in the U.S. during the 1960s.

Films commonly categorized as "pure" sci-fi or fantasy (lacking significant horror elements), as well as pictures produced during the 1960s that did not receive a U.S. theatrical release until the 1970s or later, or which were issued directly to television in the U.S., are covered in the following section ("More Movies").

For the sake of consistency, all films are referred to by the title used during their initial U.S. theatrical release. Cross-references are provided for films with alternate English language titles. Please note that following the title of each entry, the following information appears in parenthesis: The year of the film's release (when a film was released outside America first, the year of its international release is followed after a slash by the year of its U.S. release), the production company (followed by the U.S. distributor, if the film was produced internationally) and the country of origin (if not produced in the U.S.). All films are in color unless indicated as "b&w." After this parenthetical data, a list of key crew and cast members is provided, followed by the movie's original advertising tagline, when available.

Amazing Mr. H see ***Madmen of Mandoras***

The Angry Red Planet (1960; AIP) Director: Ib Melchior; Producer: Sid Pink and Norman Maurer; Screenplay: Ib Melchior and Sid Pink; Cinematographer: Stanley Cortez. Cast: Gerald Mohr, Nora Hayden, Les Tremayne, Jack Kruschen.

Spectacular adventure beyond time and space — tagline

The Angry Red Planet was one of the first genre films of the decade, reaching screens in February, 1960. Yet it seems even older, a throwback to the time of *Destination Moon* and, especially, *Rocketship X-M* (both released in 1950). It's clunky, slow-footed and cliché-riddled, populated by wafer-thin characters and plotted by rote. Despite these glaring flaws, however, the picture remains a favorite of many sci-fi and horror fans because it also features a handful of the most wildly imaginative and unforgettable monsters in movie history.

Angry Red Planet resembles *Rocketship X-M* in several key respects: It's a modestly budgeted, small-cast production about a spaceship that lands on Mars and finds it populated by hostile creatures. In both films the ship carries a crew of four, with romance blossoming between the mission commander and a young female scientist, and in both tension arises regarding available fuel for the return trip. *Angry Red Planet* masks some of those similarities with a flashback structure and some additional melodrama about whether or not the commander will survive an alien infection.

Col. Tom Bannion (Gerald Mohr) is the ship's requisite granite-jawed leader and Dr. Iris Ryan (Nora Hayden) its curvaceous scientist (who cheerfully prepares dinner for the men and says things like, "Then it isn't just me, being a woman?" when she's frightened). Also on board are the brilliant but prickly Prof. Theodore Gettell (Les Tremayne) and, for comedy relief, weapons officer Sam Jacobs (Jack Kruschen), who displays all the wit of a lug wrench. Viewers have to idle through 36 minutes of deadly dull folderol (including not one but two "dramatic" 10-9-8-7-6-5-4-3-2-1 countdowns), but once the crew leaves the ship to explore Mars, the movie finally gets into gear.

This shift is marked not simply by an improved pace and some memorable action sequences, but by the introduction of a gimmick advertised as "Cinemagic," wherein the film abruptly moves from color to overexposed, red-tinted black and white. This simple and inexpensive process lends *Angry Red Planet* a distinctive look. Then the monsters show up and the real fun starts. A giant carnivorous plant tries to digest Irish. Then a towering, bizarre creature with the face of a bat, the body of a rat and the legs of a spider menaces Prof. Gettell. The crew rows across a Martian lake to discover a mysterious, ultramodern city, but are turned back by a huge, blob-like monster later identified as a giant amoeba. Finally, the planet's three-eyed natives appear — all this within about 30 minutes of screen time! Nowhere else in the science fiction films of the 1950s and 60s will viewers encounter anything quite like *Angry Red Planet*'s "rat-bat-spider," giant amoeba or three-eyed Martian creatures. Even its woman-eating plant monster is one of the more impressive examples of its breed. It's as if filmmakers Ib Melchior and Sid Pink threw all their creativity into the story's Martian menaces and had nothing left over for the other parts of the show.

The cast and crew are competent (cinematographer Stanley Cortez earned Oscar nominations for lensing *The Magnificent Ambersons* in 1943 and *Since You Went Away* in 1945, and received a Lifetime Achievement Award from the ASC in 1990; Kruschen was Oscar-nominated in 1961 for his supporting role in Billy Wilder's *The Apart-*

Dr. Iris Ryan (Nora Hayden) and her crewmates meet carnivorous plants and far weirder creatures on Mars in director Ib Melchior's *Angry Red Planet* (1959).

ment) but, other than visual effects supervisor Herman E. Townsley, nobody brings their A-game for this outing. The blame for this can safely be placed at the feet of Melchior, whose previous directorial experience was limited to a 10-minute educational short and some TV episodes. He would helm just one more theatrical feature (*The Time Travelers*, 1964), but found greater success as a writer, penning clever scripts or stories for such films as *Robinson Crusoe on Mars* (1964), *Planet of the Vampires* (1965) and *Death Race 2000* (1975). Under Melchior's uninspiring, amateurish direction, *Angry Red Planet* emerges as a numbingly ordinary film with some extraordinarily exciting moments.

The Astro-Zombies (1969; Geneni Film Distributors) Alternate Title: *Space Vampires* (video). Director/Producer: Ted V. Mikels; Screenplay: Ted V. Mikels, Wayne Rogers; Cinematographer: Robert Maxwell. Cast: Wendell Corey, John Carradine, Tom Pace, Joan Patrick, Tura Satana, Rafael Campos.

SEE BRUTAL MUTANTS MENACE BEAUTIFUL GIRLS—poster

Any movie that opens with a skull-headed killer splattering the blood of an attractive woman on the side of a classic 1960s Mustang can't be all bad. Or can it? "You will die a thousand deaths as you watch *The Astro-Zombies*," promises the film's trailer. If so, this would be the famous "thousand deaths by boredom."

The story, penned by producer-director-editor Ted V. Mikels and Wayne Rogers (yes, *that* Wayne Rogers, of TV's *M*A*S*H* fame!), has rogue scientist Dr. DeMarco (John Carradine) trying to build a race of artificial men by creating "astro-zombies" in his basement lab. A trio of foreign spies (headed by Russ Meyer alumnus Tura Satana) and a gaggle of U.S. government agents (led by down-on-his-luck Wendell Corey) are both after the doc's secrets—the biggest being an actor wearing a dime-store skull mask who goes on a killing rampage because of his bad brain (the doc only had access to criminals for his experiments).

G-man Corey looks and sounds like he's half in the bag, and he never leaves his office. Likewise, Carradine never departs his basement laboratory, and does little but spout pseudo-scientific drivel while attaching a metal colander to his subject's head and fiddling endlessly with the garage sale junk passed off as scientific equipment (including plastic tubing, water jugs, and a horizontal refrigerator standing in as the "thermal control unit").

As shown by this evocative ad, Ted V. Mikels' best-known (and most lucrative) feature was all about selling the sizzle, not the (inedible) steak.

Reflecting the film's cheapness is a ludicrous sequence in which the astro-zombie, its "solar energy storage cell" damaged in a fight, holds an ordinary *flashlight* to its forehead in order to "recharge" itself! But cheapness alone does not a clunker make; it's the poor pacing and lack of action that "kills" this *Astro-Zombie*. One long scene, for instance (one of many, actually), has the heroine, set up as bait, waiting for the monster to appear—and waiting and waiting and waiting—which perfectly encapsulates the film itself.

The movie tries to redeem itself by offering some cheesy gore at the climax as the astro-zombie goes berserk with a machete, decapitating one cop (cue the bouncing painted Styrofoam head) and burying it in the skull of another (complete with bright orange stage blood). But it's too little, too late. With so little astro-action (the zombie only features significantly in *four* scenes, and the monster's demise comes literally with a mere flick of a switch!), *The Astro-Zombies* is an astro-snoozer.

Atom Age Vampire (1963; Leone/Topaz; France/Italy) Original Language Title: *Seddok, l'Erede di Satana*; Alternate Titles: *Atomic Age Vampire*; Director: Anton Giulio Majano (English version: Richard McNamara); Producer: Mario Fava; Screenplay: Alberto Bevilacqua, Gino De Santis, Anton Giulio Majano, Piero Monviso (English dialogue: John Hart); Cinematography: Aldo Giordani. Cast: Alberto Lupo, Susanne Loret, Sergio Fantoni, Franca Parisi, Andrea Scotti, Rina Franchetti, Roberto Bertea, Ivo Garrani.

A SPINE-TINGLING MOTION PICTURE
only the atom age could produce!—poster

Filmed and released in Italy in 1960, it took three years for this *Vampire* to fly across the Atlantic to America. Given the result, such an effort hardly seems worthwhile.

Alberto Lupo stars as an off-kilter medico researching an "anti-cancer vaccine" in his basement laboratory, aided by his beautiful and adoring (but ignored) assistant Monique (Franca Parisi). Somehow this ties in with restoring damaged tissue ("the secret of spontaneous reproduction of living cells"), and a beautiful nightclub singer (Susanne Loret), whose face has been scarred in an auto accident, becomes their human guinea pig. When the doctor falls for his patient and must murder women to procure the glands he needs to complete the treatment, he makes use of an earlier failed serum that transforms him into an oatmeal-faced monster so that he can acquire his "materials" without being recognized.

American one-sheet poster for 1963's *Atom Age Vampire.*

Despite its American title, no vampires (atomic or otherwise) appear in this dull, crass knock-off of Georges Franju's poetic 1959 trendsetter *The Horror Chamber of Dr. Faustus* (aka *Eyes Without a Face*). Nor does a single likable (much less believable) character populate this interminable import, from the boorish, overbearing doctor to his jealous, clingy assistant to the whining, self-pitying, faint-at-the-drop-of-a-chapeaux heroine. Far too many scenes of the bickering medical couple, the self-absorbed heroine, dull (and tame) nightclub dance routines and the going-nowhere police investigation make this an Atom Age Bore. It's 45 minutes before the titular terror even shows his ugly mug (his crusty face, flared nostrils and acromegalic features contrast bizarrely with the hooded coat drawn tightly over his head, making him look like some overgrown deformed schoolboy).

Most of the "horror" (the few monster attacks) takes place off-screen, and director Majano offers only dull staging with little build-up and no suspense. What's left is an abundance of statically shot and flatly lit talking head scenes (with the hackneyed dialogue made even more ridiculous by the alternately banal and strident dubbing).

On the plus side, the doc operates in a rather spiffy '60s-style "modern" lab, complete with bubbling beakers, large banks of equipment (full of dials, gauges and flashing lights) and a circular, glass-domed, steam-emitting one-man radiation chamber. And the film finally comes to life at the end when the monster-doc tells his recalcitrant love object of the horror and madness and sacrifice he's made—right as he's transforming before her very eyes—and pleads with her to profess her love and so "save" him from his horrible fate. But it's too little and too late for the doc—and for the viewer as well, who's just wasted 87 minutes of his or her life.

The Atomic Brain see ***Monstrosity***

Atragon (1963/65; Toho; Japan.) Director: Ishiro Honda. Producer: Tomoyuki Tanaka. Screenplay: Shinichi Sekizawa (from novels by Shunro Oshikawa and Shigeru Komatsuzaki). Cinematographer: Hajime Koizume. Cast: Jun Tazaki, Ken Uehara, Yoko Fugiyama, Tadao Takashima, Kenji Sahara, Akihiko Harata, Eisei Amamoto, Tetsuko Kobayashi.

An adventure beyond your wildest dreams—tagline

Like *Gorath* (1962/64), Toho's *Atragon* is a pulp science fiction film with a cameo appearance by a giant monster, and not a true *kaiju eiga*.

The long-forgotten Mu Empire, an Atlantis-like undersea kingdom that once dominated the surface world, threatens to reclaim mastery of the earth. Japan's only hope rests with Captain Jinguji (Jun Tazaki), a World War II naval hero who vanished during the war. When he learns that Jinguji still lives, retired Admiral Kosumi (Ken Uehara) undertakes a mission to retrieve him from a remote island where the captain has been stranded for 20 years. Jinguji's daughter, Makoto (Yoko Fugiyama), accompanies the Admiral. They discover that Jinguji, stranded with his entire crew, has developed a new super-submarine, the Atragon. This vessel appears to be the surface world's best defense against the mighty Mu, who open giant underground craters that consume entire cities. But Jinguji, who cannot believe his country lost World War II, refuses to employ the Atragon except in defense of the Japanese Empire. He also proves incapable of reconnecting emotionally with his daughter. Finally, when the Mu kidnap Makoto, Jinguji agrees to launch the Atragon—which can travel under water, through the air and bore through the earth, and which is equipped with a freeze ray known as the Zero Cannon. Toward the end of the film, the Atragon wages a brief, perfunctory battle with Manda, a sea serpent that defends the Mu's underwater city. (Manda returned for another cameo in *Destroy All Monsters* [1968/69].)

Although it remains essentially a mishmash of familiar elements dating as far back as the serial *Undersea Kingdom* (1936), as well as Jules Verne's oft-filmed novel *20,000 Leagues Under the Sea*, *Atragon* offers a few notable flourishes all its own. There's poetry behind the idea of pitting two lost empires against one another—the Mu vs. Jinguji (as a vestige of Imperial Japan). Some critics have accused *Atragon* of being a pro-Imperialist film, but they miss the point: Jinguji, who reluctantly moves forward and joins the post–Imperial world, triumphs, while the intractable Mu are destroyed.

The relationship between Jinguji and his daughter is the kind of thing viewers would expect to find in one of director Yasujiro Ozu's family dramas, not in an Ishiro Honda sci-fi epic. This emotional core lends *Atragon* a different texture than most of Toho's other genre efforts and enables Tazaki, usually cast as an expressionless military type, to deliver the performance of his career. The role of Jinguji was originally intended for the great Toshiro Mifune, but he proved unavailable due to Akira Kurosawa's *Red Beard* (1965). *Atragon* also features first-rate visual effects and one of composer Akira Ifukube's finest scores.

Unfortunately, the film plods along at a dirge-like pace. Although *Atragon* runs just 94 minutes, including a music-only overture, it feels more like 194. Its action scenes are few, and mostly contained in the final act. Jinguji doesn't appear until nearly a third of the movie has elapsed. Even then, the simplistic father-daughter conflict isn't compelling enough to carry the long, talky stretches in between effects sequences. *Atragon* also suffers

Manda, a giant sea serpent, attacks *Atragon*'s eponymous super-submarine during the climax of Toho's 1963 underwater sci-fi chiller.

from colossal lapses in simple logic, such as: If Jinguji and his men are capable of building this super-vessel, why didn't they build a simple boat and go home years ago? When the Zero Cannon fires underwater, why doesn't the sea turn into a giant iceberg? And so on.

Since *The Mysterians* (1957/59), Toho had alternated between giant monster films, generally aimed at younger audiences, and strait-laced sci-fi pictures, targeted at adults. But the consecutive box office disappointments of *Gorath* and *Atragon* ended that cycle. From this point forward, the studio's fantasy efforts would focus exclusively on the *kaiju eiga.*

Attack of the Mayan Mummy (1964; Mexico-U.S.; b&w)

Original Language Title: *La Momia Azteca* (The Aztec Mummy); Directors: Jerry Warren (new footage), Rafael Portillo (original version, uncredited). Producers: Jerry Warren, Guillermo Calderon (original version, uncredited). Screenplay: Gilbert Solar (Guillermo Calderon), Alfred Salimar (Alfredo Salazar), Jerry Warren (new footage, uncredited). Cinematographer: Richard Wallace (Enrique Wallace), Jerry Warren (new footage, uncredited). Cast: Nina Knight, Richard Webb, John Burton, Peter Mills, Steve Conte, Jorgi (Jorge) Mondragon, Emma Roldan, George Mitchell, Chuck Mills (Niles), Bill White, Fred Hoffman, Bruno VeSota (uncredited).

WHAT IS THERE IN THE BEYOND? DID YOU LIVE IN ANOTHER EPOCH? WILL YOU RETURN TO BE BORN?—(Mexican) tagline

In 1957, Mexican filmmaker Rafael Portillo shot a series of three related horror movies, all scripted by Guillermo Calderon, within the space of two months: *La Momia Azteca* (The Aztec Mummy), *La Maldicion de la Azteca Momia* (Curse of the Aztec Mummy) and *La Momia Azteca vs. el Robot Humano* (The Robot vs. the Aztec Mummy). Enter Jerry Warren in the 1960s, that tireless transformer of horror imports into senseless time-killers. Taking *La Momia Azteca* and adding footage of Warren "regulars"—such as Chuck (*Teenage Zombies*) Niles, George (*Invasion of the Animal People*) Mitchell and Bruno (*Creature of the Walking Dead*) VeSota—sitting around talking, drinking coffee and answering the telephone, Warren unleashed *Attack of the Mayan Mummy* on an unsuspecting American public.

About half of the 70-minute feature consists of new material shot by Warren, which means that half the picture consists of lengthy exposition that explains very little, and dull, pointless soliloquies that add nothing. For these interminable interludes, Warren locks down his camera (it literally *never* moves) on threadbare sets (or in a real living room) and has his actors recite reams of "gobbledygook" (as Warren himself has labeled his dialogue). Sample speech: "As the memory of Ann Taylor had functioned to the degree of pointing to the areas unknown to her present generation, the discovery of that which had filled the minds of everyone had become a reality." (Translation: "Hey, we found it!") Designed to do nothing more than eat up running time, these tangential conversations cover everything from "regressive hypno-

In 1964 Jerry Warren took footage from *La Momia Azteca* (released to Spanish-speaking theaters in the U.S. as *La Momia*) and added new scenes to create the abysmal *Attack of the Mayan Mummy.* (Pictured in this Spanish-language American lobby card are Ramon Gay and Rosa Arenas.)

sis" to ulcer flare-ups! According to actor Bruno Ve Sota, during the shooting of these new sequences, Warren was "just sitting there waiting till his film runs out. He doesn't give a damn what you're doing. That was Jerry Warren. I swear, he is the only person I ever met in Hollywood who set out to make a bad picture on purpose."

For those scenes involving the (far superior) original *Momia Azteca* footage, Warren, rather than taking the time to dub the dialogue, simply has a character tonelessly narrate what is being said (or happening). The banal, repetitive and inappropriate canned music—coupled with the even more banal (and often pointless) narration—serves to drain every bit of suspense, thrill or even mild interest from each and every scene. Inexplicably, Warren excised much of the original film's best footage (including about *four minutes* of mummy action!). The unique and grotesque mummy (if not terribly convincing, given its obvious immobile mask) is really the film's only draw, but it appears in a mere two sequences. Even worse, Warren dispatches his titular terror *off-screen* (by having it *hit by a car*!), revealing its fate to the viewer via a newspaper headline. Sigh.

Oh yes, the story. Well, it has something to do with a female hypnotic subject whose remembrances of her past life leads a group of greedy scientists in search of treasure to a Mayan pyramid. There a mummy guarding said riches comes to life and menaces the expedition. A radio broadcast then *tells* us how the living mummy crushed the expedition leader to death, and how the rest subdued the monster with gas bombs and subsequently transported it to their lab in the city for further study. A rival scientist attempts to steal the creature, which escapes (off-screen, of course) and wanders down the street towards the heroine's house, where it kidnaps said heroine before its fateful (off-screen again) run-in with a gas-guzzler.

"Rather than get involved in a picture from start to finish, which takes a lot of work," Warren candidly confessed to interviewer Tom Weaver, "I'd find something to use as a frame and hang my hat on it. I'd shoot one day on this stuff and throw it together. At that point I was in the business to make money. I never, ever tried in any way to compete, or to make something worthwhile. I did only enough to get by, so they would buy it, so it would play, and so I'd get the few dollars. It's not very fair to the public, I guess, but that was my attitude toward this." Well, if lacking in talent, at least Warren possessed candor in abundance.

On the plus side, at least the two Aztec Mummy sequels (*Curse of* and *Robot vs.*) made it to the U.S. relatively intact (i.e. no execrable additions), since K. Gordon Murray acquired them rather than Warren. Muchas gracias, Senor Murray.

With quotes from: "It's Ve Sota!" by Barry Brown, *Magick Theater*, 1987; *Interviews with B Science Fiction and Horror Movie Makers*, by Tom Weaver.

The Awful Dr. Orlof (1962/64; Plaza Films; Spain; b&w)

Alternate Titles: *Cries in the Night*; *The Demon Doctor* (U.K.); *The Diabolical Dr. Satan*. Original Language Title: *Gritos en la Noche* (Screams in the Night). Director/Screenwriter: Jess Frank (Jesus Franco); Producers: Serge Newman, Leo Lax; Cinematographer: G. Pacheco. Cast: Howard Vernon, Perla Cristal, Richard Valley (Riccardo Valle), Diana Lorys, Conrad San-Martin, Mary Silvers (Maria Siva).

If you like to shiver and shake,
quiver and quake, there's mayhem on a
monstrous scale in the most unlawful,
really awful AWFUL DR. ORLOF—
tongue-in-cheek American trailer

Often labeled the King of Eurosleaze, Spanish-born filmmaker Jesus Franco Manera (aka Jess Franco) has made well over 150 movies in the last five decades. (Due to numerous re-titlings, re-editings and even the insertion of hard-core footage for "specialty" markets, a definitive count may never occur.)

Franco's first horror film, *The Awful Dr. Orlof* is one of the earliest imitators/spin-offs of Georges Franju's *Horror Chamber of Dr. Faustus* (1959/62; aka *Eyes Without a Face*) in the mad-doctor-grafting-women's-faces-onto-his-daughter/wife/lover's-ruined-countenance subgenre. In it, Orlof (Howard Vernon) stalks and kills young women, with the aid of his blind homicidal servant Morpho (Ricardo Valle), to obtain the skin needed to restore his comatose daughter's disfigured face.

With this film Franco showed he was not completely devoid of talent (as so many of his subsequent offerings seemed to assert), employing some evocative photography (silhouetted shots of the two villains carrying a coffin towards a forbidding castle; a murder taking place in front of an upstairs window viewed solely from the street below) and taking atmospheric advantage of the actual castle settings to add some much-needed gothic mood and verisimilitude.

Sporting pop-eyed makeup and a billowing

Christopher Lee-style Dracula cape, the blind, mute, relentless Morpho makes a unique—and disturbing—maniac. But this being a Franco film (whose *raison d'etre* often seems to be to make the viewer feel as uncomfortable as possible), Morpho, for no discernible reason, likes to *bite* his victims to death. As Orlof, Franco fave Howard Vernon adds his patented brand of unsavory menace to the mix, but the remainder of the cast are forgettable at best and annoying caricatures at worst (including *several* painfully unfunny comic relief characters).

Franco also displays here the appalling lack of pacing that so often plagues his subsequent films, as *Orlof* offers scene after scene of tepid filler (including an interminable—and pointless—sequence in which the police inspector makes a composite sketch of the killer from the descriptions of numerous witnesses). Also, attention to detail seems to have slipped past Senor Franco. While everyone drives around in a horse and carriage (setting the film near the end of the nineteenth century at the latest), some characters (including Morpho) sport modern dress (a dark suit and tie in Morpho's case).

The European version of *The Awful Dr. Orlof* contained more gruesome surgical shots and hints of necrophilia excised from the American prints in an effort to spare those with New World sensibilities (and get past the MPAA). The toned-down version played on a double bill with the far superior *The Horrible Dr. Hitchcock*. Sometimes cited as Jess Franco's best film (damning with faint praise indeed), *The Awful Dr. Orlof* doesn't quite live down to its name; but it's not that good, either.

Mexican lobby card for Jess Franco's (and Spain's) first horror film, *The Awful Dr. Orlof* (1962/64).

Back to the Killer see *Horror Castle*

The Beach Girls and the Monster (1965; U.S. Films; b&w) Alternate Title: *Monster from the Surf* (TV); Director/cinematographer: Jon Hall; Producer: Edward Janis; Screenplay: Joan Gardner (Janis). Cast: Jon Hall, Sue Casey, Walker Edmiston, Elaine DuPont, Arnold Lessing.

Beach party lovers make hey! hey! in the moonlight ... while the Monster lurks in the shadows!—ad line

---

For a brief moment in time, America's moviegoing teens became infatuated with California beaches (and the bikinis and brawn that frequented them)—thanks to American International Pictures and their "Beach Party" series (begun in 1963 with *Beach Party*). Within two years the cycle was already winding down (after having been saturated with titles like *Muscle Beach Party*, *Bikini Beach*, *Pajama Party* and *Beach Blanket Bingo*), but there were still a few grains of sand left to kick into audience faces. While AIP seemed to have put up No Trespassing signs on their cinematic shoreline, in 1964 two independent-minded producers decided to strap their surfboards onto the old Woody and race to the beach as well—chased by monsters. The first was Connecticut-based (!) filmmaker Del Tenney, whose *Horror of Party Beach* added a welcome helping of horror—and a dollop of gore—to the Beach Party formula. The other beach-bound tag-along was former TV cartoon producer Edward Janis, who hired retired matinee heart-throb Jon Hall to direct (and shoot and star in) *Surf Terror* (written by

Janis' wife, Joan Gardner), which followed Tenney's lead by adding some much-needed monster mayhem to the tired beach party scenario. (The working title "Surf Terror" metamorphosed into *The Beach Girls and the Monster* upon the film's September 1965 release, nearly a year-and-a-half after its April 1964 shoot.)

Young Richard (Arnold Lessing) has been hanging about with his beach-bunny girlfriend and their surfing companions far too long for the liking of his workaholic scientist father (Jon Hall), who insists his son follow in his lab-locked footsteps. Soon a rash of teen murders at the local beach decimates the ranks of Richard's friends, and it appears that a humanoid sea monster is responsible — or is something fishy going on?

The monster in question — with its pointy head, plastic eyes, giant frog lips, and stray strands of seaweed — is no Creature from the Black Lagoon. (It's not even a Monster from Piedras Blancas.) But director Hall treats it seriously, providing some evocative nighttime lighting that makes the most of its shaggy fish appearance, and lingering on the rather gruesome slash marks on its victims to hammer the horror home. About their Black Lagoon-reject monster, co-star Walker Edmiston told interviewer Tom Weaver (for the laserdisc liner notes), "They could rent a rubber suit from Western Costume, but somebody had stolen the head that went with it. So, being that I made puppets and all that [Edmiston starred in — and made puppets for — several early TV kiddie shows], I got the job of making a head for the monster. I sculpted it in my kitchen, as I remember. I sculpted it out of clay, and then I called Don Post, Sr. [head of a mask-making company], a dear old friend. I called him and he said, 'Well, get it over here first thing in the morning and we'll cast it.' They made a plaster cast and poured the thing, and I air-brushed it. So now we had a head for the creature."

Hall, serving as his own cinematographer, takes more care than one would expect from a cheap, non-union monster movie. He keeps the visual interest level high via frequent camera movement, some atmospheric lighting, inventive framing (shooting through the fireplace, or through a silhouetted cave mouth), and clever transitions (for example, dissolving from one limping protagonist's legs as he walks along the beach to the healthy legs of the scientist striding across a room).

Of course, this being a beach movie, there's plenty of stock surfing footage, bikini beach dancing, and silly songs (including one co-written by Frank Sinatra, Jr., who also "wrote the entire [movie] score in two days," according to the film's publicity). But beneath these sunny surface sequences surges a dark undercurrent of infidelity and murder, making *Beach Girls and the Monster* a truly adult vision of a beach party movie.

Though lacking the raw, even mean-spirited edge of *Horror of Party Beach*, its closest relative, *The Beach Girls and the Monster* offers its own brand of offbeat, adult-oriented charm. "CALL IT A BASH! CALL IT A BALL! CALL IT A BLAST!" suggested the ads. Or call it a mildly entertaining little time-killer.

The Beast of Morocco (1968; Associated British Pathe; U.K.) Alternate Title: *The Hand of Night* (U.K.). Director: Frederic Goode; Producer: Harry Field; Screenplay: Bruce Stewart; Cinematography: William Jordan. Cast: William Sylvester, Diane Clare, William Dexter, Edward Underdown, Aliza Gur, Terence de Mornay.

"I should have died with them. It's meaningless me being here without them."
— Paul Carver (William Sylvester)

The mummy was a vampire.

That's the offbeat premise behind this rarely screened low-budget British chiller, which also features an unusual Middle Eastern setting. While it boasts some novel elements, however, *The Beast of Morocco* fails to assemble these quirky components into anything resembling a satisfying narrative.

British investment broker Paul Carver (William Sylvester) travels to Morocco to meet a client, only to discover that the man has died. The news sends Carver, still reeling emotionally from the death of his wife and children in a recent car crash, into an alcoholic tailspin. He's befriended by German archeologist Dr. Otto Gunter (Edward Underdown) and his French assistant Chantal (Diane Clare) who try to revive Carver's spirits by inviting him to visit their excavation. On the way there Carver encounters a mysterious, exotic beauty named Marisa (Aliza Gur), who he begins meeting in the ruins of an ancient palace. When Carver tells his friends about his new romantic interest, Otto and Chantal are struck by the coincidence that their dig involves opening the sealed crypt of an ancient princess also named Marisa. When they learn that, according to local lore, Princess Marisa was entombed alive because she was a vampire, the scientists must spring into action to save their new friend from a fate worse than death.

The Beast of Morocco's attempt to merge the mummy and vampire mythologies, although novel in concept, proves clumsy and contrived in execution. For instance, Otto and Chantal—trained scientists unlikely to accept local superstition at face value—swiftly and enthusiastically make the transition from archeologists to vampire hunters to facilitate the story's resolution. Worse yet, the story's lone marginally interesting idea is set adrift in a sea of talky melodramatic filler as Paul grapples with survivor guilt over his dead family, grows obsessed with Marisa, and finds himself triangulated with Otto by Chantal's unrequited romantic interest in him. All of this plays out through reams of banal dialogue from scenarist Bruce Stewart. Frederic Goode's rudderless direction and Cliff Sharpe's laughable makeup effects only exacerbate the picture's problems.

William Sylvester, a dependable but unexpressive actor, lacks the charisma to redeem a project like this. Former Miss Israel (and Miss Universe runner-up) Aliza Gur certainly *looks* enchanting enough, but her flat-affect performance further damages the movie's already shaky credibility. Edward Underdown had been Ian Fleming's first choice to play James Bond in *Dr. No* (1962), but the actor's undistinguished work here as Otto demonstrates why producers Albert Broccoli and Harry Saltzman never seriously considered him for the role. Diane Clare had contributed memorable supporting turns to pictures such as *The Haunting* (1963), *Witchcraft* (1964) and *Plague of the Zombies* (1966) but isn't given much to do here, which is a shame since *Beast of Morocco* turned out to be her final screen appearance. Maybe the actress figured that if she couldn't find better vehicles than this, it was time to hang it up. Viewers could hardly blame her.

The Beast of Yucca Flats (1961; Crown International; b&w) Director/Screenwriter: Coleman Francis; Producers: Coleman Francis, Anthony Cardoza; Cinematographer: John Cagle. Cast: Tor Johnson, Douglas Mellor, Barbara Francis, Bing Stafford, Larry Aten, Linda Beilema.

COMMIES MADE HIM AN ATOMIC MUTANT!—ad line

The good news: It's only 54 minutes long. The bad news: All 54 minutes are about as exciting as watching paint dry. Devotees of *le bad cinema* hold up movies like *Robot Monster* and *Plan 9 from Outer Space* as shining examples of ineptitude as entertainment. While a case can be made for those two features possessing a healthy "fun quotient," the same *cannot* be said for *The Beast of Yucca Flats*, a Coleman Francis opus that's about as dry as the desert in which it was shot.

Written by director/co-producer Francis, *The Violent Sun* (its less-than-exciting title before it became the more exploitable *Beast of Yucca Flats* for release) opens with a pre-credit sequence in which a bare-breasted woman towels off in her bedroom before a hulking man (his face unseen) enters, then strangles and (by implication) rapes her. (According to co-producer Anthony Cardoza, said sequence was included solely because Francis liked nudity.) The film proper (using the term loosely) then begins as a small plane lands at a desert airfield and disgorges a 390-pound Tor Johnson, playing "Joseph Jaworski, noted scientist, recently escaped from behind the Iron Curtain" (as the narrator tells us). Jaworski, carrying secret data on the Russian moon-shot, is headed for Yucca Flats and "a meeting with top brass at the A-bomb testing ground." But Communist agents arrive and, after a pathetic and protracted gun-battle/car-chase, pursue Jaworski into the desert. Big Tor ambles over a hill and a bright flash occurs, followed by stock footage of a mushroom cloud. The next thing we know, Tor—with torn shirt and minimalist burn makeup (reminiscent of wrinkled toilet paper)—takes to living in a cave, carrying a stick, and strangling anyone he can find. As the narrator explains it: "Joseph Jaworski, respected scientist, now a fiend prowling the wastelands, a prehistoric beast in the nuclear age; kill, kill just to be killing." The remainder of the film consists of two lawmen driving around or flying overhead trying to spot the man-monster that's been murdering passing motorists, while a family of four has car trouble and the two boys wander off to encounter The Beast. Finally, after one of the deputies shoots the wrong man from a plane ("shoot first and ask questions later," intones the narrator), the "heroes" run across The Beast and gun him down.

Costing $34,000, according to Francis, and shot sporadically on weekends over a six-to-eight-month period in 1959, there's very little beauty in this *Beast*. You wouldn't think that a movie only 54 minutes long would need padding, but *Beast* is chock full of filler. We're "treated" to endless shots of cars driving down the desert highway; aerial views of the monotonous desert; people getting into cars and out of cars—into planes and out of planes; and even two boys feeding soda pop to some pigs! (Sadly, this last is actually a highlight.) The picture was filmed without sound, so the rule is that characters speak only while *off*-screen or with their back to the camera (though sometimes Tor slips up and we see his lips move but hear no voice). Apart from Tor Johnson, the cast is primarily made up of friends and relatives of Coleman Francis, including his then-wife (playing the mother) and two sons (playing the boys menaced by the Beast). As might be expected, there's really no "acting" going on, just bodies standing around waiting for direction and giving the camera something to focus on. A narrator occasionally pipes in with a comment. This overdramatic narration (provided by Francis himself) consists of obvious observations ("A man runs; somebody shoots at him"), "profound" interjections ("Touch a button, things happen; a scientist becomes a beast") and outright non-sequiturs ("Flag on the Moon—how did it get there?"). The *real* question should be: Movie on the screen—*why* did it get there?

Beauty and the Beast (1962; United Artists) Director: Edward L. Cahn; Producer: Robert E. Kent; Screenplay: George Bruce and Orville H. Hampton; Cinematography: Gilbert Warrenton. Cast: Joyce Taylor, Mark Damon, Eduard Franz, Michael Pate, Merry Anders, Dayton Lummis, Walter Burke.

Fans of Disney's 1991 animated musical and/or director Jean Cocteau's 1946 masterpiece *La Belle et la Bete* will hardly recognize this *Beauty and the Beast*, which bears only a passing resemblance to the oft-filmed French fairy tale (George Bruce and Orville Hampton's screenplay was "suggested by," not based on, the traditional story, according to the opening credits).

In this version, inexplicably relocated to Italy from France, "Beauty" is Iprincess Althea (Joyce Taylor), who is engaged to charming Prince Eduardo (Mark Damon), ruler of an unnamed duchy. But Eduardo turns into a wolf-like beast at sundown every night, a curse he's kept hidden from both Althea and his scheming cousin, Bruno (Michael Pate). Even when he's furry and fierce-looking, however, Eduardo retains his kindly disposition and his princely diction (free of animalistic grunts and growls). Althea and Eduardo, along with Eduardo's loyal manservant (Eduard Franz), must find a solution to the curse before Bruno's machinations result in Eduardo being deposed—and possibly burned at the stake.

These radical revisions of the fairy tale were designed to cut costs for this low-budget production, eliminating the need for animated clocks or candlesticks, and, since most of the film takes place in daylight, limiting the amount of time Eduardo spends in Beast form. But the changes are so drastic that the entire point of the yarn is lost. For instance, the Beast bears no fault for his plight; the curse is a familial one, visited upon him due to the misdeeds of his father, who buried alive an uppity castle sorcerer. The whole business falls so far afield from Jeanne-Marie Leprince de Beaumont's original story that retaining the title seems like false advertising.

Although it runs a compact 76 minutes, *Beauty and the Beast*'s refashioned plot isn't very eventful (the whole scenario easily could have been compressed into a single episode of *The Wonderful World of Disney*), not at all scary (remaining fixed in the realm of juvenile fantasy), nor particularly well-told. B-movie director Edward ("Fast Eddie") Cahn was hired for his efficiency rather than his artistry. The dialogue is stiff and the performances broad. Joyce Taylor makes a forgettable Beauty and Mark Damon a disappointingly wimpy Beast. At least Michael Pate and Walter Burko (who plays Bruno's henchman, Grimaldi) attack their stock villain roles with gusto.

The only truly notable aspects of this *Beauty and the Beast* are Gilbert Warrenton's lush Technicolor cinematography and the briefly-seen Beast makeup, created by former Universal studio great Jack Piece. It's essentially a recreation of Piece's legendary Wolf Man, with that masterpiece in spirit gum and yak hair seen here for the first time in full color. Aside from those fleeting moments of interest, there's little here worth howling about.

Berserk (1968; Columbia; U.K.) Director: Jim Connolly; Producer: Herman Cohen; Screenplay: Aben Kandel, Herman Cohen; Cinematographer: Desmond Dickinson. Cast: Joan Crawford, Michael Gough, Ty Hardin, Diana Dors, Judy Geeson.

The motion picture that pits steel weapons against steel nerves!!!—tagline

Best remembered, if remembered at all, as the penultimate picture in the lengthy filmography of star Joan Crawford, *Berserk* proves a feeble effort. Crawford, at 61, plays Monica Rivers, the sexpot owner-operator-ringmaster (ringmistress?) of a troubled traveling circus whose fortunes unexpectedly rebound when a series of mysterious killings begin to plague the caravans. As Monica ruthlessly cashes in on the free publicity provided by the murders, the circus performers begin to suspect she may be committing the crimes herself.

With only one memorable murder scene (co-star Michael Gough takes a spike through the head), *Berserk* plays more like a routine whodunit than a full-tilt horror show. But since the plot's solution involves a "cheat," the film isn't satisfying as a mystery, either. Indifferently shot, with threadbare production values, banal dialogue and stilted performances, and over-padded with footage from the Billy Smart Circus (including a high wire act, performing elephants, dancing poodles, prancing horses and a lion tamer)—not to mention a musical number!—*Berserk* seems to trundle on for twice its 95-minute length. Camp value remains the film's only "virtue," with Crawford and Gough trying to out-ham one another in the film's early scenes, and Crawford, improbably, seducing a hunky young tightrope walker (Ty Hardin). At one point, one of the circus performers says that Monica "has the gift of eternal youth." Cohen must have thought so, too, since he had the gall not only to cast her in the lead but to costume her in bikini bottoms and fishnet hose, despite her age.

Joan Crawford goes *Berserk* (1967). (Italian four-sheet poster).

Bland and boring, *Berserk* ranks as not only one of Crawford's worst films, but one of producer Herman Cohen's weakest as well (a severe indictment, considering Cohen also unleashed *Konga* on the moviegoing public). Alas, Crawford and Cohen would team once more, with even more depressing results, for 1970's *Trog*, the last and most pathetic movie the once-great star would make. After that debacle, Crawford realized it was time to retire. Too bad she didn't reach that conclusion a couple of pictures sooner.

Billy the Kid Versus Dracula (1966; Embassy Pictures) Director: William Beaudine; Producer: Carroll Case; Screenplay: Carl K. Hittleman; Cinematographer: Lothrop Worth. Cast: John Carradine, Chuck Courtney, Melinda Plowman, Virginia Christine.

THE WEST'S DEADLIEST GUN-FIGHTER! THE WORLD'S MOST DIABOLICAL KILLER!—poster

Horror Westerns are an odd breed. Their uneasy mix of gunfights, horseplay, gothic-style chills and monsters are often enough to leave a viewer shaking his or her head like a cowpoke trying to clear his rattled thoughts after a barroom brawl. Few films in this bizarre subset can be deemed successful (or even entertaining), with perhaps 1959's *Curse of the Undead* being the (relative) best of the lot. The strangest pair of ponies in this cinematic corral would have to be *Billy the Kid Versus Dracula* and its co-feature *Jesse James Meets Frankenstein's Daughter*—an outrageous double-bill that becomes almost train-wreck fascinating in its outlandish aplomb.

Billy and *Jesse* were first announced in May of 1961, with Joe Breen slated to direct the Dracula picture and Erle C. Kenton (*Island of Lost Souls*) earmarked for the Frankenstein. When finally filmed in 1966, the two were shot back-to-back (even *concurrently*, according to Howard W. Koch, Jr., who served as assistant to producer Carroll Case) under the direction of B-Western specialist William "One Shot" Beaudine. (Apart from director Beaudine and producer Case, the two movies also shared the same screenwriter, Carl Hittleman, *and* cinematographer, Lothrop Worth.) Shown together to unwary drive-in patrons across the country, the pair went down in history as arguably the most eccentric terror tandem ever produced.

Billy the Kid Versus Dracula opens on a close-up of the highly made-up, pasty-faced John Carradine *yawning*— which proves a prophetic image for the tedious 70-odd minutes to come. Carradine plays Dracula — complete with top hat, cape, satanic goatee and (saddle)bags under his eyes — for the first time on the big screen in over 20 years; 1945's *House of Dracula* being his last cinematic go-round as the Count. (Oddly, the name "Dracula" never comes up in the film — though it does appear throughout Carl K. Hittleman's script.) The King of the Undead is now roaming the Old West, where he assumes the identity of a never-before-seen relative to infiltrate the household (or, more accurately, *ranch*hold) of Betty Bentley (Melinda Plowman). The randy old bloodsucker intends to make the beautiful Betty his undead bride. Standing in his way is the reformed William "Billy the Kid" Bonney (Chuck Courtney)— Betty's foreman *and* fiancé. (Courtney shot and killed himself in January 2000 at age 69, despondent after suffering a series of strokes.)

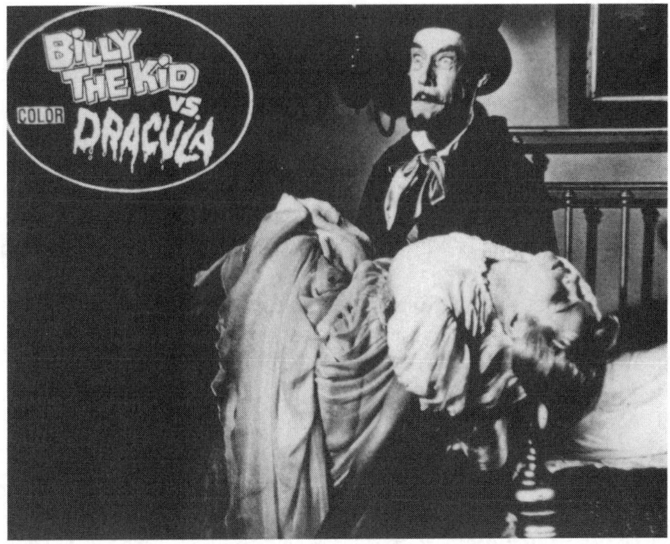

The only thing preventing Dracula (John Carradine) from making ranch owner Betty Bentley (Melinda Plowman) his undead bride is a reformed Billy the Kid(!) in this bizarre horror hybrid *Billy the Kid vs. Dracula* (1966).

"I have worked in a dozen of the greatest, and I have worked in a dozen of the worst," pronounced John Carradine. "I only regret *Billy the Kid Versus Dracula*. Otherwise, I regret nothing." The Shakespearean-spouting actor often cited this as his poorest film. Taking into account some of the I'll-take-anything-with-a-paycheck actor's other movie appearances, it has plenty of (un)worthy competition. "I needed the money, to be honest," explained Carradine about why he accepted the assignment. "Actors have to live too, you know. It was a bad film. I don't even remember it. I was absolutely numb."

Said numbness may have come from a bottle, as the heavy-drinking Carradine would frequently drown his sorrows in the nearest cantina. In *The Dracula Book*, author Donald F. Glut recalled: "When I visited the set at Producers Studio in Hollywood ... Carradine was doing a scene in which he was trying to seduce a pretty victim with his talk of a world of vampires. Carradine insisted that Count Dracula would be averse to using the term *vampire*, and substituted the word *un-dead*. When the shooting halted for lunch it was amusing to see Carradine, in full Dracula costume, relaxing in the bright sun and then crossing Melrose Avenue to enter a nearby bar."

Though he may have been "absolutely numb," Carradine's performance was anything *but* (though it is indeed numbing in its *badness*). While John Carradine produced some of the finest acting to grace the silver screen (one need only consider his sublime performances in features like *The Prisoner of Shark Island* and *The Grapes of Wrath*), he was capable of amazing excess when thrown into a take-the-money-and-run feature. Whenever Dracula notices something of interest, for example, Carradine's eyes comically widen into saucers. When confronted with the abhorred mirror, he gives a throaty "waaaaah" like some tantrum-throwing geriatric. Of course, director Beaudine and cinematographer Lothrop Worth were no help to the grand ac-*tor*. Every time Dracula uses his hypnotic powers, a colored spotlight turns his face a *bright red*, signifying the level of subtlety and sophistication employed by the filmmakers— and, no doubt, the level of embarrassment felt by Carradine.

The special effects are less than special, consisting of a bat gliding on a wire (in several silhouetted shots of the fake *fledermaus* flapping its wings it looks for all the world like the flying rodent is wearing its own miniature top hat!) and Dracula popping in and out of the scene à la a turn-of-the-century George Meliès short. At the climax, Billy empties his six-gun into the undead monster with no effect, but when the frustrated outlaw heaves the empty side iron at him, it lays the vampire low! So much for supernatural power (or dignity) in this David and Count Goliath encounter.

The picture also plays fast and loose with traditional cinematic vampire lore. Dracula walks around in broad daylight and sleeps in a bed rather than a coffin (oddly, in one scene we even get to watch him *make* the bed — the Count is nothing if not tidy, and director Beaudine is nothing if not *tedious*). The vampire drinks the blood of lambs and eats regular food (not even blood pudding), and a metal scalpel rather than a wooden stake sends him to his eternal rest at film's end. Said end is quizzical as well, for when Billy stakes Dracula, a bat flies unsteadily out of the cave to crash into some bushes while the vampire's body remains; perhaps it is the fiend's undead soul taking wing ... or something?

"We did the Dracula thing with William Beaudine, who was a wonderful guy with a fine reputation," recounted cinematographer Worth to interviewer Jack Gourlay. "But he was so old by then, he'd have to rest between taking scenes." (At the time, the 74-year-old Beaudine was the oldest active member of the Screen Directors Guild.) "Beaudine said, 'You can't make the Academy Awards with these pictures — just take 'em and get the job done.'"

When John Carradine appeared on *Late Night with David Letterman* in the 1980s, the subject of this film came up:

David Letterman: "Do you remember some of the stranger films or the stranger parts that you played?"

John Carradine: "Well, I think the worst one was something called *Billy the Kid and Dracula. Billy the Kid* Versus *Dracula* — that makes it even worse!"

Letterman: "That was a true story though, right?"

Carradine: "No, no, I don't think so."

With quotes from: *John Carradine: The Films*, by Tom Weaver.

The Birds (1963; Paramount) Director/Producer: Alfred Hitchcock; Screenplay: Evan Hunter (Story: Daphne du Maurier); Cinematographer: Robert Burks. Cast: Rod Taylor, Tippi Hedren, Jessica Tandy, Suzanne Pleshette, Veronica Cartwright.

The Birds is coming — tagline

Upon its initial release in 1963 *The Birds* was widely considered a disappointment. But almost anything Alfred Hitchcock had issued as a successor to the cultural phenomenon that was *Psycho* (1960) would have seemed like a letdown. In the decades that followed, *The Birds*' reputation deservedly soared. Viewed in historical perspective, it stands as one of the last great Hitchcock pictures and, arguably, the most terrifying entry in the legendary director's filmography.

Newspaper heiress Melanie Daniels (Tippi Hedren) travels from San Francisco to tiny Bodega Bay, California, to deliver a pair of lovebirds to attorney Mitch Brenner (Rod Taylor). It's a birthday gift for Mitch's kid sister (Veronica Cartwright), and a ploy to try to win the hunky lawyer's heart, but Melanie faces unforeseen obstacles in the form of Mitch's jealous mother Lydia (Jessica Tandy) and his ex-girlfriend Annie (Suzanne Pleshette). As Melanie begins trying to disentangle these interpersonal difficulties, she and the Brenners are suddenly struck with a far different and more terrifying problem: Birds — sea gulls, crows, even sparrows — begin attacking and killing the people of Bodega Bay.

Perhaps *The Birds* was just too weird for 1963 audiences. It still leaves some viewers flat. Hitchcock biographer Donald Spoto calls *The Birds* "perhaps Hitchcock's least accessible motion picture, since it reveals it richness like a demanding art novel or a complex symphony, only after considerable effort." But if the film is difficult, that is by design. After *Psycho*, Hitchcock had carte blanche, and he made the least compromising movie of his entire career. *The Birds* is a collection of daring, even radical, artistic choices. Federico Fellini called it "an apocalyptic poem." It is that and more.

Hitchcock purchased Daphne du Maurier's short story "The Birds," initially, with the idea of adapting it for his *Alfred Hitchcock Presents* TV series. But in his search for a follow-up to *Psycho*, the director eventually recognized that du Maurier's tale had greater possibilities — although it would also present daunting challenges. Filming the yarn's attack scenes would involve hundreds of special effects shots — far more than any other Hitchcock picture — using live birds, mechanical birds and optically matted-in birds. Since live birds were used in many shots, representatives of the American Society for the Prevention of Cruelty to Animals were often on-set during production. To eliminate the blue haloing that was common to traveling matte effects of the era,

Hitchcock acquired specialized sodium light blue screen equipment pioneered by the Disney studio.

Since du Maurier's original story was very short and included almost no characterization, Hitchcock and screenwriter Evan Hunter also faced problems developing the screenplay. In key respects, the final scenario resembles *Psycho*. Once again, Hitchcock leads viewers "down the garden path." *The Birds* opens with a "meet cute" scene at a pet shop. The first 52 minutes of the two-hour film are devoted to romantic piffle, intended to emulate the screwball comedies of the 1930s (that's why Melanie is an heiress — a stock screwball character). Audiences, Hitchcock said, "come to the theater and they sit down and say, 'All right. Now show me!' And they want to be one jump ahead of the action. 'I know what's gong to happen.' So I have to take up the challenge. 'Oh, you know what's going to happen? Well, we'll just see about that!' With *The Birds* I made sure the public would not be able to anticipate from one scene to another."

But *The Birds*' extended introductory sequence was intended not only to keep audiences guessing, but to help viewers bond with the characters so that the unprovoked, literally out-of-the-blue carnage which unfolds throughout the second half of the film would have meaning and impact. "The pattern of *The Birds* was deliberately to go slow," Hitchcock said. "I felt it was vital that we take our time, get absorbed in the atmosphere before the birds come. Once more, it is fantasy. But everything has to be as real as possible — the surroundings, the settings, the people." Nevertheless, the leisurely pace of the film's first half puts off some viewers, as does another controversial but equally powerful decision — to not explain the reason for the bird attacks. "We decided that it would be science fiction if we explained why the birds were attacking," said screenwriter Hunter. "It would have greater meaning if we never knew." And, finally, Hitchcock and Hunter gave *The Birds* a haunting, open ending — one that offered some hope but not a tidy resolution to the mystery. (Hitch planned but jettisoned a bleak, ominous final shot of the Golden Gate Bridge covered in birds, waiting to descend on San Francisco.)

In addition to its "garden path" opening, *The Birds* features a meticulously edited montage sequence when Melanie is attacked and nearly killed by birds near the climax of the movie. Like *Psycho*'s famous shower scene, this sequence took

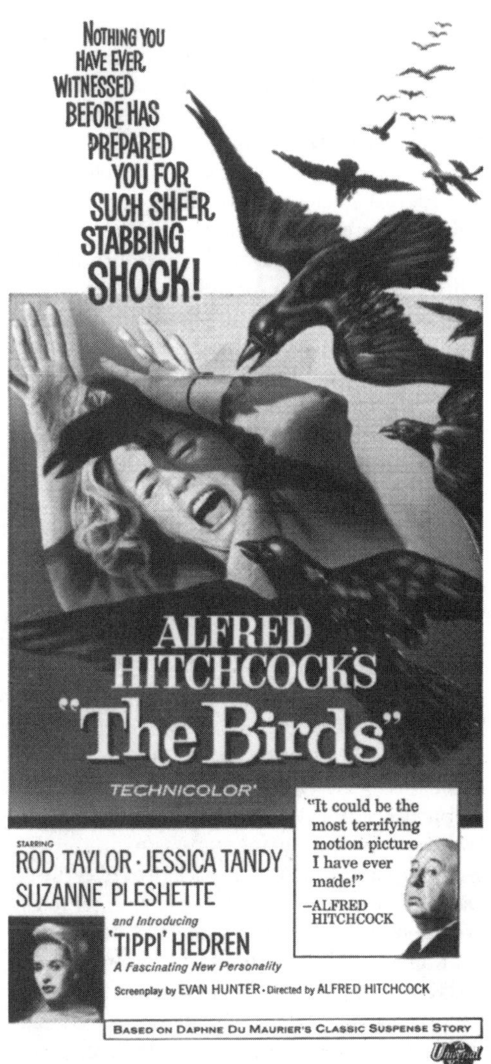

Ad for "the most terrifying motion picture [Alfred Hitchcock] ever made!" (1963).

five grueling days to shoot. Afterward, Hedren was so exhausted that she was briefly hospitalized. All the bird attack scenes prove intense and unnerving. In one particularly harrowing sequence, a flock of huge, demonic-looking crows attack panicked children on their way home from school. Even *Psycho*'s stunning murders can't top the stark terror of this and similar moments.

Unexpectedly, *The Birds* took the famously intractable, story-boarded, over-prepared Hitchcock into the uncharted realm of on-the-spot improvisation. "I've always boasted that I never look at a script when I'm shooting," Hitchcock said. But "something happened [on *The Birds*] that was altogether new to my experience: I began to study the scenario as we went along, and I saw that there were weaknesses in it. This emotional siege I went through served to bring out an additional creative sense in me. I began to improvise. For instance, the whole scene of the outside attack on the house by birds that are not seen was done spontaneously, right on the set. I'd almost never done anything like that before, but I made up my mind and quickly designed the movements of the people inside the room."

In devising this sequence, Hitch called upon his memories of the Blitz in World War II England. "The helplessness of the people is no different in that sequence than people in an air raid with nowhere to go," he said. "Now, that's where the idea came from. I've been in raids ... in London and the bombs are falling, and the guns are going like hell all over the place. You don't know where to go. Where can you go? Can't go down to the basement. That's kind of sissy, you know."

Another brave decision on Hitchcock's part was to eschew a traditional score for *The Birds*. Despite the outstanding contribution composer Bernard Herrmann had made to *Psycho*, Hitch elected to employ only electronically enhanced bird calls and other sound effects here—and to use no sound whatsoever during some sequences. Once again, this unorthodox approach proved eerily effective. The film's casting also ran counter to expectations. In the leads, Hitchcock cast Tippi Hedren, a model with very limited acting experience, and Rod Taylor, a lantern-jawed heroic type miles removed from both of Hitchcock's preferred leading men, the suave Cary Grant or the everymannish James Stewart. Both Hedren and Taylor turn in performances a cut above anything else in their careers, but Jessica Tandy steals the film with her carefully layered, deeply moving portrayal of Lydia, Mitch's clinging, grief-stricken mother. (Her horrified reaction, upon discovering the dead farmer's body, is far more frightening than Howard Smit's pecked-out-eye-socket makeup effects; she also delivers the film's emotional high point when, during one of bird attacks, she screams to Mitch, "If your father were here...!" then chokes up and breaks off in mid-sentence.) Suzanne Pleshette, playing Mitch's old flame, and Veronica Cartwright, as his terrified younger sister, are also outstanding.

Over the years, critics have proffered all manner of theories regarding the deeper, thematic meaning of *The Birds*. Even Hitch himself found the answer mercurial. He told one interviewer, "All you can say about *The Birds* is nature can be awful rough on you, if you play around with it. Look what uranium has done. Man dug that out of the ground." Later, speaking with filmmaker Peter Bogdanovich, Hitchcock suggested an entirely different reading of the film: "Generally speaking, that people are too complacent. The girl represents complacency. But I believe that when people rise to the occasion—when catastrophe comes—they are all right. The mother panics because she starts off being so strong, but she is not strong: it is a face—she has been substituting her son for her husband. She is the weak character in the story. But the girl shows that people can be strong when they face up to the situation." Both of these are valid interpretations, but neither is definitive. Like many fine works of art, *The Birds* may mean something different to every viewer.

On a more basic level, *The Birds* can be seen as the grand-daddy of all animal-attack thrillers. It's also worth noting that there are significant similarities in dramatic structure between this film and another watershed 1960s shocker, George Romero's *Night of the Living Dead* (1968): Both feature protagonists confined to a remote, boarded-up farmhouse fighting off inhuman attackers. Neither picture spends much time explaining why these attacks occur, and neither one has a happy ending. With the exception of *Frenzy* (1971), Hitchcock would never again approach the brilliance of *Psycho* or *The Birds*. This marked the end of the director's most illustrious period, a series of commercial and critical triumphs that began with *Strangers on a Train* (1950) and also included classics such as *Rear Window* (1954), *Vertigo* (1958) and *North by Northwest* (1959). Difficult and inaccessible as it may be, *The Birds* belongs in the company of those masterworks. It's one of Hitchcock's greatest achievements.

With quotes from: *The Art of Alfred Hitchcock*, by Donald Spoto; *Hitchcock on Hitchcock*, edited by Sidney Gottlieb; *Hitchcock/Truffaut*, by François Truffaut; *Who the Devil Made It*, by Peter Bogdanovich; and *All About The Birds*, DVD documentary from MCA/Universal Home Video.

The Black Cat (1966; Falcon International/Hemisphere; b&w) Director/screenwriter: Harold Hoffman; Producer: Patrick Sims; Cinematographer: Walter Schenk. Cast: Robert Frost, Robyn Baker, Sadie French, Scotty McKay, George R. Russell, George Edgley, Anne MacAdams, Jeff Alexander ... and *introducing* Pluto as the black cat.

WHAT FORCE DRIVES HIM TO COMMIT ACTS *AGAINST NATURE* ... ? TO *TERRIFY* ... TO *TORTURE* AND *TORMENT*...!!—ad line

This low-budget drive-in obscurity from Texas updates Edgar Allan Poe's classic short story to the 1960s. A disturbed, alcoholic writer (Robert Frost) becomes morbidly obsessed with the black cat given him by his wife (Robyn Baker) as an anniversary present. He maims it (by gouging out its eye) and then kills it, but this (or another) cat comes back. The homicidal husband nearly gets away with murdering his wife and walling her up in the basement until the wailing of the cat, which he had accidentally bricked up with the body, gives the crime away to the police.

Though more faithful to the storyline than previous efforts, this third full-length feature based on Poe's "The Black Cat" really does the author no favors (even misspelling his name on-screen as Edgar *Allen* Poe). Poe's tale of obsession, addiction, guilt and madness is undermined by the cheap production at every turn (which offers tinny sound, inappropriate stock music, and pedestrian pacing and direction), and even more so by the inane characterizations and awful acting. (The only technical plus is some evocative black-and-white photography, courtesy of former Russ Meyer cameraman Walter Schenk, which manages to occasionally conjure up a creepy mood.)

As the verbose, drunken, deranged husband, Robert Frost overacts up a storm, while Robyn Baker, as his vapid, bouffant-bearing wife, can't seem to change expression (when she 'cries' it looks like she's smiling). It's no wonder this animal-obsessed wacko would rather spend time with his menagerie (consisting of a toucan, monkey, raccoon, parrot and, of course, black cat named Pluto ["Ploo-tow" in Frost's Texas drawl]) than his insipid spouse.

To stretch the story out to feature length, we're treated to several bar interludes, in which the no-goodnik drinks, smokes, dances crazily (to the songs "Bo Diddly" and "Brown-Eyed Handsome Man," performed by Scott McKay and his band), and starts a fight. Later he drunkenly races around in his snazzy sports car with surf guitar music blaring. He also plays with, drinks with, and even *dances with* his cat at home, while his worried (and jealous) wife cries herself to sleep. Of course, his happy-go-lucky pet-and-alcohol-filled haze takes a dark turn when he gouges out his beloved cat's eye in a drunken rage. "If thine eye offends thee, pluck it out," he says, while in close-up his hand opens to reveal a mass of gore with an eyeball sitting in the middle—a gruesomely shocking sight, and a disturbing portent of things to come.

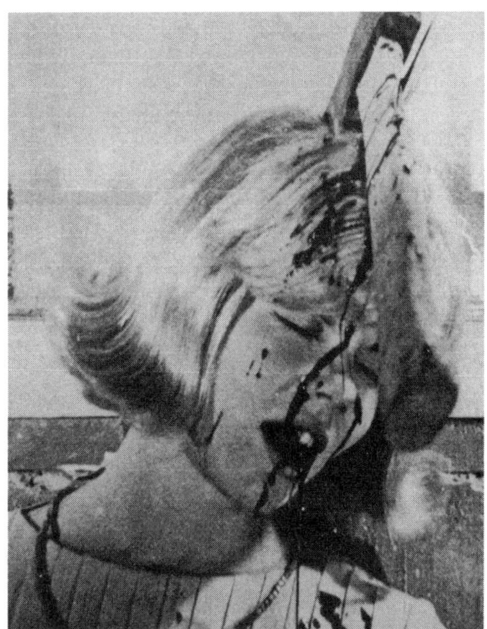

The shockingly effective murder sequence from the otherwise impoverished 1966 version of Edgar Allan Poe's *The Black Cat* (Robyn Baker pictured).

The animal cruelty scenes—pouring scalding coffee on his caged pet monkey (when he suspects the simian is "laughing" at him) stands as the mildest representative—that follow are pretty hard to take. (It's a well-known phenomenon that viewers frequently respond more strongly to images of violence against animals than to scenes of abuse against their own species—a comment, perhaps, on the nature of "humanity"?) Not only does the drunken villain subsequently strangle the ill-fated cat with a noose made of frayed electrical cord, he *plugs it in* and fries the feline as well. (This sets the house afire, represented by the ridiculous shot of an unconvincing model consumed by a giant gout of flame.)

Continuing in the gory vein, the film's gruesome centerpiece arrives when the husband buries a hatchet in the head of his long-suffering wife. Convincingly bloody, it's a shockingly strong scene. Then, of course, comes the poetic justice/money shot of the cat perched atop his wife's decomposing corpse.

A few bits of levity momentarily alleviate the

unsavory tedium (such as the absurdly-heavy-handed-yet-still-amusing post-eye gouging bar interlude in which the band all wear eye patches and sing "Sinner Man" to the hallucinating husband sitting there feeling guilty). And, this being a Texas no-budgeter, it's good to see the oversized Lone Star Stater and Larry Buchanan regular Bill Thurman put in an appearance (as a bartender). But it's too little and too late. Offering a bit of grue, a general air of unpleasantness and little else, *The Black Cat* remains a black *mark* on the cinematic name of Edgar Allan Poe.

The Black Pit of Dr. M (1959/61; Alameda Films/United Producers Releasing Organization; Mexico; b&w)

Original Language Title: *Misterios de Ultratumba.* Director: Fernando Mendez; Producer: Alfredo Ripstein, Jr.; Screenplay: Ramon Obon; Cinematographer: Victor Herrera. Cast: Gaston Santos, Rafael Bertrand, Mapita Cortes, Carlos Ancira, Carolina Barret, Luis Aragon, Beatriz Aguirre, Antonio Raxel.

PLUNGES YOU INTO A NEW CONCEPT OF TERROR ... and SUDDEN SHOCKS!!—ad line

One of the few Mexican horrors that crossed the border *without* the help of K. Gordon Murray (it was released Stateside in 1961 by United Producers Releasing Organization, who generally handled nudie-cutie fare), *The Black Pit of Dr. M* disappeared after a few years and remained unseen for four decades. Rediscovered and issued on DVD in 2006 (in its Spanish-language/English-subtitled form anyway, as the original English dubbing track has remained lost), one of the best Mexi-horrors of the 1960s is now back among us.

"Take equal parts of an insane violinist, a doctor experimenting in black magic, and a crazed Gypsy woman, and shake well in an insane asylum, and the result has to be one of the most hair-raising suspense stories ever filmed." While the hyperbolic "hair-raising" adjective employed by this American pressbook article may not be the most accurate descriptor, insert "unusual," "eerie," or just plain "weird" and you'd be right on the money. The film opens with sanatorium head Dr. Masali (Rafael Bertrand) reminding his dying colleague, Dr. Aldama (Antonio Raxel), of the pact they'd made a year earlier: "The one who dies first must find the way so that the other one could go and come back from the other world without dying." Dr. Masali uses a medium to contact Aldama's spirit, who warns Dr. M of "the horrible price to pay." Masali remains adamant, however, and Aldama's shade sets in motion a chain of events that ends in a tangled web of death, resurrection, madness and horrific irony.

The film's striking set design and art direction (all misty courtyards, Gothic-styled stone archways, and heavy ornate furniture), aided by some evocative camerawork and shadowy lighting, establishes an uncanny atmosphere so thick you'd need a headsman's axe to cut through it. During an opening burial sequence, for instance, the backlighting of the surrounding woods combines with the blazing foreground torchlight at the gravesite to give the proceedings a decidedly hellish cast—as if caught between two worlds. Director Fernando Mendez (who also helmed the Mexican *The Vampire* and *The Vampire's Coffin*) and cinematographer Victor Herrera (*The Vampire's Coffin, Castle of the Monsters*) takes us further into this macabre milieu via a disquieting ground-level camera shot of the pallbearers lowering the coffin into the grave, before cutting to

Pressbook cover for one of the few Mexican horrors of the 1960s released in the U.S. (in 1961) by someone *other than* K. Gordon Murray.

a close-in overhead shot of the casket disappearing into the dark hole — emphasizing the isolation, fear and (ironically, as it turns out) finality of death. Later, shadowy movements and subtle changes in lighting heralds the appearance of the supernatural, so that even when Aldama's ghost is visually absent from the screen, its preternatural presence remains. Additionally, the gruesome acid-burn makeup on the doctor's assistant (horribly scarred while trying to subdue a violent patient) — reminiscent of Lionel Atwill's twisted, ruined visage from *Mystery of the Wax Museum* (1933) — hammers home the horror on a more visceral level. All these technical elements artistically combine to brilliantly establish the film's macabre mood and enhance the complex, eventful and otherworldly story unfolding.

Unfortunately, this *Pit* is not completely devoid of, er ... pitfalls. The ingénue and nominal leading man (Mapita Cortes and Gaston Santos) make for a vapid and uninteresting pair, while the "lovers' destiny" angle seems mawkish and out-of-place. Likewise, the sudden shot from cupid's arrow into Dr. M's bosom appears so abruptly that it screams Lazy Plot Device. And the finale devolves into a rather standard mad villain moment that appears disappointingly mundane after the previous 70 minutes of deliriously macabre originality. But even with these few minor missteps, a viewer would do well to gaze into this *Pit*, as it offers a startlingly unique and creepily atmospheric look into the strange and wonderful world of Mexican horror cinema.

Black Sabbath (1964; AIP; Italy/U.S.) Original Language Title: *I Tre Volti della Paura* (The Three Faces of Fear); Director: Mario Bava; Producer: Paolo Mercuri; Screenplay: Marcello Fondato, with the collaboration of Alberto Bevilacqua and Mario Bava; Cinematographer: Ubaldo Terzano. Cast: Boris Karloff, Mark Damon, Jacqueline Soussard, Michele Mercier, Susy Andersen, Lydia Alfonsi, Gustavo De Nardo.

The most gruesome day in the calendar! — ad line

Boris Karloff's disembodied head appears on the screen and intones: "Come closer please, I've something to tell you. Ladies and gentlemen, how do you do. This is *Black Sabbath*. You are about to see three tales of terror and the supernatural. I do hope you haven't come alone!" So begins one of the best horror films to spring from Italian shores in the 1960s, and one of the most frightening horror anthologies ever released.

After the success of Roger Corman's Poe-based Vincent Price anthology *Tales of Terror* (1962), AIP cast about for another omnibus vehicle in which they could use their *other* contract horror star, Boris Karloff. Teaming up with Galatea and Emmepi Film of Rome, and Societe Cinematographique Lyre of Paris, AIP obtained the services of director Mario Bava, instructing him to base his movie on "classic" terror tales (re: public domain and, consequently, *free*) by someone other than Edgar Allan Poe (to avoid treading on Corman's territorial toes). Bava, who, according to his son Lamberto, was an avid reader and was especially fond of Russian literature ("he prided himself on having read the complete works of Dostoevsky six times") then commissioned writers Marcello Fondato and Alberto Bevilacqua to flesh out his ideas into a screenplay.

The result was *I Tre Volti della Paura* ("The Three Faces of Fear"), a trio of terror tales. In the first story, "The Drop of Water," a greedy nurse (Jacqueline Soussard) steals a ring from the

Boris Karloff as "The Wurdulak" in Mario Bava's masterful omnibus *Black Sabbath* (1964) (American lobby card).

corpse of an old woman, a spiritualist. Soon the nurse is haunted by the continual sound of dripping water and the ghost of the old woman, which literally scares her to death. In the next segment, "The Telephone," a woman (Michele Mercier) is terrorized by a phantom phone caller. The last episode features Boris Karloff in a period piece as a Russian patriarch who's transformed into a vampire known as "The Wurdalak," a creature that seeks the blood of those it loves most.

Shot in Italy in 1963, the picture became *Black Sabbath* when released by AIP in America in 1964 (possibly in a nod to that film company's earlier Bava-directed Italian import and box-office hit, *Black Sunday*). AIP re-ordered the three tales (Bava's original cut had "The Telephone" first, then the lengthiest episode—"The Wurdalak"—in the middle, and finishing up with the strongest of the trio, "The Drop of Water") and added a series of onscreen introductions by "host" Karloff along the lines of his popular *Thriller* television anthology. Said intros, though rather silly ("As you will see from one of our tales, vampires—Wurdalaks—abound everywhere. Is that one sitting behind you now?! You can't be too careful you know"), are also somewhat endearing for Karloff fans, allowing Boris to indulge his too-often-suppressed sense of humor.

Bava achieved an anthological miracle with *Black Sabbath* by constructing a multi-story movie whose tone remains constant, despite the changes in characters and story lines—a real rarity in this frequently problematic cinematic subset. Each of the three tales, though not equally effective, builds a palpable sense of dread over the course of its short running time. Their carefully measured tempos gradually build suspense until each story finishes with a satisfying flourish, avoiding the hurried pacing and often abrupt endings that plague many an omnibus.

The film's sumptuous sets would be the envy of any Hammer production. Bava (a former cameraman himself) works with cinematographer Ubaldo Terzano to wring every ounce of atmosphere from these meticulously dressed and cluttered settings, lighting them via flickering firelight or cleverly-placed spot-lighting, strategically illuminating certain portions of a room while leaving others in deepest shadow.

While the camera prowls in and around these sets to maximum effect, Bava also makes potent use of sound. In "The Drop of Water" (a perfectly-paced and absolutely terrifying vignette—and the film's most chilling segment) the relentless noise of dripping water, the startling bang of unfastened shutters, and a howling wind that alternately sounds like a sharp intake of breath and the wail of some inhuman beast all add to the tension and eerie mood.

Bava punctuates his malevolent atmosphere with some cleverly placed visceral shocks—exclamation points for his visual poetry. At the beginning of "The Drop of Water" the nurse pulls back the bed sheet from her patient to reveal a hideously emaciated corpse—lips stretched taut over a rictus grin, and bulging eyes staring. It's a gruesome and unexpected sight, particularly startling because the viewer had no expectation of seeing a *corpse*, much less such a horribly grotesque one. The nurse closes the ghastly eyes, but a moment later the camera reveals them open and staring again—with a crescendo on the soundtrack as potent punctuation—generating a moment of true *frisson*. (Mario Bava's father, sculptor Eugenio Bava, provided the hideous mask worn by the "corpse," as well as a severed head for "The Wurdalak.")

Later, when the nurse nervously wrestles the ring from the corpse's finger it skitters under the bed. As she rummages around next to the bed, the cadaver's hand suddenly drops into the frame and onto the nurse's *head*, causing the woman—and the viewer—to start violently. The tension builds steadily to the story's admittedly foregone conclusion, but in this instance getting there is *all* the shuddery fun. While "The Wurdalak" may be the best-remembered segment (due primarily to Karloff's commanding presence), for artful suspense-building and sheer fright, the tightly played "Drop of Water" proves to be liquid gold.

After the delicious opening terror of "The Drop of Water," the movie's next segment (in the AIP version) proves somewhat less enthralling. This is not due to any missteps on Bava's part—for the original version of "The Telephone" is an engrossing, multi-layered vignette of unease and mounting suspense—but to AIP's nonsensical tampering. AIP (thankfully) left the movie's other two segments alone, but felt that "The Telephone" needed juicing up in the supernatural department. Originally a Hitchcockian "psychological thriller" tale of a woman tormented via telephone by a vengeful former lover, AIP decided to redub the dialogue and make the phantom phone caller a former *dead* lover. So scenes of a pair of eyes peeking through the blinds, and the man himself creeping into the room only to be stabbed and killed by the terrified woman, make a confusing hash of the (new) premise. (The studio also deleted lesbian overtones in the woman's relationship with the "friend" from whom she seeks solace, thereby eliminating an entire subtext.)

Fortunately, the final segment, "The Wurdalak," raises the bar once again. It begins with an evocative and expansive exterior shot of a silhouetted rider on horseback at sunset that dispels the claustrophobia engendered by the first two tales' interior settings. After this brief moment of picturesque respite, however, Bava immediately moves onto the fog-shrouded sets as the rider arrives and the living nightmare begins. And a waking nightmare it is, with its dreadful theme, malevolent atmosphere, tension-filled characters and a powerful performance by that legend of horror himself, Boris Karloff.

Karloff's performance as the Wurdalak is the only time in his 60-year film career that he played a vampire, and the King of Horror does not disappoint. His wild, curly hair and gray moustache gives him a dangerous, unkempt, Cossack-like appearance, which the veteran bogeyman matches with his demeanor and delivery. "I'm hungry," he announces at one point, and breaks into a sinister smile whose menace conjures up images of films gone by. A moment later he refuses conventional food — obviously hungry for something *else*.

Unfortunately, the story of "The Wurdalak" is rather predictable, and the audience identification characters — Mark Damon as the hero and Susy Andersen as the heroine (whose radiant beauty is both wholesome and seductive) — are as shallow as that earlier drop of water. So we're left with Karloff's menace (which is considerable) and Bava's eerie atmosphere (which is all-pervasive). It makes for a stylish ride.

Bava considered this film his personal favorite, and it's easy to see why. Without question, *Black Sabbath* stands as the best horror anthology of the decade, superior to the various Amicus entries and even to Corman's *Tales of Terror*. Given its strong visuals, suspenseful build-ups, startling shocks and some genuine moments of fright (not to mention presenting a real treat for all Karloff fans by giving the King of Horror one last shot at something genuinely scary), *Black Sabbath* is a day all lovers of terror will want to circle on their cinematic calendars.

With quotes from: *Black Sabbath* DVD liner notes, by Tim Lucas, Image Entertainment, 2000.

Black Sunday (1960; AIP; Italy; b&w) Original Language Title: *La Maschera del Demonio* (Mask of the Demon). Director: Mario Bava; Producer: Massimo Derita; Screenplay: Ennio De Concini, Mario Bava, Marcello Coscia, Mario Seranore; Cinematographers: Mairo Bava, Ubaldo Terzano. Cast: Barbara Steele, John Richardson, Ivo Garrani, Andrea Checchi, Arturo Dominici, Enrico Olivieri, Clara Bindi, Antonio Pierfederici, Tino Bianchi, Germana Dominici.

THE UNDEAD DEMONS OF HELL TERRORIZE THE WORLD IN AN ORGY OF STARK HORROR! — poster blurb

"THE MOST FRIGHTENING MOTION PICTURE YOU HAVE EVER SEEN" trumpeted the Allen Theater marquee in Cleveland for *Black Sunday*'s "world premier" in 1960. While such hyperbole is not uncommon in the movie biz, truth in advertising *is* — and *Black Sunday* was one film that actually lived up to its ballyhoo. While it may no longer be the "most frightening" film for today's viewers, in 1960 there were few that could argue

Barbara Steele, as Princess Asa, receives a terrifying shock when her vampirized father (Ivo Garrani) awakens in his coffin on *Black Sunday* (1960) (American lobby card).

the point. Britain's Hammer Films were glorifying in the gothic, but, though often colorful and engrossing, few of Hammer's Draculas or Frankensteins or Mummys could truly be termed terrifying (perhaps the closest the studio came to making a seriously scary film was *The Plague of the Zombies* in 1966). In America, Roger Corman's Price/Poe cycle was just beginning (and again, though well-mounted and enthralling, these American Gothics weren't all that frightening either).

Enter 45-year-old Mario Bava, who for 20 years had toiled as a cameraman in the Italian film industry. After taking over the directorial reins on two different Galatea productions (*The Giant of Marathon* and *Caltiki the Immortal Monster*) when the directors walked out on the projects half-way through production, the Italian film company gave Bava the green light to choose anything he wished for his full directorial debut. Enamored of Russian literature, Bava chose Nikolai Gogol's ghost story *The Vij*. "The genius of the screenwriters—myself included," admitted Bava, "saw to it that almost nothing remained of Gogol's tale." (Of course, this didn't stop AIP from bandying about the literary heavyweight's name in its advertising.)

Originally titled *Mask of the Demon* (and called *Revenge of the Vampire* in England—when it finally made it past the British censors *eight years later*), *Black Sunday* begins literally on Black Sunday, the day on which legend says the dead may walk the earth, as Princess Asa Vaida (Barbara Steele) and her satanic lover Javutich (Arturo Domenici) are condemned as witches and vampires in 17th century Moldavia. Before being executed in a particularly horrific fashion (the executioner hammers a metallic mask lined with spikes onto their faces!), Asa places a curse on the house of her accuser—her own brother. (The deadly mask was sculpted and cast in bronze by the director's father, Eugenio Bava.) Two centuries later, a pair of doctors (John Richardson and Andrea Checchi) traveling to a medical conference stumble upon the crypt holding Asa and inadvertently revive the witch, who vampirises the elder doctor and resurrects her undead lover. The witch intends to possess the beautiful Princess Katia (Steele again), Asa's lookalike descendent. It is up to the young physician and a well-versed local priest to stop the evil vampiress/witch before she can change places with Katia and so live another 100 years until the next Black Sunday.

Galatea urged Bava to shoot *Black Sunday* in Technicolor, but he refused. Bava's experienced cinematographer voice told his fledgling director's persona that the atmosphere he wanted to convey could only be captured in black and white. Said sentiments were echoed by the film's star, Barbara Steele. "I think that black and white movies are much more subjective," Steele opined to interviewer Christopher Dietrich. "They reach the unconscious on a much more profound level than films in color, especially in [the horror] genre. You put your own reading into black and white, whereas color is so literal that it's less intimate." (In the late 1960s, an American producer offered Bava the opportunity to remake *Black Sunday* in color. The maestro refused.)

Black Sunday certainly is intimate. Bava builds his nighttime atmosphere and imagery into a shadowland of doom and dread. Steele told interviewer Mark Miller that because Bava "was a fabulous director of cinematography, he actually chose that script, I think, so that he could show all of his visual tricks." Bava's prowling camera and silhouetted images conjure up shuddery images (such as a lantern suspended in total blackness or a face suddenly appearing out of the darkness) that both startle and chill. "[Bava] really geared it to play out all of his cinematographic visual fantasies," opined Steele, "and I think that the strongest point of the movie is its visual look." Indeed.

"Bava was a shy, elegant man," continued Steele, "like a very quiet businessman in a way, and unobtrusive but nurturing. There was a very kind mood around him that was unaggressive. He was really lovely."

"YOUNG STARS MAKE AMERICAN FILM DEBUT IN 'BLACK SUNDAY'" read a headline in AIP's *Black Sunday* pressbook. It's an amusing claim considering the film is one-hundred percent *Italian*—AIP only picked it up for American distribution after the movie was completed. One of these "young stars" referenced was Barbara Steele. Though she'd been seen in a number of small-scale British movies, this was the actress' first starring role. It's an iconographic performance (at least visually—since her voice was unfortunately dubbed by another actress), one that would come to embody Steele's mix of beautiful innocence and smoldering sensuality. Such a persona codified the good and evil that could drive men to their nirvana or to their doom (sometimes simultaneously—as with *Black Sunday*'s Dr. Kruvajan, whom Asa orders to "embrace me; you will die, but I can bring you pleasures mortals cannot know").

"I was very young when I did *Black Sunday*," noted Steele in *Film Comment* magazine, "it was right at the beginning of my career, and so I was terrified on that set. Maybe some of that terror and intensity translated onto the screen." *Black Sunday* proved the beginning of an intense association for Steele with European horror, as she went on to star in nine more terror tales (most of them from the Continent) over the next six years. Though she'd prefer to be remembered for her work in art house fare like Fellini's *8½* and *Young Torless*, it is her image as the ultimate Siren of the Scream that lingers.

Filming *Black Sunday* was no Sunday picnic. "We were all dying during the shooting of Black Sunday," recalled Steele to interviewer Dietrich. "It was freezing. We shot for three or four weeks in December. There was no heat, and it was one of those arctic Roman winters. Everyone had some terrible virus, and everyone was totally asphyxiated by all the dry ice! It's just as well that the film was dubbed later, because everyone was utterly nasal."

While perhaps lacking the obvious impact of today's modern gore-fests (though the mask-nailing and reanimation sequences still pack a visceral wallop), *Black Sunday* weaves its potent spell to draw the viewer into a shadowy world of palpable evil, making it one of the most atmospheric, eerie and frightening horror films of the 1960s. "The producers of *Black Sunday* recommend that it be seen only by those over 12 years of age!" warned the posters. Indeed, those of us who visited this world at an impressionable age were not soon to forget—as Barbara Steele herself learned: "I remember a nightmare experience when [my son] Jonathan was very young, about three, when we were living in New York. He was in a terrible state because his babysitter let him watch *Black Sunday* on television. There was that terrible scene, you know, where I got that awful mask lined with nails pounded on my face. This was really traumatic for Jonathan. Little children think television's real when they're three. I wanted to kill that babysitter." Babysitters—and viewers—beware.

With quotes from: "Karma, Catsup, & Caskets: The Barbara Steele Interview," by Christopher S. Dietrich with Peter Beckman, *Video Watchdog* 7, September/October 1991; "An Interview with Barbara Steele, Diva of Dark Drama," by Mark A. Miller, *Filmfax* 51, July/August 1995; "The Dark Queen," by Alan Upchurch, *Film Comment*, January/February 1993.

The Black Zoo

The Black Zoo (1963; Allied Artists) Director: Robert Gordon; Producer: Herman Cohen; Screenwriters: Aben Kandel, Herman Cohen; Cinematographer: Floyd Crosby. Cast: Micheal Gough, Jeanne Cooper, Rod Lauren, Virginia Grey, Elisha Cook, Jr., Jerome Cowan, Edward Platt.

FANG AND CLAW KILLERS ... RULED BY A MASTER MIND OF *HORROR*!—ad line

Michael Gough once again chews the scenery as a private zoo owner who sends his various animals out to do his murderous bidding. Gough, left to his own devices (as here and in his two previous Herman Cohen-produced films, *Horrors of the Black Museum* [1959] and *Konga* [1960]), can overact up a storm, indulging in mad histrionics that would make even Bela Lugosi blush. Sometimes this can be to the film's advantage, such as in the morbidly effective *Horrors of the Black Museum*. Other times it becomes laughable, as in the pathetic *Konga*. (The none-too-convincing gorilla suit from that giant ape movie is recycled here—though it's limited to "normal" size.)

In *The Black Zoo* Gough seems to vacillate from one scene to the next, sometimes underplaying (such as in the absurd yet bizarrely unsettling sequence in which he ushers his big cats into his living room to play the organ for them) and sometimes going over the top (such as when he escalates an argument with his wife into a ridiculous screaming fit). Gough's unevenness in this context is actually a plus, because you never know quite how he's going to react next, and this fits in well with his domineering character who loves his animals above all else (definitely more than any pesky human). It's obvious his character is at least one can shy of a six-pack, and this makes him all the more intriguing.

"Michael Gough," said producer/screenwriter Herman Cohen to interviewer Tom Weaver, "who I brought here from London to do the film, loved animals, and the animals took to him beautifully." (Gough told *Scarlet Street* magazine that he would lie down next to the mountain lion, rest his head on the animal's chest and eat a sandwich—and the big cat would be purring!) "But we had to be very careful on *Black Zoo*," continued Cohen. "When I interviewed any female in the picture, I had to ask when they had their periods. And right away, they shouted, '*What*?!' But if an animal smells blood ... there can be trouble."

"The best experience I had on a film produced

Michael Gough (holding tiger cub) and Oren Curtis (in headdress) preside over a cult of animal worshippers (here trying to "pray the soul" of a dead animal into the cub) in *Black Zoo* (1963).

by Herbert Cohen," related Gough to interviewer David Del Valle, "was *Black Zoo*, which was made wonderful because of those animals that I worked with that made filming absolutely unforgettable. The trainer who owned them was a fearless soul with a total understanding of just how to get these animals to work in front of a camera.... The most amazing scene was the one where I summon all my creatures into the parlor where I play the organ, and they all came in one at a time and sat around me. Let me tell you I was completely at the mercy of their owner, who, as I said, was truly a genius with God's creatures great and small. He loved them and had no use for circuses and zoos that exploited animals; he was well ahead of his time. I will always have a fondness for that film out of all of those thrillers I did for Herman [the others being *Horrors of the Black Museum*, *Konga*, *Berserk*, and *Trog*]."

"Fondness" is definitely *not* the word Gough would choose to apply to producer Herman Cohen himself. "Herman Cohen was the boss on all that he produced and not in a positive way either," recalled Gough. "Cohen was a showman — first, last and always; his manner was always overbearing and his opinions sacrosanct."

While *The Black Zoo* drags a bit in the middle, it picks up nicely at the climax, which features a surprising plot twist as well. Though not the most logical of storylines, Gough's presence smoothes over most of the rough spots, and the animal kills are handled well. ("[The animal trainer] also played the victim in our film," stated Gough, "he would dress up like the character about to be killed and actually roll around with the lions as if they were attacking him.") And where else can you see a midnight funeral for a tiger(!)—complete with graveyard atmosphere that would make any 1930s Universal horror film proud — and attended not only by people, but by lions, pumas and cheetahs as well (friends of the deceased)?

With quotes from: *Attack of the Monster Movie Makers*, by Tom Weaver; "Konga — Put Me Down! In Conversation with Michael Gough," by David Del Valle, *Little Shoppe of Horrors* no. 23, October 2009.

Blackbeard's Ghost (1968; Disney/Buena Vista) Director: Robert Stevenson; Producer: Bill Walsh; Screenplay: Bill Walsh and Don Da Gradi (Book: Ben Stahl); Cinematography: Edward Colman. Cast: Dean Jones, Peter Ustinov, Suzanne Pleshette, Elsa Lanchester, Joby Baker, Richard Deacon, Michael Conrad, Hank Jones.

Ghost-to-Ghost Laughs!—tagline

Until an upstart named Steven Spielberg arrived in the mid–1970s, Robert Stevenson held the distinction of being the highest-grossing director in movie history. Although little celebrated today, Stevenson helmed 19 widely popular and highly profitable family films for Walt Disney beginning with *Johnny Tremain* (1957), continuing through *The Shaggy D.A.* (1976) and including *Old Yeller* (1957), *The Absent-Minded Professor* (1961), *Mary Poppins* (1964) and *The Love Bug* (1968). The rollicking supernatural farce *Blackbeard's Ghost* is prime Stevenson.

New track coach Steve Walker (Dean Jones) arrives in the New England village surrounding tiny Godolphin College and immediately finds himself embroiled in a dispute between a group of kindly old ladies (the "Daughters of the Buccaneers"), who want to preserve a historic inn once owned by the notorious pirate Blackbeard, and a gang of ruthless mobsters who want to take over the place and turn it into a casino. The Daughters, led by dotty Emily Stowecroft (Elsa Lanchester), believe the pirate's spirit still haunts the inn. Steve is dubious until, after stumbling across an ancient book of magic spells, he accidentally invokes the spirit of Blackbeard (Peter Ustinov). The pirate's mischievous ghost hounds Steve's every step, swilling rum and causing a ruckus wherever he goes—trouble which is blamed on the coach, since Blackbeard remains invisible to everyone else. Blackbeard is cursed to remain in limbo between this world and the next until he can prove he's not all bad; Steve is cursed to coach the most pathetic track team in history. But together the two hatch a plot to reverse both hexes and, in the process, save the inn from the gangsters.

Born in Buxton, Derbyshire, England, Stevenson began his career churning out "quota quickies" and ended it cranking out episodes of the *Disneyland* TV series. He was Oscar-nominated as Best Director for his work on *Mary Poppins*. Early in his career the filmmaker displayed a flair for macabre material with *The Man Who Lived Again* (aka *The Man Who Changed His Mind*, 1936), starring Boris Karloff and Anna Lee (Stevenson's first wife), and with the gothic romance *Jane Eyre* (1944), starring Orson Welles and Joan Fontaine. *Blackbeard's Ghost* serves as a quintessential example of Stevenson's work for Disney. It's a lively, lighthearted story told deftly but without showy camera movements or any sort of artistic pretensions, and it features two hilarious set pieces. In the first of these, Godolphin triumphs at a track meet thanks to the unseen intervention of Blackbeard, who causes a series of unlikely disasters to befall Godolphin's rivals (slicing a rival vaulter's pole in half with his sword, for instance) and equally preposterous good fortune to find the Godolphin team (like snatching a falling shot put out of the air and carrying it several yards further). The second is the climactic confrontation between Steve and the mobsters, during which the invisible buccaneer performs a similar series of stunts to out-cheat a rigged roulette wheel and out-punch a roomful of thugs. By this point in his career, Stevenson could pull off such elaborate sequences, full of complicated special visual effects and delicate comic timing, with apparent ease.

Another key to the director's success was his ability to elicit winning performances from his cast. Here, both Jones as the plucky but frequently exasperated track coach, and Ustinov as the irascible but endearing pirate, contribute likeable, amusing performances. The duo receive able support from Suzanne Pleshette as Steve's love interest (a psychology professor assigned to keep an eye on the coach because the administration thinks he may be crazy), Joby Baker as oily villain Silky Seymour, Michael Conrad as a blowhard football coach and Elsa Lanchester as the loopy Miss Stowecroft. It's no wonder Stevenson's work was so popular. Funny, imaginative pictures like *Blackbeard's Ghost* make enjoyable family viewing even today.

Blind Beast (1969; Daiei International; Japan) Original Language Title: *Moju*. Director: Yasuzo Masumura; Producer: Kazumasa Nakano; Screenplay: Yoshio Shirasaka (Story: Rampo Edogawa); Cinematographer: Setsuo Kobayashi. Cast: Eiji Funakoshi; Mako Midori; Noriko Sengoku.

"If it doesn't hurt, it doesn't satisfy me."—Aki Shima (to her masseur)

The disturbing, repellant *Blind Beast* is less a horror movie than a particularly gruesome and twisted art film—after the fashion of Hiroshi

Teshigahara's *Woman in the Dunes* (1964), only far more brutal and with a sado-erotic bent.

Assisted by his mother (Noriko Sengoku), blind sculptor Michio (Eiji Funakoshi) kidnaps model Aki Shima (Mako Midori), locks her away in his warehouse studio and forces her to pose for him. At first, Aki tries to escape, playing mind games to try to turn her captors against one another. But this tactic goes awry and, trapped in the dark studio, she starts to lose her eyesight. She also begins to fall in love with Michio, and to discover a latent masochist fetish. At first the couple beat each other with ropes and chains, but they soon graduate to cutting one another with knives. Finally, Aki begs Michio to amputate her arms and legs (without benefit of anesthetic).

Although clearly aiming for the critical acclaim afforded Teshigahara or Shohei Imamura, director Yasuzo Masumura lacks those filmmakers' deft touch with shocking material. *Blind Beast* is an artless art film, full of ham-fisted symbolism (Michio's studio is full of giant sculpted body parts—he and Aki have sex between an enormous pair of breasts) and riddled with Freudian psychobabble. Masumura never simply lets events play out and allow viewers to draw their own conclusions; instead, he beats every idea into the audience's heads with a 10-minute conversation between Aki and Michio. Worse yet, most of the film's deep philosophical-thematic concepts are actually harebrained or wrongheaded. Particularly revolting is the way the scenario seems to correlate blindness with insanity.

Even Teshigahara or Imamura would have had trouble handling a scenario as ghastly and ultimately vapid as this one. Then again, those filmmakers would have been smart enough to steer clear of any picture as tasteless and stupid as *Blind Beast*.

Blood and Black Lace (1964/65; Emmepi Cinematigrafica/Allied Artists; Italy.) Original Title: *Sei Donne per l'Assassino* (*Six Women for the Murderer*). Director: Mario Bava; Producers: Alfredo Mirabile and Massimo Patrizi; Screenplay: Giuseppe Baarilla, Marcel Fonda, Marcello Fundato and Mario Bava; Cinematography: Ubalso Terzano. Cast: Cameron Mitchell, Eva Bartok, Thomas Reiner, Claude Dantes, Mary Arden, Ariana Gorini, Lea Lander, Dante DiPaolo, Franco Ressel.

A fashion house of glamorous models becomes a terror house of blood!—tagline

Although it would take nearly a decade to fully flower, the seed director Mario Bava planted with *Blood and Black Lace* eventually would transform the horror genre—for better or worse. Its legacy aside, however, the film remains riveting entertainment.

A young model, Isabella (Francesca Ungaro), on her way home from the haute couture salon where she works, is strangled to death by a mysterious assailant in a black trench coat, gloves, wide-brimmed hat and a faceless mask. When one of her coworkers discovers that Isabella kept a diary, the black figure returns to kill other models—those who come into possession of the diary or are believed to know about its contents—often in a bizarre or brutal manner. One, attacked in an antique store, is slashed with the spiked glove from a nearby suit of armor. Another's face is pressed against a red-hot stove. At first, police believe that one of four men employed at the studio may be behind the crimes, but authorities are baffled when the murders continue even though all their sus-

Police investigate the double-homicide handiwork of a fashion-model killer in Mario Bava's seminal giallo *Blood and Black Lace* (1964/65) (U.S. lobby card).

pects are in custody. Could the killer be a sex maniac, or is there another explanation for the sadistic crimes?

Blood and Black Lace is an engrossing, well-plotted whodunit — briskly paced, with dramatic tension sustained throughout and a satisfying "twist" resolution to the mystery. But those are the least of the film's merits. The story itself pales in comparison to the artistry with which Bava tells the tale. Every frame of the movie is beautifully composed (with plenty of foreground silhouettes and symmetrically balanced two-shots, among other eye-catching devices) and lovingly photographed, full of smooth pans and fluid tracking shots that take full advantage of the picture's evocatively appointed sets (including such details as the eerily faceless, red velvet mannequins in the fashion studio, or the ghostly, sheet-covered furniture at a model's country house, or the creepy miscellany of the antique shop). Bava's mastery of expressionist color provides the finishing touch, bathing nearly every scene in eerie green, red and/or violet gels.

By design, the director's most inventively and attractively staged sequences are the murders. At one point a victim is drowned in her bathtub — a scene many directors might present in a coy or perfunctory manner. Not Bava. He plunges viewers into the scene without warning, opening with the killer in the middle of the crime, holding a model's head under water — shot from what appears to be the bottom of the tub, the camera pointed upward into the terrified face of the gasping, dying woman, seen in close-up. The dead body sinks to the bottom of the tub, and the killer slits the victim's wrists to make the death look like a suicide. Fire engine red blood billows out, covering the body like a rolling storm cloud. Meticulous color balancing further enhances this striking image, as the red blood matches the victim's lipstick, and the model's white brassiere matches the now coffin-like bathtub.

The story's characters are well defined, but the acting is merely adequate. Bava typically provided little guidance to his actors and seldom elicited outstanding performances from his cast — the notable exceptions being Barbara Steele in *Black Sunday* (1960) and Daliah Lavi in *What!* (aka *The Whip and the Body* [1963/65]). Cameron Mitchell and Eva Bartok are top-billed as the owners of the fashion salon, but the scenario has no true lead. It's more of an ensemble piece, with the cast divided between suspects and victims, but Ariana Gorini, Lea Lander and Mary Arden along with Bartok, all make good impressions. The script's male characters are more thinly written than its females, and the performances of Dante DiPaolo, Franco Ressel, Thomas Reiner and others suffer as a result. Only Mitchell truly stands out among the male cast.

Today, *Blood and Black Lace* is widely recognized as the first "giallo" thriller, a particularly bloodthirsty brand of murder mystery originating in Italy, with singular stylistic and thematic conventions, most of which originate with this film. In developing the giallo style, Bava was profoundly influenced by Alfred Hitchcock (especially *Psycho* [1960]), West German "krimi" crime films and then-popular lurid, pulpy Italian mystery novels with yellow covers ("giallo" is Italian for yellow). Bava had introduced elements of the giallo style in earlier films, such as *The Evil Eye* (aka *The Girl Who Knew Too Much* [1963/64]) and "The Telephone" segment in *Black Sabbath* (1963/64), but he assembles all the form's signature components for the first time for *Blood and Black Lace*: a masked, knife-wielding killer; a "target-rich" setting (like a fashion salon, girls' school or dance studio); a high body count; and, most importantly, brutal murders filmed with bravura visual style (and often sexualized). Bava's approach would be widely imitated, especially after the breakthrough international success of director Dario Argento's *The Bird with the Crystal Plumage* (1970), which ushered in a flood of Italian giallo thrillers. In the early 1970s the gialli were nearly as plentiful as Italy's earlier torrents of spaghetti Westerns and peplum sword-and-sandal adventures. Bava made a few more gialli himself, including *Bay of Blood* (aka *Twitch of the Death Nerve*, 1971/72), which served as a pivotal influence on *Friday the 13th* (1980). *Friday*, in turn, precipitated the rise of the slasher sub-genre — slasher films being, essentially, dumbed-down, Americanized gialli lacking the artistic stylization of their progenitors.

Blood and Black Lace also presents one of Bava's clearest and most unequivocal statements of a frequently recurring thematic message — the soul-destroying nature of greed. In many of the director's movies characters that put personal gain ahead of compassion for other people are consumed and ultimately undone by their own selfishness. To say more would give away the ending, but in *Blood and Black Lace*— as in most Bava films— money (at least when valued more than human life) truly is the root of all evil.

Blood and Black Lace was shot on a six-week schedule in late 1963 and early 1964 (shortly after the assassination of President John F. Kennedy) at two Roman villas on a modest budget of about $125,000. According to Mitchell, Bava achieved the film's slick, stylized look despite major deficiencies in resources. "Do you remember that wonderful dolly shot through the fashion house?" asks Mitchell, recalling one of the film's most graceful camera movements. "Well, our dolly on that shot was a *kid's red wagon*! And when we had to do a crane type shot, we didn't have a crane. They literally took something like a seesaw and counterbalanced the camera by sitting crew people on the other end! But wasn't that elegant? Didn't that film have style?"

Yes it did. And it still does.

With quotes from: *Mario Bava: All the Colors of the Dark*, by Tim Lucas.

Blood and Roses (1960/61; Documento/Paramount; France/Italy) Original Language Title: ... *Et Mourir de Plaisir*. Director: Roger Vadim; Producer: Raymond Eger; Screenplay: Roger Vadim and Roger Vailland (Story: Claude Martin and Claude Brule, from a story by Sheridan Le Fanu); Cinematographer: Claude Renoir. Cast: Mel Ferrer, Elsa Martinelli, Annette Vadim.

It plunges you into the midnight zone beyond the grasp of reason!—tagline

The idea of director Roger Vadim, the notorious purveyor of saucy art house fare like *And God Created Woman* (1959) and *Dangerous Liaisons* (1960), adapting Sheridan Le Fanu's Sapphic vampire yarn *Carmilla* must have posed a titillating prospect for moviegoers. Yet Vadim's *Blood and Roses* proved to be an unaccountably tepid affair, taking a surprisingly chaste approach to the story's lesbianism, and even its vampirism.

Vadim's modernization of Le Fanu's novella, set in contemporary Italy, centers on a wealthy young woman, Carmilla (Annette Vadim), who's secretly in love with Leopoldo (Mel Ferrer), who is engaged to mutual friend Georgia (Elsa Martinelli). To celebrate the impending nuptials, Leopoldo and Georgia host a costume party with fireworks. But the fireworks accidentally explode previously undiscovered Nazi land mines, and the resulting tremors open the grave of Carmilla's ancestor, Milarka, a vampiress who also had been trapped in a romantic triangle. Milarka possesses Carmilla and sets out to destroy the bond between Leopoldo and Georgia, then restart her vampiric reign of terror.

Bidding for critical respectability, Vadim softpedals nearly every exploitable element in the scenario. He leaves the story's lone murder offscreen; discreetly cuts away from Carmilla's seduction of Georgia; and offers a possible psychological (rather than supernatural) explanation for Carmilla's "possession." The screenplay, by Vadim and Roger Vailland, telegraphs every plot turn well in advance, further negating any dramatic tension, let alone suspense.

Instead of thrills and chills, Vadim focuses on visual stylization. Unfortunately, aside from a few isolated moments (such as a gorgeous shot of Carmilla kneeling to gaze at her reflection in a pond as fireworks light up the sky above), *Blood and Roses* remains fairly prosaic in its imagery. That is, at least until its final reel, when Vadim delivers an impressionistic dream sequence clearly envisioned as a *tour de force* finale. But this scene, too, falls flat, in part because it so obviously emulates Jean Cocteau's surrealist classic *Blood of a Poet* (1930). Although the rest of the film is in Technicolor, Vadim shoots the dream sequence in black-and-white with red-tinted blood.

The film's cast also proves problematic. Ferrer and Martinelli remain stiff and unconvincing; but

Carmilla (Annette Vadim, then-wife of director Roger) meets a gruesome fate at the conclusion of the otherwise surprisingly tame *Blood and Roses* (1961).

they look like Oscar winners compared to Annette Vadim (the director's wife), whose blank non-performance hangs like a millstone around the movie's neck. The lone bright spot is Jean Prodromides' superb score, including a haunting piano sonata, which gives viewers something to hang onto as this picture meanders along. Although it runs just 87 minutes (slashed to 74 for its U.S. release), *Blood and Roses* seems far longer. Despite its brevity, this snoozer will try the patience of all but the most indulgent or easily amused viewers.

Blood Bath (1966; Deal/Fox; b&w). Alternate Title: *Track of the Vampire* (TV, home video). Directors: Jack Hill, Susan Rothman; Producer: Jack Hill; Screenplay: Jack Hill, Stephanie Rothman; Cinematographer: Alfred Taylor. Cast: William Campbell, Marissa Mathes, Sandra Knight, Karl Schanzer, Biff Eliot, Sid Haig, Jonathan Haze.

The SHRIEKING of MUTILATED VICTIMS CAGED in a BLACK PIT of HORROR!—tagline

Given its scruffy origins, it's a wonder that *Blood Bath* is even watchable.

Executive producer Roger Corman hired Jack Hill to cobble together an "original" film around footage from a Hungarian picture Corman bought on the cheap. Displeased with Hill's progress, Corman sacked the director in mid-production and replaced him with Susan Rothman. Inevitably, the results are mixed (and at times incoherent), yet *Blood Bath* features some arrestingly effective moments, too.

The plot (such as it is) revolves around beatnik painter Tony Sordi (William Campbell), who rises to prominence with a series of "dead red nudes"—gory paintings of brutalized women. As young women continue disappearing and Sordi continues producing paintings, rival artist Max (Karl Schanzer) begins to suspect that Sordi is the reincarnation of ancestor Erno Sordi (also Campbell), a medieval artist accused of vampirism. But no one takes this fantastic theory seriously, in part because of Max's jealousy over Sordi's financial success, and the fact that Max fancies Sordi's ballet dancer girlfriend (Sandra Knight).

The film's basic premise is solid albeit unoriginal, recycled from Corman's *A Bucket of Blood* (1959) and H.G. Lewis' *Color Me Blood Red* (1965). But the film's episodic structure and haphazard construction—plot threads are picked up, then dropped; characters appear then inexplicably vanish—precludes any sort of sustained tension. A satiric undercurrent present in the film's early scenes quickly dissipates. The picture comes to a screeching halt for a fistful of filler scenes, including an extended, split-screen sequence where the bikini-clad Knight simply dances on the beach, accompanied by a tinkling piano. Due to moments like this, *Blood Bath* plays like a padded-out *Night Gallery* episode.

However, *Blood Bath* boasts isolated moments that prove highly effective. The story's finale, in which Sordi's victims return from the dead to claim their revenge, almost makes up for all the nonsense which precedes it. Most of the film's murders are executed (pun intended) with panache and a dollop of dark humor. For example, in one early scene, Campbell pretends to neck with a dead girl to avoid detection. There's also a remarkably effective, Salvador Dali-like dream sequence.

The film's messy production history makes it difficult to assign credit (or blame) for these wildly disparate sequences. Technically, as in virtually

Murder-mad artist Antonio Sordi's victims (including a jealous husband played by David Miller) rise from the dead to claim vengeance during the climax of *Blood Bath* (1966).

every other respect, the film is all over the map. The lighting, for instance, alternates between the evocative and the perfunctory. The performances of the cast are just as uneven, but the good-humored Campbell — who also starred in the Corman-produced *Dementia 13* (1963) — makes an unusually appealing villain.

Bottom line: *Blood Beast* isn't a good film, but it contains enough intriguing elements to make it worth a look.

Blood Beast from Outer Space (1965; Armitage; U.K.; b&w) Alternate Titles: *The Night Caller* (U.K.), *The Night Caller from Outer Space.* Director: John Gilling; Producer: Ronald Liles; Screenplay: Jim O'Connolly (based on the novel *The Night Callers* by Frank Crisp); Cinematographer: Stephen Dade. Cast: John Saxon, Maurice Denham, Patricia Haines, John Carson, Jack Watson.

SPACE CREATURES SNATCH GIRLS TO MYSTERIOUS PLANET!— poster

This intelligent, suspenseful sci-fi/horror film from genre specialist John Gilling (*Shadow of the Cat, Mania, The Plague of the Zombies,* etc.) was released in 1965 in England as the more literate *The Night Caller*, but had to wait a year before being picked up by an American distributor. The fact that it's shot in moody black and white when, at the time, even low-budget efforts were almost invariably in color consigned it to the bottom half of a double bill with the awful (but color) *Castle of Evil*, while being re-titled the awful (but colorful) *Blood Beast from Outer Space.* It's a fate few films deserve, especially one so engrossing as *Blood Beast.*

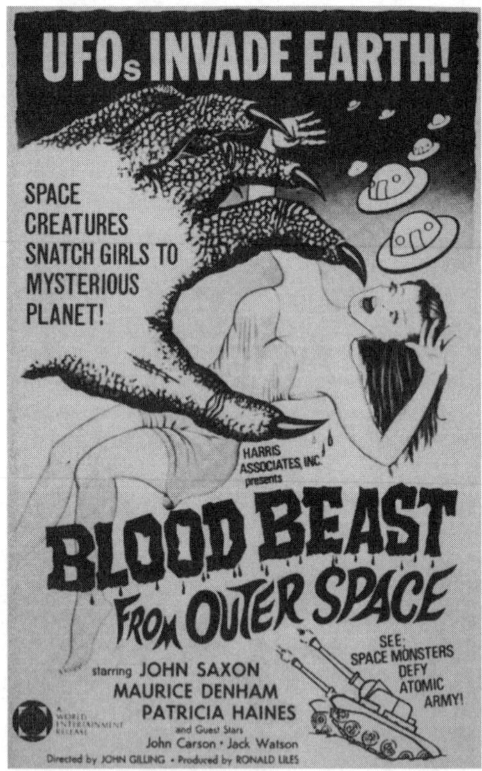

Ad for the luridly-titled but surprisingly literate *Blood Beast from Outer Space* (1965).

"The Night Caller casts a hypnotizing spell/ Fools that try to fight it never live to tell," croons singer Mark Richards in the movie's opening theme song (whose pseudo-pop sensibilities prove to be one of the production's few missteps). Indeed, said Night Caller turns out to be a mutated humanoid alien from Ganymede, Jupiter's third moon, who's come to London (via a matter transmitting sphere) to seek young females for his dying world's gene pool. On the trail of this mysterious "Mr. Medra" (whose modus operandi is luring girls to a Soho office via a modeling advertisement, planting hypnotic suggestions and then later transporting them to his home world) are scientists John Saxon and Patricia Haines (Michael Caine's first wife), as well as much of Scotland Yard and the military.

Director Gilling starts the film off in a straightforward, almost documentary-like mode, harkening back to the sci-fi films of the previous decade. But once Medra is out and about, Gilling's Gothic sensibilities come to the fore, and he quickly establishes an air of mystery and menace, making judicious use of shadows and camera movement, and building the suspense by keeping Medra largely unseen except for a hideous clawed hand and an indistinct yet forbidding shadowy outline.

Apart from token American John Saxon, the film features uniformly excellent actors, which helps keep the unlikely proceedings rather down to earth, so to speak. (Saxon, whose wooden demeanor would give Pinnochio a run for his money, performs his usual earnest-yet-dull routine here.) John Carson (*The Plague of the Zombies, Taste the Blood of Dracula*), as the beleaguered Army Major assigned to the weird case, provides just the right dose of subtle, self-deprecating humor to leaven the otherwise serious scenario. The film offers several unexpected twists and turns, including the brutal disfigurement/killing of the heroine(!), and an unusually philosophical climax rather than the expected slam-bang monster-meets-his-fate standard.

Despite its appalling American re-titling, *Blood Beast from Outer Space* stands as a superior (though largely forgotten) member of that rarest of 1960s cinema subspecies—the literate horror/sci-fi hybrid.

The Blood Beast Terror see *The Vampire-Beast Craves Blood*

The Blood Demon (1967/69; Constantin/Hemisphere; West Germany) Original Language Title: *Die Schlangengrube und das Pendel*; Alternate Titles: *The Torture Chamber of Dr. Sadism*; *Castle of the Walking Dead*; *Blood of the Virgins*; Director: Harold Reinl; Production Supervisor: Erwin Gitt; Screenplay: Manfred R. Kohler; Cinematographers: Wernest W. Kalinke and Dieter Liphardt. Cast: Christopher Lee, Lex Barker, Karin Dor, Karl Lange, Christiaane Rucker, Vladimir Medar, Dieter Eppler.

A MATURE PERSON'S TRIP THROUGH THE ULTIMATE IN HORRIFIC WICKEDNESS—ad line

Shot between May 16 and July 7, 1967, and advertised (correctly) as Germany's first Gothic horror film made since World War II, *Blood Demon* stars Christopher Lee as alchemist/Satanist Count Regula, who's drawn and quartered for killing a dozen young virgins. Thirty-five years later he rises from the dead (with the help of his faithful—and also undead—servant) to claim his thirteenth victim and so secure his immortality. Regula lures a young lawyer (Lex Barker) and a young woman (Karin Dor), both descendents of those who condemned him, to his ruined castle, intending to torture and murder them, and so complete the ceremony that will give him eternal life.

With trap doors, pet vultures, elaborate torture contraptions, knockout gas, magical portals that open and close by themselves, a medieval alchemy lab, and a servant who bleeds green hemoglobin, *Blood Demon* offers up horror hokum by the coffinful. In fact, it becomes difficult to take anything seriously in this cinematic Halloween funhouse.

That said, its wonderfully macabre set design (underground medieval hall; torture chamber strewn with a dozen naked bodies, all demurely posed in various devices; cave-like corridor covered in human skulls) and several shuddery set-pieces make this a tasty piece of ghoulish eye candy. Highlights include a surreal coach journey through a fog-shrouded magical forest festooned with hanging human figures and body parts; a sequence in which the heroine meets one horror after another (including an alcove crawling with spiders and scorpions, and the dreaded snake-filled pit); and the sweating hero enduring the torture of the pendulum. (Unfortunately, the hero's ridiculously improbably escape—involving a well-thrown rock!—drags the scene down to the level of a Saturday matinee serial.)

Lex Barker makes for a broad-shouldered, stalwart hero, and Karin Dor (wife of director Harold Reinl) screams in all the right places. Christopher Lee, however, looks tired and less (re)animated. He only seems to, ahem, come alive at the end when the hero threatens to foil his plans by waving a hated crucifix in his face. (Though an alchemical potion is responsible for Regula's resurrection, the everything-but-the-graveyard-sink story also turns on the supernatural nature of the proceedings.) Lee tipped his less-than-enthusiastic hand in a letter to his fan club: "I am leaving on Monday 19 June for Munich, where I shall be playing a rather revolting aristocrat in a rather weird semi-surrealistic German film entitled at the moment *The Pendulum*. I really have no idea whether this film will ever be shown outside of Europe, and it is just possible that this might be an advantage."

Blood Feast (1963; Friedman-Lewis) Director/Cinematography: Herschell Gordon Lewis; Producer: David F. Friedman; Screenplay: A. Louise Downe. Cast: William Kerwin (as Thomas Wood), Connie Mason, Mal Arnold, Lyn Bolton, Scott Hall.

Nothing So Appalling in the Annals of Horror—tagline

If nothing else, *Blood Feast* deserves kudos for truth in advertising. A landmark of its peculiar idiom, this pioneering splatter film indeed proves appalling—both in the sense intended by its tagline and also for its slipshod moviemaking.

Detective Pete Thornton (William Kerwin) seems baffled by a series of murders involving brutally mutilated young women. Little does he know that his girlfriend's mother (Lyn Bolton) has hired the killer, an Egyptian caterer named Faud Ramses (Mal Arnold), to prepare a birthday banquet for her daughter Suzette (former *Playboy* model Connie Mason). Ramses, a follower of the ancient cult of Isis, plans to make Suzette the main course of a cannibalistic feast honoring the Egyptian goddess.

With *Blood Feast*, for better or worse, exploitation director Herschell Gordon Lewis stamped his indelible thumbprint on the horror genre. Recognizing the salacious interest generated by blood-spattered scenes in hits like *Psycho* (1960) and the early Hammer color gothics (which now seem tame but were edgy in their day), Lewis decided to shoot a picture that would up the ante for screen violence. He overloaded *Blood Feast* with gore sequences that went far beyond anything previously unleashed on movie audiences and completely disregarded the boundaries of good taste. While the film's murders are generally suggested rather than shown (usually through subjective shots from the victim's perspective, followed by a quick cutaway), Lewis' camera lingers on scenes of dismemberment and cannibalism, showing the killer chopping off legs, tearing out his victim's tongue, slicing out an eyeball and, later, baking severed limbs in an oven and stirring a pot of grue stew. All of this would be sickening if Lewis' filmcraft wasn't so inept.

Previously, Lewis had traded in no-budget softcore porn. He shot *Blood Feast* with the same crew and much of the same cast as his most recent nudie-cutie, operating the camera himself while producer David Friedman ran sound. As a result, *Blood Feast* operates on the same level as one of Lewis' raincoat specials, with gore sequences simply replacing the sex scenes. Its dialogue is banal, its performances amateurish and stilted, and its production values nonexistent. *Blood Feast* is so cheaply made that Lewis doesn't even bother to drop in a siren sound effect during its climactic police chase — instead, the sound is mimicked by a trombone. As a result, the *only* point of continuing interest in this film is its gore scenes. Yet, even those are badly botched. The makeup effects are so poor, so obviously fake, that they undercut any potential power to shock. As a result, *Blood Feast* remains far more likely to inspire gales of derisive laughter than wholesale vomiting (even though, as a promotional gimmick, barf bags were distributed to moviegoers at some cinemas during the film's initial theatrical run). Nevertheless the course of horror cinema was changed. Although it took years for graphic bloodletting to become a mainstay of the genre, its emergence was inevitable after *Blood Feast*, which proved astoundingly profitable.

The Blood Drinkers (1966; Philippines; b&w and color) Alternate Title: *The Vampire People* (TV); Director: Gerardo de Leon; Producer: Danilo H. Santiago; Screenplay: Cesar Amigo (story by Rico Bello Omagap); Cinematographer: Felipe J. Sacdalan. Cast: Amalia Fuentes, Eddie Fernandez, Eva Montes, Celia Rodriguez, Renato Robles, Mary Walter, Ronald Remy.

THE BLOOD DRINKERS WILL SINK THEIR TEETH INTO ANYTHING THAT MOVES!— ad line

---

It's refreshing to see a Filipino horror movie that *doesn't* star the vapid former teen heartthrob John Ashley (who made a second career out of walking through a half-dozen horrors from the Philippines in the late '60s/early '70s), especially one with such admirable atmosphere and a strikingly unusual plot.

"Death is a final word," begins the narrator (a priest) as the Gothic gates of a fog-shrouded cemetery open. Well, not in *The Blood Drinkers* ... Marco (Ronald Remy) is a bald-headed, sunglasses-and-cape-wearing aristocratic vampire whose undead lover Katrina (Amalia Fuentes, who played a bloodsucker yet again in 1970's *Creatures of Evil*, a semi-sequel to *The Blood Drinkers*) lay dying — in need of a heart transplant! Marco (who seems to be the cinema's first cardiac surgeon-turned-vampire) intends to transplant the heart of Katrina's twin sister Cherito (also Fuentes) into his lover. At Cherito's village the local priest (who bears an uncanny resemblance to an elderly John Carradine) and Cherito's boyfriend (Eddie Fernandez) must find a way to stop Marco and his minions (who include a sexy, lingerie-clad vampiress, a hunchback named Gordo, a dwarf, and a bat-familiar called Vasla who bobs up and down and growls like a puma!).

The amazing thing about this low-budget oddity is the fact that not only does it hold one's interest (how could it *not*, given such a bizarre storyline?), but it offers up fine atmospherics (an appropriate graveyard ambiance, complete with horse-drawn hearse and plenty of fog) that enhances its romantic-tragic-horrific elements.

The imposing and frightening Marco is also rather tragic, as he's committing his heinous acts out of love (an admittedly obsessive, all-consuming, perverted form of love — but love, nonetheless). There's even a singular scene in which "the power of prayer" seemingly cures both Marco and his lover, allowing the two to walk (in romantic slow-motion) through the woods in the sunshine (though there's still plenty of fog to filter the rays). But, alas, as the priest relates, "The Devil does not give up, ever..." and Katrina catches her leg on a snag and bleeds—causing the couple to revert to their undead condition. Nonsensical, but arresting.

Also arresting is the film's photography. "In blood-curdling color!" promised the ads. Well, sort-of, since *Blood Drinkers* is actually in full color only *part* of the time. Many of the scenes are black and white but tinted either red (when the vampires are around) or blue (for no discernable reason). One assumes that the filmmakers used up all the color film stock they could afford and then fell back to the cheaper black and white. The tinting, at times, seems arbitrary, but occasionally it achieves its desired effect, such as when, during a vampire attack, it fades from red to purple as the nosferatu begins to feed.

Granted, there's plenty to sneer at here. Apart from the (expected) awkward dubbing and sometimes off-putting tinting, *The Blood Drinkers* offers up a stop-the-film-I-wanna-get-off Filipino love ballad, the old wobbly bat-on-a-stick trick, abrupt editing and some overlong expository scenes filled with nonsensical dialogue (one has the priest postulating that the vampires' bodies are filled with "fluid similar in chemical composition to that of hot glue, [and] the hot glue renders the bullets harmless, but wood turns the glue to water" [!]).

But the climax is as novel as the rest of the picture, with the hero inciting the torch-wielding villagers to turn out en masse for a rumble with the vampire hordes (all half-dozen of them). Ever resourceful, he shoots flares into the air to halt the fleeing bloodsuckers, since "vampires fear light."

Director Gerardo de Leon had previously helmed the moody *Terror Is a Man* (1959), a small-scale but evocative adaptation of H. G. Wells' *The Island of Dr. Moreau*, and subsequently paired up with Eddie Romero to co-direct *Brides of Blood* (1968) and *The Mad Doctor of Blood Island* (1969), neither of which are as atmospheric — or entertaining — as *The Blood Drinkers*.

If you can watch only one Filipino horror movie (heaven forbid!), this should be the one.

Blood Fiend (1967; London Independent/Hemisphere; U.K.) Original Title: *Theatre of Death* (U.K.). Director: Samuel Gully; Producer: M. Smedley Aston; Screenplay: Ellis Kadison and Roger Marshall; Cinematography: Gilbert Taylor. Cast: Christopher Lee, Julian Glover, Leila Goldoni, Jenny Till, Evelyn Laye, Ivor Dean.

The BLOOD FIEND will disgust and repel those too weak to share a living nightmare of the BIZARRE!! — tagline

---

Actually, there's disappointingly little disgusting or repellent about *Blood Fiend*, a standard issue whodunit tricked out with a lot of horror trappings rather than a full-tilt chiller.

Dr. Charles Marquis (Julian Glover), a Parisian police surgeon on medical leave, is called in to assist with the investigation of a series of baffling murders. Three young women have been killed, their throats opened with an unusual triangular weapon and their bodies drained of blood. Marquis' suspicions fall on Philippe Darvas (Christopher Lee), the tyrannical director of the Theatre de Mort, which specializes in horror stories depicting torture, murder and mayhem. Marquis' girlfriend, Dani (Leila Goldoni), is a star in the Theatre de Mort, and the surgeon notices that prop knives from one of the company's skits have the distinctive triangular shape of the murder weapon. Meanwhile, Dani is concerned that her roommate, Nicole, is getting too deeply involved with Darvas, who begins hypnotizing the girl to (the director claims) remove Nicole's inhibitions and unlock her acting talent. Then Darvas suddenly disappears, but the murders continue. Has he gone into hiding to continue the crime spree? Is Nicole carrying out the murders under his hypnotic influence? Or could Dani, a former mental patient, be the killer?

Screenwriters Ellis Kadison and Roger Marshall go out of their way to dress up *Blood Fiend*— now better known under its original British title, *Theatre of Death*— with horror imagery. Their scenario is a crazy quilt of fright film clichés, including its Grand Guignol-like setting, vampiric killings and Darvas' spooky old house (full of sliding panels and paintings with peepholes for eyes). The plot involves both hypnotism and madness, and briefly suggests the supernatural. But, at its core, the story remains a mundane murder mystery, and one with too few credible suspects to make an intriguing whodunit.

This fundamental weakness undermines solid work by the picture's cast and crew. Samuel Gully's direction (full of extreme high- and low-angle compositions and smooth tracking shots) is expressive, and cinematographer Gilbert Taylor's color-splashed lighting designs are atmospheric. Art director Peter Proud's sets (especially the baroque Darvas home) are also first-rate. Christopher Lee is in his element playing Darvas, the cruel, egocentric *artiste*. It's a tribute to Lee's compelling work that Darvas remains a viable suspect in the crimes—and as a possible malign influence over Nicole—for the balance of the film, particularly since the character vanishes from the story midway through. Glover, who went on to an acclaimed career with the Royal Shakespeare Company, holds the film together with his emotionally charged performance as Charles Marquis, an injured police surgeon who latches onto the case as something worthwhile to invest himself in while unable to operate. Unfortunately, since they're playing the other two prime suspects, Leila Goldoni and Jenny Till are less convincing in their roles as Dani and Nicole, respectively. Most of the rest of the cast are consigned to glorified bit parts, like Ivor Dean as do-nothing Inspector Micheaud and Evelyn Laye as flinty theater owner Madame Angelique.

For his part, Lee—a renowned amateur operatic vocalist as well as an actor—isn't enamored with the picture but has fond memories of its production. "Strange film, *Theatre of Death*," Lee muses. "What really appealed to me about it, at the beginning, was the fact that the director, Sam Gully, informed me that he had sung tenor with Toscanini. So, of course, off we went into opera right away. We sang at each other all throughout the film."

A better plot might have given audiences something to sing about as well.

With quotes from: "Sinister Theatrics: An Interview with Christopher Lee," DVD bonus feature (Anchor Bay Entertainment).

Blood of Dracula's Castle (1969; Crown International) Director: Al Adamson; Producers: Al Adamson, Rex Carlton; Screenplay: Rex Carlton; Cinematographer: Leslie Kovaks. Cast: John Carradine, Paula Raymond, Alex D'Arcy, Robert Dix, Gene O'Shane, Barbara Bishop, Vicki Volante, Ray Young.

HORROR BEYOND BELIEF ... LIES WAITING FOR ALL WHO DARE ENTER THE VAMPIRE'S DUNGEON!—poster

Replace the word "horror" with "boredom," and the above tag-line would be far more accurate. That said, at least this slow-moving low-budgeter is better than its even cheesier co-feature, *Nightmare in Wax*. (Damning with faint praise.) And *Blood of Dracula's Castle* is also one of producer-director Al Adamson's (*Dracula vs. Frankenstein*, *Blood of Ghastly Horror*, etc.) better-looking efforts. (Damning with even *fainter* praise.)

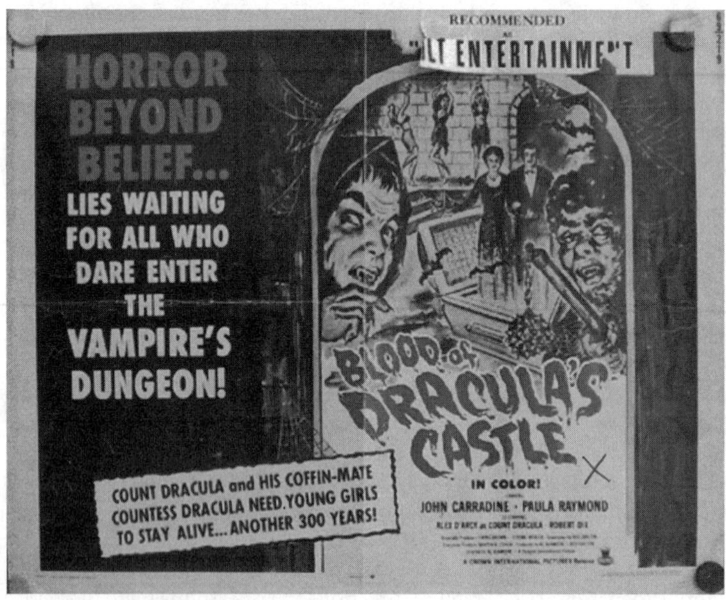

Despite this half-sheet poster's claim, there's very little horror and even less belief in *Blood of Dracula's Castle* (1969)..

A professional photographer (Gene O'Shane) inherits a castle out in the California desert(!) and takes his fiancée (Barbara Bishop) to inspect his new property. There he ultimately learns that the castle's genteel renters (Alex D'Arcy and Paula Raymond) are a pair of vampires (Count and Countess Dracula actually, though they employ the alias Townsend) who, along with their butler George (John Carradine), deformed hunchback caretaker Mango (Ray Young) and escaped psychopath helper Johnny (Robert Dix), kidnap young girls to keep in the dungeon as their own personal hemoglobin taps. They also occasionally sacrifice one of the captives to the Moon god 'Luna.'

Despite its reported eight-day schedule, the picture looks fairly professional (thanks to the competent lighting and solid photography of Leslie Kovaks [*Easy Rider*, *Ghostbusters*, *Two Weeks Notice*]), and is generally well-acted, both by old pros Carradine, D'Arcy (*Horrors of Spider Island*) and Raymond (*Beast from 20,000 Fathoms*)—each of whom add a touch of class and some droll humor to the silly proceedings—*and* by likable newcomers O'Shane and Bishop. (Adamson originally wanted Carradine for the Dracula role, but the production's money men demanded that D'Arcy play the Count, so Adamson had to settle for Carradine as the butler.)

Consisting mostly of talk, or long stretches designed solely to eat up some much-needed running time (a photo shoot at Marineland; the protagonists swimming in the ocean; two lengthy driving-in-the-car sequences; an even longer convict-escapes-down-a-creek interlude, etc.), the film offers little in the way of action. Admittedly, some of the dialogue *is* amusing (Count to Johnny: "How about your psychotic desire to kill?" Johnny: "Oh well, we all have our little shortcomings"), but most sounds simply banal. And worst of all, the picture's one "money" shot (the dissolution of the vampires) was filmed for pennies. Too cheap even for some dissolves and a couple of prop skeletons, Adamson keeps the camera locked down on the hero and heroine as they stare and exclaim, "They're getting old" and "They turned to dust"—without ever *showing* it.

While the movie's exteriors (filmed at a real castle purportedly shipped over from Ireland and rebuilt in Lancaster, California) appear impressive, the interior sets (shot at the Santa Monica Sound Stage) look shoddy in comparison, including what has to be the world's tidiest plywood-and-styrofoam castle dungeon (two token rats appear; but, despite the captive girls' screams of disgust, the rodents make little impact when they scurry across a floor so clean you could eat off it).

"Al was not what you would call a good director," concluded John "Bud" Cardos, who served as *Blood*'s production manager (and had a small role as a security guard). "He could raise the money for these little shows, and put them together, but he shot everything so fast he could have made 'em a lot better ... [they were] sloppy." (Cardos later went on to direct his own features, including the entertaining William Shatner-starrer *Kingdom of the Spiders*.) Retired from moviemaking since the early 1980s, Adamson was murdered in 1995 and his body entombed in cement under his own Jacuzzi (allegedly by a live-in contractor remodeling Adamson's Indio, California, home). It proved a tragic denouement bizarre enough for one of the filmmaker's own tawdry movies.

With quotes from: "Motorcycle Maniacs, Fantastic Fights: John 'Bud' Cardos," by Bob Plante, *Psychotronic Video* 24, 1997.

The Blood of Nostradamus (1963; Estudios America/Trans International Films; Mexico; b&w)

Original Language Title: *La Sangre de Nostradamus*; Director: Frederick Curiel, Stim Segar (English language version); Producer: Victor Parra, K. Gordon Murray (English version); Screenplay: Charles E. Taboada, Alfred Ruanova; Cinematographer: Ferdinand Colin. Cast: Germán Robles, Julio Aleman, Domingo Soler, Aurora Alvarado, Manuel Vergara.

> "That beast was able to fool us like children."
> —Prof. Dolan

Insert the name "K. Gordon Murray" after the word "beast" in the above quotation and you've a pretty good account of what a viewer feels after sitting through this fourth and final installment in the Mexican-lensed "Nostradamus" series. Florida-based theater builder-cum-movie mogul Murray snatched up a fistful of South-of-the-Border horror films and released them as Saturday matinees in the early sixties before sending them off to television (though in some cases he *reversed* the process and sent out theatrical double bills of movies he'd already sold to TV!). While he gave American audiences the chance to see such offbeat and entertaining Mexi-movies as *The Witch's Mirror*, *The World of the Vampires* and the notorious *The Brainiac*, he also schlepped such subpar fare as *Spiritism*, *Curse of the Aztec Mummy* and the four Nostradamus movies.

Anyone stumbling across this feature at some Saturday matinee (or bleary-eyed 1:00 a.m. TV showing) would be utterly nonplussed had they not seen the series' previous entries. Adapted from the final three episodes of a 12-chapter serial about a nefarious vampire named Nostradamus (Germán Robles), *The Blood of Nostradamus* begins with the vampire's disembodied voice taunting his arch-nemesis, Professor Dolan, who'd thought he'd destroyed Nostradamus in the *last* picture (*The Genie of Darkness*) by tossing his ancestor's ashes to the winds (since a vampire must sleep on his progenitor's ashes during the day or die ... yes indeedy). Apparently, in the best—or worst—Saturday matinee serial fashion, Nostradamus "substituted the ashes for those of one of [his] victims," and so the show can go on. And it does go on ... and on ... and on ... as the boorish bloodsucker resumes his mundane modus operandi of announcing to the Professor who he'll kill next and then doing just that. Victims this time around include a grotesquely overbearing police commissioner and a flighty songstress. Finally, Nostradamus can stomach the pontificating professor no longer (understandable after *four* movies) and points his fangs in Dolen's direction—with the expected "pointed" result. Yes, the world is now safe from Nostradamus' evil, and, more importantly, any further features.

There's little to differentiate this entry from the other three, apart from the fact that Nostradamus *really* dies this time. *Blood* does possess one impressively atmospheric set-piece, however, as a female victim-to-be flees in terror through the deserted, fog-shrouded streets. Pursued at first by the shadow of a huge bat, she's then attacked by the impressively mobile beast itself, which (after a judicious cut to a horrified onlooker) transforms into the caped Nostradamus. Then, in close-up, the bloodsucker's fangs seemingly sink into his victim's throat—a shockingly progressive sight not seen in American films of this time.

But such moments come so few and far between that they disappear under the weight of the picture's going-nowhere plotting and pathetic palaver. Though slightly better than the similarly serialized *Aztec Mummy* movies (at least there's no nondescript masked wrestling hero here), the Nostradamus films remain some of the weakest of the '60s Mexican monster movies. As far as this final entry goes, simply put, *The Blood of Nostradamus* is bloody awful.

Blood of the Man Devil see *House of the Black Death*

Blood of the Virgins see *The Blood Demon*

Blood of the Zombie see *The Dead One*

Blood Rites see *The Ghastly Ones*

The Blood Suckers see *Dr. Terror's Gallery of Horrors*

Bloodlust! (1961; Westhampton Distribution; b&w) Director/Producer/Screenwriter: Ralph Brooke; Cinematographer: Richard E. Cunha. Cast: Wilton Graff, June Kenny, Walter Brooke, Robert Reed, Gene Persson, Joan Lora, Troy Patterson, Lilyan Chauvin.

HE HUNTED HUMANS for the sheer sport of killing ... and made his island paradise into a Hell on Earth!—poster

Here's your chance to see the father of *The Brady Bunch* hunted down like a wild animal (and who among us that grew up in the 1970s could resist such a satisfying concept?). Long before Robert Reed became a household name and face on television via "a story of a man named Brady," he was chased through a forest of potted plants by a crossbow-wielding madman thirsting for his blood.

Two young couples—Johnny and Betty, and Pete and Jeanne (Robert Reed, June Kenny, Gene Persson, Joan Lora)—on a chartered boat stumble across a private island owned by Mr. Balleau (Wilton Graff). Says Balleau, "I've developed a kind of passion for hunting." Indeed, he hunts *humans*, and plans to make the boys his next prey in this low-rent version of "The Most Dangerous Game."

As *Bloodlust*'s unit manager Bri Murphy (who later married *Bloodlust!* writer-producer-director Ralph Brooke) related, "[*Bloodlust!*] was a remake of [1932's] *The Most Dangerous Game*—Ralph figured that was one of the best horror pictures he'd ever seen, so why not do it again?" To that end, Brooke adapted the story to his decreased ($80,000) budget. For instance, he dispensed with the rather costly use of trained dogs from the original film, replacing them with a few extra actors (that could be had on the cheap), one even serving as the antagonist's tracker. Brooke also transformed the original film's two adult protagonists into a quartet of attractive young people, no doubt in a savvy effort to ride the coattails of the teen-targeted horror films then ruling the drive-ins (led by AIP and their teenage monster movies like *I Was a Teenage Werewolf*, *I Was a Teenage Frankenstein*, and *Blood of Dracula*). In fact, it's rather surprising that *Bloodlust!* wasn't titled something like "I Was Teenage Prey."

First-time director Brooke, aided by cinematographer Richard E. Cunha (a director in his own right, whose credits include *She Demons, Giant from the Unknown, Missile to the Moon*, and *Frankenstein's Daughter*—all from 1958!), seems remarkably self-assured in the visuals department, utilizing varied camera angles and evocative lighting to augment what little resources he had (though no amount of clever trickery can disguise the faux cave walls of Balleau's underground lair as anything but what they really are—crumpled construction paper). For example, the goateed, rifle-bearing Balleau first appears in a low-angle shot (accompanied by a dramatic chord sounding on the music track) that suggests the man's menacing power. The scene then fades to a roaring lion's head, with the camera pulling pack to reveal the animal as a stuffed and mounted trophy in Balleau's study—the sudden juxtaposition of Balleau and the predatory beast furthering the unsettling feeling surrounding this ominous "host."

"The Most Dangerous Game" hits the '60s in *Bloodlust!* (1961). Left to right: Wilton Graff, Gene Persson, Joan Lora, June Kenny, and Robert Reed (of *The Brady Bunch* fame) (American lobby card).

Unfortunately, Brooke the Screenwriter fares worse than Brooke the Director. The four clean-cut "kids" (actually 20-something adults) are far too *Leave It to Beaver*-ish, with their bland politeness and gee-wiz demeanor, to take seriously. The banal dialogue they spout further scuttles their already-sinking credibility. When told by Balleau of their impending doom, Johnny blandly retorts: "Listen, Mr. Balleau, fun's fun, but if you think we're going to be the day's pigeons in your shooting gallery, you're just a little far out."

Happily, the stylish playing of the more seasoned Wilton Graff as Balleau helps offset such banalities. Graff receives the script's best lines—and delivers them with aplomb. When Balleau displays his trophies—his victims posed at the moment of death—Betty screams. At this, Graff gives a wry smile and observes, "I see that my latest trophy has *really* impressed you. I'm glad, because I think it's the best thing I've done—" here Graff pauses ever so slightly, and the smile fades to a malevolent coldness as he pointedly adds "—so far."

Lengthy sequences of Archie and Betty and Jughead and Veronica ... er, Johnny and Betty and Pete and Jeanne creeping about the house trying to Find Out What's Going On quickly engenders an unwelcome feeling of juvenilia. It gets to the point where one almost expects Erich Von Zipper to pop up on his way to some AIP beach party movie. (And the fact that Balleau's nondescript henchmen all sport striped shirts—like some landlocked Disney pirate gang—doesn't up the maturity level any.)

But just when you tire of the Hardy Boys/Nancy Drew-like shenanigans, Brooke and company toss out some genuine shocks, including the macabre sight of a henchman retrieving human body parts from a tank in Balleau's hellish workroom—first a foot, then what looks like a patch of human skin, then a head (but with the skull removed, so that he promptly starts filling the baggy skin with packing material before carefully setting the gruesome relic on the table). The human taxidermy show concludes with the man dumping a load of offal into a second tank, the bubbling mist rising from it indicating its acidic nature. This was strong stuff for 1961 (two years before Hershell Gordon Lewis introduced the "gore film" via *Blood Feast*'s animal intestines and sheep's tongue). Combine such unexpected grue with some evocative camerawork and a well-played villain worthy of the title, and *Bloodlust!* often manages to escape from the many traps set by its scripting and budgetary deficits.

With quotes from: *Monsters, Mutants and Heavenly Creatures: Confessions of 14 Classic Sci-Fi/Horrormeisters*, by Tom Weaver.

Bloodsuckers see *Island of the Doomed*

Bloody Pit of Horror (1965; Pacemaker Pictures; Italy) Alternate Titles: *The Crimson Executioner*; *A Tale of Torture*. Original Language Title: *Il Boia Scarlatto*. Director: Max Hunter (Massimo Pupillo); Producer: Francesco Merli; Screenplay: Robert Christmas (Roberto Natale), Robert McLorin (Romano Migliorini); Cinematographer: John Collins (Luciano Trasatti). Cast: Mickey Hargitay, Walter Brandt, Louise Barrett (Luisa Baratto), Ralph Zucker, Alfred Rice, Femi Martin (Femi Benussi), Rita Klein, Barbara Nelli, Moha Tahi, Nick Angel.

Never before so much paralyzing terror as in this hair-raising orgy of sadism...— trailer

In this mostly dull but occasionally shocking exploitation horror, ex–Mr. Universe (and then-husband of Jayne Mansfield) Mickey Hargitay plays an unbalanced ex-actor who lives in seclusion at an isolated castle to perfect his narcissistic dream of developing his "perfect body." When a group of photography models (including his former lover) stumble upon his castle, he goes mad and in his mind becomes the "Crimson Executioner," a sadistic medieval torturer.

The film is basically an excuse to show scantily clad women (it lacks any actual nudity) tortured in a myriad of admittedly ingenious ways. For instance, apart from the expected iron maiden, rack, and some uncomfortably exploitative moments of torment (hot oil sizzling a maiden's back; blades drawn across heaving bosoms), there's the bizarrely diabolical but admittedly arresting giant spider web contraption rigged to dozens of bows placed along a wall (making rescue impossible)—with a poisonous mechanical spider dancing inexorably towards its ensnared victim.

This *Pit* is not just for those enamored of the female form in peril, however. The focus on Hargitay's well-oiled torso and his frequent ramblings about his "perfect body" (not to mention the presence of his various muscle-bound henchmen) make this a homoerotic fantasy "safely" circumvented by the torture of women. Having rejected the world and its conventions (including his former heterosexual lover), Hargitay slips into nihilistic madness and deviance, becoming the Crimson Executioner who must punish those enticing temptresses. But is that because he feels desire for them and seeks to burn it out of himself (since he's so obviously male-form oriented)? Or is it because he subconsciously loathes his homoerotic feelings and so escapes himself by becoming the Executioner, channeling his sexual energies away from his homoerotic impulses into torturing the "useless" sex? Or maybe this is simply too much subtext for a crass exploitation horror film...

The impractical but amusingly bizarre mechanical spider torture device from *The Bloody Pit of Horror* (1965).

Apart from its misogynistic set-pieces, *Pit* offers some lackluster big-time wrestling-style fight scenes with the Executioner's beefy minions; an impressive but grossly over-lit (and, consequently, atmosphere-less) real castle (full of out-of-place bright colors and furnishings—including fire-engine red railings); poor pacing punctuated by dull interactions between the various caricatures—er, characters; and an amazingly inappropriate jazz-organ-bongo musical score.

What makes this poorly produced and mean-spirited movie at all tolerable is the comic book performance of bodybuilder-cum-actor Hargitay, who staggers about shouting maniacally in such an over-the-top fashion that one can't take him—or the film—seriously. "I wasn't any more of an accomplished actor than a taxi driver!" admitted Hargitay. "So, to me, it was a good performance. The first time you see the movie, though, I'm sure it is shocking." Indeed, it's ironically fortunate that this slice of beefcake turned out to be so much ham.

With quotes from: "The Hungarian Hercules," by Michael Barnum, *Filmfax* 93/94, October/November 2002.

The Bloody Vampire (1962/65; Internacional Sono-Film/Tela Talia Films S.A./Trans-International Films; Mexico; b&w) Alternate Title: *Count Frankenhausen*; Original Language Title: *El Vampiro Sangriento*; Director/Screenwriter: Michael Morayta; English language version director: Manuel San Fernando; Producer: Raphael Perez Grovas, K. Gordon Murray (English version); Screenplay: Michael Morayta; Cinematographer: Raoul Martinez Solares; Cast: Begona Palacios, Erna Martha Bauman, Raoul Farell, Bertha Moss, Charles (Carlos) Agosti.

Weirdos! Bring a *fiend* to a night of terror.
—radio spot

A young doctor and student of the famous vampire-hunter Count Cagliostro, along with the doc's fiancée (Cagliostro's daughter), infiltrate the house of Count Frankenhausen(!) to determine if he is the vampire depleting the local populace during the full of the moon. Frankenhausen is indeed an undead fiend—with grandiose plans ("The day will soon arrive when all the men and women on earth are at last my loyal slaves," he rants) and a crypt full of "dormant" vampire minions. "There are only two kinds of vampires," explains Cagliostro. "Some of them walk around, some remain dormant." Also, Cagliostro has invented a new method to exterminate vampires, a machine that will "inject the heart, the arteries and the veins of vampires, *and* their victims, with this unique acid [made from a special plant]. It's the only way we can abolish this bloodcurdling infirmity and stop the danger of contagion also."

This rather dull Mexican horror movie starts strongly enough with an eerie shot of a coach at twilight, the silhouetted horses (silently) galloping in slow motion as a bell tolls mournfully and the wind howls on the soundtrack (a technique later used so effectively by Amando de Ossorio in his Spanish *Blind Dead* films). At the scene's conclusion, the camera suddenly dollies in to reveal the cloaked driver to be a grinning skull—death itself. It's a haunting opening, both surreal and startling.

Unfortunately, nothing else in the picture equals this moody moment; and, though blessed with some imposing sets and atmospheric lighting (courtesy of Raoul Martinez Solares), the film soon settles down into a series of overlong expository scenes. "Let us go on talking about the famed subject," suggests Cagliostro early on, and this seems to be the movie's anthem, as the picture frequently surrenders its atmospherics to long stretches of dull (and awkwardly dubbed) palaver. Much of the talk comes in the form of impromptu lectures by Cagliostro, but the Count's wife and servants, as well as the vampire himself, get in on the act at intervals as well.

Spanish one-sheet for *The Bloody Vampire* (1962/65).

The "vampire-killing machine" angle goes absolutely nowhere (we never get to see it used); and throughout the film the various vampires do indeed remain disappointingly "dormant." They must wait until this film's sequel, *Invasion of the Vampires* (shot back-to-back with *The Bloody Vampire* in December 1961-January 1962) to rise to the occasion (so to speak).

As Frankenhausen, Carlos Agosti looks imposing enough, but the harsh and raspy (dubbed) voice that issues from his lips belongs more to a teamster than an aristocratic vampire. In one of the most irresolute non-endings of the time, Frankenhausen gets away! "The vampire lives on and he's still at liberty," intones Cagliostro, as the Count, in bat form, flies through the trees. But never fear, Frankenhausen returned the following year in the superior (re: faster paced) *Invasion of the Vampires* (also written and directed by Michael Morayta, photographed by Solares, and starring Bauman, Moss and Agosti)—and this time he meets his match.

Though ponderously paced, *The Bloody Vampire* does manage to inspire a few unintentional guffaws, the loudest of which results from a priceless scene of the Count flapping about (or gliding at least, since the oversized stuffed *fledermaus* is about as stiff and unwieldy as the movie's dialogue) as an hysterically funny-looking bat sporting the biggest rabbit-like ears this side of *Night of the Lepus.* This bat-bunny hybrid almost makes *The Bloody Vampire* worth watching ... almost.

Bluebeard's 10 Honeymoons (1960; Allied Artists, b&w) Director: W. Lee Wilder; Producer: Roy Parkinson; Screenplay: Myles Wilder; Cinematographer: Stephen Dade. Cast: George Sanders, Corinne Calvert, Jean Kent, Patricia Roc, George Coulouris.

The Man with the Do-It-Yourself Murder Kit!—tagline

From 1914 to 1918, Frenchman Henri Landru swindled and murdered 10 wealthy widows, dismembering their bodies and incinerating them in the kitchen stove of his Parisian villa. After a spectacular trial he was convicted on 11 counts of murder (including the teenage son of one of the widows) and guillotined. The press nicknamed Landru "Bluebeard" after the title character of a French fairy tale about a wicked king who kills his wives.

Almost immediately, novels, plays and movies inspired by the Landru case began to appear. Despite the grisly nature of the crimes, however, many of the works which emerged were comedies—including the most celebrated films to arise from the case, Ernst Lubitsch's *Bluebeard's Eighth Wife* (1938) and Charles Chaplin's *Monsieur Verdoux* (1947). *Bluebeard's 10 Honeymoons* takes a similarly tongue-in-cheek approach and offers star George Sanders a perfect vehicle for his acidic screen persona.

In this telling, Landru (Sanders), a lonely heart antiques dealer, is lured into a life of crime by a gold-digging young seductress, Odette (Corinne Calvert). He preys on brokenhearted women—romancing them, gaining their trust (and access to their bank accounts), bringing them to his villa and then poisoning them and burning their bodies—all to raise money to woo Odette. He rents her an apartment and keeps her in jewels and furs, yet she holds him at arm's length, constantly milking him for more money while she maintains a young boyfriend on the sly. Eventually, frustration, jealousy and greed inspire Landru to turn on Odette.

W. Lee Wilder, the less-accomplished brother of the legendary Billy Wilder, handles the film's quirky blend of horror and dark humor nimbly, displaying wit and sophistication utterly lacking

George Sanders as the notorious killer embarking on *Bluebeard's 10 Honeymoons* (1960).

in his previous projects, which included *Phantom from Space* (1953), *Killers from Space* (1954), *The Snow Creature* (1954) and *Manfish* (1956). The screenplay by Myles Wilder (Lee Wilder's son) is a minor gem, far and away his best. Indeed, it's *so* much better than his other work (again, including *Phantom from Space, Killers from Space, The Snow Creature* and *Manfish*) that viewers may wonder if he ran this one past Uncle Billy for an uncredited polish. The characters are well delineated, the pace is brisk and the dialogue is sharp. It's also full of priceless little throw-away bits of business, like when one of the women Landru is wooing marvels at the large tip he leaves after dinner. "Success is nothing if not shared," Landru opines, as he reaches behind his back to pick up the money and stuff it back in his pocket. Although the Odette character and the frustrated romantic subplot are fictions, the script includes many factual details, such as Landru's habit of keeping a ledger recording the names of his victims and the alias he used for each (to avoid confusion).

The picture benefits greatly from the presence of Sanders in the lead role. His droll, cynical performance fits the part like a finely tailored suit. This Landru could be a murderous cousin of Addison de Witt, the caddish drama critic from *All About Eve* (1950). Sanders won an Oscar for that role, and while *Bluebeard's 10 Honeymoons* is certainly no *All About Eve*, Sanders proves no less delightful here. Plus, he's onscreen almost constantly. Sanders' towering performance overshadows the rest of the cast, with the notable exception of the luminous Corinne Calvert as Odette, Landru's sultry temptress. Playing a character even more vicious and amoral than Landru himself, at points she threatens to out–Sanders Sanders. Calvert is wickedly funny and undeniably sexy.

Bluebeard's 10 Honeymoons is a picture ripe for rediscovery, but it's not an easy one to see. So far, it hasn't been issued on home video, and it seldom shows up on television. It's well worth tracking down, however, especially if you're a fan of George Sanders (and who isn't?).

Body Snatcher from Hell (1968; Shochiku; Japan) Alternate (international) Title: *Goke, Body Snatcher from Hell.* Original Language Title: *Kyuketsuki Gokemidoro.* Director: Hajime Sato; Producer: Takashi Inomata; Screenplay: Susumu Takaku, Kyuzo Kobayashi. Cast: Teruo Yoshida, Tomomi Sato, Hideo Ko, Eizo Kitamura, Masaya Takahashi.

A fiendish vampire from a strange world in outer space drains his victims' blood and turns them into weird corpses!—tagline

Although it shares some plot points in common with Toho's *Attack of the Mushroom People* (1963), and contains elements from the often-imitated *Invasion of the Body Snatchers* (1958), Shochiku Films' *Body Snatcher from Hell* isn't much like any other fantasy film of its era—or any other era. It owes less to the popular *kaiju eiga* (monster movie) genre or traditional Japanese ghost stories than to the plays of Jean-Paul Sartre or the "cubist" art films of Alain Resnais (such as *Hiroshima mon Amour,* 1959). The Japanese pictures it most resembles are the eerily allegorical films of Hiroshi Teshigahara, such as *Woman in the Dunes* (1964) and *The Face of Another* (1966). Ambitious, creepy and thought provoking, *Body Snatcher from Hell* is also self-consciously arty and ultimately compromised by its threadbare budget.

American one-sheet poster for the unique Japanese horror/sci-fier *Body Snatcher from Hell* (1968; aka *Goke, Body Snatcher from Hell*), released in the States on a double-billed with the wacky reissued Euro-import *Bloody Pit of Horror* (1965).

From its unnerving and breathlessly paced opening sequence, the film keeps viewers off balance, never sure of what's coming next: A passenger jet on a routine flight enters a bank of ominous-looking orange clouds. Suddenly, panicked birds begin crashing into the plane, splattering the windows with blood. Then comes word from ground control that one of the passengers left a suicide note and may be carrying a bomb. The co-pilot, Sugisaka (Teruo Yoshida), and a flight attendant Kazumi (Tomomi Sato) begin a discreet search for explosives. Instead, they discover that another passenger is an assassin fleeing the murder of an ambassador. To avert capture, the assassin (Hideo Ko) tries to hijack the plane. He forces his way into the cabin, but then a UFO appears. Finally, a bird flies into one of the engines and causes the plane to crash. The pilot and the assassin are killed, but nearly everyone else survives—at least, initially.

The contentious group of survivors function less as fully developed characters than as metaphors for a host of societal ills: There's a sniveling, amoral arms manufacturer (representing greed) and his unfaithful wife (the embodiment of eroding moral and sexual values), a greedy congressman (political corruption incarnate), a broken-hearted American war widow (self-explanatory), a coldly clinical psychiatrist (standing in for cynicism and the loss of compassion) and the would-be suicide bomber (a voice of despair and madness). Sugisaka and Kazumi also survive, and continue to serve as the story's point-of-view characters.

This motley assortment of malcontents, huddled inside the crippled plane atop a rocky mountain with no food or water, argue bitterly about how to proceed. Suddenly, the suicidal passenger tries to blow up what's left of the plane. But the attempt fails, and the bomber flees. Not far from the downed plane, however, he discovers the UFO, which has landed nearby. He enters the mysterious ship, and is promptly taken over by a blob-like alien entity, which splits his forehead open and oozes into his skull. Later that night, he returns to the downed aircraft and begins a series of vampire-like attacks on the survivors.

The narrative includes so many curveballs and out-of-nowhere plot twists that it becomes disorienting, almost surreal. At its best, however, the film generates the same kind of tense, interpersonal situations that fuel George Romero's classic *Night of the Living Dead* (also released in 1968). As in *Night*, the truly horrific moments in *Body Snatcher from Hell* arise from the way people treat one another. The panicked passengers soon turn on each other, and then, in desperation, try using the American widow as a human sacrifice. At one point the alien-possessed vampire creature states the picture's theme bluntly: "Mankind is on the verge of destruction.... It is your own fault.... You have already turned your world into a monstrous battlefield." The film's finale proves equally striking, ironic and bizarre.

All too clearly, the purpose of this often heavy-handed production is to make a statement about the state of the world, circa 1968 (one of the most turbulent years of the 20th century, which saw the Tet Offensive in Vietnam, the assassinations of Martin Luther King and Robert Kennedy in the U.S., the collapse of the de Gaulle government in France, and numerous other political upheavals). The film's "statement" isn't exactly refined or even entirely coherent—it's more like a primal scream—but it seems to be deeply felt. Like the anguished version of "The Star Spangled Banner" that Jimi Hendrix began playing at around this time, *Body Snatcher from Hell* expresses in an oblique but visceral way the fear, tension and rage harbored by many young people. So, on that level, it works.

On a purely cinematic level, however, *Body Snatcher from Hell* has some glaring problems. Most of the issues stem from the production's skimpy budget, which restricts the action almost entirely to the not-very-convincing airplane set, and forced director Hajime Sato to settle for even-less-convincing special effects, which undermine key moments. Sato could have done a better job of disguising these limitations, but otherwise performs commendably. Nothing in Sato's previous genre film, the formulaic *Terror Beneath the Sea* (1966/71), suggested the filmmaker was capable of anything as audacious or compelling as this. The cast's performances are one-note, but since the movie is populated mostly by allegorical types rather than lifelike characters, this isn't a severe handicap.

Despite its faults, *Body Snatcher from Hell* remains one of the most fascinating and original Japanese chillers of the 1960s.

The Brain That Wouldn't Die (1962; AIP; b&w) Director/Screenwriter: Joseph Green; Producer: Rex Carlton; Cinematography: Stephen Hajnal. Cast: Herb Evers, Virginia Leith, Leslie Daniel, Eddie Carmel, Adele Lamont.

ALIVE ... WITHOUT A BODY ... FED BY AN UNSPEAKABLE HORROR FROM HELL!—poster

While not the first Disembodied Head movie, and not the best (1985's *Re-Animator* wins that title), *The Brain That Wouldn't Die* is undoubtedly the most offbeat and entertaining of its ilk. Filmed in thirteen days in 1959 (but not released until 1962 by American International Pictures), the New York lensed *Brain* remains a treasured guilty pleasure for many a horror/sci-fi afficianado.

AIP's publicity department called the picture "an adventure into a terror-filled world of science gone mad where anything and everything can—and does—happen." For once, the PR crew was guilty of understatement. Arms ripped from sockets, flesh bitten from necks, decapitation, reanimation, misogyny ... *The Brain That Wouldn't Die* is indeed a film in which anything can—and does—happen.

Inspired by producer Rex Carlton's suggested title of *I Was a Teenage Brain Surgeon* (this was right after Herman Cohen's "Teenage" monster films had come out), writer-director Joseph Green pounded out his outlandish script, now titled *The Head That Wouldn't Die*, in only three days. (AIP ultimately changed it to *The* Brain *That Wouldn't Die* before release).

The strange storyline has Dr. Bill Cortner (Herb Evers) keeping alive the severed head of his fiancée, Jan (Virginia Leith), after she's decapitated in an auto accident. Cortner then goes on a hunt for the perfect body, prowling sleazy nightclubs and "body beautiful" contests to find prime pulchritude. Aiding him in his heady plan is his warped (both in mind and body) assistant, Kurt (Leslie Daniel), who's deathly afraid of 'the thing in the closet'—a horrible creature made from grafted tissues, the result of countless failed experiments. Jan is less than pleased with her current situation and merely wants to die. She develops a link with the unseen closet monster and, at the propitious moment, exhorts him to kill Kurt and break out of his cell. The mutant knocks over some chemicals which promptly burst into flame and then bites a chunk of flesh out of his creator's neck, tossing Bill's writhing body to the floor. As the flames rise higher, the creature scoops up Bill's intended body donor (a photographer's model) and carries her out while Jan cackles hideously from inside the conflagration.

First-time director Joseph Green does wonders

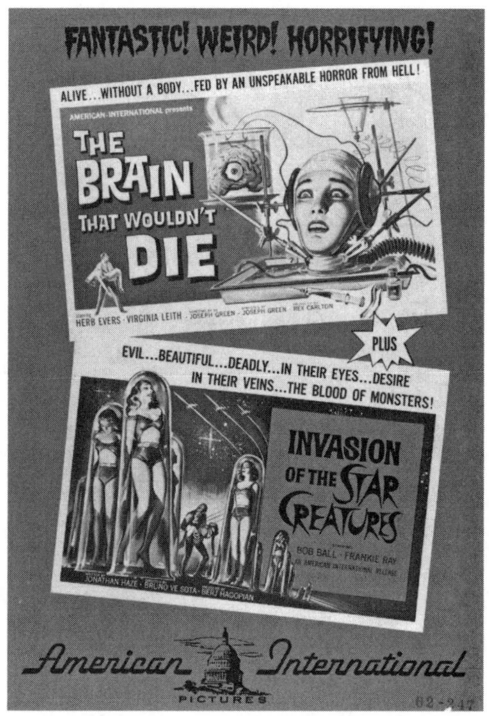

"FANTASTIC! WEIRD! HORRIFYING!" *The Brain That Wouldn't Die* (1962) is one of those rare pictures that actually lives up to its advertising (pressbook cover).

with a tight budget and little time. (In one interview Green put the cost at $62,000, though he later explained to this writer that the final budget was "about $125,000 to $150,000" with the $62,000 figure being "for certain preliminary work." Right.) The fatal car crash sequence, for instance, shows just how inventive a low-budget filmmaker can (and must) become. In close-up, Bill shouts in alarm and we see his foot frantically stamp on the brake before the camera runs directly into the guardrail and seemingly flips up into the air in a sudden, violent motion. Next we see Bill rolling over and over down a hill. He sits up and a pained look of horror crosses his face. The camera cuts to a close-up of the car's shattered side window, viewed from inside the automobile. Flames burn in the left foreground while a hand seemingly reaches upwards for help from the right. Bill staggers forward and reaches over the jagged glass toward the hand, but it collapses and falls out of the shot. Bill takes off his jacket and lowers it into the car out of camera range. When he draws it back again, there's *something* wrapped up inside.

Green shows some real ingenuity here, using camera angles and p.o.v. shots to give the feel of a fatal car crash without the expense (none of those overpriced stuntmen and pyrotechnicians with specialty vehicles here — just a junkyard car door, a hand-held camera, and some lighter fluid). Amazingly, it does the job by allowing our imagination (rather than money) to do the work. "It was all suggestion," recalled Green. "The picture was not a big-budget picture so I had to pick out ways to *suggest* a violent automobile crash and her head being severed from her body." Sometimes a suggestion is worth a thousand greenbacks.

Of course, the next sequence turns almost comically absurd as Bill dashes with his gruesome package through the landscaped woods (the manicured grounds of North Tarrytown's Detmer Estate) like an NFL running back. For a full minute and a half, the camera jogs alongside and in front like some macabre blocker intent on seeing his teammate carry the pigskin across the goal line. It is strange juxtapositions like these (inventive sequences alternating with moments of amusing preposterousness) which create much of the film's bizarre charm and make it so enjoyable.

The characters continually bicker and needle each other, setting up scene after scene of verbal friction that effectively distracts the viewer from the occasional spells of inactivity. Talk is cheap, and Green fills his low-budget picture with plenty of it. Fortunately, the frequently over-the-top conversations make for some fascinating moments of intense absurdity, with the disembodied head blathering away to the unseen monster in the closet ("I've *got* to see your hideousness; you've got to see *mine* ... Nothing you can be is more terrible than I am — a head without a body — a head that should be in its grave") or the high-strung lab assistant petulantly sniping back at the insulting cranium ("I'm getting fed up with you and your *insidious talk*! He should have cut out your tongue while he was at it!").

The picture sports some downright priceless moments, such as when Bill, annoyed at Jan's vociferous objections, *tapes her mouth shut*! And the film boasts one of the most unintentionally amusing death scenes in the annals of cinema. After the closet creature pulls Kurt's arm from its socket, the maimed man staggers about for *two solid minutes*, running his mutilated shoulder into doors and walls so he can drag it along the surface and leave a gory snail-track of blood. (AIP cut this extended sequence, along with a few other gruesome tidbits, upon the film's initial release. Fortunately, the missing footage has been restored and can now be viewed in all its gory glory.)

"Heading" up the cast was actress Virginia Leith. Publicity articles claimed that *The Brain That Wouldn't Die* was Virginia's "bid for renewed stardom." Sadly, the cerebral role didn't exactly take the actress to the head of her profession, for she only appeared in one more film, *First Love* (1977), and a few sporadic television shows. Much of *Brain*'s enjoyment factor, however, comes from her game performance as the bitter disembodied head.

Herb (later Jason) Evers, making his big-screen debut, does equally well, possessing a smooth manner and comfortable charm while mixing in quiet smirks and subtle leers to give his obsessed mad surgeon a human (if slightly sleazy) quality. (One wonders if starring in *Brain* had anything to do with Evers' subsequent name-change.)

Apart from these two players, most of the other *Brain* thespians emote as if they're performing nineteenth century grand guignol (which may not be so inappropriate after all, since they are, in fact, doing a cheesy form of *twentieth* century grand guignol!). As Kurt, Leslie Daniel (who worked primarily as a dubbing actor) reaches new heights in melodramatics, speaking his ludicrous lines with a near-violent fervor while sighing and gesturing with boundless theatricality. Daniel's painful sincerity and over-the-top mannerisms, while far from any sense of normalcy, are indeed *fun* to watch. (And since nothing in this picture is "normal," Daniel's hyperdrive performance works.)

The arm-removing "giant pinhead closet monster" (Green's appellation) was played by the exceedingly tall Eddie Carmel. A sometime Ringling Brothers and Barnum & Bailey Circus giant, Carmel's publicity listed him at 500 pounds and nine feet tall! While these stats may have been 'heightened' just a bit, there's no denying the imposing impression he made as the hideous mutant behind the door. "He was a very fine young guy," remembered Green. "Every actor should be that easy to work with on the set. It was a shame he had this glandular problem." Sadly, this glandular problem, which made Carmel so suitable for his gigantic role in *Brain*, led to his early death in 1972 at the age of 36. (His director survived him by nearly three decades; Joseph Green succumbed to liver failure on September 1, 1999.)

While not particularly realistic looking, the creature's appearance certainly is *unusual*, with its oatmeal face, pointed bald head, off-kilter eye, and flaps of scarred, wattled flesh under its chin that make the poor wretch appear to sport some monstrous turkey-neck. "[Make-up man] George Fiala did a very good job," opined Green, "using a rubberized mask and regular makeup directly applied. I was very happy with the result."

Call it what you will, but *The Brain That Wouldn't Die* remains about as far from boredom as a film can get — despite the fact that it is indeed the ultimate "talking head" movie. For those viewers with a sense of cinematic fun and love of the outlandish, *The Brain That Wouldn't Die* will forever remain *The* Movie *That Wouldn't Die.*

With quotes from: *The Brain That Wouldn't Die/Invasion of the Star Creatures* pressbook, American International Pictures, 1962; "The Brain That Wouldn't Die," by Bryan Senn, in *Son of Guilty Pleasures of the Horror Film*, Gary and Susan Svehla (eds.).

The Brainiac (1961/69; Cinematografica A.B.S.A./Trans-International Films; Mexico; b&w) Original Language Title: *El Barón del Terror*; Director: Chano Urueta, Paul Nagel (English version); Producer: Abel Salazar, K. Gordon Murray (English version); Screenplay: Aldolpho Lopez Portillo, Frederick Curiel; Cinematographer: Jose O. Ramos. Cast: Abel Salazar, Ariadne Welter, David Silva, Germán Robles, Louis Aragon.

Trapped in a whirlpool of shrieking fear!
— radio spot

In the early 1960s, former carnival owner and drive-in theater builder K. Gordon Murray acquired a number of low-budget horror films and children's movies from Mexico's Churubusco-Azteca Studios (where *Honey, I Shrunk the Kids* was later filmed). After making a fortune with his various "kiddie matinees," Murray turned his showman's sights toward TV and sold the syndication rights to American International Television. Along with a string of vampire films starring Germán Robles, and a bevy of Aztec Mummy movies, the package included one deliriously bizarre celluloid abnormality titled *El Barón del Terror*, which Murray re-christened *The Brainiac*. (Several years *after* the film had played on television, Murray packaged it with another of his better Mexi-movies, *The Curse of the Crying*

The Brainiac **(Abel Salazar) arrives on a soundstage forest ready to suck brains in the most (in)famous of all 1960s Mexican horror movies.**

Woman, and premiered the double-bill theatrically on April 9, 1969, in Trenton, New Jersey!)

Far from being the standard south-of-the-border celluloid junk, *The Brainiac* (shot in two weeks in February of 1961) is something special when it comes to *le bad cinema*. The story begins with Baron Vitalius (Abel Salazar, who also produced the film), a "sorcerer and heretic," being burned at the stake during the Inquisition. Engulfed in superimposed flames, Vitalius looks up and sees a comet moving across the heavens (actually a painfully unrealistic painting) and utters this curse to his executioners: "I shall return to your world in 300 years when that [comet] completes its cycle and is once again in these latitudes ... I will kill each and every one of your descendants and I shall expunge your foul lineage from this earth." And he means it. Suddenly it's 1961 and the comet is spotted. Cut to a soundstage landscape, upon which drops a huge papier-mâché rock (conjuring up images of the oft-used "10-Ton-Weight" gag from a Monty Python skit). The comet fragment dissolves to reveal ... the Brainiac!

Possessing an oversized, puffy head that inflates and deflates for horrific emphasis, a long pointed nose, an even longer 12-inch forked tongue, and lobster pincers for hands, this is one of the most ludicrously fun monsters ever to suck brains. And that is just what he does with that unwieldy protruding tongue of his, sucking his victims' gray matter out through their necks. Moreover, he can change into human guise to hypnotize and lure his victims into range. Clever Brainiac that he is, he also keeps a bowlful of brains in a locked cabinet, which he can daintily spoon out whenever in the mood for an in-between-meal snack.

The cast's deadly earnestness only increases the unintentional hilarity, especially Salazar as the brain-sucking Baron. (Among the Baron's victims are Germán Robles, *The Vampire* himself, and Ariadne Welter, sister of *The Devil's Hand* star Linda Christian.) "[The on-set mood was] serious, very serious!" recalled Robles. "But when the director said, 'cut,' everybody laughed! But they didn't approach the film as a joke — they were very serious about it, treated it with respect."

If the film's boffo plot doesn't grab you, how about an endless array of painted paper backdrops? *The Brainiac* features absolutely no outdoor shots; it is completely studio-bound. Location shooting consists of having cast members stand in front of various blown-up photographic backdrops of an observatory, bridge, night sky, cityscape, etc. (Even Roger Corman, on his two-and-a-half-day wonder *The Little Shop of Horrors*, went outside to shoot once in a while!)

Further dubious assets include some wonderful "bad" dialogue ("I wish they'd find some way to control the subject of Man's studies — a maniac with a lot of knowledge is a threat!"), laughable effects, name problems (with characters alternately calling him *Baron* Vitalius and *Count* Vitalius) and a pair of inspectors who inexplicably show up with flame throwers to wrap it all up.

Unfortunately, the film also sports an abundance of boring lectures and banal conversations that frequently slow things down. And missing is the evocative Thirties-style horror atmosphere (mist-enshrouded graveyards, dripping dank crypts) usually found in even the cheesiest of Mexican horror productions from this time.

But when the title terror shows up, it's no-holds-barred guffaws for bad cinema lovers everywhere — sort of a *Plan 9 from South-of-the-Border*. In the right frame of mind, even those not enamored of "golden turkeys" can enjoy this one-of-a-kind imported oddity.

With quotes from: "El Vampiro Speaks! An Interview with Mexican Horror Star Germán Robles," by Bryan Senn, Richard Sheffield and Jim Clatterbaugh, *Monsters from the Vault* 24, February 2008.

Brides of Blood (1968; Hemisphere; Philippines/U.S.) Alternate Titles: *Brides of the Beast* (video); *Grave Desires* (reissue); *Island of Living Horror* (TV). Directors: Eddie Romero, Gerardo de Leon; Producer: Eddie Romero. Cast: John Ashley, Kent Taylor, Mario Montenegro, Beverly Hills (Powers), Eva Darren.

FOR PEOPLE WITH NERVES OF IRON ONLY!!! — ad line

Blood Island and Hemisphere. For late-night fright-flick fanatics, the place name and company moniker go together like, well, some mutant horse and carriage, carrying off the startled viewer to a realm of jungle beauties, mad doctors and bizarre chlorophyll man-monsters. And Blood Island lived up to its name, with plenty of the red stuff spattering the palm fronds. Then there were the native (and imported) femmes, who'd drop their tropical tops at the mere sight of American former teen-heartthrob John Ashley (star of all three Blood Island features).

Brides of Blood was the first in the loosely connected "Blood Island" trilogy shot in the Philip-

The first of the Filipino "Blood Island" films: *Brides of Blood* (1968) (Italian one-sheet poster).

pines and released Stateside by Hemisphere (notwithstanding 1959's *Terror Is a Man*, which introduced the name Blood Island but was unrelated to the subsequent trio). Each of the three proved cheesily (and sleazily) entertaining (warts and all), but *Brides of Blood* was the first.

The story has a small Peace Corp-like band—engineer Jim Farrel (Ashley), dour biologist Dr. Henderson (Kent Taylor) and Henderson's slutty young wife Carla (Beverly Hills)—land on Blood Island to both help the natives improve their lot (Jim teaches them the rudiments of irrigation) and investigate the possible effects of radiation on the flora and fauna from past atomic testing near the island. Greeted on the beach by a native funeral procession, the trio watches as one of the litter bearers slips in the sand, resulting in a bloody disembodied leg and head falling from underneath the bier's covering! We're not in Kansas anymore, Toto; and this shocking intro portends more gruesomeness to come. Soon the protagonists must deal not only with mutated land crabs, mobile killer banana trees and a vicious oversized butterfly(!), but a native lottery that sacrifices young girls to placate the island's lustful monster known as "the Evil One" (more radiation results).

Said creature is an ugly, green, gloppy Michelin Tire Man mutant with big lips and pointed teeth that sexually assaults the sacrificed girls and literally rips them apart. ("It is *his* way of satisfying himself," says the resigned native girl heroine). The beast's appearance is always presaged by its overloud raspy, grunting breathing that reverberates throughout the jungle like some monstrous obscene phone caller on the loose—which is pretty much accurate (well, barring the phone).

One of the film's less gruesome highlights came in the form of Beverly Powers (here using her burlesque name of Beverly Hills, which she also employed for her "grieving widow" cameo in 1963's *The Comedy of Terrors*). Despite her silly sobriquet, Ms. Hills could act as well as look good in low-cut dresses. She brings her underwritten character of the love-starved, cheating wife to life—the only one in the cast who could make such a claim. Ashley is his usual whitebread wooden self, while veteran Kent Taylor walks through his part with a pasted-on dour look.

And it's too bad that the heretofore fast-moving and jaw-droppingly bizarre picture can't seem to sustain its psychotronic pace, and ends with a rather perfunctory climax, followed by a long ceremonial dirty dancing session that drags on and on and on. Fortunately, a plethora of oogy (and ogling) monster business up to then helps gloss over its limp finish.

Without a hint of irony, Hemisphere went all out in their *Brides of Blood* promotional trailer: "Are you ready for the ultimate GIFT OF LOVE?" the screen reads as romantic music dramatically swells on the soundtrack. "FREE Imitation ENGAGEMENT and WEDDING RINGS will be given to every UNMARRIED FEMALE at All Showings of *BRIDES OF BLOOD*!" *Brides of Blood*: the ultimate date movie...

Brides of Dr. Jekyll see *Dr. Orloff's Monster*

The Brides of Dracula

(1960; Hammer/Universal-International; U.K.) Director: Terence Fisher; Producer: Anthony Hinds; Screenplay: Jimmy Sangster, Peter Bryan and Edward Percy; Cinematographer: Jack Asher. Cast: Peter Cushing, Yvonne Monlaur, Freda Jackson, David Peel, Andree Melly, Miles Malleson, Martita Hunt.

THE MOST EVIL, BLOOD-LUSTING DRACULA OF ALL!—tagline

The Revenge of Frankenstein (1959), Hammer's

Baron Meinster (David Peel, standing) is about to put the bite on Professor Van Helsing (Peter Cushing) in *Brides of Dracula* (1960), arguably Hammer's finest horror film of the 1960s.

first sequel to the groundbreaking *Curse of Frankenstein* (1957), had taken the unexpected tack of continuing the story of the titular scientist rather than (like Universal Pictures' long-running Frankenstein series) chronicling the further exploits of the misshapen monster. *Brides of Dracula*, the much-anticipated sequel to *Horror of Dracula* (1958), took a similar approach, starring the vampire-slaying Dr. Van Helsing (Peter Cushing) and — advertising taglines aside — not featuring Dracula at all. In the case of *Brides*, however, this innovation was a product of necessity rather than artistic choice.

Christopher Lee, catapulted to stardom by his sensational performance in *Horror of Dracula*'s title role, declined to appear in *Brides of Dracula*. Lee claims he turned down *Brides* because he feared becoming typecast, but producer Anthony Hinds remembered that Lee "was asking too much money.... We decided we could do without him." In any case, Lee's departure from the project necessitated delays and rewrites (three screenwriters receive script credit, an unusually high number for a Hammer picture). The final product, however, proved well worth the wait.

Marianne Danielle (Yvonne Monlaur), a naïve student-teacher traveling to her first assignment, becomes stranded in a remote Transylvanian village. The (apparently) kindly Baroness Meinster (Martita Hunt) offers to let her stay at her chateau. There, Marianne discovers the handsome young Baron Meinster (David Peel) chained to the wall of his room. He convinces gullible Marianne that he is being held prisoner by his evil mother, the Baroness. Marianne impulsively sets him free, then (after the Baron reveals himself as a vampire) realizes she has made a terrible mistake. She flees the castle and, luckily, falls in with Van Helsing (Peter Cushing), who had been called by the local vicar to investigate a growing vampire plague stemming from Chateau Meinster, where the Baroness had been feeding young girls to her son. Van Helsing immediately sets about demolishing the Meinster monsters, beginning with the baroness and, after a series of hair-raising encounters, concluding in spectacular fashion with a showdown with the baron and his "brides" in an old windmill.

The scenario isn't perfect. Questions remain unanswered (for instance, if Baron Meinster can change into a bat, why does a simple leg restraint trouble him?), and other plot threads are left unresolved (including the final disposition of the two vampire "brides" of the film's title), lapses likely introduced during rewrites. The movie could also do without the untimely introduction of an intrusive comedy relief character, the greedy hypochondriac Dr. Tobler (Miles Malleson), whose unwelcome presence is especially distracting since he arrives at the beginning of the final act, just as *Brides of Dracula* begins racing toward its breathless finale.

Ultimately, however, these flaws seem inconsequential. Director Terence Fisher's urgent storytelling and bold compositions (with figures placed in the frame so that they pack the same sort of dramatic punch as a Jack Kirby comic book layout) sweep the viewer along and sustain tension throughout. Bernard Robinson's sets were never more beautifully designed or decorated than here. (The effort that went into some of these sets is simply amazing, especially the main hall of Chateau Meinster, which features dozens and dozens of blazing white candles—all of which had to be carefully lit prior to each shot.) Cinematographer Jack Asher's evocative lighting proves no less remarkable, making subtle use of green, blue, yellow and pink gels, as well as deep shadows carefully draped for maximum impact.

Fisher was horror cinema's answer to C.S. Lewis—a spinner of tales that can be enjoyed on a surface level as spellbinding fantasy, but can also be read as an allegory for the cause of Christian evangelism. In film after film, Fisher's Christian heroes propagate the faith by vanquishing pagan-satanic adversaries. Other than *The Devil's Bride* (1967), *Brides of Dracula* represents the boldest expression of this theme in the director's canon. Van Helsing states the case overtly when he describes vampirism as "a strange sickness ... partly physical, partly spiritual" and "a survivor of one of the ancient pagan religions in its struggle against Christianity."

Fisher's Van Helsing (a "doctor of philosophy and doctor of theology," according to his calling card) is not merely a swashbuckling vampire killer but a super-powered evangelist, successor to apostolic fathers such as Saints Peter and Paul who, according to the bible, invoked the power of Christ to cast out demons, heal the blind and lame, and perform other miracles. Through learned use of Christian iconography—a crucifix and a flask of holy water (not to mention a handy hammer and stake)—Van Helsing is able to conquer the undead and even heal himself when he falls victim to Baron Meinster in the final reel. In one unforgettable scene, the baroness (after confessing her sins to Van Helsing) willingly submits to being destroyed—smiling with relief as he drives in the stake that releases her from Satan's grip and restores her to a righteous relationship with God.

Originally, an entirely different conclusion was conceived for *Brides* in which Van Helsing used black magic to invoke the powers of evil, sending a plague of bats against the Baron and his brides. Fisher rejected this ending (later resurrected for *The Kiss of the Vampire* [1963/64]), both because he was unwilling to trust the finale of his film to Hammer's visual effects team (valid concerns, based on the subsequent results in *Kiss*) and because an evil-defeating-evil resolution would have completely contradicted the basic moral paradigm that ruled his fantasy movies. "If my films reflect my own personal view of the world, it is in their showing the ultimate victory of good over evil, in which I do believe," Fisher said. Cushing (himself an ardent Christian) also lobbied for a different ending. Throughout both *Brides* and the preceding *Horror of Dracula*, the actor seems fully invested in Fisher's vision, as his reverent delivery of lines such as "Only God has no fear" attests.

Cushing's masterful, meticulous work as Van Helsing had been one of *Horror of Dracula*'s greatest strengths. At least until the story's action-packed finale, Cushing ratchets down his hyper-animated Van Helsing for *Brides*, taking a more pensive, wary approach than in the first film—which seems natural given the good doctor's previous encounters with the undead. Yet, as ever, the actor finds a number of physical bits of business to round out his character (for instance, he brings life and veritas to a potentially dry, expository sequence by delivering it while packing a suitcase).

Brides of Dracula boasts several other excellent performances as well. Peel, in his only starring film role (he retired from acting to pursue other interests shortly afterward), brings an unsettling blend of effete dandyism and seething menace as the pansexual Baron Meinster. It's an altogether different quality than Lee's Count Dracula, and it proves especially effective in the early scenes at the chateau. Monlaur's wide-eyed, endearing portrayal as Marianne strikes another perfect note. Freda Jackson (playing Greta, a sort of distaff Renfield) and Andree Melly (as one of the Baron's "brides") also deliver memorable turns. Hunt threatens to steal the film with her affecting, multi-layered performance as the once-proud, now broken-hearted and repentant baroness.

Most fans and critics rank *Brides of Dracula* among the very best Hammer Films productions, and why not? It's thrilling entertainment, nearly immaculate moviemaking, a key work in the Fisher filmography and it only improves with repeated viewings. Its place among the decade's best-loved chillers is richly deserved.

With quotes from: *Hammer Films: An Exhaustive Filmography*, by Tom Johnson and Deborah Del Vecchio; and *The Men Who Made the Monsters*, by Paul Jensen.

Brides of the Beast see *Brides of Blood*

Bring Me the Vampire (1961; Trans-International Films; Mexico; b&w) Original Language Title: *Échenme al Vampiro* (Throw Me to the Vampire); Director: Alfred B. Curevenna, Manuel San Fernando (English language version); Producer: Mario Garcia Camberos, K. Gordon Murray (English language version); Screenplay: Alfred Ruanova (story: Mario Gracia Camberos); Cinematographer: Ferdinand Colin. Cast: Mary (Maria) Eugenia Saint Martin, Charles (Carlos) Riquelme, Hector Godoy, Raymond Bugarini, Celia Viveros.

"You earned all of this through sweat and a lot of fear, and that's work in any man's language."

Among Florida-based entrepreneur/distributor K. Gordon Murray's many Mexican acquisitions released in the 1960s (the Nostradamus films, the Aztec Mummy movies, Samson vs. the Monster-of-the-Week, etc.) was this bizarre mystery-horror-comedy. Its nonsensical plot (a silly pastiche of *The Cat and the Canary*, *Ten Little Indians* and *Seven Keys to Baldpate*) centers on a group of unrelated (and artistic) individuals chosen by a recently deceased millionaire to be his heirs (the eccentric apparently valued creativity above all else). The heirs must spend several days and nights in the man's spooky old mansion in order to collect, while the deceased's sinister (and disappointed) brother Julius makes thinly veiled threats. One by one the heirs meet their doom until the run-around-with-their-heads-cut-off finale in which everybody disguises themselves in black robes and hoods and scampers about, trying to avoid the machine-gun toting(!) villains until we learn ... well, that would be giving it away (though "it" turns out to be so ludicrous a denouement that it scarcely bears repeating).

Bring Me the Vampire offers a decent Old Dark House setting (including a creepy cobwebbed cellar and underground catacombs), a mysterious housekeeper who talks with spirits and intimates she's a witch (even carrying a broom at times), and the ghost of the deceased who turns up to alternately aid and insult the protagonists ("You're all idiots!" shouts the exasperated specter periodically). The film also boasts the occasional inventively bizarre set-piece (e.g., the head of one victim ends up underneath a dinner platter, then turns transparent and floats off through a wall, leaving a bloodstain behind!).

But given the fact that nearly all the heirs are played by Mexican and Argentine comedians, there's far too much broad acting, silliness and pointless buffoonery to sustain the infrequent moments of weirdness. A "boinging" on the soundtrack often punctuates the comedy moments (just in case the viewer hadn't noticed something was supposed to be funny), illustrating the movie's level of comedic sophistication.

And despite the title, there's no real vampire (though Julius, a simple, greedy madman, does sleep in a coffin and, at one point—for no discernable reason—sports fake fangs).

In fact, *Bring Me the Vampire* proves to be as nonsensical as its title, with the thrills as scarce as the moniker's missing bloodsucker.

Burn, Witch, Burn (1962; Anglo-Amalgamated/American International; U.K.; b&w) Alternate Title: *Night of the Eagle* (U.K.). Director: Sidney Hayers; Producers: Albert Fennell and Samuel Arkoff; Screenplay: Richard Matheson, Charles Beaumont and George Baxt (novel: Fritz Leiber); Cinematographer: Reginald Wyer. Cast: Janet Blair, Peter Wyngarde, Margaret Johnston, Anthony Nichols, Colin Gordon, Kathleen Byron.

Do the undead demons of hell still arise to terrorize the world?—tagline

Up-and-coming sociology professor Norman Taylor (Peter Wyngarde), acclaimed for debunking witchcraft, psychic phenomena and other "silly superstitions," is shocked to discover his wife, Tansy (Janet Blair), secretly practices black magic. She learned the craft under the tutelage of a witch doctor while the Taylors were on a research trip to Jamaica, where Norman suffered a near-fatal injury. Tansy insists that her magic has propelled Norman to success despite jealousy and hostility from the insular intellectual establishment of the provincial college where he now teaches. Incredulous (and convinced that his meteoric rise should be credited solely to his own brilliance), Norman forces Tansy to destroy all her magic charms.

Soon afterward, however, a series of personal and professional setbacks suddenly befall Norman, threatening his career and perhaps his life. Slowly, Norman's skepticism, his devotion to science and his bloated ego all begin to crumble, and he grows to believe that some dark force may indeed be working against him. This suspicion is confirmed during a spine-tingling climax in which a decorative stone eagle springs to life from the university roof and swoops down upon the terrified scholar.

Burn, Witch, Burn is a difficult film to dissect critically because its success stems from how beautifully cohesive it is. While the picture's component parts remain impressive when considered individually, they prove far more powerful working in synthesis with one another. There's nothing flashy about *Burn, Witch, Burn,* and yet it emerges as a terrific film — engrossing, believable and chilling.

The tone of the entire production (including Peter Lamont's sets and Reginald Wyer's lighting) is subtle and naturalistic. Its sound design is particularly potent, making unnerving use of music, sound effects (including a memorable bit of business with a reel-to-reel tape of one of Norman's lectures) and cleverly calculated silences. The screenplay, adapted from Fritz Leiber's novel *Conjure Wife* by Richard Matheson, Charles Beaumont and George Baxt, invests as much in compelling human drama as in supernatural chills. Indeed until the final reel the scenario leaves room for doubt as to whether or not actual witchcraft is in play. The story's fantastic elements, once they come to the fore, seem all the more credible because the script builds toward them so meticulously.

This is also a marvelously acted picture. Leads Wyngarde and Blair both provide richly nuanced and at times achingly authentic performances as Norman and Tansy, a dedicated, loving couple who see tiny cracks in their mostly happy marriage suddenly grow into chasms of fear and mistrust. The rest of the cast performs impeccably, as well. Judith Stott, for instance, seems almost eerily un-

Ad for the chilling *Burn Witch Burn* (1962).

affected in her small but pivotal role as a student who accuses Norman of sexual misconduct.

Director Sidney Hayers orchestrates all these elements with uncanny precision, allowing tension to build patiently but inexorably. It's a masterful job. Yet, ironically, Hayers may be the primary reason why *Burn, Witch, Burn* languishes among the lesser known great horror films of the 1960s. Had it been the work of a "name" director, instead of a guy who enjoyed his greatest popular success with episodes of TV shows like *Knight Rider* and *The A-Team, Burn, Witch, Burn* would enjoy a far higher profile today. (Fright fans should also thank Hayers for the gloriously trashy 1959 chiller *Circus of Horrors.*)

In 1944, *Conjure Wife* was adapted for the screen with far less satisfying results as *Weird Woman*, starring Lon Chaney, Jr., and Evelyn Ankers, part of Universal Pictures' series of dismal Inner Sanctum mysteries. The 1962 version was shot in England, where it was distributed by Anglo-Amalgamated under the title *Night of the Eagle.* For its U.S. release, American International Pictures changed the title to the more exploitable *Burn, Witch, Burn* and added an asinine voiceover introduction. Prior to the opening credits, as the audience stares at a black screen, narrator Paul Frees intones a minute's worth of mumbo jumbo to "cast a protective shield" over those in the audience to guard against the evil spells invoked during the picture. This cheap gimmick seems entirely out of place with the literate, tasteful, thought-provoking film it precedes.

Despite these minor compromises, *Burn, Witch, Burn* stands alongside pictures such as Robert Wise's *The Haunting* (1963) and Roman Polanski's *Rosemary's Baby* (1968) as one of the most compelling adult-oriented horror films of its decade.

The Cabinet of Caligari (1962; Twentieth Century–Fox; b&w) Producer/Director: Robert Kay; Screenplay: Robert Bloch; Cinematographer: John L. Russell. Cast: Glynis Johns, Dan O'Herlihy, Richard Davalos, Lawrence Dobkin, Constance Ford, Estelle Winwood.

No one permitted out or in during the last thirteen nerve-shattering minutes!—tagline

Despite its title, this film bears little relation to Robert Weine's German expressionist masterpiece, *The Cabinet of Dr. Caligari* (1919). It is, instead, one of the many early-Sixties psychological thrillers calculated to attract the audience that made *Psycho* (1960) a box office bonanza. In fact, the advertising tagline for *The Cabinet of Caligari* proves more revealing than its title. Posters warned, "No one permitted out or in during the last thirteen nerve-shattering minutes!" This admonition was calculated to recall *Psycho*'s advertising: "No one will be admitted to the theatre after the start of each performance of Alfred Hitchcock's *Psycho*!"

The similarities don't end with the poster. In an unusual (and telling) move, screenwriter Robert Bloch (who wrote the novel upon which *Psycho* was based) receives above-the-title billing—higher than *Caligari*'s director or any of the picture's stars. Whether producers asked Bloch for something *Psycho*-like, or he was simply out of fresh ideas, his *Caligari* script reprises many devices and plot points from *Psycho*, albeit rearranged and often used to different effect: The story features a troubled young blonde (Glynis Johns, standing in for Janet Leigh) driving cross country and forced to stop for the night. She's glimpsed in a white bra during her early "good girl" scenes and in black lingerie later. There's a surprise ending involving a false identity, and a coda wherein a psychiatrist explains the film's resolution for those who may not have fully understood what just happened.

Unfortunately, recycling these and other familiar elements hardly makes *Caligari* the equal of *Psycho*. It runs a wearisome 106 minutes (at least 20 longer than needed), and remains turgidly acted and indifferently staged. *Caligari* is one of those movies where every time something exciting threatens to happen, a conversation breaks out.

The film's leads only worsen matters. Although best remembered for musical performances—she introduced the song "Send in the Clowns" and won a Tony for Stephen Sondheim's "A Little Night Music," and played the suffragette in *Mary Poppins* (1964)—Johns' performance here is tone-deaf, and her squeaky speaking voice grates on the nerves. (A few years later, Johns would appear on the album cover for *Led Zeppelin II*.) Dan O'Herlihy was an accomplished actor, notable for his work in director Carol Reed's *Odd Man Out* (1947), Orson Welles' *Macbeth* (1948) and Oscar-nominated for the title role in Luis Bunuel's *The Adventures of Robinson Crusoe* (1954). But—perhaps be-

Belgian poster for the Robert Bloch–scripted *The Cabinet of Caligari* (1962).

cause *Caligari* director Robert Kay was no Reed, Welles or Bunuel — his work here proves undistinguished. O'Herlihy would go on to appear in several more horror and sci-fi films, including *Fail Safe* (1969), *Halloween III: Season of the Witch* (1983), *The Last Starfighter* (1984), *Robocop* (1987) and *Robocop 2* (1990).

Still, *The Cabinet of Caligari* boasts some interesting visual flourishes— especially during its bravura finale, the only sequence where the film attempts to recreate the expressionist production design of Weine's silent classic. The original score by Gerald Fried pales next to Bernard Herrman's masterful *Psycho* score, but proves far more effective than most music for films of this type and budget. And Estelle Winwood — a fine comedic character actress who also appeared in such films as *Camelot* (1967) and *The Producers* (1968), as well as countless TV shows, including *Twilight Zone*, *Thriller* ("Dialogues with Death") and *Batman*—contributes an amusing supporting performance. So this *Caligari* is not without marginal interest.

Two more *Caligari*s would eventually reach movie screens— the avant-garde *Dr. Caligari* (1989), which was "inspired" by Weine's film, and finally an actual remake, *The Cabinet of Dr. Caligari* (2005). Neither of those films left much of an impression, but both are more interesting than the '62 *Caligari*.

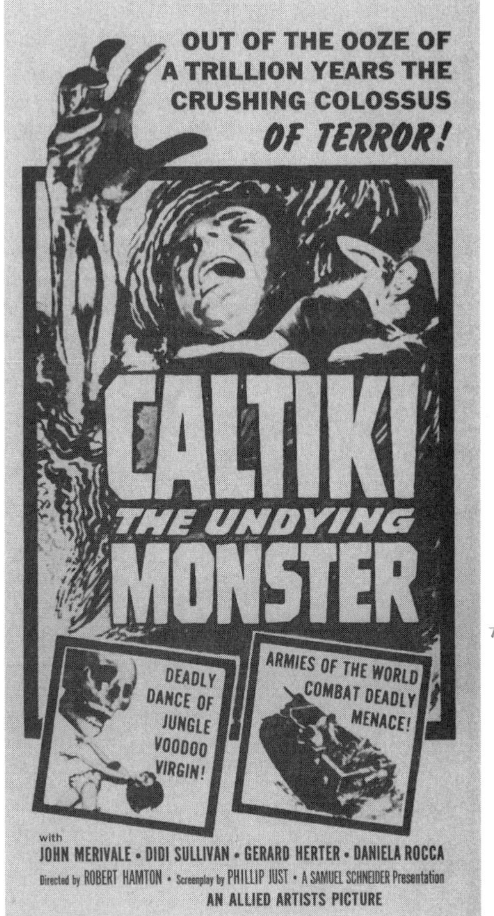

Allied Artists apparently held a low opinion of its target audience's literacy, since they changed *Caltiki the Immortal Monster* (1959/60) to the more prosaic *Caltiki the* Undying *Monster* for some of its advertising (courtesy Ted Okuda).

Caltiki, the Immortal Monster (1959/60; Lux/Allied Artists; Italy; b&w) Original Language Title: *Caltiki, il Monstro Immortale.* Directors: Riccardo Freda (as Robert Hamton) and Mario Bava (uncredited); Producers: Sam Schneider and Bruno Vailati; Screenplay: Philippo Sanjust (as Philip Just); Cinematography: Mario Bava (uncredited). Cast: John Merivale, Didi Perego (as Didi Sullivan), Gerard Herter, Danila Rocca, Giacomo Rossi-Stuart.

Will the first life on Earth be the last terror of man?— tagline

In 1956, director Riccardo Freda and cinematographer Mario Bava teamed to make *I Vampiri*, the first Italian-produced horror movie in over 35 years. The film sank like a stone, drawing poorly in Italy and worse elsewhere in Europe; it wouldn't be released in the U.S. until 1963, and then only in a bastardized, heavily edited form under the title *The Devil's Commandment.* But Freda blamed its failure on the audience, not the product, claiming that patrons were turned off when they saw Italian names on the movie posters. "They [Italian moviegoers] assumed that Italians didn't know how to make films of this kind," Freda said. So, in 1959, Freda and Bava mounted another horror show — a sci-fi chiller called *Caltiki, the Immortal Monster* that (with most of the cast and crew credited under pseudonyms) met with greater success than *I Vampiri.*

Somewhere in the Mexican jungle, a team of scientists, led by Dr. Fielding (John Merivale), discovers a priceless cache of gold Mayan artifacts; unfortunately, these treasures are at the bottom of a lake inside a cave and protected by a maneating, gelatinous monster, which the Mayans named Caltiki and worshipped as a god. (Note to armchair archeologists: This movie's "Mayan legend" is a complete fabrication.) When one of Fielding's greedy colleagues (Daniele Vargas) tries to recover the loot, he's eaten alive by the monster and reduced to a steaming, slime-covered skeleton. Afterward, the creature goes on a rampage, injuring Max (Gerard Herter), a third member of the expedition, before being burned to death. Fielding manages to preserve some Caltiki samples, however, and subsequently learns that the creature was brought to life when a comet passed near the Earth hundreds of years ago. By sheer chance, the same comet is returning in just a few days, threatening to revive the blob-beast yet again. Meanwhile, Max, in the wake of Caltiki's attack, comes unhinged, kills a nurse and escapes from the hospital.

While Freda was probably right that audience prejudices worked against *I Vampiri* (at least in Italy), the primary reason for that picture's failure was that it simply isn't a very good movie (and is a far worse one in its U.S. versions). Although handsomely designed and artfully shot, *I Vampiri* was a predictable and timid effort. By the same token, *Caltiki* fared better not only because its credits Anglicized the names of the cast and crew (Riccardo Freda, for instance, became "Robert Hamton"), but because it's a solid, if minor, sci-fi monster movie. Although even more overly imitative than *I Vampiri, Caltiki* is much harder-hitting and features some at-times spectacular (for their era) special effects.

Bava called *Caltiki* "a take-off on *The Quatermass Xperiment*," but its scenario is more a mélange of both *The Creeping Unknown* (aka *The Quatermass Xperiment*, 1955) and a second Hammer Films production, *X the Unknown* (1956), with a dash of jungle melodrama added for spice. Not all this material works— the film's tedious "native ritual dance" number is painfully obvious filler, and an ill-timed comedy relief sequence (in which Fielding is apprehended by Barney Fife-like local police while racing to save his wife and child from the monster) plays even worse, since it compromises the momentum of the picture's finale — but the good stuff proves exceptionally good. Highlights include a couple of jolting scare sequences; Gerard Herter's edgy performance as Max (clearly modeled on Richard Wordsworth's haunting performance in a similar role in *The Creeping Unknown*); and Bava's chiaroscuro jungle photography, with menace looming behind every thickly draped shadow. But clearly the picture's biggest selling point was its plentiful, generally convincing and sometimes startlingly brutal visual effects (also overseen by Bava). The monster's flesh-eating attacks are far more gruesome than anything found in similar but better-remembered films such as *X the Unknown* or *The Blob* (1958). *Caltiki*, a 76-minute film, features more than a hundred trick shots, which took three weeks to shoot. The titular menace was, in actuality, literally a pile of tripe, animated by various mechanical and optical methods.

As with *I Vampiri*, once again Bava finished a film started by Freda — only this time it was by design. Freda claims that he intentionally handed *Caltiki* over to Bava in mid-production to try to jump-start his friend's directing career. "I don't claim it as my own," said Freda, who nevertheless received sole (pseudonymous) screen credit. Bava, conversely, wasn't even credited for his work as director of photography. Nevertheless, the picture's best moments are pure Bava, like the early scene in which an archeologist, full of gold-lust, dives back into the murky cave lake for more treasure despite his friends' warnings of danger. "I don't mind risks when I can bring back this!" he says, shaking a fistful of gold necklaces. Moments later, he's a steaming pile of gooey bones, and Bava has made the first in an endless series of cinematic statements on the folly of greed.

Caltiki was picked up by Allied Artists for its U.S. release and issued to drive-ins and lower grade "hard-top" theaters in 1960, where it earned a modest profit. This success, qualified though it was, helped pave the way for the third Italian horror film of the era, which proved to be the charm. Soon, Mario Bava's sensational *Black Sunday* would help established Italian horror as a brand fans would seek out, rather than shun.

With quotes from: *Mario Bava: All the Colors of the Dark*, by Tim Lucas.

The Cape Canaveral Monsters (1960; CCM/Republic; b&w) Director/Screenwriter: Phil Tucker; Producer: Richard Greer; Cinematographer: Merle Connell. Cast: Scott Peters, Linda Connell, Jason Johnson, Katherine Victor, Billy Greene.

"We need more earthlings for our experiments, especially females." — Alien invader

Filmmaker Phil Tucker will forever live in the hearts of bad movie enthusiasts, thanks to his *Robot Monster* (1953) and its ape-suited, diving-helmeted, antenna-sporting Ro-Man alien. After many trials and tribulations (detailed below) Tucker returned to his space-roots in late 1959 to film yet another low-budget alien invader disaster, *The Cape Canaveral Monsters.* This time Tucker crossed over into horror territory with his sci-fi scenario (which he penned himself, reportedly because of his dissatisfaction with Wyatt Ordung's writing on *Robot Monster* ... go figure) by having his aliens, represented by two little white dots(!), inhabit dead bodies. No expensive monster suits here (nor even any cheap gorilla costumes this time), just some scar makeup and an actor with his arm stuffed in his shirt; it just doesn't get any simpler (or cheaper) than that.

Two aliens (appearing as tiny, bright circles of light) come to Earth, cause a couple's car to crash, and then take over their dead, reanimated bodies. (The male half of the alien zombie duo has trouble with his arm — it keeps falling off, supplying some unintentional, though welcome, humor.) Their mission is to sabotage the rocket program at Cape Canaveral. The two young science students(!) working on the top-secret project must find a way to foil the alien plot.

Though no *Robot Monster* (compared to that cinematic disaster, this is *Citizen Kanaveral*), *Cape Canaveral Monsters* is *not* a good movie. It's also not a bad *enough* movie to elicit the ridiculously high fun quotient of Tucker's earlier opus. Competently, if uninterestingly, shot, the movie effectively incorporates some great missile disaster stock footage and offers one or two moments of creepy excess, such as when, during the opening car crash, the woman's face bounces off the windshield before displaying its gruesome cuts and gashes; or when an M.P. brings the alien zombie's freshly-severed arm (torn off by guard dogs) into the base's control room for a bit of grotesque show-and-tell. (Amusingly, none of the personnel in the room even bats an eye at the dripping, gory mess!)

But then there's the completely colorless hero and heroine, played by Scott Peters (*Panic in Year Zero!, They Saved Hitler's Brain*) and Linda Connell (daughter of the cinematographer); the expected cheesy sets (the aliens' teleportation device consists of a developing tray filled with bubbling liquid!); and the *de riguer* dismal dialogue ("I think with a little help we can lick these freaks"). And Tucker's idea of science has the hero adding plastic wallet inserts and table salt to the "hydrogen-like" liquid in the transporter device to generate a mountain-moving explosion!

Actress Katherine Victor (who goes way over the top as the scheming alien named "Nadja"— take *that*, you Commies!) remembered that, "A group of dentists or doctors were putting up the money for *Cape Canaveral Monsters*; it was going to be shot in color and there was a nice budget. But then, just the day before shooting started, they cut the budget in half." Even so, "it was a very pleasant group, and it was sad that we ran out of money and had to cut back and make all those compromises." (Victor ended up applying her own scars halfway through shooting, when the production could no longer afford the makeup man.) "Phil paid me $420 or $450 [a week]," continued Victor. "Phil was broke about that time, and he came with me to the bank after he gave me the check and borrowed back half of it [*laughs*]. The poor guy, he was really flat broke."

Tucker's entire early career seems to have been one long hard-luck story. After completing *Robot Monster* (his directorial debut) and being cheated out of the film's profits (Tucker claims, rather dubiously, that it made over a million dollars), Tucker became despondent, ending up in the mental ward at the Los Angeles Veterans Administration Hospital, and even attempted suicide via an overdose of sleeping pills. After his recovery Tucker continued on with his film career (at the urging of his doctors, who felt it would be good therapy), and, with the help of his friend Lenny Bruce, made *Dance Hall Girl* and several other low-budget movies. After *Cape Canaveral Monsters* Tucker abandoned directing and went to work as an associate producer in television. He also worked as post-production supervisor on Dino de Laurentiis' *King Kong* (1976) and *Orca, the Killer Whale*, and served as editor on *The Nude Bomb* (1980). Given the quality of these big-budget stinkers, his career may have gotten bigger, but not much better.

And while (marginally) bigger and (slightly) better than *Robot Monster, Cape Canaveral Monsters* remains an obscure curio in the '60s horror/sci-fi cinematic cabinet, neither good enough nor bad enough to really stand out.

With quotes from: *Science Fiction Stars and Horror Heroes*, by Tom Weaver.

Carnage see *Corruption*

Carnival of Souls (1962; Hertz-Lion; b&w) Director/Producer: Herk Harvey; Screenplay: John Clifford; Cinematographer: Maurice Prather. Cast: Candace Hilligoss, Frances Feist, Stanley Berger, Art Ellison, Stan Levitt.

The story of a girl caught between reality and the unknown — tagline

---

Young church organist Mary Henry (Candace Hilligoss) miraculously survives a car crash that claims the lives of two friends, but she seems curiously affected by the accident. Mary feels unaccountably ill at ease and is vexed by recurring visions of a mysterious, white-faced man. She drives through the night to take a new job in Salt Lake City, where she becomes fascinated by a broken-down, long-closed amusement park. Aloof and withdrawn, Mary spurns friendly overtures from her kindly landlady (Frances Feist), social invitations from her new boss (Art Ellison) and sexual advances by a wolfish neighbor (Sidney Berger). But after a bizarre experience at a department store — where everything falls silent and, for a while, no one can see or hear Mary — the young organist turns to a doctor (Stan Levitt) for advice and to her neighbor for companionship. Finally, she gives in to her curiosity and drives out to the abandoned carnival, where she reaches a spine-tingling revelation.

The atmospheric *Carnival of Souls* (1962), one of the most enduring low-budget horror shows of the 1960s, continues to cast its eerie spell over audiences. Like any quickly and cheaply made movie, *Carnival of Souls* has its flaws, of course — some small (minor continuity gaffes and sometimes clunky dialogue) and others not-so-small (the narrative screeches to a halt every time the doctor appears, and minutes of laborious exposition ensue). Yet most viewers tend to forget those faults and to remember the way *Carnival of Souls* makes them *feel*— the unique, unearthly ambiance of the piece, punctuated by moments of startling frisson (for example, the shocking first appearance of the white-faced phantom, reflected in the glass of Mary's passenger door window). For a horror film, being scary atones for a lot of sins, and *Carnival of Souls*— unlike many more expensive thrillers of its era — retains its power to raise the hair on the back of viewers' necks.

Carnival's creepy atmosphere arises from producer-director Herk Harvey's skillful fusion of location footage (shot at the disused Saltair amusement park outside Salt Lake City) and haunting music (Gene Moore's mysterioso organ solos). Since the protagonist is an organist, Moore's creepy score sounds like the music of Mary's imagination, revealing her state of mind more eloquently than clumsy devices like voiceover narration commonly used in other low-rent chillers. These elements are further enhanced by Maurice Prather's chiaroscuro lighting. Harvey appears on screen as the pale phantom that haunts Mary, but delivers an even better performance behind the camera. For the most part the director's visual storytelling is straightforward and efficient (often with clever transitions), but his work becomes more baroque — employing more extreme high angle shots and off-kilter compositions — during the film's weird silent sequences.

Although it contains some awkward dialogue, for the most part John Clifford's screenplay is remarkably effective. (Its twist ending is so good that it still seemed fresh when M. Night Shyamalan ripped it off for *The Sixth Sense* in 1999.) Clifford intentionally isolates Mary Henry; or rather, he creates a character who intentionally isolates herself. Throughout the film, Mary remains acutely alone. Although when afraid she sometimes reaches out to other people for protection, she never tries to form a lasting bond with anyone. As a result, there's no one to care about her — no one except the audience who, because the story unfolds from her point of view, unconsciously bonds with her, sharing her isolation and paranoia.

Candace Hilligoss' stiff, slightly flat delivery might be a liability elsewhere (she's not good at all in Del Tenney's *Curse of the Living Corpse* [1964]), but her subdued portrayal here perfectly suits the cold, remote Mary Henry. The rest of the film's performances prove wildly uneven: Frances Feist is a delight as the busybody landlady, and Stanley Berger contributes a memorable turn as Mary's lusty neighbor, but the tin-eared work of Stan Levitt as the doctor and Art Ellison as the minister seriously damage the movie's believability.

Harvey — who, like most of the *Carnival* crew, was employed by Centron Films, a maker of industrial and educational pictures — was inspired to create *Carnival of Souls* when he spotted the abandoned Saltair amusement park while returning home from a business trip. "With the sun setting and with the lake in the background, it was the weirdest-looking place I'd ever seen!" Harvey said. As soon as he got back to Centron, he asked coworker Clifford for a horror script that would revolve around Saltair, including a climactic scene featuring ghosts rising from the lake and dancing in the old pavilion. Two weeks later the script was ready. Harvey took three weeks off to shoot the picture (on a paltry $30,000 budget), mostly on location in Salt Lake or in Lawrence, Kansas, where Centron was located.

Initially, studio executives and even the premiere audience in Lawrence didn't quite know what to make of *Carnival.* "I thought it was kind of far-out for its time," Harvey said. "Most horror films, even then, really weren't that far-out as far as an inter-dimension, the character Death coming back to reap his just reward and things like that." Although he had hoped to sell the picture to a major studio, no offers were forthcoming. So Harvey entered into a fateful distribution deal with the new Herts-Lion distribution company. Herts-Lion cut the film from 84 to 78 minutes and issued it on a double-bill with *The Devil's Messenger* (1962). But Harvey (and his financial backers— mostly personal friends from Lawrence) never saw any money from Hertz-Lion, which quickly folded. Burned by his one foray into feature filmmaking, Harvey never made another commercial movie. Yet, *Carnival* refused to die, becoming a late-night TV movie favorite. It was remade in 1998 as *Wes Craven's Carnival of Souls.*

Although Harvey told interviewer Tom Weaver that *Carnival* was merely "an exercise in weirdness," he clearly harbored artistic aspirations for the project. Harvey famously stated that he and Clifford aimed for a picture "with the look of a Bergman and the feel of a Cocteau." Amazingly, given the film's paltry budget, he very nearly hit the target. *Carnival* bears visual similarities to contemporary Ingmar Bergman pictures such as *Through a Glass Darkly* (1961) and *Winter Light* (1963), and recreates the dreamlike texture of Jean Cocteau fantasies like *Beauty and the Beast* (1946) and *Orpheus* (1950). In his liner notes to the Criterion Collection DVD of *Carnival,* film scholar Bruce Kawin draws comparisons between Harvey's film and the work of Michelangelo Antonioni. And indeed, Mary Henry (who at one point says, "I don't belong in the world, that's what it is. Something separates me from other people") would fit right with the characters from any of Antonioni's searing 1960s classics, such as *L'avventura* (1960) and *The Eclipse* (1962), all of which feature emotionally numb protagonists who stumble through life, unable to form meaningful connections with one another. If *Carnival of Souls* has an underlying theme, it seems to be that emotional separation from other people is tantamount to separation from life itself. Whether or not viewers elect to read it so deeply, however, *Carnival of Souls* remains a relentlessly unsettling viewing experience.

With quotes from: *Science Fiction Stars and Horror Heroes,* by Tom Weaver.

Carry On Screaming!

Carry On Screaming! (1966/67; Warner-Pathe/Sigma III; U.K.) Director: Gerald Thomas; Producer: Peter Rogers; Screenplay: Talbot Rothwell; Cinematography: Alan Hume. Cast: Harry H. Corbett, Kenneth Williams, Jim Dale, Fenella Fielding, Joan Sims, Angela Douglas, Bernard Bresslaw, Peter Butterworth, Tom Clegg, Billy Cornelius, Jon Pertwee, Charles Hawtrey.

Carry On Screaming with the Hilarious CARRY ON gang!— tagline

Carry On Screaming! is a typically frenetic entry in the long-running, high energy, lowbrow Carry On comedy series. It was the twelfth of 31 Carry On films, and fans of the series generally count it among the better ones. Your mileage may vary.

When during a romantic rendezvous in Hocombe Park his girlfriend Doris (Angela Douglas) mysteriously disappears (whisked away by a furry, flat-headed creature that looks like a cross between the Wolf Man and the Frankenstein Monster), Albert (Jim Dale) rushes to the police for assistance. Unfortunately, the police in this case are dim-witted detective Sidney Bung (Harry H. Corbett) and constable Slobotham (Peter Butterworth). Doris is the sixth woman to have disappeared from the park in the past six months. "There may be a connection," Bung deduces. Indeed, there is: All were kidnapped by the loony Dr. Watt (Kenneth Williams) and his nymphomaniac sister Valeria (Fenella Fielding, made up to resemble Vampira). Watt has discovered an electrical process for reanimating the dead (beginning with himself and also including the creature). But to make ends meet, he and his sister have been kidnapping young women, encasing them in plastic and selling them as mannequins. Whether or not the blundering Bung and Slobotham can uncover this secret, however, remains a mystery.

The humor in the Carry On films is hardly the dry, sophisticated English wit popularized by Ealing Studios. It's more akin to Benny Hill than Alec Guinness, a crude but lively mash-up of parody and farce, full of double-entendres and puns, with a lot of material about sex-starved and/or henpecked men and plenty of random silliness. *Carry On Screaming!* serves as a prime example of the approach. Many of its gags fall flat, but Talbot Rothwell's screenplay keeps them flying at such a breakneck pace that even if two or three jokes in a row bomb, something funny will arrive shortly. There's an Abbott and Costello-like exchange be-

Fanella Fielding (center) as the nymphomaniacal Valeria, and Kenneth Williams (left) as the reanimated Dr. Watt, provide most of the laughs in *Carry On Screaming!* (1967). In this scene, Valeria dispatches the monstrous Oddbod (Tom Clegg) to round up another victim.

tween Bung and Slobotham as they try to question Dr. Watt (Bung: "Watt's the doctor's name." / Slobotham: "That's what I'm trying to find out!"), a scene between Valeria and Bung (in which she asks if she can "blow his police whistle") that's so explicit it's practically a *single*-entendre, an incessant string of quips by Dr. Watt ("Oh, I feel half dead!"), and on and on.

Although ostensibly a parody of Hammer Films chillers, the plot and style of *Carry On Screaming!* owe more to American movies such as *House of Wax* (1953). Producer Gerald Thomas likely didn't want to spend the money it would have taken to recreate the look of a Hammer picture for this typically low-budget Carry On spoof. While the film's sets and costumes look absurdly cheap, production values were beside the point. Fans were paying for the series' signature brand of manic comedy and its repertory of comedians. Indeed, one of *Carry On Screaming!*'s glaring weaknesses is that it lacks series stalwart Sidney James (who appeared in 19 entries). Unavailable due to a scheduling conflict, James ordinarily would have played the Bung character. Harry H. Corbett is passable, but not a patch on the irascible James. The film's sharpest performances come from Kenneth Williams (who, with 26 appearances, starred in more Carry On comedies that any other performer) as the twitchy, effete Dr. Watt and Fanella Fielding as his oversexed sister Valeria. The name "Dr. Watt," of course, is a pun on the popular British sci-fi series *Dr. Who*. Ironically, Jon Pertwee, who plays a kooky police scientist in *Carry On Screaming!*, would go on to play Dr. Who from 1970 to 1974. Frank Thornton, who plays the owner of a women's dress shop in the film, gained fame in a similar role as Captain Peacock on the TV series *Are You Being Served?* Charles Hawtrey, added to the cast at the last minute at the request of the film's American distributor, has a memorable cameo as eccentric restroom attendant Dan Dann.

Carry On Screaming! will satisfy fans of the perennially popular comedy series. Viewers who prefer a more refined style of comedy may be less impressed.

Castle of Blood (1964; Woolner Brothers; France/Italy; b&w) Original Language Title: *La Danza Macabra*; Alternate Titles: *Castle of Terror* (TV), *Coffin of Terror*, *Dimensions in Death*, *The Long Night of Terror*, *Tombs of Horror*; Director:

Anthony Dawson (Antonio Margheriti); Producers: Frank Belty (Marco Vicario), Walter Sarch (Giovanni Addessi); Screenplay: Jan Grimaud (Gianni Grimaldi), Gordon Wilson, Jr. (Sergio Corbucci); Cinematographer: Richard Kramer (Riccardo Pallottini). Cast: Barbara Steele, Georges Riviére, Margaret Robsahn, Henry Kruger, Montgomery Glenn (Silvano Tranquili), Raoul H. Newman (Umberto Raho), Sylvia Sorente.

THE LIVING AND THE DEAD CHANGE PLACES IN AN ORGY OF TERROR!—ad line

Journalist Alan Foster (Georges Riviére) meets Edgar Allan Poe and Lord Blackwood in a tavern. Blackwood owns a haunted castle and challenges the impetuous reporter to spend a night at the castle on All Souls Eve ("the Night of the Dead"). Despite Poe's warnings, Alan accepts and witnesses several ghosts reenact their murders. He also falls in love with Elizabeth Blackwood (Barbara Steele) and discovers she has no heartbeat—she too is a ghost inhabiting the castle. The spirits need the blood of the living so that they may rise yet again on the next All Souls Eve. With the specters clamoring for Alan's blood, Elizabeth, who's fallen in love with him, tries to help the young man escape.

One of the weaker Continental horrors Barbara Steele made in the Sixties, *Castle of Blood* plays like a campfire ghost story that's outstayed its welcome. Though chilling at first, with Foster tentatively exploring the admittedly creepy castle (filled with sinister shadows, cobwebs and archaic furnishings), these I-mustn't-succumb-to-my-frightened-imaginings sequences stretch endlessly, quickly becoming tedious. And very soon after the flesh-and-blood "ghosts" show up, it becomes painfully obvious to everyone but the protagonist that these oddly behaving "people" are not what they seem to be. The one-note story is too thin to sustain a full feature, and padded scenes begin popping up more frequently than the apparitions.

Barbara Steele's dark beauty and odd mannerisms make her both alluring and dangerous, but she's undone by the banal dubbing and lack of real characterization (her "heroine" declares her love for the living stranger mere minutes after they meet!). "How I love you Alan—uselessly, absurdly," she avows. Absurdly indeed.

Filmed in 10 days using the three-camera technique common in television, *Castle of Blood* was "exhausting," recalled Steele. "It meant sometimes working eighteen hours a day!" The movie was advertised as being based on the Edgar Allan Poe story "Dance Macabre," but no such story exists. Obviously the distributors felt they could gain a few extra box-office dollars by riding the coattails of AIP's Poe series. In the U.S. the Woolner Brothers released *Castle of Blood* on the top half of a double bill with *Hercules in the Haunted World.*

A few moments of *frisson* (such as when Foster rests his head on Elizabeth's breast and discovers

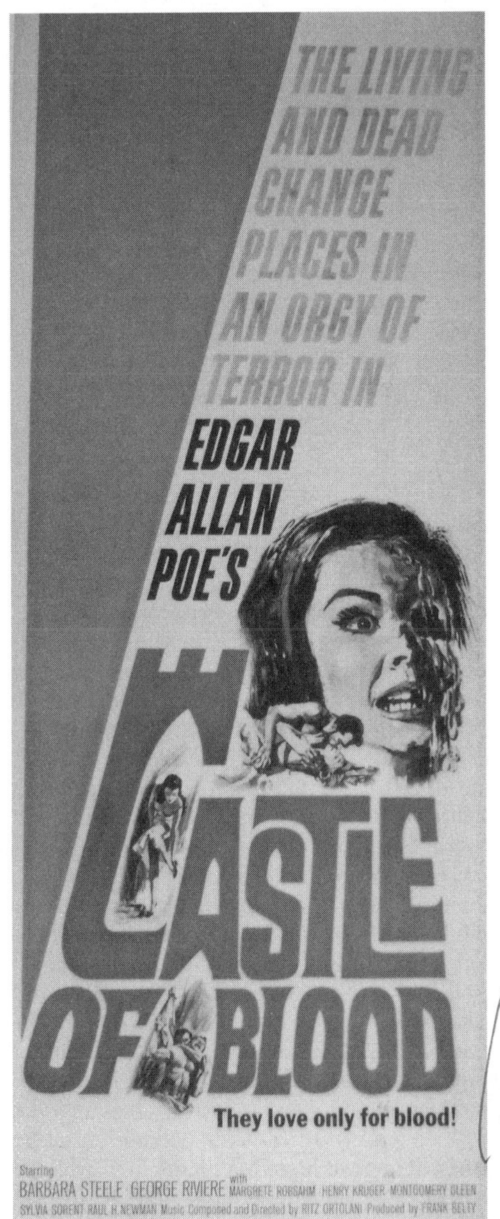

American insert poster (1964).

that his lover has no heartbeat, or when a gruesome entombed corpse suddenly begins to breathe) and an ironic ending help make a visit to this *Castle* at least bearable, but the viewer, like the film's desperate protagonist, is ready to leave long before the show's over.

Director Margheriti remade this film in color as the rather more energetic yet still unnecessary *Web of the Spider* in 1970.

With quotes from: "An Interview with Barbara Steele, Diva of Dark Drama," by Mark A. Miller, *Filmfax* 51, July/August 1995.

Castle of Bloody Lust see *Castle of the Creeping Flesh*

Castle of Evil (1966; United Pictures) Director: Francis D. Lyon; Producer: Earle Lyon; Screenplay: Charles A. Wallace; Cinematographer: Brick Marquard. Cast: Scott Brady, Virginia Mayo, David Brian, Lisa Gaye, Hugh Marlowe, Shelley Morrison.

WE HAVE RESERVED YOUR COFFIN! ...
IF YOU D.D. [DROP DEAD]
WHILE WATCHING—poster

"Funeral expenses guaranteed by a Major North American Insurance Co.," promised the ads for *Castle of Evil*. While it's highly unlikely that the distributors of this low-budget entry *really* took out a policy, it's even more improbable that anyone ever collected, since there's not much chance that a viewer will "D.D." from watching *Castle of Evil*—unless they expire from extreme boredom.

Originally shot as *The Evil at Montego Castle*, the story has a group of people arriving at disfigured industrialist/scientist Kovic's island castle just in time to hear a reading of his will. The deceased's motive for gathering together this dubious bunch of friends/enemies is to posthumously discover, with the aid of a look-alike robot he's built, which of the 'guests' is the one responsible for his bad looks and slow, lingering death. The scientist's long-serving housekeeper (Shelley Morrison) has plans of her own, however, and reprograms the robot, who starts picking them off one by one.

Male model-turned-actor William Thourlby (the original Marlboro Man himself) played the killer robot. "God, we shot that film so fast!," recalled Thourlby. "The director, Francis Lyon [*Cult of the Cobra, Destination Inner Space*, in which Thourlby also appeared], was the kind of guy who could find a set and make a whole film around it."

This impressive castle set was indeed the film's primary—*only*, actually—asset, with its imposing main hall, stone-walled passageways and medieval set decorations setting an appropriately ominous tone. Unfortunately, cinematographer Brick Marquard (*Destination Inner Space, Foxy Brown*) turns up the house lights far too bright in order to show off both the sets and the dated '60s color schemes. Couple this with an overblown and inappropriate music score, and whatever ambiance the set might have generated rapidly dissipates.

Though sporting some admittedly gruesome makeup, the mute, expressionless, business suit-wearing robot ("his brain is a computer filled with all the evil that was Kovic") does little but walk around the various corridors, making him appear more lost than "evil." Charles Wallace's talky script desperately tries to inject some horror into the sci-fi hokum via a Dark Stormy Night, a séance-like intro and, of course, the hideous android. It's all in vain, however, as director Lyon's

Ad for 1966's *Castle of Boredom*... er, *Evil*.

slow pacing and mundane staging sink whatever potential this Ten-Little-Indians-Meet-the-Monster scenario possessed. Fifth-billed Hugh Marlowe (*Earth vs. the Flying Saucers*) gives a personable turn as a naïve doctor, but the rest of the cast, headed by a take-the-check-and-just-say-the-lines Scott Brady, are forgettable at best and laughable at worst.

Despite its garish Technicolor, *Castle* appears ironically colorless next to its far superior co-feature, the literate and suspenseful (but black and white) *Blood Beast from Outer Space* (aka *The Night Caller*). Indeed, this *Castle of Evil* is, more aptly, a *Castle of Boredom*.

With quotes from: "The Marlboro Man Meets the Creeping Terror!" by Paul and Donna Parla, *Filmfax* 68, September 1998.

Castle of Horror (1964) see *Castle of the Living Dead*

Castle of Horror (1963) see *Horror Castle*

Castle of Horror (1964) see *Castle of Blood*

The Castle of Terror (1963) see *Horror Castle*

Castle of the Creeping Flesh (1968; Constantin Film, West Germany)

Original Language Title: *Im Schloss der Blutigen Begierde*. Alternate Titles: *Castle of Bloody Lust*; *The Castle of Unholy Desires*. Director: Percy G. Parker (Adrian Hoven). Producer: Pier A. Caminneci. Screenwriters: Percy G. Parker, Eric Martin Schnitzler. Cinematographers: Jorge Herrero, Franz Hofer. Cast: Janine Reynaud, Howard Vernon, Michael Lemoine, Elvira Berndorff, Claudia Butenuth, Jan Hendricks, Pier A. Caminneci, Vladimir Medar.

A HAUNTED GOTHIC TALE OF MADNESS, LUST AND BLOOD — ad line

Since it was made by the same man (Adrian Hoven, using the alias Percy G. Parker) who brought us the unpleasant and mean-spirited *Mark of the Devil* (1970) and *Mark of the Devil 2* (1972), one should not be surprised that *Castle of the Creeping Flesh* is as nasty as it is. The story concerns a small group of hedonistic partygoers, headed by a brutal Baron (Michael Lemoine), who stumble into the castle of the reclusive Count von Saxon (Howard Vernon — *The Awful Dr. Orlof* himself). The Count is trying to revive his dead daughter through some kind of mad medical operation and chooses one of the visiting girls as an unwilling donor. "Life and death — *they* are alike; but there is also love," justifies Von Saxon in a bit of off-kilter, homespun philosophy. "Love creates life; love has a right to kill. But he who kills for revenge will be cursed." Good to know.

With an overly talky script (not helped by atrociously dubbed dialogue) populated by unlikable characters, this piece of celluloid eurotrash's only real asset is an overpowering sense of decadence that gives the proceedings a sleazy sort of attractiveness. The photography and sets are lushly Gothic, and there are some truly erotic sequences involving actress Janine Reynaud, a sensuous beauty often found in the films of Jess Franco. There are also endless unpleasant close-ups of real-life open heart surgery as the Count (a surgeon) tries to revive his dead daughter using "borrowed" organs; an unconvincing man-in-a-bear-suit inflicting ridiculous face slaps on a cast member with its, er, faux paws; several gratuitous rape scenes; and a gratingly bad piano-bar jazz score. Though not for everyone, *Castle of the Creeping Flesh* possesses a repellant albeit fascinating air that makes it (almost) watchable.

Castle of the Dead see *Castle of the Living Dead*

The Castle of the Living Dead (1964; Woolner; Italy/France; b&w)

Original Language Title: *Il Castello dei Morti Vivi*; Alternate Titles: *Castle of the Dead*; *Castle of Horror*; Director: Warren Kiefer; Producer: Paul Maslansky; Screenplay: Warren Kiefer, Micheal Reeves (uncredited) (story by Paul Maslansky and Warren Kiefer); Cinematographer: Aldo Tonti. Cast: Christopher Lee, Gaia Germani, Philippe Leroy, Mirko Valentin, Donald Sutherland.

He lured beautiful women to his evil castle and induced them into a state of living death until Infinity! — poster

Castle of the Living Dead could very well be called *Castle of Wax*, for it's really a variation on the old *House of Wax*/*Mystery of the Wax Museum* story. But while its main theme may be the same, the movie's sensibilities are something else entirely, given its European flavor and macabre humor.

In the chaotic aftermath of the Napoleonic

Wars ("there was no war, but the killing had not stopped," informs the film's narrator), a traveling troupe of actors journey to the castle of Count Drago (Christopher Lee) for a private performance. Along the way an old hunchbacked witch-woman (Donald Sutherland in drag) warns, "Beware the castle—of the living dead." It proves to be a warning worth heeding, for the protagonists soon discover that the Count, who's something of a mad scientist, has perfected the art of taxidermy. No messy entrail-pulling and sawdust-stuffing here; instead, Drago uses "an acid secretion from a tropical plant [which] injected under the flesh ... will stiffen the entire body." Having already transformed all the local wildlife into perfect statues, the Count sets his sights on bigger game, intending to add the actors to his "collection."

British poster for one of the better Eurohorror double-bills of the 1960s.

Though the film's direction is officially credited to Herbert Wise (Luciano Ricci's pseudonym) for quota reasons, the picture was actually helmed by co-screenwriter Warren Kiefer. (Donald Sutherland, who made his screen debut here—in a dual role and of both sexes, no less—named his son Kiefer after the writer/director.) And a very young and enthusiastic Michael Reeves, who went on to helm *The She Beast* (1965), *The Sorcerers* (1967) and the classic *The Conqueror Worm* (1968), co-wrote and shot second unit material for the film (though he was officially credited only as assistant director).

Kiefer fills his movie with unusual and unsettling touches. For instance, he closes a suspenseful stalking sequence by cutting from the Count's sinister servant slashing at his fallen victim with a huge scythe to an up-angle shot of the servant later cutting the grass with this self-same tool, making for a startling and disconcerting transition.

In another sequence Kiefer cleverly builds suspense by cutting back and forth between a funeral, presided over by the Count, out on the castle grounds and an actor investigating the scene of the deceased's murder *inside* the castle. We see a hand load a miniature crossbow before the scene shifts back to Drago reading over the grave: "We shall not all sleep but we shall all be changed, in a moment, in the twinkling of an eye..." The camera then cuts back inside to the crossbow, which fires, and the dart-like arrow imbeds itself in the man's *eye*. The dialogue outside, juxtaposed with the carnage inside, infuses this disturbing moment with a macabre humor.

A cold, imperious, menacing Christopher Lee plays the cold, imperious, menacing Count to perfection, his rapid, strident delivery giving way to a kind of held-in-check mania when speaking of his character's "work." And a young Donald Sutherland shows both his burgeoning flair for comedy (as a slightly buffoonish gendarme) and his impressive acting talent (as the unsettlingly convincing old witch-woman who speaks in riddles and rhymes).

Despite its recycled theme, this *Castle* stands as one of the better Continental horror films of the 1960s. In the U.K. *Castle* played on a double bill with *Terror Creatures from the Grave*, yet another worthy European horror.

The Castle of Unholy Desires see *Castle of the Creeping Flesh*

Castle of the Walking Dead see *The Blood Demon*

Cave of the Living Dead (1964; Objective Film Ltd./Modern Sound Pictures Inc.; West Germany/Yugoslavia; b&w) Original Language Title: *Der Fluch der Grünen Augen* ("The Curse of the

Green Eyes"); Director/Producer: Akos V. Ratony (Rathonyi); Screenplay: C. V. Rock; Cinematographer: H. Saric; Cast: Adrian Hoven, Carl Mohner, Erika Remberg, Wolfgang Preiss, Karin Field, John Kitzmiller.

Beyond the black mouth of the cursed cave lurk the unfleshed...— ad line

In the 1960s, executive producer Richard Gordon (who oversaw such fine fare as *Fiend Without a Face* and *Island of Terror*) brought to America over 50 West German films, most of them Edgar Wallace *krimis* (criminal mysteries) or Schnitzel Westerns (the Teutonic equivalent of Italy's *Spaghetti* Westerns). Among them was this surprisingly effective German-Yugoslav horror coproduction, an overlooked gem among so much Euro-dross.

An inspector (Adrian Hoven) journeys to a small village to investigate the mysterious deaths of six girls near "the grotto" (a series of caves under the local castle). He slowly comes round to the locals' view that *vampires* are responsible, with the reclusive owner of the castle (a "professor" doing blood research!) as the prime undead suspect.

Hungarian-born veteran director (with nearly 30 years of filmmaking experience behind him) Akos Ratony's artistic use of shadows, as well as shuddery shots of long-nailed hands clawing at windowpanes, help set the mood early on — or at least help *off*-set the hero's "modern playboy" introductory image and the soundtrack's pop jazz music score. Fortunately, the jarring jazz soon gives way to naturalistic sound effects, dominated by sinister echoing footsteps, the baleful howling of dogs and the mournful wail of the wind (as well as a weird, resonating — and unnerving — sound that always accompanies the vampires' appearance).

Despite its modernist "crime" structure (reflective of the then-popular *krimi* cycle in German cinema), *Cave of the Living Dead* soon fulfills the promise of its title by settling down into a full-blooded, Gothic-style horror tale. The moody lighting (cinematographer H. Saric often illuminates the actors so that a portion of their face remains in shadows, adding a touch of mystery); hushed talk of vampires ("Each night at midnight they leave the grotto, gliding over their graves, to visit sleeping ones in their beds"); real castle and cave setting (evocatively lit by flickering torchlight); and even the characters themselves (the mysteriously surly doctor, the all-knowing witch-woman, the "Professor" whose touch is cold as ice) all combine to generate an otherworldly atmosphere ripe with dread.

This supernatural tone both contrasts with and compliments the very worldly lead character, an inspector whose modern wardrobe, humor and skeptical attitude makes him an obvious audience identification figure. Star Adrian Hoven (who later stepped *behind* the camera to produce the notoriously sadistic exploitation films *Mark of the Devil* [1970] and *Mark of the Devil 2* [1972]) makes for a likable, confident hero with a welcome sense of humor ("Either coffins are cheap around here," he observes upon finding the vampire's lair, "or they haven't got enough beds").

Beyond its more obvious merit, *Cave of the Living Dead* broke new ground in the horror arena by addressing an issue that came to a head in 1960s America yet remained largely ignored by genre filmmakers, an issue even more insidious than vampirism itself: racism. The Professor's sympathetic black servant, John (John Kitzmiller), is friendly, helpful and likable (the Inspector finds him so, as well), yet most of the backwards populace shun him because of his dark skin, even suspecting him of vampirism ("He gives me the willies," spits one dullard). In one scene a local ruffian refuses to drink with John at the Inn and manhandles him out the door in an ugly display. It makes for a tidy little subplot that's handled with a few well-placed lines and well-integrated scenes, adding a whole other dimension to this simple "horror" tale.

In the U.S. *Cave of the Living Dead* was released on a double bill with the deadly dull Italian snoozefest *Tomb of Torture*, a film possessing none of *Cave*'s atmospheric charm or thematic richness. Vampires, atmosphere and social consciousness—1960s Eurohorror fans would be well advised to do a bit of cinematic spelunking in this *Cave*.

Cemetery of the Living Dead see *Terror Creatures from the Grave*

Chamber of Horrors (1966; Warner Bros.)

Director/Producer: Hy Averback; Screenplay: Stephen Kandel (story: Ray Russell, Stephen Kandel); Cinematographer: Richard Kline. Cast: Cesare Danova, Wilfrid Hyde-White, Laura Devon, Patrice Wymore, Suzy Parker, Patrick O'Neal.

A film with many scenes so terrifying, a built-in audio-visual warning system has been devised.— poster

Originally shot as a television pilot for a series to be called *House of Wax*, *Chamber of Horrors* was deemed too shocking for the small screen. Consequently, the studio ordered a few additional scenes (not to mention a gimmicky "Fear Flasher" and "Horror Horn"—the screen flashing red to the sound of a beeping noise as a warning of upcoming violence) and released it theatrically. The result is a fairly intriguing, moderately charming, but ultimately overlong and unsatisfying tale centering on the two gentleman proprietors (Cesare Danova and Wilfrid Hyde-White) of a turn-of-the-century Baltimore wax museum, both of them amateur criminologists. When the police are unable to locate the mad killer Jason Cravatte (Patrick O'Neal), who escaped hanging by cutting off his own hand with an axe(!), the authorities enlist the aid of the two amateur sleuths to track down the deranged, oh-so-clever killer, who is now employing various nasty implements attached to his stump to take revenge on those who condemned him.

The picture opens with the well-dressed and quietly mad Cravatte forcing a minister to marry him to the corpse of his fiancée, whom he just strangled with her own hair! Unfortunately, little else in the film lives up to this macabre beginning. "At the start of certain scenes that many may consider too shocking, a red light will begin its signal on the screen to alert you to the terror ahead," announced the film's poster. Of the four "certain scenes" preceded by said "Fear Flasher" (and Horror Horn), only the first really lives up to the hype of such a device—when Cravatte, on his way to the gallows, jumps from the train into a river and, while underwater, cuts off his own hand to escape (he's handcuffed to a heavy gear wheel that's dragging him to the bottom). Though devoid of gore per se—just a billowing cloud of red blood accompanying Cravatte's silent, watery scream of pain—it's an intense scene nonetheless.

The hook-handed "Butcher of Baltimore" (Patrick O'Neal) hovers over Laura Devon in *Chamber of Horrors* (1966).

Though Danova and Hyde-White make appealing and clever protagonists, aided and abetted by their charming midget assistant Pepe, played by "Tun–Tun" (aka Jose Rene Ruiz), and O'Neal makes a strong impression as the quiet yet dangerously mad Cravatte ("But you're dead!" says one incredulous victim-to-be when confronted with the vengeful killer, to which O'Neal politely yet coldly replies, "Yes, I am; won't you join me?" before dispatching the terrified man), the story bogs down in the middle with too much drawing-room palaver and romantic intrigue. Warner's pledged their not-inconsiderable resources to the project, providing opulent costumes and convincing period sets, as well as studio stars Marie Windsor and Tony Curtis in "guest cameos" (undoubtedly with an eye towards future episodes of the proposed series). And it's gruesome fun to see the various nasty attachments (hook, cleaver, scalpel, even a modified pistol) Cravatte employs in place of his missing hand. But the meandering pacing and too-genteel TV-style restrictions mark this *Chamber* as one of *Intermittent Interest* rather than outright *Horror*.

Children of the Damned (1964; MGM; U.K.; b&w)

Director: Anton Leader; Producer: Ben Arbeid; Screenplay: John Briley; Cinematographer: Davis Boulton. Cast: Ian Hendry, Alan Badel, Barbara Ferris, Alfred Burke, Sheila Allen, Ralph Michael, Patrick Wymark.

So young, so innocent, so deadly—tagline

To his credit, screenwriter John Briley, in writing this sequel to *Village of the Damned* (1960), didn't settle for a simple rehash of that film. Instead, he takes the concept in a radically different direction. Unfortunately, his approach may or (more likely) may not entirely satisfy fans of the original picture.

Psychologist Tom Llewellyn (Ian Hendry) and geneticist David Neville (Tom Badel) discover Paul (Clive Powell), a young English boy with superhuman intelligence and amazing psychic abilities (telepathy and mind control). But before they can begin to study him, political and military leaders intervene. They take Paul to join five other extraordinary children from around the globe with similar abilities. When the six governments realize the extent of the children's powers, however, they attempt to bring the youngsters home. But the children refuse to be separated, and flee together to an abandoned church, where a standoff develops between the kids and the British army.

While *Village of the Damned* was a near-perfect blend of horror and science fiction, *Children* runs closer to pure sci-fi, with a greater emphasis on Cold War social commentary and far fewer (and less effective) scare sequences. Also, while it revives the basic concept that made *Village* so successful — and so frightening — *Children* turns those ideas inside-out. Here, the super-powered kids are victims rather than villains: they represent a new generation who want to live together peaceably despite their ethnic differences, without subscription to the outmoded nationalistic prejudices and suspicions of their parents. The military and scientific leaders, treated heroically in the original film, here are portrayed as power-mad puppetmasters who want to turn the youngsters into living weapons. None of this is in and of itself bad (it's a perfectly valid approach to the material), but it stands in stark contrast to *Village* — so much so that it can be jarring to watch both movies in close succession.

The sequel boasts many of the same strengths as the original — a smartly written scenario, low-key but slick direction (from television veteran Anton Leader), and convincing performances. But *Children*'s narrative unfolds much more methodically and contains none of the spine-tingling set pieces that made *Village* so unnerving — in large part because Briley (who went on to earn an Oscar for *Gandhi* [1980]) wants viewers to fear *for* the children rather than be afraid *of* them. Ian Hendry's heartfelt performance as the sympathetic Dr. Llewellyn, who tries to save the children from the clutches of his fellow scientists and government men, headlines a uniformly sound ensemble cast. Other standouts include Alan Bedel as Llewellyn's comrade and eventual adversary, Dr. Neville, and Sheila Allen as Paul's terrified (and doomed) mother. (She memorably seethes at her son, "I should have crushed you the moment I held you to my breast!")

Children of the Damned would likely be better regarded if it had been titled something else and left to stand on its own merits. Considered apart from its predecessor, *Children* remains a solid, well-crafted, thought-provoking picture; as a sequel to *Village of the Damned*, however, it leaves something to be desired — namely, thrills.

City of the Dead see *Horror Hotel*

City Under the Sea see *War-Gods of the Deep*

Coffin of Terror see *Castle of Blood*

Color Me Blood Red (1965; Friedman-Lewis) Director/Cinematography/Screenplay: Herschell Gordon Lewis; Producer: David F. Friedman. Cast: Gordon Oas-Heim (as Don Joseph), Candi Conder, Elyn Warner, Patricia Lee, Scott H. Hall, William Harris.

It will leave you aghast! — tagline

Actually, it's more likely to leave you unconscious.

Color Me Blood Red, the final entry in an unofficial trilogy of seminal splatter films directed by Herschell Gordon Lewis and produced by David Friedman, contains all the flaws of its predecessors (*Blood Feast* and *Two Thousand Maniacs!*) plus another, more damaging defect: It's *boring*. Languidly paced, overstuffed with tedious filler and surprisingly short on gore, *Color Me Blood Red* serves as cinematic Sominex for all but the most ardent admirers of Lewis' offbeat oeuvre.

Painter Adam Sorg (Gordon Oas-Heim) enjoys financial success, thanks to the patronage of bourgeois trophy wives, but yearns for the acceptance of art critics who revile his work. In a moment of inspiration (or perhaps desperation), Sorg paints a canvass using blood flowing from the fingertip of his indulgent girlfriend, who had cut herself on a tack. His blood-soaked painting finally earns him critical admiration; but to stay in favor, Sorg must produce similar works. Acquiring all the blood he needs will mean murder — beginning with his clueless girlfriend.

After swiping the premise of *Brigadoon* (1954) for *Two Thousand Maniacs!* (1964), Lewis shamelessly imitates Roger Corman's *A Bucket of Blood* (1959) with this seriocomic story of a maniacal artist. Unfortunately, *Color Me Blood Red* lacks the satirical sophistication of Corman's film, deriving its humor from eye-rolling one-liners (for instance, after discovering a woman's body on the beach, a "hip" teenager exclaims, "Dig that crazy driftwood!").

The picture is plagued by the technical problems (bland and immobile camera setups, harsh lighting, tinny sound, etc.) and mostly amateurish acting endemic to the Lewis filmography. Yet, given its preposterously cheap budget (six days and $30,000), it's a minor miracle that *Color Me Blood Red* is even coherent. Indeed, its poor craftsmanship might be overlooked if it were simply more entertaining. But Lewis allows the narrative to limp along at a dirge-like pace (it takes nearly half an hour to get to the first murder) and pads out the picture's 79-minute running time with more than 15 minutes worth of pointless footage of teenagers frolicking on the beach. While the stage blood flows profusely, the film's scant murder scenes lack the deranged genius present in *Two Thousand Maniacs!*

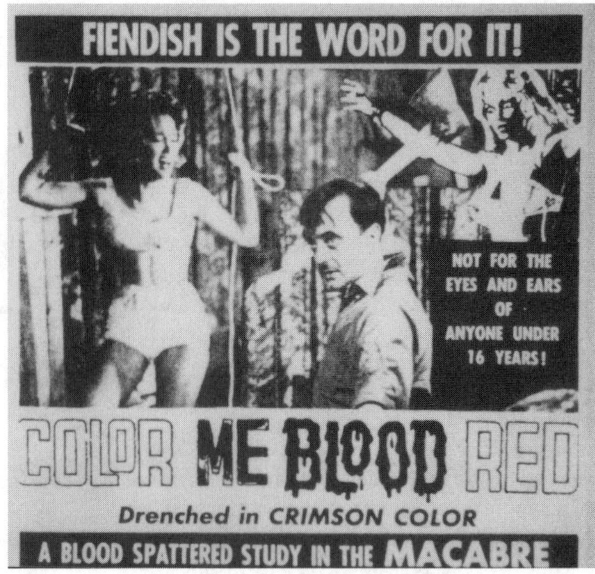

Advertising for Herschell Gordon Lewis' *Color Me Blood Red* (1965) were long on hyperbole, but the film runs short on action.

Oas-Heim's arch theatrical performance as troubled artist Adam Sorg provides the sole point of interest in *Color Me Blood Red*. However, it was not accomplished without considerable grief on Lewis' part. Oas-Heim "was an exceptionally good actor but not really a team player," Lewis said. "Gordon would constantly second guess my suggestions for direction. Apparently he had some directing experience on the stage.... [But] I can't fault the way the guy threw himself into his work." Indeed, despite the on-set tension, Lewis hired Oas-Heim again for his next project, the hillbilly feud picture *Moonshine Mountain*.

After *Color Me Blood Red*, Lewis and Friedman parted ways over a financial dispute and Lewis' career veered off in a different direction. The director moved on and tried other exploitation angles before returning to the gore genre he had created with *A Taste of Blood* and *The Gruesome Twosome* in 1967. Perhaps Lewis (seeing something of himself in Adam Sorg) didn't want to be pigeon-holed as a goremeister. Or maybe disappointing box office returns had something to do with it. Unlike the first two Lewis-Friedman films, *Color Me Blood Red* was not a commercial success— or, at least, not initially, when it played in only about 20 theaters. It was seen more widely in the early 1970s when *Blood Feast, Two Thousand Maniacs!* and *Color Me Blood Red* were released as a drive-in triple bill. By then, Lewis was back in the blood business.

With quotes from: *Color Me Blood Red* DVD commentary with H.G. Lewis and David Friedman.

The Comedy of Terrors (1964; AIP) Director: Jacques Tourneur. Producers: James H. Nicholson & Samuel Z. Arkoff. Screenwriter: Richard Matheson. Cinematographer: Floyd Crosby. Cast: Vincent Price, Peter Lorre, Boris Karloff, Joyce Jameson, Beverly Hills, Basil Rathbone, Joe E. Brown, Rhubarb the cat.

YOUR FAVORITE CREEPS TOGETHER AGAIN!—poster blurb

When producer-director Roger Corman and screenwriter Richard Matheson began injecting humor into their period horror films (first with the omnibus *Tales of Terror* and its comedic segment "The Black Cat," then with the full-length comedy of *The Raven*), American International Pictures took notice—at least after eyeing the healthy box office receipts. After this, AIP decided to give its horror films "more production values and a comedy slant in keeping with current audience response" (as announced by *The Holly-*

wood Reporter in September 1963). To this end, the company procured term contracts or multi-picture commitments from Vincent Price, Boris Karloff, Elsa Lanchester, Basil Rathbone and Peter Lorre, "all with the talent and stature to impart class and prestige to chill-and-thrill entertainment."

The Comedy of Terrors, the first of AIP's all-out horror-comedies, went into production on September 4, 1963, at Producers Studio under the working title *Graveside Story* (a moniker AIP later used for the film when it reissued *The Comedy of Terrors* in 1965 on a double bill with *The End of the World*— a re-titled *Panic in Year Zero!*). While the "comedy slant" was definitely there, AIP must have been saving the "more production values" for a future project, since *Comedy of Terrors* carried an even smaller price tag than the Corman-Poe pictures that inspired it. The fifteen-day shooting schedule and tight budget (Director Jacques Tourneur even reused the graveyard set from *The Premature Burial*) meant that there was little time for luxuries.

In a small New England town sometime before the turn of the century, underhanded undertaker Waldo Trumbull (Price) has hit on hard times. Trumbull loathes his beautiful wife (Joyce Jameson), doddering father-in-law (Boris Karloff) and mild-mannered, bumbling assistant, Gillie (Peter Lorre). When business is slow, Trumbull (with the aid of the reluctant Gillie) drums up new clients via murder. After Trumbull's boorish landlord, Mr. Black (Basil Rathbone), threatens eviction for non-payment of back rent (Boris Karloff was originally cast in this larger role of Mr. Black, but the 75-year-old actor, suffering from arthritis, could not manage the physical action the part required, and the more robust Rathbone switched roles with him), Trumbull sets his sinister sights on Black himself, resulting in a comical free-for-all that includes a sword fight, strangulation and even some mistakenly administered poison.

Suspense and noir specialist Jacques Tourneur (*Cat People* [1942], *I Walked with a Zombie* [1943], *Out of the Past* [1947], *Curse of the Demon* [1956], etc.) seems an unlike candidate to helm a farcical comedy, and the choice indeed turned out to be a rather unfortunate one. While Tourneur's direction is competent, and he generates some appropriately macabre mood at times (particularly in the graveyard sequences), his periodic injection of slapstick comedy and reliance on physical humor (one almost expects Lorre to come out with a few "nyuk, nyuk, nyuk's" before the night is through) jars harshly with his penchant for atmosphere and leisurely build-ups. Whatever *effective* humor can be found in this *Comedy* is due more to Richard Matheson's dialogue and what the actors do with it than to any directorial touches or pacing. Tourneur uses speeded-up photography (complete with Silent era-style piano music) and a plethora of "zany" physical gags to hammer his point home that this is indeed a horror-COMEDY. He even has the *cat* (played by the legendary feline thespian Rhubarb) get in on the act by including a shot of the animal swallowing—complete with audible gulp on the soundtrack—when Trumbull makes one of his frequent poisoning threats. Time and again Tourneur returns to Rhubarb for a feline reaction in a desperate attempt to wring a cheap laugh out of the moment.

The advertising for *Comedy of Terrors* (1964) emphasized comedy over terror (one-sheet poster).

Vincent Price receives all the best dialogue (some of it quite clever), and he's obviously enjoying himself, infusing the erudite but black-hearted Trumbull with his trademark buttery charm and enthusiasm. Peter Lorre, on the other hand, seldom becomes truly animated, though on one or two occasions his impish humor does manage to shine through.

Though it did make money, *The Comedy of Terrors* was less successful at the box office than *The Raven*, a result blamed on both the title and the advertising's emphasis on humor. Consequently, AIP scrapped any plans for further horror-comedy installments.

The Conqueror Worm (1968; AIP; UK) Alternate Title: *Witchfinder General* (UK); (Note: On American film prints themselves the title actually appears as *Matthew Hopkins, The Conqueror Worm*). Director: Michael Reeves; Producers: Louis M. Heyward, Philip Waddilove, Arnold Miller; Screenplay: Tom Baker, Michael Reeves (additional scenes by Louis M. Heyward; from the novel *Witchfinder General* by Ronald Bassett); Cinematographer: John Coquillon. Cast: Vincent Price, Ian Ogilvy, Robert Russell, Nicky Henson, Hilary Dwyer, Rupert Davies, Patrick Wymark.

LEAVE THE CHILDREN HOME! ... and if YOU are SQUEAMISH STAY HOME WITH THEM!!!!!!!—ad line

---

Witchfinder General (renamed *The Conqueror Worm* in America), based on Ronald Bassett's historical novel of the same name, began with producer Tony Tenser, head of Tigon British Film Productions (a cut-rate competitor of England's Hammer Films). "I thought it would make a wonderful film," recalled Tenser, "but a lot more expensive than my other pictures, so I would have to look for a partner." Tenser found said partner in American International Pictures, who kicked in £32,000 to enhance the £50,000 Tenser had already raised. One condition the Americans imposed was to insist that their current contract star, Vincent Price, play the title role. "AIP felt that it would enhance their market if Vincent Price played Matthew Hopkins," explained Tenser. "They paid for his salary [reportedly £12,000]. I was totally happy with that, because Price would enhance my market as well."

"All screen villainy is fun," declared Price in the film's American pressbook. "That is why I enjoy doing it so much. It gives me as big a kick as comedy, which I also love doing, besides being so much easier." On *The Conqueror Worm*, however, nothing apparently was "easy" for Price. While *Worm* stands as one of his finest cinematic moments, it also proved to be one of the actor's most disagreeable filming experiences. For instance, on the first day of shooting, Price was thrown from his horse and had to spend the rest of the day in bed recovering from the various bumps and bruises. But the pain inflicted by an uncooperative animal was nothing compared to the mental anguish inspired by *The Conqueror Worm*'s disgruntled director—a headstrong, 24-year-old Michael Reeves. Reeves emphatically did not want Price in the title role (Donald Pleasance was the director's initial choice) and was not at all circumspect about it. "When I went on location to meet [Reeves] for the first time," recalled Price in 1990, "he said, 'I didn't want you and I still don't want you, but I'm stuck with you!' ... [He] made me so self-conscious that I was poker-faced—and, as it turned out, he was right! He wanted it that concentrated, so it would be that much more menacing. He could have been a wonderful director ... such a sad, sad death." (Reeves died of an overdose of barbiturates and alcohol in early 1969; whether accident or suicide remains a mystery.)

Price put the unpleasant fric-

Vincent Price (left) gave one of the finest performances of his long and varied career playing "Witchfinder General" (the film's British title) Matthew Hopkins in *The Conqueror Worm* (1968). Pictured with him in this lobby card is his assistant John Stearne (Robert Russell).

tion between himself and his young director down to Reeves' inexperience (Reeves had only directed two previous features, *The She Beast* and *The Sorcerers*). "He hadn't the experience, or talked to enough [actors] to know how," Price later stated (in *Cinefantastique*). "Afterwards, I realized what he wanted was a low-key, very laid-back, menacing performance. He did get it, but I was fighting with him almost every step of the way. Had I known what he wanted, I could have cooperated." Willing to give credit where credit is due, Price admitted that, "I realized only after I saw the finished film how talented [Reeves] was."

Billed as Price's 92nd film (it was actually his 75th), *The Conqueror Worm* began shooting on September 17, 1967, and wrapped on November 13. "The year is 1645," intones an off-screen narrator. "England is in the grip of bloody civil war. On the one side stand the Royalist party of King Charles; on the other, Cromwell's Parliamentary party, the Roundheads. The structure of law and order has collapsed.... In a time where the superstitions of country folk are still a powerful factor, [Matthew] Hopkins preys upon them, torturing and killing in a supposed drive to eliminate witchcraft from the country—and doing so with the full blessing of what law there is." The cleverly-constructed story that follows is dual-pronged, one branch following the brutal activities of "witchfinder" Matthew Hopkins (Vincent Price) and his assistant John Stearne (Robert Russell), while the other follows the (also sometimes brutal) activities of neophyte Parliamentary soldier Richard Marshall (Ian Ogilvy). The two story threads soon cross and become inexorably intertwined when Hopkins descends upon the village of Marshall's fiancée, Sarah (Hillary Dwyer). Hopkins not only tortures and kills Sarah's uncle, the local Priest, but also seduces Sarah by (falsely) promising to go easy on the old man if she acquiesces. Visiting on leave, Richard learns from the traumatized Sarah what has happened and swears vengeance, then sets about tracking down the pair of witchfinders. Once found, however, Hopkins turns the tables and accuses Richard and Sarah of consorting with the Devil. In the shocking climax, Hopkins meets his bloody fate at the hands of Richard—but not without cost to both the hero and heroine.

"Grim" is the watchword for *The Conqueror Worm*. "By far it was our most violent—and least humorous—Poe picture," remarked AIP head Sam Arkoff. "There wasn't much funny about torture, hangings, and burnings at the stake. But it was effective." Effective indeed, thanks to an unflinching approach by director Michael Reeves. Rather than softening the edges of violence, Reeves displays it for the brutish and ugly thing it is. "Mike always believed violence should be seen to be horrible," explained Ian Ogilvy to *Cinefantastique*'s Bill Kelly, "to put people off, not to glorify it." And the violence seen in *The Conqueror Worm* is indeed horrible, from the intimately sickening sight of Stearne thrusting a long needle into the bare back of the old priest (searching for "the Devil's mark") to the horrific scene of a screaming woman tied to a wooden ladder lowered face first into a blazing fire.

Such an unshrinking approach generated a lot of heat from the critics of the day. Britain's *Sunday Telegraph*, for instance, denounced the film as "a sadistic extravagance," while the *London Sunday Times* labeled it "peculiarly nauseating." Even Tinseltown reviewers seemed offended, as the *Hollywood Citizen News* called it "a film with such bestial brutality and orgiastic sadism, one wonders how it ever passed customs to be released in this country." But these critics missed the point; by not turning away from the violence inherent in the story, Reeves forces the viewer to see it for the sickening act it is. The brutality in *The Conqueror Worm* is never appealing (much less "orgiastic" as the *Hollywood Citizen News* labeled it) but repugnant in its realism. Perhaps it was the discomfort caused by this unsentimental approach to something that has so often been glossed over and stylized beyond recognition that so offended the reviewers. (Ironically, all this critical outrage became a prominent factor in the film's financial success; co-producer Deke Heyward related to interviewer Tom Weaver that, though a resounding success in the U.S., the film only became a hit in England "after all the horrified letters came in to *The London Times*.")

Director Michael Reeves responded to the critical attacks on his film with newspaper letters of his own. In one he wrote, "Violence is horrible, degrading and sordid. It should be presented as such—and the more people it shocks into sickened recognition of these facts the better."

Despite the critics' complaints, *The Conqueror Worm*'s ultimate tone is one of *anti*-violence, as evidenced not only by the repulsive depiction of the act, but by the effect it has on the story's characters, particularly the hero and heroine. The climax hammers home the notion that from violence (even though it may seem like a just retribution) springs only horror and madness. Both

Richard and the watching Sarah (upon whose hysterically screaming face the film freezes and ends) cannot participate in such ferocious violence and escape with their sanity intact. By showing the awful wages of brutality, *The Conqueror Worm* carries an effective message.

Beyond its overt anti-violence stance, *The Conqueror Worm* holds further thematic relevance for modern viewers. Though ostensibly about the archaic subject of the persecution of witches, the film raises the broader issue of the abuse of authority. It's not much of an imaginative stretch to go from the lawfully empowered Mathew Hopkins and his assistant brutalizing and torturing an innocent woman in 1645 to a group of Brooklyn policemen brutalizing and torturing a Haitian immigrant in 1997 (as detailed in relatively recent headlines). One reason *The Conqueror Worm* remains so disturbing (and it does disturb, as evidenced by the occasional critical backlash even today) is that it touches on the horrors of power brutally misused.

What makes such an uncompromising and disturbing treatment palatable are the well-drawn characters and the efficacious acting that draws the viewer into their cruel world. "I was surprised how terrifying Vincent was in that," commented AIP head Sam Arkoff. Indeed, Price does terrify with his cold presence and forbidding manner, bringing his character to full malevolent life. Garbed in black hat and cloak, sporting a long and luxuriant mane of graying chestnut hair and a close-cropped, well-combed silver beard, wearing spotless white gloves and mounted on a white steed, Price cuts an extremely imposing figure.

Matthew Hopkins may be Price's finest characterization in a terror film. It is certainly one of his most unusual portrayals in that he eschews the buttery charm and smooth flamboyance for which he had become so well known (and loved) to deliver a steely, subdued, and intensely menacing performance that becomes utterly convincing. While it may not be every Price fan's favorite role, it is undoubtedly his most powerful.

Reeves' sure-handed direction and squeeze-every-pound-attitude creates a realistic stage upon which the players can move. *The Conqueror Worm* looks much more lavish than its meager £82,000 pound (roughly $250,000) budget should allow—thanks to the ingenuity and creativity of Michael Reeves and his production crew. For instance, during a witch-burning sequence, Reeves found that they couldn't afford an expensive camera crane, so for a mere £10 he rented a cherry picker from the local utility company instead. Also, rather than rent costly studio space for the interiors, the production leased two abandoned aircraft hangers outside of St. Edmunds for the bargain rate of £1,500 a month. (Of course, since the tin roofs caused an echo sound, this necessitated significant dialogue re-dubbing later on; but it still proved far cheaper than shooting in a film studio.) And filming at actual historic locations (such as Orford Castle in East Anglia) not only saved on set construction, but added immensely to the realism.

In America, of course, AIP re-titled the more literate-sounding *Witchfinder General* as *The Conqueror Worm* (after a poem by Edgar Allan Poe) to ride the tail end of their ongoing Poe series. It proved a financial boon for AIP, grossing over $1.5 million in domestic rentals (no doubt buttressed by all the inflammatory reviews complaining of excessive violence and bad taste).

"Although the story had a Poe flavor to it," explained Sam Arkoff, "we had worried that *The Witchfinder General* [sic] was an English tale that wouldn't have much appeal on this side of the Atlantic.... However, we came across an Edgar Allan Poe verse which included a line that spoke of a 'conqueror worm.' We weren't exactly sure what it meant [Poe uses the term as a metaphor for death], but it was pure Poe and seemed to fit with *The Witchfinder General*'s story line. We felt if we had Vincent recite the poem at the beginning of the film, we could legitimately call the picture a Poe movie."

Price himself, however (as well as just about everyone else), failed to see the "legitimacy" of calling *Witchfinder General* a Poe picture, opining that "*The Conqueror Worm* was the most ridiculous title for *Witchfinder General*. It took me six months to find the goddamn poem!"

Commenting on his co-star, Ian Ogilvy said, "I remember [Vincent Price] was a funny, funny guy, but a lot of it was fairly unprintable, the stuff he came out with. He was extremely forbearing. I had to kill him with an axe, and we had this very hard rubber axe. I hit him and Vincent died gracefully."

Though a "funny, funny guy" off-screen, Vincent Price (under Michael Reeves' fractious hand) delivered a deadly serious performance as Matthew Hopkins. His powerful portrayal, combined with Reeves' inventive direction and hard-line approach to violence, turned this tale of a *Witchfinder General* into a film of significant thematic and artistic integrity.

With quotes from: "Titan of Tigon Terror," by Steve Swires, *Fangoria* 129, December 1993; *The Conqueror Worm* pressbook, American International Pictures, 1968; Vincent Price appearance at the "*Fangoria* Weekend of Horrors," Los Angeles, 1990; "Vincent Price: Looking Back on Forty Years as Horror's Crown Prince," by Steve Biodrowski, David Del Valle and Lawrence French, *Cinefantastique*, January 1989; *Flying Through Hollywood by the Seat of My Pants*, by Sam Arkoff, with Richard Trubo; "Michael Reeves: Horror's James Dean," by Bill Kelly, *Cinefantastique*, August 1991; "Vincent Price: The Merchant of Menace," by Michael Orlando Yaccarino, *Scarlet Street* 7, Summer 1992; "What Price Glory!" by Bruce G. Hallenbeck, *Scarlet Street* 13, Winter 1994.

Corridors of Blood (1958/63; Amalgamated/MGM; U.K.) Alternate Title: *Doctor from Seven Dials* (U.K.); Director: Robert Day; Producers: John Croydon, Charles Vetter; Screenplay: Jean Scott Rogers; Cinematographer: Geoffrey Faithful. Cast: Boris Karloff, Betta St. John, Finlay Currie, Francis Matthews, Adrienne Corri, Francis DeWolfe, Basil Dignam, Christopher Lee.

A N-E-R-V-O-R-A-M-A SHOCKER!—trailer

Though filmed in England in 1958, *Corridors of Blood* went unreleased in the United States for nearly five years "because MGM didn't know quite what to do with it; they didn't have a picture to go with it," according to executive producer Richard Gordon.

In 1840, before the discovery of anesthesia, Mr. Bolton (Boris Karloff) is working on a drug that can be used as an anesthetic (curiously, Bolton, a surgeon, is referred to throughout the film—as are his medical colleagues—simply as "Mr." rather than "Dr."). After an initial demonstration to prove that "pain and the knife are *not* inseparable" goes badly, Bolton is eventually dismissed from the hospital. In the course of his research, Bolton has become addicted to the drugs, and now finds his way to a seedy tavern where innkeeper "Black Ben" (Francis DeWolfe) and his partner, grave robber "Resurrection Joe" (Christopher Lee), use the doctor's addiction to blackmail him into signing phony death certificates—for lodgers they have murdered in order to sell their bodies to anatomists.

"You'll take shock after shock after shock!

Left to right: Boris Karloff, Christopher Lee, Adrienne Corri, and Francis De Wolff in *Corridors of Blood* (1963).

Don't hold in your terror; shriek if you must!" warned the film's misleading trailer. Actually, there are few "shocks" (an antagonist taking a face full of acid; another falling to his death-by-impalement on iron posts) and even fewer moments of "terror" in this serious-minded historical melodrama.

"We were looking for another subject for Karloff," recounted Gordon about the film's genesis, "and [producer] John Croyden came up with the original story idea for *Corridors of Blood*. A woman named Jean Scott Rogers wrote the screenplay. Her idea was to make a very serious picture about surgery in the days before anesthetics, which of course wouldn't have made a very commercial picture. So we tried to inject horror and melodramatic elements into it."

Basically an historical drama with a few horror trappings (mainly the murderous Burke and Hare/body snatching angle), *Corridors* offers a sumptuously-set, authentic-minded tale of a fascinating time in medicine's history.

Corridors is exceedingly well-acted, from Francis DeWolfe's ingratiating yet murderous Black Ben and Christopher Lee's cold-as-a-snake Resurrection Joe (obvious stand-ins for Burke and Hare), to Adrienne Corri's beguiling yet pitiless barmaid. In fact, it's Lee's chillingly calm delivery and convincing cockney accent—combined with a look of intensity-cum-madness in his eyes—that provides the movie with its little bit of "horror." The only thespian misstep is (surprisingly) Boris Karloff's overly melodramatic portrayal of the kindly Bolton trapped in horrible circumstances. His constantly furrowed brow, dramatic gestures, and plaintive tones contrast jarringly with the more naturalistic playing of the rest of the cast.

With financial backing from MGM came that studio's substantial resources, allowing shooting at the plush MGM Studios in London, and the utilization of the MGM wardrobe and carpentry departments. As a result, *Corridors of Blood* features impressive (and authentic) costuming, and splendid sets far beyond what would be expected in a budget film of this nature.

Director Robert Day (aided by Geoffrey Faithful's evocative lighting and mobile camerawork) nicely captures the back-alley squalor of the Seven Dials district. For instance, a seedy tavern-set scene opens with a close-up of the filthy legs and muddy feet of a sleeping street urchin — an attention to detail that brings the squalid settings vividly to life.

"I think the problem with *Corridors of Blood* is that it's really a hybrid film which isn't one thing or the other," concluded Gordon. "It's not enough of a horror film like, let's say *The Haunted Strangler*, and yet it's too much of a horror film to be regarded as a picture dealing seriously with surgery and with the medical profession in that era."

When finally released in America in 1963, *Corridors* was ignominiously paired with the cheap, tepid Italian import *Werewolf in a Girls' Dormitory*. Sold as an out and out shocker to the horror crowd, *Corridors* was destined to disappoint. "The whole thing was a disaster," recounted Gordon. It was a fate undeserving of the well-crafted and engrossing *Corridors of Blood*.

With quotes from: *Interviews with B Science Fiction and Horror Movie Makers*, by Tom Weaver.

Corruption (1968; Columbia; Great Britain) Alternate Title: *Carnage*. Director: Robert Hartford-Davis; Producer/Cinematographer: Peter Newbrook; Screenplay: Donald and Derek Ford. Cast: Peter Cushing, Sue Lloyd, David Lodge, Noel Trevarthen, Anthony Booth, Kate O'Mara.

Corruption is not a woman's picture; therefore, no woman will be admitted alone to see this supershocker.— radio spot

Eminent surgeon Sir John Rowan (Peter Cushing) feels partly responsible for the disfiguring of his fiancée, Lynn (Sue Lloyd); Sir John got into a fight with fashion-model Lynn's crass photographer, resulting in a photographic lamp crashing down and burning one side of her face. Determined to eradicate her scars, Sir John combines his laser surgery technique with pituitary gland extracts to affect a cure. But the cure is only temporary, and, at Lynn's frantic urging, he turns to decapitating young women to secure the needed glands.

This mad medico scenario was far from groundbreaking in 1968, with such Continental horrors as Georges Franju's poetic *Horror Chamber of Dr. Faustus* (aka *Eyes Without a Face* (1959/62) and Jesus Franco's exploitative but lively *The Awful Dr. Orlof* (1962) having previously paved the gruesome path.

What the British *Corruption* brings to this cinematic operating theater is a startlingly harsh realism — both in its modern-day, prosaic setting and its naturalistic acting. Without a doubt, *Corruption* is one of the most impeccably acted "thrillers" of its day. And leading the thespian pack is arguably the finest actor ever to wield a

Following in the mad medico footsteps of *The Horror Chamber of Dr. Faustus* and *The Awful Dr. Orlof*, Peter Cushing (left), playing a surgeon trying to restore his fiancée's ruined face, succumbs to *Corruption* (1968).

horror-movie scalpel, Peter Cushing. Whether playing the coldly calculating Baron Frankenstein, the determined Van Helsing or the haughty Dr. Knox, Cushing imbues his roles with an unshakable conviction, bringing these sometimes fantastic characters to vivid life. So when he's taken out of the one-step-removed safety of Gothic period pieces and plunked down into the harsh realism of "modern day" brutality, his potent brand of verisimilitude becomes almost unbearable — particularly as we watch him stab a prostitute to death and cut off her head(!), with his disgust and self-loathing at the act all-too-apparent on his horrified face.

In Germany *Corruption* was released as *Die Bestie mit dem Shalpell* (*The Beast with the Scalpel*), but Cushing's character is anything *but* a beast. Cushing goes from a quiet guilt and determined obsession to becoming a reluctant murderer and ultimately to a sort of resigned madness with the utmost poignancy. He is both antagonist and *pro*tagonist, and while we're horrified at his brutal acts, so is *he*, so we never lose touch with the tragedy of the character. It's a brilliant portrayal that, admittedly, deserved a better vehicle than that provided by Donald and Derek Ford's "mod"-flavored script and director Robert Hartford-Davis' exploitative approach.

The film is also a clever character study, not only of Cushing's guilt-wracked doctor but of his beauty-obsessed fiancée. Early in the picture, before her disfigurement, Lynn tells a friend that she's giving up modeling to marry Sir John — not for money but "for love." "Marriage lasts, a career doesn't," she wisely pronounces. But after her accident she can think of nothing but regaining her beauty. Though John loves her despite her scars, she cannot see past her surface image, and so uses her "love" to exhort him to murder. It all culminates in madness and death — a telling statement on the lure and danger of superficiality.

"It was gratuitously violent, fearfully sick," concluded Cushing in *The Films of Peter Cushing* by Gary Parfitt. "But it was a good script, which just goes to show how important the presentation is." While Hartford-Davis (*Bloodsuckers*, 1969) stages the murder scenes with plenty of odd angles and quick cutting (no pun intended) that generate a frantic immediacy, these techniques serve to intensify the horrific excitement of the acts. It's only Cushing's playing that makes these moments at all bearable — and only just. And the incredibly downbeat, nihilistic ending makes the film even more unpalatable.

Filmed during July and August of 1967 (the "Summer of Love"), there's a bit too much of "Swinging London" (of the desperate party atmosphere variety that only existed in 1960s cinemas) peppered throughout the picture, complete with brightly-colored "pads" populated by paisley prints, miniskirts and Nehru jackets.

Bill McGuffie's wildly inappropriate manic pop-jazz musical score adds to the vulgarity. It becomes so intrusive at times that it unintentionally serves as a bit of (comic) relief for some of the more intense unpleasantness.

By no means could *Corruption* be labeled an enjoyable film (nor, for that matter, could it really be called a "good" one), but it's a picture that, thanks primarily to Cushing and his fellow thespians, says a few things about the nature of guilt and the dangers of narcissism. Though little more than a well-acted and exceedingly grim exploitation piece, *Corruption* remains a curiously affecting anomaly from the 1960s.

Former Miss Iceland Sirry Steffan screams upon discovering *The Crawling Hand* (1963) in this Mexican lobby card.

Count Frankenstein see *The Bloody Vampire*

The Crawling Hand (1963; Hansen Enterprises; b&w)

Director: Herbert L. Strock; Producer: Joseph F. Robertson; Screenplay: William Edelson, Herbert L. Strock; Cinematographer: Willard Vander Veer. Cast: Peter Breck, Kent Taylor, Rod Lauren, Arline Judge, Richard Arlen, Alan Hale.

The remains of an astronaut destroyed in space fights for life! — trailer

"The Crawling Hand *demands* to live! — demands *you* to see it!" shouts the film's promotional trailer; but it just demands too much. Budgeted at $100,000, the movie was brought in by director Herbert L. Strock for "ninety-eight some-odd." Some-odd is right.

What a bizarre story line: An astronaut on his way back from an historic moon landing is taken over by some kind of evil space organism that just wants its host to "Kill! Kill! Kill!" So said spaceman, with what remaining will he has left, contacts mission control and begs them to detonate the self-destruct button for him, since his own arm won't obey. This sequence gives the film one of its few exciting moments, with some pretty scary make-up — blackened eyes, a pasty white complexion, sweat pouring down his face, and the poor soul screaming, "Push the red button! Push iiiiiit!!!" Yes, ground control pushes it and the rocket blows up over California, but his arm (the uncooperative one) falls to Earth and is promptly found by pre-med student Paul (Rod Lauren), who, naturally, takes it home and puts it on a shelf in the basement(!). Bad move Paul, since that nasty space organism is still inside the arm and ready to take *you* over now. Into the mix come two scientists (Kent Taylor and Peter Breck) from "Space Operations" to investigate, while Paul tries to find the ambulatory arm, clear himself of a murder charge, and keep himself from killing his friends and fiancée (former Miss Iceland Sirry Steffen).

The remainder of the running time is filled with scenes of the unconvincing arm crawling around (either a fake-looking mechanized prop or the director's own appendage), the two scientists running afoul of the obstinate local law (personified by sheriff Alan Hale), Paul becoming possessed, Paul fighting off the possession, and talk. Too much talk — in the office, on the phone, on the beach...

With its absurd plot line, *Requiem for an Astronaut* (its original title — which was changed to *The Crawling Hand* to make it more commercial) could have been a low-budget, unconventional winner. But a preponderance of inaction and a talky, blatantly stupid script (by William Idelson and director Strock) sink it. Lines like, "In space, life might mutate or even fully evolve in a matter of hours or even minutes" proliferate. When one of the scientists goes on (and on *and on*) about this theory, he advises, "Throw out the logic pills when you swallow it." That pretty much goes for the viewer as well.

Director Strock brought the same adequate-but-uninspired sensibilities to *The Crawling Hand* that he evinced on his other low-end sci-fi/horrors (*How to Make a Monster*, *Gog*, *Blood of Dracula*, *I Was a Teenage Frankenstein*, *The Devil's Messenger*). "I was able to stage things the way I had envisioned them in writing the script," stated the director, "but I found that interpretations and subtleties were missing because the actors really didn't have the experience.... I could have had Burt Reynolds, who read for a part, but I didn't think Burt was good enough; at that time, he was a stuntman. So we wound up with Kent Taylor, who was a bit of a problem. He was never on time and he never knew his lines." With dialogue such as, "Does a living cell from Earth romance a cosmic ray and give birth to an illegitimate monster?" one could hardly blame him.

While juvenile leads Rod Lauren and Sirry Steffen absurdly overplay and underplay respectively, the picture's main problem is *not* the acting but its dull and unlikely script — as evidenced by the admittedly bizarre but action-less climax in which the arm is partially devoured by stray cats(!), thus freeing Peter from its control.

"It *is* a minor film," concluded Strock. "It was made for peanuts, as I said, but it was a lot of fun to do." Too bad it's not a lot of fun to *watch*.

With quotes from: *Interviews with B Science Fiction and Horror Movie Makers*, by Tom Weaver.

Creature from the Haunted Sea (1961; Filmgroup; b&w)

Director/Producer: Roger Corman; Screenplay: Charles B. Griffith; Cinematographer: Jack Marquette. Cast: Anthony Carbone, Betsy Jones Moreland, Robert Towne (as Edward Wain), Robert Bean, Beach Dickerson.

What was the unspeakable secret of the sea?— tagline

The third time wasn't a charm for producer-director Roger Corman, whose *Creature from the Haunted Sea* (1961)— the final entry in an informal trilogy of black comedies, following *A Bucket of Blood* (1959) and *The Little Shop of Horrors* (1960)— remains the rickety leg of its metaphorical tripod.

Shortly after Fidel Castro's takeover of Cuba, American gangster Renzo Capetto (Anthony Carbone), assisted by his moll (Betsy Jones Moreland) and a couple of dim-witted henchmen (Robert Bean and Beach Dickerson), agrees to use his yacht to help a band of renegade Cuban generals, along with a chest full of gold from the nation's treasury, escape to the U.S. En route to the States,

Misleading one-sheet poster for *Creature from the Haunted Sea* (1961).

Capetto plans to bump off the Cubans and steal the loot. But first he needs to thin the ranks of the Cuban troops brought along to protect the treasure. Capetto invents a tall tale about a deadly sea monster to explain the soldiers' disappearances. To his surprise, however, the monster turns out to be real. This zany yarn is told from the perspective of a CIA agent (Robert Towne) disguised as one of Capetto's crewmen.

In 1960, Corman brought a single cast and crew to Puerto Rico (where he could take advantage of "certain tax laws that were extremely advantageous") to shoot two films—the post-apocalyptic thriller *The Last Woman on Earth* and the World War II drama *Battle of Blood Island* (both 1960). Once in Puerto Rico, however, Corman decided to stay an extra week and make a third picture—specifically, a black comedy in the tradition of *Bucket* and *Little Shop*. He called screenwriter Chuck Griffith, who had written his two previous horror-comedies, and the two roughed out the plot, loosely adapted from Griffith's earlier *Beast from Haunted Cave* (1959). The schedule allowed one day for preproduction—work that included making the titular Creature out of a wetsuit, moss and Brillo pads, with tennis ball eyes and pipe cleaner claws—and one week of shooting. Originally, Corman planned to act in *Creature from the Haunted Sea*. "I mentioned to Chuck that he could write a minor part for me and he deliberately came up with Happy Jack Monohan, without question the most complex acting role Chuck ever created," Corman wrote in his autobiography. "In every scene, Happy Jack had to express a different, powerful emotion.... I know Chuck did this to drive me crazy." It was too big a role for Corman, who gave the part to Bobby Bean, a young actor working on the crew.

Although from all reports Corman and company had a ball making this film, and even though Corman wrote that preview audiences "laughed and applauded just as they had with *Little Shop*," *Creature* never rises to the level of its two hilarious predecessors. It certainly has its moments, like when Capetto comforts the passengers on his sinking yacht with, "Relax, everybody, the boat's insured." Later, one of the characters vows, "I'll love you 'til the day I die," and is immediately killed by the monster. Plus, the Creature itself (in which Corman invested a measly $150) is quite amusing-looking. Overall, however, Griffith's work isn't as strong here as in either *Bucket* or *Little Shop*. The manic scenario seems jumbled, the characters are unappealing and too many of the jokes fall flat. Also, the actors who made *Bucket* and *Shop* so enjoyable—especially Mel Welles and Dick Miller—are sorely missed. Anthony Carbone isn't bad as Capetto, but neither Jones-Moreland nor Towne show any flair for comedy. (Towne, in fact, wasn't even an actor, he was a screenwriter; Corman brought him along to play the third lead in *Last Woman* because production was about to begin but Towne had not yet finished the script.) On the positive side, Bean has a field day playing over-emotional simpleton Happy Jack, and Beach Dickerson seems to be channeling Harpo Marx as Capetto's first mate, who speaks primarily in animal mating calls (via the overdubbed roars of lions, howls of monkeys, etc.).

Despite its considerable faults, *Creature from the Haunted Sea* contains enough laughs to make it worth a look for Corman diehards, or anyone who loves *A Bucket of Blood* and *The Little Shop of Horrors*. Just don't expect anything quite as much fun as either of those kooky cult classics.

With quotes from: *How I Made a Hundred Movies in Hollywood and Never Lost a Dime*, by Roger Corman with Jim Jerome.

Creature of the Walking Dead (1965; ADP Productions; Mexico; b&w)

Original Language Title: *La Marca del Muerto*; Director: Frederic Corte (Fernando Cortes); Producers: Alfred Ripstein, Jerry Warren (English version); Screenplay: Alfredo Varela, Jr., Fernando Cortes, Joseph Unsain (English Version); Cinematographer: Richard Wallace. Cast: Rock Madison (Fernando Casanova), Ann Wells (Sonia Furio), George Todd, Katherine Victor (English version), Bruno Ve Sota (English version).

A FLAMING HOLOCAUST OF HORROR!
—trailer

Here's another incoherent mess from ultra-cheap producer Jerry Warren. Warren had a habit of buying low-budget film footage—or even whole features—and adding new scenes, usually of actors sitting around talking (e.g. *Invasion of the Animal People, Attack of the Mayan Mummy*, among *many* others). The Mexican *Creature of the Walking Dead* (shot in 1960 but not released—by Warren—in the U.S. until 1965) may be the worst of the lot.

The plot centers on a doctor (Fernando Casanova) who discovers how to retain his youth by extracting a special fluid from young girls. He is found out and hanged, but many years later his

DRAW POWER WHILE IN THE GRAVE!
AN EXPERIMENT OF TERROR! A RESULT OF HORROR!
CREATURE OF THE WALKING DEAD
STARRING
ROCK MADISON • ANN WELLS
WILLARD GROSS • GEORGE TODD
Original Screenplay by JOSEPH UNSAIN
Directed by FREDERIC CORTE
Produced by ALFRED RIPSTEIN
A JERRY WARREN ADP PRESENTATION

Ad for *Creature of the Walking Dead* (1965) (courtesy Ted Okuda).

descendent, who happens to look *exactly* like him (undoubtedly due to budgetary restrictions), finds his notebooks, digs him up, and brings him back to life. Pretty soon the evil ancestor has imprisoned his 'good' descendent and begins menacing the young man's fiancée (Sonia Furio). Nothing new here. The film opens with a narrator (the protagonist) asking us, "Is the world real, or thought essentially a true reflection or merely an illusion brought about by a mind separate from the ultimate reality? Thus is the question of man." Huh?! Did the aptly named scripter Joseph Unsain (probably a pseudonym for Warren himself) really write that, or was the narrator just winging it? And this is one of the more coherent passages.

Scenes of people talking about things often only vaguely related to the story pad the running time. One long Warren-added sequence has Warren regular Catherine Victor discussing with a detective the merits of the use of mediums in police work. This has nothing to do with the plot, nor are these two characters ever seen again! Most of the remaining footage has the narrator telling us what is taking place on the screen, even relating what the people are saying as they silently mouth the words. And the heavy-handed, incredibly obtrusive music doesn't help.

An occasional gruesome shot of a corpse, and a bizarre scene of an operation on a dog cadaver, add a bit of liveliness to the proceedings, but when the unimaginative climactic conflagration rolls around, the only emotion inspired is relief that it's finally over. Even Bad Movie aficionados may find this incoherent mess too long a *Walk* to take.

The Creeping Terror (1964; Crown International; b&w) Director/Producer: A.J. Nelson; Screenplay: Arthur Ross; Cinematography: Andrew Janczak. Cast: Vic Savage (A.J. Nelson), Shannon O'Neil, William Thourlby, John Caresio, Norman Boone.

"Despite Brett's inquiries about what Martin had seen in the spacecraft, he avoided specific details for fear of disturbing her more than she was. If the truth were known, Martin was more than a little disturbed himself."—omnipresent narrator

A blob-like creature creeps out of a wrecked spaceship and eats everyone in its laborious path, while a newlywed sheriff's deputy (Vic Savage, aka director A.J. Nelson), a handsome scientist (male model-turned-actor William Thourlby, the original "Marlboro Man"), and a military platoon tries to figure out a way to stop it.

Living down to its reputation as one of the worst films of all time, *The Creeping Terror* is so jaw-droppingly awful that it becomes almost snake-fascinatingly entertaining. Sure, you could harp on the flat lighting, inept camerawork, toneless non-acting and endless padding, but then you'd miss the sublimely irrational chuckles gleaned from such sights as a bikini-clad victim screaming and thrashing as she wriggles her way *into* the monster's maw, or a folk singer attempting to beat off the monster with his acoustic guitar!

The infamous mottled shag-carpet monster needed five people inside it to make it ... er, move. Looking like a mangy, dreadlock-wearing Care Bear dragging an oversized throw rug behind it (from the back it resembles a blotchy tea cozy), this *Creeping Terror* does literally creep ... slooowly. (All one need do to evade the lumbering lump is *walk away*; amazingly—and amusingly—few in this movie ever think to do that.) In one scene, members of what must be the most inept platoon in the United States Army all huddle close together about five feet away from the monster to fire their pistols. The creature crawls slowly forward to push them all over like bowling pins and then ingest them!

Shooting took place in 1963, "in the heat of summer," recounted co-star William Thourlby. "And we got some local kids to get inside this thing and make it move and operate. The kids had a ball trying to make it move through the forest, but when some of them started passing out, I got worried and thought, 'how in the world did I get mixed up in all this?!' No one was getting paid, either."

By his own account, Thourlby, who invested his money as well as his acting talent in the movie, ended up "saving" the picture when producer-director-star-*shyster* (according to Thourlby) Arthur J. Nelson disappeared before the production was finished. "I gave $25,000 to get the picture going, but Nelson spent the money on everything else but the picture!" claimed Thourlby. "At one point, we stopped shooting—for a few days or a week—and I was waiting to hear from Nelson to resume shooting, but still no call from this guy ... [so] I decided to pay him a visit. When I arrived at his house, there was a group of guys removing his furniture and other belongings and loading them onto a moving van. Nelson was nowhere to be found, so I walked into the house, and in the corner stood two boxes, which I opened. Inside was the film itself and the negative. I picked them up and drove back to my home."

But the footage was a shambles: "In some spots there was audio and in other segments there wasn't.... It was a mess. I got a bunch of my friends together; we put blankets up all around the room to help absorb some of the acoustics and then we practically lip-synched the rest of the film.... The narration had to be injected into the film to give it some kind of story line, but that didn't work too well either." Indeed, there's so much narration (we watch people converse, while the narrator *tells* us what they're saying) that the few moments of actual dialogue seem abrupt and out-of-place!

"I tried saving the film," concluded Thourlby, "but to no avail.... I hope that fans of this type of film will try and imagine what it might have been if things were different. It's so bad that I don't think many will have difficulty imagining just how much better it could have been." Well, it's those very "so bad" qualities—resulting in inspired moments of accidental hilarity—that, like with *Plan 9 from Outer Space* and *Robot Monster* before it, endear *The Creeping Terror* to its fans.

With quotes from: "The Marlboro Man Meets the Creeping Terror!" by Paul and Donna Parla, *Filmfax* 68, September 1998.

Cries in the Night see *The Awful Dr. Orlof*

Crimes in the Wax Museum see *Nightmare in Wax*

The Crimson Executioner see *Bloody Pit of Horror*

The Curse of Nostradamus (1961; Estudios America/Trans-International Films; Mexico; b&w) Original Language Title: *La Maldición de Nostradamus*; Director: Frederick Curiel; Producer: Victor Parra; Screenplay: Charles Taboada, Alfred Ruanova, Frederick Curiel; Cinematographer: Fernando Alvarez Garces. Cast: Germán Robles, Julio Aleman, Domingo Soler, Aurora Alvarado, Manuel Vergara.

From the depths of an evil mind came a diabolical plan of conquest ... INCREDIBLE ... UNBELIEVABLE—ad line

The Curse of Nostradamus is a truly terrible south-of-the-border vampire film with few redeeming values. For late-night movie enthusiasts, even those enamored of Mexican monster movies, it is indeed a *Curse*.

For some reason, the son of the son of the famed sixteenth century French physician-cum-prognosticator Nostradamus is a vampire (played by Mexico's answer to Bela Lugosi and Christopher Lee, Germán Robles) who's trying to establish a cult following for his dead grandfather. He attempts this by confronting a "Professor" (Domingo Soler) who campaigns against superstitions (such as the belief in vampires). The vampire (who, by the way, calls *himself* Nostradamus as well) predicts murders, which he then carries out, and generally makes a nuisance of himself. The Professor, now convinced of the vampire's veracity, is still too pigheaded to give in to Nostradamus' demands. The climax, using the term loosely, has the Professor's male secretary (Julio Aleman) chasing the bloodsucker through catacombs waving a pistol loaded with platinum bullets (apparently good old silver was just too gauche). He fires seven of those bullets (missing every time)—quite a trick considering he's using a *six-shooter.* Despite being such a lousy shot, Our Hero gets a break when the roof caves in and buries the vampire, leaving only his withered hand showing.

The good news is that this is THE END; the bad news is that there are three—count 'em, *three*—sequels. You see, this is actually only the first of four theatrical features made from a 12-chapter serial (the very first straight *horror* serial, by the way) and released in Mexico in 1961–63. (The "features" made their way North via Florida-based entrepreneur/producer K. Gordon Murray, who packaged them into a series of matinee movies and then dumped them onto the hungry television market.) By the late 1950s the serial as a commercial venture had died in the U.S. (thanks largely to the influx of television), but it was still a thriving medium in Mexico. *The Curse of Nostradamus* is comprised of the serial's first three chapters, translated as "The Finger of Destiny," "The Book of the Centuries" and "Night Victims."

***The Curse of Nostradamus* is vampirism in this cinematic cure for insomnia, the first of *four* Nostradamus features (Mexican lobby card).**

According to star Germán Robles, the "serial" format was all simply a ruse by the production company, who never intended to release it in episodic form. "They misrepresented themselves to me," complained the actor. "They told me they were filming 30-minute episodes—like fill-in shorts for theaters. When I finished the filming of these episodes, they put three episodes together to make one full-length picture. It ended up as being four full-length motion pictures. It is really uncomfortable to even think about this—it was a very unpleasant situation, because they actually cheated me.... It hurts that they would take advantage of me—make fun of me, literally. Because I always try to do things right."

The one bright spot in this *Curse*d production comes in the form of an amazingly impressive bat (superior to the often ungainly Universal and Hammer bat-on-a-string variety)—with wings that actually move (unfortunately, it is the only thing that *does* in this celluloid cure for insomnia).

Next up was *The Monsters Demolisher*, followed by *The Genie of Darkness* and *The Blood of Nostradamus.* Predicting that these "sequels" are no better than the dismal original takes no great prognostication ability.

With quotes from: "El Vampiro Speaks! An Interview with Mexican Horror Star Germán Robles," by Bryan Senn, Richard Sheffield and Jim Clatterbaugh, *Monsters from the Vault* 24, February 2008.

Curse of Simba see *Curse of the Voodoo*

Curse of the Aztec Mummy

(1957/62; Cinematografica Calderon S.A./Trans-International Films; Mexico; b&w) Original Language Title: *La Maldición de la Momia Azteca*; Director: Rafael Portillo, Paul Nagel (English language version); Producer: William Calderon Stell, K. Gordon Murray (English version); Screenplay: Alfred Salazar; Cinematographer: Enrique Wallace. Cast: Ramon Gay, Rosita Arenas, Crox Alvarado, Luis Aceves Castaneda, Jorge Mondragon.

AN ANCIENT AZTEC PRIEST'S CURSE IS DEFIED ... HIS MUMMY ARISES FROM THE GRAVE TO FULFILL HIS VENGEANCE!—ad line

---

A masked wrestler hero, a criminal mastermind, bad dubbing, a deadly snake pit, small-time hoods, fistfights, bad dubbing, an Aztec treasure, bad dubbing, oh — and an ancient Aztec mummy come to life — all in the space of 65 minutes. With elements such as these, this south-of-the-border cheapie (filmed in 1957, but not released in America until 1962) couldn't possibly be boring. Guess again.

Looking like nothing more than a low-grade serial, complete with cliff-hanging escapes and endless rounds of fisticuffs, this first sequel to *La Momia Azteca* (which was released — in altered form — in the U.S. by the shameless Jerry Warren as *Attack of the Mayan Mummy*) occupies its brief running time with the exploits of a hammy master criminal dubbed "the Bat" and his gang of suit-and-fedora-clad thugs trying to find an ancient Aztec treasure guarded by the living mummy Popoca. Popoca wears an ancient breastplate and bracelet that are the keys to locating the treasure. The Bat tries to get to the mummy through a scientist's fiancée, who is the reincarnation of Popoca's lost love. Opposing the criminals is a masked crime-fighting hero who calls himself "the Angel."

About the only enjoyment that can be gleaned from this tedious trial (which, in time-honored Universal Mummy fashion, trots out the flashback footage from the original *Momia Azteca* to pad its threadbare plot) are a surprisingly brutal fight sequence (in which one of the protagonists has his head repeatedly pounded into the floor!) and the rather imposing appearance of the desiccated mummy itself (no bandages here, just some tattered Aztec garb and a hideous dried-apple mummy mask). Unfortunately, said mummy only appears near the very end, in two brief scenes.

Even so, with all its faults, at least this sequel proved a step up from its bastardized progenitor, the utterly unwatchable *Attack of the Mayan Mummy*. Next up: *The Robot vs. the Aztec Mummy*.

Curse of the Blood-Ghouls (1962/69; Pacemaker; Italy; b&w) Alternate Title: *The Slaughter of the Vampires*; Original Language Title: *La Strage dei Vampiri*; Director/screenwriter: Roberto Mauri; Producer: Dino Sant'Ambrogio; Cinematography: Ugo Brunelli. Cast: Walter Brandy (Brandi), Dieter Eppler, Graziella Granata, Paolo Solvay, Gena Gimmy, Alfredo Rizzo, Edda Ferronao, Maretta Procaccini.

A group of torch-wielding villagers chase two fleeing vampires through the night. The female bloodsucker trips and falls, while the male escapes. She lies there screaming in terror as the angry mob surrounds her, shouting as they poke at her with sticks and pitchforks. So begins this "golden age" gothic Italian horror film from 1962 (released Stateside in 1969 on a double bill with the British *The Vampire-Beast Craves Blood*), which, disappointingly, offers little else in the way of excitement after this non-sequitur opening.

The (19th century-set) story proper has an unnamed undead (Dieter Eppler)—possibly the surviving vampire from the pre-credits sequence (though this remains hazy; the fact that U.S. prints were shorn of 10 minutes undoubtedly impacted continuity)—crash a genteel party hosted by Austrian nobleman Wolfgang (Walter Brandi) and his beautiful wife Louise (Graziella Granata). The seductive bloodsucker determines to introduce Louise to his nocturnal world, and Wolfgang must enlist the aid of a Van Helsing-like doctor (future director Louigi Batzella [*The Devil's Wedding Night*] acting under the name Paolo Solvay) to combat the evil in their midst.

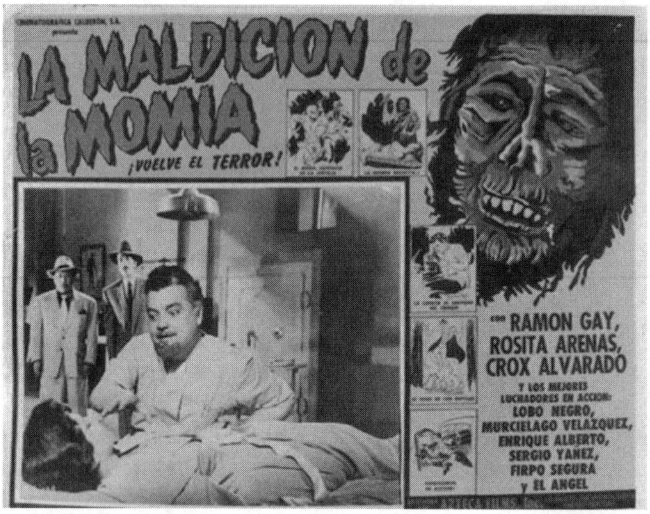

The Aztec treasure-seeking master criminal "the Bat" (Luis Aceves Castañeda) hypnotizes heroine Rosita Arenas and thus invokes the *Curse of the Aztec Mummy* (1957/62) (U.S. lobby card aimed at Spanish-speaking theaters).

Though pretty standard vampire fare, *Curse of the Blood-Ghouls* offers more visual panache than most, thanks not only to the impressive, expansive and authentic castle settings (a trademark of Italo-gothic), but to Ugo Brunelli's mobile camerawork. Smooth tracking shots, varied angles, and stark moody lighting add some much-needed visual interest to the mundane story.

Also in the visual interest department stands the gorgeous Graziella Granata as Louisa. Director Roberto Mauri takes every opportunity to focus on her unholy, erotically-charged longings; heaving bosom, (barely) held in check by a plethora of low-cut gowns; and ecstatic sighing.

Dieter Eppler, on the other hand, makes for a decidedly feeble vampire. Sporting the standard evening clothes and cape, his slight frame poses little in the way of physical threat (in fact, he must resort to attacking the hero with a mace at one point, and even then is overpowered). This rather bloodless bloodsucker does little but run around in the dark, peep through windows, and seduce young women. No wonder the film's original language title was "Slaughter of the Vampires" (as opposed to "Slaughter of the Humans"), since all these weakling wurdalaks manage to do is get themselves staked.

The banal dubbing; awkward (and overlong) dialogue; leisurely pacing; and unconvincing, primitive lap-dissolve effects (not to mention the oh-so-dramatic piano and violin music score right out of the Silent era) further work against the film.

A simplistic, nondescript, and ultimately forgettable vamper, *Curse of the Blood-Ghouls* offers only one buxom starlet and the occasional camera flourish to the intrepid '60s gothic film lover. The actors, with the exception of the stunning Granata (whose thespian attributes almost match her more obvious ones), are as bland and banal as the story, with little emoting or even reaction (beyond the seemingly endless discourse) in evidence. (Male lead Walter Brandi did better in his other vampire outings, *The Playgirls and the Vampire* and *The Vampire and the Ballerina.*) At the end, the doctor intones, "Life has many secrets ... but I think I'm talking too much." Amen.

The Curse of the Crying Woman (1962/69;

Cinematográfica A.B.S.A.-Clasa Mohme/Young America Productions; Mexico; b&w) Original Language Title: *La Maldición de la Llorona*; Director: Raphael Baledon, Stim Segar (English language version); Producer: Abel Salazar, K. Gordon Murray (English version); Screenplay: Raphael Baledon, Fernando Galiana; Cinematographer: Joseph Oritiz Ramos. Cast: Rosita Arenas, Abel Salazar, Rita Macedo, Carlos Lopes Moctezuma, Henry Lucero, Mario Sevilla, Julissa del Llano, Foy Fletcher.

See nightmare after nightmare in the most terrifying picture *ever* to be shown!—TV spot

Mexican horror movies of the 1950s and '60s were something of a throwback to the Universal Gothics of the 1930s and '40s, in that they seemed to be trying to recapture the dark, brooding atmosphere of those earlier classics. Often saddled with gonzo plots and over-the-top acting, this little subculture of horror cinema possesses its own unique charm, largely due to the graveyard ambiance coupled with the more gruesome shocks that the less restrictive time period allowed. One of the better entries in the south-of-the-border

Rita Macedo and her hounds prowl the night in *The Curse of the Crying Woman* (1962/69), one of the decade's most atmospheric Mexi-horrors.

horror sweepstakes was *The Curse of the Crying Woman* (which premiered theatrically in the U.S. in 1969 as a co-feature with *The Brainiac*).

Shot during the last two weeks of November 1961, *Curse*'s story centers on "La Llorona" (the Crying Woman), a prominent figure in Mexican folklore. A sinister woman named Thelma summons her estranged niece Emily, along with her oblivious husband Herbert, to her isolated mansion, revealing that she is a descendent and follower of "the Wailing Witch." With the aid of her ugly, murderous, Ygor-like servant—complete with stiff neck, limping gait and a reference to being saved from the gallows—named Fred, the evil aunt intends to use her young niece in a plan to resurrect the legendary witch and thus cement her own diabolical powers and immortality.

Given its creepy soundstage forest and (Spanish-style) castle (with its cobwebbed, rat-infested interiors that'd make any Universal art director proud), and low-key lighting and evocative photography (courtesy of cinematographer Joseph Oritiz Ramos), *Curse* looks the part of a genuine Gothic horror. It also contains a number of arresting images. When exercising Thelma's evil powers, for instance, actress Rita Macedo wears appliances over her eyes that transforms them into large, shiny, black orbs—a simple but disturbing effect. In the film's most startling scene, the witch flies, bat-like, directly at the camera only to abruptly change from a hideous corpse-like crone into the slightly less repulsive Thelma with her oversized, blackened eyes.

Producer Abel Salazar cast himself as the hero, Herbert; and to play his new bride, Emily, he chose Venezuelan-born actress Rosa (Rosita) Arenas—which wasn't much of a stretch, since the two were married in real life. Arenas also played the heroine in *The Witch's Mirror*, *Face of the Screaming Werewolf* and a trio of Aztec Mummy movies. Keeping it all in the family, villainess Rita Macedo's real-life daughter, Julissa del Llano (who went on to become a popular movie actress herself), has a small role as the young girl in the pre-credits sequence who's crushed under a coach wheel (a brutally shocking scene).

Granted, as with most of these south-of-the-border oddities, the film sports some awkward dubbing and occasional bouts of monotony, and the overly-protracted and lackluster fight scene at the end between Herbert and Fred (what a name for a sinister sidekick!) drags on interminably.

But if you can get past the occasional tedium and those hilariously banal names, then *The Curse of the Crying Woman* will make any Mexican horror aficionado smile ... and the rest, well, at least it won't inspire too many tears of pain.

Curse of the Dead see *Kill, Baby ... Kill!*

The Curse of the Doll People (1961/68; Cinematografica Calderon S.A./Trans-International Films; Mexico; b&w) Original Language Title: *Muñecos Infernales*; Director: Benito Alazrahi, Paul Nagle (English version); Producer: William Calderon Stell (Pedro A. Claderon and Guillermo Calderon), K. Gordon Murray (English version); Screenplay: Alfred (Abel) Salazar; Director of Photography: Henry (Enrique) Wallace. Cast: Elvira Quintano, Raymond (Ramon) Gay, Robert (Roberto) G. Rivera, Quintin Bulnes, Alfonso Arnold, Jorge Mondragon, Xavier Loya, Nora Veryan, Luis Aragon.

GHOULS! *SEE* IF YOUR BOY FIENDS CAN TAKE IT!—ad line

Like the loopy south-of-the-border bad movie "classic" *The Brainiac*, *The Curse of the Doll People* is one of a clutch of Mexican monster movies that carnival owner-cum-theater builder K. Gordon Murray acquired from Mexico City's Churubusco–Azteca Studios, selling them to American International Television (the TV distribution arm of AIP) as well as sending them out as theatrical double-features (sometimes years *after* they appeared on the tube!). AIP dumped these dubbed disasters onto the unsuspecting American air waves where they've resided ever since (and still pop up occasionally on Saturday afternoons).

One of the more unique entries in the package (though far from the best), this killer doll oddity follows the machinations of a voodoo sorcerer who (accompanied by his prune-faced, wide-brimmed hat-wearing zombie) sends out his life-like dolls to take vengeance upon those who stole an idol from his Haitian temple. The sorcerer creates his demonic dummies in his victims' images and traps their souls inside, then sends the "medium-sized dolls" (as one character describes them—though, in truth, they are actually about three feet tall) out to do his evil bidding. As a result, midgets dressed in half-pint business suits and doll masks (resembling homely middle-aged men—one even sports a gray goatee!) creep about with long nasty needles. A woman doctor (an expert on the occult) and her fiancé (another doctor — who seems to have trouble telling if a victim is alive or dead!), along with some *very* stupid policemen, try to stop them.

Talky and slow, and lacking the large doses of 1930s and '40s-style atmosphere (crumbling castles, dank crypts, fog-shrouded graveyards) featured in the best Mexican horror movies of the period, the main enjoyment gleaned from *The Curse of the Doll People* comes from the (unintentional) laughs it generates. For instance, when the voodooist calls the soul of his latest victim to enter the body of a doll he's constructed, said spirit flitting about the darkened chamber looks for all the world like a flying handkerchief! Other chuckles come when the heroine explores the sorcerer's lair and the zombie opens its sarcophagus lid while her back is turned — only to quickly close it again when she wheels about to see what was behind her (Abbott and Costello would have been proud). But best of all, the villain hypnotizes the heroine by using a large disco-style revolving glitter ball! Shake your boogey — er — booty.

A voodoo sorcerer (Quintin Bulnes), aided by his prune-faced zombie slave, invokes *The Curse of the Doll People* (1961/68) in this Mexican lobby card scene.

The script was written by Abel (Anglicized as "Alfred" for the dubbed version) Salazar, a familiar name (and face) to those enamored of Mexican monster movies. An actor (who initially specialized in light comedy) in Mexico since 1941, Salazar soon turned his hand to producing and even formed his own company in 1957. He sometimes scripted, and often acted in, his own features (including taking the title role in *The Brainiac*) as well as those made by others (such as this one, produced by Pedro A. Calderon and Guillermo Calderon, which was combined into "William Calderon Stell" for American viewers).

As with most K. Gordon Murray jobs, the dubbing is generally toneless but the dialogue is often quite funny. "Your young fiancé," remarks the sorcerer to the heroine, "who denies the existence of all he is unable to measure or place under a microscope, is assuredly a drooling idiot!" Zing.

As far as the acting goes, however, the cast would be better suited to a film entitled *The Curse of the DULL People*. The picture is padded with scene after scene of people standing around talking, sitting around talking, even *laying* around talking. The dolls themselves manage to contribute one or two shuddery moments as they creep ever so slowly toward their intended victim, their face expressionless, needle in hand, sinister malice in every move.... But don't get your hopes up; this is still your typical south-of-the-border celluloid junk — good for a few laughs, one or two shudders and some atrocious dubbing. But hey, at least nobody *wrestles* in this one.

Murray released *The Curse of the Doll People* theatrically in 1968 on a double bill with the far superior *The Vampire* (Mexico's take on *Dracula*), advertising the duo as "A psychedelic trip into the 5th dimension!" Well, it *was* the sixties, after all...

Curse of the Fly (1965; 20th Century–Fox; b&w) Director: Don Sharp; Producers: Robert L. Lippert and Jack Parsons; Screenplay: Harry Spalding; Cinematographer: Basil Emmett. Cast: Brian Donlevy, George Baker, Carole Gray, Yvette Rees, Burt Kwouk, Michael Graham, Mary Manson.

What Made Them Half-Human Creatures From The 4th Dimension? — tagline

This final installment in a series that began with the 1958 blockbuster *The Fly* sometimes is derisively referred to as "the Fly movie without the Fly." True enough, viewers who tune in only for the familiar insect-headed creature in a lab coat will leave disappointed. However, anyone willing to meet *Curse of the Fly* halfway will discover a suspenseful, character-driven, adult-minded science fiction thriller.

A generation after the events depicted in *The Fly*, Henri Delambre (Brian Donlevy) has become obsessed with perfecting father's experimental matter-transportation device. His two adult sons, Martin (George Baker) and Albert (Michael Graham), share in the work but not in Henri's Ahab-like fixation on the transporter. Both yearn to move on with their lives, despite making fantastic advances. The Delambres can now transport people and objects from Quebec to London and back, but such progress has been made at a steep price, including three deformed human "mistakes" now kept behind locked doors at the Delambres' Canadian manor.

Henri turns apoplectic when he learns that Martin has married a young woman named Patricia (Carole Gray), who he met and fell in love with on a short vacation in Toronto. Worse yet, Pat didn't reveal to Martin that she's an escaped mental patient. Soon the police, looking for Pat, come snooping around Chateau Delambre. To hide evidence of the secret experiments, Henri sets in motion a series of events that lead to calamity.

A disfigured victim of the *Curse of the Fly* (1965).

For *Curse of the Fly*, producers Robert L. Lippert and Jack Parsons reunited director Don Sharp and screenwriter Harry Spalding, the team behind the unfairly neglected 1964 chiller *Witchcraft*. While not as rewarding a discovery as that hidden gem, *Curse of the Fly* remains underrated. Smartly written, stylishly directed and believably performed, it's the thinking person's Fly film.

Spalding's screenplay blends super-science and star-crossed lovers, recreating the undertone of romantic tragedy that served the original *Fly* so well. Sharp handles both elements deftly, and appears equally invested in pastoral romantic interludes between Martin and Patricia and in the film's bracing shock moments.

The picture is strewn with arresting sequences, beginning with its opening credits, which are intercut with striking, slow motion footage of Pat, wearing only a bra and panties, escaping through an asylum window and racing into the woods. Sharp's prowling camera and Basil Emmett's evocative lighting design create a sense of mounting tension throughout. In one exemplary scene, Pat is awakened by the sound of off-key piano playing lilting up from the sitting room of the Delambre mansion. She leaves her bed to investigate and discovers a strange woman seated at the family's baby grand. When Pat enters, the woman turns her head and reveals that one side of her face is horribly scarred (it appears half-melted, thanks to Harold Fletcher's simple but jarringly effective makeup).

While it includes enough shock moments to satisfy the film's core audience, Spalding's scenario also offers more subtle tensions. For instance: To hide the nature of the family's secret experiments from his new wife, Martin tries to convince Pat that her meeting with the melted-face woman was only a nightmare. But this leads Pat to fear that she may be suffering a relapse of her (unspecified) mental illness. Martin agonizes over what would be more harmful, revealing the true nature of the family business or allowing Pat to question her fragile sanity. He's also torn between his loyalties to his new bride and to his domineering, manipulative father. ("Send her back," Henri pleads. "You can't do this to us!") These are well-sketched, carefully shaded characters placed in complex situations—something rarely found in bottom-of-the-bill B-movies like this one.

Baker and Gray display good chemistry and deliver unaffected and touching portrayals as the doomed lovers. Donlevy essentially reprises his patented irascible scientist shtick from his two appearances as Dr. Quatermass (in *The Creeping Unknown* [1955/56] and *Enemy from Space* [1957]), which is either good or bad depending on how you feel about Donlevy's Quatermass work. (Your authors approve.) Graham doesn't have much screen time as Martin's brother Albert, but comes through in the chilling final act, providing the most emotionally harrowing moments in the entire picture.

Producers Lippert and Parsons hoped some residual marquee value remained with the *Fly* brand name, even though six years had elapsed since *Return of the Fly* (1959), the quickie sequel Fox rushed into production while box office receipts were still pouring in from the first *Fly*. Ultimately, *Curse of the Fly* debuted on the lower half of a twin bill with the modern-dress vampire yarn *Devils of Darkness*, a co-feature it thoroughly outclassed. The duo failed to make a dent at the box office. Seldom shown on TV, *Curse of the Fly* sank into relative obscurity until finally revived with a U.S. DVD release, part of a boxed set with the original *Fly* and *Return of the Fly* (1959), in 2007. It remains a picture overdue for reappraisal.

The Curse of the Living Corpse (1964; Deal/Fox; b&w).

Producer/Director/Screenplay: Del Tenney; Cinematography: Richard Hilliard. Cast: Roy Scheider, Helen Warren, Robert Milli, Margot Hartman, Hugh Franklin, Linda Donovan, Candace Hilligoss.

> "More terrifying than Frankenstein!
> More deadly than Dracula!"—trailer

But not as much fun as *The Horror of Party Beach* (1964).

The Curse of the Living Corpse may be best remembered as the *other* movie that debuted on the double feature with *Party Beach*. But it wasn't intended that way. *Living Corpse* was the first of the two pictures written and filmed. *Party Beach* was a last-minute inspiration to fill out the twin bill. Filmmaker Del Tenney must have figured that *Living Corpse* was the safe bet of the duo. Where *Party Beach*—the first movie to blend the horror and beach party genres—was a shot in the dark, *Living Corpse* was a known commodity: a strait-laced chiller, complete with a spooky old house, a curse, a masked killer (or is it a ghost?) and other proven elements. Ironically, however, it pales next to *Party Beach* because it seems *too* familiar, stale and formulaic, especially when viewed side-by-side with its original and energetic companion feature.

In turn-of-the-century New England, the Sinclair family—including vain, philandering Bruce (Robert Milli), besotted Philip (Roy Scheider), timid Abigail (Helen Warren) and creepy-looking groundskeeper Seth (J. Frank Lucas), among others—gather for the reading of patriarch Rufus Sinclair's will. There's some question as to whether or not Sinclair died of natural causes since (in a lift from Poe) the old man was prone to cataleptic fits and had a morbid fear of premature burial. In his testament Rufus vows to return from the grave and kill anyone who violates the terms of the will—and to do so in a manner fulfilling the victim's darkest fears. Even before the reading, everyone has broken those terms. Soon afterward, a masked, cloaked figure appears and launches a murder spree, beginning with

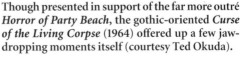

Though presented in support of the far more outré *Horror of Party Beach*, the gothic-oriented *Curse of the Living Corpse* (1964) offered up a few jaw-dropping moments itself (courtesy Ted Okuda).

pretty maid Letty (Linda Donovan), Bruce's galpal. In the film's most memorable scene, her severed head is served to Bruce on his morning breakfast tray!

Unfortunately, nothing else in the film matches the *frisson* of that moment. While not altogether bad, *Living Corpse* remains a tepid body-count mystery — quite similar to the dozens of assembly-line "krimis" coming out of Germany at the time (but lacking the continental style and exotic flair that made some of those films quirkily entertaining whodunits). Tenney devotes virtually no screen time to the idea that the killer might actually be Rufus returned from the grave, so any possible supernatural spark is extinguished quickly. The acting is mostly in the stilted, precisely enunciated, costume drama style, although Milli makes a first-class heel as the caddish Bruce. Future *Jaws* star Scheider, making his film debut, isn't too bad as the drunken, sardonic Philip. *Living Corpse* also features the only other movie appearance of Candace Hilligoss, star of *Carnival of Souls* (1962). She has very little to do here, and makes the least of her limited screen time.

As if having "the world's first horror-monster musical" on the bill wasn't attraction enough, the *Party Beach/Living Corpse* double feature premiered with a promotional gimmick — the "Fright Release." The theatrical trailer warned, "Remember — you will not be admitted unless you release this theater from all responsibility for death by fright!" Patrons were handed a "Fright Release" certificate as they walked (or, more often, drove) into the theater. In actuality, no theater manager could have worried overmuch about "death by fright" liability for the indifferent *Living Corpse*.

Curse of the Living Dead see *Kill, Baby ... Kill!*

The Curse of the Mummy's Tomb (1964; Hammer; U.K.)

Director/Producer: Michael Carreras; Screenplay: Henry Younger (Michael Carreras); Cinematographer: Otto Heller. Cast: Terence Morgan, Fred Clark, Ronald Howard, Jeanne Roland, Bernard Rebel, George Pastell, Jack Gwillim.

HALF-BONE HALF BANDAGE AND ALL BLOOD-CURDLING HORROR!— poster blurb

Hammer's second mummy movie has little of the energy and excitement of their first, *The Mummy* (1959), and a much less impressive title character. Initially, the project (slated to be co-financed and distributed in America by Universal) was going to be a rather unusual one. As described in the *Daily Cinema*: "A group of archaeologists on a routine expedition into the Sahara Desert ... discover an ancient tomb containing the mummy of a Pharaoh. Dabbling in things they don't understand, they bring to life a monstrous twenty-foot giant which goes on a murder rampage in Cairo. When the gigantic Creature escapes into the desert, aircraft and parachute troops go in pursuit." This rather grandiose Giant Monster concept was quickly dropped (though, curiously, the pre-production art showing a gargantuan mummy holding a screaming girl was retained for the British posters), with producer-director Michael Carreras ultimately penning the scaled-down screenplay (under his pseudonym "Henry Younger"). Shooting began on February 28, 1964, and concluded May 8, with the feature slotted as support for Hammer's *The Gorgon*.

A 19th century expedition financed by crass American showman Alexander King (Fred Clark) uncovers the mummy of Prince Ra-Antef, with King intending to exploit the find via a money-making world tour. The Mummy (Dickie Owen) awakens from its long sleep and begins murdering those who defiled its resting place. The enigmatic Adam Beauchamp (Terence Morgan) appears on the scene, and it's soon revealed that Beauchamp is actually the brother of the Mummy(!) and had

Ad for *The Curse of the Mummy's Tomb* (1964).

been cursed with eternal life by his Pharaoh father for murdering Ra-Antef: "[Rameses] cursed him to everlasting life—unless he could die by the hand of his own brother." Beauchamp used an amulet containing "the sacred Words of Life" to revive his sibling and so provide the means to end his eternal suffering ("Life without end is the only pain I can no longer bear," he laments). It's up to archeologist John Bray (Ronald Howard) to discover the truth and save his fiancée (Jeanne Roland) from the clutches of Beauchamp (who's become smitten with her and wants her to join him in the afterlife) and the Mummy.

With its convoluted and overcrowded scenario (the first hour is scattered with subplots involving the various archeologists and participants), its obvious cost-conscious corner cutting and its overfed, underworked monster, *The Curse of the Mummy's Tomb* is a rather disappointing follow-up to Hammer's initial venture into cinematic Egyptology. As the Mummy, stuntman Dickie Owen, wearing makeup by Roy Ashton, looks both uncomfortable and ungainly in his barrel-bellied suit of bandages. Ra-Antef must have enjoyed his Tana juice, since he's acquired quite a thick midsection. The prominent prosthetic temples and angular cheekbones Ashton added to Owen's gaunt face after an early makeup test was deemed unsatisfactory only serve to make the Mummy look like a walking piece of dirty plaster of Paris. And it's nearly an hour before the Bandaged One is up and stalking about, leaving us to make do with the various squabbling amongst the Brits, Egyptians and Americans.

Fortunately, the cast, for the most part, is good, and the film's main asset. American comic actor Fred Clark plays the brash but likable American showman Alexander King with a P.T. Barnum-esque enthusiasm and good humor that proves a breath of fresh colonial air in the rather stuffy Victorian atmosphere. Ronald Howard (son of *Gone with the Wind*'s Leslie Howard) as the hero-archeologist (looking a little like Patrick Macnee) also makes the most of his rather limited role. Jeanne Roland (a Burmese-born model named Jean Rollins whom Carreras had met at a party), however, is vapid and uninteresting as the typical nightgowned heroine (and her voice had to be dubbed by another actress).

To save costs (the film was budgeted at only £103,000), the production was completely set-bound, with *no* exteriors. Though the supposedly "outdoor" desert scenes are as about as convincing as an original *Star Trek* set, the interiors are up to Hammer's usual opulent standards. Michael Carreras, in only his second directing job, proved unimaginative as a director, and builds very little suspense. Once the Mummy gets rolling, however, the action picks up as he engages in some impressive set-bashing.

Still, though *The Curse of the Mummy's Tomb* is ostensibly little more than another (overlong) mummy-on-the-loose movie, its story line features a truly distinctive and novel concept: An immortal, weary of the burden of immortality, revives the mummy as a means *to commit suicide*. Full marks for originality if not for (ahem) execution.

Curse of the Stone Hand (1964; A.D.P. Productions.; Chile; b&w) Directors: Hugo Christensen, Jerry Warren; Producers: Carl Gallart, Andrew Edwards; Screenplay: F. Amos Powell, Marie Laurent; Cinematographer: Richard Younis. Cast: Ernest Walch, John Carradine, Sheila Bon, Charles Cores, Catherine Victor, Lloyd Nelson, Bruno Ve Sota (narrator).

What lurid secret lied [*sic*] beyond that hidden door?—ad line

---

"You will not forget this adventure into chills!" So claimed the ads for a triple bill consisting of *Face of the Screaming Werewolf*, *My Son the Vampire* and this film, the Chilean-lensed, Jerry Warren-tampered-with *Curse of the Stone Hand*. This triple-bill was memorable, all right—but for all the wrong reasons. The hapless viewer lured to the cinema back in the Sixties might indeed have a hard time driving this terrible trio of tripe out of his or her mind.

Grade-Z filmmaker Jerry Warren (*Face of the Screaming Werewolf*, *Attack of the Mayan Mummy*, etc.) made a career out of buying up foreign horror films, excising exposition scenes to avoid extensive—and expensive—dubbing (and generally dubbing only those scenes in which characters are turned *away* from the camera so as to get around having to match their mouth movements), adding voice-over narration and inserting cheaply-shot sequences with low-rent actors in which the new characters do nothing but talk. Of course, this usually left him with about half a movie, so Warren would splice in scenes from yet another import to bring his "new" feature up to (barely) feature length. Consequently, a "Warren" film is invariably a jumbled mess of vaguely related sequences mixed with tedious, ridiculous, and even tangential "original" footage that rarely makes more than rudimentary sense.

Curse of the Stone Hand is comprised (apart from the terrible inserts Warren filmed with the likes of John Carradine and Catherine Victor) of footage from two Chilean omnibuses from the 1940s—*La Dama de la Muerte* (directed by Carlos Hugo Christensen) and *La Casa Esta Vacia* (helmed by Carlos Schlieper). Oversized sculpted hands situated "in every single room of the house as well as outside of it" apparently bring down a curse upon whoever occupies a large seaside estate. The first story has a newlywed gentleman in financial difficulty seek relief in a private gambling establishment that turns out to be a suicide club. The second tale follows the nefarious activities of a young boy who falls under the Hands' evil spell and grows into a domineering tyrant who lords it over his family, leading to tragedy.

Admittedly, the film looks good—at least in parts (particularly in Christensen's "Suicide Club" half, which, being strong in visual storytelling, is thankfully free of any mismatched Warren footage)—with some mobile camerawork and evocative lighting making the most of the opulent interiors and foggy, gaslit, horse-drawn-carriage milieu. Of course, it doesn't *sound* good, with the poor dubbing and inappropriate canned music (of the 1940s Monogram variety) laid haphazardly over scenes (courtesy of the haphazard Mr. Warren). Still, some of the impressive visuals makes one long to see the original film before Warren got his hands on it, as exemplified by one sequence in which the protagonist, marked for death, sees in his fevered mind danger in every approaching figure—even recoiling from a grinning deaths head transposed over the face of a passing woman in a startlingly eerie scene.

The second story, the slow and meandering "House of Gloom," fares worse, since it relies more on dialogue than visuals, resulting in the various Warren inserts bringing the already leisurely pace to a grinding halt. And it features little in the way of horror, apart from the final scene awkwardly bringing in the old Dorian Gray-like self-portrait angle to reveal the degeneration of the main character's soul, but in an almost nonsensical—even non sequitur—manner.

"Those were just patch jobs," admitted Catherine Victor (in *Science Fiction Stars and Horror Heroes*, by Tom Weaver) about the Warren pictures. "I remember *Curse of the Stone Hand* because we did that with John Carradine. We shot that in a beautiful home in the Los Feliz area; these people were friends of Jerry's. I remember talking to John Carradine and I asked him, 'Why do you *do* pictures like this?' and he said, 'The color of the money's the same.'" And getting paid is about the only reason ever to go near *Curse of the Stone Hand*.

One-sheet poster for the half-baked *Curse of the Stone Hand* (1964).

Curse of the Vampire see *Playgirls and the Vampire*

Curse of the Voodoo (1965; Allied Artists; U.K.; b&w) Alternate Titles: *Curse of Simba* (U.K.); *Voodoo Blood Death*; Director: Lindsay Shonteff; Producer: Fred Slark; Screenplay: Tony O'Grady (additional scenes and Dialogue by Leigh Vance); Cinematographer: Gerald Gibbs. Cast: Bryant Haliday, Dennis Price, Lisa Daniely, Ronald Leigh Hunt, Mary Kerridge, John Witty.

THE HORROR AND BESTIALITIES OF VOODOO IN A STORY THAT REACHES ACROSS FOUR CENTURIES AND CONTINENTS...—ad line

"There was a script called *The Lion Man* that was brought to us by a man name Tony O'Grady, who had written it on speculation," recalled executive producer Richard Gordon about this film's genesis. (Note: Tony O'Grady is actually an early pseudonym used by Brian Clemens, who went on to write for and produce *The Avengers* TV series as well as such features as *Dr. Jekyll and Sister Hyde* and *Captain Kronos, Vampire Hunter*.) "Despite the fact the setting of the story was mostly in Africa, we felt it could be done very well in England with a little bit of luck in finding the right locations. So we did some little rewriting on the screenplay to fit the locations we'd selected and went right ahead with it." What resulted was an earnest but rather sluggish low-budget tale of African black magic (with London-area woodlands standing in for the Dark Continent).

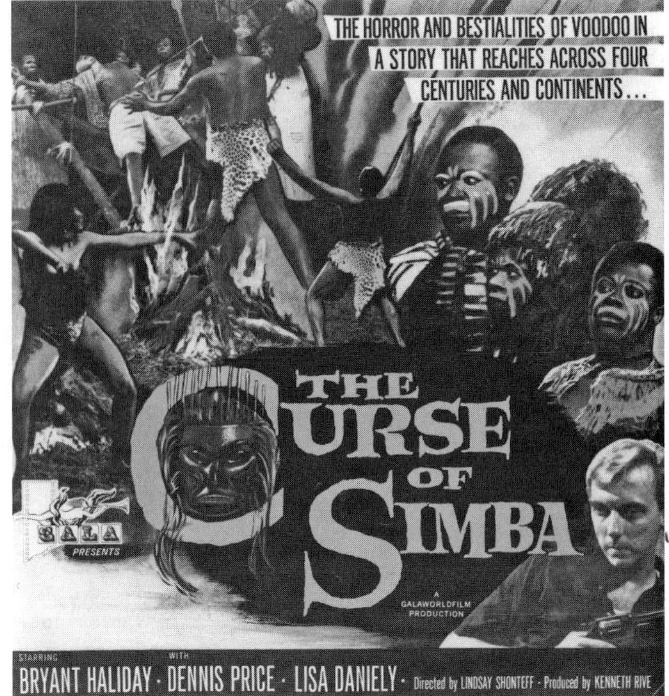

British ad for *Curse of the Voodoo* (1965), titled *The Curse of Simba* in the U.K.

In Africa, big-game hunter and safari guide Mike Stacey (Bryant Haliday) breaks taboo by following a wounded lion into the land of the dreaded Simbaza, a lion-worshipping tribe. He kills the beast but receives a mauling in the process. Stacey flies to London to attempt a reconciliation with his wife (Lisa Daniely), while back in Africa the Simbaza use voodoo to magically reopen Stacey's lion-inflicted wound. Frightening images plague Stacey, as he feels the stalking presence of a lion or flees through the woods pursued by spear-wielding warriors. His only hope is to return to Africa and slay the witchdoctor who cursed him.

It's difficult to dislike *Curse of the Voodoo*, mostly because of its sheer earnestness. It is a deadly serious film with no touch of whimsy or camp about it. The participants play their parts and treat their subject with a grim solemnity (whose somber tone is only enhanced by the gray skies and dark photography)—no doubt due, in part, to the lousy weather and uncomfortable conditions that prevailed during shooting.

Yet it's also nearly just as difficult to *like* the film, for its slow pace and cranky characters possess little appeal. Not only does the picture sport seemingly endless scenes of Stacey lying in bed suffering nightmares or of his dysfunctional attempts to reconcile with his wife, director Lindsay Shonteff includes numerous filler sequences (such as tepid nightclub scenes) that do nothing to advance the story or mood. Even worse, Stacey makes for a rather unlikable protagonist as the alcoholic, self-pitying hunter. Humorless and continually scowling, Stacey's condescension and arrogant attitude inspires little sympathy in the viewer—a pathos vital in order to make the "curse" scenario come to life for the audience. Though playing a rather cold fish, Bryant Haliday (who spent most of his acting career in France and made only four English language pictures—*Devil Doll, Curse of the Voodoo, The Projected Man* and *Tower of Evil*) does what he can, bringing an intense assuredness to the role of Stacey that adds efficacy and (some) poignancy to the plight of a man bedeviled by forces beyond his control.

Curse was budgeted at (35,000, but due to weather-related delays it ballooned to (50,000 (still less than $150,000). Visually, it looks like all of its production dollars ended up on the screen, thanks in no small part to the clever use of some impressive stock footage. "We got some pretty good black and white stock footage to pump up the African scenes," remembered Gordon. Indeed they did, and the well-integrated shots of African animals add a bit of authenticity lacking in the closer jungle scenes (with English forests standing in for the African bush).

Originally announced as *The Lion Man*, the film became *The Curse of Simba* in the U.K. and *Curse of the Voodoo* in the U.S., where it was double-billed with *Frankenstein Meets the Spacemonster*. Though rather somber and leaning toward the dull side, *Curse of the Voodoo* stands as an offbeat, occasionally intriguing '60s British horror entry.

With quotes from: *Drums of Terror: Voodoo in the Cinema*, by Bryan Senn.

The Curse of the Werewolf (1961; Hammer/Universal-International; U.K.) Director: Terence Fisher; Producer/Screenplay: Anthony Hinds (as John Elder); Cinematographer: Arthur Grant. Cast: Oliver Reed, Clifford Evans, Yvonne Romain, Catherine Feller, Anthony Dawson, Richard Wordsworth, Justin Walters, John Gabriel, Martin Matthews, John Gabriel.

He fought the hideous curse of his evil birth, but his ravished victims were proof that the cravings of his beast-blood demanded he kill ... Kill ... KILL!—tagline

Oliver Reed in full (wrinkly) regalia for *The Curse of the Werewolf* (1961).

Hammer Films' unorthodox *Curse of the Werewolf* marked a radical departure from previous wolf man entries in its mythology and tone, recasting lycanthropy as a struggle between good and evil within the soul and transforming subject matter normally relegated to B-budget quickies into the stuff of a sprawling epic. As a result, the picture remains divisive; most viewers either love it or loathe it.

A bedraggled beggar (Richard Wordsworth) shambles into the wedding feast of a despised despot (Anthony Dawson), where the poor man is humiliated and (after making a careless joke at the expense of the Marquis) locked away in the palace dungeon. Forgotten, he wastes away in the dungeon for decades, cared for by the jailer and his mute daughter, who grows into a lovely young servant girl. When the mute woman spurns the advances of the Marquis, she is locked in the dungeon with the now-mad beggar, who rapes her. Freed from the dungeon to service the Marquis, the servant instead stabs the tyrant to death and flees into the countryside, where she is found barely alive and taken under the wing of kindly Professor Carrido (Clifford Evans). The mute woman gives birth to a son (the product of the dungeon assault) and dies, leaving Carrido to raise the child, who he names Leon.

Flash forward: Goats begin turning up with their throats ripped out. Young Leon complains of strange nightmares and confesses to an affinity for the taste of blood. Carrido consults the village priest (John Gabriel), who explains that an evil wolf-spirit has taken residence in the child's body and now battles the boy's immortal soul for control. Those things like prayer and loving kindness, which strengthen the soul, weaken the wolf-spirit; things like anger and lust, which weaken the soul, strengthen the wolf-spirit. Flash forward again: Now a young man, Leon (Oliver Reed) strikes out on his own, landing a job bottling wine and launching an ill-fated romance with his employer's already-engaged daughter (Catherine Feller). Then a debauched night out with a coworker unlocks Leon's inner wolf and sets in motion a series of events that leads to tragedy.

The movie's detractors complain that *Curse of the Werewolf* is too slow and doesn't include enough monster action. Yet in fact its pace is quite brisk. If anything, *too much* happens in the course of the film — even the lengthy summary provided above leaves out several prominent supporting characters and subplots. However, *Curse* may indeed *seem* slow to viewers simply waiting around for the werewolf to show up. Reed doesn't appear until nearly 48 of the film's 93 minutes have elapsed, and the werewolf is first glimpsed at the 63-minute mark.

This could have been avoided through some structural revisions to the script—for instance, by beginning the story *in media res* with the werewolf on the prowl, and by tightening the elaborate back-story about Leon's unfortunate mother for use as a later flashback sequence. But such changes would have materially altered the style of picture and undermined its epic, multi-generational scope. As it stands, *Curse* (adapted from French novelist Guy Endore's *The Werewolf of Paris*) plays like something out of Alexandre Dumas or Victor Hugo. It's a sweeping, wide-angle yarn teeming with well-drawn characters and packed with melodramatic tension.

Once the werewolf finally appears, monster lovers get their money's worth. Roy Ashton's creature makeup is a masterpiece of fur and greasepaint, the most ferocious-looking lycanthrope in movie history. Under the makeup Reed snarls and growls with bulging-eyed, feral intensity. Director Terence Fisher and cinematographer Arthur Grant pull no punches in the film's two extended werewolf sequences—which, thanks to shrewd composition and shot selection, seem incredibly vicious. One shot, panning across the remains of the monster's first victim, her bedroom covered in splattered blood and shattered glass, plays like something from the Dario Argento *oeuvre*—extraordinarily powerful stuff for 1961.

While intimidating as the werewolf, Reed remains sympathetic and endearing as the tormented Leon. Hammer intended *Curse* to be a breakout role for Reed, and the actor gave it his best, even though true stardom would elude him a few years longer. His work stands out even though the film is practically bursting with excellent performances. The screenplay (written by producer Anthony Hinds under his usual "John Elder" pseudonym) sketches the supporting characters with great care, and the cast realizes them brilliantly. Especially impressive are: Dawson as the cruel, lecherous Marques; Wordsworth as the befuddled beggar; Romain as the courageous, mute servant girl; Justin Walters as the timid, confused young Leon; Warren Mitchell as Pepe, the beleaguered but intrepid watchman; and Matthews as Jose, Leon's *bon vivant* friend (and second victim). This peppering of unforgettable secondary characters lends the picture much of its appeal.

As usual for Hammer productions of this vintage, *Curse of the Werewolf* boasts outstanding production values—top drawer sets, costumes, makeup and lighting. The film's setting was hastily rewritten from France to Spain to make use of expensive sets built for *The Rape of Sabena*, a swashbuckler set during the Spanish Inquisition which was abandoned after the Catholic Church threatened to ban the film. Although this change was born of convenience, the Spanish setting lends *Curse* another distinctive touch, setting it apart from most gothic chillers typically set in Eastern Europe or in gaslit London or Paris.

The film's only major demerits, from a technical perspective, are an embarrassing man-to-werewolf transformation scene, which relies on a pair of absurdly fake-looking hands and crude stop-motion animation (fortunately, all the other transformations occur off screen), and its reliance on often-redundant voiceover narration, delivered in the same cooing, "once upon a time" style as a Walt Disney animated feature.

Fisher, years later, named *Curse of the Werewolf* as his personal favorite among his films. "It is certainly the deepest of all my films, in emotional content and in the inter-relationship of the characters.... All the performances were tremendous," Fisher said. "I love the film because it is my only one with the core of a true love story in it."

Fisher was also pleased with the way the film addressed his recurrent theme of Christian good defeating pagan-satanic evil. Even though, after his death, Leon remains in werewolf form (another departure from previous screen lycanthropes), Fisher believed that the moral remained clear. "The silver bullet, melted from a cross, is only symbolic for the power of Good, which as always destroys the power of Evil in the end," he said. "The physical body of the werewolf remains, but the message is just the same.... The body of the werewolf was irrelevant. It was just the vehicle in which his soul was trapped. If you come to think of it all like this, it is a very religious picture."

It's also a very enjoyable one, even if at times it seems more like *Les Miserables* than *The Wolf Man*.

With quotes from: "Terence Fisher in Conversation" by Jan Van Genechten, from *Little Shoppe of Horrors* No. 19.

Dance of the Vampires see *The Fearless Vampire Killers*

Dark Intruder (1965; Universal; b&w) Director: Harvey Hart; Producer: Jack Laird; Screenplay: Barre Lyndon; Cinematography: John F. Warren. Cast: Leslie Nielsen, Mark Richman, Judi Meredith, Gilbert Green, Charles Bolender, Werner Klemperer.

He killed with the power of demons a million years old!—tagline

A top-hatted, cloaked, Ripper-like killer stalks the streets of 1890 San Francisco, slashing women and leaving strange ivory statues—figures of some ancient god—at the crime scene. After the fourth murder, the exasperated police call in occult expert and amateur detective Brett Kingsford (Leslie Neilsen), a free-spirited playboy who lives with a dwarf servant named Nikoli (Charles Bolender) and a giant mandrake plant that shivers in the presence of supernatural forces. Soon Kingsford ascertains that the ivory figures represent a Sumerian demon, which is said to take possession of human beings and force them to commit ritual slayings. Meanwhile, antique dealer Robert Vanderberg (Mark Richman), who's engaged to Kingsford's dim-witted gal pal Evelyn (Judi Meredith), has been suffering mysterious blackouts; Robert fears he might be the killer. But the truth, Kingsford discovers, is more complicated—and more frightening, since the killer turns out not to be a run-of-the-mill maniac, but a Hyde-like, inhuman monster.

The little-known *Dark Intruder* began as a pilot for a proposed TV series titled *The Black Cloak*, produced by Alfred Hitchcock's Shamley Productions at Universal City. When the series failed to sell, Universal expanded and renamed the pilot for release as a short (59-minute) theatrical feature. The picture's small-screen origins are apparent in its daytime and interior scenes, which are shot in the flat, over-lit style of most 1960s TV shows, but its nighttime exterior sequences are far more atmospheric, full of thickly draped shadows and drifting fog.

Although far-fetched even by the standards of supernatural horror, Barre Lyndon's scenario is lively and suspenseful, effectively balancing action, mystery and old-fashioned monster sequences. Only its (thankfully brief) comedy relief bits falter, and then mostly because they center on the attractive but unfunny Judi Meredith as the ditsy Evelyn. Brett Kingsford (sleuth, occultist, master of disguise and notorious rake) is a fascinating character, endearingly portrayed by Neilsen. Richman also fares well, albeit in a more conventional role as Robert. The film's action sequences are furious and flashy, especially a scene in which Kingsford is attacked by the monster in Robert's antique shop, fighting off the creature with his sword-cane. The monster makeup (credited to Bud Westmore), with gnarled claws and a deformed, ape-like face, isn't up to 1965 big-screen standards in terms of realism but at least looks appropriately grotesque.

Dark Intruder proves effective enough to inspire viewers to imagine what *The Black Cloak* might have been: a unique 19th century action-horror series with a likeable and dynamic lead in Neilsen, like a cross between Robert Conrad in *The Wild, Wild West* and Darren McGavin as *Kolchak, the Night*

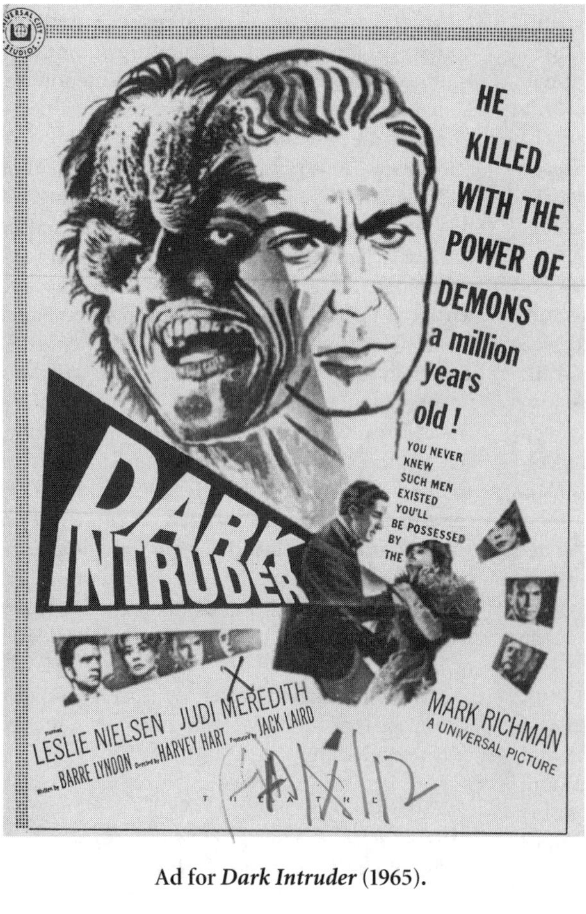

Ad for ***Dark Intruder*** **(1965).**

One-sheet poster for the surprisingly eerie *The Day Mars Invaded Earth* (1963).

Stalker. The possibilities are tantalizing, but fans will have to settle for this one-off treat.

The Day Mars Invaded Earth (1963; 20th Century–Fox; b&w) Director/producer: Maury Dexter; Screenplay: Harry Spalding; Cinematographer: John Nickolaus, Jr. Cast: Kent Taylor, Marie Windsor, William Mims, Betty Beall, Lowell Brown, Gregg Shank, Henrietta Moore, Troy Melton, George Riley.

SUDDENLY THEY WERE HUMAN SHELLS ... THEIR BODIES AND BRAINS DESTROYED BY SUPER-MINDS OF ANOTHER WORLD!—poster

---

Here's a horror film disguised as science fiction in order to ride out the end of the sci-fi wave still cresting from the 1950s. Though lensed in Cinemascope and distributed by major studio 20th Century–Fox, *The Day Mars Invaded Earth* has more of a low-budget AIP feel, which is not surprising considering it was made by Robert Lippert's Associated Producers, who contracted with Fox to make cheap black-and-white 'Scope movies to support the studio's bigger pictures on double bills.

Written by Harry Spalding (*Witchcraft* [1964], *The Earth Dies Screaming* and *Curse of the Fly* [both 1965]), *The Day Mars Invaded Earth* begins with a cheesy robot probe moving across the barren surface of Mars for a few seconds before it stops dead amid a puff of smoke. At a loss to explain it, Cape Canaveral rocket scientist Dr. Fielding (Kent Taylor) heads to a relative's soon-to-be-sold Beverly Hills mansion to reunite with his family and try to save his disintegrating marriage. The family, isolated on the huge estate, soon begin seeing doppelgangers of themselves, and they discover that the bodiless inhabitants of Mars ("We have intelligence in the abstract, much like your electricity here," explains Fielding's alien double) used the probe to "transmit [their] intelligence" to Earth, where they intend to impersonate Fielding and his family in order to halt the exploratory invasion of their planet.

Constructed more like a haunted house movie than a sci-fi flick, *Day* generates a creepy ambiance (aided by some surprisingly effective day-for-night photography) as the principals wander about the huge, isolated estate and keep seeing each other in places they simply cannot be. The doppelgangers initially appear more like apparitions than aliens, emerging unexpectedly to simply stare and look sinister (observing their "hosts" in order to emulate their behavior, we later learn), exuding an air of icy menace. Their terrifying power, however, is revealed when they make a meddlesome family friend spontaneously combust with just a glance and an accompanying high-pitched tone. The dry ice smoke pouring from the terrified man's clothing (before he's reduced—after a coy cutaway—to a vaguely man-shaped pile of ashes on the flagstones) is cheap but chilling.

The cost-conscious production requires con fining its small cast to almost a single setting, but this ultimately adds to the general sense of unease and isolation. Fortunately, the cast proved up to the task, particularly Kent Taylor (whose career stretched back to the early 1930s), who in the 1960s tended to walk through his roles (offering somnambulistic turns in such sixties shockers as *The Crawling Hand*, *Brides of Blood* and *The Mighty Gorga*) but here provides some unexpected animation and warmth as the likable workaholic scientist trying to balance his calling with his family life. Marie Windsor (*Chamber of Horrors* [1966], *Salem's Lot* [1979]) appears both natural and believable as

Fielding's long-suffering wife, whose ambivalence about their relationship shines through in her gloomy yet still affectionate interactions. (This marriage-on-the-rocks subtext adds a more adult flavor to the proceedings than that usually found in lower berth sci-fi/horrors of the time.)

Of course, talk is cheap, and a Lippert budget dictated that most of the running time be filled with it. The lack of action causes the film to sag in spots, but the likable characters and apprehensive atmosphere helps paper over the cracks, and Harry Spalding's truly chilling downbeat finale (unusual for a production from the early '60s) makes *The Day Mars Invaded Earth* a day worth remembering.

The Day of the Triffids (1962/63; Rank/Allied Artists; U.K.) Director: Steve Sekely; Producer: George Pitcher; Screenplay: Philip Yordan (Novel: John Wyndham); Cinematographer: Ted Moore. Cast: Howard Keel, Nicole Maurey, Janette Scott, Kieron Moore, Janina Faye.

Man eating plants!
Spine chilling terror!—tagline

Naval officer Bill Masen (Howard Keel), hospitalized with an eye injury, awakens to discover that nearly the entire population of London (and as he later learns, the world) has been struck blind after watching a spectacular shower of green meteors the night before. Since his eyes were bandaged, Masen's vision is saved. In addition to the plague of blindness, however, the meteors brought something even worse to earth: triffids—walking, carnivorous plants who prey on the suddenly helpless humans. Masen saves the life of a young sighted girl (Janina Faye) and together they flee from London to Touloun, France, and on to Cadiz, Spain, through the groping masses and killer plants. Meanwhile, alcoholic marine biologist Tom Goodwin (Kieron Moore) and his long-suffered wife Karen (Janette Scott) find themselves stranded and surrounded by triffids on an island lighthouse off the Cornish coast. As they fight for survival, Tom struggles to find a way to kill the seemingly indestructible alien plants.

Pressbook cover for *The Day of the Triffids* (1963).

Posters for *The Day of the Triffids* boasted, "From the greatest science fiction novel of all time!" but failed to mention that screenwriter Philip Yordan disposed with nearly the entirety of John Wyndham's acclaimed book. Wyndham's post-apocalyptic chiller focuses less on the killer plants and more on the terrifying breakdown of social structures (and basic human decency) that results when nearly everyone on the planet is suddenly blinded, suggesting that in order to survive the human race must set aside longstanding moral and behavioral conventions (including monogamy). The titular plant monsters are accidentally unleashed biological weapons rather than extraterrestrial invaders, and don't become the story's primary concern until its final few chapters. The novel ends on a ray of hope, but is far more downbeat than the film.

Since Production Code restrictions rendered key plot elements of the novel unfilmable in 1962, and because the scope of Wyndham's book would have necessitated an epic on the scale of a David Lean production, Yordan's adaptation reshapes *The Day of the Triffids* into a smaller and more conventional monsters-from-space yarn. But it's a rip-snorting, action-packed monsters-from-space yarn. The pace is brisk, and Yordan's lighthouse sequences (which do not originate with Wyndham) enable the narrative to cut to monster action whenever a lull threatens during Masen's trans-European trek. The isolated lighthouse subplot involving Moore and Scott battling the triffids was not in the original script, and all that footage was shot after principal photography had wrapped. "The lighthouse sequences were written in conjunction with the existing footage," explained (uncredited) *Triffids* producer Bernard Glasser, "and directed [uncredited] by Freddie Francis at MGM Elstree. Freddie was a former lighting cameraman, and he understood the difficulties inherent in lighting the Triffid sequences." Added Francis, "When they finished the film, they didn't think it stood up. I believe the distributors would not accept it. I think that what went wrong with the film was that they thought this was a special effects film, so they'd just crash off the live action, get rid of the live action, and stress the special effects—but they hadn't done their homework on the special effects." Producer Glasser agreed that they had difficulty "getting the triffids to perform action called for in the script," and so ended up with too short a film after being forced to drop "the special effects sequences that did not play." But it all worked out in the end, as Francis' 25 minutes of additional footage, with its evocative lighting and exciting, suspenseful staging, generates many of the movie's highlights.

Credited director Steve Sekely's visual storytelling is fluid but unobtrusive. He's aided by Ted Moore's moody lighting designs, which make eye-catching use of colored gels and deep shadows. Aside from Keiron Moore, who operates in a more elevated register, the cast delivers uniformly credible, low-key performances, lending the kind of gravitas necessary to pull off a yarn about killer plants from outer space. But the film's biggest selling point remains the triffids themselves, which rank among the movies' most original space invaders—giant, demonic rotadendrums with tentacle-like vines and blooms that fire poison darts.

With the Production Code long gone and computer animation now available, *The Day of the Triffids*—perhaps more than any other classic chiller from the early 1960s—is ripe for a remake, which hopefully would adhere more closely to Wyndham's chilling original vision. As it stands, however, *Triffids* remains one of the better sci-fi thrillers of its era.

With quotes from: *Science Fiction Stars and Horror Heroes*, by Tom Weaver; *The Men Who Made the Monsters*, by Paul M. Jensen.

The Dead One (1961; Favorite Films)

Alternate Title: *Blood of the Zombie*; Director/Producer/Screenwriter: Barry Mahon. Cinematography: Mark Dennes. Cast: John Mackay, Linda Ormond, Monica Davis, Clyde Kelly, Darlene Myrick.

WHEN THE DRUMS START ...
HE WALKS AND KILLS—trailer

"THE GREATEST VOODOO FILM EVER MADE!" shouted the ads for *The Dead One*. This grandiose claim was, until recently, difficult to dispute, since for four decades *The Dead One* remained a lost film. Its rediscovery (and subsequent DVD release), however, finally put paid to *that* notion. Made by exploitation/nudie veteran Barry Mahon (*Nude Scrapbook*, *Sex Club International*, etc.), the story centers on a woman who uses voodoo to raise up the corpse of her dead brother in an effort to keep a property inheritance from going to her newly-married cousin.

The picture, shot in and around New Orleans, jumps feet-first into its supernatural waters by showing the titular zombie rising from its tomb under the opening credits. Unfortunately, the over-bright lighting and pedantic staging preva-

The exceedingly well-dressed *Dead One* (1961).

lent in this grade-Z production dispels any sense of creepiness this sequence could have inspired. Adding insult to injury, it's another *forty-five minutes* before the Dead One shows its ugly mug again. In the meantime we're treated to "THE EXCITEMENT OF A NIGHT IN NEW ORLEANS," as the trailer puts it (consisting of our newlywed protagonists checking out a white jazz quartet in one Bourbon Street club, watching a belly dancer in another, and listening to a black jazz group in yet a third), and much palaver between the principals regarding their inherited "plantation" (which, from all we see of it, consists of two cramped bedroom sets, a stairway, and one corner of a cheaply-furnished sitting room).

When the Dead One finally reappears, and we "SEE the voodoo princess call on the dead ones to Kill! Kill! Kill!" (as the ads promise), he only makes one "Kill!"—and that *off-screen*, no less—before returning to his sarcophagus once again. And the banal climax moves as slowly as, well, the shuffling zombie itself, ending abruptly and disappointingly in a literal puff of smoke.

Said zombie (named "Jonas," by the way) is a particularly well-dressed specimen, sporting a bow tie and tuxedo (like some undead maitre d'), which seems none-the-worse-for-wear from all those years in a dank crypt (obviously Mahon couldn't afford the damage deposit on the rental tux, and so made sure his zombie kept it neat). On the plus side, the zombie makeup, all yellowish parchment skin, blackened eyes and mouth, and claw-like fingernails, appears appropriately cadaverous (though an unfortunate choice of rock-star-style fright wig makes him look a bit like an undead, raven-haired Rod Stewart).

But at a scant 68 minutes, this bargain-basement cheapie still feels far too long. Yes, *The Dead One* is really The *Dull* One.

The Deadly Bees (1967; Amicus; U.K.) Director: Freddie Francis; Producers: Max J. Rosenberg, Milton Subotsky; Screenplay: Robert Bloch, Anthony Marriott; Cinematographer: John Wilcox. Cast: Suzanna Leigh, Frank Finlay, Guy Doleman, John Harvey, Catherine Finn, Michael Ripper.

The stings of death!—ad line

Bzzzzzz ... minus the "B," that's just the sound you'll hear coming from the audience after a few minutes of viewing this boring British misfire. In the 1960s and '70s, Amicus, Hammer's biggest rival in the English horror movie arena, specialized in terror anthologies. *The Deadly Bees* was one of their few single-story efforts. Given the tepid results, they should never have gotten off that omnibus.

Adapted by Robert (*Psycho*) Bloch and Anthony Marriott from the novel *A Taste of Honey* by H. F. Heard, *The Deadly Bees* became the very first Killer Bee movie, a threadbare subgenre that includes such losers as *The Savage Bees* (1976), *The Bees* (1978) and *The Swarm* (1978). Not only is *The Deadly Bees* the first of its type, it is also quite possibly the dullest.

When pop singer Vicky Robbins (Suzanna Leigh) has a nervous breakdown, her doctor sends her for a few weeks rest to an out-of-the-way farm owned by his friend, Ralph Hargrove (Guy Doleman). Hargrove, who seems to get along with no one (including his disaffected wife), keeps bees, and so does his distrustful neighbor, Manfred (Frank Finlay). When a swarm of bees kills first a dog and then Mrs. Hargrove, it appears that Hargrove has concocted a chemical by which he can induce his killer insects to attack anyone who

Not only is *The Deadly Bees* (1967) unsuitable for children (as this Australian poster claims), it's unsuitable for anyone wishing to stay *awake*.

comes in contact with the substance. But things are not quite what they seem, as Vicky ultimately discovers.

Unlike so many British horrors of the 1960s, *The Deadly Bees* is a rather poorly acted specimen. Though Suzanna Leigh (*The Lost Continent*, *Lust for a Vampire*) is unquestionably lovely to look at, she fails to flesh out her character; and her overused expression of bewilderment, which is supposed to pass as terror, quickly becomes tiresome. She's just a handy heroine to become imperiled. (Even worse, the picture starts by forcing us to watch Ms. Leigh mouth the words to a painfully bad pop song.)

Scripter Bloch intended that the two male lead roles go to Christopher Lee and Boris Karloff. Such casting might have salvaged the project; but, alas, it was not, ahem, to bee. As Hargrove, Guy Doleman is as dour as they come, and he spends the whole film faintly frowning—as if he's just caught a whiff of some mildly unpleasant odor. Frank Finlay's tweed-wearing, tea-drinking, stuttering bee expert (with impossibly-colored faux gray hair) possesses less screen presence than his bugs.

Poor process shots of bees buzzing around in slow motion while actors flail about behind them (occasionally with a few plastic insects—which, oddly, look more like beetles than bees—pasted onto their faces) distance us further from the protracted proceedings. Strangely, considering the movie was directed by Oscar-winning cinematographer Freddie Francis, *The Deadly Bees* looks flat, with uninspired photography and a drab color scheme to match its equally drab mood. The film's low budget becomes oh-so-obvious in the artificial studio "farm" set and the painfully noticeable painted backdrop of the "English countryside" tacked up behind the farm's apiary. And the story's see-it-coming-from-a-mile-away "surprise" at the end carries no, er ... sting in its tail.

In the U.S. *The Deadly Bees* was paired with *The Vulture* for a decidedly desultory double-bill. The only thing "deadly" about *The Deadly Bees* is its deadly dullness.

Death Curse of Tartu (1967; Thunderbird International Pictures) Director/Screenwriter: William Grefe; Producers: Joseph Fink, Juan Hidalso Gato; Cinematographer: Julio C. Chavez. Cast: Fred Pinero, Babbette Sherrill, Bill Marcus, Mayra Gomez, Sherman Hayes, Gary Holtz, Maurice Stewart, Douglas Hobart, Frank Weed.

THIS IS HORROR!—ad line

Every decade wastes its share of film stock, and the sixties were no exception. One of the strongest arguments for celluloid conservation (preserving the *raw* stock, that is) came in the form of this Florida-lensed no-budget independent.

Written (in 24 hours!) and directed (in seven days for $27,000!!) by William Grefe, the man who brought us *Hooked Generation* (1968), *Stanley* (1972) and *Mako: The Jaws of Death* (1976), not to mention *Tartu*'s co-feature—*Sting of Death* (about a jellyfish-man!!!), *Death Curse of Tartu* follows a group of archeology students into the Florida everglades to excavate an ancient Seminole Indian burial site. "My grandfather and the elder members of my tribe say that 400 years ago a witchdoctor named Tartu had power to turn himself into a wild creature," warns their native guide. "When he died, he swore if anyone would disturb the burial ground he would change himself into a wild beast and kill them." And Tartu proceeds to do just that—as a snake, alligator and shark.

Composed mostly of lengthy sequences of canoeing, airboating and hiking through the Everglades, *Tartu* sports so much padding it could play in the NFL. The movie's pace is summed up by a sequence in which a man is stalked by a *snake*! (Then, when the slithering serpent finally catches up with its intended victim, the creature is obviously *thrown* at the actor at the pivotal moment, flying through the air in a most un-snake-like manner.) Admittedly, this does provide one of the film's few effective scenes: As the large constrictor wraps itself around the struggling man's neck, you start to actually fear for the actor.

The amateurish performances by a cast of unknowns, and the less-than-scintillating dialogue ("Man, this is groovy," enthuses one student when they find a carved stone tablet), do nothing to alleviate the tedium. At one point the obviously hip youngsters even start their own mini-beach party, complete with bad music, bad dancing and bad camerawork.

But all this could be (at least partially) saved by some energetic Indian vengeance from beyond the grave. Wishful thinking. All Tartu does is lie in his sarcophagus and occasionally rock back and forth. At the climax he actually *sits up*!—but then transforms into an ordinary-looking, flesh-and-blood Indian brave before engaging in a fistfight with the hero. So much for Tartu. "What disappointed me most about my shots were that I did not have much movement in the film," recounted spook show actor/stuntman/amateur makeup artist Doug Hobart (who not only played the mummified Tartu but designed the makeup as well), "just getting up and down, and that hampered the look somewhat." It also seriously hampered the entertainment value.

Director Grefe originally intended that Hobart wear a phony rubber mask, but Hobart felt he could come up with something better. And he did: phony makeup. Tartu's appearance is admittedly striking — if not particularly convincing — with wrinkled, dried skin; heavy shoe polish around the eyes; and skull-like teeth protruding from (or, more accurately, pasted on) the mouth. Hobart literally dreamed up Tartu's look. "I went to sleep one night thinking about this project," remembered the actor, "and it weighed on my mind, and low and behold Tartu came to me in this horrific nightmare.... The face was hideous and I woke up and said, 'Hey, that's me!' This was about five in the morning, and I went into my dining room and into my makeup box and created Tartu, and so Grefe had his monster and he loved it!" That makes one.

At an hour and twenty-three minutes, *Death Curse of Tartu* is about an hour too long, its pace as sluggish as an Everglade current. "The film played nationwide in 1967 and did fairly well on the double-bill with *Sting of Death*," reported Hobart. *THIS*, indeed, IS HORROR!

With quotes from: "Jellyfish-Man ... an Interview with Doug Hobart," by Paul Parla, *Scary Monsters* 26, March 1998.

Dementia 13 (1963; American International; b&w) Alternate Title: *The Haunted and the Hunted.* Director/Screenplay: Francis Coppola; Producer: Roger Corman; Cinematographer: Charles Hanawalt. Cast: William Campbell, Luana Anders, Bart Patton, Mary Mitchel, Patrick Magee, Ethne Dunn.

You Must Pass the "D-13" Test To Prepare You for the Horrifying Experience of *Dementia 13*. If You Fail the Test ... You Will Be Asked to Leave the Theater! — tagline

Dementia 13 remains best known as the first feature from future Oscar-winning writer-director Francis Ford Coppola, which is as it should be. Without Coppola, *Dementia 13* would be just another *Psycho* rip-off. But, thanks to Coppola's dexterity with dialogue and flair for visuals, it emerges as a stylish and enjoyable *Psycho* rip-off.

Louise Haloran (Luana Anders) fears she will be cut out of her wealthy mother-in-law's will after her husband dies of a heart attack, so she decides to cover up his death and pretend her spouse was called away on a business trip. She travels to her in-laws' family estate in Ireland and discovers that the Halorans, especially Lady Haloran (Ethne Dunn), are haunted (perhaps literally) by the memory of John's younger sister, Kathleen, who drowned in a pond six years earlier. The family — including John's brothers Richard (William Campbell) and Billy (Bart Patton) — ritualistically reenacts the girl's funeral every year, even carrying umbrellas with them because it was raining the day Kathleen was buried. Louise tries to take advantage of the Halorans' obsession with the dead girl, but finds she's in over her head.

Featuring a *Psycho*-like paradigm-shifting plot twist about halfway through and promoted with a salacious advertising campaign, *Dementia 13* was one of several low-budget, black-and-white psychological thrillers rushed to market in the early 1960s in the wake of Alfred Hitchcock's watershed shocker. The qualities that set it apart from its mostly lackluster contemporaries can almost all be credited to Coppola, who both directed and wrote the script.

As a screenwriter, Coppola displays command of the conventions and plot devices characteristic of an emerging subgenre, as well as the keen ear for naturalistic dialogue that would become a

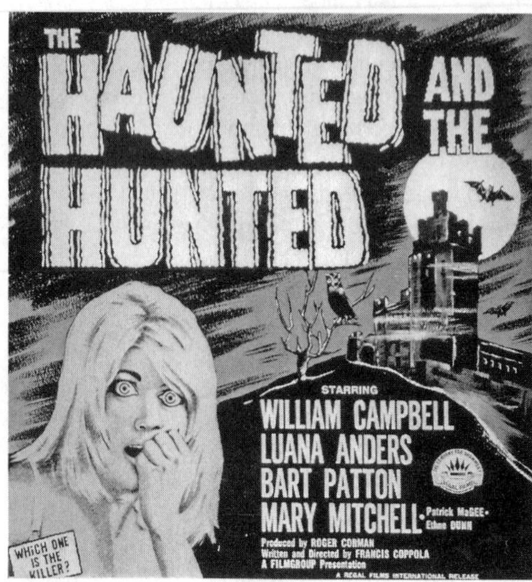

The nonsensically-titled *Dementia 13* (1963) was re-christened the more descriptive *The Haunted and the Hunted* in the U.K.

hallmark of later triumphs such as *The Godfather* (1972) and *The Conversation* (1974). As a director, he demonstrates extraordinary acumen for visual storytelling — right from the eye-catching opening shot of a pier stretching out into the inky blackness of a lake at night. John suffers his fatal heart attack while rowing Louise around the lake and arguing about the rock music blaring from his transistor radio. Afterward, Louise shoves John's body over the side of the boat, then tosses the radio in after him. Coppola offers a final, underwater shot of John's body sinking to the bottom, trailed by the radio, still playing, the music muffled and distorted by the lake water.

Coppola also mounts a pair of remarkable set pieces, one in which the film's first victim discovers what seems to be Kathleen's body, perfectly preserved at the bottom of the Haloran family pond. Startled, the swimmer emerges from the water, gasping for air, and is summarily axed to death by an unseen assailant. In another harrowing sequence Lady Haloran, visiting a makeshift shrine to her dead daughter, is menaced by the same unidentified ax-wielding fiend.

With more moments like this *Dementia 13* might have been truly outstanding instead of merely intriguing. But unfortunately, after the film's major plot twist, the story morphs into a fairly standard whodunnit (or who'sdoinnit, since the attacks continue). The cast, although professional and credible, seldom make the most of Coppola's script or bring any inner life to their roles. Anders comes off best, seeming delightfully saucy and unscrupulous (although she's not at impressive here as in her key supporting role as the sister of Don Sebastian (Vincent Price) in *The Pit and the Pendulum* [1963].) Campbell, who Trekkers may recognize from two memorable guest appearances on *Star Trek,* also acquits himself well, walking a narrow line between engendering pathos and serving as a viable suspect. Stalwart veteran Patrick Magee proves as capable as ever playing a family doctor who attempts to unravel the family's dark secrets. Most of the other players fade into the woodwork. The movie also suffers from the cut-rate production values characteristic of early-60s Roger Corman productions not directed by Corman himself.

According to Coppola, *Dementia 13* was shot for a paltry $20,000 — although the director's atmospheric use of actual Scottish locations partially mitigates its shoe-string budget. Coppola had traveled to Europe with Corman to run sound and serve as second unit director on the Grand Prix melodrama *The Young Racers* (1963). "We all knew that when Roger went to Europe or Hawaii or Puerto Rico for a picture that he always made a second picture with his own money," Coppola said. "When Roger decided not to direct a second movie himself, I went to him and said, 'I'll do the other film. Let me take the camera and some of the equipment and staff and make a low-budget psychological thriller.' So I immediately went home that night after the shoot and wrote the big horror scene — a Hitchcock-type ax murder sequence — and showed it to him. He came back, with some changes, and said, 'All right, if you can do the rest of the script like that you can do it for $20,000.'"

Despite its weaknesses, there's enough of merit in *Dementia 13* to make it well worth a look, especially for curious fans of Coppola's later, more distinguished efforts.

With quotes from: *How I Made a Hundred Movies in Hollywood and Never Lost a Dim,* by Roger Corman with Jim Jerome.

The Demon Doctor see *The Awful Dr. Orlof*

Demon Hunter see *The Legend of Blood Mountain*

Demon Planet see *Planet of the Vampires*

Destination Inner Space (1966; Magna Pictures) Director: Francis D. Lyon; Producer: Earle Lyon; Screenplay: Arthur C. Pierce; Cinematographer: Brick Marquard. Cast: Scott Brady, Sheree North, Gary Merrill, Mike Road, Wende Wagner, John Howard.

TERROR from the DEPTHS
of the SEA! — poster

From the beginning credits sequence, which looks like any number of late-1960s TV adventure show openings, one gets the feeling that this poor man's *Creature from the Black Lagoon* is nothing more that an overlong *Voyage to the Bottom of the Sea* episode.

A rather pudgy Scott Brady (there's an embarrassing moment in which Brady really struggles to hook his wet suit belt across his ample midriff — presumably we're not supposed to notice) plays no-nonsense Navy Commander Hugh Wayne, who is dispatched to a submerged "Aqua-sphere" (an underwater lab) to investigate a mysterious undersea craft lurking nearby. Exploring the mysterious ship (which turns out to be an uninhabited, automated flying saucer!), Wayne and divers Hugh Maddox (Mike Road, best known as the voice of "Race" Bannon on *Jonny Quest*) and Sandra Welles (Wende Wagner, co-star of TV's *The Green Hornet*) discover a cylindrical tank that, back at the lab, "hatches" into an amphibious creature. The monster (Ron Burke) grows quickly and, without any apparent motivation, begins terrorizing the lab and killing the oceanauts.

Such a scenario is prime territory for some claustrophobic monster scares. Not so here. Director Francis D. Lyon and art director Paul Sylos, Jr., apparently thought it better to arrange the submerged lab as a group of large, brightly lit rooms, with no corridors or shadowy recesses within which a decent monster could lurk. The wonderful opportunities for atmosphere and suspense, used so successfully in such winners as *The Thing* (1951), *It! The Terror from Beyond Space* (1958) and, later, *Alien* (1979), are completely ignored. (Someone who *was* paying close attention to those earlier classics, however, was scripter Arthur C. Pierce, who slavishly "borrowed" many of the plot points from both *The Thing* and *It! The Terror* for his thinly-disguised aquatic copy.) Instead we're treated to lengthy undersea travelogue footage; an I've-been-a-coward-but-am-now-a-self-sacrificing-hero subplot; and an over-lit, garishly colored, cartoonish monster whose presence is telegraphed reels in advance. Admittedly, the fish-creature itself is at first kind of fun, with audaciously bright red fins, huge black bug-eyes, a large frowning mouth and blue skin. But it is so overexposed and devoid of personality, and moves (even underwater) in such a lumbering and graceless manner ("It was very heavy to move in," remembered Monster actor Burke), that one soon loses all interest in it.

The monster was built by Richard Cassarino (who also constructed *The Hideous Sun Demon*), a former toy designer for Mattel and staff animator for Disney, where he worked on such features as *Lady and the Tramp*, *Sleeping Beauty* and *101 Dalmatians*. "For that costume," related Cassarino, "I mixed a sea creature with dragon-like proportions and gave it the head of a demonic serpent." (From its comically perpetual frown, it was obviously a very *cranky* demonic serpent.) Said sea creature suit took about two months to create and weighed nearly 140 pounds.

Beyond its ungainly aqua-beast, the film's effects are worse than anything found in even the cheapest TV series of the time. For the shots of the disappointingly simple miniature models of the saucer and sea-lab, the filmmakers didn't even bother to use slow-motion photography, making the too-rapid-to-be-real movements of the spacecraft and the lab's diving bell betray them for what they are—cheap models. Nor did "special effects" technician Roger George bother to clear away or dress up the normal-sized coral and sea growth that, next to the models, totally destroys any illusion of size.

The characterizations are merely caricatures (Chinese cook: "You no like black dragon tea Miss Anna?") and the dialogue hackneyed ("You know, Hugh," says the leading lady, "until a few minutes ago I couldn't find much in you I really liked; now I think I could fall in love with you").

Even on its obviously low budget, with the proper low-key lighting, a smoother build-up and better use of the situation's possibilities, this could have been a passable "Amphibious Monster" movie. But due to the obvious lack of care on the part of the filmmakers, *Destination Inner Space* is just destined to disappoint.

This Italian photobusta featuring Sheree North shows off *Destination Inner Space*'s monster to good(?) effect.

With quotes from: "Monster Man: 'Destination Inner Space' Creature Ron Burke, and "Hideous Monster Maker from Inner Space," by Paul and Donna Parla, *Filmfax* 62, August/September 1997.

Destroy All Monsters (1968/69; Toho/AIP; Japan) Original Language Title: *Kaiju Soshingeki* (Monster Invasion); Alternate Title: *Operation Monsterland* (U.K.). Director: Ishiro Honda; Producer: Tomoyuki Tanaka; Screenplay: Ishiro Honda and Takeshi Kimura; Cinematographer: Taiichi Kankura. Cast: Akira Kubo, Jun Tazaki, Yukoko Kobayashi, Yoshio Tsuchiya, Kyoko Ai, Andrew Hughes.

The battle cry that could save the world!
— tagline

As the 1960s wound down, Toho's once-mighty Godzilla series clearly had lost its way. Budgets had been slashed and, with director Jun Fukuda replacing Ishiro Honda, the movies grew more kid-friendly and comedy-oriented (akin to Daiei's puerile Gamera pictures). Not surprisingly, box office returns suffered. Fukuda's first two G-films, *Godzilla vs. the Sea Monster* (1966) and *Son of Godzilla* (1967), failed to earn a U.S. theatrical release, and 1965's *Monster Zero* wouldn't be released stateside until 1970. To try to put the series back on track, Toho came up with two good ideas: first, throw virtually every rubber suit giant in the studio's history together for a monster rally to end all monster rallies; and second, bring back Honda.

Unfortunately, neither of these gambits played out as expected.

The biggest problem was that the studio remained unwilling to invest capital in the series. Shooting all the giant monster footage necessitated by the story would have made *Destroy All Monsters* the most expensive *kaiju eiga* since the original *Gojira* in 1954 (the costliest Japanese movie of its day). To reduce expenses, Toho bosses forced Honda to utilize stock footage for the monster attack scenes. As a result, *Destroy All Monsters* plays more like *Godzilla's Greatest Hits* than an original production. The storyline also proves highly derivative, recycling elements from earlier films like *Battle in Outer Space* (1960) and *Ghidrah, the Three-Headed Monster* (1964).

The year is 1999, and all the Earth's monsters have been rounded up and caged behind "scientific walls" on a remote island known as Monster Land. From a subterranean lab, a team of scientists monitors the creatures, which include Godzilla, Rodan, Mothra (in caterpillar form), Minya (the Son of Godzilla) and several others. Suddenly, the entire island (above and below ground) is enveloped in a strange yellow gas cloud, rendering everyone — and every monster — unconscious. Freed from Monster Land, the beasts begin attacking the great cities of the world. (Godzilla takes Manhattan; Baragon will, ahem, always have Paris.) Investigation by the United Nations Scientific Council reveals that the monsters— as well as the Monster Land scientists— are now under the mental control of the Kilaak, aliens out to conquer the Earth. Eventually, the intrepid scientist-heroes of the UNSC destroy the Kilaak mind-control mechanism, and the monsters (not happy about being played for suckers) attack the aliens *en masse*. The Kilaak call in their defender from outer space, Ghidrah, and the stage is set for a final showdown.

If nothing else, *Destroy All Monsters* ranks among the most action-packed of all Toho's rubber suit monster epics. Although the human characters are either simple types or else completely

Mothra, Godzilla and Rodan face off against *Ghidrah the Three-Headed Monster* (1964/65).

indistinguishable from one another, there are none of the usual mundane homo sapien subplots to gum up the works. And, for *kaiju* fans, there's an undeniable thrill in seeing virtually all Toho's monster stars appearing together, including some who had been absent from the screen for years: Manda (from *Atragon*, 1963/65), Baragon (from *Frankenstein Conquers the World*, 1965), Gorosaurus (from *King Kong Escapes*, 1967/68), Angilas (from *Gigantis, the Fire Monster*, 1955) and even, briefly, Varan (from *Varan the Unbelievable*, 1958/62). Another plus is that the annoying Minya receives very little screen time.

Yet, *Destroy All Monsters* simply isn't everything it could have been. Its key concept—a monster rally to end all monster rallies—wouldn't be fully realized until the highly entertaining *Godzilla: Final Wars* (2004). *Destroy All Monsters* wastes too much time with the UNSC scientists, either on the trail of the Kilaak or wringing their hands back at the lab. The overuse of stock shots lends a hang-dog air to the production. Honda, unhappy to be forced into using so much retread footage, fails to instill the vitality and sense of wonder he brought to his earlier *kaiju* classics. Hamstrung by low budgets, and with the loss of visual effects specialist Eiji Tsuburaya (who died suddenly in 1970), Honda would never again direct a great monster movie. His remaining *kaiju eiga* work included *Godzilla's Revenge* (1969/71), *Yog, Monster from Space* (1970/71), *Terror of Mechagodzilla* (1975/77) and a few episodes of the *Ultraman* TV series.

Recognizing a highly exploitable concept and title, American International Pictures purchased *Destroy All Monsters* for release in the U.S., making this the only G-film to receive a timely stateside theatrical run between *Ghidrah, the Three-Headed Monster* in 1964 and *Godzilla vs. the Smog Monster* in 1972. The glory days for the Japanese giant monsters had reached their end.

Devil Doll

Devil Doll (1965; Galaworld/Gordon Films; U.K./U.S.; b&w) Director/Producer: Lindsay Shonteff; Screenplay: George Barclay (Ronald Kinnoch), Lance Z. Hargreaves (Charles Vetter, Jr.), from an original story by Frederick Escreet Smith; Cinematographer: Gerald Gibbs. Cast: Bryant Haliday, Willaim Sylvester, Yvonne Romain, Frances De Wolff, Sandra Dorne.

WHAT IS THE STRANGE, TERRIFYING EVIL SECRET OF THE DUMMY ... and why is it locked in a cage every night?—ad line

"Can a beautiful woman be enslaved against her will?" asked the ads to this oddly disquieting yet at the same time rather torpid exploitationer. Unusual camera angles and techniques (including dummy's-eye-view shots, still-frames and even positive-to-negative film changes) and unsettling moments (did the doll's eyes just move or didn't they?) never quite jell with overlong stretches of exposition and obvious padding.

When newspaperman Mark English (Willaim Sylvester) covers "the Great Vorelli" (Bryant Haliday), a mesmerist and ventriloquist whose act has been selling out in London, he determines to get to the bottom of Vorelli's "fakery" (which includes his dummy, Hugo, actually standing up and *walking* across the stage). To this end, Mark enlists the aid of his wealthy socialite girlfriend, Marianne (Yvonne Romain), to serve as a "volunteer" in Vorelli's act. But Vorelli's hypnotic powers are real (and so is Hugo), and the mad mesmerist sets his lascivious sights on hypnotizing Marianne into marrying him. He then plans to place her soul in a doll and abscond with her wealth. But little, wooden Hugo, Vorelli's first soul-stealing victim, has other ideas.

Shot in two weeks in April of 1963 at the low-rent Merton Park Studios in London for the paltry sum of $50,000, *Devil Doll* didn't see release until June of 1965, when it went out as support for the straight melodrama *Sylvia*. *Devil Doll* was originally to be directed by Canadian Sidney J. Furie.

Ad for 1965's *Devil Doll.*

But shortly before production, Furie was offered the (infinitely more prestigious) assignment of directing *The Ipcress File* with Michael Caine and backed out of *Devil Doll*. In his stead, Furie offered his then-protégé (and fellow Canadian) Lindsay Shonteff as director, with the promise that Furie would closely supervise Shonteff, guiding him (uncredited) from behind the scenes. (In fact, executive producer Richard Gordon attributes *Devil Doll*'s success more to Furie than Shonteff.)

Though *Devil Doll* manages to wring several shudders from its preposterous but admittedly creepy premise, the movie can't avoid falling into its low-budget trap on occasion. "The Great Vorelli," for instance, engages in the lamest of hypnotism acts: The big moment comes when he hypnotizes the heroine into thinking she can *dance*— and has an "expert in modern dance" come onstage and do the twist with her (to the vigorous applause of the apparently astounded — and amazingly un-hip — audience)! It's astounding all right — astounding in its banality.

The acting in *Devil Doll* is about what one can expect from a low-budget production — uneven. Oakland-born William Sylvester (*Gorgo, Devils of Darkness, The Hand of Night, 2001: A Space Odyssey*) offers a general pleasantness but not much presence, though his steady, unassuming "hero" contrasts nicely with Vorelli's malevolent intensity and dour demeanor. The gorgeous, French-born Yvonne Romain (*Circus of Horrors, Curse of the Werewolf*) appears rather vapid and makes little impression, apart from a strictly decorative one.

Bryant Haliday (*Curse of the Voodoo, The Projected Man, Tower of Evil*), on the other hand, carries the film with his rather one-note but highly effective performance as the intense, never-smiling, always smoldering hypnotist. Moving — and speaking — slowly and deliberately, his penetrating gaze and unsmiling antagonism makes the viewer believe that he can indeed control the wills of others. "The tension between Vorelli and that dummy — it was there — everybody felt it," remarks English. Thanks to Haliday's forceful performance, the viewer readily believes it. "Bryant Haliday was chosen to play the lead because he had money in the project," recalled Shonteff. "But in spite of that financial muscle he was perfect for the role." Yes he was.

The dummy, Hugo (played by female circus midget Sadie Corre), generates some genuine chills, with its creepy wooden child-face and slowly shifting eyes. Its measured, awkward advance, as it obeys its "master's" command to walk to the footlights and apologize to the audience for some verbal slight, is nearly as disturbing as its quick lunging with a knife in several deadly (and cleverly edited) sequences. Hugo encapsulates that uneasy fear generated by oversized dolls— especially those of the faux-sentient ventriloquist variety.

Though unevenly paced and indifferently acted (apart from Haliday's forceful presence), *Devil Doll* remains moderately effective due to Shonteff's (or Furie's?) unusual techniques and some genuinely shuddery sequences involving one rather creepy three-foot doll. "It was a very low-budget film," said Gordon. "I flatter myself that it doesn't show it..." Well, not *much*, anyway.

With quotes from: *Interviews with B Science Fiction and Horror Movie Makers*, by Tom Weaver.

The Devil Rides Out see *The Devil's Bride*

The Devil's Bride (1968; Hammer/20th Century–Fox; U.K.) Alternate Title: *The Devil Rides Out* (U.K.) Director: Terence Fisher; Producer: Anthony Nelson Keys; Screenplay: Richard Matheson (from a novel by Dennis Wheatley); Cinematographer: Arthur Grant. Cast: Christopher Lee, Charles Gray, Leon Greene, Patrick Moyer, Nike Arrighi.

> The beauty of woman — the demon of darkness— the unholy union of "The Devil's Bride!"— tagline

With a finely wrought screenplay, crackling direction, excellent production values and outstanding lead performances, this picture boasts all the major elements that characterize Hammer Films' best gothic chillers. But the devil's in the details— or, in this case, in the visual effects.

The Duc de Richleau (Christopher Lee) and his friend Rex (Leon Greene) casually drop in on Simon (Patrick Mower), the son of a deceased war comrade, and discover that the young man has fallen in with a coven of devil-worshipers led by a powerful necromancer named Mocata (Charles Gray). After commanding, then pleading with Simon to leave "The Circle," de Richleau coldcocks Simon with a right cross and hauls him away in a fireman's carry. ("You fool! I'd rather see you dead than meddling with black magic!" de Richleau growls, grabbing Simon by the lapels.) But Simon, under Mocata's hypnotic influence, soon escapes and returns to the coven. Undaunted, de Richleau and Rex try to free Simon from Mocata's control and come face-to-face with a vision from Hell — the first of several demonic apparitions and other supernatural encounters they will endure in what becomes a life-or-death struggle with the evil sorcerer.

Nearly all director Terence Fisher's horror films contain variations on a single theme: The triumph of Christian good over pagan/Satanic evil. Sometimes, as in his Frankenstein movies, this idea remains hidden beneath other elements. But *The Devil's Bride* depicts this struggle literally. The result is one of the director's boldest and most personal efforts, the cinematic equivalent of a fire-and-brimstone sermon. It's hardly subtle but undeniably potent. For instance, just prior to the final fade-out, when Simon exclaims, "Thank God!" de Richleau replies, "Yes, He is the one we must thank."

One indicator of how seriously Fisher took his recurrent God-versus-Satan theme is that he didn't consign *The Devil's Bride* to the realm of fantasy (at least, not entirely). "The whole thing is based on fact and it is consequently one of the most difficult ones to make," he said. Fisher explained that he and screenwriter Richard Matheson were trying to depict Satanism (and its dangers) authentically, which lends special gravitas to passages such as de Richleau's explanation of the power of darkness ("It is a living force that can be tapped at any given moment of the night").

Fisher, of course, was never a screenwriter, nor did he have enough clout (even at Hammer) to pick and choose movies on the basis of thematic continuity or any other artistic consideration. He simply directed whatever films he was assigned, like everybody else at the studio. Yet he managed in film after film to find ways to bring his personal vision to the screen by underscoring elements that reflected his beliefs, both in his presentation of scripted scenes and sometimes (as with the finale of *Brides of Dracula*) through rewrites. However, he seldom received a script so perfectly aligned with his personal vision as *The Devil's Bride*, adapted by Matheson from Dennis Wheatley's 1934 novel *The Devil Rides Out*. Clearly, Fisher was enthused about the project and his excitement lights up the finished film, which is almost overstuffed with his trademark dynamic compositions.

Matheson's script is a marvel — concise and urgent in its storytelling, without surrendering to simple stereotypes or clichés. In de Richleau and Mocata, the scenario offers a pair of perfectly matched foils, both of them powerful, resourceful and implacable. And in those roles, Christopher Lee and Charles Gray deliver (arguably) the finest performances of their respective careers. Certainly Lee's imperious but benevolent de Richleau ranks among the most nuanced and compelling portrayals in the actor's lengthy filmography. Together, he and Gray are electrifying. The rest of the cast perform capably, as well, particularly Moyer as Simon, who realizes he is in over his head but feels powerless to do anything about it. The film also benefits from the usual impeccable Hammer production values, particularly Bernard Robinson's richly appointed sets and James Bernard's rousing score.

Unfortunately, all these treasures are nearly squandered by the film's lone deficiency:

The evil Mocata (Charles Gray) prepares to sacrifice young Tanith (Nike Arrighi) as director Terence Fisher's *The Devil's Bride* (1968) races to a breathless climax.

Michael Stainer-Hutchins' atrocious special effects. For starters, the visuals are unimaginative and not at all menacing. The first satanic apparition, conjured up in Simon's observatory, is a chunky, glassy-eyed black man wearing what looks like a red diaper. This guy might pass for some sort of cut-rate genie, but as an emissary from Hell he is simply laughable. While the movie's other demonic figures (a goat-faced man, a giant spider, a skull-faced knight on horseback) aren't as risible as its first, they consistently undercut the dramatic power of the story. Years later, Matheson expressed exasperation with the movie's visuals. "They always go for the goddamned spider!" he said. "That wasn't in my script." Not only are the effects disappointingly ordinary in design, they are also clumsy in execution. Even relatively simple rear-projection shots during a car chase sequence look awkward and unconvincing. Fortunately the rest of *The Devil's Bride* is so well done, it's possible (if at times difficult) for viewers to overlook this significant failing.

With this picture, Hammer found itself at the forefront of an emerging trend. Previously, the most popular movie monsters had been vampires, werewolves and monsters of all sorts. But horror heroes would face off against the devil himself in a new wave of films including *Rosemary's Baby* (1968), *The Exorcist* (1974) and *The Omen* (1976), among many others. Ironically, although it was produced first, *The Devil's Bride* wasn't released in the U.S. until after *Rosemary's Baby* and suffered from unfair comparisons with Polanski's masterpiece. Even today it's not as well-remembered by general audiences, but Hammer devotees generally rank *The Devil's Bride* among the studio's finest efforts of the 1960s.

Aside from its poor visual effects, it's a hell of a good show.

Sources: "Terence Fisher in Conversation" by Jan Van Genechten, *Little Shoppe of Horrors* No. 19 and *The Men Who Made the Monsters* by Paul Jensen.

The Devil's Commandment (1957/1963; Titanus/RCIP; Italy; b&w)

Alternate Titles: *I Vampiri* (*The Vampires*, Italy), *Der Vampir von Notre Dame* (*The Vampire of Notre Dame*, West Germany), *Lust of the Vampire* (alternate U.S. version). Directors: Riccardo Freda, Mario Bava (uncredited), Ronald Honthaner (uncredited, U.S. versions only); Producers: Ermando Donati and Luigi Carpentieri; Screenplay: Piero Regnozi (as Rijk Sjostrom), Mario Bava (uncredited) and R.V. Rhems (uncredited, U.S. versions only); Cinematography: Mario Bava. Cast: Gianni Maria Canale, Carlo d'Angelo, Dario Michaelis, Wandisa Guida, Antoine Balpetre, Paul Muller, Al Lewis (U.S. version only).

BEAUTIFUL GIRLS WERE VICTIMS OF HIS EVIL MIND!—tagline

The Devil's Commandment—now better known under its original Italian title, *I Vampiri*—is a film of momentous historical significance but only middling quality, especially in its butchered American versions.

Inspector Chantal (Carlo d'Angelo) and reporter Pierre Lintin (Dario Michaelis) are both investigating a series of mysterious Parisian abductions and murders, all involving young women whose bodies are surgically drained of blood by a perpetrator that newspapers have nicknamed "The Vampire." Pierre believes a junkie named Joseph Signoret (Paul Muller) may have kidnapped at least one of the victims but can't convince police of his theory. He has an even harder time selling his next idea, that Signoret is somehow

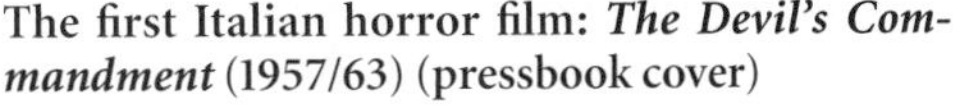

The first Italian horror film: *The Devil's Commandment* (1957/63) (pressbook cover)

linked with Duchess Margherita (Gianni Maria Canale in old age makeup), a reclusive noblewoman who once had an unrequited infatuation with Pierre's father. (Now the duchess' niece, Giselle [Canale, *not* in old age makeup], has a crush on Pierre — but like his father, the younger Lintin remains wary.) "Giselle," it's soon revealed, is actually Margherita, her youth restored by a blood-based potion concocted by her mad scientist husband, Prof. Julian du Grand (Antoine Belpetre). To keep his vain wife young and beautiful, however, du Grand must continue killing.

The Fascist government of Benito Mussolini prohibited Italian studios from making horror movies during its rule, from 1922 to 1943. Meanwhile, highly restrictive Catholic censors at both the national and local levels banned the exhibition of imported fright films for decades. Classic Universal chillers, including *Dracula* and *Frankenstein* (both 1931), reached Italian theaters in the early 1950s once the Fascists were gone and censorship codes finally began to relax. Still, when director Riccardo Freda undertook making *I Vampiri* in 1956, Italy hadn't produced a horror film since *Il Monstro di Frankenstein* in 1920. As a result, *I Vampiri* was carefully calibrated to evade censorship concerns: despite its title, the story involves no vampirism or witchcraft; despite its romantic subplot it contains no kissing (often excised by local Italian censors); and it's set in decadent Paris rather than devout Rome.

However necessary these compromises may have been, they inevitably weaken the final product. Especially in comparison with later Italian gothic horrors, *I Vampiri* seems extremely tame. Its plot also proves disappointingly familiar, echoing elements from such dated and uninspiring fare as *The Vampire Bat* (1933) and *The Corpse Vanishes* (1942), although since horror films were so hard to see in Italy at the time, these similarities may be coincidental. The film's principal assets are Beni Montressor's baroque sets and Mario Bava's moody, high-contrast black-and-white cinematography, which together defined what would become the signature look of the Italian gothic thriller. The picture also boasts some spectacular visual effects, also supervised by Bava. The showiest of these are Giselle/Margherita's transformations from young beauty to aged hag, which Bava realized using the same technique that had transformed Fredric March from Dr. Jekyll to Mr. Hyde in the 1931 Rouben Mamoulian version of that tale. Canale was painted with red old-age makeup which appeared invisible under red lights. As the lights were dimmed, the makeup became visible to the camera — and the actress appeared to age. Bava probably learned this gimmick not from the Mamoulian film (which had not yet been released in Italy), but from Fred Nilbo's *Ben-Hur* (1925), which used the same effect (in reverse) during its "Christ heals the lepers" scene.

I Vampiri remains only intermittently engaging, not only due to its general aversion to anything scary or salacious, but because it's noticeably uneven in tone and suffers from glaring lapses in logic — problems that stem from the picture's troubled production history. Freda fell hopelessly behind schedule as the shoot progressed, due in part to difficulties with the cast. "Freda knew his job very well, he was gifted, but his behavior was unacceptable," Bava said. "He was convinced ... that most actors have their heads up their asses. Maybe I agree, but Freda took this notion to extremes. Just imagine: he would only walk onto the set after each new scene had been completely blocked and rehearsed [by Bava]. Then he would arrive, sit down in his chair and shout 'Si gira!' ('Roll 'em!') After the take was finished he would turn to me and ask if we should print. Well, after a few days of that, the actors were at their wit's end."

I Vampiri was scheduled for 12 days of production, but after 10 days Freda had filmed only half the script. Then he stormed off, leaving Bava to finish the picture in the two remaining days. "I quit working on the film due to an argument between myself and the producers," Freda admits. In order to finish on time, Bava radically altered and streamlined the story, expanding the Lintin character, decreasing the importance of the inspector and abandoning entire subplots. In the original screenplay, for instance, Joseph Signoret was not merely a drug addict but an executed killer revived from the dead by a chemical agent formulated by Professor du Grand. This explains the Frankenstein Monster-like surgical scars around Joseph's neck (where his guillotined head had been reattached). Bava somehow managed to complete the film on time and on budget, but *I Vampiri* failed miserably at the box office. Italian audiences stayed away in droves, which Freda marked up to simple prejudice ("They assumed that Italians didn't know how to make films of this kind," he said). French audiences found the picture's faux Parisian setting laughable.

The movie languished unreleased in the U.S. until 1963, when it was purchased by the Releasing

Corporation of Independent Producers, a low-rent importer of grindhouse fare. The company hired Ronald Honthaner, who had edited Robert Clarke's *The Hideous Sun Demon* (1959), to shoot new material to be inserted into *I Vampiri*, which RCIP issued in two retitled versions—the "all-audiences" *Devil's Commandment* and the "adults only" *Lust of the Vampire*, which contained nudity. *The Devil's Commandment* runs eight minutes shorter than *I Vampiri* yet contains 11 minutes worth of new material originating from neither Freda nor Bava. Key sequences from *I Vampiri* were truncated or deleted, rendering an already choppy film virtually incomprehensible. The new scenes were intended to amp up the thrill quotient but are so ineptly staged, performed and photographed that they only reduce the dramatic impact. *The Devil's Commandment* features a different opening scene — in this version, a black-gloved killer strangles a woman while she takes a bubble bath. Audiences are treated to cheesecake footage of the victim undressing, as well as a quick glimpse of her bubble-covered bosom. The most notorious of these newly created scenes arrives near the end of the film, when Al ("Grandpa Munster") Lewis, playing one of Professor du Grand's henchmen with a gleam of deranged lust in his eye, attacks a blonde prisoner, ripping open her blouse to reveal her brassiere. The original, uncut version of *I Vampiri* wasn't shown in the U.S. until 1993, at a Bava retrospective in New York. In 2001 it was issued on DVD, where it finally supplanted *The Devil's Commandment*.

Fortunately, the failure of *I Vampiri* did not derail, but only delayed, the arrival of Italy as an influential player in the development of horror cinema. Freda and Bava joined forces again, with greater success, for *Caltiki, the Immortal Monster* (1959/60) before Bava scored the major breakthrough with *Black Sunday* (1960/61).

With quotes from: Mario Bava: All the Colors of the Dark, by Tim Lucas.

Devil's Doll see *The Devil's Hand*

The Devil's Hand (1962; Crown International; b&w)

Alternate Titles: *Devil's Doll, Live to Love, The Naked Goddess, Witchcraft*; Director: William J. Hole, Jr.; Producer: Alvin K. Bubis; Screenplay: Jo Heims; Cinematographer: Meredith Nicholson. Cast: Linda Christian, Robert Alda, Ariadna Welter, Neil Hamilton, Gene Craft, Jeannie Carmen.

THIS IS THE HAND OF TERROR!—ad line

The Devil's Hand is a deservedly obscure entry in the horror cinema sweepstakes whose only real point of interest lay in the astounding beauty of its star, Linda Christian. Christian plays Bianca Milan, an enticing temptress who sets her sights on Rick Turner (Robert Alda). Bianca, a prominent member of a modern-day voodoo cult that worships Gamba ("the devil-god of evil"), uses her powers of thought transference to invade Rick's dreams. When the leader and "high executioner" of the cult (Neil Hamilton) uses a voodoo doll to send Rick's fiancée to the hospital, Bianca lures Rick to her and ensnares him with her captivating beauty. He agrees to join the cult so that they can be together, and so "renounces goodness and virtue." After an introduction to the cult's sacrificial version of Russian Roulette (using a rotating hanging wheel mounted with swords), Rick's conscience ultimately overcomes his infatuation with Bianca and Rick ultimately rescues

Despite its title and tag-line ("This is the hand of terror!"), there's no "hand" and precious little "terror" in *The Devil's Hand* (1962). In this lobby card, Bianca (Linda Christian, center) initiates her newfound beau Rick (Robert Alda, right) into a voodoo cult.

Donna from the cult's clutches, resulting in the coven's destruction by fire ... or does it?

This obviously threadbare production sports only cramped and minimalist sets. William J. Hole, Jr.'s direction is adequate, but only just, with a heavy reliance on the master shot and nothing extra in the way of evocative angles or mood-enhancing photography (it's about what one should expect from the director of *Ghost of Dragstrip Hollow*. Jo Heims' rambling screenplay offers absolutely no depth of character anywhere, ignoring whatever tortured reasons caused these people to seek out this "devil-god of evil." None of the bland characters seem as if they've lost their souls (they don't appear interesting enough to have even had one in the first place), and the coven comes across as nothing more than a rather silly and dull after-hours club.

As Lamont, Neil Hamilton makes a truly one-dimensional (or, more precisely, *non*-dimensional) villain. His smug, one-note performance, in which his tone never changes and he never even gets excited, makes one long for a bit of his Commissioner Gordon histrionics to liven things up. (Hamilton later achieved fame as the perpetually surprised and spluttering police commissioner on the *Batman* television series.)

Robert Alda is just as toneless and lacking in charisma as he was in *The Beast with Five Fingers* (1947), and it's hard to fathom what Bianca sees in this rather seedy middle-aged man. (This was the last American film the former Broadway star and father of Alan Alda made before abandoning Hollywood for the sunny climes of Rome and fifteen years of European productions.)

Fortunately, Linda Christian as Bianca, with her sultry, come-hither looks and breathy, sexy voice, makes Rick's impetuous decision to devote his life to a devil-god cult just to get laid seem *almost* reasonable. Lounging provocatively in nearly see-through negligees, Christian creates a heady air of seething sensuality. Of course, her acting can't match her looks, and her character, despite an obsessive nymphomania, seems no more evil than a spoiled fashion model.

Born Blanca Rosa Welter in Mexico, Linda Christian, daughter of a Dutch oil man, grew up in exotic locales such as Venezuela, South Africa and Palestine (where, for a time, she attended medical school). She entered movies in the mid–1940s in films like *Holiday in Mexico* (1946), *Green Dolphin Street* (1947) and *Tarzan and the Mermaids* (1948) but never really made it as a leading lady. She was better known for her numerous off-screen romances (including Hugh O'Brien, Errol Flynn and Turhan Bey) than for her on-screen performances. Among her husbands were actors Tyrone Power and Edmund Purdom. She eventually moved to Spain, where she continued her romantic pursuits among the European aristocracy.

Though completed in 1959, *The Devil's Hand* wasn't released until 1962; unsurprising, since it is a singularly unremarkable — and unmemorable — production, save for the sultry presence of Linda Christian. Instead of a firm grip on horror, *The Devil's Hand* offers only a limp wrist.

The Devil's Messenger (1962; Herts-Lion International; Sweden-U.S.; b&w) Directors: Herbert L. Strock, Curt Siodmak (uncredited); Producer: Kenneth Herts; Screenplay: Leo Guild, Curt Siodmak (uncredited); Cinematographer: William Troiano. Cast: Lon Chaney, Karen Kadler, Michael Hinn, Ralph Brown, John Crawford, Bert Johnson.

Be Careful What You Wish For! — ad line

The Devil's Messenger began as a proposed television horror anthology called *No. 13 Demon Street*, written and directed by Curt Siodmak in Sweden, and starring Lon Chaney as the host. But when the American half of the production, Herts-Lion, showed the dozen or so episodes to CBS, the network balked. Producer Kenneth Herts then contracted director Herbert L. Strock to go to Sweden and re-shoot several of the episodes, then link them together into a theatrical feature (writing and filming a new wraparound with Chaney as the Devil). According to Curt Siodmak, "Herts-Lion double-crossed me — they took three of the shows, put them together, put a frame around 'em and put Herbert Strock's name on it as the director.... I wasn't even mentioned in the credits, but I'm glad of that. I never saw it." Strock maintains that he "reshot, put some exteriors and action in, put a live score in and so on. I remade four of the messes that Siodmak had left." If said "messes" were even poorer than the tepid results on offer in the revamped feature, then it's little wonder that *No. 13 Demon Street* never hit the television airwaves.

As is, the anthology pastiche opens with a fleshy-faced, shirt-sleeved Lon Chaney (obviously just your average working-stiff Joe Satan) chuckling over his rolodex in Hell's antechamber as he checks in some new tenants. A girl named Satanya (Karen Kadler, then-wife of producer Herts), a suicide, arrives, and the Devil decides to make her his "messenger" (with a name like "Satanya," how could he *not*?), sending her back to Earth to deliver three different objects to a trio of likely prospects. When she protests that she doesn't want to ruin peoples' lives and lure them into Hell, Satan reasonably responds, "People ruin their own lives; all we do is help them a little."

First up is the delivery of a "special camera" to a womanizing photographer who ends up killing (and, it is implied, raping) a woman, only to be haunted by her ever-advancing image in a photograph he took. The second story involves a scientist becoming obsessed with the 50,000-year-old body of a (beautiful) woman found encased in ice at the bottom of a mineshaft. The final tale features a man with a recurring nightmare encouraged to face his fears by his psychiatrist, resulting in a fortune teller predicting the man's death at midnight — by her own hand.

Neither Rod Serling (*The Twilight Zone*) nor John Newman (*One Step Beyond*), nor even Boris Karloff (*Thriller*), need have worried about competition from this Land-of-the-Midnight-Sun TV horror anthology. While the three stories (presumably the best of the bunch) offer a few intriguing premises (particularly the first rather novel tale), and the final segment was well-acted and cleverly constructed (with the figurative noose tightening about the protagonist's neck as time ticks away), none of them (especially the middle episode, which offers only stilted acting and a silly non-ending) can hold a candle to even the sub par installments of the three portmanteau series mentioned above. The wrap-around with Chaney's Devil may please fans of the obviously-on-the-skids actor (who, admittedly, looks like he's having a good time), but the cheesy sets (faux cave walls, ordinary office desk, shelves filled with Halloween bric-a-brac — including a skull, tiki statuette and pitchfork!) only underlines the production's cheapness. Though lovers of camp might enjoy the film's mildly amusing atomic-scare coda, in the end *The Devil's Messenger* delivers only a shabby package.

With quotes from: *Interviews with B Science Fiction and Horror Movie Makers*, by Tom Weaver.

The Devil's Mistress (1966; Holiday Pictures)

Director/Screenplay: Orville Wanzer; Producer: Forrest Westmoreland (as Wes Moreland); Cinematography: Teddy Gregory. Cast: Joan Stapleton, Robert Gregory, Forrest Westmoreland, Douglas Warren, Drew Williams, Arthur Resley.

So young ... So bewitching ... So EVIL! — tagline

While not a major rediscovery, the obscure Western chiller *The Devil's Mistress* — an ultra-low-budget, semi-professional production that played mostly at drive-ins and lower tier "hard-top" theaters in the Southwest — proves far more thoughtful and effective than most films of its breed.

Four cowboys — Will (Drew Williams), Frankie (Robert Gregory), Charlie (Forrest Westmoreland) and Joe (Douglas Warren) — are traveling through Apache territory when they chance across a hardscrabble homestead. Against the advice of cautious Will, the other three cowpokes decide to drop in on the locals in search of food and water. Weird, reclusive homesteader Jereboam (Arthur Resley) and his beautiful young bride Leah (Joan Stapleton) share a meal of stew, cornbread and coffee. Charlie and Joe — who, around the campfire the night before, were joking about raping "squaws" — repay the couple for their generosity by gunning down Jereboam and kidnapping Leah. But the pair gets more than they bargained for, since it turns out that Jereboam was a practitioner of black magic and Leah has supernatural powers. She kisses Charlie and drains his life-force; the next day he topples off his horse, dead. Next she lures Joe to his death by rattlesnake bite. Will realizes that Leah is evil but can't convince Frankie of the danger or escape her vengeance.

Like Herk Harvey's *Carnival of Souls*, *The Devil's Mistress* appears to have been a one-off; producer Forrest Westmoreland and writer-director Orville Wanzer have no additional screen credits. Made on a shoestring budget near Las Cruces, New Mexico, *The Devil's Mistress* never approaches the level of artistry found in Harvey's cult masterpiece, but it's much more ambitious and compelling than the better-known movies of schlock merchants such as Larry Buchanan, who churned out bargain basement drive-in fodder in neighboring Texas.

Wanzer's scenario is a minor marvel of film-making economy. Its Western setting and small cast help disguise the picture's tiny budget (all that's needed are some six-guns, a few horses and a shack — the cast probably wore their own cowboy hats and boots). Emulating the scruffy, ragged look of the spaghetti Westerns further reduced expenses while also enhancing the picture's credibility. Wanzer's low-key approach (the story's supernatural elements slip in almost unnoticed at first) and authentic-sounding dialogue represent additional strengths. Yet, the movie's biggest weakness also belongs to Wanzer's screenplay—namely, that Leah's nature remains poorly defined. She literally kisses the life out of Charlie like a succubus, she magically commands animals to kill Joe and Will like a witch, and she tries to bite Frankie's neck like a vampire. So which is she? The resulting confusion creates a distraction. The film's reflective pace, self-consciously arty flourishes (cutaways to crows looking on from barren trees, etc.) and surreal, what-does-it-all-mean? ending may put off some viewers as well. But it seems wrongheaded to fault an underdog production like *The Devil's Mistress* for being too artful in its approach.

The work of the picture's mostly amateur cast proves predictably uneven. Joan Stapleton, likely cast due to her slight resemblance to horror icon Barbara Steele, comes off best in her speechless role as the alluring Leah. Both Robert Gregory as Frankie and Oren Williams as Will give unaffected, naturalistic performances. Douglas Warren and Forrest Westmoreland are shakier as Joe and Charlie, respectively. Arthur Resley's hambone antics as Jeroboam sink his scenes, but fortunately his role is the smallest.

Nearly forgotten and extremely difficult to find, *The Devil's Mistress* may not be worth the effort of tracking down, but it's worth a look if you happen to stumble across it.

Devils of Darkness (1965; Planet Film/Twentieth Century–Fox; U.K.) Director: Lance Comfort; Producer: Tom Blakeley; Screenwriter: Lyn Fairhurst; Cinematographer: Reg Wyer. Cast: William Sylvester, Hubert Noel, Carole Gray, Tracy Reed, Diana Decker, Rona Anderson, Peter Illing.

What Was This Sinister Evil That Robbed The Dead ... And Killed The Living?—tagline

Panned by the few critics who have bothered to review it and ignored by most genre fans, *Devils of Darkness* lingers among the least-loved British chillers of the decade—a fate it doesn't fully deserve. While it's no forgotten classic, it boasts some worthwhile elements and remains a perfectly painless way to waste 87 minutes.

Author Paul Baxter (William Sylvester) is vacationing in Brittany when two of his traveling companions mysteriously die. Dissatisfied with the explanations for these deaths provided by local police, Baxter orders the bodies shipped to England for autopsy. He also puzzles over a curious amulet featuring a figure of a bat and a snake, which he discovers near the scene of his friend's disappearance. Unknown to him, the amulet is a powerful talisman used by the evil Count Sinistre (Hubert Noel), a 400-year-old vampire-guru whose satanic cult rules the tiny village. Baxter's actions force Sinistre and his minions expand their operations to London, to try to recover the talisman and snuff out the meddling writer.

Devils of Darkness marked the final big-screen directorial credit for former cinematographer Lance Comfort, whose work here is competent but undistinguished. The film's cinematography and production design are even less impressive. This was a cheap production and it shows, which may rankle British horror buffs accustomed to the glossy output of the Hammer and Amicus studios.

Lyn Fairhurt's screenplay suffers from some serious structural problems. Too many abrupt changes of time and locale (its seven-minute precredit prologue seems superfluous) make the narrative seem disjointed. Disappointingly, most of the story's bloodshed occurs off screen. And at

In America, Twentieth Century–Fox paired the obscure *Devils of Darkness* (1965) with the better known *Curse of the Fly*.

times the screenwriter resorts to clumsy narrative devices (like having a book fall open to reveal the vampire as "Count Sinistre").

But Fairhurst's scenario also contains some intriguing ideas. The scenes in rural Brittany, where Baxter runs up against an entire village full of Renfields, have an unnerving paranoia about them that presages later, superior 60s shockers like *Rosemary's Baby* (1968). Once the scene shifts to London, the film amusingly depicts Satanism/ vampirism as an intellectual vogue practiced by jaded Swinging London dilettantes. And *Devils of Darkness* retains the distinction of being the first British vampire movie with a modern-day setting.

Kay Walsh as the Satanic High Priestess lording over *The Devil's Own* (1966).

Among the picture's other merits are a winning lead performance by the ever-reliable Sylvester, whose genre credits also include *Gorgo* (1961), *The Devil Doll* (1965), and *2001: A Space Odyssey* (1968). Hubert Noel's eely Count Sinistre provides a perfect counter-point to Sylvester's likable hero. Carole Gray contributes a memorable supporting turn as Sinistre's jealous vampire queen.

In the U.S., *Devils of Darkness* originally played on the lower half of a double bill with *Curse of the Fly*, another underrated English export.

The Devil's Own (1966; Hammer; U.K.) Alternate Title: *The Witches* (U.K.); Director: Cyril Frankel; Producer: Anthony Nelson Keys; Screenplay: Nigel Kneale (based on the novel *The Devil's Own* by Peter Curtis); Cinematography: Arthur Grant. Cast: Joan Fontaine, Kay Walsh, Alec McCowen, Duncan Lamont, Gwen Ffrangcon-Davies, John Collin, Ingrid Brett, Leonard Rossiter, Michele Dotrice, Carmel McSharry, Martin Stephens, Ann Bell.

Black witchcraft as real as an African nightmare!—trailer

"WHAT DO *The Devil's Own* DO AFTER DARK?" asks the poster for this dull British import. The answer: Not much. In fact, what little excitement that can be gleaned from this tepid tale of modern-day (or at least 1966) witches in a small English village comes during the brief two-and-a-half minute pre-credit prologue. In it, a schoolteacher (Joan Fontaine) at an African missionary compound hurriedly packs up her books while deafening drums beat ominously all around her. Suddenly, a weird knife with its hilt fashioned into a voodoo doll flies through the door to thud into the room's table. The schoolmarm frantically blocks up the door as her two terrified native helpers bolt. Abruptly, the door smashes inward and a figure wearing a huge, horrific primitive mask enters. The woman screams and the screen fades into the credit sequence.

The rest of the film deals with this same woman coming to a small English village (after recovering from the nervous breakdown she suffered because of her African experience) to teach school. Once there she finds that much of the town is involved in witchcraft (of the standard Satanic variety), which culminates in her attempt to stop a human sacrifice.

As might be expected (since it's a Hammer film), *The Devil's Own* is well-acted but slow, with little happening until the story winds down to its rather uninteresting conclusion. (Hammer did eventually make one good witchcraft movie, 1968's *The Devil's Bride.*) *The Devil's Own*'s witchery and supposedly "wanton" coven activity appear dreadfully tame, and the evil high priestess is vanquished with a whimper rather than a scream. Scripter Nigel Kneale (*Enemy From Space, The Abominable Snowman of the Himalayas, First Men in the Moon*, et al.) would have done better to expand the voodoo-themed prologue rather than abandoning it in favor of the dull small-town witchcraft scenario, since the tense opening two minutes prove to be the film's sole highlight. Director Cyril Frankel complained that, "They went a little potty by writing a semi-orgy scene at the end which I was not quite happy with." Screenwriter Kneale, on the other hand, griped, "There's nothing as funny as people imagining they're witches. It's naturally comic. I think a cleverer director would have faced that possibility of it all turning into laughs and he would have managed to make it really horrible, creepy and threatening."

Apart from Hammer's casting coup of corralling Academy Award winner Joan Fontaine for the lead role, *The Devil's Own* is noteworthy only because it turned out to be child actor Martin Stephens' (star of both *Village of the Damned* [1960] and *The Innocents* [1961]) final screen appearance.

The Devil's Own failed miserably at the box office, and Joan Fontaine (who had purchased the screen rights to Nora Lofts' [writing under the pseudonym Peter Curtis] novel herself in 1962 and eventually brought the story to Hammer's attention) reportedly was devastated by the movie's poor showing. With only a few sporadic TV appearances left ahead of her, *The Devil's Own* proved a poor finish to the illustrious actress' big-screen career.

With quotes from: *The Hammer Story*, by Marcus Hearn and Alan Barnes.

The Diabolical Dr. Satan see *The Awful Dr. Orlof*

The Diabolical Dr. Z (1966/67; Spain/France; b&w)

Original Language Title: *Miss Muerte*; Director: Henri Baum (Jess Franco); Producers: Serge Silberman, Michel Safra; Screenplay: Jesus Franco, Jean-Claude Carriere; Cinematographer: Alejandro Ulloa. Cast: Howard Vernon, Mabel Karr, Estella Bain, Guy Mairesse, Fernando Montes, Antonio J. Escribano.

NOTHING EVER STRIPPED YOUR NERVES SCREAMINGLY RAW LIKE... "THE DIABOLICAL DR. Z"—poster blurb

This Spanish/French co-production from the diabolical director Jess Franco (using the pseudonym "Henri Baum") may be that prolific Spanish filmmaker's finest film. Best known to English-speaking audiences for his 1970 version of *Count Dracula*, starring Christopher Lee, Klaus Kinski and Herbert Lom, Franco has been turning out the European equivalent of drive-in fare since 1959 (reportedly over 150 features to date!).

The Diabolical Dr. Z centers on Dr. Zimmer (Antonio Jiminez Escribano), who has developed a strange machine that blends acupuncture and hypnosis to transform people into obedient slaves. Dr. Z explains his reasoning like this: "Thanks to me, all the killers, all the abnormal, all the sadists, all the maniacs could be transmuted into wise and good persons." Unfortunately, the poor physician never has a chance to prove his theory, for he dies of a coronary induced by his ridicule at a scientific convention. Consequently, his rather cold daughter (Mabel Karr) decides to avenge his death by destroying the three prominent scientists whom she feels were responsible. The instrument of her vengeance is a gorgeous exotic dancer with two-inch fingernails that goes by the stage name of "Miss Death" (played by the strikingly beautiful Estella Blain). Miss Zimmer kidnaps Miss Death, subjects her to the mind-control machine, treats her remarkable fingernails with the "poison" curare, and sends her out to exact vengeance.

Running throughout this unique film is an undercurrent of Sadean sensuality, largely due to the presence of Estella Blain (who, sadly, committed suicide in 1981) and Franco's voyeuristic approach.

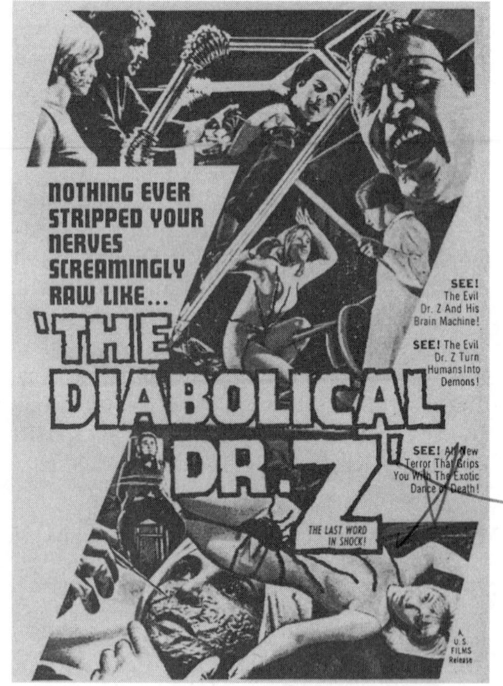

From the diabolical director Jess Franco comes *The Diabolical Dr. Z* (1966/67).

Blain's bizarrely erotic "dance of death" in the nightclub sequence is worth the price of admission alone. After being turned into an unwilling killer, she still manages to inspire flashes of sympathy, however, making the audience actually care about what happens to her — a rare occurrence in subsequent Franco films.

Franco peppers his odd-yet-clever scenario with striking set pieces, including a suspenseful chase through village back-alleys; a sudden and vicious murder-by-auto; some wince-inducing facial self-surgery; the surreal mind-control machine, with its spider-like mechanical "arms" and oversized acupuncture needles, at work; a brutally realistic fight sequence; and, of course, Miss Death's unforgettable nightclub performance (involving her writhing about on a huge, stylized spider web). Aided by cinematographer Alejandro Ulloa's atmospheric lighting and gorgeous black-and-white photography (transforming stately manor homes and village streets into ominous dens of shadow and darkness), Franco here updated 1960s Continental horror with a striking eroticism and deliciously bizarre ambiance. (And watch for the filmmaker himself in an amusing cameo role as a sleep-deprived police inspector.) *The Diabolical Dr. Z* is a remarkably polished achievement for an off-kilter filmmaker who, in a few short years, would come to be seen largely as a perverted hack, when seen at all.

Diary of a Madman (1963; United Artists)

Director: Reginald Le Borg; Producers: Robert E. Kent and Edward Small; Screenplay: Robert E. Kant (Story: Guy de Maupassant); Cinematographer: Arthur Ibbetson. Cast: Vincent Price, Nancy Kovack, Chris Warfield, Elaine Devry, Ian Wolfe, Mary Adams.

The most diabolical pages ever written become THE MOST TERRIFYING MOTION PICTURE EVER CREATED!— tagline

Diary of a Madman is a tastefully done, literary-minded chiller. In fact, it's too tasteful. Its stately, high-toned approach drains much of the life out of a ripping good story before recovering with a very satisfying third act.

In gaslight-era Paris, a crusading magistrate, Simon Cordier (Vincent Price), visits the cell of a man awaiting execution for murder. The prisoner pleads for mercy and contends the crimes were committed by an invisible alien entity which gained hypnotic control over him. Cordier dismisses the fanciful story, but over the course of the next few weeks realizes that the entity (which calls itself the Horla) is real and is now haunting him. Under the influence of the Horla, Cordier begins a dalliance with a gold-digging young artist's model, Odette (Nancy Kovack), and then kills her. The woman's husband (Chris Warfield) stands accused of the murder, and Cordier is assigned to preside over the man's trial.

The fundamental flaw with *Diary of a Madman* is that, in a misguided attempt to capture a wider audience, producers Robert Kent and Edward Small hedge their bets, clinging to the story's literary origins (it's loosely based on the short story *The Horla* by Guy de Maupassant) and soft-pedaling its more exploitative elements. For instance, after his visit with the condemned man, the film spends nearly 20 minutes establishing that the Horla is now pursuing Cordier, a fact that could

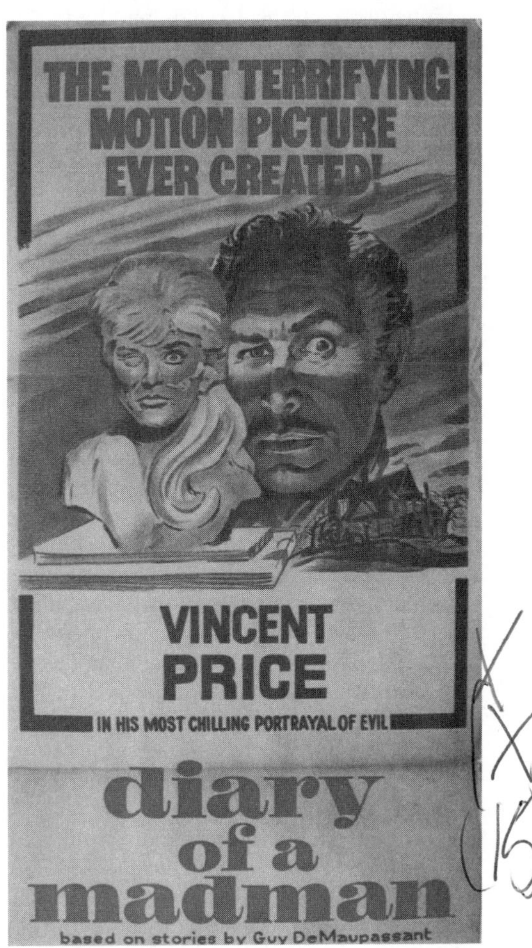

Australian daybill poster for *Diary of a Madman* (1963).

have been established with a single visual effects shot in the prisoner's cell. (Besides if it were not, there would be no movie!) While these scenes, with Cordier questioning his own sanity and finally realizing that the Horla exists, derive from the original story, de Maupassant's spellbinding yarn is structured as a mystery. By adding a flashback framing sequence and the expository scene with the condemned man, *Diary of a Madman* tips its hand immediately, rendering Maupassant's scenes painfully obvious and dull. Robert E. Kant's screenplay also takes pains to explain in copious detail the origin of the Horla and why it chose to persecute Cordier, elements de Maupassant wisely elected to leave unexplained or ambiguous. All this contributes to the movie's lethargic 96-minute running time.

Diary finally comes to life with Odette's murder, which is put over with surprising verve and intensity — a blank-faced, hypnotized Price striking with repeated, vicious stabs, then returning home, glassy-eyed, the murder-knife dripping blood as he ascends the stairs. From this scene onward the pace quickens and tension mounts, building to a fiery climax when Cordier tries to turn the tables and kill his invisible antagonist. *Diary of a Madman* would have been far more rewarding if it had gone for the jugular from the get-go.

If nothing else, however, the picture serves as a fine star vehicle for Price. He's onscreen nearly the entire film and given a wide range of compelling moments to play. Price is sympathetic in the otherwise forgettable early scenes as he struggles to come to grips with the existence of the Horla; endearing as a bereaved widower grasping at a chance for new romance; and menacing as the Horla's somnambulist-like murder-drone. This was the second of three films Price made for Admiral Pictures. Distributed through United Artists, *Diary* was preceded by *Tower of London* (1962) and followed by *Twice Told Tales* (1963), both of which remain better known than this often-overlooked production. In fact, *Diary of a Madman* may be better recognized as the title of a triple-platinum-selling album by former Black Sabbath vocalist Ozzy Osborne.

Among the supporting cast, Ian Wolfe and Mary Adams provide delightful turns as Cordier's befuddled but loyal servants, and Novack makes the most of her plum role as the two-timing Odette. The film also boasts handsome sets, designed by Victor A. Gangelin, who also decorated sets for director Roger Corman's Edgar Allan Poe movies. Unfortunately, beyond the lone bravura murder scene, director Reginald Le Borg's composition and shot selection remains pedestrian. Cinematographer Arthur Ibbetson over-lights everything, lending this Technicolor film a disappointingly flat look.

Despite its considerable demerits, *Diary of a Madman* boasts an exciting final half-hour and an under-appreciated performance by Price, which gives viewers something worth watching until the fun starts. Although hardly an unsung classic — more like a noble failure — it's worth a look for Price devotees.

Die! Die! My Darling (1965; Hammer/MGM; U.K.) Original Title: *Fanatic* (U.K.) Director: Silvio Narizzano; Producer: Anthony Hinds; Screenplay: Richard Matheson (from a novel by Anne Blaisdell); Cinematographer: Arthur Ibbetson. Cast: Tallulah Bankhead, Stephanie Powers, Peter Vaughan, Maurice Kaufmann, Yootha Joyce, Donald Sutherland.

The ultimate in stabbing suspense! — tagline

Hammer Films' series of *Psycho*-inspired black-and-white psychological thrillers, which began promisingly with the excellent *Scream of Fear* (1961), and continued with the worthwhile *Maniac* (1963) and *Paranoiac* (1964), veered toward creative oblivion with the lackluster *Nightmare* (1964) and *Hysteria* (1965). Clearly, a new direction was needed. *Die! Die! My Darling* tries to plot that course, but can't decide where it wants to go.

Screenwriter Richard Matheson stepped in to replace the written-out Jimmy Sangster, who had penned Hammer's first five pseudo *Psychos*, and positioned this film as an entry in the burgeoning "horror hag" sub-genre. To emphasize this connection, the film — called *Fanatic* in England — was renamed *Die! Die! My Darling* for U.S. audiences, a title that duplicated the meter of *Hush ... Hush, Sweet Charlotte* (1964). However, director Silvio Narizzano envisioned the film as a dark comedy. Indeed, the animated, cat-and-mouse opening credits suggest something on the order of Blake Edwards' *Pink Panther* films. Yet Matheson's story remains only occasionally and at best mildly funny. The cast's performances are similarly uneven — some played straight, others for laughs. Neither fish nor fowl, *Die! Die! My Darling* inevitably emerged muddled, but not without its merits.

One major strength is the enchanting perform-

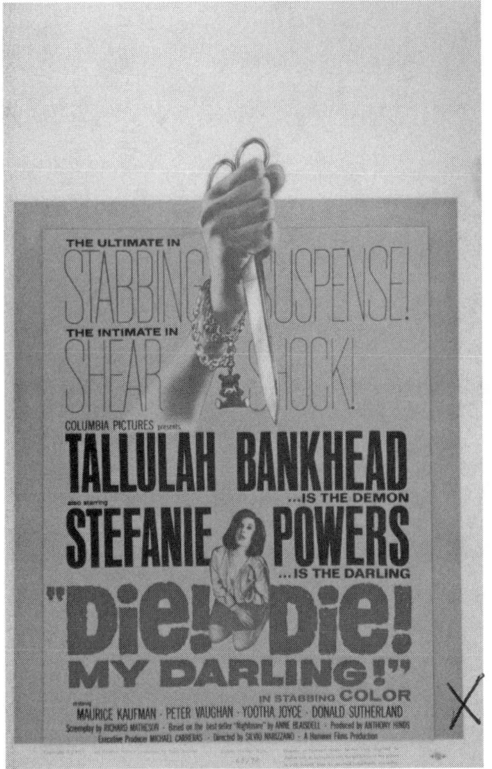

Window card highlighting the psycho-terrors of *Die! Die! My Darling!* (1965).

ance of Stephanie Powers, who stars as Patricia Carroll, a young woman paying a courtesy call on the family of her dead fiancé and finds becomes trapped by her would-be mother-in-law, Mrs. Trefoile (Tallulah Bankhead), a religious fanatic who wants to "cleanse" her of her worldly "sins" so the young woman can be reunited with her dead son when she dies. Mrs. Trefoil spends hours daily reading aloud from her Bible, and has removed all the mirrors from her house, since they promote vanity. She also demands that Patricia wipe the lipstick from her mouth, and refrain from wearing anything red.

The legendary Bankhead, making her final screen appearance, hisses and seethes with convincing lunacy. But Powers more than holds her own; likeable and relaxed in her early scenes, she becomes progressively frazzled as the story unfolds. Powers expertly handles several demanding physical bits of business, as Patricia endures all sorts of abuse at the hands of the crazy old woman and her equally creepy servants. Donald Sutherland contributes an amusing comedic performance as one of those servants, a simple-minded handyman, but his approach seems out of step with that of Powers and Bankhead, both of whom seem deadly serious.

The movie suffers from a slow first act, and its conclusion isn't entirely satisfying, but in between — during the lengthy battle of wills between Patricia and Mrs. Trefoile —*Die! Die! My Darling* proves engrossing and suspenseful. To further differentiate this film from its predecessors, *Die! Die! My Darling* was shot in color, and cinematographer Arthur Ibbetson's bold, glossy palate lends a distinctive visual style to the picture.

While not entirely successful, *Die! Die! My Darling* delivered the jolt of creative energy badly needed to jump-start Hammer's psycho-thriller series. If nothing else, it remains far preferable to either *Nightmare* or *Hysteria.* Hammer would fare even better next time out, when it returned to horror hagdom with *The Nanny* (1965).

Die, Monster, Die! (1965; Anglo Amalgamated/American-International) Director: Daniel Haller; Producers: Pat Green; Screenplay: Jerry Sohl (Story: H.P. Lovecraft); Cinematographer: Paul Beeson. Cast: Boris Karloff, Nick Adams, Freda Jackson, Suzan Farmer, Patrick Magee, Terence de Marney.

Can you face the ULTIMATE in DIABOLISM ... can you stand PURE TERROR?— tagline

Die, Monster, Die has a great deal going for it: an appealing cast headlined by the great Boris Karloff; a classic story by H.P. Lovecraft; handsomely appointed sets; atmospheric cinematography. Unfortunately, the picture squanders most of those assets and winds up as something less than the sum of its parts— tepid, plodding and mediocre.

Young American Steven Reinhart (Nick Adams) travels to a remote English estate to meet the family of his girlfriend, Susan (Suzan Farmer). Susan's father, Nahum (Karloff), tries to run him off, while her mother, Letitia (Freda Jackson), begs Steven to take Susan away immediately. Letitia's maid has disappeared, and she's afraid her husband may be going insane. After much snooping around (and protracted exposition), Steven and Susan discover that Nahum is keeping a strange, glowing meteorite in the basement. Radiation from the meteor is turning the estate's plants and animals into bizarre mutations and having a disturbing effect on Nahum.

Although Jerry Sohl based his screenplay on Lovecraft's short story "The Colour Out of

Die, Monster, Die! **(1965): Boris Karloff (or, at this point, his special effects dummy stand-in) does just that.**

Space," there's nothing very Lovecraftian about this scenario. Sohl retains little beyond the basic premise of a radioactive meteor that lands in a secluded farmstead. In most aspects, from its introduction of a romantic subplot to its house-burning finale, Sohl's screenplay owes more to Roger Corman's Edgar Allan Poe movies than to its literary source. Maybe the screenwriter deserves a mulligan here, considering that Lovecraft's work seldom translates well to the screen (perhaps because so much of its power arises from the author's brilliant wordcraft). Still, it's disappointing that Sohl begins with a story as intense and unnerving as "The Colour Out of Space" and winds up with something this limp and predictable, a movie that plays like a worn-out retread of Corman's *House of Usher*.

Die, Monster, Die marked the directorial debut of former production designer Daniel Haller. Predictably, Haller takes full advantage of Colin Southcott's beautifully crafted and decorated sets, as well as Paul Beeson's moody cinematography. But Haller allows the narrative to limp along, especially during the picture's overlong opening act, without generating credible tension or suspense. By the time the meteor is discovered and things actually start to happen, nearly 50 of the film's 80 minutes have elapsed. Then, just when it seems *Die, Monster, Die* may be redeemed with a rousing finale, shoddy, laughable visual and makeup effects undercut its credibility. Especially damaging is the emergence of a radioactive monster that looks like a stunt man with his head wrapped in aluminum foil.

Haller also proved ineffective at eliciting a committed performance from his star. Karloff, who spends most of his limited screen time in a wheelchair, doesn't seem particularly engaged here. This is a cookie-cutter performance, full of almost sing-song line readings and lacking the sense of inner life that mark the actor's best work. While he does nothing to damage the film, Karloff doesn't significantly help it, either. The same can be said for his likable co-stars, including Nick Adams and Hammer Films veterans Freda Jackson and Suzan Farmer. They seem somewhat more invested in *Die, Monster, Die* than Karloff, but their since their roles are simple stereotypes there's not much they can do to inject any degree of dramatic gravitas.

Haller took another swing at Lovecraft (and missed again) with *The Dunwich Horror* (1969) before retreating to television, where he enjoyed a long and productive career on shows like *Ironside, Kojak* and *The Fall Guy*. In retrospect, considering all the resources available, *Die, Monster, Die* looks like a missed opportunity.

Dimensions in Death see *Castle of Blood*

Dinosaurus! (1960; Universal) Director: Irvin S. Yeaworth, Jr.; Producers: Jack H. Harris and Irvin S. Yeaworth, Jr.; Screenplay: Dan E. Weisburd and Jean Yeaworth (from an idea by Jack H. Harris); Cinematographer: Stanley Cortez. Cast: Ward Ramsey, Paul Lukather, Kristina Hanson, Alan Roberts, Fred Engelberg, Gregg Martel.

The most amazing adventure since the beginning of time!—trailer

For the 13-and-under crowd, or even those young-at-hearts among us, *Dinosaurus!* offers everything one could want in a giant monster movie: an orphaned boy protagonist with an evil stepfather (who ultimately gets his comeuppance); a "good" monster (brontosaurus) battling a "bad" one (tyrannosaurus); a friendly fatherly hero and his motherly girlfriend; a comical caveman who befriends the boy (and even teaches him to ride the bronto's back!); and a climactic triumphant battle between machine and monster.

Monster vs. machine in *Dinosaurus!* (1960).

Shot in five weeks (excluding the stop-motion effects) on location at St. Croix in the Virgin Islands (with studio work done in Hollywood) for $450,000, *Dinosaurus!* tells the tale of harbor demolition work on a small Caribbean island dislodging two frozen dinosaurs (a brontosaurus and tyrannosaurus rex), along with a Neanderthal caveman. Brought to shore, the preserved bodies quickly thaw, and a lightning strike restores them to life, leading to all manner of menace as the island inhabitants try to avoid being eaten, ultimately taking refuge in an old ruined fortress.

This straightforward *Boys Own*-style monster movie is aimed squarely at the kids, with the villain being thoroughly villainous, the hero completely heroic, and the fish-out-of-water caveman cavorting in near-slapstick fashion (with gags involving a flushing toilet and even a pie in the face!). Such humor may tickle the average prepubescent funny bone, but it becomes rather tedious for the older crowd. "*Dinosaurus!* did have a humorous central portion," related producer Jack H. Harris. "[Director] Irvin Yeaworth and his [screenwriter] wife, Jean, came up with that. I was on the fence about it, but it tickled me so much that I gave in.... Looking back, it would have been better if we didn't do it." Indeed.

There *are* moments of horror in this children's fantasy, however. Many of the dinosaur scenes take place at night, enhancing the fright factor, including a sequence in which the tyrannosaur carries off a screaming man in his claws and later viciously attacks a bus (which features a shot, from inside the vehicle, of the Rex peering in that obviously inspired Spielberg for his *Jurassic Park*).

The dino models were built by Marcel Delgado, the man who crafted the creations seen in Willis O'Brien's *The Lost World* (1925) and *King Kong* (1933). While they fail to live up to the marauding monsters of those earlier classics (looking rather ungainly in comparison), they're serviceable enough. The animation, executed by Wah Chang and Gene Warren (who worked on *The Time Machine* this same year), though lacking the unique personality of an O'Brien or even Ray Harryhausen creation, again proves passable.

The (human) leads perform their undemanding roles adequately, and even Alan Roberts, as the precocious boy Julio, rates fairly low on the annoyance meter. Producer Harris originally planned to star Steve McQueen as the hero in *Dinosaurus!*, "but he was such a royal pain [on Harris' earlier *The Blob*] and I hated him so much I didn't use him." Of course, after McQueen became a huge star, Harris regretted this decision to no end. (In 1964 Harris paired *Dinosaurs!* with *The Blob* for a reissue double-bill; had McQueen made *Dinosaurus!*, it could have been a huge McQueen-double-feature money-spinner.)

With quotes from: *Interviews with B Science Fiction and Horror Movie Makers*, by Tom Weaver.

Dr. Blood's Coffin (1961; United Artists; U.K.) Director: Sidney J. Furie; Producer: Gene Fowler; Story and screenplay: Nathan Juran (as Jerry Juran) (Adaptation: James Kelly, Pete Miller); Cinematographer: Stephen Dade. Cast: Kieron Moore, Hazel Court, Ian Hunter, Kenneth J. Warren.

We dare you to look into ... Dr. Blood's Coffin!—tagline

Young doctor Peter Blood (Kieron Moore) returns from medical school to the tiny British village of his youth and embarks on a series of secret experiments aimed at reviving the dead. He's able to fool his father, Dr. Robert Blood (Ian Hunter), and young widowed nurse Linda (Hazel Court), but when villagers begin to go missing, local police investigate. Peter assists in the investigation and throws authorities off track, but Linda grows suspicious and eventually discovers him harvesting a heart from one of his victims. Indignant that she fails to appreciate the value of his brilliant research, Peter decides to resurrect the young widow's late husband, with catastrophic consequences.

Dr. Blood's Coffin bumps along without making much of an impact until its final 20 minutes or so, when this disappointingly timid chiller finally delivers on its blood-and-thunder title. During the film's earliest moments, the face of the doctor performing these brutal (but mostly unseen) medical procedures remains hidden, suggesting that the misanthropic medical man might or might not be Peter—but then, after about a half-hour of cat-and-mouse camera business, this element is inexplicably abandoned and Peter is clearly revealed as the villain. From that point forward, the picture devotes much screen time to Peter rushing back and forth between the abandoned mine, where he has built a makeshift laboratory (and hidden his human guinea pigs), and the village, where he is trying to woo Linda. Peter's misguided attempt to impress Linda by reviving her husband fails horribly. His subject, after rotting in the grave for an entire year, is a grotesque, zombie-like specimen. "You haven't brought Steve Parker back to life," Linda cries. "that's something out of Hell!"

That late-arriving spellbinder aside, Nathan Juran's screenplay offers too few thrills and too much heavy-handed moralizing ("You want me to kneel down to a new god: science," Linda says—while standing in front of a crucifix, no less). Sidney Furie, who directed this vapid, predictable low-budget picture, went on to direct vapid, predictable big-budget pictures such as *Superman IV: The Quest for Peace* (1987) and the *Iron Eagle* series. Like those later films, *Dr. Blood's Coffin* is slick and professional, but devoid of nuance or personality. It's cookie-cutter filmmaking.

For much of its running time, the film's only real selling point is a wonderful performance by Hazel Court. As Linda, she has some terrific moments—describing the auto accident that killed her husband, playfully ribbing Peter about his driving, eventually growing suspicious of her new beau. *Dr. Blood's Coffin* showcases the actress' talents better than any picture other than Roger Corman's *Masque of the Red Death* (1964). Keiron Moore is acceptable but, compared to Court, flat and one-dimensional in the title role. The rest of the cast, including Ian Hunter as Peter's father and Kenneth J. Warren as a police sergeant, is equally forgettable. But, if only for Court's fine work (and for a humdinger of a finale), *Dr. Blood's Coffin* remains worth a look.

A reanimated corpse (Paul Stockman) attacks Dr. Peter Blood (Kieron Moore) in *Doctor Blood's Coffin* (1961).

Doctor from Seven Dials see *Corridors of Blood*

see *Corridors of Blood*

Dr. Jekyll's Mistress see *Dr. Orloff's Monster*

Doctor of Doom (1962/65; Cinematografica Calderon S.A./Young America Productions; Mexico; b&w) Original Language Title: *Las Luchadoras vs. el Médico Asesino*; Alternate Title: *Rock 'n' Roll Wrestling Women vs. the Aztec Ape* (Rhino Video altered reissue version); Director: Rene Cardona; Manuel San Fernando (English language version); Producer: William (Guillermo) Calderon Stell, K. Gordon Murray (English version); Screenplay: Alfred (Alfredo) Salazar; Cinematographer: Henry (Enrique) Wallace. Cast: Lorena Velazquez, Armand Silvestre, Elizabeth Campbell, Robert Canedo, Sonia Infante, Chucho Salinas.

"This case is enough to make a madman sane!"
—Detective Tommy

And so's the movie. The first of the Female Mexican Wrestler movies to come north of the Border in the 1960s (released Stateside in 1965), *Doctor of Doom* centers on a mad doctor (Roberto Canedo) who hides his identity beneath Ku Klux Klan-style hood and robes(!), and is obsessed with transplanting brains. To this end he sends out Gomar (Gerardo Zepeda), a man with the brain of a gorilla who wears a bullet-proof metal suit(!!), to kidnap women for his experiments. When the doctor chooses as his next 'donor' the sister of a professional female wrestler named Gloria Venus (Lorena Velazquez), Gloria and her partner in the ring, the Golden Ruby (Elizabeth Campbell), join up with a pair of police detectives (Armando Silvestre, Chucho Salinas) to stop the madman and his pet gorilla-man.

Whew! *Doctor of Doom* comes off more like a boffo episode of the old *Superman* TV show than a real movie. The mad doctor behaves like a deranged comic-book crime-lord, operating out of a secret lair (complete with a "room of death"—a chamber with moving, spiked walls), and sending out his gang of thugs to do his bidding (and augment Gomar's activities). The two policeman "heroes" even wear radio wristwatches straight out of *Dick Tracy*! (In a charming role reversal, the wrestling heroines must rescue these "heroes" from said "room of death.") Throw in a handful of ringside scenes (which feature obvious—and chunky—*real* female wrestler doubles stepping in for Our Battling Beauties), some serial-like fisticuffs, bargain basement sets, ludicrously dubbed dialogue, and a secret identity mystery that's no mystery at all (there's only *one possible suspect*!), and *Doctor of Doom* becomes a naively charming guilty favorite among Mexican Wrestling Horror Movie aficionados.

Director Rene Cardona (unofficially) remade this feature in 1968 as the nudity-and-gore-filled exploitationer *Night of the Bloody Apes*. Ironically, Armando Silvestre, who stars as the heroic detective Mike Henderson in *Doctor of Doom*, took on the transplant-happy mad doctor role in *Bloody Apes*.

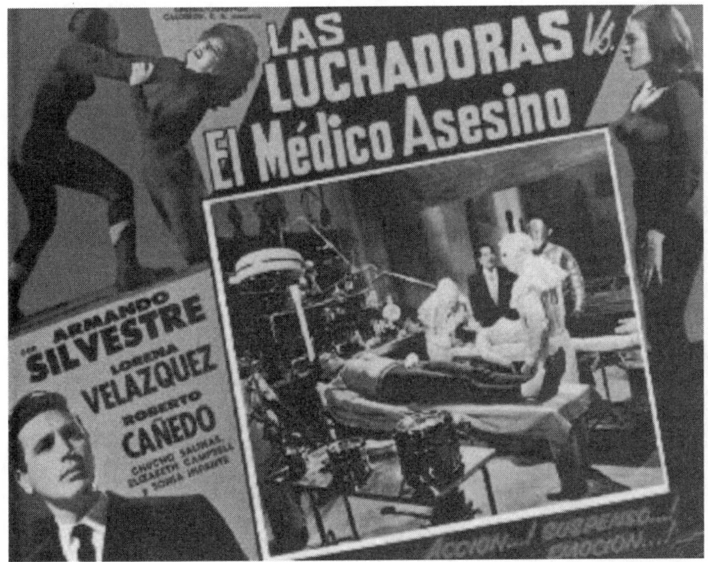

The 1962 Mexican-wrestling-women-meet-the-monsters feature *Las luchadoras vs. el medico asesino* became *Doctor of Doom* when dubbed into English in 1965 (U.S. lobby card for Spanish-speaking theaters).

Dr. Orloff's Monster (1964; Cooperativa Cinematografica/Leo Films Spain; b&w) Alternate Titles: *Brides of Dr. Jekyll, Dr. Jekyll's Mistress, Mistresses of Dr. Jekyll, The Secret of Dr. Orloff*, Original Language Title: *El Secreto del Dr. Orloff*; Director: John Frank (Jess/Jesus Franco); Screenplay: Nick Frank (Ricardo Franco); Cinematographer: Alfonse Niell. Cast: Agnes Spaak, Joseph Raven (Jose Rubio), Pearl (Perla) Cristal, Patrick Long, Mike Arnold (Marcello Arroita-Jauregui), Daniel Plummer (Blumer), Hugh White (Hugo Blanco).

"You hold the key to the greatest scientific secret of our time."—Dr. Orloff

A sequel in name only to Jess Franco's commercially successful *The Awful Dr. Orlof* (1962), *Dr. Orloff's Monster* (with "Orloff" mysteriously acquiring a second "f") centers on Professor Fisherman (Marcello Arroita-Jauregui), a castle-dwelling scientist who has developed the means to control people via sound waves. (The only tenuous tie to the earlier film comes when an investigating inspector says of the case: "I'm reminded of the work of Dr. Orloff; he experimented with a robot which responded to ultrasonics.") Twenty years ago Fisherman caught his wife cheating on him with his own brother, Andros (Hugo Blanco). The professor murdered Andros and transformed him into a robot-like zombie, whom he now sends out to strangle nightclub singers (an apparent fetish of Fisherman's). The professor's niece Melissa (Agnes Spaak), the zombie's daughter, arrives for a visit and, along with her newfound cabdriver boyfriend, starts to unravel the mystery. When Fisherman orders his zombie to kill the girl, vestiges of paternal feelings arise in the walking automaton, and the monster turns on its maker. (But just how Andros could recognize the now-grown daughter that he had never seen—he 'died' just after she was born—remains a mystery only the screenwriter, the late Ricardo Franco [the director's nephew], could have answered.)

While *The Awful Dr. Orlof* offered some impressive castle settings and isolated moments of creepiness, this 'sequel' offers some impressive castle settings. Moments of creepiness need not apply. Instead, it's a steady flow of tedium from beginning to end (starting with the opening, which consists of interminable slow zooms into staring faces as Fisherman recalls his wife's infidelity—sort of a Franco Does Bergman sequence). Franco spends far too much time in a dreary jazz club (which he returns to *three more times*). The jazz-loving 'maestro' himself can be seen, wearing his trademark dark glasses, tickling the ivories in one of these never-ending scenes.

The film's slow pace isn't helped by dull dialogue sequences, long stretches where absolutely nothing happens, and unfunny comic relief characters (the cracked castle caretaker and a supercilious police inspector). The robotic zombie Andros moves at about the same pace as the film, and the sketchy makeup makes him look more like a man with a slight case of eczema than a walking corpse. Hugo Blanco does what he can with the role, even eliciting sympathy at times, such as when he escapes the castle and stands forlornly over his own "grave" (one of the few effective moments in the film). The mind-controlled, death-dealing monster/person theme turned up again in Franco's next film, the far superior *Diabolical Dr. Z* (1965).

Dr. Terror's Gallery of Horrors (1967; American General) Alternate Titles: *The Blood Suckers, Gallery of Horror, Return from the Past* (TV). Director: David L. Hewitt; Producers: David L. Hewitt, Ray Dorn; Screenplay: David Prentis (David L. Hewitt), Gary R. Heacock (original stories by Russ Jones); Cinematography: Austin McKinney. Cast: Lon Chaney, John Car-

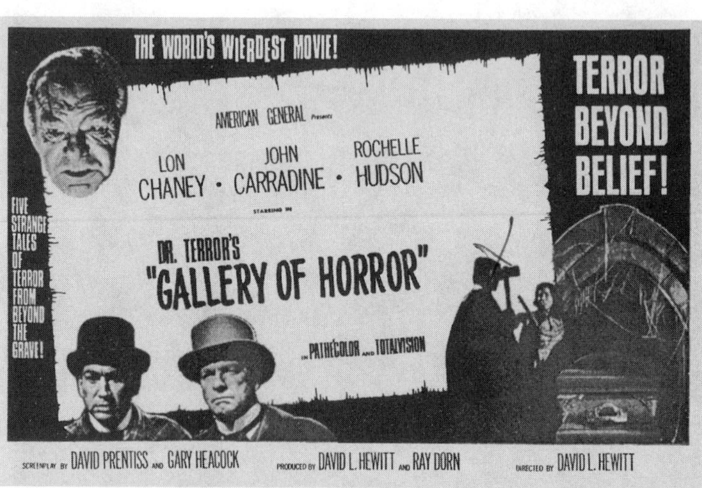

Ad for the amateurish anthology *Dr. Terror's Gallery of Horror* (1967)—not to be confused with the far superior *Dr. Terror's* House *of Horrors* (1965).

radine, Rochelle Hudson, Roger Gentry, Ron Doyle, Karen Joy.

SEE STRANGE TERRORS BEYOND BELIEF
—poster

John Carradine once cited *Billy the Kid vs. Dracula* (1966) as the worst movie he ever made. He must have forgotten about *Dr. Terror's Gallery of Horrors.*

Not to be confused with the superior Amicus anthology film *Dr. Terrors* House *of Horrors* (which undoubtedly the distributors of this pathetic portmanteau intended), *Dr. Terror's* Gallery *of Horrors* features five short tales of the supernatural, each introduced by on-screen narrator Carradine, and each offering (silly or predictable—or both) twist endings.

The first tale, "The Witch's Clock," has a young couple buy a castle in Massachusetts(!) and find a cursed clock with the power to raise the dead (Carradine appears in this one as a revived 17th century warlock). The second segment, "King Vampire," follows two 19th century police inspectors as they try to stop a vampire killer. In "The Monster Raid," a researcher returns from the grave thanks to a special "formula" to revenge himself on his cheating wife and murderous colleague. Story four, "The Spark of Life," stars Lon Chaney as a doctor delving into the power of electricity whose experiments revive a flabby, middle-aged executed murderer. The final tale, "Count Alucard," becomes a micro-retelling of *Dracula*, with Mr. Harker arriving at the Count's castle to conclude the deal on Carfax Abbey, only to run afoul of a vampiress and the Count himself.

Statically shot on cheap plywood sets constructed on a cramped soundstage (with "exteriors" consisting of castle matte shots and coach-driving footage stolen from the Roger Corman Poe films *House of Usher*, *The Pit and the Pendulum* and *The Raven*), *Gallery* looks more like a collection of high-school skits than a feature film. The acting matches the sets in amateurish awfulness, though both Carradine and Chaney give it the old college try, with Chaney (who reportedly earned $1500 for his half-day's work) in particular plowing his way through his underwritten role like a thespian bull in a cinematic china shop. Sadly, this proved to be the ailing horror star's final speaking part in a horror movie.

Carradine's poorly-written, rambling monologues leading into the poorly-written, rambling stories were actually an afterthought. When director-producer-writer David L. Hewitt (*The Wizard of Mars* [1965], *The Mighty Gorga* [1969]) realized his script was too short, he contracted his friend and associate Gary R. Heacock to write intros for each story. "They told me, 'Make 'em as long as you *can*!'" laughed Heacock to interviewer Tom Weaver. "So if John Carradine's introductions to the different scenarios seem a little bit wordy—well, they were, because we had to have [say] 80 minutes, or whatever the running time was, and there just simply wasn't enough in the scenarios." For his long-winded efforts, Carradine received $3,000 of the film's reported $20,000 budget.

Those involved with the wretched project held little illusions about it. Interviewed by Jack Gourlay, co-star Ron Doyle, who appeared in three of the five segments, labeled the film "a piece of shit—pretty disastrous." Another actor, Ron Brogan (from the "King Vampire" story) opined (again to Gourlay), "It was pretty much on the camp side—phony thing.... [W]e didn't go back and correct mistakes as there was no time for retakes."

At least the actors occasionally had some fun with the film (unlike the hapless viewer), as recounted by Doyle: "We were doing a take, and I was supposed to look under a sheet at this dead body. Lon [Chaney] got underneath the sheet and I didn't know it. When I pulled it back, Lon yelled 'Aaarrr' and scared the hell out of me!" That makes *one* person scared by *Dr. Terror's Gallery of* Horridness.

Dr. Terror's House of Horrors (1965; Amicus; U.K.) Director: Freddie Francis; Producers: Milton Subtosky and Max J. Rosenberg; Screenplay: Milton Subotsky; Cinematographer: Alan Hume. Cast: Peter Cushing, Christopher Lee, Michael Gough, Neil McCallum, Roy Castle, Donald Sutherland, Bernard Lee.

SUSPENSE THAT CLAWS AT EVERY FIBER OF BODY AND SOUL!—poster blurb

Dr. Terror's House of Horrors proved to be the first (though not the best) in a long line of Amicus anthology films, which included *Torture Garden* (1967), *The House that Dripped Blood* (1971), *Tales from the Crypt* (1972), *Asylum* (1972), *The Vault of Horror* (1973) and *From Beyond the Grave* (1973). Headed by frequent scriptwriter Milton Subotsky and his partner Max J. Rosenberg, Amicus proved to be Hammer's biggest competitor in the British horror arena of the 1960s.

Amicus' first anthology feature was originally going to be shot in 1962 in black and white with financial backing from Columbia Pictures, but Columbia dropped out when they deemed it too expensive (at a mere $94,000!). It took another two years to obtain alternate financing for the (now-color) project, and even after production finally got underway, the difficult dollar (or, more accurately, problematic pound) reared its ugly head yet again. After two weeks of shooting, the production nearly shut down when part of the American financing was withdrawn (British co-financier Joe Vegoda ponied up the extra cash needed).

Dr. Terror's House of Horrors relates five tales of the supernatural, tying the disparate stories together via Dr. Schreck (Peter Cushing), a mysterious "doctor of metaphysics" who, with a deck of tarot cards, tells the futures of the five men sharing his train compartment. (Subotsky had originally written the five stories back in 1948 as scripts for a planned TV series that never materialized.) The first episode, entitled "Werewolf," is a rather muddled lycanthrope tale (complete with poorly-lit manor house, skulking servants and easily whipped-up clip of silver bullets); while the second yarn, called "Creeping Vine," has an intelligent mobile plant inexplicably cut phone wires, put out fires, strangle people and trap a family inside their house. The third tale, named "Voodoo," details what happens when a jazz musician (Roy Castle) steals the "sacred music of the great god Damballah." The fourth (and best) segment has pompous art critic Franklin Marsh (Christopher Lee) humiliated by artist Eric Landor (Michael Gough). The spiteful critic then runs down Landor with his car, causing the artist to lose his hand. After the despondent Landor commits suicide, his disembodied hand haunts Marsh, leading to the critic's demise in a bit of poetic justice. In the fifth and final story, Donald Sutherland plays a small-town doctor whose new French bride turns out to be a vampire. As the piece de resistance, the film ends with the train pulling into the station. Schreck has disappeared and the platform is dark and deserted. A newspaper wafts down to the confused travelers which reads "5 dead in train wreck." They see the figure of Dr. Schreck across the platform, but his gaunt bearded countenance has transformed into that of a grinning skull. The Grim Reaper then leads his five "guests" away.

Peter Cushing as the mysterious Dr. Schreck (which translates as "Dr. Terror") in *Dr. Terror's House of Horrors* (1965), the first in a long line of Amicus anthologies.

"I like anthology films," opined Subotsky, "because I feel that in SF and horror the short story format works better than either the novel or novelette." Subotsky's preference notwithstanding, the downside of the anthology format is that there's very little time to develop characters or build and sustain mood—two key components in successful horror films. It's very difficult to fashion a believable milieu or create intriguing characters in less than 30 minutes. When given only about fifteen minutes, as with most of *Dr. Terror's* segments, it's nearly impossible. In *Dr. Terror's*, the fantastical notions are too abrupt as characters seemingly take these unlikely happenings as a matter of course (since there's no time for any doubt), allowing for no real credibility.

Fortunately, Subotsky and Rosenberg gathered together a cadre of fine actors who managed to invest some realism in their somewhat stereotypical roles. Peter Cushing, Christopher Lee, Michael Gough, Neil McCallum and Donald Sutherland in particular all bring a believable quality to the unbelievable situations.

In talking of his various anthology movies, director Freddie Francis explained that "my approach to these films is that no one is really going to believe that these sort of things happen ... so I believe that though people may find it horrid for a while, they find it horrid in a giggly sort of way." Of all the segments, "Voodoo" possesses the most of this "giggly" quality. "To my mind," admitted Francis, "it was a fun thing, obviously not to be taken seriously." So while "Voodoo" remains a musically and comedically effective segment (thanks largely to Roy Castle's amiable attitude and Bob Hope-style asides), it fails to generate any real scares. Of the four other segments, only the "Disembodied Hand" episode really works well. "Werewolf" is rather dull, while the "Creeping Vine" remains ridiculously unconvincing, with a poor build-up leading to a weak (anti)climax. Despite the ever-quirky presence of a young Donald Sutherland (in only his third film), "Vampire" also fails to satisfy thanks to its perfunctory plotting and all-too-ready staking (though it does possess an unexpected and amusing final twist). Fortunately, the film's wrap-around is a creepy, suspenseful, well-constructed story unto itself, with the passengers becoming more and more uneasy as Dr. Schreck relates their horrific fates one by one. Of the omnibus format, Francis felt, "The only thing one has to do is to make sure you have a good link. And I think the link has to be able to stand on its own. I think the link we had with Peter Cushing in *Dr. Terror's* was one of the best." Indeed it was.

Thanks to its clever connecting device, the superbly acted and genuinely scary "Disembodied Hand" segment and (to a lesser extent) the flawed but still entertaining "Voodoo" story, *Dr. Terror's House of Horrors* remains a fairly solid entry in the notoriously uneven Anthology subset.

With quotes from: "The Vault of Subotsky," by Philip Nutman, *Fangoria* 32, 1983; *Drums of Terror: Voodoo in the Cinema*, by Bryan Senn.

Dracula Has Risen from the Grave (1968/69; Hammer/Warner Bros.; U.K.)

Director: Freddie Francis; Producer: Aida Young; Screenplay: Anthony Hinds (as John Elder); Cinematographer: Arthur Grant. Cast: Christopher Lee, Rupert Davies, Veronica Carlson, Barry Andrews, Barbara Ewing, Ewan Hooper, Michael Ripper.

You just can't keep a good man down.
—tagline

Perhaps because it was the first entry in Hammer Films' long-running Dracula series not directed by the great Terence Fisher, or maybe due to a controversial plot element, or possibly as a result of its campy advertising campaign, *Dracula Has Risen from the Grave* is seldom celebrated by critics or fans. Yet, this breathtakingly designed and beautifully photographed picture, packed with endearing characters and peppered with harrowing suspense sequences, stands as one of Hammer Films' most underrated productions.

Even though Dracula has been dead for 10 years, the tiny village at the foot of the mountain where the Count once lived remains figuratively and literally in the shadow of Castle Dracula. When Monsignor Mueller (Rupert Davies) arrives to inspect the local church, he finds the town's priest (Ewan Hooper) has retreated into alcoholism and despair, shattered by Dracula's former reign of terror. To assuage the villagers' fears, the Monsignor forces the priest to assist him with an exorcism of Castle Dracula. But the troubled cleric isn't up to the task and inadvertently revives the Count from the frozen river into which the vampire plunged at the conclusion of *Dracula, Prince of Darkness* (1966). The enraged Dracula claims the faithless priest as his would-

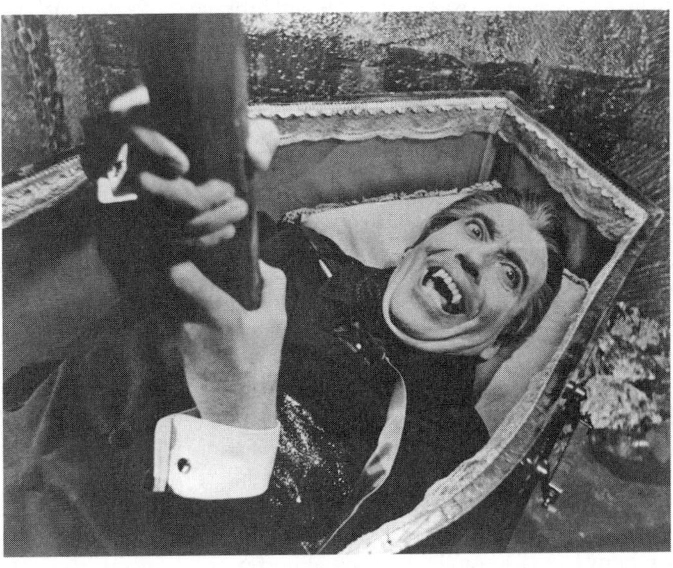

Despite the stake, Christopher Lee rises from the grave yet again in *Dracula Has Risen from the Grave* (1969).

be Renfield and sets out to take revenge on the Monsignor for "desecrating" his ancestral home and barring its doors with a giant cross.

Dracula pursues Mueller to his hometown of Keinenburg then plots to kill the bishop and take his lovely niece, Maria (Veronica Carlson), as a vampire "bride." Maria's beau, a free-thinking student named Paul (Barry Andrews), tries to destroy Dracula and rescue Maria, and in the film's most memorable scene, drives a stake into the Count's heart as he sleeps in his coffin. But since Paul is an atheist, he is unable to invoke Christ through prayer to sanctify his actions. So instead of dying, Dracula simply pulls the stake out of his chest.

Many viewers object to this sequence since it seems, on the surface, to violate the established "rules" of vampirism. But the idea that faith is essential to vanquish the undead had been a core concept of Fisher's Dracula films, dating all the way back to *Horror of Dracula* (1958). (After all, it's Van Helsing's faith that transforms two candlesticks into a makeshift cross during that film's finale.) Consistently, Fisher had framed the battle with the forces of darkness as a contest between Christian good and Satanic evil. In *Has Risen*, for Maria to be saved, either Paul must become a believer or else Dracula's henchman, the former clergyman, must recover his faith.

Has Risen ranks among the most satisfying directorial efforts from Freddie Francis, who joined the project after Fisher (who was originally slated to helm this picture) was hit by a car and broke a leg. Francis, himself an Oscar-winning cinematographer, works with director of photography Arthur Grant to maximize the impact of Bernard Robinson's imaginative sets, particularly the *Caligari*-like rooftops and balconies of Keinenburg, and the dank cellar of an inn, where Paul stakes Dracula. Francis takes painterly care with these meticulously designed sets and with Grant's atmospheric lighting (sickly greens, icy blues, eerie yellows). He also keeps the pace brisk and elicits uniformly naturalistic and likable performances from his cast.

Andrews and Carlson may be the most endearing pair of romantic leads of any Hammer chiller. Davies' self-assured, unflappable Monsignor makes a fitting foil for Lee's imperious, relentless Dracula. Hooper excels as the weak-willed, besotted priest. All the actors benefit from one of Anthony Hinds' most vivid scripts, almost overstuffed with well-drawn characters. Even the film's minor roles—such as Michael Ripper's fatherly innkeeper and Barbara Ewing's saucy barmaid—seem authentic and engender sympathy. Unfortunately, as usual, Dracula is kept off-screen for long stretches. Still, *Has Risen* makes far better use of the character than *Prince of Darkness* (1966)—at least Lee has dialogue in this one!

Unfortunately, this carefully crafted, thoughtful film was promoted with an incongruously tongue-in-cheek ad campaign during its initial American release. For instance, one movie poster showed a close-up of a woman's neck with two strategically placed Band-Aids. "*Dracula Has Risen from the Grave* ... obviously," went the tagline. Such posters erroneously suggested a spoof along the lines of Roman Polanski's *The Fearless Vampire Killers* (1966), which may have confused audiences and critics.

Hammer's Dracula movies declined sharply after *Has Risen*. Next up was the mediocre *Scars of Dracula* (1970), directed by Roy Ward Baker. Then Hammer tried shifting the series to a contemporary setting with disastrous results. Director Alan Gibson's *Dracula A.D. 1972* (1972) remains a notorious debacle. The studio reunited Lee and Peter Cushing for Gibson's *Count Dracula and His Vampire Brides* (aka *The Satanic Rites of Dracula*), but the results proved so dismal that afterward Lee abandoned the Dracula role permanently. It took four years for *Satanic Rites*, released in England in 1974, to find an American distributor. Hammer's ignominious final Dracula entry, the offbeat Dracula-kung fu hybrid *The Seven Brothers Meet Dracula* (aka *The Legend of the Seven Golden Vampires*, 1974), was an ill-fated co-production with Hong Kong's Shaw Brothers.

It's only wishful thinking, of course, but fans might prefer to simply pretend that the series ended with *Has Risen*. It would have been a far more fitting conclusion to what had been, up to that point, the studio's best and most beloved collection of films.

Dracula, Prince of Darkness (1966; Hammer/20th Century–Fox; U.K.) Director: Terence Fisher; Producer: Anthony Nelson Keys; Screenplay: Jimmy Sangster (as John Sansom), from a story by Anthony Hinds (as John Elder), based on characters created by Bram Stoker; Cinematographer: Michael Reed. Cast: Christopher Lee, Barbara Shelley, Andrew Keir, Francis Matthews, Suzan Farmer, Charles Tingwell, Thorley Walters, Philip Latham.

Bloodthirsty Vampire Lives Again!—tagline

The vampirized Helen (Barbara Shelley) is about to get the point—at the hands of stake-wielding monks—in *Dracula, Prince of Darkness* (1966) (American lobby card).

Almost anything would have paled in comparison to the nearly perfect *Horror of Dracula* (1958) and *Brides of Dracula* (1960), but Hammer Films' third Dracula entry seems unaccountably anemic. All the pieces for another superb shocker are present, but screenwriter Jimmy Sangster and director Terence Fisher appear unable to assemble them properly. Consequently, *Dracula, Prince of Darkness* adds up to less than the sum of its parts.

Four English tourists ignore the stern advice of Father Sandor (Andrew Keir), an eccentric rifle-toting Carpathian monk, and end up stranded in the forest, forced to spend the night at Castle Dracula. Dracula has been dead for 10 years (since being reduced to ashes by Van Helsing at the end of *Horror*), but his faithful servant Klove (Philip Latham) has preserved the Count's dusty remains in a box. During the night, Klove kills one of the travelers (Charles Tingwell) and uses his blood to revive Dracula (Christopher Lee) from the dead. (After spreading the remains into a coffin, Klove hangs the victim upside down and slashes his throat; blood gushes onto Dracula's ashes and *voila*—rehydrated vampire.) Dracula takes the dead man's wife (Barbara Shelley) as his first victim, and she joins him as a vampire "bride." The other two travelers (Francis Matthews and Suzan Farmer) flee to the nearby monastery, where Father Sandor takes them in and formulates plans to destroy Dracula. Before Sandor can make a move, however, Dracula strikes—taking hypnotic control of a weak-minded scribe (Thorley Walters) and kidnapping the remaining English woman. This sets up a climactic race to the rescue.

With the studio's best director, an accomplished (if inconsistent) screenwriter, a fine cast (including Lee as Dracula), composer James Bernard and the rest of Hammer's high-performing team of craftsmen and technicians in tow, *Prince of Darkness* would seem to have everything that worked so beautifully in the first two Hammer Draculas. Plus, in its resurrection scene, *Prince of Darkness* boasts a (rare, for Hammer) powerful and convincing visual effects set piece, enhanced by some crafty touches by Fisher (for instance, after the process is complete, Lee's hand rises into view, fingers crawling across the lip of the coffin like a giant spider).

Unfortunately, the film falls short on two elements essential to any Dracula story: Dracula and a story.

Sangster's disjointed, nearly plotless scenario breaks the film into two halves: the first, set primarily at Castle Dracula and climaxing with the Count's revival, is a methodically paced but unnerving preamble; the second, set primarily at the monastery and on the road back to the castle, feels rushed and jumbled and amounts to little more than an extended chase. During the latter half of the film, characters such as the Renfield-like scribe Ludwig are introduced but not developed, so their behavior seems arbitrary and contrived. The film's unusual method of dispatching Count Dracula also stretches its credibility. Sangster was so displeased with the screenplay that he signed it with the pseudonym "John Sansom." Executive producer Anthony Hinds received story credit under his usual "John Elder" nom de plum, leaving Bram Stoker's as the only real name listed among the movie's writing credits.

Christopher Lee, who high-handedly refused to appear in *Brides*, returned to fill the title role.

Unfortunately, *Prince of Darkness* completely wastes its star. Not counting a stock footage recap of the *Horror* finale, Lee doesn't appear until nearly the 48-minute mark, has only about nine minutes of screen time and no dialogue in the entire film. Lee later claimed that he was given lines but refused to deliver them. "I didn't speak because I was given, originally, nothing to say worth hearing," he said.

While it fails to coalesce in a fully satisfying whole, *Prince of Darkness* remains diverting enough and contains some outstanding individual sequences and performances. Shelley steals the show as Helen, a prissy, repressed Englishwoman who morphs into a ravenous bisexual predator after being vampirized by Dracula. Keir also provides a memorable turn as the film's swashbuckling cleric. And Matthews and Farmer also give a good accounting of themselves, bringing intelligence and sensitivity to their thinly written roles.

Although *Brides* suggested that Hammer's Dracula series would follow the adventures of vampire-slaying Professor Van Helsing (Peter Cushing), the character does not appear in *Prince of Darkness* and would not return to the series until *Count Dracula and His Vampire Brides* (aka *Satanic Rites of Dracula* [1974/78]). However, replacing Van Helsing with Father Sandor brings the Christian-good-versus-pagan/satanic-evil theme of Fisher's previous Dracula films into sharper relief. By making its hero a clergyman, *Prince of Darkness* brings the church itself into the fight against vampirism. Notably, the travelers run into trouble when they ignore the advice of a priest, and later find aid and comfort in a monastery.

During its initial U.S. release, 20th Century–Fox paired *Prince of Darkness* with *The Plague of the Zombies* and marketed both with a gimmicky ad campaign in the William Castle tradition. Movie posters exclaimed, "Boys! Fight back ... bite back with Dracula fangs! Girls! Defend yourself with Zombie eyes! Get yours free as you enter the theater." Fortunately, the twin bill didn't need such hucksterism. *Plague of the Zombies* proved to be a minor classic, and *Prince of Darkness*, while less impressive than the king and queen of Hammer's Draculas (*Horror* and *Brides*), extends the royal bloodline entertainingly.

With quotes from: *The Christopher Lee Filmography*, by Tom Johnson and Mark A. Miller.

Drops of Blood see *Mill of the Stone Women*

Duel of the Space Monsters see *Frankenstein Meets the Spacemonster*

The Dungeon of Harrow (1964; Herts-Lion)

Alternate Title: *Dungeons of Horror*; Director: Pat Boyette. Producers: Russ Harvey, Don Russell. Screenwriters: Pat Boyette, Henry Garria. Cinematographer: James Houston. Cast: Russ Harvey, Helen Logan, William McNutty, Michelle Buquor, Maurice Harris, Eunice Grey, Lee Morgan.

PAT BOYETTE'S UNDERGROUND CLASSIC — tag line (DVD)

Hardly.

During (presumably) the 19th century, an aristocratic young man named Mr. Fallon is shipwrecked, along with the ship's captain, on a deserted island. The island, however, is not so deserted after all, as our two protagonists soon find a castle and encounter the five inhabitants, including the mad lord of the castle (named, incredibly, Count Lorente DeSade) and his leprous wife locked away in the dungeon. After much uninteresting by-play between the characters, the captain is tortured and murdered, while Our Hero falls in love with the only eligible female in the household and kills the evil Count. We then learn the ironic fate that has befallen the young man (now no longer young as he narrates the tale). You see, Our Hero is now contaminated with the hideous disease leprosy and is doomed to live out the rest of his days on the island, taking the place of the mad Count as he, too, now slowly sinks into the madness of the horrible disease.

The Dungeon of Harrow (filmed in San Antonio, Texas) is one of those semi-professional shoestring pictures that gives the word "cheap" a bad name. Tacky, garish sets; terrible non-acting; and poor lighting and sound are the standard. However, what really sinks this production is its slow, ponderous pace and heavy-handed pretentiousness. There's too much talk about ominous events soon to happen, too much talk describing how characters are feeling (probably because the amateur actors were incapable of any effective emoting), and too much talk by the annoying, whispering narrator. The camera doesn't do anything interesting either, with the lens lingering on unimportant movements, watching people walk about the room just to kill some running time. The over-obvious musical score is too overused to be effective — even to the point of overlaying the characters' speech, making it difficult to hear the dialogue. Granted, the film offers one or two minor chills, such as when Fallon, now chained in the dungeon with the hideous, leprous Countess, sees her disfigured form coming towards him with the intention of consummating their "wedding night." But bad taste can't cover up the awesome dullness of this little loser. Avoid *The Dungeon of Harrow* like you'd avoid a leper colony.

Dungeons of Horror see *Dungeon of Harrow*

The Dunwich Horror (1969; AIP) Director: Daniel Haller; Producers: James H. Nicholson, Samuel Z. Arkoff; Screenplay: Curtis Lee Hanson, Henry Rosenbaum, Ronald Silkosky; Cinematographer: Richard C. Glouner. Cast: Sandra Dee, Dean Stockwell, Ed Begley, Sam Jaffe, Lloyd Bochner.

H. P. LOVECRAFT'S CLASSIC TALE OF TERROR AND THE SUPERNATURAL!—poster blurb

H. P. Lovecraft has proven very elusive for filmmakers. His terror tales involving a complicated mythos of "Old Gods" and primal evil have a unique atmosphere of decay and corruption that doesn't yield well to the film medium (so far). This effort directed by Daniel Haller (Roger Corman's former art director) attempts to capture the Lovecraft feel with psychedelic lights and exposure effects, but misses the mark completely. (Haller had delved into Lovecraft territory once before with 1965's *Die Monster Die*—and with just as little success.)

In *The Dunwich Horror* Wilbur Wheatley (Dean Stockwell) steals the *Necronomicom*, a book of pure evil, and plans to sacrifice Sandra Dee to usher the "Old Gods" back into the world of Man. Sam Jaffe, as his grandfather, and Ed Begley, Sr. (in his final role), as a college professor, try to stop him. There's also a Thing-Behind-The-Door (Stockwell's monstrous twin), which breaks out and goes on an (off-screen) rampage.

Stockwell is so vapid and listless that you just can't take him seriously as the embodiment of evil. Jaffe, best remembered by genre fans as the wise, sympathetic scientist in *The Day the Earth Stood Still* (1951), is wasted in his few moments of doddering histrionics. Begley is bug-eyed, and Sandra Dee is so limp one hopes for demonic possession—or *anything* that'll inject some life into her. Barboura Morris (the beatnik love-interest from Roger Corman's *A Bucket of Blood* [1959]) provides a nice turn, though, as a frightened housewife. The unnamable monster receives an effective buildup at the start, as we see only glimpses of writhing tentacles and a horrible shape suggestive of unimaginable ancient horrors. But there's no payoff—since that's *all* we see—and it's ultimately disappointing. And the climax (or, more aptly, *anti*-climax) is swift, painless and unexciting. Lovecraft will have to wait.

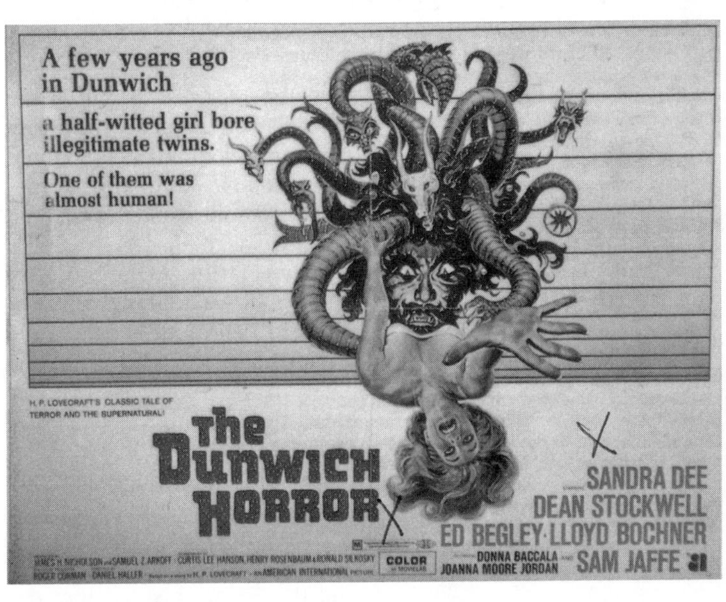

A few years ago
in Dunwich
a half-witted girl bore
illegitimate twins.
One of them was
almost human!
H.P. LOVECRAFT'S CLASSIC TALE OF TERROR AND THE SUPERNATURAL!
The Dunwich Horror
SANDRA DEE
DEAN STOCKWELL
ED BEGLEY · LLOYD BOCHNER
DONNA BACCALA
JOANNA MOORE JORDAN
SAM JAFFE
COLOR

The far-more-interesting-than-the-movie poster for the desultory *Dunwich Horror* (1969).

The Earth Dies Screaming (1965; Lippert/20th Century–Fox; b&w) Director: Terence Fisher; Producers: Robert L. Lippert, Jack Parsons; Screenplay: Henry Cross; Cinematographer: Len Harris. Cast: Willard Parker, Virginia Field, Dennis Price, Thorley Walters, Vanda Godsell, David Spenser, Anna Palk.

THE EARTH DIES SCREAMING ... AND A NEW TERROR REIGNS!—trailer

Great title, lousy movie.

Some unknown force has wiped out nearly the entire human population. Robots with silver heads and dressed in spacesuits roam a small English village where a handful of people who escaped the "gas attack" (including real-life husband and wife Willard Parker and Virginia Field) are trying to figure out what is going on. What's worse, robots are reviving the dead as white-eyed, mindless zombies. With elements like these (not to mention a real grabber for a name), *The Earth Dies Screaming* should be a sure-fire hit. But, sadly, you can't judge a film by its title. The production is obviously of very small scale. With only seven cast members, no special effects to speak of (we're never shown where the robots originate, for instance), and only two robots (looking like cut-rate escapees from an early *Dr. Who* episode), it's difficult to create a believable scenario through which our intrepid band can fight for their lives against insurmountable odds.

Terence Fisher, Hammer Studio's best resident director (who helmed such classics as *The Curse of Frankenstein* and *Horror of Dracula*) never takes advantage of the possibilities inherent in the story. We don't see any eerie shots of deserted towns, or kettles boiling over unattended, or any other trappings of a world suddenly devoid of people. Everything is filmed in a straightforward, almost casual manner.

Likewise, the horror and menace to be found when faced with walking corpses is never fully exploited. They move so slowly, and there are so few of them, that they fail to pose any real threat (particularly since they easily "die" a second time; no need to "shoot 'em in the head"—anywhere will do). It's almost as if their inclusion was an afterthought—"Right, some zombies would make for a jolly good show." The climax contains no surprises and little excitement. The two heroes formulate a plan to destroy the transmitter through which the robots and zombies are directed. They locate the transmitter and blow it up. That's it—straight to the point without any undue drama or suspense.

In the end, *The Earth Dies* not with a scream but a whimper.

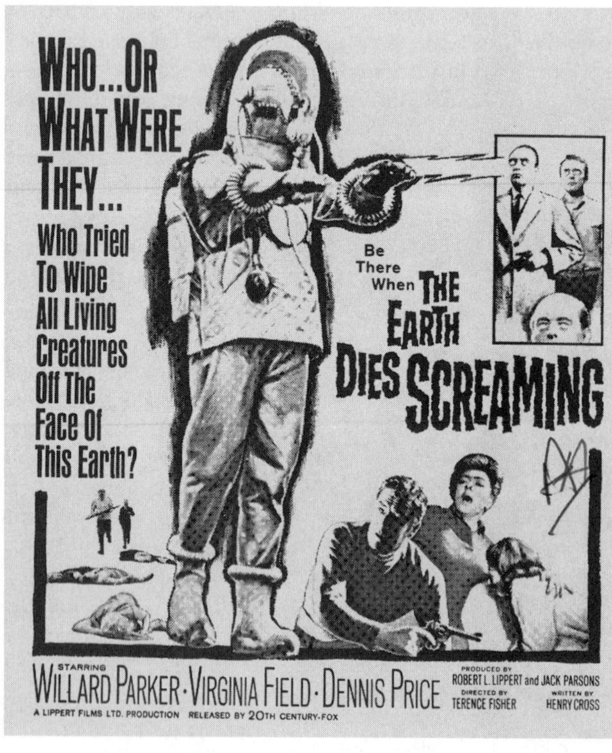

When *The Earth Dies Screaming* (1965), the viewer only yawns.

Eegah (1962; Fairway International). Director/Producer: Arch Hall, Sr. (as Nicholas Merriwether); Screenplay: Bob Wehling and Arch Hall, Sr. (as Nicholas Merriwether); Cinematographer: Vilis Lapenieks. Cast: Arch Hall, Jr., Marilyn Manning, Arch Hall, Sr. (as William Watters), Richard Keil.

The Crazed Love of a Prehistoric Giant for a Ravishing Teenage Girl!
—tagline

Widely regarded as one of the worst films ever made, this inane caveman melodrama doesn't quite live down to its lowly reputation—which, ironically, makes *Eegah* even harder to watch.

Roxy (Marilyn Manning) accidentally hits a hulking caveman (Richard Keil) with her car while driving home across the desert one night. At first, her rock singer boyfriend Tom (Arch Hall, Jr.) and adventure novelist father Mr. Miller (Arch Hall, Sr.) are understandably skeptical of her story. But when Tom discovers huge footprints in the sand, Mr. Miller decides to try to find the "giant" his daughter described. Mr. Miller soon goes missing, so Tom and Roxy rush to save

Caveman love and Arch Hall, Jr.—two of the dubious delights of *Eegah* (1962).

him, only to have Marilyn carted away by the caveman, who calls himself Eegah. It seems that Eegah is a prehistoric throwback kept alive by drinking sulfur water (huh?). The last of his lineage, he lives in a cave, surrounded by his mummified ancestors. Eventually, Tom rescues Roxy and her father and brings them back to town. Afterward, however, Roxy realizes she has developed romantic feelings for Eegah, setting the stage for a finale highly imitative of *King Kong* (only not nearly as exciting).

Given its daffy scenario, meager budget ($35,000), and semi-pro cast, the most viewers can reasonably hope for from this film is a few unintentional chuckles. Indeed, *Eegah* delivers a few of those—most of them generated by Hall's brainless pop songs and spectacularly coiffed hair, or else Manning's dumbfounding romantic interludes with the titular troglodyte—but not enough to make *Eegah*'s overlong 93 minutes anything less than a chore to sit through. This would be a far more entertaining picture if it were more poorly made. Although patently ridiculous, *Eegah* never sinks to the level of hysterical incompetence that makes movies like *Plan 9 from Outer Space* and *Robot Monster* unintentional laugh fests. Director Arch Hall, Sr., and crew are simply too professional for that. The result is a film that is simply tiresome.

Arch Hall, Sr., and his team mount a production of far better quality than, for instance, similarly budgeted productions by filmmakers such as Herschel Gordon Lewis or Andy Milligan: The lighting, sound and other technical work is perfectly adequate. But the acting is mostly atrocious, especially the tortured emoting of Keil (best remembered for his role as James Bond villain "Jaws"). The movie also contains too much blatant filler, including a lengthy footage of Tom and Roxy tooling through the desert in a dune buggy, and two banal pop ditties performed by Hall Jr.

Eegah was the second feature produced by Fairway International Pictures, a tiny outfit founded by Hall Sr., a former B-Western villain turned exploitation movie maven. He not only produced, directed and starred in the film (under various pseudonyms to try and disguise the film's minuscule budget), he also wrote the two pop tunes his son performs and dubbed the voice of Eegah. Amazingly, just a year later Fairway International produced the superb low-budget thriller *The Sadist* (1963), also co-starring Hall Jr. and Manning. It's difficult to imagine two more different films, both in tone and quality, than *Eegah* and *The Sadist*. Viewers are advised to seek out that minor masterwork and give this caveman caper a miss.

E.T.N.: The Extra Terrestrial Nasty see *Night Fright*

The Evil of Frankenstein (1964; Hammer; U.K.). Director: Freddie Francis; Producer: Anthony Hinds; Screenplay: Anthony Hinds (as John Elder); Cinematographer: John Wilcox. Cast: Peter Cushing, Peter Woodthorpe, Sandor Eles, Katy Wild, Kiwi Kingston.

> He's never been more shocking!
> Shocking! Shocking!—tagline

Actually, he's never been more boring! Boring! Boring!

Peter Cushing returns in the title role, but the sluggish, derivative *Evil of Frankenstein* (1964) represents a major drop-off in quality following Hammer Films' groundbreaking *Curse of Frankenstein* (1957) and superb *Revenge of Frankenstein*

British poster for Hammer's weakest Cushing/ Frankenstein entry (1964)

(1958). Although Cushing remains fun to watch, an addle-brained script requires him to act like a ninny half the time. Director Freddie Francis, pinch-hitting for *Curse* and *Revenge* director Terence Fisher, introduces some attractive visuals, but lets the story crawl along without generating credible dramatic tension.

The film opens with the bankrupt Baron and his assistant, Hans (Sandor Eles), sneaking incognito back to Frankenstein's abandoned chateau in Karlstadt to recover his valuables and hock them for laboratory equipment. Even though he's been in exile for 10 years, Frankenstein is shocked to discover his home has been vandalized and looted, and to find his self hung in effigy in the ransacked living room. Later, dining at a local tavern, Frankenstein blows his cover trying to recover a pilfered ring, now worn by the local burgomaster (David Hutcheson). Forced to flee, Frankenstein and Hans fall in with another Karlstadt outcast, carnival hypnotist Zoltan (Peter Woodthorpe), and a mute beggar (Katy Wild). Together, they make haste to a mountain cave, where they discover Frankenstein's Monster (Kiwi Kingston) frozen in a glacier. Frankenstein revives the creature, but Zoltan mesmerizes the Monster and dispatches him to seek vengeance against the townsfolk of Karlstadt, with predictably cataclysmic consequences.

None of this adds up to much, in terms of suspense or thrills. Francis' eye for beautiful compositions remains sharp, especially during a flashback sequence to the Monster's creation, full of flashing electrodes and arcs of electricity. Nevertheless, *Evil* sorely misses Fisher's narrative precision. Aside from Cushing, most of the cast proves forgettable. The sole exception is Kingston, who's memorably awful, laboring beneath an atrocious Monster makeup.

Back in 1959, Hammer inked a deal with Universal to obtain exclusive remake rights to Universal's horror classics, including permission to recreate the famous Jack Pierce Frankenstein makeup. (The immediate fruit of this pact was Hammer's excellent *The Mummy* [1959]—actually a remake of *The Mummy's Hand* [1940].) Unfortunately, makeup artist Roy Ashton's inept attempt to update Pierce's design makes the Monster look more like Peter Boyle (from *Young Frankenstein* [1974]) than Boris Karloff.

Anthony Hinds' script, which completely abandons the continuity established by *Curse* and *Revenge*, suffers from rehashing too many elements from Universal's Frankenstein movies: the electrified creation scene (as in the 1931 *Frankenstein*), a Frankenstein protégé who uses the monster for his own nefarious purposes (a la Ygor in *Son of Frankenstein*), a handicapped "friend" for the monster (like the blind hermit from *Bride of Frankenstein*), the monster's fear of fire (every entry in the Universal series), the discovery of the monster frozen in ice (recycled from *Frankenstein Meets the Wolf Man*), and on and on. Fortunately, after this misfire Hammer returned to making Hammer Frankenstein movies instead of trying to make Universal Frankenstein movies. Executives also had the good sense to recall Fisher, who returned to direct all of Hammer's subsequent Frankenstein films, with the exception of the 1970 spoof *Horror of Frankenstein*.

Exorcism at Midnight see *Naked Evil*

The Exotic Ones (1968; The Ormond Organization) Alternate Title: *Monster and the Stripper*. Director/Screenplay: Ron Ormond; Producers: Ron & June Ormond; Cinematography: Sid O'Berry. Cast: Georgette Dante, Edward B. Moates,

Donna Raye, Gordon Terry, Tim Ormond, Jimmy & Mildred Mulcay.

WARNING!! Unless you can stand VIVID REALISM ... IT MIGHT *SNAP* YOUR MIND!—ad line

---

Contrary to popular belief, H. G. Lewis was not the only enterprising individual to make a cottage industry out of producing independent no-budget gore movies in the 1960s. There was also Tennessee's Ron Ormond (and his co-producer wife June, not to mention their actor-son Tim, who appeared in nearly all of his parents' movies—usually as a character named, er, "Tim"). Ormond got his start in Hollywood, producing and later directing a slew of Lash Larue B-westerns in the late 1940s and early '50s, but ultimately turned to exploitation, delivering the likes of *Please Don't Touch Me* (1959; which offers graphic surgery footage) and various hick flicks (e.g. *Forty Acre Feud,* 1965). In 1968 the Ormonds reached the pinnacle of their checkered career with the bizarre amalgam known as *The Exotic Ones,* which they distributed themselves through their "Ormond Organization" to drive-ins and grindhouses throughout the South.

The jaw-dropping mix of skin and gore that is *The Exotic Ones* (1968; aka *The Monster and the Stripper*) (U.S. one-sheet poster).

One part monster movie, two parts gore flick and three parts burlesque show, *The Exotic Ones* begins like a "hip" 1960s travelogue of New Orleans (complete with historic-minded narration and swingin' upbeat horns-and-drums music). "New Orleans ... the Crescent City," the narrator (Ormond himself) observes, "sleepy by day, psychedelic by night." Yeah baby. However, the tone abruptly changes when he concludes: "But our story doesn't begin on Bourbon Street; instead, it begins in the swamps of Louisiana." In said swamp (actually Waycross, Georgia's, Okefenokee Swamp Park) a fisherman is pulled from his pirogue by a huge, misshapen arm — one belonging to "the Swamp Thing" (no, not the DC comic book character, but a wild giant of a man with bad teeth, dark circles around his eyes, and frizzy fright wig—played by rockabilly performer Sleepy La Beef). After this shocking opening we find ourselves inside a sleazy Bourbon Street nightclub, watching an exotic dancer twirling her *flaming* tassels. For the next 40 minutes we follow the travails of an innocent singer conned into a life of sin by the nightclub's mobster owner, Nemo (Ron Ormond again, sporting bangs, sunglasses and loud threads, and acting under the name Vic Naro); a cop trying to put a stop to the local drug trafficking; and myriad teasing girly acts. Suddenly, it's time to hit the swamps again, and a teenage boy (Tim Ormond) stumbles across a (real) headless, eviscerated cow carcass (victim of the swamp monster), bloody innards exposed to the world! (Talk about juxtapositions of the damned...) Nemo sends his flunkies to the bayous to track down the Swamp Thing for use in his nightclub act, employing the teen as a guide. Now firmly in H.G. Lewis territory, we watch the beleaguered bayou beast demonstrate that the would-be hunters have more guts than brains—literally (he kills one, leaving a corpse with a torn-open belly). The creature next tracks down another member of the panicked party, throws him to the ground, grabs him by the arm, plants his foot on the screaming man's chest, and pulls ... ripping the victim's arm from its socket! The monster then repeatedly bitch-slaps the man with his own bloody stump until he dies!! The astounding audacity and black humor of this what-the-hell-was-that? moment manages to out-Lewis H. G. himself. After this gore-filled interlude, it's back to the strip club for another tame number—this one with the now-captive, caged monster as backdrop (though we're soon treated to the onstage geek show of the wild man biting the neck of a live chicken and drinking its blood)—before the gruesome finale, involving the creature's escape and brief rampage.

On the technical side, *The Exotic Ones* proves surprisingly adept. While no Oscars came the way of anyone working on this bizarre regional indy, the film possesses a passable level of acting and technical competence usually missing from the Lewis oeuvre and its ilk. While true subtlety and artistry become conspicuous solely by their absence, the lighting is solid, the camera moves on occasion, and the (mostly amateur) actors look relatively comfortable.

On the distaff side, time-(and pace)-killing sequences (including an excruciating stage number by a husband-and-wife *harmonica* team) pop up at regular intervals, but Ormond offers enough outrageous moments to keep the slack-jawed viewer on the hook.

To shoot his interiors, Ormond took his fake blood and real strippers to a Nashville studio (the same one in which Elvis recorded "Heartbreak Hotel") owned at the time by the United Methodist Church! But it all balanced out in the end, for both Ron and June soon found Jesus, became born-again Christians, and started a new career making religious films of the "Soul Winner" variety (45-minute fire-and-brimstone movies shown at revival meetings in order to scare patrons into coming to the Lord), their first being 1971's *If Footmen Tire You, What Will Horses Do?*

Eye of the Devil

Eye of the Devil (1967; MGM; UK; b&w) Director: J. Lee Thompson; Producers: Martin Ransohoff, John Calley; Screenplay: Robin Estridge, Dennis Murphy (from the novel *Day of the Arrow* by Philip Loraine); Cinematographer: Erwin Hillier. Cast: Deborah Kerr, David Niven, Donald Pleasence, Edward Mulhare, Flora Robson, Emlyn Williams, Sharon Tate, David Hemmings.

> This is the climax in mind-chilling terror!—poster

Here's an anomaly—a relatively big-budgeted, studio-backed, star-studded horror film that has seemingly dropped off the radar, even among devout horror fans. Forgotten and/or ignored for over four decades, the intriguing, disturbing and highly cinematic *Eye of the Devil* deserves better than the overlooked niche it occupies today.

Predating the similarly-themed but far more famous and revered *The Wicker Man* by five years, the story (based on the novel *Day of the Arrow* by Philip Loraine) has wealthy French aristocrat Phillipe de Montfaucon (David Niven) mysteriously summoned back to his family estate at Bellenac after the vineyards have failed for three years running. His concerned wife Catherine (Deborah Kerr) takes her two small children and follows her troubled husband, only to be drawn into a sinister web of pagan conspiracy, leading to what might become the ultimate sacrifice.

Veteran director J. Lee Thompson (*The Guns of Navarone*, 1961, *Cape Fear*, 1962) cleverly weaves moments of unease into a cinematic tapestry of malevolence as Catherine, bit by bit, draws nearer to the truth. Thompson fully exploits the gorgeous chateau setting (the French Chateau de Hautefort), showing its regal beauty as one stands outside looking in, but emphasizing the sometimes stark and shadowy and even forbidding interior once one enters the structure (and story). Mobile camerawork and point-of-view shots capture the immediacy of several frightening sequences, such

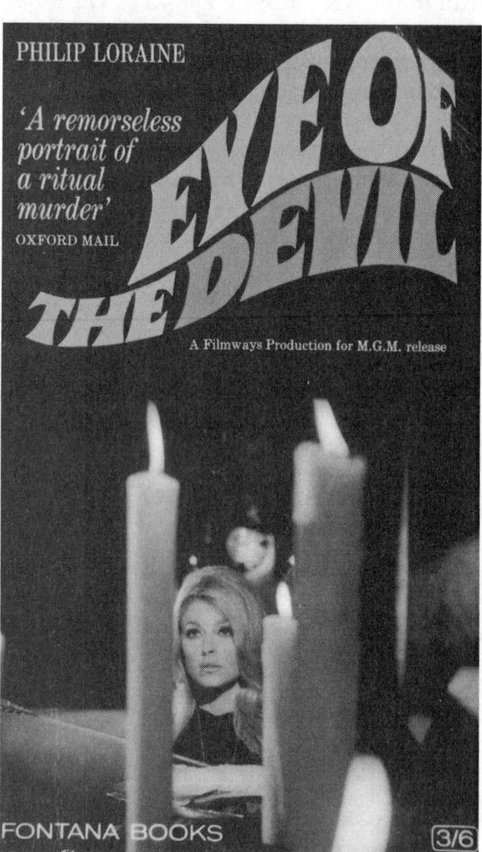

Paperback novel tie-in for MGM's *Eye of the Devil* (1967), with Sharon Tate pictured on the cover.

as when Odile (Sharon Tate) hypnotically attempts to lure Catherine to her death from atop the parapets, or when black-robed and seemingly faceless figures inexorably close in on Catherine in the woods. It all coalesces into a race-against-time climax in which direction, editing, acting and sound combine to form a sequence of almost unbearable suspense. Thompson soon seemingly abandoned the subtlety he brought to *Eye of the Devil*— if his subsequent genre credits are any indication: *Conquest of the Planet of the Apes* (1972), *Battle for the Planet of the Apes* (1973), *The Reincarnation of Peter Proud* (1975), and the slasher entry *Happy Birthday to Me* (1981).

The acting proves just as important as the technical elements in *Eye of the Devil*, perhaps more so, as it's truly a character-driven story. Deborah Kerr, a last-minute replacement for Kim Novak (injured early in the shoot in an on-set horseback riding accident — though some sources claim she was simply not up to the acting job, with the mishap simply an excuse to replace her), does exceptionally well, harkening back to her somewhat similar turn of rising hysterics mixed with determination seen in *The Innocents* (1961). David Niven strikes the right balance between his love for his family and his inner struggle to do what he feels is "right" (with his face and eyes occasionally revealing the barely-suppressed fear breaking through the cracks of his grim resolve). When Phillipe, trying to explain his actions to Catherine, quietly says, "It's our belief in something that makes that thing, for a moment — or forever, divine," one almost admires, or at least sympathizes with, this misguided man.

Donald Pleasance, as the priest and supposed spiritual leader of the community, with his bald head, penetrating eyes, and cold unsmiling demeanor, cuts anything *but* a succoring and reassuring figure. And David Hemmings and Sharon Tate, as the angelic-looking but sinister siblings Christian and Odile, appear to function as the cult's instruments, the living vessels of the barbaric religion. The hypnotic calmness and quiet malevolence of Odile, and the implied menace of the almost mute Christian (no doubt named in irony) and his ever-present deadly bow and arrows, personify the setting's dichotomous nature. Nothing is quite as it seems in the quiet and peaceful village of Bellenac. The siblings' surface beauty masks the danger lurking beneath, just as the serene chateau and surrounding countryside hides the dark secret of death and human sacrifice needed to preserve that loveliness.

MGM produced an 11-minute promotional short called "All Eyes on Sharon Tate" to coincide with the release of their starlet's *Eye of the Devil* motion picture debut. Tate's luminous, almost painfully perfect beauty (curiously, her voice appears to have been dubbed by another actress in *Eye*), combined with the knowledge of the horrible fate that lay in store for her at the hands of the Manson Family only three years later, adds a bitter poignancy to this unfairly forgotten piece of cinematic poetry.

Eyes Without a Face see *The Horror Chamber of Dr. Faustus*

The Face of Another (1966/67; Toho/Janus; Japan; b&w) Original Title: *Tanin no Kao.* Director/Producer: Hiroshi Teshigahara; Screenplay: Kobo Abe; Cinematographer: Hiroshi Segawa. Cast: Tatsuya Nakadai, Machiko Kyo, Mikijiro Hira, Kyko Kishida, Miki Irie.

"Are you more interested in rejoining society or in escaping it?" — psychiatrist to Okuyama

The Face of Another, Hiroshi Teshigahara's eagerly awaited follow-up to his art house sensation *Woman in the Dunes* (1964), was considered a profound disappointment during its initial U.S. release, when it was lambasted by critics and mostly ignored by audiences. After four decades of obscurity, however, *The Face of Another* seems overdue for reevaluation.

Okuyama (Tatsuya Nakadai), a "salary man" whose face was horribly disfigured in an industrial accident, confides to his psychiatrist (Mikijiro Hira) that he feels increasingly alienated from other people and even from his own emotions. After walking around for months with his face bandaged like Claude Rains in *The Invisible Man*, he believes he is becoming a different person and a stranger to his wife (Machiko Kyo). The doctor agrees to create for Okuyama a super-advanced, experimental mask that will give him a face — not Okuyama's own, but that of a donor from whom the mask will be molded. Once the mask is complete, Okuyama rents a second apartment, begins a double life and sets out to seduce his own wife. As his behavior grows more unpredictable, his psychiatrist muses that "masks like this could destroy human morality" by providing everyone with a second identity capable of acting out his or her secret desires.

From there, the story takes on overtones of *Dr. Jekyll and Mr. Hyde*, but *The Face of Another* is not a simple sci-fi chiller. It's an existential meditation on the nature and meaning of personal and societal identity, very much of a piece with contemporary works by Ingmar Bergman (*Persona* [1966]), John Frankenheimer (*Seconds* [1966]) and Michelangelo Antonioni (*The Eclipse* [1962] and *Red Desert* [1964]). Admittedly, however, *The Face of Another* proves far less effective than any of those pictures.

The two standard criticisms of the film — that it is slow and arty — are not inaccurate but seem misguided. As a term of derision, "arty" typically indicates the work of an uppity movie director with aspirations beyond his station. Teshigahara, however, was an artist who happened to make films. His other pursuits included pottery, calligraphy, opera and *ikebana* (the ancient Japanese art of flower arrangement), and he was an innovator in every field. Running 124 minutes and moving at a pace that may charitably be described as methodical, *The Face of Another* is certainly slow. But Teshigahara's intent is to underscore the duality of human existence — the mask of social propriety that disguises our true, animalistic selves— through constant doubling of visual motifs, musical cues and plot points. Nearly every element in the film is coupled with an echo, rhyme or duplicate, including one scene entirely replayed (once with Okuyama's face wrapped in bandages, and a second time with him wearing the mask). All this takes time, both to set up and to sink in.

If nothing else, *The Face of Another* is an eye-popping, jaw-dropping visual *tour de force.* Kiyoshi Awazu's ultra-modernistic production design (especially the unearthly antiseptic lab where the mask is created — all blank white walls and glass), cinematographer Hiroshi Segawa's daring lighting effects (including dramatically dropping all background lighting during two key scenes) and Teshigahara's painterly attention to composition and framing are all above reproach. So is composer Toru Takemitsu's unsettling score, which juxtaposes *avant garde* electronic music with an eerie-sounding traditional waltz.

Teshigahara, an avowed devotee of pioneering movie surrealist Luis Bunuel, also peppers *The Face of Another* with frequent breaks from reality. In one scene a woman seated on a bed begins zooming above the city, via obvious rear projection. In another a door in the background of the psychiatrist's clinic opens to reveal matted-in footage of a woman's flowing black hair waving in water. Perhaps most strikingly, during the film's finale Okuyama and his psychiatrist move through a literally faceless mob — extras wearing smooth, blank masks. Teshigahara also employs countless radical editing and photographic techniques, including zooms, freeze frames, swish-pans, jump cuts, extreme close-ups, wipes and even (in the opening scene) x-rays. The merits of such dramatic directorial flourishes may be debated, but these devices keep viewers engaged despite the film's length and leisurely tempo. Meanwhile, the subtle, naturalistic performance of the cast, particularly Nakadai as Okuya, help ground the film so it never becomes cartoonish or grotesque.

The movie's most significant flaws are rooted in its willfully difficult-to-follow script, adapted (with uncredited assistance from Teshigahara) by Kobo Abe from his own novel. Particularly problematic is the introduction of a parallel story line, which never intersects with the primary narrative, about a scar-faced young woman who has a sexual encounter with her brother and commits suicide. As it nears its conclusion, the film intercuts between these two stories so that the subplot comments on the main story with all the subtlety of a lead pipe to the skull.

To some extent, 1967 critics were correct in their assessment of *The Face of Another.* It's arguably more challenging than ultimately rewarding, and certainly a steep letdown after the brilliant, disquieting *Woman in the Dunes.* Yet *The Face of Another* remains a far more impressive and compelling picture than critical consensus would indicate. It's hard to love, but easy to admire.

Face of Fire see *The Mask*

Face of the Screaming Werewolf (1959/64; A.D.P. Pictures, Inc.; b&w)

Original Language Title: *La Casa del Terror*; Director: Jerry Warren, and (uncredited) Gilberto Martinez Solares (werewolf footage) and Rafael Portillo (mummy sequences); Producer: Jerry Warren; Screenplay: Gilbert Solar (Gilberto Martinez Solares, werewolf scenes), Alfred Salimar (Alfredo Salazar, mummy sequences); Cinematographer: Richard Wallace (Enrique Wallace, mummy scenes), Raul Martinez Solares (werewolf sequences, uncredited). Cast: Landa Varle (Yolanda Varela), Lon Chaney, Donald Barron, Raymond Gaylord (Ramon Gay), Steve Conte, Jorge Mondragon, Emma Roldan, George Mitchell, Chuck Niles, Bill White, Fred Hoffman.

A TERROR-CADE IN THRILLS!
A NIGHTMARE IN CHILLS!
—trailer

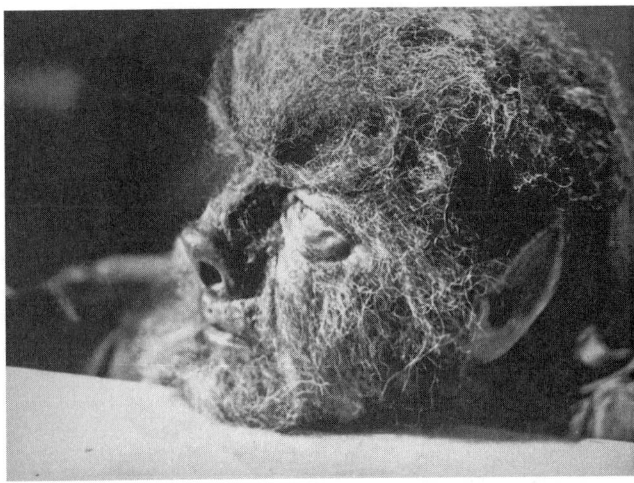

Lon Chaney, Jr., dons his famous Wolf Man makeup one last time in the south-of-the-border pastiche *Face of the Screaming Werewolf* (1959/64) (Photofest).

In the early 1960s, American fringe filmmaker Jerry Warren (*Man Beast, Teenage Zombies*) acquired the rights to a 1959 Mexican horror comedy, starring the popular Latin comedian Tin Tan (*and* featuring Lon Chaney, Jr., as a werewolf!), called *La Casa del Terror*. Warren excised nearly all of Tin Tan's scenes (thus eliminating the original movie's *star*) and inserted footage from the 1957 *La Momia Azteca* (which he'd already cannibalized to create the atrocious *Attack of the Mayan Mummy* in 1963). But Warren didn't stop there; *Face of the Screaming Werewolf* is really a combination of *four* different film snippets: In addition to the *Momia Azteca* and *Casa del Terror* footage, Warren recycled some of his own scenes shot with American actors for *Attack of the Mayan Mummy*, and included a few scraps of *new* footage lensed specifically to bridge some of the expository gaps in *Face*.

As might be expected from such a patchwork pastiche, *Face of the Screaming Werewolf* makes little sense and provides even less entertainment, offering only a few nostalgic moments of Lon Chaney in his trademark Wolf Man make-up (though a bit shaggier here than usual) for those diehard fans desperate enough to sit through this painful 60 minutes (which feels like *twice* that length).

The story has a young woman, the reincarnation of an Aztec maiden, lead a scientific expedition to an ancient pyramid on the Yucatan peninsula, where they find two bodies—that of an ancient mummy and that of a modern man in some sort of mummified condition ("placed in the pyramid only recently after an exchange of body fluid with the mummy in an effort to achieve an apparent state of death," as one character 'explains'). The Aztec mummy comes to life, but the expedition subdues the creature and brings it—and the still-dead 'modern' mummy—back to the city for study (all, disappointingly, off-screen). A rival scientist steals the modern mummy and restores it to life, only to find that the man (Lon Chaney, Jr.) is actually a werewolf! Meanwhile, the living mummy escapes, abducts the reincarnated girl, and is promptly killed when hit by a car (again, off-screen).

The two story lines have literally nothing to do with one another, and a paucity of dialogue (synching the dubbing was obviously too big a strain on Warren's grade-Z budget) insures that the viewer often has no idea who is doing what to whom. Many of the scenes appear to be thrown in at random just to eat up the running time (and the few new shots of Warren regulars—like Chuck Niles and Steve Conte—answering the telephone or delivering radio broadcasts further eat up time without adding anything appreciable to the confusing proceedings).

The first 20 minutes (a full third of the picture's short running time) consists of *La Momia Azteca* footage lifted (again) from Warren's earlier *Attack of the Mayan Mummy* (1963). It didn't improve with age, for the looong ceremonial flashback sequence quickly grows tiresome, and the mummy only pops up in the last minute.

The *Casa del Terror* footage provides *Face*'s few highlights, including seeing Chaney Jr. in his black-shirt-and-trouser Lawrence Talbot get-up once more (he even leaps over a lab table at one point with a bit of the old Wolf Man ferocity); atmospherically-lit and unsettling insert shots of creepy wax figures (the villains' secret lab is at a wax museum—though this isn't made clear in *Face*, resulting in more confusion); and the boffo lab set itself, with a giant pressure cooker/tanning bed contraption (used to try and revive the mummy), various banks of electrical equipment, bubbling beakers, and a giant spinning apparatus of undetermined origin.

In an interview with Tom Weaver, Jerry Warren referred to his doctoring of Mexican imports as "a natural, easy way to make movies without an exceptional amount of work." Well, with *Face of the Screaming Werewolf*, Warren put in even less work than usual — and it shows.

The nonsensical (but not in a good — or even entertaining — way) *Face of the Screaming Werewolf* is chock full of people we don't know doing things for reasons we don't know involving other characters we don't know. Why watch *Face*? I honestly don't know.

With quotes from: *Interviews with B Science Fiction Stars and Horror Heroes.*

The Faceless Monster see *Nightmare Castle*

Fanatic see *Die! Die! My Darling*

Fangs of the Living Dead (1968; Europix International; Spain/Italy) Alternate Title: *Malenka, the Vampire*; Original Language Title: *Malenka, la Sobrina del Vampiro*; Director/Screenwriter: Amando de Ossorio; Producers: Aubrey Ambert, Rosann Yanni; Cinematographer: Fulvio Testi. Cast: Anita Ekberg, John Hamilton (Gianni Medici), Diana Lorys, Adriana Ambesi, Rosanna Yanni, Julian Ugarte.

Vampire vixen: "Is your blood very warm?"
Male victim-to-be: "I'm Italian!"

Considering it was made by the same man, Amando de Ossorio, who brought us the innovative and disturbingly creepy *Blind Dead* quartet (beginning with 1971's *Tombs of the Blind Dead*), *Fangs of the Living Dead* remains a disappointingly tepid sixties prelude to those seventies shockers. (Of course, de Ossorio also subjected moviegoers to the god-awful *Night of the Sorcerers* in 1974, so maybe the substandard *Fangs* should come as no real surprise).

In *Fangs of the Living Dead*, Anita Ekberg plays a beautiful model, Sylvia, who unexpectedly inherits a spooky castle — and a vampire uncle to go with it. Here the Swedish bombshell clearly demonstrates why she never made it big as an actress, running about in a laughable Shirley Temple ringlet coiffure and acting, well, about on the level of her hairdo. The convoluted plot matches Ms. Ekberg's thespian in banality, and there are no special effects to speak of to relieve the tedium (surprising, considering De Ossorio's self-confessed love of makeup effects, which he often did himself on his later films).

Fangs is not entirely without interest for '60s Eurohorror fans, however. Cinematographer Fulvio Testi contributes some beautiful, moody color lighting to the authentic castle settings and sinister-looking crypt (the flickering torchlight in the latter augmented by an otherworldly bluish hue). But while the movie is fine to look at, as are a bevy of gorgeous Continental starlets (such as Diana Lorys [*The Awful Dr. Orloff*, 1962; *Night of the Blood Monster*, 1969], Adriana Ambesi [*Terror in the Crypt*, 1963] and *Fangs*' co-producer Rosanna Yanni [*Frankenstein's Bloody Terror*, 1968; *Kiss Me Monster*, 1969]), not enough happens to warrant such atmospheric attention.

The film slows to a crawl when Sylvia's fiancé comes to investigate, taking forever to discover what the audience already knows. And the viewer quickly tires of watching wishy-washy Sylvia trying to decide whether or not to give in to the family "curse." The nonsensical ending initially exposes it all as a hoax, a plot concocted by the uncle to drive Sylvia insane. But then why does this "fake" vampire turn to bones when killed? To add

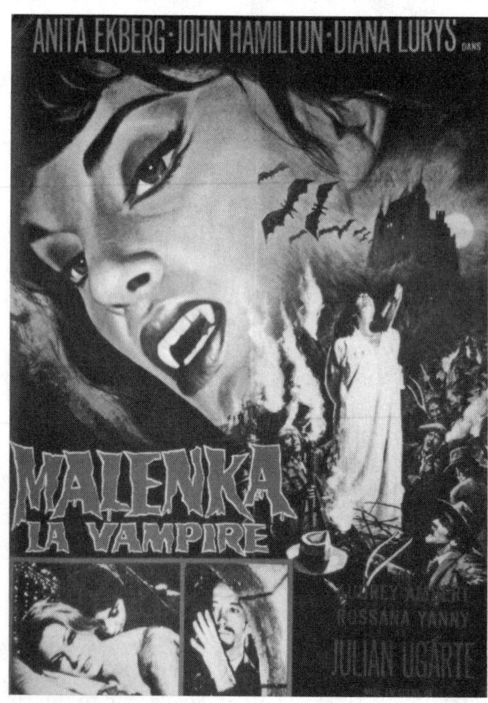

Striking French poster for the less-than-striking 1968 Eurohorror *Fangs of the Living Dead* (aka *Malenka, the Vampire*).

insult to injury, the movie closes with a painfully forced final "camp" humor scene. Indeed, these *Fangs* lack bite.

The Fearless Vampire Killers (Or, Pardon Me but Your Teeth Are in My Neck)

The Fearless Vampire Killers (Or, Pardon Me but Your Teeth Are in My Neck) (1967; MGM) Alternate Title (U.K.): *Dance of the Vampires.* Director: Roman Polanski; Producer: Gene Gutowski; Screenplay: Gerrard Brach and Roman Polanski; Cinematographer: Douglas Slocombe. Cast: Jack McGowran, Roman Polanski, Sharon Tate, Alfie Bass, Ferdy Mayne, Terry Downes.

> Who says vampires are no laughing matter?
> —tagline

Director Roman Polanski's spoof of Hammer horror films boasts many strengths, including A-budget production values and gorgeous cinematography from future Oscar nominee Douglas Slocombe. But it lacks the one element essential to any comedy: Laughs.

Dotty Professor Abronsius (Jack McGowran) and his nebbish apprentice Alfred (Polanski), on the hunt for vampires, stop for the evening at a rural Transylvanian inn. During the night the undead Count von Krolock (Ferdy Mayne) kidnaps the innkeeper's daughter Sarah (Sharon Tate) and spirits her away to his castle. Professor Abronsius and Alfred make haste to rescue the young woman, only to become trapped themselves. Soon they discover that the three of them will serve as the buffet table at a Vampire Ball hosted by Count von Krolock.

Unfortunately, it takes nearly two hours for that simple plot to play out. The film's leaden pace undoes what was intended to be a frothy farce, full of broadly played slapstick (including one scene, involving a cannon, shot in under-cranked, Mack Sennett style) along the lines of *The Pink Panther* (1963) and its sequels. Perhaps Polanski and screenwriter Gerrard Brach hoped to do for horror films what the Pink Panther pictures did for (or to) movie mysteries. If so, their plan contained a fatal flaw: *The Fearless Vampire Killers* does not star Peter Sellers.

Instead, moviegoers must make do with the cartoonish mugging of Jack McGowan (whose Abronsius is to Dr. Van Helsing what Sellers' Clouseau is to Inspector Poirot). The rest of the cast—with the notable exception of Polanski himself—turn in equally broad, caricatured portrayals. Polanski, on the other hand, projects stone-faced, Buster Keaton-like stoicism, or else seems mildly befuddled. His low-watt approach makes everyone else (especially McGowran) seem even more over the top. Perhaps this was even intentional.

The Fearless Vampire Killers boasts gorgeous location photography (including stunning nighttime snow scenes, with the Alpine landscape bathed in eerie blue moonlight), magnificent sets and elegant period costumes. The picture has some very impressive set pieces, especially the climactic Vampire Ball (which lampoons the finale of Hammer's *Kiss of the Vampire* [1963]). It even has a couple of clever comedic elements, notably a Jewish vampire who scoffs at crosses but cowers before the Star of David, and a gay vampire who wants to turn Alfred into his undead boy-toy. But such moments are too few and far between, languishing amid much aimless wandering around and botched gags (like the cannon scene). Several of Polanski's early short films (especially *Two Men and a Wardrobe* [1958]) display a gift for keenly

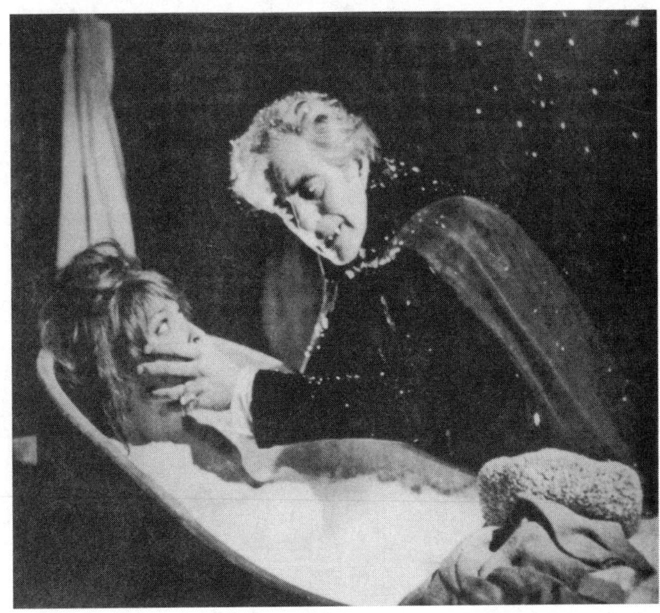

Count von Krolock (Ferdie Mayne) menaces a bathing Sarah (Sharon Tate) in _The Fearless Vampire Killers_ (1967).

observed dry comedy. Perhaps *The Fearless Vampire Killers* would have fared better if played in that register.

Viewed today, the film also suffers from the morbid, eerie shadow cast by future events. This was the film on which Polanski met future wife Sharon Tate, destined to be sadistically killed (along with Polanski's unborn child) by the Manson Family. While it's no fault of the movie itself, knowledge of this gruesome destiny casts a pall over Polanski and Tate's timidly romantic scenes.

The Fearless Vampire Killers was a troubled production from the start. Star Jill St. John dropped out at the last minute and was replaced by the virtually unknown Tate. Shortly before filming began, the Alpine location work, originally scheduled for Austria, relocated to Italy, so the entire shooting schedule had to be revised. Finally, in mid-production, Polanski decided to switch to the 2.35:1 widescreen Panavision process, which meant all previously shot footage had to be reframed and cropped.

For its U.S. release, MGM made several alterations to the film, none of which sat well with Polanski. The most obvious of these was changing its title from *Dance of the Vampires* to *The Fearless Vampire Killers (Or, Pardon Me But Your Teeth Are in My Neck)*, making it painfully obvious that the picture was supposed to be funny. The studio also slashed the movie's length and added cartoonish sound effects to "goose" some scenes. Finally, MGM threw together a cheesy trailer that played up the picture's slapstick moments, as well as a goofy one-reel promotional short, *Vampires 101*, featuring clips interspersed with unfunny shtick from English comedian Max Wall (who does not appear in the film) as "Professor Cecil Havelock-Montague, Ph.D., LL.D., B.A.T." Despite (or perhaps because of) these efforts, *The Fearless Vampire Killers* became Polanski's first commercial and critical failure.

Although it has garnered some belated critical respect in recent years, for horror buffs *The Fearless Vampire Killers* seems like a wasted opportunity. After all, it's tantalizing to think what the results could have been if Polanski had invested the same resources and his towering talent into making a *real* vampire movie. Or, at least, a parody that was actually funny.

Dr. Quatermass (Andrew Keir) and Dr. Roney (James Donald) discover what turn out to be telepathic, insectoid Martians in Hammer's superb science fiction-horror hybrid *Five Million Years to Earth* (1967/68).

The Fiendish Ghouls see *Mania*

Five Million Years to Earth

(1967/68; Hammer/Seven Arts; U.K.) Original Title: *Quatermass and the Pit.* Director: Roy Ward Baker; Producer: Anthony Nelson Keys; Screenplay: Nigel Kneale; Cinematographer: Arthur Grant. Cast: Andrew Keir, James Donald, Barbara Shelley, Julian Glover, Bryan Marshall.

FORCE MORE POWERFUL THAN 1,000 H-BOMBS UNLEASHED TO DEVASTATE EARTH ... World in Panic! Cities in Flames!—tagline

Before introducing its trademark Technicolor gothic chillers with *The Curse of Frankenstein* (1957), Hammer Films' biggest moneymakers (and best pictures) had been its adaptations of two BBC science fiction miniseries—*The Creeping Unknown* (aka *The Quatermass Xperiment* [1955]) and *Enemy from Space* (aka *Quatermass 2* [1957]). So naturally the studio quickly snatched up the movie rights to the BBC's third Quatermass epic, *Quatermass and the Pit* (1958).

Yet it took nearly a decade to bring the yarn to the big screen, in part because the studio chose to focus on the supernatural shockers that had become its bread and butter, and in part due to budgetary trepidation. *Quatermass and the Pit* boasted the largest scope and most sophisticated plot of all three Quatermass miniseries. A true sci-fi/horror hybrid, its story incorporated black magic, demons, telepathy and telekinesis (all eventually accounted for through super-scientific explanations), as well as traditional science fiction elements. And it climaxed with all of London consumed in a fiery tumult. This would not be an easy or inexpensive production, and other complications exacerbated the inherent difficulties. Due to overcrowding at Hammer's home studio in Elstree, the project had to be moved to MGM's facilities in Borehamwood. And the originally assigned director (Val Guest) and star (Peter Cushing) both bowed out due to schedule conflicts.

Despite these woes, however, *Five Million Years to Earth* (as the picture would be retitled for its U.S. release) emerged as one of the more satisfying Hammer products of the late 1960s. Though far from perfect, it's an intelligent, fast-paced sci-fi chiller and a worthy successor to the earlier Quatermass entries.

While excavating for a subway expansion in the old Hobbs End section of London, workers unearth mysterious misshapen skulls, which anthropologist Dr. Roney (James Donald) identifies as a previously unknown species of ancient anthropoids, millions of years older than any similar species. Further digging at the site yields an even more fantastic discovery—a mysterious missile of unknown (and possibly unearthly) origin. Since the object is originally identified as an unexploded bomb, the military is called in, led by the dunderheaded Col. Breen (Julian Glover). Dr. Bernard Quatermass (Andrew Keir), a brilliant but irascible rocket scientist, comes along for the ride and quickly discerns that the object is a five-million-year-old alien spacecraft.

Soon several giant insects (they look like yard-long, thirty-pound locusts) are discovered in a sealed compartment within the space capsule, and workers begin complaining of bizarre and frightening visions when they approach the craft. Playing a hunch, Quatermass and Roney's assistant, Barbara Judd (Barbara Shelley), begin investigating local legends regarding Hobb's End—a place with a centuries-long reputation for terrifying, unexplained, apparently supernatural phenomena. Quatermass and Roney eventually work out that: (1) the capsule originated on Mars and crashed on earth five million years ago; (2) the strange anthropoids were genetic mutations created by the Martians; (3) the ship is an organic being—dormant but not lifeless; and (4) the ship was piloted by the alien insects, which were telepathic. Now the spacecraft has "awakened" and is trying to make telepathic contact with humans, with potentially catastrophic consequences.

Five Million Years to Earth is action-packed—in fact, it's a bit *too* action-packed. Although screenwriter Nigel Kneale does an admirable job condensing his elaborate, idea-rich BBC teleplay from three hours to 97 minutes, the movie's final act feels rushed. In rapid succession, audiences are hit with a great deal of information—for instance, that humans have untapped telekinetic powers (except a few who don't), that those powers are the result of ancient Martian genetic experiments, that the mysterious capsule can form a telepathic link with humans (except a few who are immune) and can unlock those untapped psychic abilities, and on and on—and all this data must be properly processed for the viewer to understand what's going on and why the characters behave as they do. Anyone who isn't paying rapt attention is apt to get lost, and even the alert viewer may require a second screening to fully comprehend it all. *Five Million Years* would have played better with a running time closer to two hours, but its tightly compressed narrative gives the film a frenetic pace, rocketing from one scene to the next with urgency and mounting tension.

The film's visual effects have long been an object of derision, perhaps because this picture made its U.S. debut the same year as the game-changing *2001: A Space Odyssey*. In actuality, *Five Million Years'* effects aren't *that* bad and in no way undermine the impact of the story. Overall, the show's production values are strong. If nothing else, the film's sets, props, costumes and other technical merits represent a quantum leap forward from the no-budget BBC original.

Unfortunately, the same cannot be said for the film's cast. Although they perform credibly, nearly all of them are outshined by their BBC counterparts. Keir's performance suffers in comparison to Andre Morrell's portrayal in the BBC *Quater-*

mass and the Pit (his is generally regarded as the authoritative interpretation of the character) and to the imaginations of fans who may wonder how Cushing might have handled the role. Morrell was asked to reprise his role for *Five Million Years*, but the actor declined, opening the door for Kier. Most observers credit Keir as an improvement over Hammer's original Professor Quatermass, American Brian Donlevy, but that is open to debate. Donlevy played Quatermass as an iron-willed, dictatorial genius who refused to suffer fools— a man who had reached the pinnacle of his profession based on his formidable talent and his willingness to brush aside or crush anyone or anything that stood in his way. This approach was both fresh (compared to the typical Mr. Perfect 1950s sci-fi hero) and realistic (since many leaders achieve great stature even though, or because, they do not play nicely with others). Keir's kinder, gentler Quatermass seems like a milquetoast in comparison, put-upon and even panicky when he should be indignant and righteously outraged.

Like Kier, Donald and Glover prove perfectly serviceable but somewhat bland. Only Shelley (in a role beefed up from the original BBC script) outperforms her television counterpart, bringing intelligence, sensitivity and charm to her rangy part as Miss Judd — seeming eager, bright and courageous early on as she investigates the dark past of Hobb's End, and genuinely menacing during the film's climax when she poses a threat to Quatermass and Roney. Shelley was always a strong addition to any cast, but this remains her best work for Hammer.

The film also represents a relative high point for director Roy Ward Baker. After his 1958 classic *A Night to Remember* earned international acclaim, Baker spent most of his career alternating between television assignments and modestly budgeted horror and exploitation pictures. While it's hardly *A Night to Remember*, *Five Million Years to Earth* stands as his finest fantasy film.

Even though *Five Million Years* wasn't an outstanding financial success, afterward Hammer approached Kneale about creating a Quatermass project specifically for the silver screen. At the time, however, the writer had no interest in revisiting the character. Eventually Kneale penned a fourth BBC miniseries, titled simply *Quatermass* (1979), as well as a BBC radio serial, *The Quatermass Memoirs* (1993), and an unproduced prequel, *Quatermass and the Third Reich*. By 1979, however, Hammer had closed shop. Although he had saved the world three times already, Professor Quatermass didn't arrive in time to rescue the failing studio.

The Flesh and the Fiends see *Mania*

see *Mania*

The Flesh Eaters

The Flesh Eaters (1964; Vulcan/Cinema Distributors of America; b&w) Director: Jack Curtis; Producers: Terry Curtis, Jack Curtis and Arnold Drake; Screenplay: Arnold Drake; Cinematographer: Carson Davidson. Cast: Martin Kosleck, Byron Sanders, Barbara Wilkin, Rita Morley, Ray Tudor.

Absolutely nothing will prepare you for what you will see!— tagline

---

Throughout the 1960s, as drive-in theaters proliferated and Hollywood's studio system disintegrated, many upstart filmmakers saw an opportunity to break into the business by making low-budget genre movies. Some of these maverick productions, like *Carnival of Souls* (1962) and *Night of the Living Dead* (1968), now are revered as horror classics. *The Flesh Eaters* never rises to that level, but stands head and shoulders above most other low-budget, independent shockers. Although clearly designed to shock and titillate, it displays uncommon sophistication and craftsmanship.

All the film's earmarks— gore and a hint of sex, as well as skillful direction — are encapsulated in its unforgettable opening sequence: Bikini-clad Ann (Barbara Wilson) is lounging on the deck of her boyfriend Freddy's speedboat, when Freddy (Ira Lewis) begins to pester her to take a swim. Horseplay ensues, and Freddy winds up with Ann's bikini top. Ann dives into the sea to protect her modesty. Freddy dives in after her, but never surfaces. Instead, clouds of blood billow up through the water. Then, tiny silver flashes appear around Ann. She screams and is dragged beneath the waves. The sea begins to bubble like acid as the credits appear. A decade later, Steven Spielberg would open *Jaws* (1974) with a remarkably similar sequence, and to equally powerful effect.

Flesh Eaters' main narrative opens with Jan Letterman (Barbara Wilkin) chartering a seaplane to fly her boss, Laura Winters (Rita Morley), a drunken movie star, to the island location of her latest film. Pilot Grant Murdock (Byron Sanders) is leery of accepting the job due to an approaching tropical storm, but agrees when Jan offers to triple his regular fee. Unfortunately, mechanical problems force Murdock to land on a deserted island, where he and his passengers seek shelter from the storm. To their surprise, they find that the island is inhabited — by creepy marine biologist Peter Bartell (Martin Kosleck). Next, they're horrified to discover Ann's body (now merely a skeleton in bikini bottoms) washed ashore. After the storm passes, the shore is covered in fish skeletons. Bartell reports that the water surrounding the island is full of shimmering microscopic parasites that feed on living flesh. But Murdock grows suspicious of Bartell, who seems to be withholding information. What sort of experiments is Bartell doing on this island, anyway?

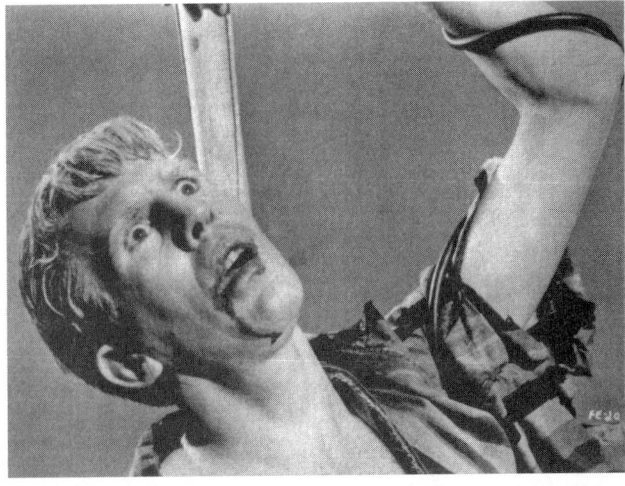

The beatnik Omar (Ray Tudor) falls victim to *The Flesh Eaters* (1964).

First-time director Jack Curtis displays a solid grasp of film technique and employs some imaginative camera angles (including a shot looking outward from inside the mouth of a monster) to maximize dramatic impact, while keeping the pace brisk. The script, from former comic book author and rookie screenwriter Arnold Drake, is tight and punchy, full of believable characters and snappy dialogue.

The only sour note in this pitch-perfect tale is the unwelcome arrival of Omar (Ray Tudor), a dimwitted beatnik who appears out of nowhere, apparently crossing the open sea on a rickety handmade raft, carrying a phonograph but no food or water. Rescued from the Flesh Eaters by Murdock and friends, Omar hangs around long enough to spout inane lines like, "Why do you think they [the Flesh Eaters] do it [eat flesh]? Ya think maybe they're just kooky?" Presumably, Curtis and Drake felt the picture needed a little comedy relief. That's just what Omar provides— little relief. Fortunately, his stay on the island proves short. Bartell tricks Omar into drinking a glass of beer spiked with Flesh Eaters. The beatnik's demise proves the most gruesome of the film's handful of gory death scenes— Omar screams, writhes in agony and clutches his stomach, blood oozing over his hands as the monsters eat him from the inside out. In another ghastly sequence, the creatures splash onto the face of a victim.

Drake's finale, involving a giant monster Flesh Eater, was a bit more ambitious than advisable given the picture's budget, and Roy Benson's cut-rate visual effects aren't entirely convincing. Still, they're no worse than what viewers might encounter in a Bert I. Gordon production — on balance, acceptable for a movie in this weight class. Viewers will likely forgive Benson's effects (and even Omar's dialogue), given the film's many other virtues, which include solid work from the cast. Kosleck, a veteran whose career stretched back to the silent era and included some of the classic Universal chillers, was seldom better than here, as the cold, calculating Bartell. Sanders, a TV actor then known for the soap opera *The Doctors*, makes a fine, granite-jawed hero. Wilkin, who had only a few TV guest spots on her resume, holds her own. And Morley, another soap star (from *The Edge of Night*), nearly steals the show playing the imperious, alcoholic starlet.

In the DVD liner notes for *The Flesh Eaters*, Drake reveals that the idea for his screenplay originated with a news report that millions of dead fish had washed ashore along the coasts of Florida, Georgia and South Carolina. "It took scientists years to find the guilty virus," he writes. "It took me minutes to find the story of *The Flesh Eaters*." Drake joined with the husband-and-wife team of Jack and Terry Curtis to bring this tale to the screen, with a planned budget of $60,000. Unfortunately, as Drake recalls: "While filming on location at Montauk, New York, a hurricane flattened the sets and took our equipment with it. Completion was delayed a year and the budget soared to $105,000." It seemed the film might never be completed, until Terry Curtis appeared on a TV quiz show, *High Low*, and won $72,000.

Despite its generally fine craftsmanship and future status as a cult favorite, *The Flesh Eaters* did nothing to further the careers of its makers and remains the lone film produced by Drake or the Curtises. Drake's only subsequent screenwriting credit was the Sal Mineo drama *Who Killed Teddy Bear?* (1965). Jack Curtis worked primarily as a voice artist, and could be heard on many cartoons, including the American dubbing for *Speed Racer*. Sadly, considering the promise he showed with *The Flesh Eaters*, he never directed another movie.

With quotes from: *The Flesh Eaters* DVD (liner notes) by Arnold Drake (DarkSky Films).

Frankenstein Conquers the World (1965; Toho; Japan) Original Title: *Furankenshutain tai Chitei Kaiju Baragon* (Frankenstein vs. the Subterranean Monster Baragon). Director: Ishiro Honda. Producer: Tomoyuki Tanaka; Screenplay: Takeshi Kimura, Jerry Sohl, from a story by Reuben Bercovitch, based on a novel by Mary Shelley. Cinematographer: Hajime Koizume. Cast: Nick Adams, Tadao Takashima, Kumi Mizuno, Koji Furuhata, Jun Tazaki, Takashi Shimura.

He rolled the Seven Wonders of the World into one!— tagline

Frankenstein Conquers the World ranks among Toho's must frustrating *kaiju eiga* (giant monster) movies, simply because it never should have been a *kaiju eiga* in the first place. If allowed to follow its own course, this colorful, outlandish mad science yarn might have turned into a very entertaining picture — something along the lines of *The Manster* (1962), perhaps. Instead, Toho channels the story into its well-worn giant monster rut. As a result, *Frankenstein Conquers the World* begins promisingly but soon falters due to its numbingly predictable, paint-by-numbers second and third acts.

The film opens with a frenetic pre-credit sequence set during the final days of World War II. Nazi storm troopers burst into Dr. Frankenstein's laboratory and confiscate his experiments— including the still beating, disembodied heart of the Frankenstein monster. A Nazi submarine transports the heart to Hiroshima, where Imperial Japanese scientists are examining it when the A-bomb falls.

Flash forward to postwar Japan. Residents near Hiroshima discover a strange-looking feral boy with a protruding brow (a new Frankenstein monster, spontaneously regenerated from the disembodied heart following the atomic blast) feeding on local pets and other small animals. Police capture the monster (Koji Furuhata), in this film simply referred to as "Frankenstein," and place him under the care of scientists James Bowen (Nick Adams), Sueko Togami (Kumi Mizuno) and Yuzo Kawaji (Tadao Takashima). Sueko immediately takes a motherly interest in Frankenstein.

Suddenly the child-monster begins to grow at an alarming rate. He doesn't mature physically, but simply balloons in size, eventually becoming a 100-foot colossus. Once he begins to grow, Kawaji decides that Frankenstein presents a threat and attempts to destroy him. But the scientist botches the job and the giant boy escapes. Meanwhile, a four-legged, subterranean monster named Baragon tunnels out of the earth and begins wreaking havoc. The military blames Frankenstein for the destruction caused by Baragon. James and Sueko must prove Frankenstein's innocence before the Japanese army finds and destroys him. All of which

Ad for *Frankenstein Conquers the World* (1965/66) (courtesy Ted Okuda).

leads to an inevitable confrontation between Frankenstein and Baragon.

Setting aside the ludicrous "science" of this tale, *Frankenstein Conquers the World* leaves numerous major questions unresolved, paramount among them: Why does Frankenstein grow into a giant? Because this movie was made by Toho remains the only apparent answer. The entire production takes a nosedive as soon as the monster begins to mysteriously increase in size. The energetic, wildly imaginative (albeit goofy) set-up gives way to a succession of *kaiju eiga* clichés.

The buildup to the final showdown between Frankenstein and Baragon seems interminable, and the fight itself proves anti-climactic. Part of the problem lies in the picture's lackluster visual effects, but the greater issue is the listless, let's-just-get-this-over-with staging of the sequence. In an alternate ending, never released to theaters but available on Japanese home video versions of the film, after dispatching Baragon, Frankenstein battles a giant octopus. But this scene, which suffers from the same uninspired staging and chintzy effects, hardly improves matters.

This movie's Frankenstein — an overgrown, gap-toothed 12-year-old with a Jack Pierce-inspired prosthetic forehead — ranks among the least impressive giant monsters in cinema history. Baragon, however, looks even sillier. He galumphs around on all fours, his face sculpted into a permanent smile, with a glowing yellow horn on the end of his nose, looking like something Jim Henson might have created for Sesame Street (except that Big Bird is far more intimidating than Baragon.)

The picture's best moments arrive in the early going. In addition to the wild and wacky pre-credit sequence, the film's first act also includes some disarming character-development moments involving James and Sueko. In one charming sequence, James visits Sueko's house, where she prepares a traditional Japanese meal; later, she visits his apartment, where he dons an apron and cooks old-fashioned American hamburgers. Adams, a teen idol gone to seed, trades effectively on his boyish likeability and finds great chemistry with Mizuno, Toho's most appealing *kaiju* actress. Apparently, their rapport didn't end on the set. "He proposed to me," Mizuno told interviewer Stuart Galbraith IV. "I already had a fiancé, so I had to refuse."

Takashima has considerably less success in his unsympathetic role. Furuhata won't make anyone forget Boris Karloff, but engenders much-needed pathos in the film's early scenes. With a less endearing monster, this film would be completely unwatchable.

Even as it stands, *Frankenstein Conquers the World* may conquer the patience of all but the most ardent Tohophile.

Frankenstein Created Woman (1967; Hammer/20th Century–Fox; U.K.)

Director: Terence Fisher; Producer: Anthony Nelson Keys; Screenplay: Anthony Hinds (as John Elder); Cinematographer: Arthur Grant. Cast: Peter Cushing, Suzan Farmer, Thorley Walters, Robert Morris, Peter Blythe, Barry Warren.

> Now Frankenstein has Created the Ultimate in Evil — A BEAUTIFUL WOMAN WITH THE SOUL OF THE DEVIL! — tagline

The engrossing and surprisingly poignant *Frankenstein Created Woman* represented a badly needed course correction for Hammer Films' long-running Frankenstein series, following the misguided *Evil of Frankenstein* (1964).

The story finds Frankenstein engaged in a new series of experiments focused on nothing less than gaining control of the immortal soul. Frankenstein's young assistant Hans (Robert Morris) loves the scarred and crippled Christina (Susan Denberg), daughter of a local innkeeper. When three wealthy young men try to take advantage of Christina, Hans defends her honor. Later the trio returns and kills her father — a crime for which Hans is convicted and executed. However, Frankenstein recovers the body and uses a gizmo that looks like a sort of cosmic tuning fork to capture the young man's soul. When the anguished Christina commits suicide, Frankenstein steals her corpse, repairs its physical defects and places Hans' soul into her now-beautiful body. Afterward, Christina is consumed by Hans' thirst for revenge, and one by one kills off the young men who murdered her father.

Director Terence Fisher rejoins the series (Freddie Francis had helmed *Evil*) for this outing, and with him returns the dynamic compositions and clean visual storytelling which had marked *Curse of Frankenstein* (1957) and *Revenge of Frankenstein* (1959). Fisher maximizes the impact of Jack Asher's evocative lighting scheme, full of bloody reds, sickly greens and icy blues. Composer James Bernard contributes one of his most haunting scores.

The script, written by executive producer Anthony Hinds under his "John Elder" pseudonym, is both well-constructed and emotionally gripping. As in *Revenge*, the sociopathic Frankenstein's undoing is his inability to sympathize with other people or comprehend their emotional motivations. Since he has no conscience, he can only look on with frustration and fury as Christina, torn by guilt and her split personality, brings his experiment to an abrupt end.

Nearly all of Fisher's fantasy films are at their core morality tales where Christian good opposes satanic evil, but this theme is less obvious in his Frankenstein pictures since the conflict plays out within the Baron himself. As Fisher later explained, Frankenstein's motivations are good but he is tempted by Satan into performing evil deeds: "The devil said to him, 'Go on with your work. You're wonderful. Do anything. Create a creature better than God's. You're better than God.' That, I think, comes out marvelously in Peter's performances."

Cushing is marvelous as ever in *Frankenstein Created Woman*. He's animated, meticulous and passionate, his enthusiasm for the role unabated even after three previous appearances. In anyone else's hands the film's soul-capturing device would seem patently ridiculous, but with Cushing at the controls viewers accept it. If there's any knock on his performance, it's that there's simply not enough of it. While Cushing had been onscreen virtually every minute of his previous Frankenstein pictures, this time around, to cut costs, Hammer reduced the actor's screen time (and number of work days).

Fortunately, the rest of the cast come through, so the film doesn't suffer grievously. Morris and Denberg are endearing as the star-crossed lovers. Also, Denberg, a former *Playboy* centerfold, looks ravishing — perhaps too ravishing in the early scenes, when she's supposed to be ugly. Thorley Walters nearly steals the film with his warm, seriocomic turn as Hertz, Frankenstein's befuddled surgical assistant. Initially the character seems like mere comedy relief, but as the picture wears on, Hertz, a genuinely nice person despite the company he keeps, seems to represent the picture's moral center, daring to ask questions like (as they prepare to capture Hans' soul) "Is it right?" Predictably, Frankenstein replies, "What does right have to do with it?"

Neither as historically significant as *Curse*, nor as flat-out brilliant as *Revenge* or the later *Frankenstein Must Be Destroyed* (1969/70), *Frankenstein Created Woman* languishes among Hammer's lesser celebrated series entries. Nevertheless, it's a picture that wears its age well and seems overdue for critical reassessment. Even its director admitted he had initially underestimated the movie. "I saw it again on the box the other day and I quite liked it," Fisher said. "At the time I didn't, that's true. I didn't care for it so much until I saw it again and I liked it. Just like the one with David Peel [*Brides of Dracula*]. I saw it again on the box and I loved that one."

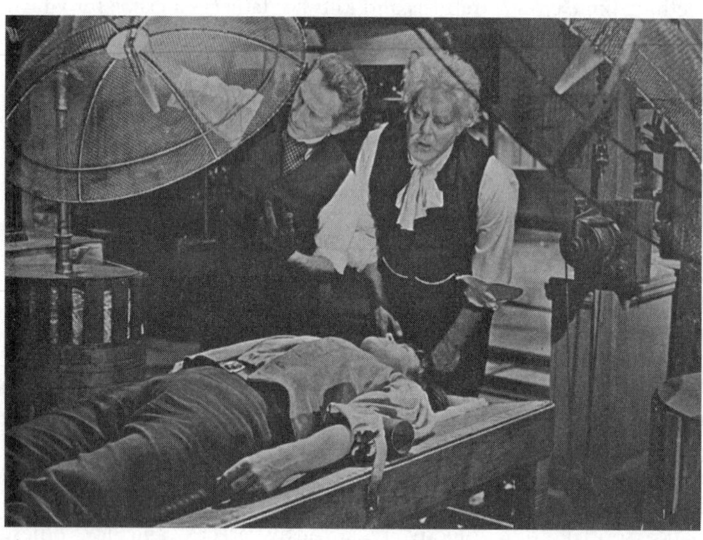

A more accurate title for 1967's *Frankenstein Created Woman* would have been "Frankenstein Transfers Souls." Here Baron Frankenstein (Peter Cushing, adjusting the machinery), aided by his assistant Dr. Hertz (Thorley Walters), does just that.

Fisher's epiphany aside, *Frankenstein Created Woman* remains the most underrated of Hammer's Frankenstein films.

With quotes from: "Terence Fisher in Conversation" by Jan Van Genechten, *Little Shoppe of Horrors* No. 19.

Frankenstein Meets the Spacemonster

(1965; Futurama) Alternate Titles: *Duel of the Space Monsters*, *Mars Invades Puerto Rico*; Director: Robert Gaffney; Producer:

Robert McCarty; Screenplay: George Garret; Cinematographer: Saul Midwall. Cast: Jim Karen, Marilyn Hanold, Lou Cutell, Robert Reilly, Nancy Marshall, David Kerman.

FREE! THE MANAGEMENT WILL SUPPLY YOU FREE SPACE SHIELD EYE PROTECTORS TO PREVENT YOUR ABDUCTION INTO OUTER SPACE!!—poster promise

When a movie's opening line, delivered by an effeminate, bald-headed, pointy-eared, mascara-wearing alien is, "We continue to hear a modulated hydrogen frequency signal of 21 centimeters, Princess," you know you're in for a cinematic trash treat. But when the aforementioned "Princess" asks, "What does that mean?" and receives the reply, "We're not quite sure, Princess," it's evident that you've found the '60s answer to *Robot Monster.*

Frankenstein Meets the Spacemonster has absolutely nothing to do with Mary Shelley's classic creation. (In fact, the only tie-in is this closing credit: "And featuring ROBERT REILLY as L. Frank Saunders and Frankenstein.") But forget the name stealing; this one has it all: Ed Wood-style invading aliens looking for "good breeding stock" (i.e. bikini-clad bathing beauties), impressive Army stock footage (the shooting script was titled *Operation San Juan* so the U.S. Department of Defense wouldn't mind lending the footage), a bad '60s folk/rock music soundtrack (by the Poets and the Distant Cousins), a very young James Karen (*Poltergeist, Return of the Living Dead*) as the scientist-hero, Puerto Rico beach locations (where filming is cheap!), a cheesy mutant monster (sort of a hairy, no-budget *It! The Terror from Beyond Space*), and an android named Frank Saunders (aka Frankenstein) who has half his face turned into oatmeal by an alien ray gun—and then gets mad.

An alien spaceship, commanded by Princess Marcuzan (Marilyn Hanold) and her toady Dr. Nadir (Lou Cutell), hovers outside Earth's atmosphere. When NASA launches a manned mission to Mars, the aliens mistake it for a missile and shoot it down. The rocket's pilot, Colonel Frank Saunders (Robert Reilly), a half-man/half-android, ejects and lands in Puerto Rico. The aliens, fearing their plan of "optimum pollenization" will be discovered (survivors of a nuclear war, they've come "to acquire good breeding stock to repopulate our planet"), follow the escape pod in order to destroy the "witness"—as well as abduct women from beaches, pool parties and off of mopeds.

Ad for the shot-in-Puerto Rico wackiness that is *Frankenstein Meets the Space Monster* (1965).

"We were doing a send-up," explained director Robert Gaffney. "Look at the story line. They come from outer space, and where do they land to steal women to repopulate their planet? Puerto Rico!" Shot in December 1964 ("that's why we wrote it for Puerto Rico, because where the hell were we gonna go?" observed Gaffney) on a budget of $60,000, *Frankenstein Meets the Spacemonster* featured such cost-saving methods as turning a hot dog stand dome into a spaceship ("we painted it silver, erected it on stilts and stuck it out in the middle of the swamp," laughed Gaffney), inserting copious stock NASA and military footage ("half the picture is stock footage"), turning cheap toys into alien weapons ("the ray guns were nothing more than Wham-O air guns and a flashlight body with a mirror on the end of it") and writing scenes for specific locations ("we found some caves down on the seashore and all this weird-looking lava rock, so I designed all the sequences around that, and we went back and wrote them").

If you're looking for good science fiction or anything to do with the Frankenstein legend, you'll have to look elsewhere. But for inept and amusing thrills, don't miss *Frankenstein Meets the Spacemonster*.

With quotes from: "Frankenstein Meets the Space Monster: When Genres Collide," by Tim Ferrante, *Fangoria* 138, January 1995.

The Frozen Dead (1966; Seven Arts/Warner Bros.; U.K./U.S.) Director/producer/screenwriter: Herbert J. Leder. Cinematographer: David Boulton. Cast: Dana Andrews, Anna Palk, Philip Gilbert, Karel Stepanek, Kathleen Breck.

Chiller of the year!—ad line

Star Dana Andrews, whose career took a steep nosedive in the 1960s, still must have thought he was making the likes of *Laura* (1944) or *Curse of the Demon* (1956) when he signed on the dotted line for this odd British-American co-production, for he takes the ridiculous proceedings *very* seriously and gives his all, even affecting a slight German accent—which was far more than this pathetic production warranted. Unfortunately, none of the other (no-name) actors in this film can match Andrews' level of professionalism. For example, when the hero (Philip Gilbert) prattles on to an obviously-not-listening heroine (Anna Palk) and finally says (blandly), "You must think me a bore," the viewer can only nod vigorously in agreement. And a bore is exactly what this movie turns out to be.

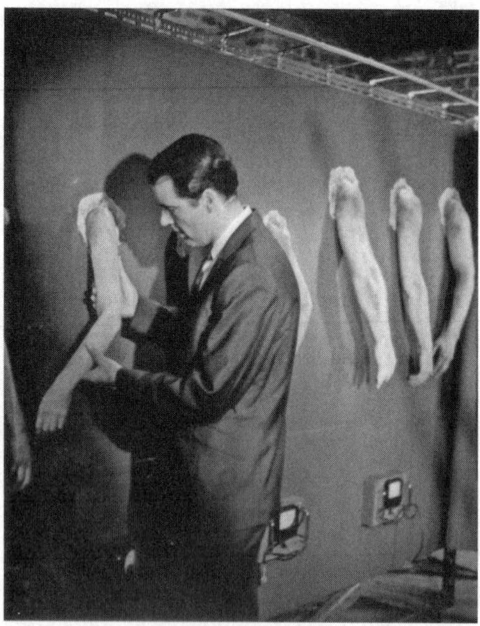

Philip Gilbert lends a hand to *The Frozen Dead* (1966).

Andrews plays a Nazi scientist who developed a method to freeze humans and place them in suspended animation. Unfortunately, in the 20 years since the war, he hasn't quite figured out how to thaw them out without damaging the brain, and his basement is full of imbeciles and half-wits—the formerly frozen Hitler henchmen on whom he's been experimenting. It's all got something to do with restoring "the Party" (led by several aged and *un*frozen Nazis) to its earlier greatness. In the meantime, the scientifically-minded Andrews, who may be the first *sympathetic* Nazi in horror film history, is dismayed to find his beloved niece arriving unexpectedly. Duped by his nefarious Brownshirt helpers, Andrews ends up performing an experiment in which he keeps alive the disembodied head of his niece's murdered companion! (Exactly *what* this has to do with defrosting his Stormtrooper-sicles remains rather vague, except that he wants a "living brain" to study.) The mad medico also has a wall of disembodied arms(!!) hooked up to an electric current and begins a new experiment intended to establish a link between head and hands. Of course, this turns out to be a mistake, and the embittered cranium learns to control the arms all too well, resulting in the doctor and his evil associates being (literally) strangled by the hand of fate.

While a wall covered with arms, a freezer full of Nazis and a head on a table (with ghastly blue makeup and a plastic dome for a skull to expose the gray matter) keep this film firmly entrenched in the bizarre, endless (and pointless) scenes of talk, talk, talk sink it in a quagmire of apathy. In fact, the movie's mid-section is about as exciting as watching a TV dinner thaw. And though the disembodied head contributes a few shudders with its horrific—and pitiable—appearance, *The Brain That Wouldn't Die* (1962) did it all much better. The production values are fairly high for such a subject, with a luxurious English country mansion sprucing up the silliness. But an opulent setting and a head on a table can't overcome triple-threat producer-director-screenwriter Herbert J. Leder's meandering script and deadly dull direction.

Released as the bottom half of a double bill with the slightly less-tedious *It* (again produced, directed and written by Leder), *The Frozen Dead* should indeed remain in the deep freeze.

Gallery of Horror see *Dr. Terror's Gallery of Horrors*

Gamera see *Gammera the Invincible*

Gammera the Invincible (1965/66; Daiei; Japan; b&w) Original Title: *Daikaiju Gamera.* Home Video Title: *Gamera.* Director: Noriaki Yuasa and Sandy Howard (U.S. version); Producer: Masaighi Nagata; Screenplay: Nizo Takahashi and Richard Kraft (U.S. version); Cinematographer: Nobuo Munekawa and Julian C. Townsend (U.S. version). Cast: Albert Dekker, Brian Donlevy, Diane Findlay, Eiji Funakoshi, Michiko Sugata, Harumi Kiritachi, Yoshiro Unchida.

The super-monster even the H-bomb cannot destroy...—tagline

This indifferently produced low-budget Godzilla knock-off seems like an unlikely genesis for the only film series to threaten Toho's hegemony on *kaiju eiga* (giant monster) movies. Yet, in spite of itself, *Gammera the Invincible* proved to be exactly what Daiei Studio executives hoped for: The debut of a new rubber suit-monster superstar and the sire of long line of sequels.

Gammera remains a bland, almost generic *kaiju eiga* picture. Its threadbare, overly familiar plot seems almost beside the point: nuclear bomb tests in the Arctic awaken a sleeping, prehistoric creature, which, despite the military's best efforts, rampages from the frozen north to Japan. Clearly trying to imitate the success of *Godzilla, King of the Monsters*, Daiei produced a separate U.S. version of the film with extensive (but pointless) new footage featuring past-their-prime American stars Albert (*Dr. Cyclops*) Dekker and Brian (Dr. Quatermass) Donlevy. The American scenes consist of Dekker, as the Secretary of Defense, and Donlevy, as General Arnold, sitting in claustrophobic meeting room sets (supposedly the Pentagon and the U.N.) and wringing their hands over events occurring off-screen, thousands of miles away. Producers also added a kitschy pop title song for the American version.

This was the final Japanese giant monster movie shot in black and white, and the first issued in this format in several years. It's unclear whether this was part of Daiei's effort to imitate the black-and-white *King of the Monsters*, or simply another cost-saving measure for a project with appallingly cheap production values and visual effects.

The film contains only two imaginative elements, but those two were enough to ensure its success. First, there's Gammera himself—a giant, snaggle-toothed, fire-breathing, flying turtle—a more fanciful creation by far than any of Toho's monsters, which tended toward reanimated dinosaurs and overgrown versions of common animals. Second, the film places a young boy in a central role. Yoshiro Uchida plays Toshio, a schoolboy fascinated by turtles. During one of Gammera's raids, the giant turtle saves Toshio's life. This convinces the boy that Gammera "doesn't mean to be dangerous. He's just so big and clumsy.... If people were kind to Gammera, I bet he could be trained to be nice and quiet, like other turtles." (It never occurs to Toshio that Gammera wouldn't have had to save his life if the monster hadn't attacked his family's home in the first place. The boy also overlooks Gammera's penchant for barbecuing fleeing extras.) With its cartoony monster and sympathetic juvenile lead, *Gammera* went over extremely well with young viewers, who would become the fledgling series' primary audience.

These movies performed well enough at Japanese box offices for Daiei to produce a new Gamera (the second "m" was dropped after the first

Spanish poster for the first giant flying turtle(!) movie, *Gammera the Invincible* (1966).

picture) installment every year until 1971, when the company went belly-up. *Gammera the Invincible* was the only entry in the series released theatrically in the U.S. The rest went straight to TV. In the 1980s, when the Gamera pictures were released to home video in America, this film was re-edited by producer Sandy Frank, who excised most of the Dekker and Donlevy footage and retitled the picture simply *Gamera.*

The character was revived with *Gamera: Guardian of the Universe* in 1995, and the remake spawned two sequels. Ironically, although the "classic" Gamera films of the 1960s and '70s fell far below the standard set by the Godzilla series, many monster fans consider the Gamera pictures of the 1990s superior to Toho's G-films of the same era.

The Genie of Darkness (1962; Estudios America/Trans-International Films; Mexico; b&w) Original Language Title: *Nostradamus, el Genio de las Tinieblas*; Director: Frederick Curiel, Stim Segar (English language version); Producer: Victor Parra, K. Gordon Murray (English version); Screenplay: Charles E. Taboada, Alfred Ruanova; Cinematographer: Ferdinand Colin. Cast: Germán Robles, Julio Aleman, Domingo Soler, Aurora Alvarado, Manuel Vergara, Jack Taylor.

"My hate is endless."

Though the above sentiment is voiced by the villainous vampire Nostradamus (Germán Robles), this could very well be the attitude of the exasperated viewer after sitting through this third installment in the *Nostradamus* quartet.

Actually, of the four "features" culled from the 12-chapter Mexican serial (begun with *The Curse of Nostradamus*, continued with *The Monsters Demolishers* and this entry, and finishing up with *The Blood of Nostradamus*), *The Genie of Darkness* may very well be the best (which is damning with faint praise indeed).

Genie starts right where *The Monsters Demolishers* left off, as Leo (Nostradamus' dimwitted hunchbacked henchman) helps the fallen vampire to his feet. (The previous film closed abruptly with Nostradamus collapsing — in a vampire's version of sympathetic labor pains— when the protagonists stake his undead underling.) Nostradamus then hypnotizes Professor Dolen's assistant, Anthony ("I own your soul now and you are my servant"), in order to find out what his adversaries are up to. The Professor, Anthony and Igor (a mysterious vampire-hunter who popped up in the previous film) are searching for a centuries-old parchment that holds the secret of Nostradamus' power. "Destroy the document and annihilate the vampire," instructs the Professor.

One of the things that gives this *Genie* its magic (at least comparatively speaking) is its focus on the enigmatic, sorcery-practicing Igor (played authoritatively by subsequent Eurotrash horror star Jack Taylor), who's far more interesting a character than the dour Professor or bland Anthony. It culminates in an impressively staged confrontation (a rarity in this series) between Igor and his hated enemy Nostradamus, with the camera zooming in on each in turn to punctuate the duel of wills.

Genie also proves superior in the atmosphere department, in that most of the film takes place either at Nostradamus' crypt-like lair, Igor's castle-like house, Rebecca's (Leo's crone-like mother, who's the keeper of Nostradamus' precious parchment) witch-hovel or the Professor's archaic-looking basement lab (where he tinkers with bats and sound waves in a subplot that goes absolutely nowhere).

But the film bogs down in a lengthy, boring interlude involving Nostradamus' pedestrian plot to turn a woman against her lover, with the bloodsucker laughing maniacally and declaring — without the slightest hint of irony — "Now is a great triumph for Nostradamus!" Too bad the same can't be said for Mexican horror cinema.

The Ghastly Ones (1968; J.E.R. Pictures Inc.) Alternate Title: *Blood Rites* (U.K. video title); Director/Cinematographer: Andy Milligan; Producer: Jerome-Fredric; Screenplay: Hal Sherwood, Andy Milligan. Cast: Veronica Radburn, Maggie Rogers, Hal Borske, Anne Linden, Fib La Blaque, Carol Vogel.

An experience so sensually shocking that it will be the stomach-shocker of your life!— trailer

When the soft-core sexploitation subgenre turned hard in the late 1960s and early '70s (with the arrival of such pictures as 1969's *I Am Curious Yellow* and 1970's *Sexual Freedom in Denmark*), low-rent filmmakers who made their professional home on New York's notorious 42nd street needed to change with the times. Producer-director Andy Milligan, a fringe player among fringe players, declined to go the hard-core route and so turned his sweaty sights towards horror and gore. *The Ghastly Ones* was the first of his $1.98 homegrown

Ghastly Mexican lobby card for Andy Milligan's *The Ghastly Ones* (1968).

horror productions, quickly followed by *Torture Dungeon* and *Bloodthirsty Butchers* (both filmed in 1969 but not released until 1970). Milligan would pay his actors $25 a day, shoot in his own run-down Victorian-style home in the wilds of Staten Island, make the costumes himself (using his "Raffine" pseudonym), and shoot on short ends with a 25-year-old 16mm newsreel camera. The question is not why his pictures are so bad, but why they are watchable at all. And the answer is that Milligan's movies contain a raw, often perverse energy that's never conventional, as he wears his misanthropic, misogynistic, conflicted heart on his sleeve. (By all accounts Milligan had a horrible childhood and loathed his mother, angrily shouting out "Bitch!" at her funeral; such anti-family vehemence frequently breaks through in his films.)

Set in the nineteenth century, the story follows the ill-fated reunion of the three Crenshaw sisters. When their wealthy absentee father finally dies, the fractured family is brought back together for the reading of the will, which carries an odd proviso: "Each of you [heirs] and your husbands shall reside at the Crenshaw house in sexual harmony for the period of three days.... This house must know married love in those three days, a love that it had never known from your mother and I." Soon a mysterious figure adds a sour note to said "harmony" by murdering the principals one by one in various, er, ghastly ways.

Writing for *Film Bulletin*, future director Joe Dante (*Gremlins*) reported that *The Ghastly Ones* "looked like a home movie from Bedlam." It's an apt description, given the picture's no-budget ambiance swirling about its twisted characters and depraved scenarios. As production values go, it just doesn't get any lower than an Andy Milligan movie. *The Ghastly Ones* (made for $13,000—which was Milligan's *biggest* budget up to that time!) is filled with shaky, hand-held, sometimes focus-challenged camerawork (courtesy of Andy himself); lighting that's at one point garish and unflattering, and at another so dim the scene appears lit by flashlight; garden shear-style editing; amateurish acting from the coffee-house regulars and street hustlers Milligan employed; tinny, often garbled sound; inappropriate canned music; and cheesy, fake-looking gore (the film was banned in Britain as a "video nasty" when released there on tape as *Blood Rites* in the early 1980s). About the only thing that's truly convincing are the period costumes, created by Milligan himself (a former dress shop owner). What sets *The Ghastly Ones* (and the rest of the Milligan oeuvre) apart from such other low-end dreck as *The Beast of Yucca Flats* (1961) or *Manos, the Hands of Fate* (1966) is a manic energy and unconventional, cynical, almost avant garde sensibility. For instance, Milligan often offers off-kilter, ultra-tight close-ups even during mundane talking-head scenes, making the viewer feel slightly uncomfortable—like the camera was an awkward adolescent standing too close and invading your personal space.

Distributor Sam Sherman came up with the film's title and promotion campaign ("in CRANIUM-CLEAVING *COLOR*"). "I thought truth in advertising wouldn't be bad because the picture really was ghastly, so I called it *The Ghastly Ones*," Sherman laughingly admitted to writer Jimmy McDonough in his fascinating biography *The Ghastly One: The Sex-Gore Netherworld of Filmmaker Andy Milligan*.

Though often containing isolated moments of boredom (i.e. long talky stretches), rarely does a Milligan film seem dull, thanks to their offbeat weirdness. And Andy's first horror opus, though certainly not for everyone (and for *no one* seeking a straightforward, competent horror film), will reward those cineastes willing to dumpster-dive for their fix.

The Ghost (1963/65; Panda/Magna; Italy) Original Language Title: *Lo Spettro*; Director: Robert Hampton (Riccardo Freda); Producer: Louis Mann (Luigi Carpentieri, Ermanno Donati); Screenplay: Robert Davidson (Oreste Biancoli), Robert Hampton (Riccardo Freda); Cinematographer: Donald Green (Rafaelle Masciocchi). Cast: Barbara Steele, Peter Baldwin, Harriet White (Medin), Leonard G. Elliot (Elio Jotta), Carol Bennet, Charles (Carlo) Kechler, Raoul H. Newman (Umberto Raho), Reginald Price Anderson.

Horror ... sharp as a razor's edge!—tagline

Made in 1963 in Italy, but not dubbed and released in the U.S. until 1965, *The Ghost*, an unofficial sequel to writer-director Riccardo Freda's earlier *The Horrible Dr. Hichcock*, has Dr. H. return as a cuckolded cripple who is killed by his wife (Barbara Steele) and her lover (the doctor's own physician). But the ghost of the vengeful Hichcock seemingly returns to torment the faithless couple ... or does he?

Large French poster for Riccardo Freda's *The Ghost* (1963/65), an unofficial semi-sequel to *The Horrible Dr. Hichcock.*

Barbara Steele claims *The Ghost* was made on a bet (likewise *The Horrible Dr. Hichcock*). "Freda made a bet one day at lunch with a producer, Pietro Pupillo," reported the actress. "He said he could write a script *and* shoot a movie in a week. He wrote it in a day; we had a day of preproduction, and he shot it in three days. One night I slept on the set, because I knew we would be shooting again in four hours."

Despite the obvious pressures such a rushed production put on its cast and crew (such as the actors having to literally learn their lines between scenes as the crew hurriedly set up for the next shot), Steele didn't see that as necessarily a bad thing: "I like working with a certain sense of urgency. It has its pluses because it creates an interesting energy, a kind of nerving sort of charge, a crisis energy on the set which I really think the film picks up on. I think that film on some subconscious level picks up this magnetism, this energy, when it's really happening. Somewhere I think it translates."

If so, than in *The Ghost* something was *lost* in translation, as it suffers from a decided *lack* of energy. Though opulently presented (with its wonderfully Gothic set dressings and old manor house setting), and possessing occasional moments of atmosphere and shock (such as a ghastly-lit face slowly emerging from the shadows; or an eerie visit to a twilight-lit, fog-enshrouded graveyard; or a vicious, well-edited straight-razor murder, complete with blood splattering the camera lens), the film's pacing matches the principals' turn-of-the-century garb—stately and demure.

The small cast do a superb job with some demanding roles, led by Steele, who does what she does best—seductive in one scene, terrified in the next, and totally mad at the end.

Filled with shots of billowy curtains, chess pieces that suddenly scatter from the board, drops of blood mysteriously appearing, disembodied ghostly laughter, and Charles' eerie voice issuing from the housekeeper medium's mouth, *The Ghost* offers up sporadic Gothic-flavored chills, but its measured tread and predictable ending (the poetic "twist" is anything *but* unexpected) make this *Ghost* a rather pale entry in the Italo-Gothic sweepstakes of the 1960s.

With quotes from: "Princess of Darkness," by Bill Warren, *Fangoria* 102, May 1991.

The Ghosts of Hanley House (1968; Victoria Productions; b&w) Director/Screenwriter: Louise Sherrill; Producer: Joesphe S. Durkin, Jr.;

Cinematographer: Claude Fullerton. Cast: Elsie Baker, Barbra Chase, Wilkie De Martel, Roberta Reeves, Cliff Scott, Leonard Shoemaker.

"I don't believe in ghosts—and I don't think there's anything wrong with the Hanley place that a good bucket of paint won't fix."
—doubting protagonist

A group of people spend the night in a notorious haunted house in this seldom-screened and nearly forgotten *Haunting* wannabe. There they are confronted by (unseen) ghosts who first frighten, then aid them in uncovering the horrible secrets behind the hauntings. After a brief (and very limited) release in 1968, *The Ghosts of Hanley House* dropped from sight, remaining as invisible as the house's occupants until the video boom of the 1980s prompted some enterprising fringe distributors to release it on videotape.

The film's low-budget ambiance and stark black-and-white photography enhance the creepiness of its simple scenario, much in the way that these same gritty attributes helped make *Carnival of Souls* and *Night of the Living Dead* so memorable. Though *Ghosts* begins with a generic organ-and-guitar rock 'n' roll score, once the protagonists arrive at the house, the inappropriate music gives way to a disturbing, ominous low bass motif that, along with moody shots of the empty house—both inside and out—generates an unsettling atmosphere. The aural impressiveness continues, as much of the subsequent shudders arise from bizarre and startling sound effects (á la *The Haunting*).

Ultimately, however, the movie falls well below the admittedly lofty mark set by the better-known films it strives to imitate. Most of the blame for this would appear to rest with rookie director Louise Sherrill, who apparently never directed another picture, though she did appear *before* the camera in small roles on at least two occasions—*Blood and Lace* (1971) and *Speak of the Devil* (1991). Sherrill's camera rarely moves, and she relies heavily on the medium shot, abruptly inserting the occasional close-up to break the monotony (in some of these the actor stares directly into the camera—an amateurish no-no).

Some judicious editing would have helped. Sherrill holds on scenes too long, which doesn't help the obviously uncomfortable (and obviously non-professional) actors appear any more at ease. She occasionally inserts moody shots of empty rooms full of pregnant menace, but again locks the camera down for far too long. And much of the running time consists of dull filler. Audiences must endure lackluster scenes of the group playing cards and dancing, or their later attempt to escape the house by walking through the woods after their cars mysteriously won't start. Though the paths all somehow lead them *back to the house* (a creepy concept exploited more fully two decades later in *The Blair Witch Project*), the sheer length of this poorly-lit walking-down-the-trail sequence transforms the shudders into tedium.

Capping it off is a disappointingly banal climax in which, after all the sundry spooky phenomenon (clock hands spinning, paintings falling, the sound of galloping hooves thundering through the house), a "ghostly" voice behind a door spells everything out for the dim-witted protagonists. Though Sherrill attempts to put a final twist in the tale, it all just peters out in the end as the group simply does what the spirit asks (the wraiths merely wanted a decent burial for their murdered bodies).

While no rediscovered classic, *The Ghosts of Hanley House* remains a strangely compelling curio in the haunted cinema cabinet, despite its amateurish lapses.

Girls of Spider Island see *Horrors of Spider Island*

Godzilla vs. Mothra see *Godzilla vs. the Thing*

Godzilla vs. The Thing (1964; Toho; Japan)

Original Title: *Mosura tai Gojira.* Alternate Title: *Godzilla vs. Mothra* (US video). Director: Ishiro Honda. Producer: Tomoyuki Tanaka; Screenplay: Shinichi Sekizawa. Cinematographer: Hajime Koizume. Cast: Akira Takarada, Yuriko Hoshi, Hiroshi Koizumi, Yu Fujiki, Emi Ito, Yumi Ito, Yoshibumi Tajima, Kanji Sahara.

WHAT IS IT ... How much terror can you stand?—tagline

American-International Pictures played it coy with that tagline, hiding the identity of Godzilla's sparring partner in Toho's latest super-monster slugfest. AIP re-christened the film *Godzilla vs. The Thing*, perhaps to suggest some nonexistent connection with the Howard Hawks sci-fi classic *The Thing* (1951), and removed all images of Mothra from its advertising. Despite this tactic, Americans now commonly refer to the movie by its U.S. home video title, *Godzilla vs. Mothra.*

By any name, however, this remains one of the keynote *kaiju eiga* (giant monster) pictures. With this fourth entry in the series, Toho's Godzilla saga hits its stride. Many fans consider *Godzilla vs. Mothra* the best G-film of them all. In retrospect, a Godzilla-Mothra showdown seems inevitable. Following the electrifying commercial success of *King Kong vs. Godzilla* (1962), Toho wanted to pair Godzilla with another high-profile beastie. A year earlier, *Mothra* (1961) had jump-started the studio's moribund *kaiju eiga* cycle with a similar box office jolt. Putting the two together didn't require Buddha-like wisdom.

Reporter Ichiro (Akira Takarada) and photographer Yoka (Yuriko Hoshi) are at the shore, covering the damage caused by a massive hurricane, when local fishermen haul in a giant egg discovered floating at sea. A shady character named Kumayama (Yoshibumi Tajima) buys the egg from the fishermen and plans to charge admission to see it. He partners with the even less scrupulous Torahata (Kenji Sahara) to build an amusement park around the egg. Soon the two Infant Island fairies (Emi and Yumi Ito), heroines of the original *Mothra*, arrive to plead for the return of the egg, which belongs to Mothra. But Kumayama and Torahata, who have invested heavily in their would-be egg-stravaganza, refuse and send the fairies home empty-handed.

In the course of their hurricane reportage, Ichiro and Yoka discover unusually high radiation levels near an industrial building site. They return to investigate. Suddenly Godzilla erupts from beneath the earth, emerging tail-first and mad as hell. The monster immediately begins a fresh rampage and, as ever, the Japanese military proves incapable of stopping him. The journalists hit on the idea of enlisting Mothra's aid against Godzilla, and travel to Infant Island to enlist the twin fairies' assistance. But the twins refuse, because the giant moth is near the end of its life cycle. Nevertheless, once Godzilla begins to threaten the giant egg, Mothra zooms to the rescue. The two monsters battle to a standstill before Mothra dies. Godzilla is incapacitated momentarily, but soon revives. In the short interim, the giant egg hatches to reveal two larval Mothras—essentially, giant silkworms. In a climactic second battle, the larvae work together to cocoon Godzilla into submission. Godzilla tumbles into the sea, and the young Mothras swim away toward Infant Island.

The characters in *Godzilla vs. Mothra* exist primarily to bring Mothra into the story, and provide little interest in and of themselves. The dastardly Kumayama and Torahata remain the only characters with distinct personalities. The wafer-thin plot serves as little more than connective tissue between special effects sequences. Fortunately, those effects sequences are spectacular, especially the two fight scenes, which rank as the most imaginative and thrilling of all Toho's giant monster showdowns.

Godzilla vs. The Thing (1964) turned out to be "Godzilla vs. Mothra" (one of the film's alternate titles).

Maybe AIP hid Mothra's identity because executives feared fans wouldn't pay to see Godzilla fight an oversized butterfly. Yet, it's just this oddball pairing that makes the film's monster battles work. Unlike *King Kong vs. Godzilla*, in which the creatures grapple like professional wrestlers, in this film, the monsters use their unique abilities to combat their opponent: Mothra waylays Godzilla by releasing a cloud of dusty yellow poison; Godzilla fires back with a burst of atomic breath; and the twins eventually prevail due to their cocooning goo.

In short, these scenes play out like a contest between two animals, not between two guys in rubber suits. The battles are notable for their dramatic structure, as well: At first glance, Mothra seems pitifully overmatched. This is David and Goliath, Monster Island-style — the "King of the Monsters" dethroned by two baby caterpillars.

After a subpar outing with *King Kong vs. Godzilla*, Toho's visual effects department delivers one of its finest efforts with *Godzilla vs. Mothra*. In addition to the two monster-v-monster tilts, there are numerous scenes of Godzilla battling the military, plus additional sequences involving Mothra and the fairies. All are strikingly executed and composed. At one point, sunlight streams through Mothra's gossamer red, yellow and brown wings— one of the more beautiful shots of any *kaiju eiga*.

As another plus, *Godzilla vs. Mothra* reached U.S. audiences without extensive re-editing. Except for the inevitable dubbing, Americans saw virtually the same film that played Japanese theaters. This film also remains memorable as the final film in which Godzilla would appear as the bad guy, until Toho restarted the series in 1984.

Goke, Body Snatcher from Hell see *Body Snatcher from Hell*

Goliath and the Dragon

(1960; AIP; Italy) Original Language Title: *La Vendetta di Ercole*; Alternate Title: *Vengeance of Hercules*. Director: Vittorio Cottafavi, Lee Kressell (English language version); Producers: Achilli Piazzi, Gianni Fuchs; Screenplay: Marcello Baldi, Mario Ferrari (Story: Marco Piccolo, Archibald Zounds, Jr.); Cinematographer: Mario Montuori. Cast: Mark Forest, Broderick Crawford, Eleanora Ruffo, Gaby Andre, Philippe Hersent.

"I forbid you to work on any more of these plots that don't make sense, you *moron*!"— exasperated villain to his inept henchman after yet another failed attempt to kill the hero

Though dozens of pepla (Italian-made muscleman films set in ancient Greece or Rome) washed ashore in America during the sword-and-sandal flood initiated by the surprise success of 1957's *Hercules* (released by Joseph E. Levine in the U.S. in 1959), only a handful contained significant fantasy elements, most being concerned with palace intrigue, heroic romance, and small-scale battles. (Note: by the time the genre's popularity began to wane in 1964, over 170 pepla had been produced in Italy.) Even fewer offered any real horror along with the muscles and swordfights. *Goliath and the Dragon* is one of those few.

Always on the lookout for a trend, AIP heads Jim Nicholson and Sam Arkoff decided to jump on the beefcake-and-brawn bandwagon by acquiring two pepla: *Sign of Rome* (changed to the more exploitive *Sign of the Gladiator*— despite there being no gladiator in the picture!) and a Steve Reeves Hercules movie, which became a "Goliath" film because, as Arkoff wrote in his autobiography *Flying Through Hollywood by the Seat of My Pants*, "we did not want to seem as though we were trying to exploit Levine's success with his Hercules movies." (Given Arkoff's penchant for, let's say, coloring the issues, it was more likely fear of a lawsuit that prompted the change.) That film, *Goliath and the Barbarians*, subsequently became a huge hit for AIP.

"After the success of *Goliath and the*

Broderick Crawford(!), as the evil King Euetus, places a damsel in distress in one of the few horror-themed peplums (Italian muscleman movies) of the 1960s, *Goliath and the Dragon* (1960) (Mexican lobby card).

Barbarians, Jim and I decided we needed another 'Goliath' movie," wrote Arkoff, "and we signed contracts in Italy to co-produce a new film, *Goliath and the Dragon*. Lou Rusoff wrote a script for us, and we flew Debra Paget to Italy as one of the leads in the new picture.... Just days before production was set to begin, however, the movie was put on hold. The Italian filmmakers decided they needed to make some changes— most significantly, they wanted to double the budget of the film." AIP balked and walked away from the project. Fortuitously, Nicholson and Arkoff soon learned of another in-production Hercules movie that had run out of money after four weeks of shooting. Providing the necessary completion financing, AIP transformed it into their proposed *Goliath and the Dragon.*

While Hercules remains the best-known Italian action hero (and headlines the best peplum ever made: *Hercules in the Haunted World*), numerous other classical champions (played by a variety of chiseled-physique — and stony-faced — body builders) donned the leather loincloth to hurl Styrofoam rocks at soldiers and occasionally battle unwieldy monsters. Maciste, Samson, Atlas, and even Ulysses oiled their torsos and bulged their biceps across American screens in the 1960s. AIP added Goliath to the peplum pack, featuring him in five films from 1960 to 1964. Three of these entries were (ahem) "straight" adventure pepla (*Goliath and the Barbarians, Goliath and the Sins of Babylon*, and *Goliath and the Conquest of Damascus*), while another, *Goliath and the Vampires*— despite its title — offered only brief, half-hearted fantasy elements.

Goliath and the Dragon, on the other hand, shows its blood-red colors as a true horror peplum in its first ten minutes, in which the titular titan, played by Mark Forest (actually, American gymnast Lou Degni; Nicholson and Arkoff felt his name didn't sound American enough, so they persuaded him to adopt the new moniker), faces a three-headed, fire-breathing dog monster; a stop-motion dinosaur-like dragon (which he lets pass for the moment, saving it for a later confrontation); and a man-sized flying bat-creature. Unfortunately, the monsters (apart from the impressive dino-dragon) look like oversized Steiff stuffed animals, with the devil-dog sporting mangy heads and floppy paws that move up and down in an awkward wave, and the bat-beast looking stiff and unwieldy in its fake fur and Bigfoot feet.

The plot introduces "Emilius the mighty, Goliath of Thebes" (thereafter referred to simply as "Goliath" in the English export version), who must journey to the Cave of Hell to return to Thebes their precious "Blood Diamond" and appease the gods. The evil King Euetus (a slumming Broderick Crawford, who looks for all the world like he'd rather be *anywhere* else), ruler of a neighboring kingdom, has stolen the gem in order to lure Goliath to his death at the hands/talons of his monsters. But, of course, Goliath overcomes all (including dealing with his own brother's Romeo-and-Juliet-like love affair and the kidnapping of his beloved wife Dejanira by a randy centaur!).

With a long stretch of monster-less "action" in the film's middle, this *Dragon* slows to a crawl after its exciting opening, before waking up again when the G-man finally battles the dragon. The sparse but lively stop-motion inserts of said beast (provided to AIP by Project Unlimited, a company owned by Tim Barr, Wah Chang and Gene Warren, who'd won an Academy Award for their work on 1960's *The Time Machine*) are nearly ruined by juxtaposing them with scenes of the silly papier mache head used in the up-close-and-personal shots of Goliath whacking at the monster. But just as the chuckles arise, Goliath gruesomely gouges out the creature's eye with his sword (leading to a nice stop-motion shot of the dragon rearing up in pain). Rather than ending here, there remains another 15 minutes of mundane mayhem typical of the genre (hero leads attack on evil ruler, battle ensues). At least this climactic conflict offers an impressive scene of the castle walls collapsing as Goliath destroys the support pillars in the cave beneath.

Though not a perfect peplum by any means, *Goliath and the Dragon* stands as a passable, intermittently exciting entry in the he-man horror sweepstakes.

Goliath and the Vampires (1961/64; AIP; Italy) Original Language Title: *Maciste Contro il Vampiro.* Alternate Title: *The Vampires* (TV). Directors: Sergio Corbucci, Giacomo Gentilomo; Producer: Paolo Moffa; Screenplay: Sergio Corbucci, Duccio Tessari; Cinematographer: Alvar Mancori. Cast: Gordon Scott, Gianna Maria Canale, Jacques Sernas, Leonora Ruffo, Mario Feliciani.

MONSTER vs. GOLIATH ... ALL NEW ... THE MIGHTIEST BATTLE OF THEM ALL!— ad line

Imported by AIP in 1964, *Goliath and the Vampires*, along with Mario Bava's *Hercules in the*

Haunted World, ranks among the best and most eventful horror-pepla to hit the big screens of America (not surprising, perhaps, since it was co-directed and co-written by Sergio Corbucci, creator of some of the greatest Spaghetti Westerns ever made, including *Django*, *The Mercenary*, and *The Great Silence*). Gordon Scott stars as Goliath (changed from "Maciste" in the original Italian version), the "strongest man in the world." When a band of raiders from Salmanak attack and burn Goliath's village, killing the men and abducting the women, Goliath vows revenge. Journeying to Salmanak, Goliath aligns himself with a race of mysterious "Blue Men" to battle the evil sorcerer Kobrak and free both the kidnapped women and the oppressed people of Salmanak.

Goliath and the Vampires takes a more brutal approach than most sword-and-sandal flicks. Rather than the usual ration of sword thrusts and arrows to the chest, *Goliath* offers up a feast of throat slashings, arrows to the *eye*, and bodies dropped head-first into a raging inferno. And there's the inventively cruel torture of forcing one unfortunate to climb a greased pole above a platform of spikes— with the expected pointed result. The film even kills off Goliath's pre-teen friend in a shockingly unexpected (and rather poignant) death scene.

Then there's the supernatural angle. Kobrak requires blood, which, during his first appearance, he reaches for from behind a curtain with his horrible, monstrous arm. After grasping the gory chalice, a hellish wind and eerie fog suddenly springs up to swirl about the room, terrifying even Kobrak's own servants. Corbucci and co. keep Kobrak's appearances sporadic and brief, never fully exposing the monstrous magician, thereby letting the viewer's imagination fill in the grotesque blanks. Until the end, Kobrak only appears out of a red mist as a transparent, ghostly image (though his hideous arm and clawed hand turn corporeal in order to slash and strangle disobedient underlings). At the climax the sorcerer transforms himself into the very likeness of Goliath (with the "evil" Goliath played by none other than Steve "Hercules" Reeves!) to go one-on-one with our real hero.

The underground "Kingdom of Blue Men" offers some impressive cavern settings, complete with massive sliding-rock doorways and a pit housing a giant beetle-monster (a disappointing spindly-legged puppet of *Queen of Outer Space* caliber). And Goliath leads his Blue Men allies through a creepy, misty swamp setting — only to have Kobrak appear and destroy them with fire, resulting in screaming stuntmen set aflame as burning tree trunks fall upon them.

Though no master thespian, Gordon Scott was still one of the more expressive peplum stars, even displaying some genuine anguish here when he finds the lifeless body of his lady love. Former Tarzan Scott also performs some impressive stunt work himself, such as jumping from a 10-foot wall only to spring forward and launch himself at a group of soldiers— all in one continuous motion (and take).

On the downside, *Goliath* is loaded with the expected awkward (dubbed) dialogue, though

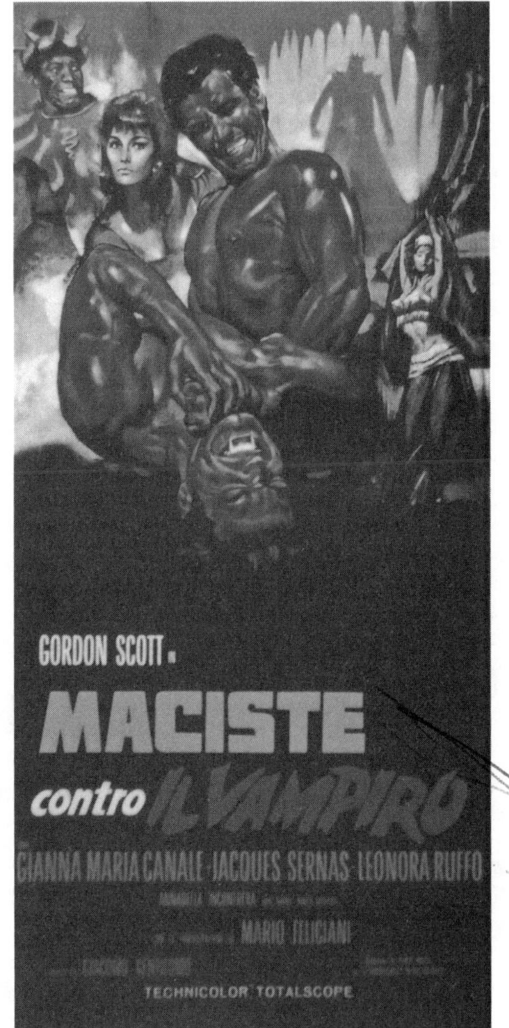

Italian poster for *Goliath and the Vampires* (1961/64).

some of it proves rather colorful (such as: "There exists here a beast who's more evil than a fiend!"). The film also features not one, not two, but *four* Goliath-vs.-soldiers confrontations, adding a sense of mundane repetition to the otherwise bizarre scenario. Upping the banality factor are two dancing-girl sequences—one a showstopper (in the literal sense of the term, since it halts the movie dead in its tracks), but the other proving rather more entertaining due to some Turkish-tinged 60s surf guitar music playing on the soundtrack!

Despite its (inevitable) faults, *Goliath and the Vampires* offers enough inventive and chilling moments to keep both horror and peplum fans happy, making this one of the few truly successful horror/he-man hybrids of the 1960s.

Gorath (1962/64, Toho, Japan) Director: Ishiro Honda. Producer: Tomoyuki Tanaka. Screenplay: Takashi Kimura. From a story by Jojiro Okami. Cinematographer: Hajime Koizume. Cast: Ryo Ikebe, Yumi Shirakawa, Takashi Shimura, Kumi Mizuno, Ken Uehara, Akira Kubo.

> See! the world doomed by an invading wild sun 6000 times bigger than earth!
> —Advertising tagline

Gorath will sorely disappoint monster fans who approach it in hopes of finding another Godzilla or Ghidrah. Despite its monstrous-sounding title, this is a straight science fiction yarn with a giant monster shoehorned in, not a true *kaiju eiga*.

Obviously inspired by George Pal's *When Worlds Collide* (1951), the plot involves a rogue star that threatens to destroy all life on Earth as it passes through our solar system. The nations of the world unite to build a network of gigantic, nuclear-powered thrusters, which shift the planet's orbit and allow the Earth to dodge the passing star. The thrusters are built in Antarctica, and their heat awakens a sleeping monster that looks like a giant prehistoric walrus. Gorath, for the record, is the name of the star, not of the walrus.

This film, which continued the lineage of *The Mysterians* (1957) and *Battle in Outer Space* (1960), was intended to be the grandest of Toho's sci-fi epics. And in some respects, it is. *Gorath* is ambitious in scope and adult in tone. It features a large and accomplished cast, as well some astoundingly detailed, eye-catching miniature F/X sequences, among the best Toho ever produced. Unfortunately, like the Pal film that inspired it, *Gorath* bogs down in hackneyed subplots involving underwritten characters. It incessantly pounds the viewer over the head with its Call for Global Unity, which however noble, quickly grows tiresome. And the story's "science" is laughable in the extreme, which is a difficult to overcome when a movie takes itself so seriously. The awkward-looking walrus-monster's brief appearance adds little to the proceedings, and was edited out of the picture for its American release.

In fact, *Gorath* was butchered almost beyond recognition for U.S. audiences. Not only were some scenes deleted, but others were re-ordered. The American version also suffers the usual atrocious dubbing and re-scoring, this time with robotic beeping noises and other "science fictiony" sounds inserted at random. Viewers are advised to seek out the original Japanese cut of *Gorath*, if they bother to see it at all.

Gorgo (1961; King Bros.; UK) Director: Eugene Lourie. Producer: Herman King. Screenwriter: Robert L. Richards (as John Loring) and Daniel Jams (as Daniel Hyatt). Cinematographer: Freddie Young. Cast: Bill Travers, William Sylvester, Vincent Winter, Christopher Rhodes, Joseph O'Conor, Bruce Seton.

> Like nothing you've ever seen before!—tagline

Gorgo is the kind of movie that's easy to love when you're a kid, but hard to revisit as a grownup.

Uncluttered by romance, comedy relief or boring subplots, starring one of the coolest-looking of all giant monsters and concluding with an epic, city-smashing finale, *Gorgo* boasts everything preteen viewers could want. On the other hand, its script seems cobbled together out of leftover elements from earlier, better films. Its characters remain thinly developed "types," and its visual effects are woefully inconsistent—limitations likely to try adults' patience.

When their salvage ship is damaged in a violent storm, sailors Joe (Bill Travers) and Sam (William Sylvester) find themselves stranded in a small Irish fishing village. To pass the time during their vessel's repair, they venture down in a diving bell, hoping to find something worthy of salvaging. Instead they discover and capture an authentic, living dinosaur. Despite the pleas of a local lad, Sean (Vincent Winter), who urges them to let the creature go, Joe and Sam transport the beast, which they dub Gorgo, to London, and put it on display in a circus. Sean stows away aboard their ship so he can continue to pester them about releasing the monster.

Scientists examine the creature and inform the surprised sailors that their 65-foot monster is a mere infant. Sure enough, 200-foot Mama Gorgo soon emerges from the sea. She appears at the 43-minute mark of this 76-minute movie, and her unstoppable march to retrieve her captive child, battling the Royal Air Force, Navy and Army all the way, consumes the remainder of the film.

Gorgo **(well, his mother, actually) takes out a famous London landmark (1961).**

Unfortunately, the concept of a mommy monster protecting her young is the film's only original thought. Despite its advertising tagline ("Like nothing you've ever seen before!"), *Gorgo* remains little more than a collection of swipes. For instance, the scene in a diving bell derives from *The Beast from 20,000 Fathoms* (1953). A photographer's flash bulbs send the Baby Gorgo on a homicidal rampage, a la *King Kong* (1933). A verbose radio reporter (Maurice Kaufmann), who prattles inanely throughout the final battle evokes the fonder memory of Raymond Burr in *Godzilla, King of the Monsters* (1954/56).

Although it's fun to watch virtually every world-famous British landmark (Tower Bridge, Big Ben, Parliament, Picadilly Circus) fall before the monster's wrath, the film's 30-minute, city-stomping military-versus-monster finale ultimately grows tiresome. *Gorgo*'s wildly uneven visual effects, sometimes quite poor, are further hampered by clumsily integrated stock footage. Filmmakers even intercut of jet fighters zooming across a cloudy daytime sky with *night* footage of the rampaging Mama Gorgo. When mother and child finally reunite, the proportions are all wrong. Baby Gorgo barely reaches his mother's ankle. If he stands 65 feet tall, then Mama must be closer to 2,000 feet than 200.

This was director Eugene Lourie's third giant monster movie, following the seminal *Beast from 20,000 Fathoms*, as well as *The Giant Behemoth* (1959). He signed on to helm *Gorgo* reluctantly, and producers Frank and Maurice King rejected most of his ideas. Perhaps as a result, his work here often seems perfunctory. Ironically, while Lourie wanted no city-smashing sequences at all, he does a masterful job in the scenes of raw destruction, conveying the stark terror of Londoners fleeing at the approach of monsters.

Unlike Lourie's *Beast* and *Behemoth*, which featured stop-motion animated creatures, Gorgo was portrayed by a stunt man in a rubber suit. Luckily, it's a great-looking costume, one of the best in movie history. The fearsome Gorgos are Tyranosaurus-like creatures with bulbous red eyes and distinctive, wing-like fins that jut from the sides of their skulls.

Gorgo also benefits immeasurably from the work of cinematographer Freddie Young, whose evocative Technicolor photography lends the film an air of respectability. An excellent craftsman, Young had worked previously with Michael Powell and Emeric Pressburger, and would subsequently film two of David Lean's greatest pictures, *Lawrence of Arabia* (1962) and *Dr. Zhivago* (1965). If not for Young and that terrific monster suit, *Gorgo* might well be forgotten today.

The Gorgon (1964; Hammer; U.K.) Director: Terence Fisher; Producer: Anthony Nelson-Keys; Screenplay: John Gilling, John Elder [Anthony Hinds] (based on a story by J. Llewellyn Devine); Cinematographer: Micheal Reed. Cast: Peter Cushing, Christopher Lee, Barbara Shelley, Richard Pasco, Michael Goodliffe, Patrick Troughton.

She Turns Screaming Flesh Into Silent Stone
—ad line

Hammer Films, who made versions of nearly all the great monster stories, here tackles Greek mythology—setting it (as they did most of their better films) in the 19th century. Peter Cushing plays the local doctor employing Barbara Shelley, who just happens to be possessed by the spirit of Megera (one of the three gorgons) during the full moon. It seems that everybody but Shelley and the milktoast hero/love interest knows it—including the audience (although the plot is ostensibly set up as a mystery).

Beginning production on December 9, 1963, and wrapping on January 16, 1964, *The Gorgon* cost a mere £150,000. Given Hammer's two biggest stars, Cushing and Lee, the studio's top director, Terence Fisher (who helmed all of Hammer's best entries from the previous decade, including *Curse of Frankenstein*, *Horror of Dracula* and *The Mummy*)—not to mention leading lady Barbara Shelley (arguably the best actress ever to appear as a Hammer heroine), one would expect great things from *The Gorgon*. Sadly, one would be disappointed.

"*The Gorgon*," co-scripter John Gilling told *Little Shoppe of Horrors* magazine, "was a writing assignment from Hammer that I considered one of my best screenplays." However, Gilling felt that Anthony Hinds, who "re-wrote the opening and changed much of the dialogue," ruined the script—and the film.

The Gorgon has two things going for it—the lush, colorful photography and sets (a trademark of many Hammer outings), and the performance of Christopher Lee as the strong-willed Professor Meister, determined to get to the bottom of things even if the truth may prove unpleasant for our love-smitten hero. Meister is not your typical book-bound professor; no, he has no compunction about climbing out a two-story window to evade interfering police or breaking into a lab to peruse some revealing records. Lee's powerful screen presence is given free reign in the form of this no-nonsense, forceful figure who dominates every scene he's in.

Not so the title character, however. The Gorgon itself does nothing even remotely menacing, its greatest exertion being stepping out of the shadows. The unconvincing make-up doesn't help; and the only tremors produced by the dime-store rubber snakes in her wig are the result of viewers' belly laughs.

In *The Films of Christopher Lee*, by Poole and Hart, Christopher Lee called *The Gorgon* a "beautiful-looking picture, but the whole thing fell apart because the effect of the snakes on Megera's head was not sufficiently well done for the climax of the film. Not a memorable picture, but it could have been terrific." Indeed.

Christopher Lee takes aim at *The Gorgon* (Prudence Hyman) (1964).

Grave Desires see *Brides of Blood*

The Green Slime

The Green Slime (1969; MGM; U.S./Japan) Director: Kinji Fukasaku; Producers: Walter Manley, Ivan Reiner; Screenplay: Charles Sinclair, William Finger, Tom Rowe; Cinematographer: Yoshikazu Yamasawa. Cast: Robert Horton, Richard Jaeckel, Luciana Paluzzi, Bud Widom, Ted Gunther, David Yurstun, Robert Dunham.

The Green Slime are coming!—
bumper sticker promo

What kid growing up in the 1960s could resist such a title? And what adult going to the video store nowadays could resist *sniggering* at such an absurd appellation? For all those "camp" followers out there, however, *The Green Slime* has become something of a mainstay, thanks to its encased-in-amber sixties sensibilities. In the words of the film's star, Robert Horton, "It's so bad it became a cult film." Well, actually it's not *that* bad.

The first half of the movie is basically *Armageddon* (1998), though not nearly as laugh-out-loud funny as that overblown and overpriced unintentional comedy. Orbiting space station Gamma III must dispatch a crew to land on an asteroid, drill holes into its surface, and plant bombs that will blow it to smithereens before it collides with the Earth and destroys the human race. Horton plays the trouble-shooting specialist dispatched to the station to head the asteroid mission. Richard Jaeckel is the well-meaning but weak space station commander and former friend of Rankin — until he stole Rankin's girl, the beautiful space station medico (former *Thunderball* Bond girl Luciana Paluzzi). Although the mission is successful, one astronaut inadvertently brings back to the station a tiny amount of green substance that grows into one-eyed walking slime monsters that feed on electricity and electrocute their victims. It's up to Rankin and Elliot to set aside their differences and find a way to defeat the ever-growing and seemingly unstoppable monsters.

According to *The Hollywood Reporter*, Robert Taylor was originally scheduled to star in this first ever Japanese-U.S. co-production. But when cameras rolled in late 1967 just outside Tokyo (with a Japanese crew and Caucasian cast), it was a *different* Robert — Horton, of TV's *Wagon Train*, *Alfred Hitchcock Presents* and *As the World Turns* fame — in the heroic hotseat. Horton does fine in his square-jawed, underwritten role of a hard-line military man-of-action. And Richard Jaeckel (*The Dirty Dozen*, *Grizzly*, *Starman*) does equally well in the part of the nice-guy-but-no-leader space station commander. The film's main bit of human interest comes from the friction between these two characters and their different approaches to the responsibility of leadership.

(Really) big laser guns and *Star Trek* sensibilities (shoot first and ask questions later) are the order of the day. And the monsters, with their squat green bodies, giant solitary red eye, and impossibly long (and ungainly) tentacles, are unique, if nothing else. "I have a photograph of me feeding one of the monsters a *cookie*, because that's what I thought of the monsters," laughed Horton. "I thought they were ridiculous." Even so, thanks to some frantic staging by director Kinji Fukasaku (as well as some heroically straight-faced playing by the principals), these Little Green Globs on Gamma III do generate a few moments of suspense, with Our Heroes desperately weaving and dodging the waving appendages whose touch means instant (and gruesome) death by electrocution.

Arguably the most amazing thing about this film is the fact that the movie's title song ("Is it just something in your head? / Will you believe it when you're dead? / Greeeeen Sliiiiime!") came out as a 45 single.

MGM's (yes, *that* MGM) PR boys went all out in their promotional ploys. "All over Manhattan," recalled Horton, "on the curbs all up and down Manhattan, were printed '*The Green Slime, The Green Slime, The Green Slime*'! I remember we went down to see it on 34th street, and about three minutes before I knew the film was going to be over with, I said, 'Let's get out of here; I have no desire to have anybody see me!' [*Laughs*] The picture was dreadful."

Ray guns vs. ***The Green Slime*** (1969).

Dreadful ... but in a *good* way. With its comic-book iconoclastic cyclopean monsters, plasticine rockets, bright color schemes, "mod" wardrobes (and go-go dancing!), and fabulously campy theme song, *The Green Slime* remains an entertaining bit of late-sixties kitsch. It's a pulp horror/sci-fi cover come to life.

With quotes from: "Mini-skirts, Lasers, and Monsters, Oh My!: Robert Horton Remembers The Green Slime," by Bryan Senn, *Filmfax* 92, August/September 2002.

The Gruesome Twosome (1967; Mayflower)

Director/Producer/Cinematography: Herschell Gordon Lewis; Screenplay: Louise Downe. Cast: Elizabeth Davis, Gretchen Wells, Chris Martell, Rodney Bedell.

The most barbaric humor since the guillotine went out of style — tagline

By the time *The Gruesome Twosome* reached movie screens, director Herschell Gordon Lewis, originator of the splatter film, hadn't directed a full-tilt gore fest in nearly two years (since *Color Me Blood Red* [1965]). Lewis had issued two chillers earlier in 1967 (*Something Weird* and *A Taste of Blood*), but both toned down the violence. Now he was feeling pressure to deliver one of his patented blood baths.

"One reason we did this this way was because some of the exhibitors had said, 'What's going on? Your pictures don't seem to have the amount of blood they used to,'" Lewis said. In an attempt to please the naysayers while still breaking new ground, Lewis decided to combine "black humor with gore." The result was one of his quirkiest efforts, a film by turns wildly amusing, stomach-churning and (for long stretches) deadly dull.

The plot is simple enough: Batty old Mrs. Pringle (Elizabeth Davis) and her half-wit son Rodney (Chris Martell) run a tiny wig shop near a college campus. A sign in the window proudly boasts, "100% Human Hair Wigs for Sale." Care to guess where the hair comes from? That's right—from gullible coeds who Mrs. Pringle lures into the shop and Rodney scalps. After a third girl goes missing, one determined student, Kathy (Gretchen Wells), decides to try to solve the mystery. Her boyfriend (Rodney Bedell) reluctantly tags along.

When Lewis wrapped production on *The Gruesome Twosome* and assembled the rough cut, he realized that (due to a mathematical error) the picture had come in 10 minutes too short. The cast and crew had disbanded so he was forced to improvise, coming up with two sequences that he calls "absolutely classic example[s] of desperation-type filler." The first was a bizarre, four-minute introduction in which two wig blocks decorated with paper eyes, noses and lips (like something from a Mrs. Potato Head doll) exchange catty remarks in a thick Southern drawl. The second expanded a throwaway sequence in which Kathy and Dave attend a drive-in movie by cutting in a scene from the "art film" they are supposedly watching.

As a result, Lewis once named *The Gruesome Twosome* as the lone film among all those on which he had complete creative control that he dislikes. "Those were devices we had to add in later to make the film a respectable length," he said. "It sickened me at the time. In fact, even now, it bothers me.... My heart sank because there was so much more we could have done. In fact, there was one whole effect we didn't do because we thought we had plenty of length there." This gag—pushing a victim's face down into a vat of boiling French fries—was later revived for *The Gore Gore Girls* (1972).

Despite Lewis' self-recriminations, the oddball wig-block intro and the art film parody remain perhaps the film's most memorable moments, and certainly further Lewis' desire to inject some humor into the proceedings. The biggest problem with the film isn't that these elements were added, but rather that other sequences of no interest whatsoever (co-eds sharing a bucket of fried chicken in their dorm room, for instance) could not be trimmed. In one agonizing *nine-minute* sequence, Kathy follows the college's janitor home and accuses him of being a serial killer—only to discover he was merely bringing home a soup bone for his dog.

The film could have used more footage of Mrs. Pringle and Rodney, characters who are both funny and well-played by Elizabeth Davis and Chris Martell. In another of the film's most striking scenes, Mrs. Pringle forces her pathetic son to recite the following oath: "I promise to be a good boy always and listen to mother so I can live with her forever and never have to go away to the place for bad boys." As a reward for his devotion, Mrs. Pringle gives her son an electric knife, which he promptly uses on their next victim. The film's other characters are simple props. Kathy, for instance, has no apparent motivation for her obsessive snooping other than a possible overdose of Nancy Drew mysteries. *The Gruesome Twosome* functions on the same low level as every Lewis picture in terms of production values, cinematography, sound design and dialogue, although it's marginally better acted than most.

Despite exhibitors' obvious appetite for such material, *The Gruesome Twosome* proved to be Lewis' final gore film of the 1960s. He spent the rest of the decade on other exploitation fare — biker flicks, hillbilly comedies and sex farces. He returned to the peculiar idiom he had pioneered just twice more, with *The Wizard of Gore* (1972) and *The Gore Gore Girls* (1972). Nevertheless, for better or (usually) worse, the stamp he left on the horror genre proved indelible.

With quotes from: *A Taste of Blood: The Films of Herschell Gordon Lewis,* by Christopher Wayne Curry; *The Gruesome Twosome* DVD audio commentary with H.G. Lewis.

Hand of Death (1962; Twentieth Century–Fox; b&w) Producer: Eugene Ling; Director: Gene Nelson; Screenplay: Eugene Ling; Cinematographer: Floyd Crosby. Cast: John Agar, Paula Raymond, Stephen Dunne, Roy Gordon, John A. Alonzo, Joe Besser.

No one dared come too close! — tagline

Issued on the bottom of an agonizing twin bill with *The Cabinet of Caligari, Hand of Death* virtually vanished following its brief theatrical run. Never revived theatrically, nor included in any Fox television package, *Hand of Death* went unseen for decades, and as a result took on a patina of mystery and promise. Stills from the film, showing star John Agar in a monster makeup that strongly recalled artist Jack Kirby's The Thing from the Fantastic Four comic book, looked intriguing. Then, more than 30 years after its debut, *Hand of Death* finally turned up on cable's Fox Movie Channel, where it was seen by thousands (and copiously bootlegged). Audiences quickly figured out why Fox hadn't bothered with this picture for three decades: It stinks.

Agar plays Alex Marsh, a scientist developing a new form of nerve gas designed to temporarily paralyze the enemy. Alas, prolonged exposure to the various chemicals used in the production of the gas renders Alex's touch deadly — which he discovers by placing his hand on the shoulder of his unfortunate lab assistant. After inadvertently bumping off a couple more innocents— including former Stooge Joe Besser, playing a luckless gas station attendant — Alex holes up at a friend's house. As the ailment progresses Alex begins to transform physically, turning black (!) as his body swells and cracks. While working furiously to find an antidote, Alex's pals realize their friend is also going insane.

The "death touch" scenario has potential and remains relatively fresh (although it's similar to the 1936 Boris Karloff-Bela Lugosi vehicle, *The Invisible Ray*). Alas, screenwriter/producer Eugene Ling seems to have no idea what to do with this rich premise. *Hand of Death* proves talky and uneventful, building to a "climax" that is, to be charitable, perfunctory. Although it runs a paltry 58 minutes, there's barely enough story for a decent *Outer Limits* episode, let alone a feature film. *Hand of Death* isn't even bad in an amusing way. Unlike similar, low-budget, experiment-gone-wrong shockers such as *The Hideous Sun Demon* and *The Alligator People* (both 1959), there's little fun to be had here.

Bob Mark's monster makeup looks OK in still photos but isn't convincing in action. Cinematographer Floyd Crosby lends the picture a professional look despite its threadbare budget, but has nearly nothing to work with. The two most in-

Ben Grimm from *The Fantastic Four*? No, it's a mask-wearing John Agar proffering the *Hand of Death* in 1962.

teresting aspects of the production may be Sonny Burke's offbeat, jazzy score, featuring prominent bongos, piano and theremin, and the jaw-dropping device of having Agar turn black to evidence his dehumanization. While it's doubtful the filmmakers intended to send such a message, this ploy speaks volumes about the way many whites viewed African American men in the early 1960s. Call it a cinematic Freudian slip.

Armchair psychoanalysis aside, *Hand of Death*'s obscurity proves well-earned.

Mexican lobby card for *The Beast of Morocco* (1968; aka *Hand of Night*).

The Hand of Night see *The Beast of Morocco*

Hands of a Stranger (1962; Allied Artists; b&w) Director/Screenplay: Newt Arnold; Producers: Newt Arnold and Michael DuPont; Cinematographer: Henry Crowjager. Cast: James Stapleton, Paul Lukather, Joan Harvey, Michael Rye, Larry Haddon.

They gave him the hands of a killer!—tagline

This otherwise tepid and forgettable variant on the familiar *Hands of Orlac* theme has the dubious distinction of being one of the most hysterically overwritten and overacted chillers of its era. It's so absurdly gaseous and campy that it may appeal to viewers who enjoy a good, old-fashioned terrible movie.

When concert pianist Vernon Paris (James Stapleton) loses his hands in an auto accident, crusading physician Gil Harding (Paul Lukather) replaces them with the hands of an unidentified murder victim. Dr. Harding takes a personal interest in the case—and in Vernon's doting sister, Dina (Joan Harvey). But Vernon, who has always been phobic about his hands, can't adjust to the transplants; he snaps and sets about exacting brutal revenge against everyone be believes has wronged him.

Hands of a Stranger is a hangdog, low-budget affair with minimalist production values and a no-name cast. The scenario is an uncredited rip-off of the often-remade and frequently imitated *Hands of Orlac* (1924), in which a pianist receives the transplanted hands of a killer. The best known (and just plain best) version of this story remains director Karl Freund's *Mad Love* (1935), co-starring Colin Clive and Peter Lorre. Would-be auteur Newt Arnold, whose only other directorial credits are the Philippine-made *Blood Thirst* (1971) and the Jean-Claude Van Damme vehicle

Publicity photograph of Joan Harvey for *Hands of a Stranger* (1962).

Bloodsport (1988), adds little to the Orlac legacy. He keeps the picture in focus and hides the boom mikes, but demonstrates little acumen for visual storytelling.

Yet *Hands of a Stranger*'s biggest liability—or its greatest asset, depending on your point of view—remains its slow-moving and verbose screenplay, co-written by Arnold and Michael DuPont. Vernon doesn't even become aware he has new hands until a solid hour of this 85-minute film has elapsed. Even then, most of the thrill sequences are pretty tame. (The lone exception, however, is indeed shocking: In the middle of what appears to be a warm-and-fuzzy scene with a piano-playing, 10-year-old boy, Vernon suddenly turns, crushes the child's hands and chokes the kid to death!) Most of the way, though, *Hands of a Stranger* plays less like a thriller and more like a soap opera, overstuffed with preposterous dialogue. The script veers from hardboiled snappy patter (a homicide detective refers to his department as "the local office of bullets and bodies") to purple prose (as when Dr. Harding marvels, protractedly, at the wonders of the human hand) to maudlin sentimentality (especially in its seemingly endless sappy romantic interludes). The overwrought word craft extends even to the closing credits: instead of a simple "The End," Arnold opts for the windy valedictory, "The Past is Prologue."

The only thing to do with material this overcooked is to chew the hell out of it, and that's exactly what the unfortunate souls appearing in this picture do. The principle players seem bent on out-emoting one another. Paul Lukather's over-earnest grandstanding as the noble Dr. Harding is matched by Joan Harvey's tremulous histrionics as the self-sacrificing Dina. James Stapleton's faux-maniacal scenes aren't as scary as his hambone speechifying on the subjects of Art and Beauty. And Richard LaSalle's over-the-top score is just as arch as the script and acting. It all adds up to a movie so astonishingly theatrical that it becomes sort of fascinating—or at least amusing. It's not quite *Robot Monster* (1953) or *Plan 9 from Outer Space* (1959), but for fanciers of camp, *Hands of a Stranger* should hit the spot.

The Hands of Orlac (1960/64; Britannia/Continental; U.K.) Director: Edmond T. Greville; Producers: Steven Pallos and Donald Taylor; Screenplay: John Baines and Edmond T. Greville (Additional dialogue: Donald Taylor; Novel: Maurice Renard); Cinematographer: Desmond Dickinson. Cast: Mel Ferrer, Christopher Lee, Dany Carrel, Lucille Saint Simon, Donald Pleasence.

Melody ... or murder in these hands?—tagline

This bland retelling of Maurice Renard's frequently filmed novel *The Hands of Orlac* languishes among the least memorable of the story's many screen incarnations. A remarkable supporting appearance by Christopher Lee only partially redeems this narcoleptic dud.

Concert pianist Steven Orlac (Mel Ferrer) badly injures his hands in a plane crash. As he slips in and out of consciousness, Orlac is rushed to the same hospital that's receiving the body of a just-executed strangler. His fiancée Louise (Lucille Saint Simon) takes Orlac to her home in the French countryside to recuperate from delicate surgery, but the pianist is haunted by the suspicion that his hands have been replaced by those of the strangler. After fending off a sudden urge to strangle Louise, Orlac rushes away to a

British quad poster for *The Hands of Orlac* (1960/64).

nearby village, where he crosses paths with Nero (Lee), a small-time magician/con man, and his assistant/accomplice Li Lang (Dany Carrel). Nero discovers Orlac's fears about his hands and torments the pianist as part of an extortion scheme. But does Orlac truly have a killer's hands, or is it all in his head?

Writer-director Edmond T. Greville's tame, psychological approach serves *Hands of Orlac* poorly. The screenplay, co-written by Greville and John Baines, never suggests that Orlac was anything other than a perfectly normal, well-adjusted guy — why then should he suddenly become prone to paranoid fantasy? The entire scenario is absurdly contrived and deadly dull, devoid of dramatic tension or excitement of any sort. The lone murder in the film, however, is a good one — after Li Lang tries to help Orlac, Nero "accidentally-on-purpose" kills his assistant during their magic act — but it arrives 90 minutes into this 95-minute movie. Prior to this, audiences are privy to many heart-to-hearts between Orlac and Louise, and, later, Orlac and Li Lang, plus scenes of Orlac fidgeting nervously and wringing his hands, or else boozing it up in his hotel room.

Ferrer, a serviceable but undistinguished actor, supplies a serviceable but undistinguished portrayal in the title role. Lucille Saint Simon and Dany Carrel provide little more than visual interest. Donald Pleasence is wasted in a one-scene bit part as a sculptor who wants to use Orlac as a hand model. Fortunately, as the devious, misanthropic Nero, Lee delivers a gleefully sadistic performance that ranks among his best of the early 1960s. It's a showy part; the actor attacks it with relish. Every time his character makes an appearance, *The Hands of Orlac* receives a badly needed jolt of energy. But Lee alone can't overcome the picture's many fundamental problems. "I thought the film was destroyed in many ways by many people but I had a good part and, I think, played it well." Lee said. "In fact, it's one of my best of the period. Nero was an interesting character — very odd, very sick, very angry." Lee devotees may want to seek out *Hands of Orlac*, but are advised to make sure their fast-forward button is in good working order.

With quotes from: *The Christopher Lee Filmography*, by Tom Johnson and Mark Miller.

The Haunted and the Hunted see *Dementia 13*

The Haunted Palace

(1963; American International) Director/Producer: Roger Corman; Screenplay: Charles Beaumont; Cinematographer: Floyd Crosby. Cast: Vincent Price, Debra Paget, Lon Chaney, Jr., Frank Maxwell, Leo Gordon, Elisha Cook, Jr.

What was the terrifying
thing in the PIT that
wanted women?— tagline

Charles Dexter Ward (Vincent Price) and his wife Ann (Debra Paget) arrive in a remote New England village to take possession of a castle he has inherited. To their surprise, the couple is shunned by the townspeople. The local physician (Frank Maxwell) explains that Ward's ancestor, Joseph Curwen, was burned alive by the villagers for practicing witchcraft. Many of the villagers have inherited bizarre deformities and mutations, which they claim are the result of Curwen's attempts to mate the women of the village with demons Curwen had conjured up within the castle. Soon Ward begins to succumb to the evil influence of Curwen — who, before his death, vowed to return from the grave and revenge himself. The warlock possesses Ward's body and restarts his experiments, while meting out vengeance against those who burned him alive.

Although posters and even screen credits refer to it as "Edgar Allan Poe's *The Haunted Palace*," this movie is not based on Poe was never intended to be part of producer-director Roger Corman's lengthy series of Poe adaptations. Nevertheless, at the eleventh hour, American International Pictures executives James Nicholson and Sam Arkoff demanded the picture be renamed so it could be promoted as another Poe film. Some voiceover narration by Price from the titular Poe poem was hastily added, and the movie's credits were adjusted accordingly.

"We were running out of good Poe stories to use and I wanted to take a break from Poe, anyway," Corman said. "Jim Nicholson knew [H.P.] Lovecraft's stories and really liked his work. I thought Lovecraft was a good writer, but I didn't think he was of the same complexity and nuance that Poe was, but I felt 'The Case of Charles Dexter Ward' would be fine for a movie. Then, after the film was finished, Jim [Nicholson] and Sam [Arkoff] changed their minds and decided somehow they wanted to integrate the picture into the Poe series. I always felt calling it a Poe picture made absolutely no sense. It was really something that was done simply for box office ap-

Warlock Joseph Curwen (Vincent Price) is about to be burned at the stake by irate villagers, only to return years later to possess his lookalike descendent and inhabit *The Haunted Palace* (1963) (American lobby card).

peal, because all the Poe pictures had made a lot of money for AIP."

Even the movie's re-vamped screenplay credit (by Charles Beaumont, "based on a poem by Edgar Allan Poe and a story by H.P. Lovecraft") doesn't really tell the whole story of the picture's origins. The scenario, based primarily on Lovecraft's novella "The Case of Charles Dexter Ward," also incorporates elements from other Lovecraft stories, including "The Shadow Over Innsmouth," but nothing at all by Poe (aside from the title and Price's concluding voiceover). Corman said he and Beaumont decided to "bring elements in from other Lovecraft stories to give it more depth." Also, Francis Ford Coppola, then Corman's top assistant, provided an uncredited dialogue polish on Beaumont's script.

However, if *The Haunted Palace* remains bogus as a Poe movie, it's one of the more effective adaptations of Lovecraft, a notoriously difficult author to translate to the screen. The film captures Lovecraft's lingering sense of dread, and the looming presence of ancient, implacable evil. This is suggested in part by its visual style. Compared to the preceding Poe pictures, cinematographer Floyd Crosby lends *The Haunted Palace* a darker, almost Dutch Masters look, with lots of deep, velvety blacks and a more subdued color palate. "I envisioned, and I think I got, a slightly different look for Lovecraft than I had used for Poe," Corman said. "I used a somewhat starker lighting pattern because I felt that was intrinsically the difference between Lovecraft and Poe, and we should have a slightly more realistic, starker look." This turned out to be Crosby's most impressive work of the entire series.

Two other key Corman collaborators, production designer Daniel Haller and composer Ronald Stein, also make superlative contributions. Haller's sets are the largest-looking and most imposing of all those he had designed for the Poe films thus far. In some cases, their screen impact was enhanced by camera trickery. For instance, the film's street set was built in perspective, laced with dry ice fog and then shot with a wide angle lens to make it seem larger and deeper. For *The Haunted Palace*, the prolific Stein composed what is generally regarded as his finest score, including a title theme that is majestic yet ominous and brooding.

Vincent Price, back for his sixth Corman Poe feature, delivers one of his more convincing performances of the series in what amounts to a dual role, as Charles Ward and as Joseph-Curwen-possessing-Charles-Ward, finding distinctive deliveries for both characters—softer and more naturalistic as the former, more forceful and theatrical as the latter. The radiant Debra Paget spends most of the movie weeping, screaming or furrowing her eyebrows as the perplexed Mrs. Ward; she's fine as far as the role allows. Lon Chaney, Jr.'s dull, slightly dopey performance as Simon the castle caretaker (and fellow warlock) presents a more significant issue. The rest of the cast—including Frank Maxwell as Dr. Willett, and Leo Gordon and Elisha Cook, Jr., as spooked villagers—doesn't leave much of an impression.

Aside from uneven performances, *The Haunted Palace*'s biggest liabilities are a ponderously slow second act and the story's numbing predictability. Despite its literary pedigree, the basic narrative remains very similar to numerous other films, ranging from the sublime (*Black Sunday* [1960]) to the ridiculous (*The Brainiac* [1962]). Another minor but irksome problem is that not only are the same actors are used for a pre-credit sequence that takes place 110 years earlier than the main story, but when they reappear, playing their own descendents in "present day," they all look *exactly* the same — right down to their identical hair styles. Price even wears the same beard. (This is a missed opportunity: Why not let Ward arrive clean-shaven, then grow a beard — like the one Curwen wears in a castle painting — to outwardly symbolize his inner transformation?) Also, the picture's climax plays like something out of James Whale, torch wielding villagers and all. It adds up to a solid but less than scintillating picture — one well worth seeing, but unlikely to become a great favorite.

Corman says that the last-minute switcheroo that turned a Lovecraft movie into an ersatz Poe flick didn't scuttle a possible Lovecraft series. "I wasn't envisioning a Lovecraft series of films," Corman said. "I thought I would go back to Poe, but I just wanted break the cycle, as it were, for one picture." Indeed, Corman was soon back to (true) Poe adaptations with the penultimate, and best, entry in the series, *The Masque of the Red Death* (1964).

With quotes from: "California Gothic: The Corman/Haller Collaboration," by Lawrence French, from *Video Watchdog* No. 138; and "A Change of Poe" DVD interview with Corman, *Midnite Movies Double Feature: The Haunted Palace/Tower of London*, MGM Home Entertainment.

The Haunting (1963; MGM; U.S./U.K.; b&w) Producer/Director: Robert Wise; Screenplay: Nelson Gidding (based on the novel *The Haunting of Hill House* by Shirley Jackson); Cinematographer: David Boulton. Cast: Julie Harris, Claire Bloom, Richard Johnson, Russ Tamblyn, Fay Compton, Rosalie Crutchley, Lois Maxwell, Valentine Dyall.

FEEL ... Your Throat Grow Tight with Fear, Your Hands Twitch with Growing Terror — ad line

Ghost Cinema, like horse racing, has its own "triple crown." The first leg comes in the form of a truly haunting tale of love and hate from beyond the grave, *The Uninvited* (1944). The next big event in the apparitional arena is a terrifying study of repressed hysteria and supernatural possession, *The Innocents* (1961). But the undisputed jewel in the ghostly crown, the Kentucky Derby of spectral cinema, is Robert Wise's chilling masterpiece of understated terror, *The Haunting.*

For economical reasons, producer-director Wise shot the film in England (thereby reducing the projected budget from $1,400,000 to $1,050,000), but he retained the story's American setting. "I did keep the New England background of Shirley Jackson's original story [*The Haunting of Hill House*]," related Wise, "because I thought that haunted houses were *fresher* there than the haunted houses around England and London, which are a dime a dozen, you know. So I managed to shoot it over there but keep it located in New England." The director remembered that it was no more difficult to transform Olde England into New England than having to "block off the road for a mile or two so I could have [Julie Harris] driving on the right side — that kind of thing. It was very simple, wasn't hard at all."

The five leads of the decade's greatest ghost film: Claire Bloom, Russ Tamblyn, Julie Harris, Richard Johnson, and Ettington Park (as the terrifying Hill House — site of *The Haunting*, (1963)).

The Haunting's story follows four psychic investigators (three of them non-professionals) who journey to the infamous Hill House, a house that was "born bad," in order to probe the depths of the supernatural forces said to walk there. Soon, horrible sounds and deafening poundings assail the quartet in the dark of night, while by day they experience sudden chills and "cold spots." During one of the audio assaults, the parlor door begins to bow inward—as if some monstrous force was pushing against it from the other side. (Wise achieved this frightening effect simply enough by having a burly prop man push on cue against the other side of the laminated wood with a two-by-four, causing it to bend inward and create a "breathing" effect.) As the hours pass, the hauntings seem to focus on Eleanor (a troubled woman sensitively played by Julie Harris) who becomes more and more ensnared by the dark forces inhabiting Hill House, ultimately leading to the film's tragic conclusion.

"It was such a good script," opined Rosalie Crutchley (who played Hill House's morose housekeeper). "As you know, we're all ninety percent as good as our script, most of us. And that *was* a good script." Robert Wise concurred: "I thought Nelson Gidding did just a *fine* job on the screenplay."

The film itself plays much better than a brief synopsis reads. Through realistic and complex characters, superb acting, creative direction, inventive cinematography and terrifying sound effects, the picture deftly sidesteps a gaping pit of haunted house clichés to take the viewer down a darkened path on which every shadow, every unexplained sound, every movement out the corner of one's eye conjures up frightful terrors of The Unknown. On a deeper level, the film works as a carefully drawn character study in which the disparate personalities interact—and react—with both the turbulent forces within themselves and the terrifying forces surrounding them in Hill House. *The Haunting* is so much more than a simple (and effective) ghost story; it is a story of human needs, motivations and frailties.

At one point a character states, "Ghosts are a visible thing." Not at Hill House. *The Haunting* is perhaps the only ghost film in which the specters are never seen. "I can't tell you," remarked Wise, "how many people have said to me, 'Mr. Wise, you made the scariest picture I've ever seen and you didn't show anything!'" Time after time Wise places his audience in literally hair-raising situations, not by exposing us to pasty-faced ghouls but by playing upon the terrors of our own individual imaginations. Through clever use of lighting, camera movement, sound and actor reactions, Wise terrifies with pure atmosphere, frightening us with what is *not* seen.

This writer remembers viewing the film as a pre-adolescent and feeling cheated because he never saw a single ghost, especially at the very end when Eleanor seemingly struggles with a disappointingly *invisible* force inside her car. Fortunately, *The Haunting* wasn't made for children and there's nothing childish about it. Now, as an adult, he can fully appreciate Wise's restraint and applaud the artistry with which he applies it. For some viewers, however, this lack of visual confirmation of the supernatural becomes a major stumbling block, not realizing that it is the ambiguous, mysterious, *unseen* nature of the inhabitants of Hill House that gives the film its chilling power. To put it bluntly, sometimes what is *not* shown makes the most impact, an axiom modern filmmakers have seemingly forgotten. Wise's mentor, producer/screenwriter Val Lewton, in his string of subtle chillers from the 1940s, forged a career out of employing this principle in films like *Cat People* (1942), *The Leopard Man* (1943) and *Isle of the Dead* (1945). Wise, having broken his directing teeth under Lewton's tutelage on *The Curse of the Cat People* (1944) and *The Body Snatcher* (1945), knew full well the power of this 'fear of the unseen.' "It's kind of an homage to Val Lewton," declared the director.

Though a superbly acted picture (with its cast made up of primarily classically-trained and well-respected stars of the stage, including English Shakespearean actors Richard Johnson and Claire Bloom, and American Broadway star Julie Harris), the movie's biggest "star" proved to be Hill House itself—a centuries-old English manor named Ettington Park. Now a very posh hotel, Ettington Park is itself purportedly haunted, with half a dozen different specters having been seen walking its halls over the years.

"There was supposed to be a ghost around there," declared the director, "supposed to be a young lady a century or two before who was kept from her lover and all—another tragic love story—and she jumped out the tower window or something. I didn't experience her myself."

In fact, during the week in which cast and crew stayed at Ettington Park shooting exteriors, none of the company ran across any resident specters. "The only ghostly goings-on was our acting," laughed Rosalie Crutchley.

When this author visited the site in 1997, he

was shown the house's "haunted book." The mansion's library had been converted into a bar, and, according to the staff, every so often one particular book (*St. Ronan's Well* by Sir Walter Scott) is thrown to the floor by an unseen hand, always opened to the same page, which reads: "A merry place, 'tis said, in days of yore; but something ails it now — the place is cursed."

As a photographic experiment, Wise used a special film stock in order to obtain the dark, moody, and (pardon the expression) truly haunting image of the house itself. "I made it look a little bit more monstrous than it might have been," explained the director, "because I shot all the exteriors with infra-red film, which brought out the kind of exaggerated striations of the rock and turned the skies blacker and turned the clouds whiter. It added an eerie feeling to it."

Wise's experimentation extended even to the camera lens. "*The Haunting* was filmed in Panavision anamorphic — that's the wide screen," the director recalled. "And at that time, the widest angle that they had was about a 35mm, and I was just wishing I had something wider for some more extreme angles. So from London I called Bob Gottschalk, who was the head of Panavision and whom I knew very well. I said, 'Bob, don't you have anything wider than 35 that I could use in the film to get some special angles?' He said, 'Well, we're working on a 28mm but it's still got distortion in it.' I said, 'Jesus, that's just what I *want*! I want that distortion.' He finally, after much persuading on my part, agreed to send it over to me. But I had to sign a document saying that I would not come back at him and complain about distortion in the lens. I used that for some of the shots down the long hallway, up stairs, along the stairwell — the spooky shots. That lens really helped me to milk those sets and create atmosphere."

With Eleanor's (and the viewer's) first clear sight of Hill House, Wise's wide angle lens creates a subtle distortion that gives the towers and turrets a bent, off-kilter appearance. The house looms over us, its edges seeming to curve inward slightly like the encircling arms of some monstrous beast. Coupled with the stark texture and dark hues produced by the infra-red film stock (in which the recessed gothic windows become solid black masses, like the empty eye sockets of some gigantic skull), the sight becomes a subliminally unsettling vision. Upon seeing the grotesque structure, the alarmed Eleanor thinks, "It's staring at me! Vile, vile!" Due to Wise's innovative techniques, the viewer feels the very same thing. "One of the things I liked about the house," stated the director, "and I was able to really use it that way to make a character out of it, was that it had that tower there with those windows. So I could cut to the windows and then down to Julie getting out of her car and going in, like the *house* was watching you. I tried to capitalize and use the house just as much as I could."

Since sound (and the actors' reactions to it) was so very critical to the picture's success, Wise spared no expense in that department. The filmmaker sent a six-man sound crew, headed by dubbing editor Allan Sones, to an empty 17th-century manor house where (related a studio article), "working in shifts day and night for a week, they recorded every sound which developed, as well as a few synthetic secrets of their own. Doors, they reported, do slam for no apparent reason and floorboards do creak when no one treads on them."

"I remember working with Robert Wise as an excellent experience," remarked Rosalie Crutchley. "He was a very brilliant director. And I seem to remember he was terribly kind and friendly. I think we all felt it was rather like working in a theater company, we were all working together, you know what I mean? You didn't just turn up and do your bit and disappear. I mean we all kind of worked together."

"I have to be immodest and say I really like *The Haunting* because that's one of my best directorial jobs," declared the creator of such classics as *The Body Snatcher* (1945), *The Day the Earth Stood Still* (1951), *West Side Story* (1961) and *The Sound of Music* (1965). "I really think it worked well." Indeed it did — and still does.

With quotes from: "The Haunting," by Bryan Senn, in *Cinematic Hauntings*, by Gary J. and Susan Svehla (eds.).

The Head (1959/62; Trans-Lux; West Germany; b&w) Original Language Title: *Die Nackte und der Satan*. Alternate Title: *The Screaming Head*. Director/Screenwriter: Victor Trivas; Producer: Wolfgang Hartwig; Cinematographers: Otto Reinwald, Kurt Rendel. Cast: Horst Frank, Michel Simon, Karin Kernke, Helmut Schmid, Paul Dahlke, Dietter Eppler, Kurt Muller Graf, Christiane Maybach.

It just won't lay down and stay dead! — ad line

"Meet the scientist with the detached point of view," camped up the ads for this atmospheric

West German oddity (whose publicity amusingly urged theater owners to have local barbers give "head jobs" to lucky contest winners). Ironically, there's nary a smirk to be had for the kitsch-loving viewer, as *The Head*, filmed in 1959 and released Stateside three years later, remains a gloomily effective and deadly serious early entry in the Eurohorror sweepstakes.

The aptly-named (and very odd) Dr. Ood (Horst Frank) comes to work for the ailing Professor Abel (respected Renoir regular Michel Simon), who's been experimenting with keeping disembodied dog heads alive. When a proposed heart transplant fails to save the professor's life, Ood uses Abel's "Serum Z" to preserve the Professor's living head. Then, reveling in his God Complex, Ood sets about finding a sexy new body to graft onto the head of the beautiful hunchbacked nun/nurse Irene (Karin Kernke), whom he's become obsessed with.

Despite its medical science premise, *The Head* looks backwards towards nightmarish horror rather than forwards towards the shiny sci-fi future. Though shot during the science fiction boom of the late 1950s, it nevertheless focuses on that old horror chestnut from two decades earlier warning against Man tampering in God's domain (one of Abel's assistants even voices this sentiment outright). Yet, conversely, *The Head* also overlays its Fifties sci-fi sensibilities with a heady dose (pun lamentably intended) of sexuality that both betrays its Continental roots and looks ahead to the less repressed decades to come. Given the original language title, which translates as "The Nude and the Devil," it's no wonder a general air of lasciviousness permeates the film, with the randy scientist seducing his "creation" in order to "possess her, body and soul," and Irene exploring her "restored" body by fondling her new breasts (though clothed, actress Karin Kernke exudes eroticism as well as curiosity).

Reflecting its Germanic roots is the somber, almost dour tone the film takes. Devoid of all humor, *The Head* offers a pervasive air of gloom, heightened by the shadowy photography and the fact that nearly every scene plays out at night. Dimly-lit rooms (even the well-equipped modern operating theater offers planes of light and pools of darkness) and moon-illumined exteriors (full of denuded trees and thick stone walls) are the order of the day. Contrasting with this Gothic ambiance are the expressionistic interiors and furnishings, all sliding panels, circular stairways, angular sculptures, and metal and glass tables. Such impressive attention to detail should come as no surprise, since *The Head* features art direction by Herman Warm, who designed both the 1919 *The Cabinet of Dr. Caligari* and Carl Dryer's *Vampyr* (1932). Warm reportedly came out of retirement to provide the modernist nightmare settings and bizarre Teutonic atmosphere for *The Head*, his final film.

On the downside, the pacing of this literal talking head movie flags at times, with much of the central portion eaten up by Irene discovering what the viewer already knows—she now has the body of the murdered stripper Lily. This prompts her to ask, "Which is my past—the past of Lily's body, or the past of my head?" Though a risible question on the surface, it raises a very real point long contemplated by religious and metaphysical philosophers: Does humanity, or the "soul," reside in the mind (head) or the body (heart)? And just what is it that truly defines a "person"?

But before one becomes lost in philosophical musings, *The Head* brings us back to its own ghoulish reality with another scene of the unhappy professor's disembodied head on a table. Filmed with some impressive effects trickery, the Professor is not the usual hokey head atop a podium with the actor's body stuffed inside. Here the Professor's cranium sits on a surgical cart with a clear aquarium tank, half full of bubbling liquid, on the open shelf beneath, tubes and wires trailing from it like mechanized tentacles. It makes for a bizarre—and convincing—sight.

With its pulp plotting, alarming ambiance, simmering sexuality, and the juxtaposition of hoary horror clichés and forward-looking science and sensuality, *The Head* remains a transitional and unique Sixties Shocker.

Hercules Against the Moon Men (1964;

Governor Films; Italy/France) Original Language Title: *Maciste e la Regina de Samar*; Alternate Title: *Hercules vs. the Moon Men*; Director: Giacomo Gentilomo; Producer: Luigi Mondello; Screenplay: Arpad De Riso, Nino Scolaro (story by Arpad De Riso, Nino Scolaro, Giacomo Gentilomo, Angelo Sangermano); Cinematographer: Oberdan Trojani. Cast: Alan Steel, Jany Clair, Anna Maria Polani, Nando Tamberlani, Delia d'Albertini, Jean Pierre Honore.

The supernatural and the real clash in a world of horror!—trailer

---

A race of evil aliens (presumably from the Moon, given the movie's title—though this is

The leader of the Moon Men (the *only* Moon Man seen in the film, actually) intends to resurrect their dead queen in *Hercules Against the Moon Men* (1964).

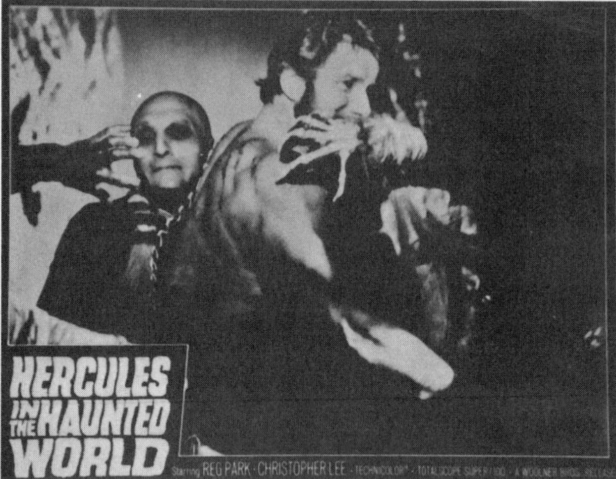

Walking (and flying) corpses attack *Hercules in the Haunted World* (1961/63) (U.S. lobby card).

never made clear) land in ancient Greece and take up residence in the "Mountain of Death," demanding children for sacrifice. The evil queen of nearby Samar (Anna Maria Polani) joins forces with the Moon Men in a bid to rule the world, and it's up to muscleman hero Maciste (changed to Hercules in the American dubbed version) to stop the monsters and put an end to the evil queen's tyranny.

Alan Steel (real name: Sergio Ciani) dons Steve Reeves' leather mini-skirt for this unique but ultimately disappointing peplum (Italian muscleman movie). Despite the novelty of its concept, most of the picture consists of the standard, tedious conflict between Hercules and various soldiers/guards/bandits, etc. (showcasing the usual boulder throwing, tree uprooting and iron bar bending). Only twice does the Mighty One face off against less mundane opponents, once briefly battling a large-tusked, pointy-eared ape man kept in the Queen's dungeons, and then meeting up with an army (well, about ten, anyway) of rock monsters, servants of the Moon Men. Though not particularly convincing, these "Stone-Men" certainly present a striking appearance — as they totter forward like gigantic mottled stalagmite Gumbys. Unfortunately, what should have been the movie's exciting centerpiece goes over like a lead balloon. Instead of beginning a battle of behemoths, Hercules simply sidesteps the lumbering rock monsters, pushes the Moon Man leader off a platform, and topples the alien's idol-cum-moonbeam energy generator, causing gouts of flame to shoot upwards and (presumably, as we don't actually *see* it) destroy the Moon Men forever in a decidedly *anti*-climactic conflagration.

This Hercules outing definitely belongs to the small-scale species of spectacle, as no more than a dozen soldiers or civilians ever appear together in one shot — even when the citizens "storm the palace." And, as far as we can see, the entire population of Moon Men consists of the solitary leader, hidden behind a silver mask and robes.

The soundstage "Mountain of Death" set offers an eerie, forbidding landscape, full of gnarled denuded trees, howling wind, blowing sand, and drifting fog that changes color from blue to red to amber. But even if one viewed *Hercules Against the Moon Men* through rose-colored gels, it would still appear as a pale specimen of Italian musclemania. (Appropriately enough, this lackluster, lugubrious peplum was released on a double bill with *The Black Torment*. Torment indeed.)

Hercules Against the Vampires see *Hercules in the Haunted World*

Hercules in the Center of the Earth see *Hercules in the Haunted World*

Hercules in the Haunted World (1961/63; Omnia SPA Cinematografica/Woolner Brothers; Italy)

Alternate Titles: *Vampires Versus Hercules, Hercules Against the Vampires, Hercules in the Center of the Earth*; Director: Mario Bava; Producer: Archille Piazza; Screenplay: Alessandro Continenza, Mario Bava, Duccio Tessari, Franco Prosperi; Cinematographers: Mario Bava, Ubaldo Terzano. Cast: Reg Park, Christopher Lee, Leonora Ruffo, Giorgio Ardisson, Marisa Belli, Ida Galli.

> An all new height in fright
> and might!—ad line

One of the few sword-and-sandal movies to feature a significant horror element, *Ercole al Centro Della Terra* (*Hercules in the Center of the Earth*, which served as the film's British title) told the story of—you guessed it—Hercules (Reg Park) and his buddy Theseus (Giorgio Ardisson), who journey to Hades to find the means to break a spell placed upon Hercules' love, Princess Deianira (Leonora Ruffo), by the vampiric Lico (Christopher Lee), "the very spirit of evil on Earth."

Released in Italy in 1961, it took two more years (and a title change) before *Hercules in the Haunted World* washed up on American shores, courtesy of the Woolner Brothers (and it was three years after that before this leather-loined demi-god invaded Great Britain). Thanks to director Mario Bava's visual sensibilities, this particular piece of flotsam rose to the top.

"It was an unserious film," wrote Christopher Lee in his autobiography *Tall, Dark and Gruesome*, "widely liked by the Italians, had pretty Leonora Ruffo in it and Mario Bava for director, who looked liked Toto and mugged before the camera before saying, 'Cut!'"

Director Bava (a brilliant cinematographer who co-photographed this film with his long-time collaborator Ubaldo Terzano) brought his mastery of mood to play on this admittedly unworthy vehicle, lifting it above the mythological mediocrity of the typical Italian he-man epic. Granted, it offers the usual convoluted "quest" scenario (Hercules needs to find a magic ship in order to find a magic golden apple that will allow him to enter Hades and find a magic stone that will cure the Princess...); a wobbly, ridiculous-looking man-in-a-suit rock monster; acting as stone-faced as the aforementioned fiend; and an annoying "comedy relief" character. In addition, Christopher Lee's sonorous voice was dubbed, dampening much of the aural menace Mr. Lee could have brought to the role. (Even so, the actor seemed to have enjoyed his Italian "working vacation." In *The Films of Christopher Lee*, by Robert Pohle, Jr., and Douglas Hart, Lee called his co-star Reg Park, a former Mr. Universe, "a most delightful man. I'm afraid we disgraced ourselves by giggling in certain scenes.")

And so, too, does the discerning viewer. Bava counters these sniggers with swirls of dry-ice fog; garish, otherworldly color schemes and lighting; and bizarre, unsettling sets full of weird rock formations, blackened trees and dead-looking vines that bleed when cut ("blood from the souls of the damned").

The film shakes off the mantle of fantasy (and banality) to don the cloak of horror toward the end, when an army of corpses rises from their graves—literally flying out of their sarcophagi in a terrifying attack. The eerie blue lighting, ghastly silhouetted forms, and grasping disfigured arms of the shrouded walking dead are as frightening as anything in a George Romero movie.

Thanks to Bava's "Herculean" efforts to generate some otherworldly atmosphere and a truly chilling finale, *Hercules in the Haunted World* stands as one of the best Hercules/Atlas/Goliath/Maciste he-man entries of the decade. That said, to those not enamored of beefy brawn in leather loincloths, it's still not a very good movie.

Hercules vs. The moon men see *Hercules Against the Moon Men*

The Hidden Room of 1,000 Horrors see *The Tell-Tale Heart*

Homicidal (1961; Columbia)

Director/Producer: William Castle; Screenplay: Robb White; Cinematographer: Burnett Guffey. Cast: Glenn Corbett, Patricia Breslin, Jean Arless, Eugenie Leontovich, Richard Rust.

> There will be a special FRIGHT BREAK during
> the showing of "Homicidal." All those too timid
> to take the climax will be welcomed to the
> COWARD'S CORNER!—poster

William Castle, the brazen, Barnum-esque showman behind *The Tingler* (and its electrically wired theater seats), *The House on Haunted Hill* (which offered a plastic skeleton that zoomed out over the audience) and *13 Ghosts* (with its free "Ghost Viewer" handed out to every patron) pays homage to (cashes in on) the Hitchcock classic *Psycho*. Ironically, Hitchcock filmed Psycho in part as a reaction to the success of Castle's early films. Castle's gimmick this time around was a 60-second "Fright Break" just before the climax. At this time all those too petrified to face the terrors of the last reel could slink away to the "Cowards Corner," following the yellow streak to the box office where their money would "sneerfully" be refunded. "Of all the films I had made, *Homicidal* was the most fun," Castle wrote in his autobiography *Step Right Up! I'm Going to Scare the Pants off America*. "When we finally got the kinks out of the money-back guarantee, less than one percent of the audiences asked for a refund."

Fun gimmicks aside, Castle's films were usually entertaining (*House on Haunted Hill*), often ridiculous (*The Tingler*), and occasionally engrossing (*Mr. Sardonicus*). With *Homicidal*, Castle steals the luridness and shocks from *Psycho* without borrowing the finesse and subtlety of that far superior production. We're left with an outlandish plot, banal characters and an unconvincing Norman Bates stand-in (only this time it is a woman who plays the character of a man in order to obtain an inheritance). Revealing this crucial plot point is spoiling absolutely nothing, since Jean Arless (real name: Joan Marshall), when playing her male role, is so effete looking (and the male voice-over so obviously dubbed) that she fools no one — except the story's unobservant protagonists.

"*Homicidal* was the story of a transvestite," Castle wrote about turning actress Joan Marshall from a beautiful woman into a man. "The transformation was amazing. Coming on the set dressed in men's clothing and speaking in a deep voice, she fooled everyone, even the crew." Given Castle's well-known penchant for confabulation — and, more tellingly, the results on the screen — this seems *highly* unlikely.

Robb White, Castle's longtime collaborator, wrote *Homicidal*. (White penned the screenplays for four other Castle films: *Macabre*, *House on Haunted Hill*, *The Tingler* and *13 Ghosts*.) "Bill gave me the idea for *Homicidal*," White told interviewer Tom Weaver (in *Science Fiction Stars and Horror Heroes*). "After I worked on that screenplay he worked on it, more than I did — more than he had on any other script that I did for him. It just felt very funny to me that he was helping out so much, and that he wanted it exactly this way and that way and so on. One day, after working at the studio, I was on my way home when I saw that *Psycho* was playing somewhere in Santa Monica. I'd heard about the picture, so I went in there and, Jesus Christ, I was afraid I was going to get arrested before I could get out! I was so embarrassed! He had stolen everything! And *Homicidal* was already in production by that time. But apparently nobody gave a shit that he had stolen it from Hitchcock."

A master showman but apparently unable to grasp the concept of irony, Castle said of *Homicidal*: "I consider it one of the most original of my motion pictures." In fact, it's his most derivative. Yet, there's enough here to hold viewers' interest. Castle generates more than his fair share of shudders, manages to build some edge-of-the seat suspense in a few scenes and adds one or two deft tricks calculated to make audiences jump. In one scene, for instance, the heroine is shown sleeping peacefully in her bed, safe and secure. The camera slowly pulls back to suddenly reveal a

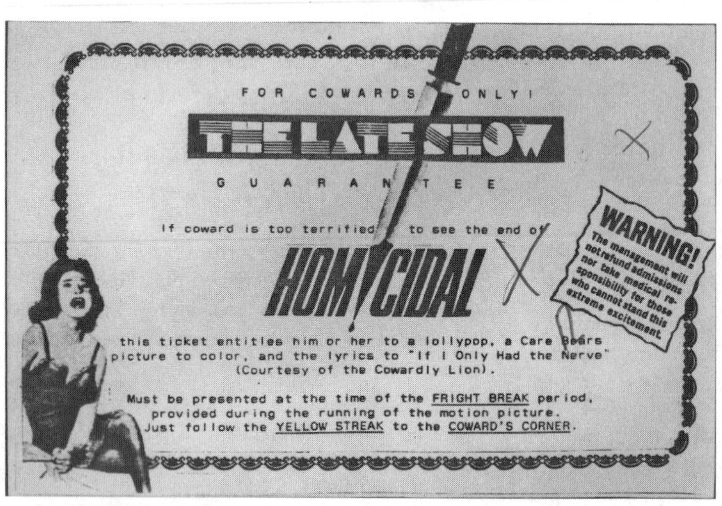

FOR COWARDS ONLY!

THE LATE SHOW

GUARANTEE

If coward is too terrified to see the end of

HOMICIDAL

this ticket entitles him or her to a lollypop, a Care Bears picture to color, and the lyrics to "If I Only Had the Nerve" (Courtesy of the Cowardly Lion).

Must be presented at the time of the FRIGHT BREAK period, provided during the running of the motion picture. Just follow the YELLOW STREAK to the COWARD'S CORNER.

WARNING! The management will not refund admissions nor take medical responsibility for those who cannot stand this extreme excitement.

Old-style handout highlighting *Homicidal*'s "Fright Break" and "Coward's Corner" gimmick for a 1980s revival showing (courtesy of Lynn Naron).

menacing figure sitting in a chair staring at the slumbering girl. The appearance of the malevolent intruder is so unexpected that it creates a moment of true *frisson.*

All in all though, *Homicidal* remains a crude, only partially successful attempt to cash in on the success of *Psycho*, and one that's not nearly as enjoyable.

The Horrible Dr. Hichcock (1962/64; Sigma III/Panda; Italy) Original Language Title: *L'Orribile Segreto del Dottor Hichcock*; Alternate Title: *The Terror of Dr. Hichcock* (U.K.); Director: Robert Hampton (Riccardo Freda); Producer: Louis Mann (Luigi Carpentieri, Ermanno Donati); Screenplay: Julyan Perry (Ernesto Gastaldi); Cinematographer: Donald Green (Raffaele Masciocchi). Cast: Barbara Steele, Robert Flemyng, Montgomery Glenn (Silvano Tranquilli), Teresa Fitzgerald (Maria Teresa Vianello), Harriet White (Medin).

The candle of his lust burnt brightest in the shadow of the grave!—ad line

After *Black Sunday*, this may be the most famous (and most notorious) of Barbara Steel's Italian gothic horrors from the 1960s (a fairly substantial subset, with eight titles to its credit). It's also one of the best.

Shot as *Raptus*, the story begins in 1885 London, where the brilliant, wealthy surgeon Dr. Hichcock (Robert Flemyng) displays one little quirk—he's a necrophile ("His secret was a coffin named DESIRE!" shouted the not-so-subtle ads). Hichcock's wife Margherita (Maria Teresa Vianello) willingly submits to her husband's funereal sex games by playing dead—helped along by the doc's experimental anesthetic. Their happy home life comes to an abrupt end when Hichcock accidentally kills Margherita with an overdose. The grief-stricken doctor abandons his ancestral manor house (and, apparently, his sick sexual proclivities), but returns twelve years later with a new (and unknowing) wife, Cynthia (Barbara Steele). Soon Cynthia is terrorized by the seeming specter of Margherita, and then by the now-unhinged doctor himself, who appears to have fallen under the spell of his adored, dead former wife and intends to make a corpse out of his live current one.

Cinematographer Raffaele Masciocchi's gorgeous Technicolor photography and lighting sets the uneasy tone. Deep graveyard blues in exterior scenes contrast starkly with the warm yellow interior light; while the occasional spot-specific red tint (pointedly appearing when the doctor's lust rises) creates a feeling of danger and heat, and the white of the phantom Margherita's gauzy gown fairly glows. Such illuminated imagery would do even Mario Bava proud. "The good thing about this picture, it's beautifully shot," observed star Robert Flemyng to interviewer Alan Upchurch. Indeed it is.

The entire film was lensed at the rented Villa Perucchetti in the district of Parioli in Rome. The villa's baroque architecture and archaic furnishings perfectly complement the picture's bizarre theme and gothic atmosphere. "You know, that villa was absolutely the only thing that was used," recalled Flemyng. "The kitchen of the house was all tile, so the various pantries and such-like had been turned into the mortuary. We shot everything in that villa."

"We were all influenced by the films of [Alfred]

This striking Mexican lobby card for *The Horrible Dr. Hichcock* (1962/64) shows the necrophilic doctor (Robert Flemyng) engaging in funereal love-games with his soon-to-be-dead-for-real spouse (Maria Teresa Vianello).

Hitchcock, who was the master of masters," admitted screenwriter Ernesto Gastaldi. Gastaldi filled his screenplay with borrowings from several Hitchcock films, including a (possibly) poisoned glass of milk from *Suspicion*, and the new wife haunted by the memory of the dead wife from *Rebecca* (not to mention the doctor's sinister housekeeper, played by Harriet White Medin: "[Here] I was definitely thinking of *Rebecca*," Gastaldi stated). In a brilliant masterstroke of exploitability, Gastaldi gave his necrophile antagonist the same name as the Master of Suspense (though dropping the "t" in "Hitchcock" to ward off any potential lawsuit).

English actor Robert Flemyng paints a startling and commanding portrait of obsession, of a man battling his inner demons. His powerful presence infuses every frame of the perverse picture. The subtle struggle in Flemyng's face as the "respectable" doctor fights against his compulsion (after seeing a woman's corpse wheeled by at the hospital at which he works), or the intent gaze with which he fixes a female cadaver in the autopsy room, speak volumes. Such moments of strain and barely-held-in-check "passion" contrasts starkly with his generally clipped, cold speech patterns and formal manner. "I just hammed away at it and hoped for the best," the actor recalled; and "the best" is exactly what he delivered.

Flemyng admitted that he took the part simply because he wanted to go to Rome. "I thought, 'What the hell, no one will ever see it.'" The allure of Rome also secured the services of Barbara Steele. Having come to the city to work on Fellini's *8½*, Steele told Upchurch: "I did [*Hichcock*] because I'd found a glorious little apartment with fabulous terraces and I was determined to stay there."

"That's the movie that [director] Riccardo Freda did on a bet, you know," continued Steele. "Freda said, 'I bet I can write and shoot a film in ten days,' and one of his friends bet him a race horse that he couldn't. And he shot it in ten days. He wanted this horse very badly, and we all felt obliged to help him. We were running at top speed through the entire movie." (Note: It was actually a 14-, rather than 10-day shoot.)

Steele does well enough in what, unfortunately, turns out to be a sorely underwritten role that asks little more of her than to look frightened and scream at the appropriate moment. Freda fails to exploit that sinister, dangerous quality in Steele that made her so alluring, leaving her to play a standard, put-upon heroine who faints at the drop of a hat (after the third fainting-from-terror episode, it becomes rather comical). Even so, Freda and Masciocchi's masterful visuals and moody build-up keep the air of menace thick in the heavy gothic air.

A rather tangential sequel-of-sorts, *The Ghost*, followed a year later, again starring Steele (in a far meatier role) and directed by Freda. Though intriguing in its own right, it's not quite up to the delirious gothic perversion that is *The Horrible Dr. Hichcock*.

With quotes from: "Raptus: The Making of The Horrible Dr. Hitchcock," by Alan Y. Upchurch, with Tim Lucas and Luigi Boscaino, *Video Watchdog* 49, 1999; "What Are Those Strange Drops of Blood in the Scripts of ... Ernesto Gastaldi?" by Tim Lucas, *Video Watchdog* 39, 1997; "Raptus" op cit.

The Horrible Mill Women see *Mill of the Stone Women*

Horror Castle (1963; Zodiac/Woolner; Italy/W. Germany) Original Language Title: *La Vergine di Norimberga*; Alternate Titles: *The Castle of Terror* (U.K.), *The Virgin of Nuremberg* (video), *Castle of Horror*, *Back to the Killer*; Director: Anthony Dawson (Antonio Margheriti); Producer: Marco Vicario; Screenplay: Ernesto Gastaldi, Edmond T. Greville, Antonio Margheriti (based on a story by Frank Bogart); Cinematographer: Richard Palton (Riccardo Pallottini). Cast: Rossana Podesta, George Riviere, Christopher Lee, Jim Dolen, Lucille St. Simon, Patrick Walton.

THE EVIL TORTURE — THE SHRIEKING FEAR — poster blurb

Released in Europe in 1963 (and finally arriving on American shores in 1965), *Horror Castle* (aka *The Virgin of Nuremberg*) remains one of the more unusual — and engrossing — Italian horrors of the 1960s. Though set in the (then) present, and employing as an integral plot point the Nazi atrocities of World War II, *Virgin*'s setting and tone is one of deep, dark Gothicism, making it a unique bridge between classical and "modern" horrors.

German aristocrat Max Hunter (George Riviere) brings his American bride Mary (Rossana Podesta, real-life wife of producer Marco Vicario) on a visit to his ancestral castle home. One night Mary hears noises coming from the Castle's "Torture Museum" and investigates—only to find a dead girl in the Virgin of Nuremberg, a medieval iron maiden-like torture device. She faints, and the next day everyone (including Max) tries to convince her she imagined it. But soon other torture victims turn up, and Mary herself is pursued by a hooded figure who calls himself "the Punisher"—the living embodiment of a 200-year-old ancestor obsessed with torturing women. The sinister sadist turns out to be Max's own unhinged father, a former Nazi general whose punishment for trying to assassinate Hitler was to be turned into a hideous "living skeleton" by Nazi surgeons. Aided by his loyal servant Erich (Christopher Lee), Max rescues Mary from the horrors of the Virgin, while the Castle—and his mad father—go up in flames.

The grotesquely mutilated (by Nazi surgeons) madman calling himself "the Punisher" carries another victim through his *Horror Castle* (1963).

Horror Castle may very well be the ultimate "imperiled heroine" (a Gothic staple) movie of the 1960s, as nearly the entire picture follows Mary as she wanders uneasily through dark castle hallways, torture chamber and crypt; or hides, terrified, from her assailant; or even tries to flee through the grounds outside (in a marvelously photographed sequence in which the camera moves with her in a disorienting up-angle shot, intercut with dizzying scenes of protruding branches whizzing by). In fact, Mary spends nearly the whole of the picture clad in her nightgown! Though occasionally slow, the first hour of *Castle* is one long, uneasy—and often suspenseful—Gothic nightmare.

The disquiet turns into outright shock at times, when we see a female victim with red, oozing holes where her eyes should be (complements of the titular torture device), or another woman (still alive) with half her nose gruesomely chewed away by rats! In addition, a black and white flashback sequence shows the Nazi doctors clinically removing a man's face bit by bit in antiseptic detail. (In Germany, this Nazi subplot and its attendant imagery was reportedly expunged from the film prints—with the German ads even misleadingly claiming the story was based upon the works of Edgar Allan Poe!)

This *Virgin*, however, is not altogether untainted. Riz Ortolani's '60s jazz score becomes irritatingly inappropriate at times. And it's a real disappointment to find someone else's dubbed voice issuing from the mouth of Christopher Lee (whose vocal characteristics are arguably one of that actor's greatest assets).

But the impressive castle sets, cluttered torture chamber, cobwebbed crypt, and truly remarkable "living skull" makeup revealed at the end help smooth over the rough spots. Lee recalled, "The Yugoslav Mirco Valenin [who played the disfigured "Punisher"] went through extraordinary tortures in makeup. It was quite relaxing, for once, to be able to look at somebody else getting the sticky end of the wedge."

Lee almost came to a "sticky end" himself during filming. "I was very nearly burned alive," he said. "I had to rush down a corridor that was going up in flames. The roof of the studio caught fire." Given the impressive fire footage and Lee's obvious proximity—and alarm (not all of it play acting, evidently)—one can readily believe it.

With quotes from: *Tall, Dark and Gruesome: An Autobiography*, by Christopher Lee.

The Horror Chamber of Dr. Faustus

(1959/62; Lux; France, b&w) Original Language Title: *Les Yeux Sans Visage*. Alternate Title: *Eyes Without a Face* (UK). Director: Georges Franju; Producer: Jules Borkon; Screenplay: Pierre Boileu and Thomas Narcejac (dialogue by Pierre Gascar, from a novel by Jean Redon. Cinematographer:

Eugen Shuftan. Cast: Pierre Brasseur, Edith Scob, Alida Valli, Beatrice Altariba, Juliette Mayniel, François Guerin.

A macabre masterpiece — U.S. trailer

During its initial release, *The Horror Chamber of Dr. Faustus* (now better known under its original title, *Eyes Without a Face*) quickly grew notorious for its stomach-churning gore. When it was shown at the Edinburgh Film Festival, seven viewers fainted, prompting director Georges Franju to quip, "Now I know why Scotsmen wear skirts."

This movie has lost none of its power to make viewers squirm. And yet, its most striking attribute remains its sensitivity — its sometimes-poetic visuals, and the empathy it grants its emotionally and physically damaged characters. Few horror movies are this brutal, or this gentle.

As the opening credits roll, we watch Louise (Alida Valli), assistant to the esteemed Dr. Genessier (Pierre Brasseur), dump the body of a young woman into the Seine. When they find the body, police are aghast to discover the victim's face literally peeled from her head. Genessier, we soon learn, has undertaken a series of desperate, secret medical experiments to try to restore the face of his daughter, Christiane (Edith Stob), who was disfigured in a car crash.

Louise helps Genessier trap another victim, Edna (Juliette Mayniel). In the film's most notorious scene, Genessier performs a grotesque "face lift" operation on Edna, using a scalpel and forceps to remove the skin from the still-living patient's face. Genessier labors with medical precision and without emotion. Franju documents every step of the procedure in sickening detail and icy clinical detachment. The matter-of-fact presentation only makes the sequence more difficult to watch.

Genessier also experiments on a kennel full of caged dogs. But between experiments, he continues his bustling medical practice and remains a pillar of the community. Meanwhile, Louise tends to Christiane, tenderly brushing her hair and trying to keep her in good spirits. Christiane, for most of the film, wears a mask Genessier has crafted in the likeness of her own, lost face. The expressionless mask lends her the unsettling appearance of an animated mannequin. Briefly, it seems that her father's treatment has succeeded, but Christiane's body soon rejects the skin graft from Edna's face, and the cycle must begin again. Franju presents the grotesque deterioration of Christiane's face in a series of clinical photographs, accompanied by deadpan voiceover from Brasseur.

In the end Christiane turns on her would-be benefactors, stabbing Louise in the throat and then freeing her father's next intended victim, as well as the trapped dogs and several caged doves. In a shocking conclusion that recalls the classic *Island of Lost Souls* (1932), the dogs, at least a dozen of them, snarling and barking, fatally maul Genessier.

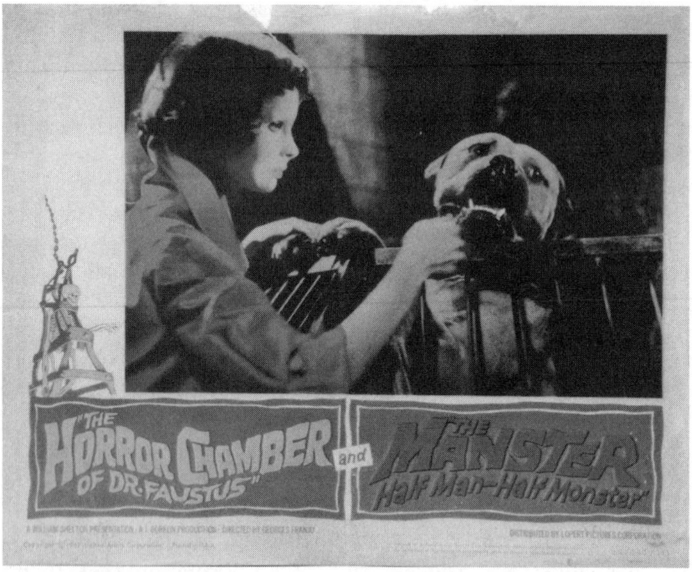

On a basic level, there's nothing special about this scenario. The obsessed-doctor-trying-to-save-his-loved-one premise seemed shopworn even a half-century ago. The beauty of *Eyes Without a Face* lies not in the tale but in the telling. And the closer you examine it, the better it gets.

Franju had scandalized the French film community 10 years earlier with his slaughterhouse documentary *Blood of the Beasts* (1949), which

The disfigured Christiane (Edith Stob) must wear a mask, since she only has *Eyes Without a Face* (re-titled *The Horror Chamber of Dr. Faustus* for its 1962 U.S. release, where it was double-billed with *The Manster*).

juxtaposed footage of animals being butchered with scenes of children at play. He uses a similar device in *Eyes Without a Face*, by placing the graphic medical sequences adjacent to introspective, character-focused scenes. For instance, just prior to the "face lift" gorefest, Christiane visits the caged dogs, petting them and lovingly scratching their ears. She understands their torment, because she, too, is a trapped medical specimen.

The only music heard in the film is a swirling carnival theme, like something from one of Nino Rota's Federico Fellini scores. This theme recurs periodically, usually to provide an ironic counterpoint to the visuals. Large tracts of the film, including all the medical sequences, feature no music at all. However, Franju makes evocative use of natural sound—birds chirp during contemplative moments, while barking dogs signal danger ahead. The director integrates visual symbols, as well, and composes every frame with painterly care. The eerie finale, in which the masked Christiane walks past her dead father as the newly freed doves flutter around her, could *only* originate from a French film.

A more conventional film would portray Genessier as a heartless maniac and Christiane as a helpless pure-heart. But the central characters of *Eyes Without a Face* have complex motivations, and suffer inner turmoil. Genessier's obsessive quest to heal his daughter stems not from mad determination to achieve a medical breakthrough, but from guilt. He was driving the car at the time of the accident that ruined his Christiane's face. At his clinic, Genessier continues to care for his patients with skill and compassion. Lonely Christiane yearns to have her face back so she can return to her fiancé (François Guerin). While Genessier prepares to operate on Edna, Christiane steals into the laboratory and covetously strokes the soft skin of the unconscious woman's cheek. Christiane understands what's about to happen and could stop it if she wanted to, but she doesn't. Nevertheless, Christiane recognizes the evil of her father's experiments, and eventually realizes their futility. Ultimately, guilt and despair overwhelm her. She cannot allow Genessier to continue.

Most critics consider 1959 the greatest single year in the history of French film. That year ushered in the *Nouvelle Vague*, and saw the release of several movies now considered classics of world cinema, including Jean-Luc Godard's *Breathless*, François Truffaut's *The 400 Blows*, Alain Resnais' *Hiroshima, Mon Amour*, Robert Bresson's *Pickpocket*, Claude Chabrol's *Les Cousins* and Roger Vadim's *Dangerous Liasons*. *Eyes Without a Face* also belongs on the short list of France's 1959 masterworks.

American audiences, however, didn't see it until 1962. Unsure of how to handle what was, essentially, a blood-spattered art film, the U.S. distributor dubbed it, changed its title to the gaudy *Horror Chamber of Dr. Faustus*, and issued the picture on the bottom half of a double-bill with (of all things) the oddball Japanese-American coproduction *The Manster* (1962). The film's bloodiest sequences were trimmed or deleted for its U.S. release, including most of the "face lift" operation. Scenes at Genessier's clinic, which help humanize the doctor, were also removed.

Along with Henri-Georges Clouzot's *Diabolique* and Alfred Hitchcock's *Psycho*, *Eyes Without a Face* profoundly influenced the subsequent generation of European horror movies. Too often, however, its imitators would duplicate only the copious gore of *Eyes Without a Face*, never realizing that what made the original film special was the beauty that accompanied its ugliness.

Horror Hotel (1960; Britannia/Trans-Lux; U.K.; b&w) Alternate Titles: *City of the Dead* (U.K.), *Doctor Bloodbath* (home video); Director: John Moxey; Producer: Donald Taylor; Screenplay: George Baxt (story by Milton Subotsky); Cinematographer: Desmond Dickinson. Cast: Dennis Lotis, Christopher Lee, Betta St. John, Patricia Jessel, Venetia Stevenson, Tom Naylor, Valentine Dyall, Ann Beach.

Just ring for doom service!—ad line

While AIP were winding down their mutant-laden double bills at the end of the 1950s in favor of their soon-to-be-launched gothic-style Poe series, and as Britain's Hammer Studios left off their sci-fi-oriented black and white features to plunge headfirst into the color-drenched Gothicism of *Curse of Frankenstein*, *Horror of Dracula* and *The Mummy*, the independent producer team of Milton Subotsky and Max J. Rosenberg set up shop in England and took their first fledgling steps into screen terror under the "Vulcan Productions" banner. (The pair later formed Amicus Productions, arguably Hammer's biggest U.K. competitor in the fright field of the 1960s and '70s.) What resulted was one of the most atmospheric offerings of the decade, perhaps second only to *Black Sunday* in its evocative otherworldliness.

"*Horror Hotel*—the guests are over 300 years

old...” warns the film’s trailer. Indeed, the story begins in 1692 in Whitewood, Massachusetts, as the townspeople prepare to burn the witch Elizabeth Selwyn (Patricia Jessel) at the stake. Her secret accomplice, Jethro Keane (Valentine Dyall), calls upon Lucifer to help her, and a violent storm arises as the witch curses the villagers and warns of her return. Flash forward to a modern-day college course, as Professor Driscoll (Christopher Lee) invokes the chant of the terrified townsfolk: “Burn witch, burn witch, burn!” One of Driscoll’s students, Nan Barlow (Venetia Stevenson), decides to use the upcoming semester break to research her class thesis on witchcraft in New England. Driscoll directs her to Whitewood, a reclusive town seemingly blanketed in a perpetual fog. At the Raven’s Inn Nan meets Mrs. Newless (Patricia Jessel again) — a phonetic anagram of Selwyn — and Jethro. She also promptly falls victim to the ancient coven’s sacrificial rites. Her disappearance leads Nan’s brother (Dennis Lotis) and fiancé (Tom Naylor) to Whitewood, where their search ends in a fiery confrontation with the 300-year-old witches (Driscoll among them!) who intend to sacrifice one more maiden on Candlemass Eve to preserve their unnatural lives.

Critics have often dismissively pointed out *Horror Hotel*’s similarities to the same year’s *Psycho* (“the film’s framework is modeled on *Psycho* lines,” observed *Daily Cinema*). The movie’s female protagonist stops at an out-of-the-way hotel where she’s brutally murdered a half-hour into the movie; the woman’s lover comes looking for her, accompanied by a concerned sibling; and there’s even a final shot of the seated, charred corpse of Elizabeth Selwyn that conjures up images of Mrs. Bates in the cellar. But *Horror Hotel* actually began shooting at Shepperton Studios on October 12, 1959, whereas *Psycho* didn’t begin filming in Hollywood until a month-and-a-half *later*, on November 30, 1959.

When asked about killing the female lead halfway through the picture, screenwriter George Baxt (*Circus of Horrors*, *Shadow of the Cat*, *Burn Witch Burn*) admitted (to interviewer Matthew R. Bradley), “I think I killed her because I couldn’t figure out what else to do with her. This script was put together from whole cloth! I wrote it in about a week.”

The British-made *City of the Dead* (its name was changed to *Horror Hotel* when released by Trans-Lux in the United States in 1961) was filmed in three weeks by first-time director John Moxey on an incredibly tight £45,000 budget. Though much of the movie takes place outdoors, it was shot entirely on sound stages at Shepperton Studios. “They built the entire *village*!” exclaimed Moxey. “It was a stage that hadn’t been used for some years, a big old stage that was barely soundproof.” (Baxt recalled that, because of the soundproofing problems, all the dialogue had to be looped in later.)

Christopher Lee (second from right), flanked by fellow coven members Patricia Jessel and Valentine Dyall, look on in terror as two of their own go up in flames after being exposed to the shadow of a cross in *Horror Hotel* (1960).

Filmed on an English sound stage, the story’s *New* England setting required the British cast to ape American accents. For the most part they do well (though Tom Naylor’s inflections seem to waver a bit at times) — particularly Christopher Lee, who seems quite proud of his affected accomplishment. “I think my greatest achievement was my American accent,” announced the actor. “It is a very difficult thing for a British actor to do. They usually exaggerate it beyond belief, and vice versa.”

“I believe that you have to leave a lot to the audience’s imagination because you can never be quite as horrific as what people can dream up in their minds," explained Moxey. "That's what we did with *Horror Hotel*, we tried to *suggest* some of it." Moxey and his cast and crew succeeded admirably. When Nan gives a ride to a tall, sepulchral-voiced stranger (Jethro) on the dark road to Whitewood, the man stares straight ahead and only cryptically answers her queries. After she stops the car to gaze out her window at the ominous Raven's Inn, she turns back to say something to the stranger — only to find *he is not there*. Later, walking through the town's solitary street, Nan passes a few townspeople (clad all in black) who stop their measured progress to turn and stare coldly — one even giving the hint of a knowing, malevolent smile.

A series of clever twists and eerie moments build an atmosphere of uneasy dread. Going to her room, Nan sees several couples dancing in the inn's lobby to some low-key jazz (though, oddly, the dancers remain utterly silent, moving to the rhythms as if in a play — or a dream). Then, when Nan finally decides to join the "party," she dresses (all the while hearing the music, since her room adjoins the lobby) and opens the door — at which point the music abruptly stops— to find the lobby empty, with only the ticking of a clock to be heard. It is an unsettling moment in which it is what is *not* seen that evokes the chill.

Moxey paces his picture perfectly, building up to the early — and disturbing —climax of Nan's death. It begins when Nan uncovers a hidden trapdoor in the floor of her room, from which she hears odd chanting. As she listens to the ominous chorus, the window shade suddenly rolls up, startling her (and the viewer), fortuitously revealing a metal handle attached to its string with which she can lift the heavy trapdoor. Venturing down the cobwebbed stone passage, she's suddenly overtaken by several black-robed figures, and her screaming form is laid upon a stone altar. Mrs. Newless approaches and coldly announces to the shrieking and struggling Nan, "I am Elizabeth Selwyn." Counting down the midnight tolling of the clock, Newless raises her knife and, when the clock strikes *thirteen*, plunges it downward. At this, the scene abruptly cuts to a knife slicing into a birthday cake (at a birthday party Nan was expected to attend back home). It's a clever release of tension, allowing the film to build once again to its second and final climax; while at the same time it shocks the viewer and heightens the feeling of dread, infusing the movie's second half with an almost unbearable level of ominous anticipation.

Horror Hotel could easily have been called *Fog Hotel*, since Moxey turned up the fog machines full blast to bathe his village set in dank mist, creating an otherworldly eerieness that makes it one of the most creepily atmospheric pictures of the 1960s. "The fog was my idea," Moxey proudly proclaimed, before adding, "The only problem with that —*always*— is the time it takes to lay it on. Once you start using it, it doesn't *go away*, and if you do more takes and you lay in some *new* fog, in the end you find you can't see across the stage, there's so much fog in there [*laughs*]! So then we'd have to get the extractor fans and clear the stage. By the way, I don't know whether you noticed in the film, but we tried to lay it in layers, not just in a mass on the floor like you often see it. By changing the heat on the guns that fired it, we found that we could lay it in layers. That worked very well." Indeed it did.

Moxey works with cinematographer Desmond Dickinson (*The Importance of Being Earnest*; Olivier's *Hamlet*) to invest this "American Gothic" (as Christopher Lee labeled it) with a spectral sense of foreboding. The old wooden buildings of the town become malevolent sentries whose shadowy recesses seem to stare with malignant eyes. The deep fog continually blanketing the streets melds with the cover of night to transform the town into an unhealthy miasma of evil. Characters step from the shadows to suddenly appear, while people are there one minute and, impossibly, gone the next.

"It was a great experience for a young director to work with such an experienced cinematographer," recounted Moxey. "He taught me a lot and we had great fun working together.... He *knew* what he was doing and he was very helpful to me, and he did a wonderful job." After *Horror Hotel*, John Moxey worked extensively in television (though he did take a side trip back to the big screen in 1966 with *Psycho Circus*). In England he helmed episodes of *The Saint* and *The Avengers*, and then came to America in the late 1960s to toil in TV-land for the next two decades, overseeing episodes of such series as *Mission Impossible* and *Hawaii Five-O*, and directing literally dozens of Made-for-TV movies (including the ultra-popular *The Night Stalker* in 1972).

Horror Hotel's cast also does quite well, from Christopher Lee's strident, humorless professor to Valentine Dyall's mysterious and malevolent stranger ("I shall be resting [at the Raven's End]," he intones— not "staying," but "*resting*"— adding a nicely archaic and slightly funereal touch).

Venetia Stevenson (daughter of director Robert Stevenson and actress Anna Lee, and former wife of Russ Tamblyn and future wife of singer Don Everly) makes a convincing (doomed) heroine as she determinedly sets about her research and investigations—only to find she's dug a bit too deeply. As her brother, Dennis Lotis' derisive skepticism turns into near-panic as the truth reveals itself to him. But top honors go to stage star Patricia Jessel (a one-time Lady MacBeth for Donald Wolfit) as Elizabeth Selwyn/Mrs. Newless, with her haughty self-assuredness, chilly demeanor and icy laugh. (While working on *Horror Hotel* during the day, Jessel also acted in the play *The Sound of Murder* at the Aldwych Theatre at night—alongside Peter Cushing.)

"It really was a very good picture in many ways," opined Lee, "insofar as it did combine ancient superstition and ritual with modern American University life. It had very much the witch-haunted flavor of Lovecraft's stories."

"One thing we *didn't* want to do was to make a Hammer film!" exclaimed Moxey when that famous film company's name came up for comparison. "We wanted to make something *better*, we wanted to make something with a little *class*, and I think that we went a long way towards it." While some of Hammer's output possesses its own brand of "class," the atmospheric, streamlined and suspenseful *Horror Hotel* is indeed "better" than much of its more-famous British competition.

With quotes from: "Baxt Stabs Back," by Matthew R. Bradley, *Filmfax* 50, May/June 1995; *Science Fiction and Fantasy Film Flashbacks*, by Tom Weaver; *The Films of Christopher Lee*, by Robert W. Pohle, Jr., and Douglas C. Hart.

The Horror Man see *The Tell-Tale Heart*

The Horror of Party Beach (1964; Deal/Fox; b&w).

Producer/Director: Del Tenney; Screenplay/Cinematographer: Richard Hilliard (Additional dialogue: Ronald Gianettino and Lou Binder). Cast: John Scott, Alice Lyon, Allan Laurel, Augustin Mayor, Marilyn Clarke.

The first ever horror-monster musical!—trailer

This idea should *never* work. And yet, it does.

Crossing a monster movie with a beach party comedy sounds like a recipe for disaster. About the only thing these two genres have in common is that, in the early 1960s, teenagers flocked to

Promotional photograph-magazine recounting *The Horror of Party Beach* (1964).

both types of pictures. Yet, in the deft hands of maverick filmmaker Del Tenney, *The Horror of Party Beach* emerges as a wildly entertaining romp, with enough rock 'n' roll, babes and beau-hunks to satisfy the beach party set, and plenty of shocks to please horror fans.

Wholesome Hank (John Scott) drives his trashy girlfriend, Tina (Marilyn Clarke), to the beach, where an argument ensues. Hank wants a more serious relationship, but Tina only wants to drink and "party." While Hank tells his troubles to good girl Elaine (Alice Lyon), Tina begins flirting and dancing with biker-dude Mike (Augustin Mayor). Hank and Mike square off in a fight scene so elaborately choreographed that it looks like something out of *West Side Story*. Meanwhile, a boat surreptitiously dumps radioactive waste in the bay, where it falls onto human remains from a shipwreck, causing the skeletons to instantly reanimate, transformed into scaly, fanged fish-monsters.

Except for the fish-monster interlude, the first 23 minutes or so of *The Horror of Party Beach* is strictly beach blanket brand soap opera and dancing (to the peppy tunes of the Del-Aires). Then the story takes a hard left turn into horror territory, as Tina swims out into the bay and promptly becomes the first victim of the fish-monsters. Her death is bloodier and more brutal than viewers might expect from a picture that begins as light and frothy as this one. The movie stays in Horrorville the rest of the way, and includes one sequence — in which the creatures crash a slumber party — that's actually a little scary. In an interesting twist on the typical monster movie formula, the struggle isn't to devise a way to destroy the beasts (that's discovered fairly quickly), but to locate the creatures so they can be destroyed. The fishy fiends have a habit of attacking and then vanishing back into the ocean.

Naturally, *The Horror of Party Beach* has some problems. Its dialogue includes too many bad one-liners, and its second act is consumed by a handful of disconnected episodes, losing track of the main characters for long stretches. The acting is, at best, forgettable. But those faults are mostly beside the point, since nobody went to beach party movies or low-budget horror flicks expecting a finely structured script or scintillating performances from the cast. Audiences came looking for fun and thrills, and in those respects *The Horror of Party Beach* delivers the goods. In addition to the slumber party massacre, most of the other monster attacks are effectively staged (especially a scene involving three bimbos in a convertible). Despite its sometimes surprising level of bloodletting, this picture doesn't take itself too seriously, as evidenced by the zany, ping-pong-ball-eyed monster suits. ("They are funny and ridiculous in a way, but that's what the movie is supposed to be," Tenney explains in a DVD audio commentary.) Even the Del-Aires are enjoyable.

Tenney hit on the idea of combining the horror and beach party genres while trying to come up with a second feature to be twin-billed with his already-completed *Curse of the Living Corpse*. But *The Horror of Party Beach* proved to be much more than a bottom-of-the-bill throw-away, and remains the most original and entertaining picture of Tenney's career, which also includes *Violent Midnight* (1964) and *I Eat Your Skin* (1964/71). It was also Tenney's greatest box office success— a smash hit that surprised even its distributor, 20th Century–Fox. Originally, Fox requested 50 prints of *Party Beach* and *Living Corpse*. After seeing the opening weekend grosses for the twin bill, the studio increased its order to 500.

Rival filmmakers realized that Tenney was on to something, and several more beach party-horror hybrids soon reached movie screens, including *Beach Girls and the Monster* (1965), *Dr. Goldfoot and the Bikini Machine* (1965), its sequel *Dr. Goldfoot and the Girl Bombs* (1966; both starring Vincent Price) and *The Ghost in the Invisible Bikini* (1966; with Boris Karloff). Predictably, however, none of its imitators could match the appeal of the original. Most of them put the emphasis on the "Beach Party" aspect and included only a few token, comedic horror flourishes. Perhaps *Party Beach* stands out because it alone didn't short-change the audience on the "horror" part of the bargain.

Horror of the Stone Women see *Mill of the Stone Women*

Horrors of Spider Island (1960; Pacemaker Pictures, Inc.; W. Germany/Yugoslavia; b&w) Alternate Titles: *It's Hot in Paradise*, *Girls of Spider Island* (video), *The Spider's Web* (video); Original Language Title: *Ein Toter Hing im Netz*; Director/Screenwriter: Jaime Nolan (Fritz Bottger); Producers: Gaston Hakim, Wolfgang Hartwig; Cinematographer: Georg Krause. Cast: Alex D'Arcy, Barbara Valentine, Allen Turner, Temple Foster, Donna Ulsike, Norma Townes.

BLOOD-CURDLING! HAIR-RAISING! SPINE-CHILLING! — poster

"One bite from a giant spider," screamed the ads, "turned him into the world's most hideous monster with a diabolical lust to kill!" While the "world's most hideous monster" part is definitely an exaggeration, the rest basically covers the movie in a nutshell. A dance troupe from New York on their way to Singapore ends up stranded on a remote South Pacific island when their plane crashes. The troupe's manager, Gary (Alex D'Arcy, a looooong way from his supporting role in *How to Marry a Millionaire*), is bitten by a giant (well, foot-long anyway) radioactive spider and instantly transforms into a hairy-faced, claw-handed, three-fanged monster. He occasionally pops up to disrupt the girls' skinny-dipping and skimpy-outfit modeling sessions by strangling one of them — until a pair of hunks arrive on the island to lead the girls in lighting torches and chasing their manager-turned-monster into some quicksand.

Given that the movie carried two titles with completely different slants— the straightforward *Horrors of Spider Island* vs. the racy *It's Hot in Paradise* (depending on whether the distributor targeted the drive-in or raincoat crowd) — it's obvious the film couldn't decide whether to be a (tame) sexploitation flick or a horror movie, so it failed at both. First we have myriad (and tedious) scenes of the girls lounging in their underwear, skinny-dipping (though obviously wearing panties and bodysuits) and taking a (teasing) shower — all accompanied by a sleazy saxophone score. The movie even begins with a protracted "audition" sequence set in New York in which the girls try out for the troupe — some dance (one performs ballet, but most just shake their groove thing), some strip (though only down to their unmentionables), and some simply stand and show off their gams.

Then comes the "horror" — in the form of the goofiest looking oversized spider (with its plastic eyes, grinning mouth and front leg pincers) this side of *Sesame Street*. After Gary transforms, we're treated to the old Reaching Hands (or, in this case, claws) chestnut (in which a pair of paws reach out towards the heroine's neck from behind a curtain, wall, tree, whatever) that was already creaking back in the 1930s. And the filmmakers do it *twice*! So much for horror.

Though director/screenwriter Fritz Bottger filled his movie with beautiful females, he seemed to possess a rather misogynistic attitude towards his subject. The various "bad" girls in the troupe throw themselves (almost literally) at the men, while the (few) "good" girls instantly fall in love with them! And, of course, *all* the girls are simply helpless until led by a male (first Gary, then the two late arrivals).

Bottger's technical prowess proves no more progressive than his anti-feminist politics. Uneven and suspect lighting, glacial pacing and nonexistent special effects are the order of the day. (The troupe's plane crash consists of stock footage of what looks like a flaming *bomber* nosediving into the ocean and *exploding*— with the next scene showing Gary and his dance troupe, slightly disheveled, paddling their inflatable raft. Right.)

Though released in West Germany in 1960, *Horrors of Spider Island* didn't escape to America until 1963. Too bad it escaped at all.

Silly sexploitation (*Horrors of Spider Island*) combines with grim realism (*The Fiendish Ghouls* aka *Mania*) in this mismatched double-feature from 1960.

House of Dreams (1963; Melpomini; b&w)

Director/Producer/Screenwriter: Robert Berry; Cinematographers: Lance Bird, Robert Berry, Stewart R. Sanders. Cast: Pauline Elliott, Robert Berry, Charlene Bradley, Lance Bird.

A unique psychological journey into terror! — tag line

For the dedicated cineaste constantly on the lookout for that elusive genre gem, finding a film that had never even crossed his or her radar can be an exciting moment. Unfortunately, more often than not, that hoped-for precious cinematic stone turns out to be just another worthless agate. Well, *House of Dreams*, a no-budget '60s obscurity that resurfaced in the new millennium, is *not* just another rough-hewn rock. Nope, it's more like a deceptive clod of dirt that crumbles to dust in your hand.

First of all, it's a bad sign when the crude credits (chalk letters drawn on the floor and walls of an abandoned house) list only four actors before moving on to the technical acknowledgments. And it's an even worse sign when three of those four names crop up again and again (and, in the case of producer/director/screenwriter/co-cinematographer/editor/star Robert Berry, *again*) under different job titles. For instance, one thespian (Lance Bird) did double duty not only as part-time cameraman, but also as the assistant director *and* continuity person. Need a "set designer"? Just ask your female lead to pitch in.

Second, the first quarter of this barely-over-an-hour movie consists of such exciting scenes as

(1) Man lying in bed; (2) Man and woman having coffee in kitchen; (3) Man sitting at typewriter; (4) Man getting into car, starting car, then driving down road; etc. You just *know* you're in trouble when a movie *starts* with filler scenes.

The paper-thin plot has a writer, struggling with writer's block, begin dreaming about a nearby abandoned (and supposedly haunted) house. When he dreams that he finds a person dead in the house, they die for real the next day. After tragedy strikes close to home, he must go himself to the malevolent mansion and confront the evil.

Filmed in Decker, Indiana, *House of Boredom* ... er, *Dreams* has absolutely nothing to recommend it. Little of import happens onscreen. We only *hear about* the deaths afterwards, rather than see them (or their aftermath). We don't even see what happens to our protagonist when he finally goes inside the house, as the film limps to its foregone conclusion in the most desultory fashion possible. Filled with overlong scenes in which nothing happens (including a mostly-silent bus depot sequence highlighted by an entire bus unloading), *House of Dreams* stands as a poster child for the fast forward button. Abrupt edits with little thought given to time or space, out-of-focus close-ups that come off as annoying rather than eerie, atonal dubbing (the movie was obviously shot without sound), an almost complete lack of sound effects, and poor framing that sometimes cuts off the bottom half of an actor's face (even while he's speaking) point up the total ineptitude in all departments. Even the potentially uncanny dream sequences inside the haunted house are sunk by pathetically ill-thought-out attempts at "art" (e.g., at one point the protagonist sees himself, shirtless, pretending to climb the walls in slow motion!). And to label the acting amateurish would be to give amateur thespians everywhere a bad rap, as the most expressive actor in the movie is the (admittedly creepy-looking) abandoned house. Worst of all, and the structural weakness that causes this *House* to collapse under the weight of its own ennui, is the slightness of its script: As written, *House of Dreams* is a 15-minute backyard movie drawn out to 68 tedious minutes.

Move over *Manos, the Hands of Fate*, there's a new challenger vying for the title of Worst Sixties Shocker.

House of Fright (1960/61; Hammer/Columbia; U.K.) Original Title: *The Two Faces of Dr. Jekyll.* Director: Terence Fisher; Producer: Michael Carreras; Screenplay: Wolf Mankowitz (Based on Robert Louis Stevenson's *The Strange Case of Dr. Jekyll and Mr. Hyde*); Cinematographer: Jack Asher. Cast: Paul Massie, Dawn Addams, Christopher Lee, David Kossoff, Norma Marla.

A completely different version of the classic story ... A new Dr. Jekyll ... A handsome, evil Mr. Hyde!—tagline

---

By 1961, Hammer Films was riding the crest of a wave of commercial and creative triumphs. But with *House of Fright* (now better known under its original British title, *The Two Faces of Dr. Jekyll*) the studio's tide of success began to ebb. This would be the first of the studio's trademark color gothic chillers to stumble at the box office, and it remains one of Hammer's least loved horrors of the era.

Yet, while seriously flawed and certainly a letdown from the heights of *Horror of Dracula, The Revenge of Frankenstein* (both 1958), *The Mummy* (1959) and *Brides of Dracula* (1960), *The Two Faces of Dr. Jekyll* deserves more respect and attention than it usually receives. It's hardly a neglected classic, but it contains some clever concepts and outstanding acting.

As the film's American posters warned, *Two Faces* re-imagines Mr. Hyde as a sociopathic Adonis rather than a simian-faced fiend, an innovation intended to underscore the thematic message that evil is seductive rather than repellent. This gambit enables director Terence Fisher and screenwriter Wolf Mankowitz to refresh some of the more shopworn elements in the story by turning clichés on their heads. Unfortunately, this ploy failed to wow audiences, who simply considered *Two Faces* a monster movie without a monster.

Dr. Henry Jekyll (Paul Massie), obsessively devoted to his experiments, neglects his wife Kitty (Dawn Addams), who finds comfort in the arms of Jekyll's best friend, Paul (Christopher Lee). Despite the ridicule of his colleagues, Jekyll remains bent on discovering a serum that will release the "perfect inner man" who exists "beyond good and evil." Naturally, he tests the potion on himself, and the homely, repressed, reclusive Dr. Jekyll transforms into the handsome, hedonistic, outgoing Edward Hyde. As Hyde, he discovers his wife's infidelity. First, Hyde tries to seduce Kitty away from Paul. When that fails, he takes a mistress of his own and plots revenge against his faithless spouse and underhanded "friend."

Unfortunately, Mankowitz's static, overly chatty script runs short on fright sequences (or action of any sort), and the scenes depicting Jekyll's revenge fall flat. The film opens with three consecutive dialogue sequences, beginning with a tedious, exposition-packed exchange between Jekyll and his colleague, Dr. Litauer (David Kosoff). Next up is a scene in which Kitty informs Litauer that she recently heard a strange man's voice (clearly, Hyde's) coming from her husband's laboratory. Why not show this episode rather than simply relating it in dialogue? (For instance: Kitty pauses outside the locked door of her husband's lab, her head cocked, wondering at the unfamiliar voice heard behind the door. She knocks. Pause. The door opens. But the face belonging to the strange voice is nowhere to be seen; only Jekyll is present.) This—or almost anything else—might have made a more involving, atmospheric opening. Instead, the film limps out of the gate with 12 minutes worth of talking heads.

After much buildup, Jekyll's revenge on Kitty and Paul disappoints, seeming too contrived and far-fetched. He murders Paul by trapping him in a room with a giant constrictor snake (hardly a reliable murder weapon). Then he rapes Kitty and abandons her. Afterward, she gathers the strength to get out of bed and walk across the room, but then suffers a fatal (and mighty convenient) swoon off a balcony and through a glass ceiling.

In the lead, Massie proves problematic. For starters, he lacks the matinee idol looks the part demands. Given the film's premise, its Hyde should be devastatingly handsome, yet both Lee and Oliver Reed (who enjoys a memorable walk-on bit) cut more dashing figures in their period garb than Massie. Also, while Massie's animated, slightly effete Hyde remains fascinating, his near-comatose underplaying as Jekyll registers barely any impact at all. Massie isn't helped by Roy Ashton's "ugly" Jekyll makeup, featuring a bushy beard and eyebrows that make the doctor look a little like Abraham Lincoln. Nor is he aided by the script, which presents Jekyll as self-righteous yet insecure, self-pitying, whiny and dour. In short, he's a total schmuck, and it's no wonder his spouse has tired of him.

Fortunately, *Two Faces* also contains many admirable elements that provide some compensation for the film's flaws. Its finale, for instance, represents an ironic inversion of the typical *Jekyll and Hyde* resolution (Hyde is exposed when he changes back into Dr. Jekyll). It's a satisfying finish and fully in keeping with the film's thematic point. The picture also boasts characteristically clean, efficient visual storytelling by Fisher and all the expected Hammer production gloss. Bernard Robinson's sets and Mayo's costumes are top-drawer, and Jack Asher's lighting is gorgeous. Best of all, the film boasts two outstanding supporting performances. Addams enchants as the manipulative, pleasure-seeking Kitty. And Lee delivers one of the most underrated performances of his career as Paul, a weak and shameless cad, but also the best-written and most likable character in the film—the kind of jaded bounder so often played by George Sanders. Addams and Lee have wonderful chemistry, and together they prevent their characters from becoming stock villains by convincing viewers that, despite their behavior toward everyone else (and even each other), Kitty and Paul truly love one another.

Lee's excellent work helps viewers overcome the sinking sensation that the actor should have taken the lead role instead of Massey—a feeling shared by Lee. "I'll admit that, initially, I was put off by not playing Jekyll and Hyde," Lee said. "Who wouldn't be? I thought I deserved the opportunity. In retrospect, I'm grateful because I got a very good part." Lee finally received his chance to play Jekyll and Hyde in *I, Monster* (1973), unfortunately a far weaker film than *Two Faces*. If not a success, *The Two Faces of Dr. Jekyll* remains an intriguing failure.

With quotes from: *The Christopher Lee Filmography*, by Tom Johnson and Mark A. Miller.

House of the Black Death

House of the Black Death (1965; Taurus Productions, Inc.; b&w) Alternate Titles: *Night of the Beast* (shooting title), *The Widderburn Horror*, *Blood of the Man Devil*; Directors: Harold Daniels, Jerry Warren (uncredited); Producers: William White, Richard Shotwell; Screenplay: Rich Mahoney, based on the novel *The Widderburn Horror* by Lora Crozetti; Cinematographer: Murray De Atley. Cast: John Carradine, Lon Chaney, Jr., Andrea King, Tom Drake, Dolores Faith, Sabrina.

SHOCK! MALE WITCHCRAFT IN EVIL TERROR!—poster blurb

In this obscure, no-budget tale of witchcraft, John Carradine and Lon Chaney, Jr., play Andre and Belial Desard, two rival warlock brothers. Carradine is the good warlock and Chaney the evil one, and they engage in a Satanic struggle for control of their ancestral home. Mixed into the mess—er, story—is a subplot about werewolves, in which Belial and his coven place a lycanthropic curse on one young member of the Desard family. (The film's budget was so low that there was no cash for werewolf makeup; we simply see his back as he escapes the room in which he's been imprisoned, and then his normal face again after he's been killed. Sad.)

Lovers of *Le Bad Cinema* maintain that the only truly bad movie is a boring movie; given that, *House of the Black Death* is a *terrible* movie. Anything remotely exciting is talked about rather than shown — and often talked to *death*. A better title would have been *House of the Unending Gabfest*. Add to this static photography; dim, uneven lighting; amateurish acting; choppy, often nonsensical editing; and continuity that seems to have sprung from another dimension (despite frequent looooong scenes of exposition added by schlockmeister Jerry Warren in a desperate attempt to plug some of the plot holes), and the film becomes an unwatchable pastiche. This may be the absolute nadir of 1960s horror.

To add insult to injury, it embarrasses two of the screen's classic horror icons, for Carradine and Chaney hit rock bottom with this pathetic crime against celluloid. Chaney plays Belial as a rather simple-minded devil worshipper (as if Lenny had sold his soul for a rabbit hutch), all amiable grins and obvious expressions. Carradine spends most of his screen time in bed; when up (and awake), he puts on his patented authoritative, crotchety old man persona.

Apparently, making the film was nearly as painful a process as *watching* it. When producer William White ran into problems, with personnel leaving like rats deserting a sinking ship, the investors turned the half-finished project over to no-budget moviemaker Jerry Warren. "They had a terrible mishmash of a movie," recalled Warren. "It *wasn't* a movie, it was a bunch of film. Somebody took over the project, contacted me and asked if I could make a movie out of it.... The whole thing was laid in my lap and I functioned as *everything*— as producer, as director, as editor, putting music in it, the whole works. It came out *bad* but it came out playable, too, and it did pull out some money for the people who backed it."

When *Jerry Warren* (*Teenage Zombies* [1960], *The Incredible Petrified World* [1961], *Frankenstein Island* [1981], ad infinitum, ad nauseum) has to rescue a film, you *know* you're in trouble. Actress Katherine Victor (who Warren brought in for some additional expository scenes) commented: "[Somebody] made a picture called *House of the Black Death* and it wasn't cohesive. So [Warren] took it over and I think he made it *less* cohesive!" Indeed.

Next up for poor John Carradine: *Billy the Kid vs. Dracula*— believe it or not, a step *up*.

With quotes from: *Interviews with B Science Fiction and Horror Movie Makers*, and *Science Fiction Stars and Horror Heroes*, by Tom Weaver.

House of the Damned (1963; 20th Century–Fox; b&w) Director/Producer: Maury Dex-

Erika Peters (pictured in this cheesecake publicity photograph) is by far the most interesting thing found in the *House of the Damned* (1963).

ter; Screenplay: Harry Spalding; Cinematographer: John Nickolaus, Jr. Cast: Ronald Foster, Merry Anders, Richard Crane, Erika Peters.

13 Keys open the doors to the house haunted by the living dead!–poster

Obviously patterned after the 1959 William Castle horror hit *House on Haunted Hill*, the low-budget, small-scale (with only half a dozen speaking roles) *House of the Damned* pales in every department. The story has an out-of-work architect and his wife (Ronald Foster and Merry Anders) hired by their lawyer friend (Richard Crane) to survey an isolated castle-like mansion up on a hill near the California coast. The owners of the house are the wealthy and reclusive Rochester family, whose elderly heiress is in a mental hospital. For the last ten years the house has been leased by an old hermit-like man known as "the Captain." But the lease is up, the Captain has disappeared, and the Rochesters want the bizarre structure refurbished and sold.

What ensues is an hour (and three minutes) of the two couples (the lawyer brings his distrusting wife) wandering about the structure, with the tedium only alleviated by the occasional odd occurrence, such as a hulking silhouette following their movements; a shadowy and grotesque figure invading their bedroom to steal the house keys; a giant of a man (Richard Kiel) advancing menacingly on the lawyer's spouse (Erika Peters); and the architect's wife opening a door to see a headless woman sitting in the room. It's all explained away — without undue distress— at the film's (anti)climax in which it's revealed that a quartet of former circus freaks (fat lady, giant, a legless man and legless woman) were given haven by the Captain (a former circus owner), who has died in his bed. The quartet of human misfits (played by real-life "human oddities") just wanted to scare away the "normal" folks, and meant no real harm.

The only remarkable thing about this decidedly unremarkable film is the use of real "freaks" to portray the former sideshow performers (something that hadn't been done since Tod Browning's *Freaks* was lambasted for the practice over thirty years earlier). "Frieda Pushnik was the little legless girl and she was so sweet," remembered co-star Merry Anders. "She came on the set with her mother.... Johnny Gilmore was the legless man and he used to walk on his hands. And he just loved to play tricks."

Lacking the wit, craftsmanship, and campy scares of *House on Haunted Hill*, as well as the outré resolution and intriguing characters (with the bitchy, deadly, and oh-so-entertaining backbiting between Vincent Price and Carol Ohmart replaced by the dull marriage problems of a po-faced Richard Crane and a petulant Erika Peters), the bloodless and action-less *House of the Damned* should be boarded up and condemned.

With quotes from: "Merry-Go-Round: An Interview with Actress Merry Anders," by Paul Woodbine, *Filmfax* 63/64, October/January 1998.

House of Usher (1960; American International) Director/Producer: Roger Corman; Screenplay: Richard Matheson; Cinematographer: Floyd Crosby. Cast: Vincent Price, Mark Damon, Myrna Fahey, Harry Ellerbe.

Edgar Allan Poe's overwhelming tale of EVIL & TORMENT — tagline

This is the *House* that Roger built, the movie that ushered in one of the most successful horror

Star Vincent Price goes right to the source in this clever publicity shot for *House of Usher* (1960).

franchises of the 1960s, catapulted its director and star to new heights and turned an American literary master into a bankable box office draw.

Philip Winthrop (Mark Damon) rides to the secluded, dilapidated Usher mansion in search of his beloved Madeline Usher (Myrna Fahey) but is rebuffed first by the family butler (Harry Ellerbe) and then by Madeline's moody, withdrawn older brother, Roderick (Vincent Price). Roderick is horrified when Philip announces his intentions to marry Madeline and raise children. The Usher line is "tainted" by madness and criminal tendencies, Roderick claims; he wants to ensure the family does not survive another generation. After Madeline suddenly falls dead from a mysterious ailment, Philip suspects Roderick may have murdered his sister to prevent the marriage. Roderick, now half-crazy, believes his sister's ghost haunts the Usher house. Weeks pass. Eventually, Philip discovers that Madeline was accidentally entombed alive — a revelation which drives guilt-ridden Roderick beyond the edge of sanity.

With *House of Usher*, director Roger Corman and star Vincent Price launched a series of profitable and critical acclaimed Edgar Allan Poe adaptations that became emblematic of their careers. But that wasn't the plan at the time. "*House of Usher* was a story I read in high school and always loved," Corman said. "I had no thoughts of a Poe series at the time; it was just a picture I wanted to make."

As 1960 dawned, Corman had established himself as a reliable purveyor of money-making, low-budget exploitation features. But the restless producer-director wanted to branch out into bigger, more ambitious productions. Instead of delivering two more black-and-white horror films, with two-week shooting schedules and budgets of $100,000 apiece, Corman asked American International Pictures' Sam Arkoff to consider approving a single color feature, to be shot in Cinemascope on a three-week schedule for $200,000. The project Corman had in mind was an adaptation of Poe's "The Fall of the House of Usher," with Price in the lead. After some haggling (a dubious Arkoff asked, "Where's the monster?" ; Corman replied, "The *house* is the monster"), Arkoff green-lighted *Usher*, with a $240,000 budget and a 15-day shooting schedule. It was a major gamble for AIP, by far the costliest feature the company had yet financed.

Much of the budget went to Price's salary. Corman also spent $5,000 to engage acclaimed author and screenwriter Richard Matheson to pen the screenplay, and another $5,000 for sets, decorations and props. "The real star of the show may have been my art director Daniel Haller," Corman wrote in his autobiography. "He went over to Universal and for $2,500 brought back stock sets and scenery — large, well-built units we couldn't otherwise afford." As a result, *Usher* boasted by far the highest production values of any Corman picture to date. With the skilled Floyd Crosby behind the camera making judicious use of colored gels, dry ice fog and matte effects, Corman and Haller were able to create the impression of a massive, decaying mansion, and a pervasive ambiance of gloom and madness. Matheson's script also proved to be a wise investment. Despite a slow and talky first act (a weakness that Corman tries to mitigate with fluid dollies and pans, and by having characters move while speaking), *Usher* remains an effective expansion of Poe's brilliant but brief story, steadily building tension toward a harrowing finale. Of all Corman's Poe films, this remains most faithful to the source material. Later entries reflect more the spirit of Poe than the letter of the author's prose.

Corman, who had recently entered psychoanalysis, weaved Freudian concepts into the narrative. "I felt that Poe and Freud had been working in different ways toward a concept of the unconscious mind, so I tried to use Freud's theories to interpret the work of Poe," explained Corman in his autobiography. "Put together correctly, the classic horror sequence is the equivalent of the sexual act. The sharp, shocking event at the end that releases the tension is the equivalent of the orgasm." Fortunately, most of *Usher*'s Freudian symbolism remains subtle. These concepts emerge most visibly in an eerie, purple-tinted dream sequence — one of the movie's most effective scenes. Surreal flashbacks and dreams quickly became a staple element in the series.

Usher's primary weakness, beyond its languid first act, remains the uneven performances of its supporting cast. Mark Damon is bland and boring as Philip, and Myrna Fahey seems a bit too robust and chipper as the sickly, death-obsessed Madeline. Harry Ellerbe is quite good as the Ushers' skittish manservant, Bristol. Ultimately, however, the film's fortunes would pivot on Price's performance alone. From his striking entrance, wearing dyed-white hair and a blazing red jacket, Price is mesmerizing as the effete, unhinged Roderick Usher. His finely shaded performance wins viewer's sympathy while remaining quietly menacing. His outstanding work here capped a minor comeback; after starring in *House of Wax* in 1953, the actor had worked primarily in television for several years but was enjoying a big-screen renaissance thanks to *The Fly* (1958), *House on Haunted Hill* and *The Tingler* (both 1959)—and his association with Corman's Poe series cemented Price's status as a horror icon. *Usher* also marked the beginning of the actor's long association with AIP, which would produce and/or distribute most of the actor's vehicles for the next 15 years, including nearly all of his most enduring work.

Usher also enhanced Corman's reputation, demonstrating that he could deliver product of a markedly higher standard than his earlier pictures. Part of the reason Corman wanted to make *Usher* was the prestige associated with the story's literary pedigree (as Corman calculated, many critics did, in fact, treat Usher with greater respect due to these origins). At first, Arkoff was dubious. Would teenagers go see a movie based on a story they were forced to read in school? But the success of *Usher* and Corman's later Poe features turned the author himself into a marquee attraction. When Corman decided to adapt a Lovecraft story, Arkoff insisted the movie be retitled (to *The Haunted Palace*) so it could be sold as a Poe picture. And when AIP acquired director Michael Reeves' *Witchfinder General* (1968), Arkoff demanded a new title and the inclusion of a few lines from a Poe poem, so it could be marketed as "Edgar Allan Poe's *The Conqueror Worm.*"

Arkoff's gamble on *Usher* paid off handsomely. The movie far exceeded expectations, raking in over $2 million and becoming one of the most profitable releases of 1960. A follow-up was inevitable. Arkoff and partner Jim Nicholson placed Price under exclusive contract and quickly green-lit Corman's next Poe picture, *The Pit and the Pendulum* (1961). As triumphant as *Usher* had been, the best of the Poe series—in both artistic and commercial terms—was still to come.

With quotes from: "California Gothic: The Corman/Haller Collaboration," by Lawrence French, from *Video Watchdog* No. 138; and *How I Made a Hundred Movies in Hollywood and Never Lost a Dime* by Roger Corman with Jim Jerome.

The Human Vapor (1960/64; Toho; Japan) Director: Ishiro Honda. Producer: Tomoyuki Tanaka. Screenplay: Takeshi Kimura. Cinematographer: Hajime Koizume. Cast: Tatsuya Mihashi, Kaoru Yachigusa, Yoshio Tsuchiya, Keiko Sata, Fuyuki Murakami, Bokuzen Hidari

Something Evil Has Drifted Into the City
—tagline

The Human Vapor concluded a trilogy of Toho thrillers that mixed gangsters and shape-shifting menaces. The cycle began with *The H-Man* (1958), about a criminal with the ability to melt into a kind of radioactive goo, and continued with *Secret of the Telegian* (1960), which featured a villain capable of broadcasting himself from place to place like a TV signal. This time around, the titular character transforms into a rolling mist.

The film hits the ground running with a title sequence depicting a bank robbery and murder, then cuts literally to the chase, with police in high-speed pursuit of the fleeing thief. The getaway car crashes, but the cops can't find the criminal's body. A series of other baffling crimes follow. Detective Okamoto (Tatsuya Mihashi) suspects that a down-on-her-luck dancer, Kasuga

The Human Vapor **(1960) does his stuff.**

(Kaoru Yachigusa), who lives near the site of the bank robber's car crash, may be mixed up in all this. Okamoto's girlfriend, Kyoko (Keiko Sata), a newspaper reporter, shares his suspicions and insists on "helping" him investigate. Okamoto discovers some of the stolen money in Kasuga's home and arrests the dancer, forcing the real culprit to reveal himself.

This proves to be Mizuno (Yoshio Tsuchiya), a mild-mannered librarian with a Phantom of the Opera-like romantic fixation on Kasuga. He gained his shape-shifting power as a result of a bizarre government experiment, and began a wave of robberies to fund Kasuga's return to the stage. Mizuno cares only about Kasuga and her career, and harbors no remorse for his crimes. "I am no longer a human being, therefore I am no longer subject to human law," he reasons. Even though, by his own admission, Mizuno is an inhuman sociopath, Kasuga loves him. However, she's not willing to let him continue to harm others, and in the end makes the ultimate sacrifice to stop his crime spree.

Although better plotted and paced than its predecessors, *The Human Vapor* lacks the moody, noir ambiance of *The H-Man* and *Secret of the Telegian*. The visual effects in *The Human Vapor* remain competently crafted, but clouds of mist simply aren't as compelling an oozing blob-man or the shimmering, ghostly "Telegian." It also lacks the human interest of the first two films. The first act of *The Human Vapor* focuses too much on the saccharine romantic rivalry between Kyoko and Okamoto. The bigger problem, however, rests with the other pair of lovers, Kasuga and Mizuno. Yachigusa and Tsuchiya have zero screen chemistry, and the screenplay fills in none of the blanks behind their unlikely, doomed romance. So little sympathy is generated for the couple, the picture's tragic finale carries little emotional impact.

Released in Japan in 1960, *The Human Vapor* failed to reach American shores until 1964, when it debuted on the lower half of a double-bill with *Gorath* (1962/64), Toho's answer to *When Worlds Collide* (1951). Like *Gorath*, *The Human Vapor* was extensively re-edited for its U.S. release. Mizuno's identity is revealed immediately in the American version, negating the mystery component of the picture's first act. Inevitably, the film was also dubbed and re-scored, and its exciting title sequence replaced.

After offering villainous liquids, murderous TV signals and criminal gasses, Toho's short-lived cycle of altered-state sci-fi thrillers ran out of steam. *The Human Vapor* remains the last and least of the lot.

Hush ... Hush, Sweet Charlotte (1964;

Twentieth Century–Fox; b&w) Producer/Director: Robert Aldrich; Screenplay: Henry Farrell and Lukas Heller (from a story by Henry Farrell); Cinematographer: Joseph Biroc. Cast: Bette Davis, Olivia de Havilland, Joseph Cotten, Agnes Moorehead, Cecil Kellaway, Mary Astor, Victor Buono, Bruce Dern.

The ultimate in suspense!—trailer

The box office and critical triumph of *What Ever Happened to Baby Jane* (1962) made a follow-up inevitable. A direct sequel was out of the question, since *Baby Jane* ended with one of its protagonists dead and the other hopelessly insane, so producer/director Robert Aldrich and writer

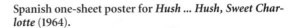

Spanish one-sheet poster for ***Hush ... Hush, Sweet Charlotte*** **(1964).**

Henry Farrell concocted the next best thing—a sister film with the working title *What Ever Happened to Cousin Charlotte*, structured like the original, echoing its central themes, and reuniting its two stars, Bette Davis and Joan Crawford. At least, that was the plan. Eventually, both the title and Crawford had to be replaced.

Like *Baby Jane, Hush ... Hush, Sweet Charlotte* (as the picture was ultimately named) opens with a protracted pre-credit sequence. The scene is an opulent ball at the antebellum mansion of "Big" Sam Hollis in Hollisport, Louisiana, 1927. Sam (Victor Buono) has learned that his only child, lovely young Charlotte, has been carrying on with a married man, John Mayhew (Bruce Dern), and that the two plan to run away together. John, shamed when he learns that his wife, Jewel, also knows about his affair, agrees to break up with Charlotte—and does so, in the quiet of the Hollis carriage house. Charlotte leaves in tears. Shortly afterward, an unidentified person enters the room and murders John with a meat cleaver. This scene is shockingly graphic for an early-sixties major studio production, including one shot in which John's hand is chopped off at the wrist. (We later learn that John was also beheaded.) Moments later, Charlotte enters the ballroom, her party gown spattered with blood.

The story then flashes forward to 1964. Charlotte (Bette Davis) is an aged, shut-in spinster and the Hollis mansion is scheduled for demolition to make way for a state bridge-building project. Charlotte has never recovered from the loss of her beloved John and seems unnaturally fixated on her late father. Although never charged with John Mayhew's murder (due to "lack of evidence"), everyone in town considers her a murderess, and most think she's insane. Her crusty housekeeper, Velma (Agnes Moorehead), is Charlotte's only companion—that is, until her cousin Miriam (Olivia de Havilland) arrives from Back East, ending a decades-long separation. Miriam also renews acquaintances with old flame Dr. Drew Bayliss (Joseph Cotten), now Charlotte's physician. Charlotte is convinced the destruction of Hollis House was somehow engineered by Jewel Mayhew (Mary Astor), and believes that her lover's widow has been tormenting her for years. Did Charlotte kill John Mayhew? Or was it someone else? Are Velma, Miriam and Drew protecting Charlotte or plotting against her? And how does Jewel Mayhew fit into all this?

That's only the first wave of mysteries posed by the sprawling, 132-minute *Sweet Charlotte*, which remains in nearly every respect a more ambitious production than *Baby Jane*—boasting a wider scope, larger cast, richer setting and more complicated plot. But while *Sweet Charlotte* tries to do more than its predecessor, it accomplishes less. Aldrich drenches the film in shadowy Southern Gothic ambiance and uses unorthodox camera setups to unnerving effect—for instance, employing a high number of overhead shots to suggest a ghost's-eye-view. But after that stunning opening he allows the tension to dissipate, and the movie bogs down in a succession of repetitive dialogue scenes, never catching fire again until its final 35 minutes—beginning with an eerie, expressionist dream-sequence flashback to the fateful 1927 ball (shot in glowing, overexposed black-and-white by cinematographer Joseph Biroc). Although the story's major plot twist proves disappointing—it's a near-verbatim lift from director Henri-Georges Clouzot's often-imitated thriller, *Diabolique* (1954), *Sweet Charlotte* finishes with a satisfying climax. Whatever its faults, *Sweet Charlotte* remains a hard film to dislike, because it's such fun watching Davis, de Havilland, Cotten and Moorehead strut their stuff.

Davis plays Charlotte like a rusted-out version of Julie Marsden, her character from the Civil War melodrama *Jezebel* (1938), for which she earned her second Oscar. Although Charlotte is a rangier and more sympathetic role than "Baby" Jane Hudson, she doesn't make the impact here she did in the previous film. Even though her part was written for Crawford, de Havilland (also a two-time Oscar winner) seems tailor-made to play Miriam and turns in a stronger performance than Davis. For 1964 audiences, the casting of the two leads created some misdirection that enhanced the mystery. With *Baby Jane* in fresh memory, viewers were fully prepared to accept Davis as an unhinged psycho. On the other hand, de Havilland remained forever identified with her role as the virtuous Melanie Wilkes from *Gone with the Wind* (1939), so moviegoers were likely to accept Miriam's apparent selflessness at face value.

The film reunited Davis with Cotten, who had co-starred with her in the notorious bomb *Beyond the Forest* (1949). Although his career was in decline—he would soon begin popping up in low-rent Japanese and European fare like *Latitude Zero* (1969), *Lady Frankenstein* (1971) and *Baron Blood* (1972)—his skills remained sharp, as he proves here. Cotten, of course, began his acting career as part of Orson Welles' Mercury Players, along with Agnes Moorehead, who steals *Sweet*

Charlotte (and won an Oscar nomination) for her spunky supporting performance as the crass, grubby Velma — a character miles apart from her role as the glamorous, charming Endora on TV's *Bewitched*, which also premiered in 1964. *Sweet Charlotte* marked the final screen appearance for Astor, yet another former Oscar winner.

When shooting began on what was then *What Ever Happened to Cousin Charlotte*, Crawford had the role of Miriam. But the production had to be suspended several times while Crawford checked herself in and out of Cedar Sinai Hospital. Reports vary as to whether Crawford was truly ill or simply sickened by the prospect of being upstaged again by her hated rival Davis, as she had been in *Baby Jane*. The project fell further and further behind schedule until finally the insurance company underwriting the production gave Aldrich an ultimatum: Replace Crawford or shut down for good. After Barbara Stanwyck, Loretta Young and Vivien Leigh all rejected the part, Aldrich flew to Switzerland and sweet-talked de Havilland into playing Miriam. A few brief shots of Crawford (glimpsed from behind, and in the distance) survive in the finished film. Due to all this, *Sweet Charlotte* wrapped production nearly a half-million dollars over-budget, at a final cost of $1.9 million. Originally planned for release in November, 1964, the film was rushed into a few theaters in December to qualify it for Oscar consideration, but its general release had to be delayed until March, 1965. Still, audience anticipation was so great that *Sweet Charlotte* earned back production costs in a single week. Although it falls below the lofty standard set by *Baby Jane*, mostly due to its unfocused and overly chatty midsection, *Sweet Charlotte* remains a fascinating and fun near-miss, thanks to its riveting opening and closing sequences, gothic atmosphere and razor-sharp performances.

The Hypnotic Eye (1960; Allied Artists; b&w)

Director: George Blair; Producer: Charles B. Bloch; Screenplay: Gitta and William Read Woodfield; Cinematography: Archie Dalzell. Cast: Jacques Bergerac, Merry Anders, Marcia Henderson, Allison Hayes, Joe Partridge.

BEWARE OF THE EYE! Its hypnotic power turns human flesh into robots! — poster

A beautiful woman rubs shampoo into her hair and, instead of approaching the kitchen sink, walks to the stove, lights the gas burner, and bends down to the flame. She raises up with her head and arms ablaze, and, suddenly realizing what she's done, screams in pain and fear. The scene goes black and the credits roll for *The Hypnotic Eye*, a rather grisly, ahead-of-its time gimmick-thriller.

The story concerns the Great Desmond (Jacques Bergerac), a successful stage hypnotist who uses a small hypnotic device resembling an eye to entrance young women onstage and plant post-hypnotic suggestions that induce them to later mutilate themselves in various ways. His motivation: his beloved assistant (Allison Hayes) is herself disfigured (but wears a very convincing mask), and wants to destroy the beauty of all those around her.

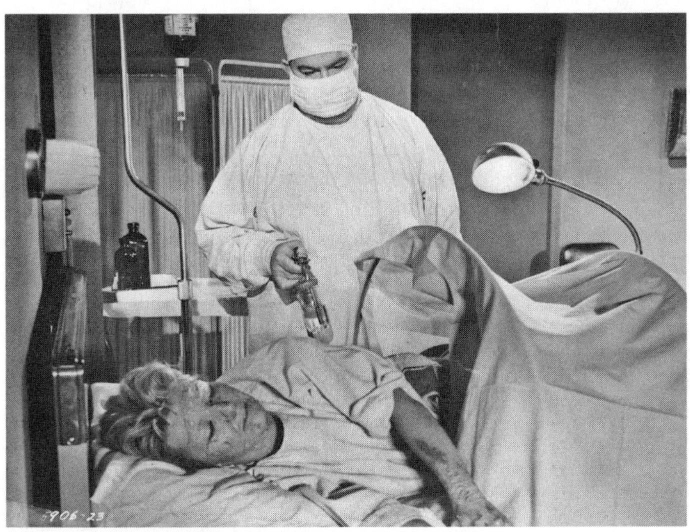

Victim of *The Hypnotic Eye* (1960) Mary Anders is treated by Fred Demara ("the Great Imposter").

"Oh, that was such fun," recalled Merry Anders, who plays a victim that washes her face with acid (and who received top femme billing, despite filling only a supporting role). "And it was such a weird picture." Weird indeed. Not only does the film contain the bizarre mutilation scenes (and some particularly gruesome makeup), it offers beatnik coffeehouse "cool, man, cool" poetry (delivered by real-life beatnik Eric "Big Daddy" Nord), the strikingly beautiful Allison Hayes, Fred "the Great Imposter" Demara as a doctor(!), and, of course, "HypnoMagic."

"HYPNOMAGIC: It makes *YOU* part of the show!" proclaimed the posters, while the movie's pressbook exhorted exhibitors to "sell HypnoMagic big and it will pay off big for you!" This "big sell" turned out to be a William Castle-style gimmick in which, just before the movie's climax, Bergerac, performing his stage show, asks that the house lights be turned on (which was the cue for the projectionist to raise the lights about 40 percent). At this point Bergerac speaks directly to the camera, merging the audience in the movie with the audience in the theater. Bergerac then demonstrates the "power of the mind" by squeezing the juice from a "bitter, bitter" lemon and informing the viewer how s/he can't help but salivate (which, amusingly, is true). Next comes a plethora of party tricks (one involving a balloon — handed out to each patron at the start of the show — supposedly becoming a lead weight in the viewer's lap) that, unlike the simple lemon bit, *don't* work and only serve to slow down the hitherto quick-paced proceedings. (Of course, the entertainment value of observing a theater full of people all rapidly raising and lowering their arms for one of these silly hypno-games would have been worth the price of admission alone!) "The potentialities of this new technique are tremendous," enthused producer Charles Bloch in the film's press materials. "HypnoMagic opens up whole new vistas to the director and is bound to work an organic change throughout the medium — something like when pictures first learned to talk." These "new vistas" were apparently limited ones, as nobody rushed to implement any "organic changes," and HypnoMagic became yet another obscure footnote in cinema showmanship history.

On the distaff side, poorly developed characters (there's little interaction — much less affection — between Desmond and his assistant, for whom he's supposedly doing it all) and too many onstage sequences sometimes bring the story to an abrupt hypno-halt. Still, Allison Hayes' intense demeanor (and beauty), some shocking setpieces, and an intriguing (though admittedly hokey) story line make *The Hypnotic Eye* worth a look.

At the film's close, a protagonist comes onstage and delivers this warning to Desmond's audience (and to the viewer): "Hypnosis, although an important and invaluable medical tool, can be extremely dangerous when improperly used by untrained or unscrupulous practitioners. Therefore, never allow yourself to be hypnotized by anyone who is not a medical doctor or who has not been recommended to you by your doctor — not even in a motion picture theater." Not just another amusing entertainment, *The Hypnotic Eye* serves as a public service announcement!

With quotes from: "Merry-Go-Round: An Interview with Actress Merry Anders," by Paul Woodbine, *Filmfax* 63–64, October/January 1998; *The Hypnotic Eye* pressbook, Allied Artists, 1960.

Hysteria (1965; Hammer/Columbia; U.K.; b&w). Director: Freddie Francis; Producer/Screenplay: Jimmy Sangster; Cinematographer: John Wilcox. Cast: Robert Webber, Anthony Newlands, Jennifer Jayne, Maurice Denham, Leila Goldoni.

TERRIFYING SUSPENSE ... it will knock you out of your seat! — tagline

Cheaply made, static and cliché-riddled, *Hysteria* is a film without ambition or imagination. It feels like what it is: The end of the line for Hammer Films' once-thriving series of *Psycho*-inspired black-and-white psychological thrillers.

"Chris Smith" (Robert Webber) suffers from amnesia following a car crash. An anonymous benefactor pays his hospital bills and provides him with a posh London flat. But the only clue to his identity is a photograph of a young woman (Jennifer Jayne) ripped from the pages of a magazine. His doctor (Anthony Newlands) warns him that his mind may "play tricks" on him until his memory returns. And, sure enough, after he moves into the apartment, he begins hearing voices acting out a violent domestic dispute. He learns that the girl in the photo was stabbed to death months before — but then sees her a few minutes later. Is he losing his mind? Is he remembering a murder that he committed? Is someone trying to frame him for the killing? Or is some other sinister plot afoot?

The biggest mystery is whether or not audiences will remain awake to find out.

As with Hammer's preceding pseudo-Psycho entry *Nightmare* (1964), producer-screenwriter Jimmy Sangster shoulders most of the blame for this misfire. The amnesia plot device was hackneyed long before the 1960s and *Hysteria* offers nothing new. (Alfred Hitchcock's 1945 thriller *Spellbound* remains the final word on the subject.) Indeed, Sangster's approach to amnesia seems unpardonably lazy, since after months of struggle "Smith" suddenly recovers his memory for no apparent reason other than to further additional plot contrivances. *Hysteria*'s fright elements are marginal at best, so it plays like watered down *film noir* than horror. But there are too few suspects for the film to function well as a mystery.

Perhaps Sangster, who had penned excellent scripts for earlier entries in the series, was letting his duties as producer interfere with his responsibilities as screenwriter. He nearly admitted this later. "If you're writing a script purely as a writer, you dress it up as you would want to see it," Sangster said. "But if you're going to produce it as well, you often find yourself pulled in two directions." In other words, you find yourself scrapping ideas if they might be difficult or costly to shoot.

Sangster leaves director Freddie Francis precious little to work with. Although slick and professional, *Hysteria* does not approach Francis' best effort. Cinematographer Don Wilcox's work is sufficient but unremarkable. Don Banks' brassy jazz score isn't bad. Most of the cast proves serviceable, although charisma-challenged star Webber drags down the rest of the ensemble.

After this flop, it was clear that Hammer needed to either get out of the psychological thriller business altogether or find an entirely new approach. They opted for the latter course and delivered the flawed yet far more satisfying *Die! Die! My Darling* (in color and without Sangster) in 1965.

For its part, *Hysteria* remains an amnesia story well worth forgetting.

With quotes from: *Hammer Films: An Exhaustive Filmography*, by Tom Johnson and Deborah Del Vecchio.

One-sheet poster for *Hysteria* (1965).

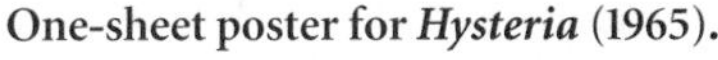

"There is no such thing as happiness"
— The ghost of Oiwa

I Married a Werewolf see *Werewolf in a Girls' Dormitory*

Illusion of Blood (1965/1968; Toho/Frank Lee) Original Language Title: *Yotsuya Kaidan* (*Yotsuya Ghost Story*). Director: Shiro Toyoda; Producers: Ichiro Sato and Hideyuki Shiino; Screenplay: Toshio Yasumi (Story: Nanboku Tsuruya); Cinematography: Hiroshi Murai. Cast: Tatsuya Nakadai, Mariko Okada, Junko Ikeuchi, Mayumi Ozora, Keiko Awaii, Eitaro Ozawa, Masao Mishima, Mikijiro Hira.

While not without points of interest, *Illusion of Blood* represents a major disappointment for a project that involved a well-respected director and one of Japan's best leading men.

In feudal Japan, master less (and penniless) samurai Iyemon (Tatsuya Nakadai) has reached his nadir — he's resorting to making umbrellas to scratch out a meager existence, his wife Oiwa (Mariko Okasa) has been called home by her father (Yasushi Nagata) in shame and now he's on the verge of selling his sword for a paltry few ryo. But Iyemon has a last-minute change of heart; he decides to keep his sword and use to regain what he's lost, beginning with his wife. He confronts Oiwa's father and discovers that his father-in-law (another poor ronin) has sold Oiwa into prostitution to support himself. Enraged, Iyemon kills his father-in-law and reclaims Oiwa from the brothel. But the killing sends Iyemon into a moral tailspin and he soon turns on his wife and infant son. When the opportunity arises to marry into a wealthy family with connections to help him gain a position with a new lord, he poisons his wife and allows his child to die as well. But Oiwa returns from the grave to sabotage his plans, tricking Iyemon into killing his new bride and generally wreaking havoc on his life.

Illusion of Blood has several issues, but the most problematic of these are its painfully contrived and needlessly convoluted plot and its dearth of likeable characters. The protracted set-up for this haunting/revenge story consumes nearly the first hour of this overlong 105-minute movie. (And the synopsis provided above doesn't include an elaborate subplot involving Iyemon's best friend, who lusts for Oiwa's sister and, coincidentally, kills her husband the same night!) Although Iyemon's first crime seems understandable, considering that he's facing starvation and his father-in-law is a total scumbag, Iyemon doesn't so much slip into evil as power-dive into it. Just a few minutes after retrieving his wife from a life of prostitution, he's plotting to end her existence altogether. He's inexplicably cruel toward both her and to his newborn son (who dies of malaria because Iyemon insists on hocking the mosquito netting around the baby's crib). In fact, the only remotely sympathetic character in the film is Oiwa.

The career of director Shiro Toyoda, which had begun in the silent era and reached its zenith in the mid–1950s with a series of well-received literary adaptations (including *The Mistress* [aka *Wild Geese*, 1953] and *Marital Relations* [1955]) was tapering off by the time he made *Illusion of Blood* in 1965. Although slick and professional, *Illusion* is nowhere near the director's best work and also lacks the poetic visuals of classic Japanese ghost stories such as Kenji Mizoguchi's *Ugetsu* (1953) or Misaki Kobayashi's *Kwaidan* (1964). *Illusion* suffers further damage due to its laughably poor special makeup effects.

Star Tatsuya Nakadai, still active as of this writing, remains one of Japan's foremost actors and was a favorite of esteemed directors Kobayashi (he starred in the *Human Condition* trilogy [1959–1961], *Harakiri* [1962] and of course *Kwaidan* [1964]) and Akira Kurosawa (who cast the actor in *Yojimbo* [1961], *Sanjuro* [1962], *High and Low* [1965] and *Ran* [1985], among other projects). Nakadai tries to use his role as Iyemon to showcase his range but winds up taking the idea too far. In the film's early moments, Nakadai underplays so severely that he seems nearly comatose; by the end of the picture he's become a frothing, grunting, quivering mass of bug-eyed lunacy. Needless to say, this isn't the actor's finest portrayal, but it's by far the best performance in the movie.

Diehard J-horror fans and devotees of Toyoda and/or Nakadai will find worthwhile moments here — the story's bitterly ironic conclusion is nicely accomplished — but neophytes are advised to begin their exploration of classic Japanese ghost yarns someplace else, like *Kwaidan*.

The Illustrated Man (1969; Warner Bros./Seven Arts) Director: Jack Smight; Producers: Howard B. Kreitsek and Ted Mann; Screenplay: Howard B. Kreitsek (Book: Ray Bradbury); Cinematographer: Philip H. Lathrop. Cast: Rod Steiger, Claire Bloom, Robert Drivas, Tim Weldon, Christine Matchett.

Don't Dare Stare at the Illustrated Man — tagline

Forget staring — don't even waste a glance on *The Illustrated Man*, a pretentious, ponderous misfire that wastes a wealth of source material.

Young Willie (Robert Drivas) is hitch-hiking form New York to California during the Great Depression when he chances across a strange drifter named Carl who's tattooed from his neck to his toes. Carl tells Willie that his "skin illustrations" were given to him by a woman from the future, and that if you stare into them, the pictures come alive and tell stories. Willie doesn't believe this but can't resist looking at Carl's fascinating body art, which begins to tell its tales.

It was a fine idea to make an anthology movie derived from the genre-bending short stories of Ray Bradbury and based on *The Illustrated Man* in particular, since it comes with a ready-made framing device to link the segments. Unfortunately, producer-screenwriter Howard Kreitsek's 1969 adaptation bungles the job, failing miserably to capture the melancholy grace of Bradbury's storytelling and sometimes missing the author's point entirely. Even though he and director Jack Smight clearly want *The Illustrated Man* to be taken as a serious literary adaptation, Kreitsek dumbs down the material, rendering it less poetic and more exploitative. (Not surprisingly, Bradbury hates this movie.)

Kreitsek's first mistake is stretching to absurd lengths Bradbury's simple framing device. It takes an astounding 27 minutes to begin the first short story. Subsequent, between-segment interludes also drag, as does the movie's final (lame) wrap-up. If the frame were handled more efficiently, *The Illustrated Man* could have included at least

Rod Steiger, looking the worse for wear, is *The Illustrated Man* (1969)

one more and maybe two more episodes into its 103 minutes. As it stands, the picture includes just three tales: "The Veldt," a reasonably faithful but talky version of Bradbury's story about a mother and father worried that their children are spending too much time in their holographic playroom; "The Long Rain," which tries to sex up Bradbury's story about astronauts stranded on the planet Venus; and worst of all, "The Last Night of the World," which completely rewrites Bradbury's subtle, poignant end-of-the-Earth yarn, turning it into an E.C. Comics-style shocker. *The Illustrated Man* marked Kreitsek's screenwriting debut. Tellingly, he went on to pen another failed literary adaptation (John Updike's *Rabbit, Run* [1970]) and a trio of brainless action flicks (*Breakout* [1970], *Walking Tall Part II* [1975] and *Final Chapter: Walking Tall* [1977]).

Smight, who worked primarily in television (where he made *Frankenstein: The True Story* [1973]), does a steady but unremarkable job behind the camera. The film's only noteworthy technical aspects are negatives: cinematographer Philip Lathrop's curious obsession with yellow and pink gels, which recur in several scenes; and the production's abominably cheap-looking sets, especially for "The Last Night on Earth," which inexplicably takes place in a tent. Bradbury essentially hand-picked Steiger for the title role—he sold the screen rights to Kreitsek and co-producer Ted Mann on the condition that the Illustrated Man be played by either Steiger, Burt Lancaster or Paul Newman. Sure enough, Steiger's brooding, intense portrayal as Carl is spot-on. Steiger, who won an Oscar the year before for *In the Heat of the Night* (1968), deserved some sort of award for enduring the 10 hours per day he spent in the make-up chair while countless tattoos were painstaking painted on his body. Unfortunately, for budgetary reasons, and perhaps as another arty touch, Steiger was also assigned the male leads in all three of the segments, and he's not quite as effective in some of those roles (he seems especially flat as the troubled father in "The Veldt"). Claire Bloom plays opposite Steiger in all three episodes, as well as in flashback sequences during the extended frame. Her performances are more consistently convincing than Steiger's, but the picture would have been better served by expanding the cast and hiring different performers to star in each of the three stories. Then again, there's so much wrong with this movie, it would have been better to scrap the whole thing and start over from scratch. A new version of *The Illustrated Man* was in production in 2010.

The Incredibly Strange Creatures Who Stopped Living and Became Mixed Up Zombies!!?

(1964; Fairway International) Producer/Director: Ray Dennis Steckler; Screenplay: Gene Pollock and Robert Silliphan (story by E.M. Kevke); Cinematographer: Joseph Mascelli. Cast: Ray Dennis Steckler (as Cash Flagg), Brett O'Hara, Atlas King, Sharon Walsh, Pat Kirkwood (as Madison Clarke), Carolyn Brant.

Not for sissies!—tagline

If you like sleazy, Z-grade productions set in seedy burlesque clubs and fleabag carnival sideshows, *Incredibly Strange Creatures* could be your kind of movie. If you enjoy watching balding 30ish men with Eastern European accents try to pass for typical American teenagers, *Incredibly Strange Creatures* might be your kind of movie. But if you want all of the above, plus go-go music, rampaging zombies and ballroom dancing interludes, then *Incredibly Strange Creatures* is *definitely* for you.

The story—told in drips and dabs between numerous burlesque routines—follows Jerry (Steckler), a teenager who dumps his girlfriend, Angela (Sharon Walsh), gets mixed up with a sideshow exotic dancer (Erina Enyo) and falls prey to an evil gypsy fortune teller (Brett O'Hara) who turns wayward young men into hideously deformed, hypnotically-controlled automatons. Under hypnosis, Jerry commits one, and then another, murder and even tries to strangle Angela. Finally Jerry's friends, while trying to free their pal from the psychic's control, accidentally let loose a basement full of frenzied, bloodthirsty zombies. (At some screenings, at this point performers in monster masks— sometimes including Steckler himself—would run into the theater.)

This picture is a kind of magnum opus in the career of producer/director Ray Dennis Steckler, the notorious purveyor of grind house schlock like *Rat Pfink a Boo Boo* (1966) and *The Horny Vampire* (1971). *Incredibly Strange Creatures* (as the film's 12-word title is commonly abbreviated) is schlock, too— but it's wildly amusing schlock. Despite a paltry $38,000 budget, Steckler seems bent on making sure there's something entertaining happening onscreen every second of the film's 82 minutes— even if any given scene has nothing to do with the preceding one, or with anything else. In addition to the zombie murders, Steckler includes a surprisingly effective, surreal dream sequence, a strip-tease, numerous musical performances (including a couple of meager production numbers), standup comedy, amusement park footage and, of course, ballroom dancing. His direction proves equally manic, frequently employing unconventional camera angles and whirling handheld shots.

By investing so much energy, Steckler and friends earn a measure of forgiveness for the production's litany of flaws: amateurish acting, hackneyed dialogue, nonsensical plot, grainy photography, atrocious sound (so poorly recorded that at times the dialogue is virtually unintelligible), and on and on. Tom Scherman's mush-faced zombie makeup looks hokey, too, but the character designs have a certain crude effectiveness— they are at least memorable. And once the zombies finally break free, Steckler doesn't reign in the mayhem, even letting the monsters crash one of the musical set pieces and attack the dancers!

Incredibly Strange Creatures owns the (dis)honor of being named the worst film of all time in the 2004 documentary *The 50 Worst Movies Ever Made.* It also endured the *Mystery Science Theater 3000* treatment in 1997. But legendary rock critic Lester Bangs wrote an appreciation of the movie in 1973. "This flick doesn't just rebel against, or even disregard, standards of taste and art," Bangs wrote. "In the universe inhabited by *The Incredibly Strange Creatures Who Stopped Living and Became Mixed-Up Zombies*, such things as standards and responsibility have never been heard of.... It will remain as an artifact in years to come to which scholars and searchers for truth can turn and say, '*This* was trash.'"

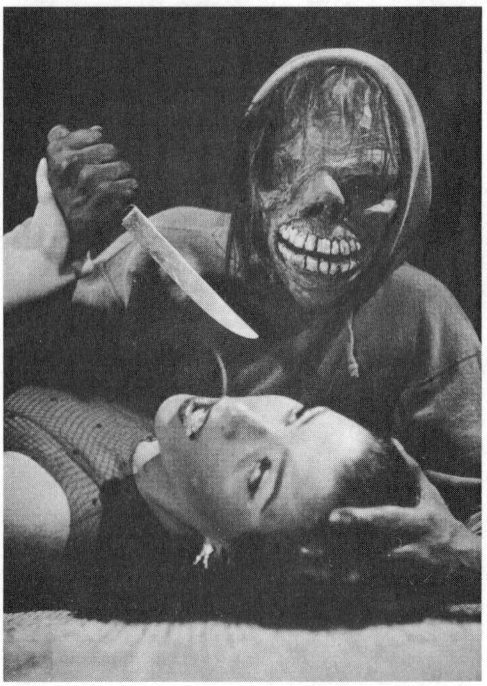

One of the *Incredibly Strange Creatures Who Stopped Living and Became Mixed-Up Zombies* menaces Marge (Carolyn Brandt).

Unintentionally hilarious and willfully bizarre, it's nearly impossible to take your eyes off this incredibly strange, mixed-up movie.

With quotes from: *Psychotic Reactions and Carburetor Dung*, by Greil Marcus (ed.).

Incubus (1965; Daystar; b&w) Director/Screenwriter: Leslie Stevens; Producer: Anthony M. Taylor; Cinematographer: Conrad Hall. Cast: William Shatner, Allyson Ames, Eloise Hart, Robert Fortier, Ann Atmar, Milos Milos.

"LOOK ON with Bewilderment as William Shatner Speaks in *Tongues*!"—(reissue) trailer

Bewilderment indeed, as (according the trailer again) *Incubus* is "the only film shot entirely in the artificial language of Esperanto." A failed experiment, Esperanto was designed to be a universal language that would unite the peoples of the world. Well, though a reported seven million individuals throughout the globe spoke this synthetic tongue in 1965, it never really caught on. And while director/screenwriter Leslie Stevens (creator of TV's *The Outer Limits*) was banking on these seven million rushing out to see the only movie made in "their" language, he forgot to take into account the fact that he could not get these scattered millions together for significant-sized theater screenings. As a result, *Incubus* failed to secure a distributor and, following a few film festival showings (Roman Polanski and Sharon Tate attended the movie's San Francisco premier), disappeared from the cinema scene to become a "lost" film. Thirty years later producer Anthony Taylor finally located a damaged print in Paris and restored it; and *Incubus* was ready for the world again ... but was the world ready for *Incubus*?

A beautiful succubus named Kia (Allyson Ames) tires of tempting already-lost souls to Hell and sets her demonic sights on corrupting a "good" man. Enter William Shatner as Marc, Kia's intended victim. When Kia becomes "tainted" by the love of this noble man, she vows revenge and summons up an incubus (Milos Milos) to corrupt and destroy Marc's sister. Marc must then battle the demon and his love for Kia for his very soul.

According to Shatner, Esperanto was spoken on-set at all times—as ordered by director Stevens, even though this meant nobody really understood anybody else (none of the actors actually knew Esperanto; they had the script's text in English on one side of the page and Esperanto on the other so they could recite it phonetically). Onscreen, this translated (no pun intended) into a dreamy, disconnected, almost otherworldly interplay between the actors. Since they really didn't know what they were saying to each other, their reactions are often oddly muted, almost surreal.

Even apart from the obvious novelty of Esperanto, *Incubus* remains a one-of-a-kind '60s film. One part *Outer Limits* (cinematographer Conrad Hall photographed that groundbreaking TV series—before winning two Academy Awards, for *Butch Cassidy and the Sundance Kid* and *American Beauty*), one part *Carnival of Souls* and two parts Ingmar Bergman, *Incubus* generates a timeless ambiance in its allegorical tale of good vs. evil. The internal struggles; the stark photography; the vaguely Scandinavian clothing (not to mention the overtly Scandinavian blonde succubae); and the use of Esperanto itself (with its faint Northern European flavor) all heighten the movie's Bergmanesque qualities. Whether this is a plus or a minus in a horror film — since *Incubus* also shares with Bergman a leisurely pace and overabundance of dull stretches (as the camera follows characters walking through the woods, reading, etc.) — remains a matter of taste.

In any case, Stevens and Co. managed to create a substantial something out of next to nothing, with its minuscule $100,000 budget and tight 10-day shoot. Particularly impressive (given its no-frills schedule) are some unique camera angles—shooting through water up at characters, tipping the camera upside down to follow a figure running past — and evocative lighting (including fog-shrouded back-lighting to generate some ominous atmosphere). And the incubus resurrection sequence, in which the (human-looking) demon literally rises from the earth in the dark of the night, is as frightening and eerie a scene as can be found in '60s cinema.

Incubus was William Shatner's last movie before *Star Trek*. Though a — little bit — of — Captain — Kirk creeps into his performance towards the end, he makes for a good-humored, likable protagonist. And Allyson Ames' ethereal beauty casts her as a convincing temptress (off-screen as well as on — she married, but later divorced, director Stevens).

Unfortunately, this atmospheric and surreal film becomes both prosaic and ridiculous at the end when the incubus transforms into an oversized *goat* (a baaaaad effect) to attack Kia as she tries to defect to "the God of Light" and aid the wounded Marc. Such a banal — and unconvincing —climax flies in the face of the movie's eerie, lyrical mood.

Though not exactly the self-described "lost cult classic" it claims to be ("lost" and "cult" apply, but "classic" definitely overstates), *Incubus* offers enough atmosphere, chills and just plain novelty to make it a lost movie worth finding.

In a bizarre life-imitates-art postscript, Milos Milos (Yugoslavian-born actor Milos Milosevicz), who plays the demonic incubus sent to seduce and destroy Marc's sister, later mirrored this plot in real life when in 1966 he murdered his lover, Barbara Rooney (wife of Mickey), and then committed suicide. (In addition, actress Ann Atmar, who plays the sister ravaged by the incubus, also committed suicide shortly after the film wrapped.)

The Innocents (1961; Fox; b&w) Producer/Director: Jack Clayton; Screenplay: William Archibald and Truman Capote (Based on "The

Turn of the Screw" by Henry James; Additional Scenes and Dialogue: John Mortimer; Script Editor: Jeanie Sims); Cinematographer: Freddie Francis. Cast: Deborah Kerr, Martin Stephens, Pamela Franklin, Megs Jenkins, Michael Redgrave, Peter Wyngarde, Clytie Jessop.

Do THEY ever return to possess the living?—tagline

Better horror films than *The Innocents* were made in the 1960s, but not many, and none of greater subtlety or pictorial beauty. Advertised as a ghost story for grownups and boasting a prestigious literary pedigree (based on Henry James' novella *The Turn of the Screw,* adapted by Truman Capote), *The Innocents* is a resolutely tasteful chiller — a triumph of suggestion over shock.

In gaslight era England, Miss Giddens (Deborah Kerr) signs on to serve as governess for two wealthy orphans, Miles (Martin Stephens) and Flora (Pamela Franklin), and moves into a secluded country estate along with the children and a few servants, including housekeeper Mrs. Gross (Megs Jenkins). It's the first job for Giddens, a sheltered minister's daughter, and her first time away from home. At first, she's enchanted by the large, opulently furnished home and picturesque grounds, as well as the precocious children. But soon she begins to sense a sort of lingering evil hanging over the place, and fears that something isn't quite right with the children. Flora, for instance, asks an odd question after reciting her bedtime prayer: "If I weren't [good], wouldn't the Lord leave me here to walk around? Isn't that what happens to some people?" Miles returns home after being expelled from boarding school for unspecified reasons, events he refuses to discuss.

While playing a game of hide-and-seek with the children, Giddens steps behind a heavy window drape. She turns to look outside and suddenly comes face-to-face with a ghostly-looking visage of a young man. Later, she finds a photograph of the man, but when she shows it to the housekeeper, Mrs. Gross informs Giddens that the man in the picture, a former valet named Peter Quint (Peter Wyngarde), is dead — murdered. Eventually Mrs. Gross also reveals that the previous governess, Miss Jessel (Clytie Jessop), was having an affair with the abusive Quint, who drove her to suicide. When, later, Jessel appears, weeping, in Giddens' classroom, Giddens becomes convinced that the spirits of Quint and Jessel still roam the estate. The children, she believes, are pawns in some wicked game being

Questioning poster for the questioning ghost story *The Innocents* (1961).

played by these evil apparitions. "They can only reach each other by entering the souls of the children and possessing them," she explains. "The children are possessed."

However, nothing in *The Innocents* can be taken at face value — every scene can be interpreted in two or more different ways. Is the house truly haunted, or are Quint and Jessel figments of Giddens' imagination? Is Miss Giddens the children's only hope, or their greatest danger? The film's conclusion remains ambiguous— open to both paranormal and psychological explanations. Ultimately, each viewer must decide.

Jack Clayton directs with restraint worthy of legendary RKO producer Val Lewton. *The Innocents* is a masterpiece of insinuated menace and ethereal horrors—creeping shadows, flickering candles, flapping curtains, howling wind and distant voices. All of which are enhanced by cinematographer Freddie Francis' evocatively lit, deep-focus black-and-white photography. Francis, who would go on to direct several horror films himself, clearly had an affinity for the material and it shows— especially in Giddens' candlelit midnight walk through the mansion, a photographic *tour de force*. This remains perhaps the most gorgeous film ever lensed by Francis, a two-time Oscar winner. Together, Clayton and Francis keep the film forever in that twilight zone between waking and dreaming, between sanity and madness. Along the way, they work in a couple of startlingly effective "jumps," like the face-outside-the-window moment, the highlight of the most spine-tingling game of hide-and-seek ever filmed.

Clayton also coaxes sensational performances from the cast. The picture turns in large part on Kerr's spellbinding, carefully calibrated lead performance. She's extremely quiet and restrained in the film's early stages—both in her tone of voice and in her gait and body language. This enables her, throughout the course of the film, to visibly unravel—gradually allowing her voice to become more strident, even jagged, her movements quicker, her gestures more fraught. Kerr's is the kind of portrayal viewers expect from a six-time Oscar nominee. But perhaps even more impressive are the standout performances of the two child actors. Tone-deaf line readings by young actors have sunk many films (call it the Donnie Dunagan Effect), but Franklin and especially Stephens (who appeared the year prior in *The Village of the Damned*) are convincing throughout, even when they're called upon to break down emotionally.

Clayton and his cast alike benefit from Georges Auric's atmospheric score, as well as from the finely hewn script, which, without making significant changes to the events of James' story, adds the underlying supposition that the "ghosts" may be delusions, products of Giddens' repressed sexual desires. Capote set aside work on his "nonfiction novel," *In Cold Blood*, to adapt this screenplay from William Archibald's stage play, *The Innocents*, which ran in London's West End and on Broadway in 1950.

In 1959, John Frankenheimer directed a TV version of *The Turn of the Screw* starring Ingrid Bergman, but *The Innocents* marked the first big-screen treatment of the James novella. Several more unremarkable movie and television versions have followed. Director Michael Winner delivered a bizarre prequel, *The Nightcomers* (1971), starring Marlon Brando as Peter Quint. *The Innocents* also served as a major influence on the hit chiller *The Others* (2001), starring Nicole Kidman. Clayton went on to direct one more upscale chiller with literary origins, *Something Wicked This Way Comes* (1983), although the results proved far less impressive in that instance.

Although Oscar didn't smile on *The Innocents*, others did. It earned two British Academy Award nominations, including one for Best Picture, and the National Board of Review named Clayton Best Director. All those honors—and more—were richly deserved.

The Innocents proves that horror films can be made with class and still deliver chills. It belongs alongside *The Uninvited* (1944), *Ugetsu* (1953), *Carnival of Souls* (1962) and *The Haunting* (1963) on any list of cinema's greatest ghost stories.

Invasion of the Animal People (1962; Sweden/U.S.; b&w)

Alternate Title: *Terror in the Midnight Sun* (U.K.); Director: Virgil Vogel. Producer: Bertil Jernberg. Screenwriter: Arthur C. Pierce. Cinematographer: Hilding Bladh. Cast: Barbara Wilson, Robert Burton, Stan Gester, Bengt Blomgren, John Carradine.

GIANTS OF THE AGES RUN AMUCK IN ICY DEATH ATTACK CONTROLLED BY ALIEN BRAINS!—ad line

Shot in Sweden in 1958 as *Terror in the Midnight Sun* (a moniker retained for its British release), with a Swedish title of *Rymdinvasion i Lapland* ("Space Invasion of Lapland"), *Invasion of the Animal People* is a unique oddity that can produce both pleasure and pain in the viewer—in about equal measure. This cinematic version of S&M offers some of the most mind-numbingly dull "narration" found this side of an Ed Wood film (at least the occasional "Woodism" proved unintentionally *funny*; no such luck here) while at the same time displaying some truly unique, beautiful and atmospheric visuals, with a half-decent giant creature and enigmatic aliens thrown in for good measure.

American character actor Robert Burton (*I Was a Teenage Frankenstein, The Manchurian Candidate, The Slime People*) plays Dr. Wilson, the head of a scientific team investigating a strange object that landed in northern Sweden. Among the team is Erik Engstrom (Stan Gester) and Wilson's daughter Barbara (Diane Wilson). As the team discovers a round flying saucer (looking similar to the spaceship from *It Came from Outer Space*) in the frozen waste, Erik and Diane hit it off. But the saucer has unleashed a 20-foot tall shaggy monster (Lars Ahren) that sets about ravaging the countryside (destroying a Lapp village and eating some reindeer). The creature carries off Barbara, and it's up to Erik and a mob of skiing Laplanders to rescue the girl and destroy the monster. The saucer then departs, taking its mysterious inhabitants (hooded aliens who, apart from high foreheads and dour demeanors, look just like humans) with it.

Budgeted at a mere $40,000 (with half coming from American and half from Swedish investors), the film was shot in Northern Sweden where, according to director Virgil (*The Mole People*, *The Land Unknown*) Vogel, the temperatures reached 60 degrees below zero! Despite the weather, some atmospheric night shooting and impressive (for the time) ski sequences (though Warren Miller need not worry), along with the grandeur of the frozen north, make this an *Invasion* of cinematic beauty.

Since there's only one monster (a few silent alien observers aside), a more accurate appellation would be *Invasion of the Animal PERSON*. Said creature is fairly effective, with its shaggy bulk and frightening face (complete with a unique set of tusks!), and Vogel shoots it from low angles to give it a menacing, gigantic appearance. (The beast costume was worn by a Swedish newspaperman, one of the investors on the film.)

The movie fizzles at the end, with a mob of torch-bearing villagers—er—nomadic Laplanders (on skis!) easily dispatching the giant beast by setting its shaggy fur alight. At this, the aliens reverse their landing procedure (via the filmmakers simply running the admittedly impressive landing sequence backwards—a comical cost-cutting effect) and leave.

The hero (Stan Gester) is handsome and the heroine (Barbara Wilson, who also appeared in *The Man Who Turned to Stone*) beautiful, but there's not much significant emoting to be found above this cinemArctic Circle. Understandable, perhaps, since the film was shot entirely in English, with many of the Swedish actors learning their lines phonetically.

Though released immediately in Europe, the movie could not find an American distributor until Jerry Warren finally bought the U.S. rights in 1962 for $20,000. And once Warren gets his hands on a movie ... "abandon all hope ye who enter here." In Hollywood Warren pared away much of Vogel's ski and scenery footage (as well as some nudity, according to one European review), shot some new nonsensical footage of Barbara Wilson running down the street in terror from an (offscreen) UFO (or something), and inserted shots of John Carradine in a vaguely lab-like setting (with an ordinary switchboard standing in for high-tech research equipment!) as the onscreen narrator calmly delivering tangential drivel like, "The main functions of science can be termed as primarily function and control," and, "Without a future, there would be no present."

Vogel claims his original version was "a great piece of artistic work." Well, doubtful; but it's odds-on that Warren's re-editing didn't improve it, and a *dead certainty* that his added scenes made it worse. In fact, said scenes stink like rotten herring. Fortunately, there's still enough visual interest and monster mayhem to make this offbeat *Invasion* worth watching.

With quotes from: *Science Fiction Stars and Horror Heroes*, by Tom Weaver.

Director Virgil Vogel and friend take a break during location filming in Lapland on *Terror in the Midnight Sun* (1962), renamed *Invasion of the Animal People* for U.S. release (courtesy Ted Okuda).

The Invasion of the Vampires

(1963; Internacional Sono-Film/Tela Talia Films S.A./Trans-International Films; Mexico; b&w) Original Language Title: *La Invasión de los Vampiros*; Director/Screenwriter: Miguel Morayta; Producer: Rafael Perez Grovas; Cinematographer: Raoul Martinez Solares. Cast: Erna Martha Bauman, Rafael del Rio, Carlos Agosti, Tito Junco, Fernando Soto, Berta Moss, David Reynoso, Enrique Garcia Alvarez.

"I'll think of something to avoid the invasion of the vampires."
— Dr. Ulysses Alberan

Dr. Alberan (Rafael del Rio, far right) attempts to protect Erna Martha Bauman and Fernando Soto from the *Invasion of the Vampires* (1963) (Mexican lobby card).

Actually, you could do much worse than run across this cinematic *Invasion*; and those enamored of that special subset of cinema, the "Mexi-horror," will find plenty here to enjoy: eerie atmosphere and evocative lighting; a creepily effective musical score (a real rarity in South-of-the-Border productions of this time); and even some mobile camerawork. Of course, there's also the usual preposterous dialogue and rapid, clipped, unnatural-sounding dubbing; overlong expository scenes; and ridiculous "special" effects— but these are all par for the course in a Mexican monster movie.

A direct (and superior) sequel to *The Bloody Vampire*, *Invasion* takes place at the "haunted hacienda" owned by a clueless Marquis. A young alchemist, Dr. Ulysses Alberan ("I'm sorry, I've only studied alchemy and the occult sciences, not medicine," the "doctor" answers when asked for some medical advice), arrives to investigate the mysterious deaths in the nearby village. There he matches wits with the vampiric Count Frankenhausen and his minions. Alberan eventually uses something called "clammic acid," made from a special plant, to destroy the vampires— though he employs the tried-and-true stake-through-the-heart method to dispatch the Count himself, pinning him to the wall in bat form with a javelin!

This gives us a good look at arguably *the* most amusing movie bat ever to flap across a piece of celluloid. Very large and *very* unwieldy, it sports Bugs Bunny-sized ears and visible wires. About on the level of the *Devil Bat* or, even worse, the *Flying Serpent*, this rabbit-with-wings looks most ridiculous when it literally bounces on a string outside a window. And the climactic battle with Dr. Alberan consists of the wascally wabbit—er—bat making pass after pass *after pass* (eight, to be exact!) as the doc ducks each time it "flies" by.

Fortunately, there's a few chills to go along with the chuckles. Raul Martinez Solares' evocative lighting casts mysterious pools of shadow across the impressive Gothic-style sets, and one scene has a sinister face abruptly appear at a window— complete with a startling zoom and cacophonous concussion on the soundtrack.

The most impressive sequence in the film, however, comes after Frankenhausen's demise. Apparently, upon the death of the head vampire, all of his victims (who've remained in a dormant state) rise up to stalk the night. Though such topsy-turvy vampire lore may be short on logic, it provides a real *Night of the Living Dead* moment, as dozens of corpses shuffle through the fog— with stakes protruding from their chests! (Alberan had previously staked all these "dormant vampires" as a precaution, but, according to the chagrined doctor, sometimes stakes work and sometimes they do not...)

Likewise, sometimes this *Invasion* works and sometimes it does not; but it rarely fails to entertain.

Invasion of the Zombies (1962; Azteca/ Panamericana; Mexico; b&w) Alternate Title: *Santo vs. the Zombies*; Original Language Title: *Santo Contra los Zombies*; Director: Benito Alazraki; Producer: Alberto Lopez; Screenplay: Benito Alazraki, Antonio Orellana; Cinematographer: Jose Ortiz Ramos. Cast: Armando Sylvestre, Lorena Velasquez, Carlos Agosti, Ramon Bugarini, Jaime Fernandez, Dagoberto Rodriguez, Irma Serrano.

"He'd rather see the Saint wrestle than have supper with Anita Ekberg."— Lt. Savage

While the above statement refers to this film's admiring protagonist, it could very well apply to the legion of rabid Santo fans, both south *and* north of the border.

Rudolfo Guzman Huerta (1917–1984), aka El Santo, aka Samson, aka the Saint, became the biggest Mexican wrestling star of the last century. He became such a popular icon (his *El Santo* comic book, for instance, sold over a million copies each month!) that he continued to live the roll outside the ring. Few knew his real name, and fewer still ever saw his face, for he wore his famous silver mask almost constantly (as a result, his facial skin became hyper-sensitive and his ears were permanently pinned back to his head).

It seemed inevitable, therefore, that El Santo should invade the celluloid arena as well. His debut came in 1958 with two low-budget features shot in Cuba, *Santo Contra el Cerebro del Mal* (*Santo vs. the Evil Brain*) and *Santo Contra los Hombres Infernales* (*Santo vs. the Infernal Men*). However, Santo made no further big-screen appearances for three years (possibly due to the horribly corrupt film industry at that time—in which, it was said, three-quarters of a film's allotted budget would disappear into someone's pocket). In any case, Santo came roaring back with a vengeance with this, his third, feature, *Invasion of the Zombies* (for which El Santo received a mere $1,700), beginning a trend that lasted two decades and nearly 50 films. Apart from *Invasion*, however, only two further Santo movies made it to America in dubbed form (*Samson vs. the Vampire Women*, 1962, and *Samson in the Wax Museum*, 1963).

In essence, all Santo movies are tales of good vs. evil set in a wrestling ring, meaning that every entry features numerous protracted wrestling bouts. For those appreciative of the finer points of an over-the-shoulder body slam, this poses no problem. For viewers not so enamored of a deftly executed scissors-hold, however, such spectacle quickly becomes tiresome.

In *Invasion of the Zombies*, "the Saint" (in the two subsequent dubbed pictures he became "Samson") faces off against a madman who has kidnapped a professor versed in the lore of Haitian voodoo and zombies. The villain (who sports a black cape and executioner's hood[!] in a vain attempt to keep his identity a seen-it-coming-from-a-mile-away secret) has developed a serum and machine that creates zombies. (Why he needs the professor remains hazy, since apparently it's not the supernatural but science—including a remote-control device attached to their belts—that powers his undead automatons.) The villain sends his zombies (who, rather than walking cadavers, look like brawny young men in tunics and tights that move slowly and are impervious to bullets) to rob jewelry stores and kidnap further experimental subjects. The perplexed police call on the Saint ("He's not only a wrestler," observes one character, "he's kind of a crimefighter") for help.

Spanish poster for the Mexican Santo feature *Invasion of the Zombies* (1962).

Invasion starts with a *ten-minute* wrestling bout—and then goes downhill from there. Interspersed with the lackluster zombie activities are several *more* repetitious wrasslin' matches (including one against a zombified wrestler). Strident, awkward dubbing and incongruous events do nothing to alleviate the ringside tedium, and a general lack of atmosphere and suspense surrounding these decidedly *un*zombie-like walking dead make this *Invasion* one for Santo completists only. Fortunately, things would improve for his two subsequent American-released outings.

Island of Living Horror see *Brides of Blood*

Island of Terror (1966; Universal; U.K.) Director: Terence Fisher. Producer: Tom Blakeley. Screenwriters: Alan Ramsen, Edward Andrew Mann. Cinematographer: Reg Wyer. Cast: Peter Cushing, Edward Judd, Carole Gray, Eddie Byrne, Sam Kydd, Niall MacGinnis.

Out of an experiment on life came a devastating death!—trailer

---

"*Island of Terror* came to me when Gerry Fernback sent me a screenplay called *The Night the Silicates Came*," recalled executive producer Richard Gordon. "I read it and really thought it was one of the best finished science fiction/horror screenplays that I'd read for a very long time." It was indeed a good yarn, and, thanks mostly to the suspenseful script and solid acting (highlighted by Peter Cushing's witty portrayal), *Island of Terror* remains one of the more entertaining sci-fi/horror hybrids of the 1960s.

"Fiction or fact?" asked the film's trailer. "This could really happen." Well ... doubtful, but you be the judge: On an isolated island off the Irish coast, a prominent scientist has set up a sophisticated cancer research lab. In "trying to create some form of living matter to counteract the cancer cells," the doctor has instead produced a silicon-based life form that sucks bone from its victims and replicates itself by division every six hours. When a local farmer is found dead (and denuded of all bone matter), the puzzled village doctor calls in eminent pathologist Brian Stanley (Cushing) and bone disease specialist David West (Edward Judd). Learning what they're up against from the scientist's notes (the doctor and all his assistants were killed by the creatures), Stanley and West must find a way to destroy the ever-advancing "silicates."

Principal photography on this English production began on November 22, 1965, at Pinewood Studios, where the entire film was made (with the studio's back lot and lake standing in for the island exteriors). Without an expensive location shoot, the production could remain within its extremely economical budget of £75,000 (about $200,000).

The script is intelligent and well-paced (with the menace remaining a mystery for the first half, setting up the ever-mounting tension of the latter portion), and peppered with believable and often wryly amusing dialogue. "Are you all right?" asks one concerned character after a particularly close encounter. "No!" is the emphatic—and reasonable—response.

Adding to the credibility quotient is the incisive playing of the cast, particularly Edward Judd as West and Peter Cushing as Stanley, who both bring a natural intelligence and believability to their characters. Though Judd had the reputation of sometimes being "difficult," he exhibited no such behavior here. "With Peter Cushing's general 'benign' influence," recalled Gordon, "it was a happy shoot."

Despite its science-oriented premise, *Island of Terror* possesses more horror/suspense than sci-fi/gadgetry. Director Terence Fisher, Hammer Films' mainstay during their Gothic horror revival period in the late 1950s and early '60s, creates some eerie set-pieces—particularly early on when the creatures are kept largely unseen. The silicates, with their slimy, bubbly turtle shell-like bodies and long protruding tentacles, are unique little monsters. Admittedly, the creatures (animated "mostly with wires being pulled along the ground," revealed Gordon) sometimes appear rather plastic and less than convincing (looking particularly slow and ungainly in long shot), but

The unfortunate Dr. Stanley (Peter Cushing) comes to grips with the tentacle of an unstoppable "silicate" on the *Island of Terror* (1966) (American lobby card).

the high-quality acting and professional demeanor of the principals sells the illusion. (Edward Judd relayed to interviewer Steve Swires an amusing story of how a stray dog wandered onto the shoot one day and "actually tried to make love with one of the silicates. He found an opening and started to mount it. That poor dog must have gotten the *surprise* of his life.")

While some might consider it just another creature feature, the film's literate script and intelligent acting make this *Island* a worthy destination for discerning fans of 1960s horror and sci-fi.

With quotes from: *Interviews with B Science Fiction and Horror Movie Makers*, by Tom Weaver.

Island of the Burning Damned (1967; Planet Company; U.K.)

Alternate Titles: *Night of the Big Heat* (U.K.), *Island of the Burning Doomed* (U.S. TV); Director: Ternence Fisher; Producer: Tom Blakeley; Screenplay: Ronald Liles, Pip and Jane Baker; Cinematographer: Reg Wyer. Cast: Christopher Lee, Peter Cushing, Jane Merrow, Patrick Allen, Sarah Lawson, William Lucas.

SHOCK AND TERROR — FOR THOSE STRONG ENOUGH TO TAKE IT!
— poster blurb

Based on John Lymington's novel *Night of the Big Heat*, the story centers on the inhabitants of a small inn on the remote British island of Fara during an inexplicable winter heat wave. Among the characters are the inn's owners, novelist Jeff Callum (Patrick Allen) and wife Frankie (Sarah Lawson, Allen's real-life wife), the level-headed local doctor (Peter Cushing), "slut" Angela (Jane Merrow), who came to the island to try and rekindle the illicit tryst she had enjoyed with Jeff (and which Jeff bitterly regrets), and a solitary, no-nonsense scientist named Hanson (top-billed Christopher Lee), who's conducting a secret investigation. As the temperature climbs ("108 degrees and still rising," reports one character), it comes to light that the island is a staging ground for an invasion from outer space. The blob-like aliens traverse a heat ray trained on the island from another planet and set about sucking energy sources dry (including car engines and acetylene tanks), while also frying any of the indigenous population they run across. It's up to the protagonists to find a way to stop the invaders before they spread to the mainland and ultimately turn Earth into a burned-out cinder.

In Britain the film retained its literary title of *Night of the Big Heat*, but the U.S. distributor (United Productions of America) renamed it the more exploitative *Island of the Burning Damned*—which was then changed to *Island of the Burning Doomed* for its television debut (to avoid offending the children — and Bible thumpers— one supposes).

Something of a companion piece to the previous year's *Island of Terror* (both were British sci-fi/horror productions directed by Terence Fisher, both starred Peter Cushing, and both involved creatures laying siege to a remote island), *Island of the Burning Damned* is less successful as a creature feature (with the unlikely but inventive tentacled monsters of *Terror* inspiring far more shudders and excitement than the disappointing, slow-moving blobs of *Burning Damned*) but more impressive as a character study. In fact, *Night* is a well acted, character-driven drama draped over a rather shaky alien monster framework.

"The idea is an excellent one," enthused star Christopher Lee in *The Films of Christopher Lee* by Robert Pohle, Jr., and Douglas Hart, "and it's a good picture right until the very end, when they

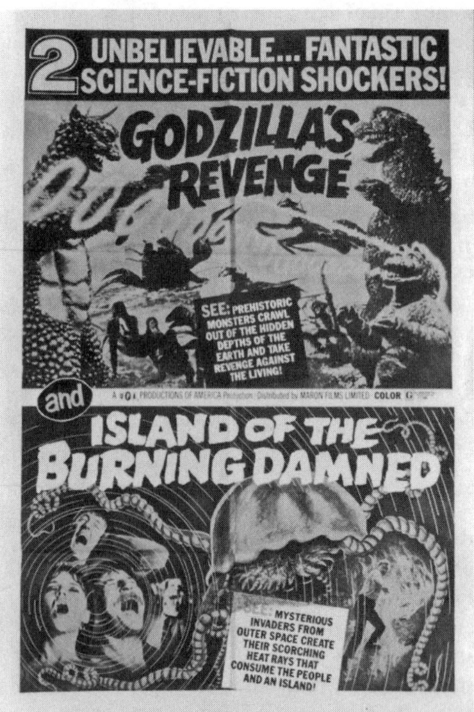

Cinematic odd couple: The juvenile thrills of *Godzilla's Revenge* paired with the adult issues (and alien blobs) found on the *Island of the Burning Damned* (1967).

made the mistake of introducing the aliens. They were supposed to represent pieces of protoplasm. To me, they looked like badly fried eggs." Indeed, it's the interactions and tensions between the characters, as the rising temperature makes temperaments rise, that prove to be the film's strong point and *raison d'etre*. The cast does marvelously well, with the standout perhaps being Jane Merrow. As Angela, she is desirability incarnate, using her sexuality to entice and torment. As the terror unfolds, however, her narcissistic front crumbles into a panicky, almost self-destructive self-loathing.

Making the movie was no picnic in the park for the actors, considering it was filmed during the height of the English winter. "The whole point of the story is that this freak heat wave happens in the winter," explained Lee in Mark Miller's *Christopher Lee and Peter Cushing and Horror Cinema*. "Now, there's no problem involved in that if you're shooting interiors, but if you're shooting exteriors— and we shot a lot — you have to show trees without leaves on them. So this film was shot in February, about the coldest month of the year, and we did a lot of night shooting on that, wandering about and running about with practically nothing on, pretending to sweat and saying how hot it was when, in fact, we were freezing to death because it was probably down to zero centigrade. That was murderous, as you can imagine, and it was amazing we survived it. I don't think anybody even got a cold. The main problem was the smoke of one's breath. We got around that by sucking ice cubes."

Director Terence Fisher does an admirable job of juggling the character development and interactions with the initial mystery build-up and early (and thankfully monsterless) "encounter" scenes, using sound, atmosphere and actors' reactions to convey the terror that showing the creatures would have negated.

"Terence really was the ultimate professional," praised Jane Merrow to Miller. "With him, it was let's get on with the job, use what we have at hand, and don't let us cry about spilt milk if they [the effects] aren't absolutely right. Obviously, if they'd been absurd he would have, I'm sure, fought to have them as right as they possibly could be. But the British directors were very good at working with what they had, and we were working with very limited means. You just got on with what you were given, really." Oversized fried eggs and all.

Well written, well acted and well directed (with a good, mysterious build-up and several suspenseful set-pieces), *Island of the Burning Damned* is a cracking good yarn — until the glowing glops show up. Still, it remains one of the better adult-oriented sci-fi/horror films of the decade.

Island of the Burning Doomed see *Island of the Burning Damned*

Island of the Doomed (1965; Orbita-Tefi; Spain/West Germany) Original Language Title: *La Isla de la Muerte*; Alternate Titles: *Maneater of Hydra*; *Bloodsuckers*; Director Ernest Von Theumer (Mel Welles); Producer: George Ferrer; Screenplay: Stephen Schmidt, Ira Meltcher; Cinematographer: Cecilio Paniagua. Cast: Cameron Mitchell, Elisa Montes, George Martin, Kay Fischer, Herman Nelson, Matilde Sampedro, Richard Valle, Mike Brendel, Ralph Naukoff.

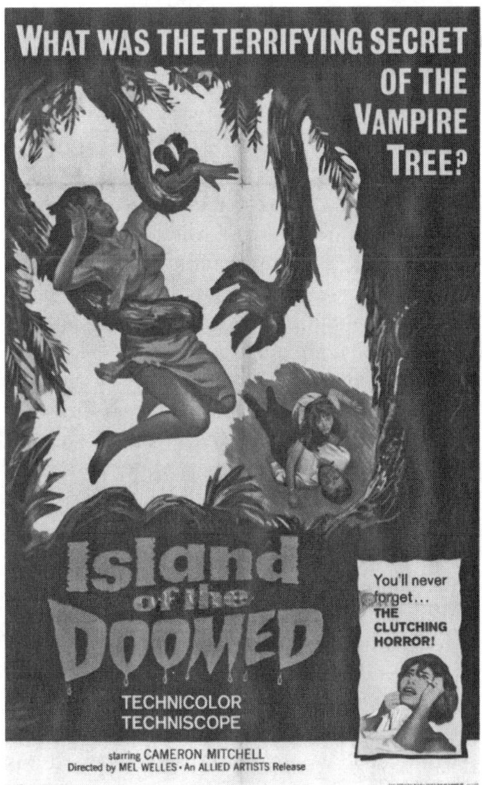

This one-sheet poster promises far more activity than what's actually seen on the *Island of the Doomed* (1965), a deserted atoll, entertainment-wise.

WHAT WAS THE TERRIFYING SECRET OF THE VAMPIRE TREE?—poster blurb

On his own private island, nobleman Baron Von Weser (a woefully miscast Cameron Mitchell) creates new species of plant life, including a large tree that wraps its tendrils around its victims and sucks their blood. A group of tourists lured to the island becomes plant food.

Shot on a huge private estate near Barcelona (the producers paid the owners $5,000 for the use of their villa), *Island of the Doomed* certainly lives up to its name: Whoever falls under the spell of this celluloid monstrosity is indeed doomed—doomed to an hour and a half of unrelieved boredom. Scenes of the annoying characters (cuckolded husband; slatternly wife—named "Mrs. Robinson"!; bookish botanist; brash middle-aged matron; handsome hero; innocent ingenue; etc.) eating, walking, talking, arguing and engaging in illogical behavior (thinking there's a killer loose on the island, several characters go out walking *by themselves*) go on and on and on...

The only thing that might save this bland cinematic salad would be a generous helping of horror inspired by the movie's only intriguing character—the tree. "WHAT WAS THE TERRIFYING SECRET OF THE VAMPIRE TREE?" asks the movie's advertising. The Answer: IT DOESN'T WORK. "We built a tree that was supposed to run electronically," recounted director Mel Welles. "It cost $30,000 in Spain to build it. And then it didn't work. So we wound up using the old-fashioned trick of pulling the branches with wires." The film is an hour and fifteen minutes old (having looooong overstayed its welcome) by the time the viewer glimpses said sinister shrub. Granted, it *is* rather disturbing, with its vaguely obscene proboscis waving about in the middle of oversized flowers attached to the ends of long, thick vines—all the while accompanied by sickening slurping noises (which are more than a little reminiscent of flatulence!)—but it's too little, too late.

Welles intended to finish the film with a bang by having lightning strike the tree, setting both monster and master alight. But the special effects technicians ("who had not accomplished *anything* correctly up till then," griped the director) had bought magnesium *salt* instead of powder. "It was enough laxative for three movie companies," laughed Welles. "We ended the picture without the fire because I didn't want to go an extra day, and there was no way to get magnesium powder late on a Sunday night." So instead, the tree just bleeds to death after being chopped at by the axe-wielding hero. By this point, the viewer's interest has been bled dry as well.

"It's a dreadful film," admitted Cameron Mitchell, "but it's made a lot of bucks.... I enjoyed playing the villainous Baron, although I didn't think the dubbing was very good." Indeed, it's particularly disconcerting to hear the actor's distinctive, gravelly voice replaced by an aristocratic-tinged, upper-crust accent totally incongruous with Mitchell's gruff persona.

Incidentally, this same year Cameron Mitchell filed for bankruptcy.

With quotes from: *Interviews with B Science Fiction and Horror Movie Makers*, and *Attack of the Monster Movie Makers*, by Tom Weaver.

It! (1966; Warner Bros./Seven Arts; U.K./U.S.) Director/Producer/Screenwriter: Herber J. Leder. Cinematographer: Davis Boulton. Cast: Roddy McDowall; Jill Haworth, Paul Maxwell, Aubrey Richards, Ernest Clark, Oliver Johnston.

HOW CAN WE DESTROY *IT* BEFORE *IT* DESTROYS US?—ad line

Typically dismissed as another boring British misfire (if even considered at all), the much-maligned *It!* is not altogether unworthy of attention. Impeccably acted (particularly by star Roddy McDowell) and possessing several worthy themes, not to mention a unique (for the 1960s anyway) monster, *It!* remains an unusual entry in '60s British horror (and one far superior to its co-feature, the flaccid *The Frozen Dead*).

When a museum warehouse catches fire, the only item untouched by the flames is a mysterious stone statue. After several inexplicable deaths occur near the figure, milquetoast curator's assistant Arthur Pimm (Roddy McDowell) discovers that it's actually the cursed Golem created by Rabbi Loew in the 16th century to protect his persecuted people. Pimm reactivates the statue and sets it to serving his own ends, including murdering a superior to secure a promotion and destroying a bridge (a misguided attempt on Pimm's part to impress his would-be girlfriend with his new-found power). Finally gone completely mad, Pimm kidnaps his reluctant lady love (Jill Haworth) and takes the Golem to a remote estate owned by the museum. There the police—and, eventually, the army—attempt to stop the stone leviathan.

Two things make *It!* worth watching: Roddy McDowell and the grotesque Golem. McDowall has a rather low opinion of this picture: "The film just went totally to pieces," remarked the actor, "and I really don't remember chapter and verse on it." Which is too bad considering it's the biggest part McDowall ever played (though far from the best), with the actor onscreen in nearly every scene. He makes the most of it, with his mild manner and blend of bemused distraction making him appear both harmless and likable — which makes it doubly effective when the worm turns. Despite Pimm being a few biscuits shy of a full tin, the actor transforms the bizarrely written character into a real person, diverting his eyes in horror when he orders his first murder, for instance, and seeming genuinely sorry when someone stumbles upon his secret and must be eliminated.

_It!_ carries off Jill Hayworth.

Ads called *It* the "monster of the year!" and it's a hard point to argue. When the heroine comments, "There's something uncanny, frightening about it," she's not far wrong. With its conical-shaped head, vaguely skull-like features and rough-hewn texture, *It* cuts a hideous and imposing figure.

The problem with the film — and this is a big one — is its meandering, half-baked script. Unfortunately, producer/director Herbert. J. Leder felt his screenwriter could do no wrong. Who was said screenwriter? Why, Herbert J. Leder. (Leder also wrote the highly enjoyable *Fiend Without a Face* in 1958, which *someone else* produced and directed.) Leder's script earns an A for effort but only a C- for execution. "Power destroys," says one character, delineating a theme that could have made this a truly intriguing story — had not Pimm's character been shown as petty, deceitful and outright *psychotic* from the get-go. (The very first scene, in which the devoted Momma's boy goes home to give his mum a necklace 'borrowed' from the museum, reveals her to be a preserved corpse, à la *Psycho*!) Power corrupting the already corrupted doesn't generate the same impact.

Then, of course, there's the outright lapses in logic, the most glaring of which has the Army dropping a *nuclear bomb* on the English countryside! (To be fair, the film's nominal hero protests this as absurd; but it's explained that the Army's conventional weapons have failed and they need to save face ... or something.)

"It should have been rather good, actually, but it was very badly done," concluded McDowell. Not really. Though the story had its problems, there is still enough here to make it a diverting — if not wholly engrossing — 95 minutes (or 70 minutes anyway, as the film is indeed too long to truly sustain *It*self).

With quotes from: "From Collies to Werewolves: Roddy McDowall," by Danny Savello, *Scarlet Street* 26, 1997.

It's Hot in Paradise see *Horrors of Spider Island*

Jack the Giant Killer (1962; United Artists)

Director: Nathan Juran; Producer: Edward Small; Screenplay: Orville H. Hampton, Nathan Juran; Cinematographer: David S. Horsley. Cast: Kerwin Mathews, Judi Meredith, Torin Thatcher, Walter Burke, Robert Mobley, Don Beddoe.

THE MOST AWESOME SPECTACLE THAT EVER STUNNED THE IMAGINATION!
— poster blurb

Well ... not really. Unless you're a prepubescent cinematic neophyte, it's unlikely — even back in 1962 — that your imagination would be much affected, much less "stunned," by this "AWESOME SPECTACLE." Said spectacle follows the adventures of one medieval farmer-turned-hero named Jack (Kerwin Mathews) who, after killing a giant who had kidnapped a princess (Judi Meredith), is knighted by the King of Cornwall and appointed the official Princess Protector. When the evil wizard Pendragon (Torin Thatcher), who sent the giant, manages to recapture the princess, Jack, a plucky cabin boy, a Viking fisherman and a leprechaun in a bottle(!) must journey to the sorcerer's castle to battle various monsters and rescue the girl. Some of the formidable foes faced by Jack include a bevy of witch-demons (one of which sports a giant lizard head from whose gaping maw spews a gale-force wind), huge zombie warriors, a two-headed ogre and a winged dragon.

After producer Edward Small turned down Ray Harryhausen and his fabulous sketches for a proposed Sinbad movie, the stop-motion animation wizard took his ideas to producer Charles H. Schneer, who collaborated with Harryhausen to produce the box office winner *The Seventh Voyage of Sinbad* in 1958. Obviously coming to regret his hasty decision, Small belatedly made *Jack the Giant Killer*, hiring the two key stars from *Sinbad* (hero Mathews and villain Thatcher, playing nearly identical roles as they had in *Sinbad*), as well as that previous film's director, Nathan Juran. Unable to afford the animation master himself, however, given Small's—er, small budget, the producer turned to up-and-comer Jim Danforth for the film's stop-motion monster effects.

Though Danforth later proved his talent by earning an Oscar nomination for his Visual Effects work on *When Dinosaurs Ruled the Earth* (1970), his awkward designs and crude technique on *Jack* looks substandard compared to anything done by Harryhausen.

"[Director Nathan Juran] rewrote [*Jack the Giant Killer*]—and made me sick with what he did to it," complained scripter Orville H. Hampton (*The Alligator People*, *The Atomic Submarine*, *The Four Skulls of Jonathan Drake*). While there's little innovation and even less depth in the straightforward story, it remains serviceable enough as a simple adventure fantasy strewn with horror elements. Competent—if unspectacular—in most departments (though disappointing in the poorly animated monster scenes), *Jack* makes for an undemanding *Time Killer*.

Viewer beware: There are two versions of this film. One is a straight horror/fantasy aimed at a young-adult audience, while the other is a cloying musical intended to soften the film's frightening aspects for the children. The footage remains basically the same in both, but the musical version dubs "cute" songs over the dialogue (and many of the monster scenes!)—this latter aberration becoming the *true* horror.

With quotes from: "The Write Approach: An Interview with Screenwriter Orville H. Hampton," by Paul Woodbine, *Filmfax* 66, April/May 1998.

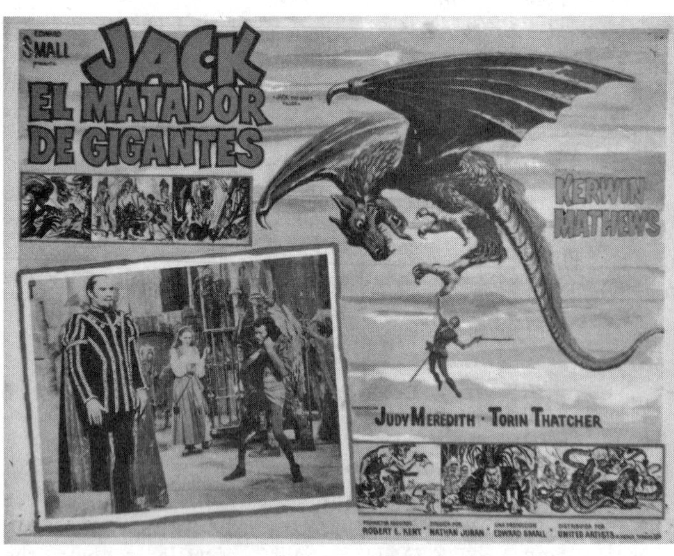

The evil wizard Pendragon (Torin Thatcher, at left) and his minions in *Jack the Giant Killer* (1962) (Mexican lobby card).

Jack the Ripper (1960; Embassy/Paramount; U.K.; b&w/color) Directors/Producers/Cinematographers: Robert S. Baker, Monty Berman; Screenplay: Jimmy Sangster (original story: Peter Hammond, Colin Craig). Cast: Lee Patterson, Eddie Byrne, Betty McDowall, Owen Solon, John Le Mesurier.

THE MOTION PICTURE SCREEN SCREAMS WITH EXCITEMENT!—tagline

Though this British import (filmed at Shepperton Studios in November 1958 and released in America in February 1960) may not be the best cinematic take on "Saucy Jack"—1944's *The Lodger*, starring Laird Cregar, wins that top honor—it certainly makes a strong case for runner-up.

"London—1888" the screen tells us, as a tipsy streetwalker staggers through the dark, foggy lanes of Whitechapel, only to be confronted by a black shadow who menacingly rasps, "Are you Mary Clarke?" before a gleaming blade silences whatever response she could have made through her terrified gasps. It's a stark and startling pre-credits sequence that sets the ominous, atmospheric tone (and would become something of a template for similar scenes in numerous television and filmic Jack the Ripper adaptations to come).

Hammer veteran Jimmy Sangster's screenplay, based on a story by Peter Hammond and Colin Craig (who "borrowed" the intriguing theory espoused by Leonard Matters in his investigative book *The Mystery of Jack the Ripper*), focuses on Scotland Yard Inspector O'Neill's (Eddie Byrne) and his American friend and colleague, Detective Sam Lowry's (Lee Patterson), fruitless pursuit of the maniacal Jack the Ripper, with both their superiors and the terrified populace up in arms at the department's inability to stop the killings. (Note: Before this film, almost all Ripper movies had been based on either *Lulu* or *The Lodger*—both having fictional origins. *Jack the Ripper*'s use of an authentic—if no longer authoritative—theory was a first in Ripper cinema.) Sangster provides a plethora of likely suspects, from the haughty head of the local hospital to the tentative young physician on staff, from the cranky and furtive Dr. Tranter (John Le Mesurier) to a disfigured hunchbacked assistant. The immediacy of the horror, as well as the (nicely understated) love interest, is brought home with the arrival of Trantor's niece, Anne (Betty McDowall), who ultimately crosses paths with the Ripper.

Besides the suspenseful mystery and horrific killings themselves, Sangster's script highlights the mob mentality and hysteria that arise from the fear and paranoia engendered by the seemingly unstoppable crimes, resulting in brutal and disturbing attacks on several innocents. This adds a further, more expansive layer to the horror, as well as a bit of sociological insight and historical accuracy (London's East End became a veritable powder keg during the Ripper murders, with mob anger often aimed at Jews).

The producing/directing/cinematography team of Robert S. Baker and Monty Berman take full advantage of the cleverly constructed story, emphasizing the foggy, shadowy street settings, and maximizing, via tilted angles, close shots, reactions and judicious use of shadow, the horror of the murders themselves. The duo were responsible for such literate and atmospheric British terrors as *The Crawling Eye*, *Blood of the Vampire* (both 1958) and *Mania* (1960, another sixties shocker based on real-life historical horror).

Film distributor Joseph Levine (the man who made Steve Reeves a household name in America by importing the Italian muscleman feature *Hercules* and starting the Stateside peplum craze in the late 1950s) bought the U.S. rights to *Jack the Ripper* and struck a releasing deal with Paramount. "My sole thought upon acquiring the film was that here was the type of 'chiller' the British do so very well," Levine stated in a publicity piece. "With their acting company in fine fettle, Mr. Baker and Mr. Berman bring their camera to bear on a lengthy scene and let it grind away. There are none of the short 'takes' and obvious cuts which characterize so many hastily made movies. The mood is created and the actors are given full opportunity to sustain it." Indeed it was, and they did. (To up the shock value, Levine also inserted a brief color shot into the climax of the black-and-white film that drove home the

Atmospheric Belgian poster for the excellent *Jack the Ripper* (1960).

killer's gory demise with the startling sight of oozing red blood.)

Backed by Paramount, Levine launched a huge marketing campaign, sinking over $700,000 into promoting the picture (including buying extensive TV spots and striking over 600 prints for saturation bookings). The strategy paid off in almost $2 million in gross ticket sales in the U.S. and frequent holdovers at theaters across the country. Of course, the fact that it was an atmospheric, engrossing, well-acted and at times shocking Jack the Ripper movie helped tremendously. Curiously, the film subsequently appeared to drop out of circulation, with few television showings and no official video release to date, unfairly leaving *Jack the Ripper* in the cinematic equivalent of a London fog.

Jason and the Argonauts (1963; Columbia)

Director: Don Chaffey; Producer: Charles H. Schneer; Screenplay: Jan Read and Beverley Cross; Cinematographer: Wilkie Cooper. Cast: Todd Armstrong, Nancy Kovac, Gary Raymond, Laurence Naismith, Niall MacGinnis, Honor Blackman, Patrick Troughton, Nigel Green.

THE EPIC STORY THAT WAS DESIGNED TO STAND AS A COLOSSUS OF ADVENTURE — tagline

Jason and the Argonauts remains one of the most beloved fantasy films of all time. Among other things, it's special effects legend Ray Harryhausen's personal favorite among his own films. This lofty reputation is well-earned, but *Jason* isn't flawless, nor is it Harryhausen's best picture (sorry, Ray).

The evil Pelias betrays his king and attempts to murder the entire royal family and claim the throne for himself. However, the infant prince Jason is spirited away to safety. Twenty years later, Jason (Todd Armstrong) returns to overthrow Pelias, but is duped by the wily despot into taking on a quest to "the end of the world" to capture a legendary Golden Fleece that brings peace and prosperity. Jason assembles a crew of Greece's greatest athletes, including Hercules (Nigel Green), and — aided by the goddess Hera (Honor Blackman) — sets about the arduous quest, which involves encounters with horrific adversaries such as Talos, a giant bronze statue come to life; Hydra, the fabled seven-headed snake; and an army of living skeletons (all of these and other terrors created in stop-motion "Dynamation" by the great Harryhausen).

There's no denying that *Jason* is an enthralling spectacle, and Harryhausen's visual effects sequences — particularly the skeleton battle — rank among the most thrilling and iconic of his career. Better still, unlike many Harryhausen pictures, *Jason* doesn't stop dead in its tracks between its animated set pieces. However, Jan Read and Beverley Cross' screenplay has problems with pacing and dramatic construction, and its conclusion proves less than satisfying. While not completely without interest, the film's opening act, which establishes Jason's relationship with the Greek gods and chronicles the assembly of his ship and crew, rambles on considerably. The Argos doesn't set sail until 26 minutes have elapsed. A bigger issue is that, after setting up Pelias as a truly reprehensible villain (we see him viciously murder a defenseless young woman, running his sword through her back), the story ends before Jason completes his mission and dethrones the evil usurper. While clearly we are intended to gather that, carrying the fleece, Jason will now succeed

Possibly the most thrilling fantasy sequence of the decade: the amazing skeleton attack in *Jason and the Argonauts* (1963), starring Todd Armstrong.

in this endeavor, such knowledge does not make an entirely adequate substitute for seeing the villain vanquished. The picture would have had ample time to portray this climactic confrontation had it not spent so long noodling around during its first 20 minutes. Perhaps the ending was left open for a never-realized sequel (Zeus ventures that "I am not yet done with Jason"), but in any case it's a letdown. While still highly enjoyable, and certainly his best work of the 1960s, *Jason* proves less gratifying as an overall viewing experience than earlier Harryhausen classics such as *The Beast from 20,000 Fathoms* (1953), *Earth vs. the Flying Saucers* (1956) and *The Seventh Voyage of Sinbad* (1958).

As in most of Harryhausen's fantasy epics, the story is populated by types rather than fully developed characters, but Armstrong makes a particularly appealing and likeable hero. Honor Blackman, who would gain immortality a year later for her role as Pussy Galore in *Goldfinger* (1964), and Niall MacGinnis offer amusing turns as the meddling Hera and Zeus. The movie also benefits greatly from a rousing score by the great Bernard Herrmann. All of which makes *Jason and the Argonauts* a rollicking fun adventure — if not quite a perfect one.

Jesse James Meets Frankenstein's Daughter

(1966; Embassy Pictures) Director: William Beaudine; Producer: Carroll Case; Screenplay: Carl K. Hittleman; Cinematographer: Lothrop Worth. Cast: John Lupton, Cal Bolder, Narda Onyx, Estelita, Steven Geray, Jim Davis.

ROARING GUNS AGAINST RAGING MONSTERS! — ad line

Though *Jesse James Meets Frankenstein's Daughter* played second fiddle to its top-lining co-feature *Billy the Kid Versus Dracula* (with which it was filmed back-to-back, and even concurrently, by the same crew), it's actually the superior half of this peculiar pairing (perhaps damning with faint praise?). In it the famous outlaw (John Lupton) and his muscle-bound (and muscle-headed) sidekick Hank (Cal Bolder) flee to Mexico after a stage holdup goes sour. There the pair stumble upon Maria Frankenstein (Narda Onyx), granddaughter of the infamous doctor, conducting her experiments in a Mexican mission (whose interiors, with their huge stone block walls, oversized nail-studded doors and ornate wall sconces, look more like a Transylvanian castle than a south-of-the-border monastery). Apparently, Maria and her weak-willed brother had been chased out of Vienna for her unorthodox experiments and have taken refuge in this little out-of-the-way corner of Mexico. Maria has been using the local peasants in an attempt to transplant the "artificial brains" her grandfather had created years before into new bodies. So far, the villagers have proven too weak physically to make her experiments a success, but Maria sees just what she needs in the buffed-up Hank. Maria's passion runs to more than her work, however, and she makes advances to the handsome Jesse. To her annoyance, the outlaw rebuffs her, having fallen in love with a local girl named Juanita (Estelita). Meanwhile, Marshall McVie (Jim Davis of TV's *Dallas* fame) tracks Jesse to the village but runs afoul of Hank who, thanks to Maria's successful experiment, has been transformed into a bald, shirtless automaton (and rechristened "Igor") under Maria's control. In the

The strangest double-bill the '60s ever saw.

end, Igor turns on his female master and must finally be shot down by his former friend.

Just like its *compadre* did with vampire lore, *Jesse James Meets Frankenstein's Daughter* takes ludicrous liberties with its legends. Maria Frankenstein's experiments center on trying to successfully transplant the "artificial brains" her grandfather had created into new bodies—*not* in piecing together disparate body parts to create a new being. (Quite a comedown for a Frankenstein actually—rather than "playing God" and creating life, Maria's burning ambition is simply to insert a surplus organ she found laying about her grandfather's old lab into an already living body. I don't think grandpappy would have been impressed.)

As to Jesse James, this film turns the notorious thief and murderer into an Old West Robin Hood! At one point, the Marshall admits, "Well, folks say Jesse James steals from the rich and gives to the poor." Right. Then the ending has Jesse ride off willingly with the lawman to stand up and take what's coming to him, presumably reformed by the love of a woman. (Or perhaps battling man-made monsters in a Mexican monastery has made prison seem less unattractive?)

As expected, the film's grade-Z budget shows through frequently, such as in the unconvincingly flat, painted scenery viewed outside a set door or the disappointing lack of special makeup for the "monster" (excepting a thin scar encircling Hank's shaved head). To veteran Western director William "One Shot" Beaudine's credit, however, he takes his cast and crew outside to shoot on occasion, so that the gun battles and stagecoach scenes look relatively realistic (or at least up to the level of a 1960s Western TV series—which this film resembles more than a little for the first half-hour).

Ms. Frankenstein's "lab" also disappoints with its small-scale machinery and minimalist mad doctor equipment. Unable to afford even the most rudimentary pyrotechnics for the big "creation" sequence, Frankenstein's granddaughter must make do with placing a ridiculous piece of headgear on her monster (nothing more than a red and yellow motorcycle helmet with lightning-shaped neon rods attached) and waiting for the creature to sit up.

The picture's saving grace (apart from a wacky appeal inspired by the sheer audacity of it all) is the entertainingly energetic performance of Estonia-born actress Narda Onyx (whose career highlights consist of guest spots on TV's *One Step Beyond* and *The Man From U.N.C.L.E.*) as the female mad scientist. In the best Bela Lugosi/Monogram tradition, nothing will stop this maniacal medico from her warped, scientific goal. She bullies her brother mercilessly into helping with her "work" (it is Maria who obviously wears the pants in this Franken-family), employs (and kills) the locals in her experiments with a callous zeal, and even finds time to fall for the heroine—er—hero (as all the best madmen—and, apparently, mad-*women*—do). When Ms. Onyx enthuses, "I'm on the verge of a great experiment, and I know I will succeed this time!," her passionate delivery breathes some much-needed fire into the time-worn dialogue.

Jesse James Meets Frankenstein's Daughter proved to be William "One Shot" Beaudine's last feature. Beginning in 1915, Beaudine's directorial career spanned fifty years(!) and nearly every genre, including comedies (several Bowery Boys entries), detective films (various Philo Vance and Charlie Chan features), numerous horror movies (*The Ape Man* [1943], *Ghosts on the Loose* [1943], *Voodoo Man* [1944], *Face of Marble* [1946], *Bela Lugosi Meets a Brooklyn Gorilla* [1952]) and, of course, Westerns. Though his baton held sway over myriad genres, all his pictures shared one thing in common—they were all low-budget "B" movies, often made for poverty-row studios. As usual, on *Jesse James Meets Frankenstein's Daughter*, old "One Shot's" direction is plagued with dull staging, a heavy reliance on the medium shot, and an apparent aversion to interesting angles. Though he may not have been good, Beaudine was certainly prolific, directing over 175 features, 325 one- and two-reelers, and 350 episodes for various television series before his death in 1970 at age 78.

While *Jesse James Meets Frankenstein's Daughter* may not be the ideal meeting of Wild West and Gothic Horror, its outrageous premise, absurd genre blending and Monogram-style mad scientist (female, no less) make it a moderately engaging cinematic curio. Partner it with the somewhat stodgier but no less offbeat *Billy the Kid Versus Dracula*, and this terrible twosome rides off into the sunset as the most unforgettable (for all the wrong reasons) double feature in sixties cinema history.

Kill, Baby ... Kill! (1966/68; MGM/Europix Consolidated; Italy) Alternate Titles: *Operazione Paura* (*Operation Fear,* Italy), *Curse of the Dead* (U.K.), *Curse of the Living Dead* (U.S. reissue).

Director: Mario Bava; Producers: Nando Pisani and Luciano Castenacci; Screenplay: Romano Migliorini, Roberto Natale and Mario Bava (Story: Romano Migliorini and Roberto Natale; Additional dialogue: John Hart); Cinematography: Antonio Rinaldi. Cast: Giacomo Rossi-Stuart, Erika Blanc, Fabrienne Dali, Piero Lulli, Luciano Catenacci (as Max Lawrence), Giuseppe Addobbati, Giovanna Galletti, Valerio Valeri.

Eerie, horrific, bloodcurdling!—tagline

Mario Bava directed many outstanding horror films, but none whose greatness was more purely a reflection of his own genius than *Kill, Baby ... Kill!* Compared to earlier masterworks such as *Black Sunday* (1960/61), *Black Sabbath* (1963/64), *What!* (aka *The Whip and the Body*, 1963/65) and *Blood and Black Lace* (1964/65), *Kill, Baby ... Kill!* seems deceptively slight, with a feathery-light plot, no spectacular set pieces and few characters. What the picture has instead is buckets of that ethereal quality known as atmosphere. *Kill, Baby ... Kill!* is a mood piece of the highest order, a gossamer creation of images and music that's both deeply unsettling and strikingly beautiful. It's a mournful rumination on loss and guilt. And it's also the best directed movie in Bava's legendary filmography.

At the request of Inspector Kruger (Piero Lulli), Dr. Paul Eswai (Giacomo Rossi-Stuart) travels to the isolated, backward hamlet of Karmingen to perform an autopsy on a young woman who died mysteriously. Nurse Monika (Erika Blanc), a Karmingen native who recently returned to the village after many years away, assists with the autopsy, where it's discovered that, post mortem, the victim's chest was cut open and a silver coin inserted into her heart. After Inspector Kruger turns up dead, Ruth (Fabrienne Dali), the town sorceress, tells Paul and Monika that Karmingen is haunted by the ghost of a seven-year-old girl named Melissa Graps who was killed decades earlier during a village celebration. Legend has it that Melissa's ghost lures all that lay eyes on her to their death. To keep Melissa's victims from returning as new ghosts, the villagers place silver coins in the corpses' hearts. Neither Paul nor Monika readily accept this fantastic explanation and decide to visit Baroness Graps (Giovanna Galletti), the dead girl's mother, to learn more. But Ruth warns them that no one ever returns from the Graps villa alive.

As *Kill, Baby ... Kill!* unfolds, it's seldom entirely clear what's going on (although the story's resolution provides a fully satisfactory explanation). But a more straightforward story would work against the picture's singular charms. Its nebulous narrative enhances the movie's dreamlike ambiance and encourages viewers to simply soak in a succession of gorgeously designed and photographed sequences that demonstrate Bava's total command of both *mise en scene* and cinematography. Working hand in glove with cinematographer Antonio Rinaldi and set decorator Alessandro Dell'Orco, the director crafts a film of stunning visual splendor. Almost any frame from *Kill, Baby ... Kill!* could be blown up, framed and hung in the Louvre. Its exterior shots are not only perfectly composed, but every element is richly textured—mossy, weather-beaten or dilapidated, often shrouded in fog—and bathed in curiously evocative colors (thanks to Bava's signature green, yellow and violet gels). Meanwhile, interiors such as the Graps villa are superbly decorated, with cobweb-strewn candles, drapery and assorted bric-a-brac, mirrors and portraits strangely shrouded in black linen and long hallways with candleholders sculpted to resemble human arms (an image Bava borrowed from Jean Cocteau's *Beauty and the Beast* [1946]).

This visual stylization extends even to Bava's presentation of the villagers—especially the secretive burgomaster (Luciano Catenacci) and dejected innkeeper (Giuseppe Addobbati)—whose craggy, forlorn faces the director employs more for composition rather than characterization, shooting them more like a still life than a portrait. Using faces in this manner was a favorite technique of Federico Fellini. But if Bava was attempting to emulate Fellini here, Fellini in turn copied Bava, swiping *Kill, Baby ... Kill*'s most startling image—the ghostly Melissa, often seen playing with a large white ball—for his short film "Toby Dammit" (included in *Spirits of the Dead*, a 1969 anthology of Edgar Allan Poe adaptations). Melissa is an otherworldly, blonde-haired, blue-eyed vision of death, whose sudden, jolting appearances (at a window pane, amidst a pile of stuffed animals) signal impending danger. To enhance the subtle weirdness of the character, Bava cast a young boy as Melissa, seven-year-old Valerio Valeri, costuming the lad in a dress and long blonde wig.

The other essential ingredient in the film's success is its ragtag but surprisingly resonant musical score. Although credited to Carlo Rustichelli, it was not an original composition but rather a compilation of library cues composed by Rustichelli and others, including recycled themes from *I Vampiri* (1956), *The Ghost* (1963) and Bava's own *What!* (aka *The Whip and the Body*), among other earlier Italian gothics. Once again, however, what could constitute a weakness actually works in the film's favor, since time and again each carefully selected (albeit familiar) theme perfectly melds with Bava's images. Much of *Kill, Baby ... Kill!*'s chilling ambiance results from a sort of chemical reaction between these two critical elements. No other genre film of the 1960s, apart from Stanley Kubrick's *2001: A Space Odyssey* (1968), so astutely and powerfully marries music and pictures.

Kill, Baby ... Kill! is serviceably acted. While none of its performers in any way damage the film, none of them particularly distinguish themselves either. Giovanna Galletti in the small but showy part of the Baroness Graps makes the boldest mark. Fabrienne Dali has some effective moments as Ruth. In the leads, Giacomo Rossi-Stuart and Erika Blanc are adequate. The only real problem with *Kill, Baby ... Kill!* is its inane title. The picture was issued (and reissued) under several titles, none of them worthy of the film's brilliance. In Italy it was known as *Operazione Paura* (*Operation Fear*), which made it sound like a James Bond rip-off. In England it was issued under the bland moniker *Curse of the Dead*. In Germany it became the misleading *Die Toten Augen des Dracula* (*The Dead Eyes of Dracula*). It was later re-released in the U.S. under the equally deceptive name *Curse of the Living Dead*. As *Kill, Baby ... Kill!*, the movie made its American debut on a twin bill with an ultra-cheap Spanish chiller called *The Sound of Horror* (1964), which notoriously featured an *invisible* dinosaur. Such history, combined with its snicker-inducing title, left *Kill, Baby ... Kill* to languish among the most underrated chillers of the 1960s.

Kill, Baby ... Kill! (or whatever you choose to call it) was shot mostly on Roman soundstages, with primary exteriors filmed at Calcata, a crumbling medieval village in Tuscany so remote that it didn't gain electricity and running water until the 1990s. Bitter cold (the production ran through November and December of 1965) worsened these privations. But the real trouble began when, two weeks into the shoot, the money ran out. Astoundingly, the cast and crew agreed to continue shooting without pay while producers Nando Pisani and Luciano Castenacci secured additional funds. As a result, *Kill, Baby ... Kill* was completed on time for the paltry sum of about $50,000. Bava claimed he was never paid for his work. "At least they left me with a film I love," the director said.

It's a picture worthy of adoration.

With quotes from: *Mario Bava: All the Colors of the Dark*, by Tim Lucas.

King Kong Escapes (1967/68; Toho/Rankin-Bass; Japan) Original Title: *King Kong no Gyakushu* (King Kong's Counter-attack). Director: Ishiro Honda; Producers: Tomoyuki Tanaka and Arthur Rankin, Jr.; Screenplay: Takeshi Kimura and William J. Keenan (based on the Rankin-Bass animated television series *King Kong*); Cinematographer: Hajime Koizume. Cast: Rhodes Reason, Mie Hama, Linda Miller, Eisei Amamoto, Akira Takarada.

Two King Kongs fight to the DEATH!
—tagline

Despite its strait-laced title, this picture bears closer kinship with the Rankin-Bass animated horror-comedy *Mad Monster Party?* (1967) than with Merian C. Cooper's classic *King Kong* (1933). Tellingly, *King Kong Escapes*—a Toho/Rankin-Bass co-production based on a Saturday morning cartoon series—made its American debut double-billed with the Don Knotts juvenile comedy *The Shakiest Gun in the West*. *Escapes* is a sequel to neither the original *King Kong* nor Toho's *King Kong vs. Godzilla* (1962). Taken for what it is, however—namely, a live action kiddie cartoon—*Kong Escapes* proves an enjoyable romp, superior to many of Toho's "serious" *kaiju eiga* (giant monster) pictures of similar vintage.

At a secret laboratory above the Arctic Circle, evil scientist and "international Judas" Dr. Who (Eisei Amamoto) has constructed a giant robot replica of the legendary Kong and is using the android ape to dig for a rare radioactive element that will be used to create a nuclear arsenal for an unnamed Asian power. Meanwhile, submarine Commander Carl Nelson (Rhodes Reason) leads a joint American-Japanese expedition to Mondo Island and discovers the true Kong. Nelson leaves the island to report Kong's whereabouts to the U.N., then returns and finds that Kong has disappeared—kidnapped by Dr. Who and spirited away to the North Pole. The RoboKong, hindered by the Arctic cold, wasn't able to finish the task of digging out the radioactive element, forcing Who to try using the real McCoy instead. He attempts to hypnotize Kong and force him to complete the work, but Kong breaks free and dives into the sea, with his mechanical twin in hot pursuit. Kong swims for (where else?) Tokyo for (what else?) a climactic Kong-versus-Robo Kong clash of the titans.

Director Ishiro Honda keeps the pace brisk and the tone light. The performances are appropriately broad, with Amamoto particularly enjoyable as the gleefully underhanded Dr. Who (no relation to the British TV character). The creature designs and visual effects, typically for a late-sixties Toho production, prove uneven. The Kong robot remains one of the most memorable and attractive creations in the entire Toho filmography, but the living Kong looks far less impressive. Although it's a marked improvement over the embarrassingly shabby ape suit used in *King Kong vs. Godzilla*, it's hardly convincing and appears far too cuddly. In one of the film's surprisingly few allusions to the 1933 original, Kong and a T-Rex-like "gorosaurus" battle, in what plays like a judo match. Kong also fights off a rather pathetic-looking sea serpent.

In the 1970s, Toho would return to the robot-monster idea to create the wildly popular "Mechagodzilla," featured in *Godzilla vs. Mechagodzilla* (1974) and a sequel, *Terror of Mechagodzilla* (1975), as well as a 1993 remake of *Godzilla vs. Mechagodzilla* and its sequels, *Godzilla Against Mechagodzilla* (2003) and *Godzilla, Mothra and Mechagodzilla: Tokyo S.O.S.* (2004). Unfortunately, the studio never had the idea of having Mechagodzilla battle the Robo Kong!

While it doesn't approach the best of Toho's rubber suit-monster epics, the studio could — and did — do far worse than *King Kong Escapes*.

King Kong Escapes ... along with audience interest (1967).

King Kong vs. Godzilla (1962; Toho, Japan)

Director: Ishiro Honda and Thomas Montgomery (American version footage); Producer: Tomoyuki Tanaka; Screenplay: Shinichi Sekizawa and Bruce Howard and Paul Mason (American version). From a story by Willis O'Brien, uncredited. Cinematographer: Hajime Koizume. Cast: Tadao Takashima, Kenji Sahara, Yu Fujiki, Ichiro Arishima, Mie Hama, Jun Tazaki, Akihiko Hirata.

The most colossal conflict the screen has ever known! — tagline

This movie made Godzilla what he is today — or at least what he was throughout the 1960s and Seventies.

Toho's not-yet-jolly green giant had been frozen under an avalanche of ice since the conclusion of *Gigantis the Fire Monster* (aka *Godzilla Raids Again*, 1955) seven years earlier. Encouraged by the success of *Mothra* (1961/62), the studio decided to re-launch what would become its signature *kaiju eiga* (giant monster) franchise with a yarn in the whimsical vein of *Mothra*, as opposed to the grim tenor of Godzilla's first two pictures.

Not everyone was enthusiastic about charting this new course. "Toho decided to make him more heroic and less scary," Director Ishiro Honda told interviewer Stuart Galbraith IV. "I didn't like the idea, but I couldn't really oppose it. We didn't have many rights then."

The vehicle for Godzilla's reappearance originated with, of all people, Willis O'Brien, the stop-motion animation genius behind the original *King Kong* (1933). O'Brien authored a treatment for a proposed a sequel, *King Kong vs. Frankenstein*, which producer John Beck optioned. After much financial wrangling and several rewrites, Beck struck a deal between Toho, RKO, who owned the rights to the Kong character, and Universal-International, the film's U.S. distributor. In the end, Toho not only replaced Frankenstein with Godzilla, but also threw out everything else from all previous incarnations of the project. They were buying the Kong brand name, and it proved to be a wise investment.

The final narrative follows parallel stories. An American atomic submarine collides with an iceberg — the very iceberg in which Godzilla, frozen

False advertising: This lobby card pastiche features an image of the original stop-motion *King Kong* (1933), which is far more impressive than the mangy man-in-a-suit monkey that actually shows up in Toho's *King Kong vs. Godzilla* (1962).

but still alive, has been trapped for the past seven years. Godzilla breaks free, attacks a nearby Arctic air base and begins swimming for Japan. Meanwhile, Mr. Tako (Ichiro Arishima), a television executive desperate to improve his network's ratings, organizes an expedition to "Pharaoh Island," rumored to be the home of a giant monster (guess who?). Tako intends to capture the monster and put it on TV.

King Kong vs. Godzilla remains one of the few Toho giant monster epics to feature stop-motion photography—but, ironically, it's a giant octopus that's animated, and not Kong. This movie's Kong is a stunt man wearing the shabbiest-looking ape suit in history. The appalling lameness of this godawful suit cannot be overemphasized.

Godzilla looks different here, too. The rubber costume was redesigned, the size of the head increased, the eyes made larger and more bulbous. The effect was a more amiable-looking monster. Also, it's in this film that Haruo Nakajima, who played the Godzilla in every film from 1954 to 1972, begins to integrate the kind of anthropomorphic gestures and comic bits of business that would later become trademarks of the character (flapping his arms in rage, shadow-boxing like Rocky Balboa, etc.).

To make a long, and inane, story short, Kong is captured and brought to Japan, many buildings are stomped by both monsters, and eventually the two titans meet for a much-ballyhooed smackdown. Contrary to popular myth, *King Kong vs. Godzilla* did *not* feature different endings for the American and Japanese markets. In both versions, the climactic battle ends in a draw. However, the film endured several major alterations for its American release. Universal cut entire sequences from the Japanese version, and inserted new ones, featuring American actors Michael Keith, Harry Holcombe and James Yagi.

Both versions suffer from an overabundance of unfunny, over-the-top comedy relief. The primary culprit is Arishima, who, in eyeglasses and a phony mustache and with his eccentric gesticulations, resembles Talking Heads singer David Byrne wearing a Groucho Marx funny-nose-and-glasses. *King Kong vs. Godzilla* features little of the human drama that made *Mothra* so memorable. Its plot amounts to a juvenile collection of contrivances. Even its visual effects, from that moth-eaten Kong suit on down, fall well below Toho's previous standard.

Despite these glaring flaws, however *King Kong vs. Godzilla* emerged as a colossal hit. It was seen by more than 19 million moviegoers in Japan alone during its initial release, and was by far the highest grossing of all Toho's *kaiju eiga*. Unfortunately, its box office triumph sent the message that audiences would pay to see these types of films even if they contained infantile plots and indifferent visual effects. The obvious drawing card, which trumped everything else, was the climactic confrontation between two monster-superstars.

"It was very successful, and after that the Godzilla series became one monster vs. monster movie after another," Assistant Director Teruyoshi Nakano told Galbraith. "After that particular film, the flow of Godzilla movies and *kaiju eiga* completely changed. It had been hard, but after that, Godzilla movies became soft."

On the other hand, if *King Kong vs. Godzilla* had flopped, this probably would have been the end of the line for the character, and might have dealt a serious blow to Toho's newly revived giant monster series. In the event, this film cemented Godzilla's place in the firmament of horror cinema, jumped-started a film series that continued, off and on, to this day and insured that many more *kaiju eiga* would follow. Many of those films would far exceed this film, artistically speaking.

Kiss of Evil see *Kiss of the Vampire*

see *Kiss of the Vampire*

The Kiss of the Vampire

The Kiss of the Vampire (1963/64; Hammer/Seven Arts; U.K.) Alternate Title: *Kiss of Evil* (TV). Director: Don Sharp; Producer/screenplay: Anthony Hinds (screenplay as John Elder); Cinematographer: Alan Hume. Cast: Edward de Souza, Jennifer Daniel, Noel Willman, Clifford Evans, Barry Warren, Jaquine Wallis, Isobel Black, Vera Cook.

GIANT DEVIL BATS ... SUMMONED FROM THE CAVES OF HELL TO DESTROY THE VAMPIRES!—tagline

The balance sheet for *The Kiss of the Vampire* reflects several admirable assets and a couple of galling liabilities. In the final accounting, it's a minor but stylish and diverting product from the Hammer Films fright factory.

Honeymooners Gerald and Marianne Harcourt (Edward de Souza and Jennifer Daniel) are stranded in rural Bavaria when their horseless carriage runs out of petrol, forcing them to spend the night at a decrepit local inn. As the couple settle into their dusty room, a dinner invitation arrives from Dr. Ravna (Noel Willman), a wealthy aristocrat who lives in an imposing mountaintop chateau overlooking the village. Despite the desperate warnings of the hotel's only other customer, the eccentric Dr. Zimmer (Clifford Evans), the Hartcourts' dinner at chez Ravna concludes without incident, so they think nothing of returning for a masked ball. What they don't know is that Dr. Ravna is the leader of a cult of vampires. During the party Gerald is drugged and Marianne kidnapped. The next day Gerald is ejected from the premises while Marianne is "initiated" into the cult. The young man joins forces with Zimmer, who turns out to be an expert on the occult, to rescue Marianne. Zimmer then performs a black magic ceremony intended to pit evil against evil, and—as advertised on the movie's posters—send a legion of hell-spawned bats against Ravna and his disciples.

The screenplay, written by producer Anthony Hinds under his "John Elder" nom de plum, suffers some lapses in logic. (Why doesn't Ravna simply kill Gerald while the young man is incapacitated at the party? For that matter, why hasn't the cult done away with Zimmer, the only person for miles around who poses any sort of threat?) But the story moves briskly, contains several well-sketched characters and features a bravura set piece in the elegant yet eerie masked ball, later

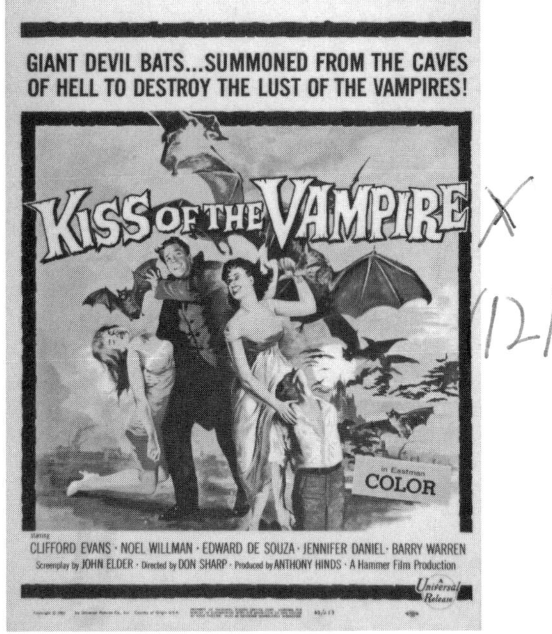

American window card (1963).

parodied by director Roman Polanski in *The Fearless Vampire Killers* (1967). One of the scene's most arresting images—a room full of men in Mardi Gras-like headpieces resembling animals and demons—may have influenced similar visuals in *The Wicker Man* (1973/75).

Journeyman director Don Sharp doesn't receive the degree of respect or affection accorded other Hammer helmsmen, such as Terence Fisher, Val Guest and Freddie Francis. Yet Sharp was a formidable talent whose carefully crafted, tightly wound films—including the underrated *Witchcraft* (1964), *Curse of the Fly* (1964) and *Rasputin, the Mad Monk* (1966)—seldom disappointed. *Kiss of the Vampire* is no exception. Sharp's camera remains fluid throughout, making evocative use of pans, dollies and subjective camera angles (including a particularly ghastly one of Ravna's fangs, shot from the point of view of his victim). Whenever Gerald and Marianne are on screen, and particularly when they appear separately, Sharp makes clever, expressive use of unbalanced compositions, leaving large empty spaces to the left, right or top of the figure to underscore the characters' isolation.

This technique has the added benefit of giving viewers a good look at production designer Bernard Robinson's splendid sets, including the sumptuous chateau and the ramshackle inn. James Bernard contributes one of his most effective scores, including a beautiful yet unnerving piano interlude.

For the most part, the production values are pristine — the notable exception, unfortunately, being Les Bowie's visual effects during the bat attack finale. An establishing shot with a horde of animated bats circling the (matte painting) chateau is acceptable, but once the action cuts to the castle's interior, viewers must accept pathetically obvious rubber bats on wires — lots of them — not to mention a few phony bats not wired, but simply being held to the neck by their shrieking "victims." On paper, Hinds' climax (originally envisioned for *Brides of Dracula* [1961] but rejected by director Terence Fisher) must have seemed like a second grand set piece. But the execution is so botched, so downright laughable, that it takes the entire movie down a notch.

The cast acquits itself well — with, again, one unfortunate exception. Jennifer Daniel is radiant as Marianne — enchanting and believable throughout, whether luring her new husband away from breakfast and into bed or later (vampirized) spitting in her spouse's face. De Souza's fiery, heartfelt portrayal of Gerald provides the movie's emotional center. Evans, as Zimmer, and Barry Warren and Vera Cook, as the terrorized proprietors of the inn, also perform commendably. Alas, Noel Willman's work as Dr. Ravna leaves much to be desired. Willman is not only a precipitous step down from Hammer's previous screen vampires (Christopher Lee in *Horror of Dracula* and David Peel in *Brides of Dracula*) but a virtual non-entity. Flat, humorless and never remotely intimidating, Willman sleepwalks through the role and — like Les Bowie's bat effects — drags the film down with him.

With more credible visual effects and a more engaging Dr. Ravna, *Kiss of the Vampire* might have emerged as a top-shelf Hammer chiller. Compelling but compromised, the picture must instead be consigned to a lower tier in the studio's horror pantheon.

Konga (1961; Anglo Amalgamated/AIP; UK) Director: John Lemont; Producers: Herman Cohen, Nathan Cohen and Stuart Levy; Screenwriter: Herman Cohen and Aben Kandel; Cinematographer: Desmond Dickinson. Cast: Michael Gough, Margo Johns, Jess Conrad, Claire Gordon, Austin Trevor, George Pastell.

Not since "KING KONG" has the screen exploded with such mighty fury and spectacle! — tagline

Not since *Konga* have ticket-buyers been so miffed.

Patrons who walked into theaters based on the poster art, tagline and title of this picture, expecting to see a rampaging giant gorilla, must have

The "mighty fury and spectacle" of this insert poster is far more exciting than anything seen in the risible film itself (1961).

been sorely disappointed with this tepid, talky misfire. *Konga* plays more like the ridiculous *Gorilla at Large* (1954) than *King Kong*.

Dr. Decker (Michael Gough), an eccentric professor of botany, returns to London after surviving a plane crash and spending a year in the Ugandan jungle. With him he brings a chimp named Konga (who Decker pets and scratches compulsively while chatting with reporters) and several species of African "insectivorous" plants, which he believes possess fantastic properties. They are "the missing link between vegetable and animal life!" proclaims the nutty professor. From these plants, Decker distills a serum that transforms Konga from a friendly chimp into a menacing gorilla (or, rather, a stunt man in a gorilla suit). He then hypnotizes Konga and commands the ape to dispose of various thorns in his side, including the skeptical dean of his university, a rival researcher also experimenting with insectivorous plants and the beau of a blonde college student, Sandra (Claire Gordon), who Decker tries to seduce.

The botanist's romantic proclivities result in his downfall. When his clinging assistant and sometimes-lover Margaret (Margo Johns) spies Decker with Sandra, she administers an additional dose of the secret serum to Konga and orders him to kill the student. Instead, Konga grows to giant proportions and goes out of control, killing Margaret and seizing Decker.

The brief giant monster sequence at the conclusion of the film proves to be a bitter disappointment. After waiting 80 minutes for this snooze-fest to live up to its *Kong*-tastic ad campaign, viewers see the outsized gorilla wander around for a minute or two before stopping beside Big Ben to wait for the British army to shoot him dead. That's it. The entire sequence seems listless and perfunctory—but, then, so does the rest of *Konga*.

Wacky pseudo-botany, hypnotized gorillas, lecherous college professors—this is not the stuff from which great cinema arises. However, it might have made for a rollicking fun monster movie had this material been handled skillfully. Unfortunately, it wasn't. The script, by Aben Kandel and Herman Cohen, bogs down in one static, chatty sequence after another: a lecture, a dinner party, a police interrogation, a *tête-à-tête* between Decker and Margaret, and on and on. All this dialogue is banal and poorly delivered. Gough, as usual, over-emotes with reckless abandon, but at least his scenery-chewing antics are entertaining, after a fashion. The supporting players either fade into the woodwork (Johns) or seem completely inept (Gordon). Director John Lemont allows the film to limp along with no sense of tension or suspense.

The visual effects are, at best, laughable. The clumsy rolling matte used to superimpose Gough into the paw of the giant Konga, for instance, functions on a sub–Bert I. Gordon level. Cohen himself seemed unaccountably proud of the effects, claiming he spent "18 months, over a year and a half, to get those bloody special effects done perfect. It just went on and on, because it was trial and error." (Mostly error, apparently.) The reader can take Cohen's claims with a grain of salt, since he also reports that *Konga* cost 500,000 pounds—nearly a million dollars. It looks far cheaper.

Any confusion with The Eighth Wonder of the World was purely intentional, according to Cohen. "[That] was fine, [that] was what I wanted," said the producer, who claimed to have paid RKO $25,000 to use the *King Kong* brand name in the advertising for *Konga*. "I paid RKO because I didn't want them to think we were stealing it."

Instead, Cohen was merely ripping off audiences.

With quotes from: *Attack of the Monster Movie Makers*, by Tom Weaver (McFarland, 1994).

Kwaidan (1965; Toho/Continental) Producer: Shigeru Wakatsuki; Director: Masaki Kobayashi; Screenplay: Yoko Mizuki (based on a book by Lafcadio Hearn); Cinematographer: Yoshio Miyajima. Cast: Rentaro Mikuni, Michiyo Aratama, Misako Watanabe, Tatsuya Nakadai, Kaiko Kishi, Katsuo Nakamura, Takashi Shimura, Tetsuro Tamba, Kanemon Nakamura.

A poem on a grand scale—Original Japanese trailer (translation)

If it's possible for an internationally renowned, critically decorated movie to be under appreciated, then director Masaki Kobayashi's *Kwaidan*, a compendium of four eerie and magnificently told ghost stories, is that film. Even though it won a special jury prize at the 1965 Cannes Film Festival, and earned a Best Foreign Language Film nomination at the 1966 Academy Awards, it inspires, at best, tempered enthusiasm from many critics and scholars who prefer to wax philosophical about Kobayashi's earlier work. For casual monster movie fans, *Kwaidan* often proves daunting, given its extreme length, deliberate pace and subtitles. Editor Phil Hardy's *Film Encyclopedia: Horror* goes so far as to label the picture "over-rated" (while granting that it contains "some astonishingly beautiful sequences").

Nevertheless, intrepid viewers will discover in *Kwaidan* a veritable wonderland of cinematic delights. This is a show capable of inspiring pop-eyed wonder at its meticulously designed visuals, of invoking great empathy for its characters and of making the hair stand up on the back of your neck — sometimes all at once. Like Stanley Kubrick's *2001: A Space Odyssey* (which also leaves some viewers cold), *Kwaidan* is a thought-provoking film of epic length, outstanding pictorial beauty and flawless craftsmanship.

In "The Black Hair," the first of *Kwaidan*'s four segments, a poor samurai leaves his devoted wife to advance his career through marriage to the daughter of a wealthy official from another region. His financial fortunes improve, but his cold and selfish second wife brings him only misery. After years of anguish and recrimination, he divorces her and returns to his original spouse. He begs her forgiveness, and they spend the night together — but in the morning he realizes she is long dead, and he has been in the company of her ghost.

Next up is "Woman of the Snow," in which an apprentice woodcutter and his master find themselves trapped in a terrifying snowstorm. During the night, huddled in a small hut, the apprentice, Minokichi (Tatsuya Nakadai), watches as a mysterious woman with snow-white skin and blue lips appears and kneels over his companion. When her icy breath touches his face, the elder woodcutter dies. Then she approaches Minokichi. But since he is young and handsome, she decides to let him go, provided he never tells anyone about her; if he breaks his promise, she will return and claim him. Later, Minokichi falls in love with a beautiful young woman (Keiko Okada) who bears him three children and proves to be an ideal wife. One evening, he realizes his bride bears a striking resemblance to the Woman in the Snow. He decides to finally break his long silence and tell her about that fateful, snowy night...

The third and longest story, "Hoichi the Earless," begins with an elaborate prologue depicting a historical sea battle that ended in the bloody rout of the Heike Clan. As the fighting winds down, the nursemaid to the infant emperor takes the young ruler in her arms and plunges into the blood-red water, drowning herself and the child. Flash forward hundreds of years to a remote temple where a young, blind musician, Hoichi (Kazuo Kakamura), has taken refuge. One evening a samurai appears and demands that Hoichi perform a ballad for his powerful lord based on the ancient battle. Eventually, the temple priest (Takashi Shimura) discovers that Hoichi is performing for the ghosts of the Heikie (including the baby emperor). To protect the young musician from the spirits, he orders a monk to paint Holy Scripture over Hoichi's entire body. But the monk forgets to paint Hoichi's ears.

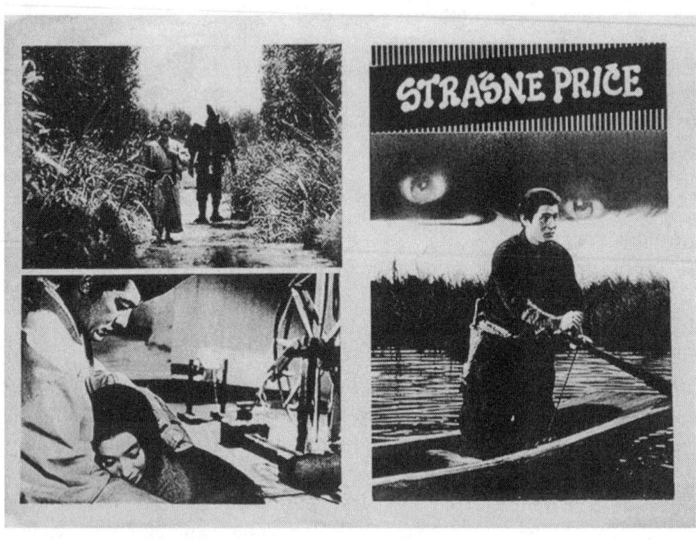

Yugoslavian movie program for the Japanese horror anthology *Kwaidan* (1965).

The film concludes with "In a Cup of Tea," the shortest and only tongue-in-cheek entry, which ponders the fate of characters from stories never finished by their authors.

"The Woman in the Snow" and "Hoichi the Earless" proves to be the film's most effective and memorable segments. "The Black Hair" is nearly as satisfying, but seems a bit too familiar, its scenario resembling Kenji Mizoguchi's sublime *Ugetsu* (1953). "In a Cup of Tea," whose brief story seems underdeveloped, disappoints mildly, at least in relation to the other three segments. All four yarns originate from *Kwaidan: Stories and Studies of Strange Things*, a 1902 book written by Lafcadio Hern, a Greek-Irish writer who came to the U.S. in 1869 and later emigrated to Japan. Upon its release, *Kwaidan* must have seemed more like something out of Hearn than out of Kobayashi—which is just the way executives wanted it.

Kobayashi had emerged as one of the leading lights and most controversial figures of Japanese cinema during the postwar years, when he directed a series of increasingly incendiary pictures that excoriated the traditional Japanese values, including the samurai honor code known as *bushido*. In pictures such as his *Human Condition* trilogy (1959–61) and *Harakiri* (1962), Kobayashi suggested that these traditions were rooted in hypocrisy and had led his nation towards military, economic and moral catastrophe in World War II.

Such anti-establishment sentiments didn't sit well with studio bosses, who, after all, were part of the establishment. Between 1952 and '62, Kobayashi directed 14 films, but the scathing, cynical *Harakiri* was viewed as a last straw. Even though his pictures remained profitable, he found it difficult to get new projects green-lighted, and made just seven more movies (plus a TV miniseries) during the balance of his career, which stretched until 1985. Following *Harakiri*, Toho executives demanded the director deliver a less confrontational, more "traditional" product. Kobayashi responded with *Kwaidan*, which represented a major departure from his earlier work in terms of both theme and, especially, style. Thematically, only "The Long Hair" and the prologue to "Hoichi the Earless" bear any obvious kinship with Kobayashi's previous masterpieces. And, whereas his earlier efforts were gritty and naturalistic, *Kwaidan* is highly stylized, even impressionistic.

Its widescreen "Tohoscope" compositions are symmetrical and carefully color-balanced, making every frame a work of art. Shot entirely on enormous sets built in a disused airplane hanger, the film's artificial "exteriors" and painted backdrops are completely obvious. In the "Woman in the Snow," for example, the winter sky is dotted with giant eyeballs instead of stars! Cinematographer Yoshio Miyajima's lighting and color scheme proves equally exotic and evocative (especially the blood-red sea and inky-blue night in "Hoichi the Earless"). Toru Takemitsu's sound design is no less eccentric. Kobayashi and Takemitsu eschew a traditional score and uses sound effects in atypical ways, sometimes employing complete or near-total silence. Many normally expected sounds—such as footsteps crunching through the snow, or the roaring wind of the blizzard in "the Woman in the Snow"—are withheld. All this combines to make viewing *Kwaidan* a truly otherworldly experience.

The single aspect of the production that remains realistic is its acting. As usual, Kobayashi takes the time (even in the restrictive "portmanteau" format) to flesh out his leading characters and inspire touching, believable performances from his actors. Kakamura, as Hoichi, and Nakadai (previously, the star of *The Human Condition* and *Harakiri*) as Minokichi, are especially convincing. Even Okada, as the mythical Woman of the Snow, brings a sense of inner life to her character.

Unfortunately, American audiences didn't see the film in all its glory during its initial release. The original Japanese version of *Kwaidan* ran a staggering 183 minutes. For the U.S. market the picture was shortened to 125 minutes by removing "The Woman in the Snow" in its entirety. (This excellent segment was probably selected for excision in part because it contained a topless romantic interlude.) In the 1990s, U.S. home video and DVD releases of the film restored "The Woman in the Snow" (minus nudity), in a 162-minute edit. The complete, uncut Japanese version was issued subsequently on DVD in England and Australia, but still awaits an authorized American release.

In the meantime, any version of *Kwaidan* is well worth seeing.

The Last Man on Earth (1964; Produzioni La Regina/Associated Producers Inc.; Italy/U.S.; b&w) Original Language Title: *L'Ultimo Uomo della Terra*; Directors: Ubaldo B. Ragona, Sidney Salkow (dubbing supervision); Producer: Robert L. Lippert; Screenplay: Logan Swanson (Richard Matheson), William F. Leicester; Cinematography: Franco Delli Colli. Cast: Vincent Price, Franca Bettoia, Emma Danieli, Giacomo Rossi-Stuart.

DO YOU DARE IMAGINE WHAT IT WOULD BE LIKE TO BE THE LAST MAN ON EARTH ... OR THE LAST WOMAN?—poster

Screenwriter Richard Matheson has nothing good to say about *The Last Man on Earth* (which is based on his own classic horror novel *I Am Leg-*

end). "The [story's] initial sale was to Hammer Films," related Matheson. "I went over there [to England]; I was living there for about two-and-a-half months working on the script for *I Am Legend*. They told me later on that the censor would not pass it ... it was too horrific. So they sold it back to the United States, to producer Robert Lippert." Matheson maintains that Lippert promised him acclaimed filmmaker Fritz Lang (*M*, *Scarlet Street*) as a director, but delivered only Italian neophyte Ubaldo B. Ragona and TV-journeyman Sidney Salkow (*77 Sunset Strip*, *The Addams Family*). Not only that, "they had some guy named William Leicester do a revision on [the script]. I hated it." As a result, Matheson employed the pen name "Logan Swanson" (derived from his mother-in-law's and mother's maiden names) for his screen credit. Of the finished film, Matheson concluded, "I thought it was pretty bad." He was wrong.

Set in the "near future" of 1968, the story centers on Los Angeles-based scientist Robert Morgan (Vincent Price), seemingly the only person in L.A. left alive (thanks to some kind of natural immunity) after a mysterious plague annihilates the population, transforming its victims into vampire-like zombies. Morgan spends his days hunting down the sleeping creatures (who possess an aversion not only to sunlight, but to garlic and mirrors as well) and driving wooden stakes through their hearts, and his nights holed up in his boarded-up home trying not to go crazy as the monsters weakly attempt to get at the "last man on earth" ... but is he?

Atmospheric ad for *The Last Man on Earth* (1964).

"It's the only time I haven't liked Vincent Price," opined Matheson (who penned a number of Price vehicles in the 1960s, including *House of Usher*, *The Pit and the Pendulum* and *The Comedy of Terrors*). "I didn't think it was his kind of thing at all." While it may not have been Price's usual "thing," the actor rose to the occasion admirably. Onscreen nearly every second, Price paints an effective and poignant portrait of a man going through the motions of living while sinking deeper and deeper into loneliness and despair. Price excels at revealing his character's near-breaking-point anguish, such as when he watches home movies of his family shot at a circus and begins to laugh, his giddy laughter gradually degenerating into agonizing sobs.

Critics latch onto the film's admittedly cheap production values, as exposed by some poor day-for-night shots and flashbacks that show little European cars buzzing around the obviously-not-Los Angeles location. "The problem was that it was supposed to be set in Los Angeles, and if there's a city in the world that doesn't look like Los Angeles, it's Rome!" laughed Price. "We would get up and drive out at five o'clock in the morning, to beat the police, and try to find something that didn't look like Rome."

While the bleak Italian location fails miserably to replicate Los Angeles (particularly when an early establishing shot of the deserted city shows a wide natural river running through the landscape — a feature the City of Angels decidedly lacks), the setting isn't really important. The sense of desolate isolation *is*, and the shots of deserted, litter- and corpse-strewn streets capture that feeling to a shuddery tee.

And the horror quotient rises steadily from there, with a disturbing montage of Morgan searching out and staking the sleeping vampires, then the nighttime assault on his home by the walking dead (who beat weakly on the house and tonelessly cry, "Morgan, come out, come out..."), while Morgan drinks wine and listens to jazz records in a vain attempt to both recapture some sense of normalcy and drown out the horror.

Admittedly, the film falters during its later stages (after Morgan learns he is not alone), resulting in a tepid action "chase" sequence, and an ill-conceived and rushed wrap-up. But the frightening images of the walking dead, combined with Price's convincing portrayal of loneliness and despair, make *The Last Man on Earth* both involving and horrific.

"I think it was better than *The Omega Man* [the second adaptation of Matheson's *I Am Legend*], which Charlton Heston did later," opined Price. "It had a kind of amateur quality about it. We worked in a studio that was so cold we had to put ice water in our mouths so you wouldn't see our breath!"

The Leech Woman **(Coleen Gray) about to claim another victim.**

This unpolished aspect actually serves the story well, lending a gritty edge and air of immediacy to the proceedings that the bigger-budgeted, glossier *Omega Man* lacks. And the despondent, sport jacket-wearing Price makes a far more believable "everyman" than the two-fisted, bare-chested Heston.

With quotes from: *Famous Monsters of Filmland* convention, Crystal City, VA, 1993; *Fangoria* Weekend of Horrors convention, Los Angeles, 1990; Interview with Vincent Price, by Lawrence French, in *Midnight Marquee Actors Series: Vincent Price*, by Gary and Susan Svehla (eds.).

Last Victim of the Vampire see ***Playgirls and the Vampire***

The Leech Woman (1960; Universal-International; b&w) Director: Edward Dien; Producer: Joseph Gershenson; Screenplay: David Duncan (Story: Ben Pivar, Francis Rosenwald); Cinematographer: Ellis W. Carter. Cast: Coleen Gray, Grant Williams, Philip Terry, Gloria Talbott, John Van Dreelen, Estelle Hemsley.

Forever young! Forever deadly!—tagline

The Leech Woman (1960) is a diverting, albeit minor, old school horror show with a solid lead performance and a refreshing proto-feminist perspective.

Cynical, misogynistic medical researcher Paul Talbot (Philip Terry) drags his disenchanted, middle-aged wife June (Coleen Gray) with him to Africa in search of a miracle drug derived from a rare flower, with the power to make old women young and beautiful again. Thanks to an elderly native woman, Malla (Estelle Hemsley), they discover the secret—but also learn the drug only works when mixed with a hormone derived from the human cerebellum (extracting the hormone is invariably fatal). Dr. Talbot forces June to serve as a human guinea pig to test the youth serum, but she turns the tables on her conniving husband by extracting the poison from him—gaining revenge, along with youth and beauty (and ending the couple's loveless marriage). Soon after, however, she learns that she must continue killing, not just to stay young, but merely to remain alive. She returns to America and, impersonating her own niece, sets her sights on hunky young attorney Neil Foster (Grant Williams). Problem is, Neil's already engaged—to the late Dr. Talbot's nurse (Gloria Talbott), whose jealousy threatens to wreck June's plans.

Although made in 1960, *The Leech Woman* seems considerably older. It's a throwback to overheated safari melodramas of the 1940s. Under the direction of Edward Dien, who previously helmed the cowboy vampire picture *Curse of the Undead* (1959), *Leech Woman* remains pedestrian in every technical aspect. But mediocrity represents a step up for Dien, who, as a screenwriter, was responsible for three of Universal's weakest chillers—*Calling Dr. Death* (1943), *Jungle Woman* (1944) and *The Cat Creeps* (1946). *The Leech Woman*'s biggest problem is its glacial pace. Viewers watch the pith-helmeted cast plod endlessly through a soundstage jungle with cut-in stock footage of lions, elephants, crocodiles and other wildlife, and then must endure an embarrassingly dated "native" ritual dance. Forty-five of the film's 77 minutes elapse before June first drinks the magic potion — and the picture never really picks up steam until she returns to the U.S., 53 minutes along.

The cast includes several veteran genre players, most of whom had their best moments in other pictures. Former *Incredible Shrinking Man* Grant Williams (who also starred in *The Monolith Monsters* [1957]) is OK here as lusty lawyer Neil Foster. Gloria Talbott proves acceptable as Neil's jealous fiancée. Her performance doesn't approach her brilliant work in *I Married a Monster from Outer Space* (1958), but remains preferable to her wooden appearances in *The Cyclops* and *Daughter of Dr. Jekyll* (both 1957). Veteran character actor Philip Terry fares better with his he-man, woman-hating turn as Dr. Paul Talbot. But the film's best performance, hands down, comes from Coleen Gray, who turns bitter alcoholic June Talbot into a multi-dimensional character — broken-hearted yet clinging to hope for reconciliation in the early scenes, and doomed but still fighting for happiness later in the film. Gray recalls the role as one of her most difficult: "Not only because each day of shooting I'd be in a different age bracket with different motivations, but with every age change my mannerisms, gestures and speaking voice had to change also," she said. "Some days things became so confusing for me my hands would be trembling like an old woman's, my voice would be a youthful 20-year-old's and my character would be 45."

Beyond Gray's winning characterization, the main element in *The Leech Woman*'s favor is its bold feminist theme. All the male characters in David Duncan's screenplay are chauvinist pigs who objectify women and try to exploit them in one way or another: Dr. Talbot wants to use his wife as a lab rat; African guide Garvay (John Van Dreelen) jumps June's bones while she's young and beautiful, then leaves her to die when the youth serum wears off; con man Jerry Landau (Arthur Batanides) seduces then robs elderly women; and even straight-arrow attorney Neil Foster is ready to throw over his fiancée when a younger, hotter prospect appears. Malla, the old African woman, makes the point crystal clear: "For a man, old age brings rewards," she says. "His gray hairs bring dignity and he's treated with honor and respect. But for the elderly woman there is nothing. At best she is pitied. More often, her lot is of contempt and neglect."

Sure, *The Leech Woman* delivers this message in obvious, even clumsy ways. Still, while it's hardly high art, unlike most B-budget chillers, this movie at least attempts to be *about* something. That may not make up for the film's numerous failings, but such uncommon ambition, combined with Gray's standout performance, make *The Leech Woman* worth a look.

With quotes from: Interview with Coleen Gray, by Tom Weaver, quoted in *A Year of Fear: A Day-by-Day Guide to 366 Horror Films*, by Bryan Senn.

The Legend of Blood Mountain (1965; Craddock Films)

Alternate Title: *Demon Hunter* (video). Director: Massey Cramer; Producer: Don Hadley; Screenplay: Bob Corley; Cinematographer: Joseph Shelton. Cast: George Ellis, Erin Fleming, Edward Yastion, Ernest D'Aversa, Glenda Brunson.

When the Mountain Bleeds, Terror Reigns!
— ad line

This regional Southern horror-comedy filmed at Stone Mountain and Lake Spivey, Georgia, begins with a three-minute pre-credit sequence in which the film's supposed "producer" (George Ellis, playing a country hick come to Hollywood carrying a suitcase literally bulging with money who's been duped into financing a movie starring his cousin...) directly addresses the audience. "Now they say this picture is a horror picture," he drawls into the camera. "There ain't no question 'bout that, I can tell you. They also say it's a comedy, but I don't think they found *that* out until after they finished the picture."

Oh, if only it were so. It's one thing when a movie tries to be serious and inadvertently becomes funny; it's quite another when it tries to be funny and fails miserably. *The Legend of Blood Mountain* falls into that latter category, robbing the viewer of whatever camp entertainment might have been generated had the filmmakers played it straight.

Bestoink (pronounced "be stoic") Dooley (George Ellis again) is a middle-aged copyboy at a city newspaper who dreams of becoming a real reporter. Dooley wears a bowler hat, frock coat and spats— all that's missing is a red rubber nose to complete the clown ensemble. ("Bestoink Dooley" was a character Ellis created for a Saturday morning Atlanta-area children's program, and Ellis reportedly played the film Dooley exactly as he did the TV show character.) When Dooley hears that the rocks on Blood Mountain are bleeding again, signifying the reappearance of the legendary monster that supposedly lives within the mountain, Dooley sees it as his big chance and decides to investigate.

Soon we're watching Dooley reading in bed, eating cookies and milk, attempting to exercise (he's too fat to finish more than two push-ups), and even brushing his teeth! An early "highlight" has Dooley dreaming that he's "the world's greatest newspaper reporter" who is "besieged by ravishing women" (well, two mildly attractive girls on an empty soundstage, anyway).

Dooley's producer cousin periodically breaks in now and again to ... well, to do not much of anything, really. During one interruption he pleads, "Don't you all leave the theater.... Anybody leaves the theater is *chicken*! You paid for your tickets, you may as well stay." By this point, undoubtedly many patrons decided to cut their losses and ignore his advice.

Now, 50 minutes into this clunker, we finally glimpse the monster — in silhouette. It's another 20 minutes before we get our first good look. Unsurprisingly, this heart-ripping terror of Blood Mountain is *not* worth the wait, looking like a flabby, bare-chested man with shaggy goatskin legs, two(!) tails hanging off its rump, and what looks like a hornets nest on its head (though it does sport an impressive set of snaggle-teeth). Suggesting the obvious — that this monster outfit was whipped up in somebody's garage — would be an insult to garages everywhere.

At the film's climax, when this Teletubby with mange finally menaces the heroine, Dooley hits it with his hat and runs, then comically plays hide and seek with it among three sparse trees. (Here the "producer" cuts in again, and not only mocks the monster's slow speed, but tries to sell the viewer some "papier mache rocks and pine trees.... We spent about 5000 dollars making this picture, and 4000 on those papier mache rocks and pine trees...") Dooley even sneaks up and kicks the creature in its two-tailed posterior at one point!

Appropriately enough, the "producer" has the last word. "You have just seen a *rank* production," he deadpans before hitting a gong with a feather (in imitation of the famous Rank Films symbol). And he's dead right.

Amazingly, this tatty *Legend* didn't simply fade away after its spotty regional release. Eleven years later, spook-show magician and drive-in entrepreneur Donn Davison decided to cash-in on the "Bigfoot" craze by replacing *Legend*'s monster scenes with shots of a Bigfoot-like creature, and inserting himself into the film as a "world traveler, lecturer and psychic investigator" talking about primates and interviewing supposedly real people who'd seen the supposed real Bigfoot! He then released it in 1976 under the title *Legend of McCullough's Mountain* and advertised it as a documentary!! Now *that's* chutzpah. After Davison's death, producer Jeffrey C. Hogue acquired this bastardized version and reissued it under the more exploitive title *Blood Beast of Monster Mountain.*

The Little Shop of Horrors (1960; Filmgroup; b&w) Director/Producer: Roger Corman; Screenplay: Charles B. Griffith; Cinematographer: Archie Dalzell. Cast: Jonathan Haze, Jackie Joseph, Mel Welles, Dick Miller, Myrtle Vail, John Shaner, Jack Nicholson, Wally Campo, Jack Warford.

Seymour Krelboin (Jonathan Haze, wearing cap) shows off his bloodthirsty plant "Audrey Junior" to, among others, Mr. Mushnik (Mel Welles) and Audrey (Jackie Joseph, far right) in Roger Corman's three-day wonder *The Little Shop of Horrors* (1960).

The funniest picture this year!— tagline

The Little Shop of Horrors remains best known as the movie that producer-director Roger Corman, on a dare, made in two and a half days. But that in and of itself isn't so remarkable. What's truly impressive is that the movie Corman made so quickly remains as enduring and enjoyable as *Little Shop*.

Bumbling Seymour Kelboin (Jonathan Haze) is on the verge of getting fired from his job at a skid row flower shop when he reveals that he has crossbred a new species of plant for his boss, Gravis Mushnick (Mel Welles). Seymour has named the plant Audrey Jr. after his girlfriend (Jackie Joseph). A quirky but seemingly knowledgeable customer (Dick Miller) convinces Mushnick that the plant could attract customers, so the florist agrees to keep Seymour on the job— as long as Audrey Jr. stays alive. Unfortunately, the plant, Seymour learns, can only survive by feeding on human blood. Initially Seymour nurses Audrey Jr. by nicking his fingertips, but as the plant grows, greater quantities of food are required. When he accidentally causes the death of a skid row drunk, Seymour feeds the body to Audrey Jr. The plant soon grows to giant proportions, begins to speak ("Feeed meee!") and even exert hypnotic influence over its creator. The fantastic plant brings in big-money business for Mushnick and turns Seymour into a minor celebrity. But after a dentist, a burglar and a hooker are fed to Audrey Jr., the police begin to take an interest.

Little Shop served as Corman's follow-up to *A Bucket of Blood* (1959), a wickedly amusing lampoon of beatnik culture which scored with both critics and audiences (and stands as one of the director's best films). When the filmmaker learned that a nearby studio had a standing office set, left over from another production, Corman rented the studio—set and all—for a week (three days of rehearsals followed by two days of shooting) between Christmas and New Year's 1959.

Then, according to Corman's autobiography, the director then phoned screenwriter Chuck Griffith, who had written *Bucket*, and ordered another black comedy, "a variation on the *Bucket* story line." That's precisely what Griffith delivered. Like *A Bucket of Blood, Little Shop* is the story of a likeable misfit who, with all good intentions, stumbles into a life of crime and horror. The major difference between the two films is tone. *Little Shop* is an off-the-wall farce, lacking the social satire that gave *Bucket* its biting edge. Nevertheless, Griffith's script is riotously funny, and the primary reason why the movie became a cult favorite. It's overflowing with bizarre, extreme characters (caricatures, really)—including not only the story's leads but minor roles, such as Seymour's alcoholic-hypochondriac mother (played by Griffith's real-life mom, former radio actress Myrtle Vail), a sadistic dentist (John Shaner) and his masochistic patient (Jack Nicholson), and even Audrey Jr. (an outsized puppet voiced by Griffith himself). Griffith's scenario also incorporates a spot-on parody of the TV hit *Dragnet*, complete with dry, "just-the-facts"-style narration from Detective Joe Fink (Wally Campo).

Shooting at breakneck speed, Corman and cinematographer Archie Dalzell couldn't worry about niceties of lighting and composition. As a result, their work here remains professional but nondescript. Aside from Griffith's screenplay, the film's real strength lay in its acting. The wisest investment Corman made proved to be those three days of rehearsal, which bought him strong performances from most of his cast, including Mel Welles' winning turn as the irascible, exasperated, and English-language-challenged Gravis Mushnick; Jack Nicholson's giddily over-the-top portrayal as the pain-loving dental patient; and Dick Miller's side-splitting deadpan delivery as a flower-eating patron of Mushnick's shop. Jonathan Haze and Jackie Joseph may be a bit out of their depth as the film's nerdy romantic leads, but their awkwardness perfectly suits their characters. "We adhered very closely to the script," Corman wrote in his autobiography. "Any changes made were worked out in the three days of rehearsal before rolling. Everybody just came in very prepared." Later , Griffith, doubling as second unit director, picked up the film's exterior shots on actual skid row locations, including "the world's largest used-tire yard and the world's largest used-toilet yard," featured in the film's police-chase climax.

Although it previewed very well (Nicholson remembers being taken aback by the audience's response to the picture, and to his performance: "I got all embarrassed because I'd never really had such a positive response before," he said), *Little Shop* was only moderately successful at the box office during its initial theatrical release. Its status as a cult favorite and cultural phenomenon grew over time, aided by frequent showings on television and the rise of Nicholson as a major Hollywood star in the 1970s. In 1982, composer Alan Menken and writer Howard Ashman premiered an off-Broadway rock musical adaptation of *Little Shop of Horrors*, which became a smash, toured the U.S., and has enjoyed revivals on Broadway, in London's West End and throughout the world. In 1986 the musical was adapted for the screen by puppeteer-turned-director Frank Oz. The budget for Corman's *Little Shop* wouldn't have covered the catering bill for the 1986 version, which starred Rick Moranis as Seymour. There was even a Saturday morning cartoon series based on *Little Shop of Horrors*, which ran on Fox Kids in 1991.

Many of those versions—especially the play—have their merits, but none of them boast the free-wheeling, underdog spirit of Corman's original picture, which turned out to be The Little Movie That Could. A year later, Corman whipped up a third black comedy, *Creature from the Haunted Sea* (1961), with far less satisfactory results.

With quotes from: *How I Made a Hundred Movies in Hollywood and Never Lost a Dime,* by Roger Corman with Jim Jerome.

Live to Love see *The Devil's Hand*

The Liver Eaters see *Spider-Baby*

The Living Coffin (1959/65; Trans-International Films; Mexico) Original Language Title: *El Grito de la Muerte.* Director: Fernando Mendez; Producers: Alfred Ripstein, Jr., Cesar Santos Galindo. Cinematographer: Victor Herrera. Cast: Gaston Santos, Maria Duval, Pedro d'Aguillon, Carlos, Ancira, Carolina Barret, Antonio Raxel, Horensia Santovena, Quintin Bulnes.

Fear, Greed and Murder!
—ad line

Another of the Mexi-horrors imported and dubbed by K. Gordon Murray in the mid–1960s, *The Living Coffin* stands out for two reasons (unfortunately, neither has anything to do with quality): It's one of the few South-of-the-Border horrors shot in color; and it's a horror-*Western*. A melding of two popular genres in Mexico, the *ranchero* (the Latino version of the B-Western) and Gothic-styled horror, *The Living Coffin* combines the native legend of La Llorona (the Crying Woman or Wailing Witch) with serial-Western sensibilities to create a hybrid that's one part Edgar Allan Poe (spotlighting the theme of burial alive), one part Tom Mix (featuring a super-intelligent horse that senses danger, rescues his master from quicksand, and even takes out the villain at the climax!) and one part Scooby-Doo (complete with not one, but *two* unmasking-the-phantom moments). In place of the "meddling kids" we have famous bullfighter-turned-actor (well, sort of) Gaston Santos and his perpetually sleepy comic-relief sidekick Pedro d'Aguillon (whose grating comments and annoying antics are frequently accompanied by "funny" noises on the soundtrack), who journey to a beleaguered hacienda plagued by mysterious deaths and the apparent ghost of "the Crying Woman" (whose pasty, cracked-and-peeling cadaverous countenance, coupled with cinematographer Victor Herrera's low-key lighting, generates most of the film's memorable moments). Decidedly human villains searching for a hidden gold mine in the nearby "Skeleton Swamp" are behind all the spectral shenanigans, and it's up to Santos to uncover the truth—after the requisite (substandard) fistfights and gunplay. Santos' horse even gets in on the act, pulling a string connected to a stationary firearm contraption to make the bad guys think there's a whole posse firing at them rather than just one lawman!

Director Fernando Mendez (*The Vampire, The Vampire's Coffin, The Black Pit of Dr. M*) builds

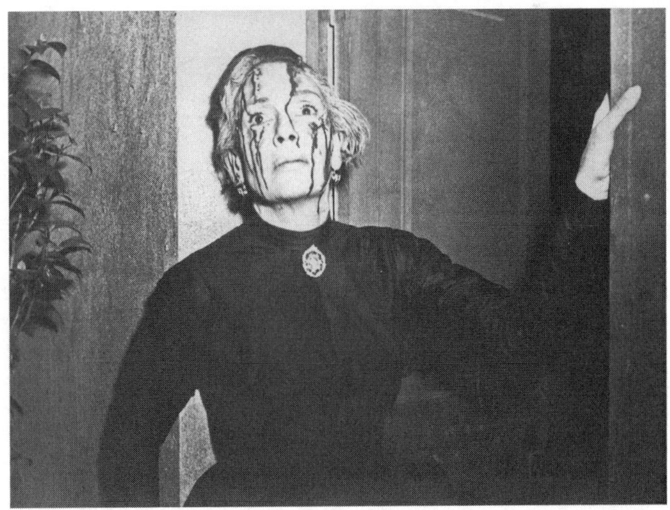

A bloody victim (Hortensia Santovena) of "the Crying Woman" staggers out of the darkness in the Mexican mixing of La Llorona, Edgar Allan Poe and Scooby-Doo known as *The Living Coffin* (1959/65).

an appropriately atmospheric mood, utilizing Herrera's layered lighting to turn the hacienda into a warren of torch-lit corridors and shadow-filled rooms (including an in-house mausoleum whose stone sarcophagi and iron-barred gate would be right at home in a Corman Poe entry). Unfortunately, the mood is shattered at regular intervals by the various riding, shooting and brawling scenes involving the brave-and-bland hero (not to mention his comical sidekick's continual search for a place to sleep, leading to innumerable scenes of him pulling chairs together to make a bed or climbing hay bales to lie down). And then there's the seriously unsatisfying Scooby-Doo ending that leaves the viewer feeling more cheated than enlightened—particularly since the cheesy masks removed from the faux phantoms bear only a passing resemblance to the previously highlighted spectral make-ups. Ruh-roh!

As an unofficial companion piece to the deadly dull *The Swamp of the Lost Monsters* (another color Mexican horror-Western starring Santos and d'Aguillon that featured an explain-it-all-away ending), the intermittently creepy *Living Coffin* far surpasses its compatriot. But when compared to most "straight" Mexican horrors of the 1960s, *The Living Coffin* seems disappointingly lifeless.

The Living Head (1963/68; Cinematografica A.B.S.A./Trans-International Films; Mexico; b&w) Original Language Title: *La Cabeza Vivente*; Director: Chano Urueta, Manuel San Fernando (English language version); Producer: Abel Salazar, K. Gordon Murray (English version); Screenplay: Frederick Curiel, A. Lopez Portillo; Cinematographer: Joseph Ortiz Ramos. Cast: Abel Saalzar, Ana Luisa Peluffo, Maurice Garces, Germán Robles, Antonio Raxel.

Can a decapitated head perpetrate a horrible crime?!—TV spot

There are bad movies, and then there are baaaaaad movies. Well, *The Living Head* is an *awful* movie. Though made by the same producer-director team (Abel Salazar—who also stars in this picture—and Chano Urueta) who brought us the deliriously bizarre *The Brainiac* (filmed a mere month before this feature), *The Living Head* offers none of the outré fun to be had in that boffo "classic."

The story is basically a Mexican reworking of the Universal Mummy movies, as a team of archeologists (including *The Vampire* himself, Germán Robles) break into the tomb of an ancient Aztec chief/sorcerer whose head is preserved and, apparently, still living (hence the title). The leader of the expedition takes the head and the perfectly preserved (and rather beefy) mummy of a protective priest back to his home for study. Of course, the mummy revives and, under (apparently telepathic) orders from the head, sets about dispatching all those who defiled the tomb.

Unlike so many of its fellow Mexi-monster movies, *The Living Head* has little in the way of atmosphere. After a brief sojourn to the (rather Spartan) Aztec tomb, it offers only modern apartments and big-city backgrounds (of the pathetic rear-screen projection variety). And the monstrous mummy stalking through these banal sets looks like nothing more than the Aztec version of a flabby linebacker. No desiccated flesh or grinning-skull visage here, just a big guy with some jewelry and a stone knife. Sad. And all the "Living Head" ever does is open its eyes for an instant before closing them again. It's the "mummy" that engages in all the long-winded conversing.

Mexican lobby card for the brainless *The Living Head* (1963/68).

And that's about all the *film* does as well, since *The Living Head* bombards the viewer with scene after dull scene of talk, talk and more talk—consisting of ludicrously banal dubbing and unwieldy dialogue. For example: "It's an infantile theory and you really must forget it—do me that favor." Substitute the word "movie" for "theory," and the viewer would do well to heed this advice.

The Living Head premiered theatrically on May 29, 1968, in Maryland on a double bill with the far more entertaining *The Witch's Mirror*. Reportedly, American distributor (and cut-rate showman) K. Gordon Murray included a "personal appearance" (of sorts) to promote the picture—by promising patrons they would "See and talk to the living head in person!"

The Long Hair of Death (1965; Cinegay; Italy; b&w) Original Language Title: *I Lunghi Capelli della Morte*; Director: Anthony Dawson (Antonio Margheriti); Producer: Felice Testa Gay; Screenplay: Robert Buhr (Bruno Valeri), Julian Berry (Ernesto Gastaldi); Cinematography: Richard Thierry (Ricardo Pallottini). Cast: Barbara Steele, George Ardisson, Halina Zalewska, Robert Rains, Laureen Nuyen (Laura Nucci).

"I curse the shrew who brought her into this castle of hell!"—Kurt Humboldt

Set in the fifteenth century, the Italian-lensed *I lunghi capelli della morte* (The Long Hair of Death) tells the story of a woman wrongly accused of murder and burned at the stake as a witch, witnessed by her daughter (Barbara Steele). The daughter is murdered but seemingly returns from the dead to torment and finally engineer the death of the real killer (via the aforementioned burning), the son of a powerful nobleman.

Co-screenwriter Ernesto Gastaldi admitted that his film's ending (with the murderer trapped and helpless inside the wicker effigy of Death as the locals unknowingly set it alight to celebrate the passing of the plague) was inspired by the shock conclusion of a popular 1961 Roger Corman Poe film. "*The Pit and the Pendulum* had a big influence on Italian horror films," explained Gastaldi. "Everybody borrowed from it." Too bad Gastaldi and Co. didn't borrow *more* from that American horror classic, since *The Long Hair of Death* turned out to be a slow, ponderous, only intermittently entertaining Italo-Gothic.

In 1994 director Antonio Margheriti said, "*The Long Hair of Death* was done in three weeks, but I don't like that one too much. I don't like the story. The screenplay we had was very badly written and a lot of things were not really fixed in it. On the set, a lot of things turned out to be stupid or impossible, so we had to invent a lot and improvise every day. We shot only a few days in the studio, with the rest done on location at the *castello* in Anzio. There was hardly any time to think, to invent, or write something down properly, because we had to shoot, shoot, and shoot. Something is wrong with that film."

Indeed. Though Margheriti keeps his camera mobile, prowling about the marvelously dressed castle setting and cobweb-drenched catacombs, and even offers the occasional chill (such as when a lightning strike blows the lid off a stone tomb, exposing the skeleton within—which then, amidst the rain and mud, begins to take on flesh), he can't overcome the rambling, tedious script. The film spends far too much time on the antagonist's convoluted scheme to murder his unwanted wife, and the subsequent is-she-dead-or-isn't-she? shenanigans. The evil Kurt proves so unlikable that no suspense or real interest arises from the "haunting" proceedings. An unexpected

With 1965's *The Long Hair of Death* (sported by Barbara Steele, left, accompanied by George Ardisson, right), director Antonio Margheriti offers gothic mood but little else.

sting in the ghost tale relieves some of the previous tedium (but only some), and Barbara Steele does what she does best—first entices, then terrifies. Even so, when it comes to entertainment value, *The Long Hair of Death* is really nothing more than a Continental buzz cut.

With quotes from: "What Are Those Strange Drops of Blood in the Scripts of ... Ernesto Gastaldi?" by Tim Lucas, *Video Watchdog* 39, 1997; "Margheriti: The Wild, Wild Interview!" by Peter Blumenstock, *Video Watchdog* 28, 1995.

The Long Night of Terror see *Castle of Blood*

The Lost Continent (1968; Hammer/Twentieth Century–Fox; U.K.) Producer/Director: Michael Carreras; Screenplay: Michael Nash (based on a novel by Dennis Wheatley); Cinematographer: Paul Beeson. Cast: Eric Porter, Hildegard Knef, Suzanna Leigh, Tony Beckley, Nigel Stock, Neil McCallum, Benito Carruthers.

Man ... Woman ... and Prehistoric Beast Battle for the Survival of the Fittest in the Living Hell That Is ... THE LOST CONTINENT—tagline

Although indefensible on the basis of its cinematic merits *The Lost Continent* remains irresistible, inspiring the same sort of knee-jerk fascination that compels motorists to slow down and gawk at traffic accidents. It's a burning four-car-pileup of a movie.

Captain Lansing (Eric Porter) sails out of Johannesburg carrying a secret cache of illegal explosives and an equally combustible collection of passengers, including Eva (Hildegard Knef), ex-lover of a military dictator; Ricaldi (Benito Carruthers), an emissary of the dictator; a doctor (Nigel Stock) being sued for malpractice; and his nymphomaniac daughter (Suzanna Leigh); as well as an alcoholic piano player (Tony Beckley) and a crew full of scurvy malcontents. In a distinctly *Wages of Fear*-like turn of events, the ship sails into a storm, which threatens to set off the highly volatile cargo.

Several turns of events later, the vessel becomes entangled in tendrils of giant, man-eating seaweed. Although the title suggests a lost kingdom (perhaps Atlantis), there's no large land mass involved, only a few tiny islands conjoined by the carnivorous seaweed, and a collection of luckless ships trapped there. Survivors—including the inbred descendents of Spanish conquistadors still prosecuting the Inquisition—live among the wrecks, moving about by attaching hot air balloons to their arms to avoid the seaweed and other monsters that inhabit the area.

The story, told in flashback, breaks into two distinct halves and lacks any sort of cohesive plot. Events collide with one another without regard for cause and effect, let alone niceties like narrative structure. The first half of the film is a constellation of every cliché known to maritime melodrama, including a hurricane, a mutiny, a shark attack, and even a lifeboat-survival sequence that ends, improbably, with the lifeboaters climbing back aboard the ship they abandoned! All this seems even more frenzied since the scenario also introduces (and establishes conflicts between) various members of the ship's crew and passengers. It's like watching one of the epic disaster movies of the 1970s compressed into 45 minutes.

The latter half of the film proves just as manic and jumbled, involving killer seaweed, giant crabs and other monsters, plus the Conquistadors That Time Forgot, while resolving all the interpersonal conflicts established

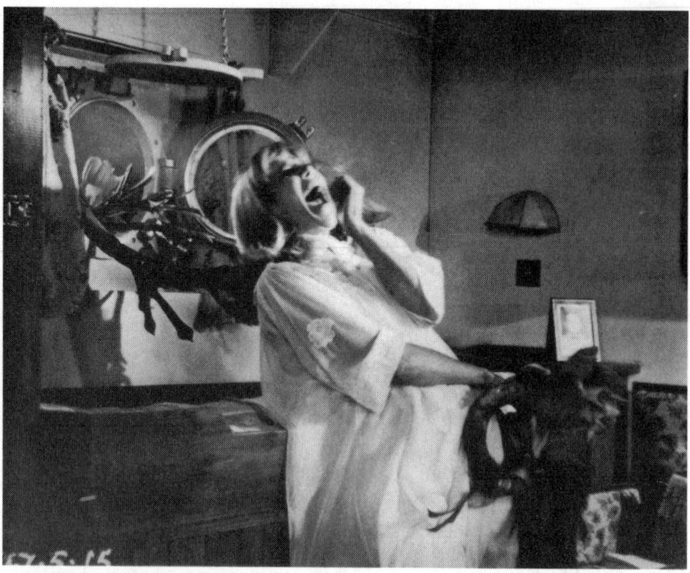

Suzanna Leigh meets the killer seaweed of *The Lost Continent* (1968).

among the characters during the early going. Some of these elements are intriguing but none of them are developed in a satisfying manner; they are simply thrown against the wall in hopes that something will stick. Fortunately, there's so much whizzing past that it's impossible to get bored.

Initially, Hammer announced that *Lost Continent* (based on Dennis Wheatley's novel *Uncharted Seas*) would be an upscale-budget production on the order of the studio's *She* (1965) and *One Million Years B.C.* (1967). Ultimately, however, *Lost Continent* was produced on a typical Hammer budget, which proved inadequate for its more ambitious concepts. Michael Carreras was a gifted producer and writer but an undistinguished director (see *Prehistoric Women* or *Shatter* for further evidence of his limitations), and he seems out of his depth here, dealing with a complex story, large cast and numerous production challenges. Cinematographer Paul Beeson does what he can to distract viewers from the film's flimsy production values with a striking, orange-sky lighting scheme and liberal use of dry ice fog. The monsters, designed by Robert Mattey (who later created the mechanical shark for *Jaws*) are unconvincing but imaginative—lots of squishy, tentacled things with prominent fangs and eyeballs. The characters are all stock types, but the cast performs acceptably, particularly Porter as the iron-fisted captain.

The term "guilty pleasure" was coined for movies like the loopy and lively *Lost Continent.* Like a gory traffic accident, it's awful but you can't take your eyes off it.

The Lost World (1960; 20th Century–Fox)

Director/Producer: Irwin Allen; Screenwriters: Irwin Allen, Charles Bennett; Cinematographer: Winto Hoch. Cast: David Hedison, Claude Rains, Michael Rennie, Jill St. John, Fernando Lamas, Richard Haydn, Ray Stricklyn, Jay Novello, Vitina Marcus, Ian Wolfe.

Your Mind Won't Believe ... What Your Eyes Tell You!—trailer

Fox's *Journey to the Center of the Earth* (1959) was an underground exploration that not only discovered subterranean wonders but also struck box-office gold. When exhibitors clamored for a half-alike follow-up, producer-director Irwin Allen obliged with *The Lost World*, the second screen version of Sir Arthur Conan Doyle's 1912 dino-novel (the first being the 1925 Willis O'Brien silent classic).

Unfortunately, Allen's tepid Saturday matinee filler doesn't deserve to share the same name with O'Brien's 1925 adaptation. O'Brien filled his version with nearly 50 excitingly realistic stop-motion animation dinosaurs (O'Brien is the same special effects genius who eight years later created *King Kong*). In this weak remake, Allen decided a few dressed-up lizards would do just fine. What's worse, in an unkind bit of irony, the talented (and down-on-his-luck) O'Brien worked on this version as an "Effects Technician" but was *not* allowed to work his stop-motion magic.

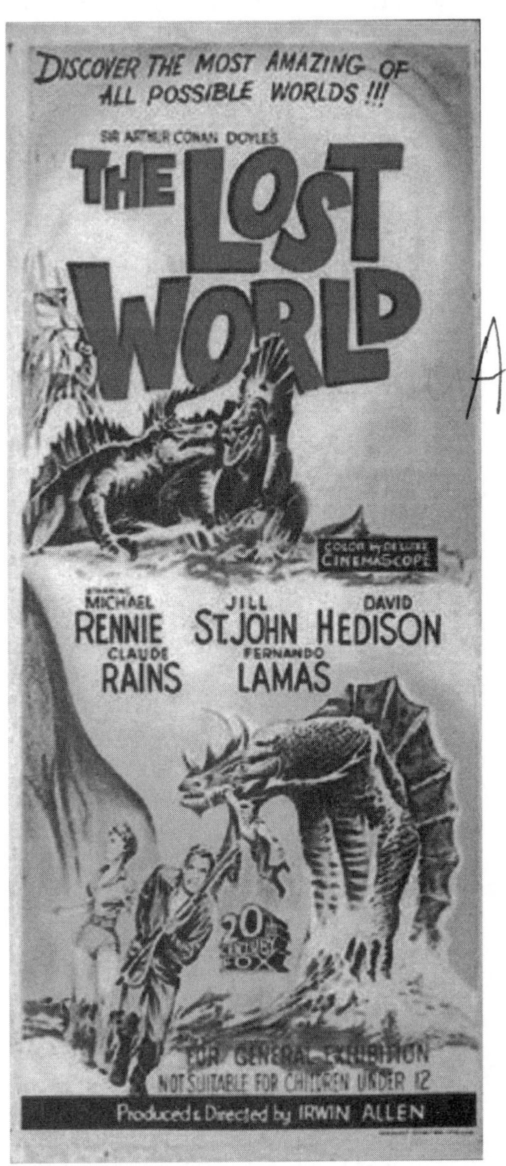

Australian daybill for the 1960 version of *The Lost World.*

The story is the standard one of a small group of disparate individuals looking for a lost prehistoric plateau, being stranded there, encountering dinosaurs and primitive peoples, and making their escape before it all blows up; not to mention the various human love interests and conflicts. There's nothing new in this version except that Allen had the resources to cast some decent actors. Claude Rains plays Professor Challenger, the leader of the expedition; Michael Rennie ("Klaatu" from *The Day the Earth Stood Still*) is big-game hunter Sir John Roxton (who seems just as interested in "bagging" fuchsia pants-wearing Jill St. John as one of the dangerous dinos); David ("Help meeeee!") Hedison (*The Fly*, 1958) struts about as the hero/love interest; and Fernando Lamas plays the experienced local helicopter pilot. Unfortunately, Allen is not a good enough director to get the most out of this interesting and talented cast. Rains goes over the top with his eccentric, blustery portrayal; Rennie seems to be just walking through his role; Lamas isn't given much to do except glower; and Hedison, though seeming sincere, is obviously trying too hard.

Despite its colorful trappings and extravagant premise, *The Lost World* is heavy handed and dreary, its "humor" is overstated and intrusive, and all sense of pacing is absent. Even worse, the effects (ostensibly the film's *raison d'etre*) are pitiful, complete with terrible matting and unconvincing miniatures. And live lizards passed off as dinosaurs are disappointing at best and ludicrous at worst, putting the dinosaur scenes here on a par with low-budget dreck like *King Dinosaur* or *The Cyclops* rather than on the elevated plain (pun intended) of the original. Allen only makes things worse when he has Rains label a lizard with a frill a "Brontosaurus" and a baby alligator with horns glued to its head a "Tyrannosaurus Rex"! This kind of thing just shows contempt for the audience — especially the younger audience out there who recognize even more than adults the difference between a newborn 'gator and the great "thunder lizard." Credit, though, must be given to art directors Duncan Cramer and Walter M. Simonds, especially in one scene when the group walks through the ribcage of some giant beast's bleached skeleton in an underground cavern — using the giant vertebrae as stepping stones. And the film *is* colorful. But a few interesting sets can't save a movie, and this one is sunk by either the filmmakers' ignorance (to be kind) or outright disregard for the material and audience.

Even so, Twentieth Century–Fox laughed all the way to the bank. The movie simultaneously opened in 400 theaters throughout the U.S. on July 13, and just over a week later the studio was already heralding it in the trade paper ads as "A Bigger Blockbuster Than *Journey to the Center of the Earth*." In the first five weeks of domestic release, it grossed $2,000,000.

Sometimes there's just no accounting for taste.

Lust of the Vampire see *The Devil's Commandment*

Maciste in Hell see *The Witch's Curse*

Macumba Love (1960; United Artists) Director/Producer: Douglas V. Fowley; Screenplay: Norman Graham; Cinematographer: Rudolph Icsey. Cast: Walter Reed, Ziva Rodann, William Wellman, Jr., June Wilkinson, Pedro Paulo Hayherer, Ruth de Souza.

Blood-Lust of the VOODOO QUEEN!— ad line

Macumba Love was filmed in Brazil, making it (along with *Curucu, Beast of the Amazon*) one of the few American-made horror films shot in South America. However, unless you're a fan of Brazilian beaches (upon which this picture spends an interminable amount of time) or June Wilkin-

Voodoo in Brazil: the tepid terrors of *Macumba Love* (1960).

son's dubious talents, the film's glacial pacing and dull dramatics leave little to recommend to the discerning viewer.

On an island off the Brazilian coast, American "novelist, lecturer and general debunker of mankind" Peter Weils (Walter Reed) runs afoul of the local voodoo cult headed by Mama Rataloy (Ruth de Souza). When Peter threatens to write an exposé of the cult, Mama Rataloy soon begins menacing those close to Peter: drugging his girlfriend (Ziva Rodann); frightening his daughter (June Wilkinson) by appearing as some kind of snake-woman; and kidnapping Sara's new husband (William Wellman, Jr.) for sacrifice in a voodoo ceremony.

Macumba Love's leaden pace and endless filler leave little room for excitement. About the best it can do is a moment of visceral shock when Mama Rataloy jabs a hatpin into a man's eye. The man screams and the screen then cuts to a literal victim's-eye-view as bright red blood suddenly gushes over the camera lens—as if we're seeing from behind the punctured orb itself. It's a gruesomely inventive (though arguably tasteless) bit of camerawork that remains one of the few memorable things in the picture.

Not surprisingly, the movie's level of acting perfectly matches its technical (non)proficiencies. Though easy on the eyes, the two young leads, June Wilkinson (known as "the most photographed nude in America" and, more amusingly, as simply "The Bosom" in the pages of *Playboy* magazine) and William Wellman, Jr. (son of famed director William A. Wellman), are both excruciatingly bland. Ironically, the film's pressbook noted that "In *Macumba Love*, Wellman has his most challenging role to date, calling for a full display of dramatic emotion." The young actor must have simply forgotten to *answer* that call.

The film's one bright spot comes in the form of Israeli actress Ziva Rodann. Not only is she sexier than the grossly pulchritudinous June Wilkinson, she out-acts her (and everyone else in the picture) as well. In reviewing *Macumba Love*, *Variety*'s Holl (who had little good to say about the production) praised Ms. Rodann's "outstanding performance" and called her "an attractive and fiery performer who has a chance to make an important impact in future films." Sadly, such a chance never materialized, for, after half a dozen more unimportant and gimmicky pictures like *Giants of Thessaly* (1961) and *Three Nuts in Search of a Bolt* (1964; her last), she dropped from sight. Rodann's presence also enlivened one other exotic horror, *The Pharaoh's Curse* (1957).

Macumba Love was the directorial debut of actor Douglas Fowley. As such, it proved a very inauspicious one, as Fowley fails in his pacing, staging (apart from the two aforementioned shocks) and direction of actors. It's little wonder that he was never entrusted with the director's baton again and, for the remainder of his career, worked only in front of rather than behind the camera.

Though successful financially (reportedly earning $3,000,000 in the U.S. alone), it failed aesthetically. *Macumba Love*'s final sequence epitomizes the picture's level of ineptitude. It begins when Mama Rataloy's face dissolves into an obviously papier mache mask with wrinkled skin and misshapen cardboard lips in one of the most amateurish makeup jobs ever seen in 35mm. Then, after an awkward (and very noticeable) jump cut, the fake head bursts into flame—just as the viewer bursts out laughing.

Mad Doctor of Blood Island (1969; Hemisphere; Philippines/U.S.) Alternate Title: *Tomb of the Living Dead.* Directors: Eddie Romero, Gerardo de Leon; Producer: Eddie Romero; Screenplay: Reuben Candy; Cinematographer: Justo Paulino. Cast: John Ashley, Angelique Pettyjohn, Ronald Remy, Alicia Alonso, Bruno Punzalan.

Do you have the GUTS to come and join the WEIRD RITES of GREEN BLOOD?—ad line

This crude and exploitative American-Filipino horror was the second installment in Hemisphere Pictures' loosely-connected "Blood Island" trilogy shot in the Philippines between 1968 and 1970. They each starred John Ashley opposite a different American actress and were directed (or co-directed) by Eddie Romero, whom *Castle of Frankenstein* magazine once labeled "a Filipino Edward L. Cahn" (ouch). The first entry was *Brides of Blood* and the last was *Beast of Blood* (a direct sequel to *Mad Doctor of Blood Island*). Each cost about $120,000 to make and are pretty much interchangeable, with little to chose between them in terms of quality.

The story of *Mad Doctor of Blood Island* has American government pathologist Bill Foster (John Ashley) investigating the weird goings-on on the remote Blood Island, where a monstrous madman has been murdering the locals. Also arriving on the island is Shelia (Angelique Pettyjohn—who later made porno films under the name Heaven St. John), looking for her expatriate father. As if Shelia and Bill don't have enough problems, they discover that the island's resident scientist, Dr. Lorca (Ronald Remy), has been doing "research on the medical uses of chlorophyll." While this sounds benign enough, in fact, Lorca has been trying to discover that old standby — "eternal youth" — and using the natives as guinea pigs, turning one into a hideous, green-blooded chlorophyll monster who's escaped and gone on a rampage. Complicating matters are various love triangles (one even involving the creature!) and the doctor's murderous servant. It all wraps up in the expected creature-creator confrontation and subsequent conflagration.

Totally absent from this Filipino production is any sense of conviction. The principle actors (excepting Ronald Remy as the obsessed Dr. Lorca, who indeed seems to relish his mad scientist role) all emote as if on Valium (maybe it was the Filipino heat), so that one simply can't take the proceedings seriously. Particularly wooden is the late John Ashley, a former teen heartthrob (and Beach Party movie regular) who literally walks through his role without changing expression. Ashley claims to have enjoyed filming in the Philippines and went on to make about a dozen movies there (many of which he co-produced as well). From his unenthusiastic acting in *Mad Doctor of Blood Island*, however, one could never tell — but then it's not much different from his typically bland performances in American films (*How to Make a Monster*, *Frankenstein's Daughter*, *The Eye Creatures*, etc.). Ashley later stepped behind the camera for good when he went into television production, overseeing the hit show *The A-Team*, among others.

Tito Arevalo's loud, intrusive and painfully overdramatic music score (full of blaring horns and crashing cymbals) doesn't help matters. (Oddly, schlockmeister Al Adamson lifted the entire score for his awful *Brain of Blood* in 1972 ... on second thought, maybe that's *not* so odd.) Cinematographer Justo Paulino's underexposed photography gives everything a murky look, and a tawdry air of sexploitation (characters ogle skinny-dipping island girls; one young nymph fleeing from the monster is inexplicably nude; and the native ceremony intended "to drive out evil spirits" turns into a Filipino take on 'Dirty Dancing') permeates the picture. But the absolute worst aspect of this Filipino frightfest is co-directors Gerry De Leon (*The Blood Drinkers*) and Eddie Romero's (*Terror Is a Man*) reliance on the zoom lens. *Every* moment the monster is onscreen (and even during the creature's frequent point-of-view shots) has the zoom lens working overtime. And it doesn't just zoom *in*— it zooms back *out* ... and back *in* ... and back *out* ... in a rapid, headache-inducing motion that ultimately leaves the viewer as green as the chlorophyll monster.

Manic zooms aside, *Mad Doctor of Blood Island* is not without its entertainment value. The bizarre premise (and monster) certainly is *unique*, and the Filipino jungle settings can be quite beautiful (on those rare occasions when Paulino actually provides enough light to *see* them). But the best bit of boffo fun comes from the pre-credit sequence Hemisphere tacked onto the film as a promotional gimmick and showed to patrons who were given a vial of green liquid before the screening. "*Now* THE MAD DOCTOR OF BLOOD ISLAND invites YOU to join him in taking the OATH of GREEN BLOOD," reads the screen over shots of a small group of teens/young adults drinking test tubes of "mystic emerald fluids." "Now, take

The strikingly bizarre Filipino "chlorophyll monster" created by the *Mad Doctor of Blood Island* (1969).

your sample of Green Blood," exhorts the narrator, "and it is guaranteed that you can never turn into a *green-blooded monster*!"

Mad Monster Party? (1967; Embassy) Director: Jules Bass; Producer: Arthur Rankin, Jr.; Screenplay: Harvey Kurtzman and Leo Korobkin; Cinematographer: Tad Mochinaga. Cast: Boris Karloff, Allen Swift, Gale Garnett, Phyllis Diller.

It's the Silliest Party of the Year ... and you're all invited!—tagline

Although beloved by a generation of monster movie fans who fell head over heels for it during Halloween season TV broadcasts, the charms of *Mad Monster Party* may escape those who don't view it through the rose-colored glasses of childhood nostalgia.

Rankin-Bass Productions shot this offbeat children's movie in its trademark "Animagic" process, using stop-motion puppets like those seen in its timeless Christmas specials (*Rudolph the Red Nosed Reindeer, Santa Claus Is Coming to Town*, etc.). The puppets, in and of themselves, remain far and away the most endearing element in *Mad Monster Party*: amusing, kid-friendly caricatures of Boris Karloff (in mad scientist garb), the Frankenstein Monster, Dracula, the Wolf Man, the Mummy, the Invisible Man, Dr. Jekyll and Mr. Hyde, the Creature (as in *Black Lagoon*), the Hunchback of Notre Dame, a Kong-like giant gorilla and Phyllis Diller (as the Bride of Frankenstein), as well as a horde of zombies and sundry other ghouls and goblins. Designed by Mad Magazine artist Harvey Kurtzman, these figures averaged about eight inches in height and cost about $5,000 apiece to create.

Dr. Frankenstein (voiced by Boris Karloff), mad scientist extraordinaire and president of a global confederation of monsters, calls a special meeting of all the world's monsters to unveil his latest creation (a disintegrator potion) and to announce his retirement. Frankenstein plans to hand over the family business to his nephew (and only living relative), Felix Flankin, who is also invited to the gathering. Alas, Felix knows nothing of his uncle's work and even less about dealing with monsters. Meanwhile, Frankenstein's curvaceous assistant, Francesca, conspires with Dracula to eliminate Felix so they can gain control of Frankenstein's "secrets."

Unfortunately, *Mad Monster Party* lacks the wit and catchy songs that make the better Rankin-Bass holiday specials treasured classics. *Mad Monster Party*'s tunes—"Do the Mummy," "One Step Ahead," etc.—are less than memorable, and most of its jokes fall flat. Also, while *Mad Monster Party* might have worked as a 50-minute Halloween television special, there simply isn't enough plot here to sustain a feature-length narrative. To pad the film out to its 95-minute runtime, executive producer Joseph E. Levine demanded the addition of a musical number featuring Frankenstein's butler, Yetch, and his chef, as well as a protracted sequence involving antique biplanes, neither of which do anything to advance the story.

The most striking moments in the picture are mildly subversive sex gags that somehow snuck into the proceedings (and past censors). For instance, as the chef sings "a pinch of this and a pinch of that," he pinches Yetch's bottom. Later, Francesca and Frankenstein's bride rip each other's dresses off and begin to wrestle in their underwear (to a soundtrack of caterwauling felines, no less). And when Felix slaps the hysterical Francesca, she swoons into his arms in masochistic delight and suddenly declares her love for him.

Narrative shortcomings aside, *Mad Monster*

Felix Flankin (left, voiced by Allen Swift, who also vocalized Dracula, the Invisible Man, Jekyll and Hyde, and others) and "Uncle Boris" (voiced by Boris Karloff) in the animated puppet monster mash *Mad Monster Party?* (1967).

Party (or *Mad Monster Party?*, since the on-screen title includes an inexplicable question mark at the end) remains well-crafted. The herky-jerky "Animagic" process may seems crude by 21st century standards, but retains a warmth lacking in modern computer animation. The film's vocal talent also performs capably. Karloff, of course, is the main attraction, and his playful, sing-song reading fits the tone of the production like a gleefully ghoulish glove. Impressionist Allen Swift lends all the other male characters the instantly recognizable delivery of a different movie star: Jimmy Stewart for Felix, Bela Lugosi (who else?) for Dracula, Peter Lorre for Yetch, Sidney Greenstreet for The Invisible Man, etc. Singer Gale Garnett voices Francesca with conviction and does what she can with her share of the film's disappointing songs. Diller is, well, Diller—cackling and hamming it up as always as Frankenstein's bride, whose screen time is (thankfully) limited.

Mad Monster Party earned a brief theatrical release, almost exclusively playing kiddie matinees. It sank without a trace at the box office but resurfaced on TV, to the unending delight of its faithful devotees. Those include movie maker Tim Burton, whose animated feature films *The Nightmare Before Christmas* (1993) and *Corpse Bride* (2005), as well as his short *Vincent* (1982) all owe major debts to *Mad Monster Party*. If nothing else, those less enchanted by *Mad Monster Party* should tip their hat to the Rankin-Bass picture for inspiring Burton's vastly superior productions.

Note: For a dissenting opinion, the author consulted his 4-year-old daughter. "I like *Mad Monster Party*!" she reported, gleefully jumping in place with the DVD held high. Why do you like it? "Because it's about monsters and I *like* monsters!" she replied. So let us grant that the film works well when approached on this level.

Madmen of Mandoras (1964; Crown International; b&w) Alternate Titles: *Amazing Mr. H*; *They Saved Hitler's Brain* (TV). Director: David Bradley; Producer: Carl Edwards; Screenplay: Richard Miles (original story by Steve Bennett); Cinematographer: Stanley Cortez. Cast: Audrey Caire, Walter Stocker, Carlos Rivas, Dani Lynn, Scott Peters, Marshall Reed.

WHAT UNKNOWN FORCE was created in the diabolical minds of the ... "*MADMEN OF MANDORAS*"—poster

As this film's alternate TV title so subtly suggests, they saved Hitler's brain! More than that—they saved his whole head!! That's the premise of this worst-film-of-all-time candidate that's actually better than its dire reputation allows. Not *much* better, but...

This bizarre exercise in outré political paranoia (bolstered by some evocative, noir-style lighting from cinematographer Stanley [*The Magnificent Ambersons*] Cortez) has a group of Nazis spiriting away Hitler's still-living disembodied head to the tiny South American country of Mandoras. Eighteen years after the war they have taken over the local Mandoran government and are poised to perpetuate a plot concocted by their (ahem) head man to rule the world using deadly nerve gas. Several American agents become involved and join with some locals to foil the nefarious plans of the Fourth Reich.

Released (briefly) in 1964, *Madmen of Mandoras* lapsed into a cinematic coma until revived four years later for television sales. But with a running time of barely an hour, Crown International decided to add a 30-minute "prologue" of sorts (à la Jerry Warren—and about at that same lousy level), focusing on a pair of bickering American CID agents investigating the death of a scientist involved in developing the gas. Crown also re-christened it the more exploitive (and explanatory) *They Saved Hitler's Brain*. Unfortunately, this poorly-paced, badly-shot and atrociously-acted addition (featuring the two most uninteresting and amateurish agents this side of *Dr. Goldfoot and the Girl Bombs*) adds nothing but tedium to the already lackluster proceedings. Admittedly, it *is* startling when both agents—the film's (smarmy) hero and (plain-Jane) heroine up to this point—meet their deaths, but it's also something of a relief to have their annoying presence removed. (The best thing about this added footage is the impressive car crash that prematurely concludes the protagonists' investigation—a shot lifted from 1958's *Thunder Road*!)

Of course, this pathetic preamble only serves to make the original footage look that much better (or at least less dowdy). But there's still plenty of tedious talk and silly spy shenanigans to fill the remaining hour. The rapidly-blinking Hitler head in a glass jar gets trotted out from time to time to liven things up, but he/it does little but sneer on occasion and bark out, "Mach schnell!" Fifties sci-fi fans will be pleased to see the always-welcome Nestor Paiva (Lucas from *Creature from the Black Lagoon*) playing the corrupt Mandoran Chief of Police. (And Nestor must have felt right at home, given that the filmmakers "borrowed" the distinctive *Creature* music for their film's climax!) It all concludes with a few low-rent superimposed explosions at the ubiquitous Bronson Canyon (as all the best bad movies do).

With less mundane spy stuff and more surreal weirdness (such as when a Nazi minion attaches a handle to the glass container and carries off Hitler's head like some bizarre handbag), *Madmen of Mandoras* could have become a moderately entertaining cult item. As is (particularly with the added footage), *They Saved Hitler's Brain* is not really *worth* saving.

Majin (1966/68; Daiei; Japan) Original Language Title: *Diamajin* (Giant Majin), U.S. Television Title: *Majin, the Monster of Terror*. Producer: Masaichi Nagata; Director: Hisashi Okuda; Screenplay: Tetsuro Yoshida; Cinematographer: Fujio Morita. Cast: Miwa Takada, Yoshihiko Aoyama, Jun Fujimaki, Ryutaro Gomi.

Majin. Terror Monster. He Could Love or Destroy Anything He Wanted!—tagline

For decades, the *jidai-geki* (period drama) reigned as the most popular genre among Japanese moviegoers. As the Sixties wore on, however, the traditional *jidai-geki* began losing its audience in favor of its more violent offspring, the *chambara eiga* (swordplay movie), and to the upstart *yakuza eiga* (gangster movie). The commercial appeal of the *kaiju eiga* (monster movie) also was beginning to sag. Executives at Daiei hit on the idea of producing a series of films that, it was hoped, would attract fans of both slumping genres.

The result was a trio of films—*Majin* (1966/68), *Return of the Giant Majin* (1966/68) and *Majin Strikes Again* (1966)—made in short order, none of which scored the hoped-for box office breakthrough. Only the first of the three received a (limited) theatrical release in the U.S. The second installment was picked up by AIP for American television, and the third went unreleased in the States until it finally reached DVD in 2005. Despite their disappointing reception, however, the *Majin* films rank among the most distinctive and well crafted of all Japanese monster shows.

The initial entry in the series sets the template for the following two features: In feudal Japan, Samanosuke (Ryutaro Gomi), an unscrupulous samurai, overthrows the beloved lord of a prosperous and peaceful village. Kogenta (Jun Fujimaki), one of the slain lord's faithful retainers, escapes with his master's two children and hides them on the sacred mountain of Majin, home to a giant stone samurai statue, which the villagers believe is inhabited by the spirit of a powerful warrior-god. Over the next 10 years, Samanosuke turns the lives of the townsfolk into a hell of deprivation, war and forced labor. When he learns that the rightful heirs to the lordship are still alive, Samanosuke captures the fugitives and prepares to execute them. All seems lost. "Only the God of the Mountain can save us!" one villager laments. In the final reel, that's precisely what happens. Majin, the stone colossus, comes to life and wreaks vengeance on Samanosuke and his followers.

The period setting allowed Daiei to reuse its existing *jidai-geki* sets and costumes, which are quite impressive, especially in comparison with typically chintzy *kaiju eiga* production values. And Majin's limited screen time enabled technicians to devote greater attention to detail during the film's special effects-laden finale. The resulting visuals prove far more convincing than those in Daiei's slipshod Gamera series, and at least as impressive as any conceived by rival Toho in the Sixties, and are greatly enhanced by Hisashi Okuda's inventive direction, which frequently utilizes extreme angle shots from the victim's point of view. These foreshortened perspectives make Majin seem truly colossal and terrifying. Cinematographer Fujio Morita shoots the film in a muted color palate, which contributes to the somber, dead-serious tone of the story. Daiei even went to the trouble of bringing in composer Akira Ifukube, Toho's specialist in *kaiju eiga* music, to write the score, which is one of his best.

The *Majin* films aren't *kaiju eiga* stories set in the past; they are *jidai-geki* stories that happen to involve a giant monster. In addition to the period costumes and settings, the fundamental structure and central themes of the *Majin* films are those of a traditional period drama (the inequities and abuses of the feudal era, the importance of honor as exemplified in the code of *bushido*). The only difference is that in a standard *jidai-geki* the hero would be a valiant flesh-and-blood samurai, not a Godzilla-sized stone one. The titular giant doesn't come to life until 68 of the film's 84 minutes have elapsed, which may try the patience of *kaiju eiga* fans expecting loads of goofy rubber-suit monster shenanigans. However, more open-minded viewers may find *Majin* enchanting.

Malenka, the Vampire see ***Fangs of the Living Dead***

The Maltese Bippy (1969; MGM) Director: Norman Panama; Producers: Robert Enders, Everett Freeman; Screenplay: Everett Freeman, Ray Singer; Cinematography: William H. Daniels. Cast: Dan Rowan, Dick Martin, Carol Lynley, Julie Newmar, Mildred Natwick, Fritz Weaver.

DAN: "Dick, it sure was fun making a flick with you!"
DICK: "Well, ring my chimes! I thought we were posing for a center-spread in Playboy!"—poster

---

Pop culture history is strewn with catch-phrases that were enormously popular in their day and are now extremely difficult to defend, let alone explain. Radio audiences of the 1930s lapsed into convulsions whenever Joe Penner quipped, "Wanna buy a duck?" Then Baron Munchausen's (i.e., Jack Pearl's), "Vas you dere, Charlie?" became a national catch-phrase. And every living-room jester insisted on favoring the gathered crowd with his or her drunken interpretation of Billy Crystal's "You look mah-velous." The popular '60s comedy show *Rowan and Martin's Laugh-In* produced its own seemingly endless parade of catch-phrases, including "Sock it to me," "Verrrry interesting," and "You bet your sweet bippy." Critics lauded *Laugh-In* for its revolutionary approach—revolutionary, assuming one had never seen Ernie Kovacs or Olsen & Johnson—of piling one madcap, outrageous gag, verbal and visual, upon another at a furious pace. Despite its obvious debt to previous comic styles, *Laugh-In* took the approach a step further (or backwards, depending on your point of view) by essentially eliminating set-ups, exposition, and characterization, and rushing straight to the punchline. What the pundits (and, evidently, most of the nation) failed to grasp is that without set-ups, exposition, and/or characterization, there can be no real punchline. You wind up with an empty form of humor with no lasting resonance; but if you're lucky, you can devise a term or phrase that's just goofy enough to momentarily catch the public's fancy. *Laugh-In* managed to capture the public's fancy for a few seasons before its luck ran out.

Ad for Rowan and Martin's big-screen horror-comedy (sort of) *The Maltese Bippy* (1969).

With the popularity of *Laugh-In*, Rowan and Martin got the chance to star in a feature film (they'd made one together before—1958's *Once Upon a Horse*— but few remembered it). The fact that "bippy" was part of the title speaks volumes about the patronizing, cashing-in-on-a-fad mentality that doomed this project from the start. *The Maltese Bippy* opens with a faux historical sequence of slaves carrying out tortuous physical tasks under the oppressive rule of Irving the Horrible. Then an onscreen title informs us that none of this has any relation to the actual movie we're about to see, which is set in Flushing, New York. It doesn't take long to (sadly) realize that this pre-credit bit is one of the cleverest gags in the picture. The plot, such as it is, then commences: Nudie-moviemakers Sam Smith (Rowan) and Ernest Grey (Martin) are busy working on their latest erotic epic, *Lunar Lust*, when they're evicted from their offices (and film set). Meanwhile, a dead body is discovered in a cemetery, while a neighbor reports that she was pestered by a man who howled like a wolf. Sam and Ernest pile their gear into a moving truck and head to the boarding house Ernest owns. Coincidentally, the house is located next to the cemetery in question. And just as coincidentally, Ernest has been suffering from strange "spells" during which he howls like a wolf.

Even the most charitable viewer will have to admit that an air of desperation sets in pretty quickly. A variety of plot elements are tossed into the mix, perhaps in the hopes of generating narrative interest, if not laughs. Ernest thinks he's become a werewolf, an idea reinforced by his psychologist (David Furst). A pair of odd Hungarian neighbors—the remote Ravenswood (Fritz Weaver) and the loopy Carlotta (Julie Newmar), brother and sister—might actually be werewolves too. Or vampires (the scripters don't seem to know the difference). After a string of aimless plot twists, red herrings, and lewd sex jokes (sans nudity—the film was rated "G" for general audiences!), it all boils down to various parties preparing to slice open the murder victim so they can retrieve a valuable diamond inside the corpse.

Like many films that attempt to be several things at once, *The Maltese Bippy* fails on every count: as a horror-movie farce, as a satire of (and homage to) mystery films, as an attempt to revive the audacious humor of *Hellzapoppin'*, or even as a piece of no-brainer entertainment. Chief among the film's problems are the stars. Dan Rowan and Dick Martin simply didn't have what it took to be viable movie comedians. Television and nightclubs seemed to be better venues for their debatable skills, though *Laugh-In* probably would have been successful without them, given such talented regulars as Goldie Hawn, Arte Johnson and Judy Carne. Rowan and Martin were occasionally amusing but undeniably bland (they never had the spark of superior duos like Abbott & Costello and Hope & Crosby), and the big screen only served to magnify their lack of tangible comic personalities. In their stand-up act, Rowan was the straight man and Martin the goofy comic, and their identities weren't defined much beyond that. Yet *The Maltese Bippy* even botches that by splitting them up much of the time. Rowan plays a craftier (and, oddly, more dimwitted) character than usual. Martin's one-note "scared reaction" clowning only goes to show how much better Bob Hope essayed these sorts of cowardly-hero roles. The (deserved) financial failure of *The Maltese Bippy* resulted in MGM pulling the plug on another proposed Rowan & Martin movie, *The Money Game*, and the two comedians faded into TV land history.

Perhaps the most entertaining thing about *The Maltese Bippy* has nothing to do with anything in the actual movie. At the film's Hollywood premiere, a TV reporter cornered Art Linkletter, who had just come out of the screening, and asked him his opinion of the picture. In addition to being a very successful television host (*Art Linkletter's House Party* ran for years), Linkletter had appeared in a couple of movies himself (most notably *Champagne for Caesar*, opposite Ronald Colman and Vincent Price). Watching the relaxed, gentlemanly, and usually upbeat Linkletter struggle to find something—*anything*—positive to say about the train-wreck he just witnessed was more amusing than *The Maltese Bippy* could ever hope to be: "Well ... it's full of wild gags ... and crazy stunts ... and all sorts of stuff ... people should love it." Linkletter earned a fortune as a commercial spokesman, but this movie had to have been the hardest sell of his career.

The Maltese Bippy is so dull and so unrelentingly awful that it makes a putrid parody such as *Haunted Honeymoon* (1986), starring Gene Wilder, seem like a *brilliant* parody such as *Young Frankenstein* (1974), starring Gene Wilder. They should have stuck with the tale of Irving the Horrible instead.

—Ted Okuda

The Man and the Monster (1958/65; Cinematografica A.B.S.A./Trans-International Films; Mexico; b&w) Original Language Title: *El Hombre y la Monstruo*; Director: Raphael Baledon, Paul Nagle [Nagel] (English language version); Pro-

The Man becomes the Monster in the Faustian Jekyll-and-Hyde tale of *The Man and the Monster* (1958/65). Pictured in this Mexican lobby card are Enrique Rambal and Ofelia Guilmáin.

ducer: Abel Salazar, K. Gordon Murray (English version); Screenplay: Alfredo Salazer (story: Raoul Centeno); Cinematographer: Raoul Martinez Solares. Cast: Henry (Enrique) Rambal, Abel Salazar, Martha Roth, Ofelia Guilmain.

A "thing" of unspeakable horror ... terrorizes the universe...—ad line

This third offering from producer/actor Abel Salazar's A.B.S.A. film company (after *The Vampire* and *The Vampire's Coffin*) is something of a south-of-the-border Faust-Meets-Jekyll-and-Hyde-by-Way-of-the-Phantom-of-the-Opera.

Mediocre pianist Samuel (Enrique Rambal) sells his soul to the Devil (and murders his beautiful and talented rival, Alejandra, to seal the deal) in order to become the world's greatest ivory tickler—the only hitch being that whenever he plays he transforms into a Hyde-like monster! Horrified by his monstrous alter-ego, Samuel intends to free himself from this curse by training a talented protégé, Laura (Martha Roth), to become the greatest pianist in the world ("I'll replace what I destroyed at last!" he proclaims). But the Maestro's evil piano-playing Mr. Hyde becomes jealous of Laura's phenomenal ability and attempts to kill her. Fortunately, the music promoter/hero (Abel Salazar), who has fallen for Laura, discovers the devilish doings, leading to the demise of both man and monster.

Apart from its tragic, tortured-soul story line, *The Man and the Monster* offers some fine production values and visuals, including fairly elaborate sets (creepy, cobwebbed hacienda contrasting with art deco-style, spacious apartments), evocative lighting (deep blacks and long shadows creating pools of light and dark), and fluid photography (the camera smoothly following the heroine, for instance, through the eerie hacienda as she frantically flees in terror from the homicidal monster). Directed by Raphael Baledon (who helmed another of the better Mexi-horror imports from the 1960s, *The Curse of the Crying Woman*) and photographed by Raoul Martinez Solares (*The Bloody Vampire, Invasion of the Vampires*, various Santo outings), *The Man and the Monster* remains one of the more visually impressive horrors to cross our Southern border.

Unfortunately, "visually impressive" doesn't readily spring to mind when one sees the Monster itself. With his bulbous nose, oversized buck teeth (that seem to be constantly on the verge of falling out), mutton-chop whiskers and wild fright wig, he looks like a cross between W.C. Fields and the Wolf Man. But at least, like Mr. Hyde, he's devoted to murder and mayhem (even killing a child—something *not* seen in Hollywood horrors of the time); and the believable cast handles it all with deadly seriousness (including hero Abel Salazar, who often portrayed a likable *comic* character but here plays it straight).

Unlike with the ludicrous makeup, director Baledon handles the pivotal deal-with-the-Devil sequence with both subtlety and panache (no horned, pitchfork-sporting Satan here; just a fervent wish and a clap of thunder on a bizarre, eerily-lit backstage set to signify the unholy bargain being struck). And, upping the macabre quotient, the slightly unhinged Samuel keeps the corpse of his murdered rival (and implied unrequited love object) in a closet of his music studio—and regularly *talks* to it.

To the tortured Samuel, playing the piano is like a drug—he must have his "fix" periodically. Though he tries to resist (and so hold his evil Id at bay), his hands shake and he pleads like an addict, ultimately succumbing to temptation. This addiction aspect imbues the proceedings with a weightier subtext than that found in the average Mexican monster movie.

If one can overlook the over-the-top makeup, the (not unexpected) unwieldy dubbing, and (ironically) some inappropriate, bombastic music cues, *The Man and Monster* becomes a unique and satisfying foray into Mexican horror.

The Man with the X-Ray Eyes see *X—The Man with the X-Ray Eyes*

Maneater of Hydra see *Island of the Doomed*

Mania (1960/61; Triad; U.K.; b&w) Alternate Titles: *The Flesh and the Fiends* (U.K.); *The Fiendish Ghouls* (reissue); *Psycho Killers*; Director: John Gilling; Producers: Robert S. Baker, Monty Berman; Screenplay: John Gilling, Leon Griffiths; Cinematographer: Monty Berman. Cast: Peter Cushing, Donald Pleasence, June Laverick, Dermot Walsh, Renee Houston, George Rose, Billie Whitelaw, John Cairney, Melvyn Hayes.

VILE GRAVEROBBERS! DEPRAVED MURDERERS! DEFILERS OF THE DEAD! SHOCK UPON SHOCK!—poster blurb

"This is the story of lost men and lost souls. It is a story of vice and murder. We make no apologies to the dead. It is all true." So begins the opening written narration to one of the finest (and most overlooked) English horror films of the 1960s. Shot in May 1959 at Shepperton Studios as *The Flesh and the Fiends*, it went into release in the UK in February 1960, making its way to American shores a year later under the new title *Mania*. Subsequent re-issues saw the movie's name changed to *Psycho Killers* and *The Fiendish Ghouls* (under which moniker it was ignominiously paired with the bizarre titillating terror of *Horrors of Spider Island*). Despite its poor treatment at the hands of callous exhibitors, *Mania* remains an intelligent, well-acted, gritty, realistic and *disturbing* portrayal of one of the most infamous criminal incidents in history.

William Hare (Donald Pleasence) about to silence breezy prostitute Mary (Billie Whitelaw) in the big screen's best retelling of the Burke and Hare horrors, *Mania* (1960/61).

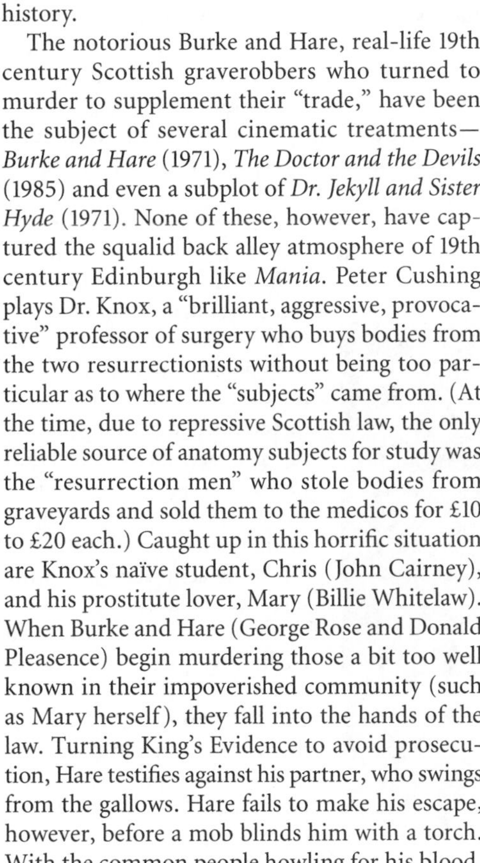

The notorious Burke and Hare, real-life 19th century Scottish graverobbers who turned to murder to supplement their "trade," have been the subject of several cinematic treatments—*Burke and Hare* (1971), *The Doctor and the Devils* (1985) and even a subplot of *Dr. Jekyll and Sister Hyde* (1971). None of these, however, have captured the squalid back alley atmosphere of 19th century Edinburgh like *Mania*. Peter Cushing plays Dr. Knox, a "brilliant, aggressive, provocative" professor of surgery who buys bodies from the two resurrectionists without being too particular as to where the "subjects" came from. (At the time, due to repressive Scottish law, the only reliable source of anatomy subjects for study was the "resurrection men" who stole bodies from graveyards and sold them to the medicos for £10 to £20 each.) Caught up in this horrific situation are Knox's naïve student, Chris (John Cairney), and his prostitute lover, Mary (Billie Whitelaw). When Burke and Hare (George Rose and Donald Pleasence) begin murdering those a bit too well known in their impoverished community (such as Mary herself), they fall into the hands of the law. Turning King's Evidence to avoid prosecution, Hare testifies against his partner, who swings from the gallows. Hare fails to make his escape, however, before a mob blinds him with a torch. With the common people howling for his blood, a now-more humane Dr. Knox finds support and strength from his students, who rally behind their beleaguered teacher.

Cushing turns in a bravura performance as the forceful doctor, unwavering in his conviction that the end justifies the means. Cushing shines in his portrayal of a man driven by his convictions to overlook his own morality. In the end, when it all catches up with him, we see a changed man—bent but not broken, still strong in his beliefs of what is right but more human and more *humane* in those beliefs. The moment comes as he wanders the back streets, brooding ("I've been walking around all night—excellent for the constitution but terrifying for the soul," he confesses). The doctor meets a little girl who asks him for money. "I haven't any with me," he answers, and then offers, "but if you'll come with me to my house I have some there." The child replies, "No thank you, you might send me to Dr. Knox." At this moment you can see in Cushing's eyes a man shattered by facing the truth, and to that great actor's credit, this is truly heartbreaking to watch. ("And for this scene he shed real tears," recounted director John Gilling. "Tremendously professional, Peter!")

Further praise should go to George Rose as Burke and especially to Donald Pleasence as Hare. Their characterizations are both quirky and disturbing, fitting oh-so-easily into the heartless, humanity-robbing poverty of Edinburgh. (Tony award-winning Rose met a tragic real-life death when he was brutally murdered in 1988 by the father and uncle of a teenage boy then living with Rose.)

John Gilling's clever script, aided by his deft direction, adds immeasurably to the film's subtlety and power. (The writer/director labeled this film "my best horror picture"—high praise, considering some of his others were *Shadow of the Cat*, *Blood Beast from Outer Space*, *The Reptile*, and *The Plague of the Zombies*.) Gilling augments and emphasizes his story's real-life horror with sly bits of black humor that fit in well with the movie's horrific topic and squalid ambiance. When an old man dies at Burke's lodging house, for example, Burke's wife complains to the undertaker about leaving the coffin in the front room, noting, "it makes the place look untidy."

Belying its lurid, ridiculous original title, *The Flesh and the Fiends*/*Mania* is a highly literate and thought-provoking look into the horrors created by the mores of an oppressive and backward society. This too-often overlooked gem truly deserves to be "resurrected."

With quotes from: "'Don't Call Me a Horror Film Director...'—The Great John Gilling Interview," *Little Shoppe of Horrors*, no. 23, October 2009.

Maniac (1963; Hammer; U.K., b&w) Director: Michael Carreras; Producer/Screenplay: Jimmy Sangster; Cinematographer: Wilkie Cooper. Cast: Kerwin Matthews, Nadia Gray, Donald Houston, Liliane Brousse, George Pastell.

Kerwin Matthews reaches for Nadia Gray in *Maniac* (1963).

The Maniac stalks his wife ... his daughter ... their lover!—tagline

---

Maniac was Hammer's second *Psycho*-like black-and-white psychological thriller, following *Scream of Fear* (1961). While not as enthralling as its predecessor, *Maniac* remains an engaging picture, thanks mostly to Jimmy Sangster's wily, twist-filled script.

Artist Geoffrey Farrell (Kerwin Matthews) splits with his wealthy girlfriend in the middle of a trip to Nice and finds himself stranded in rural France. He's befriended by a local barkeep, Eve (Nadia Gray), and her stepdaughter, Annette (Liliane Brousse), and takes up residence with them. Geoff inherits the room of Eve's husband, Georges, who was confined to an asylum four years earlier for exacting brutal revenge against a man who assaulted Annette—George killed the molester with an acetylene torch. Initially, Geoff is attracted to Annette and attempts to strike up a romance with her. But Eve intervenes and seduces Geoff, and Geoff falls in love with her. The lovers hatch a scheme to help Georges escape from the asylum, since he will only grant Eve a divorce if she helps free him. But things go awry when, following the escape, Geoff discovers Georges left the body of a murdered nurse in the trunk of Eve's car. After that, the plot twists come fast and furious—including two especially wicked ones in the final five minutes.

With someone like *Scream of Fear* director Seth Holt calling the shots, *Maniac*—with its decidedly noirish scenario, rich in kinky romantic intrigue—might have emerged as a minor classic. Unfortunately, Michael Carreras took on *Maniac* as his second directorial assignment (following *The Steel Bayonet* in 1957) for Hammer. Carreras was a visionary producer, and helped bring some of the studio's crowning achievements to the screen, including its early Frankenstein, Dracula and Quatermass pictures. But he remained a lackluster director, and went on to helm some of the weakest films in the Hammer filmography, including *Prehistoric Women* (1967), *The Lost Continent* (1968) and *Shatter* (1974). Although he contributes a few nicely composed shots and manages the tempo capably, *Maniac* never rises above the prosaic.

Stanley Black's jazzy, Henry Mancini-like score aids Carreras' cause. So does the performance of former Sinbad Matthews (star of *The Seventh Voyage of Sinbad* [1958]), who displays unsuspected dramatic chops. He's not entirely believable when professing his love to Eve, but this is more a flaw of Sangster's script. Given his randy behavior earlier on, sexual obsession would have provided a more convincing bond between Geoff and Eve than true love. Gray and Brousse both perform acceptably, but are hindered by phony-sounding French accents. (Matthews, playing an American, faces no such stumbling block.)

Maniac may be the least Hammer-like of Hammer's early-60s productions. Its small cast features none of the familiar Hammer supporting players. It includes a great deal more exterior and location footage (shot in the Camarge region of Southern France) than was typical. And its interiors were shot at MGM's studios at Boreham Wood rather than Hammer's familiar confines at Bray (unavailable because production of William Castle's remake of *The Old Dark House* ran long).

The commercial and critical success of *Scream of Fear* created the demand for more Hammer pseudo-*Psycho*s, and Sangster rushed to fill the breach, quickly completing scripts for three more psychological thrillers, all of which were filmed in 1962. Although *Maniac* was the first picture shot, it was the second one released, reaching British screens in May, 1963, on a twin bill with *These Are the Damned*, and American theaters (via Columbia) in October, 1963, double-featured with Castle's *The Old Dark House*. *Paranoiac*, the second Sangster psycho-thriller lensed in 1962, reached U.S. screens first, launching in America in May, 1963, via Universal. Both films have their merits, but *Maniac* proves the more consistently rewarding of the pair, and the second-best of the series, following *Scream of Fear*.

The Maniacs Are Loose see *The Thrill Killers*

see *The Thrill Killers*

Manos, the Hands of Fate (1966; Emerson Film Enterprises) Director/Producer/Screenwriter: Harold P. Warren; Cinematographer: Robert Guidry. Cast: Tom Neyman, John Reynolds, Dian Mahree, Hal Warren, Stephanie Nielson, Sherry Proctor, Robin Redd, Jackey Neyman.

A cult of weird, horrible people who gather beautiful women only to deface them with a burning hand!—tag line

When El Paso fertilizer salesman Harold P. Warren decided to make a movie, he pulled out all the stops, serving as producer, director, scripter *and* 'star.' That's when the ... fertilizer hit the fan.

A vacationing family (father, mother, little girl and poodle named Peppy) makes a wrong turn in the desert and ends up at the run-down house of "the Master" (Tom Neyman), a pasty-faced, mustachioed, black-and-red-robed devil worshipper with supernatural powers who prays to "Manos, god of primal darkness." Aided by his six nightgown-clad "wives" and his twitching, stuttering, limping servant Torgo (who looks like a cross between Joe Cocker and Vincent Van Gogh—and sports the most ludicrously oversized/deformed thighs outside of an Olympic speedskating rink), the Master determines to sacrifice the interlopers to (the unseen) Manos.

Nothing happens in this movie, reportedly shot for $19,000. It begins with a painfully protracted "travel" sequence in which the family drives ... and drives ... *and drives* past fields and up dirt roads and down dirt roads and across dirt roads and.... Even the climactic confrontation, when the father and the Master go, ahem, Manos-a-Manos, has the protagonist emptying his revolver at the fiend while the Master simply stands and stares as the scene fades out.

The film's "highlight" is a half-speed faux catfight between the six nightgowned wives. Or it might be when the Master, displeased with his servant, forces Torgo's hand into the sacrificial fire, then breaks it off and waves the flaming member about for awhile. (But this gruesome jolt completely fizzles due to the pathetically phony prop.)

Inept in all departments, from the tinny sound (it was obviously shot silent, with dialogue—such as it is—dubbed in later); alternately overlit and muddy—yet always flat—photography (which lacks even simple establishing shots and, at times, even proper focus); Motel-6 style sets; stilted acting that gives the term "amateurish" a bad name; and editing by Sominex, *Manos* is the cinematic equivalent of an open sore.

This sorry waste of celluloid came with a sad epilogue: John Reynolds, the 25-year-old "actor" (he appears to have no other credits) who plays Torgo, committed suicide shortly after filming.

"He killed himself about six months after the movie was finished," remarked cinematographer Bob Guidry to interviewer Richard Brandt. "John was a troubled kid; he didn't really get along with his dad, who was an Air Force colonel, and he got into experimenting with LSD. It's a shame, because he was really a talented young actor."

In the end, Harold P. Warren hadn't moved far from his original profession of fertilizer salesman after all, since with *Manos* he was once again selling a load of manure.

With quotes from: "The Hand That Time Forgot," by Richard Brandt, http://jophan.org/mimosa/m18/brandt.htm.

The Manster (1961; United Artists; Japan/U.S.; b&w) Directors: George Breakston and Kenneth Crane; Screenplay: Walt Sheldon (story by George Breakston); Producer: George Breakston; Cinematographer: David Mason. Cast: Peter Dyneley, Jan Hylton, Satosi Nakamura, Terri Zimmern, Van Hawley, Jerry Ito.

Half man, half monster!—ad line

This is the eyeball-on-the-shoulder movie.

In the film's most startling moment, foreign correspondent Larry Stanford (Peter Dyneley), struggling against a nameless entity that's trying to take control of his mind and body from within, looks in the mirror and sees that a third eye has suddenly appeared on his shoulder. It may sound silly on paper, but this sequence is guaranteed to raise the hairs on the back of your neck—especially if you see it before your fourteenth birthday. Michael J. Weldon's *Psychotronic Video Guide* calls this scene "a high point of screen surrealism." Take that, Luis Bunuel!

The Manster was not born of any such grandiose artistic aspirations. United Artists tossed off this low-rent shocker to fulfill contractual obligations, which required the company to co-produce a certain number of films in Japan. Producer/co-director George Breakston's original story, upon which the script is based, was both distinctly American and noticeably creaky—hoary old mad doctor stuff, the kind of thing Bela Lugosi might have starred in for Monogram 20 years earlier. Yet a certain Japanese-ness seems to have seeped into the picture. *The Manster* holds the same disregard for naturalism, and the same heartfelt commitment to the outlandish, normally found only in Toho's rubber suit monster extravaganzas.

During its first act, *The Manster* plays like a cross between *The Lost Weekend* and *Return of the Ape Man*. Stanford's final assignment in Japan is to visit the laboratory of the reclusive Dr. Suzuki (Satoshi Nakamura). The reporter can't wait to wrap up the story and return home to his fiancée (Jan Hylton) after a lengthy and rocky separation. But Dr. Suzuki slips Standford a mickey and injects him with a mysterious enzyme. In order to monitor his unwitting test subject, Suzuki befriends Stanford and shows him the wilder side of Japan, beginning with its geisha bars. Suzuki then instructs his attractive young assistant (Terri Zimmern) to cozy up to Stanford. The journalist's demeanor and behavior change, and he begins to undergo a physical transformation as well: one hand grows hairy and deformed. He suffers blackouts, during which he goes on homicidal rampages. Despite the best efforts of his editor and his fiancée, Stanford spirals downward into drunkenness and despair (not to mention monsterism). The adult situation and unusually well defined characters provide these scenes with an emotional punch rarely found in a film of this type and budget.

Then the eyeball appears on Stanford's shoulder. It soon grows into a full second head. The murders continue. Finally, the man and the monster split into two completely separate beings and square off against one another for a climactic showdown. Although patently ridiculous, the film's latter stages don't lack for either imagination or action.

All this would play much better if not for a few glaring weaknesses. Dyneley's role called for an actor capable of delivering a performance with some degree of subtlety—or at least someone who could play drunk convincingly. Dyneley fails on all counts. The rest of the cast proves equally inept, with the exception of the charismatic Nakamura. A few more parts like this and he could have become Japan's answer to George Zucco. The technical merits of the picture appear just as dubious. Most of the film is indifferently shot, although the few sequences filmed with care register an almost visceral impact. The editing is also haphazard. Although *The Manster* runs only 73 minutes and builds momentum nicely in its final act, a few dialogue-heavy scenes in the picture's midsection could have been tightened or even dropped. The chintzy monster makeup, sets and costumes don't help, either. (How do you say "Poverty Row" in Japanese?)

Nevertheless, for its scattered moments of brilliance, it's worth casting an eye toward *The Manster*.

Mars Invades Puerto Rico see *Frankenstein Meets the Spacemonster*

see *Frankenstein Meets the Spacemonster*

The Mask (1961; Beaver-Champion/Warner Bros.; Canada; b&w and color) Alternate Title: *Face of Fire* (reissue). Director: Julian Roffman; Producers: Julian Roffman and Nat Taylor; Screenplay: Franklin Delassert, Sandy Haver and Frank Taubes (Dream sequences: Skavko Vorkapich); Cinematography: Herbert S. Alpert. Cast: Paul Stevens, Claudette Nevins, Bill Walker, Anne Collings, Martin Lavut, Leo Leyden, Norman Ettlinger.

Look through The Mask ... if you can't take it ... take it off!—tagline

Although cheap and gimmicky, the Canadian-made, part-3-D oddity *The Mask* (1961) contains moments of inspiration and some chilling ideas.

Archeologist Michael Radin (Martin Lavut) rushes to psychiatrist Dr. Allen Barnes (Paul Stevens) with a desperate tale about an ancient ritual mask that gives him nightmares and compels him to kill. Barnes doesn't believe Radin's wild story, but after the archeologist commits suicide, the psychiatrist comes into possession of the mask. Barnes can't resist trying it on — the mask calls to him telepathically — and is transported into a dream world populated by figures of death and filled with other horrific imagery. Soon he becomes addicted to wearing the mask and consumed by the desire to commit murder. He turns to his fiancée (Claudette Nevins) and a former professor (Norman Ettlinger) for help, but no one believes *his* wild story, either.

The Mask employed a promotional gimmick very similar to the "Illusion-O" ghost viewers producer-director William Castle had distributed at showings of his feature *13 Ghosts* the previous year. As *Mask* patrons entered the theater, they were issued cardboard masks with polarized lenses over the eyeholes. When characters in the film put on the mask, audience members would don their facsimiles and watch the dream sequences in 3-D.

The idea of a mask that brings its wearer's deepest, darkest hidden impulses to the surface and compels that person to act on them is genuinely unsettling, since it forces viewers to ponder what secret evils might be locked away within them. *The Mask* builds on this unnerving idea with its lengthy and eerily imaginative dream sequences. The last of these scenes is typical. Running four minutes, it depicts Barnes being rowed

Hallucinatory imagery from the early Canadian horror film *The Mask* (1961).

down a river of dry ice by a skeletal boatman. Spectral visions of floating skulls drift through the air, while the "water" is filled with human bones. The boat — revealed to be a coffin — drifts to a giant likeness of the mask, which shoots out multicolored (red, white and blue) flames. Suddenly Barnes finds his fiancée, unconscious on a stone slab; then she's wearing the mask; and finally she's transformed into a skeleton. Although *The Mask*'s dream sequences are credited to artist Skavko Vorkapich, most of his designs were too elaborate for the movie's budget and were replaced by simpler ones from director Julian Roffman. Whoever authored them, however, they remain without question the film's strongest material. In fact, the plot of the film (thin enough to serve as a *Twilight Zone* episode) is little better than a framework on which to hang these arresting, surrealistic interludes. It's as if Roffman and company had little creativity left for the rest of the film, which otherwise is presented and performed in a professional but perfunctory manner. Paul Stevens' portrayal of the doomed Dr. Barnes tends toward the baroque but at least provides some color, in contrast to the drab work by the rest of the cast.

While it's not an acknowledged inspiration, the basic concept of *The Mask* (1961) is remarkably similar to the idea behind the darkly comedic Dark Horse comic book series *The Mask*, which was adapted into a 1994 feature film starring Jim Carrey. (The film spawned a sequel and a Saturday morning cartoon series.) Shot in Toronto, *The Mask* is generally credited as the first Canadian horror film and the only Canadian 3-D movie. It was also the first Canadian picture to receive wide distribution in the U.S., and Warner promoted it with a blood-and-thunder advertising campaign. "Management is not responsible for nervous breakdowns!" posters declared.

It won't cause any nervous breakdowns, but *The Mask* may raise the occasional goose-pimple.

Mask of the Demon see *Black Sunday*

The Masque of the Red Death (1964; Anglo Amalgamated/American International; U.K.) Director/Producer: Roger Corman; Screenplay: Charles Beaumont and R. Wright Campbell; Cinematographer: Nicholas Roeg. Cast: Vincent Price, Hazel Court, Jane Asher, Patrick Magee, David Weston, Nigel Green, Skip Martin.

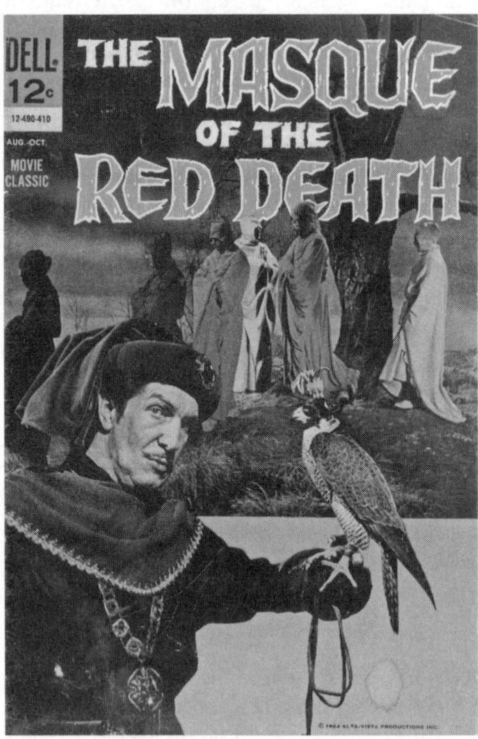

Comic book Poe: the Dell comic book tie-in for 1964's *Masque of the Red Death* (Vincent Price pictured on cover).

SHUDDER ... at the blood-stained dance of the Red Death!—tagline

With the masterful *Masque of the Red Death*, producer-director Roger Corman's series of Edgar Allan Poe adaptations reached its creative zenith. An emotionally resonant screenplay, pulse-quickening pace, impeccable production values and outstanding acting help make *Masque* exciting, unsettling and at times even poetic — in short, the finest film of Corman's prolific career.

Naïve, young Francesca (Jane Asher) catches the eye of jaded Prince Prospero (Vincent Price) while he visits a peasant village to invite the starving townsfolk to grovel for scraps from an extravagant feast he's throwing for the local nobles. Prospero is on the point of executing Francesca's fiancé and her father when he discovers the plague of the Red Death has struck the village. He whisks Francesca, along with her fiancé and her father, away to his castle and orders soldiers to burn the village to the ground. At the castle, Prospero—a confirmed Satanist—tries to seduce Francesca into not only his bed, but his cult. Prospero's jealous consort, Juliana (Hazel Court), attempts to shore up her own place in the prince's favor, first by attempting to set her rival free and later by undertaking Satanic vows in order to impress Prospero. The prince lords over a bacchanal fete with the other assembled nobles (who arrived before the Red Death was discovered in the vicinity) but, in fear of the disease, refuses to admit anyone else — even striking down one late-arriving guest with a crossbow. Despite such extraordinary measures, however, the Red Death himself—a walking, red-robed embodiment of human mortality—crashes the party.

Corman had considered making *Masque of the Red Death* the follow-up to his original Poe film, *House of Usher* (1960), but feared the story had too many similarities to Ingmar Bergman's *The Seventh Seal*, made in 1956 but not released in the U.S. until 1958. "Both films were set in the middle ages, and both had death personified, so I felt if I did *Masque*, people would think I had taken some of the story from Ingmar Bergman," Corman said. "That was partially the reason we ended up making *Pit and the Pendulum* as the second Poe film." By 1964, however, Corman figured enough time had elapsed that it was safe to take on

Masque. Besides, he had already adapted most of the other top-tier Poe stories.

Corman commissioned a screenplay from Charles Beaumont but wasn't entirely happy with it, so he asked scenarist Bob Campbell for a rewrite. Beaumont's script introduced Prince Prospero's Satanism (an element not present in the Poe story); Campbell incorporated a subplot involving the carefully plotted revenge of a dwarf jester (Skip Martin), taken from Poe's story "Hop-Frog." "That was Bob's idea, which I thought was good because it gave an additional dimension to the picture," Corman said. "I always thought Bob did an excellent job on the rewrite." Between the two of them, Beaumont and Campbell crafted a marvelous script, brimming with action (more happens in the first 30 minutes of *Masque* than occurs in the entirety of most entries in the series) yet remaining thoughtful and emotionally resonant. Part of the appeal of the film is that its three major characters, in their own ways, are simply searching for security in a time of fear and despair: cynical Prospero turns to Satanism, emotionally needy Juliana clings to Prospero, while simple Francesca places her trust in family and Christianity.

All Corman's preceding Poe films were shot in Hollywood, but, for financial reasons, *Masque* was filmed in Britain. AIP, which had a co-production agreement with Anglo-Amalgamated, wanted to take advantage of an England subsidy that refunded 20 percent of the production cost for films made in the U.K. using English cast and crews. "We were happy to go over, because it meant we were able to increase our budget for *The Masque of the Red Death*," Corman said. Instead of the typical three-week (15-day) shooting schedule, *Masque* was shot on a relatively luxurious five-week (25-day) schedule. To qualify for the subsidy, the entire cast and crew (except for the director and one star) had to be British. As a result, production designer Daniel Haller worked without credit on the film, and cinematographer Floyd Crosby was replaced. Haller nevertheless made a significant contribution to the picture, locating standing sets (left over from the multi-million-dollar historical epic *Becket* [1964]) far beyond anything previously available to Corman. Nicholas Roeg, who had shot *Lawrence of Arabia* (1962) and would soon graduate to directing critically acclaimed films of his own, replaced Crosby. Roeg lends the film a sophisticated look, making splashy use of a bold color palate (rich in yellows, purples, greens and, of course, reds). *Masque*'s closing scene, set in a studio "countryside" with a gathering of rainbow-hued Deaths, lingers in the memory, a haunting piece of visual artistry.

Although Corman complained that the English crew worked more slowly than their American counterparts (five weeks' shooting in the U.K., Corman wrote in his autobiography, "was actually closer to four U.S. weeks"), the level of craftsmanship displayed here is far beyond that found in any other Corman picture. The director's prowling tracking shots were never smoother, his subtle pans and dolleys never more fluid and graceful. President John F. Kennedy was assassinated while *Masque* was under production, and, in the fallen leader's honor, Corman halted shooting "for a few minutes."

The cast is uniformly superb as well, headlined by Vincent Price's oily malevolence as the debauched Prospero, a portrayal that ranks among the best of his legendary career. Co-star Hazel Court was never better than as the clingy, insecure Juliana — a woman who brands her own breast with an inverted cross, willing to consign herself to Hell in order to maintain a grip on her man. Jane Asher's role as the plucky Francesca is less flashy than Court's, but her convincing portrayal provides the story's emotional center. (Asher was the real-life girlfriend of Beatle Paul McCartney, who visited the set during production.) The supporting cast proves equally impressive. Patrick Magee's leering turn as the lascivious Alfredo serves as the perfect foil for Skip Martin's endearing performance as the wily, revenge-driven dwarf, Hop-Toad.

Masque gave Corman another critical and box office triumph, and whetted AIP's appetite for more Poe. Although he had begun to tire of the series, Corman complied with a final entry, *The Tomb of Ligeia* (1964). But never again would he create a film as poignant or perfectly constructed as *Masque of the Red Death.*

With quotes from: "California Gothic: The Corman/Haller Collaboration," by Lawrence French, from *Video Watchdog* No. 138; and *How I Made a Hundred Movies in Hollywood and Never Lost a Dime*, by Roger Corman with Jim Jerome.

The Master of Horror (1965; Argentina Sono Film/Gates-Torres Productions; Argentina; b&w) Alternate Titles: *Short Stories of Terror*; *Masterworks of Horror*. Original Language Title: *Obras Maestras del Terror*. Director: Enrique Carreras; Producer: Nicholas Carreras; Screenplay: Louis Penafiel (based on stories by Edgar Allan

Poe); Cinematographer: Americo Hoss. Cast: Narcisco Ibanez-Menta, Oswald Pacheco, Carlos Estrada, Inez Moreno, Stevan Serrador, Mercedes Carreras.

TWO CHILLERS to turn your DREAMS to SCREAMS!—ad line (when double-billed with *Master of Terror*)

Made in 1960, a year before Roger Corman's similarly-themed Poe omnibus *Tales of Terror*, the Argentinean *The Master of Horror* features three stories by Edgar Allan Poe: "The Facts in the Case of M. Valdemar," "The Cask of Amontillado" (both adapted by Corman in *Tales*) and "The Tell-Tale Heart." American producer Jack H. Harris (best known for such fan favorites as *The Blob* and *Dinosaurus!*) bought the distribution rights, jettisoned the third story, "The Tell-Tale Heart" (thus drastically reducing the running time from 115 to 61 minutes), and paired it with his own 1959 feature *The 4D Man* (retitled *Master of Terror*) for a 1965 double-bill.

Though lacking the inestimable talents of Vincent Price (with the adequate though rather nondescript Narcisco Ibanez-Menta starring in all three segments, à la Senor Price), and shot in black and white rather than Corman's rich color schemes, the all-but-forgotten *Master of Horror* still measures up rather well against its more famous American cousin.

The "Valdemar" story in *Master* bypasses the unnecessary—and somewhat distasteful—soap operish embellishments of Corman's film, becoming a straightforward—and atmospheric—telling of Poe's chilling tale of a mesmerist who hypnotizes his friend at the moment of death and keeps the tortured soul 'alive' for months. While missing the rather hammy yet always welcome presence of Basil Rathbone and Price from *Tales of Terror*, this version features a much more convincing—and terrifying—denouement, in which the finally-released Valdemar transforms into a withered, skeletal "mass of putrefaction" that's much more frightening than the Kayro syrup monster Price becomes in *Tales*.

The second story in *Master*, "The Cask of Amontillado," on the other hand, falls short of Corman's amusing take in *Tales* (which is greatly aided by Peter Lorre's—and Price's—presence). With much of the story consisting of padded preamble (featuring tiresome scenes of the burgeoning adulterous love affair) before the business of the cuckolded husband walling his rival up alive in his wine cellar finally commences, it tends to drag. Once we reach the cellars, however, *Master* offers a few shudders (courtesy of Ibanez-Menta's deadly-calm taunting and Carlos Estrada's disbelief-turned-panic) and even an unexpected shock.

As is usual with south-of-the-border imports, the awkward dubbing often leaves something to be desired. For instance, in the film's wraparound segment, a bored French maid picks up a volume of Poe and reads in the introduction that, "[Poe] was a genius as a poet and as a writer, and uniting both talents he created a **gender** [sic] that made him forever famous." Let's hope that something was lost in the translation.

Some atmospheric black-and-white photography and adequate performances, plus its faithful renderings of Poe's famous stories (which—even in *Tales*—are typically folded, spindled and mutilated beyond all recognition in the transition from page to screen), make *The Master of Horror* an above-average (if short) sixties import.

Masterworks of Horror see *The Master of Horror*

The Mighty Gorga (1969; American General Pictures) Director: David L. Hewitt; Producers: Robert O'Neil, David Hewitt; Screenplay: David Prentiss, Jean Hewitt; Cinematographer: Gary Graver. Cast: Anthony Eisley, Megan Timothy, Scott Brady, Kent Taylor, Gary Kent, Graydon Clark, Sheldon Lee, Lee Parish.

The Greatest Horror Monster Alive! —(grossly duplicitous) tagline

There's nothing "Mighty" about *The Mighty Gorga*, except perhaps that it's *Mighty Bad*. Clumsy camerawork, dull direction, a silly screenplay ("Mighty Gorga, I know that your thirst for the blood of young virgins is great, but leave our village in peace," entreats the local witchdoctor while exercising his powers of persuasion with a 50-foot ape) and amateurish acting are the highlights of this no-budget grade-Z *King Kong* wannabe.

The worst part of this production (using the term loosely here) are the insulting effects, which should be the primary *raison d'etre* of this shoddy piece of celluloid. Gorga is a 50-foot gorilla who lives on a plateau in deepest Africa—or so the script tells us, since in actuality Gorga is director David L. Hewitt wearing a homemade gorilla suit, complete with immobile face and plastic eyes; and we can't really tell if he's 50 feet tall or not, since there are no miniatures to be seen, and the big ape is shown only with the sky or treetops as background. (This was because Hewitt, low on funds, decided to build only the top half of the suit!).

The story follows Anthony Eisley as the owner of a down-and-out circus come to Africa to capture the mighty monkey. He meets a female animal trapper (Megan Timothy) and they set off with nothing more than a couple of backpacks and one small land rover to retrieve this hostile 50-foot monstrosity from a Lost World-like plateau in the heart of an uncharted jungle. Thrown in there somewhere are those low-budget stalwarts, Scott Brady and Kent Taylor, to try and add at least a modicum of professionalism to the proceedings (unfortunately, they're onscreen for so short a time they add virtually nothing). The protagonists run afoul of a lost tribe, find the ridiculous-looking Gorga and an equally ludicrous Tyrannosaur, stumble upon a cache of King Solomon's treasure, and rush past a stock footage Jim Danforth-animated dragon from AIP's *Goliath and the Dragon*. After a few awful rear-screen projections; a battle between the Absurd — er — Mighty Gorga and the worst plastic-looking dinosaur ever to cross the silver screen (actually a hand puppet!); some high school-level dramatics from the overweight witch doctor (Bruce Kimball, who also — aptly — plays a clown in the opening scenes set at the circus); and the expected volcanic eruption (which we're only *told* about, since it happens off-screen), this mess finally comes to a close.

Special effects man turned director Hewitt was also responsible for the equally inept *Wizard of Mars* (1964), *Dr. Terror's Gallery of Horrors* (1966 — not to be confused with the far superior *Dr. Terror's* House *of Horrors*) and *Journey to the Center of Time* (1967), making Hewitt a strong candidate for the title: "The Ed Wood of the 1960s."

"I can't believe this thing's real," exclaims the heroine as *The Mighty Gorga* spools out before our disbelieving eyes — and neither can the viewer. The more you watch, the more you're convinced that this is actually an expanded 8mm high school project. *The Mighty Gorga* offers no budget, no sense and no thrills. The one or two unintentional laughs are only respite from the rest of the painfully bad experience.

Mill of the Stone Women (1960/63; Galatea/ Parade; France/Italy) Alternate Titles: *Drops of Blood*; *The Horrible Mill Women*; *Horror of the Stone Women*. Original Language Title: *Il Mulino delle donne di Pietra*. Director: Giorgio Ferroni; Producer: Gianpaolo Bigazzi; Screenplay: Giorgio Ferroni, Remingio Del Grosso, Ugo Liberatore, Giorgio Stegani, from a short story in *Flemish Tales* by Pieter Van Weigen (English dialogue and dubbing supervised by John Hart and Richard McNamara); Cinematographer: Pierludovico Pavoni. Cast: Pierre Brice, Scilla Gabel, Wolfgang Preiss, Danny Carrell, Herbert Boehme.

SEE A BEAUTIFUL GIRL CHANGED INTO A *PETRIFIED MONSTER* BEFORE YOUR VERY EYES! — ad line

"Trouble began with a woman..." begins the opening narration. In 1912, Hans (Pierre Brice) journeys to a small town in Holland to do a story on the famous "carousel" located in what the locals call the "Mill of the Stone Women." Professor Wahl (Herbert Boehme), a famous sculptor, attends (and adds) to this display of female statues of gruesome torture and death — all on a moving track powered by the windmill. Hans

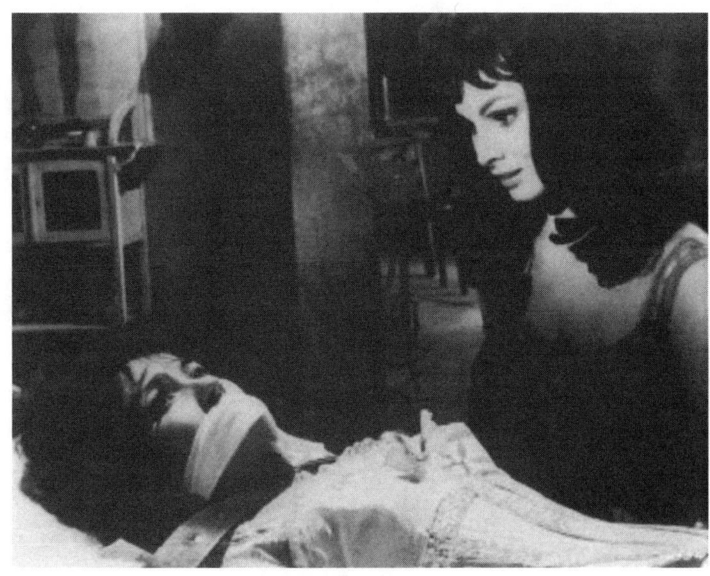

Scilla Gabel leans over a bound Dany Carrel in the *Mill of the Stone Women* (1960/63).

succumbs to the charms of the Professor's beautiful, mysterious daughter, Elfi (Scilla Gabel), who is not allowed to leave the mill due to a rare blood disease. Hans also ultimately learns the terrible truth of how the Professor, aided by his furtive assistant Dr. Boles (Wolfgang Preiss), keeps his daughter alive ... while adding to his collection of statuary.

Though possessing a novel setting (a Dutch windmill) and some impressive atmospherics, *Mill of the Stone Women* has little else to recommend it. The derivative story offers nothing new (it being little more than a combination of *Eyes Without a Face* and *Mystery of the Wax Museum*) and fills its time with the forced and unconvincing romance angle. While some moody lighting and evocative shots of the windmill, not to mention a judicious use of rich colors on the splendidly dressed sets, generate some visual ambiance and an occasional sense of foreboding, the picture's pace moves slower than the mill's blades on a windless day.

Filler and repetition abound. At one point Hans, in the grip of a hallucinatory drug given him by the Professor, goes to the cemetery to see if Elfi's body is there (he saw her die). Then later he and his friend do the *very same thing*, which, to the viewer, becomes a tedious waste of time. Add to this tepid characters, colorless leads and poor model effects of the burning mill, and this mostly forgotten import offers little to belie its obscurity.

Released in Europe in 1960, *Mill of the Stone Women* didn't open in the U.S. until three years later. Though the ads promised "A CHILLING EXPERIENCE," this *Mill* offers a mostly BORING one.

Mr. Sardonicus (1961; Columbia; b&w) Producer/Director: William Castle; Screenplay: Ray Russell; Cinematographer: Burnett Guffey. Cast: Ronald Lewis, Audrey Dalton, Guy Rolfe, Oskar Homolka, Audrey Dalton.

The Only Picture with the Punishment Poll!
—tagline

In an onscreen introduction to this movie, producer-director William Castle describes *Mr. Sardonicus* as "old-fashioned," and indeed it is, although not in a bad way. With its gaslight-era setting and a melodramatic plot reminiscent of Victor Hugo, *Mr. Sardonicus* represents Castle's lone attempt at a traditional gothic chiller—the sort of picture Universal popularized 30 years earlier—and the results prove effective enough to make viewers wish the filmmaker had returned to this idiom.

Crusading physician Sir Robert Cargrave (Ronald Lewis) rushes from his London dispensary to a distant Carpathian barony at the urgent request of his former sweetheart, Maude (Audrey Dalton), now a baroness. Cargrave finds that Maude is trapped in a loveless marriage to the sadistic Baron Sardonicus (Guy Rolfe), who wears an eerie, blank-faced mask to hide his hideously disfigured face—frozen in a permanent grin as a result of psychological trauma. The Baron threatens to have henchman Krull (Oskar Homolka) carve Maude's face into a similarly hideous visage unless Dr. Cargrave performs a radical experimental procedure to try to cure Sardonicus.

Unable to speak, *Mr. Sardonicus* (Guy Rolfe) uses alternate means to make his wishes known.

Mr. Sardonicus stands apart from most of Castle's low-rent horror shows—not just because of its period setting, but because it's so well made. Nearly everything here is first-rate: Ray Russell's screenplay is well-structured and consistently compelling; the acting is uniformly convincing (especially Ronald Lewis as Sir Robert, Guy Rolfe as Sardonicus and Oskar Homolka as Sardonicus' one-eyed henchman, Krull); Burnett Guffey's lighting schemes are moody and atmospheric, with lots of deep shadows and misty fog; and the production values are the highest for any Castle picture other than *The Old Dark House* (1963), which was shot in partnership with Hammer Films. (*Sardonicus*' forest of bare trees and dry ice virtually recreates Jack Otterson's iconic set from *The Wolf Man* [1941].) In terms of sheer film craft, *Mr. Sardonicus* trails only *House on Haunted Hill* (1959) among those pictures directed by Castle.

With a product this good, Castle didn't need any of his usual promotional gimmicks—but he included one anyway, the "Punishment Poll." Moviegoers were handed a card with a thumbs-up/thumbs-down image as they entered the theater. Near the climax of the film, Castle reappeared onscreen to ask if viewers believed that Sardonicus had been punished enough, or if he deserved "further punishment." They were instructed to hold their cards thumbs-up to let the villain live, or thumbs-down to consign him to a gruesome fate. Castle even pretended to count the votes (mumbling to himself, "carry the three"), but the result was always the same: Death to Sardonicus. That's because only one ending was shot; the "Punishment Poll" was a put-on. Ironically, although it's fun to watch Castle trying to pull the wool over viewers' eyes, *Mr. Sardonicus* would play better without the "Punishment Poll," which brings the picture to a screeching halt just prior to its climax. Also, Sardonicus' ironic fate is handled so subtly that it seems like a letdown after the additional build-up.

Castle was on a roll, with a half-dozen horror hits in a row, beginning with *Macabre* (1958). But, following *Mr. Sardonicus*, the filmmaker abruptly turned away from his bread-and-butter genre and launched a series of intermittently entertaining comedies—*Zotz* (1962), *13 Frightened Girls* and *The Old Dark House* (both 1963). Castle wouldn't make another full-blooded fright flick again until *Strait-Jacket* (1964), and would never again direct a picture as polished and satisfying as *Mr. Sardonicus*. As a producer, however, his greatest accomplishment still lay ahead.

Mistresses of Dr. Jekyll see *Dr. Orloff's Monster*

Monster A-Go Go (1965; B.I. & L. Releasing Corp.; b&w) Director: Bill Rebane; Producers: Sheldon S. Seymour (H.G. Lewis), Bill Rebane; Screenplay: Jeff Smith, Dok Stanford, Bill Rebane (additional dialogue by Sheldon Seymour [H.G. Lewis]); Cinematographer: Frank Pfeiffer. Cast: Phil Morton, June Travis, George Perry, Henry Hite.

> Never in your life have you seen such a combination of happy, sad, good, bad, rock 'em sock 'em action!—trailer

The film's poster sports the following "quote" from NASA: "THIS PICTURE COULD SET OUR SPACE PROGRAM BACK AT LEAST FIFTY YEARS!" Doubtful, but had it escaped the Southern Drive-in circuit into a wider release, it may well have set the *motion picture industry* back half a century.

The debut feature of Wisconsin-based indie filmmaker Bill Rebane (*The Giant Spider Invasion* [1975], *The Capture of Bigfoot* [1979], etc.), *Monster A-Go Go* began as a film called *Terror at Halfday*. Herschell ("Godfather of Gore") Gordon Lewis, whom Rebane had met when they both were making shorts and commercials in Chicago, needed a co-feature for his hillbilly comedy *Moonshine Mountain*. Lewis took Rebane's unreleased (and reportedly unfinished) movie, added new scenes and narration, and unleashed it on an unsuspecting public. "When I finally saw the picture," recounted Rebane, "I hardly recognized it. All that was left was some of the original bad acting from the scientists that I shot. Herschell added the rock music, the narration and all the scenes of the monster attacking the girls." Good thing, too, since without these addendums, *Monster A-Go Go* would have been even *less* watchable than it currently is.

In a plot borrowed from 1959's *First Man Into Space* (with a bit of *The Giant Behemoth* thrown in for good measure), a space capsule returns to earth carrying a deranged, oversized, deadly radiation-spewing (the *Behemoth* bit) astronaut who goes on a rampage. It's up to the space program and military authorities to locate and stop this "monster."

Said fiend is really a tall, slow-moving bald guy in minor burn makeup and a silver suit (played by 8-foot-4-inch Henry Hite, of the former vaudeville act Low, Stanley & Hite). The height (so to speak) of the film's monster "action" has one character *back into* the creature's oversized hands.

The echoing sound against bare-walled rooms,

static camerawork, poor lighting (with the contrast so high at times that facial features disappear — and so low at others that *everything* disappears), and even poorer pacing make this *Monster* one of the ugliest of the decade. (It's so cheap that at one point someone makes an off-screen phone noise before a character answers the "ringing" phone! Sad.) And it's one of those movies where the actors (and narrator) *talk* about what has happened in order to save the trouble of showing it.

But nowhere does this project's low budget — and even lower imagination level — show more clearly than at its pathetic non-ending. The "climax" has the two lead-suited military men (leisurely) pursuing the monster through a sewer tunnel simply stop, as the narrator chimes in: "Suddenly there was no trail. There was no giant, no monster, no *thing* called Douglas to be followed." The End. Apparently (since, of course, we don't *see* it happen) the monster simply — and inexplicably — vanishes.

"You've Never Seen a Picture Like This," touted the ads. Nor, indeed, would you *want* to. While it may not be the worst the 1960s had to offer (*Manos, the Hands of Fate* wins that dubious distinction), *Monster A-Go Go* comes in a close second.

TRIVIA(L) NOTE: Director/co-producer/co-scripter Bill Rebane's father invented the formula for beer nuts.

With quotes from: "The Rebanes of the Day," by Keith Bearden, *Fangoria* 158, November 1996.

Monster Among the Girls see *Werewolf in a Girls' Dormitory*

Monster and the Stripper see *The Exotic Ones*

Monster from the Surf see *The Beach Girls and the Monster*

The Monsters Demolisher (1962; Estudios America/Trans-International Films; Mexico; b&w) Original Language Title: *Nostradamus y el Destructor de Monstruos*; Director: Frederick Curiel, Stim Segar (English language version); Producer: Victor Parra, K. Gordon Murray (English version); Screenplay: Frederick Curiel (Story by Charles Taboada, Alfred Ruanova); Cinematographer: Ferdinand Colin. Cast: Germán Robles, Julio Aleman, Domingo Soler, Aurora Alvarado, Manuel Vergara, Jack Taylor.

Creatures of evil — an army of vampires—arise from their crypts ... to carry out a maniacal scheme ... the destruction of the civilized world!–ad line

This second entry in the infamous Mexican Nostradamus quartet follows right on the heels of *The Curse of Nostradamus*. Germán Robles (who popularized Mexican vampires in the late 1950s with *The Vampire* and *The Vampire's Coffin*) returns once again as the black-cloaked, homburg wearing, goatee sporting vampire Nostradamus when his half-wit hunchback servant (Manuel Vergara), complete with dumb ("duh...I'm coming, Master") goofy voice, digs the bloodsucker out of the rubble in which he was buried at the close of the first movie. Mr. N. then continues his tedious task of trying to force Professor Dolen to "revindicate [*sic*] the memory of my illustrious ancestor" (the real Nostradamus, the famous French prognosticator).

The movie's first half just retreads the same old ground as the original, with the vampire appearing (seemingly nightly) in the Professor's study to inform him of the identity of his next victim; then the Professor and his assistant Anthony (Julio Aleman) try to foil Nostradamus' plan — over and over again.

The second half at least offers some novelty, as Nostradamus turns a criminal into a vampire slave, and a mysterious man named Igor(!) shows up to offer aid to the Professor. Igor (a young Jack Taylor, who later carved a career in Spanish horror movies working for the likes of Jess Franco, Paul Naschy and Amando de Ossorio) comes from a long line of vampire hunters and uses "the magic arts" to track the fiend (by looking into a bubbling chalice and magic mirror). It all ends (or, more precisely, peters out) with Igor staking Nostradamus' minion — at which point Nostradamus himself clutches his chest and falls motionless to the floor, before an abrupt THE END signals a final relief for the viewer (until, that is, the next installment, *Genie of Darkness*).

Monsters of the Night see *The Navy vs. the Night Monsters*

Monstrosity (1964; Emerson Film Enterprises; b&w) Alternate Title: *The Atomic Brain* (TV); Director: Joseph Mascelli; Producers: Jack Pollexfen, Dean Dillman, Jr.; Screenplay: Vy Russell, Sue Dwiggins, Dean Dillman, Jr.; Cinematographer: Alfred Taylor. Cast: Marjorie Eaton, Frank Gerstle, Frank Fowler, Erika Peters, Judy Bamber, Lisa Lang, Xerxes the cat.

Chained ... to the devil's love lab!—tagline

In 1964 Joseph Mascelli, Ray Dennis Steckler's cinematographer from *The Incredibly Strange Creatures ...* (1963) and *The Thrill Killers* (1964), decided to step up and direct his *own* low-budget horror movie; and the results, while far from impressive, beat Steckler's dubious oeuvre by a country mile.

Of course, it may have helped that Mascelli had a *real* (albeit low-budget) Hollywood producer in Jack Pollexfen (maker of such '50s fare as *The Man from Planet X*, *The Indestructible Man* and *Daughter of Dr. Jekyll*), who was able to secure, if not first rate, than at least competent actors with *some* experience (as opposed to Steckler's usual cast of friends, family and amateur wannabes). This, coupled with a decent cinematographer in Alfred Taylor (*Spider Baby* [1964], *Blood Bath* [1966], *Killer Klowns from Outer Space* [1988]), and location shooting at an impressive old mansion (including one effective sequence filmed on the structure's ornately gabled roof), gave Mascelli's pet project a fighting chance to at least *look* like a real movie. Said chance took flight, however, after a glance at the amazingly boffo script. This is not to say it's not an *entertaining* story....

To wit: A rich old woman (Marjorie Eaton) hires a mad scientist (veteran character actor Frank Gerstle [*The Neanderthal Man*, *The Wasp Woman*, *The Four Skulls of Jonathan Drake*, etc.]) to transplant her brain into a young girl's body. The scientist has plans of his own, however, including giving a woman (Lisa Lang) the brain of a cat!

The brain—(and *species*)—swapping plotline proffers some amusingly original moments (many of them involving the cat-brained woman meowing and hissing and batting at the air). There's also a man with the brain of a dog (and, oddly, a rather hairy countenance and a huge set of fangs to go with it), the aforementioned woman with a cat's brain (who at one point eats a live mouse and literally scratches somebody's eyes out), and a revived female corpse with basically *no* brain. (A cat with a *human* brain even pops up at the end!)

Given this bizarre scenario, some competent cinematic technique (at least it's lit properly and in focus) and generally decent acting (though dizzy blonde Bea is played with an appallingly inconsistent Cockney accent by Judy Bamber—the dizzy blonde model from 1959's *A Bucket of Blood*), and *Monstrosity* comes off better than it should. Even so, there's still plenty of dull stretches; talk, after all, *is* cheap. ("I went in for an interview and they wanted somebody with an English accent," recounted Bamber about her winning the role of a Cockney beauty. "So, naturally, you say you can do it. But I'd never done an English accent in my life." And she still hasn't.)

The film's fairly racy (sleazy?) tone also—for better or worse—ups the interest level. The beautiful "bodies" stolen by the doctor are nude; no coy sheet coverings here—though strategically placed steel bands keep it on the PG level. And the leering-voiced narrator (an uncredited Bradford Dillman[!], whose father, Dean Dillman, Jr., co-produced) makes observations like, "so firm, so nicely rounded in places men like," and, "Well, sometimes it's convenient to have a man, especially when he comes cheaper than servants."

When compared to other Grade-Z independents of the time, such as *Monster A-Go Go*, *Manos the Hands of Fate*, or anything by Steckler, Jerry Warren or even H. G. Lewis, the offbeat and moderately entertaining *Monstrosity* looks like a million bucks. But compare it to just about any Grade-B (or even C) Hollywood horror, and *Monstrosity* lives up to (or, more precisely, *down to*) its name.

With quotes from: "All About My Little Sister: Judy Bamber," by George Bamber, *Filmfax* 121, Summer 2009.

The Most Dangerous Man Alive (1961; Columbia; b&w) Director: Allan Dwan; Producer: Benedict Bogeans; Screenplay: James Leicester, Philip Rock. Cinematographer: Carl Carvahal. Cast: Ron Randell, Debra Paget, Elaine Stewart, Anthony Caruso, Gregg Palmer, Morris Ankrum.

IN THE HEART OF AN ATOMIC TESTING AREA IT TAKES ONLY 10 SECONDS TO TURN A HUMAN INTO THE ... MOST DANGEROUS MAN ALIVE—poster blurb

The Most Dangerous Man Alive is a gritty blend of the sci-fi, horror and gangster genres. A framed gangster (Ron Randall) escapes from prison and wanders into the test site of a new type of cobalt bomb. The bomb detonates but he's not killed. Instead, he becomes a "man of steel"—his flesh absorbs metal. Randall uses his newfound talent to revenge himself on the gang that sent him up the river. To the mobsters' dismay, bullets won't stop him, electricity won't stop him, apparently nothing will stop him. Randall finally meets his match, however, when a battalion of police and national guardsmen runs him to earth and then fries him with a flame-thrower.

The tone of the picture is grim realism, with the principals playing their parts well. Beautiful Debra Paget, as the gangster's mistress, assays her role in a sensuous, daring manner (especially for 1961). Her seduction scene, in which she entices Randall to remove her shoe and stocking, is charged with a subtle erotic energy. Even though Randall plays a no-good gangster, he manages to arouse sympathy in the audience and put them on his side. One feels pity for him as the changes going on in his body begin to affect his mind ("I'm not human anymore.... All I can feel now is hate!").

The script becomes rather simplistic and vague in its explanations (referring to a mysterious "Element X" contained in the cobalt and showing us some shabby "mutated" lab animals as explanation), but the plot does possess some effective twists, such as extending some hope to Randall in the form of scientific help only to dash that hope when the bad guys interfere at the wrong moment. The climax proves to be a major disappointment, however, with terrible flame effects poorly superimposed over shots of Randall shouting hysterically about ruling the world. And the obvious stock footage of flamethrower troops completely erases the film's sense of realism. Here the low budget becomes painfully apparent.

Still, *The Most Dangerous Man Alive* remains one of the more unusual sci-fi/horror entries from the early '60s and deserves better than its current status as one of *The Most Unseen Films Today*.

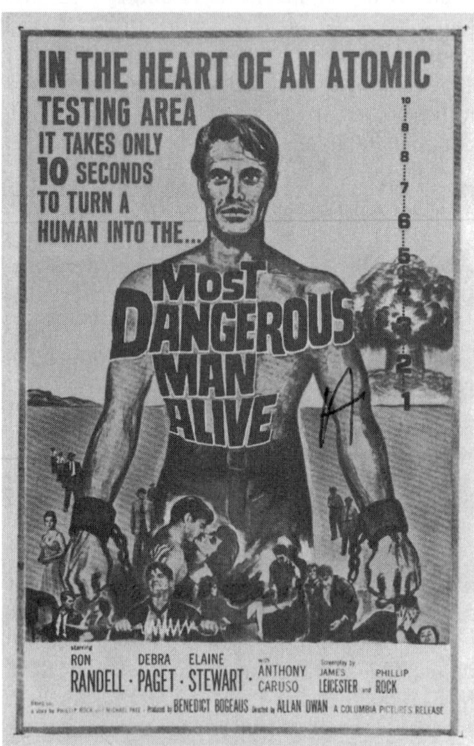

One-sheet poster for *The Most Dangerous Man Alive* (1961).

Mothra (1961/62; Toho, Japan) Original Language Title: *Mosura.* Director: Ishiro Honda; Producer: Tomoyuki Tanaka; Screenplay: Yoshie Hotta, Shinichiro Nakamura and Shinichi Sekizawa (from a novel by Takehiko Fukunaga); Cinematographer: Hajime Koizume. Cast: Frankie Sakai, Hiroshi Koizumi, Kyoko Kagawa, Emi Ito, Yumi Ito, Jerry Ito, Takashi Shimura, Satosi Nakamura.

Mightiest Monster in All Creation!—tagline

Following the breakthrough success of *Godzilla, King of the Monsters* (1954/56, aka *Gojira*) Toho produced three similar films, *Gigantis the Fire Monster* (1955, aka *Godzilla Raids Again*), *Rodan* (1956) and *Varan the Unbelievable (1958/62).* All were cast in the template set by American sci-fi monster movies such as *The Beast from 20,000 Fathoms* (1953) and *Them* (1954). The results, both artistic and commercial, were mixed. This approach reached a dead end with the dismal *Varan*, made in 1958 but not released in the U.S. until 1962. Clearly, the studio needed to reinvent its *kaiju eiga* (giant monster) movies if its fledgling film cycle was to survive.

Enter *Mothra.*

With this picture, director Ishiro Honda jettisoned the quasi-documentary tone of the previous films, along with all other American-style trappings. In a sense, *Mothra* was the first fully Japanese *kaiju eiga*. The director had completely assimilated the foreign model and was ready to go off in a more whimsical, and singularly Japanese, direction. More fairy tale than science fiction, *Mothra* is a color-splashed fantasia brimming with wildly imaginative, and sometimes downright bizarre, ideas. It's a more kid-friendly film than the previous pictures, yet it includes a scathing indictment of economic imperialism clearly intended for grownups. And, for the first time, the titular monster is not the villain.

Mothra, in giant caterpillar form, lays siege to a TV tower (a not-so-subtle commentary perhaps?) in *Mothra* (1961/62).

As a rule, Toho's subsequent giant monster movies would integrate some or all of these same elements, but seldom would the results prove so enjoyable.

A handful of shipwreck survivors wash up on the shore of a remote atoll previously used for atomic bomb tests. Miraculously, given the radiation levels on the island, they survive to tell of strange natives who have concocted an elixir that protects against radiation. An international scientific team, led by the unscrupulous Clark Nelson (Jerry Ito), sail to the island to investigate. A tenacious young reporter (Frankie Sakai) nicknamed "Bulldog" (or, in the original Japanese version, "Snapping Turtle") sneaks aboard. On the island, scientists discover a pair of tiny women (Emi and Yumi Ito), identical twins about a foot tall. Nelson kidnaps the twins and brings them back to Japan, where he and a henchman (Satosi Nakamura) hold them prisoner and force them to perform a nightclub act.

What Nelson doesn't realize is that the tiny twins are native priestesses, and the islanders don't take kindly to their removal. The natives call upon their god, Mothra, to rescue the twins. Mothra begins its life as a giant egg, which hatches to reveal a colossal caterpillar. Drawn to the twins by a telepathic link, Mothra swims to Japan in her caterpillar form. "Bulldog" and his friends realize the only way to save Japan is to free the twins from Nelson and deliver them to their monster protector. Despite their best efforts, however, Mothra arrives in Japan, wreaks havoc, cocoons herself and then emerges as a gigantic moth. Bulldog and friends deliver the twins to Mothra and avert further destruction.

Honda enjoyed an ample budget for this film, and the money is visible on the screen. The production values are high, the cast larger than usual, and the special effects superb. Which is to say that they look beautiful, not that they look real. This represents another major break from the previous films, with their more Americanized, naturalistic effects. *Mothra*'s more stylized approach — although it may seem "hokey" to American audiences— aligns with most other Japanese art forms, which tend away from naturalism. The ancient Japanese theatrical traditions of the Noh and Kabuki, for instance, are almost ritualistic, completely at odds with more naturalistic Western dramatic forms.

The plight of Bulldog and his friends, as they try to rescue the tiny twins, provides an emotional context for the film's requisite monster-versus-military/smashup-the-city sequences— human interest sorely missed in many later *kaiju eiga*. Without such context, even the best-executed monster effects scenes generate no real tension or drama. Although their roles are more caricatures than characters, the cast proves likeable. But most of the film's entertainment quotient is provided by its striking, evocative visuals and its nonstop supply of charmingly kooky variations along familiar themes. For instance, rather than working furiously to devise a way to destroy the monster, the scientists in *Mothra* try to *communicate* with it. In the final act, Bulldog realizes that prayers and songs operate on the same wavelength as the Twins' telepathic link — an idea that's utter nonsense and yet oddly poetic.

It's no wonder that this remains one of the most beloved of Toho's monster epics. Hitting an artistic high note, and earning some serious coin at the box office, *Mothra* not only rescued the Ito twins, but also saved the *kaiju eiga*.

The Mummy's Shroud (1967; Hammer/ 20th Century–Fox; U.K.) Director/Screenplay: John Gilling; Producer: Anthony Nelson Keys; Cinematographer: Arthur Grant. Cast: Andre Morrell, John Phillips, David Buck, Elizabeth Sellars, Michael Ripper, Catherine Lacey, Maggie Kimblerley.

Beware the beat of the cloth-wrapped feet!
—tagline

Although widely (and deservedly) considered one of the most defect-riddled products to emerge from the Hammer Films fright factory, *The Mummy's Shroud* is not entirely dysfunctional. It's derivative, slow-paced and indifferently crafted, but it includes isolated sequences that work well and a matched set of outstanding performances that almost make it worth the slog.

Stanley Preston (John Philips), the wealthy financier of an Egyptian archeological expedition, arrives in Cairo to organize search parties for his team of archeologists, feared lost in a sandstorm. The self-promoting Preston, with media fanfare orchestrated by his nebbish press secretary Longbarrow (Michael Ripper), joins in the search personally. But by the time they reach the expedition the archeologists are safe and have discovered the hidden tomb of a deposed boy pharaoh, Kah-to-Bey. The tomb, naturally, is cursed, and protected by a band of zealots who cling to the ancient Egyptian religion. Once Kah-to-Bey's mummy is removed to Cairo, Preston has the expedition's leader, Sir Basil (Andre Morrell), committed to a sanitarium and tries to take credit for the discovery himself. Meanwhile, an Egyptian cultist, reciting magic words from a shroud that covered the pharaoh's body, reanimates the hulking mummy of Kah-to-Bey's protector, Prem (Eddie Powell). Prem begins murdering everyone who entered the tomb, beginning with Sir Basil.

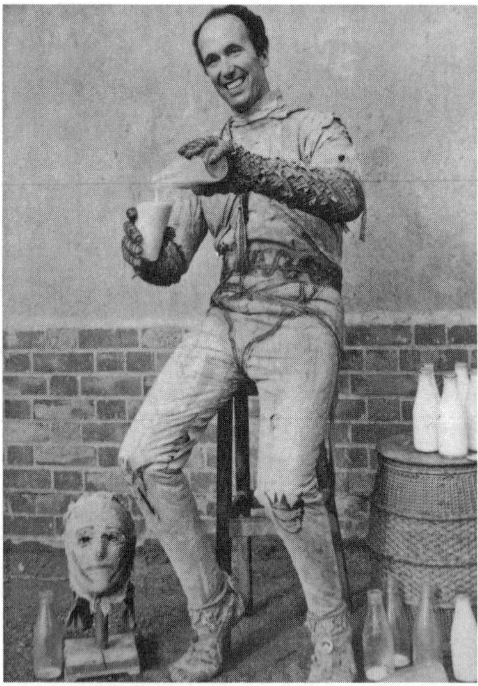

"Milk—it does a mummy good." Stuntman Eddie Powell takes a refreshment break during filming of *The Mummy's Shroud* (1967).

The Mummy's Shroud trots out every cliché in the history of mummy movies, from its cursed tomb to its magic artifact capable of restoring life to the mummy to its murderous band of Egyptian cultist holdouts, and on and on. The picture might have succeeded if its hackneyed hokum were executed in some fresh or particularly stylish way. Unfortunately, director John Gilling fails to muster any of the visual flair he brought to films such as *Mania* (1960) and *Plague of the Zombies* (1966). His work here is strictly by the dog-eared book. Production values fall a notch or two below the usual Hammer standard, especially the cut-rate sets and costumes employed during a protracted, 8-minute flashback to ancient Egypt that opens the film, as well as Powell's blank-faced, generic-looking mummy mask. (The studio could have found more convincing masks for sale in the back pages of *Famous Monsters* magazine.)

Nevertheless, once Prem finally sets about his gruesome business (45 minutes into this 86-minute film), *Shroud* finally begins to pick up steam. A couple of the murders are chillingly effective—especially that of Longbarrow, who (without his glasses) can't see the mummy and doesn't understand what's happening.

However, the movie's most enjoyable element by far are the amusing Punch-and-Judy portrayals of John Phillips and Michael Ripper as the cold, domineering Preston and the fidgety, browbeaten Longbarrow. Even though Preston is, essentially, the story's villain, he makes an excellent comic foil for his nervously chatty, easily intimidated assistant. Although playing a primarily comedic part, Ripper enjoys some touching moments later in the film when Longbarrow becomes almost giddy at the prospect of returning to England, only to have those dreams crushed by the heartless Preston. Along with his work in *The Reptile* and *Night Creatures*, this is one of the ever-reliable Ripper's very best performances. Phillips is equally impressive as the ruthless, headline-grabbing Preston. The two play off one another marvelously.

Shroud wastes the gifted Morrell in a do-nothing role and then kills him off at the close of the story's first act. (It's perplexing that Morrell accepted this inglorious assignment but rejected Hammer's infinitely superior *Five Million Years to Earth.*) Catherine Lacey leaves an appropriately bizarre impression in her small role as a weird, drooling gypsy fortune teller. None of the rest of the cast stands out.

Aside from the performances of Phillips and Ripper, and a few rare moments of frisson, *The Mummy's Shroud* contains little even for diehard Hammer devotees to cling to. At least the picture's advertising tagline ("Beware the beat of the cloth-wrapped feet!") was catchy. Does that count?

Munster, Go Home! (1966; Universal) Director: Earl Bellamy; Producers: Joe Connelly, Bob Masher; Screenplay: George Tribbles, Joe Connelly and Bob Masher; Cinematographer: Benjamin H. Kline. Cast: Fred Gwynne, Yvonne De Carlo, Al Lewis, Butch Patrick, Debbie Watson, Terry-Thomas, Hermione Gingold; Robert Pine, Maria Lennard, John Carradine.

America's Funniest Family in their FIRST FULL-LENGTH FEATURE — tagline

---

The Munsters, a situation comedy produced by Universal Studios and featuring cartoonish parodies of its classic monster characters, made its television debut on CBS in 1964. After a successful first season, the series was clobbered by ABC's new hit *Batman* during its second campaign and cancelled after 70 episodes. *Munster, Go Home!*, a Technicolor theatrical feature, was Universal's first attempt to resurrect the franchise.

The film reunites a houseful of amiable creatures: Herman Munster (Fred Gwynne), aka the Frankenstein Monster; Lily Munster (Yvonne De Carlo) and Grandpa (Al Lewis), a pair of vampires; Herman and Lily's son Eddie (Butch Patrick), a werewolf; and Lily's niece, Marilyn (Debbie Watson), the only non-monstrous Munster. Despite all its macabre trappings, conceptually *The Munsters* strongly resembled *The Beverly Hillbillies* (another CBS series), with nearly all its humor arising from the displacement of an eccentric but loving, multi-generational family into an environment ill-prepared to cope with them. Like the Clampetts, the Munsters consider themselves normal, well-adjusted citizens. They try to be good neighbors and often wonder why other people act so strangely in their presence. *Munster, Go Home!* brings this similarity to *The Beverly Hillbillies* into sharper relief with a plotline that involves Herman Munster (like Jed Clampett) coming into unexpected wealth, then loading up his family and moving — not to Beverly Hills, but to an English manor.

A wealthy, distant British uncle dies and leaves Herman the family estate and title of Lord Munster. While Herman, Lily, Grandpa, Eddie and Marilyn board a transatlantic liner, Herman's English cousins— Lady Effigie (Hermione Gingold), Freddie (Terry-Thomas), Millie (Maria Lennard) and their butler Cruickshank (John Carradine)— plot to bump Herman claim the fortune for themselves. During the ocean voyage Marilyn strikes up a romance with Roger (Robert Pine), a British race car diver who turns out to be the son of Squire Moresby (Bernard Fox), who is embroiled in a generations-long feud with the Munster clan. Later, Herman and Grandpa discover that someone is operating a counterfeit ring out of Munster Manor. The whole business concludes with a slapstick auto race.

The film plays like an elongated episode of the TV series, albeit with somewhat higher production values, most notably Benjamin H. Kline's splashy color lighting scheme. The comedy relies mostly on juvenile word play (Lily gets "vulture bumps" instead of goose bumps) and sight gags (like Eddie's coffin-shaped surf board). Gwynne, De Carlo, Lewis and Patrick simply carry forward their shtick from the show, and Debbie Watson, replacing TV's Pat Priest as Marilyn, remains as forgettable as her counterpart. Among the performers added for the film, only Terry-Thomas stands out as the infantile but homicidal Freddie, who throws tantrums and sucks his thumb, yet sleeps with a revolver beneath his pillow. Keen-eyed fans of classic TV will spot Richard Dawson (Corp. Newkirk from *Hogan's Heroes*) in a minor role.

Perhaps because the series had so recently flopped, or more likely because it's simply not very funny, *Munster, Go Home!* sank like a stone at the box office. Yet, despite the film's failure and the brevity of their life on CBS, the Munsters refused to stay dead. The series gained great popularity in syndication and enjoyed numerous other revivals, beginning with the animated movie *The Mini-Munsters* (1973) and continuing with *The Munsters' Revenge* (1983), which reunited the original cast of the series. The success of that telefilm prompted Universal to produce *The Munsters Today*, a syndicated series featuring a new cast, which ran from 1988 to 1991. While generally considered inferior to the original *Munsters*, *The Munsters Today* ran two episodes longer than the first series and also spawned two TV movies, *Here Come the Munsters* (1995) and *The Munsters' Scary Little Christmas* (1996).

If you're a Munsters devotee, you'll probably enjoy *Munster, Go Home!* If not, this picture is unlikely to convert you. Your authors confess a preference for *The Addams Family*.

Murder Clinic (1966/68; Europix; Italy) Original Title: *La Lama nel Corpo* (*The Knife in the Body*); Alternate Title: *Revenge of the Living Dead* (U.S. reissue). Director/Producer: Elio Scardamaglia; Screenplay: Ernesto Gastaldi (as Julian Barry) and Luciano Martino (as Martin Hardy) (Novel: Robert Williams); Cinematography: Marcello Masciocchi. Cast: William Berger, Françoise Prevost, Mary Young, Barbara Wilson, Philippe Hersent, Harriet Medin (as Harriet White).

The obscure *Murder Clinic*— which the authors of this book were unable to locate for review— appears to combine elements of the Italian gothic and giallo horror styles. Although set in a classic gothic location (1870s London), the plot (about a hooded, razor-wielding maniac who murders helpless hospital patients) remains pure giallo. Those who have seen the film hardly lavish it with praise, but usually find kind remarks for Marcello Masciocchi's Technicolor cinematography or other isolated elements. "Although nowhere near as lyrical as Riccardo Freda, Mario Bava or even Antonio Margheriti's work the film does show some flair in the editing," reports editor Phil Hardy's *Overlook Film Encyclopedia: Horror*. *Murder Clinic*, based on Robert Williams' novel *The Knife in the Body*, was successful enough to earn a re-release in 1972 under the misleading title *Revenge of the Living Dead*.

With quotes from: *The Overlook Film Encyclopedia: Horror*, Phil Hardy, editor.

Mutiny in Outer Space (1965; Woolner Brothers; b&w) Director: Hugo Grimaldi; Producers: Hugo Grimaldi, Arthur C. Pierce; Screenplay: Hugo Grimaldi (original story: Arthur C. Pierce, Hugo Grimaldi); Cinematography: Archie Dalzell. Cast: William Leslie, Delores Faith, Pamela Curran, Richard Garland, Harold Lloyd, Jr.

"Discover the monstrous horror from the Moon threatening to destroy everything it touches, the fiendish force that ignited the loves, the hates, the passions of the explorers in space!"— trailer

Though produced in the mid–1960s, *Mutiny in Outer Space* looks— and acts— like it was made 10 years earlier. Perhaps it's the derivative "borrowings" from various 1950s horror flicks that make the supposed futuristic *Mutiny* (set in the far-flung 1990s!) look backwards rather than forward. Or perhaps it's the black-and-white photography, coming at a time when even low-budget features such as this one were turning to color. Or perhaps it's the sexist 1950s-style attitudes of the male space-crew towards their female counterparts. In any case, *Mutiny in Outer Space* feels like it sprang not so much from the Age of Aquarius as the Age of Eisenhower.

Ice samples found on the Moon are brought back to the orbiting Space Station X-7 for study. Unfortunately, a deadly fungus that consumes living cells tags along. (This provides the film's single startling moment— a gruesome shot of the one-

Despite its psychedelic sixties poster, *Mutiny in Outer Space* (1965) feels like a throwback to the previous decade.

and-only fungus victim, one dead eye staring from the ghastly spongy mass that has become his face.) Meanwhile, the station's commander (stodgily played by the dour Richard Garland), suffering from the effects of prolonged weightlessness, develops a persecution complex, hallucinates, threatens the safety of the station, and ultimately scampers about committing sabotage (prompting the "mutiny" of the film's title). But *The Caine Mutiny* this ain't, and shunting aside the all-consuming fungus for long stretches to deal with the commander gives the film a disjointed — and prosaic — feel. Ultimately the fungus (Spanish moss, actually) takes over the station, both inside and out, and the crew must come up with a way to combat the deadly intruder.

Though officially credited to director/producer Hugo Grimaldi, *Mutiny*'s script was actually penned by low-budget horror/sci-fi veteran Arthur C. Pierce (at least according to Pierce himself, who also at one point claimed credit for the film's *direction* as well!). Given Pierce's track record (*The Cosmic Man, Invasion of the Animal People, Beyond the Time Barrier, The Human Duplicators, Destination Inner Space, Women of the Prehistoric Planet*), it's no wonder *Mutiny*'s screenplay looks like it was cobbled together from bits stolen from earlier films, with *The Blob* and *Space-Master X-7* being two of the most obvious victims. Pierce even lifts the Blob's Achilles heel, cold (and includes a completely random demonstration with a fire extinguisher!), and shamelessly names his space station "X-7"!

Misleadingly goofy American poster for the superior horror peplum *My Son, the Hero* (1962/63).

The totally inadequate 6-day shooting schedule allotted only one day for all the miniature work. It shows. If the cheap, plastic-looking model of the spinning-wheel space station was any indicator, one would never guess that the realism of *2001: A Space Odyssey* was just around the corner.

Director Grimaldi (or Pierce, if he is to be believed) tries to hide his cheesy sets' many shortcomings by utilizing some wholly inappropriate but occasionally atmospheric low-key lighting. While such dim illumination seems ridiculous on a working space station, the shadowy atmosphere does help prop up the paper-thin wall of suspense and menace.

Still, it's a good bet that many viewers will nip this cut-rate *Mutiny* in the bud before it ever gets rolling — not by any power of the court, but by the power of their own remote.

My Son, the Hero

My Son, the Hero (1962/3; Vides Cinematografica/United Artists; Italy/France) Original Language Title: *Arrivano i Titani*. Alternate Titles: *The Titans*; *Sons of Thunder* (UK). Director: Duccio Tessari; Producer: Alexandre Mnouchkine; Screenplay: Ennio De Concini, Duccio Tessari; Cinematographer: Alfio Contini. Cast: Pedro Armendariz, Giuliano Gemma, Antonlla Lualdi, Serge Nubret, Jacqueline Sassard.

> Smarter than a fox! Braver than a lion!
> Cuter than a pussy cat! — poster

The silly tagline on the *My Son, the Hero*'s cartoonish American poster rather overstates the case for this unique take on the Italian muscleman movie. While it does offer a lighter tone than most pepla, and spotlights a hero who relies more on his wits than his biceps (though he still holds his own in the palace guard-tossing department), it's no mere live-action cartoon. In fact, *My Son, the Hero* is refreshingly rife with often-creepy supernatural elements (many right out of Greek mythology), making it one of the more entertaining entries in this generally moribund subgenre.

When Cadmo (Pedro Armendari), the evil king of Crete murders his wife in order to marry his mistress, the gods take notice and send an oracle to warn him that he will die once his infant daughter grows to womanhood and falls in love. (As insurance, they stipulate that should he kill his child, his heart will cease to beat when hers does.) Some 18 years later, the sequestered princess has never seen a man. Now the gods decide to release from hell the youngest (and smartest) of the demi-god Titans, Krios (Giuliano Gemma), to exact (belated) vengeance on Cadmo. Krios is made mortal and instructed to bring about the demise of Cadmo. Krios subsequently insinuates himself into the king's court, and even falls in love with the forbidden princess, before he's aided by his fellow Titan brothers in a final battle against the king and his invincible soldiers.

Unlike most musclemen heroes, such as Hercules, Maciste, Goliath, et al, Krios utilizes his brain more than his brawn, and displays a definite sense of humor about things (which peplum purveyors like Steve Reeves, Kirk Morris and Gordon Mitchell generally lacked). As a result, the classical storyline takes on a breezier tone, which serves to bring the darker elements into sharp relief when they arise. And arise they do, in the form of such supernatural horrors as two separate trips to hell (complete with classical Greek torments), a cadre of invincible soldiers (bloody, mortal sword wounds miraculously disappear as they rise to continue the fight), and a tense confrontation with a Gorgon. (Despite the mythical monster's disappointingly mundane appearance — looking like nothing more than a mildly unattractive woman with a few garter snakes woven into her hair — director Duccio Tessari generates some horrific atmosphere and genuine suspense through low-angle camerawork and clever editing). Then there's the horrific "Most Dangerous Game" interlude in which Cadmus hunts down a human prisoner like an animal for sport.

Giuliano Gemma (nee "Montgomery Wood") makes for a far more engaging hero than the standard Muscle Beach denizens generally cast in pepla. Gemma, who traded in his leather loincloth for a pair of six-guns a few years later to become a staple in Spaghetti Westerns (including several *Ringo* titles), possesses not only a pleasing screen presence, but genuine acting ability, as demonstrated over his nearly five-decades-long career in Italian cinema. His natural charm, relaxed demeanor before the camera (many peplum purveyors look stiff and uncomfortable on-camera, even the supposed sword-and-sandal "king," Steve Reeves) and surprising litheness (including some impressive trampoline-style acrobatics on market awnings as he amusingly eludes pursuing soldiers) helps make *My Son, the Hero* one of the more enjoyable Euro He-Man movies of the decade.

Mysterious Island (1961; Columbia; U.S./U.K.) Director: Cy Endfield; Producer: Charles H. Schneer; Screenplay: John Prebble, Daniel Ullman, Crane Wilbur; Cinematographer: Wilkie Cooper. Cast: Michael Craig, Gary Merrill, Michael Callan, Percy Herbert, Herbert Lom, Joan Greenwood, Beth Rogan, Dan Jackson.

YOU ARE PLUNGED INTO PREHISTORIC ADVENTURE AMID MONSTROUS FLORA AND FAUNA AS AN EPIC OF EXCITEMENT ERUPTS BEFORE YOUR STARTLED EYES!
— ad line

Had this movie's protagonists known where they would end up — facing the terrors and tribulations of the titular *Mysterious Island*— they would undoubtedly have abandoned their plan to escape their Richmond, Virginia, Confederate prison camp. Based on the 1874 Jules Verne novel *L'lle Mysterieuse* (a sequel to the author's *20,000 Leagues Under the Sea*), the film's story has a group of Civil War soldiers steal a hot-air balloon during a howling storm. After a long airborne voyage, they end up on a tropical island inhabited by gigantic animals (created by Captain Nemo and his advanced science). There they must use their ingenuity to survive not only the more mundane natural elements, but also marauding pirates; colossal crabs, birds and bees; and even an erupting volcano.

An exciting, colorful, and straightforward fantasy-adventure aimed squarely at the juvenile set, *Mysterious Island* has it all: a thrilling prison break; an exciting and perilous balloon journey; Robinson Crusoe-like exploits (including fending off an attack by pirates!); a race against time involving an erupting volcano; assorted fantastic Ray Harryhausen stop-motion creations; the ruins of a lost civilization; and even Captain Nemo himself and his amazing submarine, the *Nautilis*. Besides this surfeit of exhilarating activity, what sets *Mysterious Island* apart from — and above — its contemporaries is its serious attitude (courtesy of then-blacklisted Hollywood director Cy [*Zulu*] Endfield) and beautiful attention to detail (thanks to Harryhausen's meticulous influence). While the film's intended audience may be juveniles, the movie's tone never stoops to that level. There's no precocious and irritating pre-teen; no simplistic pat plot devices; and no out-of-place puerile humor (what laughs arise do so naturally out of the situations). *Mysterious Island* is a mature-minded fantasy that appeals to pre-teens and adults alike.

Courtesy of Ray Harryhausen's amazing stop-motion animation techniques, Gary Merrill, Michael Craig and Michael Callan (left to right) are menaced by one of the giant denizens of the *Mysterious Island* (1961) (courtesy Lynn Naron).

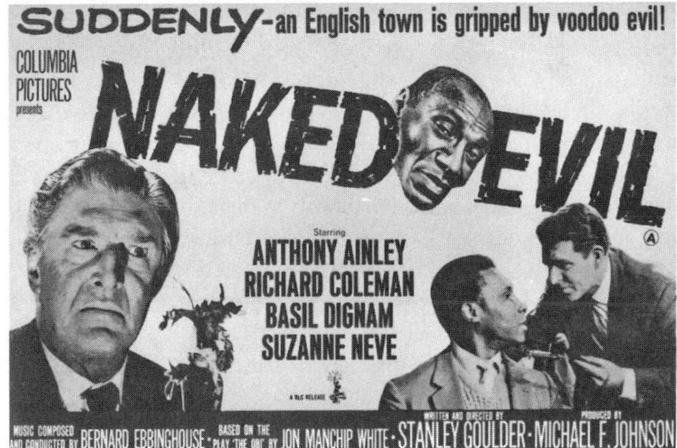

An atmospheric amalgam of British gangsters and Jamaican voodoo (1966).

Though the characters are largely cut from stock cloth, the players dress them up with enough personality to make them memorable, particularly Gary Merrill as the cynical and world-weary war correspondent, and Herbert Lom as the supremely confidant and cultured Nemo. And while many of the miniatures (the balloon, the volcano, the undersea ruins) appear to be just that (with the never-quite-convincing insertion of stock footage of real eruptions detracting further from the verisimilitude), the picture never loses its charm or aura of exotica—a fantastical aura built upon the backs of Harryhausen's wonderful creatures. Harryhausen originally intended to populate his mysterious island with dinosaurs, but abandoned this Lost World concept to update the story via Nemo and his experiments with gigantism. To this end, Harryhausen created set-pieces involving a giant crab (a real crab shell—bought at Harrod's department store—with a stop-motion armature placed inside), a giraffe-sized hopping bird (a holdover from the "prehistoric" concept, as it's really a "phororhacos"), a huge bee trapping some protagonists inside a colossal honeycomb, and a mammoth cephalopod (another prehistoric throwback)—all staged with Harryhausen's trademark flair for action and convincing attention to detail. (Harryhausen labeled the thrilling crab sequence as "one of my favorites.")

Of the phororhacos, Harryhausen wrote in his *Film Fantasy Scrapbook*: "Originally, the bird was to have an antediluvian background, but owing to some script deletions its origin was discarded. Most reviewers and audiences assumed it to be an overgrown chicken. Its awkward movements turned it into a 'comedian.' However, a good laugh in the story was a pleasant relief from all of the melodramatic thrills of the rest of the film."

Chock full of "good laughs" and "melodramatic thrills," *Mysterious Island* remains a real treat for the adventure-loving 12-year-old inside all of us.

Naked Evil (1966; Columbia/Hampton International; U.K.; b&w and tinted) Alternate Title: *Exorcism at Midnight* (U.S. TV); Director/Screenwriter: Stanley Goulder (based on the play *The Obi* by Jon Manchip White); Producer: M. F. Johnson; Cinematographer: Geoffrey Faithful. Cast: Basil Dignam, Anthony Ainley, Suzanne Neve, Richard Coleman, Olof Pooley, George A. Saunders, Lawrence Tierney (*Exorcism at Midnight* version only).

... Your nightmares are suddenly alive and shove you screaming to the bottomless pit of Hell ... There is No Escape!—ad line

Rarely seen and even less talked about, the British *Naked Evil* is a diamond-in-the-rough that has slipped pass the notice of genre fans. It's a pity, since *Naked Evil* is an original, suspenseful and engaging horror offering from the 1960s, one that holds the viewer's interest with intelligent handling and atmospheric staging.

The film was designed as a low-budget (about £60,000) British program filler to be shot in four weeks. "This was made as a quota picture," explained executive producer Richard Gordon, "to fulfill a certain requirement by Columbia to fill a certain slot because they needed to have a certain amount of British product in distribution."

Though based on a play called *The Obi*, Gordon didn't feel that that rather non-threatening moniker lent itself well to exploitation, and his partner, Steve Pallos, came up with *Naked Evil*. "I thought it was a very good title," said Gordon. Indeed it was, for as well as being mildly titillating, it captured the tone of the film very well—the idea of a raw, overpowering force of malignancy.

In the black section of an English town, a drug-dealing gangster uses Jamaican Obeah (a variation of voodoo) to decimate his competitor's ranks. To accomplish this, he sends his intended victims a dreaded obi (a bottle filled with graveyard dirt and "muck," topped with feathers). "With an obi, smash the bottle and you unleash the devil," explains one character. Three men have succumbed to the evil magic already ("a fall from a window of a locked room, a frightened man dashing in front of a bus, and yet another found in the canal"). Meanwhile, at a nearby university hostel for "colored students," its operator, Mr. Benson (Basil Dignam), receives a dreaded obi. It soon comes to light that the mysterious "obi-man" is the hostel's unsavory Jamaican caretaker, who's been selling his magic to the gangster (and applying it to Benson as well, since he knows the headmaster is about to fire him). Things soon go awry, culminating in death, possession, and exorcism.

Director Stanley Goulder's clever staging and cinematographer Geoffrey Faithful's atmospheric lighting and camerawork weave a palpable spell of evil around the sinister events. Goulder fills *Naked Evil* with eerie touches. When one character drops an obi bottle into the basement furnace, the cellar door suddenly slams shut and the dangling light swings as if pushed by an unseen force. Even the credits sequence builds a macabre atmosphere when, as the credits roll, the camera silently prowls through a church graveyard at night, coming to rest at a graveside where we see a mysterious hand placing fistfuls of dirt into a shoebox.

British movies from this period are generally very well acted, and *Naked Evil* is no exception. Worthy of note is Basil Dignam as Benson. His natural and authoritative delivery does much to lend conviction to the strange events. Dignam's familiar face and steady presence added to such pictures as *The Creeping Unknown* (1955), *Corridors of Blood* (1958), *Gorgo* (1961) and *Lawrence of Arabia* (1962).

Unfortunately, *Naked Evil*'s rather schizophrenic construction tends to weaken the film's overall impact and undermines Goulder and Faithful's careful staging. The more mundane gangster scenes and subplot (with the wiseguys complaining about their "business" troubles on cheap nightclub sets) seem dull and out of place next to the more fantastical Obeah angle.

"I'd thought it would be a real horror picture, and that there would be much more use made of the voodoo stuff and less of the gangsterism and all that," lamented Gordon. "It's not what I would really call a genre picture in its present form. It's sort of neither fish nor fowl." Despite Gordon's regrets, it's still a fairly tasty bird.

In England, Columbia released *Naked Evil* as intended (as a supporting feature in black and white). In the United States, however, things didn't go quite as planned. Robert Saxton of Hampton International took the film and *tinted* it, coloring scenes variously red, green, blue and amber. "Saxton's release publicity said it was in 'Evil Color,'" laughed Gordon, "which I thought was a nice gimmick. It promised a lot but didn't guarantee anything." Nor did this unfortunate and unnecessary tinting *deliver* anything—except occasional confusion and eyestrain. Hampton International soon went bankrupt, and, after some initial spotty distribution, *Naked Evil* ended up on drive-in triple features put out by Sam Sherman's Independent International. In the late 1970s Sherman further bastardized the film by adding some new, full-color footage (starring a terribly miscast Lawrence Tierney as a psychiatrist[!] and shot in one day for about $5,000) before selling it to television as *Exorcism at Midnight*.

With quotes from: *Drums of Terror: Voodoo in the Cinema*, by Bryan Senn.

The Naked Goddess see ***The Devil's Hand***

The Naked Temptress see ***The Naked Witch***

The Naked Witch (1964; Alexander Enterprises) Directors/screenplay: Larry Buchanan and Claude Alexander; Producer: Claude Alexander; Cinematographer: Ralph Johnson. Cast: Jo Maryman, Robert Short, Libby Hall, Denis Adams, Charles West, Jack Herman, Howard Ware, Marilyn Pope, Der Saengerbund Children's Choir.

THE STORY OF THE WITCH WHO BECAME RESTLESS IN HER GRAVE — ad line

Don't confuse this no-budget indy, the first horror movie by Texas-based schlockmeister Larry Buchanan, with that *other Naked Witch* from 1964, the first horror movie by Staten Island-based schlockmeister Andy Milligan. (Yes, believe it or not, two naked witches were seen cavorting on the big screen in 1964; unfortunately, neither of them were much to look at.)

Buchanan's film begins with an eight-minute prologue in which a narrator (an unbilled Gary Owens!) oh-so-dramatically provides a discourse on witchcraft using period Bosch and Brueghel paintings as illustration, and soap opera-style organ music as punctuation. Once the time-eating intro concludes, the story proper, set in "the hill country of central Texas," commences, as a college student (Robert Short) journeys to the (real) German-themed Texas town of Luchenbach (in which the lederhosen- and dirndl-wearing locals speak pidgin Deutsch and live the simple life of German farmers) to research local customs and legends. Inadvertently reviving "the Luchenbach Witch" (by digging up her grave and removing the stake from her corpse out of "curiosity"), the student falls under her spell as she seeks vengeance on the descendants of those who condemned her to death over a century before.

As might be expected from the inaugural effort of the man who brought us *Zontar the Thing from Venus* and *Mars Needs Women*, *The Naked Witch* offers little beyond amateurish acting (particularly from the bland male lead), a locked-down camera, laughable special effects (a few crude stop-camera shots of a plastic fright mask for the big "resurrection" scene), toneless narration (negating the need for live sound or post-production looping), and a snail's pace (the movie is half over before the witch rises; she then, apart from committing two coyly-shot murders, does little but walk, bathe, and dance seductively — or tries to, anyway).

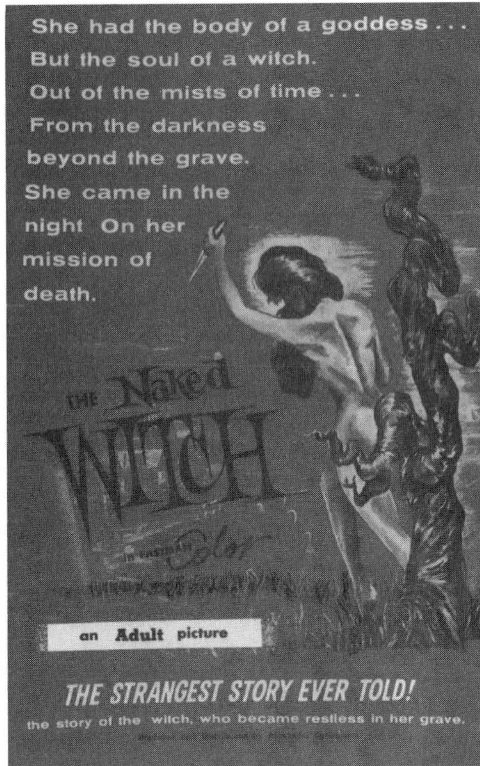

Salacious advertising for Larry Buchanan's debut feature, *The Naked Witch* (1964).

And while said witch (Libby Hall, wearing Tammy Faye-style glamour makeup, all penciled-in eyebrows and bright red lipstick) does initially walk about naked, a fuzzy black censor bar (added by the distributor) obfuscates the salacious spots. She soon steals a black nightie anyway, becoming the Nightgowned Witch. However, *some* truth in advertising shines through, as a later sequence of her bathing in a pond offers a few teasing glimpses of her less-than-ample charms.

One bit of interest arises when the heroine asks the student, "But what pleasure can you get from studying about all this [witchcraft]?" To this he replies: "To better understand the witch hunts we have today. You would think that after the delusions of New England and early Texas, the urge to hunt witches would have disappeared from the Western world, but nothing of the kind. The medieval idea of witchcraft was replaced by things like race and nationality." But this brief snippet of topical social commentary is as far as it goes.

In a conversation with video entrepreneur Mike Vraney (of Something Weird Video), producer Claude Alexander repeatedly dismissed *The Naked Witch* as "Larry's home movie," and he's not far wrong. On the film's DVD commentary track, Buchanan himself called it "one of those desperate movies we make when we want to be movie makers and we have nowhere to go, and no funding, and no *nothing*." While one can applaud Buchanan's determination, it takes a far more forgiving soul to applaud the result. About the kindest thing one can say of *The Naked Witch* is that it lasts a mere 59 minutes.

Filmed in color in 16mm for a mere $8,000 in 1961, *The Naked Witch* didn't see release until 1964, and then usually in *black and white* (since it was far cheaper to strike monochromatic prints than full-color ones). Years later, on the drive-in circuit, Buchanan's no-budget opus frequently played the lower half of a double bill with the far superior *The Legend of Witch Hollow* (a retitled *The Witchmaker*).

The Naked Witch (1967) Alternate Title: *The Naked Temptress*. Director/Producer/Cinematographer: Andy Milligan, Screenplay: Clay Guss. Cast: Beth Porter, Robert Burgos, Bryarly Lee, Lee Forbes, Maggie Rogers.

Clothes cramped the style of the Naked Witch!—tagline

Not to be confused with Larry Buchanan's 1961 shocker also titled *The Naked Witch*, this ultra-low-budget nudie chiller—produced, directed and photographed by schlock maven Andy Milligan—appears to be lost. The film seems to have played like an X-rated rip-off of *The Hunchback of Notre Dame*. An attractive young woman named Beth (Beth Porter) is shunned by local townsfolk because her mother conducted orgiastic ceremonies and was burned at the stake as a witch. Beth carries on a secret affair with a sailor (Robert Burgos) and befriends a mute hunchback known only as the Dumb One (Lee Forbes). When a devious rival, Bella (Bryarly Lee), falsely convinces villagers that Beth is continuing her mother's Satanic debauchery, the enraged townspeople try to burn her at the stake but the Dumb One comes to her rescue. Milligan shot the film entirely on location in tiny Manasquan, New Jersey, with a skeleton crew and a semi-professional cast. "Those who saw the film claim it was Milligan's most visually arresting," writes Milligan biographer Jimmy McDonough. "Adding to the stark quality was the fact that it was shot in the middle of a bitter snow and rain storm, which made the coastal location look even more foreign and remote." Co-star Robert Burgos reports that Beth Porter had "the biggest tits in the world," which might have been the most significant visual for the film's intended audience.

With quotes from: *The Ghastly One: The Sex-Gore Netherworld of Andy Milligan*, by Jimmy McDonoough.

The Nanny (1965; Hammer/Seven Arts; U.K.; b&w) Director: Seth Holt; Producer/Screenplay: Jimmy Sangster (from a novel by Evelyn Piper); Cinematographer: Harry Waxman. Cast: Bette Davis, Wendy Craig, Jill Bennett, James Villiers, William Dix, Pamela Franklin.

Another memorable Davis portrait!—tagline

Immaculately crafted and beautifully performed, *The Nanny* marked a truly grand finale for Hammer Films' on-again, off-again series of black-and-white psychological thrillers.

Ten-year-old Joey (William Dix) returns home after spending two years in a mental institution for allegedly drowning his younger sister. Joey's parents (James Villiers and Wendy Craig) fear their son may be unbalanced; he seems antisocial and

When *The Nanny* (1965) is an unhinged Bette Davis, you'd do well to trust the boy...

is given to paranoid-sounding accusations against the family's kindly and dutiful nanny (Bette Davis). Joey blames Nanny for his sister's death, and claims that the servant is now trying to kill him. He refuses to eat any food she prepares out of fear of poisoning and won't bathe unless Nanny swears not to sneak into the bathroom and try to drown him.

Then his mother is poisoned, and the evidence points to Joey. Nevertheless Joey again blames Nanny — and this time his Aunt Penelope (Jill Bennett) and Joey's friend, Bobbie (Pamela Franklin), a 14-year-old upstairs neighbor, wonder if he might be telling the truth. The film's spine-tingling final 20 minutes include a flashback that reveals Nanny as a more conflicted and motivationally complex character than at first it appears.

The Nanny's virtues are many, but chief among them are its finely tuned script (among the career-best for prolific producer-screenwriter Jimmy Sangster) and the uniformly outstanding performances of its cast.

Sangster's screenplay, adapted from Evelyn Piper's novel, establishes credible dramatic tension — not only between Joey and Nanny, but also between the boy and his parents—from the outset and sustains it throughout. The lone questionable aspect of the scenario is its unorthodox finale. While it's original and transforms Nanny from a stock villain into a three-dimensional personality, it may seem somewhat anti-climactic after so much sustained suspense. Although the Nanny character would have suffered, a more conventional resolution might have better served the film. As it stands, *The Nanny* remains a movie packed with rich, believably sketched characters and pitch-perfect dialogue. The scenes in which Joey and Bobbie strike up their friendship are especially impressive, since writing young characters well always presents special difficulties. This is an altogether marvelous outing for Sangster, all the more so since his creative well appeared to have run dry after his substandard, unimaginative scripts for *Nightmare* (1964) and *Hysteria* (1965).

The cast recognized what a golden vein Sangster's script represented, and they mine it for all its riches. The supporting players are all excellent: Villiers as Joey's domineering, aloof father; Wendy Craig as his simpering, child-like mother; Jill Bennett as the free-spirited but sickly Aunt Penelope; and Pamela Franklin as Bobbie, beginning to grasp the power of her blossoming womanhood. The title role offered Davis the rangiest of all the "horror hag" parts she would undertake following *What Ever Happened to Baby Jane?* (1962). Her quietly sinister demeanor grounds the entire feature. Davis' Nanny remains one of the best portrayals ever by an actress in a Hammer film. But, improbably, Dix proves her equal as young Joey. His likable, touching performance — full of childish bravado barely masking stark terror — was the finest to date by a child actor in a horror film, and would not be surpassed until Chris and Martin Udvarnoky's chilling work in *The Other* (1972).

Seth Holt's taught, efficient direction and Harry Waxman's exquisite, moody cinematography also deserve commendation. Holt later complained that Davis was a terror on the set. "Oh, it was hell!" he said. "She was always telling me how to direct. When I did it her way, she was scornful. When I stood up to her, she was hysterical." Sangster remembered it differently, and called Davis "the most professional actress I ever worked with." Sangster and Davis reunited (without Holt) for the painfully unfunny and deadly dull dark comedy *The Anniversary* (1968), in which Davis wore an eye patch — which is only appropriate since this misfire remains a black eye on the resumes of its writer and star.

Promoted as a Bette Davis vehicle rather than a Hammer chiller, *The Nanny* garnered glowing reviews and gangbuster box office. Despite its unqualified success, however, *The Nanny* proved to be the final Hammer psycho-thriller of the 1960s. During the first half of the decade, Hammer had split its genre output between its trademark glossy color gothics and smaller-budgeted black-and-white thrillers. But *She*, also released in 1965, represented the (curvaceous) shape of things to come. For whatever reason, the studio began to balance its gothic bread and butter with a steady diet of color fantasy pictures (*One Million Years B.C., Prehistoric Women, The Vengeance of She, The Lost Continent*, etc.), many of which prominently featured scantily clad starlets. Hitchcockian suspense was out; "Hammer glamour" was in. The studio wouldn't attempt another psychological thriller until *Crescendo* (1970/72).

None of that, however, dims the brilliance of *The Nanny*, which stands as one of Hammer's and Davis' most satisfying productions of the 1960s.

With quotes from: *Hammer Films: An Exhaustive Filmography*, by Tom Johnson and Deborah Del Vecchio.

The Navy vs. the Night Monsters (1966; Realart) Alternate Title: *Monsters of the Night* (U.K.); Director/Screenwriter: Michael Hoey; Producer: George Edwards; Cinematographer: Stanley Cortez. Cast: Mamie Van Doren, Anthony Eisley, Pamela Mason, Bill Gray, Bobby Van, Walter Sande.

Insert poster highlighting what happens when it's *The Navy vs. the Night Monsters* (1966).

TERRIFYING ACID BLEEDING MONSTERS READY TO CREMATE THE HUMAN RACE!!—ad line

---

A long-time staple of late-night TV, *The Navy vs. the Night Monsters* is a cut-rate color monster movie that remains more entertaining than it should be. Though filled with jarring edits, dialogue that comes out of nowhere, and cheesy studio "jungle" sets that look like rejects from a *Voyage to the Bottom of the Sea* episode, *Night Monsters* has gone on to become a fairly popular cult film.

Based on the 1959 pulp novel *The Monster from Earth's End* by Murray Leinster, the film was shot back-to-back (and on some of the same sets) with *Women of the Prehistoric Planet.* The story begins as a plane carrying a load of primitive carnivorous plants found in "the warm lakes area" of Antarctica crash lands at the naval base on Gow Island in the South Seas. There the trees flourish and go on a rampage, picking up their roots and moving about to eat as many cast members as they can lay their fronds on. Said members are led by fallen *Hawaiian Eye* TV star Anthony Eisley (as Lt. *Charlie Brown*!), blonde bombshell Mamie Van Doren, former MGM musical comedy star Bobby Van, and former child star Billy Gray (*The Day the Earth Stood Still*, TV's *Father Knows Best*).

The Navy vs. the Night Monsters is a strikingly visual film — not because of any efficacy on the part of first-time director/screenwriter Michael Hoey (son of character actor Dennis Hoey), whose straightforward staging could best be described as "mundane," but because of its amazingly garish color scheme. Vivid orange dirt, bright blue walls and cherry red oil drums predominate, and bizarrely intense red lighting turns this tropical island into a Mecca for Sixties-style sensibilities. To be fair, cinematographer Stanley Cortez (a loooong way from his heyday shooting films like *The Magnificent Ambersons*) does occasionally tone down the bright hues to create effectively low-key lighting in some of the more suspenseful sequences.

According to Anthony Eisley, the film was ruined by some severe tampering that took place after principal photography wrapped. Executive producer Jack Broder expected a 90-minute movie, and Hoey only delivered 78 minutes. So he had Arthur Pierce, the director of *Women of the Prehistoric Planet*, come in and shoot added scenes, including some boring banter between the plane's pilots and an unfunny sequence in which an inept sailor tries to inflate a weather balloon.

Former matinee idol Jon Hall also shot some additional monster scenes and a new finale.

"That picture, as Michael Hoey wrote and directed it," opined Eisley, "would have been a very good little thriller." Even without Broder's tampering, however, such a claim seems rather dubious. First off, in a movie about killer plants, said vegetation needs to be frightening. Sadly, these *Night Monsters* look more like barrel-shaped automated car-wash mechanisms (complete with long, limp strips hanging down) than terrifying tree-creatures. They're never really menacing—until a hapless victim *backs into one* (which happens at amazingly frequent intervals).

Character-wise, a love-triangle between the three principals (upon which Hoey spends an inordinate amount of time) never goes anywhere nor develops any real tension.

Sprinkled in with the banalities, however, are a few memorable moments—most of them centering on gruesome makeup (such as an acid burn victim courtesy of low-budget veteran Harry Thomas) or gory activity (in one scene Billy Gray's arm is torn from its socket and he staggers screaming into the jungle). And Hoey does manage a few instances of genuine suspense as various characters creep warily through the killer tree-infested jungle after dark.

The film was shot in 10 days for $178,000, according to Hoey, under the title *The Nightcrawlers* and released in the U.K. as *Monsters of the Night*. Whatever its moniker, it remains a risible yet oddly entertaining (in a snake-fascinating way) late-hour entry to the monster movie heyday of the 1950s and '60s.

With quotes from: *Interviews with B Science Fiction and Horror Movie Makers*, by Tom Weaver.

The Night Caller see *Blood Beast from Outer Space*

The Night Caller from Outer Space see *Blood Beast from Outer Space*

Night Fright (1967; independent) Alternate Title: *E.T.N.: The Extra Terrestrial Nasty* (home video). Director: James A. Sullivan; Producer: Wallace P. Clyce, Jr.; Screenplay: Russ Marker; Cinematographer: Robert C. Jessup. Cast: John Agar, Carol Gilley, Bill Thurman, Ralph Baker, Jr., Dorothy Davis, Roger Ready.

"I'll never forget the sight of those horrible mutations!"—Prof. Alan Clayton (Roger Ready)

For everyone who's ever endured a Larry Buchanan snooze-fest wondering, "What could be worse than this?" there is *Night Fright*.

Made in Dallas by several protégés of Buchanan, the Texan schlockmeister responsible for such awful films as *Free, White and 21* (1963) and *Zontar: The Thing from Venus* (1966), *Night Fright* functions on an almost unthinkably poor, sub–Buchanan level. Rookie director Jim Sullivan had served as Buchanan's production manager on *The Eye Creatures* (1965) and *Curse of the Swamp Creature* (1966), and cinematographer Bob Jessup shot Buchanan's *Mars Needs Women* and *In the Year 2889* (both 1967). Actor Bill Thurman, Roger Ready and Carol Gilley each appeared in multiple Buchanan productions. It's as if Buchanan's repertory company got fed up and decided, "Jeez, we can do better than this on our own!" Yet, against all odds, they failed.

When college lovebirds Chris (Ralph Baker, Jr.) and Judy (Dorothy Davis) discover two mutilated bodies near the site of a crashed NASA rocket, they call on Sheriff Clint Crawford (John Agar) and Deputy Ben Whitfield (Thurman) to investigate. Meanwhile, a bunch of Chris and Judy's classmates decide to throw a party at a secluded cabin also near the crash site. Finally, a professor from the local college (Roger Ready) reveals that the crashed spacecraft carried animals mutated by exposure to cosmic rays. One of the creatures remains at large.

Following in the Buchanan tradition, anything that might cost money to film—such as the crashed spaceship and bodies of the victims—is kept off screen. Instead, *Night Fright* gives us endless cheap-to-produce filler: romantic blather from Chris and Judy, scientific babble from Prof. Clayton, interminable shots of Crawford and Whitfield walking around in the woods, plus copious footage of dancing partygoers (grooving to the surf-rock instrumentals of "the Wildcats"). Even though early on Clayton and Crawford describe the monster as looking "like an alligator," once the creature finally appears, it turns out to be a guy in a ratty-looking gorilla suit and a jagged-fanged mask. Technically, the picture is substandard in every department, and the acting is mostly of the Amateur Hour variety. Gilley's tone-deaf portrayal of Crawford's love interest proves especially grating. Agar, looking thin and worn out here, lends his fading marquee value to the picture but little else; this may be his worst film. Only Thurman brings any sort of credibility to his (minor) role.

The credits for *Night Fright* don't list a production or distribution company (perhaps no one wanted to claim it), but the picture seems to have played drive-ins in the South and Southwest in the late 1960s. According to an entry on the All Movie Guide website, *Night Fright* was a remake of an earlier, even more obscure film (also penned by screenwriter Russ Marker) titled *The Devil from Demon Lake* (1964). That movie—if it ever existed—has vanished without a trace. But *Night Fright* resurfaced in the 1980s on home video under the title *E.T.N.: The Extra Terrestrial Nasty*, advertised as if it were a gory rip-off of Steven Spielberg's *E.T.* (1982). It was subsequently released to DVD (under its original title) by Alpha Video. By any other name, however, *Night Fright* would smell as foul.

Night of Bloody Horror (1969; Howco International) Director/Producer: Joy N. Houck, Jr. Screenplay: Robert A. Weaver, Joy N. Houck, Jr. Cinematographer: Robert A. Weaver. Cast: Gerald McRaney, Gaye Yellen, Herbert Nelson, Evelyn Hendricks.

A blood psycho goes berserk (at least according to this one-sheet poster) on the *Night of Bloody Horror* (1969).

Filmed in VIOLENT VISION—poster

"Filmed in GRAINY VISION" would have been more apt a descriptor for this low, low, low-budget *Psycho*-esque knock-off. To be fair, *Night of Bloody Horror* does present a trio of violent visions: a needle to the eye, an axe to the chest, and a cleaver to the wrist (with attendant limb separation). It also offers poor pacing and overlong scenes (one interminable close-up sequence of the protagonist kissing his latest conquest gives us far too much information about the pair's dental work); dim lighting; murky photography; tinny sound; over-the-top acting; and a tedious wind-down to an abrupt and perfunctory conclusion (which became obvious way back at minute 20).

The story follows young "stud" Wesley (the film opens with Wes and his girlfriend du jour doing the horizontal mamba, promising panting patrons more than the film ultimately delivers via its one teasing glimpse of feminine flesh), who has a problem—the girls he hooks up with end up murdered in gruesome fashion (cue the orb-piercing needle and torso-penetrating axe). With all fingers pointing at Wes himself (you see, he has headaches and blackouts and psychedelic spirals spinning over him to symbolize his tortured psyche, not to mention the fact that he spent 13 years in an *asylum* after accidentally shooting his younger brother to death!), his doting mother calls in Wes' former psychiatrist to help. Things go from bad to worse, however (in more ways than one), until the expected revelation wraps it all up in a nice, derivative bundle.

Producer/director/co-writer Joy N. Houck, Jr. (who's biggest claim to fame is perhaps another low-budget horror, the 1976 Bigfoot movie *Creature from Black Lake*), manages a few kitschy and questionable flourishes (the cheesy psychedelic spirals; the image of a sixties rock band [The Bored] switching back and forth between positive and negative while the zoom lens goes berserk; one scene transition looking like dripping blood; another scene closing on a pool of blood, with the next sequence opening on a bowl of tomato soup!). Then there's the beach scene in which an unseen assailant slams an axe into a bikini-clad woman's chest, with Wes coming upon the still-living victim moments later, only to squishily *remove* said axe (while crying and cradling his dying girlfriend in his arms), resulting in a pool of bright orange stage blood dripping down onto the sand.

Of course, Houck Jr. also fails to take advantage of the exotic visuals offered by the New Orleans setting (spending most of his time shooting in dim, tackily-furnished interiors or nondescript nighttime exterior locations), while letting his lead actor (first-timer Gerald McRaney) grimace and groan and pull faces at the drop of a hat. Amazingly, McRaney went on to establish a successful acting career in television, appearing on everything from *Night Gallery* and *Police Story* to *The West Wing* and *Deadwood*, and starring in eight seasons of *Simon & Simon* and four seasons of *Major Dad*. Obviously, he improved.

Night of Bloody Horror is so bloody awful that viewers may well wonder how this turkey ever made it to movie screens in the first place. The answer is simple: It was distributed by Howco International, which, coincidentally, was owned by Joy N. Houck, Sr.

Night of the Big Heat see *Island of the Burning Damned*

Night of the Doomed see *Nightmare Castle*

Night of the Eagle see *Burn, Witch, Burn*

Night of the Living Dead

Night of the Living Dead (1968; Continental; b&w) Director/Cinematographer: George A. Romero; Producers: Russell W. Streiner and Karl Hardman; Screenplay: John Russo and George Romero; Cast: Duane Jones, Judith O'Dea, Karl Hardman, Marilyn Eastman, Keith Wayne, Judith Riley, Kyra Schon, Russell Streiner, Charles Craig, George Kosana, Bill Hinzman.

THEY WON'T STAY DEAD!
—tagline

... and neither will this movie. More than 40 years since its original release, director George Romero's *Night of the Living Dead* refuses to molder in the grave, remaining fresh, relevant, influential and utterly terrifying, even while it serves as a celluloid time capsule, brilliantly reflecting the tensions and anxieties of its moment. This is not merely the best low-budget monster movie of all time but one of the finest chillers ever made at any cost, and arguably the most culturally significant horror film since *Dracula* (1931).

Barbara (Judith O'Dea) and her brother Johnny (Russell Streiner) have driven hundreds of miles from Pittsburgh into rural central Pennsylvania to place a wreath on their father's grave. But as they leave the cemetery, a pale, dazed-looking assailant (Bill Hinzman) lurches after them and kills Johnny. Panicked, Barbara flees and takes refuge in a nearby farmhouse, unoccupied except for the half-eaten remains of a dead woman. Moments later Ben (Duane Jones), running from a band of murderous ghouls, arrives in a stolen pickup truck that's nearly out of gas. As Barbara lapses into near-catatonic shock, Ben hurriedly boards up the house, discovers a rifle and ammunition and plugs in an old radio. Through radio (and later TV) broadcasts, he learns that all over the country the unburied dead are spontaneously reanimating to kill and devour the living. Five more survivors, led by Harry Cooper (Karl Hardman), emerge from the farmhouse's cellar, where they have been hiding. Young, African American Ben and middle-aged, white Harry take an immediate dislike to one another and bicker over what to do next—retreat to the cellar or defend the first floor ("The cellar's the safest place!" Harry bellows; "The cellar's a death trap," Ben replies). Tensions steadily mount as Ben and one of Harry's friends, Tom (Keith Wayne), decide to try to refuel the pickup at a gas

The seminal flesh-eating-ghoul classic *Night of the Living Dead* (1968) spawned not only a raft of direct sequels but an entire cinematic subgenre.

pump located behind the house and make an escape, a daring scheme that will require the two men to leave the relative safety of the farmhouse and pass through dozens of flesh-eating zombies who now surround the place. When the plan goes awry, the occupants of the farmhouse are plunged into even greater horror.

The plays of William Shakespeare often take place in the rarified environs of English, Danish or Scottish castles and involve romances and intrigues among kings and their royal courts. Yet despite settings and characters that seem remote from everyday life, the Bard's work remains vital because his stories are driven by timeless human foibles such as ambition, jealousy, vanity and indecision. *Night of the Living Dead*, despite its outlandish apocalyptic setting, owes much of its durability to a similar emphasis on evergreen human weaknesses. The scariest part of *Night*—and of Romero's later pictures—is how people treat one another. Unable to overcome selfishness, fear and prejudice, humankind (represented by Ben and Harry) chooses self-destruction rather than cooperation.

This is not to minimize the bone-chilling concept of the dead rising from their graves to feed on the living, which also retains its unnerving power. Indeed, the flesh-eating zombie has emerged as one of horror's most iconic and wildly popular terrors, rivaled only by vampires and serial killers. Today novels like Max Brooks' harrowing *World War Z* (2006) and Seth Grahame-Smith's spoofy *Pride and Prejudice and Zombies* (2009) earn spots on the New York Times Bestseller List, and Romero-esque living dead films, horrific and comedic alike, do monster box office business (*Zombieland* alone earned more than $102 million in 2009). The Zombie Movie Database, a website fashioned after the Internet Movie Database but devoted specifically to zombie films, includes more than 4,400 entries—and is not complete. Plus, there are scores of video games in which players do battle with the virtual undead. *Night of the Living Dead* not only introduced the cannibalistic zombie idea but popularized it in the same way that director Tod Browning's *Dracula* (1931) established vampirism as a fright film staple.

Night sired this massive legacy, first and foremost, because it was written, produced and performed with amazing skill and originality. The screenplay, by Romero and John Russo, is a fascinating combination of the traditional and the revolutionary. "The film has a nostalgic quality which recalls the horror films and the E.C. comics of the fifties," Romero wrote in his preface to Russo's *Complete Night of the Living Dead Filmbook*. True, the eerie, shadow-draped farmhouse creates an old school gothic backdrop for the story, which concludes with a bitterly ironic twist that E.C. publisher William Gaines would have loved. Yet in most respects, *Night of the Living Dead* rejects genre conventions. The picture offers no comedy relief, no romantic subplots, no all-knowing scientists or heroic military leaders and no happy ending. "Our way of thinking ... led us away from formula," Romero wrote. In lieu of comedy, romance and other time-honored diversions, *Night* offers horror and more horror, ever-escalating dramatic tension broken only by spasms of (then) shocking violence and gore. None of these are more notorious or groundbreaking than the zombie "cookout" scene, in which the undead gnaw on the entrails and severed limbs of two victims killed in the pickup truck refueling debacle. Although surpassed by shock sequences from later pictures by Romero and other filmmakers, in its day this sequence (in which extras pretend to gulp down lamb intestines and sawed-off bits of mannequins) went far beyond anything shown before, even in the oeuvre of gore pioneers such as Herschel Gordon Lewis. The screenplay's lone nod to convention was to supply a tentative explanation for why the dead were rising, provided through television broadcasts: A space probe, returning from Venus carrying high levels of "mysterious radiation," was destroyed by NASA; radioactive debris falling through the Earth's atmosphere apparently caused "a mutation" that awakened the dead. The filmmakers were of two minds about whether or not to include this material (Russo was against it), and Romero's sequels eliminated this science fictional back story.

Although made inexpensively (the total budget ran to $114,000), *Night* never looks *cheap*, mostly due to Romero's polished technique—rich in chiaroscuro lighting designs and atmospheric compositions. His footage of the dead in various states of undress and decomposition, shuffling toward the farmhouse, in and out of the moonlight and the shadows of the trees, remains equally beautiful and bone-chilling. The film features a succession of brilliant directorial choices, right down to the decision to let its gut-wrenching final scene play out in a series of still images, over which the closing credits appear. Romero's work seems all the more extraordinary because most of

Night was shot with a single, bulky, 80-pound camera and without the benefit of a dolly or crane. The director also elicited mostly impressive performances from his inexperienced and often nonprofessional cast. Judith O'Dea's overly theatrical portrayal of Barbara (the movie's only poorly written character) is the weakest among the principle cast but still passable. Karl Hardman's tightly wound work as Harry hits all the right notes, and is matched perfectly by Marilyn Eastman's affecting turn as Harry's disgruntled wife, Helen. The picture is dotted with pitch-perfect bit performances, too, including Charles Craig as the incredulous TV announcer, Bill Hinzman as the implacable cemetery zombie, and George Kosana as a no-nonsense sheriff leading a posse of zombie hunters. The sheriff's famous description of his quarry ("They're dead, they're all messed up") was an ad-lib by Kosana.

Clearly, however, the film's finest acting — and one of horror cinema's greatest performances— is Duane Jones' haunting, multifaceted portrayal of Ben. His unaffected, rangy performance (which requires displays of fear, courage, anger, compassion, shock and determination, among other emotions) is so convincing that it makes everything else seem believable, too. At one point Ben disassembles a dining room table (he needs the wood to board up the windows) and relates to Barbara his first encounter with the undead at a place called Beekman's Diner; Jones' delivery of this lengthy monologue is spellbinding. The mere presence of an African American actor in the role adds additional layers of meaning to the narrative. For instance, in an early scene Ben slaps the hysterical Barbara to try to bring the woman to her senses. What would have been a hackneyed moment must have seemed jolting for 1968 audiences because it showed a black man striking a young white woman. Similarly, Ben's possession of the scepter-like rifle places him in a then-unusual (for a black character) position of power, one he readily makes clear to Harry ("Get the hell down in the cellar," Ben says. "You can be the boss down there. I'm boss up here."). The conflict between Harry and Ben is not merely, as scripted, intergenerational but becomes interracial as well. Suddenly, with the zombie apocalypse standing in for the Vietnam war, *Night of the Living Dead* almost inadvertently begins to play like a fun house mirror reflection of the boiling tensions that threatened to rip America apart in 1968, the year of the Tet offensive in Vietnam, the anti-war riots at the Democratic National Convention in Chicago and the assassinations of Robert Kennedy and Dr. Martin Luther King, Jr. After the King assassination, race riots erupted all across the country; meanwhile, Alabama governor George Wallace ran as a third-party candidate for president on a pro-segregationist platform.

Nevertheless, Jones' casting was just one of many fortuitous accidents— or, in Romero's words "kismet factors"— that happened during the making of the film. "We cast a black man not because he was black, but because we liked Duane's audition better than the others we had seen," wrote Romero. These and other smaller but equally fortunate decisions "elevated the film from the ordinary and because of its realistic presentation, an allegorical interpretation becomes possible." The first of these "kismet factors" was the decision to make *Night of the Living Dead* instead of Romero and Russo's first idea, a science fiction comedy about unruly teenagers from outer space, which never got beyond the treatment stage. Romero and Hardman (who co-produced as well as co-starred) were partners in a company called The Latent Image, which made commercials and industrial training films. *Night* was the first commercial feature anyone at Latent Image had made, but Romero and company were wise enough to hold out for a more promising scenario.

Although *Night* eschews comedy relief, there were plenty of laughs off-screen while it was made. During a discussion of how to conclude the film (whether or not anyone should survive), Hardman and Eastman "joked that maybe at the climax of the film when the ghouls swarm en masse into the house, Ben could discover that they die when they're hit in the face with a Boston cream pie," Russo writes in his *Filmbook*. "Then, at the wrap-up, a pie truck could arrive and save the day." Romero must have remembered this idea, because he included a pie-in-the-face gag in his sequel *Dawn of the Dead* (1978). The devastatingly downbeat finale of *Night of the Living Dead* was no laughing matter, however. It nearly prevented the picture from getting released. Columbia considered purchasing *Night* but ultimately passed, in large part due to the ending. AIP also declined, citing the film's defeatist conclusion. "American International turned the picture down on the basis of being too unmitigating," Romero told *Cinefantastique* magazine. "They told us if we would re-shoot the end of it, they would distribute it for us." Eventually, Romero and his partners entered a distribution agreement with Continental Pictures, a respected supplier of art house product such as Peter Brook's *Lord of the Flies* (1963) and John Cassavetes' *Faces* (1968). Continental wanted five minutes trimmed from the film (mostly from the mock TV footage shot in Washington, D.C.) but did not demand a new ending. As a promotional stunt, Continental purchased a $50,000 policy from Lloyd's of London, payable to any audience member who died of fright while watching *Night of the Living Dead.* This, of course, was advertised on the movie's posters, much to the dismay of Romero and Russo, who believed that the gimmick cheapened their film. The filmmakers were also disappointed in the way Continental marketed the film, with staggered regional releases rolling out over more than a year rather than a larger scale national release. But in the end, nothing could stop *Night of the Living Dead.* It did record business and earned generally favorable reviews everywhere it played, and remained a favorite "midnight movie" at art house and revival theaters for decades.

An eerie, strange and macabre one-sheet poster for the eerie, strange and macabre *Night Tide* (1961) (courtesy Ronald V. Borst/Hollywood Movie Posters).

Romero returned to the zombie world for a series worth of sequels, beginning with the masterful *Dawn of the Dead* (1978)—which proved even more violent and gory than its predecessor and was widely imitated, especially by European filmmakers—and continuing with diminishing artistry through *Day of the Dead* (1985), *Land of the Dead* (2005), *Diary of the Dead* (2007) and *Survival of the Dead* (2010). Eventually Romero's living dead epics would be eclipsed by those of his disciples. Danny Boyle's *28 Days Later* (2002), Edgar Wright's comedic *Shaun of the Dead* (2004) and even Zack Snyder's *Dawn of the Dead* remake (2004) for instance, all overshadowed Romero's *Diary*, which did not receive a major theatrical release in the U.S. But none of that lessens the genius of the original *Night of the Living Dead*, a towering achievement that remains shocking, spellbinding and scary as hell.

With quotes from: *The Complete Night of the Living Dead Filmbook*, by John Russo.

Night Star, Goddess of Electra see *War of the Zombies*

Night Tide (1961; Phoenix/AIP; b&w) Director/Screenplay: Curtis Harrington; Producer: Adam Kantarian; Cinematographer: Vilis Lapenieks. Cast: Dennis Hopper, Linda Lawson, Gavin Muir, Luana Anders.

Temptress from the sea ... loving ... killing!
—tagline

Writer-director Curtis Harrington made a splashy debut with the stylishly eerie *Night Tide*, one of the more memorable low-budget chillers of the 1960s.

Johnny (Dennis Hopper), a young sailor, gets more than he bargains for when he picks up the beautiful but aloof Mora (Linda Lawson) in a boardwalk jazz café. Naïve, lonely Johnny, who joined the navy to see the world but has yet to sail on his first voyage, falls instantly for Mora despite stern warnings from the young woman's neighbors, who believe she may have murdered her two previous boyfriends, both of whom mysteriously drowned. Eventually Mora, who dons a fish tail skirt to impersonate a mermaid in a sideshow, reveals that she thinks she's a real-life mermaid—a murderous siren being called back to her watery home by the denizens of the sea.

In its approach, *Night Tide* blends techniques from European art films and from the thrillers of Alfred Hitchcock, Harrington's self-confessed biggest influences. The film is strikingly composed, moves well and makes great, atmospheric use of the story's seedy boardwalk setting. However, Harrington's work as a screenwriter proves even more impressive than his direction. Not only does he seamlessly meld several seafaring legends into a cohesive mythology, he populates his script with likeable, well-sketched characters and supplies them with realistic-sounding dialogue. Harrington's subversive sense of humor, which would feature prominently in his later work—especially *Who Slew Auntie Roo?* (1971)—here is limited to a slyly amusing bathhouse scene. (As Johnny receives a massage, his burly masseuse asks another patron, "Would you like me to pound you later?")

As the timid, love-struck Johnny, Dennis Hopper delivers an appealing performance miles removed from his maniacal screen persona in movies like *Blue Velvet* (1986) and *Speed* (1994). But Linda Lawson's portrayal of the haunted Mora provides the film's real lynchpin, delicately balancing pathos and menace. Unlike Hopper, Lawson never found movie stardom, but she enjoyed a long career as a character actress on television. *Night Tide* marked the final big-screen appearance of Gavin Muir, whose career began in the 1930s and included more than 50 films. He brings a world-weary gravitas to a pivotal supporting role as Mora's carnival barker and father figure, Captain Murdock.

Night Tide boasts many strengths and only one weakness, but it's a critical one: an anticlimactic and unnecessary cop-out ending. Not only is the film's finale a letdown, but it's static, expository and un-dramatic in the manner of the Simon Oakland scene at the conclusion of *Psycho* (1960)—Harrington perhaps opting for one too many Hitchcock-isms.

This lame conclusion doesn't negate the excellence which precedes it, but it prevents *Night Tide* from joining *Carnival of Souls* (1962), *The Sadist* (1963) and *Night of the Living Dead* (1968)—and *The Flesh Eaters* (1964) and *Spider Baby* (1968), for that matter—among the most enjoyable low-budget horror shows of the decade. Yet *Night Tide* still remains an overachiever—an extremely atmospheric and intriguing picture, far better than most movies in its budgetary weight class. Unfortunately, Harrington would surpass this remarkable debut only once during the remainder of his career, with the playful suspense pastiche *Games* in 1967. Outside of that picture, *Night Tide* would remain his career high water mark.

The Night Walker (1964; Columbia; b&w)

Producer/Director: William Castle; Screenplay: Robert Bloch; Cinematographer: Harold E. Stine. Cast: Barbara Stanwyck, Robert Taylor, Hayden Rorke, Judith Meredith, Lloyd Bochner.

Are you afraid of the things that can come out of your dreams ... LUST, MURDER, SECRET DESIRES?—tagline

Flushed with the success of *Strait-Jacket*, released in January of 1964, producer-director William Castle rushed to churn out a follow-up, and managed to get *The Night Walker* written, shot, edited and released by December. Castle again retained the services of screenwriter Robert Bloch and secured an aging female star to headline the production—the great Barbara Stanwyck, making her final big-screen appearance. In a bit of stunt casting, Castle signed Stanwyck's ex-husband, Robert Taylor, to co-star.

Like *Strait-Jacket*, *The Night Walker* ranks among Castle's least histrionic productions. Even the movie's advertising campaign was (by Castle standards) low-key, playing up the more salacious possibilities of dreams, nightmares and sexual fantasies but eschewing his trademark gimmicks (electrified theater seats, flying skeletons, "ghost viewer" glasses, etc.). Unless you count an extended voiceover prologue in which Paul Frees

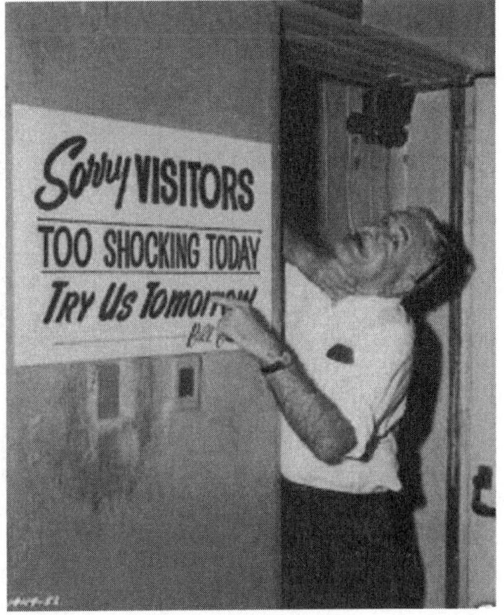

Master showman William Castle in a gag shot taken on the Universal lot to promote *The Night Walker* (1964).

bombastically delivers a heaping load of pseudo-Freudian psychobabble about dreams, *The Night Walker*, like *Strait-Jacket*, has no gimmick.

What it has instead is one of Bloch's more cleverly crafted scenarios (including one bravura fright sequence), a convincing lead performance by Stanwyck and better production values than those typically found in a Castle project.

Irene (Stanwyck), trapped in a loveless marriage to a blind millionaire, dreams every night of a handsome young lover. After her husband is killed in a mysterious fire, the family attorney (Robert Taylor) attempts to comfort her, but may have designs on her inheritance. Then the young man from her dream (Lloyd Bochner) appears (or does he?) and begins to court her. In a standout sequence, her lover takes her out for an evening on the town, which concludes with a nightmarish wedding ceremony held in a deserted church where the preacher and the witnesses all appear to be mannequins. Then Irene's horribly burned husband (whose body was never found) bursts in. It all seems to have been a dream, yet Irene is convinced of its reality. What's really going on?

The secret of the film's success is its ability to keep viewers off balance — never sure what's real and what's a dream. Howard Stine's lighting scheme, draping the sets in deep shadows, goes a long way toward creating the picture's nightmare ambiance. Castle uses slow tracking shots prowling through empty corridors, lingering looks into deserted rooms and crawling dry ice fog to set viewers on edge, wondering what may be lurking in Stine's shadows. Composer Vic Mizzy provides the finishing touch — a creepy score with a slinky guitar motif like something out of Ennio Morricone.

Stanwyck usually worked in a lower register than *Strait-Jacket* star Joan Crawford, and that's certainly true here. Her subtle, naturalistic portrayal prevents *The Night Walker* from descending into camp. This may be a mixed blessing, since Crawford's over-the-top theatrics were a major drawing card for the previous film. But Stanwyck's more sober approach enables *The Night Walker* to be, at times, genuinely weird and unnerving. She extended her career through the mid–1980s on television, but *The Night Walker* marked Stanwyck's silver screen swan song. Taylor comes off a little flat in comparison, but does what he can with a more thinly written part. Lloyd Bochner's eerily unctuous performance as Stanwyck's Dream Lover is pitch-perfect.

While it won't make fans forget about Castle classics like *House on Haunted Hill* and *The Tingler* (or *Strait-Jacket* for that matter), *The Night Walker* remains a minor but welcome addition to the William Castle filmography.

Nightmare (1964; Hammer/Universal; U.K.; b&w). Director: Freddie Francis; Producer/Screenplay: Jimmy Sangster; Cinematographer: John Wilcox. Cast: Jennie Linden, David Knight, Moira Redmond, Brenda Bruce, Irene Richmond.

It will haunt, haunt,
haunt your dreams!
— tagline

Hammer Films' series of *Psycho*-like black-and-white psychological thrillers written by Jimmy Sangster, which began promisingly with *Scream of Fear* (1961) and wobbled a bit through *Maniac* and *Paranoiac* (both 1963), finally reached the point of diminishing returns with *Nightmare*, a lethargic, unimaginative dud.

Sangster's script creates most of the film's problems. It lacks enough ideas to carry even *Nightmare*'s pithy 80-minute running time, and its "surprise" ending is visible a mile away. Sangster gives director Freddie

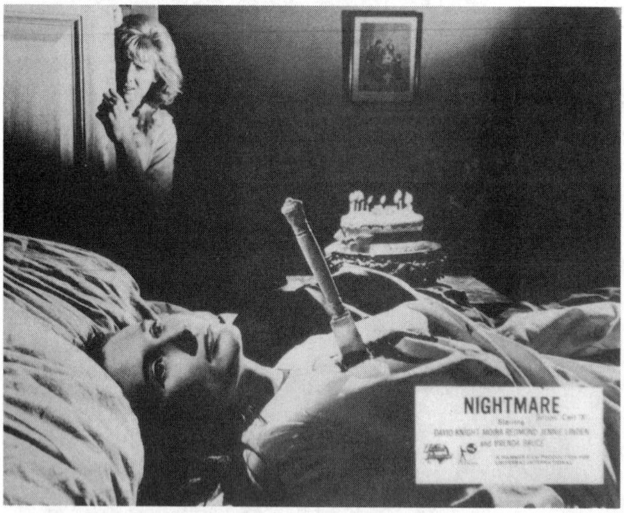

Lobby card for Hammer's disappointing psychological thriller *Nightmare* (1964), starring Jennie Linden (background). Has she stumbled onto a murder, or is it all a dream? And will the audience remain awake to find out?

Francis, who displayed so much promise with *Paranoiac*, almost nothing to work with. The result is a one-way ticket to Dullsville.

High-strung Janet (Jennie Linden), tortured by a recurring nightmare in which she discovers her mother is locked away in a padded cell, is sent home from boarding school because her teacher (Brenda Bruce) fears for the girl's sanity. When she arrives home, the housekeeper (Irene Richmond) informs her that her nightmare stems from a real-life experience she had blocked from her memory. As a girl, Janet walked in on her mother in the act of stabbing her father to death. Janet returns to school, but is plagued by an even worse nightmare involving a mysterious woman in a shroud. She's sent home again, her sanity still in doubt, but her guardian, Henry (David Knight), refuses to send the girl to a psychiatrist. Janet attempts suicide and fails. Then Henry's wife arrives—and she looks exactly like the woman in the shroud.

A murder and a couple of plot twists follow, but by that point (more than halfway through), most viewers will have long since lost interest due to the film's leaden pace, overabundance of dialogue and indifferently executed dream sequences. Linden tries for the kind of twitchy brilliance that Julie Harris brought to *The Haunting* (1963), but she's no Harris (and *Nightmare* is no *Haunting*). The rest of the cast proves equally forgettable.

Nightmare was the last and least of three Sangster-penned psychological thrillers filmed by Hammer in 1962, following *Maniac* and *Paranoiac*. The generic-sounding *Nightmare* was a substitute for the picture's working title, *Here's the Knife, Dear—Now Use It*. Producers decided that that moniker provided too big a clue to the film's "shock" ending. Indeed, the working title recalls the Brazilian title for *Psycho*, which (translating literally from the Portuguese) was *The Son Who Was the Mother*. Talk about giving away the ending!

Even though the series was clearly running out of gas, Hammer would allow a final Sangster pseudo-*Psycho* to limp into theaters, *Hysteria* (1965). It would prove equally dismal.

Nightmare Castle

Nightmare Castle (1966; Emerci-SRL/Allied Artists; Italy; b&w) Original Language Title: *Amanti d'Oltretomba* (Lovers Beyond the Tomb); Alternate Titles: *The Faceless Monster* (UK), *Night of the Doomed*; Director: Alan Grunewald (Mario Caiano); Producer: Carlo Caiano; Screenplay: Fabio de Agostino, Mario Caiano; Cinematographer: Enzo Barboni. Cast: Barbara Steele, Paul Miller (Muller), Helga Line, Lawrence Clift, John McDouglas (Giuseppe Addobbati), Rik Battaglia.

SO WEIRD, SO TERRIFYING ... DO *YOU DARE* SEE IT?—trailer

Between 1960 and 1966 the iconic Sixties horror movie "scream queen" Barbara Steele starred in 10 terror titles, most of them of European origin. After *Black Sunday*, (1960) and perhaps *The Pit and the Pendulum* (1961), the Gothic Italian period horror film *Nightmare Castle* may very well be the best, as well as being the entry that best serves Steele the actress, allowing her far greater range than most (even *Black Sunday*).

Steele plays Muriel, the sexy but shrewish wife of sadistic scientist Stephen (Paul Miller), who likes to experiment with electricity. When Stephen finds his wife in the arms of her lover, he tortures them both to death (dripping burning acid on Muriel, and using a red-hot poker on her paramour). Learning that Muriel left all her wealth to her stepsister Jenny (Steele again), Stephen woos the naïve, high-strung girl. (Amazingly, these two "stepsisters" appear to be identical

Paul Miller takes matters into his own hands in this gorgeous Mexican lobby card for *Nightmare Castle* (1966).

in every way except hair color!) Stephen plots to drive his new bride mad, and soon Jenny is wearing Muriel's clothes, playing Muriel's music, drinking Muriel's brandy, and behaving as if possessed by the dead woman's ghost. Is it delirium, or has the dead wife returned to seek retribution?

As the heartless Muriel, Steele is at her coldest *and* most alluring. With Muriel's death and Jenny's arrival, the actress transforms herself into a nervous and ultimately terrified victim — before turning terrifying herself at the end as she gleefully exacts Muriel's gruesome revenge. "I loved the duality of it," enthused Steele. "First to play the victim and then use that energy to turn it into the revenge part, that's good. It's got power. It's good to have both, because we all need justification in our lives.... Duality makes drama, and not just in horror films."

Veteran Swiss character actor Paul Muller's (*Fangs of the Living Dead*, 1968; *Count Dracula*, 1970; *Lady Frankenstein*, 1971) cold, assured, arrogant portrayal of Stephen matches Steele's impressive playing scene-for-scene, making him a calculating villain you love to hate.

One of the film's few missteps comes in the form of some poor old-age make-up on the duplicitous housekeeper Solange (Helga Line), making her look like a cut-rate she-mummy. Fortunately, she soon transforms into the young and beautiful Ms. Line (explained with a simple offhand comment from Stephen about having "restored your youth"!). The film later takes an intriguing detour into *Awful Dr. Orloff Eyes Without a Face* territory via a subplot in which Stephen uses a serum derived from the murdered Muriel's blood to scientifically sustain his new mistress' youth (youth in danger of fading again without the infusion of *more* blood).

Fortunately, the rest of the make-ups prove disturbingly effective, beginning with the bloody, scarred visage of Muriel's lover after Stephen smashes in his face with a metal poker. Following their torture (and electrocution), Stephen coolly and scientifically cuts the hearts from Muriel and her lover and drops them into a small tank in full gory view — the blood spreading slowly, almost poetically, through the clear water. Stephen cremates their bodies and places the ashes in an ornate pot — which we next see the maid *watering*, as it now houses a potted plant! It's a cold, cruel and startlingly macabre moment, perfectly summing up the film as a whole.

Shocking and chilling moments abound in this *Nightmare Castle*, such as Jenny watching in horror while the aforementioned plant mysteriously drips blood, or hears the frightening disembodied sound of twin heartbeats, or jumps when the wind blows open a door to the sound of diabolical laughter. And the climactic appearance of the ghosts remains one of the eeriest sequences in Sixties horror cinema. As Muriel slowly approaches the disbelieving Stephen, her raven tresses hang down, obscuring her beautiful face. Stephen abruptly pulls back the hair to reveal a horribly ruined countenance — the gruesome shock augmented by Muriel's demonic laughter. (And this over three decades before Japanese entries like *Ringu* made such an image a horror movie staple).

With its mix of gruesome shocks and shuddery Gothic atmosphere (augmented by the opulent — and authentic — castle setting, mobile camerawork, intriguing angles and evocative lighting), *Nightmare Castle* truly lives up to its name, standing as one of the best Italo-horrors of the decade.

With quotes from: "Barbara Steele: On the Set of Fred Olen Ray's 'Prophet,'" by Brad Linaweaver, *Filmfax* 63–64, October/January 1998.

Nightmare in Wax (1969; Crown International) Alternate Title: *Crimes in the Wax Museum*. Director: Bud Townsend; Producers: Herbert Sussan, Martin B. Cohen; Screenplay: Rex Carlton; Cinematographer: Glenn Smith. Cast: Cameron Mitchell, Anne Helm, Scott Brady, Barry Kroeger, Victoria Carroll.

PEOPLE PUPPETS ... AT THE MERCY OF A *FIENDISH MADMAN* IN A *CHAMBER OF TORTURE*! — ad line

Filmed at the Movieland Wax Museum in Los Angeles in 1966 (but not released until 1969), this low-rent take on *Mystery of the Wax Museum/House of Wax* stars Cameron Mitchell as Vince Renard, a one-time make-up artist at Paragon Studios until a fight with studio boss Max Black (Barry Kroeger) leaves him scarred for life (sporting an eye patch and rather mild burn make-up). Bitter over the loss of his livelihood and fiancée (Anne Helm) — whom he self-pityingly sends away, Renard turns his talents to creating wax figures. He also invents a serum that paralyzes people and controls their will, using this to populate his wax museum with living zombies (focusing on those he feels have wronged him — including several Paragon actors who dared to date his ex-fiancée).

"*Nightmare in Wax* was one of the lowest-budget movies I've ever been in," noted Anne Helm. (And this from the woman who starred in Bert I. Gordon's *The Magic Sword*!) "It was *really* low! That was a difficult movie to do, just because they didn't have very much money. The sets were tacky, and we were all pretty silly.... It's probably one of the worst movies I've ever seen. Everything was done in one take — that was it! Because we didn't have time. I think it was shot in a week!"

Unlike Lionel Atwill and Vincent Price in *Mystery* and *House*, Cameron Mitchell Makes Renard a very unsympathetic villain, his motives coming not from a love of art and creation, but from petty petulance and vengeance (turning all those who dare to love his ex-fiancée into zombie-statues). Plus, Renard is simply a sick puppy who enjoys terrorizing his victims. "Why didn't you scream," he whines after stabbing a girl to death, "I wanted you to scream." It all makes for a rather cheap and sleazy exercise.

The unpleasantness finally ends when Renard apparently awakens from the dream we've just been watching (further drawn out via a montage of scenes we've already seen) — a pathetic non-ending to a pointless hour-and-a-half. Mitchell claims to have come up with this hoary old cop-out himself: "That saved the picture," boasted the actor, "because it could not have been made the way it was written." Actually, the only thing it "saved" was any need for rational character actions or motivations (hence the nonsensical finale wherein one of Renard's victims-to-be inexplicably begins laughing maniacally while suspended over a vat of boiling wax, taunting Renard into lunging at the heckler and plunging into the deadly cauldron himself).

"That was a real shockeroo," noted Mitchell. "I wanted to call it *Nightmare*. The *in Wax* made it a B movie." Well, Mitchell's assertion aside, it was more the sleazy script, dull direction and poor production values that made it a B movie.

Nightmare in Wax was released on a double bill with Al Adamson's *Blood of Dracula's Castle*. According to Adamson, screenwriter and executive producer Rex Carlton killed himself after borrowing money from mobsters to help finance this picture and *Blood of Dracula's Castle*. This becomes doubly sad given the final results of these two desultory duds.

With quotes from: *I Was a Monster Movie Maker*, by Tom Weaver; *Attack of the Monster Movie Makers*, by Tom Weaver; "Cameron Mitchell: Star of Tomorrow," by David Del Valle, *Psychotronic Video* 19, 1994.

Wonderful Italian four-sheet poster for the decidedly less-than-wonderful American cheapie *Nightmare in Wax* (1969).

The Oblong Box (1969; AIP; U.S./U.K.) Director/Producer: Gordon Hessler; Screenwriter: Laurence Huntington (additional dialogue by Christopher Wicking); Cinematographer: John Coquillon. Cast: Vincent Price, Christopher Lee, Rupert Davies, Uta Levka, Sally Geeson, Peter Arne, Alister Williamson, Hilary Dwyer.

Where beatless hearts still hunger and
dead hands twitch and tremble
with desire — ad line

Perhaps because it is not one of Roger Corman's Edgar Allan Poe movies and sports a markedly different texture, the Vincent Price Poe vehicle *The Oblong Box* has long been looked upon as a weak afterthought in AIP's Price/Poe cycle. Such a superficial assessment, however, does a great disservice to both Price and Poe. Thanks to a well-crafted script, deft direction and effective playing, *The Oblong Box* remains a worthy addition to both the Poe and Price cinematic canons.

When originally announced, *The Oblong Box* was to be shot in Spain as a Spanish/Anglo co-production under the supervision of veteran writer/director Lawrence Huntington (who penned the film's original screenplay). Unfortunately, Huntington died less than a month before shooting was to begin. The project was then rescheduled for filming in Ireland under wunderkind director Michael Reeves (*The She Beast* [1965], *The Sorcerers* [1967], *The Conqueror Worm* [1968]). When Reeves, who was having severe mental problems at the time (he died of an overdose of alcohol and barbiturates shortly thereafter), dropped out at the last minute, producer Gordon Hessler took over the directorial reigns himself. With the project now moved to the more familiar environment of England's Shepperton Studios, the three-week shoot (on a budget of about $175,000) began on November 20, 1968.

In 19th century Ghana the natives perform a horrible voodoo rite that disfigures the face and unhinges the mind of white plantation owner Edward Markham (Alister Williamson). When he returns to England, Edward's brother Julian (Vincent Price) keeps his unbalanced sibling chained in a room. Meanwhile, Edward's friends conspire to secure the afflicted man's escape from Julian's imprisonment by employing a witchdoctor's potion to make it appear that Edward has died. But when Julian unwittingly has his brother buried alive, the friends abandon Edward to his horrible fate. Graverobbers free the madman, who sets a course of vengeance against those who wronged him, leading to a surprise denouement infused with poetic justice.

"*The Oblong Box* is the fifth Edgar Allan Poe subject to be made by AIP in England," reported the film's pressbook (with the other four being *The Masque of the Red Death*, *The Tomb of Ligea*, *War-Gods of the Deep* and *Witchfinder General*). Like its two latter sister productions, *The Oblong Box* takes nothing from Poe but the name. Still, as AIP publicity takes such pains to point out, "It is typical of Edgar Allan Poe terror-territory, where the atmosphere is one of impending doom, where every awful happening is the harbinger of something worse." While not quite as good as its excellent Anglo predecessors (the muddled misfire *War-Gods of the Deep* excepted), *The Oblong Box* manages to generate a substantial and melancholy atmosphere that does indeed conjure up the mood of America's greatest 19th century terror scribe.

Director Hessler (*Scream and Scream Again* [1970], *Cry of the Banshee* [1970], *Murders in the Rue Morgue* [1971]), along with cinematographer John Coquillon, creates an atmosphere of macabre claustrophobia, as if the characters are trapped within an ever tightening noose — or a certain "oblong box." Even during the pre-credit sequence, the frantic hand-held camera, distorting close-ups of painted natives, and moody flickering lighting create a terrifying scene of voodoo ritual as the natives chant and dance and shout to the relentless drumbeats, culminating in a man's crucifixion. (Price himself felt that "Gordon [Hessler] did a very good job with it, because he only took on the film a couple of days before we started shooting.")

Star Vincent Price (left) chats with "Special Guest Star" Christopher Lee between takes on *The Oblong Box* (1969).

Despite a critical reception that could charitably be labeled "mixed," *The Oblong Box* did well at the box office, earning AIP just over a million dollars in film rentals (six times its cost!). Long thought of as the "poor relation" to AIP's Poe family, *The Oblong Box* deserves respect from both Poe lovers and Price fans alike.

The Old Dark House

(1963/66; Hammer/Columbia) Producer/Director: William Castle; Screenplay: Robert Dillon (from a novel by J.B.

Priestley); Cinematographer: Arthur Grant. Cast: Tom Poston, Robert Morley, Janette Scott, Joyce Grenfell, Mervyn Johns, Fenella Fielding, Peter Bull, Danny Green.

READY! SET! LAUGH! Join the fun in a nuthouse of terror!—tagline

Joyce Grenfell's needles do more than knit in *The Old Dark House* (1963/66).

In 1962, two of the decade's most prolific producers of screen chillers, American William Castle and England's Hammer Films, forged an unlikely alliance. Stylistically, the Castle and Hammer approaches could hardly have been more disparate. Castle specialized in scrappy, low-budget black-and-white productions that succeeded through promotional gimmicks and sheer chutzpah. Hammer remained best known for its finely crafted, high-gloss color gothics.

In hindsight this collaboration seems fated for failure, but, had the right project been selected, it could have worked. Hammer's impeccable production values would have greatly enhanced Castle's previous *Mr. Sardonicus* (1961), for instance. Unfortunately, *The Old Dark House* proved to be a poor choice.

Tom Penderel (Tom Poston), an American car salesman, drives a new convertible through a furious rainstorm to the secluded family estate of its eccentric buyer, Casper Femm (Peter Bulls). By the time he arrives, Casper is dead. With roads now impassible due to the deluge, Penderel is forced to spend the night with the bizarre Femm family, each of whom has some odd fixation (for instance, one of them is building a full-size replica of Noah's Ark, complete with menagerie). He soon learns that the Femms are being murdered one by one. To survive the night, he will have to expose the killer. Along the way, he must also deflect the advances of nymphomaniac Morgana Femm (Fenella Fielding) and the homicidal rage of her over-protective father (Danny Green).

Director James Whale had adapted J.B. Priestley's novel *Benighted* under the title *The Old Dark House* 30 years earlier. The result had been one of the crown jewels of the Universal horror treasury, an idiosyncratic masterpiece of quirky, dry, dark humor, overstuffed with superb performances from its spectacular ensemble cast (Boris Karloff, Charles Laughton, Melvyn Douglas, Ernest Thesiger, Gloria Stuart, et al.). Alas, Castle and screenwriter Robert Dillon reduce the scenario to broadly played bedroom humor and cheap slapstick. Saying they dumb down *The Old Dark House* doesn't go far enough—they lobotomize it. Dillon's painfully unfunny script bears only passing resemblance to either the Whale film or the Priestley novel, playing more like Agatha Christie's *Ten Little Indians* crossed with a ribald farmer's daughter joke.

Although Poston was a gifted comedian, he seldom played lead roles, and *The Old Dark House* reveals the limitations of his one-dimensional persona. Poston performed best in secondary parts where he could play off other talented comics, as he did in Castle's earlier comedy, *Zotz!* (1962) and, most famously, in his role as George Utley, the numbskull handyman on TV's *Newhart*. He's in over his head here, especially saddled with Dillon's clunker-filled script and a spotty supporting cast. Robert Morley, an accomplished and versatile player, serves the film well as gun-crazy patriarch Roderick Femm, and so does Joyce Grenfell, who benefits from most of the film's few good lines as the knitting-obsessed Aunt Agatha. The rest of the ensemble seems bent on out-mugging one another, although some of the blame for this belongs to Castle, who clearly urged his actors to "play it up."

Although his films never took themselves too seriously and were frequently very amusing, Castle's outright comedies usually fell flat. *The Old Dark House* serves as a prime example. Composer Benjamin Frankel worsens matters with his grating, overripe score. Otherwise, Hammer's technicians and artisans— especially production designer Bernard Robinson — hold up their end of the bargain, but their best efforts are wasted on this dimwitted flop. It also squanders an animated title sequence created by cartoonist Charles Addams, by far the most charming element in the entire picture.

During production, both Castle and Hammer executive producer Michael Carreras seemed enthusiastic about *The Old Dark House.* "It will take the mickey out of horror pictures in a most original and entertaining way," predicted Carreras, apparently victimized by a crystal ball malfunction. As it turned out, Hammer was so displeased with the final product that they let *The Old Dark House* gather dust until 1966, finally foisting it on British audiences nearly three years after its American release. The Castle-Hammer partnership , however, ended immediately.

With quotes from: *Hammer Films: An Exhaustive Filmography*, by Tom Johnson and Deborah Del Vecchio.

One Million Years B.C. (1967; Hammer/ 20th Century–Fox; U.K./U.S.) Director: Don Chaffey; Producer: Michael Carreras; Screenplay: Mickell Novak, George Baker, Joseph Frickert, Michael Carreras; Cinematographer: Wilkie Cooper. Cast: John Richardson, Raquel Welch, Robert Brown, Percy Herbert, Martine Beswick, Jean Waldon.

MAN VS. WOMAN VS. BEAST ... IT WAS SURVIVAL OF THE FITTEST!— ad line

Caveman Tumak (John Richardson) is ousted from his savage "Rock Tribe" by his ruthless chief (his own father!). After emigrating across dinosaur-infested regions, he is taken in by Loana (Raquel Welch) and her civilized, fair-haired companions (the "Shell People"). While learning the tribe's strange new customs, Tumak fends off a dynamic attack by a small allosaurus, killing the beast single-handedly. Unfortunately, those primitive savage habits die hard in Tumak, and the gentle shell people are forced to expel him after he attempts to steal the spear of— and then use it on — Loana's former cave-mate. Loana, smitten by the ousted Tumak, follows him back through the rugged terrain where his brutal brother Sakana (Percy Herbert) awaits in ambush. Ultimately, a fierce battle ensues between Sakana's rock men and the Tumak-led shell people before an erupting volcano settles the dispute in the fiery climax. Tumak and Loana survive, and primitive cave-love conquers all.

Despite its rather hackneyed story, *One Million Years B.C.* ranks as one of the best prehistoric/dinosaur films ever made (and certainly far superior to its 1940 model, the Hal Roach–produced *One Million B.C.*). While the drawing card may have been the stunning face and figure of Raquel Welch (whose generous pulchritude is the most prominent feature in the posters and ads), the real star of the show is stop-motion superstar Ray Harryhausen, whose meticulous animation work took nearly nine months to complete. Harryhausen's pre–*Jurassic Park* dinosaurs are so exciting and lifelike that something new can be seen with each successive viewing, as he brings to vibrant life a lumbering brontosaurus, a startlingly realistic giant sea turtle, a lithe and deadly allosaurus, a thrilling and bloody battle to the death between

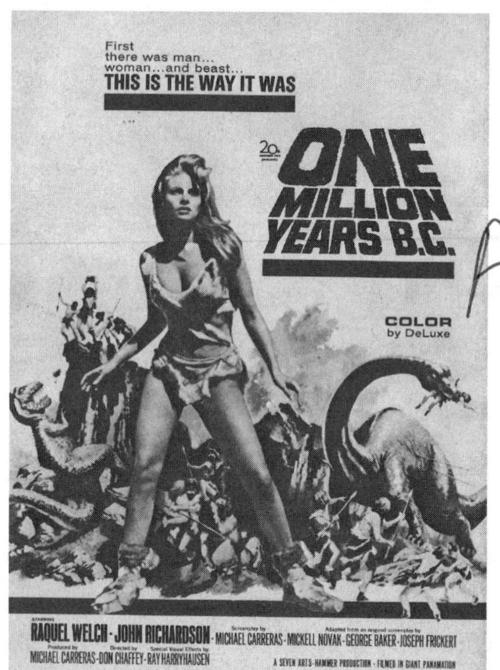

"The anatomy of dinosaurs used in *One Million Years B.C.* [1967] had to be basically correct," said stop-motion animation genius Ray Harryhausen. In the film's advertising, however, Harryhausen's life-like dinosaurs took a back seat to the anatomy of Raquel Welch.

a triceratops and ceratosaurus, and a swooping and diving pterodactyl who carries off the heroine as food for her hatchlings—though, fortuitously, it drops her in the surf in order to combat another pterodactyl in an exciting aerial dinofight.

One aspect that greatly contributes to the film's primitive atmosphere is the fresh Africanesque percussional music score by Mario Nascimbene. That, combined with credible makeup work and solid cinematography by Wilkie Cooper (filming in the stark environs of the Canary Islands) helps bring the illusion of a prehistoric world to life—disregarding, of course, the fallacy of integrating the dinosaur age with homo sapiens. But hey, as Ray Harryhausen said: "I feel it is far more important to create a dramatic illusion rather than be hampered by detailed accuracy simply for the sake of detailed accuracy." So who's to quibble about a little thing like 65 million years?

While having one of the most beautiful women in the world portraying a primitive cave girl stretches the bounds of believability almost as far as Raquel Welch stretches the limits of her fur and doeskin bikini, her acting proved more than adequate. (Hammer Films originally sought Ursula Andress for the role after her success with that company's earlier *She*, but the former She-Who-Must-Be-Obeyed declined the offer.) Since Loana speaks only a few words of gibberish (primitive cave-speak), Ms. Welch had to rely on a strictly non-verbal method of acting—facial expressions, body language, etc. (Of his *One Million Years B.C.* screenplay, writer/producer Michael Carreras once joked, "I may be the only member of the Writers Guild who continues to get royalty checks for a script containing *no dialogue*.") She does an excellent job in such a demanding physical role and manages to bring real personality to her character. The same can be said for John Richardson as Tumak, whose actions and personality draw us into this primitive, brutal and frightening world.

Though the cast performs admirably, too many petty struggles over food, spears, women, men, etc. quickly become tiresome. It seems as though whenever human beings meet, a fight sequence is sure to follow (a bit of social commentary perhaps?). One or two exciting (and brief) conflicts would have been quite sufficient, but apparently Carreras felt the more human violence the better, and the picture suffers for it. Fortunately, there's sure to be a Harryhausen creation lurking just around the next outcropping to replace the human tedium with some saurian thrills.

Costing about a dollar for every year in its title, *One Million Years B.C.* grossed over $8,000,000 worldwide, making it Hammer's biggest commercial success ever. For both stop-motion animation and dinosaur fans, it is not to be missed.

With quotes from: *Film Fantasy Scrapbook*, by Ray Harryhausen.

Operation Fear see *Kill, Baby ... Kill!*

Operation Monsterland see *Destroy All Monsters*

Panic see *The Tell-Tale Heart*

Paranoiac (1963; Hammer/Universal; U.K.; b&w). Director: Freddie Francis; Producer: Anthony Hinds; Screenplay: Jimmy Sangster; Cinematographer: Arthur Grant. Cast: Oliver Reed, Janette Scott, Sheila Burrell, Alexander Davion, Liliane Brousse, Maurice Denham.

A harrowing excursion into terror that takes you deep into the twisted mind of a ... Paranoiac!—tagline

Paranoiac, one of a series of black-and-white psychological thrillers released by Hammer Films in the early 1960s, remains notable primarily as an early directorial credit for former cinematographer Freddie Francis and for its standout leading performance by Oliver Reed.

The film opens with a memorial service for wealthy John and Mary Ashby, who died in a plane crash 11 years earlier, and for their son, Tony, who committed suicide shortly afterward. In attendance are the surviving Ashby children—jittery Eleanor (Janette Scott) and rowdy Simon (Reed)—as well as their guardian, Aunt Harriet (Sheila Burrell). During the ceremony, Eleanor thinks she sees her deceased brother standing in the shadows near the church. When Eleanor reports this to the family, Simon begins angling to have the high-strung Eleanor declared insane, so he can take her share of the family fortune—money he desperately needs to cover his massive bar tab and gambling debts. Driven to despair, Eleanor attempts to commit suicide, but is rescued by "Tony" (Alexander Davion), who explains that he faked his own suicide to escape from the family. Tony moves back into the Ashby mansion and soon an apparently incestuous romance begins to blossom between he and Eleanor. In actuality, "Tony" is an imposter who's also after the Ashby fortune. His feelings for Eleanor force him to reveal his true identity.

Soon, even more twisted deceptions come to light, involving Simon and Aunt Harriet. At times it stretches credibility to the breaking point, but *Paranoiac*'s story remains a ripping good yarn—until its conclusion. In the interest of not revealing any of the remaining plot twists, suffice to say that after a great deal of buildup, the finale fizzles when it should sizzle. Although the entire cast performs capably, Reed steals the show with a riveting, charismatic performance as the drunken, lusty, underhanded Simon. It's a showy part and at times Reed careens wildly over the top, but he remains a joy to watch throughout.

Hammer had tried to film this story (based on Josephine Tey's novel *Brat Farrar*) twice before in 1955 and 1959, only to cancel production both times. Screenwriter Jimmy Sangster, on the lookout for similar material following the commercial and critical success of *Scream of Fear* (1961), resurrected *Brat Farrar* and turned in a fresh adaptation under the new, *Psycho*-like moniker *Paranoiac*. This was the second of three Sangster psychological thrillers filmed in 1962. The slightly superior *Maniac* (1963) preceded it in production and the vastly inferior *Nightmare* (1964) followed. However, *Paranoiac* was the first of the trio released in the U.S., where Universal launched it in May 1963. It didn't reach British theaters until January 1964.

In his first directorial assignment for Hammer, Francis, an Oscar winner for his photography on *Sons and Lovers* (1960), devises some spectacular images, including an unforgettable shot from the corpse's eye-view of a drowning victim, the killer's face obscured by rippling water. Francis would continue to work as a cinematographer on mainstream pictures, and won a second Academy Award for *Glory* (1989). But his directorial efforts would be confined almost exclusively to the horror genre, including such excellent chillers as *Dr. Terror's House of Horrors* (1965), *Tales from the Crypt* (1972) and *The Creeping Flesh* (1973). He directed a four more films for Hammer: *Nightmare* (1964), *The Evil of Frankenstein* (1964), *Hysteria* (1965) and *Dracula Has Risen from the Grave* (1968). Although too uneven to rank as a top-tier film for either Francis or Hammer, *Paranoiac* remains a worthwhile attempt.

Peeping Tom (1960/62; Anglo-Amalgamated/Astor; U.K.) Director/Producer: Michael Powell; Story and Screenplay: Leo Marks; Cinematographer: Otto Heller. Cast: Carl Boehm, Anna Massey, Moira Shearer, Maxine Audley, Brenda Bruce, Esmond Knight, Jack Watson, Nigel Davenport, Miles Malleson.

WARNING! Don't see *Peeping Tom* unless you are prepared to see the screaming shock and raw terror in the faces of those marked for death!—tagline

No movie was ever more savagely brutalized by critics than *Peeping Tom* (1960), and no director's reputation was ever so damaged by a single project. One critic wrote, "The only really satisfactory way to dispose of *Peeping Tom* would be to shovel it up and flush it down the nearest sewer. Even then the stench would remain." Another declared it "the sickest and filthiest film I remember seeing." After playing less than a week, *Peeping Tom* was withdrawn from British theaters. To continue his career, Powell—up to this point considered a leading light of the English film industry—was forced to immigrate to Australia.

The intensity of Oliver Reed in *Paranoiac!* (1963) (American lobby card).

That was 1960. Fifty-one

years later, *Peeping Tom* is considered a masterpiece.

Cameraman Mark Lewis (Carl Boehm) works as a focus-puller at a British movie studio by day and moonlights shooting nudie films. But he's secretly fixated on filming fear — recording women's shrieking faces as he murders them with the sharpened leg of his camera's tripod. His kind-hearted neighbor, Helen Stevens (Anna Massey), takes a shine to the shy photographer, and the two begin a tender romance. Helen learns that as a child Mark was abused by his father, a fear-obsessed psychiatrist who used his son as a guinea pig—filming bizarre experiments such as dropping a lizard on his sleeping child and recording the young Mark as he looks over the corpse of his dead mother. These revelations only make Helen more sympathetic toward Mark, but her blind, alcoholic mother (Maxine Audley) suspects the worst of her daughter's new beau, especially when one of his studio coworkers turns up murdered. Even though both Scotland Yard and Mrs. Stevens is closing in on the truth, Mark cannot stop killing and filming; his compulsions are too powerful.

Peeping Tom is a work of genius, but it's hardly a comfortable film to watch. It was designed to shake viewers to the core and remains one of the most disturbing of all classic motion pictures. The scenario not only asks audiences to sympathize with a perverted killer, but since this is a movie about making movies, it makes obvious the intrinsic voyeurism of the cinematic experience — it renders shockingly overt the vicarious, nearly pornographic thrill of watching onscreen violence. British critics hated *Peeping Tom* because it brought those bastions of good taste face to face with their own hypocrisy. *Peeping Tom* also dared show sides of England seldom revealed on movie screens at the time — places where two-quid hookers walked the streets, where respectable gentlemen bought pornographic photos under the counter at the corner pharmacy, and where nice old ladies quietly drank themselves to death. It all seemed even more shocking coming from Powell, the director of national treasures such as *Black Narcissus* (1947) and *The Red Shoes* (1948).

Yet, *Peeping Tom* displays the same impeccable craftsmanship of those revered classics. Powell's mastery of scene construction and cinematic technique remains apparent in every frame, right from the unnerving opening sequence, which is shot from the camera's-eye view as the killer murders a prostitute and photographs her cries of anguish and terror. Powell and screenwriter Leo Marks designed several sequences where the killer risks exposure by indulging his uncontrollable compulsions, not only to kill but to film. In the most acclaimed of these scenes, Mark sleathily climbs onto an overhead lighting rig while, far below, detectives inspect a soundstage where a body was discovered. As he surreptitiously films the policemen, three red pencils slip out of his pocket and fall to the floor. The pencils tumble through the air in slow motion, wringing every drop of tension from the scene.

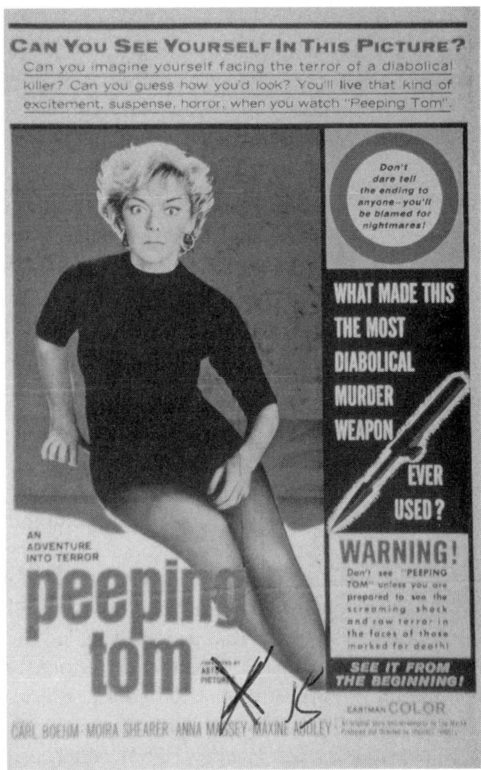

One-sheet poster (courtesy Ronald V. Borst/Hollywood Movie Posters).

The picture also benefits from superb acting. Anna Massey lends a warm, feathery touch to her romantic scenes but seems genuinely mortified as the story speeds to its conclusion. In less skilled hands, Maxine Audley's character might have seemed laughable, like some modern day Oracle of Delphi. Instead, the actresses' deft performance underscores Mrs. Stevens' overriding concern for her daughter's well-being; rather than an all-seeing blind woman, she's simply a devoted, instinctively worried mom trying to save her daughter from a broken heart — or worse. The linchpin of the cast's success, however, is German-born Carl Boehm's heart-wrenching portrayal of Mark Lewis. Rather than a psychopathic monster, Boehm saw Mark as a damaged soul, compelled to violence by unfathomable inner pain. "I identified myself totally with this figure," Boehm said. "I had such an enormous pity for this young man. One of the reasons people refused this film was the fact that I played him in such a sympathetic way."

Two years after its disastrous British release, scruffy Astor Films issued *Peeping Tom* in the U.S., promoting the picture as salacious exploitation fare. Finally, in the late 1970s—too late to rescue Powell's career, which never fully recovered—*Peeping Tom* was rediscovered and reevaluated, thanks in large part to Martin Scorsese and Francis Ford Coppola. Both filmmakers spoke and wrote glowingly about Powell in general and *Peeping Tom* in particular, and Scorsese paid for a print to be brought to the U.S. as part of a Powell retrospective in 1979. Critics promptly hailed the movie as an overlooked classic and frequently compared it with Alfred Hitchcock's *Psycho* (1960). (In truth, the Hitchcock film *Peeping Tom* most resembles is *Rear Window* [1954], which also deals with voyeurism, albeit in a much more playful and audience-friendly manner.) Today, *Peeping Tom* is much studied and written about, especially by feminist and psychoanalytical film theorists. It remains a unique and uncompromising masterwork, one of the finest efforts from one of England's greatest filmmakers, the best thriller ever made in Britain and a jarring, in-your-face viewing experience.

With quotes from: *A Very British Psycho* BBC television documentary, *Peeping Tom* DVD liner notes by Laura Mulvey.

The Phantom of the Opera (1962; Hammer/Universal-International; U.K.) Director: Terence Fisher; Producer/Screenplay: Anthony Hinds (as John Elder, based on the novel by Gaston Leroux); Cinematographer: Arthur Grant. Cast: Herbert Lom, Edward de Souza, Heather Sears, Michael Gough, Thorley Walters, Ian Wilson.

THE GREATEST *THRILL* CLASSIC OF ALL TIME!—tagline

There are worse screen adaptations of Gaston Leroux's oft-filmed novel than Hammer Films' bungled 1962 version—but not many. Hammer's *Phantom of the Opera* gets everything wrong. Among other failings, it moves at a glacial pace, includes too little horror and completely misses the point of its source material.

The Paris Opera's latest production, *Saint Joan*, is forced to shut down due to a series of mishaps and murders. The cast and crew believe *Saint Joan* was sabotaged by a mysterious Phantom who haunts the opera house, and the terrified star vocalist resigns. Director Harry Hunter (Edward de Souza), theater manager Lattimer (Thorley Walters) and composer Ambrose D'Arcy (Michel Gough) press on with the production and hire a talented unknown, Christine Charles (Heather Sears), to take over the lead. In her dressing room, the unseen Phantom promises to turn Christine into the world's greatest opera singer. When she refuses his assistance, the Phantom's mute, hunchbacked henchman (Ian Wilson) kidnaps Christine and carts her off to a secret lair in the catacombs beneath the theater. Meanwhile, Hunter, tipped off by a stray sheet of music, discovers that "D'Arcy's" opera is the stolen work of a talented unknown, Professor Petrie (Herbert

British quad poster for Hammer's 1962 updating of the Universal classic.

Lom), who was horribly disfigured in a fire at a music publishing house and believed dead. Hunter's investigation leads him to the underground hideaway of the Phantom, who Hunter now recognizes as Petrie. The repentant Phantom frees Christine, but pleads to help the young singer prepare to play Saint Joan. Hunter and Christine agree, but a tragic accident mars the opera's finale.

The film plods through all this at a leaden pace, often doubling back on itself. Twice, Christine recounts for Hunter events the audience already watched unfold. Much of the movie's second act is consumed by Hunter's investigation of Professor Petrie and the publishing house fire, which is spelled out in painstaking detail. Yet, seven of the picture's final 20 minutes are devoted to a flashback sequence illustrating these already laboriously explained events.

Unfortunately, such redundancies are the least of the issues with *Phantom*'s screenplay, written by producer Anthony Hinds under his "John Elder" pseudonym. Originally penned with — of all people — Cary Grant in mind for the title role (Grant had approached Hammer about appearing in a horror movie, but later came to his senses and withdrew from the project), the picture for the most part soft-pedals the story's violence and horror elements. (The lone exception is a bizarre scene in which for no apparent reason the Phantom's hunchback suddenly leaps into frame and stabs the opera's amiable rat-catcher in the eye.) Hinds places the famous unmasking and chandelier-drop scenes in entirely different contexts that change their meaning and rob them of their dramatic impact. The unmasking, shot so that viewers can't even see the Phantom's scarred visage, seems like a pointless throwaway — something tossed in at the last minute because viewers would miss it otherwise. And in another appalling lapse, the conniving D'Arcy never receives his overdue comeuppance.

The script's most pervasive problem is that Hinds reduces Leroux's complex, conflicted characters to one-note stereotypes. The timeless appeal of Leroux's Phantom is that he is both sympathetic *and* diabolical. By offloading all the violence onto the animalistic hunchback and painting the venal, underhanded D'Arcy as the story's true villain, Hinds turns the Phantom into a pathetic cipher. Leroux's Phantom tempts Christine into a dangerous relationship by playing on the young singer's vanity and professional ambition. But Hinds' Christine remains a simplistic, pure-hearted, doe-eyed victim.

Even Hammer's ace director, Terence Fisher, could not redeem this misbegotten mess. For example, in an attempt to inject a badly needed sense of menace into the proceedings, Fisher litters the first hour of the film with insert shots of Lom's right eyeball, filmed ultra close up — a device that loses its limited power (and even begins to seem comic) through incessant repetition. Although competently directed, *The Phantom* remains one of Fisher's least distinguished efforts.

Taking Hinds' disastrously muddled script into account, the cast doesn't perform too badly. Discounting ocular close-ups, Lom has relatively little screen time and spends most of it behind a mask that hides his face and muffles his voice. His best moments are confined to the pointless flashback sequence. Sears and de Souza prove endearing, if forgettable, in their underwritten parts as Christine and Hunter. Improbably, Michael Gough comes off best, gleefully preening and mugging his way through his role as the slimy, smug D'Arcy.

Production values remain high; as well they should, since the studio gave *The Phantom* the largest budget of any Hammer project to date. Part of that expense went toward commissioning an original operetta from composer Edwin Astley, which consumes seven of the film's final ten minutes. Unfortunately, it was money poorly spent, since Astley's work sounds like a collection of corny, *faux*-operatic show tunes. In any case, the "opera" is clumsily staged (Fisher was no choreographer!), including a wildly gesticulating conductor whose frantic arm motions are completely out of time with the music.

Not surprisingly, Hammer's *Phantom* bombed miserably at the box office. It was only natural for such a tone-deaf production to end on a sour note.

Picture Mommy Dead (1966; Embassy) Director/Producer: Bert I. Gordon; Screenplay: Robert Sherwood; Cinematography: Elsworth Fredricks. Cast: Don Ameche, Martha Hyer, Zsa Zsa Gabor, Susan Gordon, Wendell Corey, Maxwell Reed, Anna Lee.

An Inferno of Terror! — tagline

Producer-director Bert I. Gordon — best remembered for low-budget, high-camp giant monster movies such as *The Beginning of the End* and *The Amazing Colossal Man* (both 1957) — made this weak and formulaic psychological thriller, which languishes among his most forgettable productions.

After spending three years in a convent following the death of her mother, who died in a mysterious house fire, young Susan (Susan Gordon) returns home with her father, Edward (Don Ameche), and her new stepmother (and former governess), Francine (Martha Hyer). When they arrive home, a cynical attorney (Wendell Corey) explains to Susan that she has inherited $500,000, but the money must remain in trust until she reaches age 25; her father — who has blown his $100,000 inheritance during the past three years on his gold-digging young bride—cannot touch Susan's funds unless his daughter dies or is declared insane. Susan's weird cousin Anthony (Maxwell Reed), whose face was horribly scarred in the deadly fire, also stands to benefit if the girl dies or goes crazy. That very night Susan begins to suffer nightmares and visions of her dead mother (Zsa Zsa Gabor). Is she being visited by a ghost? Is she going mad? Is someone trying to drive her mad? Or is she simply remembering what happened that fateful night, events that her mind has blacked out?

Robert Sherwood's screenplay answers the questions posed by its shopworn premise in the most predictable manner possible. There's plenty of backbiting and skullduggery — including a belabored subplot about a missing diamond necklace — a little madness, a hint of the supernatural but almost no real horror. The adult characters are simplistic stereotypes, broadly played by Ameche, Hyer and Reed. Sherwood's bungled attempt to write "childlike" dialogue for Susan instead makes the poor girl seem either incredibly stupid or possibly retarded.

Terror indeed catches fire when you *Picture Mommy Dead* (1966) (one-sheet poster).

It was hardly the most flattering role, but at least the part enabled Susan to work with her director father, who, Susan Gordon reports "was very stern as a father, very protective of his daughters.... There's a sequence [in *Picture Mommy Dead*] where I set fire to the bedroom, and of course, it was real fire.... If you recall the scene, I light a candle and use it to set everything in the room on fire before my stage father, Don Ameche, and I walk slowly out of the room. The operative word here is 'slowly.' We were leaving the room as if we weren't bothered by the fire raging behind us. Well, let me tell you, the heat was so intense that I was sure my back must've been on fire. The only thing that kept me from breaking character and dashing out of the room — and ruining the scene that, for obvious reasons, could only be shot once — was the knowledge that both my parents were standing by and would surely not allow me to be consumed by the flames! My mother admitted to me afterward that she almost screamed, 'Get out of there!' during the scene."

Bert I. Gordon's usual penchant for visual effects is restrained here, although the film's best moments are the dead mother's eerie appearances, sometimes seen with superimposed, hellish flames lapping at her head and arms. The only other element that truly works in this picture is Susan Gordon singing an eerie children's ditty under the opening credits: "The worms crawl in, the worms crawl out/ in you stomach and out your mouth." The tune may stick in your head, but the rest of *Picture Mommy Dead* will quickly fade from memory.

With quotes from: "Daughter of Horror: Susan Gordon," by John Wooley, *Fangoria* 218, 2002.

The Pit and the Pendulum (1961; American International)

Director/Producer: Roger Corman; Screenplay: Richard Matheson; Cinematographer: Floyd Crosby. Cast: Vincent Price, John Kerr, Luana Anders, Anthony Carbone, Barbara Steele.

The Greatest Terror Tale Ever Told!—tagline

After the box office triumph of *House of Usher* (1960), you can't blame producer-director Roger Corman for attempting to duplicate that film's success. But, unfortunately, Corman's second Poe adaptation duplicates a bit too much from its predecessor.

Francis Bernard (John Kerr) arrives at the seaside castle of Don Nicholas Medina (Vincent Price) to inquire about the death of his sister Elizabeth (Barbara Steele), Nicholas' wife. Francis grows suspicious when Nicholas and his younger sister, Catherine (Luana Landers), prove evasive on the specifics of Elizabeth's death. He's particularly suspicious of Nicholas, the mentally unstable, guilt-plagued son of a notorious inquisitor who retains his dead father's torture devices in the castle's dungeon. Catherine reveals that as a child, Nicholas watched as his father, Don Sebastian Medina, tortured his unfaithful mother and then entombed her alive. Finally, local physician Dr. Leon (Anthony Carbone) arrives and clumsily reveals that Elizabeth died of fright. Still not satisfied, Francis insists his sister's body be exhumed so the true cause of death can be determined. When the tomb is opened, it appears that Elizabeth was accidentally interred alive—a revelation that pushes Nicholas over the edge.

Two pictures into the film cycle that would become virtually synonymous with its producer-director, there was still no conscious plan to create an ongoing series of Poe adaptations. "*House of Usher* had been a big success, bringing in over $2 million for AIP," Corman said. "So Jim [Nicholson] and Sam (Arkoff) asked me to do another Poe picture. I had always liked 'The Pit and the Pendulum,' so I said, 'All right.' At that point it wasn't evident that I was going to do a whole series of Poe pictures; I simply thought, 'Now there will be two Poe films instead of one.'"

And the second entry would look even better than the first. *The Pit and the Pendulum* is beautifully designed (by Daniel Haller) and photographed (by Floyd Crosby), with a larger, more imposing look, even though Corman and company utilized many of the same sets and props from *Usher*. "We saved everything from the first picture and stored it in the scene dock," Corman writes in his autobiography. "If we had the same art department budget for the second picture, we had, say, $20,000 of sets stored from the first, so it became a $40,000 design. For the third film we had, say, $40,000 in stock and spent another $20,000 on the design. It wasn't quite that mathematical, because there is money spent to strike sets and store them, and you do rebuild each time. But it explains how the Poe films looked increasingly more elaborate without increasing the production budgets or shooting schedules." Indeed, as the series progressed, Corman's Poe films steadily grew larger and more impressive, eventually approaching the level of craftsmanship found in the lush productions of England's Hammer Films.

But in other respects *Pit* proved harder to develop than *Usher* (1960). "*The Pit and the Pendulum* was one of the most difficult of the Poe pictures to write, because Poe's original story had almost no characterization at all," Corman said. "With *Pit and the Pendulum*, the original story was about a man in a room being tortured. So we simply utilized that, by having John Kerr come to Vincent Price's castle and then putting him under

Vincent Price and Barbara Steele in a pivotal scene from Roger Corman's impressive 1961 adaptation of the classic Edgar Allan Poe story "The Pit and the Pendulum" (American lobby card).

the pendulum for the climax of the story. You could think of it as our creating a two-act prologue that leads up to the third act — which contains the actual Poe story. But in creating the first two acts, [screenwriter] Richard Matheson attempted to use concepts and themes Poe developed in his other stories."

True enough, Matheson's *Pendulum* script integrates elements from Poe's "The Cask of Amontillado" and "The Premature Burial." But the scenario remains a thinly disguised retread of *Usher*. Among the many similarities: Both films feature a young man who descends on the home of a half-mad older brother and his lovely young sister; both films chronicle the mental disintegration of a character played by Vincent Price, which in both cases is exacerbated by guilt over the premature burial of a loved one. In addition, both movies contain surreal flashbacks or dream sequences and a fiery finale, staples elements common to many entries in the series. Alas, the similarities between the two pictures also include a static and overly chatty opening act. On the positive side, however, the flashback sequence in which young Nicholas watches his father murder his mother and her lover is more powerful than a similar dream sequence in *Usher*, and *Pit*'s electrifying final 20 minutes, full of brutal violence and wickedly ironic plot twists, are better than anything in Corman's first Poe picture.

Vincent Price's s finely nuanced performance as Roderick Usher was essential to the first film's success, but Price slices the ham quite a bit thicker as Don Nicholas in *Pit*. Although still enjoyable — in a scenery-munching sort of way — his work here is nowhere near as believable or affecting as in *Usher*. Although his mental health is supposed to be crumbling throughout the film, Nicholas seems pretty maniacal from the start. The movie's other major horror star, Barbara Steele, has very limited screen time as Elizabeth. John Kerr makes a far more convincing juvenile lead than Mark Damon from *Usher*, but Francis remains a one-note character. Catherine and Dr. Leon are also thinly written, leaving little for Luana Anders and Anthony Carbone to work with.

Despite its flaws, however, *The Pit and the Pendulum* earned even higher grosses than its predecessor. Corman followed with a third Poe adaptation, *The Premature Burial* (1962).

With quotes from: "California Gothic: The Corman/Haller Collaboration," by Lawrence French, from *Video Watchdog* No. 138; and *How I Made a Hundred Movies in Hollywood and Never Lost a Dime,* by Roger Corman with Jim Jerome.

The Plague of the Zombies (1966; Hammer/20th Century–Fox; U.K.) Director: John Gilling; Producer: Anthony Nelson Keys; Screenplay: Peter Bryan; Cinematographer: Arthur Grant. Cast: Andre Morell, Diane Clare, John Carson, Alex Davion, Jacqueline Pearce, Brook Williams, Michael Ripper, Marcus Hammond.

See ... the undead slaves driven from their graves and forced to labor for the masters of *evil*! — trailer

When someone mentions Hammer movies, one's thoughts naturally turn to monsters. In the annals of Hammer horror, the classic figures of Frankenstein and Dracula loom large. With seven entries each (not to mention a passel of vampire variations, including the Karnstein trilogy), these two figures have proved to be the monstrous cornerstones of Britain's Hammer Films. But these were not the only film franchises staked out by

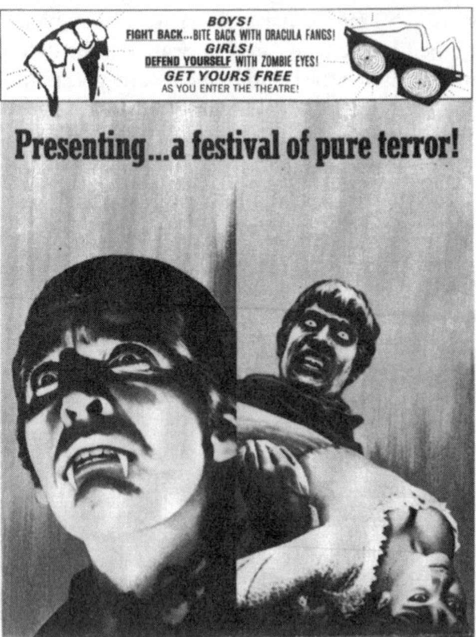

Free "Dracula Fangs" and "Zombie Eyes" for patrons of this 1966 double-bill!

the studio. Hammer continued in its "series" mentality with the Mummy theme (four features to its bandaged credit), a prehistoric subset (consisting of *One Million Years B.C.* ,1966; *When Dinosaurs Ruled the Earth*, 1970; and *Creatures the World Forgot*, 1971), the Quatermass triad, and innumerable post–*Psycho* "psychological thrillers" (such as *Taste of Fear*, 1961; *Maniac*, 1963; *Nightmare*, 1964; ad infinitim, ad nauseum). Hammer was nothing if not repetitious.

Over the years, however, the studio occasionally left off beating their stable of (un)dead horses to venture outside the fiscal safety of its popular monster corral. Unique one-shot productions such as *The Abominable Snowman* (1957), *The Devil's Bride* (1968), and *Countess Dracula* (1970; a "Dracula" in name only) are worthy efforts that have largely been overshadowed by the studio's various series, remakes, and clusterings. Among Hammer's originals are the two "Cornwall Classics" (as some devotees have overzealously labeled them), *The Reptile* and *The Plague of the Zombies*. The two were filmed back-to-back (*Plague* first and then, with only a week's break, *The Reptile*) utilizing many of the same sets and much of the same personnel (both in front of and behind the camera). Though similarly themed (exotic foreign deviltry invades a rural English village to spawn monsters that decimate the xenophobic locals), the two pictures are miles apart in efficacy. *The Reptile* is a slow-moving, predictable, sleep-inducing misfire while *The Plague of the Zombies* stands as a visually exciting, occasionally frightening, and thoroughly entertaining horror yarn.

In turn-of-the-century England, Medical professor Sir James Forbes (Andre Morell) journeys to a remote Cornish village to help his former pupil, Dr. Peter Tompson (Brook Williams), discover the cause of a mysterious rash of deaths plaguing the sleepy hamlet. When Peter's wife Alice (Jacqueline Pearce) dies of the malady, she rises from the dead (in a harrowing scene) as a zombie. Ultimately, the doctors discover that the local lord, Squire Hamilton (John Carson), is using voodoo to create a zombie labor force to work his tin mine. With Sir James' daughter Sylvia (Diane Clare) now imperiled, the doctors must do battle with Hamilton and his undead coterie.

"Horror, as we at Hammer films know the word," pontificated producer Anthony Nelson Keys in *The Plague of the Zombies* pressbook, "has nothing to do with nastiness or cruelty or sadism for its own sake.... We try to make horror films with a sense of taste and style, but whether we did or didn't, audiences still recognize that a horror film in period costumes is pure, honest-to-goodness fantasy."

Filming for a mere 28 days in late July-early August 1965, Keys and co. did indeed succeed in infusing *Plague* with "a sense of taste and style." Director John Gilling (*Mania*, 1960; *Shadow of the Cat*, 1961; *Blood Beast from Outer Space* 1966; etc.), working with cinematographer Arthur Grant (whose steady hand and artful eye enhanced such Hammer productions as *The Curse of the Werewolf*, 1960; *Dracula Has Risen from the Grave*, 1968; and *Frankenstein Must Be Destroyed*, 1969) films scenes with an eye toward composition, movement, and atmosphere. When Alice comes upon the old tin mine during her fateful nocturnal walk, for instance, the camera shoots through a huge disused gear wheel, enclosing her image so that she looks small and trapped within the confines of the massive metal structure. Suddenly, the shadow of a hand rises up from the bottom of the screen. As the unseen figure advances towards her, the silhouette moves steadily up Alice's body before the shadow's bulk finally blots out her whole image with its ominous darkness. The staging and camera position, combined with the use of the sinister and intrusive shadow (further augmented by Jacqueline Pearce's uneasy demeanor), creates a moment ripe with dread.

Gilling stages the first appearance of a zombie (obviously a pivotal moment in something called *The Plague of the Zombies*) for maximum impact. It begins when Sylvia passes the same giant gear wheel that Alice had come by earlier (with Sylvia's image momentarily framed behind it just as the doomed Alice had been). She rounds it and advances toward the camera (just like Alice) so that her worried face is backed by the dark sky and forbidding mine silhouetted behind. Then she suddenly whirls around and the scene cuts so that the camera looks down upon her now-shocked visage. In the next shot the camera starts from behind her and swiftly zooms past, tilting upwards to reveal what she sees hovering on the rise above her — the horrible figure of the walking corpse holding Alice's lifeless body in its arms. A rapid zoom reveals the hideous grinning countenance in all its ghastly glory. Then, after a quick reaction shot of Alice cringing behind the gear wheel, we see the creature gleefully dump its burden, which falls out of the frame seemingly at our very feet. Enhanced by careful positioning and camera movement, this scene, both shocking and terrifying, becomes one that, once seen, is not soon forgotten.

As with most Hammer productions, the acting in *Plague* is first-rate. Andre Morell is simply a joy to watch, playing the elegant, no-nonsense Sir James with a twinkle in his eye and a droll half-smile on his lips. "I don't know why I put up with you at all," he offhandedly tells his daughter when she interrupts him, "I should have drowned you at birth." At this, Morell gives the hint of a soft smile at his feigned annoyance and gruff joke. When Hamilton angrily demands of Sir James, "Are you mad?!," Morell answers, "I almost wish I was, this business is so appalling," with just the right mix of throwaway glibness and introspective sincerity to make the rather unlikely line work.

Morell adds further depth to his character by making Sir James' assured, take-charge facade human enough to give way during the odd unguarded moment. Cleaning up after dinner, he tells Peter of his plans to illegally exhume a corpse. When the shocked Peter voices his objection, Sir James answers, "Why not? It's a full moon, couldn't be better. We'll start about midnight." Morell then promptly fumbles with and drops the plate he'd been drying, his unsteady action and the slightly vexed look on his face belying his nonchalant words.

Born André Mesritz in London in 1909, Morell turned to amateur acting in 1930 and made his professional debut in 1934. Four years later he joined the illustrious Old Vic company and simultaneously started his screen career. After serving as a Major in the Royal Welsh Fusiliers during World War II, his stage and screen career flourished. Among Morell's seventy-plus film credits (which span forty years— right up until his death in 1978) are such prestige pictures as *Bridge on the River Kwai* (1957), *Ben Hur* (1959), *Julius Caesar* (1970), *QB VII* (1974), *Barry Lyndon* (1975) and *The Great Train Robbery* (1978). Morell's presence graced a number of genre features as well, including *1984* (1954), *The Hound of the Baskervilles* (1959; in which he created what some consider to be the screen's definitive Dr. Watson), *The Giant Behemoth* (1959), *Mysterious Island* (1961), *Shadow of the Cat* (1961), *She* (1965), *The Mummy's Shroud* (1967) and *The Vengeance of She* (1968). Of special note to Hammer fans is his marvelous turn in the little-seen crime thriller *Cash on Demand* (1962); in it, Morell plays a perfect foil to Peter Cushing, who gives one the finest performances of his long career.

As *Plague of the Zombie*'s head villain, John Carson possesses the appropriately aristocratic bearing and cool charm of a James Mason (he even sounds like Mason), adding both weight and dignity to the rather ill-defined roll. (Sadly, the character of Squire Hamilton remains both one-dimensional and underdeveloped, and we're left simply to wonder at the motivations and root of his heinous actions.) Carson went on to appear in two other Hammer horrors, *Taste the Blood of Dracula* (1970) and *Captain Kronos, Vampire Hunter* (1973).

Of the female leads, Jacqueline Pearce (who essayed the title role in *The Reptile*) is the more effective of the two, for she is both attractive and affecting. In her introductory scene, her obvious relief at seeing her old school friend Sylvia seems subtly tempered by a guilty nervousness. She appears skittish and secretive, refusing to let Sir James look under her bandage (as if somehow knowing it's an unholy wound yet at the same time feeling protective of it). Pearce speaks rapidly, her eyes and head often downcast, though she frequently glances up as she talks in a furtive, almost pleading manner. The actress's demeanor immediately pulls the viewer in and arouses sympathy.

Diane Clare, though possessing a larger role, makes less of an impression. She appears rather stilted and never quite convinces, even in her potential showcase scenes of fear or anger. (No doubt the fact that Hammer dubbed her voice with that of another actress didn't help her cause any.) In any case, next to Pearce, the chubby-cheeked Clare looks girlish and passionless.

Regarding zombies, *Plague* features some of the most effective in the pre–*Night of the Living Dead* pantheon. Dressed in sackcloth shrouds, these walking dead appear quite frightening with their dead-gray pallor, flaking skin, wide-staring filmy eyes, and evil grins and smirks (admittedly a ridiculous trait for a creature with no will of its own — but a visually chilling one nonetheless).

The film's horrific highlights center on these "undead" creatures (as Sir James labels them). The famed dream sequence, in which mottled hands thrust up through the newly dug graves as the zombies rise from their earthen tombs to close upon the frightened Peter (who stands motionless, seemingly rooted to the spot), may well be one of the most memorable (and chilling) scenes in the Hammer canon. The off-kilter camera angles, eerie flowing mist, gruesome makeup, and the inherent terror of death (symbolically represented by these perambulating corpses) make this shuddery sequence a justifiably revered one among horror enthusiasts in general and Hammerheads in particular. Macabre details, such as the rainwater lying on the raw, red earth looking like puddles of blood, combine with the horrific appearance and slow-but-inexorable movements of the hideous host to make the hackles stand on end. It's a brief, relentless, and frightening scene, and one that probably inspired George Romero in filming his *Night of the Living Dead* (and surely served as a blueprint for Bob Kelljan's effectively creepy opening for *The Return of Count Yorga*). (Note: This sequence is *not* tinted green as some uninformed writers have erroneously claimed, but features an effective use of *full* color — as exemplified by the blood-red puddles.)

Castle of Frankenstein's Russ Jones visited Hammer's Bray studios during the filming of *The Plague of the Zombies* and related how quickly and efficiently the production team worked. Lunching with Tony Keys, Jones wrote that "across the room sat Andre Morell and the rest of the cast of *Plague of the Zombies*, deeply engrossed in discussing the afternoon shooting schedule. After our meal, Reg [Williams, who worked in the publicity department] was to take us to an interior set for a fight scene in which Andre Morell battled one of the zombie leaders. We walked to the set. Here an astonishing thing occurred. In the room were nothing but four walls and a bare floor. Within twenty minutes it was an English pub with a bar, bookcase, chairs, tables, carpets, pictures and various bric-a-brac. The cameras and crew came in, and the scene was put in the can after three takes."

Plague of the Zombies was placed on the bottom half of a double bill with *Dracula, Prince of Darkness* (which is rather unfair because *Plague* certainly moves faster, and is arguably the more entertaining of the two). In the United States, the films were ballyhooed as "The Greatest All New Fright Show in Town!" and patrons were blessed with promotional giveaways: "Boys! Fight back ... Bite back with Dracula Fangs! Girls! Defend Yourself with Zombie Eyes!" (cheap cardboard cutouts with small eyeholes).

Poor pairings and grotesque giveaways aside, *The Plague of the Zombies* stands near the top of zombiedom's cinematic ladder and, indeed, if not on the top *Hammer* rung as well, then at least solidly positioned on its second step.

Planet of Blood see *Queen of Blood*

Planet of the Vampires (1965; Castilla/Allied Artists; Italy)

Alternate Titles: *Terrore Nello Spazio* (*Terror in Space*, Italy), *Demon Planet* (TV). Director: Mario Bava; Producer: Fulvio Lucisano; Screenplay: Mario Bava, Alberto Bevilacqua and Castillo Cosulich (U.S. version: Louis M. Heyward and Ib Melchior); Cinematography: Antonio Rinaldi and Antonio Perez Olea. Cast: Barry Sullivan, Norma Bengell, Angel Aranda, Evi Marandi, Stelio Candelli, Franco Andrei, Fernando Villena.

> This was the day the universe trembled
> before the demon forces of
> the killer planet! — tagline

Although often categorized as science fiction, director Mario Bava's *Planet of the Vampires* might more accurately be described as a horror film that happens to be set in outer space. After all, it's about the dead rising from their graves to prey on the living — only instead of at some fog-shrouded Carpathian castle or an isolated Penn-

Director Mario Bava poses with a giant alien skeleton on a *Planet of the Vampires* (1965) set.

sylvania farmhouse, these events take place on an eerie and desolate alien world.

The spacecraft Galliot crashes while responding to a distress signal from a previously unexplored planet, so her sister ship, the Argos, follows her to the planet's surface. Immediately upon landing, astronauts slip into a trance and turn violently against one another. But Captain Markary (Barry Sullivan), seemingly unaffected, is able to bring his crew to its senses. When a landing party reaches the wreck of the Galliot, they discover the ship's crew has killed one another, apparently under the same hypnotic spell that befell the Argos. Markary's men bury the dead, but later that night an astronaut claims to see one of the bodies walking around. Then members of the Argos crew begin disappearing. Next, two Galliot crewmen show up, claiming to have miraculously survived the crash — but they are soon revealed to be walking corpses reanimated by a species of non-corporeal symbiotes native to the planet, which have seized control of the dead in an attempt to flee their dying world. It's up to Markary and a handful of other survivors to stop them.

Whether you label it horror of sci-fi, *Planet of the Vampires* remains one of the most atmospheric and visually dazzling genre entries of the 1960s. Gabriele Mayer's costumes, including the astronaut's black leather uniforms (eschewing the usual silver spandex, they look more like something from an S&M shop than from any other SF flick of the era); Giorgio Giovannini's wildly inventive sets (full of bubbling red volcanic pits and weird, jagged rock formations like something out of a Chuck Jones Road Runner cartoon); and Antonio Rinaldi and Antonio Perez Olea's cinematography (closely overseen by Bava, and full of his signature red, green and violet gels, often shining on faces of the walking dead) all contribute to the film's pictorial brilliance and chilling ambiance. Although he goes a little zoom-happy at times, Bava's compositions remain dynamic and his restless camera movements fluid. *Planet of the Vampires* also benefits from first-rate special effects (likewise overseen by Bava). Although its miniatures are not entirely convincing, the film's mattes and other optical effects remain outstanding, especially by pre-*2001* standards.

Planet of the Vampires also boasts a few moments of spine-tingling frisson involving its titular menaces. While certainly "undead," the creatures faced by the Argos crew are more like high-functioning zombies than vampires in the Bela Lugosi sense of the term. But if anything this makes them even more disconcerting, since although they speak and think, they shuffle around with the 30-yard stare of the living dead. The scenes in which the dead — some of them damaged, disfigured and even decaying—climb out of their graves prove extremely unnerving.

Yet, despite these undeniable strengths, *Planet of the Vampires* remains one of Bava's more flawed products. As is typically the case with Bava, who provided little guidance to his casts, the film's acting is merely so-so, and further hindered (in the picture's English-American version, at least) by screenwriter Ib Melchior's stilted, techno babble-heavy dialogue. As a result — apart from Barry Sullivan as Markary and Norma Bengell as Sanya, his first mate — the astronauts seem interchangeable. The scenario's slow-moving second act (with astronauts endlessly running back and forth between the Argos and the Galliot) presents another problem, as does its lame attempt at a "surprise" ending, which cheapens the entire story. Many of these issues stem directly from the movie's troubled production history, which was marked by bickering between Bava and his American producers and screenwriters.

Bava, eager to get back onto familiar turf after a couple of missteps in the burgeoning spaghetti Western genre, commissioned a screenplay based on Renato Pestriniero's short story "Una Notte di 21 Ore" ("One Night of 21 Hours"), which had appeared in the Italian science fiction magazine *Interplanet No. 3.* American International Pictures, which had scored major hits with Bava's *Black Sunday* (1960/61) and *Black Sabbath* (1963/64), was excited to secure another Bava chiller. Executive producer Jim Nicholson expressed interest in the project but balked at the initial scenario provided by the director, asking sci-fi author and screenwriter Ib Melchior for a complete rewrite. To prepare, Melchior watched *Black Sunday.* "I came away very impressed by Bava's visual sense and his command of atmosphere," Melchior said. "So that's what I played up in my screenplay, the atmosphere, which is also present in the original story." However, Melchior jettisoned many of the ideas from the short story that appealed to Bava in the first place, including the concept of alien creatures that appear childlike. (Bava revived the idea of a child-like evil for his subsequent masterpiece *Kill, Baby ... Kill!* [1966/68].) Melchior also added a twist ending in which Markary and Sanya, unable to reach their home planet, land on Earth in prehistoric times and become Adam and Eve.

Bava despised this ending, and sent Nicholson detailed notes with suggested changes and improvements to Melchior's script. His notes include ideas that would be developed into some of the movie's best moments: "With the thought that we want to make a 'Fantasy-Science-Terror' sort of thing, I would have the dead of the Galliot buried ... in order, later in the night, to see the ground swell out, and see the dead ones walking out one by one with their ghostly faces, while strange clouds whorl around them. I would show the wonder and the terror of those who find the empty graves." Finally, Bava brought in screenwriters Alberto Bevilacqua and Castillo Cosulich to rewrite Melchior's rewrite. "We basically read it [Melchior's script] and then ignored it," Cosulich said. Production began, budgeted for six weeks and about $200,000 at the Cinecitta studio in Rome. When he learned that Bava was working from a script other than their agreed-upon version, Nicholson sent Deke Heyward from AIP's London office to Rome to make sure Bava wasn't straying too far from the approved concepts. Finally, Melchior himself flew to Rome to iron out the sticky issue of the film's ending. Melchior claims that, after batting ideas around with Bava, Italian producer Fulvio Lucisano and star Barry Sullivan, he helped devise the final (nearly as bad) conclusion. Bava was more dismissive of Melchior's contribution. "There was an American screenwriter on the set, rewriting the script, changing the dialogue," the director said. "Eventually, I stopped paying any attention to him."

Throughout these trials and tribulations, the film changed titles numerous times. Known at various points as *The Haunted Planet, The Shadow World, The Outlaw Planet, Warlords of the Outlaw Planet* and *Warlords of Outer Space*, it was eventually released as *Terrore Nello Spazio* (*Terror in Space*) in Italy and as *Planet of the Vampires* in the U.S., where AIP issued it on a twin bill with the Boris Karloff vehicle *Die, Monster, Die! Planet of the Vampires* was renamed yet again, to *Demon Planet*, when AIP distributed the film to television.

Although Gino Marinuzzi, Jr.'s dated, derivative electronic score, done in the style of *Forbidden Planet* (1956), makes *Planet of the Vampires* seem old-fashioned, it was nothing of the sort. In retrospect, it seems prescient. Director Ridley Scott's blockbuster *Alien* (1979) owes a major debt to *Planet of the Vampires*, from which it borrows key plot points (astronauts land on a dangerous, unknown world in response to a distress call), concepts (most notably, the symbiotic alien menace) and images (viewed from certain angles, the curvy, asymmetrical Argos resembles the foundered space ship encountered by *Alien*'s Nostromo crew). While it's a far less satisfying movie than *Alien*— which also appropriated elements from Edward L. Cahn's *It! The Terror from Beyond Space* (1958) and John Carpenter's *Dark Star* (1974)—*Planet of the Vampires* remains fascinating, mostly due to Bava's genius imagery. That's why, despite the glaring imperfections of its screenplay, this film exerted a tidal pull on the imaginations of later filmmakers.

With quotes from: *Mario Bava: All the Colors of the Dark*, by Tim Lucas.

Playgirl Killer (1968; Brookdale Productions; Canada) Alternate Title: *Portrait of Fear.* Director: Erick Santamaria; Producer: Maxwell A. Sendel; Screenplay: Erick Santamaria (story by Harry Kerwin and William Kerwin); Cinematographer: Roger Moride. Cast: William Kerwin, Jean Christopher, Andree Champagne, Neil Sedaka, Mary Lou Collins, Linda Christopher.

Artist or killer? Temptress or playgirl?— tag line

Both, actually — on both counts— since in the Montreal-shot *Playgirl Killer* the artist *is* a killer,

A dart-to-the-heart victim of the *Playgirl Killer* (1968).

and the gorgeous playgirls he encounters definitely fall into the "temptress" category (Quebec must have been swimming in potential *Playboy* models in the 1960s). The story: A goatee-sporting drifter named Bill (well played by the reliable William Kerwin) likes to sketch beautiful women. Unfortunately, he loses control whenever his "models" fail to sit still for him and violently murders them. After escaping the scene of one of his impromptu crimes (in which the frustrated artiste grabs up a handy spear gun[!] to "quiet" his subject), he stumbles across a spoiled rich girl staying at her father's summer house. Using the mansion as a base (and the debutante as an unfortunate "model"), he sets about finding the right subjects for his work-in-progress (capturing a traumatic, obsessive dream on canvas) and storing their properly-posed corpses in the walk-in basement freezer. Of course, it all comes to a rather poetic—and violent—end.

This Canadian import plays a bit like an H.G. Lewis opus, but without the tongue-ripping, limb-lopping, entrail-pulling cheap gore effects (apart from the pre-credits spear-gun killing, the murders are all handled rather demurely, some even taking place off-screen). The small-scale cast, the mad artist with violent proclivities, the beautiful women as victims—all are staples of the Lewis oeuvre. Reinforcing the notion is the star turn by frequent Lewis actor William Kerwin, who also co-wrote, with his brother, *Playgirl Killer*'s story (perhaps a little of H.G. rubbing off?). Kerwin starred in a trio of the goremeister's best-known '60s horrors—*Blood Feast* (1963), *Two Thousand Maniacs* (1964) and *A Taste of Blood* (1967). In *Playgirl Killer*, Kerwin makes for a likable antagonist, one who sees through the phony, conniving "temptresses" and actually inspires sympathy for the imbalanced artist. It's too bad that Kerwin never made the jump to big-screen stardom; but he did make a decent living as a jobbing actor in television (both in series and TV movies), beginning back in the 1950s and working right up until his death in 1989.

Though missing the dubious delights of H.G. Lewis-styled splatter, the low-budget (reportedly $150,000 Canadian, or about $100,000 American) but professional-looking *Playgirl Killer* surpasses Lewis' films in every other department—acting, writing, sound, and photography (the last thanks to the work of veteran Quebecoise cinematographer Roger Moride, who provides some evocative lighting for the various night scenes and murder sequences). And while it's never going to be accused of being a pace-setter, there's enough intrigue in the story and adequate acting on the screen to keep the viewer engaged between Bill's kinetically-obsessed murderous outbursts.

Also of interest is a rare onscreen appearance by '60s songster Neil Sedaka, playing the doughy, wandering-eyed fiancée of the debutante's sister. Sedaka disappears after the first few minutes, never to be seen again (no doubt due to budgetary reasons)—which is just as well, since his brief turn here indicates his vocal talents far outstripped his dramatic ones. "Guest Star" Sedaka (of "Breaking Up Is Hard to Do" fame and about 1000 other songs) performs one onscreen number at a pool party, "Waterbug." It's about as close as Canada ever came to a Frankie and Annette moment.

Though *Playgirl Killer* certainly won't make anyone's Top Ten Sixties Horror lists, its one of those mildly pleasant little rediscoveries for those looking for something off the beaten horror path.

The Playgirls and the Vampire (1963; Nord Film Italiana/Fanfare; Italy; b&w) Alternate Titles: *Curse of the Vampire* (TV), *Last Victim of the Vampire*; Original Language Title: *L'Ultima Preda del Vampiro* ("The Vampire's Last Victim"); Director/Screenplay: Piero Regnoli; Producer: Tiziano Longa; Cinematographer: Aldo Greci; Cast: Lyla Rocco, Walter Brandi, Maria Giovannini, Alfredo Rizzo.

5 PLAYGIRLS WALKED INNOCENTLY INTO HIS ARMS ... only to meet the devil in the flesh!—poster

Though advertised as "An unusual story of unnatural love and desire ... so bold, so shocking ... it must be shown to ADULTS ONLY!" this early Italian pseudo-sexploitation/horror flick appears tame in both its sex *and* horror. In fact, unlike with the best vampire films (which effectively combine sex and death in an attraction/repulsion dichotomy), Eros and Thanatos seem to be at odds with each other here. For every atmospheric horror-tinged sequence (inventive POV shots keeping the fiend's first appearance hidden while focusing on the victim's mounting terror, for instance; or a funeral scene in which the low-angle camera moves from one mourner to the next in a 360 degree pan from *within the open grave*), there's several absurdly banal sequences of the "playgirls" pathetically practicing their hoochie-koochie routines (with one pulchritudinous platinum blonde even bursting into an impromptu striptease at one point — emphasis on the "tease"). The ridiculousness of the latter (and there's no real payoff for the raincoat crowd, anyway) totally deflates the mood of the former, making it an uphill battle either way.

Director/screenwriter Piero Regnoli's (who went on to script such Italian zombie gut-munchers as *Burial Ground* and *City of the Walking Dead*, both 1980) story has a cut-rate traveling troupe of five showgirls, their manager and bus driver stumble across the sinister castle of Count Kernassy (Walter Brandi). The Count's vampiric lookalike ancestor (Brandi again, who earlier played a bloodsucker in the similar but far superior *The Vampire and the Ballerina*) lurks below in the castle catacombs, waiting to claim the scantily clad lovelies (including one, Vera, who is a dead ringer for his lost love).

The dullness of the cardboard characters; the horrible, intrusive, piano-dominated music score; the aforementioned "teasing" interludes (which include the girls ludicrously wandering about in their lacy unmentionables — a fetching sight, admittedly, but one at odds with all logic); the banal dubbed dialogue ("The strength of love is miraculous if you trust it"); and some poorly-dressed, cheap-looking sets mixed in with the actual castle location do nothing to help this tawdry production. (Said castle, reportedly owned by an impoverished aristocratic Italian family who paid their bills by renting out the villa to film companies [Paul Morrisey, who shot *Andy Warhol's Dracula* there, claims at least four other productions were filming there simultaneously!], also served as the setting for the '60s horrors *Terror Creatures from the Grave* [1965] and *Nightmare Castle* [1966].)

The admittedly exciting and energetic climax includes the film's one real grabber: the shockingly brutal staking — with a flaming torch! — of a nude (yet coyly shot) vampiress. But the picture continues to drag out in a long, protracted sequence involving Vera's reconciliation with the Count and various leave-takings. It makes for a tedious end to a failed attempt at combining titillation with terror.

Portrait of Fear see *Playgirl Killer*

The Premature Burial (1962; American International) Director/Producer: Roger Corman; Screenplay: Charles Beaumont and Ray Russell; Cinematographer: Floyd Crosby. Cast: Ray Milland, Hazel Court, Richard Ney, Heather Angel, Alan Napier.

Within the Coffin I Lie ... ALIVE! — tagline

Wealthy painter Guy Carrell (Ray Milland), a catalyptic, is tortured by a phobia of being interred prematurely, so much so that he designs and builds an elaborate, escape hatch-equipped tomb for himself. Troubled by his anxieties, Guy believes he would never make a fit husband, but his beautiful young fiancée, Emily (Hazel Court), eventually convinces him not only to marry her but, in order to overcome his fear, also destroy his elaborate tomb. However, at the wedding reception, Guy is seized by catalypsy and mistaken for dead. With the tomb destroyed, he is buried in the ground. Accidentally freed from his coffin by grave robbers, Guy — now completely mad — goes on a murderous rampage.

In 1962, producer-director Roger Corman and his distribution partners at American International Pictures were enjoying heavenly returns from the runaway success of *House of Usher* (1960) and *The Pit and the Pendulum* (1961). But there was trouble in paradise, in the form of a financial disagreement between Corman and AIP chiefs Sam Arkoff

Mexican lobby card for the (tame) Italian sex-and-horror romp *The Playgirls and the Vampire* (1963). Note the "recycled" rendering of Germán Robles from *The Vampire* (1957/68), a different film from a different continent!

and Jim Nicholson. "AIP and I had a dispute over my piece of the profits after *Pit*," Corman writes in his autobiography. "In negotiating my fee, Sam and I had an informal tradition of flipping a coin to settle, say, a $10,000 difference. I won the first time, he won the next three times and I stopped flipping."

Instead, Corman decided to finance his next Edgar Allan Poe adaptation independently and struck a deal with Pathe Labs, which wanted to enter the film distribution business. Pathe agreed to put up half the production costs in exchange for U.S. distribution rights. Corman hired screenwriter Chuck Beaumont to develop a screenplay based on Poe's story "The Premature Burial." Since Vincent Price (who had starred in *Usher* and *Pit*) was under exclusive contract to AIP, Corman signed Ray Milland for the lead in *The Premature Burial.* The first day of shooting, however, Arkoff and Nicholson unexpectedly arrived on set. "They were both smiling so I thought, 'They've come to wish me well,'" Corman said. "Then Sam came up to me and shook my hand and said, 'Congratulations, Roger! Our partnership continues.' It turned out that the night before they had bought out Pathe's interest in the picture."

Even though it was not intended to be an AIP release, the participation of Corman, cinematographer Floyd Crosby and production designer Daniel Haller kept the look and feel of *Premature Burial* very much in line with the preceding Poe pictures. The production reused sets and props from the first two films. Although *Burial* features more external scenes than *Usher* or *Pit* (which take place almost exclusively within the walls of crumbling castles), all of *Burial*'s "exteriors" were shot on soundstages (with lots of dry ice fog) and share the same carefully designed, nightmarishly unreal look of the interior sets.

If anything, *Premature Burial* is *too* similar to Corman's first two Poe features. The director wasn't entirely happy with Beaumont's script so he brought in Ray Russell to do a rewrite (both writers receive screen credit, but they did not collaborate in the traditional sense). Nevertheless, the scenario remains disappointingly akin to *Usher* and *Pit.* Like those films, *Burial* chronicles the mental breakdown of a neurotic, morbidly obsessed protagonist who's pushed into raving, murderous insanity when a character is buried prematurely—in this case, himself. Like *Usher* and *Pit, Burial* suffers from a slow-moving and overly expository opening but builds to a lively and intense finale. Like those films, it features a surreal, tinted, slow-motion dream sequence; all that's missing is the climactic house fire. Nevertheless, *Burial* remains a weaker effort than its predecessors. Compared to the first two, it's predictably plotted, glacial in pace, populated by wafer-thin characters and overstuffed with dry, starchy dialogue. Beaumont and Russell simply aren't Richard Matheson, the acclaimed (but pricier) screenwriter who had penned Corman's first two Poe pictures. Corman quickly returned to Matheson as he continued the series.

Aside from Matheson, the other key contributor to *Usher* and *Pit* missing from *Burial* was, of course, Vincent Price. However, in Ray Milland Corman found a much more amenable substitute. Milland, owner of a Best Actor Oscar for his work in *The Lost Weekend* (1945), displays terrific range as Guy, playing the early scenes with subtlety and tenderness, and then cutting loose with venomous glee for the movie's bloodthirsty climax. "Having

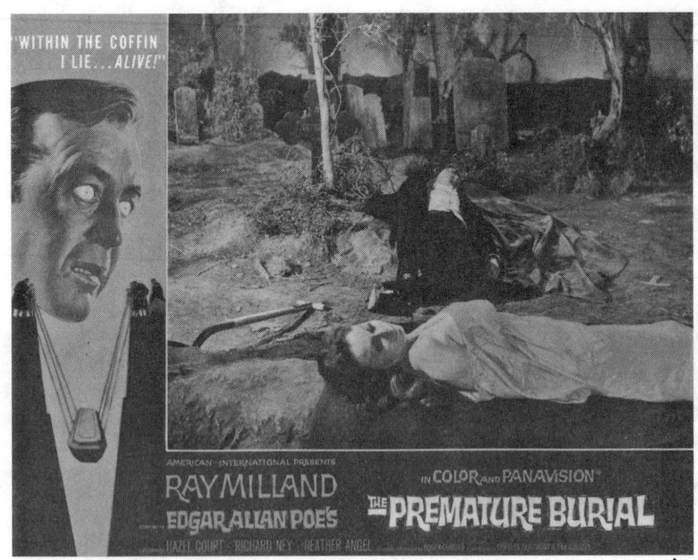

Hazel Court (foreground) about to experience *The Premature Burial* (1962) first-hand (American lobby card).

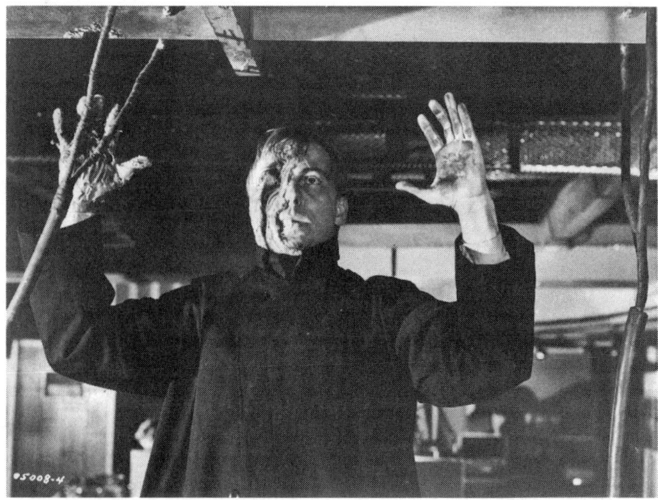

Bryant Haliday as the gruesomely-disfigured, electrically-charged *Projected Man* (1966).

Ray in *The Premature Burial* was an interesting switch because he had been a romantic leading man in the Forties, so he brought that with him," Corman said. "He played the part with a little more charm and romance." It helped that Milland had the lovely and gifted Hazel Court on board as his co-star. Court's appealing, multi-faceted performance is a major asset here, although her portrayal of Emily is overshadowed by her masterful work in Corman's later Poe entry, *Masque of the Red Death* (1964). The rest of the cast—including Richard Ney, Heather Angel and Alan Napier—are essentially along for the ride, although none of them in any way harm the picture.

Perhaps because it lacked the drawing power of Vincent Price, or maybe because audiences were growing bored with the same warmed-over plot, *The Premature Burial* did not reap the extravagant box office returns of *Usher* or *Pit*. "*Burial* generated more than $1 million in rentals but did not do as well as the first two," Corman writes in his autobiography. "It was clear the formula had to be varied." And so Corman struck out in a radically different direction with his next Poe feature, *Tales of Terror* (1962).

With quotes from: "California Gothic: The Corman/Haller Collaboration," by Lawrence French, from *Video Watchdog* No. 138; and *How I Made a Hundred Movies in Hollywood and Never Lost a Dime*, by Roger Corman with Jim Jerome.

The Projected Man (1966; Universal; U.K.)

Director: Ian Curteis; Producers: John Croydon, Maurice Foster; Screenplay: John C. Cooper, Peter Bryan; Cinematographer: Stanley Pavey. Cast: Mary Peach, Bryant Haliday, Norman Wooland, Ronald Allen, Derek Farr, Tracey Crisp.

DO YOU DARE FACE ... THE PROJECTED MAN—ad line

Double-billed with (the far more entertaining) *Island of Terror*, *The Projected Man* is a dull, dull, dull entry in Britain's sci-fi/horror sweepstakes of the 1960s. This derivative *Fly* redux, with a little *Invisible Ray* thrown in, has scientist Paul Steiner (Bryant Haliday, of *Devil Doll* and *Curse of the Voodoo* "fame") perfecting a matter transference device. The fly in the ointment (not a literal one this time) comes in the form of his stuffed-shirt boss, Dr. Blanchard (Norman Wooland), who, for some vague reason, wants Steiner to fail. To this end Blanchard sabotages the equipment, with the upshot being that Steiner makes a desperate gambit to transport himself, resulting in his becoming a horribly disfigured and electrically charged monster who uses his newfound killer touch to electrocute those who've wronged him.

About the only intriguing thing about this talky yawn-fest is its outrageously nonsensical foreign-language title: In West Germany, the film was released under the moniker *Frankenstein—das Ungeheuer mit der Feuerklaue* (*Frankenstein—the Monster with the Fireclaw*)! Long stretches of repetitive lab scenes and uninteresting talk sink the film before it even has a *chance* to swim. The movie is half over before anything resembling a (literal) shock occurs.

To its credit, the first appearance of the monstrous "projected man" *is* suspenseful, as director Ian Curteis keeps him unseen, relying on actors' reactions to the off-screen horror to pique the viewer's curiosity. When the "monster" finally steps out of the shadow into the light, a literally in-your-face close-up shockingly reveals the effectively hideous visage, with its bulging, filmy eye and blistered, road-rash half-a-face. But then, after a few brief murders, the "projected man" starts to *talk* again! (Even the expected jealous confrontation between the monstrous Steiner and the heroine, seeking solace in the strong arms of

Steiner's handsome assistant, carries no suspense, since he just *talks to them.*) And at the climax, nothing really happens—apart from him talking, of course. After deciding to destroy the projecting device, Steiner is struck by the now-deadly beam and just disappears—along with the viewer's interest (actually, *that* has evaporated *long* ago).

Though the cast does what it can with their rather tepid characters (blonde, English beauty Mary Peach, though sincere and natural in her acting, never quite convinces as a brainy pathologist; and Bryant Haliday's character is so strident as to become unlikable), they can't get past the incessant dialogue and inactivity.

According to executive producer Richard Gordon, the film was written with a Los Angeles setting in mind, but the script was ultimately rejected by AIP. (It's not hard to fathom why.) Gordon and Compton Films picked it up and changed the location to England. Even so, with its English settings and endless talk, *The Projected Man* comes across as veddy British ... and veddy dull.

Psycho (1960; Paramount; b&w) Director/Producer: Alfred Hitchcock; Screenplay: Joseph Stefano (Novel: Robert Bloch); Cinematographer: John L. Russell. Cast: Anthony Perkins, Janet Leigh, Martin Balsam, Vera Miles, John Gavin.

Alfred Hitchcock's Greatest Shocker!—tagline

Psycho changed everything. Although not a flawless movie, it stands among the most enduring and influential films of all time, and represents a tectonic shift in the horror genre.

Marion Crane (Janet Leigh) is having a torrid affair with struggling shopkeeper Sam Loomis (John Gavin), but he refuses to marry her until he's on better financial footing. As a modestly paid secretary in a realtor's office, she's in no position to help—until she's entrusted with $40,000 cash, which a wealthy client drops off to pay for a new house (a wedding present for his daughter). Marion takes the money and skips town, but grows weary of driving and is forced to stop for the night at an out-of-the-way motel. After a heart-to-heart chat with proprietor Norman Bates (Anthony Perkins), a young man tormented by his domineering mother, Marion has a change of heart and decides to return the stolen money. Before she can do so, however, Norman's mother breaks in and stabs Marion to death in the shower. Norman dutifully cleans up the mess, disposing of the body and Marion's car (and, unknowingly, the $40,000). When an insurance investigator (Martin Balsam) and, later, Sam, along with Marion's sister (Vera Miles), come looking for the dead woman—and the money—Mother must kill again.

According to screenwriter Joseph Stefano, *Psycho* was inspired by the success of other low-budget, black and white chillers (likely the early efforts of William Castle and Roger Corman). "He mentioned another company that was making very low budget movies which were not terribly good and were doing very well at the box office," Stefano said. "His feeling was, 'How would it be if somebody good did one of these low budget movies?'" However, *Psycho* wasn't the kind of movie Paramount wanted from Hitchcock. The studio wanted another *North by Northwest* or *To Catch a Thief*—glossy, high-toned Technicolor mysteries full of big stars, not some grimy black-and-white horror show. Undaunted, Hitch financed *Psycho*'s relatively modest $800,000 budget himself and shot it using the crew from his popular television show *Alfred Hitchcock Presents*.

In adapting *Psycho* for the screen, Hitchcock and Stefano retained novelist Robert Bloch's plot but made subtle revisions that dramatically altered the impact of the story. The two most significant of these were changing Norman (in the novel, an overweight, bespectacled, middle-aged

Portrait of predation: publicity shot of Anthony Perkins as Norman Bates in *Psycho* (1960).

reprobate) into a handsome, sympathetic but troubled young man, and elongating the opening sequence to further develop the character of Marion ("Mary" Crane is murdered in Chapter Two of the novel). All of this was intended to misdirect audiences. "*Psycho* was designed, first of all to lead an audience completely up the garden path," Hitchcock said. "They thought the story was about a girl who stole $40,000. That was deliberate. And suddenly out of the blue, she is stabbed to death.... You know that the public always likes to be one jump ahead of the story; they like to feel they know what's coming next. So you deliberately play upon this fact to control their thoughts.... You turn the viewer in one direction or another; you keep him as far as possible from what's actually going to happen.... I was directing the viewers. You might say I was playing them, like an organ."

If *Psycho* has a general weakness, it's that Hitchcock succeeds too well in building a cinematic thrill ride. While its power to elicit an emotional response from viewers remains undeniable, *Psycho* may seem overly mechanical, too coldly calculating. It lacks the warmth and humanity of earlier Hitchcock masterworks such as *Strangers on a Train* (1950) and *Rear Window* (1956). *Psycho* has less ethereal problems, too: Its third act is noticeably weaker than its first two; and its penultimate scene — a belabored, excruciatingly expository sequence in which a psychologist (Simon Oakland) explains the bizarre relationship between Norman and Mother — hangs like an anvil around the film's neck (although *Psycho* redeems itself with its short, blood-curdling final scene, a last visit with Mother in her jail cell).

Nevertheless, the movie's assets far outweigh its liabilities. Hitchcock, one of the most fluent storytellers in the language of cinema, was never more eloquent or powerful. As is inevitably the case with Hitchcock's films, *Psycho*'s most powerful sequences play out without dialogue. But *Psycho* may be the ultimate expression of the director's "pure cinema" concept. "I don't care about the subject matter; I don't care about the acting; but I do care about the pieces of film and the photography and the soundtrack and all of the technical ingredients that made the audience scream," Hitchcock said. "I feel it's tremendously satisfying for us to be able to use the cinematic art to achieve something of mass emotion. And with *Psycho* we most definitely achieved this. It wasn't a message that stirred the audiences, nor was it a great performance or their enjoyment of the novel. They were aroused by pure film."

More than any other Hitchcock picture, *Psycho* utilizes the montage editing techniques the director learned during the silent era. Hitchcock employs them to especially powerful effect during the famous shower scene. "*Psycho* is probably one of the most cinematic pictures I've ever made," Hitchcock said. "Because there you had montage in the bathtub killing, where the whole thing is purely an illusion. No knife ever touched any woman's body in that scene. Ever. But the rapidity of the shots, it took a week to shoot. The little pieces of film were probably not more than four or five inches long. They were on the screen for a fraction of a second." The effect was so powerful that many viewers believed they had seen a naked woman brutally murdered—complete with slashing blade and gushing blood. This, too, was by design. "Now a lot of people have complained about the excessive violence" of the shower murder, Hitchcock said. "This was purposely done, because as the film then proceeded I reduced the violence while I was transferring it into the mind of the audience.... So that the audience, by the time we got toward the end when the girl was going over the house, wandering, they didn't particularly care who she was.... They will yell LOOK OUT!"

Hitchcock also elicits career-best work from a number of key collaborators. Composer Bernard Herrmann's spiky, string-laden score is a landmark in itself, as instantly recognizable as any other element in the picture. Saul Bass' simple but visually arresting opening titles are elegance itself. Stefano's screenplay is a marvel of sustained tension. The picture's entire cast performs well, but Leigh and Perkins are sensational. She earned a Best Supporting Actress Oscar nomination. Even though he delivered one of the greatest portrayals in movie history, the Academy denied Perkins a similar honor. Perkins' work here is spectacular, alternately awkwardly appealing, mournful and menacing—changing smoothly back and forth, sometimes (like during Norman's parlor dinner with Marion) making these transitions from one line of dialogue to the next. He also laces his performance with a note of black humor that becomes evident on subsequent viewings, once viewers learn the true nature of Norman's relationship with Mother.

Few films reward repeat viewings as richly as *Psycho*, which only improves when watched more closely. For instance, careful inspection reveals the film's subtle manipulation of bird imagery and its metaphoric use of mirrors, as well as the deeply

Freudian undercurrents in the scenario. In his book *The Art of Alfred Hitchcock*, author Donald Spoto posits that the key to *Psycho*'s ongoing appeal is that the picture contains "themes, images and ideas of which we're only casually or obliquely aware until after multiple viewings. For this film is really a meditation on the tyranny of past over present. It's an indictment of the viewer's capacity for voyeurism and his own potential for depravity.... *Psycho* is also— and this doesn't exhaust the contents— a ruthless exposition of American Puritanism and exaggerated Mom-ism." It's no wonder that entire books and feature-length documentary films have been devoted to the movie's meaning and its legacy.

Despite Paramount's trepidations, *Psycho* turned out to be one of the greatest box office triumphs of the decade. Lines formed around the block at many theaters, in part because, in an unusual congruence of artistic integrity and promotional ballyhoo, Hitchcock refused to allow viewers to enter the theater after the film began (thus preserving the integrity of the story's shocking plot twists). *Psycho* remained a hot ticket even when reissued in 1961. It spawned a trio of belated sequels (*Psycho II* [1983], *Psycho III* [1986], and *Psycho IV: The Beginning* [1990]) and a 1998 remake. *Psycho* remains one of the most laurelled films ever made (it ranked No. 18 on the American Film Institute's Top 100 Movies list, and No. 1 on the AFI's Top 100 thrillers survey). But the picture's immediate impact was to inspire a flood of black-and-white psychological thrillers that poured into movie theaters throughout the early 1960s. These ranged from the prestigious (Roman Polanski's *Repulsion* [1963]) to the puerile (William Castle's *Homicidal* [1961]). Some of *Psycho*'s progeny inspired new lineages of their own. *Scream of Fear* (1961) inaugurated a long series of similar pictures from Hammer Films. *What Ever Happened to Baby Jane* (1962) launched the horror hag subgenre. More significantly, Italy's Mario Bava, inspired by Hitchcock in general and *Psycho* in particular, created films like *The Evil Eye* (1963/64) and *Blood and Black Lace* (1964), establishing the giallo oeuvre, a style of gory whodunit that would eventually be Americanized (and dumbed down) as the slasher film.

Psycho also pounded the first nail into the coffin for the classic, gothic horror film. Although it would take another 10 years or so for the style to fully wither, after *Psycho*, spooky old Carpathian castles increasingly would be replaced by suburban homes as the preferred setting for fright films. Serial killers would usurp vampires as the movies' ultimate bogeymen. Although there had been dozens of scary movies made about homicidal killers, none of them were as widely imitated or culturally resonant as *Psycho*, which can arguably be counted as the first modern horror movie. Indeed, for all these reasons, the history of horror cinema divides neatly into two eras: pre-*Psycho* and post-*Psycho*.

With quotes from: *The Art of Alfred Hitchcock*, by Donald Spoto; *Hitchcock on Hitchcock*, edited by Sidney Gottlieb; *Hitchcock/Truffaut*, by François Truffaut; *Who the Devil Made It* by Peter Bogdanovich; and *The Making of Psycho*, DVD documentary from MCA/Universal Home Video.

Psycho Killers see *Mania*

Psycho Killers see *Mania*

The Psychopath (1966; Amicus/Paramount; U.K.) Director: Freddie Francis; Producers: Max J. Rosenberg and Milton Subotsky; Screenplay: Robert Bloch; Cinematography: John Wilcox. Cast: Patrick Wymark, Margaret Johnston, Alexander Knox, John Standing, Judy Huxtable, Don Borisenko, Thorley Walters, Robert Crewdson.

A New Peak in Shriek!— tagline

Despite an excellent pedigree — by *Psycho* author Robert Bloch through gifted director Freddie Francis— *The Psychopath* is hardly a trophy-winning example of its breed. Francis does everything in his power to advance the film's cause and so does ever-reliable star Patrick Wymark, but their efforts are compromised by Bloch's lazy, uninspired screenplay.

Reinhardt Klermer, an apparently unremarkable middle-aged amateur violinist, is on his way to meet three music-loving chums who play together as a chamber quartet when a red sedan suddenly appears and runs over him — intentionally and repeatedly. The killer leaves a doll at the scene created in the exact likeness of the victim, right down to a tiny violin case. Inspector Holloway (Wymark) believes the crime may have been committed by another member of the ensemble — until they, too, are assassinated (poisoned, hanged, stabbed), with a doll left at every crime scene. Then it comes to light that all four victims gave evidence against a convicted war criminal whose eccentric, crippled widow (Margaret Johnston) lives nearby, along with her doting son Mark (John Standing). Mark and his mother (who collects dolls) become prime suspects, but so do Louise Saville (who works in a doll factory) and her penniless fiancé (Donald Loftis) because Louise's (Judy Huxtable) wealthy, recently poisoned father disapproved of their plans for marriage. Holloway presses on with the case, even after discovering a doll with *his* features.

Although it has some exceptional moments—particularly Holloway's visit to the old widow's home, strewn with thousands of dolls; a cat-and-mouse action sequence that plays out in a darkened boat factory; and the mystery's almost gratuitously icky resolution—*The Psychopath* remains a standard issue police procedural tarted up with a few horrific flourishes (such as the voodoo-like doll gimmick) rather than a full-blooded psychological thriller. The problem isn't so much that the content isn't horrific enough, but rather that Bloch's scenario presents the crimes (and even the doll business) in such a stiff, formulaic manner they fail to make much impact. Even though it's unsettling—and by far the best sequence in the film—the mystery's creepy resolution seems overly familiar; it's a simple inversion of Bloch's *Psycho* climax, followed by a particularly gruesome counterpoint to that picture's final scene.

Bloch's characters are all pat stereotypes, even Holloway. Wymark's rich, subtle performance masks the fact that his character is little more than a cipher. Holloway wanders through *The Psychopath* making about as much difference as the newsreel journalist in *Citizen Kane*. No one else in the cast is nearly as impressive as Wymark, although Margaret Johnston's unbridled scenery-chewing as the paralyzed old woman is at least fun to watch. On the other end of the spectrum, Don Borisenko's work is painfully robotic. Francis seizes on the few opportunities afforded by Bloch's screenplay. For example, the director makes symbolic use of the recurring dolls. He also introduces a second motif through his imaginative use of the color red, which from the opening scene signals danger (the murder car is fire engine red). By the end of the film, the mere sight of a character in a bright red raincoat is enough to put viewers on the edge of their seats. Francis' eye for evocatively designed shots is in full evidence at points, too—not only for the "doll house" and boat factory sequences, but also during a murder that takes place in a creepy sculptor's studio full of distorted hunks of half-sculpted metal.

It's unfortunate that such outstanding moments unfold in the context of this disappointingly routine yarn. *The Psychopath*'s flashes of brilliance make the rest of the movie look all the more lackluster.

Louise (Judy Huxtable) and Mark Von Sturm (John Standing) come face-to-face with the killer at the climax of the disappointing *Psychopath* (1966), written by Robert Bloch and directed by Freddie Francis.

Quatermass and the Pit see *Five Million Years to Earth*

Queen of Blood (1966; AIP) Alternate Title: *Planet of Blood* (TV). Director/screenplay: Curtis Harrington; Producer: George Edwards; Cinematography: Vilis Lapenieks. Cast: John Saxon, Basil Rathbone, Judi Meredith, Dennis Hopper, Paul Boon, Don Eitner, Florence Marly.

HIDEOUS BEYOND BELIEF with AN INHUMAN CRAVING—tagline

In the far-flung future of 1990, just as Earth is preparing manned spaceflights to both Mars and Venus, the human race is contacted by an alien civilization: The space people are sending an ambassador to Earth. The news causes a sensation everywhere, but especially at the international space agency, where astronauts including Allen Brenner (John Saxon), Paul Grant (Dennis Hopper) and Laura James (Judi Meredith) have been training under the direction of Dr. Farraday (Basil Rathbone). Then word arrives that the alien ship has crashed on Mars. Paul, Laura and a third astronaut, Anders Brockman (Paul Boon), are sent on a rescue mission but their rocket is damaged in a "sunburst" and stranded on the red planet. So Allen and his pal Tony (Don Eitner) blast off to rescue the rescuers. On Phobos, a moon of Mars, Allen and Tony discover a beautiful, green-skinned alien woman, who they attempt to bring back to Earth along with Paul, Anders and Laura (the rest of the aliens are dead). On the flight home, however, the alien reveals herself to be a vampire, attacking and killing Paul while the others sleep. Nevertheless, mission control considers the alien a priceless scientific specimen, and instructs the surviving astronauts to feed her blood plasma and bring her safely to Earth. But soon the plasma runs out...

Following his atmospheric and artfully crafted debut *Night Tide* (1961), writer-director Curtis Harrington found himself working for Roger Corman, cobbling together cut-rate, double-feature-filling product out of recycled footage from Russian science fiction epics—first, *Voyage to the Prehistoric Planet* (1965), an Americanization of *Planeta Bur* (*Planet of Storms*, 1962), and then *Queen of Blood* (1966), which combines scenes from both *Nebo Zovyot* (*The Sky Calls*, 1960) and *Mechte Navstrechu* (*Encounter in Space*, 1963) with newly shot scenes starring Saxon, Hopper, Rathbone and friends.

Although both films represent a major step down from *Night Tide*, *Queen of Blood* is by far the better of the two. It's more of an original production than *Voyage to the Prehistoric Planet*, containing more ideas that belong to Harrington, including its unforgettable title character. Such originality was necessary because Corman had already used *Nebo Zovyot* once—he had Francis Ford Coppola trim it and dub it for release as *Battle Beyond the Sun* (1962)—and even Corman wasn't cheap enough to have Harrington simply re-cut the same picture over again. Still, stock shots account for more than half the running time of *Queen of Blood*, with the balance of the footage quickly filmed on bargain basement spaceship and laboratory sets. These sequences look even worse in contrast with scenes from the elaborately designed, special effects-laden Soviet pictures, but at least Harrington displays some ingenuity in the way he integrates his new material with that from the two Russian movies.

The set-up is overly protracted, mostly to show off the admittedly impressive Soviet visual effects sequences, but the story finally comes to life when (with about 30 minutes left in the 81-minute feature) the astronauts begin their return trip to Earth with the alien "queen." Suddenly, *Queen of Blood* becomes a surprisingly effective science fiction-horror hybrid, with the beautiful but menacing green-skinned title character wooing first Paul (Hopper) and then Anders (Paul Boon) to their deaths with a seductive grin and her blue eyes glowing ghostly white. The story's cynical, downbeat finale also works well. It's enough to (barely) redeem a film plagued by chintzy production values, corny dialogue, clumsy dubbing and bad acting. Among the cast's stars, Saxon is passable, Hopper is flat and Rathbone is barely involved (he's occasionally seen in a lab coat, talking into a microphone to Saxon and Hopper). Hopper's performance seems especially disappointing, not only because it comes from a future major star but because he was so good in *Night Tide*. Here Hopper seems wooden, although the screenplay doesn't help (after the "sunburst" he quips, "I've got a symphony in my head and it ain't Brahms"). Florence Marly steals the film in its speechless but showy title role.

After doing penance with Corman, Harrington was rewarded with a major studio feature, the stylized Hitchcockian thriller *Games* (1967)—arguably the best work of his career—and went on to make several

Ad for ***Queen of Blood*** (1966).

horror films in the 1970s and direct numerous TV episodes in the '80s. As with *Queen of Blood*, Harrington consistently brought fresh ideas and visual panache to productions that were often beneath his talent.

Rasputin, the Mad Monk (1966; Hammer; U.K.) Alternate Title: *Rasputin*; Director: Don Sharp; Producer: Anthony Nelson Keys; Screenplay: John Elder (Anthony Hinds); Cinematography: Michael Reed. Cast: Christopher Lee, Barbara Shelley, Richard Pasco, Francis Matthews, Suzan Farmer.

> DISGUISE YOURSELF FROM THE FORCES OF EVIL! GET YOUR "RASPUTIN" BEARD *FREE* AS YOU ENTER THE THEATRE!
> —promotional giveaway

Based on the life of the mysterious and controversial historical figure Grigori Efimovich Rasputin, who held sway over the Royal family of Russia and virtually ruled the Russian Empire prior to the Bolshevik Revolution, *Rasputin the Mad Monk* is far from historically accurate but still a good fictional stab at capturing the feel of the man and his "power."

For many years, star Christopher Lee named Rasputin as his personal favorite among his many roles, and it's easy to see why. In the title role, Lee delivers a towering, intense performance as a character who is powerful, ruthless, cunning and irresistible to women. Bedecked in monk's robes, a shaggy wig and a bushy beard, he's onscreen almost constantly, and his intimidating presence looms over the picture even when he's absent. Who *wouldn't* love playing this part?

The story—a mishmash of historical factoids and elements borrowed from *Svengali*—follows Rasputin (a rogue Russian orthodox monk with hypnotic powers) as he connives his way into the Russian royal court through his mesmeric control of the Czarina and her handmaidens. But the production suffers from a cramped feeling, with very little scope given to the setting, undoubtedly due to budgetary restrictions (Hammer re-used much of the sets from their more opulent *Dracula, Prince of Darkness*, which wrapped only three days prior to the start of *Rasputin*'s shoot). The Czar doesn't even appear, and there is no depiction of court life. "[Hammer executive] Tony Hinds came to me and said we were running over budget and asked for input on scenes that had to be cut to compensate," said director Don Sharp. "So we ended up losing a whole ballroom set and cutting scenes involving the Czar's court." Consequently, *Rasputin* lacks the expansiveness necessary for an effective historical horror film

Nevertheless, Sharp keeps the hokum rolling merrily along with his prowling camera and urgent cross-cutting, and production values generally remain high, despite a couple of obvious

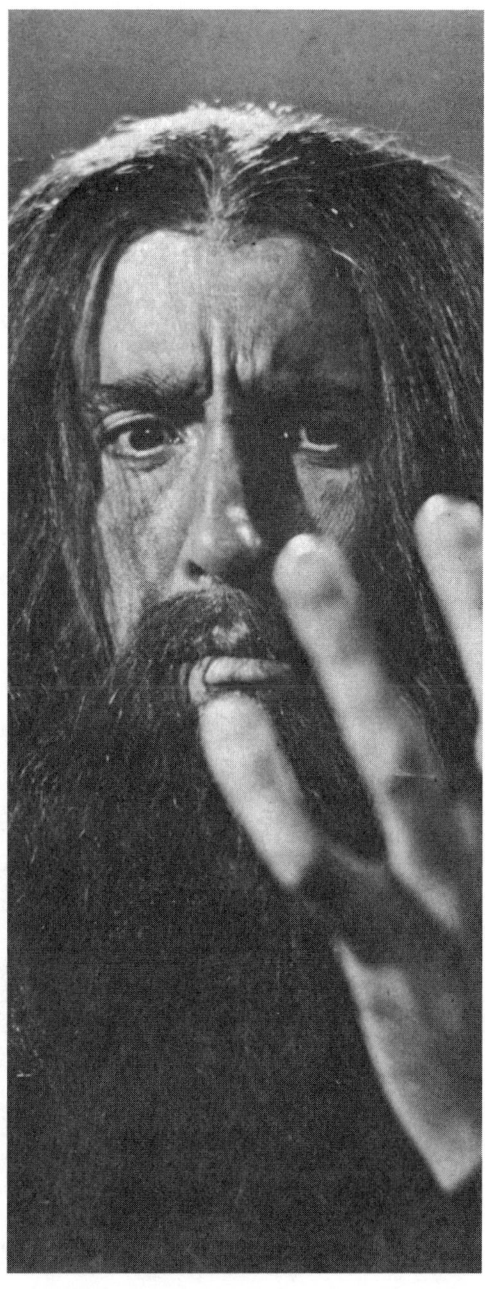

Christopher Lee as ***Rasputin, the Mad Monk*** (1966).

stock footage inserts. The supporting players also enhance the scenario's credibility (particularly Barbara Shelley). The film's main attraction, however, is Lee, who has called Rasputin "one of the best parts I've ever had" and "one of the best performances I've given."

Lee's performance has been labeled a tour-de-force, and rightly so; for when he is on the screen, all eyes are on him. "I thought he was brilliant," praised co-star Barbara Shelley (who plays a lady in waiting who's hypnotized by Rasputin into committing suicide). "If it hadn't been a Hammer film, he would have had incredible reviews for that." Unfortunately, screenwriter Hinds doesn't serve Rasputin as well as actor Lee. The script paints Rasputin as an almost inhumanly devilish narcissist rather than a complex historical figure. "The film concentrated on the diabolical side of Rasputin," observed Lee. "Apparently, that's what the world expects to see."

Rasputin remains more a historical melodrama than a full-bore horror film. That didn't stop the studio from promoting it as such, however. In the U.S., where it was issued on a twin bill with *The Reptile*, movie goers ("boys and girls" alike, according to vintage TV spots) were issued fake Rasputin beards upon admission. Regrettably, the bogus beards are long gone, but *Rasputin* retains other compensations, first and foremost Lee's barnstorming performance, which indeed ranks among the most memorable of his long career.

With quotes from: *The Films of Christopher Lee*, by Robert W. Pohle, Jr., and Douglas C. Hart; *Christopher Lee: The Authorised Screen History*, by Jonathan Rigby; *Hammer Films: The Bray Studios Years*, by Wayne Kinsey.

The Raven (1963; AIP) Director/Producer: Roger Corman. Screenplay: Richard Matheson; Cinematographer: Floyd Crosby. Cast: Vincent Price, Peter Lorre, Boris Karloff, Hazel Court, Olive Sturgess, Jack Nicholson, Connie Wallace, William Baskin, Aaron Saxon.

The HORROR BEGAN at MIDNIGHT!—ad line

When director Roger Corman's Poe anthology *Tales of Terror* earned close to $1.5 million in 1962, Corman and screenwriter Richard Matheson decided (in Corman's words) "to transform Poe's classic poem *The Raven* into a lighter comedy-horror project and use those two again." Those two, of course, were Vincent Price and Peter Lorre. Add to the cinematic broth a heavy dose of "heavy" Boris Karloff, a pinch of the oh-so-pinchable Hazel Court, and a dash of a less-than-dashing Jack Nicholson (in tights and silly hat), and *The Raven* became a tasty comedy-horror dish.

Although AIP publicity called *The Raven* "the most terrifying combination of Edgar Allen [sic] Poe story and cast ever assembled," and advertised it as a straight horror film ("The Supreme Adventure in Terror!"), it turned out anything *but* straight. *The Raven* was the fifth Poe movie directed by Corman and the fourth written by Richard Matheson, who was desperate for a change of pace. "*The Raven* was fun," recounted Matheson in John Brosnan's *The Horror People*. "The AIP executives had found out that the middle portion in *Tales of Terror*, which had been done for laughs, was very successful, so they decided to do a whole funny picture. Anyway, I couldn't have done another serious one. It would have been more than I could stand. I had to do them for laughs by then."

"Once upon a midnight dreary, while I pondered, weak and weary..." intones Vincent Price's mellifluous voice as *The Raven* opens with the

The Comedy of Poe: Peter Lorre, Vincent Price, Hazel Court, Olive Sturgess and Boris Karloff in *The Raven* (1963).

actor reciting the first stanza of the famous Poe poem. (This brief recitation, and the fact that the protagonist is pining over "the lost Lenore" [his dead wife], is about all the film takes from Poe.) The story proper, set sometime during the middle ages, begins with Dr. Erasmus Craven (Price), sorcerer extraordinaire, lamenting the loss of his beloved wife Lenore two years earlier. "Gently there came a rapping" at Craven's window and in steps "a stately raven." Said raven turns out to be more than he appears, for the bird is actually another magician, the bumbling, wine-loving Dr. Bedlo (Lorre). Bedlo had been turned into the black bird by Dr. Scarabus (Karloff), the powerful and ruthless head of the "Brotherhood of Magicians." After Craven effects a cure for Bedlo's feathery enchantment, Bedlo relates that he'd seen Craven's long-dead Lenore (Hazel Court) at Scarabus' home. Accompanied by Craven's daughter (Olive Sturgess) and Bedlo's son (Jack Nicholson), the two magicians journey to Castle Scarabus to investigate, culminating in a magical "duel to the death."

"I have always felt that *The Raven*, for a three-week shoot, is one of the more accomplished films I directed," wrote Corman in his autobiography *How I Made a Hundred Movies in Hollywood and Never Lost a Dime*. "[Art director] Danny Haller again created lavish-looking, stylized sets that gave the film great-looking production value for the money." Indeed he did. From the creepy, cobwebbed Craven crypt to the great hall of Scarabus Castle (with its towering pillars, overpowering stone staircase and blazing brazier centerpiece), Haller's sets create a grandiose, otherworldly atmosphere for this comedic, medieval-style fairy tale. Corman and cinematographer Floyd Crosby shoot to best advantage, utilizing varying angles and lighting to generate a sense of grandeur and wonder perfectly suited to the larger-than-life characters and scenario.

The undisputed star attraction of *The Raven*, however, is that "Triumvirate of Terror"—Price, Karloff and Lorre. Price is as charming as he's ever appeared on film, and he makes his self-effacing and kindly Dr. Craven a likeable and engaging character. Karloff is insincerity personified, as he deceives with wickedly false smiles and empty flatteries while hatching his devious plots. And Lorre is the comedic glue that binds it all together. His disarmingly garrulous and irascible demeanor both contrasts and compliments Price and Karloff's flowery, Old World characters. Lorre's unpretentiousness takes all the starch out of the stuffiness around him, creating some wonderfully comedic moments. And he has all the best lines, most of them of his own devising.

"Peter knew every line of the script perfectly," recalled Price, "but loved to invent his own, and sometimes his ad-libs were so humorous Corman let them stay in." Lorre tosses a quip here and an aside there so frequently that amusing ad-libs come thicker than raven droppings—of which raven-toting co-star Jack Nicholson bitterly complained. "The raven we used shit endlessly over everybody and everything," recalled Nicholson in Corman's autobiography. "It just shit endlessly. My whole right shoulder was constantly covered with raven shit."

Costing $350,000, *The Raven* reportedly earned over 1.4 million in rentals, making it a big financial success for AIP and inspiring them to continue in the horror-comedy vein with *The Comedy of Terrors* (whose much poorer box-office showing scotched AIP's plans as promptly as *The Raven* had spawned them).

In addition to the usual "midnight screening" and "bravest boy and/or girl" contest (with the winner to sit alone in the theater watching *The Raven* after midnight), AIP came up with a few unusual tie-ins (including a *Raven* paperback and comic book) and seat-selling slants. "Offer free admission to see *The Raven* for anyone who brings a real raven to the theater," suggested the pressbook. No doubt *that* wouldn't have sat too well with the theater clean-up crew.

The Reptile (1966; Hammer/Seven Arts; U.K.)

Director: John Gilling; Producer: Anthony Nelson Keys; Screenplay: Anthony Hinds (as John Elder); Cinematographer: Arthur Grant. Cast: Noel Willman, Jennifer Daniel, Ray Barrett, Jacqueline Pearce, Michael Ripper, John Laurie, Marne Maitland.

What strange power made her half woman—half snake?—tagline

Michael Ripper fans, this one's for you.

Although the stalwart supporting player appeared in dozens of productions for Hammer Films over the years, sometimes in uncredited bits, the studio never gave the beloved Ripper a more prominent role than his turn as the good-hearted innkeeper in *The Reptile*. Ripper projects vulnerability, compassion and courage in equal measure as a common man who rises to meet uncommon circumstances, coming to the aid of the nominal hero and heroine, and helping solve the riddle of the mysterious Black Death murders. Like his work in *Night Creatures* (1962) and *The Mummy's Shroud* (1967), it's the kind of performance that makes viewers wonder why Hammer so seldom entrusted the reliable and loyal Ripper with parts worthy of his ability.

Unfortunately, outside of Ripper's exemplary portrayal, there's very little of merit in *The Reptile*.

Newlyweds Harry and Valerie Spalding (Ray Barrett and Jennifer Daniel) inherit a cottage in a remote Cornish village following the mysterious death of Harry's brother, Charles. The only local to welcome the newcomers is Tom Potter (Ripper), proprietor of the local inn. The Spalding cottage sits adjacent to the sprawling estate of the reclusive Dr. Franklyn (Noel Willman), who seems overprotective (and perhaps abusive) toward his adult daughter, Anna (Jacqueline Pearce). The village drunk, "Mad Peter" (John Laurie), informs Harry that "they" killed his brother, but is unable to specify who "they" are. When Mad Peter turns up dead, his body disfigured in the same manner as Charles Spalding's, Harry asks Tom to help him uncover who or what killed his brother and the other victims of what

Ad for Hammer's *The Reptile* (1966).

the villagers call the "Black Death." Harry and Tom unearth the bodies of Charles and Mad Peter, and discover both are marked with what looks like a cobra bite.

Soon after, Harry and Valerie receive a note from Anna Franklyn begging for help, Harry rushes over and is bitten by Anna, a shape-changing snake-woman. (Anna, it seems, was transformed into a monster by a snake-worshiping Malaysian sect who objected to Dr. Franklyn's investigation of its rituals. A member of the cult, identified only as "Malay" [Marne Maitland], pursued the Franklyns to Cornwall.) Harry staggers home but survives Anna's bite thanks in part to Tom's timely intervention. Then Valerie finds Anna's note and, even though her husband hovers between life and death, strikes out for the Franklyn house, placing herself in peril and setting the film's predictable fiery conclusion into motion.

After an effective pre-credit sequence depicting Charles Spalding's death, *The Reptile* shifts into low gear and grinds there until 52 of the film's 90 minutes have elapsed, when Harry and Tom start digging up graves. The picture's final act proves livelier, but much of the action seems contrived rather than driven by any sort of internal logic or discernible character motivation. Why, for instance, does Valerie run to Anna's aid when she has seen what happened to Harry? Indeed, why would the devoted young wife leave her husband while he's fighting for his life? And just as the movie is speeding to its conclusion, the narrative screeches to a halt so Franklyn can launch into a protracted tale of woe, spelling out the picture's backstory through exposition of the most painfully obvious variety.

Production values are predictably sound — the usual Hammer polish is applied to its proper sheen. Director John Gilling relies on low camera angles, calculated use of shadows and other subtle devices to try to enliven the static scenario, but his efforts meet only intermittent success. Roy Ashton's fanged, bug-eyed snake woman makeup is both original and fierce-looking, but Gilling overuses it (and cinematographer Arthur Grant over-lights it) during the finale, reducing its impact.

Beyond Ripper's fine work, the acting is a mixed bag. Daniel, who was so impressive in *The Kiss of the Vampire* (1963/64), has less to do here as Valerie but remains both convincing and appealing. Willman, who was such a zero in *Kiss*, remains unimpressive as Dr. Franklyn (but fares marginally better this time around). Barrett has little screen presence but makes a game effort as Harry. As "Mad Peter," John Laurie delivers the kind of colorful, scene-stealing turn that fans normally expect from Ripper. Jacqueline Pearce can't muster the verve the title role requires, perhaps limited by Ashton's elaborate makeup. Marne Maitland performs capably as "Malay," the latest in a long line of enthnically vague villains portrayed by the actor.

Unintentional, perhaps, but nevertheless fascinating is the scenario's latent xenophobia. An alternate title for *The Reptile* might have been *There Goes the Neighborhood*. Villagers who frequent Tom's alehouse shun outsiders and complain that their Cornish hamlet was a delightful little place until Those People arrived with their foreign ways. The narrative posits that Dr. Franklyn brought disaster upon himself and his daughter by investigating, and eventually adopting, foreign customs and beliefs; they "went native" and corrupted their sacred Britishness. Yet Maitland's character, identified only as "Malay"—not truly a name, but rather a generic term for anything emanating from Malaysia (he might just as well have been called "Oriental")—looms as the story's true villain, an inscrutable Asian fiend who takes sadistic pleasure in prolonging the torment of Dr. Franklyn and his daughter. With "Malay" and his fellow-travelers dead and the Franklyn estate going up in flames, the village will once again become fit for good, pure–English folk, *The Reptile*'s resolution suggests.

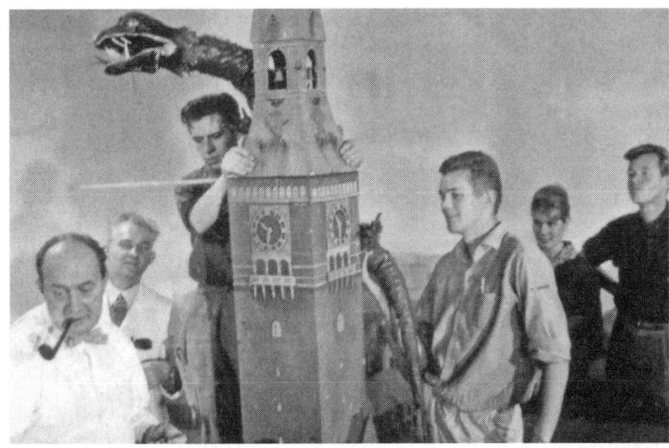

Behind the scenes on the shot-in-Denmark *Reptilicus* (1962). Among those pictured are model-builder Kaj Koed (at left, with pipe) and cinematographer Aage Wiltrup (far right) (courtesy Kip Doto).

Reptilicus (1962; AIP; Denmark/U.S.)

Director/Producer: Sidney Pink; Screenplay: Ib Melchior, Sid Pink; Cinematographer: Aage Wiltrup. Cast: Carl Ottosen, Ann Smyrner, Asbjorn Andersen, Bent Mejding, Poul Wildaker, Mimi Heinrich.

SEE Civilization Rioting with Fear!—ad line

When producer/director/co-writer Sid Pink needed an idea for a film to be shot in Denmark (Pink had production and distribution ties to that country), he turned to AIP heads Jim Nicholson and Sam Arkoff. "Jimmy suggested that we do something that could include the beauties of the Danish countryside but with a monster motif," wrote Pink in his autobiography *So You Want to Make Movies*. Though Pink claims he wrote the script in six days, it was actually penned by Pink's collaborator on *The Angry Red Planet* (1960), Ib Melchior, and *re*written by Pink. In any case, the haste certainly shows.

A drilling crew in Lapland discovers the frozen tail of a gigantic prehistoric beast, and it's shipped back to Copenhagen for study. When the tail begins to grow a new creature(!), the U.S. sends General Mark Grayson (Carl Ottosen) to supervise. During an electrical storm, the re-grown beast comes fully alive and goes on a rampage of destruction, with Grayson and the Danish military chasing it about until the monster (who spits a deadly "acid slime" and whose "armor-like" hide is nearly impenetrable) comes crashing into the heart of Copenhagen.

"INVINCIBLE ... INDESTRUCTIBLE! WHAT WAS THIS BEAST BORN FIFTY MILLION YEARS OUT OF TIME?" asked the ads. The answer: a pathetic puppet. With its tiny legs, immobile body (the only thing that ever seems to move is its long, ungainly neck and head) and silly-looking (and apparently useless) wings, Reptilicus is the dopiest giant monster this side of *The Giant Claw*. Actually, Reptilicus does fly in the Danish version, but when Arkoff saw these airborne scenes, he reportedly burst out laughing and ordered the beast grounded in the American prints. (How he kept from laughing throughout the *rest* of the movie remains a mystery.)

Reptilicus was actually filmed twice—an

English version directed by Pink and a Danish version directed by Saga Studio head Poul Bang (Saga co-financed the film with AIP, with a final budget of $133,000). "I was to shoot each scene first," explained Pink, "and after I accepted a take, Paol [sic] Bang would then rehearse and shoot until he had a satisfactory take." Things didn't go quite as planned, however. "Paol [sic] was never satisfied with my camera placements and would change them." (Of course, given the finished product, one can't really *blame* the Dane.)

Pink has no illusions about either his performance as a first-time director or the film itself. "I made every mistake in the book and then some," he admitted, concluding, "I was able to finish directing the picture without really knowing what the hell I was doing." Most of the film is taken up with goofy "comic" antics by an overall-clad night watchman (Danish comedian Dirch Passer), talking head scenes with the bulldog-like general (who e-nun-ci-ates ve-ry care-ful-ly, becoming quite comical), and plenty of footage of the Danish Army and Navy on maneuvers. (Through Saga Studio owner Fleming John Olsen, Pink secured the full cooperation of the Danish military, and was given the use of jeeps, troops, cannon and even tanks!) The "money" shots of Reptilicus trashing Copenhagen consist of the immobile marionette anchored to the unconvincing model sets, trying to knock something over with its head. Occasionally it spits its "acid slime" in a (literal) cartoon effect that would have felt right at home on the campy *Batman* TV series ("Zowie!"). Said slime was actually an afterthought on the part of AIP, who added the cartoon effects after Pink turned in his finished film.

According to Ib Melchior, AIP was less-than-satisfied with *Reptilicus*. Apart from demanding that the film be re-dubbed (though shot in English, Arkoff felt the Danish actors' "singsong" accents would have set American audiences rolling in the aisles), AIP also asked Melchior to shoot some additional scenes. This tampering led to lawsuits filed by Pink, delaying the movie's release for nearly a year and a half.

According to Pink, "*Reptilicus* went on to be a multimillion dollar grossing picture for AIP." *Caveat Emptor*! In the end, a more apt name for *Reptilicus* would have been *Ridiculus*.

Repulsion (1965; Compton Films/Royal Films International; b&w) Director: Roman Polanski; Producer: Gene Gutowski; Screenplay: Roman Polanski and Gerard Brach; Cinematographer: Gilbert Taylor. Cast: Catherine Deneuve, Ian Hendry, John Fraser, Yvonne Furneaux, Patrick Wymark.

A classic chiller of the 'Psycho' school!—tagline

Although his debut feature, *Knife in the Water* (1962), earned an Oscar nomination and enthusiastic reviews from critics throughout the West, director Roman Polanski's work remained unpopular at home, especially within the communist film bureau that Polish moviemakers relied upon for funding. Party bosses saw no use in searing psychological dramas with no propaganda value, leaving Polanski stymied. So when exploitation producer Gene Gutowski asked the director to travel to England and helm a *Psycho* clone, Polanski jumped at the opportunity.

Yet, once again Polanski defied expectations. Gutowski wanted a simple exploitation picture (something "sensational" and "as sexual as censors would allow in those days"), but Polanski wanted to "upgrade" the project to a "psychological thriller" instead of "a cheap horror film." The director's ambitions were amply fulfilled. *Repulsion* emerged as a deeply disturbing rumination on the corrosive power of loneliness. It stands as not merely the finest of the many black-and-white psycho-thrillers produced in the wake of *Psycho* (1960), but as a truly great film in its own right. In its unflinching examination of isolation and urban paranoia, *Repulsion* seems ahead of its time,

Italian photobusta showcasing the psychological terrors of *Repulsion* (1965).

prefiguring pictures such as Martin Scorsese's harrowing *Taxi Driver* (1976), as well as Polanski's own *Rosemary's Baby* (1968) and *The Tenant* (1976).

Shy, sexually repressed Carol (Catherine Deneuve) lives with her sister Helen (Yvonne Furneaux), who is having an affair with a married man, Michael (Ian Hendry). To no avail, Carol meekly voices her disapproval. With a bit more success, she tries to fend off the advances of would-be boyfriend Colin (John Fraser)—even rushing away to vigorously brush her teeth after he kisses her goodnight. When Helen and Michael leave for a vacation in Italy, Carol's mental health crumbles. She becomes withdrawn, delusional and stricken by nightmares (in which she is repeatedly raped) and hallucinations (including phantom-like hands that reach out from the walls to paw at her body). Eventually the emotionally shattered young woman bashes Colin's head in with a candlestick. Later, after her landlord (Patrick Wymark) attempts to rape her, she slices him to death with a straight razor.

Polanski builds tension slowly but inexorably throughout this deceptively simple narrative, which includes long sequences without dialogue. He provides a visual metaphor for Carol's psychological disintegration in the remnants of a half-prepared dinner: A pair of potatoes whose eyes sprout squid-like tendrils, and the decaying carcass of a cleaned and dressed, but uncooked, rabbit (which Carol later decapitates with the razor). By offering no visual differentiation between hallucinations and "reality," Polanski draws viewers into Carol's troubled mind. Gilbert Taylor's high-contrast, chiaroscuro lighting, and Stephen Dalby's innovative sound design (full of displaced mechanical creaks and moans), further sharpen the suspense. "All the time we were looking for something to make it look odd, and if it didn't look odd we would change the setup until it did look odd," Taylor said.

The result is a film as engrossing as *Psycho,* but more naturalistic (Polanski eschews bravura camera moves and flashy set pieces, such as the murders of Marion Crane and Arbogast) and less playful (Hitchcock's dark humor replaced by a sense of existential despair). Also, *Repulsion* is a psycho-chiller devoid of psychobabble. Instead of pat Freudian explanations for Carol's behavior, the film offers only one clue to her pathology: An old family snapshot that shows Carol standing apart from her parents and siblings, staring at the camera with a blank expression on her face.

None of this would work, however, without Deneuve's inspired performance as Carol. Onscreen almost constantly, with very little dialogue, Deneuve's timid, jittery body language and her extraordinarily expressive eyes make Carol's tortured inner life seem agonizingly real. Indeed, the film's only slack moments are those rare occasions when she is off-screen (namely, scenes set in a pub, where Colin's cretinous mates rib him for failing to get into his girlfriend's pants). Deneuve's performance seems all the more remarkable considering that English was not the native tongue of either the actress or her director (this being Polanski's first English language project). The script accounts for the accents of Deneuve and Furneaux by making Carol and Helen Belgian immigrants. The rest of the cast also acquits itself well, especially Hendry, who brings charm and a surprising degree of sympathy to his role as Michael, Helen's philandering lover.

Taking a page from Charlie Chaplin's playbook, Polanski (a former actor) often demonstrated the gestures and movements he wanted from his cast. "When we shoot a scene including several actors, he acts out every role," Deneuve said in a French TV interview filmed during production. "Polanski is very meticulous," said Furneaux. "He insists that you avoid conventional approaches and clichés at all costs. 'No, that's in the theater, the movies or TV but not in real life.' And his suggestions from real life are always simpler, more subtle and much more profound, psychologically."

Polanski, of course, went on to *Rosemary's Baby* (1968) and *Chinatown* (1974), two towering classics that loom over everything before them in the director's filmography. But *Repulsion* should not be overlooked. Impeccably crafted and performed, sophisticated yet hard-hitting, it remains essential viewing.

With quotes from: The Blue Underground documentary short "A British Horror Film," and "Roman Polanski Directs in London," from the *Grand Eclan* TV show (both included on the Criterion Collection DVD of *Repulsion*).

Return from the Past see *Dr. Terror's Gallery of Horrors*

Revenge of the Blood Beast see *The She-Beast*

Revenge of the Living Dead see *Murder Clinic*

The Robot vs. the Aztec Mummy

(1957/65; Cinematografica Calderon/Trans-International Films; Mexico; b&w) Original Language Title: *La Momia Azteca Contra el Robot Humano*; Director: Rafael Portillo, Manuel San Fernando (English version); Producer: William Calderon Stell, K. Gordon Murray (English version); Screenplay: Alfred Salazar (story by William Calderon Stell and Alfred Salazar). Cinematographer: Enrique Wallace. Cast: Ramon Gay, Rosita Arenas, Crox Alvarado, Luis Aceves Castaneda, Jorge Mondragon.

A MONSTROUS NIGHTMARE TERROR turned loose in a fight to the DEATH!—ad line

"They will bring you a night of terror," promised the trailer for *The Robot vs. the Aztec Mummy*. So much for truth in advertising, as the hoodwinked viewer will more likely experience a night of *boredom*. Third in the original Aztec Mummy trilogy begun with the abominable *Attack of the Mayan Mummy* and continued with the slightly-better-but-still-bad *Curse of the Aztec Mummy* (a fourth "Aztec Mummy" film, *The Wrestling Women vs. the Aztec Mummy*, was made seven years later, but is only tangentially related to the earlier trio), *The Robot vs. the Aztec Mummy* stands as a slight improvement over its lackluster progenitors (if only by dint of stealing the earlier films' few intriguing scenes while adding its own little touch of mechanical-man wackiness). Admittedly, that's not saying much.

That evil criminal scientist "the Bat" is back and once again searching for the breastplate and bracelet (which hold the secret to a fabulous Aztec treasure) guarded by the living mummy Popoca. The Bat constructs a "human robot" (a metal man with a human brain) in a convoluted plot to destroy the Aztec Mummy and obtain the treasure, which will finance his intentions to build an army of robots to conquer the world. It's up to a professor and his wife (the reincarnation of Popoca's lost love)—and Popoca himself—to once more thwart the madman's evil plan.

Over a third of *The Robot vs. the Aztec Mummy* consists of flashback scenes from the previous entries (which is fine for the neophyte viewer, but quickly turns tedious for those who've seen the other Aztec Mummy movies), while the new footage offers mostly dull, talky, static scenes in which the camera rarely movies and nothing much happens. Apart from the odd, isolated mummy flashback moments, the picture only comes to life (or a risible semblance thereof) when the "robot" does the same—in the final ten minutes.

Unfortunately (or fortunately, depending upon one's "camp" sensibilities), said robot belongs to the goofy painted-cardboard-box-and-bucket variety. Laughably, the suit-wearer's face is fully visible behind the monster's faceplate—even though the mechanical monster supposedly houses merely a human *brain*. The (brief) climactic battle between the robot and the Aztec Mummy has the two titular terrors taking turns awkwardly pushing each other back against a wall, before the Mummy finally tires of the game and dismantles his silly opponent.

***The Robot vs. the Aztec Mummy* (195765): enough said (Photofest).**

For its U.S. theatrical premiere (on November 17, 1965, in Cincinnati, Ohio), *Robot* was billed with *The Vampire's Coffin* (itself a sequel—to the Germán Robles starrer *The Vampire*). To ballyhoo the release of his double feature, importer/distributor K. Gordon Murray included in his ads an endorsement by the "Young America Horror Club," a totally fictitious organization! Murray also tacked onto his prints a phony process called "Hypnoscope," which, according to the trailer, consisted of a whirling spiral that induced a hypnotic state of pure terror! Right.

Rosemary's Baby (1968; Paramount) Director/Screenplay: Roman Polanski (from a novel by Ira Levin); Producer: William Castle; Cinematographer: William Fraker. Cast: Mia Farrow, John Cassavetes, Ruth Gordon, Sidney Blackmer, Maurice Evans.

Pray for Rosemary's baby—tagline

Masterful in construction, flawless in execution and penetrating in cultural insight, *Rosemary's Baby* s towers above most horror films, including the lineage of Satanic shockers it sired.

Newlyweds Rosemary (Mia Farrow) and Guy (John Cassavetes) Woodhouse move into a historic New York apartment building, where they are befriended by their elderly neighbors, Roman (Sidney Blackmer) and Minnie (Ruth Gordon) Castavet. The Castavets take an interest in Guy's struggling acting career, and soon he lands a showy role in a Broadway play. (He gets the part after another actor, already hired for the play, is mysteriously struck blind.) As the Woodhouse's fortunes improve, however, Rosemary begins to question the curious behavior of both her pushy yet overly friendly neighbors and her increasingly distant husband. When she becomes pregnant (following a "nightmare" in which she is raped by a monster), Guy and the Castavets become overwhelmingly protective of Rosemary and her unborn child. Finally, thanks to a gift left by a deceased friend, Rosemary comes to suspect that the Castavets are part of a Satanic coven, and that they plan to use her baby in some unholy ritual. But the truth is even more horrific.

Filmmaker William Castle purchased the rights to Ira Levin's not-yet-published novel *Rosemary's Baby* and brought it to Paramount Pictures. Robert Evans, the studio's head of production, recognizing that the project was potentially "very important," nixed the idea of the film being directed by Castle, notorious for gimmicky, low-budget chillers like *House on Haunted Hill* and *The Tingler* (both 1959). He agreed to retain Castle as producer and allowed him to make a cameo appearance, but Evans wanted Roman Polanski to helm the project. To secure the director's services, Evans baited him with *Downhill Racer*, a project Polanski (a self-identified "ski fanatic") coveted. Once Polanski arrived in America, however, Evans asked him to read the galleys of Levin's novel. Polanski also grasped the extraordinary potential of the story and agreed to abandon the skiing picture in favor of *Rosemary's Baby*.

The coven of Manhattan Satanists reveals the truth to the mother (Mia Farrow, holding knife) about *Rosemary's Baby* (1968).

Once onboard, however, Evans and Polanski clashed over the casting of the lead roles. Initially, the director wanted Tuesday Weld to play Rosemary, while Evans suggested Farrow, then well-known from TV's *Peyton Place* and as the wife of Frank Sinatra (the couple would split during the film's production). When a compromise choice, Jane Fonda, turned down the part, Evans got his way. Both Evans and Polanski envisaged Robert Redford in the role of Guy, but Redford declined (ironically, he chose instead to star in *Downhill Racer*). Polanski suggested Cassavetes as a replacement. It was also Polanski's idea to populate the film's supporting roles with Hollywood veterans like Bellamy, Patsy Kelly and Elisha Cook, Jr. Tony Curtis makes a cameo appearance as a voice on the telephone. A cameo featuring Joan Crawford and Van Johnson was cut due to length.

This was Polanski's first literary adaptation, and he delivered a remarkably accurate transcription of Levin's book. "I've always felt that the film of *Rosemary's Baby* is the single most faithful adaptation of a novel ever to come out of Hollywood," Levin said. "Not only does it incorporate whole chunks of the book's dialogue, it even follows the colors of the clothing (where I mentioned them) and the layout of the apartment. And perhaps more importantly, Polanski's directorial style of not aiming the camera squarely at the horror but rather letting the audience spot it for themselves off at the side of the screen coincides happily, I think, with my own writing style."

In those rare instances where Polanski's movie varies from Levin's novel, his changes improve upon the source material, the filmmaker proving even more restrained and subtle than the author. Most notably, Polanski refrains from showing title character. We see Rosemary's mortified reaction to the sight of her child, but not the baby itself. Levin, on the other hand, describes a furry-pawed, horn-headed Li'l Devil (just the sort of thing Castle would have used). Polanski also tones down the novel's lacerating social satire, exchanging wry humor for paranoid suspense.

While Polanski's screenwriting is superb, his direction is even better. The film's eerie dream sequences rank among the most surreal and genuinely nightmarish ever committed to celluloid. Rosemary's half-waking, half-dreaming, ritualistic rape remains wrenching viewing. His treatment of other scenes, while far less flashy, prove no less powerful. He subtly ratchets up tension throughout, leveraging William Fraker's naturalistic yet suggestive lighting and employing symbolic visual compositions (for instance, using large, off-center open spaces in the frame to underscore Rosemary's isolation). Polanski used many of these same techniques for *Repulsion* (1965), albeit with less dexterity and finesse. The picture also benefits greatly from Christopher Komeda's subtly unnerving score and from the superb work of production designer Richard Sylbert, whose set designs and location decorations are creepy while steadfastly authentic. (The film was shot partly at the Dakota, a New York apartment building later notorious as the site of John Lennon's assassination.)

Finally, and perhaps most impressively of all, Polanski elicits uniformly naturalistic yet fascinating portrayals from his gifted cast. Farrow's performance in the title role remains a career high water mark. Her multi-faceted and carefully nuanced portrayal brilliantly realizes Rosemary's physical and mental deterioration, as well as her deceptive inner strength and devotion to her unborn child. It's difficult to imagine any performer doing more for a picture than Farrow, who ate raw liver during one scene and even sang the lullaby that plays under the opening credits. She is simply magnificent.

The film's most celebrated performance, however, was that of Gordon as likeable Satanist Minnie Castavet, which won the actress the 1969 Oscar for Best Actress in a Supporting Role. (Incomprehensibly, Farrow failed to earn a nomination in the lead Actress category.) Gordon is indeed a delight, bringing earthy good humor to the role without undercutting the essentially menacing nature of her character. Cassavetes, as the vain and duplicitous Guy, also performs memorably, as do Blackmer as Roman Castavet and Ralph Bellamy as Rosemary's inscrutable obstetrician, Dr. Saperstein.

Rosemary's Baby, like all works of fantasy that enjoy great popular successes, tapped into something of its moment, revealing ambitions and anxieties lurking just beneath the surface in the cultural zeitgeist, waiting for an outlet. It was one of the first films (along with *Repulsion*) to address urban paranoia, suggesting that even your kindly elderly neighbors could literally be in league with Satan. The story also takes expectant mothers' natural fears and carries them to their logical endpoint: Rosemary endures a torturous pregnancy and gives birth to a hideously deformed, evil child—and in the process her marriage collapses.

Rosemary's Baby also left an indelible imprint on horror cinema as the picture which popularized Satan as a horror movie villain. Movie audiences in previous decades may not have accepted this, but within the increasingly secularized culture of the late 1960s (Time magazine's famous *Is God Dead?* cover appears in the film), making the devil himself an essential character in the drama became fair game. Simultaneously, however, enough residual faith (or at least distant memories of Sunday school) lingered in the popular imagination for Satan to carry a great deal more emotional power than familiar characters such as vampires or werewolves. In future years dozens of similar movies emerged, most notably *The Exorcist* (1973) and *The Omen* (1976). *Rosemary's Baby*'s downbeat ending, with evil triumphant, which would not have been possible during the era of the Production Code, soon became a cliché.

In 2008, Entertainment Weekly named *Rosemary's Baby* the tenth scariest movie ever made. Its selection was a testament to the film's unabated power to unnerve audiences. The film's ongoing appeal comes as no surprise to Evans. "I knew it was going to be big because it shook people," Evans said. "There are no special effects, no screaming or walls crumbling down or crocodiles coming out of the walls, nothing like that. It's all in the way he [Polanski] shot it, and it works on every level. And it scares the hell out of you."

Along with *Psycho* and *Night of the Living Dead*, *Rosemary's Baby* stands among the smartest and most influential horror films of the 1960s— or any other decade.

With quotes from: Interview with Robert Evans, Rosemary's Baby DVD (Paramount Pictures); *Rosemary's Baby* (The Stephen King Horror Library edition), by Ira Levin (Introduction by Stephen King).

Samson in the Wax Museum (1963/65;

Filmadora Panamerica S.A./Trans-International Films; Mexico; b&w) Alternate Title: *Santo in the Wax Museum*; Original Language Title: *Santo en el Museo de Cera*; Director: Alfonso Corona Blake, Manuel San Fernando (English language version); Producer: Albert Lopez, K. Gordon Murray (English version); Cinematographer: Joseph Ortiz Ramos. Cast: Samson "The Sliver Maskman," Claudio Brook, Norma Mora, Rouben Rojo, Roxana Bellini.

Samson, the unconquerable, unearths weird beings in the tyrant's dungeon of horror ... — ad line

It's *Mystery of the Wax Museum* gone south, south of the border, that is— as well as south of believability, since the film's hero is that silver-masked, crime-fighting professional wrestler Santo (don't let the dubbing fool you — a Santo by any other name wrestles just as sweetly). Here Santo/Samson investigates a series of disappearances revolving around a sinister wax museum run by Dr. Karol (Claudio Brook).

The third (and last) Santo feature to be dubbed into English, *Wax Museum* is far superior to the initial Santo offering, 1961's *Invasion of the Zombies* (of course, this is damning with faint praise). First off, there's far less wrestling in *Wax Museum*. In fact, it's nearly a half-hour before Santo— er, Samson — shows up, which means a nice respite from wrasslin'. (Though a bit harsh when speaking of a Mexican *wrestling* movie, the less ringside wrangle the better — at least for those viewers not enthralled by the WWE circuit.)

Second, *Wax Museum* sports a rather intriguing mystery-motif in its first half, in which the police, Samson and the viewer receive evidence both for *and* against Dr. Karol's guilt. Along with the eerie atmosphere in Karol's cavern-like "museum" housing his weird, monstrous figures, this initial ambivalence keeps the viewer off balance and interested. Of course, after 45 minutes the picture spoils it all by revealing the identity of the villain who's transforming people into disfigured "statues" with his flesh-eroding and trance-inducing serum.

Spanish poster for *Samson in the Wax Museum* (1963/65).

Fortunately, the clichéd "mad doctor" plot takes a novel twist here, with the madman having been driven insane by his past experiences as a concentration camp victim. "I suffered such horrible things," he laments, "the only peace I know is watching other people suffer and writhe in agony." He goes on to espouse his twisted philosophy: "All humans are monsters, you know. I found that to be true the nights I was tortured. Since it is true, why not show what your soul and your conscience really are, using your face. Well, now I intend to create a world in which all humans are deformed." Occasionally, his utterances even border on the profound: "Should a man's face show his inner soul to us, demonstrating the things he hides so well, I assure you you'd see more deformity than you see in these quiet statues." Despite the frequently awkward language (courtesy of importer K. Gordon Murray and co.'s terrible "translations") and the strident yet oddly atonal delivery by the dubbing actor, such a thought-provoking diatribe is more than one expects in a Mexican wrestling movie.

Disappointingly, the "monsters" look like cut-rate *Island of Lost Souls* rejects (brawny man with unconvincing pig-snout, hairy-faced cretin, etc.). And the film makes up for its wrestling-free first third by tossing in a number of ringside scenes towards the middle and end, spoiling the picture's rhythm (but presumably giving the Santo fans what they want). Even so, compared to its predecessor, *Samson in the Wax Museum* still wins this Mexi-movie wrestling bout.

Samson vs. the Vampire Women (1962/63; Filmadora Primamaricana S.A./Trans-International Films; Mexico; b&w) Original Language Title: *El Santo Contra las Mujeres Vampiros*. Director: Alfonso Corona Blake, Manuel San Fernando (English Language Version); Producer: Luis Garcia De Leon and Alberto Lopez, K. Gordon Murray (English version); Screenplay: Rafael Garcia Travesi, Alfonso Corona Blake; Cinematographer: Jose Ortiz Ramos. Cast: Samson the Silver Maskman, Lorena Velazquez, Maria Duval, Jaime Fernandez, Augusto Benedico.

Deep in the bowels of the Earth live the most savage and vicious of all women!—TV spot

The best of the three Santo (ne Samson) movies dubbed into English in the 1960s (*Invasion of the Zombies* and *Santo in the Wax Museum* being the other two), *Samson vs. the Vampire Women* stars that most famous of all Mexican masked wrestler heroes, El Santo, as the main opposition to a coven of vampire women (led by Lorena Velasquez) who have awakened after 200 years to seek a new Queen of the Vampires (an innocent girl chosen at birth and destined to take her place among the undead upon her twenty-first birthday). Diana (Maria Duval), daughter of Professor Roloff (Augusto Benedico), is the chosen unfortunate, and it's up to Roloff's friend Samson (with a little help from the police) to take some time out of his ringside activities and foil the bloodsuckers' plans.

Actress Lorena Velasquez (who also starred with the masked wrestler in *Invasion of the Zombies*, and who played a wrestler herself in several pictures, including *The Wrestling Women vs. the Aztec Mummy*) appeared on Britain's *Incredibly Strange Film Show* in 1989. About El Santo, she said: "He represented justice. He was the Mexican Schwarzenegger. And he was a very nice man, very kind man, very good actor—well, *not* very good, but he represented justice and this was very important for the people." Indeed, one doesn't watch a Santo movie to see classical thespian, but to see an icon of Truth, Justice and the Mexican Way take out bad guys and monsters.

The picture opens in an Old Dark House as creepy as any you'll see in a classic Universal—full of cobwebs, shadows and low-key lighting. The camera prowls about until it comes to rest on an upright sarcophagus. The lid creaks open to expose a shrouded corpse whose hideous dried and cracked face suddenly comes to life as the eyes—in startling close-up—spring open. It's an eerie, atmospheric and unsettling beginning that, unfortunately, the subsequent step into the mundane modern lives of the dull protagonists can't sustain. In *Samson vs. the Vampire Women*, Evil truly is more interesting than Virtue.

Samson's (Santo's) opponents in their lair in *Samson vs. the Vampire Women* (1962/63) (Photofest).

The film presents a unique take on vampirism. When the female vampires drink blood, they transform from grotesque hags into diaphanous-gowned, leggy beauties who pray to Satan, even conjuring up the "Lord of Darkness" himself (in silhouette, anyway)—aligning vampirism to Devil worship. And this evil cult is definitely a matriarchy (with hints of lesbianism, as they seem to prefer biting women), adding a bit of subtext to the tale by pitting Samson, the ultimate defender of patriarchal society, against this aberration of matriarchal deviants.

But lest one become lost in subtextural musings, the movie periodically reminds the viewer of what it's *really* all about, as Samson tackles a vampire opponent in the ring (a male minion who's secretly taken a wrestler's place). After the vampire-wrestler fails to kill Samson ("He's using karate!" Our Hero exclaims), Samson unmasks him — revealing the hirsute face of a *werewolf*(!), who then proceeds to escape by transforming into a bat! Though odd in the extreme, this scene is nothing if not novel.

And novel may be the operative word for *Samson vs. the Vampire Women*, which provides enough offbeat entertainment to keep any Mexi-movie enthusiast satisfied. As the Professor so earnestly exclaims at picture's end: "God bless Samson!"

Santo in the Wax Museum see *Samson in the Wax Museum*

Santo vs. the Zombies see *Invasion of the Zombies*

Scream Baby Scream (1969; Westbury) Director/Producer: Joseph Adler; Screenplay: Laurence Robert Cohen; Cinematographer: Julio Chavez. Cast: Ross Harris, Eugenie Wingate, Chris Martell, Suzanne Stuart, Larry Swanson, Jim Vance.

A freaked-out horror-thriller that will really shock it to you! — tagline

Coed Janet (Eugenie Wingate), to the irritation of jealous boyfriend Jason (Ross Harris), strikes up a friendship with wealthy artist Charles Butler (Larry Swanson), who specializes in macabre portraiture. When she accepts an invitation to visit the notoriously reclusive Butler at his home, however, Janet discovers a shocking secret: The artist's work is painted from life, using women he has kidnapped and, with help from a demented plastic surgeon, disfigured to serve as models.

Unfortunately, *Scream Baby Scream*'s scare scenes are undercut by Douglas Hobart's laughable makeup effects. Worse yet, the film devotes very little screen time to the horror elements of its story. Instead, audiences endure nonstop romantic bickering between Jason and Janet (Jason wants to get married but Janet isn't ready, Janet wants to experiment with drugs but Jason isn't interested, and on and on), usually followed by a sex scene when the two briefly "make up." Viewers are also privy to the shenanigans of Jason, Janet and fellow hipster doofus art students Scotty (Chris Martell) and Marika (Suzanne Stuart). Together the foursome hang out in night clubs and coffee shops, listen to awful rock music (by the Odyssey), blather at length about art, smoke pot and drop acid (the last triggering a protracted, double-exposed "trip" sequence where the quartet go to the zoo and imagine themselves in the animal cages). Perhaps screenwriter Larry Cohen and producer-director Joseph Adler included all this material to try to emulate the recent success of *Easy Rider* (1969). If so, they failed miserably — mostly because their version of the counterculture is so boring it would make Abbie Hoffman join the ROTC.

Amateurishly acted, haphazardly shot and overstuffed with banal dialogue and unlikable characters, *Scream Baby Scream* is dull baby dull.

Scream of Fear (1961; Hammer/Columbia; U.K.; b&w). Alternate Title: *Taste of Fear* (U.K.) Director: Seth Holt; Producer/Screenplay: Jimmy Sangster; Cinematographer: Douglas Slocombe. Cast: Susan Strasberg, Ann Todd, Ronald Lewis, Christopher Lee.

Management and staff of this theatre have been pledged to an oath of secrecy concerning the electrifying climax! For maximum excitement, we earnestly recommend that you see this motion picture from the start! — poster

In the aftershock of the pop culture bombshell that was Alfred Hitchcock's *Psycho* (1960), opportunistic filmmakers rushed numerous black-and-white psychological thrillers into production. Most of these were cheap rip-offs and cynical cash-ins, but not Hammer Films' *Scream of Fear.* In this case at least, *Psycho* proved to be a source of inspiration rather than simple imitation.

The project certainly brought out the best in talented but erratic screenwriter Jimmy Sangster, whose scenario is a minor masterpiece of coiled suspense — taut and twisty, with finely embellished characters and spine-tingling set pieces. Sangster recognized the gem he had crafted and, after shopping the script around to other studios, managed to parlay it into his first assignment as a producer. In that role, Sangster hired all the right personnel to visualize his story. The final result was one of Hammer's most profitable movies to date, one that launched of a series of pseudo *Psychos* that would continue for the next four years.

Penny Appleby (Susan Strasberg), the estranged, paraplegic daughter of a wealthy businessman, receives an urgent summons home from her father. When she arrives at the family's manor house, however, her dad is nowhere to be found. She's greeted instead by her austere stepmother Jane (Ann Todd) and her amiable chauffeur Robert (Ronald Lewis). The only other person who seems to come by is the creepy Dr. Gerard (Christopher Lee), who Jane refers to as "a friend of the family." Jane grows suspicious, and—in a bravura sequence—sneaks out of the main house and over to a small cottage by the pool, where, in the flickering candlelight, she discovers her father's body, propped up in a chair. As she flees the cottage in screaming panic, her wheelchair veers into the pool. She's rescued by the chauffeur, and together the pair theorizes that Jane and Dr. Gerrard must have killed Mr. Appleby. To prove their suspicions they will have to uncover her father's corpse, which has mysteriously vanished. But Penny soon discovers that nothing is quite as it seems.

A bit of Hitchcockian ballyhoo for the Hitchcockian Hammer horror *Scream of Fear* (1961). (Australian daybill).

To direct *Scream of Fear* Sangster hired Seth Holt, who had edited some of Ealing Studios' most famous comedies (*The Lavender Hill Mob, The Ladykillers, The Titfield Thunderbolt*) but whose directorial experience was limited to one film, the thriller *Nowhere to Go* (1958), which he co-helmed with Basil Dearden. Holt rewarded Sangster's confidence with an assured and skillful turn behind the camera. His careful compositions take full advantage of cinematographer Douglas Slocombe's noirish, chiaroscuro lighting scheme. Thanks to his experience as an editor, Holt's command of the film's pace is masterful, as is his handling of the story's thrilling pool house sequence and other fright scenes. After *Scream of Fear*, critics heralded Holt as a new Master of Suspense, but health issues enabled him to complete just three more features before his untimely death in 1971 at age 48. Fortunately, one of those three films was another superb collaboration with Sangster, *The Nanny* (1965).

Holt also elicits fine performances from the film's small but gifted cast. Susan Strasberg (daughter of method acting guru Lee Strasberg) is nothing short of sensational, delivering an unaffected, subtle portrayal as the jittery but determined Penny. Ann Todd, as the mysterious Mrs. Appleby, and Ronald Lewis as the endearing chauffeur, also prove convincing. Fourth-billed Christopher Lee checks in with an equally effective turn, albeit in a glorified red herring role.

Scream of Fear—marketed in the U.S. with taglines that recalled the advertising campaign for *Psycho*—succeeded with both critics and moviegoers and spawned several more Hammer psycho-chillers, shot in black and white and written and produced by Sangster: *Maniac*, *Paranoiac* (both 1963), *Nightmare* (1964), *Hysteria* and *The Nanny* (both 1965). (*Die! Die! My Darling* [1965], shot in color, produced by Anthony Hinds and written by Richard Matheson, could also be considered part of this unofficial "series" of Hammer psychological thrillers.) For the most part, however, the white-hot heat of inspiration that radiates from *Scream of Fear* remains absent from these follow-ups. Only *The Nanny* approaches the brilliance of the original, although *Maniac* and *Paranoiac* remain diverting.

Over the years, Hammer's splashy color gothics have overshadowed *Scream of Fear*. Nevertheless, it ranks among the studio's best releases of the 1960s and delivers more thrills per viewing than most of the studio's higher profile productions.

The Screaming Head see *The Head*

Seconds (1966; Paramount; b&w) Director: John Frankenheimer; Producer: Edward Lewis; Screenplay: Lewis John Carlino (Novel: David Ely); Cinematographer: James Wong Howe. Cast: Rock Hudson, Salome Jens, John Randolph, Will Geer, Richard Anderson, Frances Reid, Jeff Corey.

What Are Seconds? The Answer May Be Too Terrifying For Words!—tagline

Seconds (1966), the final entry in director John Frankenheimer's informal trilogy of paranoid thrillers, remains the most underrated of the trio and, arguably, one of the most underappreciated great movies of the 1960s. Less political and more philosophical in theme, and more overtly horrific in style than its predecessors *The Manchurian Candidate* (1962) and *Seven Days in May* (1964), *Seconds* is profoundly scary, all the more so because its science-gone-wrong scenario brings viewers face to face with existential questions about their own lives.

Arthur Hamilton (John Randolph) is a middle-aged bank executive with a comfortable but humdrum life, complete with a dowdy wife (Frances Reid), an adult married daughter and a station wagon. He's intrigued when a mysterious phone call from a believed-dead friend alerts him to an astonishing possibility: the opportunity to fake his own death and begin a new life, with a surgically-enhanced body and a different identity—all in exchange for $30,000 up front, as well as control over his life savings. After some cat-and-mouse negotiations with a shadowy organization referred to simply as The Company, and an *Eyes Without a Face*–like surgical scene, Arthur is "reborn" as painter Tony Wilson (Rock Hudson) and relocated to a stylish beachfront studio in Malibu. Yet "Tony" struggles to adjust to his new life. He meets an attractive young woman (Salome Jens) who takes him to a wild, bacchanal wine festival—complete with orgiastic naked grape stomping. Although uncomfortable, Tony eventually gets into the spirit. But in the next scene, hosting a cocktail party for his new neighbors, Tony becomes so nervous and insecure that he gets drunk and blows his cover. He flees California and, after a short visit with his "widow," returns to the Company to request a second new identity, setting up the film's bitterly ironic—and bleak—finale.

No plot summary can do justice to *Seconds*, a picture whose impact lies as much in presentation as in content. Frankenheimer and cinematographer James Wong Howe (who earned an Oscar nomination for his work here) make *Seconds* an unrelentingly unsettling experience. Nearly every shot contains some off-kilter element—strange ultra-high or low camera angles, abrupt rack focus shifts, obvious rear-projection to create a sense of unreality, slow-motion and other techniques—all employed to powerful effect. Howe also makes heavy use of super-wide angle lenses, which slightly distort the image. Jerry Goldsmith's eerie, organ-drenched score adds a gothic touch.

The movie also benefits from (pun intended) Rock-solid performances from Hudson and John Randolph in the title role. Hudson sinks his teeth into his showy, change-of-pace role, displaying range untapped by the light comedic and heroic military parts he played almost exclusively throughout the 1950s and '60s. Veteran character actor Randolph's scenes are quietly touching, especially those depicting his burned-out marriage. The supporting ensemble also delivers uniformly credible work, especially Salome Jens as Tony's romantic interest, Richard Anderson as a plastic surgeon and Jeff Corey as a mysterious Company man named Mr. Ruby (a moniker that inevitably evokes conspiracy theories). But the film's most striking supporting performance comes from future Grandpa Walton Will Geer, playing a nameless old man who founded The Company, whose home-spun sweet-talking ultimately convinces the reluctant Arthur to go ahead with his "rebirth." Geer's warmth and folksiness makes The Company seem even colder and more inhuman.

In many ways, *Seconds*, released a year prior to the Summer of Love, was ahead of its time. Had it debuted just a couple of years later, after the counterculture had gone mainstream and more young people were exploring lifestyles like the one Tony discovers in Malibu, *Seconds* might have had greater box office and critical impact. Lewis John Carlino's screenplay (based on David Ely's novel) not only creates a typically Frankenheimerian world dominated by mysterious cabals, where no one can be trusted, but also forces Arthur/Tony (and viewers) to reconsider his (our) basic values. The protagonist has found no deep satisfaction in the pursuit of middle-class American, materialistic goals, but after his "rebirth" discovers no more happiness in a life of "free love" and hedonistic excess. "The years I've spent trying to get the things I was *told* were important, that I was *supposed* to want — things. Not people, or meaning, just *things*," Tony (Hudson) whispers plaintively to a fellow Reborn. "California was the same. They made the same decisions for me all over again, and they were the same things, really. It's going to be different from now on." Unfortunately, by the time he realizes his error it's already too late. There's no use in blaming others for our unhappiness, or in relying on someone else to rescue us. No matter how joyful or sad they may be, our lives, *Seconds* suggests, remain ours alone to author — or to erase.

The Secret of Dr. Orloff see *Dr. Orloff's Monster*

The Shadow of the Cat (1961; B.H.P. Films/ Universal; U.K.; b&w) Director: John Gilling; Producer: John Penington; Screenplay: George Baxt; Cinematographer: Arthur Grant. Cast: Andre Morell, Barbara Shelley, William Lucas, Freda Jackson, Conrad Phillips, Catherine Lacey.

WAS IT SUPERNATURAL FORCE OR PSYCHOTIC COMPULSION THAT MADE THEM WANT TO KILL?—ad line

This highly atmospheric and downright creepy Hammer film ... hold on a minute; despite it being filmed at Bray Studios (the "home of Hammer") and utilizing a plethora of Hammer personnel, both in front of and behind the camera (such as director John Gilling, cinematographer Arthur Grant, production designer Bernard Robinson, and actors Andre Morell, Barbara Shelley and Freda Jackson), *The Shadow of the Cat* is a B.H.P. Films production, *not* a Hammer movie — but it just as well *could* be (and one superior to much of that revered company's sometimes indifferent product).

"You seriously mean to tell me that one ordinary domestic cat is terrorizing three grownups?" asks one incredulous character. Indeed it is, as this terrifying tabby is the only witness to a heinous crime — the murder of the cat's beloved (and wealthy) mistress by her no-good husband (Andre Morell) and two disloyal servants (Andrew Crawford and Freda Jackson). The trio soon come to regard the now ever-present feline as "a sort of evil symbol — they hate it." Into the unhealthy mix comes the innocent, favorite niece (Barbara Shelley) and several unsavory, greedy relatives. The cunning cat sidesteps all attempts to kill it and, one by one, leads the guilty, via their mounting fears, to their deaths.

(Fore)*Shadow*(ing) *of the Cat* (1961).

From the film's creepy opening, with the victim-to-be up at the top of her Old Dark House reading Poe's "The Raven" to amuse herself and her cat, to the final queasily ironic scene in which the house's new owners opine, upon finding the felonious feline waiting at their new abode, that being greeted by a cat means good luck, *The Shadow of the Cat* generates an impressive atmosphere of unease and dread.

"The set was pretty tense — it wasn't completely pleasant on the set," recalled co-star Barbara Shelley (who put this tension down to director John Gilling's lack of humor). This off-screen tension may well have bled over into the actors' on-screen performances—to the film's benefit. Each of the principals gives a taut, edgy and wholly convincing portrayal, turning the unlikely concept of a vigilant, vengeful tabby into a believable and frightening notion via their angry fears and mounting hysteria. In less capable thespian hands, this *Shadow* would have paled.

Perhaps said tension was due (at least in part) to the film's frustrating feline star(s). "I had *several* of them working for me on the picture," recounted Gilling, "because they kept escaping to Buckinghamshire's Black Park where some of the film was shot. So I had the opportunity to learn a lot about cats: if you want them to act, or do things, don't tell them to do what you want them to do. Instead, tell them to do what you don't want them to do! You can quote me on that! [laughs] I had a so-called cat manager on the floor who was supposed to know all about the animals, but I'm here to certify that he didn't."

Screenwriter George Baxt was less than pleased with the treatment of his script. The disgruntled writer told interviewer Matthew R. Bradley, "I could kill him [Gilling] and everybody on [that picture]. There was no cat. My script did not have a cat in it at all. You saw the shadow. That was why it was called *The Shadow of the Cat*. My script was very spooky."

So, in fact, is the movie, thanks in no small part to the director. "Gilling did nothing," continued Baxt. "He just wrote four lines of dialogue while my back was turned." Gilling, in fact, did much more than "nothing." His use of close shots, up-angle camerawork and purposeful movement, along with an anamorphic lens to signify the cat's eye view, keeps things varied visually. And, along with Arthur Grant's atmospheric lighting, Gilling makes the most of the Gothic Old House setting, utilizing off-kilter angles of the cat creeping down the darkened hallways and frantic camera movements when the feline "attacks." Indeed, the quality of Gilling's other genre forays speaks for itself: *Room to Let*, *The Gorgon*, the underrated *Blood Beast from Outer Space*, *The Reptile*, *The Plague of the Zombies* and the finest Burke and Hare telling to date, *Mania* (aka *The Flesh and the Fiends*).

Some uneven pacing occasionally casts a lugubrious shadow over this *Cat*, with too much drawing room palaver interfering with the uneasy ambiance and creepy cat activities. "I came on the set and wrote more scenes to make the film longer," recounted Baxt. And it hurt the film. Apart from the various personnel, *Shadow* also shares with many of its Hammer brethren the trait of being about 20 minutes too long.

Largely ignored by fans whose focus seems limited to a certain British film studio, it's time for this *Cat* to step out of the *Shadow* of its Hammer contemporaries and be seen for the intelligent, well-crafted horror/thriller it is.

With quotes from: Barbara Shelley interview with the author, 2001; "'Don't Call Me a Horror Film Director...'—The Great John Gilling Interview," *Little Shoppe of Horrors*, no. 23, October 2009; "Baxt Stabs Back," by Matthew R. Bradley, *Filmfax* 50, May/June 1995.

The She Beast (1965; Europix-Consolidated; Italy) Original Language Title: *La Sorella di Satana*; Alternate Titles: *Revenge of the Blood Beast*; *Sister of Satan*. Director: Mike (Michael) Reeves; Producer: Paul W. Maslansky; Screenplay: Michael Byron, Charles B. Griffith (uncredited); Cinematographer: G. Gengarelli. Cast: Barbara Steele, John Karlsen, Ian Ogilvy, Mel Welles.

Deadlier than DRACULA! Wilder than the WEREWOLF! More frightening than FRANKENSTEIN!—poster

A newlywed couple (Ian Ogilvy and Barbara Steele) vacationing in Transylvania run their car off the road into a lake. Two hundred years earlier, a hideous witch named Vardella was drowned by the villagers in that same lake. When the wife emerges from the water, she is possessed by the spirit of the vengeful witch, causing her to take on the visage of an ugly old crone and embark on a murder spree.

Of the nine Continental-based Barbara Steele-starring horror films released in the 1960s, *The She Beast* ranks near the bottom. Though it offers a few arresting moments (such as the brutal, unflinching sequence in which the townsfolk tie the screaming witch to a seesaw-like contraption, drive a spike though her torso, and proceed to dunk her in the lake—a presage, perhaps, of things to come in director Michael Reeves' later *The Conqueror Worm*), this obviously cheap production (the protagonists even drive a VW bug!) ultimately becomes an uneasy blend of half-baked horror and *un*baked slapstick.

Fortunately, the likable Ian Ogilvy (who starred in all three of Reeves' films before the director's untimely death at age 25) and the alluring Barbara Steele do much to ground the proceedings in believability. And former Roger Corman stock player turned Italy-based Jack-of-all-Cinema-Trades Mel Welles (who dubbed, acted in and even directed numerous Continentals), as the bloated, buffoonish communist innkeeper, actually makes some of the ham-fisted comedy work.

"I wrote that in three days to get an airline ticket for my girlfriend," recounted Charles B. Griffith (who served as second unit director on *She Beast*, and appears in the picture as well, but ultimately received no on-screen credit for the screenplay). "That was originally a comedy about communistic Transylvania with Barbara Steele, Mel Welles and Paul Maslansky, who played a cop and produced." (Maslansky also produced the superior *Castle of the Living Dead*, on which Reeves served as uncredited second unit director.)

"Paul couldn't make up his mind whether he wanted to do it as a comedy or not," recounted Mel Welles. "It was a real farcical script, and by watering it down they kind of spoiled it. We made that entire picture in Italy and looped it there—in Italy you don't make direct-sound pictures because you can't keep an Italian crew quiet long enough [laughs]!"

Though occasionally the poke-fun-at-communists comedy works (the witch attacks and kills the corrupt innkeeper with a *hammer and sickle*!), most of it is so broad that it becomes both tiresome and incongruous given the film's otherwise dark tone. Sample exchange:

First communist official: "Is he able to talk?"
Second official: "No, he's already dead."
First official: "Then he's obstructing justice."

Add to this scenes of the Keystone Communists taking pratfalls, and a speeded-up car chase involving a Model A and moped(!), and the slapstick antics fatally undermine the more horrific themes of vengeance and possession.

She Beast's reputation rests on the fact that it was 21-year-old wunderkind director Michael Reeves' first full feature—plus, of course, the fact that it starred Barbara Steele at the height of her Eurohorror popularity. (Ms. Steel's fans must feel disappointment, however, at the actress' limited screen time here—which amounts to about 15 minutes, despite her star billing. The budget was so low that the filmmakers could only afford her for four days of shooting—at a fee of $5,000.)

Steele described Reeves as "quite shy, very gentle, and obviously very intelligent. I think he could have been a terrific talent. He was so young and a little overwhelmed doing the picture, but he had quite a lot of control. He knew exactly what he wanted."

Uneven, yet still moderately intriguing, *The She Beast* proved to be more of a promise of things to come from first-timer Reeves than a wholly successful effort in and of itself.

With quotes from: "That's Me, Charles B. Griffith!" by Dennis Fischer, Filmfax 6, March/April 1987; *Interviews with B Science Fiction and Horror Movie Makers*, by Tom Weaver; "An Interview with Barbara Steele, Diva of Dark Drama," by Mark A. Miller, *Filmfax* 51, July/August 1995.

Ad for the American release of *The She Beast* (1965), pairing it with *The Embalmer*: "THIS IS HORROR!"

She Freak (1967; Sonny Amusement Enterprises) Director: Byron Mabe; Producer/screenwriter: David F. Friedman; Cinematographer: Bill Trolano. Cast: Claire Brennen, Lee Raymond, Lynn Courtney, Bill McKinney.

FILMED ON ACTUAL LOCATIONS WHERE IT *COULD* HAVE HAPPENED!
—poster blurb

She Freak is a cheap, tacky, poorly produced knock-off of the 1932 Tod Browning classic, *Freaks*. While *Freaks* was a controversial, even reviled film upon its initial release (ultimately disowned by MGM and almost ruining Browning's career), which critics of the day accused of exploiting its subject matter, it actually shone a sympathetic light on its "freaks," making the "normals" the monstrous ones via their abhorrent behavior. Not so with the shoddy remake *She Freak*, which offers no interaction with the freaks, no exploration of their character or personality, and no scenes of their everyday lives. In fact, the film even lacks shots of their *working* lives; apart from the sword-swallower and a normal-looking snake handler, we never see the "freaks" until the film's climax — they simply show up at the end to advance threateningly on the heartless antagonist. Consequently, unlike with the Browning film, the freaks in *She Freak* do indeed come off as "monsters." Rather than exploring its topic, *She Freak* simply exploits it (and even does *that* badly, as it breaks the cardinal rule of exploitation cinema: never bore the viewer). Considering that producer/scripter David F. Friedman was an old-time exploitationer and carny worker himself, this, perhaps, should come as no surprise. (Frequent nudie and softcore movie producer Friedman developed a lucrative partnership with Hershell Gordon Lewis, the "Godfather of Gore," in the 1960s, with whom he made such drive-in milestones as *Blood Feast* and *Two Thousand Maniacs!*)

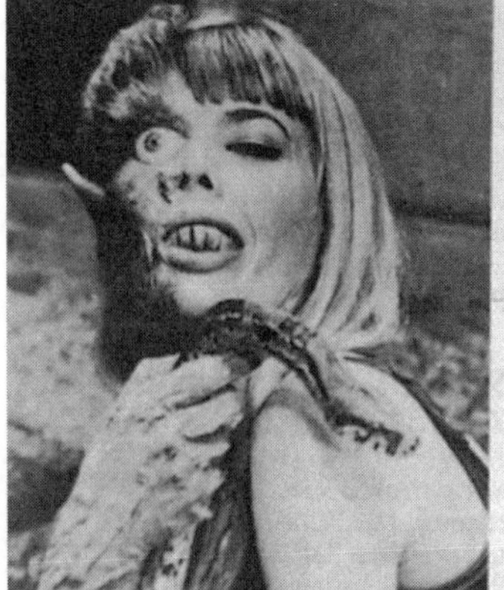

The *She Freak* (Claire Brennan), **"before" and "after (1967)."**

Shot on a $75,000 budget at the Kern County Fair in Bakersfield, California, *She Freak* begins with four minutes of carnival footage (rides, cotton candy machine, sideshow hoochie-koochie dancer, etc.) before the credits finally roll — over *more* carny shots. The movie proper then starts just like the original *Freaks* — with a carnival barker (Friedman himself) offering to show the crowd (and the viewer) the freak show's (unseen) main attraction. The film then flashes back to Jade (Claire Brennan), a money-hungry waitress at a nowheresville greasy spoon, who takes a job with the traveling carnival. There she meets Steve (Bill McKinney), the well-heeled owner of the sideshow. She entraps him with her wiles, then shows her true colors by cheating on him with one of the ride operators (Lee Raymond). (Replacing the beautiful aerialist and handsome strong man characters of *Freaks* with a white-trash hash-slinger and carny grunt demonstrates *She Freak*'s lowly ambition.) The operator kills the husband in a fight, and Jade takes over the sideshow, squeezing every penny from the operation and ousting her husband's long-serving assistant, the midget Shorty (Felix Silla). One night the freaks, led by Shorty, converge upon their new hated owner, and the scene returns to the present, where the barker directs our attention to a pit — in which the now-deformed and imbecilic Jade sits playing with a snake.

"It was an outright remake of *Freaks*," Friedman told author John McCarty in *The Sleaze Merchants*. "No picture's ever made a more lasting impression on me.... The problem when I made *She Freak* was that I had to resort to makeup tricks instead of using real freaks. When Browning made the original, there were a number of human oddities traveling around in circuses and carnivals that he was able to use in the film. But by 1966, when we made *She Freak*, that sort of exploitation was frowned upon.... So except for the dwarf character and a couple of others, all the human oddities in the film were fakes." And fake-*looking* as well — even in the pivotal lead antagonist's phony oatmeal-and-cardboard makeup after her "hideous" transformation.

Featuring amateurish acting, ugly photography and tinny sound (much of the film was obviously shot silent), *She Freak* offers nothing to those viewers not enamored of '60s carnival footage — apart from one great sixties moment: when the final credits roll, we read, "Miss Brennan's wardrobe by SASSY PANTS." You just don't see acknowledgements like that anymore...

Short Stories of Terror see *The Master of Horror*

The Shuttered Room (1968; Warner Bros./ Seven Arts) Director: David Greene; Producer: Philip Hazelton; Screenplay: D.B. Ledrov and Nathaniel Tanchuck (Novel: August Derleth and H.P. Lovecraft); Cinematographer: Kenneth Hodges. Cast: Gig Young, Carol Lynley, Oliver Reed, Flora Robson.

There are some doors that should never be opened.—tagline

Stylish direction, believable performances, superb location photography, and a moody score—*The Shuttered Room* has nearly everything going for it. The only thing missing is a story.

Newlyweds Mike Kelton (Gig Young) and Susanna Whatley Kelton (Carol Lynley) travel to Susanna's girlhood home on a remote New England island, where they plan to convert the old Whatley mill into a summer home. But the locals warn them to stay away from the place, which they claim is haunted by the Curse of the Whatleys. Already nervous about the trip (haunted by long-buried memories of a mysterious force of evil), Susanna grows even more uneasy when she becomes an object of desire for her creepy, low-life cousin Ethan (Oliver Reed).

That's about all that happens for the first hour of the film's sluggish 100-minute runtime. The final 40 minutes aren't much more eventful (the Evil Whatsit doesn't claim its first victim until the 68-minute mark). Not only is there too little narrative to justify the picture's length, but the story is also numbingly predictable. And its low-key, psychological approach will likely disappoint anyone hoping for Lovecraftian chills.

On the plus side, however, there's, well, practically everything else. *The Shuttered Room* marked the big-screen debut of veteran TV director David Greene, who employs POV shots and extreme high and low camera angles to create a sense of menace. His compositions also make evocative use of the film's atmospheric locations—a rundown lighthouse, a disused mill and hardscrabble New England village. Despite his excellent direction here, Greene continued to work primarily in television.

While short on plot, the script by D.B. Ledrov and Nat Tanchuck contains well-developed characters and fine dialogue, handled well by the strong cast. Oliver Reed (as usual) walks away with the film thanks to his showy performance as the jealous, lusty Ethan. But Lynley and Young make appealing leads, and Flora Robson contributes a memorable supporting turn as

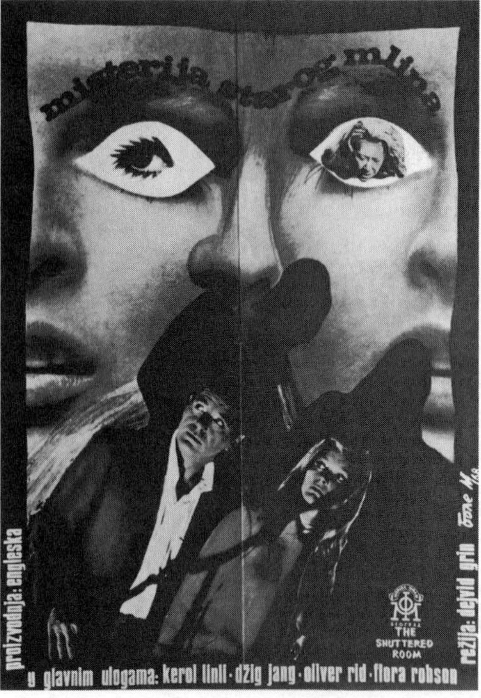

Yugoslavian poster for *The Shuttered Room* (1968).

Susanna's inscrutable Aunt Agatha. Basil Kirchin's unorthodox score, heavy on bass and percussion, underscores the suspense.

For these considerable pleasures, *The Shuttered Room* may be worth a look for patient viewers who appreciate fine acting and beautiful cinematography. Just don't expect many real thrills.

Sister of Satan see *The She-Beast*

The Skull (1966; Amicus/Paramount; U.K./ U.S.) Director: Freddie Francis; Producers: Milton Subotsky, Max J. Rosenberg; Screenplay: Milton Subtosky (from the story "The Skull of the Marquis de Sade" by Robert Bloch); Cinematographer: John Wilcox. Cast: Pter Cushing, Patrick Wymark, Nigel Green, Jill Bennett, Michael Gough, Geore Coulouris, Christopher Lee.

When the skull *strikes*—you'll *scream*!—trailer

Rather than showcasing several of author Robert Bloch's short stories in an anthology format (as they subsequently did with *Torture Garden* and *The House That Dripped Blood*), Amicus (and, specifically, co-producer/screenwriter Milton Subotsky) here stretched *one* story (Bloch's 1945 eight-page "The Skull of the Marquis de

Sade") out to feature length. Unfortunately, it shows. "[Subotsky's short, 83-page] script needed a lot of bolstering," observed director Freddie Francis, "and I put a lot of that material about black magic into it on the set." Other such bolstering measures included pace-slowing but time-eating scenes of characters leaving and entering rooms (almost to the point of absurdity, as the Skull sends its thrall to and fro on its wicked errands) and a dream sequence used for filler (admittedly *riveting* filler, however, thanks to Peter Cushing's harrowing portrayal).

Peter Cushing falls victim to *The Skull* (1965) of the Marquis de Sade in this lobby card scene.

Released in England in 1965, and in the U.S. the following year, *The Skull* stars Cushing as Christopher Maitland, a researcher/collector of occult antiquities who buys the original skull of the infamous Marquis de Sade, "the man whose name has become the symbol of cruelty and savagery in all of us" (as one character describes him). The skull is inhabited by the evil force that possessed the wicked Marquis in life, and it now attempts to seize Maitland and drive him to murder.

"The thing I like most about working with [director] Freddie [Francis]," said Subotsky, "is that he's got a fantastic visual sense, and these films need a visual style. He can give the picture a better look than any other director."

Oscar-winning-cinematographer-turned-director Francis indeed creates a stylish and visually arresting film, where the camera movement, lighting, and set design become just as important — if not more so — than the characters and (sparse) dialogue. Through the clever use of lighting, angles and judicious cuts, for instance, Francis infuses the (mostly) inanimate Skull with a malevolent life of its own.

Francis even had a special skull cowl mounted in front of the camera lens, so for certain scenes it appears as if the camera looks from inside the Skull's eye sockets, emphasizing its evil, sentient nature. For these skull's-eye-view shots Francis took over the camera operation himself, strapping on roller skates and having himself "pushed about as if I was moving and chasing Peter Cushing." (Francis later re-used this same skull's-eye-view technique for 1973's *The Creeping Flesh*). "I think Freddie Francis did a lot, considering how little he had to spend for the production," opined Robert Bloch. "The cast, of course, contributed greatly with their talented performances."

Indeed, Cushing carries the film on his skilled shoulders, since he's onscreen nearly every minute, much of the time alone and without dialogue. (All of Cushing's capable co-stars, including Patrick Wymark and Christopher Lee, contribute little more than cameos.) Through his expressions and body language, Cushing brilliantly conveys his character's desperate battle to retain control of his own will (from bemusement at his friend's concern, to his initial confusion, shocked horror, bitter anguish, and final frantic panic). It's an emotionally strenuous and simply remarkable performance.

The Skull benefits from sumptuous set decoration, the drawing rooms and studies filled with all manner of intriguing, macabre bric-a-brac (Satanic statuary, malevolent masks, sinister weaponry), enhancing the supernaturally suffused story (in which all the primary characters are either researchers, collectors or dealers in the occult). "I always like to have my sets, when I go onto them, mildly overdressed so I can pick out the best prop to use to make a particular point," commented Francis. "I could have gone on creating various scenes within Peter Cushing's study for the rest of my life and enjoying it. It was one of the things that works out just right on a picture!"

During the film's brilliant build-up, the grinning Skull several times turns up in impossible places, its unexpected, mysterious appearances adding chilling punctuation to the story's ominous tone. But the creepy implication ultimately goes by the boards when we see the Skull floating through the air, turning the initial fear of the unknown/unseen into just another banal bit of horror hokum. (Reportedly, commercial pressures compelled Francis to include these unfortunate shots.)

At one point, Maitland asks his friend, "How can a mere skull be dangerous, unless your *mind* makes it so?" offering the promise of a fascinating exploration of obsession and suggestibility. But the film heads off in a more obvious and disappointing direction, and the opportunity for something a bit more than an admittedly-atmospheric-but-straightforward horror movie was lost.

These thematic missteps aside, *The Skull* still stands as a creepy, atmospheric and thoroughly engrossing mood piece. "I had a tremendous amount of freedom and it gave me something I really love," enthused Francis, "and that's lots of nice camera moves, because so much of the picture was purely and simply atmosphere."

In France, *The Skull* was renamed *The Dreadful Crimes of the Marquis de Sade*, but a Paris court ordered the title changed after Count Xavier de Sade, a descendent of the Marquis, filed a complaint, claiming it a slur on his family's name. Now if only *Jerry Lewis* had played the Cushing role...

With quotes from: *The Men Who Made the Monsters*, by Paul M. Jensen; "Milton Subotsky," by Chris Knight, *Cinefantastique*, Summer 1973; *Christopher Lee and Peter Cushing and Horror Cinema*, by Mark Miller.

The Slaughter of the Vampires see *Curse of the Blood-Ghouls*

The Slime People

(1963; Hansen Enterprises; b&w) Director: Robert Hutton; Producer: Joseph F. Robertson; Screenplay: Vance Skarstedt; Cinematographer: William Troiano. Cast: Robert Hutton, Les Tremayne, Robert Burton, Judee Morton, Susan Hart, William Boyce.

From caves and sewers come the Slime People to *kill, kill, kill!*—theatrical trailer

The fifties are largely considered the heyday of cinematic science fiction (particularly of the low-budget variety), in which every producer and his dog had a sci-fi double feature shooting in their backyard and/or Bronson Canyon. The trend didn't stop with the close of the decade, however, continuing well into the 1960s—as evidenced by drive-in fare like *The Slime People* and its sister production, *The Crawling Hand* (both produced by Joseph F. Robertson). Surprisingly, given its bargain-basement budget and trashy title, *The Slime People* proved to be one of the more unusual and oddly entertaining low-budget sci-fi/horror entries of the time.

TV sportscaster Tom Gregory (Robert Hutton) flies his private plane through thick fog and lands in Los Angeles, only to discover the airport—indeed, the entire *city*—deserted. There he hooks up with science professor Galbraith (Robert Burton, an eleventh-hour replacement for an ill Richard Arlen; sadly, Burton died shortly after the film wrapped) and his two lovely daughters (Susan Hart and Judee Morton). Tom learns that L.A. has been evacuated following an invasion of scaly prehistoric man-beasts that have crawled up out of the sewers to attack the populace (with underground nuclear testing taking the blame for disturbing the disgusting denizens). Joined by a marine separated from his unit (William Boyce), the little band of survivors must battle the Slime People and figure out a way to penetrate/destroy

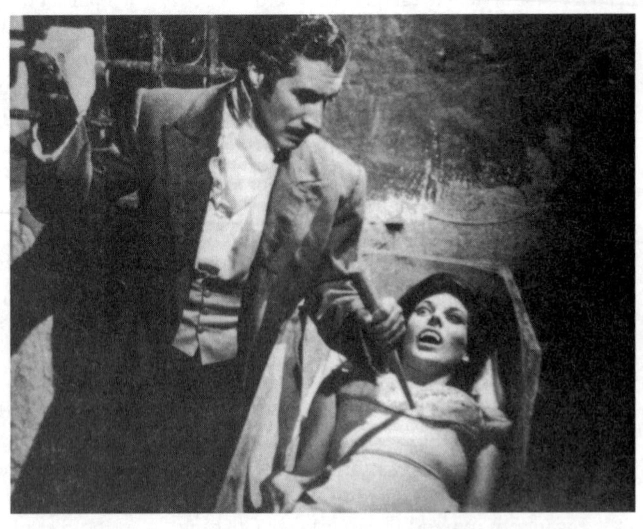

So begins the *Slaughter of the Vampires* (1962/69).

udee Morton menaced by one of *The Slime People* (1963), who crawl up out of the sewers to overrun L.A. (American lobby card).

the dome of hardened fog the creatures have thrown up over the city.

Since *The Slime People* was made for just over $51,000, according to first-and last-time director and star Robert Hutton, the mass murder and mayhem committed by the Slime Monsters on the populace of Los Angeles occurs *before* the movie ever gets rolling. We only hear about the devastating battles the losing military waged with the vicious creatures (though we do get to see a token isolated victim here and there, after the fact). Of course, it'd be pretty difficult to stage an all-out Slime assault when the production could only afford *three* Slime Monster costumes. Fortunately, the little quintet of protagonists seems to run into the creatures quite regularly, so that active skirmishes come fairly fast and furious (which, thanks to the professional stuntmen — such as Robert Herron and Fred Stromsoe — wearing the suits, also describes the rather exciting encounters themselves).

Though the Slime Monsters comically conjure up images of the "Big Fig" from the old Fruit of the Loom underwear commercials, the unique costume design is one of the movie's major assets. With their scaly, reptilian faces, oversized, deformed torsos and grotesque spinal hump, they appear both bizarre and frightening. Costing $3,000 to $4,000, these suits ate up a healthy chunk of the film's budget but proved to be money well spent.

Partially financed by the owner of a propane company and a string of launderettes, *The Slime People* ran into money problems almost as soon as it began production in January 1962; by week two, the unpaid crewmembers had begun to desert the sinking ship. "We had a makeup person the first week," recalled actress Susan Hart (Hart made her big-screen debut on *Slime People* and later married AIP co-founder James Nicholson). "All of a sudden, in the second week, we started doing our own makeup. And people started disappearing, like lighting men and carpenters. All of a sudden, the crew was down to maybe seven..." Robert Hutton even talked his father-in-law into letting the production shoot at the latter's butcher shop (where the protagonists hole up for a time against the marauding monsters) in Lancaster, California, to save money.

"*The Slime People* was a lot of fun to make," remembered Hutton. "Oh, we had a ball!" (And this from a man who says he was never even *paid* for his services!) Given the right frame of mind, *The Slime People* is "a lot of fun" for the viewer as well.

With quotes from: *Attack of the Monster Movie Makers*, and *Science Fiction Stars and Horror Heroes*, by Tom Weaver.

The Snake Woman (1961; Caralan Productions Ltd.; UK; b&w) Alternate Title: *Terror of the Snake Woman*; Director: Sidney J. Furie; Producer: George Fowler; Screenplay: Orville H. Hampton; Cinematography: Stephen Dade. Cast: John McCarthy, Susan Travers, Elsie Wagstaff, Arnold Marle, Geoffrey Denton, John Cazabon.

Teen-age beauty turns into deadly reptile at will ... spreading horror with fang and forked tongue! — poster

---

"Beauty turning into deadly reptile"? — yes. But "teen-age"? — technically no (she's 20), and "horror" most definitely not, as there's precious little of that in this cramped, low-budget, poorly acted, indifferently directed slice of British dullness.

Taking a page from *Cult of the Cobra* (1955), and pre-figuring Hammer's far-better-but-still-disappointing *The Reptile* (1966), *The Snake Woman* tells the story of a brilliant herpetologist

(John Cazabon) in a small turn-of-the-century Northumberland village who injects his wife with snake venom in order to cure her insanity. The unorthodox treatment works, but it also affects the woman's unborn baby. The wife dies in childbirth; the midwife (whom the superstitious villagers consider a friendly "witch") labels the cold-blooded, lidless newborn "the Devil's offspring"; and the fearful torch-wielding villagers set fire to the house, killing the herpetologist. Fortunately (or *un*fortunately, as it turns out), the baby is whisked away by the doctor and delivered into the hands of a friendly shepherd. Twenty years later the girl has disappeared, while the village is plagued by a rash of mysterious snakebite deaths. A young Scotland Yard detective (John McCarthy) arrives to investigate "the curse of the serpent child" (as the villagers call it) and "prove it utterly baseless" (as his superior instructs). As the torpid tale crawls along to its foregone conclusion, he runs across the beautiful and mysterious Atheris (Susan Travers), who can transform herself into a King Cobra at will.

Plagued by a pace more sluggish than a serpent in December, *The Snake Woman* just coils up and lies there for most of its (blessedly brief) 68-minute running time. Cramped sets (including sparse studio-bound "moors"), lengthy and pointless talking head scenes (in which characters blather on about what the viewer has already seen), mundane staging (Sidney Furie offers up drab direction more along the lines of his earlier *Dr. Blood's Coffin* than his later, more stylish films like *The Ipcress File* and *The Entity*), melodramatic *over*acting (particularly from Elsie Wagstaff as the cartoonish "witch"), and a predictable story (livened only by the tangential magical angle involving the voodoo-doll-wielding midwife and her prescience) do nothing to warm up this *Snake Woman*. Scenes of victims being stalked by a literal snake in the grass offer little suspense, particularly when the "special effects" consist of alternating footage of a live snake with that of a rubber one, with nary a transformation scene in sight (excepting one simple and unconvincing superimposition at the very end). And the potentially fascinating character of Atheris remains completely undeveloped, as she's given little dialogue and even less personality, denying the story much of its pathos and leaving only the "mystery" angle to engage viewer interest — of which there is none (neither mystery *nor* interest).

American one-sheet poster for *The Snake Woman* (1961).

Something Weird (1967; Mayflower)

Director/Cinematography: Herschell Gordon Lewis; Producer/screenplay: James F. Hurley. Cast: Tony McCabe, Elizabeth Lee, William Brooker, Mudite Arums, Ted Heil.

Shocks every emotion! — tagline

After a two-year hiatus from horror pictures, splatter film pioneer H.G. Lewis shot three chillers in 1967, including two of his patented gore fests (*A Taste of Blood* and *The Gruesome Twosome*) as well as this oddball supernatural thriller involving ESP, black magic and LSD.

"This is not a true gore picture as such," Lewis explained. "In gore pictures we would slash somebody with a knife or stick a pool cue through them and blood would gush and intestines would tumble out. This was not that kind of picture at all.... Nothing here would make someone's stomach to turn over."

Cronin Mitchell (Tony McCabe) is zapped by a downed power line but miraculously survives. The accident leaves him horribly disfigured but grants him incredible psychic powers (telepathy and telekinesis). Soon, Mitchell is approached by a hideous witch (Elizabeth Lee, channeling Margaret Hamilton) who offers to magically repair his face — if the young man will become her lover. Reluctantly at first, Mitchell accepts her help and becomes a renowned psychic. But things begin to unravel when he offers to help police apprehend a serial killer who has brutally murdered seven young women.

Something Weird proves a difficult film to summarize succinctly because its convoluted narrative takes so many bizarre left turns. "We truly intended to keep the audience off balance as to what's happening," Lewis said. Mission accomplished. For instance, a detective (Bill Brooker) gives Mitchell LSD to help expand his psychic abilities. (Cue surreal, red-tinted dream sequence.) In another "what the #*@%?" moment the witch magically animates the detective's blanket, which attempts to strangle him as he sleeps! The film's final act — including the revelation of the killer's identity and a climactic chase through a junk yard —fires several curveballs at the viewer.

These jaw-dropping passages, as well as the film's gore-free approach to horror, make *Something Weird* a unique and surprisingly endearing entry in the Lewis filmography, even though it suffers from all the same moviemaking demerits as every other Lewis production: flat, drab lighting; tinny, echo-stricken sound; banal, clunky dialogue; stiff, amateurish acting. It's not a good picture by any stretch (even Lewis admits, "I don't thinks *Something Weird* was the kind of movie that excited anybody"), but it shouldn't be missed by anyone interested in the director's offbeat oeuvre.

Lewis shot *Something Weird* in Chicago in less than two weeks on a budget of about $35,000. He was asked to direct the film by screenwriter/producer Jim Hurley, but Hurley (a Chicago college professor who was deeply interested in parapsychology) was displeased with Lewis' extensive rewrites of his script. So Hurley later directed his own version of the story under the title *The Psychic* (1968). *Something Weird* looks even better in comparison with Hurley's deadly dull, nearly unwatchable alternate attempt.

With quotes from: *Something Weird* DVD commentary with H.G. Lewis and David Friedman.

Sons of Thunder see *My Son, the Hero*

The Sorcerers (1967; Tigon/Allied Artists, U.K.) Director: Michael Reeves; Producers: Patrick Curtis and Tony Tenser; Screenplay: Michael Reeves and Tom Baker (From an idea by John Burke); Cinematographer: Stanley A. Long. Cast: Boris Karloff, Catherine Lacey, Ian Ogilvy, Elizabeth Ercy, Victor Henry.

He Turns Them On ... He Turns Them Off ... to live ... love ... die or KILL! — tagline

Following his awkward but intriguing debut, *The She-Beast* (1966), and before his magnum opus, *The Conqueror Worm* (aka *Witchfinder General*, 1968), wunderkind Michael Reeves directed this often-overlooked minor classic.

An aging, discredited professor of psychology, Marcus Monserrat (Boris Karloff), assisted by his wife Estelle (Catherine Lacey), has developed a fantastic machine capable of creating a powerful hypnotic link between doctor and patient. To test the device, Monserrat trawls trendy Soho, searching for a disaffected young Londoner. (Young people are "bored, taking pills to stay awake, looking for new experiences," he says.) In Mike (Ian Ogilvy), Marcus finds a willing subject; his interest is piqued when Estelle promises him "intoxication with no hangover, ecstasy with no consequences."

Boris Karloff meets the swinging sixties in *The Sorcerers* (1967) (American half-sheet).

After a top drawer psycho-freak-out sequence (full of rapid zooms in and out, splashes of colored light, lava lamp-like visuals, etc.), Marcus and Estelle realize that the device has not only given them complete psychic control over Mike, but enables them to experience everything Mike does: They see what he sees, hear what he hears, even feel what he feels. Marcus wants to use this discovery for the benefit of other elderly people, but Estelle wants to use it for her own gratification — first by forcing Mike to steal a fur coat and then indulging even darker impulses. Mike, confused and suffering from hypnotic blackouts, tries to move on with his life as Marcus and Estelle launch a battle of wills for control of his mind.

Like all Reeves' films, *The Sorcerers* has a point and makes it in compelling style. In terms of technique, it represents a quantum leap forward from *The She-Beast*. Reeves' work here is confident, even visionary. His skillful inter-cutting between Mike and the Monserrats during key sequences, such as the fur robbery, subtly stretches time and thus amps up the suspense. With a modest but adequate budget (nearly 33,000 pounds), the director makes better use of the Swinging London location than any picture of its era other than Michelangelo Antonioni's *Blow-Up* (1966). Soho practically becomes a character in the story, as its booze, rock 'n' roll and casual sex consume young hipsters like quicksand. Mike — the jaded hedonist searching for some sort of meaning to his emotionally bankrupt life — would fit perfectly into any Antonioni film.

While it lacks the visceral impact of *The Conqueror Worm, The Sorcerers* proves no less provocative or thematically complex. Taken at face value, the film serves as a timely reminder to its Flower Power generation that, in truth, there is no "intoxication without hangover" or "ecstasy without consequences." On a secondary level, however, the movie — in the tradition of Alfred Hitchcock's *Rear Window* (1954) and Michael Powell's *Peeping Tom* (1960) — explores the appeal (and danger) of voyeurism while reflexively pointing out the voyeuristic nature of cinema as an art form.

Top-billed (and top-salaried — his paycheck consumed a third of the budget) Boris Karloff gives a reliable but somewhat indistinct performance as Prof. Marcus Monserrat. The generally sympathetic scientist whose good intentions lead him to disastrous choices served as a staple role for the actor as far back as *The Man Who Lived Again* and *The Invisible Ray* (both 1936). While Karloff is by no means bad, he offers nothing fresh here. Lacey steals the film with her devilishly enjoyable portrayal of Estelle, the long-suffering wife bent on finally getting some enjoyment out of life. And Ogilvy contributes possibly the finest performance of his career as the picture's true lead. As usual, Ogilvy's character is a stand-in for Reeves, but the tragic Mike — overwhelmed by ennui and self-doubt, seeking solace in exotic pleasures — is a particularly transparent and poignant substitute (the character's full name is "Michael Roscoe"). Like so many other luminary talents of his generation (such as Jimi Hendrix, whose band the Experience was formed in Swinging London about the time this film was shot), Reeves would surrender to his own demons all too soon.

Given its status as both a Reeves picture and a Karloff vehicle, as well as its generally outstanding quality, *The Sorcerers*' relative obscurity remains puzzling. It's seldom studied or written about. And since it has yet to earn an authorized U.S. home video release and rarely turns up on cable television, it's also difficult to see. However, viewers who seek out *The Sorcerers* will find their effort richly rewarded. It's a smartly crafted, thought-provoking picture — a forgotten jewel overdue for rediscovery.

Sound of Horror (1964/67; Europix Consolidated Corp.; Spain; b&w) Original Language Title: *El Sonido Prehistórico*; Director: J. A. Nieves Conde; Producer: Gregorio Sacristan; Screenplay: Sam X. Abarbanel, Gregg Tallas, Jose Antonio Nieves Conde, Gregorio Sacristan; Cinematographer: Manuel Berenguer. Cast: James Philbrook, Arturo Fernandez, Soledad Miranda, Jose Bodalo, Ingrid Pitt, Lola Gaos, Francisco Piquer.

They can't see it, they can't escape it, they can only hear it and fear it. — trailer

This Spanish obscurity tells the tale of a group of treasure hunters in the mountains of Greece dynamiting a forbidden cave and uncovering a prehistoric egg. The egg hatches to disgorge an invisible (man-sized) dinosaur, which corners the protagonists in their isolated hacienda, slicing up everyone it can get its unseen claws on.

"It's like *Jurassic Park*, but without the dinosaurs!" laughed co-star Ingrid Pitt (here appearing in her first horror movie; Pitt went on to achieve a modicum of fame in British films like *The Vampire Lovers*, *Countess Dracula* and *The House That Dripped Blood*). "All you get to see are the big footsteps!" When pressed, Ms. Pitt (who serves as mere window dressing in the picture) had nothing further to say on the topic, except to dismiss *Sound of Horror* as "crap." An apt assessment.

Little actually happens in this low-budget exercise in tedium. Plenty of slow poking about in the cave eats up some running time; while Pitt dances the twist at one point, followed by female lead Soledad Miranda's slooow Greek-style dance interpretation, in order to pad the picture further. The "action" reaches its peak when the protagonists flee from the sound in the cave, go back, then run away *again*.

"You'll shiver and shake, quiver and quake when you hear the unearthly, uncanny sound that signals hideous death!" exclaimed the film's trailer. Admittedly, said noise is indeed rather uncanny, and provides a few moments of weird frisson. And the bloody slashes on the monster's victims (who turn ghostly pale after the creature drains their blood [a *vampiric* dinosaur?!]) offers further macabre interest.

But it's nearly half-an-hour before the sinister "Sound" makes an "appearance" (and then it's audio-only, as we hear the otherworldly groan/screech, and watch the first victim stagger about the cave screaming while bloody claw marks mysteriously appear on his body). Then it's *another* half-hour before the creature "appears" again!

Of the mystery monster, at one point someone asks, "Why is it invisible?" to which another answers, "Maybe it absorbs the color of its background and becomes invisible immediately." Or maybe the producers of this low-rent effort hadn't the pesetas for a *visible* dinosaur/monster. To be fair, at film's end the beast does finally appear — for a split-second in transparent silhouette (looking a bit like a miniature cardboard cutout T-rex).

The picture tries for that trapped/besieged feel (used to good effect in films like *The Killer Shrews* [1959], and later perfected in *Night of the Living Dead* [1968]), but only manages to produce hokum, clichés and ultimately ennui, as the underdeveloped characters mope about and experience "revelations" about their wasted lives and time misspent. The principals' heretofore greedy obsession with finding the treasure abruptly turns to bland nobility — everyone suddenly becomes oh-so-decent, which is nice and all, but makes for very poor drama. There's no cowardly sniveling or desperate self-interest here, just dull bonhomie in the face of adversity.

The few moments of suspense (such as one character using himself as a decoy so that the others can reach a girl trapped by the beast in a bedroom) sprinkled throughout the film like flour on a kitchen floor (a ploy the characters use to reveal the creature's presence via its footprints) tries to cover the lack of action, but it's spread too thin to sustain interest.

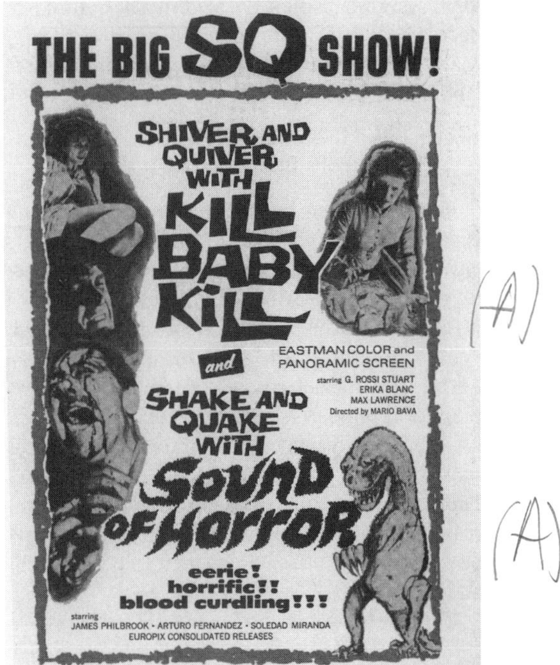

In the U.S. the tedious Spanish import *Sound of Horror* (about an *invisible* dinosaur!) played the bottom half of a double bill with Mario Bava's supremely atmospheric *Kill Baby ... Kill* (courtesy Ted Okuda).

Filmed at the Samuel Bronston Studios in Madrid, Spain, in 1964, *Sound of Horror* played the lower half of a double bill with Mario Bava's (far superior) *Kill Baby Kill* when released in the U.S. in 1967.

Ultimately, the *Sound of Horror* sounds something like "zzzzzzz..."

With quotes from: "Pitting Wits," by Howard Maxford, *Shivers* 31, July 1996.

Space Zombies see *The Astro-Zombies*

Spider Baby or, the Maddest Story Ever Told

(1964/68; American General Pictures, Inc.; b&w) Alternate Title: *The Liver Eaters* (re-issue); Director/Screenwriter: Jack Hill; Producers: Paul Monka, Gil Lasky; Cinematography: Alfred Taylor. Cast: Lon Chaney, Carol Ohmart, Quinn Redeker, Beverly Washburn, Jill Banner, Sid Haig, Mary Mitchel, Karl Schanzer, *and* Mantan Moreland.

SEDUCTIVE INNOCENCE of LOLITA, SAVAGE HUNGER of a BLACK WIDOW — ad line

From the opening theme song ("*Fiends and ghouls and bats and bones / And teenage monsters and haunted homes / A ghost on the stair, a vampire's bite / Better beware, there's a full moon tonight!*") it's obvious that *Spider Baby* is something unusual. What it *is*, exactly, can be hard to define. Is it a horror film, a black comedy, a satire, a cheap exploitation movie? (Given that Lon Chaney, Jr.'s, off-key, gravelly voice belts out the title tune, it is most assuredly *not* a musical.) Actually, *Spider Baby* is all these things and more — a film that remains completely unique, one that simply can't be pigeonholed but must be seen to be believed, and enjoyed.

Cannibal Orgy, or the Maddest Story Ever Told (the picture's shooting title) was filmed in twelve days in August 1964 for the paltry sum of $65,000 provided by two real estate developers-cum-movie moguls, Paul Monka and Gil Lasky. "They had been in dramatic school [UCLA]," explained director/screenwriter Jack Hill, "wanted to do a movie, and got a hold of a treatment I had written called *Cannibal Orgy, or the Maddest Story Ever Told*. They'd read scripts before, but never anything like this." Indeed. (When asked where he received his inspiration for such an offbeat story, Hill was nonplused. "It just came to me in a flash," he said, "and I wrote it down.... It just sounded like a good idea. I can't tell you where those things came from.")

Unfortunately, soon after the film's completion, the bottom dropped out of the California building industry and the two financier-producers wound up in bankruptcy court, resulting in the film being attached by their creditors. After four years in limbo, *Cannibal Orgy* was purchased by low-budget promoter David Hewitt, who changed the title to *Spider Baby* and released it in support of lesser color features. Then, two years later, he retitled it *The Liver Eaters* and sent it around the drive-in circuits, reaping a substantial profit (putting paid the old question of "What's in a name?").

The film centers on the Merrye family—teenagers Virginia (Jill Banner, who likes to play a deadly game of 'spider') and Elizabeth (Beverly Washburn), their older brother Ralph (Sid Haig, who acts like an overgrown toddler), and several aunts and uncles kept in a basement pit(!). Every member of the family is afflicted with the "Merrye Syndrome," a "progressive age regression" that ultimately ends in "a pre-human condition of savagery and cannibalism." Looking after this bizarre — and dangerous—family is Bruno (Lon Chaney, Jr.), the faithful chauffeur/caretaker. A group of distant relations (after the family fortune) arrive, and the disastrous meeting of the Merryes and the "normals" results in a (hilarious) family dinner of cooked cat and weeds, death by pitchfork, and an attack from the cannibals in the basement. It all ends with a bang at the explosive climax.

Director Jack Hill (left) goes over the script with star Lon Chaney, Jr., on the set of *Spider Baby* (1964/68).

By all accounts, the *Spider Baby* shoot was a happy one. "I remember just how much fun we had," recalled Beverly Washburn warmly. "We shot it very fast," added Mary Mitchel (who played the ostensibly normal heroine), "it was kind of a quick experience, but it *was* fun." Sid Haid concurred: "I *loved* going to work every day." This sense of fun and enthusiasm permeates the production, oozing out through the warped cracks to add an offbeat liveliness to the eccentric characters and bizarre situations.

Spider Baby's opening set-piece (a delivery man's demise) encapsulates the picture's tone and focus, as it's one part grotesque horror and two parts black comedy. When the courier sticks his head through the open porch window to see if anybody is home, the sash suddenly slams down on his back, pinning him like a specimen in a child's bug collection. Immediately, the teenage Virginia scuttles out into the room, hunched over, her arms crossed in front, holding two large knives in her hands like the forelegs of some huge insect. "I caught a big fat bug right in my spider web," she says gleefully and tosses a makeshift net over the astonished man's head. She then rears up and starts slashing.

Director Jack Hill (*Blood Bath*, 1966; *Isle of the Snake People*, 1968/71; *Coffy*, 1973) and cinematographer Alfred Taylor's (*Monstrosity*, 1964; *Blood Bath*, 1966) effective staging, combined with precision editing (by Hill and Elliot Fayad), emphasizes both the horror and the absurdity of the scene. POV shots from the victim's perspective as the bizarre assailant approaches her prey abruptly give way to close-ups of Virginia frenziedly slashing and shouting "sting, sting, sting!" Suddenly an ear falls to the floor and a quick zoom hammers the horror home. This gruesome sight is immediately juxtaposed with the humorous one of the man's posterior sticking out of the window on the porch side, his legs kicking comically as the vicious assault continues.

The sequence concludes with Virginia brought up short from her continued slashing by a sharp "Virginia!" uttered by her sister, Elizabeth. The camera then shows us Elizabeth: A twenty-something woman garbed in a little girl's pinafore dress with her hair up in pigtails. "Virginia, are you crazy?" she asks scornfully (and the viewer has to chuckle at this obvious question). "You're bad, *bad*," continues Elizabeth, "Bruno's going to *hate* you." Virginia looks down, momentarily cowed, and Elizabeth gives a superior smile and tilt of her head — a five-year-old chastising a misbehaving three-year-old. It's a scene both funny and chilling in its macabre absurdity.

Like another quirky and effective (and better-known) independent horror, Tobe Hooper's *The Texas Chainsaw Massacre*, the warped "family" in *Spider Baby* provides the film with its most intriguing characters. *Un*like that later terror classic, however, the "normal" people intruding into the bizarre scene in *Spider Baby* remain interesting as well, with scripter Hill taking care to write them as unusual, offbeat characters while *director* Hill makes sure his cast plays them as such. For instance, Emily (played with a wonderful biting arrogance by the sexy Carol Ohmart), who initially seems the typical greedy, disdainful relative, turns into a sensuous hedonist (enjoying twirling about in sheer stockings and black lace) in the privacy of her boudoir.

Still, *Spider Baby*'s focus is on the family. Sig Haig's expressive face and energetic portrayal turn Ralph into a perfectly realized (and effectively exaggerated) toddler. "I tried to do some muscle contraction things," said Haig, "and I just kind of played with it to see if I could make my body work the way I wanted it to. I thought, 'He's on the brink for the animal tendencies to come through,' so I tried to get that."

Jill Banner plays Virginia as a fun-loving, mischievous innocent, whose fascination with (and deadly emulation of) spiders is both amusing and horrific, making her the ultimate 'naughty little girl.' At one point she comically sticks her tongue out at her sister after Elizabeth tattles on her for killing the messenger, while at another she violently stabs the pieces of a jigsaw puzzle with the tip of her ever-present butcher knife.

As Elizabeth, the blond, pig-tailed Beverly Washburn projects a heady mixture of little-girl coquettishness and ferocious savagery. With her wide, inviting smiles and her goody-goody demeanor, she effortlessly turns from coy flirt to feral killer (her face twisted in fury as she shouts "Kill him! Kill him!" before brutally stabbing a character with a pitchfork).

Then there's Uncle Ned, Aunt Clara, and Aunt Martha kept in a pit in the cellar — the result of the Merrye Syndrome in its advanced state. (Why a pit? "Interiors were shot at a soundstage in Glendale," explained Hill, "which at one time had been an auto garage and therefore had a *pit* built into the concrete floor. This made the stage a very useful place for horror pictures, as building a set with a pit would have otherwise been prohibitively expensive.") Hill wisely keeps these mysterious figures largely out of sight, occasionally showing a filthy, grasping arm while dubbing in disturbing grunts and mewlings. The result is both frightening (for the viewer's imagination conjures up all manner of depraved terrors) and poignant (because we know that this is the inevitable fate of the three Merrye 'children').

It's a testament to both writer-director Jack Hill and to the individual actors' efforts that the three Merryes are indeed sympathetic and even likable, each possessing a weird charm that draws the viewer into their world — and their plight.

Caught between the two groups (straddling the normal and the bizarre) is Lon Chaney as Bruno. His is the only character that can seemingly function in — and relate to — both worlds, and much of the film's humor comes from Chaney's delicate balancing act as he tries to cope with the two disparate groups coming together (with disastrous results). As Chaney plays him, Bruno is an open, honest, simple man, yet one who is placed in the unenviable position of trying to maintain the charade of normalcy.

With the arrival of the 'normals,' Chaney makes the most of the opportunities presented for sly comedy. "I'm proud of you, Virginia," Bruno tells his young ward as she tries (vainly) to make a good impression at dinner, "you're doing so well." Chaney beams like a proud parent, and one can't help but feel both affection and anxiety for his character and his doomed task. Then, upon offering a dish of mushrooms to his reluctant guests, Bruno explains, "You see, [Virginia] has an uncanny knack for picking only the — uh — non-poisonous ones." Chaney's honest, smiling face and slight pause adds a welcome touch of humor.

Lon Chaney was Jack Hill's first choice for the role of Bruno. "At first," related Hill, "his agent pretended that, since it was a horror picture, Lon should receive a much higher salary; but we just didn't have the budget for it, and luckily, that same agent also represented John Carradine. So when we asked him to send the script to Carradine, Chaney quickly accepted our offer [a mere $2500] because he loved the script and really wanted to do the picture — particularly as it gave him a chance to do comedy, which he had rarely been given before — and he didn't want to lose it all to his rival Carradine." In fact, the actor was so enamored of the project that he remained on his best behavior throughout the filming (perhaps realizing that, though in a low-budget production, he was finally being offered a worthy role — at a time when such opportunities had seemingly dried up). "He was an alcoholic at the time," stated Hill, "but, since he wanted so badly to do a good job on this film, he made a truly heroic effort to stay on the wagon during the shoot, allowing himself only one glass of beer in mid-afternoon in order to get through the day." Chaney remained sober up until the very last day. ("On the last day we ran until four o'clock in the morning — " explained Hill.)

Chaney's determination held fast even under the most adverse conditions, for the shoot proved to be a physically grueling one for him. "He was very uncomfortable most of the time," remembered Hill, "suffering badly from the August heat in a non-air-conditioned building, so that someone had to stand by with a bucket of water and chamois to wipe the sweat off his face between takes.... He was a very underrated actor."

Frightening and funny, *Spider Baby* remains one of those illusive rarities in horror cinema (or *any* branch of film for that matter) — a complete original.

With quotes from: Jack Hill interviews by Jeffery Frentzen (*Fangoria*) and Michael Copner (*Cult Movies*), and correspondence with the author (for "Spider Baby, or the Maddest Story Ever Told," by Bryan Senn, in *Midnight Marquee Actors Series: Lon Chaney, Jr.*); quotes from Sid Haig, Beverly Washburn, and Mary Mitchel are from their appearance at the 30th Anniversary Showing of *Spider Baby* at the Nuart Theater in West Los Angeles.

The Spider's Web see *Horrors of Spider Island*

The Spirit Is Willing (1967; Paramount) Director/Producer: William Castle; Screenplay: Ben Starr (Novel: Nathaniel Benchley); Cinematography: Harold Stine. Cast: Sid Caesar, Vera Miles, Barry Gordon, John McGivar, Cass Daley, Ricky Cordell, Mary Wilkes, Jesse White, Robert Donner, Jill Townsend, John Astin.

Kiss-Hungry Girl Ghosts Looking for a Live Lover in a Haunted House of Mayhem — tagline

The Spirit Is Willing (1967), a faintly amusing ghost spoof, remains one of producer-director William Castle's least remembered works. While its obscurity is deserved, the picture isn't completely without charm.

The Powell family — father Ben (Sid Caesar), mother Kate (Vera Miles) and son Steve (Barry Gordon) — rent a summer vacation home which turns out to be haunted by three eternally battling ghosts (a faithless groom, along with his bride and his mistress). Sullen, teenaged Steve is continually blamed for the destruction wrought by the restless spirits, which only he can see. Eventually he decides that in order to bring peace to the house, he must find a new lover for the specter of the spurned wife.

With *The Spirit Is Willing*, Castle clearly wanted to recapture the kid-friendly appeal of his earlier horror-comedy hit *13 Ghosts* (1960). The two pictures share many common plot elements (including the central premise: a family moves into a house haunted by multiple ghosts, only visible to the young son), but *Spirit* simply isn't as endearing as its predecessor, and not simply because it lacks *13 Ghosts*' "Illusion-O" ghost viewer gimmick. A more significant problem is that, where *13 Ghosts* featured a precocious 8-year-old protagonist, *Spirit* assumes the point of view of a disaffected, horny 15-year-old — so naturally the humor tends toward the sophomoric and mildly sexual. (The film suggests that Steve loses his virginity to a ghost!) Although it's not racy enough to do justice to its better ideas (like a sex-starved female ghost preying on hormone-crazed male teenagers), it's a little too saucy to work comfortably as a children's film. Nor are its comedic set pieces, father-son verbal jousts and other bits of business executed particularly well. Aside from the offbeat *Zotz!* (1962), Castle never displayed much of a touch for farce, and most of *Spirit*'s gags are telegraphed far in advance. The film also suffers from awful visual effects (even its simple rear-screen projection scenes are atrocious) and a grating score that repeats the inane, seven-note melody of the picture's theme song ("The spirit is willing/ but the body is weak...") over and over and over again in scene after scene.

In the plus column, the picture's cast list reads like a virtual Who's Who of comedic character people (all of whom had their best moments elsewhere). TV legend Sid Caesar plays the irascible father with conviction and perfect timing, and is matched by young, toucan-beaked Barry Gordon, who looks like he really could be Caesar's kid. Former Alfred Hitchcock protégé Vera Miles fades into the woodwork in her bland role as the sympathetic mother, but several other performers contribute memorable supporting turns, especially John McGivar as the Powells' wealthy Uncle George and John Astin as an overwhelmed psychologist. Also making notable appearances in minor roles are Harvey Lembeck, Mary Wickes, Jesse White and Doodles Weaver. Too bad they weren't working with better material. Or, to put it another way, the cast is willing, but the script is weak.

Spirits of the Dead (1969, Les Films Marceau/American-International; France/Italy) Original Language Title: *Histoires Extraordinaire*; Alternate Title: *Tales of Mystery and Imagination* (U.K.). Directors: Roger Vadim ("Metzengerstein" segment), Louis Malle ("William Wilson" segment) and Federico Fellini ("Toby Dammit" segment); Producer: Raymond Eger; Screenplay: Roger Vadim, Pascal Cousin and Clement Biddlewood ("Metzengerstein"), Louis Malle and Clement Biddlewood ("William Wilson"), Federico Fellini and Bernardino Zapponi ("Toby Dammit"); Cinematographers: Claude Renoir ("Metzengerstein"), Diego Masson ("William Wilson") and Giuseppe Rotunno ("Toby Dammit"). Cast: Jane Fonda, Peter Fonda, Alain Delon, Brigitte Bardot, Terence Stamp.

The ultimate orgy of evil — tagline

Spirits of the Dead, which features an international all-star lineup of actors and directors in three adaptations of Edgar Allan Poe stories, remains an uneven but intriguing curio.

In the first segment, "Metzengerstein," directed

American one-sheet poster for *Spirits of the Dead* (1969).

by Roger Vadim, a cruel, debauched baroness, Frederique (Jane Fonda) becomes infatuated with her cousin Wilhelm (Peter Fonda). After Wilhelm is killed in a fire set by one of Frederique's henchmen, a mysterious black horse appears. She adopts the horse and soon becomes as fixated on it as she had been on Wilhelm. In director Louis Malle's "William Wilson," a sadistic, unscrupulous military officer (Alain Delon) is pursued by a doppelganger, who continually thwarts his wicked schemes. Wilson decides to eliminate his tormentor, but faces unexpected consequences. And in Federico Fellini's "Toby Dammit," a burned-out movie star (Terence Stamp) travels to Italy and, after a grueling night of public appearances, becomes lost in a village outside Rome. There, he encounters the ghostly figure of a young girl , who he believes to be the devil.

The tales chosen for *Spirits of the Dead* are lesser known (and just plain lesser) selections from the Poe bibliography. Why this trio instead of say, "The Tell-Tale Heart," "The Black Cat" and "The Pit and the Pendulum?" Perhaps producer Raymond Eger wanted to steer clear of stories already brought to the screen by Roger Corman and other filmmakers. In any case, *Spirits* is hardly designed for Poe purists. The titles for "Toby Dammit" indicate that the story was "liberally adapted" from Poe's "Never Bet the Devil Your Head." But, in truth, all three segments take substantial liberties with the source material.

Vadim hews closely to Poe's narrative, but introduces new, sexually charged elements to the story by changing Poe's Frederick to Frederique and re-imagining Wilhelm as an object of desire rather than a grandfatherly patriarch. Reinforcing these elements by the stunt casting of siblings Jane and Peter Fonda as would-be lovers, and including a sequence of Frederique riding naked on the mysterious black steed, Vadim suggests incest and bestiality, neither of which are present in Poe's story. Vadim also depicts the baroness' wanton appetites— both for power (as when she uses a young boy for archery practice) and sex (in multiple orgy scenes)— much more explicitly than Poe. Ultimately, however, while it has its compensations (including the ravishing Fonda on horseback), Vadim's segment doesn't add up to much in terms of drama. As in his previous horror film, *Blood and Roses* (1960), Vadim seems more interested in visual stylization than in storytelling. And "Metzengerstein," a simple and succinct seven-page story, simply isn't weighty enough to sustain Vadim's overblown 37-minute "short."

Malle fares better with "William Wilson." Like Vadim, he incorporates all Poe's key plot points but brings other elements into play by making minor additions and changes. Most notably, he changes the gender of a poker player who Wilson fleeces so the part can be played by Brigitte Bardot. In Malle's version, Wilson "wins" her in the game and then ritualistically whips her while the other players watch; nothing of the sort happens in Poe's tale. On the whole, "William Wilson" is a competent genre exercise by Malle, a director who dabbled in numerous cinematic forms (including noir thrillers, romances, screwball comedies, documentaries, science fiction and even a Western). Delon and Bardot assist with memorable performances.

On the surface, Fellini's "Toby Dammit" appears to be the least Poe-like of the triad. It jettisons nearly the entire original story (even the title), retaining only the tale's ironic payoff. Yet this segment comes closest to replicating the *tone* of the Poe original, hitting the same wickedly satirical note as "Never Bet the Devil Your Head" (or, as it's credited here, "Don't Wager Your Head to the Devil"). Like Fellini's *La Dolce Vita* and *Satyricon,* "Toby Dammit" is a scathing (and sometimes hilarious) indictment of vapid contemporary culture and the soul-destroying power of wealth and fame. Toby, in Rome to film "the first Catholic Western," turns to booze after being swarmed by sycophantic hangers-on and chiselers. He gives a TV interview full of amusing non sequiturs ("I'm happy and it drives me to despair") and seems more interested in obtaining the Ferrari producers have promised him than in the upcoming movie. After tearing through the Italian countryside in the convertible roadster, he becomes lost in a remote village — and "Toby Dammit" becomes truly unsettling. The ghostly figure of the devil-girl dressed in white and bouncing a large white ball Fellini admitted to "borrowing" from Mario Bava's *Kill Baby Kill.*

As usual for Fellini films of this vintage, this short plays in a skewered, impressionistic register, full of bizarre, quasi-religious imagery (at an award ceremony, Toby is presented with a golden calf) that unfolds to a creepy, carnival-like score by Nino Rota. Idiosyncratic but highly amusing and at times genuinely frightening, "Toby Dammit" stands as the most impressive and enjoyable of the film's three segments by far, even if it's more successful as a Fellini film than a horror movie. It makes the same thematic point as *Satyricon* in less than half the running time, and with more than twice the wit. Indeed, "Toby Dammit" remains one of the director's best short works, superseded only by the uproarious "Temptation of Dr. Antonio" segment from *Boccaccio '70* (1962), in which a prudish man is pursued by a giant, half-naked Anita Ekberg, who comes to life from a billboard outside his room.

For "Toby Dammit" alone, it's well worth conjuring up a copy of *Spirits of the Dead*. The film's other segments have their moments, too.

Spiritism (1961/65; Cinematografica Calderon S.A./Trans-International Films; Mexico; b&w) Original Language Title: *Espiritismo*; Director: Benito Alazraki, Manuel San Fernando (English language version); Producer: William Calderon Stell (Guillermo Calderon Stell), K. Gordon Murray (English version); Screenplay: Rafael Garcia Travesi; Cinematographer: Henry (Enrique) Wallace. Cast: Joseph L. Jimenez, Nora Veryan, Beatriz Aguirre, Alice Caro, Mary Eugenia Saint Martin, Rene Cardona, Jr.

There are many who are helplessly driven by a desire to explore forbidden phenomena; if, with this picture, we are able to squelch that unhealthy curiosity in some, we will consider *our* job well done."—closing narration

"The Monkey's Paw," by W.W. Jacobs, is a classic short story—emphasis on "short." Consequently, though it's been adapted as a cinematic short several times, it has rarely been turned into a feature. In fact, the 1933 version (currently lost) ran only a scant 58 minutes (and this with nearly a half-hour of padded prologue added). So imagine an 80-minute version, complete with cheap production values, overwrought acting and toneless dubbing—and you have imagined *Spiritism*. (Or, better yet, forget the movie and just imagine a group of cheerleaders: "We have Spiritism, yes we do / We have Spiritism, how 'bout you?!")

A middle-aged couple becomes involved with a benevolent group of spiritualists who contact the dead in order to help them pass on to their next stage. When the couple's finances fail due to the inept business dealings of their son, the wife calls upon the evil forces of witchcraft to aid her. Satan himself appears and gives her "Pandora's box" to open if she chooses. Desperately in need of money, she opens the box and finds a severed human hand (no monkey business here), upon which she makes her wish. The wish comes true, but at the cost of her son's life. She makes another wish—for the return of her son—and it also comes true, to her horror.

Full of long-winded talking heads and static photography, *Spiritism*'s banal settings (an inordinate amount of running time takes place in the couple's ordinary living room) work against the eerie theme. The picture sorely misses the graveyard ambiance that the best of the Mexican horror movies of the time possessed. (In the 1950s and '60s, Mexican horror cinema seemed to be trying to emulate the Universal look of the '30s and '40s.)

Impoverished production values don't help. When the woman impulsively "calls upon Satan" during the spiritualists' séance, the Evil One manifests himself via dimestore Halloween props floating in the air. And the unconvincing hand from "Pandora's box" that crawls about on its own is obviously set on rollers as it glides across the floor, its fingers moving in a repetitive, mechanical fashion.

Focusing on the petty problems of the protagonists—and the even pettier doings of the spiritualists—the movie is one long and tedious build-up to the final pay-off. But even this short changes the viewer, with its too-abrupt presentation and a general lack of mood.

In the end, *Spiritism* proves decidedly dispirited.

Sting of Death (1967; Thunderbird International Pictures) Director: William Grefe; Producer: Richard S. Flink; Screenplay: Al Dempsey (Executive Script Consultant: Ben Lithman); Cinematographers: Julio Chavez, Julio Roldan. Cast: Joe Morrison, Valerie Hawkins, John Vella, Jack Nagle, Doug Hobart.

Special Singing Guest Star NEIL SEDAKA—poster

Yes, *that* Neil Sedaka gives us a rousing rendition of "Do the Jellyfish" (via vinyl; the chart-topper deigns to appear onscreen) in this no-budget, Florida-lensed Sixties drive-in obscurity about a biologist in the Florida Everglades whose home/research lab is invaded not only by a group of partying young people (friends of his daughter's), but by a jellyfish-man who kills with his long, ropey stingers. According to director William Grefe, producer Richard S. Flink simply threw some quick cash at Sedaka, in Miami at the time working a nightclub gig, to come up with a song. But you gotta love lyrics like: "Wella, I'm-a saying fella / Forget your Cinderella / And do the jella / The jilla-jalla jella / It's really swella / To do the Jalla Jellyfish!"

And there's plenty more to love in this cheesy,

entertaining-in-the-right-frame-of-mind throwback to the Fifties' mutant monster movie craze. Enhancing the ambiance: Beach Party-style poolside dancing, complete with close-ups of jiggling bikinied rear-ends; a semi-nude scene involving a cutie and a barely opaque shower door; and the nihilistic notion that nearly all of the gyrating groovers end up *dead*! *Sting of Death* opens with an unseen creature (apart from its crusty "hand") pulling a sunbathing co-ed off a dock, then swimming along underwater, towing the dead girl by her hair(!) as the credits roll. Later, we meet a disfigured scientist's helper named Egon (John Vella doing his best crazed Cameron Mitchell impersonation) whose deformed eye-socket alternately contains and lacks an orb from shot to shot; a boatload of partying University students twisting, arm-waving and chicken-clucking to the aforementioned dance-craze-sensation-that-failed-to-sweep-the-nation; and the jelly-fish man lurking in the pool during the dance party ... with *nobody noticing*! "Highlights" include the partygoers attacked by a school (herd, pride, gaggle?) of little colored plastic bags (a.k.a. jellyfish) floating on top of the water; a paper mache underwater cave

Sting of Death (1967): the first (and only) horror movie about a jellyfish-man.

set (built in a local TV station studio) filled with out-of-date, obviously-not-up-to-code electrical(!) equipment; and one of the goofiest, laugh-out-loud monsters since *The Brainiac*.

"What we did when we designed the costume was copy from photographs of an actual Portuguese man-of-war, a very deadly jellyfish," related creature-creator (and wearer) Doug Hobart. "We combined images of a man with the jellyfish, and it was a super concept indeed.... The monster suit cost around 300 dollars to make. We made it in a two week period, and it looked quite good for the time and funds involved." Well, *that's* debatable. In fact, it looks just like what it is—a man in a crusty, dirty wetsuit and flippers, with plastic cords hanging from his shoulders and a clear hefty-bag inflated over his head (the human face shows nice and clear through the jellyfish casing).

Director Grefe (*Death Curse of Tartu*, 1967; *Stanley*, 1972; *Mako: The Jaws of Death*, 1976) obviously recognized his creature's shortcomings, and wisely limited the monster's appearance to shots of legs, hands and dragging tentacles until the film's finale, when he was forced to reveal the jellyfish-man in all its not-so-impressive glory. Meanwhile, Grefe, with the aid of cameramen Julio Chavez and Julio Roldan, offers some surprisingly competent underwater photography (shot at Rainbow Springs, the same site utilized by the makers of *Creature from the Black Lagoon*).

On the downside, an overabundance of mundane dialogue and amateurish acting float through the production like student bodies after a jellyfish attack. The film's idiotic science seems more magical than scientific, with the solitary sop to explanatory exposition being one line about "sea water, electricity and human blood mixed with chemicals" explaining how the human antagonist dipping his head into a tank containing a Portuguese man-of-war magically transforms him into a jellyfish-monster. And the laughable climax has the hero dancing about the tiny cave set waving a flare at, and grappling with, the menacing monster. He accidentally drops the flare into the small aquarium housing the *real* jellyfish, and this somehow causes the cave's electrical equipment to start smoking *and* the monster's bubble-head to deflate! Then it all blows up (signified by a pathetically small column of compressed air rising from the sandy bottom of the lagoon)—right in the face of the bemused viewer.

Setting such "minor" quibbles aside, the world's first (and only) jellyfish-monster movie manages to entertain through sheer audacity and the fact that it's not nearly as dull as its better-known double-bill co-feature, the dreadful *Death Curse of Tartu*.

With quotes from: "Jellyfish-Man ... an Interview with Doug Hobart," by Paul Parla, *Scary Monsters* 26, March 1998.

Strait-Jacket (1964; Columbia; b&w) Producer/Director: William Castle; Screenplay: Robert Bloch; Cinematographer: Arthur Arling. Cast: Joan Crawford, Diane Baker, Leif Erickson, Howard St. John, John Anthony Hayes, George Kennedy.

> Just keep saying to yourself: It's only a movie ... It's only a movie ... It's only a movie...—tagline

Producer/director William Castle, who never met a bandwagon he wasn't willing to climb aboard, helped shape the emerging "horror hag" sub-genre with this thriller, calculated to capitalize on the blockbuster success of *What Ever Happened to Baby Jane* (1962). Castle went all-out on this picture, hiring *Psycho* scribe Robert Bloch to pen the screenplay and *Baby Jane* co-star Joan Crawford to headline the cast. If that wasn't insurance enough of success, he also dreamed up one of filmdom's best-ever advertising taglines (which was later ripped off to promote Wes Craven's *Last House on the Left*) and even distributed toy cardboard axes to patrons at some showings.

Gimmicks aside, however, *Strait-Jacket* remains one of Castle's most dramatically credible films. In many respects, *Strait-Jacket* (not surprisingly) apes *Baby Jane*—opening with a pre-credit flashback, for instance. But it also includes significant elements that would be echoed in director Robert Aldich's *Baby Jane* follow-up, *Hush ... Hush, Sweet Charlotte* (1964): *Strait-Jacket* opens with an axe murder, *Sweet Charlotte* with a meat-cleaver murder. As in *Sweet Charlotte*, the central mystery is whether or not the protagonist is insane. And of course, the fear-of-aging undercurrent remains a constant, as it does throughout all the "horror hag" films.

In an effective opening sequence, "young" Lucy Harbin (a heavily made-up Crawford) returns home to discover her husband (a truly young Lee Majors) sharing their marital bed with another woman, in post-coital slumber. Enraged, Lucy grabs an axe and lops off both their heads. Secretly, Lucy's three-year-old daughter, Carol, looks on.

Flash forward. Lucy returns home to Carol after 20 years in an asylum, her psyche still fragile. Soon Lucy's behavior begins to change. At first timid and shy, she grows increasingly assertive and brazen. She even tries to seduce her daughter's fiancé—pawing him shamelessly and putting her fingers in his mouth! Then a new series of axe murders begins. All this builds to a "surprise" climax that won't fool anyone who has ever seen a *Scooby Doo* cartoon, followed by one of Bloch's patented "now-let's-explain-what-you-just-saw" monologues. But if the ending falls flat, the twists and turns along the way provide enough suspense and grue to keep audiences on their toes. The film's greatest virtue, however, is Crawford.

Like Vincent Price, Crawford could be led to a

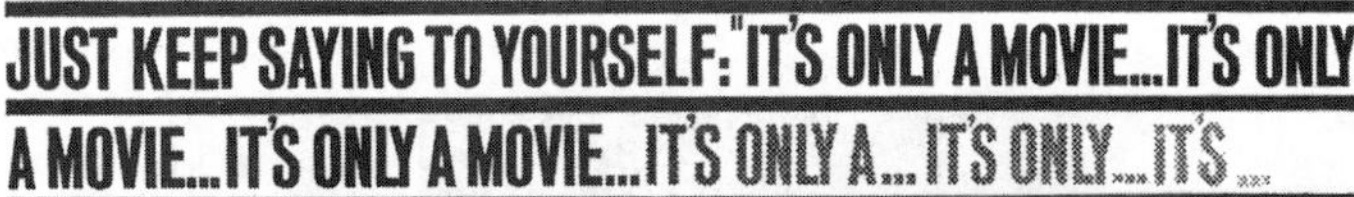

This 1964 William ("King of the Gimmicks") Castle entry was the first feature to make use of the classic "It's only a movie" ad-line later "borrowed" most famously to promote films such as *The Last House on the Left* (1972).

subtle, nuanced performance, but left to her own devices she tended to paint in broad strokes. *Strait-Jacket* finds her in Jackson Pollack mode. She rips through this film like a tornado, blowing bland co-stars Diane Baker and Leif Erickson off the screen with one bravura grandiloquent moment after another. In one unforgettable bit of business, Crawford lights a match on a spinning phonograph record! Only future Oscar winner George Kennedy manages to hold his own, playing a crude and creepy farmhand.

Castle brought Crawford on board to replace another aging former starlet, Joan Blondell, who dropped out of the project for health reasons. Once she was involved, however, *Strait-Jacket* became Crawford's show. She demanded (and received) approval of script, cast and cinematographer, as well as a product placement for Pepsi Cola (a six pack of bottles sits on the counter in Carol's kitchen). Crawford must have relished the chance to play this showy part, especially after being upstaged in *Baby Jane* by rival Bette Davis. Davis followed up *Baby Jane* with a relatively tame noir melodrama, *Dead Ringer* (1964), which earned better reviews at the time than *Strait-Jacket*. At this distance, however, *Strait-Jacket* proves the more entertaining picture.

Portrait in madness: Victor Buono is *The Strangler* (1964) (courtesy Ted Okuda).

The Strangler (1964; Allied Artists; b&w) Director: Burt Topper; Producers: Samuel Bischoff and David Diamond; Screenplay: Bill S. Ballinger; Cinematography: Jacques Marquette. Cast: Victor Buono, Ellen Corby, David McLean, Davey Davison, Baynes Barron, Russ Bender.

Based on the terror that has shocked the nation!—tagline

The Strangler (1964) wants to have it both ways. It's half ripped-from-the-headlines docu-drama and half psychological thriller. The picture's police procedural material seems dated and flat, but its fright sequences remain fresh and engrossing.

Leo Kroll (Victor Buono), the dutiful but browbeaten son of a clinging, passive-aggressive mother (Ellen Corby), is lonely, bitter and overweight. He vents his pent-up anger and sexual frustration by watching women undress and then strangling them with their own stockings. He's claimed eight victims so far, and the police, led by Lt. Frank Benson (David McLean), remain stumped. But when Leo decides to change his modus operandi and target his invalid mother's nurse, he leaves a clue that puts the cops on his trail.

Producers Samuel Bischoff and David Diamond designed *The Strangler* to capitalize on sensational national news coverage of the Boston Strangler, a serial killer who took the lives of 19 women from 1962 to 1964. In late 1964, Edward DeSalvo confessed to these murders, but the crimes remained unsolved when *The Strangler* premiered in April. At fist Bischoff and Diamond planned to shoot the movie (originally titled *The Boston Strangler*) in Boston on the actual locations of the real-life strangler's crimes! When those plans were jettisoned, the picture was retitled and the story's action relocated to an unnamed Anytown USA. Even so, given the sensitive nature of the subject matter, the film takes pains to present law enforcement in a favorable light. Its cops are hard boiled hero types who seem to be on the job around the clock, ferreting out clues, chasing down leads and staking out suspects. The narrative slows to a crawl during these dry sequences and screeches to a halt whenever Lieutenant Benson consults police psychologist Dr. Sanford (Russ Bender), who spews wrongheaded psychobabble (for instance, he suggests that all schizophrenics become dangerous criminals).

Those regrettable interludes aside, however, *The Strangler* is compelling viewing—imaginatively composed by director Burt Topper and beautifully lit by cinematographer Jacques Marquette, with startling performances by Buono and Corby. The opening shot shows a woman undressing, reflected in the eye of the killer as he watches her disrobe. Leo steps out of the shadows and throttles his victim as she attempts to answer the phone. The picture then cuts to a shot of the murderer pulling the clothes off a kewpie doll and placing the toy in a desk drawer full of other kewpie dolls—all without a word of dialogue. It's a powerful beginning, one Alfred Hitchcock might have admired, and it's only the first in a series of striking murder scenes.

Corby is brilliant as Kroll's domineering mother, who simpers for her son's affection one minute then viciously lambastes him a moment later. She warns him that all women (except her) are no good. Besides, she asks, what would any girl want with him? "You're not good-looking, you're fat. Even as a little boy, nobody liked you." Ouch! Buono's Leo Kroll proves no less spectacular—he's unctuous and effete, weirdly dainty despite the actor's imposing size, like a demented Oliver Hardy. Through his performance alone, Buono introduces a creepy sexual element to the material, leering at his prospective victims with lascivious intent and gasping in ecstasy as he strangles them. (Ironically, in reality Buono—a devout Christian—was squeamish about the more lascivious elements of the story and demanded that the killer's victims put on robes or other clothing rather than appear on the screen nearly nude.) Yet Buono also brings a surprising degree of pathos to his scenes with Corby and especially to a heart-wrenching sequence in which he proposes to a young woman (Davey Davison) who runs the ring-toss concession at a local arcade. Inevitably she rejects him, a perceived betrayal that seems to validate his mother's judgments and sends Leo into a rage that seals his doom.

With more scenes like that one, and less humdrum detective work, *The Strangler* might have been a classic. Instead, it's merely a good little movie.

Succubus (1969; Aquila Film Enterprises; West Germany) Original Language Title: *Necronomicon*; Director: Jess Frank (Jesus Franco); Producers: Adrian Hoven, Pier A. Caminnecci; Screenplay: Pier A. Caminnecci. Cinematographers: Franz Lederle, Georg Herrero. Cast: Janine Reynaud, Jack Taylor, Howard Vernon, Michel Lemoine, Nathalie Nort, Pier A. Caminnecci, Adrian Hoven, Rosanna Yanni, Chris Howland, Amerigo Coimbra.

THE sensual experience of '69—poster blurb

"She loved the games men played with death, when death must win." Indeed. This nearly unwatchable mess is prolific European director Jess Franco's attempt at an erotic art film (and the first mainstream horror movie to receive an X rating in America). Unfortunately, because it *is* Franco, there is nothing "arty" about it—it's just a sleazy, slow-paced, overly pretentious bore.

The nearly incoherent narrative deals with a woman (Janine Reynaud) who performs sado-erotic acts on stage, pretending to kill her victims/lovers. She starts to hallucinate and actually begins carrying out her act for real.

The premise sounds intriguing, but Franco botches it with his snail-like pacing and pretentious non-sequitors. "The serpent is poison to us all," somebody says for no particular reason. This type of thing happens regularly throughout the film. At one point the woman goes to a party and all the guests start advancing on hands and knees, barking like dogs!

The occasional scene does hold one's interest, and there are the odd (usually *very* odd) flashes

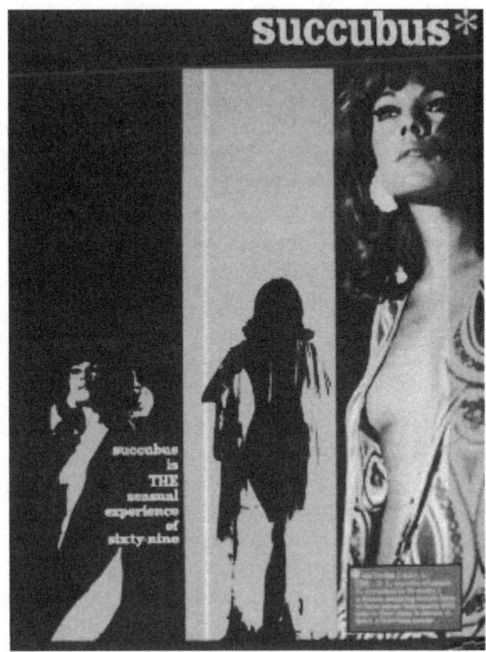

Promotional brochure for Jess Franco's erotic horror film *Succubus* (1969).

of competence from Franco, but these infrequent moments are overshadowed by the remaining boring dreck. For instance, who wants to watch a tepid love scene with the camera (for no particular reason) pointed through a fishtank, so distorting the picture that the two groping actors look more like big-time wrestlers than lovers?

At the risk of stating the obvious—in a word, *Succubus* sucks.

The Swamp of the Lost Monsters (1957/65; Trans-International Films; Mexico)

Original Language Title: *El Pantano de las Ánimas.* Alternate Title: *Swamp of the Lost Souls* (TV). Director: Rafael Baledon (English language version: Stim Segar); Producer: Alfredo Ripstein, Jr. (English version: K. Gordon Murray); Screenplay: Ramon Obon; Cinematography: Raul Martinez Solares. Cast: Gaston Santos, Pedro d'Aguillon, Manola Saavedra, Manuel Donde, Sara Cabrera, Salvador Rodriguez, Lupe Carriles.

IN THE STILL OF THE NIGHT, IT'S THE ONLY THING AWAKE—(video) tag line

The above ad line is a pretty accurate summation, since any late-night viewer hapless enough to venture into this *Swamp* will indeed have a difficult time staying conscious. Here, that inimitable importer of Mexi-trash, K. Gordon Murray, brings us Mexico's version of *The Creature from the Black Lagoon*—set in the Old West and costarring a dancing horse.

Famous bullfighter and horseman Gaston Santos plays famous cowboy detective(!) Gaston, who, along with his loyal, trick-performing steed "Moonlight" and loyal, song-performing comic sidekick "Squirrel Eyes" (Pedro d'Aquillon), investigates the strange disappearance of a corpse right out of its coffin, and the subsequent attacks by the mysterious beast (or "bist" as one dubiously dubbed dude calls it) of "the Haunted Swamp." It all boils down to an insurance scam and a "twist" ending that would make Scooby-Doo blush.

Basically a "ranchero" (Mexican Western) with a monster added to the mix, *The Swamp of the Lost Monsters* (despite its title, only one "monster" makes an appearance) offers very little to the horror fan, focusing instead on such Western staples as cantina brawls, horse riding, pony tricks (including Moonlight "dancing"—well, prancing anyway—to music), and (generally harmless) gunplay.

Periodically, the "bist" swims by or prowls around the hacienda (creating a rare moment of atmosphere when its webbed feet or hands emerge from the shadows), but once fully revealed, the baggy, reddish suit (complete with obvious air-tank hump), overlarge grouper head, and pathetic swimming ability (as it awkwardly tries to stay submerged) brand this beast a poor provincial cousin to its famous American model. And the filmmakers let the phony fish out of the bag far too early, when 20 minutes into the movie the creature takes aim at the hero with a spear gun(!), and later taps out a telegraph message in Morse code(!!).

The film offers some impressive, crystal-clear underwater photography (shot in a dressed-up swimming pool)—which only serves to point out its utter incongruousness with the muddy, Montezuma's Revenge-inducing swamp water seen while above the surface (not to mention revealing the obviously rubber nature of the wobbly knife the hero wields while lamely grappling with the creature underwater). Very quickly, *The Swamp of the Lost Monsters* becomes the Movie of the Lost Interest.

Swamp of the Lost Souls see *Swamp of the Lost Monsters*

A Tale of Torture see *Bloody Pit of Horror*

Tales of Mystery and Imagination see *Spirits of the Dead*

Tales of Terror (1962; American International)

Director/Producer: Roger Corman; Screenplay: Richard Matheson; Cinematographer: Floyd Crosby. Cast: Vincent Price, Peter Lorre, Basil Rathbone, Maggie Pierce, Leona Gage, Joyce Jamison, Debra Paget, David Frankham.

A Trilogy of Shock and Horror!—tagline

Producer-director Roger Corman scored spectacular successes with his first two Edgar Allan Poe adaptations, *House of Usher* (1960) and *The Pit and the Pendulum* (1962), but disappointing returns for *The Premature Burial* (1962) suggested the series was headed toward a dead end. *Tales of Terror* (1962) represented an abrupt change in course and, after three repetitive and formulaic entries, set the series on a far more adventurous path.

Usher, Pit and *Burial* shared many common story elements and the same basic construction (with the actual Poe tale reserved for the final act, while an elaborate, two-act set-up consumes the rest of the narrative). *Tales of Terror*, an anthology featuring three short films adapted from Poe stories, enabled Corman to jump directly into the Poe stories, without the protracted and talky "prologues" found in his earlier adaptations. Along with screenwriter Richard Matheson, Corman also brought two new elements into the series: comedy and the supernatural. As a result, *Tales* seems fresh — more like the beginning of a new series than the continuation of an old one. And, indeed, from this point forward Corman's Poe films became much more varied in both structure and tone.

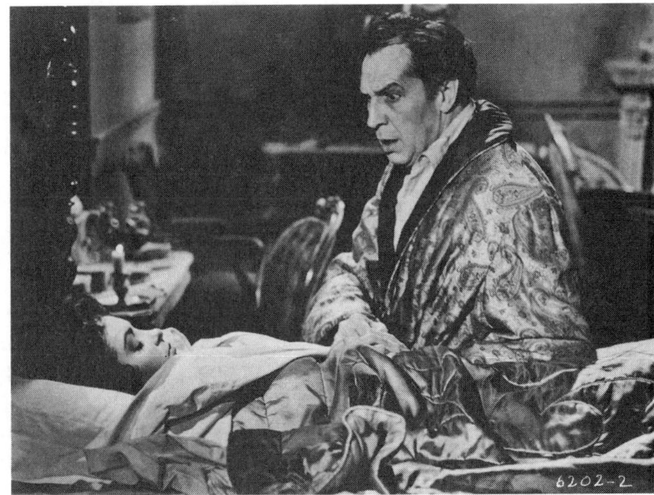

Vincent Price and Maggie Pierce in the "Morella" segment of the Roger Corman–Edgar Allan Poe anthology *Tales of Terror* (1962).

In the first of the *Tales*, "Morella," young Lenore (Maggie Pierce) returns to the home of her father (Vincent Price), a bitter alcoholic who blames his daughter for the death of his beloved wife, Morella (Leona Gage), whose desiccated corpse he keeps with him. Eventually Lenore and her father reconcile, but Morella returns from the dead to take her own revenge. In "The Black Cat" (which is actually an amalgam of "The Black Cat" and "A Cask of Amontillado"), a penniless drunkard, Montresor (Peter Lorre), challenges a snooty sommelier, Fortunato (Price), to a wine-tasting contest and wins. Afterward, Fortunato strikes up a romance with Montresor's wife. When Montresor learns of the affair, he plans a grisly revenge, but fails to account for his wife's pesky pet cat. Finally, in "The Case of Mr. Valdemar" (based on "The Facts in the Case of M. Valdemar"), a cunning hypnotist, Carmichael (Basil Rathbone), convinces the kindly but fatally ill Valdemar (Price) to submit to being hypnotized at the moment of death. The experiment works beyond all expectations. Although Valdemar is dead, Carmichael retains a hold on his consciousness; only he can release Valdemar's soul and free him from the agony of death. When Carmichael tries to use this control to extort a marriage promise from Valdemar's lovely young widow (Debra Paget), Valdemar strikes out from the Great Beyond to defend his bride.

Tales was shot on Corman's typical (for this series) three-week schedule, with one week's worth of production devoted to each 25-minute short. All the key technicians and artisans who worked on the earlier Poe pictures were on board again, including cinematographer Floyd Crosby and production designer Daniel Haller. Their work remains as impressive as ever. Also back was Price, who had starred in the first two entries but, for contractual reasons, not in *Burial*. Corman wanted each segment to have a distinctive style and personality, and decided to do something truly radical with the middle third of the picture. "Since we were doing a trilogy of Poe stories, we decided to break things up a bit and bring something totally different into the film," Corman said. "So 'The Black Cat' is a full comedy. Actually, I shouldn't say full comedy; it's really a comedy with some horror."

Corman, who just prior to launching the Poe series completed an informal trilogy of amusing black comedies (*A Bucket of Blood* [1959], *Little Shop of Horrors* [1960] and *Creature from the Haunted Sea* [1961]), hadn't lost his flair for such material. "Cat," highlighted by the uproarious wine tasting competition between Price and Lorre, remains *Tales*' most celebrated episode. But the other two segments also remain extremely enjoyable. The moody "Morella" plays like a Reader's Digest condensation of the series' first three entries, with all those pictures' strengths and none of their weaknesses. The wild and woolly "Valdemar," with its spectacularly gruesome finale, makes an ideal closer. Price contributes a trio of excellent and distinctive performances— slicing it thick as the pathetic, drunk Locke from "Morella;" hamming hilariously as the prissy, ridiculous Fortunato; and underplaying effectively as the devoted but tortured Valdemar. He receives able support, most notably from Lorre in "Cat" (he's so funny here that Corman quickly re-teamed him with Price for his next Poe film) but also from Pierce in "Morella" and both Rathbone and Paget in "Valdemar." Although few critics count it among the best of Corman's Poe films, few other pictures from the series (or anywhere else in the director's filmography) are as consistently entertaining as *Tales of Terror*.

Tales raked in over $1.5 million in rentals, less than *Usher* and *Pit* but more than *The Premature Burial*. Corman was sufficiently encouraged to make his next Poe picture, *The Raven* (1963), a full-on horror-comedy.

With quotes from: "California Gothic: The Corman/Haller Collaboration," by Lawrence French, from *Video Watchdog* No. 138.

Targets (1968; Paramount) Director/Producer: Peter Bogdanovich; Screenplay: Peter Bogdanovich (story: Peter Bogdanovich and Polly Platt). Cinematographer: Laszlo Kovacs. Cast: Boris Karloff, Tim O'Kelly, Nancy Hsueh, James Brown, Sandy Baron, Arthur Peterson, Bogdanovich.

> I just killed my wife and my mother. I know they'll get me. But before that, many more will die...— ad line

The climactic scenes from old-time horror star Byron Orlock's newest Gothic movie (oddly familiar, since it consists of footage from Roger Corman's *The Terror*) unspool in a studio screening room. The tired Orlock (Boris Karloff) is not amused: "I'm an anachronism," he sighs. "Look around you, the world belongs to the young. Make way for them — let them have it."

A clean-cut young man named Bobby (Tim O'Kelly) checks out a rifle in a gun shop by catching Orlock (standing across the street) in its crosshairs (the young indeed taking the world from the old). Polite and cheerful, the boy buys the gun, walks out to his car in the bright California sun, and opens the trunk to deposit his purchase, revealing an unsettling sight: neatly laid out on a blanket are an assortment of rifles, handguns and ammo clips, a veritable arsenal to which he adds his latest acquisition. It's a somber and disturbing opening for the thought-provoking, realistic, modern-day horror portrayed in *Targets*, the last truly worthy film to star the grand old man of horror himself, Boris Karloff. Though Karloff made four more (awful) movies after this, *Targets* was his spiritual swan song.

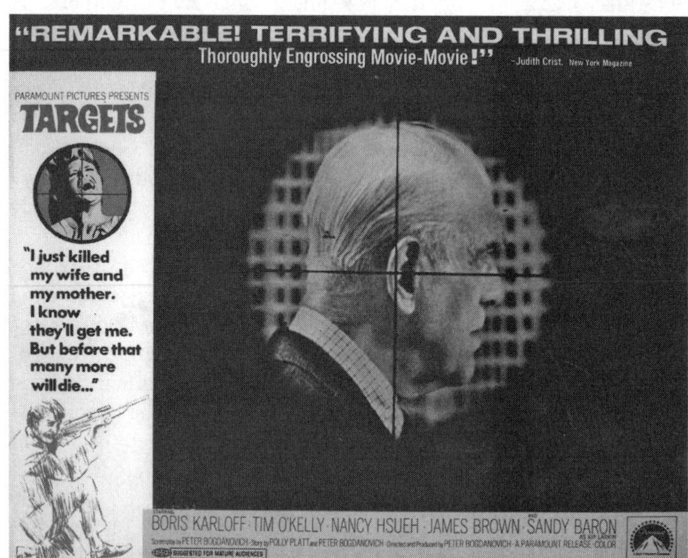

Modern realistic horror collides with traditional gothic horror in the topical *Targets* (1968), the last truly worthy vehicle for the iconic Boris Karloff (pictured in this lobby card).

"*Targets* was my first picture ... and Boris owed Roger Corman two days work," recalled director Peter Bogdanovich at the 1988 Academy of Motion Picture Arts and Sciences tribute to Karloff. (Note: *Targets* was actually Bogdanovich's *second* film, his first being *Voyage to the Planet of Prehistoric Women*, also released in 1968.) "And Roger is known to use every moment. So he said, 'I made a picture with Boris called *The Terror*. I want you to take 20 minutes of Karloff footage out of *The Terror*, then shoot 20 minutes with Boris in two days. You can shoot 20 minutes in two days; I've shot whole pictures in two days. Then you'll have

40 minutes of Karloff. Then I want you to go out and shoot 40 more minutes of stuff with some other actors and then we'll have a new 80-minute picture!' At some point along the way I had an idea it would be interesting if Boris played himself, so to speak: an aging horror movie star who wanted to quit because the random violence in the '60s—which hasn't left us yet—was more terrifying than the kind of Victorian monster he'd been playing."

Taking his inspiration from the 1966 Texas sniper killings (in which Charles J. Whitman, after murdering his wife and mother, barricaded himself in a tower at the University of Texas with a rifle, killing 14 and wounding 31 before being shot by police), Bogdanovich and his production designer (and then-wife) Polly Platt wrote the original story, with Bogdanovich penning his first draft in 11 days. The film follows Orlock as he wrestles with his outmoded image and self-imposed retirement; while concurrently showing the outwardly normal Bobby shooting his wife and mother, and then sniping at passing cars from a water tower. The two storylines converge at a drive-in where Orlock is making his final personal appearance.

"The first thing [Karloff] said after reading the script," Bogdanovich told *Dear Boris* author Cynthia Lindsay, "was, 'I believe in this picture, but you can't do it in two days.' I said that regrettably nobody was coming up with more salary for him, so I'd have to. He simply answered, 'Take as long as you like.' He worked five days.... The film would have been impossible without him."

Filmed in 25 days in December 1967 on a paltry budget of $130,000 (to save money, Bogdanovich did double duty as an actor, playing the apt part of Sammy, Orlock's director), *Targets* is an engrossing, subtly powerful, and horrifying comment on alienation and its terrible consequences. Orlock feels alienated because the world has passed him and his brand of entertainment by. Bobby, outwardly the all-American boy, also feels isolated, though Bogdanovich only drops hints at its cause: his interactions with his family (including his pretty but vapid wife) are painfully superficial (he even addresses his father as "Sir").

In one memorable scene, Bogdanovich demonstrates that Orlock may be wrong in thinking that the old horrors hold no further sway. It comes when Orlock prepares for his upcoming personal appearance by telling a scary story ("Appointment in Samara," in which a man flees from the specter of death) he plans to share with the audience. "The speech is two pages long," remembered Bogdanovich, "and I was going to break it up by panning around the room while he was speaking. Boris said, 'I want to do this without a script.' I asked him if he wanted cue cards instead. He said, 'No.' We rehearsed the mechanics of the scene—he was letter perfect. I realized I was an idiot not to stay on him. The camera was at the end of a long table. I said to the cameraman, 'Stay on him. Start with a long shot, we'll sneak the table away as you dolly in.' It was electrifying. Boris did the whole two pages in one take! Then the entire crew burst into applause. Boris was pleased." It's a testament to that great actor's abilities—and the fact that a simple story, well-told, still has the power to enthrall and frighten—that this remains one of the film's most riveting scenes.

With *Targets*, Bogdanovich wisely avoided making an overt "message" picture, choosing instead to simply put the events on the screen without preaching or pontificating. Paramount, the film's distributor, however, had different ideas, and, in light of the recent assassinations of Martin Luther King, Jr., and Robert Kennedy, tacked a gun-control prologue onto the film (over Bogdanovich's objections). Thankfully, this heavy-handed intro has been removed from most subsequent release versions.

Perfectly acted (Karloff, given his first truly worthy role in over a decade, regains the subtlety and power of his craft that seemingly had gone missing; while newcomer Tim O'Kelly is distressingly likable, making his heinous actions that much more disturbing) and well directed (Bogdanovich seamlessly weaves the two story threads together into a cohesive whole, culminating in a harrowing climax in which Bobby, hidden within the drive-in screen, takes aim at patrons in their cars), *Targets* stands as a topical—yet still timeless—treatise on modern-day horror. And it marks a fitting end to the career of horror cinema's greatest on-screen contributor, Boris Karloff.

With quotes from: "Remembering Boris: Academy of Motion Picture Arts & Sciences Tribute," by Kris Gilpin, *Deep Red* 4, 1987.

A Taste of Blood (1967; Mayflower) Director/Producer/Cinematography: Herschell Gordon Lewis; Screenplay: Donald Stanford. Cast: Bill Rogers, Elizabeth Wilkinson, William Kerwin (as Thomas Wood), Otto Schlessinger, Eleanor Vaill.

Will Dracula's avenger turn loose his wrath into the 1970s?—tagline

---

Petit bourgeois businessman John Stone (Bill Rogers) receives a mysterious parcel from London, which informs him that he is the sole heir to a Continental fortune including an English estate, works of art and other treasures. The package even contains two bottles of the family's private label brandy, with which he is instructed to toast his good fortune. This he does, without realizing that the fortune is that of the Dracula family, and the brandy contains the blood of the long-dead count. Soon Stone transforms into a bloodthirsty vampire, committed to hunting down the descendents of those who killed the original Count decades earlier. Stone's wife, Helene (Elizabeth Wilkinson), stumbles onto the truth and turns to family friend Hank Tyson (William Kerwin) for assistance. But Hank proves of little help until, finally, Dr. Helsing (Otto Schlessinger), himself a target of Stone's vengeance, arrives from Europe.

A Taste of Blood was one of three horror films made by goremeister Herschell Gordon Lewis in 1967, following a two-year hiatus from the genre. Aspiring screenwriter Donald Stanford brought the script to Lewis, who agreed to produce and direct it even though the project would stand apart from the typical Lewis horror product in its lack of gore, upgraded production values (including a three-week shooting schedule, unheard of for Lewis) and longer running time (nearly two hours). "This movie had the greatest amount of production value of any movie I ever made," Lewis claims.

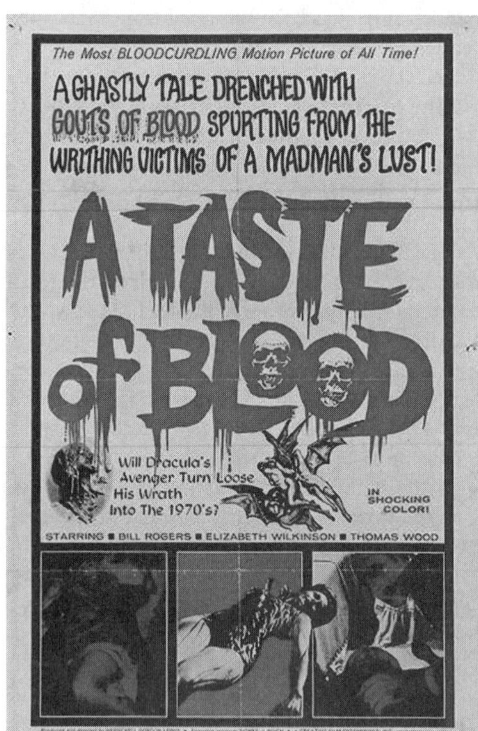

Herschell Gordon Lewis meets Dracula: *A Taste of Blood* (1967) (one-sheet poster).

However, not all of these differences were by design, and not all of them serve the film well. Take its two-hour length (please). Originally, Lewis said, "I thought the movie would run around 90 minutes ... but as [it] took form and you see the amount of time a scene lasts, it became clear to me that running at a furious pace was totally out of key with the kind of picture we were building here. So each scene took longer than the script suggested it would."

Lewis said the slower pace was dictated in large part by the thoughtful, deliberate approach of star Bill Rogers, whose work he admired. "He could *be* Dracula," Lewis said. "He's thin, his features are rugged. He knows how to play a scene.... Christopher Lee and Bill Rogers have a certain similarity to them."

Lewis is right — Rogers is thin. Unfortunately, the rest of his analysis remains suspect. Sure, Rogers' performance is entertaining in a hambone sort of way, but no more so than that of previous Lewis leads such as Gordon Oas-Heim in *Color Me Blood Red* (1965) or even Mal Arnold in *Blood Feast* (1963). And as Draculas go, he pales next to Francis Lederer (*The Return of Dracula*, 1958), let alone Chris Lee. Nothing in Rogers' work justifies the film's agonizing sluggishness. Its woefully predictable story grinds along at a sleep-inducing crawl.

The whole enterprise lacks the maniacal originality that fuels Lewis' better efforts (such as *Two Thousand Maniacs!* and *Something Weird*). The basic premise (an ancient terror returning from the grave to wreak vengeance on the descendents of those who once defeated it) was hackneyed even in 1967, explored previously in such films as *Black Sunday* (1960), *Blood and Roses* (1960) and *The Brainiac* (1962), among many others. *A Taste of Blood*'s relatively subdued murder sequences will almost certainly disappoint fans expecting something on the order of the director's earlier splatter fests. And although production values are indeed higher than those of any other Lewis picture (the lighting is more effective, the sound richer and the cast almost entirely competent), this alone hardly makes for a compelling viewing experience.

Not surprisingly, *A Taste of Blood* did not rank among Lewis' greatest commercial successes. Its length drove up print costs and precluded the film from playing the usual double-feature circuit. Instead, it was forced to compete with real movies for screen time at mainstream theaters running one feature twice per night. However, the production proved rewarding in a different way for members of its cast and crew. Soon after production wrapped, starlet Wilkinson married Lewis' camera operator, Andy Romanoff. Eleanor Vaill (who gives the film's most unaffected performance as Stone's long-suffering secretary) and Schlessinger, who also appeared together in Lewis' *The Girl, the Body and the Pill* (1967) and K. Gordon Murray's *Shanty Tramp* (1967), also eventually married.

Viewers, however, are unlikely to fall head over heels for *A Taste of Blood.*

With quotes from: *A Taste of Blood* DVD audio commentary with H.G. Lewis; .

Taste of Fear see *Scream of Fear*

Pressbook cover for *The Tell-Tale Heart* (1963).

The Tell-Tale Heart (1960/63; Warner-Pathe/Brigadier Films; U.K.; b&w) Alternate Titles: *Panic*; *The Horror Man*; *The Hidden Room of 1,000 Horrors*. Director: Ernest Morris. Producers: The Danzigers (Edward J. and Harry Lee Danziger). Screenplay: Brian Clemens, Eldon Howard (based on the story by Edgar Allan Poe); Cinematographer: Jimmy Wilson. Cast: Laurence Payne, Adrienne Corri, Dermot Walsh, Velma Vaz Dias, John Scott, John Martin, Pamela Plant.

THE BEAT OF HIS DEATHLESS HEART ...
RIPPED INTO MY TORTURED BRAIN.
—poster

A written "FORWARD" appears on the black screen, as a sonorous voice reads the words: "TO THOSE WHO ARE SQUEAMISH OR REACT NERVOUSLY TO SHOCK, WE SUGGEST THAT WHEN YOU HEAR THIS SOUND ... [loud heartbeat] ... CLOSE YOUR EYES AND DO NOT LOOK AT THE SCREEN AGAIN UNTIL IT STOPS." But then you'd miss all the gory fun. And this British 1960 (released in the U.S. in '63) adaptation of the famous Poe tale is indeed gruesome, particularly for the early Sixties, with the filmmakers apparently attempting to out–Hammer Hammer in the moist-and-meaty department.

The first half of the movie plays out as a rather slow character study, with nervous librarian Edgar Marsh (Laurence Payne), who appears addicted not only to cocaine and the bottle, but to 19th-century pornography as well, falling instantly in love with newly arrived neighbor Betty (Adrienne Corri). Unfortunately, the socially inept Edgar's fumbling attempts at courtship pale in comparison to his more worldly friend Carl's (Dermot Walsh) charm, which captivates Betty. Though Carl, out of deference for his friend, initially resists, he ultimately gives in to temptation. And when Edgar spies Betty and Carl consummating their love ... murder, madness and an ever-beating heart are the result.

Stretching Poe's intense short story into an 80-minute feature required some straining on the part of scripters Brian Clemens (*The Avengers*) and Eldon Howard, resulting in the disappointing *Peyton Place*-pacing of the film's first half. While it is something of a chore to get through the first 40 minutes (though the impressive period costumes and set decorations provide some visual interest), with so much time devoted to the fawning Edgar and his awkward dates with Betty (not to mention the frequent longing stares and pained glances from the various members of the love triangle), the patient viewer ultimately receives his or her just rewards after the murder occurs (a particularly brutal sequence involving a fireplace poker and much blood). At this point the picture takes a darker turn as we enter Edgar's world of obsessive insanity, in which the maddeningly rhythmic sounds of a ticking clock, a dripping tap, and even a swaying crystal chandelier bedevils his guilt-wracked mind. When these noises coalesce into the beating of the dead man's heart, the frantic Edgar rips up the floorboards under which he's stashed the body and performs some impromptu surgery, removing the still-beating organ (in all its gory glory) and burying it in the back garden. But it just won't stop, leading to Edgar's ultimate demise and a gruesome impalement — before a *Dead of Night*-style denouement.

Much of the film's impact can be laid at the feet of Laurence Payne (*The Crawling Eye*, *Vampire Circus*), whose contagious nervousness and tormented expressions make the scenes work (his mad sincerity even selling such ridiculous sights as the carpet over his floorboards rising and falling to the rhythmic beat). Director Ernest Morris creates a haunted, even frightening ambiance to augment Payne's engrossing playing, employing mobile (and even subjective) camerawork and moody lighting (courtesy of 30-year-veteran cinematographer Jimmy Wilson), not to mention the shuddery sounds, to reveal the deterioration of a man's mind.

Though beating slowly at first, this *Tell-Tale Heart* ultimately picks up the horrific rhythm and races to the gruesome finish, making the viewer's own heart beat just a little faster along the way.

The Terrible Dr. Hitchcock see *The Horrible Dr. Hichcock*

Terrified (1963; Crown International; b&w) Director: Lew Landers. Producer/screenplay: Richard Bernstein; Cinematographer: Curt Fetters. Cast: Rod Lauren, Steve Drexel, Tracy Olsen, Stephen Roberts.

Buried alive! How much Shock can the human brain endure before it CRACKS! — tag line

Terror snaps a boy's mind; another character's own *terror* kills him; *terror*, maintains one protagonist, is what "drives the world." The word "terror" becomes the macabre mantra of this obscure, all-but-forgotten independent (one character even writes a psychology term paper on the topic); but talk is cheap — and so is this picture. Consequently, there's very little actual "terror" onscreen.

The film starts promisingly enough with a pre-credit sequence set in a creepy graveyard in which a hooded (and suit-and-tie-wearing) madman laughs maniacally as he buries a young man alive in wet cement. Unfortunately, nothing else in the film ever quite reaches the same (modest) level of intensity, as the story focuses on heroine Marge (Tracy Olsen) and her rival boyfriends David (Steve Drexel) and Ken (Rod Lauren), who go to the "Old Ghost Town" to see if Crazy Bill the caretaker knows anything about the pre-credit events (the victim being Marge's brother, who ultimately survived but was driven insane by — you guessed it — the *terror* of his ordeal). Finding Bill brutally murdered, David and Marge go for the sheriff (played by *Dukes of Hazard*'s Denver Pyle) while Ken stays behind and ends up being stalked and terrorized by the hooded killer (who locks him in a room filling with water, shoots at him, taunts him with a hangman's noose, and finally proceeds to bury him alive). It all wraps up just as one expects, with the killer revealed as ... just whom one expected.

While the Ken-stalking sequences offer a modicum of suspense and creepy atmospherics (as he

Ad for the final feature of veteran director Lew Landers (1935's *The Raven*), who died before this low-budget film's release in 1963.

wanders warily around the dilapidated buildings, starting at cobwebs and spiders), it drags on far too long (nearly half-an-hour). "Boy, they're sure taking a long time calling that sheriff," Ken says to himself after the third repetitive attack-and-escape-from-the-madman incident, and the viewer can only chuckle and nod in agreement.

Moody lighting and some evocative nighttime photography (the entire film takes place during one evening), coupled with some above-average acting (particularly from Rod [*Black Zoo*, *The Crawling Hand*] Lauren as the brooding Ken), gives the film a more polished sheen than that usually seen in no-budget films of the early '60s.

A young Jack Nicholson (right) confronts an aged Boris Karloff in this lobby card scene from the Roger Corman throwaway *The Terror* (1960/63).

Lew Landers (whose directorial career stretched all the way back to the 1935 Karloff-Lugosi vehicle *The Raven*) generates some moody atmosphere, but the obvious budget constraints and talky script (much of the "action" is relayed through dialogue, with the characters *talking* about what has happened rather than the camera *showing* it) work against him, resulting in a film reminiscent of an overlong, mediocre *Thriller* episode.

The Terror (1963; American International) Director/Producer: Roger Corman; Screenplay: Leo Gordon and Jack Hill; Cinematographer: Floyd Crosby. Cast: Boris Karloff, Jack Nicholson, Sandra Knight, Dick Miller, Dorothy Neumann, Jonathan Haze.

A new classic of horror comes to the screen!—tagline

While *The Terror* isn't officially part of producer-director Roger Corman's Edgar Allan Poe series, it remains forever linked with those films due to its colorful and highly irregular production history. Unfortunately, the story of the making of *The Terror* is far more entertaining than the film itself.

Andre Duvalier (Jack Nicholson), a "weary and disillusioned" French army lieutenant separated from his regiment, collapses on the beach and is aided by a mysterious, beautiful woman named Helene (Sandra Knight). Then Helene walks into the sea and disappears; when Andre attempts for rescue her, he is attacked by a falcon and loses consciousness. He awakens in the cottage of a reclusive old woman (Dorothy Neumann) who claims that there is no young woman nearby, and that "Helene" is the name of her pet falcon. A brutish simpleton (Jonathan Haze) informs Andre that to discover the secret of the young woman he must travel to the castle of the Baron von Leppe (Boris Karloff). Andre does so, and learns that the woman he's seen bears an uncanny resemblance to the Baron's long-dead wife, Ilsa, who the baron believes haunts him. Duvalier becomes consumed with solving the riddle of the girl's identity.

"I was getting so familiar with the standard elements of Poe's material — or at least of our adaptations— that I tried to out–Poe Poe himself and create a gothic tale from scratch," Corman explained in his autobiography. "*The Terror* began as a challenge: to shoot most of a gothic horror film in two days, using leftover sets from *The Raven* (1963). It turned into the longest production of my career — an ordeal that required five directors and nine months to complete." Karloff and Nicholson, along with Nicholson's wife Sandra Knight and Corman favorite Dick Miller, worked on *The Raven*'s imposing castle sets for two very long days. The problem was that these scenes were shot without a completed script, so it was up to Corman and a succession of uncredited directors (including Francis Ford Coppola, Monte Hellmann, Jack Hill and even Nicholson, who led one day's worth of shooting) to cobble together some kind of comprehensible story around the castle footage. The haphazard manner in which *The Terror* was written and filmed remains woefully obvious in the finished product. It looks cheap, rushed and clumsy, especially in comparison with Corman's proper Poe pictures. Even its title is unimaginative and bland.

The Terror's story never fully coheres. Subplots are left dangling, and events occur without any clear motivation. The resolution to the film's mystery appears conventional (even predictable) until two final plot twists—one utterly contrived and nonsensical—throw the entire narrative askew. All this makes *The Terror* hard to follow, a problem exacerbated by its tedious pace; after an eventful start, the tempo slows to a dirge. Viewers endure seemingly endless filler scenes of Nicholson wandering through the woods, or down the halls of Castle von Leppe. The movie sorely misses Corman's trademark restless camera—the gliding dolleys, smooth pans, subjective inserts and varied angles and compositions associated in particular with his Poe films. This is not only because so much of the film was not helmed by Corman, but because the footage he directed was shot at such a frenetic pace. Cinematographer Floyd Crosby's lighting is uncharacteristically flat and uninteresting as well. "You just don't get super lighting when you're shooting thirty pages a day," Corman admits.

Inevitably, the cast's performances suffered as well. "We had a roughed-out story line, but no one really knew what their characters' motivations were because we didn't exactly know what was supposed to happen to them," Corman wrote. That may explain why, even though it stars a pair of screen legends, *The Terror* remains surprisingly poorly acted. Karloff delivers a paint-by-numbers turn, full of the kind of sing-song delivery he often resorted to when he was less than enthused about a project. Nicholson's accent and delivery seem all wrong for a period picture (let alone for a Frenchman)—a problem that also afflicts the usually reliable Dick Miller, who sounds like a German from Brooklyn. And those are the better portrayals.

It could have been worse. At least no one died during the production, even though Karloff refused to continue after being submerged chest-deep in water while shooting the film's finale, and Nicholson nearly drowned while filming a scene on location at Big Sur. "The water never gets deep," Nicholson said. "So in order to look disappeared ... I sort of crouched down to my knees so that when the first white water waves hit me, it did not hit me in the dick but all over.... And the water knocked me under. When I went under with Lieutenant Duvalier's huge Fifth Chasseur uniform on, I felt I couldn't stand up. I was pinned to the ground from the weight of this uniform. I had that split second of panic because I was a ways out already. I came flying out of there and threw that fucking costume off as I ran."

Despite this mishap Nicholson has fond memories of the shoot.

"I had a great time. Paid the rent," Nicholson said. "They don't make movies like *The Terror* anymore."

That's probably a good thing.

With quotes from: *How I Made a Hundred Movies in Hollywood and Never Lost a Dime,* by Roger Corman with Jim Jerome.

Terror in the Midnight Sun see *Invasion of the Animal People*

Terror of the Snake Woman see *The Snake Woman*

Terror-Creatures from the Grave (1965/67; Pacemaker; Italy; b&w)

Original Language Title: *Cinque Tombe per un Medium* (Five Graves for a Medium); Alternate Titles: *Cemetery of the Living Dead, The Tombs of Horror*; Director: Ralph Zucker; Producer: Frank Merle, Ralph Zucker; Screenplay: Robert Nathan (Roberto Natale), Robin McLorin (Romana Migliorini); Cinematographer: Charles Brown (Carlo Di Palma). Cast: Barbara Steele, Walter Brandt (Walter Brandi), Marilyn Mitchell, Alfred Rice (Alfredo Rizzo), Richard Garrett (Ricardo Garrone), Alan Collins (Luciano Pigozzi), Edward Bell.

They rise from dank coffins in the DEAD OF NIGHT to inflict AN EVIL CURSE OF DOOM, murdering their victims in an ORGY OF SLAUGHTER!—ad line

In 1911 a lawyer (Walter Brandt) journeys to a remote villa (a former 16th century plague victim hospital) only to find that the man who sent for him has already been *dead* for a year. Soon mysterious deaths begin occurring around the village, and it comes to light that the dead man (who was well-versed in the occult) was murdered, and his spirit has summoned the plague victims from their graves to exact his vengeance.

While *Terror-Creatures from the Grave*'s American distributor tacked on the credit "Inspired by

Edgar Allan Poe" in a desperate attempt to ride the coattails of the then-lucrative AIP Poe cycle (*Terror-Creatures*' story has *nothing* to do with Poe), the claim may not be that far wrong — at least in *spirit* if not actuality. Much like the putrid atmosphere brought by the plague itself, a macabre pall hangs over *Terror-Creatures*, with death (literalized by the restless plague victims) permeating every frame of the picture. The wonderfully Gothic castle setting, some eerie nighttime photography and hand-held camerawork (courtesy of cinematographer Carlo Di Palma, who went on to lens several Woody Allen movies, including *Hannah and Her Sisters* and *Bullets Over Broadway*), and somber/frightened acting by the principals (including Barbara Steele as the ... er, steely widow) generate a creepy — and downright malevolent — atmosphere.

Taking a page from Val Lewton's book, director Ralph Zucker employs some subjective camerawork that keeps the ghosts/zombies of the ancient plague victims unseen (with only a shadowy outline visible, or a bubbly, deformed hand entering the frame), raising the film's *mysterioso* level and allowing the viewer's imagination to do the shuddery work. (But this being a 1960s horror movie, it's not all shadows and suggestion; Zucker throws a few gruesome scenes into the spine-chilling mix as well — such as the shocking sight of a man's intestines oozing out a small hole in his belly after he impales himself on a sword.)

Though the film's direction has been erroneously credited to Massimo (*Bloody Pit of Horror*) Pupillo (aka Max Hunter), *Terror-Creatures* (according to film historian Alan Upchurch *and* the movie's co-star, Walter Brandi) was actually helmed by a 25-year-old American named Ralph Zucker. It was his first — and last — directing job. Zucker worked in many other film capacities in Italy, however: as an actor in Pupillos's *Bloody Pit of Horror* (1965), as technical director on *Star Pilot* (1966), as producer of *King of Kong Island* (1968), and as scenarist and executive producer of *The Devil's Wedding Night* (1973), not to mention working on the English-dubbed export versions of other Italian movies and as a distributor of foreign films in Italy. Zucker died in Los Angeles in 1982 of a heart attack, age 42.

Given its novel and intriguing storyline, Lewtonesque sensibilities (spiced with a few shuddery shocks), effective acting (including the presence of the Continental Scream Queen herself, Barbara Steele), and its pervasive atmosphere of dread, *Terror-Creatures from the Grave* can be counted among the best of the Italo-Gothics from the 1960s.

The horrific handiwork of the *Terror-Creatures from the Grave* (1965/67).

Theatre of Death see *Blood Fiend*

They Came from Beyond Space (1967; Amicus/Embassy, U.K.). Director: Freddie Francis; Producers: Max J. Rosenberg and Milton Subotsky; Screenplay: Milton Subotsky (Novel: Joseph Millard); Cinematographer: Norman Warwick. Cast: Robert Hutton, Jennifer Jayne, Zia Mohyeddin, Bernard Kay, Michael Gough.

They turn women into robots ... enslave men ... and make cities into places of terror! — tagline

A team of British astronomers descends on a remote English village to investigate the fall of several strange meteorites. The team's leader, Dr. Curtis Temple (Robert Hutton), must stay behind because he's recuperating from a serious car crash that left him with a metal plate in his head. So he sends his assistant (and love interest) Lee Mason (Jennifer Jayne) who, along with the rest of the team, is quickly taken over by disembodied aliens which burst forth from the meteorites. Next, villagers near the crash site begin falling victim to a mysterious "crimson plague." Temple investigates and, after considerable folderol, discovers the alien plot, deducing that the metal plate in his skull makes him immune to both alien mind control and the plague. It's up to him, aided by his old friend Farge (Zia Mohyeddin), to free Lee and save the world.

They Came from Beyond Space opens well, with a tried-and-true premise straight out of previous sci-fi chillers such as *It Came from Outer Space* (1953) and *Invasion of the Body Snatchers* (1956). But the picture loses momentum while Temple drives around Cornwall playing cat-and-mouse with the aliens, and then takes a turn toward the ridiculous in its final act, when Farge dons an inverted colander to fend off mind-control rays, and both he and Temple strap on absurd-looking Coke bottle goggles to help them spot the invaders. The big finale — a rocket ride to the moon for a face-to-face encounter with the alien leader (Michael Gough) — proves anti-climactic in the extreme. Cash-strapped production designer Bill Constable's space ship and lunar set look like leftovers from a high school play. Gough's egregiously overripe performance as "The Master of the Moon" further tanks the sequence.

Other than Gough's hambone antics, the acting is mostly wooden, although Jayne displays some range playing the affectionate girlfriend, the icy alien and, finally, the affectionate girlfriend pretending to be an icy alien. Director Freddie Francis, best known for gothic chillers such as *The Skull* (1965) and *Dracula Has Risen from the Grave* (1968), seems out of his element here. *They Came from Beyond Space* seems antiseptic and impersonal, lacking the stylized compositions and evocative lighting that create Francis' stylistic signature. The picture's clumsy special effects also present a major stumbling block. Forget about the miniature space ship, even simple rear-screen projection car scenes look phony.

England's Amicus Films — best known for its series of horror anthologies, such as *The House That Dripped Blood* (1971) and *Tales from the Crypt* (1972) — scored hits with a pair of Dr. Who films starring Peter Cushing (*Dr. Who and the Daleks* [1965] and *Daleks: Invasion Earth 2150* [1966]), but the twin failures of *They Came from Beyond Space* and the even more feeble *The Terrornauts* (also 1967) put the studio off sci-fi until the mid–1970s, when it achieved one of its biggest successes with *The Land That Time Forgot* (1975).

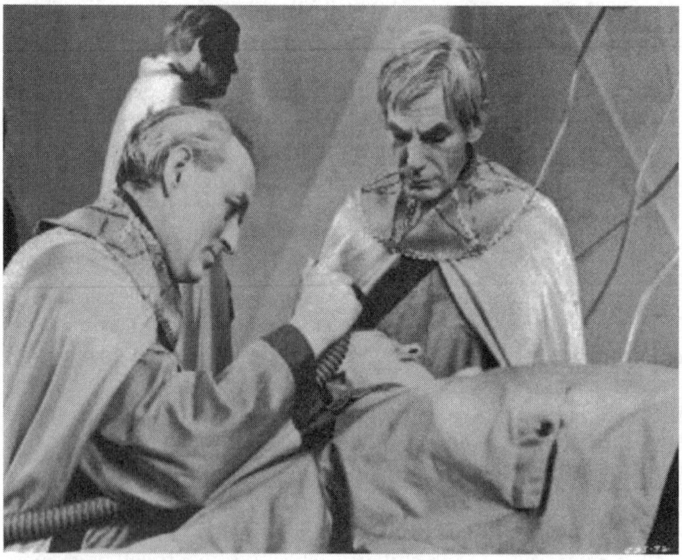

The malevolent alien leader (Michael Gough, right) and a henchman try to bend a captive to their will in Amicus' cut-rate sci-fi chiller *They Came from Beyond Space* (1967).

They Saved Hitler's Brain see *Madman of Mandoras*

13 Ghosts (1960; Columbia; b&w) Director/ Producer: William Castle; Screenplay: Robb White; Cinematographer: Joseph Biroc. Cast: Donald Woods, Charles Herbert, Jo Morrow, Martin Milner, Rosemary DeCamp, Margaret Hamilton.

13 Times the Thrills! 13 Times the Chills! 13 Times the Fun! — tagline

Thrills and chills may be in short supply, but at least producer-director William Castle's *13 Ghosts* doesn't shortchange viewers in the fun department. Although tamer and more kid-oriented than Castle's previous horror shows — *Macabre* (1958), *House on Haunted Hill* and *The Tingler* (both 1959) — *13 Ghosts* remains a diverting amusement, especially when viewed in "Illusion-O," one of the last of Castle's notorious promotional gimmicks.

Poorly paid professor Cyrus Zorba inherits a spooky old mansion from an eccentric uncle and moves in with his family: wife Hilda (Rosemary DeCamp), daughter Medea (Jo Morrow) and son Buck (Charles Herbert). Legend holds that Zorba's uncle, an expert on the occult, collected ghosts, and Cyrus' inheritance also includes a strange pair of goggles that enable wearers to see such apparitions. Even without goggles, the family soon sees plenty of evidence of the supernatural — strange creaking sounds, disembodied moans and groans, objects moving through the air of their own volition, etc. While

Elaborate promotional ploy for William Castle's *13 Ghosts* (1960).

playing with a ouija board, Buck and Medea learn that the house is haunted by 13 different specters. A creepy housekeeper (Margaret Hamilton), who refuses to move out when the Zorbas move in, and attorney Ben Rush (Martin Milner) both urge the family to abandon the house at once, but the Zorbas cannot afford to live anywhere else.

Robb White's paint-by-numbers screenplay trots out every old dark house cliché in the book, including a few recycled from his earlier, better *House on Haunted Hill* scenario. It's pure hokum, but it's lively and appealing hokum, quickly paced and laced with humorous tongue-in-cheek flourishes (like the ghost of Shadrack the Great, a decapitated lion tamer, who materializes along with the lion that bit off his head). There's also some deviously funny inside business involving former Wicked Witch of the West Margaret Hamilton.

Told principally from Buck's perspective, *13 Ghosts* aimed for a younger audience than Castle's previous fright flicks. Like most of the cast, Charles Herbert, who plays the precocious Buck, had a long (by child actor standards) 15-year career on television, although he's best remembered for playing young Philippe in *The Fly* (1958). Martin Milner, star of the hit series *Route 66*, was the biggest name in the *13 Ghosts* cast at the time, and here he plays effectively against his nice-guy image. Featuring a cast filled with television actors and shot in the same straightforward, flat style as an early 1960s sitcom, *13 Ghosts* plays like a Halloween episode of *Leave It to Beaver*. Although pedestrian in most technical aspects, the film's sound design is first-rate—Castle well understood how to rattle an audience with booming sound effects and screams.

In its original theatrical exhibition, *13 Ghosts* was presented in "Illusion-O," a simple but clever process utilizing tinted film and a cardboard "Ghost Viewer" containing strips of red and blue cellophane. When a character picks up the Ghost Viewer goggles in the movie, the picture would suddenly shift from standard black-and-white to tinted blue. Then red-hued "ghosts" would appear. Audience members could look through the blue cellophane of their Ghost Viewers to see the ghosts more clearly, or (if they became too scared) look through the red lens to make the ghosts disappear. Standard black-and-white television prints of *13 Ghosts* excluded this gimmick, but "Illusion-O" was revived when the picture was released to DVD in 2001 (discs included a reproduction of the original Ghost Viewer).

"Illusion-O" followed on the heels of "Emergo" (the plastic skeleton which flew over audiences' heads during the climax of *House on Haunted Hill*) and "Percepto" (wired theater seats which delivered an electrical shock during a key sequence from *The Tingler*), but never again would Castle utilize a gimmick as elaborate as this. *Homicidal* (1961) included a "Fright Break," and *Mr. Sardonicus* (1961) featured its "Punishment Poll," while other Castle films would include giveaways (souvenir coins for *Zotz* [1962], cardboard axes for *Strait-Jacket* [1964]), but none of those required costly customization of theaters or specialized printing processes for the film itself. From here on, his pictures would succeed or fail based primarily on their quality (or lack thereof) rather than Castle's ingenious promotional ballyhoo.

Three Faces of Fear see *Black Sabbath*

The Thrill Killers (1965; Hollywood Star Pictures; b&w) Alternate Title: *The Maniacs Are Loose*. Director: Ray Dennis Steckler; Producer:

George J. Morgan; Screenplay: Ray Dennis Steckler and Gene Pollock (additional dialogue: Ron Haydock); Cinematographer: Joseph V. Mascelli. Cast: Cash Flagg (Ray Dennis Steckler), Liz Renay, Brick Bardo, Carolyn Brandt, Gary Kent, Titus Moede, Atlas King, Herb Robins, Keith O'Brien.

The world's first horror movie ever made in hallucinogenic hypnovision.— radio spot

While the above hypno-hyperbole may be considered dubious at best, *The Thrill Killers* is definitely the first (and last) horror movie ever made by no-budget schlockmeister Ray Dennis Steckler that's any good at all. Coming from the man whose biggest claim to cinematic fame is the execrable *The Incredibly Strange Creatures Who Stopped Living and Became Mixed-Up Zombies* (1964) and the puerile *Rat Pfink a Boo Boo* (1965), *The Thrill Killers* stands as a remarkably competent achievement. Granted, the film suffers from Steckler's usual foibles and inadequacies, including uneven acting, occasional lapses in pacing, and a path-of-least-resistance attitude towards shooting action scenes. But it also offers up some genuine suspense and rather brutal shocks for the time.

Surprisingly, there are plenty of both (thrills and killers) in this moderately suspenseful 1965 low-budget offering that is far more competent than one expects from shoestring auteur Ray Dennis (*Incredibly Strange Creatures*) Steckler.

The storyline (or lines, actually, as two different tales converge at the end) centers on "psychopathic killer" Mort "Mad Dog" Click (Steckler himself, using his Cash Flagg alias), who shoots and kills a motorist for his car, then knifes to death a dance hostess because "People are no good; I hate people!" Cut to Joe Saxon (Brick Bardo), a would-be actor whose wife (former gangster's moll Liz Renay, fresh out of prison) has had enough of his stardom chasing. They end up at a small diner in Topanga Canyon, where a trio of escaped mental patients, after having murdered (with an axe) a young couple (including Steckler's real-life girlfriend, Carolyn Brandt), show up and terrorize the patrons. Violent confrontations and desperate chases ensue, as Click, the brother of one of the escapees(!), arrives on the scene.

With its *cinema verite* camerawork (i.e. Steckler couldn't afford a dolly so did his own hand-held shots), slightly seedy/down-on-its-heels ambiance, and some truly shocking violence (including two decapitations— though it's painfully obvious that the *same* mask-covered Styrofoam head was used for both victims), *The Trill Killers* is reminiscent of the intense, hard-hitting low-budgeter *The Sadist*. Given *Killers*' unconvincing acting, however (Brick Bardo, a still photographer who desperately wanted to be an actor, truly lives up to his name), and the occasional slow spots (including an overlong, cut-rate Hollywood party sequence), it stands as more of an anemic cousin than a full blood brother.

Even so, Steckler manages to invest the proceedings with enough suspense, helped along by the fact that the viewer has no idea who'll live and who'll die, to grab and hold viewers' interest. Steckler introduces characters (such as the newlywed couple or a friendly salesman) who may or may not be the main protagonists, then lets his maniacs viciously slaughter them. This anyone-can-die-at-any-time sensibility makes for an unsettling — and memorable — ride. "I just wanted to make a horror film, a shock film," the filmmaker recounted in an interview featured on the film's DVD release, and he did just that. He also added a few bizarre touches, such as having his brutal antagonist Click stumble across a cowboy in the hills, callously shoot him down in cold blood, and jump on the man's horse to flee from a pursuing motorcycle cop! "I got carried away at the end with the horse chase," laughed Steckler. While an unlikely scenario, it certainly makes for a novel final chase sequence. (Incidentally, according to Steckler, the horse came from the nearby Spahn Ranch, home of the Manson Family.)

Though *The Thrill Killers* won't be topping anyone's Best of the '60s list, it remains a competent and even engrossing surprise from one of the decade's most notorious cinematic bottom-feeders.

With quotes from: *The Thrill Killers* DVD.

The Titans see *My Son, the Hero*

The Tomb of Ligeia

(1964; Anglo Amalgamated/American International; U.K.) Director/Producer: Roger Corman; Screenplay: Robert Towne; Cinematographer: Arthur Grant. Cast: Vincent Price, Elizabeth Shepherd, John Westbrook, Derek Francis, Oliver Johnston, Richard Vernon.

CAT or WOMAN or a Thing Too Evil to Mention?— tagline

The nearly flawless *Masque of the Red Death* (1964) would have made the perfect endpoint for producer-director Roger Corman's series of Edgar Allan Poe adaptations. But American International wanted still more Poe, and even though, after seven films in five years, he was tiring of the series, Corman relented. The final results were mixed.

Lady Rowena (Elizabeth Shepherd) takes a shine to Verden Fell (Vincent Price), despite his dismissive attitude toward her and morbid fixation on his dead wife, Ligeia (also Shepherd). The more Verden rejects her, the more she wants him. Persistence pays, and eventually Rowena and Verden wed. When they return from their honeymoon, however, Verden begins acting strangely — and so does a black cat, which may or may not be the reincarnation of Ligeia. Rowena soon begins to fear that either her husband or the cat, or possibly both, are trying to kill her.

Like *Masque*, *Ligeia* was shot in England to take advantage of a British government subsidy. Longtime Corman production designer Daniel Haller (not credited here) found a stunning location — the crumbling, white stone ruin of an ancient monastery — around which much of *Ligeia* is set. Since so much of the picture was shot there, *Ligeia* has a drastically different, more naturalistic look than any other film in the series, with more exterior and daylight footage here than in all the other films combined. The studio interiors also have a more realistic look, courtesy of cinematographer Arthur Grant, a Hammer Films veteran. As with *Masque*, *Ligeia*'s craftsmanship is impeccable — its lighting and camerawork are top drawer.

Unfortunately, the picture's script isn't nearly as impressive, a surprising weakness given the writers involved. The problems begin with Poe himself. Although chillingly written, "Ligeia" remains one of the author's slightest narratives in terms of plot and character. Gifted screenwriter Robert Towne, who later penned *Chinatown* (1974), attempts to flesh this reedy narrative out to feature length, but winds up with a scenario that's simultaneously too thin and overly complicated, with a ponderously slow-moving first two acts and a convoluted finale. Although confusing, the finale nevertheless includes moments of genuine frisson, including a hair-raising sequence in which Rowena, believed dead, seems to have risen again — as Ligeia.

Vincent Price clutches at Elizabeth Shepherd in a dramatic moment from *The Tomb of Ligeia* (1964), Roger Corman's final foray into Poe territory.

Aside from its gorgeous location photography, *Ligeia*'s greatest assets are the outstanding work from the picture's leads. As Verden Fell, Price contributes one of his most restrained and naturalistic performances. His nervous, tightly coiled delivery suggests a man buffeted by an internal maelstrom of emotions, which eventually breaks free during the story's climax. Shepherd makes the most of her colorful, rangy role as the headstrong Lady Rowena, who goes from mischievous and seductive to disillusioned and terrified. The actress earns bonus points for her brief, unnerving appearance as Ligeia. The rest of the cast has little screen time and proves forgettable, with the exception of Derek Francis, whose droll portrayal of Rowena's shallow, fox hunting-obsessed father provides some minor comic relief.

Initially, Corman wanted to cast Richard Chamberlain as Verden ("Vincent was really too old for the part," the director explains), but AIP bosses Jim Nicholson and Sam Arkoff insisted on Price, who had headlined all of Corman's most successful Poe features. Despite Price's fine work, however, *The Tomb of Ligeia* was a box office disappointment. "All of the Poe films made money, but *Ligeia* made the least amount," Corman said. "I think it was because the series was just running out of steam and also because it [the story] was overly complicated." Lackluster profits convinced Corman that it was finally time to pull the plug, and so his Poe cycle concluded. Nevertheless, having turned Poe into a marquee attraction, AIP continued to release films branded with the author's name, even when some of them had little or no relationship with his work. The studio purchased Michael Reeves' *Witchfinder General* (1968), retitled it and had Price read a few lines from a Poe poem so that it could be promoted as "Edgar Allan Poe's *The Conqueror Worm.*" AIP also commissioned two Poe adaptations from director Gordon Hessler, *The Oblong Box* (1969) and *Murders in the Rue Morgue* (1971).

While *The Tomb of Ligeia* isn't one of the best of Corman's series, it's better than most of AIP's later, post–Corman Poe releases. A smattering of spine-tingling moments and a pair of outstanding performances make *Ligeia* worth a look — even if it's not the cat's meow.

With quotes from: "California Gothic: The Corman/Haller Collaboration," by Lawrence French, from *Video Watchdog* No. 138.

Tomb of the Living Dead see *Mad Doctor of Blood Island*

Tomb of Torture (1964; Virginia Cinematografica/Trans-Lux; Italy; b&w) Original Language Title: *Metempsycho*; Director: Anthony Kristye (Antonio Boccaci); Producer: Frank Campitelli; Screenplay: Anthony Kristye (Boccaci) and Johnny Seemonell (Giorgio Simonelli), story by Boccaci; Cinematographer: William Grace (Boccaci). Cast: Annie Alberti, Adriano Micantoni, Marco Mariani, Flora Carosello, William Gray, Bernard Blay.

What is the Secret of the Monster of the Castle?— ad line

U.S. half-sheet for the Italian import *Tomb of Torture* (1964).

The "Secret" answer to the above question is that this obscure, dull-as-dirt Italian import isn't worth the celluloid it's printed on.

Anna (Annie Alberti) has some mysterious link with a murdered countess (she dreams of the woman's death). Anna returns to the countess' castle and runs afoul of a giggling madman with a hideously disfigured face who likes to torture and kill young girls. It all involves a plot concocted by a greedy villain (who controls the madman and hides his/her own identity under a suit of armor!) to find the countess' hidden jewels. The countess' ghost puts in an appearance at a propitious moment to facilitate the villain's demise.

Unleashed in America on a double bill with the far superior *Cave of the Living Dead*, *Tomb* begins with a sequence in which two girls are stalked, then tortured, in a secret chamber under the castle by a misshapen beast of a man (one of his eyes rests down near his mouth!) who laughs maniacally. After this lurid opening, the film settles down into a painful exercise in tedium.

The majority of the running time consists of long stretches of people wandering about the castle and grounds, with the camera pointlessly panning across a room or moving around the torture chamber to no great purpose. Scenes of the walking suit of armor (worn by the villain) become almost comical; and the identity of said villain is as easy to spot as the tin suit s/he wears.

Romance enters the monotonous picture via a long comic interlude between a glib reporter (Marco Mariani) sent to investigate and the caught-skinny-dipping heroine. Their "love" (including talk of marriage) blossoms so abruptly that one suspects some scenes were (thankfully) excised for the export version. Though this abruptness makes the characters' actions/motivations seem ridiculous, the film would simply collapse under the weight of its own inertia had there been any more of these tiresome interludes. As it is, this *Tomb* remains nigh on *Torture* to sit through.

Tombs of Horror (1964) see *Castle of Blood*

The Tombs of Horror (1965/67) see *Terror Creatures from the Grave*

Tormented (1960; Allied Artists; b&w) Director: Bert I. Gordon; Producers: Bert I. Gordon, Joe Steinberg; Screenplay: George Worthington Yates; Cinematographer: Ernest Laszlo. Cast: Richard Carlson, Juli Reding, Susan Gordon, Lugene Sanders, Joe Turkel.

> Her lips ... cold as a tomb! Her caress ... a naked chill! ... but she is the sexiest phantom that ever haunted a man to death!—poster blurb

Tom Stuart (Richard Carlson) is *Tormented* by the ghost of his spurned lover in one of the few Bert I. Gordon movies that lacks a giant *anything* (American lobby card).

Producer/director Bert I. Gordon (Mr. B.I.G. himself) took time off from filling the screen with huge humans (*The Amazing Colossal Man*, *The Cyclops*, *War of the Colossal Beast*), enormous arachnids (*Earth vs. the Spider*), and gigantic grasshoppers (*Beginning of the End*) to make this small-scale but effective ghost story. No big bugs or mammoth anthropoids here, just Richard Carlson and one (normal-sized) vengeful ghost.

From the opening *noirish* narration, in which, over moody shots of the island setting and its rocky beaches at twilight, Richard Carlson intones, "I once loved this island ... but when the night wind rises and the fingers of fog steal in, they say you can hear voices—they say it's the dead growing restless and calling to the living," you know that this is not going to be the typical Bert I. Grotesque. Carlson plays jazz pianist Tom Stuart, who's about to marry wealthy young socialite Meg (Lugene Sanders). Tom's former mistress, Vi (Juli Reding), comes to his beachfront cottage and threatens to expose their less-than-acceptable affair if he doesn't come back to her. Fate intervenes and Vi falls to her death from atop a lighthouse. Tom *could* have saved her, however, and Vi's vengeful spirit periodically pops up to prey on his guilty conscience, leading to tragedy.

The character of Tom Stuart is quite likable, and for the most part you're on his side as he's forced to contend with the likes of ghostly footprints, disembodied hands, a talking head and bodies that turn to seaweed in his grasp. The ever-dependable Richard Carlson does a fine job playing an essentially good man who is pushed to the limit—and cracks. Carlson's genial manner quickly gives way to tortured preoccupation as his portrayal fully lives up to the picture's title. Throughout the movie the viewer sympathizes with Carlson and so becomes more involved with this story than with the typical Bert I. Gordon slice of cheese. And though the story here is an old one, it still carries impact—*and* a message: You can't escape your own conscience (even if it needs a little prodding from beyond the grave).

The story's setting (a small island community) adds to the ominous tone of the film. The lonely derelict lighthouse, the windy boardwalk and the crashing waves, all effectively photographed by Ernest Laszlo in melancholy hues of gray, create a brooding atmosphere in which to tell the tale.

Gordon himself does much to make *Tormented* a potent little thriller. He employs some subtly creepy touches (cold shadow, sudden gust of wind, etc.) to indicate the presence of the sinister specter. Gordon also utilizes off-kilter camera angles for his actor/reaction shots that enhance the shuddery feel of some scenes.

Of course, Bert being Bert, he couldn't stay subtle long, and soon superimpositions are running rampant across the screen. Gordon flirts with the ludicrous when he (for some inexplicable reason) has Vi's superimposed disembodied head taunting Tom from atop an end table. Though Carlson's sincerity nearly saves the rather laughable scene, it's completely spoiled when he picks up what is obviously a cheap mannequin head topped by a blonde wig. As usual in a B.I.G. production like this, Gordon and his wife Flora did the "Special Visual Effects" themselves. Since this is a ghost film, however, Gordon's semi-transparent process work looks just fine for the ethereal phantom (unlike for his other movies, which feature more corporeal menaces; in fact, in Gordon's *The Amazing Colossal Man* the titular titan often looks more like *The Amazing* Transparent *Man*).

Sadly, Bert soon returned to his first love (gigantism) with towering turkeys like *Village of the Giants* (1965), *Food of the Gods* (1976) and *Empire of the Ants* (1977). Though no classic, *Tormented* remains Gordon's most intelligent film; and, while not his "biggest," it is definitely his best.

The Torture Chamber of Dr. Sadism see *The Blood Demon*

Torture Garden (1967; Amicus/Columbia; U.K.) Director: Freddie Francis; Producers: Max J. Rosenberg, Milton Subotsky; Screenplay: Robert Bloch. Cinematographer: Norman Warwick. Cast: Jack Palance, Burgess Meredith, Beverly Adams, Peter Cushing, Maurice Denham, Barbara Ewing.

Jack Palance (left) and Peter Cushing are two avid Poe collectors vying for the ultimate prize in "The Man Who Collected Poe" segment of *Torture Garden* (1967).

> FREE! A package of "Fright-Seeds" for your own "TORTURE GARDEN"!
> —promotional giveaway

The British film company Amicus, who revived the anthology film format in 1965 with their highly successful *Dr. Terror's House of Horrors*, left off a string of desultory (and unprofitable) sci-fi entries (*Daleks Invasion Earth 2150 A.D.* [1966], *They Came from Beyond Space* and *The Terrornauts* [both 1967]) to return to their roots with this portmanteau production.

Amicus hired Robert (*Psycho*) Bloch to adapt four of his previously published short stories into a single screenplay: "Enoch" (which tells of a demonized cat that likes to eat human heads), "Terror over Hollywood" (about an actress who learns that the stars she idolizes are really androids), "Mr. Steinway" (which features a jealous grand piano that comes to life) and "The Man Who Collected Poe" (which stars Jack Palance and Peter Cushing as "the world's greatest collector of Poe memorabilia," whose collection houses the ultimate Poe item — the resurrected author himself). The stories are related by a carnival showman named Dr. Diablo (Burgess Meredith), who shows his patrons their hidden desires and possible futures.

Bloch was less than pleased with the result. "[Amicus] only did about 60 or 70 percent of what I had written," the author complained to John Stanley. "There is a general tendency ... to confuse visual shock with psychological buildup..."

Well, there really isn't much of either in *Torture Garden*, which proved to be one of the poorest of Amicus' many anthologies (the best of the lot being the subsequent *Tales from the Crypt* [1972]).

"We have to think of the substantial American market for our films," commented producer Milton Subotsky to interviewer Gwynne Comber, "and so we always try to include at least two actors who are well-known in America." Said stars were Jack Palance and Burgess Meredith. Unfortunately, neither brought much to the table, performance-wise, given Palance's breathless overacting in the "Poe" segment and Meredith simply doing his patented Penguin shtick (from the then-popular *Batman* TV series) while sporting a Satanic goatee. In truth, these players were forced upon Amicus by Columbia (who co-financed the feature); Subotsky initially wanted Christopher Lee in the Palance role.

As with many of Oscar-winning-cinematographer-turned-low-rent-director Freddie Francis' films, *Torture Garden* features some impressive photography (e.g. subjective shots, unusual angles, foreground focus) but a frequently lagging pace. To be fair, Bloch's script is against him from the start, with the protagonists of the first three tales so nasty and conniving that it's difficult to care what happens. Though Francis does what he can via distorting camera angles and tight reaction shots, the "Mr. Steinway" sequence in which a grand piano chases Barbara Ewing around a room is nearly laugh-out-loud in its ludicrousness. The film only really comes alive in the final segment, "The Man Who Collected Poe," an intriguing gem laden with atmosphere and featuring a wonderfully naturalistic performance by Peter Cushing (who single handedly slices through Palance's ham).

Tower of London (1962; United Artists; b&w)

Director: Roger Corman; Producer: Gene Corman; Screenplay: Leo V. Gordon, Amos Powell, James B. Grodon. Cinematographer: Arch R. Dalzell. Cast: Vincent Price, Michael Pate, Joan Freeman, Robert Brown, Bruce Gordon, Joan Camden, Richard Hale, Sandra Knight, Charles Macaulay.

DON'T COME ALONE: YOU'LL NEED SOMEONE TO HANG ONTO WHEN YOU COME FACE TO FACE WITH THE BLOOD-CHILLING TERROR IN THE TOWER!—poster blurb

Things in Hollywood had definitely changed in the near-quarter century since the original 1939 version of *Tower of London*— including big-screen terror. By the late 1950s and early '60s, the classic Teutonic-style horror spearheaded by Universal had largely given way to invading aliens and mutant bugs. Golden Horror icon Bela Lugosi was dead, while the two aging horror stars of the original *Tower of London*, Boris Karloff and Basil

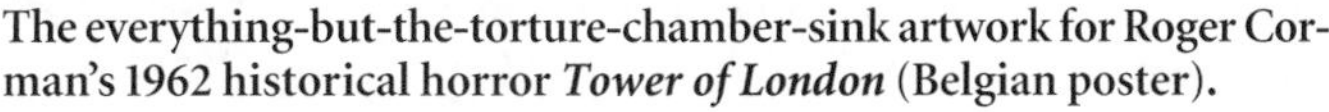

The everything-but-the-torture-chamber-sink artwork for Roger Corman's 1962 historical horror *Tower of London* (Belgian poster).

Rathbone, found themselves appearing in puerile productions like *The Black Sleep* (1956), *Frankenstein 1970* (1958) and *The Magic Sword* (1962)—when they could get movie work at all.

One *Tower of London* alumnus, however, found himself a hot horror property since his watershed year of 1958—which saw Vincent Price starring in both *The Fly* and *House on Haunted Hill.* In rapid succession, Price confirmed his "Master of Menace" title with appearances in films like *Return of the Fly* (1959) and *The Tingler* (1959), and the Edgar Allan Poe entries *House of Usher* (1960), *The Pit and the Pendulum* (1961) and *Tales of Terror* (1962). Indicative of his rise to terror prominence was Price's advancement from supporting player (Clarence) in the 1939 version to lead villain (Richard) when Roger Corman took his low-budget stab at historical horror by remaking Universal's *Tower of London.*

First announced in February 1962 as *A Dream of Kings*, the film began shooting in mid–March. "The Tower of London, a monument to the corruption of the soul..." begins the narrator (omnipresent 1950s and '60s voice-over artist Paul Frees) at the film's opening. What follows is a 15th-century tale of murder and ghosts and conscience, in which Richard III (Vincent Price) kills his brother, his political rivals, his nephews and (accidentally) even his loving wife. The ghosts of his victims appear to Richard (or at least are conjured up out of his own guilt-riddled mind) to bedevil his existence and ultimately lead him to his death at the battle of Bosworth Field.

As might be expected, Corman's version comes nowhere close to the 1939 film in production quality; but then the earlier entry was a relatively high-priced effort ($580,000) from a major studio, whereas Corman's project was a low-budget (less than $200,000—twenty-five years later) independent effort. (Corman even borrowed some of the original's battle footage to flesh out his minimalist fight scenes.) The tones of the two films are miles apart as well, the earlier variation being an historical melodrama with horrific trappings while the latter focused on the themes of madness, guilt and death—more in the vein of Edgar Allan Poe than medieval history (undoubtedly intentional, considering the personnel involved).

Corman's proved the more intimate of the two, with the weight of the film resting on the humped shoulders of Vincent Price. The role of Richard is a fascinating one, for he is a man who knows what is right and what is wrong but who chooses the path of evil anyway. "Is it what men do that darkens the sky, or do the skies blacken the souls of men?" asks this reflective villain. This makes Richard a much more intriguing figure, one who is not totally evil but who embraces it nonetheless and therefore orchestrates his own destruction (it's almost a trial run for Price's portrayal in the later *Masque of the Red Death*). Richard has a conscience, and out of it he creates his own guilt-ridden hell by conjuring up the ghosts of his victims to torment him. As a morality play, the message could not be clearer—no one, no matter how corrupt, can truly escape their own conscience. And in the end, despite the somber, often brutal trappings, the film delivers an upbeat message—that people, despite their savagery and cruelty, are basically good, and this goodness will triumph in the end, whether it be by love ... or by self-punishment meted out by one's own mind.

Praiseworthy missives aside, this *Tower* is built on shaky ground. The script is structured so that the film will rise or fall with the performance of Price (who is the focus of nearly every scene). Though at times Price sublimely points the production heavenwards, it never quite takes wing—due to that actor's uneven playing. Price (who began his career on the stage) sometimes acts as if he were back treading the boards, playing to the balcony's back row. He indulges in overblown arm-waving, lip trembling and histrionics that lessen the impact that a more subtle performance could have generated. The blame in part should rest with Corman, never noted as an actor's director, who failed to properly rein in the actor. ("He was very creative," commented Price of his director, "but more concerned with the story and effects than the actors.") Price provides a larger-than-life portrayal, sprinkling his wild-eyed, open-mouthed, full-blooded delivery with moments of subtlety and emotion. It's an enjoyable performance without doubt, but an uneven one.

1962's *Tower of London* is still an entertaining movie, filled with intrigue and shock and bizarre situations. More importantly, something worthwhile lurks beneath the garish surface. "He escaped the headsman's block, but he could not escape his own conscience." At least it's something to think about.

With quotes from: "Vincent Price: Looking Back on Forty Years as Horror's Crown Prince," by Steve Biodrowski, David Del Valle and Lawrence French, *Cinefantastique*, January 1989.

Track of the Vampire see *Blood Bath*

The before and after effects of "Dr. Heidegger's Experiment" in *Twice Told Tales* (1963). Mari Blanchard plays the bride-to-bones.

Twice Told Tales (1963; United Artists) Director: Sidney Salkow; Producer/Screenplay: Robert E. Kent (based on stories by Nathaniel Hawthorne); Cinematographer: Ellis W. Carter. Cast: Vincent Price, Sebastian Cabot, Brett Halsey, Beverly Garland, Richard Denning, Mari Blanchard, Abraham Sofaer, Jacqueline DeWit, Joyce Taylor.

NO DEMONOPHOBIACS ADMITTED!—poster

There's no getting around it; *Twice Told Tales* is the stodgy cousin of the AIP Roger Corman/Vincent Price/Edgar Allan Poe series. It's not a question of inferior source material (Nathaniel Hawthorne's stories carry as much resonance as the Poe tales), but of lackluster presentation. Corman's Poe entries are simply far more *vibrant.*

Twice Told Tales, a three-episode anthology based on two short stories and one novel written by Hawthorne, begins when skeletal hands open an old tome to reveal the title of the first segment, "Dr. Heidegger's Experiment." This first (and best) story has elderly friends Dr. Heideggar (Sebastian Cabot) and bon vivante Alex (Vincent Price) reflecting on their lives one dark and stormy night. When lightning strikes the crypt of Heideggar's 38-years-dead wife (she died on their wedding night), they investigate the damage, only to discover a mysterious liquid seeping from the rocks that has perfectly preserved Sylvia's corpse. Discovering the liquid's rejuvenating properties, Heideggar decides to use it to revive his lost love, leading to tragedy.

Price and Cabot's enthusiasm and charm catches the viewer up in the story, as they share their affection, melancholy, good humor, and eventual joy at regaining their youth. The Edwardian set dressing and bright, artificial color scheme give the episode an almost fairy-tale ambiance, an atmosphere that turns to nightmare by story's end.

Next comes "Rappaccini's Daughter," in which Price plays a bitter, possessive father who injects his daughter with sap from a poisonous plant that makes her touch lethal to all living things. Overlong and underplayed (particularly by lightweight romantic love interest/hero Brett Halsey), and completely devoid of shocks or excitement, the episode offers little but repetitive melodrama.

The film concludes with a cheesy adaptation of "The House of the Seven Gables," which stars Price in a tale of ghostly love and revenge as a man searching for a hidden fortune in his cursed ancestral home. Presenting a plethora of hoary old ghost gags (such as floating objects, bleeding paintings, doors opening by themselves, and even a reaching skeletal hand), and saddled with cheap, cramped sets (and an even less convincing model of the seven-gabled mansion itself), this ramshackle "House" is built on tatty clichés and poor theatrics rather than a solid foundation of unease and terror. And residing within is a family of missed opportunities. (Price co-starred in a much better feature-length adaptation of the same story back in the 1940s for Universal.)

Like the stereotypical country cousin, *Twice Told Tales* makes a cheap, simple, cheerful and fun first impression, but (at an overlong 119 minutes stretched over only three episodes) soon overstays its welcome and becomes tiresome. Shot as *The Corpse Makers*, the film didn't become *Twice Told Tales* until after completion. Considering the effect of its final two-thirds, a better moniker might have been *Twice* Bored *Tales.*

Australian daybill for the British Hammer horror *House of Fright* (1960/61; aka *The Two Faces of Dr. Jekyll*).

The Two Faces of Dr. Jekyll see *House of Fright*

Two on a Guillotine (1965; Warner Bros.; b&w) Director/Producer: William Conrad; Screenplay: Henry Slesar and John Kneubuhl (Story: Henry Slesar); Cinematography: Sam Leavitt. Cast: Connie Stevens, Dean Jones, Caesar Romero, Parkey Baer, Virginia Gregg, Connie Gilchrist.

> Attention: Guillotine-agers! ... If you're chopping for entertainment, here's the super-shocker of them all.—tagline

When famous magician the Great Dusquesne (Caesar Romero) dies, he leaves his entire fortune to his estranged daughter Cassie (Connie Stevens), on the condition that she remain in the house—which has been tricked out with all sorts of fright gags—for seven consecutive nights. The press gets interested because, prior to his death, Dusquesne vowed to return from the grave. To pry the story from the media-averse Cassie, reporter Val Henderson (Dean Jones) disguises his identity and strikes up a romance. He helps the skittish Cassie cope with the house's many surprises (creepy tape recordings, skeletons hung on wires, cardboard stand-ups popping out of closets) and to come to terms with the death of her father (who she believes never loved her). When Cassie's former nursemaid (Virginia Gregg) swears she's seen Dusquesne walking about, Cassie begins to wonder if her father truly has returned from the dead.

This tired and timid spooky-old-house relic doesn't generate the chills of a typical *Scooby Doo* episode, which its plot closely resembles. The hackneyed, contrived scenario not only remains utterly predictable, it doesn't even *attempt* to be scary until its final 10 minutes. *Two on a Guilllotine* (1965) makes only the most perfunctory references to the supernatural. Instead, it focuses on the budding romance between Cassie and Val (what will happen when she discovers his true identity?) to such a degree that it seems like a hastily rewritten script from a rejected Rock Hudson-Doris Day picture. Cassie is the kind of girl who says, "Oh, golly!" and Val's the kind of guy who makes wisecracks like, "I've seen better lighting in the Tunnel of Love." Jones brings the same easygoing charm to his role that made him such a likeable lead in Disney movies like *Blackbeard's Ghost* and *The Love Bug* (both 1968). Stevens is in over her head during the film's weepy dramatic moments but handles the romantic comedy material adequately. Romero's weirdly menacing performance — imagine a much more intense version of his Joker from the *Batman* television series—arrives too late to make much difference. By the time the young lovers confront the "ghost" of the late Great Dusquesne and *Two on a Guillotine* finally gets around to the would-be scary part, most viewers will have long since lost interest (and perhaps consciousness).

Two Thousand Maniacs! (1964; Friedman-Lewis) Director/Cinematography/Screenplay: Herschell Gordon Lewis; Producer: David F. Friedman. Cast: William Kerwin (as Thomas Wood), Connie Mason, Jeffrey Allen, Ben Moore, Gary Bakeman.

Madness incarnate! Ghastly beyond belief!—tagline

As they watched the proceeds pour in from their ultra low budget, ultra high gore *Blood Feast* (1963), exploitation filmmaker Herschell Gordon Lewis and his partner, producer David Friedman, realized they were on to something.

"When we saw what the result of *Blood Feast* was," said Lewis. "not just at the box office but on the industry altogether, David Friedman and I looked at each other and asked, 'Holy mackerel! What if we made a decent one?' I took *Two Thousand Maniacs!* very seriously. That was my child."

It shows. *Two Thousand Maniacs!* stands as Lewis' most ambitious and entertaining picture. Like *Blood Feast*, it remains a semi-professional production, riddled with too many fundamental flaws and clumsy mistakes to be called "good" by any reasonable standard. But Lewis' tongue-in-cheek approach softens the impact of some of those problems. The story's basic premise is intriguing, and its gruesome set pieces display a sort of demented creativity sure to satisfy gore fans.

In an unnamed Southern state, homicidal rednecks dupe Yankee tourists into taking a forgotten back road to the secluded village of Pleasant Valley (population: 2000). There, the townsfolk promise to fete the Northerners as "guests of honor" at their town's centennial celebration. But one by one the visitors are separated from one another, murdered and mutilated to reap blood vengeance for atrocities committed in Pleasant Valley by union troops during the Civil War. A clever epilogue, like something out of the musical *Brigadoon* (1947), shifts the tale into the realm of supernatural fantasy.

Two Thousand Maniacs!, like *Blood Feast*, suffers from banal dialogue, amateurish acting and a host of technical problems. The film's lighting and sound are at best passable and at worst atrocious (during one scene an actress' voice is so poorly dubbed, it sounds as if she's speaking from an echo chamber). Once again, Lewis' camera seldom moves, and his compositions remain perfunctory. William Kerwin and Connie Mason, who handled the lead roles in *Blood Feast*, seem as wooden as ever here. Jeffrey Allen offers the picture's only worthwhile performance with his broadly comedic portrayal of the unctuous Mayor Buckman.

Nevertheless, Lewis earns points for the sheer scale of this production, shot entirely on location (in St. Cloud, Florida, the future home of Disney World) and utilizing dozens of extras and bit players. He also brings a welcome dose of goofy humor to the yarn, both through his handling of the cast (in addition to Allen's smarmy antics,

Hacked-off Confederate ghosts do some hacking off of their own in Herschell Gordon Lewis' tongue-in-cheek gorefest *Two Thousand Maniacs!* (1964).

most of the bit players speak with an exaggerated, obviously fake southern drawl) and his unorthodox score, a selection of bluegrass and corn-pone folk music played by a trio of roving pickers billed as Chuck Scott and the Pleasant Valley Boys. The director even composed the movie's highly (and perhaps even intentionally) amusing theme song, a faux Civil War ballad full of references to Confederate leaders such as Robert E. Lee.

Perhaps more importantly for the film's core audience, the gore scenes in *Two Thousand Maniacs!* are staged with far more originality and slightly greater realism than those in *Blood Feast*. The sadistic imagination at work in these sequences is either impressive or disturbing, depending on your point of view. Pleasant Valley townsfolk chop off a woman's arm and then barbecue her; tie a man's arms and legs to four horses and set them bolting away in different directions; play a game that results in a giant boulder falling on another victim; and send a fourth victim rolling down a hill in a barrel full of spikes. As in *Blood Feast*, most of the actual violence is suggested rather than shown. Lewis instead shows us the bloody aftermath — bodies rent asunder, riddled with holes or smashed flat. *Two Thousand Maniacs!* actually contains less gore (at least as a per minute ratio of screen time) than its predecessor, yet it seems harsher because its sequences make far more impact.

The financial returns on this film again proved spectacular, prompting Lewis and Friedman to continue with *Color Me Blood Red* (1964). While all of Lewis' seminal splatter films are beloved by gorehounds, *Two Thousand Maniacs!* remains the one Lewis film whose appeal may extend beyond that crowd to curiosity seekers with open minds, strong stomachs and an offbeat sense of humor.

With quotes from: *A Taste of Blood*, Christopher Wayne Curry

The Undertaker and His Pals (1967; Howco) Director/Screenplay: T.L.P. Swicegood; Producer: Alex Gratton; Cinematographer: Andrew Janczak. Cast: Warrene Ott, Rad Fulton, Marty Friedman, Sally Frei, Rick Cooper, Robert Lowry, Ray Dannis.

A MACABRE STORY OF TWO MOTORCYCLE-RIDING, KNIFE-WIELDING, SHIV-SHAVING, EYE-GOUGING, ARM-TWISTING, CHAIN-LASHING, SCALPEL-FLASHING, ACID-THROWING, GUN-SHOOTING, BONE-BREAKING, PATHOLOGICAL NUTS AND THEIR PAL THE *UNDERTAKER*...— tagline

Reminiscent of an H. G. Lewis gore flick, but with goofy, tasteless, sick-and-twisted humor thrown into the mix, the low-budget *Undertaker and His Pals* follows the doings of, well, an undertaker (amusingly named "Mr. Mort") and his pals, two kooky and psychotic greasy-spoon café owners. The terrible trio don leather jackets, helmets and face masks, and venture out on their motorcycles to drum up business for the undertaker — and secure fixins for the diner. To whit: they invade the apartment of one Sally Lamb, where they stab her to death and cut off (and carry away!) her legs. The next day, while Mr. Mort buries what's left of the girl (and charges her grieving parents an, er, arm and a leg), the diner features a new special — "leg of lamb" (badda-bing!). The film wears its tongue-in-cheek heart on it sleeve from the get-go, as the camera periodically cuts from this first brutal and gruesome killing/mutilation to a tabletop picture of the victim's sailor boyfriend, with the photo having changed expression each time — from smiling blandness to open-mouthed shock to hand-on-forehead dismay! When a certain Miss Ann Poultry becomes their next victim (with the subsequent cafe special listed as— what else?— "breast of chicken"), the girl's boss/love interest puts himself on the case (though, amusingly, it's not anything *he* does, but a combination of backstabbing, clumsiness, and just plain bad luck that leads the Undertaker and His Pals to their deserved demise).

At barely an hour, this *Undertaker* has little time to outstay his welcome. Though offering the expected '60s gutter-cinema production values (cardboard and plywood sets; garish and immobile cinematography; broad, amateurish acting), it moves from goofy pratfalls and silly humor (the flustered undertaker accidentally stepping on a skateboard and taking off down the sidewalk) to brutal killings and crude gore (involving stabbings, acid and even a vicious chain-whipping) at a rapid pace.

Undertaker was reissued in the '70s alongside *The Corpse Grinders* and *The Embalmer*. The triple-feature-horror-show was accompanied by a nurse who offered blood-pressure checks and a "certificate of assurance" that released the theater from responsibility for death, coronaries or insanity inspired by the terrible terrors of the triple bill. Though the various death and mutilation sequences (including some real abdominal surgery footage) and stage-blood grue on offer might have inspired a few frowns, it's doubtful that any "death, coronaries or insanity" resulted from the wacky-and-tacky *The Undertaker and His Pals*—unless someone choked on their leg of lamb while watching.

The Valley of Gwangi (1969; Warner Bros./Seven Arts) Director: Jim O'Connolly; Producer: Charles H. Schneer; Screenplay: William E. Bast (Additional material: Julian More); Cinematographer: Erwin Hiller. Cast: James Franciscus, Gila Golan, Richard Carlson, Laurence Naismith, Freda Jackson.

COWBOYS BATTLE MONSTERS IN THE LOST WORLD OF FORBIDDEN VALLEY—tagline

In 1942, legendary animator Willis O'Brien wrote a treatment titled *Valley of the Mist*, about cowboys who discover a hidden land where dinosaurs still roam. The core concept—cowboys versus dinosaurs—was fresh and exciting, and O'Brien hoped *Gwangi* would become a second *King Kong*. But it didn't happen. O'Brien was never able to interest a major studio in the concept, which he eventually optioned to Mexican producers Edward and William Nassour. They made a tedious, low-budget version of the story (featuring a crude stop-motion T-Rex) under the title *The Beast of Hollow Mountain* (*La bestia de la montaña*) in 1956. O'Brien did not create any visual effects for that film, although he received a "from an idea by" screen credit. A dozen years later, former O'Brien protégé Ray Harryhausen took up the concept and finally did it justice—although, curiously, O'Brien didn't receive on-screen credit for the idea behind *The Valley of Gwangi*.

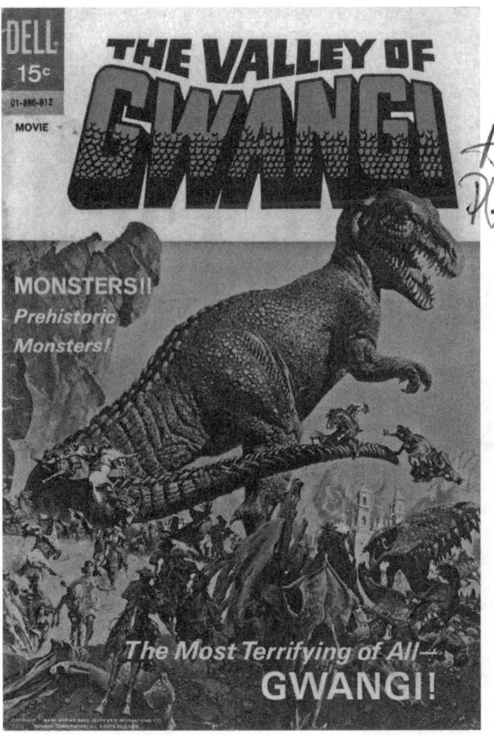

Comic book tie-in for the Ray Harryhausen cowboys-and-dinosaurs movie *The Valley of Gwangi* (1969).

Somewhere "south of the Rio Grande, at the turn of the century," rodeo talent agent Tuck Kirby (James Franciscus) discovers that his ex-girlfriend, stunt rider T.J. Breckenridge (Gila Golan), has come into possession of a fabulous attraction—a living specimen of an eohippus, the tiny three-toed "dawn horse." He shows the beast to incredulous paleontologist Professor Bromley (Laurence Naismith), who has been digging for dinosaur bones nearby. Bent on learning more about the creature, Bromley helps free the eohippus, in order to track it as it returns to its home. Tuck, T.J. and friends also leave in pursuit of the tiny horse and the lot of them find themselves in the Forbidden Valley, home of a dreaded evil spirit known as Gwangi (which turns out to be an allosaurus), as well as several other prehistoric species including a pterodactyl. Tuck and friends capture Gwangi and bring him back to civilization to put him on display. Catastrophe naturally ensues.

It's easy to understand why this project proved irresistible to Harryhausen, given his fervent devotion to O'Brien and *Gwangi*'s blatantly *King Kong*-like plot (*Kong* being Harryhausen's often-cited career inspiration). Clearly Harryhausen wanted *Gwangi* to become the movie O'Brien dreamed it would be, and devoted months of meticulous effort to create some of the most beautifully executed and imaginative sequences of his entire career. Chief among these is a breathtaking scene where Tuck and friends attempt to lasso Gwangi. Seamlessly integrating into a single frame live-action footage of cowboys on horseback throwing real ropes with stop-motion footage of the allosaur with wiry animated ropes around its neck, it's simply amazing that this episode was created in the pre–CGI era. The finale, as Gwangi rampages through a Mexican town and eventually becomes trapped in a burning cathedral, is also magnificently accomplished.

These sequences play out to Jerome Moross' exceptionally effective score. The surging and heroic title theme, reprised at key moments throughout the film, sounds like something from a John Ford cavalry epic. Instead of the cardboard cut-outs that too often populate Harryhausen pictures, William Bast's screenplay features a cast of characters sketched in refreshing detail, especially the complex and conflicted Tuck, played with charm and confidence by the underrated James Franciscus (who would move from the Forbidden Valley to the Forbidden Zone by starring in *Beneath the Planet of the Apes* in 1970). However, it takes time to establish characters in such depth and, as a result, *Gwangi*'s opening act proves sluggish. To hold audience interest until our heroes enter Forbidden Valley (about halfway through the picture), the story offers rodeo stunts, a bullfight, the charming eohippus and romantic intrigue between Tuck and T.J. The lattermost of these would work better if not for the flat, awkward performance of Golan, an Israeli fashion model who embarked on a brief and undistinguished acting career in the mid–1960s. After her role as T.J. in *Gwangi*, Golan retreated from the screen, returning only for a bit part in an Italian soccer comedy (*L'allenatore nel Pallone*) in 1984.

It certainly was not a second *Kong*, but *Gwangi* earned good returns at the box office and was reissued in 1971 on a double-bill with Hammer Films' *When Dinosaurs Ruled the Earth* (1970). And while it can't be counted among the top tier of Harryhausen pictures, *Gwangi* remains one of the most original and colorful entries in the animator's impressive filmography.

Valley of the Dragons (1961; Columbia; b&w)

Director/Screenwriter: Edward Bernds; Producer: Byron Roberts; Cinematographer: Brydon Baker. Cast: Cesare Danova, Sean McClory, Joan Staley, Danielle de Metz, Gregg Martell, Gil Perkins.

THEY GO A MILLION YEARS BACK IN TIME ... AND LAND A MILLION MILES OUT IN SPACE!—poster blurb

Based on Jules Verne's rather obscure novel *Off on a Comet* (though really little more than a variation on 1940's *One Million B.C.*), *Valley of the Dragons* begins in 1881 as two duelists (Cesare Danova and Sean McClory) prepare to defend their respective honors with pistols. But a hurricane-force wind and apparent earthquake interrupts their confrontation. When the winds subside, they find themselves in a strange, prehistoric world populated by dinosaurs (photographically enlarged lizards) and cave men. Soon they determine that "a heavenly body, a small planet or a comet perhaps, collided with the earth and bore us into space, carrying an envelope of the earth's atmosphere with us." Apparently, this happens every 100,000 years or so, hence the prehistoric flora and fauna on this planetoid "comet."

Among the cut-rate cinematic wonders encountered by the displaced duo are plastic-masked "Neanderthals"; a gargantuan mongoose vs. snake battle on a tabletop miniature set; a brief shot of an awkward flying (gliding) reptile that looks suspiciously like a *Rodan* outtake; a giant balloon-like spider prop recycled from director/screenwriter Edward Bernds' previous *World Without End* (1956); oversized armadillos (one character inexplicably labels them "ox-like animals"!); cheesy Morlock-like subhumanoids; the expected cavemen—along with the inevitable (blonde) cavegirl; and more lizard vs. baby alligator stock footage from *One Million B.C.* than you can shake a spear at.

Given this shot from *Valley of the Dragons* (1961), a more accurate title would have been *Valley of the Armadillos*.

"*Valley of the Dragons* was built around the *One Million B.C.* stock footage," admitted Bernds. "I used the Jules Verne premise of the comet scooping up the men and taking them into outer space — a pretty wild premise, but it worked all right for us. The story was then shaped around the stock stuff."

"Shaped around" seems a bit optimistic; "thrown around" seems a more accurate term for this everything-but-the-caveman-sink pastiche. While not the most coherent of story lines, at least the first portion of the picture moves from one stock footage anomaly to another in a rapid, Saturday-matinee fashion. Unfortunately, whatever fun can be squeezed from this cinematic cheese log is eclipsed by endless, dull getting-to-know-you cavemen sequences (complete with an excruciatingly drawn-out "playful swim" scene between Hector and his newfound cave love). The dead weight of these tedious time-fillers brings this comet crashing down to earth. Even the (stock footage, naturally) climactic siege by the giant lizards can't launch this comet into space again.

Bernds shot this extravaganza on a "ridiculously low budget" (Bernds' words) of $125,000. "The big lucky break we had was that we were able to use a half-million dollar mountainside set standing at Columbia that had been built for *The Devil at Four O'Clock* [1961]. That meant we didn't have to go a single day out on locations; we shot all of our exteriors on this magnificent half-million dollar set. It was a tremendous money-saver."

Then there's the utter ludicrousness of it all — which is only made worse by the protagonists trying to figure it out. One of them calls their new home "a world of the past, 100,000 years past," and labels a big lizard a "plateosaur" who "flourished on earth more than a thousand centuries ago." Scripter Bernds and his characters seemed to have dropped a few zeros, since it was closer to a *million* centuries ago when dinosaurs roamed the earth. And the film concludes with the two modern men somehow calculating that the comet will revisit earth in *seven* years! (What happened to the "every 100,000 years" theory; and what are they going to do then, anyway — just step across and go home?)

"The basis of *Valley of the Dragons* is utterly unscientific and —*ridiculous* is probably not too strong a word for that. Science really takes a beating in that picture!" laughed Bernds. "But it entertains people, and still makes money for Columbia." Well, while that last bit may be true (though it's doubtful *Valley* brings in much cash these days), the "entertains people" statement is about as accurate as this movie's scientific premise.

With quotes from: *Interviews with B Science Fiction and Horror Movie Makers*, by Tom Weaver.

The Vampire (1957/1968; Cinematografica A.B.S.A./Trans-International Films; Mexico; b&w) Original Language Title: *El Vampiro*. Director: Fernando Mendez, Paul Nagle (English language version); Producer: Abel Salazer, K. Gordon Murray (English version); Screenplay: Ramon Obon; Cinematographer: Rosalio Solano. Cast: Abel Salazar, Ariadna Welter, Carmen Montejo, Jose Luis Jimenez, Germán Robles.

FROM BEYOND THE GRAVE INTO THE AUDIENCE — THE UNDEAD AWAKEN AFTER 200 YEARS! — ad line

We primarily have two men to thank (or curse, depending upon one's perspective) for bringing us a bevy of 1960s Mexi-monsters from south of the border: actor-producer Abel Salazar, whose Cinematografica A.B.S.A. company basically *created* the Gothic-style Mexican horror movie in the late 1950s and early '60s, and theater owner-cum-producer K. Gordon Murray, who purchased the American rights to Salazar's movies (and numerous others), dubbed them into English, and exhibited them in a series of Saturday matinees before (and sometimes *after*) sending them off to television (via AIP-TV).

Salazar (who, sadly, died of Alzheimer's in 1995) started the Universal-patterned revival of Mexican horror in 1957 when he both produced and acted in the ground-breaking *The Vampire* (which Salazar described as "*Dracula* set on a Mexican hacienda") and in its 1958 sequel, *The Vampire's Coffin*. He continued the trend with *The Man and the Monster* (1958), *The Curse of the Crying Woman* (1962), *The Living Head* (1963) and the (in)famous *The Brainiac* (1961; in which Salazar abandoned his usual role of hero to play the title monster). His producer-only genre credits include *World of the Vampires* and *The Witch's Mirror* (both 1960). All eight of Salazar's horror films were released Stateside in the mid-to-late 1960s by K. Gordon Murray's Trans-International Films.

The Vampire opens as a large box of earth from Hungary arrives at the small Mexican town of Sierra Negra. Also arriving in Sierra Negra is the heroine, Martha (Ariadna Welter), there to visit her sick aunt, co-owner (with her brother and sister) of "the Sycamores" hacienda. Ten years previously, a mysterious Count Duval (Germán Robles) moved nearby, and now no one will come near the Sycamores. Duval is actually Count Lavud, a vampire, who intends to wrest the Sycamores from its rightful owners and resurrect his vampiric brother. Standing in his way is Martha and her newfound paramour, Henry (Abel Salazar), a young psychiatrist secretly summoned to the Sycamores to assess the mental condition of the ailing aunt.

"They really tried to capture the style, the mood of the old-fashioned horror movies," explained leading lady Ariadne Welter. "They kept talking about Bela Lugosi; he was the model for the part of the vampire."

In *The Vampire*, director Fernando Mendez, aided by cinematographer Rosalio Solano, captures the "old-fashioned horror movie mood" beautifully. Through its well-framed photography (a funeral procession filmed at a distance through an archway creates a forlorn tableau) and moody lighting (Lavud suddenly appears by stepping out of a misty shaft of moonlight), not to mention some of the most impressive cobwebs seen outside of a classic Universal, *The Vampire* simply drips Gothic ambiance. Evocative (and *frisson*-inducing) images abound, such as pinpoint lighting making the Vampire's staring eyes appear to glow in the blackness (an effect borrowed from — and improving upon — Universal's *Dracula*), or one low-angle shot in which the wind swirls the mist behind a statuesque, black-clad vampiress, a cruel smile on her lips and an unhealthy gleam in her wide eyes.

Enrique ("Henry" in the dubbed version), played by producer/star Abel Salazar, enters the atmospheric world of *The Vampire* (1957/68) in this Mexican lobby card.

All the players acquit themselves admirably, from the easy-mannered, likable Salazar as the skeptical hero, to Welter as the confused and vulnerable heroine who finds inner strength when needed, to Carmen Montejo as the vampirized aunt, full of dark intensity, to the crazed "good" aunt whose hollow-eyed anxiety reveals both terror and determination. Then there's Germán Robles as Count Lavud. His penetrating gaze, haughty manner, and fierce and swift attacks offer up the best of both worlds— the worlds of Universal's Bela Lugosi and Hammer's Christopher Lee. Ironically, *The Vampire* was made a year *before* Lee donned the cape for the first time in *Horror of Dracula*. (Robles claims that Lee told a mutual friend that Lee patterned *his* Count after Robles' portrayal! This seems unlikely, however, since Lee would have had little opportunity to see *The Vampire* prior to his work on *Horror of Dracula*, particularly since it wasn't even seen in its English-language version until six years later.) Though Robles doesn't quite measure up to the imposing presence of either, combining the look and intensity of Lugosi (even wearing a near-identical penguin suit) with the ferocity of Lee serves *The Vampire* well.

Ironically, Robles was not the first choice as the Vampire. Salazar originally hired well-known Mexican character actor Carolos Lopez Moctezuma to play Lavud, but soon decided "something wasn't right. The story was ready, we were ready to start, yet I was asking myself, what is it? Then I looked at American cinema again, and you know what is successful? The unknown actor! Lopez Moctezuma invariably had to be Lopez Moctezuma *before* he was 'the Vampire.' I talked to him and said, 'I'll pay off your contract because I made a mistake; I have to find an unknown actor.' Someone told me to go to a [certain] theater. I went [there, spotted Robles] and said, 'He is the Vampire!'"

By his own account, the Spanish-born Robles thoroughly enjoyed this, his first starring role. ("We had a tremendous amount of fun doing these films," agreed co-star Welter, referring to both *The Vampire* and its sequel, *The Vampire's Coffin*.) But the tight three-week shoot sometimes proved wearying. "There was a scene where I had to climb back into my coffin and close the lid over me," Robles told Parla. "So, I did the scene, but I wasn't aware of the fact that this was the last shot of the day. So, there I am, lying in this coffin, and I'm very tired. [Director] Fernando Mendez calls it a 'wrap,' and everyone left the set to go to dinner. At the restaurant, everyone asked Fernando, 'Where's German?' It suddenly dawned on him, and he ran back to the studio. When he opened the coffin, there I was, in a deep sleep!"

The former takes liberties with the latter in *The Vampire and the Ballerina* (1960/62).

Of course, this cinematic gothic castle has its share of cracks. The often banal-sounding dubbing on the American release version does the cast no favors (though Robles actually labeled the dubbing "splendid, because the voice is very similar to my own—very deep; it was a very good choice"), and some of the special effects prove either obvious and simple (the vampires abruptly appear and disappear in a crude stop-the-camera-I-wanna-get-off effect) or downright simple-minded (the ungainly and unconvincing flying rubber bats would be right at home in a Monogram movie from two decades earlier). But the engrossing story, adept playing, and wonderfully atmospheric ambiance set *The Vampire* astride the pinnacle of south-of-the-border horror cinema.

Released in Mexico in 1957, *El Vampiro* premiered theatrically in the U.S. on March 2, 1968, in Jacksonville, Florida, as a co-feature for *The Curse of the Doll People*. This came nearly four years *after The Vampire* first aired on television in 1964! (K. Gordon Murray—a pioneer in cinematic recycling...)

With quotes from: "The Vampire's Lady: An Interview with 'El Vampiro' Leading Lady Ariadne Welter," by Charles P. Mitchell and Paul Parla, *Filmfax* 67, June/July 1998; "El Vampiro Speaks! An Interview with Mexican Horror Star Germán Robles," by Bryan Senn, Richard Sheffield and Jim Clatterbaugh, *Monsters from the Vault* 24, February 2008; "El Barón del Terror: The Horror Films of Abel Salazar, by David Wilt, *Filmfax* 54, January/February 1996.

The Vampire and the Ballerina (1960/62; Consorzio Italiano Films/United Artists; Italy; b&w) Original Language Title: *L'Amante del Vampiro*. Director: Renato Polselli; Producer: Bruno Bolognesi; Screenplay: Renato Polselli, Guiseppi Pellegrini, Ernesto Gastaldi; Cinematographer: Angelo Baistrocchi. Cast: Helene Remy, Tina Gloriani, Walter Brandi, Isarco Ravaioli, John Turner, Ugo Cragnani, Maria Luisa Rolando.

BLOOD-LUSTING FIEND WHO PREYS ON GIRLS! VAMPIRE-QUEEN WHO FEEDS ON LIFEBLOOD OF MEN!—poster

Euro-hunk Walter Brandi starred in a trio of gothic-style Italian vampire flicks in the early 1960s. *The Vampire and the Ballerina* was the first—and the best. Of course, considering the other two were *Curse of the Blood-Ghouls* (1962/69) and *The Playgirls and the Vampire* (1963), that's not saying much.

The Vampire and the Ballerina's standard-issue story has a ballet troupe staying at a small village recently plagued by a rash of deaths. When several of the would-be ballerinas stumble across a mysterious castle in the woods, they run afoul of the vampires that live there. Though the generic scenario offers little of note, the fun is in the details. For instance, the lead bloodsucker sports a disfigured face, whose coarse features and gnarled, misshapen hands transform into the handsome visage and aristocratic digits of Walter Brandi only after it feeds. Also, this vampire takes the trouble to dig up his victims in the local cemetery and dispatch them, so as to prevent competition! "And this time you die, never to rise again," he tells his latest convert just before jamming a stake into her heart. "Neither you nor anyone else will ever intrude on the kingdom of the vampire." And even among the nosferatu things are not quite as they seem, for the beautiful mistress lording over the "Castle of the Damned," Countess Alda (Maria Luisa Rolando), is actually the enslaved lover/acolyte of her own servant, Herman (Brandi), who parasitically keeps her alive and eternally young by letting her drink from his own neck after he himself has fed on the blood of a victim.

Co-screenwriter Ernesto Gastaldi (who also served as assistant director on the film) told interviewer Tim Lucas that "*L'amante del vampiro* was my first official script—I was unbelievably low-paid! ... I used to write after midnight, when my young sons were sleeping. I remember, some nights, I was frightened by my own scenes and had to stop. For me, the fun of being a screenwriter is to live your stories as others live their real lives. What scared me, I realized, would scare other people too."

One such potential "scare" came in the form of a striking burial scene straight out of Carl-Theodore Dreyer's *Vampyr* (1932). As pallbearers carry the latest victim's coffin to the cemetery, the camera takes on the corpse's point of view, looking up through the glass window in the casket at the trees passing overhead, the graveside mourners gazing down, and finally the dirt raining onto the coffin itself. What makes this all the more disturbing are shots of the victim's eyes opening, as she seemingly awakens to the world of the undead, only to be buried alive!

Some atmospheric lighting, clever use of shadows (with the vampiric presence represented early on solely by a menacing silhouette) and creepy castle settings (Castello Borghese at Artena, a village near Rome) further set this *Vampire* (*and Ballerina*) apart from its Continental brethren.

"At the time I knew him, [director/co-writer Polselli] was a man of greater ambition than talent," sniped Gastaldi. Perhaps, but Polselli (who helmed yet another gothic bloodsucker in the form of *The Vampire of the Opera* in 1964, and went on to direct the delirious *Delirium*, a 1972 giallo) brought what talent he possessed to bear fully on *The Vampire and the Ballerina*. Aided by cinematographer Angelo Baistrocchi's fluid camerawork and charicusco lighting, Polselli plays up the sensual aspects of vampirism while at the same time exposing its innate horror (most obviously via the hideous visage of Brandi's blood-starved bloodsucker). When the vampire attacks, the girl's (his victims are *always* female) initial scream soon turns to a moan of pleasure, as she writhes with desire, even languorously stroking her neck wounds afterwards, as if caught up in some unholy post-coitus reverie.

Better than its meager reputation and general obscurity suggest, *The Vampire and the Ballerina* offers a few innovations on the traditional gothic vampire scenario, some macabre atmosphere and evocative camerawork, and a smooth melding of horror and eroticism. Of course, it also features several show-stopping (and not in a good way) dance numbers that would look more at home in a 42nd Street theater than the Metropolitan Opera House, and pointless filler scenes with the various vapid girls (whose buxom frames seem better suited to burlesque than ballet). But it all climaxes in an exciting flight-and-fight, and subsequent turning-to-dust, sequence (in an obvious "borrowing" from Hammer's 1958 *Horror of Dracula*, including the crossed-candlestick trick) that deftly brings the story to a satisfying conclusion. "The disintegration *was* filmed on the castle roof, by stopping the camera and making little changes, stage-by-stage," revealed Gastaldi. "We actually had to create the illusion of wind by standing around and waving newspapers."

"Our production was very cheap," continued Gastaldi, "and the director asked for some skeletons, but there weren't any to be had. The production manager proposed that we go to a cemetery and dig up some real ones! The producer had asked, very upset, 'Do you know what skeletons cost?' [Assistant director] Cirino answered, 'So we'll use the skeletons of poor people!'" Cheap producers and expensive skeletons aside, *The Vampire and the Ballerina* goes on point to stand as one of the better Continental vampire films of the 1960s.

With quotes from: "What Are Those Strange Drops of Blood in the Scripts of ... Ernesto Gastaldi?" by Tim Lucas, *Video Watchdog* 39, 1997.

The Vampire People see *The Blood Drinkers*

The Vampire-Beast Craves Blood

(1968/69; Tigon/Pacemaker Pictures; U.K.) Alternate Title: *The Blood Beast Terror* (U.K. title); Director: Vernon Sewell; Producer: Arnold L. Miller; Screenplay: Peter Bryan; Cinematographer: Stanley A. Long. Cast: Peter Cushing, Robert Flemyng,

Wanda Ventham, Vanessa Howard, David Griffin, Glynn Edwards, Roy Hudd.

A ravishing Psycho-Fiend with the diabolical power to turn into a Giant Deathshead Vampire feasts on the Blood of her lovers before clawing them to death!—poster blurb

The Death's Head Vampire (the film's shooting title) began filming on August 7, 1967, in the tiny Goldhawk Studios in Shepherd's Bush, London. Set in Victorian England, the ludicrous story has an entomologist (Robert Flemyng) seeking to create a giant (male) moth in order to pacify and curtail the bloodlust of his moth-monster daughter (whom he has also created), a beautiful girl who periodically transforms into a giant death's head moth and sucks the blood from her would-be lovers. A police inspector (Peter Cushing) and his long-suffering Sergeant (Glynn Edwards) must discover the absurd truth and lure this murderous monster moth to the flame (literally).

Made by Tony Tenser's Tigon film company (a sort of bargain basement Hammer that bankrolled such pictures as *The Conqueror Worm*, *Blood on Satan's Claw* and *The Creeping Flesh*), *The Vampire-Beast Craves Blood* (released in the U.S. on a double bill with *Curse of the Blood-Ghouls*, a re-titled *Slaughter of the Vampires*) is by far Tigon's most tepid terror offering. Slow, desultory and, oh yes, bloody awful are adjectives that readily spring to mind.

Tenser managed to secure the services of the once-great Basil Rathbone to play the mad moth-maker, but the 75-year-old actor died on July 21 and was replaced by Robert Flemyng (*The Horrible Dr. Hichcock* himself). Though Rathbone would have undoubtedly brought a touch of his trademark class to the role, there was little to work with in Peter Bryan's stolid script. Though Bryan was (partly) responsible for penning such winners as *The Brides of Dracula* and *The Plague of the Zombies*, his screenplay for *Blood Beast* falls more in line with his later efforts like the terrible *Trog* and *Seven Deaths in a Cat's Eye*. "They'll never believe this at the Yard," opines the Sergeant at film's end, to which the Inspector replies, "They'll never believe it *anywhere*." Indeed. (Note: According to Tenser, this clever retort—one of the film's few—wasn't even in the script, but was ad-libbed by star Peter Cushing. "He [Cushing] rewrote a lot of his dialogue," reported Tenser.)

While the Victorian-era costumes and settings evoke a nicely nostalgic atmosphere, nothing much of interest takes place; and Vernon Sewell's (*The Crimson Cult*) indifferent direction fails to improve the lugubrious pacing. Worst of all is the titular terror itself, which looks (in the few brief flashes Sewell dares show us) like a pathetic papier-mâché copy of the already dreadful *Wasp Woman* from that earlier Roger Corman opus.

Peter Cushing does what he can with his underdeveloped Inspector character, adding bits of business here and there in a vain attempt to liven up the proceedings, but it was obviously a lost cause. In fact, Cushing has labeled *Vampire-Beast* his worst film, and it's a tough point to argue. Author Jonathan Rigby, in his excellent *English Gothic*, quotes actor Roy Hudd (who, in two scenes, stole the show playing the irascible morgue attendant) as recalling, "I was called for make-up and there, in the next chair, was the great man himself. 'Good morning,' he said, 'I'm Peter Cushing'—as if I didn't know. 'Have you seen the script?' he asked. 'Not very good, it is?' 'Well...' I blustered. 'No, we can do better than that.' 'Can we? How can we make it funnier,' asked the great man.... That was the start. Together we rejigged the whole two scenes."

Too bad they couldn't have rejigged the entire script.

With quotes from: *Beasts in the Cellar: The Exploitation Film Career of Tony Tenser*, by John Hamilton; *English Gothic*, by Jonathan Rigby.

The Vampires see *Goliath and the Vampires*

The Vampire's Coffin (1958/1965; Cinematografica A.B.S.A./Young America Productions; Mexico; b&w)

Original Language Title: *El Ataúd del Vampiro*. Director: Fernando Mendez, Manuel San Fernando (English language version); Producer: Abel Salazar, K. Gordon Murray (English version); Screenplay: Raymond Obon (Story by Raoul Zenteno); Cinematographer: Victor Herrera. Cast: Abel Salazar, Ariadna Welter, Germán Robles, Yeyre Beirute, Alicia Montoya, Carlos Ancira.

"SMELLING SALTS" TO SAVE YOUR LIFE WHEN YOU SEE "THE VAMPIRE'S COFFIN"—ad line

While the Mexican horror classic *El Vampiro* (*The Vampire*) was still drawing patrons to Mexico City theaters in 1957, producer Abel Salazar rounded up that film's principal cast and crew and began shooting a sequel.

A direct continuation of the original, *The Vampire's Coffin* opens at the big city hospital where young psychiatrist Dr. Henry Hetherford (Abel Salazar), the hero from *The Vampire*, works, and where Martha (Ariadna Welter), *The Vampire*'s heroine, recuperates from her terrifying ordeal. A curious colleague of Henry's tracks down Count Lavud's (Germán Robles) coffin and brings the staked corpse back to the hospital for study. Naturally, the doctor's greedy, grave-robbing assistant, Manson (Yeyre Beirute), inadvertently removes the stake from Lavud's heart, bringing the vampire back to life. Lavud then sets out to "avenge myself on those who buried my slumbering soul in the awful depths of death and stole my power that night" (i.e.: kill Henry and make Martha his undead bride).

"The sequel was set in the city," observed co-star Ariadne Welter, "which did not work as well as the original, which was set in the country." Indeed, the film's first half-hour unspools upon the unconvincingly cut-rate hospital sets (consisting of a few big, white, near-empty rooms), depriving the sequel of the original's lush atmospherics. Germán Robles commented on how producer/star Abel Salazar was "a shylock, a Scrooge! He wanted to do everything with less— or as much with less. He played poor." (This "playing poor" extended to Robles' salary, which, according to the actor, was a paltry $600 U.S. on the original *The Vampire*, and a slightly-better-but-still-miserly $1040 for its sequel.) Though Salazar the producer may have "played poor," Robles enjoyed working with Salazar the *actor*, characterizing him as a "very funny guy ... very fun to work with."

Fortunately, the Vampire eventually chooses a much more appropriate (and better decorated) lair — the local wax museum, setting up shop amidst the guillotine, Virgin of Nuremberg, and creepy figures. The long, dark corridors and stone cellar, not to mention the eerie displays themselves, suits the subject far better than the stark hospital rooms and over-lit hallways.

The likable Salazar, who, despite starring in half-a-dozen horror movies, felt most at home in light comedies, does his usual comic, charming-yet-cowardly hero routine (kind of a Mexican Bob Hope but without the zingers), while Ariadne Welter makes for a fetching damsel in distress. And Germán Robles continues his imposing turn as Lavud, combining the look of Lugosi with the lunge of Lee. Unfortunately, the mundane surroundings of the film's first half make of his gothic-style Count a fish-out-of-water (or at least a vampire-out-of-crypt).

Director Fernando Mendez, aided by Victor Herrera's evocative cinematography, frequently offsets the meandering script and banal setting with eerie lighting and shuddery shadows. One well-staged vampire attack has a woman pursued down a deserted street by the Vampire's shadow, which becomes the silhouette of a bat, before she abruptly turns to find herself suddenly facing the snarling fiend and his inch-long fangs. Too bad said scene is then juxtaposed with a cheesy Guys-'n'-Dolls-style dance routine, as Martha, a professional dancer, rehearses at a theater. Fortunately, the climax offers a vigorous, exciting battle with the Vampire (and his slave) at the wax museum, marred only by some unconvincing bat-on-a-string action (but ending in a novel demise for the undead monster). Though falling short of the rich atmosphere and tight pacing of the original, *The Vampire's Coffin* still offers a passably creepy place for horror lovers to lay their heads.

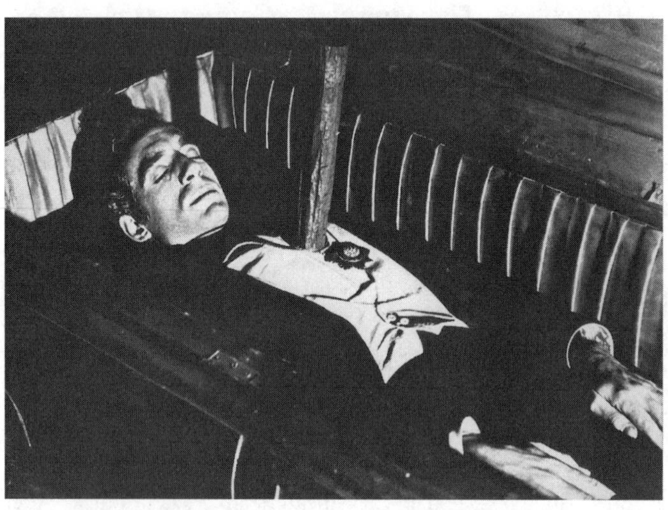

In this sequel to *The Vampire*, Germán Robles (as Count Lavud) once again occupies *The Vampire's Coffin* (1958/65).

The Anglicized version of *The Vampire's Coffin* premiered in the U.S. (in Cincinnati, Ohio) on a double bill with *The Robot vs. the Aztec Mummy* on November 17, 1965. Ironically, this sequel to *The Vampire* hit

American theaters over two years *before* the original.

With quotes from: "The Vampire's Lady: An Interview with 'El Vampiro' Leading Lady Ariadne Welter," by Charles P. Mitchell and Paul Parla, *Filmfax* 67, June/July 1998; "El Vampiro Speaks! An Interview with Mexican Horror Star Germán Robles," by Bryan Senn, Richard Sheffield and Jim Clatterbaugh, *Monsters from the Vault* 24, February 2008.

Vampires Versus Hercules see *Hercules in the Haunted World*

I Vampiri see *The Devil's Commandment*

Varan the Unbelievable (1958/62; Toho; Japan)

Original Title: *Daikaiju Baran.* Director: Ishiro Honda; Producer: Tomoyuki Tanaka; Screenplay: Shinichi Sekizawa; Cinematographer: Hajime Koizume. Cast: Kozo Nomura, Ayumi Sonoda, Fumito Matsuo, Koreya Senda, Akihiko Hirata, Myron Healey (U.S. version).

From a world below, it came to terrorize—to destroy—to revenge!—tagline

Toho's first cycle of *kaiju eiga* (giant monster) movies zoomed out of the gate with *Godzilla, King of the Monsters* (1954/56), sputtered with *Gigantis the Fire Monster* (1955) and *Rodan* (1956), and finally ran out of gas with *Varan the Unbelievable.*

The most surprising thing about this picture is its utter lack of surprises. Most Toho monster epics—even the bad ones—contain some quirky, off-the-wall flourish that presents a certain charm. Not so *Varan.* Although competently crafted, it contains no new ideas, and the elements it recycles were better executed by earlier movies. As a result, *Varan* remains bland and uninteresting, the cinematic equivalent of eating a bowl of plain white rice for dinner.

Its vaguely *Kong*-like story opens with a team of scientists hunting for rare butterflies in Siberia. In addition to butterflies, the team discovers a secluded village whose residents worship a mighty monster, Varan, who lives at the bottom of a nearby lake. The military arrive, and decide to destroy the creature before it can advance on Tokyo. (Nevermind that there's no indication Varan, who has apparently lived happily at the bottom of this lake for millions of years, plans to advance anywhere.) Once the military arrive, the story falls into a tedious pattern: Monster attack

It's *Varan the Unbelievable*—and now you know why (*TV Guide* ad).

followed by static dialogue scene (in which scientists and generals strategize for the next attack), followed by another attack, followed by another conference, and on and on, *ad nauseum.* The action scenes make extensive use of poorly matched WWII-era stock footage, which further cheapens the look of the film.

Varan himself—a four-legged, long-tailed lizard with prominent white spikes on his back—lacks the personality of Godzilla and Rodan. He looks like an overgrown iguana with racing stripes. The story's ill-defined human characters prove even less engaging. The lone aspect of this film to display any ambition whatsoever is its visual effects. Miniature effects involving water are notoriously difficult, and *Varan* features a great many of them. Although the results aren't always convincing, Eiji Tsuburaya and the rest of Toho's special effects team deserve credit for trying. The only other thing *Varan* has going for it is an excellent score. Akira Ifukube's brooding, ominous opening theme sets the mood perfectly, although that mood soon dissipates. This score also introduces the familiar "Monster March," which would be reprised in most of Toho's mid–Sixties monsteramas.

For its U.S. release, the film was dubbed and truncated from 87 minutes to 70, with additional material discarded to make room for new footage featuring American actor Myron Healey. (In this version, it's Healey who discovers Varan while conducting desalination experiments in the monster's saltwater lake.) This bastardization was christened *Varan the Unbelievable*, although a more appropriate title might have been *Varan the Unwatchable*. The original, Japanese (subtitled), uncut (and de-Myron Healeyed) film was finally released to DVD in America in 2005. Unlike the butchered American cut of the film, the Japanese version is at least comprehensible, but remains plodding, repetitive and numbingly derivative. In any language, *Varan* means boredom.

Clearly, major changes were needed to revive Toho's *kaiju eiga* series—changes that would arrive with *Mothra* (1961/62).

Vengeance of Hercules see *Goliath and the Dragon*

Village of the Damned (1960; MGM; U.K.; b&w)

Director: Wolf Rilla; Producer: Ronald Kinnoch; Screenplay: Stirling Silliphant, Wolf Rilla and George Barclay (Novel: John Wyndham); Cinematographer: Geoffrey Faithfull. Cast: George Sanders, Barbara Shelley, Michael Gwynn, Martin Stephens, Laurence Naismith.

What Demonic Force Lurks Behind Those Eyes?—tagline

Ad for one of the best British horror/sci-fi films of the decade (1960).

Unlike many chillers of its era, the offbeat, disconcerting *Village of the Damned* (1960) still retains its power to intrigue and unsettle viewers. Even 50 years on, the movie remains among the most seamless—and scariest—hybrids of horror and science fiction.

It's an ordinary morning in the bucolic English village of Midwich when suddenly the entire population falls asleep for several hours. The local telephone operator slumps over her switchboard; a farmer keels over the wheel of his tractor while plowing a field (the tractor continues running blindly until it crashes into a tree). Weeks later, every woman of child-bearing age in Midwich turns up pregnant, even teenage virgins. Those women include Althea Zellaby (Barbara Shelley), wife of professor Gordon Zellaby (George Sanders). Gordon, working with his brother-in-law, Major Alan Bernard (Michael Gwynn), and a local physician (Laurence Naismith), have been investigating the bizarre sleeping incident; they quickly surmise that the mysterious pregnancies are related.

Eventually, 12 children are born in Midwich—beautiful boys and girls, normal-looking but all with blonde hair and piercing, pale eyes. The children display superhuman intelligence and psychic powers (telepathy and mind control), as well as an icy, aloof demeanor. Led by Gordon's son David (Martin Stephens), the children lack compassion and exact pitiless, deadly vengeance for any perceived slight. After scientists theorize that the children were sired by an alien intelligence via an energy beam directed at Earth from outer space, military leaders, including Major Bernard, want to quarantine the children. Gordon pleads for their freedom, and the opportunity to teach the youngsters values and morals. But when he witnesses David and his friends using their psychic powers to force a villager to commit suicide with a shotgun, Gordon finally agrees the children must be stopped, and devises a desperate plan to do away with the super-intelligent, mind-reading boys and girls—including his own son.

Village of the Damned was derived from the best-selling British novel *The Midwich Cuckoos* (a reference to cuckoos' practice of laying eggs in the nests of other birds) by John Wyndham, who also wrote the excellent *Day of the Triffids*. *Village*'s screenplay, developed primarily by American Stirling Silliphant, streamlines Wyndham's narrative to increase dramatic impact (he reduces the size of the village, eliminates some secondary characters and makes Gordon David's father rather than the boy's grandfather), but otherwise adheres closely to the novel's plot and tone. Originally envisioned as an American picture, *Village* was shelved for a few years, then dusted off and farmed out to MGM's British unit (at which time English screenwriter George Barclay re–Anglicized the script), with a modest $225,000 budget under direction of journeyman Wolf Rilla.

Village of the Damned remains by far the finest picture in an otherwise undistinguished career for Rilla. It's a textbook example of clean, almost transparent cinematic storytelling — never showy or self-aware, but subtle and powerful, evocatively composed and full of fluid dolleys and pans. Cinematographer Geoffrey Faithfull lights the film in a gritty, pseudo-documentary style, with thickly draped shadows in key sequences. Together, Rilla and Faithfull craft a series of arresting moments, including the film's chilling opening, with the eerily silent, motionless streets and fields of Midwich strewn with dead-looking bodies. In another cringe-inducing scene, the infant David forces Althea to hold her hand in a pot of scalding hot milk as punishment for accidentally burning his tongue with a too-hot bottle. Rilla recognizes that he doesn't need elaborate camera flourishes at such moments. Rilla's low-key, straightforward approach works so well because it allows the underlying horror of Wyndham's basic concept to sink in — the idea that one's own beloved child might turn out to be a murderous, inhuman monster that must be destroyed.

Although best remembered today for playing villains and cads, like unscrupulous theater critic Addison DeWitt in *All About Eve* (1950), star George Sanders originally rose to fame playing cultured, intelligent heroes in the Saint and Falcon detective series of the 1930s and '40s; his role as Gordon Zellaby returns him to those roots. He's entirely believable as the erudite professor and doting daddy-to-be, and later heartbreakingly effective as a man facing the grim prospect of having to kill his own child. The ever-reliable Barbara Shelley contributes a similarly touching performance as the distraught Althea Zellaby, distraught over her inability to connect with her unfeeling son. Michael Gwynn, who fans may recognize as the monster from Hammer Films' *Revenge of Frankenstein* (1959), also fares well as Major Bernard, a far more sympathetic and well-rounded character than most sci-fi military types. But young Martin Stephens steals the show with his creepily placid performance as the nearly emotionless David (a slight smile appears on his face only once in the film, after the children kill one of the villagers by forcing him to drive his car into a brick wall). For *Village of the Damned* to work, the kids had to be scary as hell, and Stephens certainly is. (The young actors' impact is enhanced by a simple but powerful visual effect that makes their eyes glow when they use their mind control powers.) Stephens went on to appear in *The Hellfire Club*, *The Innocents* (both 1961), and Hammer's *The Devil's Own* (aka *The Witches*, 1966).

Village of the Damned proved very profitable for MGM, and a good but very different sequel, *Children of the Damned*, followed in 1962. *Village* also was remade, with dismal results, by director John Carpenter in 1995. Neither the sequel nor the remake recaptures the nerve-jangling spell cast by the original film.

The Virgin of Nuremberg see *Horror Castle*

Voodoo Blood Death see *Curse of the Voodoo*

The Vulture (1966; Paramount; U.K./Canada/U.S.) Alternate Title: *Manutara*; Director/Producer/Screenwriter: Lawrence Huntington; Cinematographer: Stephen Dade. Cast: Robert Hutton, Akim Tamiroff, Broderick Crawford, Diane Clare, Philip Friend.

Talons of terror! Half-man half-beastbird ... swooping on his human prey ... drinking blood ... mutilating flesh! — poster

Via some nebulous, ill-explained experiment, a scientist in a small Cornish town turns his matter transmitter device on the centuries-old grave of a 'sorcerer' who was buried alive with his pet vulture. Things go awry, resulting in a flying monstrosity that swoops down to snatch up its victims— the descendents of the family who sentenced the warlock to death.

This muddled amalgam of science and fantasy begins well enough, with a creepy opening nighttime sequence in which a bus driver warns his sole woman passenger not to cross the haunted graveyard at night. Of course she disembarks and

American one-sheet poster for *The Vulture* (1966).

promptly starts walking through the cemetery. Chillingly, we see a tombstone begin *moving*, rocking back and forth, before the ground in front of it *splits open* (accompanied by the sound of evil laughter), and the woman faints.

Unfortunately, it's a loooong time before anything *else* happens, as it takes 45 minutes for the titular terror finally to appear (and then only in the form of its impossibly stiff legs and talons—as it comically picks up the rather hefty Broderick Crawford to carry out of frame). The big bird doesn't even commit any *off-screen* murders before this, with the entire first half of the picture taken up with the police and protagonists investigating what they think is a simple grave-robbing.

Low-rent American leading man Robert Hutton (*Invisible Invaders, The Slime People, Torture Garden*) stars as a vacationing nuclear physicist whose wife's family turns out to be the target of the vengeful vulture. Hutton plays his character as an arrogant, bullying know-it-all who never smiles, orders people about, and says things like "I'm a scientist" to justify his bad manners. Cold, annoying and thoroughly unlikable, Hutton even mispronounces "nuclear" as "nu-cue-lar." Sheesh.

Producer/director/screenwriter Lawrence Huntington's dialogue is as awkward as Hutton's performance. "Some unknown scientific brain has produced a monstrous creature — half bird, half man — by means of nu-cue-lar transmutation," Hutton says by way of barmy explanation.

Leading lady Diane Clare (*Witchcraft, The Plague of the Zombies*) has little to do but act supportive of her husband (Hutton) and stand in the right spot at the right time to be picked up by the vulture claws (a rather painful harness contraption, according to Clare). Of her director, Clare said: "Lawrence Huntington was pleasant and polite, but what I remember most about him, oddly, was the amount of work he had to do. He was producer, as well as writer and director, and made changes to his own screenplay as we went along, so I have an image of a man who was sometimes abstracted, but never impatient — at least not with me."

According to Hutton, Huntington "just wanted to get the thing on film and forget it." And that's good advice for the potential viewer as well—"forget it." (*The Vulture* proved to be veteran British B-director Huntington's, er, swan song; he died in 1968.)

Apart from two grabs made by the phony oversized vulture feet, the movie consists of scene after scene of Hutton trying to convince people (the police, his wife's uncle, a professor) of his preposterous theory (which, even more preposterously — given his complete lack of hard evidence — turns out to be true). Then further scenes show *other* characters discussing it as well, generating tedium of the highest order.

"The idea wasn't bad, but I think this was one film where they needed more horror," opined Hutton. "They talked about the Vulture all the time but you hardly ever saw the damn thing. It called for less talk and more horror. But, of course, that would cost money, and talk doesn't cost as much. I think *The Vulture* took five or six weeks; we even went out on location, down to Devon and Cornwall."

The climactic payoff, when it finally comes, is a few fleeting shots of the man-headed bird (reminiscent of Peter Lorre in *The Raven*— but *that* was played for *laughs*) standing and spreading its black wings (obviously, Huntington realized how ridiculous it looked and kept its exposure to the barest minimum). In this respect, *The Vulture* truly gives its audience the bird.

With quotes from: "Directed by the Best: Diane Clare," by Mark A. Miller, *Monsters from the Vault*

10, Winter/Spring 2000; *Science Fiction Stars and Horror Heroes*, by Tom Weaver.

War of the Zombies (1963; Galatea/AIP; Italy) Original Language Title: *Roma contra Roma*. Alternate Title: *Night Star, Goddess of Electra*. Director: Guiseppi Vari; Producers: Ferruccio de Martino, Massimo de Rita; Screenplay: Piero Pierotti, Marcello Sartarelli; Cinematography: Gabor Pogany. Cast: Susy Andersen, Ettore Manni, Ida Galli, John Drew Barrymore, Mino Doro, Matilde Calman, Ivano Staccioli.

UNCONQUERABLE WARRIORS OF THE DAMNED!—poster

This unique, though ultimately unsatisfying, Roman-era Sword and Sandal offering out of Italy is nothing if not novel. John Drew Barrymore plays the evil sorcerer Adalbar, who conspires with the local Roman prelate lording over the conquered province of Salmatia to steal a horde of Roman treasure and then rebel against their Roman overlords. Adalbar accomplishes this via an army of undead legionnaires, whom he reanimates through the power of a mysterious god (or goddess— no name, including the "Electra" of the film's alternate title, is ever mentioned). Noble centurion Gaius (Ettore Manni) journeys from Rome to investigate, and must deal with various double-crosses, betrayals, and duplicitous females before finally learning the secret of the sorcerer's power (centered in the massive stone idol in Adalbar's lair).

The concept of slain legionnaires rising up to battle their living brethren sets this *War* apart from the many ancient-Greece-and-Rome-set pepla that poured forth from the Continent in the 1960s. Unfortunately, the undistinguished Guiseppi Vari's undistinguished direction, and the poorly constructed story (after an opening battle scene the film settles down into a talky tale of palace intrigue and wizard boasting), tosses it back into the peplum pit occupied by the vast majority of its boorish brethren. It does manage to climb back out for the final twenty minutes, however, in which the dead battle the living in a macabre and impressive spectacle that employed scores of horses and hundreds of dress extras. Too bad this climax loses much of its morbid punch due to either indecisiveness or an I-want-my-ghoulish-cake-and-I'll-eat-it-too attitude on the part of the filmmakers. The undead legionnaires, whom the sorcerer had pegged as zombies by showing them to be resurrected corpses "with no will of their own," rise up as superimposed spectral images moving in slow motion ("They seem like ghosts," observes one soldier, while another labels them "an army of ghosts"); but once the ghost army reaches their living foes, they appear corporeal again. Though the bluish tinting of the undead sequences, along with the weird choral voices and bizarre tonalities on the soundtrack, make for an eerie and unsettling tableau, the inconsistency remains both confusing and off-putting.

John Drew Barrymore (grandson of the Great Profile himself) in wizard's robe, black cape and dark eyeliner brings an intense gaze and deep suntan—but little else—to his villainous role. He's given some impressive sets upon which to glower, however, particularly Adalbar's cavern lair, with its dry-ice-fog carpet, shooting gouts of flame and giant cyclopean head statue. And the Roman Senate and various columned sets are more expansive and detailed than those seen in the average peplum production. It's a shame so little occurs on them (it's 40 minutes before Adalbar resurrects his first zombie in said cave, for instance, and then he does nothing with him). With a tighter script and more decisive direction, *War*

Undead Roman legionnaires fight the *War of the Zombies* (1963).

of the Zombies (or *Ghosts* or whatever) could have been so much more than the novel failure it turned out to be.

War-Gods of the Deep (1965; AIP; U.S./Great Britain) Alternate Title: *City Under the Sea*; Director: Jacques Tourneur; Producer: Daniel Haller; Screenplay: Charles Bennett, Louis M. Heyward; Cinematographer: Stephen Dade. Cast: Vincent Price, Tab Hunter, Susan Hart, David Tomlinson, John LeMesurier.

They dared the most fantastic journey that has ever challenged imagination!—ad line

"*War-Gods of the Deep* was just a disaster. Nobody knew what it was about. It was a badly produced picture. Jacques [Tourneur] was a marvelous director, but he just couldn't get around the script." So proclaimed *War-Gods* star Vincent Price, and he was right.

Director Jacques (*Cat People*, *Curse of the Demon*) Tourneur's last and weakest film, *War-Gods of the Deep* is a lackluster undersea adventure story nominally "based on" Edgar Allan Poe's poem "City Beneath the Sea." If having Tab Hunter and Susan (*The Ghost in the Invisible Bikini*) Hart as the romantic leads doesn't tip you off, then making a pet chicken the comic relief more than demonstrates this film's level of maturity. Vincent Price once again plays the cultured heavy, who this time thinks Susan Hart is his long dead wife returned to him in his city beneath the waves. There's some very poorly costumed gill-men (expressionless metallic masks erasing all sense of believability), cardboard characters (although Price does make the most of his sinister/sympathetic role) and the inevitable volcanic eruption to tie up all loose ends. At least a few interesting sets provide something to look at, possibly due to producer Daniel Haller's presence (he is best known as set designer on Roger Corman's beautifully atmospheric Poe films). Price, Touneur and Poe had all seen better days.

With quotes from: "Vincent Price: Looking Back on Forty Years as Horror's Crown Prince," by Steve Biodrowski, David Del Valle and Lawrence French, *Cinefantastique*, January 1989.

Werewolf in a Girls' Dormitory (1961/63; MGM; Italy; b&w) Original Language Title: *Lycanthropus*. Alternate Titles: *I Married a Werewolf*; *Monster Among the Girls*. Director: Richard Benson (Paolo Heusch); Producer: Jack Forrest (Guido Giambartolomei); Screenplay: Julian Berry (Ernesto Gastaldi). Cast: Barbara Lass, Carl Schell, Curt Lowens, Maurice Marsac, Mary McNeeran, Grace Neame, Lucian Pigozzi.

IF YOUR BLOOD CURDLES EASILY—*DON'T COME*!—trailer

Ditto if your eyelids droop easily. To be fair, this offbeat Euro-take on the werewolf mythos offers some atmospheric nighttime photography (courtesy of cinematographer "George Patrick," an unknown young cameraman who, according to co-star Luciano Pigozzi, died in an auto accident shortly after filming), an impressive Italian villa setting (surrounded by wolf-infested woods), the occasional shock (such as the terrified frozen stare of a young girl's bloody corpse), the bulging-eyed "Italian Peter Lorre" (Luciano Pigozzi) at his most skulkiest, and plenty of pretty girls (including doe-eyed lead Barbara Lass, Roman Polanski's first wife). But this *Werewolf* also

Double-feature "*NERVO-RAMA*" artwork for the Italian import *Werewolf in a Girl's Dormitory* (1961/63) and the British Karloff-starrer *Corridors of Blood* (1958/63).

sports awkward dialogue (and hollow dubbing), some poor minimalist makeup, and a plethora of dull stretches (including a tedious final 20 minutes that wind down to a mundane climax).

Filmed in 1961 near Rome, but released Stateside in 1963 in support of the Boris Karloff-starrer *Corridors of Blood, Lycanthropus* (its original-language title) sees a private reform school for wayward girls plagued by vicious murders. A young disgraced doctor (Carl Schell, lesser-known brother of Maximillian) comes to the school as a teacher, and must solve the case of the mysterious murders, finally uncovering a "lycanthropus" in their midst.

Structured like a mystery, the plot involves blackmail, incriminating letters, hypocritical "establishment" figures, and red herrings, as well as a few choice murders (not all at the hands of the werewolf). While this "who's-the-lycanthrope?" angle sustains interest for the film's first half, the lackluster and intermittent werewolf "action," and dull denouement only engender a sense of disappointment and tedium once the mystery bubble has burst.

Speaking of werewolves, "The pituitary gland ... causes psycho-physical transformation ... causing increasing distortion in the skin, hair and teeth." So explains the doc, who happens to be an expert on the dreaded "lycanthropus." This translates into the sparsest werewolf makeup since Henry Hull crossed yak hairs with Jack Pierce in *Werewolf of London* (1935). This werewolf in a girls' dormitory, however, with its ridged forehead (a silly and obvious prosthetic piece), oversized nose, plastic fangs and three-day beard, lacks the sinister satanic quality showcased by Pierce's minimalist makeup, resulting in what looks like a scarred man with bad teeth after a three-day drunk. It's hardly the stuff of nightmares; and the same could be said of the film as a whole.

Note: A movie pressbook can be an amazing thing, as evidenced by the following "article" printed in *Werewolf*'s campaign manual. "A lovely 17-year-old student at an exclusive girls' school outside Turin, Italy, was found pregnant during a routine physical examination. Upon questioning, she revealed that eight weeks before, under the light of the full moon, a werewolf entered her room in the girls' dormitory. Upon further questioning, she claimed that the werewolf had a long, hairy face and drooled at the lips. Local authorities are skeptical of her story, pointing out that the girl might have been influenced by the recent location shooting of the startling new horror film, *Werewolf in a Girls' Dormitory* in and near the city. However, the mayor has decided to adopt a 'wait and see' attitude for the next eight months." Life imitating Art? Right.

What (1963/65; Titanus/Futuramic; Italy) Original Language Title: *Il Frusta e Il Corpo* (*The Whip and the Body*, Italy). Director: Mario Bava (as John M. Old); Producer: Elio Scardamaglia (as John Oscar); Screenplay: Ernesto Gastaldi (as Julian Berry), Ugo Guerro (as Robert Hugo) and Luciano Martino (as Martin Hardy); Cinematography: Ubaldo Terzano (as David Hamilton). Cast: Daliah Lavi, Christopher Lee, Tony Kendall, Luciano Pigazzi (as Alan Collins), Jacques Herlin.

WHAT is her terrifying secret?? Is she the victim of a madman????
Or a dead man? You must see "WHAT"!
—tagline

When a long-unseen, nearly-lost movie reemerges, disappointment is often the result. This is understandable, since it's almost impossible for any movie to live up to the hopes and imaginations of passionate fans, especially when stoked by decades of conjecture and longing. Thankfully, this was not the case with director Mario Bava's *La Frusta e il Corpo* (*The Whip and the Body*), which, if anything, *exceeded* expectations. Previously known to American audiences only in butchered, watered-down form under the bizarre title *What*, the picture languished overlooked and underappreciated for decades until it was restored to director Mario Bava's original vision (and title) for release on DVD in 2001. Now many critics and fans count it among the director's greatest works.

Cold-hearted aristocrat Kurt Menliff (Christopher Lee) returns from exile to his ancestral home and his family, who despise him. He learns that his fiancée, Nevenka (Daliah Lavi), has married his brother. When Nevenka takes a ride along the beach, Kurt follows her, snatches the riding crop from her hand and beats her savagely. But as he whips her, Nevenka begins to writhe with pleasure. Finally, he stops beating her and the two embrace passionately. Shortly afterward, an unseen assassin creeps into Kurt's bedroom and murders him. After his death, Nevenka is plagued by visions of Kurt's ghost; he even returns in the middle of the night to whip her again. Then Nevenka's father is murdered, and the haunting takes a more sinister turn...

This is one of Bava's most complex and accomplished films, in terms of both technique and theme. The director's use of impressionist color was never more brilliant—the screen is awash with burning red, lush greens and eerie blues and yellows. He also makes deft symbolic use of these colors (specifically, the reds) and other visual motifs (most prominently, roses) as they recur throughout the film. Bava casts a sense of visceral anxiety over the picture, which is punctuated by moments of excruciating suspense. In one of these spine-tingling sequences, Nevenka awakens in the night because she thinks she hears the sound of Kurt's whip and tiptoes through the dark castle both afraid and aroused. With sequences like this one, Bava moves beyond objective realism and toward a more surreal approach. Long stretches of the film unfold from the perspective of Nevenka, who proves to be an unreliable narrator. We are seeing not "reality" but the events as she experiences them in her mind. (This isn't spelled out for the viewer until the final scene.) Bava had taken some tentative steps in this direction with parts of *The Evil Eye* (aka *The Girl Who Knew Too Much*, 1963/64) and would embrace this approach more fully in later works such as *Lisa and the Devil* (1974) and *Shock* (1977). Indeed, *The Whip and the Body* is so indelibly marked with the director's visual and thematic signatures, it seems incredible that this was a simple work-for-hire job rather than an auteur vanity project. Yet, principle screenwriter Ernesto Gastaldi's script was complete before Bava came on board, and the director made few revisions. "Bava didn't make any changes to the dialogue, the plot or the characters," Gastaldi said.

The film also benefits from an unusual number (for Bava) of outstanding performances from its cast. Producers originally wanted Barbara Steele to play Nevenka, but when the actress demurred they turned to Israeli ingénue Daliah Lavi (pronounced La-VEE). It was a fortuitous substitution. Lavi, assigned the most emotionally complex female role in any Bava film (by far), responds with an assured and unaffected performance, arguably the best by any actress in any Bava movie. Producers brought in Christopher Lee to add star power, but his contribution here goes well beyond marquee value. Lee's towering, charismatic performance casts a shadow over the movie much larger than his limited screen time (only about eight minutes). Harriet Medin also contributes a memorable turn as a red-herring housekeeper. The rest of the cast proves acceptable, as well.

According to Gastaldi, *The Whip and the Body* was intended as an imitation of director Roger Corman's popular Edgar Allan Poe adaptations. "They showed me an Italian print of *Pit and the Pendulum* before I started writing. 'Give us something like this,' they said," Gastaldi reports. While there are certainly *Pit*-like elements to the story—an isolated seaside setting, a brooding lead character tormented by a sadistic past—Gastaldi delivered a screenplay far more complex and provocative than requested. The mystery's resolution reveals the thumbprint of Alfred Hitchcock, whose influence is felt strongly throughout many Italian thrillers of the era. Like Norman Bates, Nevenka has been putting on the clothes, and assuming the identity of, a dead loved one during fits of violence (and, here, also for self-flagellation). She killed Kurt to silence her own forbidden, masochistic desires, only to become consumed by them anyway. By the end of the narrative, like Norman and Mother, Nevenka and Kurt have become inexorably intertwined.

As a result of this sadomasochistic content, the film was plagued by censorship problems. A Roman court slapped executive producer Natale Magnaghi with obscenity charges. Even though he was found not guilty two months later, this unsavory

Beautiful Belgian poster for *What* (1963/65; aka *The Whip and the Body*) (courtesy Tim Lucas).

episode kept devout Catholics away from the picture during its domestic release and cowed potential foreign distributors. *Il Frusta e Il Corpo* earned the equivalent of only $45,000 in Italy (about half of its production costs), making it one of Bava's worst box office flops. While, ultimately, Italian censors demanded surprisingly few cuts in the film (the whipping scene on the beach was abbreviated), foreign censors demanded far more extensive edits. In England, all the whipping scenes were removed and other key sequences truncated, rendering the story incomprehensible. The picture was further weakened by poor dubbing (American actor Mel Welles supervised the English language dubbing for the film, which was done without the participation of any of the original cast) and printing (although shot and released in Italy in Technicolor, international prints were made on cheap stock that quickly faded). The U.S. release version closely mirrored the butchered British version, and was also saddled with the inexplicable new title *What*.

A fine performance by Geraldine Page (pictured in this lobby card along with Jim Barbera) provides one of few points of interest in the tepid "horror hag" entry *What Ever Happened to Aunt Alice?* (1969).

For many years, the uncut version of *The Whip and the Body* was feared lost. Then, in 1993, Joe Dante provided an uncut 35 mm print from his collection for a Los Angeles Bava retrospective. In 2000, VCI Home Video undertook a complete restoration of the film, making a composite transfer from Dante's print and one from an Italian collector. Since its restoration, the picture has belatedly earned the critical respect and audience attention it richly deserves. If not Bava's best movie, *The Whip and the Body* is not far removed.

With quotes from: *Mario Bava: All the Colors of the Dark*, by Tim Lucas.

What Ever Happened to Aunt Alice?

(1969; MGM) Director: Lee H. Katzin; Producer: Robert Aldrich; Screenplay: Theodore Apstein (from a novel by Ursula Curtiss); Cinematographer: Joseph Biroc. Cast: Geraldine Page, Ruth Gordon, Rosemary Forsyth, Robert Fuller, Mildred Dunnock.

"What makes your garden grow ... wouldn't you like to know?"—trailer

When her husband dies and leaves her with little more than outstanding debts, Claire Marrable (Geraldine Page) begins swindling and murdering her live-in servants (planting their bodies under fir trees in her garden) to maintain her upper-crust lifestyle. But Claire's newest housekeeper (and latest prospective victim) becomes suspicious of her employer, setting the stage for a deadly struggle between the two women.

Producer Robert Aldrich invented the "horror hag" film with his blockbuster *What Ever Happened to Baby Jane?* (1962), and struck gold again with *Hush, Hush Sweet Charlotte* (1964). But with *What Ever Happened to Aunt Alice?*, he went to the well once too often.

In Ursula Curtiss' novel *The Forbidden Garden*, Aldrich recognized a story akin to *Baby Jane*: Two elderly women in an isolated home engage in an unlikely battle to the death. The *What Ever Happened to* ... title was calculated to underscore these similarities. For this project, Aldrich again hired two highly respected veteran actresses—Geraldine Page, a venerated Broadway performer, and the great Ruth Gordon, with her freshly-minted Oscar statuette (for *Rosemary's Baby* [1968]) in tow. But *Aunt Alice* never rises anywhere near the level of *Baby Jane* or *Sweet Charlotte*. The reasons are many.

For starters, Aldrich, who had helmed *Baby Jane* and *Sweet Charlotte* himself, turned *Aunt Alice* over to Lee H. Katzin, whose direction proves competent but unremarkable. Katzin and screenwriter Theodore Apstein had both worked primarily in television, and it shows. Apstein's screenplay offers no suggestion of the supernatural, or even (until the final reel) madness. Instead, Apstein (who had written episodes of series like *Ben Casey* and *Dr. Kildare*) dwells on a dull romantic subplot involving Alice's nephew (Robert Fuller) and Claire's neighbor (Rosemary Forsyth). The result is a relatively mundane mystery rather than a full-blown psychological chiller on par with Aldrich's previous "grande dame guinol" pictures. Cinematographer Joseph Biroc, whose evocative black-and-white cinematography was a major plus for *Sweet Charlotte*, also disappoints. His flat, overlit color lighting scheme only compounds the picture's humdrum, movie-of-the-week quality. Gerald Fried's ham-fisted score presents another problem. Full of trilling harpsichord and groaning cellos, Fried's music telegraphs instead of enhances, and inserts thundering fanfares for no apparent reason.

Fortunately, both Page and Gordon deliver spirited performances. While Page's portrayal seems a bit one-note in comparison with Gordon's winning turn as the crafty, resourceful housekeeper, both performers are fun to watch, and that's the primary appeal of all movies of this stripe. The duo doesn't produce any of the sparks that flew between Bette Davis and Joan Crawford in *Baby Jane*, or even between Davis and Olivia de Havilland in *Sweet Charlotte*, but that might be asking too much under the circumstances.

The stars muster commendable enthusiasm, especially since the formula that seemed so fresh in 1962 had grown shopworn by 1969. Nevertheless, the "horror hag" subgenre would continue into the 1970s with subsequent entries of widely varying quality, including *What's the Matter with Helen?* (1971, with Debbie Reynolds and Shelley Winters), *Who Slew Auntie Roo?* (1971, Shelley Winters again), *Blood and Lace* (1971, featuring Gloria Grahame) and *Dear Dead Delilah* (1972, starring Agnes Moorehead).

Ad for the 1962 originator of the "horror hag" subgenre (courtesy Ted Okuda).

What Ever Happened to Baby Jane?

(1962; Seven Arts/Warner Bros.; b&w) Director: Robert Aldrich; Producer: Robert Aldrich and Kenneth Hyman; Screenplay: Lukas Heller (from a novel by Henry Farrell); Cinematographer: Ernest Haller. Cast: Bette Davis, Joan Crawford, Victor Buono, Anna Lee.

Sister, sister, oh so fair, why is there blood all over your hair?—tagline

Former child star Jane Hudson (Bette Davis), now a bitter, forgotten crone, sits at her piano, drunk, and begins to tap out the melody to her schmaltzy childhood hit, "I've Written a Letter to Daddy." In a chair near the piano rests a near-life-sized doll of 12-year-old "Baby" Jane, a relic from her former celebrity. As she croaks out the lyrics to the song, she caresses the face of the doll—tracing the outlines of her own youthful features. When the song ends, she steps in front of a full-length mirror, lit by a harsh, white overhead light that makes her look impossibly ancient — shadows underscoring every wrinkle and crag in her face. At the sight of her reflection, she gasps and freezes with horror. She yelps and covers her face with her hands, sobbing.

Jane yearns desperately, insanely, to recapture the beauty, popularity and power she possessed during her youth. Beauty and popularity have long since deserted her, but she still holds one kind of power — the ability to terrorize her hated invalid sister, Blanche (Joan Crawford).

At once pathetic and stark-raving, horrifyingly mad, Jane Hudson endures as one of the richest and most memorable characters to emerge from horror cinema in the 1960s. And *What Ever Happened to Baby Jane* remains one of the most rewarding of all the sixties shockers—finely crafted, impeccably acted, thought-provoking, and at times scary as hell. *Baby Jane* inspired a whole new subgenre — the "horror hag" movie — and it stands as a troubling rumination on the perils of aging, especially in a culture fixated on youth and beauty. It also began a career renaissance for two of the greatest actresses in Hollywood history, Crawford and (especially) Davis.

The fortunes of both stars had been flagging in the late 1950s. Davis' last several films had lost money. She had been written off once before, only to stage a mid-career comeback with *All About Eve* (1950). Nevertheless, naysayers were convinced that this time, at age 54, Davis was finished for good — simply too old. Always strong-willed and iconoclastic, Davis drew attention to her plight in 1961 by placing a sarcastic "Job Wanted" ad in the Hollywood trade papers.

Then Aldrich, who had already signed Crawford, approached Davis to co-headline a project based on Henry Farrell's novel about a psychotic former child star who torments her crippled ex-movie idol sister. The material was, to say the least, outré, but Davis recognized the film's potential and not only accepted the role but threw herself into it with what can only be described as reckless abandon. If *Baby Jane* had backfired, it could easily have been the film that ended Davis' career. Never classically beautiful (Universal president Carl Laemmle once famously opined that the young Davis had "as much sex appeal as Slim Summerville"), Davis for decades carefully nurtured and protected her screen image. Now she enthusiastically dismantled it, designing for herself a startlingly grotesque make-up and wig.

It was no great stretch for Davis to act as if she despised Crawford. One of *Baby Jane*'s chief pleasures is watching two of Hollywood's most notorious enemies play out their venomous feud on screen. At Warner Brothers, where the two were under contract in the 1930s and '40s, the actresses became bitter rivals, competing for plum roles, studio publicity and sometimes men. The acid-tongued Davis once said of Crawford, "I wouldn't piss on her if she was on fire." Crawford's feelings toward Davis were no less acrimonious, and weren't helped by Davis' petty needling of Crawford throughout *Baby Jane*'s production. Among other affronts to Crawford, then a board member of Pepsi, was Davis' demand that a Coca-Cola vending machine be installed on the set. The two stars' hatred for each other radiates from almost every frame, as the on-screen tension ratchets up to pressure-cooker levels.

The film opens with a 18-minute pre-credit preamble, depicting Jane's youthful vaudeville days, and her sister's subsequent rise to fame as a movie star. Alas, Blanche's career was cut short when she lost the use of her legs in a car accident. Police suspected, but were unable to prove, that Jane intentionally ran over her sister. Blanche, apparently, has been in Jane's care ever since, despite bouts of mental illness on Jane's part. Lately, a local TV station has been playing Blanche's movies, reviving interest in her career — and stoking the embers of Jane's psychotic jealousy.

She removes her sister's call bell and telephone, giving Jane complete control over Blanche, and then visits a succession of bizarre torments upon her. She withholds food from Blanche, and then serves her a dead parakeet and, later, a drowned rat. "You wouldn't be able to do all these awful things to me if I weren't still in this chair," Blanche sobs. Jane rolls her eyes. "But ya are, Blanche! Ya *are* in that chair!" she roars, Davis' voice full of sadistic delight.

Jane plans a delusional theatrical comeback, hiring an unctuous accompanist, Edwin Flagg (marvelously played by Victor Buono), and ordering re-creations of her old costumes. She returns from the costume shop and discovers that Blanche has crawled out of her wheelchair and down a flight of stairs to reach a telephone and try to call for help. In retaliation, Jane viciously kicks her helpless sister around the floor. (Davis took advantage of this sequence to deliver some real-life kicks, resulting in minor injuries to Crawford.) When the housekeeper, Elvira (Maidie Norman), tries to intervene, Jane sneaks up from behind and bashes in Elvira's head with a hammer.

For the film's finale, Jane drags her sister to the beach. While Blanche lies rolled up in a blanket, dying, Jane walks barefoot along the water's edge, plays with a bucket in the sand, bounces a ball with a few young girls and buys ice cream cones. When Blanche begs for Jane to call a doctor, again Jane covers her ears. "Please stop!" she cries, as if *she* were the injured one. And in a way she is: a once-proud woman demolished, reduced to a pathetic and grotesque parody of girlhood.

In this aspect, *Baby Jane* and its later imitators tap into something primal — not simply fear of an aging hag wielding a hammer (or a cleaver or an ax), but fear of aging itself, the chilling truth of our mortality. The show biz backdrop of *Baby Jane* brings other grim realities into sharp relief. In Hollywood, actresses' careers usually begin to falter once they reach age 40 (if not sooner), whereas their male co-stars can work into their 60s and beyond. Hollywood movies simply aren't written for older women, a problem that has, if anything, only worsened in the decades since *Baby Jane*.

Davis' performance ranks among the greatest performances of her legendary career. As the story (and Jane's madness) progresses, her character visibly regresses. Davis begins adopting childlike speech patterns and immature gestures (such as covering her ears to avoid hearing something unpleasant), taking on the demeanor of a petulant little girl. Crawford has the less-flashy role, but never fails to elicit sympathy — even when Blanche's own dark secrets eventually come to light. Nevertheless, to Crawford's undying indignation, only Davis earned a Best Actress Oscar nomination. The Academy also nominated Buono for Best Supporting Actor.

Director Robert Aldrich gives these characters, and this story, plenty of room to breathe (a full 134 minutes of running time), without allowing the suspense to flag or losing the lingering sense of menace. Ernest Haller's Oscar-nominated, high-contrast black-and-white cinematography lends the picture a starkness perfectly appropriate to this emotionally raw material.

In addition to earning her a tenth (and final) Oscar nomination, *Baby Jane* opened up a whole new realm of possible roles for Davis. She continued making movies for another 27 years, working practically up to her death from breast cancer in 1990, including appearances in a number of horror and borderline-horror projects, such as *Dead Ringer* (1964), *The Nanny* (1965), *Burnt Offerings* (1976), *Return from Witch Mountain* (1978) and *The Watcher in the Woods* (1980). For television, she made *Madame Sin* (1972), *Scream, Pretty Peggy* (1973) and *The Dark Secret of Harvest Home* (1978). Her final film was the horror-comedy misfire *Wicked Stepmother* (1989). Crawford also appeared in several subsequent shockers, including *Strait-Jacket* (1964), *I Saw What You Did* (1965), *Berserk!* (1968), the original *Night Gallery* TV movie (1969) and *Trog* (1970).

The blockbuster box office returns for *Baby Jane* spawned numerous copycats, many with similar titles, each featuring an aging actress as a demented killer. Producer/director William Castle hired Crawford to headline *Strait-Jacket*. Davis returned to this oeuvre for Aldrich's follow-up, *Hush, Hush Sweet Charlotte* (1965), co-starring with Olivia De Havilland (after Crawford bowed out). Later, Geraldine Page appeared in *What Ever Happened to Aunt Alice?* (1969), Debbie Reynolds and Shelley Winters co-starred in *What's the Matter with Helen?* (1971) and Agnes Moorehead headlined *Dear Dead Delilah* (1972). Although that list includes some enjoyable movies, none of its successors recaptured the lightning that electrified *Baby Jane*.

The Whip and the Body see *What*

The Widdenburn Horror see *House of the Black Death*

The Witches see *The Devil's Own*

Witchfinder General see *The Conqueror Worm*

The Witch's Curse (1962; Medallion; Italy)

Original Language Title: *Maciste all'Inferno*; Alternate Title: *Maciste in Hell*; Director: Riccardo Freda; Producers: Ermanno Donati, Luigi Carpentieri; Screenplay: Oreste Biancoli, Piero Pierotti (story: Eddy H. Given); Cinematographer: Riccardo Pallottini. Cast: Kirk Morris, Helene Chanel, Angelo Zanolli, Andrea Bosic, Vira Silenti.

AFTER THE FIRES OF HADES AND THE SLASHING FRENZY OF FEROCIOUS BEASTS THERE REMAINED ONLY THE VENOM OF *THE WITCH'S CURSE*... — ad line

---

Truly one of the oddest pepla (Italian muscleman movies) ever filmed, *The Witch's Curse* starts as a period witch-hunting movie (à la *The Con-*

queror Worm or *Mark of the Devil*) set in the 16th century, abruptly takes a 90 degree turn towards an Italo beef 'n' brawn fantasy, then periodically jogs back and forth across the two disparate directions!

One hundred years after a witch was burned in the Scottish village of Loch Laird, a cursed tree stands on the spot and seemingly drives all the hamlet's young maidens mad. When the witch's innocent descendent comes to town, the villagers rise up and accuse *her* of witchcraft. As she's about to be hanged, in rides Maciste (pronounced "My-Cheese-Steak") to rescue the innocent girl. Maciste then uproots the evil tree and descends into Hell itself, with the idea of finding the witch and forcing her to lift the curse from the village.

Though not a good peplum per se, *The Witch's Curse* is not a boring one either — if for nothing else than the jaw-dropping moment when a bare-chested, oiled-up, loincloth-and-sandal-wearing Greek muscleman suddenly rides into a sixteenth century Scottish village to bend iron bars and toss aside locals before rescuing a girl accused of practicing witchcraft! And none of the villagers even

The Witch's Curse (1962): one of the oddest — and most entertaining — peplums of the 1960s.

blink at this incongruous occurrence. Astounding. Then there's this ersatz Hercules' journey through Hades (a large cavern carpeted with fire pits and colored lights), in which the hunky hero encounters (and receives aid from) the tormented souls of classical Greek mythology: Sisyphis (who Maciste helps move his ever-crushing rock) and Prometheus (who Maciste temporarily rescues from that pesky entrails-eating eagle).

Of course, it becomes a bit wearisome watching the blandly beefy Kirk Morris (as Maciste) bulging and struggling to topple a tree, lift a boulder or force open a huge door over and over again. And, disappointingly, Maciste never encounters Lucifer himself (nor any of his demon minions, either). Instead, the Brawny One battles an ordinary lion (in Hell?!), a giant named (naturally) Goliath (with a buffed-up *midget* standing in for Morris when Maciste grapples with the supposed colossus), and, most amusingly, a stampede of longhorn steers (which Machiste holds at bay with an oversized stalagmite!). Hell hath no fury like a bovine scorned...

"I've always fought against evil and always won," Maciste answers when warned against taking on Hell itself. And those viewers with a taste for the truly outré in their sword and sandal sagas will here win right alongside their Hero too.

The Witch's Mirror (1960/68; Trans-International; Mexico; b&w) Original Language Title: *El Espejo de la Bruja*; Director: Chano Urueta, Paul Nagel (English language version; with his name misspelled as Nagle); Producer: Abel Salazar, K. Gordon Murray (English version); Screenplay: Alfredo Ruanova, Carlos E. Taboada; Cinematographer: Jorge Stahl, Jr. Cast: Rosita Arenas, Armando Calvo, Isabela Corona, Dian de Marco, Carlos Nieto, Alfredo W. Barron.

FREE FRIGHT PILLS so you can take it — ad line

One of the two-dozen Mexican horror movies from the 1950s and '60s that K. Gordon Murray imported, dubbed, and then dumped on unsuspecting American audiences, first via a series of bargain matinees and then through television, *The Witch's Mirror* stands out as one of the ... well, "best" may be too strong a word — perhaps "more unusual" would be a better term. It's an everything-but-the-graveyard-sink amalgam that actually holds one's interest — a boast not all of these south-of-the-border entries can make. (Note: In some cases, like with *The Witch's Mirror* and its co-feature *The Living Head*, which had their U.S.

theatrical premiere in Maryland on May 29, 1968, Murray released the film theatrically *after* it had already played on television!)

After a famous surgeon poisons his wife, his housekeeper, a witch (who even turns into a black cat at one point!), vows revenge, since the murdered woman was her goddaughter. Later, the doctor remarries, but the housekeeper uses her witch's mirror to summon the ghost of the first wife, who torments and finally disfigures the new bride. The doctor commits murder to obtain "raw materials" that will restore his new wife's beauty, but the vengeful spirit intervenes, and the doctor meets his just fate.

The Witch's Mirror seems somewhat (ahem) reflective of a Barbara Steele Italian horror movie—but without Steele's arresting presence or Bava's/Margheriti's/Freda's artistic touches. Even so, there's much in this *Mirror* to admire.

What sets this one above its Latino contemporaries is its creepy Gothic atmosphere (though set in "modern" day, the doc lives in a candle-lit castle[!] and frequents a particularly eerie graveyard) and synthesis of various tried-and-true horror staples. Apart from the witchcraft angle (including an appearance by Satan himself—as played by a shadow puppet) and the menace of a vengeful ghost, the movie offers elements of *Eyes Without a Face* (the doctor stealing cadavers and murdering women to obtain skin grafts), *Rebecca* (the new wife tormented by the memory—and ghost—of the old), and, amazingly, *Hands of Orlac*/*Mad Love*! This crops up in a subplot involving the wife's horribly burned hands. To correct this, the mad medico transplants—in a shockingly gruesome scene for the times—a murdered girl's hands onto the arms of his wife. The ghost, however, intervenes and replaces the fresh hands with her own ghostly members. The new wife, now with the hands of the old wife, finds that her new hands have a life of their own.... At the end the hands drop off her arms(!) and crawl up the back of the doctor's lab assistant to stab him!

Granted, *The Witch's Mirror* also offers the expected stiff acting and even stiffer dubbing and dialogue; but thanks to its outré plotting, the film avoids the deadly dull drawing room palaver that plagues so many of its brethren (including its execrable co-feature, *The Living Head*). And you have to admire a movie that casts a *Satan-worshipping witch* as the good guy.

(Note: *The Witch's Mirror* was reportedly popular enough in Mexico to warrant the publication of a photo-comic book tie-in!)

Mexican lobby card for one of the most unusual and entertaining south-of-the-border horrors of the decade, *The Witch's Mirror* (1960/68).

Witchcraft (1964; 20th Century–Fox; b&w) Director: Don Sharp; Producers: Robert L. Lippert and Jack Parsons; Screenplay: Harry Spalding; Cinematographer: Arthur Lavis. Cast: Lon Chaney, Jr., Jack Hedley, Jill Dixon, Viola Keats, Yvette Rees, David Weston, Diane Clare.

After 200 years in the grave ... they returned to reap BLOOD HAVOC—tagline

Director Don Sharp's *Witchcraft* is an expertly cut jewel of a B-movie, sparkling and full of fire.

Real estate developer Bill Lanier (Jack Hedley) reignites a centuries-old family feud with the neighboring Whitlock clan with his plan to build a new housing complex over the Whitlocks' ancestral graveyard. Blustery patriarch Morgan Whitlock (Lon Chaney, Jr.) turns apoplectic when unscrupulous contractor Myles Forrester (Barry Linehan), acting against Bill's instructions, bulldozes the headstones at the Whitlock cemetery. Not only does this tick off Morgan, but it releases from the grave Vanessa Whitlock (Yvette Rees), a witch who was buried alive 200 years earlier by Bill's ancestors, from the grave. Now she and Morgan plan to take vengeance on the Laniers through black magic. Morgan, using a voodoo doll, forces Forrester to drown himself in the bathtub; Vanessa begins making spectral appearances in and around the Laniers' manor house, which once belonged to the Whitlocks. Young lovers Todd Lanier (David Weston), Bill's younger brother, and Amy Whitlock (Diane Clare), Morgan's niece, find themselves trapped between the warring factions—a sort of Christian/wiccan Romeo and Juliet. Tensions (and deaths) mount, until finally Bill and Todd race to prevent Morgan and Vanessa from making a human sacrifice of Bill's wife Tracy (Jill Dixon).

Witchcraft's virtues are many, but paramount among them are Sharp's sure-handed, keen-eyed direction and Harry Spalding's efficient, punchy screenplay. Sharp, emphasizing cinematographer Arthur Lavis' chiaroscuro lighting designs, dots the film with striking deep-focus compositions. In one memorable early scene, for instance, Bill travels to the wrecked Whitlock family plot. It's dark. As Bill moves among the broken headstones, monuments jutting into view from both sides, his parked car's headlights shine in the background, the beams disappearing into fog. This artfully crafted shot not only offers uncommon pictorial beauty, but creates a sense of gathering unease that climaxes (just after Bill leaves) with Vanessa awakening within her despoiled tomb. Sharp also mounts the most unsettling black mass committed to celluloid since director Edgar Ulmer's *The Black Cat* (1934). Shot from Tracy's perspective from a doorway some feet away, the black-hooded witches gather in a circle, chanting incantations that remain mysterious and unintelligible, their faces glimpsed in flashes of flickering torchlight.

The director also keeps the pace brisk and elicits believable performances from his cast, even the irascible, alcoholic Chaney. Sharp and his performers benefit from Spalding's lean, punchy screenplay, which introduces a sizable cast of characters, establishes the centuries-old conflict and moves from one spine-tingling sequence to the next with remarkable economy and precision. Spalding and Sharp (one of the most underrated horror directors of the decade) would join forces once more for *Curse of the Fly* (1965), again with memorable results.

Although top-billed, Chaney's role amounts to an extended cameo. After making a showy entrance, he practically vanishes from the film until the climax. But he's quite good in his limited screen time, growling and glowering with convincing indignation. This is one of the actor's best performances of the decade, surpassed only by his amusing turn as Bruno the chauffeur in *Spider Baby* (1964/68). It's even more impressive since Sharp and other crew members acknowledged that Chaney drank heavily throughout the production. "We had to make sure his dialogue scenes were completed by lunchtime," Sharp said. "He was in a haze. He wasn't in full control, either mentally or in the technical side of his performance. I had to learn when he had reached his maximum and then settle for it. Also, the more quickly we got through his scenes, the less time he had in his dressing room with his bottle.... [And yet,] his broad strokes suited the character."

Ultimately, however, *Witchcraft*'s success hinges more on the more subtle work by Hedley as Bill, Dixon as Tracy and Weston and Clare as Todd and Amy, as well as the eerie screen presence of Rees as the deathless Vanessa Whitlock (assisted ably by Harold Fletcher's subtle makeup and Lavis' spooky lighting). "They were a splendid team of non-starry people whose ordinariness lent a great strength to the situation," Sharp said. "They were a lovely cast to work with."

Shot at Shepperton Studios on a tight budget for B-movie maven Robert Lippert, *Witchcraft* seldom betrays its low-cost origins, thanks to the slick professionalism of Sharp, Lavis and production designer George Porvis. Indeed, Sharp believed the film's modest origins worked in its favor. "I have sometimes wondered if *Witchcraft* would have been so effective if I had had more time and money," the director said. "These constraints forced me to think of the most economically creative ways to shoot. This meant no special effects, no trickery, nothing that would require more time or money. We simply had to put the story on the screen and make the audience believe it. I was lucky to learn valuable lessons of invention through financial constraints."

Although *Witchcraft* earned mostly favorable reviews, it was not a box office success, perhaps because it made its debut on a twin bill with the horror-comedy clunker *The Horror of It All* (1964). And, unlike other sixties shockers that gained new popularity through TV reruns or home video, *Witchcraft* has never achieved the level of recognition it deserves. A minor marvel of quickie filmmaking, it remains one of the decade's best-kept secrets.

With quotes from: "Witchcraft" by Mark A. Miller, *Midnight Marque Actors Series: Lon Chaney, Jr.*

The World of the Vampires (1960/64; Cinematografica A.B.S.A.; Mexico; b&w) Original Language Title: *El Mundo de los Vampiros*; Director: Alfonso Corona Blake, Paul Nagel (English language version; name misspelled as 'Nagle'); Producer: Abel Salazar, K. Gordon Murray (English version); Screenplay: Alfred Salazar (story by Raul Zenteno and Jesus Velazquez); Cinematographer: Jack Draper. Cast: Maurice Garces, Erna Martha Bauman, Sylvia Fournier, William (Guillermo) Murray, Joseph Baviera, Yolanda Margain, Charles Nieto.

Incredible horror pursues victim after victim in the WORLD OF THE VAMPIRE — ad line

While, as the saying goes, "music hath charms to soothe the savage breast," it apparently also has the ability to both control and destroy vampires. At least that is the premise of this unique, atmospheric and sometimes ridiculous Mexican import. Produced by actor-filmmaker Abel Salazar (*The Brainiac* himself) for his Cinematografica A.B.S.A. film company, written by the producer's brother Alfred, and based on a story concocted by a former professional wrestler, Jesus Velazquez, *The World of the Vampires* turns out to be quite the musical one.

Vampiric Count Sergio Subotai (Argentinean actor Guillermo Murray making his Mexican movie debut) controls his legion of undead followers via music played on his grotesque pipe organ made of human bones ("They're dominated by music," observes one character). Subotai intends to "conquer all mankind" and "go forth and bring destruction to humanity." He also (less grandiosely) seeks revenge on the Kolman family, who staked his vampire ancestors years ago. To this end he vampirizes Kolman daughter Leonor (Erna Martha Baumann) and sets his sights on the father and second daughter. But family friend — and music expert — Rudolph (Maurice Garces, dubbed by voice director Paul Nagel) comes to the rescue with an "old Transylvanian melody that scares away vampires" and uses the fiend's own unholy pipe organ to defeat the undead horde.

Full marks for originality, if not necessarily for execution. For instance, the vampire vibes are often spoiled by the ludicrous, papier mache-level masks worn by Subotai's minions. (And the Count himself, when his bloodlust rises, sprouts extended fangs that a sabre-toothed tiger might envy.) After an atmospheric build-up that sees the sinister Subotai rise from his coffin and silently go about his nocturnal business, when the imposing vampire finally speaks, the banal, passionless, atonal dubbed voice that issues from his undead lips is quite a let-down. Then there's the laugh-out-loud scene in which the vampiric Leonor spies on the protagonists: In bat form (complete with visible wires) she keeps ducking behind a post whenever someone looks her way! At the close of this undead peek-a-boo session, the bat pops out once again, but on the nightflyer's body rests the (superimposed) head of Leonor — a sight both ludicrous and oddly unsettling.

Count Subotai (Guillermo Murray) controls his musically-inclined undead followers by playing a pipe organ made of human bones in *The World of the Vampires* (1960/64).

On the plus side, this *World* offers some wonderfully sinister settings, from the Count's cobwebbed castle to his dank underground cave, complete with flaming, skull-rimmed braziers and that magnificently macabre pipe organ — not to mention the expected fog-shrouded (studio) woodlands. One thing Mexican horror movies of this period excelled at was atmosphere, and *World* provides it with a capital 'A.'

One particularly memorable moment has the entranced Leonor gliding through the silhouetted forest in a disturbing midnight journey reminiscent of the classic cane field walk in *I Walked with a Zombie*. But, this being a Mexican monster movie with its own bizarre proclivities, the sequence comically closes with Leonor inexplicably ending her stately, graceful and creepy progress by breaking into a *sprint*!

But such eccentric peccadilloes are what sets Mexican horror films apart — and endears them to that special breed of aficionados enamored of these south-of-the-border oddities. For said cineastes, *The World of the Vampires* is definitely a world worth visiting.

The Wrestling Women vs. the Aztec Mummy

(1965; Churubusco–Azteca/Young America Productions; Mexico; b&w) Alternate Title: *Rock N' Roll Wrestling Women vs. the Aztec Mummy* (Rhino Video altered reissue version); Original Language Title: *Las Luchadoras Contra la Momia* (Wrestling Women vs. the Mummy); Director: Rene Cardona (English dubbing: Manuel San Fernando); Producer: William Calderon Stell (English version: K. Gordon Murray); Screenplay: Alfred Salazar. Cinematographer: Ezequiel Carrasco. Cast: Lorena Velazquez, Armand Silvestre, Elizabeth Campbell, Eugenia Saint Martin, Chucho Salinas, Raymond Bugarini, Victor Velazquez.

> Minion: "Those wrestling girls stopped us."
> Villain: "A curse on them!"
> — sample dialogue exchange

Spanish poster for the supremely odd Mexican mix of wrestling women and, well, Aztec mummies: *The Wrestling Women vs. the Aztec Mummy* (1965).

The Wrestling Women vs. the Aztec Mummy pits the wrasslin' heroines from producer William Calderon Stell's *Doctor of Doom* against the dreaded Aztec Mummy, last seen in *The Robot vs. the Aztec Mummy* (made seven years earlier by Stell, but not released in the U.S. until 1965). The combining of the two series resulted in an odd amalgam of crooks and monsters, with plenty of catfights along the way.

This entry features a Fu Manchu-wannabe called "the Black Dragon," who (along with his two evil judo-champion sisters) seeks the fabled treasure guarded by the Aztec Mummy. Our two professional wrestler beauties, Loretta (changed from Gloria in the earlier film; though still played by Lorena Velazquez) and the Golden Ruby (Elizabeth Campbell), along with their policemen boyfriends, oppose the Dragon and get to the mummy's tomb first, only to realize that the sacred breastplate which holds the secret of the treasure should remain where it belongs — under the watchful eye of the Aztec Mummy.

Much of *The Wrestling Women vs. the Aztec Mummy* moves about as slowly as, well, an Aztec mummy. In fact, it's a full hour before said monster first puts in an appearance — and then only briefly, since, upon seeing the creature rise from its tomb, the protagonists promptly run away! Fortunately, they take the sacred breastplate with them, so the Mummy follows them to the city (by transforming into a bat), where he manhandles (mummy-handles?) the Black Dragon's thugs and menaces the imperiled heroine until the coming dawn chases him back to his tomb.

The mummy has never looked better, and its unique and unsettling appearance (a vast improvement over the previous Aztec Mummy entries' rather unconvincing mask and body-suit) proves almost worth the wait, with his skull-like, parchment-skinned visage topped with wispy, matted hair, and his bony chest and leathery arms conjuring up images of the grave. And director Rene Cardona makes the most of this unique monster, offering shots of the mummy's desiccated legs and feet advancing through the darkened pyramid, shuffling inexorably through the shadows, its hideous countenance emerging from the blackness in a startling shock.

Intriguingly, this final entry in the Aztec Mummy series made several significant changes to the titular terror (besides improving upon his appearance). He is now a sorcerer, "cursed for daring to love a sacrificial virgin," who can transform himself into a (rubber) bat or a (real) tarantula (he possessed no such powers in the previous three films); and, like a vampire, he must return to his tomb to sleep during the day.

In order to finally reach the anticipated mummy mayhem, however, the viewer must wade through scene after scene of tedious talk—complete with risible dialogue ("The plan that Dr. Tracy worked out was for each of us to work alone so that we could defend ourselves." Right—*that* is clever...). Unfunny comic relief and lackluster encounters between the fist-throwing, body-blocking wrasslin' women and the Dragon's business-suited henchmen further weigh down the torpid proceedings. Two well-shot wrestling bouts—featuring varied angles, quick editing and even some hand-held photography—add a bit of excitement, but when the de rigeur staged wrestling matches prove to be a *highlight*, you know that the film is in trouble. (The gorgeous Lorena Velasquez was no wrestler, and was doubled in these sequences by a professional—which failed to please her. Interviewed for Britain's *Incredibly Strange Film Show* in 1989, she complained, "I had a double, and my double was a fat woman so I hate her [laughs]. I was just there in the close-ups.")

For the patient viewer, the picture finally kicks into gear for the last 20 minutes (after the Mummy rises), marking a vast improvement over the previous tedious hour; but in the end one can't help but wish that *The Wrestling Women vs. the Aztec Mummy* featured less Wrestling and more Mummy.

X—The Man with the X-Ray Eyes (1963; AIP)

Alternate Title: *The Man with the X-ray Eyes* (UK). Director/Producer: Roger Corman; Screenplay: Robert Dillon, Robert Russell; Cinematographer: Floyd Crosby. Cast: Ray Milland, Diana Van Der Vlis, Harold J. Stone, John Hoyt, Don Rickles.

HE STRIPPED SOULS AS BARE AS BODIES!
—ad line

There's no question that Roger Corman made a major contribution to '60s horror with his thoughtful, well-crafted Poe series. But in the midst of these Gothic horrors, Corman also created a thoughtful, well-crafted modern-day horror in the form of *X—The Man with the X-Ray Eyes*.

Ray Milland plays Dr. James Xavier, who develops a special eye drop formula to give him X-ray vision. After increasing the dosage and nearly going insane, he accidentally kills a colleague and hides out as "Mentalo" at a pier-side carnival. The show's greedy owner (Don Rickles) exploits Xavier first as a mind-reader, then as a "healer" (Xavier can see inside his patients' bodies to diagnose their illnesses). Continuing to up the dosage, Xavier ultimately sees things that Man was never *meant* to see (the very heart of the universe and "the Eye that sees us all") ... with disastrous results.

As so many AIP films did, *X* began simply as a title. "[AIP production head] Jim

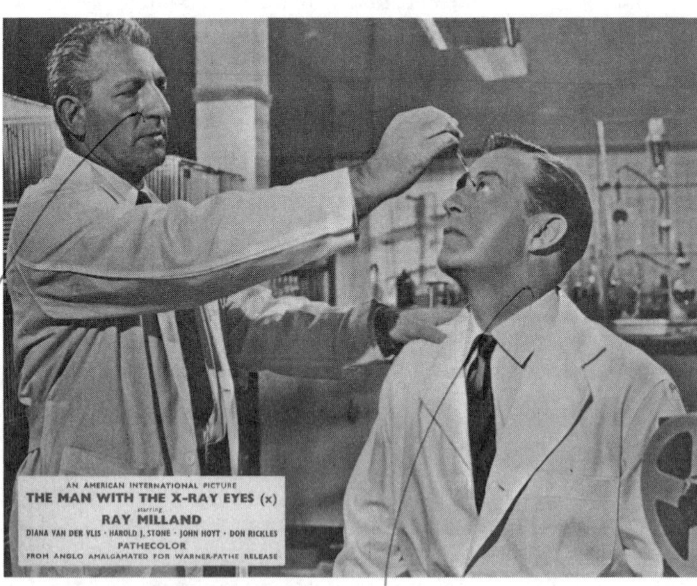

Dr. Brant (Harold J. Stone) administers the experimental eye drops that transforms Dr. Xavier (Ray Milland) into *X—The Man with the X-Ray Eyes* (1963) (British front-of-house still).

Nicholson told me, as he often did over lunch," recounted Corman in his autobiography, "that he had a title in search of a movie.... We threw ideas around over the next day or two— a jazz musician on weird drugs, a criminal who uses X-ray vision for robberies. They seemed like dead end stories. Then it hit me that the most logical direction was a medical researcher."

Corman shot for three weeks on a budget "between $200,000 and $300,000, with Ray Milland getting a big portion of the budget." Initially reluctant to accept the assignment ("I felt we were not going to be able to photograph what Xavier could see, and that the audience would be cheated," Corman told author Mark Thomas McGee), Nicholson's enthusiasm won him over. To show what "Xavier could see," Corman utilized an optical process dubbed "Spectorama." According to the film's pressbook, "Through a patented arrangement of prisms, light images are bent and color changes with the resulting distortions appearing to be impressionistic paintings in motion." Or, more aptly, out-of-focus, brightly colored blobs. Though not always convincing, the effects are at least colorfully striking. Then there's the expected party pieces, such as Xavier suddenly able to see beneath people's clothing (the nude participants strategically placed for our viewing protection, of course). Milland's bemused yet delighted attitude towards this revealing development lifts the scene out of the realm of exploitation into comedy.

Throughout the film Milland perfectly captures the mix of scientific curiosity and hubris that leads his character on his dark journey into unending light. Seeing even through his eyelids, at one point he cries, "Oh lord, I'd give anything, *anything* to have *dark*!" his hitherto self-assuredness turning to anguish.

X was "seen as an important film," wrote Corman. "Later I realized it was the concept that was important: a researcher moving through science toward a religious mystical experience." Corman compared his film to the later *2001: A Space Odyssey*, "in that there is at the end of the odyssey an hallucinogenic, mystical vision of light and motion. Kubrick's trip was through space; X's was interior." It is indeed this "odyssey" that sets the movie apart. Much like the previous decade's *The Incredible Shrinking Man*, it's the character's solitary journey into the unknown, in which ordinary objects become frightening and alien (even, in Xavier's case, other human beings—who become walking, talking horrific masses of exposed muscle and bone), that captivates the viewer. And, like *Shrinking Man*, it's the protagonist's final confrontation with the infinite that generates the film's resonance (though of a more downbeat nature in *X*— as reflecting the changing tone of cinema *and* society in the 1960s).

Anoraks can have fun playing Spot-the-Players, as Corman casts various '50s horror/sci-fi stalwarts and stock-company regulars in supporting roles and bit parts. There's Morris Ankrum (*Earth vs. the Flying Saucers*) in a blink-and-you'll-miss-him role of the cranky Hospital head; John Hoyt (*Attack of the Puppet People*) as an arrogant surgeon; Barboura Morris (*A Bucket of Blood*) in a bit part as a nurse; Dick Miller and Jonathan Haze (*Little Shop of Horrors*) as sideshow hecklers; and John Dierkes (*The Thing*) as the tent revival preacher who exhorts, "If thine eye offends thee, pluck it out!"

Thought-provoking, multi-layered and involving, *X— The Man with the X-Ray Eyes* remains a unique Roger Corman cinematic achievement.

With quotes from: *How I Made a Hundred Movies in Hollywood and Never Lost a Dime*, by Roger Corman, with Jim Jerome; *Faster and Furiouser*, by Mark Thomas McGee; *X— The Man with the X-Ray Eyes* pressbook, American International Pictures, 1963.

Yotsuya Ghost Story see *Illusion of Blood*

3

More Movies

The preceding section of this book covered all horror films (as well as fantasy and science fiction films with prominent horror elements) released theatrically in the U.S. during the 1960s.

This section provides brief overviews of movies excluded from the preceding section because they are commonly categorized as "pure" sci-fi or fantasy (lacking significant horror elements) or because the movie was produced during the 1960s but did not receive a U.S. theatrical release until the 1970s or later. Also included here are films released directly to television in America (but not *made* for TV). With a few (noted) exceptions, made-for-TV productions are not included. Also, while horror-comedy hybrids are included, science fiction–comedy hybrids have been excluded. Finally, horror films produced elsewhere in the world that never received an official (non-bootleg) U.S. release — either theatrical, television or home video— also have been omitted.

Adventure in Takla Makan (1965; Toho; Japan) Original Language Title: *Kiganjo no Boken.* Even though it stars the great Toshiro Mifune, this remains one of the most obscure Japanese fantasy films of the 1960s. Virtually forgotten today and unavailable for review, *Adventure in Takla Makan* is a period piece, filmed partially in Iran, about a shipwrecked sailor (Mifune) who assists a priest on a quest to recover the sacred remains of the Buddha. The plot apparently involves some fantasy elements, as the duo face giant birds and an evil wizard. The film appeared briefly in American theaters, where it earned a gloomy review from *Variety*, and then apparently vanished — at least from the U.S. Several key members of the cast and crew of this film, including Mifune and director Senkichi Taniguchi, also worked on *The Lost World of Sinbad* (1963/65), which suggests that the unavailability of *Adventure in Takla Makan* is not a major loss.

The Adventures of Baron Munchausen see ***The Fabulous Baron Munchausen***

Against All Odds see ***Kiss and Kill***

Alien Terror see ***The Incredible Invasion***

Along with Ghosts (1969; Daiei; Japan) Original Language Title: *Tokaido Obake Dochu* (Journey Along Tokaido Road), Alternate Title (DVD): *Yokai Monsters 3: Along with Ghosts.* This entry concludes Daiei's Yokai Monsters series, a trilogy of oddball Japanese ghost stories brimming with bizarre-looking monsters. This time, the "apparitions" help a young girl avenge the murder of her grandfather and rescue her father from captivity. *Along with Ghosts* remains too offbeat to have wide appeal, but viewers with a taste for the truly outlandish may enjoy it, along with the other Yokai Monsters features (*Spook Warfare* and *100 Monsters*). None of the trio received a general theatrical release in the U.S., but all three arrived in American via DVD in 2003.

Alphaville (1965; Athos/Janus; France; b&w) Original Title: *Alphaville, une Étrange Aventure de Lemmy Caution* (Alphaville, a Strange Adventure of Lemmy Caution). Lemmy Caution (Eddie Constantine), Secret Agent 003 from the Outlands, arrives in the capital city of Alphaville on a mission to kidnap or kill Professor Nosferatu (Howard Vernon), who has invented a death ray. While in Alphaville, Caution encounters robot-like women who offer sex the same way they dispense coffee; emotionless engineers who are programmed by their computer (instead of the other way around); and the all-powerful Alpha 60 electronic brain, which controls the city and spouts philosophy in a mechanized Cookie Monster voice. Nouvelle Vague firebrand Jean-Luc Godard dabbled in many genres during the 1960s. *Alphaville* represents the director's typically bizarre, off-kilter take on science fiction. It's a tongue-in-cheek, Orwellian tale set in a world where words such as "why" and "conscience" have been forbidden, and where a man is executed (stabbed to death in a pool by a team of knife-wielding synchronized swimmers, while onlookers applaud) because he cried over his wife's death. Despite its futuristic setting, the picture's visual sensibility is pure film noir, and its tone shifts between hard boiled and surreal, with philosophical chit-chat about poetry punctuated by spasms of violence. It also boasts an extremely unorthodox car chase sequence incorporating random negative exposures. While certainly not for every viewer (anyone adamant about logical, linear narrative will quickly grow exasperated), the quirky but compelling *Alphaville* remains one of Godard's most accessible movies. For added enjoyment, try comparing this film to *Fahrenheit 451* (1966), a similarly dystopian sci-fi thriller directed by Godard's rival, François Truffaut.

A Nation At His Mercy!!!
The Amazing
TRANSPARENT MAN
starring MARGUERITE CHAPMAN · DOUGLAS KENNEDY · JAMES GRIFFITH

The Amazing Transparent Man (1960; MCP; b&w) Edgar G. Ulmer — revered for *The Black Cat* (1934), *Bluebeard* (1944) and *The Man from Planet X* (1951) — directed this low-budget, offbeat *film noir*-science fiction hybrid. Krenner (James Griffith), a ruthless master criminal, busts an ace safecracker (Douglas Kennedy) out of prison and forces him to steal fissionable material for illegal experiments aimed at creating an army of invisible soldiers. Screenwriter Jack Lewis' scenario focuses more on its cast of back-stabbing crooks and their schemes to double-cross one another than on the sci-fi or horror possibilities of the story. More than half of the picture's skimpy 58-minute runtime elapses before the first invisible man appears (or, rather, disappears). So, despite its title, *The Amazing Transparent Man* plays more like *Kiss Me Deadly* than *The Invisible Man* (without being anywhere near as good as either of those classics). As always Ulmer's craftsmanship remains impeccable. He makes atmospheric use of high-contrast lighting, low-angle camera setups and other simple yet effective devices, but, working with flimsy material and threadbare production values, *Transparent Man* does not rank among Ulmer's most durable creations.

The Amphibian Man (1960; Ministerstvo Kinematografii; U.S.S.R.) Original Language Title: *Chelovek-Amfibiya*. This Russian sci-fi/fantasy film was released to U.S. television in 1964 where it turned up sporadically on various "creature feature" programs—despite the fact it's more a fantastical love story than a monster movie. Based on the novel of the same name by renowned Russian sci-fi author Aleksandr Belyayev, *The Amphibian Man* has a brilliant scientist cure his son of a lung disease via a shark-gill transplant, resulting in the boy's ability to breathe underwater. The locals in this coastal town (resembling Spain) label this mysterious creature (sporting a shiny, scaly wet-suit; odd pop-eyed goggles; and shark-fin headgear) "the Sea Devil." But the innocent boy (who's at a loss in the cruel, money-hungry world above) simply seeks human companionship, finding it in the love of a local girl about to marry against her will. With some beautiful underwater photography, impressive production values (including the scientist's cliff-side dwelling/laboratory, complete with a bubble-like elevator), earnest acting, and involving human drama, *The Amphibian Man* stands as a unique, romantic take on the *Creature from the Black Lagoon* theme. The story was adapted and remade in 2004 as a Russian telemovie called *The Amphibious Man*.

An Angel for Satan (1966; Italy; b&w) Original Language Title: *Un Angelo per Satana*. Barbara Steele's final (of nine!) 1960s Eurohorrors went unreleased outside of its native Italy. It's the Gothic period tale of a sculptor (Anthony Steffan) who arrives at a large estate to restore an ancient statue recovered from the nearby lake. The local villagers live in fear of the statue's 200-year-old "curse," placed upon it by a homely woman who'd murdered her own beautiful sister out of bitter

The Angel for Satan herself: Barbara Steele in a 1960s publicity photograph for *An Angel for Satan*.

jealousy. When the estate's rightful heir (Steele) returns home to claim her inheritance, the sculptor notes that she bears an uncanny likeness to the statue. Soon a rash of mysterious deaths has the villagers talking of witchcraft. Given its intriguing storyline (complete with a clever twist to the tale), beautiful cinematography and a particularly alluring—and dangerous—performance by Steele (whose provocative presence inspires lust, madness and murder), it's a pity that an English-language version didn't surface sooner (a subtitled DVD finally emerged in 2009).

Any Body ... Any Way see *Behind Locked Doors*

The Aqua Sex see *The Mermaids of Tiburon*

Around the World Under the Sea (1966; MGM) This undersea adventure film follows a small team of scientists (led by Lloyd Bridges) on an experimental submarine planting earthquake censor devices on the bottom of the sea. The team swims into horrific waters for one sequence in which a giant moray eel menaces first a diver and then the sub itself (via rear-screen projection and modelwork). Since this is an Ivan Tors production (*Riders to the Stars, Seahunt, Flipper*), it focuses more on (pseudo)science and squeaky-clean characters than excitement and suspense. Fortunately, the underwater sequences (directed by Ricou Browning, the *Creature from the Black Lagoon* himself) at least offer something pretty to look at (besides nominal female lead Shirley Eaton).

American one-sheet poster for *Assignment Outer Space* (1961).

Assignment Istanbul see *The Castle of Fu Manchu*

Assignment Outerspace (1961; Titanus/AIP; Italy) Alternate Title: *Space Men.* This early Italian sci-fi entry remains one of the decade's more serious attempts to portray space travel in a realistic fashion. Unfortunately, the budget, script and special effects aren't up to this lofty goal. The events take place entirely in space or on space stations, with the convoluted plot revolving around a reporter risking his life to stop a runaway rocket about to destroy the Earth. Via unusual camera angles and photography, first-time director Antonio Margheriti creates a tight, claustrophobic feeling, marking a sharp contrast to the vast emptiness of space. Though shot in color (fairly rare in a low-budget feature of the early '60s), it might just as well have been black and white; instead of the bright, stunning visual atmosphere often found in other Italian SF (Mario Bava's *Planet of the Vampires* being a prime example), this film opts for silvers and grays as the predominant color scheme, making it much less interesting visually. But at least the astronauts in this movie have to contend realistically with the lack of gravity in space (refreshing, since most other SF films cavalierly gloss over this serious bit of astrophysics).

Assignment Terror (1969/72; AIP; Spain/West Germany/Italy) Original Language Title: *Los Monstruos del Terror* (*El Hombre Que Vino de Ummo*). Alternate Titles: *Dracula Versus Frankenstein*; *Reincarnator*. Alien Michael Rennie (a long way from Klaatu in *The Day the Earth Stood Still*) comes to Earth from the planet Ummo on a mission to destroy the human race by unleashing all the classic monsters upon humanity: Dracula, the Frankenstein Monster, the Werewolf and the Mummy. (Spanish screenwriter/co-star Paul Naschy also included the Golem in his original script, but the production had to pare down the monster roster for financial reasons.) With such an outré plot like this, the only hope for the viewer is to squeeze a bit of boffo fun out of the bizarre proceedings—helped along by its dated go-go dancers, mini-skirts, sideburns, bright garish lights and generic psychedelic music. Unfortunately, the monsters aren't much to look at. Waldemar the Werewolf (Naschy in his third—of *eleven*—lycanthropic outings) appears acceptable in his Lon Chaney, Jr.–style getup. The Living Mummy, however, from the way his head is bandaged, looks more like a man with a splitting headache than a 3000-year-old undying monster. The Frankenstein Monster (referred to as the "Franksillian Monster" for no discernible reason) is a ridiculous ersatz copy of the Universal creation (the actor, in green face and half-closed eyes, looks more like a fatigued costume party-goer than a creature stitched together from dead bodies). One bright spot appears near the end, however, when we are treated to the novel sight

The busy artwork on this colorful Mexican lobby card for the Spanish/West German/Italian co-production *Assignment Terror* (scripted by and starring Paul Naschy, pictured at left in photo) shamelessly steals images of Boris Karloff's Frankenstein Monster, Edward Van Sloan's Dr. Waldeman (both from the 1931 *Frankenstein*), and Christopher Lee's Dracula (from *Horror of Dracula*, 1958).

of a Werewolf battling a Mummy — a first in monster history and an exciting match-up for that monster-loving inner child in all of us. The scariest part of this imported oddity (which didn't make it to American shores until 1972) is the fact that it was Michael Rennie's last genre outing. Poor Michael, let's give one last "Klaatu barada nikto" before we bring the curtain down.

At Midnight I'll Take Your Soul (1963; Paranagua Cinematografica; Brazil; b&w) Original Language Title: *A Meia-Noite Levarei Sua Alma*. In the early 1960s, Brazilian filmmaker Jose Mojica Marins wanted to make a horror movie (the first from that country), but could find no one suitable — or willing — to play the lead. So he himself donned a top hat, cape, and his best black suit to become Ze do Caixao (loosely translated as "Coffin Joe"), an evil and brutal atheist undertaker obsessed with siring an heir. Inspiring fear through tormenting and torturing all those around him, the blasphemous Ze (he rails against the idea of god, and even eats meat on Fridays!) finally meets his comeuppance on the "Night of the Dead" courtesy of his victims' vengeful spirits. Surprisingly well-photographed and extremely atmospheric, the mostly set-bound low-budget production (reportedly filmed on short ends and scraps) generates a uniquely macabre air, mixing hoary horror clichés (including a cackling witch who speaks directly at the camera) with startling brutality and blasphemies (such as Ze using his overlong fingernails to literally poke out the eyes of one victim, or lifting a miniature crown of thorns from a religious icon to smash into the face of another). The film was so popular in Brazil that it inspired a series of loosely connected pictures featuring Marins as Ze (including *This Night I'll Possess Your Corpse* and *The Strange World of Zé do Caixão*). Coffin Joe finally made his way to America nearly three decades later via video.

Atlantis, the Lost Continent (1961; MGM) In ancient times, Greek fisherman Demetrios (Sal Ponti) rescues an Atlantean princess, Antillia (Joyce Taylor), whom he discovers adrift on a raft. The spoiled, ungrateful princess forces Demetrios to risk his life to return her to her father's kingdom. They fall in love during the voyage but once they arrive in Atlantis, Antillia's jealous suitor, Zaren (John Dall), throws Demetrios into slavery. Zaren has usurped power from Antillia's weak-willed father and plans to con-

Ancient dress meets futuristic furnishings in *Atlantis, the Lost Continent* (1961). Pictured: Anthony Hall (aka Sal Ponti) and Joyce Taylor.

quer the world using Atlantis' advanced weapons, including a giant crystal that channels solar power into a laser-like death ray. It's hard to believe this corny, cut-rate fantasy came from legendary producer-director George Pal (maker of *War of the Worlds* [1953], *The Time Machine* [1960], etc.). *Atlantis, the Lost Continent* is by far Pal's worst movie — preachy, puffed-up and predictable, right down to its inescapable slave-revolt-and-volcanic-eruption finale. Aside from a couple of isolated moments — such as an alchemist turning slaves into farm animals (one bull-man is seen sporting horns and a bovine snout) or Demetrios' battle with a giant gladiator in a pit full of hot coals — the picture offers little excitement, focusing instead on palace intrigues, sappy romantic interludes and theological navel-gazing. The casts' laughable performances further undercut the picture's shaky credibility, particularly its over-emotive romantic leads (Ponti and Taylor) and a woefully miscast Edward Platt, playing high priest who pooh-poohs the graven temple gods and espouses proto Judeo-Christian beliefs. But the film's gravest failing is that its sets, costumes and even its number of extras are all far below par for a story on this scale. Pal tries to mask these deficiencies by inserting copious stock footage from *Quo Vadis* (1951), but the resulting contrasts only make *Atlantis, The Lost Continent* seem more ridiculous.

Atlas Against the Cyclops (1961/63; Medallion; Italy) Original Language Title: *Maciste nella Terra dei Ciclopi.* Alternate Titles: *Atlas in the Land of the Cyclops* (TV), *Maciste vs. the Cyclops, Maciste in the Land of the Cyclops, Monster from the Unknown World* (UK). The evil queen of Sadok must find the only surviving son of Ulysses and feed it to the Cyclops (kept in a pit on an island) in order to lift some nebulous "curse." But the infant has escaped her murdering soldiers and enjoys the protection of Maciste (the U.S. distributors changed his name to "Atlas" when they re-titled the film, but apparently neglected to tell the dubbing actors), a hero "endowed with fantastic, incredible strength." Such a scenario sounds far more exciting than the bland sword-and-sandal shenanigans that follow, since most of the film's overlong 100 minutes consist of tedious scenes of horseback riding, wrestling with a listless lion (alternating shots of an obviously drugged animal with a stuffed big cat), or Maciste displaying his prodigious strength by carrying an oversized clay pot down some stairs(!). As Maciste, Colorado-born Gordon Mitchell (who enjoyed a prolific Euro-career making gladiator movies and Spaghetti Westerns) is appropriately brawny, but his naïve expressions and stupid grins (not to mention the slow, toneless dubbing) make him seem like a simpleton. You half expect him to ask someone to "tell about the rabbits, George...." Disappointingly, the sole fantastical element — the Cyclops (looking like a one-eyed caveman) — only shows up for the last five minutes, and is easily overcome by Maciste (despite the fact that the two never appear to inhabit the same film frame!). One of the poorer pepla, *Atlas* promises so much but delivers so little.

Atlas in the Land of Cyclops see *Atlas Against the Cyclops*

Atomic Rulers (1957/64; ShinToho/AIP-TV; Japan) Alternate (home video) Title: *Atomic Rulers of the World.* The adventures of Starman (Ken Utsui) begin here. This was the first of four feature-length films compiled from nine hour-long Starman adventures originally released in Japan, where the title character was known as "Supergiant." The titular superhero battles a gang of underworld thugs who are attempting to obtain an atomic weapon. Produced on minuscule budgets and released directly to TV in America, these movies offered action, action and more action. Those interested in coherent plots, believable characters, or production values of any sort are advised to keep looking.

Atomic Rulers of the World see *Atomic Rulers*

Atomic War Bride (1960; Jadran Film/United Screen Arts; Yugoslavia; b&w); Original Language Title: *Rat* (War). Part parody (though whether intentional or not remains in question), part political polemic, and all melodrama, the Yugoslavian production *Atomic War Bride* offers horror only at the end (but what a shattering ending it is). The marriage ceremony of John and Maria, two bland yet attractive Aryan twenty-somethings, is interrupted by the announcement of war and a subsequent attack by invading aircraft (one even tries to strafe our not-quite-married couple as they flee across a field!). John is forcibly conscripted into the army, but soon develops a strong sense of pacifism, resulting in him facing a firing squad. But wait, a nuclear attack has been launched.... Is it a reprieve for John or the Final Solution for all? Filmed on still-ruined bomb sites left over from World War II, this bland and simplistic anti-war import alternates between comical scenes (government officials handing out ponchos to protect the populace from radiation — with John comically running around trying to wriggle under other people's ponchos, as his is defective[!]; John's boot-camp "camouflage training" showing the recruits sticking shrubbery into their rifle barrels and posing like trees[!!]) and serious dramatics (a man attempting suicide after the communal television reveals that his own country dropped nuclear bombs on the enemy; people wandering about the rubble-strewn wasteland). It never gels as a whole, but a few isolated scenes make an impact — such as a dazed man, searching the rubble, asking John if he's seen a leg ("It's my daughter's"), and the powerful, downbeat finale.

Attack from Space (1957–58/64; ShinToho/AIP-TV) Ken Utsui returns as Starman in the second of four feature films starring the popular Japanese superhero. This installment takes place almost entirely in outer space, as Starman foils an invasion attempt by the fearsome "Spherions." Just as action-packed and infantile as the original installment, if not more so, this entry is notable for its blatant disregard for elementary science. For example, at one point, characters walk around the exterior of a space station, without benefit of space suits! Preceded by *Atomic Rulers* (1957/64) and followed by *Invaders from Space* (1957/64).

Attack of the Monsters (1969; Daiei/AIP-TV; Japan) Alternate Title: *Gamera vs Guiron.* Original Language Title: *Gamera tai Daiakuju Giron.* The fifth installment in Daiei's Gamera series remains as puerile and slipshod as all the others, yet emerges as one of the more tolerable entries. Unlike its immediate predecessor, *Destroy All Planets* (1968), *Attack of the Monsters* makes little use of stock footage, and contains several wacky but enjoyable elements. Two boys discover a flying saucer and are whisked off to "Terra," a twin planet of Earth that revolves in synchronous orbit on the far side of the sun. Terra is a desolate world where giant monsters roam, and its only human inhabitants appear to be two beautiful young women, Barbella and Florbella, who are planning to take over Earth. They use the captured boys to lure Gamera to Terra so their *kaiju* "watchdog," Guiron, can (they hope) defeat him. Guiron is a curious-looking four-legged creature with a giant knife for a nose. For a warm-up, Guiron battles Gaos, the giant vampire bat from *Return of the Giant Monsters* (1967), who Barbella and Florbella apparently imported from Earth. Guiron not only defeats the Gaos, but decapitates him and literally chops him to bits! At 90 minutes, *Attack of the Monsters* runs about 20 minutes too long, but provides at least a smattering of fun along the way. This film was initially released to American television by AIP in a sanitized form. When producer Sandy Frank issued it on home video under the title *Gamera vs. Guiron*, he restored some choice moments (including Guiron dicing up Gaos), but also panned and scanned the film clumsily and re-dubbed it with amateurish, flat-affect vocal "performances" full of weird pauses. Daiei's Gamera series continued into the 1970s with two more movies that mercifully fall outside the scope of this book. The character reappeared in 1980 with the dreadful *Super Monster Gamera* and again in 1995 with *Gamera: Guardian of the Universe.* The 1995 film, which re-launched the franchise, is widely regarded as a latter-day *kaiju eiga* masterpiece and spawned two sequels (so far).

Attack of the Mushroom People (1963/65; Toho/AIP-TV; Japan) Original Language Title: *Matango.* The American title suggests something along the lines of *Attack of the Killer Tomatoes* (1978), but don't let that fool you. This is director Ishiro Honda's best film, a minor masterpiece of sustained suspense and eerie otherworldliness. A group of seven boaters are trapped on a remote, fog-shrouded island when their yacht is damaged in a storm. The castaways (which include a skipper, a sailor, a female movie star, a girl-next-door type, a professor and a millionaire) discover a huge, rotting research ship, which has also washed ashore. On the ship, they find a rifle and a limited supply of tinned food. The only other source of sustenance seems to be mysterious mushrooms, which grow in abundance. However, the mushrooms cause bizarre and frightening mental and physical changes in those who eat them. As hunger sets in, the tenuous social order of the group begins to break down. *Matango*, as it was known in Japan, is the kind of movie viewers would expect from George Romero, not from Honda. This is an intense, a quietly disturbing study of the way human beings turn on one another in times of crisis, and it builds to a haunting and unusual (for Toho) downbeat finale. Honda's visuals are fluid and evocative, full of darting something-or-others, barely glimpsed through the shadows and fog. And the director elicits uniformly excellent performances from his ensemble cast. The Mushroom People, who appear late in the story, look like something from the world of Sid and Marty Krofft — but in context, that only makes them seem creepier. Unfortunately, American producers didn't know quite what to make of this picture, which was so different from the kind of light-hearted giant monster fare it was used to receiving from Toho. As a result, *Matango* never received a U.S. theatrical release. Instead, it was saddled with its absurd American title and issued directly to TV, where much of its power was lost in dubbing and cropping. The original version, which was finally released to DVD in the U.S. in 2005, remains one of the finest horrors ever made in Japan.

The Bamboo Saucer (1968; World Entertainment Corp.) A hot-shot test pilot (Dan Duryea), previously "buzzed" by a flying saucer, is sent on a secret mission to rural Red China to investigate a reported alien craft that landed in a ruined monastery there. (The saucer's two "humanoid" pilots died soon after leaving the ship, presumably due to lack of natural immunities, and were cremated by the superstitious villagers, leaving the investigators—and the viewers—disappointingly in the dark about their origins and appearance.) On the way, the Americans meet up with a small band of Russians with the same idea—capture or destroy the saucer. This tedious Cold War political scare film, complete with some East-West cooperation against the hated Asian threat (not to mention a clichéd Anglo-Russo budding romance subplot), features the flying saucer merely as a sci-fi McGuffin. Dragging its political feet throughout most of the running time, *The Bamboo Saucer* only takes flight when the alien craft does (via some uneven but intermittently impressive special effects courtesy of former Universal ace John P. Fulton), as it carries our hapless hero and heroine into outer space at the end.

Barbarella (1968; Paramount; France/Italy) Based on the French comic strip by Jean-Claude Forrest, this silly sci-fi send-up strewn with sixties sexual sensibilities and psychedelica is charming in its way, thanks primarily to the alluring innocence of, and occasional comic aside from, Jane Fonda in the title role. Apart from performing a (tasteful) free fall strip tease in zero gravity, Fonda's beautiful intergalactic space agent (who travels in a shag-carpeted spaceship) must face such tongue-in-cheek perils as deadly mechanical dolls, the "Biting Bird Cage," and an orgasmic organ (of the musical variety).

Baron Munchausen see ***The Fabulous Baron Munchausen***

Battle Beneath the Earth (1967/68, MGM) Rogue red Chinese nationals with super-scientific laser drill contraptions honeycomb the U.S. with tunnels and begin attacking from below in this paranoid science fiction yarn. It's up to heroic naval commander Jonathan Shaw (Kerwin Mathews) and former laughing-stock scientist Arnold Kramer (Peter Arne) to save America. This risible premise is further compromised by appallingly cheap production values (the super-advanced Chinese drill looks like a Tonka toy) and torturously slow pacing. Most of the "action" in *Battle Beneath the Earth* consists of tense briefings with Shaw, Kramer and military brass, or Shaw and his men creeping stealthily through fake-looking underground tunnels, or Kramer poring over some technical problem in the lab. These yawn-inducing passages are occasionally interrupted by brief, poorly staged fight scenes, played out on tiny soundstages unconvincingly decorated to resemble caves. The chief villains—General Chan Lu and scientist Kengh Lee—are played by Caucasian actors (Martin Benson and Peter Elliott, respectively) in yellow-face makeup no more believable than those cave sets. *Battle Beneath the Earth* was the final film directed by Montgomery Tully, whose penultimate picture had been another sci-fi stinker, Amicus Productions' *The Terrornauts* (1967).

Battle Beyond the Sun (1959/1962; Mosfilm/AIP; U.S.S.R.) Original Title: *Nebo Zovyot.* Executive producer Roger Corman purchased the U.S. rights to the big-budget Soviet science fiction epic *Nebo Zovyot* and turned it over to his young protégé, Francis Ford Coppola, to be re-edited and dubbed for U.S. release. Coppola (on Corman's instructions) made extensive revisions. For starters, he trimmed the running time from 77 to 64 minutes. The original story had to do with heroic cosmonauts intercepting an alien space probe, but Coppola reshaped it into the tale of a race to Mars between two space programs (from the futuristic, post-nuclear war governments of North Hemis and South Hemis). Perhaps most significantly, Coppola removed the original's communist propaganda and replaced it with a message of cooperation and peace between rival nations. The dubbing and cutting is often clumsy, which might make the film hard to follow if the revised plot wasn't so predictable and formulaic. But even in this truncated and bastardized form, the *Nebo Zovyot* footage remains visually dazzling, with beautifully designed space ships and alien landscapes and special effects (mostly miniatures and traveling mattes) as skillful as—and more plentiful than—those from any classic American SF film of the 1950s or early '60s. In one unforgettable sequence, an astronaut witnesses a battle between two space monsters—one of them with what appears to be a shark's mouth arranged vertically on its belly, the other a headless creature with googly eyes at the end of long tendrils. (In fact, the sequence plays like a thinly veiled tussle between the Vagina Creature and a dangling-balled Penis Monster!) For sequences such as this, sci-fi buffs will find *Battle Beyond the Sun* worth a look.

Battle in Outer Space (1960; Toho/Columbia; Japan) Original Language Title: *Uchu Daisenso.* In *Battle*, helmed by *Godzilla*-director Inoshira Honda (with special effects by *Godzilla*-creator Eiji Tsuburaya), a series of catastrophic events are only a prelude to the impeding war waged by the alien "Natalians" in the stratospheres of Earth and the Moon with laser-like high-tech weaponry. Unfortunately, this space scenario sounds far more exciting than what shows up onscreen, as *Battle* becomes a dull, dull, dull exposition-packed, near alien-less mishmash (disappointingly, the Natalians appear only once—completely covered in bulky, human-like spacesuits). Even the much-touted battle sequences become repetitive and unconvincing. Amusingly, the alien Moon-base models resemble a big plastic pie surrounded by silver cups and saucers! Some impressive model work when a "space torpedo" hits the heart of NYC, while another takes out the Golden Gate Bridge (though this bit looks comparatively phony), are about the only respites from this *Boredom in Outer Space.*

Battle of the Worlds (1961/63; Topac Film Corp; Italy) Original Language Title: *Il Pianeta degli Uomini Spenti.* "A HOSTILE PLANET from outer space hurtling

American three-sheet poster for the Japanese import *Battle in Outer Space* (1960).

toward earth on a COLLISION COURSE!" shouted the film's poster in a one-phrase synopsis of this 1961 Italian sci-fier (released in the U.S. in '63). Antonio Margheriti (*Assignment Outerspace, Horror Castle, Castle of Blood*) directed this import programmer under his anglicized alias of Anthony Dawson. Here he had the added bonus of Claude Rains (making one of his last screen appearances) as his star. Rains plays a crotchety scientist who scribbles calculus equations on the sides of his greenhouse plant pots and ultimately solves the riddle of how to combat this invading planetoid and its automated death ray-dealing flying saucer emissaries. The laughably cheap effects often undermine the film's serious tone (tinfoil, plastic tubes and colored lights make up the planet's alien interiors; the saucers shoot literal cartoon laser beams; and the natural disasters caused by the planet's close proximity to Earth are shown solely through grainy black-and-white stock footage), but Rains manages to both create a solid character about which the film revolves *and* maintain his dignity (no easy task while wearing a silver lamé space suit).

The Beast see *Equinox*

The Beast That Killed Women (1965) One of fourteen "adults-only" features sexploitation specialist Barry Mahon made in 1965 alone(!), *The Beast That Killed Women* adds a sprinkling of horror to Mahon's typical nudist-camp antics (well, whatever "horror" can be conjured by a mangy gorilla skulking about the Florida palm fronds and attacking *one* woman anyway). Banal sequences of nudists sitting, walking, talking, swimming, square-dancing(!) or playing shuffleboard are only alleviated by slightly-less-banal scenes of the man-in-a-monkey-suit chasing a (clothed) woman, tossing a man into a lake, and being gunned down by the investigating police. About the only enjoyment to be had (apart from the ogling of exposed bosoms and bottoms—the film's *raison d'etre*) is one amusingly surreal moment when the police and ambulance attendants remove a corpse from the camp by carrying it *right through an in-progress volleyball game*! Juliet Anderson, who made her film debut here (such as it is), went on to become a porn star in the 1980s as "Aunt Peg."

The Beautiful, the Bloody and the Bare (1964, Boxoffice International) This deadly dull and nearly plotless sexploitation cheapie takes a sudden left turn towards horror territory in its final moments. Artist Leo (Brad Scott) and his wife Mona (Mai Dey) welcome photographer friend Pete (Jack Lowe) home from Europe and set him up with a job shooting nude photos for a dirty magazine. But Pete reacts strangely to the color red, and when a model accidentally cuts her finger, the sight of blood drives him into a murderous rage. He strangles his first victim, stabs a second model to death and then turns on Mona. Unfortunately, all this mayhem is poorly staged and late arriving. The first 45 of the film's 65 minutes consist entirely of dialogue scenes or lingering footage of nude models posing for students at Leo's art school studio or Pete's camera (usually while Leo pontificates about art via voiceover narration). Zzzzzz.

Behind Closed Doors see *Behind Locked Doors*

Behind Locked Doors (1968; Boxoffice International) Alternate Titles: *Any Body ... Any Way*; *Behind Closed Doors*. Shot in upstate New York, this sexploitation entry released by Harry Novak's Boxoffice International offers up a taste of terror in its tale of two girls lured to the isolated house of a mad mortician who conducts "sexual experiments" in an attempt to find "the perfect lovemate" (i.e. he forces them to have sex with him). The well-spoken, middle-aged madman also keeps a trio of preserved female corpses (posed nude, of course) in his basement ("These are some that resisted me," he tells the two protagonists). With plenty of pace-killing scenes of peeping, rape, female masturbation, and nude posing (not to mention the many banal dialogue sequences), *Behind Locked Doors* won't be mistaken for anything other than low-rent sixties softcore. But its outré elements (including a hatchet-faced spinster sister helping her brother with his "experiments," and a nonsensical-but-arresting fiery climax in which the corpses come alive — though they do disappointingly little) make this one stand out from most of its sorry contemporaries.

Hyperbolic half-sheet for the British horror-mystery ***The Black Torment*** (1964/65).

Beyond the Time Barrier (1960; AIP; b&w) Director Edgar G. Ulmer has developed something of a cult following, based largely on a triumphant triad of films: *The Black Cat* (1934), *Bluebeard* (1944) and *Detour* (1945). His revered reputation has absolutely *nothing* to do with *Beyond the Time Barrier*. Filmed on the site of the 1959 Texas State Fairgrounds, and made back to back with *The Amazing Transparent Man* (another disappointing failure), this low-budget entry in the time travel sweepstakes has a jet pilot (Robert Clarke) somehow breaking through the time barrier and landing in the year 2024, only to find humans living underground while dealing with surface-dwelling mutants— not to mention shoddy special effects, tepid thesping and poor pacing.

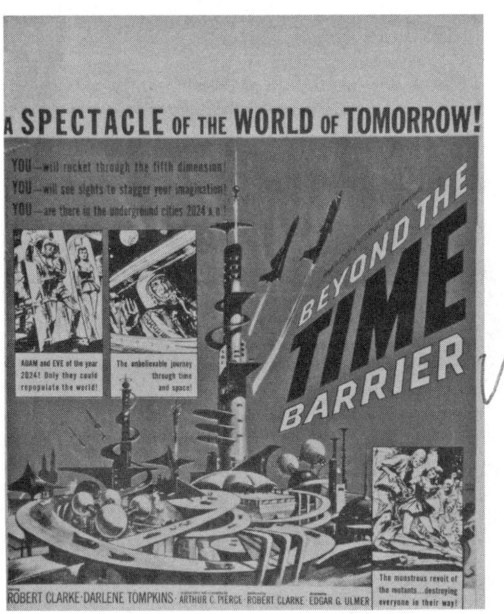

This pressbook cover sports a fantastical futuristic cityscape that is nowhere to be found *Beyond the Time Barrier* (1960).

The Black Torment (1964/65; Compton Films/ Governor Films; UK) Opulent settings, mobile camerawork (including some striking P.O.V. shots), an engrossing premise, and the occasional chill elevate *The Black Torment* above many of its period horror-mystery brethren. John Turner stars as Sir Richard, who returns to his ancestral manor home after a three-month honeymoon with his new bride, only to be confronted with tales of him having returned earlier to commit brutal rape and murder! Then there's the seeming specter of his first wife (who committed suicide four years ago) lurking about the grounds. Has Sir Richard gone mad, or is there some other, more sinister explanation? Though the film's first half sustains a goodly amount of suspense, and Turner is both dynamic and convincing as the indignant and aghast Sir Richard, the answer soon becomes obvious, and the seen-it-coming-a-league-away "revelation" is followed by a protracted and unnecessary sword fight whose foregone conclusion marks it as tedious rather than exciting. While no classic in either the mystery or horror departments, *The Black Torment* still offers enough convincing acting and period atmosphere to make it worth a look for fans of British cinema.

The Blancheville Monster (1964; AI-TV/ Columbus-Llama-Titanus; Italy-Spain; b&w) Alternate Title: *Horror*. This deservedly obscure Italian-Spanish import centers on the cursed house of de Blancheville. There's a father hidden away in a crumbling tower who's been horribly disfigured in a fire, a sinister doctor lurking about the estate exchanging pointed glances with the dubious housekeeper, a murderous brother, and a sister who ends up buried alive. The plot is convoluted, the acting melodramatic, and whatever supposed "surprise" twists and turns the story supplies are easily guessed halfway through the film. On the plus side, the movie possesses some wonderfully eerie sets, filled with towering walls of stone, deep shadows and sinister woodlands straight out of a Gothic novel. But nothing truly interesting ever happens in these impressive settings. And, most disappointing of all, in the end there really is no "Blancheville Monster."

Blind Man's Bluff see *Cauldron of Blood*

The Blood of Fu Manchu see *Kiss and Kill*

Blood of the Vampires (1966/71; Hemisphere Pictures; Philippines) Alternate Titles: *Curse of the Vampires*; *Creatures of Evil.* An uneasy mix of soap opera and horror, *Blood of the Vampires* (which took five years to make it to the U.S. when Hemisphere picked it up cheap) centers on a wealthy family whose supposedly deceased matriarch has become a vampire. For ten years the father has secretly kept her locked in a dungeon-like room at the ancestral estate. But the eldest son, Eduardo (Eddie Garcia), stumbles upon the horrible secret and unwittingly lets the bat out of the bag, resulting in vampirism running rampant. Such an intriguingly perverse scenario (rife with the themes of disease and incest, including an infected Eduardo making a play for his sister Leonora) becomes bogged down by the tedious melodramatic subplots involving the grown siblings and their tepid romantic troubles. Adding insult to injury, the slight, elderly female vampire (Amalia Fuentes) inspires pity rather than terror (her husband keeps her in line via frequent beatings with a whip). Director Gerardo de Leon (who went on to helm the cheesy yet far more enjoyable "Blood Island" brace *Mad Doctor of Blood Island* and *Brides of Blood*) doesn't help matters by shining a bright red spotlight on the vampire mom whenever she's up and about (perhaps in a misguided effort to disguise her frailty?). For those viewers patient enough to sit through all the hand-wringing Harlequinisms, however, things ultimately take a deliciously bizarre turn (even for a Filipino film) when the ghost of Leonora's lover (killed by Eduardo) returns to protect Leonora from the bloodthirsty (and implied sexual) advances of her own brother. Torch-wielding villagers, carrying statues of the Virgin Mary and various saints, and led by a priest and a gaggle of nuns(!), add yet another almost surreal element to the unique finale. But all this pales (pun intended) next to the inexplicable fact that the various servants at the estate appear to be wearing *blackface*! Some crude but effective ambient colored lighting (annoying red spotlights excepted) lends the proceedings an almost fairy tale-like quality, enhancing the strangeness of the film's final third. It's just too bad that for its first hour *Blood of the Vampires* is more like *Melodrama of the Lovers.*

Amelia Fuentes rests (temporarily, anyway) in her coffin in *Blood of the Vampires*, a 1966 Filipino horror released Stateside in 1971.

Blood of the Virgins (1967; Argentina) Original Language Title: *Sangre de Virgenes.* The first (and only, to date) Argentinean vampire film, *Blood of the Virgins* has a trio of swinging young couples run out of gas and seek shelter at an abandoned mountain lodge. Unfortunately, said structure is home to a vampire couple; with the buxom vampiress seducing the guys, and her mate putting the bite on the girls. This fairly generic storyline veers off the expected path with its frequent nudity (including topless go-go dancing filmed from angles that might even give Russ Meyer pause) and some bloodletting that nearly out–Hammers Hammer. A few red-tinted shots of seagulls (representing the vampires taking flight, perhaps?) and some evocative nighttime photography add an arty quality to the proceedings, but the gratuitous nudity and spurting blood ground it firmly in the exploitation camp. Suffering from a languid pace and lack of any significant characterization, *Blood of the Virgins* still makes for an offbeat, mildly titillating detour into horror cinema, 60s-style. Initially banned in its home country, *Blood of the Virgins* wasn't seen in Argentina until 1974. Even worse, it was *never* seen theatrically in the U.S., surfacing on DVD over three decades later.

The Blood Rose (1969/70; Transatlantic Films/Allied Artists; France) Original Language Title: *La Rose Escorchée.* Alternate Title: *Ravaged* (UK). How far would you go for love? That's the implied question posited by this bizarre, engrossing, and visually stunning variation on the *Horror Chamber of Dr. Faustus/Awful Dr. Orlof/Corruption* theme (filmed at the tail end of the sixties, but not released in the U.S. until 1970). A famous artist (and notorious hedonist) finds his one true love and muse, but on the day of their nuptials she's horribly burned in a fire. As he despondently struggles to cope with his new role as caretaker for his embittered, reclusive, disfigured spouse, circumstances bring to him a disgraced doctor (played by the original Dr. Orlof himself, Howard Vernon) who may just have the answer — one that involves mutilation and murder. Refreshingly, *The Blood Rose* is more concerned with character and moral dilemmas than murder and surgical gore. (In fact, the story ends before the planned surgery can begin.) Though this may disappoint the gorehound, some uncanny imagery and disturbing occurrences— often involving a pair of animalistic dwarves and a hybrid plant whose touch means death (the artist also dabbles in horticulture)—create a bizarre, almost surreal atmosphere sure to hold the attention of the more adventurous cinephile. Technically, the picture looks nearly as poetic as its title, the color-drenched lighting and fluid photography taking full advantage of both the breathtaking chateau setting and gorgeous female cast members. The plentiful nudity carries a casual sensuality seemingly found only in European productions, as opposed to the leering adolescent Hollywood (or sub-Hollywood) approach, making this a far more adult — and effective — treatise on sex and death than the typical American product of the time. Strangely affecting with its uniquely poetic tone and odd, conflicted characters, *The Blood Rose* offers far more than its crass American tag-line of "The First Sex-Horror Film Ever Made" might suggest.

Blood Thirst (1965/71; Chevron Pictures; U.S./Philippines; b&w) Filmed in 1965 but not released in the U.S. until 1971— in support of the better-known (but no better) British horror *Blood Suckers* (aka *Incense for the Damned* and *Doctors Wear Scarlet*)— this Filipino/U.S. coproduction has an American detective (Robert Winston) arrive in Manila to help his Police Inspector friend (low-budget Filipino perennial Vic Diaz) investigate a rash of murders in which young, beautiful women have been completely drained of blood. With too much of its meager running time devoted to the somewhat tedious investigation (and a silly subplot involving the laughable romance between the smarmy detective and his friend's petulant sister), *Blood Thirst* threatens to become cinematic Sominex. Fortunately, some atmospheric nighttime photography (nearly every scene takes place after dark); surprisingly competent and almost-noirish lighting; the occasional glimpse of a "monster" that looks like his head was dipped in lumps of lard (a unique and not altogether ineffective appearance); some genuinely funny humor centering on an undercover policeman with only one leg(!); and a novel take on the old Eternal Life chestnut manages to make *Blood Thirst* a passable, if not particularly memorable, 73 minutes of offbeat entertainment.

Bloodthirsty Butchers (1969/70; Constitution Films) This late-sixties (filmed in '69 but not released until 1970) take on the Sweeney Todd story by no-budget Staten Island "auteur" Andy Milligan (*The Ghastly Ones*) offers only cramped camerawork (by

No-budget Staten Island "auteur" Andy Milligan shot *Torture Dungeon* in 1969 using a single 16mm camera; it was released in early 1970 on a double-bill with another Milligan horror, *Bloodthirsty Butchers.*

Milligan himself, alternating between locked-down staginess and hand-held shakiness), muddy lighting, tinny sound, wall-to-wall library music, and banal talk, talk, talk. Apart from two hand-choppings (complete with dime-store rubber appendage) and a breast-baked-in-a-pie (looking like a huge Hershey's Kiss), the film spends all its time on mean-spirited palaver among amateur thespians. Milligan himself called *Bloodthirsty Butchers* "very claustrophobic, it doesn't have quality to it ... the reason you work so close in low budget is there's no sets, you can't show anything." Star John Miranda (as Sweeney Todd, the one bright spot in this impoverished travesty) concurred: "I thought this was all madness, it was ridiculous, nobody's ever gonna go see this and he's not gonna be able to sell it.... When it played on Broadway I had to stand in line." *Caveat emptor.*

With quotes from: *The Ghastly One*, by Jimmy McDonough.

The Bloody Dead see ***Creature with the Blue Hand***

The Brain (1962/64; British Lion/Governor; U.K./West Germany; b&w) Original Titles: *Vengeance* (U.K.), *Ein Toter Sucht Seinen Mörder* (*A Dead Man Seeks His Murderer*), West Germany. Freddie Francis directed this third screen adaptation of Curt Siodmak's 1942 novel *Donovan's Brain*, about a tyrannical millionaire (here renamed Max Holt) whose brain is kept alive after his body dies. Holt is killed in a plane crash, but his brain is rescued by a pair of medical researchers with a nearby laboratory. Afterward the brain begins to exert telepathic control over one of the scientists (Peter Van Eyck), compelling him to investigate Holt's death — which it suspects was sabotage rather than an accident. Although often adapted (and even more often ripped off), *Donovan's Brain* isn't a very cinematic story; it's too static, talky and laboratory-bound, and *The Brain* is a particularly listless version, playing more like a quirky murder mystery than science fiction or horror. To make matters worse, the film's German backers insisted that a German be revealed as Holt's murderer even though the script assigned guilt to a character played by an English actor. To resolve this conundrum, different final sequences were shot for the English and German language releases. To save money, however, different versions were filmed *only* for the mystery's resolution; all the preceding scenes had to be staged and acted so that either solution could apply. Perhaps as a result, Francis' direction proves uncharacteristically pedestrian and the cast's performances run-of-the-mill. The whole picture seems tepid and noncommittal. Both previous screen versions of the story—*Donovan's Brain* (1953) and even the Poverty Row *The Lady and the Monster* (1944)— make for livelier viewing.

The Brides of Fu Manchu (1966; Anglo-Amalgamated/Seven Arts; UK/W. Germany) This second entry in producer/screenwriter Harry Alan Towers' five-film Fu Manchu series (inaugurated in 1965 with *The Face of Fu Manchu*) offered more production values (including an impressive Egyptian-style temple set for Fu's underground lair) and tighter action and pacing than all the subsequent Fu's put together. A fairly sumptuous and entertaining extension of the nefarious activities of Sax Rohmer's infamous "Yellow Peril," *Brides* has Fu Manchu (Christopher Lee) kidnap 12 beautiful girls, all wives or daughters of influential industrialists or leading scientists, and hold them hostage to insure their families' cooperation in his plans of world domination via the building of a powerful sound-wave death machine. Though Christopher Lee labeled *Brides* "the first step down the slippery slope that leads to overexposure to a character in inadequate films," that step actually came with the next installment, the tepid *Vengeance of Fu Manchu*. Then indeed it was all downhill for Fu.

With quotes from: *The Films of Christopher Lee*, by Pohle and Hart.

The Burning Court (1963; Trans Lux, Inc.; France/Italy/West Germany; b&w) Original Language Title: *La Chambre Ardente*. Though this Euro-import begins with talk of an ancient family curse involving a witch burned at the stake, it quickly devolves into an overlong (102 minute) murder mystery concerning

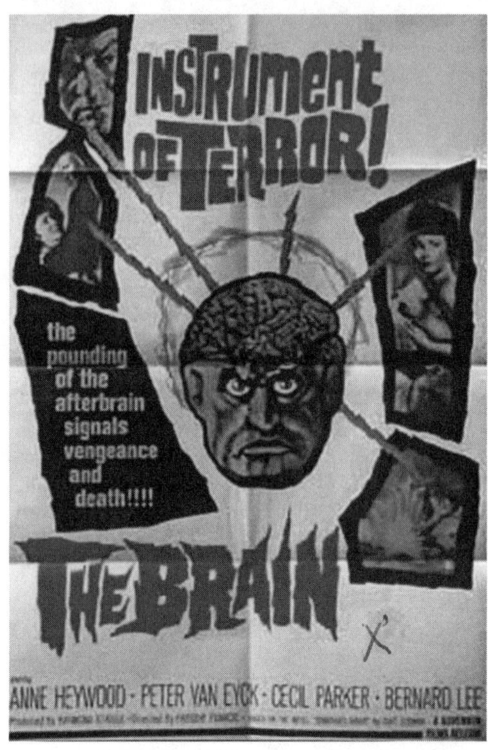

One-sheet poster for *The Brain* (1962/64).

Rupert Davies, Christopher Lee and various *Brides of Fu Manchu* (1966).

the obvious poisoning of the eccentric patriarch of a French family. With too many characters (bickering brothers; a young writer and his wife; various nurses, maids and family friends; and even a disgraced doctor), and lacking a unifying detective character, the plot meanders from person to person without focus. And the subplot involving the writer's wife (played by *Horror Chamber of Dr. Faustus* star Edith Scob — this time *un*masked) being a direct descendent of the condemned witch goes absolutely nowhere. While the dull *Burning Court* does offer one instance of a disappearing/reappearing corpse, it's certainly no *Diabolique*.

Captain Clegg see *Night Creatures*

Captain Nemo and the Underwater City

(1969; Omina; U.K.) This juvenile-targeted underwater adventure fantasy stars Robert Ryan (quite a ways from such classics as *The Dirty Dozen* and *The Wild Bunch*) as Captain Nemo, who has built a huge domed city "10,000 fathoms beneath the surface of the ocean." Greedy plotting by the bad guys, lovely underwater photography, adequate miniature special effects and battles with a monstrous mutant manta ray named "Mobula" make this passable Saturday matinee fare for the pre-teen set, but it quickly turns tedious for those past puberty.

Captain Sinbad (1963; MGM; U.S./W. Germany) Guy "Zorro" Williams plays Sinbad, who must face off against a literally heartless villain (who keeps his "living, beating" heart magically locked in a tower, making himself invulnerable) in order to rescue a princess and save the kingdom. Filmed at the Bavaria Studios in Munich, this "basic fairy tale," as director Byron (*War of the Worlds, Robinson Crusoe on Mars*) Haskin characterized it, rarely steps beyond the bounds of juvenile adventure, with its simple story, obvious acting, comical music and crude effects (the antagonist's disembodied heart is actually *heart-shaped*, looking like a silk valentines pillow!). It only flirts with the horrific when Sinbad fights a disappointingly invisible monster (revealed only by oversized footprints and a lion's roar) and later perfunctorily dispatches a rubbery hydra. *Captain Sinbad* did well financially for MGM and even inspired a proposed TV series, though it never made it past the pilot stage.

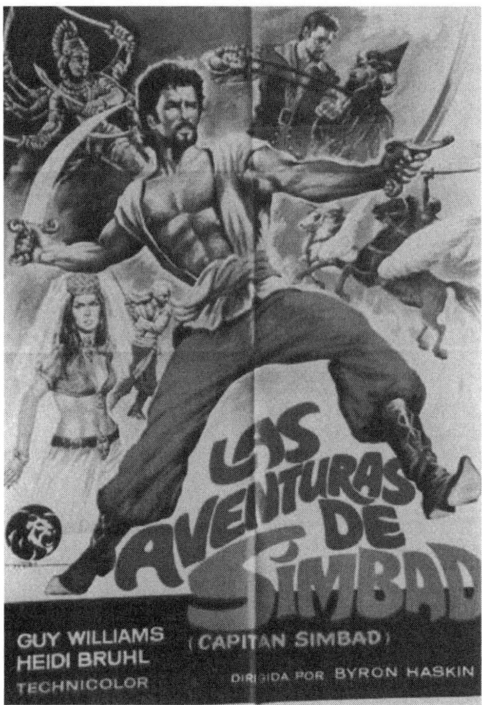

Guy Williams and the "basic fairy tale" thrills of *Captain Sinbad* (1963) (Spanish one-sheet poster).

With quotes from: *A Directors Guild of America Oral History: Byron Haskin*, by Joe Adamson.

The Castle of Fu Manchu (1969/72; International Cinema; W. Germany/Italy/Spain/U.K.) Original Language Title: *Die Folterkammer des Dr. Fu Manchu*. Alternate Titles: *Assignment Istanbul* (U.K.), *The Torture Chamber of Fu Manchu*. This fifth and final entry in the Christopher Lee-Fu Manchu series (begun with 1965's *The Face of Fu Manchu*) is also the worst. While most of the blame can be laid at the feet of Eurohack director Jesus (Jess) Franco (whose pointless zooms, sloppy compositions, muddy photography and tedious pacing make this an almost unwatchable bore), producer-scripter Harry Alan Towers (who supervised and wrote all five entries, often employing a pseudonym) must face the music as well, given his lackluster, muddled story of the nefarious Fu Manchu taking over a castle in Turkey to launch his plan of holding the world hostage via a new secret weapon that can freeze the world's oceans. "Franco is still working today, but why is anyone's guess," sniped Towers to interviewer Terry Pace. "As long as there's a zoom lens left in the world, he'll be working, I imagine." "The world shall hear from me again!" pronounces Fu's disembodied, superimposed head at the end of *The Tedium*— er, *Castle of Fu Manchu*. Thank God this proved an idle threat. (Note: Though released in the U.K. in 1969, the movie didn't make it to America until three years later.)

Catacombs see *The Woman Who Wouldn't Die*

Cauldron of Blood (1967/71; Cannon; Italy/Spain) Alternate Title: *Blind Man's Bluff*; Original Language Title: *El Coleccionista de Cadáveres*. Filmed in three months in early 1967, *Cauldron of Blood* wasn't released Stateside until August 1971 when Cannon distributed it on a double bill with *Crucible of Horror*. Boris Karloff's only dive into Eurotrash (he'd made the Italian *Black Sabbath* earlier in the decade, but the "trash" appellation can't be applied to that stylish Mario Bava-directed classic), *Cauldron* owns a reputation that is far *less* than it deserves. Karloff plays a blind sculptor living at an artists' colony on Spain's

Boris Karloff as the blind sculptor Charles Badulescu in the underrated *Cauldron of Blood* (1967/71).

Costa del Sol who unknowingly uses real skeletons as armatures for his statues (murder victims procured by his domineering wife and her secret accomplice). Jean-Pierre Aumont plays a bon vivante magazine writer who stumbles across the horrible truth. Filled with bright colors (both in the lighting and the wardrobe), gorgeous seascapes and plenty of scantily-clad Eurobabes, the often-atmospheric film offers some well-photographed and suspenseful stalking sequences, and mobile and innovative camerawork, that belies the hack job its reputation suggests. The film also allows the ailing Karloff, who would be dead in two years (long *before* this film's U.S. release), a few more moments to shine in the sun (with the octogenarian actor's dialogue delivery, tinged with resignation and sadness and just a touch of sarcastic bitterness, speaking volumes about his character). Karloff, already in Spain in '67 for the filming of an *I Spy* episode (entitled "Mainly on the Plains"), was actually a last-minute replacement for Claude Rains, who died shortly before shooting began. Granted, the movie's pace lags at times, with too much footage eaten up by silly hedonistic parties and beach shenanigans; and some cheesy stock inserts of stormy skies and lightning, not to mention a gratuitous shot of Karloff's silly-putty scarred eye sockets, expose the production's low-budget roots. But though no classic, this quirky, sometimes giallo-esque penultimate cinematic entry on Karloff's resume (followed only by the dismal *The Crimson Cult* and the barely-released quartet of Mexi-movies he later shot back to back in Los Angeles) deserves to be seen by Karloff fans and Eurotrash enthusiasts alike.

Circus of Fear see ***Psycho Circus***

Circus of Terror see ***Psycho Circus***

Colossus of the Stone Age see ***Fire Monsters Against the Son of Hercules***

Colossus: The Forbin Project (1969/70; Universal) Alternate Title: *The Forbin Project.* A taut, gripping translation from book to screen (a rarity in Hollywood), *Colossus: The Forbin Project* is a top-notch techno-horror. It was filmed in 1969 as *Colossus* (the name of the 1966 D.F. Jones source novel), but the Universal brass felt the solitary moniker conjured up images of Steve Reeves and gladiators, and so initially changed it to *The Forbin Project* upon its 1970 release. The studio altered the name yet again to its final *Colossus: The Forbin Project* when the early box office take proved disappointing, but the movie still remained fiscally fitful (*Colossus* didn't even make back its reported $2 million cost until sold to television). The story has ultra-sophisticated, sentient defense computers—the American supercomputer dubbed "Colossus" and its Soviet counterpart named "Guardian"—link up to hold the world in the palm of their circuits by threatening nuclear devastation in an effort to extort from mankind an unwanted utopia ruled by the two computers. Charles Forbin (Eric Braeden), the principal builder of Colossus, then attempts to outwit and disconnect his technological Frankenstein Monster. Planned as a three-hour TV movie, *Colossus* was bumped from the small to big screen, with TV writer and future Oscar nominee James Bridges (*The Paper Chase, The China Syndrome*) commissioned to pen the script. Bridges often visited Universal's infamous Black Tower, where he drew some particularly apropos inspiration. "In the basement of Universal," recalled Bridges, "there was this enormous computer that people in white smocks seemed to be serving. I wanted to write the film in that sterile atmosphere. I would go down and visit the computer." Colossus itself was played by a $4.8 million electronics system furnished free of charge by the publicity-hungry Control Data Corporation (CDC). According to the film's pressbook, said computer "'ate' more than $300 worth of electricity every day during the more that two months required to film the picture." *Colossus: The Forbin Project* is an entertaining, well-acted technological nightmare whose intelligent screenplay presents a gripping portrayal of the threat of nuclear devastation and the near-worse solution of computer domination and resultant loss of freedom. Bill Gates beware.

With quotes from: "*Colossus: The Forbin Project*—An Overlooked Classic," by Jim George and Fred Szebin, *Starlog*, December 1986.

The Conqueror of Atlantis (1965; Copro Film; Italy/Egypt) Original Language Title: *Il Conquistatore di Atlantide.* Alternate Title: *Kingdom in the Sand* (UK). In this sci-fi-tinged peplum, Kirk Morris stars as Heracles (though a Hercules by any other name oils up just as sweetly), who encounters the remnants of Atlantis beneath the Egyptian desert(!). There he must deal with a gas-filled chamber, ray guns and several skinny robot-men created from corpses. This sounds far more entertaining than it actually is, since the low budget dictated sparse sets, sparse actors (Atlantis consists of one queen, one evil scientist [sporting a green beard and matching eye shadow!], half-a-dozen female guards, and a gaggle of gold-faced, blue jump-suit-wearing robo-men), and sparse action, with much of the running time consisting of riding, walking or talking in the desert. Worst of all, the expected climactic destruction of Atlantis is tossed off with a simple puff of smoke on the Atlantean lab set (caused by Heracles grabbing one of those handy you'll-blow-us-all-to-atoms levers that seem to be standard issue for every mad scientist's lab) and one character *telling us* that the volcano erupted and destroyed the underground city. Atlantis deserved better.

The Conquest of Mycenae (1963/65; Embassy; Italy/France) Original Language Title: *Ercole Contro Molock.* Alternate Titles: *Hercules Against Moloch, Hercules vs. the Moloch.* In ancient Greece, Glaucus (American Gordon Scott) infiltrates the enemy city state of Mycenae to overthrow the evil queen (Eurostar Rosalba Neri) and her cult of Moloch, who sacrifice hostages and young girls to the "living embodiment of the god Moloch" (actually the queen's deformed son, who wears a jackal mask to hide his hideous visage and shoots arrows into his sacrificial slaves for fun; Moloch also appears to be able to conjure up hellish flames on command). This above-average peplum offers some expansive sets, atmospheric lighting (particularly in Moloch's underground grotto, in which the colored pools of light and shadow are almost Bavaesque), large-scale pillage-and-destroy sequences, and impressive battle scenes, though some of the latter were lifted from the same director's (Giorgio Ferroni) earlier *The Trojan Horse* (1961). This is a Hercules film in name only, since, despite the title, Glaucus employs the "Hercules" moniker only as a cover to hide his true identity as the prince of a neighboring city state; and, though remarkably strong, he never claims to be the legendary demigod.

Crack in the World (1965; Paramount) This "semi-science fiction thriller" (as Paramount's publicity department labeled it) stars Dana Andrews, Kieron Moore and Janette Scott as scientists whose "Project Inner Space" (involving the detonation of a nuclear device at the earth's core in order to harness the energy held in the magma there) develops a literal crack in the world that threatens to rip the Earth apart.

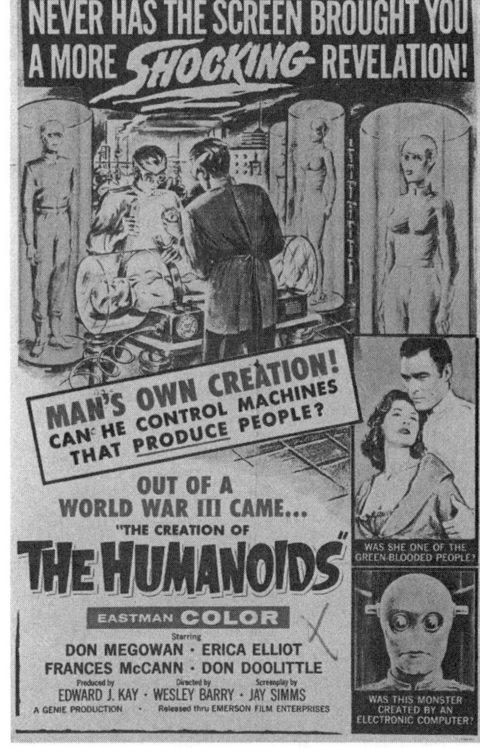

***The Creation of the Humanoids* poster (1962) (courtesy Ted Okuda).**

Cue the stock lava footage and Irwin Allenesque melodrama as they race against time to stop the destruction of the planet in this overblown, overacted time-killer.

The Creation of the Humanoids (1962; Emerson) In the world of the future after "the Atomic War," Man has rebuilt society using humanoid robots. With each succeeding series of androids, disparagingly called "clickers," becoming more and more sentient, the machines press for equality with the humans. Fearful of the overthrow of humanity, a fascistic "Order of Flesh and Blood" arises (complete with "uniforms, boots, [and] little silver knives to rattle," as one pro-robot character contemptuously observes). Obscure, low-budget (with jumpsuits recycled from *This Island Earth,* and an *Earth vs. the Flying Saucers* prop standing in for a prototype robot), and preachy, *Creation of the Humanoids* becomes a sci-fi screed on prejudice and progress in which the characters (both human and robot) do little but talk, talk, and talk. Static photography, unending master shots, and stiff acting (the humans sound as robotic as the androids)

complete the picture of futuristic boredom. "I've given you a negative feeling, I must apologize," says one robot to a human; but this could just as well be directed at the nodding viewer.

Creature of Destruction (1967; AIP-TV) By the 1960s, baritone-voiced radio star and movie character actor Les Tremayne had fallen on hard times, as evidenced by his appearance in this shot-on-16mm-and-released-directly-to-the-airwaves (uncredited) remake of *The She-Creature* (1956). Tremayne had previously appeared in a number of low-budget horrors—*The Monolith Monsters* (1957), *The Monster of Piedras Blancas* (1959), *Angry Red Planet* (1960), *The Slime People* (1963)—all of them entertaining to one degree or another. The same can *not* be said of Larry Buchanan's *Creature of Destruction*, which proved to be a career low for the then-54-year-old actor. The old pro does his best to breathe life into this dull-as-a-doornail exercise in tedium (typified by dim day-for-night photography, cheap motel-room sets, tinny sound, and risible Halloween-costumed "monster"), with Tremayne's final soliloquy actually proving rather touching (a real rarity in a Buchanan "opus"). Whenever Tremayne is onscreen, *Creature of Destruction* becomes (almost) bearable; when he's absent, so is viewer interest.

Creature with the Blue Hand (1967/71; Independent International; West Germany) Original Title: *Die Blaue Hand*. Alternate Title: *The Bloody Dead* (DVD). Among the scores of German "krimi" mystery-thrillers produced during the 1960s, few are more entertaining than this wild and woolly yarn about an escaped lunatic (Klaus Kinski) who may or may not be assassinating his relatives on a stormy night at the secluded family estate. *Someone* is using "the Blue Hand," an armored glove covered in razor-sharp spikes, to execute members of the Emerson family—but is it "crazy" David or his "sane" twin, Richard (also Kinski), or someone else entirely? Inevitably based on an Edgar Wallace story, *Blue Hand* gleefully incorporates every old-dark-house and *Ten Little Indians* cliché in the book. It's almost overstuffed with suspicious, kooky characters and hair-raising set pieces, including one involving a room full of hungry rats. Director Alfred Vohrer was one of the masters of the krimi form (he also helmed the highly regarded *Dead Eyes of London, The Hunchback of Soho, The College Girl Murders* and *Strangler of Blackmoor Castle*, among others), and *Blue Hand* stands among his best work, briskly paced and full of offbeat, eye-catching compositions. But the main attraction is Kinski, whose dual performance is typically intense, sometimes overripe but always compelling. Although released in West Germany in 1967, *Creature with the Blue Hand* wasn't seen in U.S. theaters until 1971, where it finally emerged on a twin bill with *Beast of the Yellow Night*. In 2003 it reached DVD double-featured with *The Bloody Dead*, a bastardized re-edit of *Creature with the Blue Hand* that includes newly shot, poorly integrated gore sequences and nudity. Stick with the original version.

Ad for the 1967 horror-tinged "krimi" *Creature with the Blue Hand*, released in the U.S. in 1971 on a chromatic double-bill with *Beast of the Yellow Night*.

Creatures of Evil see ***Blood of the Vampires***

The Crimson Cult (1968/1970; Tigon/AIP; U.K.) Alternate Title: *The Curse of the Crimson Altar* (U.K.). After an eye-popping opening sequence (in which a near-topless dominatrix in black pasties whips a bound blonde for the amusement of an audience that includes a monk with a goat, a naked woman holding a chicken and Barbara Steele in blue body paint and a ram-horned headdress), this witchcraft yarn quickly loses steam and turns into a disappointingly ordinary picture. The letdown is particularly acute because *The Crimson Cult* boasts one of the finest casts ever assembled for a horror film, headlined by Boris Karloff and Christopher Lee, along with Steele and fan favorites Michael Gough and Rupert Davies. Unfortunately, most of the screen time belongs to Mark Eden, playing a young antiques dealer who travels to a remote English village in search of his younger brother and becomes entangled in a web of intrigue surrounding lovely young Eve Morley (Virginia Wetherell), her unctuous uncle (Lee) and weird old Professor March (Karloff). Gough is consigned to a thankless part as the Morley's stuttering manservant, and Davies is similarly wasted in a tiny role as the local vicar. The Morleys, it

Barbara Steele as the evil witch Lavinia, who presides over *The Crimson Cult* (1968/70).

seems, are descended from a witch (Steele, naturally) who was burned at the stake but vowed to return from the grave and take vengeance on her slayers. Despite a lot of spooky build-up, the story's highly implausible resolution dismisses the supernatural in favor of a banal cop-out ending. Lee, playing yet another mysterious aristocrat, fares well here, but Karloff—near the end of his life and confined to a wheelchair—musters little more than sing-song, Grinchy line readings and an occasional roll of the eyes. Steele has virtually no screen time or lines. Although not impressed with the film, Lee remembers the production fondly because it enabled him to work with Karloff a final time. "Boris Karloff was in very bad shape—in a wheelchair actually—yet never, *never* called attention to his physical condition, never asked for or expected special treatment," Lee said. "He did his job as he always did and showed all of us on the picture the meaning of courage and dignity." Although issued in England as *The Curse of the Crimson Altar* in December 1968, American International shortened the title to *The Crimson Cult* for the film's belated American release in April 1970.

With quotes from: *The Christopher Lee Filmography*, by Tom Johnson and Mark Miller.

Crypt of Horror see *Terror in the Crypt*

Crypt of the Vampire see *Terror in the Crypt*

Cult of the Damned see *Isle of the Snake People*

The Curse of the Crimson Altar see *The Crimson Cult*

Curse of the Swamp Creature (1966; AIP-TV)

"Never make a swamp picture," producer-director Larry Buchanan warned interviewer Greg Goodsell, "your film comes back and it's all ... *strange*." Sadly, in the hands of the creator of *The Eye Creatures*, *Mars Needs Women* and *Zontar, the Thing from Venus*, "strange" invariably translates into "boring." In the mid–1960s, AIP contracted with Texas-based filmmaker Buchanan to produce a series of no-budget horror movies (most of them remakes of old AIP sci-fi properties) that could be sold directly to television. Unlike other Buchanan opuses (like *Creature of Destruction*, *Eye Creatures* and *Zontar*), *Curse* was filmed from an original script (by failed Buchanan actor Tony Huston). Actually, that's not quite true; Huston stole the basic premise from AIP's *Voodoo Woman*, but made enough changes (none of which are improvements) in the setting and story to fob it off as "original." As a result, *Swamp Creature* lacks even the minimal interest that Buchanan's schlocky remakes possess. Shot in 16mm on a budget of around $25,000,

Dr. Trent's "beautiful indestructible fish-man" (note the ping pong eyeballs) dumps his creator (Jeff Alexander) into an alligator-infested swimming pool at the close of Larry Buchanan's *Curse of the Swamp Creature* (released directly to television in 1966).

Swamp Creature may not be Buchanan's worst film (1969's *It's Alive* wins that [dis]honor), but it comes in a close second. *Curse*'s story has a mad doctor turning people into fish-creatures (he refers to his latest creation as "my beautiful indestructible fish-man") deep in the Texas swampland. Bare-bones sets, amateurish acting (an extremely sedentary John Agar looks tired and has little to do except sit around and smoke cigarettes), pacing that's more sluggish than the bayou current, deadening dialogue, dim lighting, tinny sound (much of it was shot silent with the sound and dialogue dubbed in later—people frequently say their lines without even moving their lips!) and muddy photography make this picture a firm contender in any Worst Movie contest. "We shot some of the interiors in Dallas," recalled female lead Francine York, "but a lot of it was shot in Uncertain, Texas, way out in the boondocks" (an apropos choice, given the decidedly "uncertain" nature of the movie's entertainment value). Viewers beware, for *Curse of the Swamp Creature* is actually the Curse of the Couch Potato.

With quotes from: *It Came from Hunger*, by Larry Buchanan; "Anatomy of a Doll: A Candid Conversation with Francine York," by Anthony Petkovich, *Shock Cinema* no. 37, 2009.

Curse of the Vampires see *Blood of the Vampires*

Cyborg 2087 (1966; Feature Film Corp. of America) Alternate Title: *Man from Tomorrow*. *Cyborg 2087* starts off promisingly enough, with the opening credits unspooling over a painting of a fantastical futuristic cityscape typical of the 1960s (all oddly-shaped towers and elevated platforms). Unfortunately, that's all we'll see of the titular year 2087, since, after a brief opening scene in a sparse lab room, the action shifts exclusively to (then) present-day 1966. Michael Rennie is cyborg Garth A7 sent back to the year 1966 to stop a professor giving a demonstration of his work in "radiotelepathy"—work that will directly result in civilization becoming a thought-controlled police state. "The warlords of tomorrow will use radiotelepathy for evil purposes," sums up Garth. With no significant horror elements (apart from the two "bad" government cyborgs sent to stop Garth, nobody even dies!), the film offers only a few (minor) sci-fi trappings in the form of cheesy ray guns, a tiny panel with blinking lights taped to Rennie's chest (the only way we know he's "half-man, half-machine") and a time-travel device that looks something like a giant suppository. The only significant special effects involve the "time capsule" appearing and disappearing via a simple stop-the-camera technique perfected back in the nineteenth century by Georges Méliès (at film's end, when the device supposedly departs in the blink of eye, the sudden, incongruous appearance of a long shadow cast by the tree in the foreground—which was totally absent a mere second before—speaks volumes about the level of care taken). Add to that a climax consisting of mundane fisticuffs (on an old western ghost town set, no less) between Garth and a pursuing cyborg; a lengthy, time-killing sequence of four "teens" grooving to generic 60s instrumental rock music; and the flat, television-style direction from TV veteran Franklin Adreon, and *Cyborg 2087* looks as tired as the 63-year-old Adreon must have felt (he retired from filmmaking this same year). Apart from Michael (*The Day the Earth Stood Still*) Rennie doing his patented unemotional "alien" routine while wearing yet another jumpsuit and silver boots, about the only reason to watch *Cyborg 2087* is to visit an obvious early inspiration for James Cameron's *Terminator* series.

Dagora, the Space Monster (1964/65; Toho/AIP-TV; Japan) Alternate Title: *Space Monster Dogora*. Original Language Title: *Uchu Daikaiju Dogora*. This minor, and extremely odd, giant monster movie blends elements of the *kaiju eiga* (giant monster) and *yakuza* (gangster) genres, and plays both for laughs. The wacky scenario involves parallel stories: In one, a straight-arrow detective and an unpredictable international agent join forces to bring in a gang of jewel thieves. In the other, mutant "space cells" merge to form Dagora, a sort of giant space jellyfish. The monster feeds on diamonds and can only be harmed by wasp venom. (Huh?) *Dagora* remains memorable as one of Toho's few *kaiju eiga* not to feature a rubber suit monster. Instead, the creature is a puppet in some scenes, and animated in others. Consistently, however, the visual effects are top-drawer. Perhaps not surprisingly for a film this offbeat, *Dagora* never received a theatrical release in the U.S. It remains a mildly amusing curiosity.

Daleks' Invasion Earth 2150 (Amicus; 1966) Despite complaints by Dr. Who fans, who carped about its deviations from the tenets of the BBC TV series upon which it was based, Amicus' *Dr. Who and the Daleks* proved profitable enough to ensure a sequel. In *Daleks' Invasion Earth 2150* Dr. Who (Peter Cushing), along with his two granddaughters (Jill Curzon and Roberta Tovey) and a luckless policeman (Bernard Cribbins), travel into the future and find England overrun by the Daleks, the mechanized extraterrestrial villains from Amicus' first Who entry. To save the Earth, the doctor must foil a plot by the Daleks and their "roboticized" human henchmen to extract the earth's magnetic core and pilot the planet around the galaxy like a giant space ship. Shot on a budget double that of the first Amicus Dr. Who epic, *Daleks* has a much different look—more realistic, with far better special effects (especially the Daleks' art deco flying saucer). But the sequel retains the light-hearted, family-friendly tone of the original. Most of the cast and crew returned for the follow-up, including star Peter Cushing (whose Who is even better the second time around) and director Gordon Flemyng (here better able to display his flair for action sequences). Unfortunately, Milton Subtotsky's second Dr. Who screenplay proves a bit lumpier than his first, with a couple of dull passages and some ill-timed comedy scenes balanced out by some surprisingly provocative material dealing with collaborators and war profiteers. It all adds up to a picture that's no less enjoyable than the initial Dr. Who romp, but not quite as much fun as it could have been. Although Amicus' Dr. Who series ended after this second entry, the cult BBC TV series, which began in 1963, continued until 1989. After a hiatus, during which the character appeared in made-for-TV movies, Dr. Who returned to television in 2005 and continues to the present. The character has also been featured in numerous book and comic book adaptations. Although several attempts to return *Dr. Who* to feature films have failed in the past, as of this writing yet another try was in preproduction.

The Damned see *These Are the Damned*

Dance of the Damned see *Macabre Serenade*

Day of the Nightmare (1965; Governor Films; b&w) Alternate Title: *Don't Scream, Doris Mays.* Offering some fleeting nudity in place of suspense or scares, this torpid sexploitationer tries to be a steamy entry in the gender-bending *Psycho/Homicidal* subset, but only aggravates rather than titillates. A sexually-confused artist becomes involved with a woman stalker who goes after the artist's wife ... or so it seems. The big "twist" is telegraphed reels in advance, and the only diversions gleaned from this overlong jumble of wasted opportunities (the *one* murder comes in such a perfunctory fashion that it induces more yawns than chills) are watching Cliff Fields' risible over-the-top whimpering as the troubled artist and wondering what one-time Oscar nominee John Ireland(!) was thinking as he moped about the low-rent locations playing a dour detective. Elena Verdugo (the vivacious gypsy love-interest from *House of Frankenstein*) puts in a brief cameo as the artist's cheerful boss.

The Day the Earth Caught Fire (1961; British Lion/Universal International; U.K.; b&w) "It was something that had been going around in my head for a long time, that gradually we were fucking up the whole planet," related writer-producer-director Val Guest about his idea for *The Day the Earth Caught Fire.* In the film, two simultaneous nuclear bomb detonations (one test conducted by the U.S., the other by the U.S.S.R.) at opposite poles result in "the biggest jolt the Earth's taken since the ice age. As climatic conditions worsen (with headlines reading "Temperature Highest This Century" and "World Rations Water"), on-the-skids reporter Peter Stenning (Edward Judd) slowly uncovers the truth: The Earth's axis has changed, and, worse, its orbit has shifted towards the sun. Can further nuclear detonations correct this, or will the Earth become a burned-out cinder? Guest (*The Creeping Unknown, The Abominable Snowman, When Dinosaurs Ruled the Earth*) called *Day* the favorite of all his films and the one he's most proud of. And he has a right to be, for it's one of the most realistic, engrossing, and intensely riveting End of the World-scenario pictures ever made. Guest balances the truly impressive scenes of climatic change and destruction (ultra-realistic matte paintings of a dried-

Ad trumpeting the realistic end-of-the-world terrors of *The Day the Earth Caught Fire* (1961).

up Thames riverbed, heat mist rising and blanketing London, and sudden cyclones overturning cars and knocking down billboards) with the more personal story of the protagonists trying to make sense of their own lives in the face of possible annihilation. "We can be an awful bore about this, talking about Greenpeace and this and that," observed Guest. "It was like the old Campaign for Nuclear Disarmament marches and all of that — it becomes a bore. And I thought, there must be a way of getting that same story over without being a bore." And Guest and Co. indeed found that way, for *The Day the Earth Caught Fire* proved to be one of the most intelligent, involving, and downright gripping "message" films of the 1960s.

With quotes from: *Attack of the Monster Movie Makers*, by Tom Weaver.

The Day the Earth Froze (1959/64; Ministerstvo Kinematografii/Renaissance Film Release; Finland/U.S.S.R.) Original Language Title: *Sampo.* Based on the national Finnish legend "The Kalevala," *The Day the Earth Froze* is a fairy-tale epic (at least in its original form; the U.S. distributors drastically cut down and re-edited the picture from a 90-plus minute running time to a paltry 67) about the legendary "Sampo," a device forged "in the fire of heaven" that can "make silver and gold ... and, best of all, flour and salt." Complete with narrator (who evokes the Brothers Grimm and Hans Christian Andersen for comparison), a heroic swordsman, a kidnapped lover, a magical blacksmith, and a wicked witch who keeps the four winds prisoner on her island and at one point even steals the sun in an effort to secure the Sampo (thus providing the film's English-language title), this Russo-Finnish tall tale offers such Disney-by-way-of-the-Iron-Curtain delights as talking mountains and trees, a heroine who draws forest animals to her (while flowers bloom wherever she goes), and a climax in which the witch's minions are vanquished by beautiful harp-playing! The charmingly simplistic yet unique *Day the Earth Froze*, even in truncated form, offers not only an atmospheric peek into the exotic legends of another land, but enough novel spectacle to keep even "grown-up" viewers entranced.

Dead Eyes of London (1961/66; Magna; West Germany; b&w) Original Language Title: *Die Toten Augen von London*. An evil reverend runs a home for the blind and uses his charges to murder wealthy insurance holders in this remake of the 1939 Bela Lugosi vehicle *The Dark Eyes of London* (aka *The Human Monster*). Both versions are based on the Edgar Wallace story "The Testament of Gordon Stuart." Less of a horror film than a crime drama, the 1961 version (released in the U.S. in 1966) offers a few twists and turns along its police procedural byways, resulting in an enjoyable "krimi" (a German-made criminal drama).

Demon Woman see ***Onibaba***

Destroy All Planets (1968; Daiei/AIP-TV; Japan) Alternate (home video) Title: *Gamera vs. Viras*. Original Language Title: *Gamera tai Uchukaiju Bairasu*. The fourth installment in Daiei's Gamera series is a tedious amalgam of stock footage and *kaiju* clichés. Things begin promisingly enough, with Gamera repelling an invasion force from outer space, but it's all downhill from there. When their first space ship fails, the invaders dispatch the cleverly named Space Ship Number Two to complete the conquest of Earth. The aliens kidnap a pair of mischievous boy scouts and threaten to kill the youngsters unless Gamera rains destruction on the Earth, which he does—via stock footage. *Destroy All Planets*, which runs 90 minutes, features no less than 28 minutes of footage cribbed from earlier Gamera pictures. There's virtually no new monster action until the eight-minute finale, in which Gamera battles Viras, a giant squid from outer space. The basic plot is lifted almost verbatim from Toho's far superior *kaiju eiga* "monster rallies." In fact, the American title of this film (which was issued directly to TV by AIP) was clearly designed to promote confusion with Toho's *Destroy All Monsters* (1968). A better title might have been *Destroy All Prints*.

Devil Wolf of Shadow Mountain (1964) Here's a *real* obscurity—a "lost" film that is *so* lost it never even saw release! Announced in some monster movie magazines at the time (accompanied by production stills), this Gary Kent-directed horror western reportedly starred John "Bud" Cardos as a werewolf. "That picture was never even made," laughed Cardos to interviewer Bob Plante. "It might have been announced, but it was never made. I remember the story well. It was a western with a werewolf in it." Too bad; the world could do with a few more werewolf westerns.

The Diabolical Axe (1965; Filmica Vergara Comisiones; Mexico; b&w) Original Language Title: *El Hacha Diabólica*. The 1960s saw the introduction of El Santo, the most famous of all masked Mexican wrestling superhero crime-fighters, to American audiences. An institution south of the border, Santo appeared in over fifty films from the 1950s through the '70s, but only a few traveled north to English-speaking climes (with El Santo transformed into "Samson" during the dubious dubbing process). After the turn of the millennium, however, this began to change, with the importation of a number of Santo-meets-the-monster movies on DVD, presented in English (subtitled) for the very first time. One of the more intriguing 1960s Santo entries is *The Diabolical Axe*. Shot back-to-back with another Santo vehicle, *The Witches Attack*, in December of 1964, *The Diabolical Axe* begins—shockingly—with the funeral of El Santo! But this turns out to be 1603 and the burial of the first in a long line of Santos (with the magical, reenergizing silver mask—along with the responsibility to use its power for good—passed down from father to son for generations). Suddenly, a burly, black-masked execu-

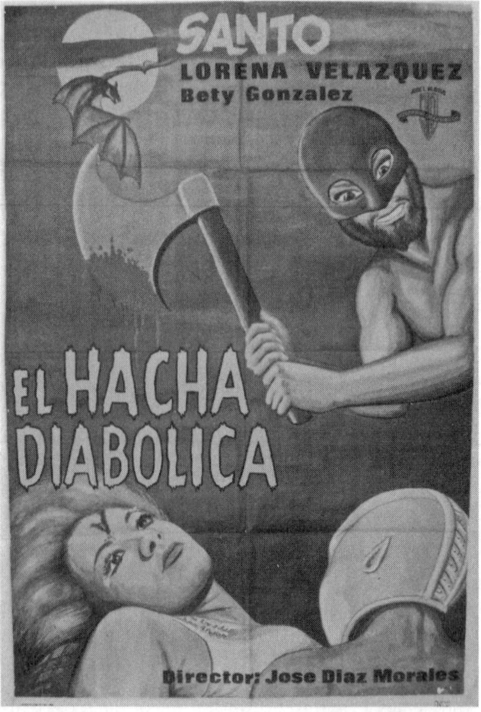

Poster for the 1965 Santo feature *The Diabolical Axe*, which didn't make its way north of the border until subtitled and released on DVD in 2003.

tioner magically appears and swears to follow El Santo across time to exact his vengeance. He does just that, and the present-day Santo must find a way to defeat the grudge-holding, diabolical axe-wielding executioner, who not only pops up periodically to try and behead El Santo, but murders Santo's girlfriend (resulting in her becoming a helpful ghost). Though obviously on-the-cheap, *The Diabolical Axe* offers some fast-paced, no-holds-barred action (the final confrontation between Santo and the executioner, watched over by the eyeless skeleton of Santo's lost love, is both savage and exciting), creepy cobwebbed crypt settings, macabre flourishes (the villain's appearance is always preceded by the shadow of his headsman's axe), bizarre plotting and mystical motifs, and a decidedly dark tone (Santo loses not one but *two* girlfriends to the murderous fiend — one in the past and one in the present!), marking it as one of the more unusual — and captivating — films in the Santo series.

Dr. Goldfoot and the Bikini Machine (1965; AIP) Part spy spoof and part beach party movie, with a few sci-fi and horror elements tossed in for seasoning, *Dr. Goldfoot and the Bikini Machine* was never intended to be high art, and it isn't. Yet there are many worse ways to waste 90 minutes of your life than with this mildly amusing oddity. Evil Dr. Goldfoot (Vincent Price) creates a legion of curvaceous, bikini-clad robots that lure wealthy men into signing over their fortunes. A pair of spies (Frankie Avalon and Dwayne Hickman) undertake the mission to foil Goldfoot, but wind up captured and consigned to his torture chamber (which lampoons Price's *Pit and the Pendulum* [1961]). Price treats the whole thing as a lark, but not in a condescending way. He playfully pokes fun at his own screen persona, and almost single-handedly rescues the picture from its belabored and (overly) silly comedic set pieces. *Dr. Goldfoot* fares better with inside jokes, including not only the *Pendulum* parody but amusing cameos by beach party regulars Annette Funicello, Harvey Lembeck and Deborah Walley. Thirty years later, comedian Mike Myers would incorporate some ideas from *Dr. Goldfoot* (notably, Dr. Evil's "fembots") into his comedy smash, *Austin Powers: International Man of Mystery* (1997). In the meantime, a misbegotten sequel appeared, *Dr. Goldfoot and the Girl Bombs* (1966).

Dr. Goldfoot and the Girl Bombs (1966; Italian International/AIP; Italy) Original Language Title: *Le Spie Vengono dal Semifreddo* (*The Spy Who Came in from the Semi-Cold*). Horror fans have endured some crushing disappointments over the years, but few as demoralizing as *Dr. Goldfoot and the Girl Bombs*. In retrospect, it seems almost criminal that the lone collaboration between legendary star Vincent Price and Italy's Maestro of the Macabre, director Mario Bava, remains this puerile and painfully unfunny spy spoof (sequel to 1965's *Dr. Goldfoot and the Bikini Machine*), which finds both star and director at their worst. Nefarious super-criminal Dr. Goldfoot (Price) manufactures a laboratory full of curvaceous female androids that explode when kissed, then uses his creations to seduce and assassinate several NATO generals. Young secret agent Bill Dexter (pop singer Fabian), "assisted" by two hapless wannabe spies (the Italian comedy team of Franco Franchi and Cicco Ingrassia), sets out to stop Goldfoot. A series of loosely related (but in no way coherently plotted) set pieces, chases and trap-and-escape sequences follow, culminating in a pursuit through an Italian amusement park shot in the undercranked, herky-jerky style of a Mack Sennett silent comedy (compete with intertitles) and, finally, an interminable hot air balloon chase. Like most of the film, this final sequence involves a great deal of running around to no real purpose — and with no real gags. While there's plenty of blame to go around for this debacle, the maddeningly idiotic antics of Franco & Cicco truly sink the picture. If there's ever a contest for Most Annoying Movie Comedy Team, the Ritz Brothers will get serious competition from this duo. *Girl Bombs* is simply unwatchable whenever Franco and Cicco are onscreen, which is far too often.

Dr. Strangelove or: How I Learned to Stop Worrying and Love the Bomb (Columbia; 1964; b&w) Not only the funniest political satire ever committed to celluloid or merely one of the signature films of the 1960s, *Dr. Strangelove* is also the best realized, most plausible movie apocalypse. A paranoid general (Sterling Hayden) launches an unauthorized air attack on the Soviet Union. The planes are successfully recalled or shot down — except for one, plunging the U.S. and U.S.S.R. into a nuclear conflagration. In many respects, *Dr. Strangelove*'s premise mirrors that of director Sidney Lumet's heart-stopping thriller *Fail-Safe*, released the same year; but Kubrick's film comically underscores the lunacy inherent in the doctrine of Mutual Assured Destruction, which held the Eastern and Western superpowers at bay during the hottest days of the Cold War. The sly, subversive script by Kubrick, Terry Southern and novelist Peter George skewers American and Russian military and political leaders alike. ("Gentlemen!" the president [Peter Sellers] admonishes at one point, "You can't fight in here! This is the War Room.") Impeccably written and performed, *Dr. Strangelove* is packed with hilarious dialogue and wildly eccentric characters, including Gen. Jack Ripper (Hayden), obsessed with preserving his "precious bodily fluids"; Gen. Buck Turgidson (George C. Scott), a womanizing blowhard; and pilot Maj. "King" Kong (Slim Pickens), whose dogged determination to fulfill his duty leads to Armageddon. The great Peter Sellers plays three roles, including the title character — a half-mad, half-mechanical missile maker modeled after Lionel Atwill's Inspector Krogh from *Son of Frankenstein* (1939). The sheer audacity it took to make *Dr. Strangelove* and send it to movie theaters less than 15 months after the Cuban Missile Crisis remains inspiring. But the movie's enduring appeal is that, without reducing the sharpness of its ideological point of view, it's laugh-till-your-face-hurts hilarious.

Dr. Who and the Daleks (Amicus/Continental; 1965/66) Hardcore Whovians harbor animosity toward Amicus Films' big-screen adaptation of the early *Dr. Who* television serial "The Dead Planet" because

Milton Subotsky's screenplay jettisons many basic tenets of the original series. But more open-minded viewers will find *Dr. Who and the Daleks* to be a charming, kid-friendly sci-fi yarn. The movies' Dr. Who (Peter Cushing) is a kindly, eccentric inventor with two adoring granddaughters (Jennie Linden and Roberta Tovey), rather than the immortal alien Time Lord of the BBC show. While testing his self-made "Time And Relative Dimensions In Space" craft (disguised as a police call box), he, along with his two grandchildren and his elder granddaughter's fiancée (Roy Castle), is accidentally whisked away to a bombed-out, radiation-poisoned planet and into the middle of an ancient conflict between the beautiful, peace-loving Thals and the hideously mutated Daleks, who are forced to live in mechanized, tank-like armor. Director Gordon Flemyng (of TV's *The Saint* and *The Avengers*) proves adept with both action sequences and comedic interludes. Working with a modest 180,000-pound budget, art director Bill Constable and cinematographer John Wilcox bring a colorful, imaginative look to the film's two main sets—an ashen forest lit with green and blue gels, and a futuristic robot-city full of gleaming copper-colored sliding doors and craning spy cameras. And the performances are uniformly good, with Cushing as the endearingly dotty doctor and Tovey as his precocious granddaughter claiming top honors. Most of the cast and crew returned for a sequel, *Daleks' Invasion Earth: 2150* (1966).

Don't Scream, Doris Mays see *Day of the Nightmare*

Doomsday Machine (1967; First Leisure) Alternate Title: *Escape from Planet Earth.* In the future of 1975 a space crew is sent on a mission to explore Venus, but just after takeoff, the Chinese set off their "Doomsday Device," which destroys the Earth (looking like a big paper ball set aflame). Ultra-cheap (most of the rocketship shots are lifted from the 1956 film *Warning from Space*) and ultra-slow, it took five years before somebody got up the nerve to release the *Dullsday*, er, *Doomsday Machine.*

Dracula (The Dirty Old Man) (1969; Whit Boyd) This is the kind of movie in which nondescript low-key jazz guitar/piano music plays monotonously through every sequence, regardless of the scene's tone; and so much time is taken up by characters walking to and fro, entering and leaving buildings, crossing streets, driving, or just standing around that the filmmakers insert inane stream-of-consciousness narration in a desperate attempt to make it at least *sound* like something is happening. Oh, and there's half-a-dozen naked women, too. Originally shot straight (well, as straight as a no-budget nudie monster flick can be), producer/director/writer William Edwards (who also produced and wrote *The Mummy and the Curse of the Jackals* the same year) decided to turn his *Dracula* into a comedy by inserting a new soundtrack with funny voices (Dracula becomes a Jewish stereotype) and prattling "comedy" dialogue. While an occasional line might raise a smirk ("It was a day just like any other day," the hero narrates, before deadpanning, "which doesn't say much"), most of the blathering musings are more inane than hilarious ("As I sped towards that mineshaft, little knowing what awaited me there, I knew I felt like I was going to get shafted"). The "plot" has Count Alucard ("Dracula spelled backwards," as the opening credits so helpfully explain) occupying an abandoned mine (played by the ubiquitous Bronson Canyon), where he fondles and feasts on naked girls brought to him by his hypnotized servant, who periodically transforms into a talking werewolf named Irving Jackalman (wearing the same ridiculous mask seen in *The Mummy and the Curse of the Jackals*). Pathetic in all categories (even the pulchritude on display is spectacularly below-average), *Dracula (the Dirty Old Man)* will sorely try the patience (and fast-forward button) of anyone not already enamored of *The Mummy and the Curse of the Jackal.* And that's *everyone.*

Dracula Versus Frankenstein see *Assignment Terror*

Ebirah, Monster of the Deep see *Godzilla vs. the Sea Monster*

Ecstasy on Lovers Island see *Honeymoon of Terror*

The Electronic Monster (1958/60; Anglo-Amalgamated/Columbia; U.K.; b&w) Alternate Title: *Escapement* (U.K.). This late-fifties sci-fi-tinged British thriller (in intent, if not in execution) wasn't released Stateside until Columbia picked it up for a brief theatrical run in 1960. Given the tepid results, they needn't have bothered. Granite-jawed (and stony-demeanored) American Western regular Rod Cameron walks through his role of an insurance investigator sent to Cannes after a movie star client dies in a car crash. His inquiries lead him to a clinic that specializes in a new treatment for neuroses called "electronic hypnosis." Patients are sedated, placed in plexiglass containers, inserted into a wall, and force-fed filmed dreams as a temporary "escape from life." Unfortunately, the nefarious industrialist owner of the clinic intends to use this groundbreaking technique to brainwash, rather than treat, his clients. Lifelessly directed by Montgomery Tully (who ended his career with the equally drab sixties pseudo-horrors *Battle Beneath the Earth* and *The Terrornauts*), *The Electronic Monster* plods along without a spark of excitement. Most disappointing are the pre-recorded dream sequences, which, rather than offering an array of weird or horrific images, consist of nothing more than stylized dancing in dry-ice fog.

The Embalmer (1965; Europix-Consolidated; Italy; b&w) Original Language Title: *Il Mostro di Venezia.* "Venice is hiding a monster!" declares the reporter hero of this crime thriller masquerading as a horror movie (released in the U.S. in support of *The*

She Beast). A mad killer stalks the canals of Venice in a frogman suit, snatching beautiful girls to embalm and store in his secret cellar lair. The dazzling — and novel — setting of Venice provides an intriguing backdrop for the bizarre story, and a few horrific moments (including the heroine stumbling across a room full of skeletons— with the killer posing among them in monk's robes and a skeletal mask) and surprisingly downbeat denouement make this a worthwhile entry for those enamored of 1960s horror-mysteries.

The End of August at the Hotel Ozone see *Late August at the*

The Epic Hero and the Beast see *The Sword and the Dragon*

Equinox (1967/70; Jack H. Harris Enterprises) Alternate Titles: *The Equinox: A Journey Into the Supernatural* (original, unreleased version); *The Beast* (home video). In retrospect, this scruffy, underdog production seems destined to become exactly what it is: a cult favorite. Four college students plan to meet a professor at his cabin retreat and enjoy a picnic in the woods nearby. But they discover the cabin has been destroyed, then come into possession of an ancient book of satanic rites. Eventually, they piece together that the professor, performing rituals described in the book, has accidentally unleashed a host of infernal terrors. With its Lovecraftian scenario and Harryhausen-esque stop-motion animated creatures, *Equinox* bombards viewers with one weird, wildly imaginative idea after another (black magic, demonic possession, trans-dimensional gateways, mythical monsters, etc.). Not all these ideas work (some prove beyond the technical capacity of the picture's semi-professional cast and crew), but their audacity and sheer volume, combined with the picture's frantic pace, render boredom impossible. For a low-budget production, the visual effects (including a winged devil and a monster that looks like a close cousin of Ray Harryhausen's Ymir) are very impressive — which was the point. In 1967, aspiring visual effects artists Dennis Muren, Jim Danforth and David Allen teamed to produce a 71-minute film titled *The Equinox: A Journey Into the Supernatural* to showcase their talents. But Muren and friends couldn't secure a distributor. So exploitation maven Jack H. Harris bought the film and hired actor/writer/director Jack Woods to rework it. Woods made major revisions, including introducing the character of Ranger Asmodeus (played by Woods himself), expanding the picture's running time to 86 minutes. Woods also replaced the film's original title theme with a haunting melody that sounds like a music box from Hell, and shortened the title to simply *Equinox*. All of these alterations worked to the benefit of the film, which was finally released in 1970. Fans of classic TV will recognize *WKRP in Cincinnati*'s "Herb Tarlek," Frank Bonner (billed here under his real name, Frank Boers, Jr.), as one of the students.

Escape from Planet Earth see *The Doomsday Machine*

Escapement see *The Electronic Monster*

An Evening of Edgar Allan Poe (1969; AIP-TV) Though made strictly for television by American International Pictures, *An Evening of Edgar Allan Poe* is included here because of its immense interest to fans of Edgar Allan Poe and/or Vincent Price. Produced, directed and co-adapted by Ken Johnson (who came from directing *Adam-12* episodes, and went on to direct/produce/write/etc. various *Incredible Hulk*, *V* and *Alien Nation* TV movies/miniseries/etc., not to mention a turn on *The Bionic Woman*— perhaps he leaves *that* one off his resume), this is a word-for-word recitation of four Poe stories by the mellifluous master of menace himself, Vincent Price. Price, the only cast member, performs faithful recitations of "The Tell Tale Heart," "The Sphynx," "The Cask of Amontillado" and "The Pit and the Pendulum." Each recital takes place on an appropriate and realistic set, ranging from 19th century drawing room to sumptuous dining hall to rat-infested dungeon. The marvelous sets are matched by equally striking costumes for Price. Price proves himself a storyteller supreme, going from drawing room civility to the passion of raging madness and all points in between. Poe's stories, macabre and fascinating, are brought to palpable life by the inflections of

A stop-motion demon from Hell in the low-budget cult classic *Equinox* (1970).

Price's resonant voice, the gestures of his hands, and the exquisite glint of madness in his eyes. The camerawork (including well-timed zooms, changes in focus, and perspectives that punctuate the frisson at hand) accents Price's movements and pointed tones, and the lighting effects and camera angles are used as effective exclamations. The full terror to be found in the dark genius of Edgar Allan Poe is made frighteningly accessible by the storytelling talent of Vincent Price. The actor labeled this little-seen and seemingly forgotten bit of small-screen uniqueness "probably the best thing I ever did in the way of Poe." *An Evening of Edgar Allan Poe* is not to be missed by fans of the particularly literate (and literal) shudder.

Evil Brain from Outer Space (1958/64; Shin-Toho/AIP-TV; Japan) The final *Starman* film, assembled for American TV from the original Japanese serial, pits Japan's superhero against a gang of colorfully costumed mutants. Fans who enjoyed the first three entries in the series won't be disappointed with this one, which is just as goofy and action-packed as the rest. Other viewers are advised to steer clear.

The Evil Eye (1963/64; Warner Bros./AIP; Italy; b&w) Original Title: *La Ragazza Che Sapeva Troppo* (*The Girl Who Knew Too Much*). Director Mario Bava's seriocomic Hitchcockian thriller is sometimes credited as the first "giallo" movie, a particularly lurid and violent sub-genre of murder mysteries (inspired by pulpy Italian crime novels with yellow covers) that became wildly popular in the 1970s and eventually spawned the American slasher film phenomenon. But while some elements of the giallo style are present in *The Evil Eye*, not enough of them are in evidence for the picture to qualify as a true giallo (the killer does not wear a mask or gloves, for instance; more importantly, the overall tone of the piece is far too light and frothy). Bava would continue to tinker with the formula in "The Telephone" segment from *Black Sabbath* (1963) before unleashing the giallo in all its gory — er, glory — with *Blood and Black Lace* (1964). While it may not be the proto-giallo some critics suggest, and despite significant flaws, *The Evil Eye* remains very entertaining. American tourist Nora Davis (Letitia Roman) witnesses a murder and then sets out to solve the crime when no one believes her story. Aided by a young doctor (John Saxon) and a kindly Roman housewife (Valentina Cortesa) who bears a striking resemblance to the murder victim, Nora suspects she's on the trail of a serial murderer known as the ABC Killer. A supernatural wrinkle forms when it seems the crime she witnessed may have actually occurred 10 years earlier, but this angle is abruptly abandoned in favor of a more conventional (yet less satisfying) solution to the mystery. Roman and Saxon make affable leads, but the script, developed by half dozen writers, is jumbled and uneven. Still, Bava manages some spellbinding moments, including the sequence in which Nora, woozy after being mugged, witnesses the killing. Although renowned for his brilliant use of impressionist color in his later films, the beautifully shot *Evil Eye* demonstrates Bava's mastery of black-and-white cinematography as well. *The Evil Eye*, issued in Italy as *The Girl Who Knew Too Much* in 1963, was judiciously re-cut by AIP for its U.S. release in 1964, with additional alterations made through dubbing (AIP also replaced the original Roberto Nicolosi score with a new Les Baxter soundtrack). The American version's revised ending improves on the cheeky Italian resolution (which included a marijuana reference) and generally plays in a more comedic fashion that the original Italian cut. In either version, however, *The Evil Eye/The Girl Who Knew Too Much* remains well worth seeing, especially for Bava fans.

This American poster for Mario Bava's proto-giallo *The Evil Eye* (1963/64) does its best to convince potential viewers that it's a supernatural horror flick. It isn't.

The Eye Creatures (1965; AIP-TV) Larry Buchanan, that grade-Z filmmaker from Texas, strikes again with this uncredited remake of the 1957 AIP winner *Invasion of the Saucer Men*. Shot in 16mm and sold directly to television, *The Eye Creatures* offers a 30-year-old John Ashley playing a teenager, a supporting cast of non-actors, static (non)direction, inconsistent day-for-night photography (black night sky alternating with shots of blue noonday sky *in the same scene*) and, worst of all, ridiculous, pitiful, ineffectual monsters. The original Saucer Men, with their huge bulbous heads, bug-eyes and leathery, veined skin, became an icon of '50s monster movies. The Eye Creatures look like the Michelin Tire Man doing a bad Frankenstein

Monster imitation. Inferior in every way, this version of the Little Green Men from Mars tale possesses none of the charm, humor or fun of the original.

Eye of the Cat (1969; Universal) More of a quirky crime thriller than a horror film, the well-shot, well-acted, and cleverly-scripted (by *Psycho* screenwriter Joseph Stefano) *Eye of the Cat* has handsome, free-spirited ladies' man Wylie (Michael Sarrazin) lured into a plot to murder his wealthy estranged "aunt," Danni (Eleanor Parker), by his aunt's seductive hair-stylist, Kassia (Gayle Hunnicutt). Danni (despite looking the short side of 40) is dying from emphysema, and intends to leave her wealth to her many cats. Kassia plans to put Wylie in the benefactor's seat, then hasten Danni's demise. Things, however, do not go quite as planned (particularly since Wylie suffers from a severe case of ailurophobia (fear of cats), nor are the characters quite what they seem (as revealed by an unexpected twist). Though somewhat slow to start, this ultimately engrossing film offers enough offbeat characterizations (Wylie's motives remain mysterious, and his actions and attitudes run the gamut from impish to malicious), hints of unhealthy relationships ("Aunt Danni was my father's mistress, not mine," explains Wylie as to why his father didn't leave *him* his money; and Danni's attentions towards Wylie smacks of more than mere maternal devotion). The San Francisco setting offers a priceless (and amusing) look at the trendy youth culture of the time (including a visit to an upscale hippie bar featuring throw pillows instead of chairs, and sitars instead of guitars), as well as a truly harrowing scene in which Danni loses control of her wheelchair and careens out of control down a steep San Francisco street (with frantic close-up shots that would do Hitchcock proud). As a straight horror film, this *Cat* offers a rather jaundiced eye (the ferocious feline "attack" comes only in the last 10 minutes, with nary a whiff of the supernatural about it); but as a character-driven, thought-provoking, twist-laden thriller, this *Eye* is definitely worth a look.

Felines strike back at Gayle Hunnicutt in *Eye of the Cat* (1969).

The Fabulous Baron Munchausen (1961/64; Ceskoslovenský Státní Film; Czechoslovakia) Alternate Titles: *Baron Munchausen*, *The Adventures of Baron Munchausen*. Original Language Title: *Baron Prásil*. This journey into the fantastic world of tall-tale spinner/adventurer Baron Munchausen by Czech filmmaker Karel Zeman (*Journey to the Beginning of Time*, *The Fabulous World of Jules Verne*, *On the Comet*) utilizes every form of special effect imaginable — block-prints, cut-outs, drawings, cartoon animation, stop-motion animation, tinting, superimpositions— to create a magical world in which gigantic fish swallow ships whole, cannonball rides are commonplace, black clouds envelope entire cities, and giant seahorses are just waiting for riders. Suffused with humor and charm, the story follows an astronaut landing on the Moon only to find Baron Munchausen already there. Mistaking the suited cosmonaut for a "moon man," the Baron takes him to Earth (aboard his space "sailing" ship), where they engage in all manner of adventures, including rescuing a princess from 10,000 angry Turks and traveling in the belly of a great beast. While the effects are about as realistic-looking as the story, they're also just as imaginative and suffused with sometimes breathtaking beauty (at times appearing almost like a classical painting come to life). *Fabulous* is indeed an apt adjective for this *Baron*.

The Fabulous World of Jules Verne (1958/61; Ceskoslovenský Státní Film /Warner Bros.; Czechoslovakia; b&w) Original Title: *Vynález Zkázy*. This offbeat, Czech-made fantasy adventure, loosely based on the little-read Jules Verne novel *For the Flag*, sometimes turned up on American television in the 1970s and '80s, where it stood out due to its striking visuals. Director Karel Zeman employed simplistic, two-dimensional animation (in the same style later used by Terry Gilliam for his *Monty Python* credit sequences) and silent era visual effects techniques (some of which dated back to Georges Melies and Edwin S. Porter) to make this movie look like a series of antiquated engraved magazine illustrations magically brought to life (a process billed as "Mysti-Mation"). The story, about a Captain Nemo-like villain who kidnaps the world's greatest scientist and tries to dupe him into helping topple the governments of the world, features hot air balloons, futuristic submarines and airships, and other typically Verne-ian contraptions but offers little in the way of characterization or dramatic tension. Its thin and ill-focused narrative makes *The Fabulous World of Jules* great fun to look at but a chore to watch. Zeman followed this picture with the visually inventive comedic fantasy *The Fabulous Baron Munchausen* (1961), which combined live action with stop-motion animation and puppetry.

The Face of Fu Manchu (1965; Seven Arts; UK/Ireland/West Germany) The evil Fu Manchu (Christopher Lee, who spent nearly three hours in the makeup chair every day to transform his occidental features into those of the Chinese super villain) concocts an airborne poison from the rare Tibetan Black Hill poppy and wipes out an entire English village of 3000 people as a demonstration (horrifically hammered home by such disturbing images as the body of a shop owner sprawled over his own window display and a young boy lying dead across his bicycle). The inscrutable madman plans to rule the world from his secret hideout below the River Thames in the heart of London itself. Lee's imposing playing brings author Sax Rohmer's famous "Yellow Peril" character to malevolent life, and his calm power makes a perfect foil for the energetic portrayal of Nigel Green as Fu's Scotland Yard nemesis, Nayland Smith. Krimi stalwart Joachim Fuchsberger adds further punch (often literally) to the scenario, which is capably handled by director Don Sharp (*The Kiss of the Vampire*, *Witchcraft*, *Rasputin the Mad Monk*). *Face* did so well for producer (and writer) Harry Alan Towers that he made four more Fu Manchus over the next four years—*The Brides of Fu Manchu* (1966, again directed by Don Sharp), *The Vengeance of Fu Manchu* (1968), *Kiss and Kill* (1968), and *The Castle of Fu Manchu* (1969)—all starring Christopher Lee, and all offering diminishing returns for viewers (particularly after Eurohack director Jess Franco took the helm for the final two).

Face of Terror (1962/64; Futuramic Releasing; Spain; b&w) Original Language Title: *La Cara del Terror*. The question (asked by this film's trailer): "Was she really a woman — or a depraved, blood-mad monster?!" The answer, disappointingly (at least for horror fans): The former, not the latter. More medical drama than horror movie, the Spanish *Face of Terror* promises to echo such Continental terrors as *The Horror Chamber of Dr. Faustus* and *The Awful Dr. Orlof* in its tale of a doctor's miraculous new surgical technique developed to restore ruined faces. But such horrific vibrations die down rather quickly when the kindly surgeon employs not the stolen skin from unwilling victims, but a special artificial plastic to repair a woman's disfigured visage. Unfortunately, said woman is an escapee from a mental institution, and her unbalanced state of mind, coupled with the eventual failure of the procedure, results in a pair of murders. Co-directed by American William Hole, Jr. (*Ghost of Dragstrip Hollow*, *The Devil's Hand*), *Face of Terror* was filmed in English. While this works for leads Fernando Rey (as the doctor) and Lisa Gaye (his patient), it makes some of the supporting performances appear stiff and stilted, since the Spanish players obviously were not comfortable in that language. Though competently filmed and acted (by the two leads, anyway), the lack of any true horror or villainy (Rey's unknowing surgeon is almost saintly; and Gaye's escapee has no greater ambitions than to regain her beauty and work as a waitress, only becoming dangerous when cornered) makes this a *Face of Melodrama* rather than *Terror*.

Fahrenheit 451 (1966; Anglo Enterprises/Universal; U.K.) François Truffaut directed this deeply flawed but fascinating adaptation of Ray Bradbury's celebrated novel set in a world where reading is illegal and "firemen" burn books instead of putting out fires. This was Truffaut's first color film, his first shot outside France and first in English. It was a project about which he cared deeply—Truffaut, an avid reader, turned down eventual blockbuster *Bonnie and Clyde* to shoot *Fahrenheit* instead—and he creates an icy, forlorn vision of a dystopian future where, without books, human thought and passion are slowly fading away. His judicious employment of authentic loca-

French poster for *Fahrenheit 451* (1966).

tions (which, nonetheless, appear remarkably futuristic) and striking use of color (bold reds are especially prominent) also serve the film well. But some of Truffaut's ideas damage the movie badly, especially the stunt casting of Julie Christie in two key roles and the presence of Oskar Werner in the lead. The German Werner, who had co-starred in Truffaut's *Jules and Jim*, was ill-suited for the part and battled with Truffaut throughout the production. Truffaut's discomfort with English created additional problems. The picture's contemplative pace and lack of bravura action or special effects sequences made *Fahrenheit 451* a box office disappointment. But it remains worth a look for fans of the director, or of Bradbury, or for anyone open to off-beat, intellectually stimulating sci-fi.

Fail-Safe (1964; Columbia; b&w) Throughout his distinguished career, director Sidney Lumet has crafted suspenseful, thought-provoking films with socially conscious themes (*12 Angry Men* [1957], *The Pawnbroker* [1964], *Network* [1976], etc.). Despite the ripped-from-the-headlines nature of some of his pictures, Lumet's movies usually age well, since his films emphasize interpersonal drama rather than political sloganeering. The grim, tightly wound *Fail-Safe*—about a computer malfunction that accidentally triggers an air strike on Moscow—is no exception. This white-knuckle thriller seems even more plausible because it's full of believable, well-rounded characters. Henry Fonda's commanding yet compassionate portrayal of the president is a primary strength of the picture, but the rest of the cast deliver solid performances, too, especially Dan O'Herlihy as a remorseful general, Walter Matthau as a war-mongering political scientist and Larry Hagman as the president's nervous young translator. While it suffers in comparison with director Stanley Kubrick's irreverent satire *Dr. Strangelove*, released the same year and with a very similar scenario, *Fail-Safe*, taken on its own merits, remains a gripping experience. Director Stephen Frears remade *Fail-Safe* in 2000 as a rare live television drama with an all-star cast, including George Clooney, Harvey Keitel and Don Cheadle, with Richard Dreyfuss as the president. The original remains superior.

Fantastic Voyage (1966; Twentieth Century–Fox) A defecting Russian scientist is shot before he can divulge crucial secrets, but clings tenuously to life. To save him, a team of doctors and scientists board a submarine, which is shrunk to microscopic size and injected into the man's bloodstream. Their mission—to destroy a potentially fatal blood clot—must be accomplished in less than hour, after which the sub and its crew will begin to return to normal size. *Fantastic Voyage*—an A-budget major studio production with Oscar-winning special effects, a respected director (Richard Fleischer) and an intriguing cast (Stephen Boyd, Raquel Welch, Donald Pleasence, Arthur Kennedy, Edmond O'Brien, etc.)—wowed audiences in its day but hasn't aged well. Part of the problem is that its miniaturization premise, although novel at the time, now plays like something left over from an episode of *The Magic School Bus*. *Fantastic Voyage* also suffers from a lethargic tempo (it takes 37 minutes for the titular journey to begin), cornball philosophical dialogue ("We stand in the middle of infinity, between outer space and inner space, and there's no limit to either," Kennedy blathers) and a tendency toward stilted edutainment (with biological processes explained *ad nauseum* as the sub moves through the heart, lungs, lymph nodes and inner ear on its circuitous route to the brain). The narrative also wastes energy on an utterly transparent subplot about a saboteur onboard the sub. Although *Fantastic Voyage* claims devoted fans, most of whom have loved this movie since childhood, less nostalgic viewers may be tempted to abandon ship.

The Fear Chamber (1968/71; Azteca/Columbia; Mexico/U.S.) Original Language Title: *La Camara del Terror*; Alternate Title: *Torture Zone*. Though this isn't the worst of the four final films Boris Karloff made in his lifetime (*Macabre Serenade* wins that [dis]honor), it's a close runner-up. (The other two are *The Incredible Invasion* and *Isle of the Snake People*; all four features were shot back-to-back in 1968 for Mexican producer Luis Enrique Vergara.) In *Fear Chamber* Karloff plays kindly-but-obsessed scientist Dr. Mandel, who finds a living-rock creature under a volcano that needs "transfusions of ferriculan" to survive, which "can only be produced in the body of a human being in a state of extreme terror." To this end, he and his helpers (including a Lennie-like hulk, a sinister Hindu, and a bald dwarf!) terrorize young women in "the Fear Chamber" (a cheap carnival-style house of horrors)

The miniaturized micronauts (and their "ship") on a *Fantastic Voyage* (1966) through the human body.

DON'T PANIC...
ONLY YOUR LIFE IS IN DANGER!
BORIS KARLOFF
JULISSA-CARLOS EAST-ISELA VEGA
FEAR CHAMBER
YERYE BEIRUTE · SANDRA CHAVEZ · EVA MULLER · SANTANON
JUAN IBAÑEZ
ENRICO C. CABIATI · JACK HILL y L. E. VERGARA
LUIS ENRIQUE VERGARA
COLOR

One of a quartet of Mexican films Boris Karloff made in 1968, just before his death (with only two, including this one, receiving a spotty theatrical release Stateside in 1971).

via spiders, snakes, skeletons and bitch-slaps before extracting the necessary hormone. Things go awry, however, when the rock gets greedy, and Mandel has to contend not only with the killer rock (who has miraculously grown a set of unwieldy tentacles), but an annoying daughter, duplicitous assistants, sadistic servants, and a show-stopping (for all the wrong reasons) strip-tease in the middle of the movie. Despite such questionable but potentially entertaining elements, the talky film moves about as fast as the rock-monster (with Karloff spending much of his screen time literally in bed). It all devolves into a tawdry, inane mess. Poor Boris.

50,000 B.C. (Before Clothing) (1963; Biolane Corp.) In this unwatchable no-budget amalgam of bad burlesque comedy and dull nudist footage, a hen-pecked sanitation worker accidentally travels back in time via his neighbor's time machine (which looks like a vintage taxi) to meet a group of cavemen (and women). Apart from the plentiful pulchritude on display, the only point of interest is the brief appearance of 7' 6" Eddie Carmel, grandiosely (and inaccurately) billed as "the World's Tallest Man," in the role of "the Giant" who threatens the cave people. He even delivers a few (poorly written) lines before he literally goes up in smoke as the butt of one of Our Hero's bad jokes. Carmel, who suffered from acromegaly, played the Closet Monster in the delirious *The Brain That Wouldn't Die* (1962).

The Finishing School see *The House That Screamed*

Fire Monsters Against the Son of Hercules (1962; Embassy; Italy) Original Language Title: *Maciste Contro i Mostri.* Alternate Title: *Colossus of the Stone Age* (UK). During the peplum craze of the 1960s (begun with the Steve Reeves Hercules pictures), Embassy bought the U.S. rights to a whole fistful of sword-and-sandal knockoffs, transformed (via the magic of dubbing) the hero du jour into a "son of Hercules" to capitalize on the more-familiar-to-American-audiences name, and released them directly to television in a "Sons of Hercules" package. *Fire Monsters* is about as far from the Hercules mold as one could get, as it's set not in Ancient Greece, but in some unnamed land at the tail end of the last ice age! The plot follows a peaceful band of nomadic, stone-axe-sporting sun-worshippers and their conflict with a tribe of brutal moon-worshipping cave-dwellers. The beefy, redheaded "Maxus, son of Hercules" (Reg Lewis) shows up out of nowhere to help the nomads rescue their women, stolen by the cave-dwellers. A more accurate title for the film would have been "*Water* Monsters Against the Son of Hercules," since no "fire monsters" appear, just one lion-faced sea serpent, a trio of skinny river-dragon hand puppets, and one lumbering rubber cave-beast. All these disappointing Sid and Marty Krofft-level "monsters" are quickly dispatched by the constantly-flexing Maxus. Lewis offers even less presence than most of his musclemen colleagues (though his duckbilled pompadour stands up impressively); and the meandering story spends most of its time on primitive love-matches and limp tribal battles. The result: *Fire Monsters* fails to spark.

First Men in the Moon (1964; Columbia) Animation legend Ray Harryhausen worked on many terrific sci-fi and fantasy pictures. *First Men in the Moon* isn't one of them. This comic fantasy, based on a novel by H.G. Wells, isn't funny, nor is it satisfying as either a Wells adaptation or a Harryhausen picture. The screenplay, by Nigel Kneale and Jan Read, smoothes over Wells' stinging social satire and replaces it with overripe farce. It also adds a pointless framing sequence set in the present day and relates its narrative in flashback. Nutty inventor Joseph Cavor (Lionel Jeffries) develops an anti-gravity paste, with which he coats a giant metal sphere and sets out to explore the moon. He's joined on this expedition by his neighbors, Kate (Martha Hyer) and her shiftless fiancé Bedford (Edward Judd). The trio reaches the moon, but fall prisoner to the Solonites, a race of insect people who live in a honeycomb of tunnels beneath the lunar surface. *First Men in the Moon* devotes nearly half its bloated 103-minute running time to the belabored antics of Cavor and Bedford as they attempt to complete the moon sphere (which doesn't launch until 45 minutes of the film have elapsed), and to its superfluous framing sequence. The movie also runs disappointingly short on stop-motion animation. The Solonites are mostly portrayed by men in bug suits. Harryhausen's only notable animated creature (which looks like a giant centipede) has minimal screen time. Although the visual effects are excellent and the climactic sequences beneath the lunar surface are nicely mounted, there simply isn't enough worthwhile material here to earn a recommendation, except to Wells or Harryhausen completists, or to devotees of the histrionic comedy stylings of Lionel Jeffries.

First Spaceship on Venus (1960/62; Crown International; East Germany/Poland) Original Language Title: *Der Schweigende Stern.* Alternate Titles: *Planet of the Dead*; *Silent Star*; *Spaceship Venus Does Not Reply.* This 1960 Soviet Bloc production (released dubbed in the U.S. two years later) is a serious spaceflight film with good effects, a great-looking rocketship, and a multi-national, multi-racial crew. In the "future" of 1985 a group of scientist/astronauts head for Venus, only to find a bizarre, dead world that is still, however, fraught with danger. Though no imported classic (a general dullness pervades the proceedings), *First Spaceship* offers effects that are well above most of its contemporary American counterparts, with convincing rocket interiors and a weird, almost surreal Venusian landscape. And there's even a black astronaut — something unheard of in American films of the time — and a rather downbeat ending, making this one of the more unusual straight sci-fi entries of the decade.

The Forbin Project see *Colossus, the Forbin Project*

Fortress of the Dead (1965/66) Frank Mason (John Hackett), the sole survivor of a World War II artillery battery, returns to Corregidor 20 years after the war to try to lay to rest the guilt he feels over failing to bring aid to his 37 companions trapped in a tunnel during a Japanese bombardment, dooming them to death by suffocation. Finally facing his demons, Frank learns that the souls of his comrades may require something more of him than simple remorse. Hackett (a dead ringer for '50s sci-fi stalwart Robert Clarke) plays his role in a low-key but believable fashion, while director/producer/screenwriter Ferde Grofé, Jr., employs limited light sources (on an even more limited budget) to enhance the eeriness and isolation of the actual ruined bunkers of Corregidor in the Philippines, making one believe that the shadows there may indeed house more than rats and dust. Unfortunately, the story offers little in the way of surprise, and it could easily be tightened to under an hour, making it more suited to a TV anthology show such as *Thriller* or *The Twilight Zone*— which makes its fate of being released directly to television a year after its production a not-inappropriate one.

Frankenstein Must Be Destroyed (1969/70; Hammer/Warner Bros.; U.K.) *Frankenstein Must Be Destroyed*, the last great Hammer horror film, and director Terence Fisher's final masterpiece, was issued in late 1969 in England but didn't reach American theaters until 1970. Frankenstein (Peter Cushing) coerces a young doctor (Simon Ward) and his fiancée, Anna (Veronica Carlson), to help him spirit former colleague Dr. Brant (George Pravda) away from an insane asylum. Then Frankenstein transplants the madman's brain into another body and tries to cure him — all to learn the solution to a medical riddle Brandt solved, but which continues to vex Frankenstein. Cleverly written, flawlessly produced and superbly performed, *Frankenstein Must Be Destroyed* blends crackling Hitchcockian suspense (including an unforgettable, heart-pounding sequence in which Anna struggles to hide a corpse unearthed in her garden by a water main break) with dollops of dark humor (mostly thanks to Cushing's dry, caustic delivery). Fisher pulls it all together beautifully and contributes some inspired flourishes of his own, such as the film's opening sequence in which the camera follows Frankenstein's feet as he walks the streets of London carrying a head in a metal case. Fisher — and many fans— disapproved of a controversial scene in which Frankenstein rapes Anna, but this ugly moment remains in character for the ruthless, sociopathic scientist used to simply taking what he wants from those under his power. *Frankenstein Must Be Destroyed* would have provided the perfect endpoint for Hammer's Frankenstein series. The studio seemed flummoxed about where to go from here. Hammer released *The Horror of Frankenstein*, a spoof directed by Jimmy Sangster, in 1970. Fisher and Cushing returned for *Frankenstein*

Arguably Hammer's finest Frankenstein, "...and Hammer says so!" A British poster for the film from 1969.

and the Monster from Hell in 1974, but that entry fell far short of expectations and brought down the final curtain on the series.

Frankenstein's Bloody Terror (1968/71; Independent International; Spain) Original Language Title: *La Marca del Hombre Lobo.* Alternate Title: *Mark of the Wolfman* (DVD). "Now, the most frightening Frankenstein story of all, as the ancient werewolf curse brands the family of monster-makers as 'Wolfstein,'" announced the opening narration tacked on by Independent International when they released the film Stateside in 1971. The company needed a Frankenstein movie to fulfill a booking obligation, and so misleadingly re-christened this 1968 import *Frankenstein's Bloody Terror* (despite the fact that no "Frankenstein" appears). This first film introducing Waldemar Daninsky (Paul Naschy) as the Wolfman has him slaying a revived werewolf and in the process becoming infected himself. In desperation, he sends for a strange couple, experts in the occult, for help. They turn out to be vampires, leading to a supernatural confrontation. Star Naschy wrote the screenplay as well (under his real name of Jacinto Molina), and wrote or co-wrote (and occasionally directed) ten subsequent films in the series. Though it sports some impressive, authentic castle and catacomb settings, and some striking, atmospheric lighting that would make even Mario Bava proud, *Frankenstein's Bloody Terror* ranks as one of the lesser Waldemar the Werewolf films due to its slow pace, predictable plotting and dearth of character development. As the 1970s progressed, Naschy's Werewolf series soon traded the rather tame Gothicism of this first entry for increasing dollops of nudity and gore (not to mention outlandish plotting), culminating in the delicious delirium of such entries as *The Werewolf vs. the Vampire Women* (1971; aka *Werewolf Shadow*) and *Night of the Howling Beast* (1975; aka *The Werewolf and the Yeti*), arguably the best—or at least most entertaining—of the bunch.

Despite its misleading ad art and title, no Frankenstein Monster appears in *Frankenstein's Bloody Terror* (1968/71). Vampires and werewolves, on the other hand...

Frozen Alive (1966; Feature Film Corp.; UK/West Germany) In this obscure sci-fi melodrama, a scientist (Mark Stevens) experiments on himself and becomes the first human to be frozen alive. The same evening, unknown to him, his wife accidentally shoots herself, with circumstances pointing to the scientist—now in suspended animation—as the number-one murder suspect. Thanks to some engaging playing by the principals, an adult approach to the material, and some witty dialogue, the drama involving a love quadrangle manages to sustain interest until the science fiction angle kicks in during the final 15 minutes (and it's sober sci-fi at that, with the human freezing handled in a realistically matter-of-fact, scientific manner), resulting in an offbeat and moderately entertaining slice of '60s cinema.

Gamera vs. Barugon see ***War of the Monsters***

Gamera vs. Gaos see ***Return of the Giant Monsters***

Gamera vs. Guiron see ***Attack of the Monsters***

Gamera vs. Viras see ***Destroy All Planets***

Games (1967; Universal) This thinly veiled and self-consciously arty remake of director Henri-Georges Clouzot's classic French thriller *Diabolique* (1955) contains some major flaws, but overcomes them with a gifted cast and expert direction. A mysterious older woman, Lisa (Simone Signoret, who starred in *Diabolique*), enters the lives of a debauched *nouveau riche* couple, Paul (James Caan) and Jennifer (Katharine Ross), who share a penchant for practical jokes. Lisa ups the ante on their dangerous games, introducing the couple to Russian roulette. Then a practical joke goes awry and Paul accidentally kills a grocery delivery boy. The film's overly stylized, tragically hip opening act may tax viewers' patience, and its "surprise" ending remains entirely predictable throughout, but in between those low points, *Games* builds suspense inexorably and generates moments of real frisson. Director Curtis Harrington (*Night Tide, Who Slew Auntie Roo?, What's the Matter with Helen?),* a Hitchcock disciple, handles this material masterfully, lending the proceedings a striking visual look and making the

Don Knotts has more to fear than fear itself (including his own reflection) in *The Ghost and Mr. Chicken* (1966) (courtesy Ted Okuda).

most of a radical production design that combines an "old dark house" set with pop art fixtures (Paul and Jennifer collect modern art). And, as in all Harrington's films, there's a heavy dose of gallows humor. The script makes some fleeting attempts at suggesting a supernatural element, but these remain perfunctory and transparent. Despite its shortcomings, *Games* proves the director's most satisfying film.

Gappa, the Triphibian Monster see *Monster from a Prehistoric Planet*

The Ghost and Mr. Chicken (1966, Universal) This disarming Don Knotts vehicle remains one of the most charming of all horror-comedies. Knotts plays Luther Heggs, a Barney Fife-like small town newspaper typesetter who dreams of becoming a reporter. He gets his chance by volunteering to spend the night in a "haunted" house where a murder was committed 20 years before. Although even the youngest members of the audience will spot the story's *Scooby Doo* finale a mile off, the film's fright sequences remain credible, thanks to Alan Rankin's straightforward direction and cinematographer William Margulies' eerie lighting. But the film's primary appeal remains its well-sketched characters and the endearing performances of its cast. Knotts was never better than here, offering a deceptively subtle and well-rounded portrait of a small man with big dreams who finds the courage to pursue his aspirations. Knotts is side-splittingly funny in small moments (eating chicken soup standing up) and in major set pieces (such as his meltdown while speaking at a chamber of commerce picnic). Perhaps because he worked so much on television, Knotts seldom earns mention among the great screen comedians. *The Ghost and Mr. Chicken* proves that he deserves to be counted in their number.

The Ghost in the Invisible Bikini (1966; American International Pictures) Boris Karloff plays the recently deceased Hiram Stokely, who is visited in his crypt by his long-dead girlfriend (Susan Hart). She tells him he must perform one good deed in the next 24 hours in order to get into Heaven. Stokely sends her ghost (wearing an invisible bikini, naturally—meaning the naughty bits become invisible) back to Earth to help his rightful heirs win out over those trying to cheat them. Saturated with puerile humor (including an *F Troop*-style Indian henchman) and a half-dozen subpar rock 'n' roll numbers (most involving dance parties around the castle's pool!), this *Ghost* scares no one. The menaces come in the form of an escaped pet gorilla, a long-haired man in a mummy suit, and one of Larry Buchanan's sorry *Eye Creatures* costumes. Basil Rathbone, playing Stokely's unscrupulous lawyer and the head baddie, adds some class to the proceedings (as well as energy—the 73-year-old Rathbone reportedly did his own fencing in a swordfight with "teen" star Tommy Kirk!); and the filmmakers thankfully confine Karloff's few scenes to his crypt, where he watches (and comments upon) the silly shenanigans through a crystal ball, thereby preserving a modicum of dignity for the octogenarian actor. *The Ghost in the Invisible Bikini*, with its admittedly impressive castle sets and well-dressed chamber of horrors, was the biggest budgeted of AIP's "Beach Party" pictures, but it failed at the box office and so became the last of the beach movies as well.

Ghosts in Rome (1961; Lux Films/Vides/Galatea; Italy) Original Language Title: *Fantasmi a Roma.* In this Italian ghost comedy, the lord of a manor house is killed when his hot water heater blows up, and he bands together with the other ghosts of the house to prevent the sale of his property. Director Antonio Pietrangeli was a qualified medical doctor before turning to a career in film.

Ghosts—Italian Style (1969; MGM; Italy) Original Language Title: *Questi Fantasmi.* Sophia Loren and Vittorio Gassman play poor newlyweds who move into a haunted house in this Italian ghost comedy. Male Lead Gassman also starred in the 1961 supernatural comedy *Ghosts in Rome.*

The Giant of Metropolis (1961/63; Seven Arts; Italy) Original Language Title: *Il Gigante di Metropolis.* "I think the time is propitious for you to begin your mission as a terrorist." You won't be hearing these words (spoken by one of the good guys to the film's hero) in post–9/11 Hollywood. The "terrorist" in question is a leather loincloth-clad muscleman named "Obro" (Gordon Mitchell) who journeys to the legendary city of Metropolis on the continent of Atlantis to chastise the power-mad King for tampering in God's domain. (The King wants to use the Atlanteans' advanced science to grant his pre-teen son immortality with some kind of brain transplant.) In any case,

Left: **One of those films that Boris Karloff generally left *off* his résumé.** ***Right:*** **The mighty Obro (Gordon Mitchell, whose name is inexplicably transposed on this American poster) takes on an Atlantean opponent in the sci-fi-tinged peplum *The Giant of Metropolis* (1961/63).**

Obro resorts to brutal hit-and-run raids on the King's guards in order to weaken the ruler's despotic control over his people. No better quality-wise than so many of its indifferent beefcake brethren, *Giant* offers the usual lackluster fight scenes with palace guards, cheesy special effects (in the form of different colored lights denoting "scalding ray," "crushing ray" and "freezing ray"), sub-par monstrous opponents (one big caveman and a quintet of smallish men denoted as "pygmies"), and small-scale scenes of destruction. The film's only distinguishing characteristic is its mix of classical imagery (Grecian costumes and weaponry) and sci-fi trappings. Set in 20,000 B.C.(!), the film sports *Star Trek*-style futuristic city sets and much talk of the power of science. Unfortunately, despite this novel approach to the sword-and-sandal genre, in the end this *Giant* is short on entertainment.

The Giants of Thessaly (1960/62; Italy/France; Medallion) Original Language Title: *Giganti della Tessaglia.* Though directed and co-written by the usually reliable Riccardo Freda (*The Horrible Dr. Hichcock, The Ghost, The Witch's Curse*), this boring sword and sandal entry is a tepid telling of the Jason and the Argonauts tale, in which Jason and his crew, in 1250 B.C., sail aboard the Argo to find the famed Golden Fleece and thus save their country of Thessaly from destruction by the angry gods (via volcanic eruptions). Filled with dull subplots revolving around palace intrigue, female stowaways, awful dancing girl numbers, pointless infighting, and an interminable anti-climactic sequence in which Jason obtains the fleece not by fighting a hydra (as in the vastly superior *Jason and the Argonauts*) but by simply climbing a big statue to grab hold of it (no muss, no fuss, no monsters), *Giants* comes up short in the entertainment department. It also falls flat in the horror arena, offering only one brief encounter with a beautiful "witch" who changes men into sheep (or so we're *told*, anyway, as we never *see* it) and an even briefer tussle with an oversized one-eyed gorilla.

The Girl Killer see ***The Sex Killer***

Belgian poster for the poor peplum *The Giants of Thessaly* (1960/62).

The Girl Who Knew Too Much see ***The Evil Eye***

Girly see ***Mumsy, Nanny, Sonny & Girly***

Godzilla vs. Monster Zero see ***Monster Zero***

Godzilla vs. the Sea Monster (1966; Toho/AIP-TV; Japan) Original Language Title: *Gojira, Ebira, Mosura: Nankai no Daiketto* (Godzilla, Ebirah, Mothra: Great Duel in the North Sea). Alternate Title: *Ebirah, Monster of the Deep* (U.K.). This seventh installment in Toho's Godzilla saga marked a major shift in direction for the series. With a reduced budget, and with a new director (Jun Fukuda, who went on to helm six G-films) and composer (Masaru Sato) taking over for stalwarts Ishiro Honda and Akira Ikufube, respectively, the look and feel of the series changed—and not for the better. The original *Gojira* (1954), the most expensive movie produced in Japan up to that point, had been a grim tale made for grownups. But with *Sea Monster*, Godzilla movies became B-budgeted kiddie fare. Instead of smashing expensive miniature cities, hereafter Godzilla's activities would be confined almost exclusively to cheaper island sets. Visual effects suffered as well, resulting in fewer and less imaginative monster sequences. The stories grew more juvenile and comedic, a switch reflected in Sato's lighthearted scores. Not that *Sea Monster* is all bad. It's silly, indifferently crafted and comes up a little short on monster action, but it's also briskly paced and frequently (although not always intentionally) amusing. Natives of Infant Island (home of Mothra, who makes a cameo appearance) are being kidnapped and forced into slave labor at the hidden island fortress of a secret society bent on world domination. The island is protected by a giant lobster (known as Ebirah in the Japanese version but unnamed in American dubbed prints) that lives just offshore. A small band of unlucky castaways trapped on the island discover Godzilla hibernating in a cave, and awaken the King of the Monsters to help thwart the bad guys and free the natives. Although it's a steep step down from the preceding *Monster Zero* (1965), *Sea Monster* proves reasonably diverting and remains far superior to any of Fukuda's subsequent Godzilla pictures. Even so, *Sea Monster* failed to earn a theatrical release in the U.S.; AIP purchased it for American TV.

Godzilla's Revenge (1969/71; Toho/AIP-TV; Japan) This is where Toho's Godzilla series, sputtering for years, finally crashed and burned. Slow-mov-

A

Godzilla's Revenge (1969/71) inflicted Minya, Son of Godzilla, on an unwary public. (Despite the Teutonic title on this German lobby card, no Frankenstein Monster appears. Nor do any thrills.)

ing, inane and juvenile, with very little original monster footage, *Godzilla's Revenge* marked a new low. It's certainly the worst G-film of the 1960s, and arguably the worst in the history of the franchise. The story concerns a lonely young boy who is fascinated by giant monsters, and daydreams about the beasts frolicking on Monster Island. When the boy is kidnapped by a pair of bumbling bank robbers, his plight mirrors that of Godzilla's radioactive rugrat, Minya, who is being bullied by a bigger monster kid, Gabera. It's difficult to say what's worse: the saccharine sentimentality, the agonizing comedy "relief," the blatant recycling of stock footage from movies like *Godzilla vs. the Sea Monster* (1966) and *Son of Godzilla* (1967), or the elevation of Minya (who receded into the background during *Destroy All Monsters*, 1968) back to star status. No wonder director Ishiro Honda, who helmed this mess, stepped away from the series for its next four entries. *Godzilla's Revenge* failed to receive an American theatrical release, but was purchased for TV exhibition by AIP. Watch at your own risk.

Goliath Against the Giants (1961/63; Medallion; Italy/Spain) Original Language Title: *Goliath Contro i Giganti*; Alternate Title: *Goliath and the Giants.* There's plenty of action in this released-directly-to-American-TV peplum, as strong-man Goliath (Brad Harris, who is more expressive than most movie musclemen) fights devious rulers, palace guards, Amazonian women(!), oversized cavemen, and an ungainly iguana (standing in for a sea serpent) to protect his lady love. Unfortunately, most of the mayhem is of the mundane human variety (protracted gladiatorial and battle scenes), with the more fantastical faction consisting of a brief encounter with the aforementioned faux "sea serpent" and a quick face-off against a couple of large fellows dressed as Neanderthals (the "Giants" of the title). On the plus side, the ambitious film (moving from palace revolution to seafaring adventures to warrior women encounters) offers some impressive production values for its weight class, including loads of dress extras and overworked stuntmen, and some expansive ancient Rome-like sets.

Goliath and the Giants see ***Goliath against the Giants***

Gomar: The Human Gorilla see ***Night of the Bloody Apes***

Haunted House of Horror see ***Horror House***

Henry's Night In (1969; Astro-Gemco; b&w) A nerdish Henry, who's finding intimacy with his wife difficult, discovers "The Diary of the Invisible Man" in an old trunk and uses the formula to become an invisible neighborhood lothario. With the (crude—in more ways than one) invisibility angle employed for laughs rather than scares (Henry even sets some invisible mice loose at a "hen party" in a ploy to get the women to shed their clothes—and it works!), and, more importantly, to give the Raincoat Brigade a chance to ogle naked female bodies writhing underneath an invisible lover, *Henry's Night In* should be just another tedious and impoverished nudie-cutie. But thanks to an amusing and genuinely likable comic performance by Forman Shane as Henry, and some competent (and even clever at times) camerawork by the uncredited film crew, *Henry's Night In* becomes one of the more watchable entries of its type—which, admittedly, isn't saying much.

Hercules Against Moloch see ***The Conquest of Mycenae***

Hercules and the Captive Women (1963; Woolner Brothers/SPA; Italy/France) Original Language Title: *Ercole alla Conquista di Atlantide.* Alternate Titles: *Hercules and the Haunted Women*; *Hercules Conquers Atlantis* (UK). Hercules (Reg Park) is shipwrecked on a living island with an appetite for humans. The island-monster, named Proteus, materializes as a snake, lion, buzzard(!), ball of fire, and man-sized, horned chameleon creature. Herc breaks off the beast's horn (with a gruesomely moist result), killing Proteus and freeing a Princess who was being consumed by the living rock itself. She takes Hercules to her home island—Atlantis! There Herc locks horns with their evil Queen, knocks off an albino army, and punches a hole near the Temple of Uranus which

Reg Park battles "Proteus" in *Hercules and the Captive Women* (1963).

causes the continent to sink. Though sporting some impressive temple and stone catacomb sets (through which Hercules races an eight-horse chariot!), there's little to separate this film from the dozens of dull pepla made during the decade. Apart from the initial island-monster encounter (the movie's only tenuous tie to terror), *Hercules and the Captive Women* focuses on the usual shenanigans of duplicitous females and palace guards—and there are *no* Captive Women. Oddly, the film's soundtrack cribs a few musical cues from *Creature from the Black Lagoon*.

Hercules and the Haunted Women see ***Hercules and the Captive Women***

Hercules and the Princess of Troy (1965; Embassy Television; U.S./Italy) Alternate Title: *Hercules vs. the Sea Monster*. This 47-minute pilot for a proposed TV series that never materialized went out over the airwaves as a stand-alone "feature." Shot in Italy (in English), it stars Gordon Scott (TV's *Tarzan*) as the famous Greek demigod, who sails to Troy to help princess Diana (Diana Hyland) rid her land of a dreaded sea monster, to whom the Trojans must sacrifice one maiden each month. Carlo Rambaldi's full-sized articulated sea beast, looking like a cross between *The Monster That Challenged the World* and one of *The Outer Limits*' "Zanti Misfits," steals the show when it meets its bloody demise at the end of Hercules' sword. With its short running time, engaging playing by Scott, some involving human drama (and villainous betrayal), and a very entertaining monster, *Hercules and the Princess of Troy* never outstays its welcome.

Hercules and the Ten Avengers see ***The Triumph of Hercules***

Hercules Conquers Atlantis see ***Hercules and the Captive Women***

Hercules, Prisoner of Evil (1964; Ambrosiana/American International Television; Italy) Original Language Title: *Ursus, il Terrore dei Kirghisi*. Released directly to American television by AIP, *Hercules, Prisoner of Evil* is a Hercules movie in name only, with a more Tartan than Grecian setting (the inhabitants call their ruler "Khan" and live in thatch huts). "Hercules" (Reg Park) is a local chieftain charged with finding and destroying the cape-wearing, demon-faced "monster" ravaging the countryside (the "ravaging" consists of making flying leaps at its victims while screeching like a bird). Hercules offers no feats of super-strength (in fact, his one encounter with the monster results in a near-fatal wounding for Herc), and (in an admittedly clever twist) it's Hercules' *brother* who turns out to be the real hero. Listless direction by the usually reliable Antonio Margheriti (under his "Anthony Dawson" pseudonym), and too much riding, walking, and just plain wandering around the forest make this *Hercules* a Prisoner of Boredom.

Hercules the Avenger (1965; Italy) Original Language Title: *La Sfida dei Giganti*. This Reg Park peplum apparently never escaped onto American theater screens—or at least its few original bits, since much of the film is footage lifted from Mario Bava's *Hercules in the Haunted World* (which *did* play in the U.S.) and *Hercules and the Captive Women*! *Avenger*'s story has Hercules journey to the Hades-like underworld lorded over by the bitter Earth Goddess Gia in order to save the soul of Zanthus, Herc's son. With the Son of Jove (strangely, the dubbing replaces the traditional Greek "Zeus" with the later Roman appellation "Jove") on his dangerous quest, Gia sends her evil son Antaius to impersonate Hercules and take over the kingdom of Syracuse as a despotic tyrant, leading to the final confrontation between the good and bad demi-god he-men. About the only thing to recommend in this tired, tedious sword-and-sandal entry are the (admittedly impressive) scenes cribbed from the Bava film, plus a few taken from *Captive Women* (including a fight with a horned lizard-monster). Just watch the originals instead of *Hercules the Plagiarizer* ... er, *Avenger*.

Hercules the Invincible see ***Son of Hercules in the Land of Darkness***

Hercules vs. the Giant Warrior see ***The Triumph of Hercules***

Hercules vs. the Hydra (1960/66; Walter Manley Enterprises; Italy/France) Original Language Title: *Gli*

Amori di Ercole. Alternate Title: *The Loves of Hercules.* The real-life husband-and-wife beauty-and-brawn team of Jayne Mansfield and Mickey Hargitay star in this awful Hercules outing. Hargitay (dubbed with an incongruous British accent that makes him sound like some prissy aristocrat!) makes for a nondescript Hercules, and offers no screen presence to go with his physique. The outrageously-proportioned Mansfield (who plays Herc's final "love" of the original language title) inspires more derisive chuckles than salacious wolf-whistles with her swooning melodramatics. A mostly action-less peplum (it's 30 minutes before Hercules does anything of note — and this simply involves wrestling one skinny bull), *Hercules vs. the Hydra* only comes alive during the brief encounter with the title creature. Disappointingly, the ungainly three-headed (the absolute *minimum* requirement for a "hydra") beast resembles a Disney version of a Chinese dragon; and, given its rooted-to-the-spot motions, one suspects it has long been suffering from a triple-migraine. In the end, the mythic monster patiently waits while Herc hacks away at one of its necks for an eternity, then it dies— as does viewer interest. This 1960 feature never saw a theater screen in America but instead went directly to television in 1966.

Hercules vs. the Moloch see *The Conquest of Mycenae*

Hercules vs. the Sea Monster see *Hercules and the Princess of Troy*

Hillbillys in a Haunted House (1967; Woolner Brothers) On their way to the "Nashville Jamboree," country-and-western singers Woody (Ferlin Husky) and Boots (Joi Lansing), along with their very nervous manager Jeepers (Don Bowman), take shelter from a storm (that never materializes) at an old abandoned mansion. Well, it's not really abandoned, since the basement houses a band of spies after a secret formula from the nearby atomic missile site — Basil Rathbone, John Carradine, dragon-lady Linda Ho, and Lon Chaney, Jr., and his pet gorilla. There ensues hijinks and hilarity (actually, tepid musical numbers and tame spook-house gags). It's really an excuse for the country stars and various guest singers to strut their stuff in a baker's dozen of musical numbers (highlighted by two songs performed by Merle Haggard — watched by Jeepers on a television set, no less!), and for the three horror stars to *waste* theirs in a trio of inane characterizations.

The Honeymoon Killers (1969; Cinerama; b&w) This fact-based account of the life and crimes of "Lonely Heart" killers Martha Beck and Ray Fernandez is, primarily, a successor to pioneering true crime docu-dramas such as *In Cold Blood* (1967). But *The Honeymoon Killers'* unflinching presentation of the duo's ghastly final murders (one victim is bludgeoned with a hammer, then strangled; the couple also drown a young child), as well as its exploitative concentration on Beck's sexual and romantic fixation on Fernandez, pushes the film toward the borders of the horror genre. Martha (Shirley Stoler), a desperately lonely, ill-tempered, overweight nurse, falls prey to Ray (Tony Lo Bianco), a two-bit con man who makes his living bilking lovelorn women. He tries to love (and rob) Martha and leave her, but Ray's resolve buckles against the power of Martha's obsessive adoration, and he accepts her as a partner. She poses as his sister, and, despite Martha's explosive jealousy, together the couple goes on a Bluebeard-style spree of robberies and murders of lonely widows across several states before eventually turning against one another. Producer Warren Stiebel originally hired Martin Scorsese to helm *The Honeymoon Killers* but dismissed the director shortly into production because he felt Scorsese was working too slowly, wasting time with elaborate, arty camera setups. Screenwriter Leonard Kastle replaced Scorsese and earned his only directorial credit. Kastle and cinematographer Oliver Wood present events in a straightforward, pseudo-documentary style. The picture's main attraction is Stoler's gloriously gut-wrenching performance as Martha Beck, who can go toe to toe with Norman Bates, Travis Bickle and Hannibal Lecter among the all-time great movie psychopaths. Like those characters, she's complex — menacing, even repellent, yet curiously sympathetic. *The Honeymoon Killers* isn't an easy film to watch because it's so emotionally raw and, at times, deeply disturbing. But Stoler's performance makes it worth the effort.

The horror of country music: *Hillbillies in a Haunted House* (1967) (courtesy Ted Okuda).

Honeymoon of Terror (1961; Sonney Amusement Enterprises; b&w) Alternate Title: *Ecstasy on Lovers Island.* This early effort by soon-to-be nudie-cutie specialist Bethel Buckalew (*Kiss Me Quick!*, *The Secret Sex Lives of Romeo and Juliet*, *Midnight Plowboy*) is more of a horror/suspense film than an adults-only feature, since the sole moment of nudity comes in one split-second of did-I-just-see-a-breast-or-didn't-I? The story concerns a newlywed couple who leave off their Las Vegas honeymoon to go camping on the deserted Thunder Island, which turns out to be not-so-deserted after all, thanks to the presence of a hulking "loco" lumberjack who "raped two girls and butchered another" eight years earlier. With the husband off getting supplies in town, the wife, left alone on the small island, must run for her life (and honor) from the limping logger. While the two leads, Doug Leith and Dwan Marlow (who apparently made their acting debut *and* swan song with this feature), display little in the way of thespian prowess, their enthusiasm and seemingly real affection for one another make them a rather endearing couple, resulting in some vested interest from the viewer (whose patience, admittedly, is sorely tried by too much puerile newlywed "banter"). And while the second half of the movie is basically one protracted chase sequence, a few inspired moments of "what would *I* do in this situation?" hold the interest. Though this cheapie is no one's ideal cinematic *Honeymoon*, at a barely-feature-length 62 minutes at least it doesn't overstay its welcome.

Horror see ***The Blancheville Monster***

Horror and Sex see ***Night of the Bloody Apes***

Horror House (1969/70; Tigon/AIP; U.K.) Alternate Title: *Haunted House of Horror* (U.K.). When a group of bored teenagers (Frankie Avalon, Jill Haworth, Mark Wynter, Mark Sewell, etc.) decide to explore a supposedly haunted house, one of them turns up dead—carved up by a knife-wielding assassin who may or may not be one of the kids. On the advice of a Scotland Yard inspector (Dennis Price), the group returns to the spooky old mansion to uncover the truth. While its scenario sounds rather tame and cozy, *Horror House*—released in England in July of 1969 but not in the U.S. until April 1970—features a pair of surprising splatter sequences in the style of the Italian "giallo" mystery-thrillers of the era (in one of these scenes, Avalon gets knifed in the crotch!). Unfortunately, however, the film never fully commits itself to this approach, devoting most of its running time to laborious, slang-filled conversations among the fashionably mod teenagers in their trendy flats. As a result, *Horror House* likely will interest only viewers fascinated with swinging London kitsch.

The Horror of It All (1963/64; Lippert/20th Century–Fox; U.K.; b&w) Terence Fisher directed this little-seen old-dark-house horror-comedy starring (of all people) Pat Boone. American salesman Jack Robinson (Boone) travels to England to ask for permission to marry his beloved Cynthia (Erica Rogers) and discovers her family is full of kooks and eccentrics (Dennis Price, Andree Melly, Valentine Dyall, Jack Bligh, Erick Chitty and Archie Duncan), one or more of whom seem bent on murdering him. Originally issued in the U.S. on a double-bill with *Witchcraft* (1964), *The Horror of It All* has become extremely scarce. The authors of this book were unable to obtain a copy for review, but those who have seen it generally regard it as one of Fisher's weakest efforts—an opinion shared by the director himself. "I don't talk about it [*The Horror of It All*] much," Fisher said. "I don't believe I will ever be very good at sending up horror." With quotes from: *The Men Who Made the Monsters*, by Paul M. Jensen.

Horrors of Malformed Men (1969; Toei; Japan) This delirious, twisted, unnerving picture plays like a psychedelic hybrid of H.G. Wells' *The Island of Dr. Moreau* and Tod Browning's *Freaks.* The convoluted scenario, told partly in flashback, concerns a young doctor falsely judged insane and then framed for murder. Fleeing police, he assumes the identity of a dead man who could be his twin (or perhaps his doppelganger), right down to a swastika-shaped scar on the bottom of his foot. This impersonation leads him to a chilling reunion with his father, a crazed scientist who looks like a Japanese Charles Manson and lives on a remote island populated by grotesquely "malformed" men and women—many of whom he has disfigured himself through ghastly experimental surgeries. Director Teruo Ishii, who specialized in exploitation fare (yakuza, *chambara* and *pinku eiga*) throws in everything but the proverbial kitchen sink, shifting abruptly from color to tinted black-and-white to negative exposure, employing slow motion and freeze frame, and utilizing all manner of unorthodox cuts and ironic transitions. Other than star Teruo Yoshida, the story's point of view character, the acting is highly stylized, further enhancing the unreal, nightmarish

Teruo Yoshida (center) confronts the *Horrors of Malformed Men.*

quality of the show. Heavily laden with nudity and gore, and often weird for weirdness' sake, *Horrors of Malformed Men* is the kind of movie that works best if you simply let it wash over you instead of trying to figure it out. Although not for every palate, viewers with strong stomachs and a taste for the exotic will find much here worth savoring. *Horrors of Malformed Men* never received a U.S. theatrical release, but was issued on DVD in 2007.

Horrors of the Red Planet see *Wizard of Mars*

The Hour of the Wolf (1968; Svenskfimindustri; Sweden) Original Language Title: Vargtimmen. Ingmar Bergman was greatly influenced by German expressionism and many of his pictures include supernatural elements, but *Hour of the Wolf* (1968) remains the closest thing the director ever made to a full-blooded horror film. Disturbed artist Johan Borg (Max Von Sydow) and his young wife Alma (Liv Ullman) move to a secluded island, where Johan spends his days painting and his nights wrestling with irrational (?) anxieties. Alma fears that her love for Johan is drawing her inexorably into her husband's madness. Johan shows Alma sketches of the "monsters" he believes inhabit their island—"spider men," "the bird man," "the cackling woman." Then Alma begins reading her husband's diary, and finds herself plunged into his world, actually seeing the characters her husband sketched. Things turn even weirder when the Borgs accept a dinner invitation from the vaguely vampiric Baron Von Merken (Erland Josephson). In the film's surreal final sequence, set in and around Castle Von Merken, Bergman employs classic horror iconography to arresting and unsettling effect. Although never known for creating lighthearted entertainments, Bergman's films of the late 1960s are the darkest, most difficult and disorienting of his career. The disturbing, methodically paced *Hour of the Wolf* jumps back and forth between the "real" world and the realm of nightmares, leaving it to the audience to sort out which is which, and to decide what it all means. The pleasure of the film—above and beyond Bergman's haunting imagery, Sven Nykvist's gorgeous black-and-white cinematography, and the superb performances of Von Sydow and especially Ullman—lies in pondering its riddles. Straightforward answers would spoil the fun.

House of Evil see *Macabre Serenade*

House of Mystery (1961; Anglo Amalgamated; U.K.; b&w) This small-scale, low-budget English ghost movie only made it to America via sporadic television airings. Directed by Vernon Sewell (and adapted by him from a play by Pierre Mills) with far more subtlety and style than his later offerings of *The Vampire-Beast Craves Blood* and *The Crimson Cult*, the film follows a young couple looking to buy a house. When they run across their ideal choice, they're flabbergasted by—and wary of—the ridiculously low asking price. The woman who shows them the cottage surmises that it may be due to the ghosts, and subsequently relates the tragic tale of murder and revenge involving the house's previous occupants. At only 54 minutes, the story has little chance to wear out its welcome, and Sewell takes full advantage of the novel hook of linking electricity to the ghostly manifestations. The denouement, though not unexpected, still carries a shivery punch due to the clever build-up and excellent playing of the engaging cast. Ghost movie aficionados could do far worse than to cross the threshold of this *House of Mystery*.

House on Bare Mountain (1962, Olympic International) This woefully unfunny and utterly unerotic horror-tinged nudie-cutie follows an undercover policewoman (Laura Eden) who infiltrates a girls' boarding school run by a bootlegging grandma (comedian Bob Cresse in drag) who keeps a werewolf captive in her cellar. The overbearing Cresse's insipid jokes are supposed to provide humor between cheesecake sequences of models taking showers, changing into nighties, dancing, jumping rope, taking more showers and even reading the dictionary(!).

The House That Screamed (1969/71; Spain) Original Language Title: *La Residencia.* Alternate Title: *The Finishing School.* In this Spanish pseudo women-in-prison feature masquerading as a horror movie (which wasn't released Stateside until 1971), the

One of the most (in)famous of the 1960s nudie-cutie horrors: *The House on Bare Mountain* (1962) (courtesy Ted Okuda).

sadistic headmistress of a European boarding school for troubled girls applies such harsh disciplinary measures that several of her charges attempt to escape—resulting in their murder by an unseen killer who seems to reside in the house. Loaded with Gothic-type atmosphere and sinister subtext, the film only strays into horror territory at the very end, whose gruesome twist in the tale definitely leaves its mark.

The Human Duplicators (1965; Woolner Bros.; U.S./Italy) "Cheesy" is the operative word for this no-budget sci-fi nonsense in which seven-foot-tall Richard Kiel ("Jaws" from the Bond films) plays an alien who beams down to earth to create android duplicates in a plot to take over the world. The effects are tacky ("our 'space ship' had been constructed by gluing four ashtrays together!" laughed Kiel in *Cinema Retro* magazine), the story thin, the dialogue silly and the direction flat. Kiel is imposing in stature but not in acting ability, and delivers the most unexciting and banal closing speech by an alien invader to date. The duplicates themselves are good for a few laughs, however. Doors can't stop them, bullets can't stop them; but if you push them over, their heads crack open like porcelain dolls. (And watch for those dressed-up hairdryers that "transfer mental capacity" from the human to the replicate.)

I Eat Your Skin (1964/71; Cinemation Industries; b&w) After producer-director-scripter Del Tenney's fiscal successes with *The Horror of Party Beach* and *The Curse of the Living Corpse* (both 1964), Tenney was on a roll. Unfortunately, this momentum couldn't quite carry his next project, *Voodoo Blood Bath*, over the distribution hill. Even in 1964, shooting a horror movie in black and white and expecting to find a decent distributor was an act of pure optimism. When *Voodoo Blood Bath* failed to sell, Tenney shelved his feature and returned to the theater, supervising plays as artistic director of the Eugene O'Neill Theater Center in New York (as well as founding a lucrative real estate business). He never made another feature. Tenney's voodoo movie might still be moldering on the cinematic shelf today had it not been for producer Jerry Gross who, in 1971, needed a second feature for his rabid hippie opus *I Drink Your Blood*. Gross purchased *Voodoo Blood Bath* and re-christened it *I Eat*

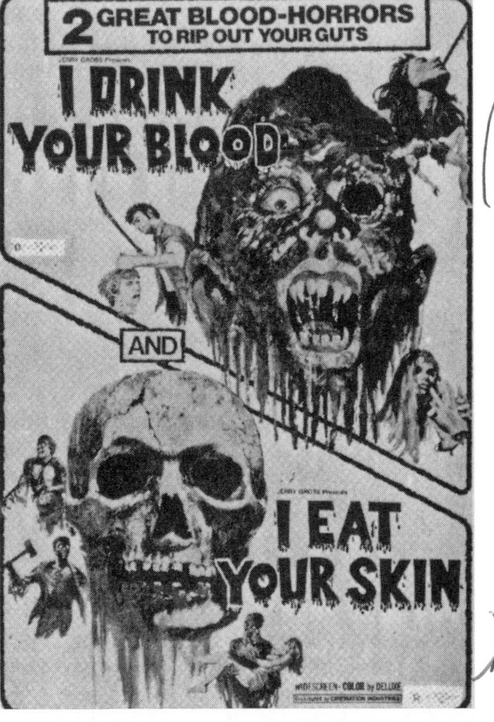

Left: **Ad for the cheesy sci-fier *The Human Duplicators* (1965). *Right:* In 1971 Jerry Gross bought Del Tenney's unreleased 1964 zombie film *Voodoo Blood Bath* and re-titled it *I Eat Your Skin* to go along with his rabid hippie opus *I Drink Your Blood.***

Your Skin. Compared to the mean-spirited *I Drink Your Blood*, Tenney's cheesy, old-fashioned tale of a mad scientist on a tropical island creating an army of zombies to conquer the world becomes downright enjoyable. Though not as fun as the wacky *Horror of Party Beach*, and not as slick as Tenney's *Violent Midnight* (1963) or *Curse of the Living Corpse*, *I Eat Your Skin* still maintains that combination of hard-edged violence (shocking decapitation, gruesome zombie faces) and raw energy (enthusiastic ceremonial sequences, lively chase scenes) that make Tenney's features as memorable as they are. In amongst the poor quality sound and flat photography (not to mention a laughable Ed Woodian model of the island blowing up at the climax) are a briskly-paced story and some genuinely creepy zombies (with their cataract-covered eyes; flaking, wrinkled skin; and tall, gaunt frames).

Australian daybill for *I Saw What You Did* (1965).

I Saw What You Did (1965; Universal; b&w) One of producer-director William Castle's weakest efforts, this limp, would-be thriller about a crank phone call gone horribly wrong is about as spine-tingling as an ABC After School Special. While her parents are out of town, 16-year-old Libby (Andi Garrett) and her pal Kit (Sarah Lane) begin calling people at random out of the phone book with the ominous message, "I saw what you did and I know who you are." Unfortunately, one of their prank victims is a man (John Ireland) who just murdered his wife. William McGivern's extremely contrived scenario relies on a one-in-a-million coincidence and a series of incredibly boneheaded and reckless choices by the two girls, neither of whom is particularly likeable. *I Saw What You Did* isn't scary and doesn't even try very hard to be scary. Van Alexander's chirpy, upbeat score would better fit a comedy, but this picture isn't particularly funny, either, making it tough to fathom what on earth Castle had in mind here. Although Castle remains best known for his gimmicky promotional ballyhoo, *I Saw What You Did* featured no such trickery, unless you count its stunt casting of Joan Crawford. Although she receives top billing, Crawford has limited screen time in her relatively minor supporting role. Anyone expecting a reprise of Castle and Crawford's wild and woolly campfest *Strait-Jacket* (1964) will be sorely disappointed. For reasons unknown, *I Saw What You Did* was remade as a TV movie in 1988.

In the Year 2889 (1966; AIP-TV) This slavish (though uncredited) remake of Roger Corman's *Day the World Ended* (1956) was part of the package of movies American International Pictures commissioned Larry Buchanan to make for their direct-to-television branch in the mid-to-late 1960s. Buchanan shot a whole fistful of genre losers from 1965 to 1969, most of them copies of 1950s AIP sci-fiers, and all of them filmed in 16mm in Texas on budgets of less than $25,000. *In the Year 2889* may very well be the best of the sad bunch — but that's damning with faint praise indeed, as it still falls well short of its Corman model in nearly every respect (the one exception being the radioactive mutant monster, which, though no more convincing in its rubberyness than Paul Blaisdell's original outrageous creation for *Day*, looks more grotesquely disturbing). The story follows a group of atomic war survivors (in obviously modern-day 1966, *not* the far-flung 2889 of the nonsensical title) who hide out in a house in a sheltered valley and face mutated monsters (well, *one* mutated monster, anyway). The cast of unknowns (with male lead Paul Peterson being the one dubious "name," having appeared regularly on TV's *The Donna Reed Show* the previous decade) acquit themselves remarkably well, far surpassing the usual thespian level of a Buchanan opus (though the amazingly wooden Neil Fletcher still manages to out-banal *Day*'s Paul Birch in the role of the humorless patriarch). Though the expected cramped sets, mundane photography and long dull stretches raise their ugly heads, Buchanan manages to avoid his usual technical gaffes (the day-for-night scenes remain consistent here, at least) and dialogue groaners (thanks to the plagiarized script, which is better than most of the others he stole from).

The Incredible Invasion (1968/71; Azteca/Columbia; Mexico/U.S.) Original Language Title: *La Invasión Siniestra*. Alternate Titles: *Alien Terror, Sinister Invasion*. In "Gudenburg 1890," a human-looking, silver pantsuit-wearing alien comes to Earth to "destroy the molecular ray" Professor Mayer (Boris Karloff) has invented, "which, if put to ill use, could destroy the universe." To this end the invader takes mental control of a Jack-the-Ripper-style psycho-killer, and then possesses the professor himself, in order to sabotage the device and discredit Mayer. It's up to the Prof's daughter and her new beau to uncover the nefarious alien plot. Of the four Mexican-American coproductions Karloff made at the end of his life for producer Luis Enrique Vergara, *The Incredible Invasion* offered the octogenarian actor the best opportunity to really act (as opposed to just sitting and reciting pointless dialogue and sci-fi gobbledygook). Karloff makes the most of the (still-limited) opportunity, effectively displaying the disturbing ambivalence resulting from the cold, calculating alien intelligence mixing with the kindly professor's human mind. And thanks to the disturbing serial-killer subplot (though under alien control, the body's brutal impulses bubble to the surface periodically), some solid period set design

Of the four Mexican horrors Boris Karloff made back-to-back just before he died, *The Incredible Invasion* (1968/71) offered the octogenarian star his best acting opportunity.

(Mayer's lab is dressed with sparking gadgets and ornate equipment that looks like it came from a Universal Frankenstein film fire sale), likable (and attractive) leads, and a few intriguing set-pieces (including a demonstration in which Mayer destroys a boulder with his new ray that conjures up a similar scene in the classic 1936 Karloff vehicle *The Invisible Ray*), *The Incredible Invasion* stands as the best of Karloff's Mexi-horrors. Admittedly, that's not saying much.

Invaders from Space (1957/64; ShinToho/AIP-TV; Japan) Yet another breathless, brainless feature cobbled together for American TV from the adventures of Japanese superhero Starman. In this one, our hero tangles with salamander men from outer space. This is the third of four pictures in the series, which concluded with *Evil Brain from Outer Space* (1958/64).

Invasion (1965; Anglo Amalgamated/Allied Artists; U.K.; b&w) *Invasion* is really a misnomer, since the entire invading force consists of one alien prisoner and two guards (Asian women dressed in white jumpsuits) sent to recapture him. They place an invisible force field around the remote country hospital where the prisoner has sought refuge. Edward Judd (*Day the Earth Caught Fire, Island of Terror*) plays the doctor hero. The script tries too hard to be "intelligent" and ends up overly talky, while the pacing is slow, the direction plodding, and the camerawork static (sometimes utilizing only a single camera setup for an entire sequence). A dull, lifeless movie, *Invasion* is one of the least interesting British sci-fi films of the sixties.

Invasion of Astro-Monster see ***Monster Zero***

Invasion of the Body Stealers (1969; Tigon/Allied Artists; U.K.) A group of British paratroopers vanish in mid-jump, their empty parachutes falling to earth. Then a team of skydivers "fade away" during an air show. When the disappearances continue, the army launches an investigation, but to keep the matter hush-hush, it hires civilian private detective Bob Megan (Patrick Allen). After many interviews, briefings and reports, a few encounters with a mysterious beauty (Lorna Wilde) whose image does not show up in photographs (hmmm...), and a lot of help from army scientists (Maurice Evans and Hilary Dwyer), Megan deduces that the paratroopers have been kidnapped by extraterrestrials. By then, however, *Invasion of the Body Stealers* is nearly over, limping to a mamby-pamby, make-nice-with-the-aliens anti-climax. This picture is a plodding, addle-brained mess from start to finish. Its plot defies logic and even common sense: Why would the aliens, if they are trying to operate in secret, snatch parachutists in mid-air rather than waiting for some (any) less conspicuous opportunity? Why does the military try to keep a lid on the investigation, considering that during the air show skydivers vanished in front of an audience of thousands? The characters here are simplistic clichés (the womanizing gumshoe, the attractive but all-business female scientist, the mysterious alien siren, the no-

nonsense general, etc.). The esteemed George Sanders is wasted in a tiny, do-nothing part as a figurehead general, and the rest of the cast perform forgetably. Since this is a cut-rate production, there are very few special effects (the single shot of the alien spacecraft is stock footage from Amicus' *Daleks Invasion Earth 2150* [1966]) and virtually no action, only conversation. There are few more grueling ways to spend 88 minutes than with *Invasion of the Body Stealers.*

Sexy ad for the not-so-sexy *The Body Stealers.* (1969).

Invasion of the Neptune Men (1961/64; Toei/AIP-TV; Japan) Alternate Title: *Space Pirate Ship.* Original Language Title: *Ucho Kaisoku-sen.* This low-budget invaders-from-space yarn remains notable only as an early starring role for future action superstar Shinichi "Sonny" Chiba.

Invasion of the Star Creatures (1962; AIP; b&w) "The gags and laughs come fast and furious in this fun-filled battle of the sexes," claims the trailer for this ultra-cheap sf/horror comedy. Well, it's half right anyway — there's plenty of gags but precious few laughs in this low-brow tale (penned by Roger Corman regular Jonathan Haze, who later summed up the picture with one word: "crappy") of two bumbling army privates who stumble upon a cave inhabited by a duo of gorgeous Amazonian space women and their vegi-men slaves (lumbering stuntmen in tights, tunics and frond-studded burlap sacks over their heads). About the only amusement gleaned from the various unfunny gags (including the "heroes" racing, Keystone Cop-like, through the same phony cave corridor over and over again; or one of them spontaneously breaking into lousy impressions of Jimmy Cagney and Peter Lorre) is an audacious bit of naming nonsense: the two sexy, well-endowed space women are named Dr. Poona and Professor Tanga! Released on the bottom half of a double bill with the far more entertaining *The Brain That Wouldn't Die*, *Invasion of the Star Creatures* is a bottom-scraper indeed.

The Invisible Terror (1963; Aero Film; W. Germany; b&w) Original Language Title: *Der Unsichtbare.* More along the lines of an (inferior) German krimi than a horror film, *The Invisible Terror* relates the tale of a scientist who discovers an invisibility serum, only to disappear (both literally *and* figuratively) during a robbery/murder at the chemical plant where he works. The man's brother, sometimes aiding and sometimes evading the police, must try to untangle the convoluted crime and subsequent murder plot(s) to try and find his missing sibling and clear his name. Though an invisible man does indeed, er ... appear, little is made of the inherent horror of the situation, as the film focuses on the mystery surrounding the invisible one's identity rather than whatever terror he might inspire. The infrequent invisibility gags are of the standard variety (doors opening and closing, objects moving through the air, etc.), and the overburdened crime plot soon wears out its welcome. Not surprisingly, the desultory *Invisible Terror* could find no takers for a Stateside theatrical release and was sold directly to American television.

Ad for ***Invasion of the Star Creatures*** (1962).

Island of the Dinosaurs (1967; Azteca Films, Inc.; Mexico; b&w) Original Language Title: *Isla de los Dinosaurios.* Released in the U.S. only to Spanish-language theaters (then ultimately in a subtitled version on DVD after the turn of the millennium), this Mexican *One Million B.C.* retread not only "borrows" the overexposed baby alligator-vs.-iguana "dinosaur" battles (and tabletop volcano eruption footage) from that 1940 film, but much of the plot as well in its tale of four scientists (two men, two women) who crash-land on an island populated by cavemen and dinosaurs (photographically enlarged lizards and oversized armadillos). One of the girls is rescued/captured by a local cave-hunk, and prehistoric love blossoms. The only things new on this Retread Island are a giant alligator-like papier-maché monster that (sort of) menaces the heroine (it looks so ungainly that director Rafael Portillo—of *Aztec Mummy* fame—wisely chose to reveal it only in long-shot) and a brief battle with a mangy ape-man (juxtaposed with some mismatched footage of an ape-suited Charlie Gamora lifted from some 1940s Hollywood production). Unless you'd care to see that oft-stolen *One Million B.C.* footage for the umpteenth time, there's no reason to ever set foot on this *Island.*

Isle of the Snake People (1968/71; Azteca/Columbia; Mexico/U.S.) Original Language Title: *La Muerte Viviente.* Alternate Titles: *The Snake People* (TV), *Cult of the Damned* (video). In early 1968, Mexican producer Luis Enrique Vergara made a deal with Boris Karloff to appear in four horror films to be shot back-to-back in Mexico. Vergara then hired Roger Corman alumnus Jack Hill to write the four screenplays. With partial financial backing provided by Columbia (in exchange for the U.S. distribution rights), Vergara learned that the ailing Karloff could not fly to Azteca's Mexico City studio due to health reasons (his emphysema prevented him from working in higher altitudes). Plans were then drawn up to shoot all of Karloff's scenes in Hollywood for all four films in only three weeks. To this end, Vergara flew the pertinent Mexican actors and crew to Los Angeles and rented the Hollywood Stages, a cheap studio that provided shooting facilities for such schlock as *The Incredible Two-Headed Transplant* and *Dracula vs. Frankenstein.* Scripter Hill directed the Hollywood scenes in four weeks in April and May 1968, going a week over schedule "due mostly to poor organization and planning on the part of the Mexican producer," according to Hill. (In addition, the $300,000 allocated for the three-week stint ballooned to a cost of nearly $400,000.) "Vergara brought the actors in from Mexico," related Hill, "and it was total chaos. The actors were not the actors who were supposed to come, they were not showing up on time, and we had to keep changing the schedule all the time. And the producer was off at Disneyland when he should have been on the set." With the chaos ended and the Karloff footage in the can, the Mexican cast and crew then returned south of the border to finish the films in their more economical homeland under Juan Ibanez' direction. The result: *The Fear Chamber, The Incredible Invasion, Macabre Serenade,* and *Isle of the Snake People,* a tale

A bit of slithery sexual suggestion from an *Isle of the Snake People* (1968/71) dream sequence (Julissa pictured).

of voodoo ceremonies, zombies and cannibal women(!) on a Pacific Island (Karloff plays a plantation owner who may be something more than he seems). Though not the worst of the quartet, *Isle of the Snake People* proved substandard in all departments. While it offers a few creepy moments (such as the ghoulish pre-credit sequence in which a black-clad dwarf re-animates a woman's corpse) and some well-dressed sets (an atmospheric cemetery full of tilted tombstones and half-exposed skeletons), a confused storyline, strained acting, poor pacing, inadequate direction, and the fact that the film's star—Karloff—is onscreen for only ten minutes make this *Isle* a deserted one as far as entertainment goes. Columbia was less than thrilled with their new Karloff features. Though it's difficult to reconstruct just what happened, two of the films, *Snake People* and *Incredible Invasion,* may have enjoyed a spotty regional theatrical release in 1971 before the studio washed their hands of them and sold the pair to television. Due to financial difficulties, complicated by producer Luis Vergara's death from heart failure, the two other pictures, *The Fear Chamber* and *Macabre Serenade,* were apparently never released to theaters at all in their English-language versions, and only came to light via the video boom of the 1980s.

It's Alive! (1969; AIP-TV) Don't confuse this inept waste of celluloid with the seminal 1970s killer-baby flick from Larry Cohen—you'll live to regret it. A *different* Larry—Larry Buchanan—made *this* execrable exercise in tedium. The obviously down-on-his-luck former Disney star Tommy Kirk plays an "assistant professor of paleontology" who, along with a bickering husband and wife pair of passing motorists, stumbles upon the secret of backwoods hillbilly Greely (burly Buchanan regular Bill Thurman): Greely keeps a prehistoric fish-creature in a cave and feeds it unwary tourists. *It's Alive!*, made for American International Picture's television division, begins like a 1960s home movie, with the camera shooting from inside a car as it drives—and drives and drives—along the highway while a narrator spouts ponderous lines like, "There is a legend in these hills that when it rains and sunshines at the same time, the Devil is kissing his wife." And nothing else that occurs serves to dispel this first impression of amateurishness, from the flat lighting and long stretches without sound (one silent flashback sequence lasts 22 minutes, with nothing but stock music cues and sporadic narration to liven it up!) to the inept acting (even old pro Tommy Kirk flails about wildly) and pathetic monster. Buchanan simply recycles his 1967 *Creature of Destruction* suit for this movie's "massasaurus, a kind of aquatic lizard" (as Tommy ludicrously labels it). *Why* is anybody's guess, since it's the poorest Creature from the Black Lagoon reject ever caught on film. Perhaps Buchanan realized this, for he keeps his green wetsuited, rubber-masked, plastic-toothed, ping-pong eyeballed beast off-screen as long as possible. In fact, the monster never really does anything—at least that we see. The big "action" sequence consists of the ridiculous creature advancing towards the camera, which abruptly goes out of focus as the victim screams, ending the scene. As far as entertainment value goes, *It's Alive!* is a dead issue.

Jigoku (1960; ShinToho; Japan) Alternate (international) Title: *Sinners of Hell.* One of two acclaimed 1960 horror films directed by Nabuo Nakagawa, *Jigoku* (Hell) chronicles the descent of a mild-mannered college student into sin, degradation and, ultimately, Hell itself. The trouble begins when Shigeru (Shiro Shimizu) and an unscrupulous classmate, out for an evening drive, accidentally run down a pedestrian and leave the victim to die. The hit-and-run casualty turns out to be a *yazuka* member, and Shigeru quickly finds himself trapped in a downward spiral of alcoholism, vice and crime. After his death, Shigeru wanders through Hell in search of his unborn child. Despite its excellent reputation, *Jigoku* can be tough sledding. The first two thirds of the 98-minute film, as poor Shigeru becomes a magnet for catastrophe and heartache, is so drawn-out and melodramatic, so weighted down with heavy-handed moralizing, that *Jigoku* nearly tips into self-parody. And the film's final third proves a bit of a letdown. Nakagawa's vision of Hell plays like something out of Herschell Gordon Lewis, with sinners literally torn in half, eyes gouged out, limbs ripped from their bodies, etc.—all rendered in unconvincing, cheap gore effects. In Nakagawa's defense, *Jigoku* (which never played American theaters during the 1960s, but reached the U.S. via DVD in 2006) is atypical of the director's oeuvre. His other 1960 chiller, the traditional ghost story *Tokaido Yotsuya Kaidan* (aka *The Ghost of Yotsuya*), is more representative. Unfortunately, *Tokaido Yotsuya Kaidan* also went unreleased in the U.S. during the 1960s, and has yet to reach America on home video or DVD. Nakagawa was a key figure in the development of Japanese horror cinema. Between 1956 and 1960 he made eight offbeat horror films, usually featuring ghosts, vampires or serial killers, two of which—*The Depths* (aka *The Ghost of Kasane*, 1957) and *Black Cat Mansion* (aka *Mansion of the Ghost Cat*, 1958)—received limited U.S. theatrical releases. After 1960, however, Nakagawa worked primarily in other genres. His only other horror film of the 1960s appears to have been *Kaidan hebi-onna* (aka *Snake Woman's Curse*, 1968), which finally emerged on DVD in 2007.

Journey Beneath the Desert (1961/67; Compangnia Cinematografica Mondiale & Fides/Transmonde Film; France/Italy) Original Language Title: *L'Atlantide.* Alternate Title: *Siren of Atlantis.* This European adventure fantasy directed (and written) by Edgar G. Ulmer has more in common with that maverick filmmaker's later low-budget output like *Beyond the Time Barrier* and *The Amazing Transparent Man* (both 1960) than his earlier innovative works like *The Black Cat* (1934) and *Bluebeard* (1944). A (model) helicopter crash-lands in the desert near an atomic testing site, and the crew are brought to the underground remnants of Atlantis (apparently the legend was wrong—the lost continent sank into the *sand* rather than the sea). There the Euro-stud crewmen (including a very young Jean-Louis Trintignant) run afoul of the amorous evil queen and spend their time dealing with the subsequent love triangle angst. Nothing too fantastical occurs (apart from one unfortunate turned into a statue for trying to escape), and the threadbare adventure winds down to its foregone conclusion (though this time via atomic explosion rather than the usual volcanic eruption).

Journey to the Beginning of Time (1955/66; CCM/Radio & Television Packagers; Czechoslovakia) Original Language Title: *Cesta do Pravěku.* Four young boys take a fanciful voyage into prehistory in this listless, poorly dubbed, Czech-produced juvenile edutainment made in 1955 but not released in the U.S. until 1966. After a visit to the American Museum of Natural History, "Doc" (Josef Lukas), Ben (Zdenek Hustak), Tony (Petr Hermann) and Jo Jo (Vladimir Bejval) rent a row boat, paddle through a cave and a strange fog, and suddenly find themselves in a mysterious river. The further downstream they go, the deeper into the past they travel, past woolly mammoths, prehistoric birds, dinosaurs and, ultimately, to the dawn of life itself. The creatures—realized through a variety of techniques, including stop-motion animation, puppetry and even a rubber suit—are impressive, but the story contains almost no dramatic tension (for example, danger seems to threaten when Jo Jo goes missing, but he is soon found quietly fishing—in fact, he lands the boys' dinner). *Journey to the Beginning of Time* is less concerned with drama than with factual accuracy, as the teenaged "Doc" explains to his younger chums the whys are wherefores of prehistoric life, with scrupulous fidelity to then-current (now mostly outdated) scientific theory, giving way to a reading from the Book of Genesis once the boys reach the Dawn of Life. Director Karel Zeman went on to make the visually dazzling fantasies *The Fabulous World of Jules Verne* (1958/61) and *The Fabulous Baron Munchausen* (1961/64).

Journey to the Center of Time (1967; American General) A time travel experiment goes haywire, sending three scientists and a ruthless businessman 5,000 years into the future, where they find Earth embroiled in *both* a devastating nuclear war *and* an alien invasion. Then, when they try to return home, they overshoot the mark and wind up in the age of dinosaurs. Unfortunately, while David Prentiss' imaginative script might have made a good, pulpy sci-fi novel, its ambitions far outstrip the production capabilities of this ultra-low-budget movie. Not only are the sets (full of voltage meters, knobs and reel-to-reel tape), costumes (spandex anyone?) and visual effects (tiny models and a bored-looking iguana) laughably cheap-looking, but its 77-minute running time includes endless static dialogue scenes (wherein scientists spout scientific doubletalk and lab techs furiously spin knobs and press buttons), stock footage montage journeys through "history" and other obvious padding. Director David L. Hewitt keeps everything in frame and in focus, and the low-rent cast (Scott Brady, Anthony Eisley, Gigi Perreau, Abraham Sofaer) delivers its stilted, cornball dialogue with precision, if little conviction. It's as if everyone involved recognized that, even though it contains some clever ideas, *Journey to the Center of Time* was a trip to nowhere.

Journey to the Far Side of the Sun (Universal; 1969; U.K.) An unmanned solar probe discovers a new planet in synchronous orbit with Earth on the far side of the sun. Two astronauts (Ray Thinnes and Ian Hendry) travel to the distant world, which turns out to be a mirror Earth, complete with look-alikes of every person and reversed duplicates of every object. *Journey to the Far Side of the Sun* was the brainchild of producers Gerry and Sylvia Anderson, creators of TV's *Thunderbirds* and *U.F.O.*, operating under the distinct influence of Stanley Kubrick's *2001: A Space Odyssey* (1968). It's a serious-minded, A-budget production with a solid cast (Thinnes, Hendry, Patrick Wymark, Herbert Lom), impressive visual effects (although not in the same league as *2001*) and imaginative production design (including believably futuristic cars, aircraft, furniture and even fashions). All the requisite components of a science fiction classic are in place — except a story. The screenplay, by the Andersons and Donald James, wastes a great deal of screen time on boring folderol about securing project funding, training astronauts and rooting out commie spies. By the time Thinnes and Hendry finally set foot on the mysterious new planet, nearly an hour of the 101-minute movie has elapsed. The story's downbeat payoff isn't worth such an elaborate buildup. At points, *Journey* tries too hard to emulate *2001*, especially with its psychedelic hyper-sleep sequences, which are clearly intended to resemble the Kubrick film's trippy "star gate." Such moments beg a dangerous comparison. While not without intriguing elements, *Journey to the Far Side of Sun* seems clumsy and vacuous next to the masterful, provocative *2001*.

Journey to the Seventh Planet (AIP, 1962) This low budget sci-fi entry, shot in Denmark by producer-director Sidney Pink from a script by Ib Melchior, plays like something warmed over from the previous decade, with elements rehashed from pictures like *Queen of Outer Space* (1958) and *Rocketship X-M* (1951). Spaceship Explorer 12 arrives on planet Uranus and surprisingly discovers an earth-like, pastoral world populated by gorgeous Scandinavian women. The astronauts eventually surmise that they are captives of a super-intelligent telepathic being (which looks like a giant brain with a big eyeball in the middle) intent on taking over their minds, then traveling to earth to subjugate the entire human race. Alas, Melchior's scenario blows any possible suspense out the airlock with an inane early scene in which the crew suddenly falls asleep and a disembodied, hypnotic voice spells out the entire plan (then tells them to remember nothing, rendering the entire sequence purposeless). Even at his best, Melchior (*Robinson Crusoe on Mars, Planet of the Vampires*, etc.) focuses on whiz-bang sci-fi gimmicks (like the Cyclops-brain monster) at the expense of dramatic structure and characterization — and *Journey to the Seventh Planet* remains far from his best work. The mostly Danish cast, handicapped by a language barrier and by Melchior's cliché-infested dialogue, turn in flat, mechanical performances. Even imported star John Agar, a stalwart of the genre, seems unusually disengaged. Pink manages a few clever directorial flourishes, including effective use of subjective camera angles, but on the whole *Journey* proves a far less satisfying effort than his first collaboration with Melchior, *The Angry Red Planet* (1960).

King of Kong Island (1968/78; Italy/Spain) Original Language Title: *La Venere Selvaggia*. Alternate Title: *Kong Island*. Shot in 1968 but not released in the U.S. until ten years later (and then just to television), this slap-dash import involves a mad scientist who lives in the jungle and inserts "brain-control" devices into the skulls of gorillas, turning them into slaves. There's no King, no Kong, nor any island (it being set in the African heartland), but there *is* a topless jungle girl (referred to as "the Sacred Monkey"!) who frolics nude in slow motion (at least in the European prints). Also present is a groovy '60s dance-party sequence, a tediously overlong (fake) gorilla brain surgery scene, plenty of stock animal footage, Halloween-style man-monkey costumes, smarmy "mood" music, and shot after shot of people following each other through the jungle. Buried beneath all this cheese is sword-and-sandal beefcake Brad Harris (*Goliath Against the Giants*) and long-time Hollywood tough-guy Marc Lawrence (*The Ox-Bow Incident, Key Largo*), who no doubt was wondering why his career had up and left without him.

Kingdom in the Sand see ***The Conqueror of Atlantis***

Kiss and Kill (1968; Commonwealth United; Spain/West Germany/U.S./U.K.) Alternate Titles:

Against All Odds, The Blood of Fu Manchu (U.K.). The fourth of five Harry Alan Towers-produced and Christopher Lee-starring Fu Manchu films may not be the worst (that "honor" belongs to the fifth and final entry—*The Castle of Fu Manchu*), but it's pretty damned close. *Kiss and Kill* has Fu and his daughter planning to rule the world by injecting a bevy of beautiful women with snake venom and sending them out to assassinate Fu's enemies (including Nayland Smith) via "the kiss of death." But it all boils down to a lot of running about in the Brazilian jungle as the protagonists search for Fu's "Lost City" hideout. The audacious concept becomes lost amidst the meandering plot and small-scale, lackluster "action" scenes. Christopher Lee's portrayal of the ultimate Yellow Peril figure remains deadly serious throughout, becoming almost unintentionally amusing as he lords it over the cheesy sets and expressionlessly delivers the often-risible dialogue. The best thing about this cheap action-adventure misfire is the tongue-in-cheek tone of the film's American trailer: "Positively recommended for the strong in heart—transplants are hard to come by." At this late stage in the Fu Manchu franchise, so was quality.

Kiss Me Monster (1967; Aquila Films; West Germany/Spain) Original Language Title: *Bésame Monstruo*. The often incoherent Jess Franco strikes again with this inevitably incomprehensible mishmash about two saxophone-playing strippers-cum-private-investigators (or something) who become embroiled in the search for a missing scientist's "nutrient formula" after the man "created two fully developed physical beings artificially." The film's tone is one of light comedy (meaning Franco abandons his usual sex-and-blood formula for poor jokes and impossibly knowing/blasé performances from the two leads, Janine Renaud and Rossana Yanni), but the result is only heavy eyelids for the baffled—and bored—viewer. It's almost like an old *Get Smart* episode, but badly dubbed and without even the minimal coherence and chuckles found in that uneven TV series. Characters come and go and disappear without explanation (as does audience interest), and by film's end one still has little insight into what the previous 78 minutes were all about. Franco has made many, many bad movies over his long career, and *Kiss Me Monster* may possibly top that list.

Kiss Me Quick (1964; Boxoffice International) Sterilox (Frank Coe, appearing under the stage name "Fatty Beltbuckle" and imitating the voice and mannerisms of Stan Laurel), an alien from the asexual planet Butliss, travels to Earth to try to procure a "perfect specimen" of female womanhood with help from the demented Dr. Breedlove (Max Gardens, appearing under the pseudonym "Manny Goodtimes" and doing a Bela Lugosi impression). This horror-themed nudie-cutie amounts to, basically, a series of stripteases accompanied by pun-filled commentary from Sterilox and Breedlove. Dracula, the Mummy and the Frankenstein Monster (Coe again, this time in an unauthorized recreation of Jack Pierce's iconic *Son of Frankenstein* makeup) make cameo appearances.

Pointless, nondescript Spanish poster for the pointless, nondescript Spanish Franco-film *Kiss Me Monster* (1967).

Many of the jokes are groan-inducing, but there is something undeniably amusing about the sight of the Frankenstein Monster surrounded by topless go-go dancers. Although more silly than sexy, scattered moments like that one help make *Kiss Me Quick* more watchable than most films of its type.

Kong Island see ***King of Kong Island***

The Last War (1961/64; Toho/AIP-TV; Japan) Original Language Title: *Sekai Daisenso*. Toho's hard-hitting, pure sci-fi, end-of-the-world epic was re-edited and released directly to American TV. This is a top-tier, big budget production, the Japanese equivalent of somber American nuclear holocaust films such as *On the Beach* (1959). *The Last War* is sometimes confused with *The Final War*, a similarly themed but smaller budgeted picture made a year earlier by rival Toei. However, *The Final War* does not appear to have received an American theatrical release and may be lost.

Last Woman on Earth (1960; Allied Artists) Harold Gern (Anthony Carbone), an unscrupulous real estate developer, along with his unhappy wife Evelyn (Betsy Jones-Moreland) and his attorney Martin (Robert Towne, acting under the pseudonym Edward Wain) emerge from scuba diving off the coast of Puerto Rico to discover they have escaped a mysterious calamity that wiped out the rest of the population of the island, and perhaps of the world. The trio hides away in a posh beach house, but tensions mount as Evelyn becomes infatuated with Martin. One of the weaker movie apocalypses of the 1960s, the punchless, predictable and preachy *Last Woman on Earth* was the first of three low-budget films producer-director Roger Corman shot (for tax reasons) in Puerto Rico. Robert Towne's debut screenplay runs long on heavy-handed symbolism and stilted dialogue but short on chills, action or even believable situations. Harold, Evelyn and Martin accept far too easily that the end of the world has arrived — they don't even bother searching for other survivors— and seem to suffer no privations as a result. There's some justice in the fact that most of the film's worst lines are delivered by Towne himself, playing the nihilistic, pseudo-intellectual Martin. Corman's earlier end-of-the-world epic *Day the World Ended* (1955) was a scruffier but, on balance, far more entertaining affair. Three years after its debut, director Monte Hellman shot additional dialogue scenes with the principal cast to pad *Last Woman*'s running time so it could be included in a package of Corman-produced films sold to television through Allied Artists. Although shot and released theatrically in color, TV prints were issued in black and white. With color or without, however, *Last Woman on Earth* quickly grows tiresome.

Late August at the Hotel Ozone (1967; National Film Archives; Czechoslovakia; b&w) Original Language Title: *Konec Sprna v Hotelu Ozon*. Alternate Title: *The End of August at the Hotel Ozone* (video). This chillingly grim post-apocalyptic film from Czechoslovakia follows a handful of teenage girls, led by the "Old Woman," as they scavenge the sparse countryside in a world apparently devoid of human life some 40 years after the nuclear holocaust (nearly everyone has died of radiation sickness). Sporting a decidedly *Lord of the Flies* sensibility (including unflinching photography that captures each brutal act the "children" commit —from needlessly shooting a dog to falling upon a cow and butchering it in a field), the film reaches its depressingly inevitable climax when the little band stumbles upon an old man (the first male they've ever seen) at an isolated mountain hotel. There, the girls' new barbarism clashes with this last pathetic vestige of the old civilization. Thought-provoking and quietly engrossing, *Late August at the Hotel Ozone* remains one of the decade's more emotionally powerful cinematic comments on What We Must Never Let Happen.

Latitude Zero (1969/70; Toho; Japan) This splashy Toho production, released in Japan in 1969 but not until 1970 in the U.S., was an undersea variant on the more successful *Atragon* (1963). Its story pits a poor man's Captain Nemo against an ersatz Dr. Moreau, with two rescued Japanese scientists (Akira Takarada and Masumi Okada) and an American reporter (Richard Jaeckel), caught in the middle. The Nemo-like Captain McKenzie (Joseph Cotten) lives in a sub-aquatic libertarian Utopia that contains the Fountain of Youth. Even though there is no government, McKenzie's ageless people live in perfect harmony, wearing clothes of spun gold. But the ruthless, power-crazed Malic (Caesar Romero) aims to rule over this paradise, and has bred a race of animal-men to help him gain control. All this should be great fun (especially with the usually reliable Ishiro Honda directing), but *Latitude Zero* never really delivers on this delirious (if derivative) scenario. Running a bloated 100 minutes, its pace is sluggish, bogged down by static dialogue scenes (most of the wonders of McKenzie's paradise are discussed rather than shown) and beautifully shot but ultimately tedious documentary-style underwater footage. Malic's creatures— including bat people, winged lions and giant rats— are laughably shoddy looking, some of the worst creature suits ever from Toho. The other costumes and sets look equally chintzy. The cast's stylized, serial-like performances (especially Romero's scenery-chewing, Joker-like antics) are enjoyable, but better suited to a much livelier film. Indeed, the impulse behind *Latitude Zero* seems to have been to recreate the appeal of a vintage chapter play — but those films were predicated on action, not on small talk and scenery.

Legend of Horror (1960/71; General Film Corporation; Argentina/U.S.; b&w) "A Double Dose of Hell Filmed in the 'Blood-Chilling' Realism of Magicmation." So promised the poster for this obscure oddity (paired with *Diabolical Wedding*) combining about 30 minutes of footage (an entertaining adaptation of Poe's "The Tell-Tale Heart") from the 1960 Argentinean Poe portmanteau film *Obras Maestras del Terror* ("Masterworks of Terror") with another 45 minutes of newer, U.S.-shot scenes to create a full feature (released in 1971). (*Obras*' two remaining Poe tales, "The Facts in the Case of M. Valdemar" and "The Cask of Amontillado," ended up released in the U.S. by Jack H. Harris in 1965 as *The Master of Horror*.) The new American footage involves a man thrown into prison for 15 years for "attempting to seduce the mayor's daughter" (tough laws in this unnamed, backwards country). There he meets a crazy old man who helps him escape, all the while relating *his* tale of woe as an extended flashback (the Argentinean footage). Amazingly, it all dovetails quite nicely in a shocking and unexpected denouement set in a misty graveyard right out of a classic Universal horror. This, coupled with the small-scale but highly atmospheric art direction of the American scenes set in the dank cell and dungeon-like, cobwebbed corridors of the primitive prison (not to mention the structure's exterior represented by a seaside castle matte painting cribbed from Roger Corman's Poe series!), makes *Legend of Horror* a welcome throwback to earlier times— with a few moments of unexpected gore to shock one's nostalgic sensibilities. The young lead of the Argentinean-lensed Poe story was played by Narcisco Ibanez Serrador, who became a respected director in Spain, most notably for helming the shocking *The House That Screamed* (1969) and the disturbing *Who Can Kill a Child?* (1976). The much-ballyhooed "Magicmation," by the way, consists of three gory instances of startling, though not altogether convincing, stop-motion animation (involving two throat piercings and a throat slitting) in the U.S. footage.

Lila see ***Mantis in Lace***

Little Red Riding Hood and the Monsters see ***Tom Thumb and Little Red Riding Hood***

The Living Corpse (1967; Pakistan; b&w) Original Language Title: *Zinda Laash.* From the opening credit stating that this Pakistani vampire flick is "adopted" from the Bram Stoker tale, you know that *The Living Corpse* will be straying far from the beaten path — not necessarily by intent, however. For instance, it employs Hammer's *Horror of Dracula* (1958) as a blueprint: several scenes, including the Chris Lee entrance and the *vampiress interruptus* sequence (in which the Count brutally saves Harker from the lady bloodsucker), are outright steals (though *Corpse* adds a disturbing touch to the latter by having the male vamp toss a baby to the delighted vampiress and telling her to "feast on this" as she scampers happily away — an incident taken from Stoker's book but rarely seen onscreen). The film also borrows dialogue ("children of the night") and atmosphere (giant spider web, anyone?) from the 1931 Lugosi *Dracula.* But plenty of unique and bizarre touches make this *Corpse* stand out from the vampiric crowd. For example, when a hefty, size-16 female bloodsucker attempts to seduce the Harker-like character by spontaneously erupting into an "erotic" dance (a strange bit of 1960s "performance art" that looks like a cross between the Hula and the Swim!), the viewer's jaw can't help but hit the floor. Then there's several traditional Indian-style musical numbers (one in which the heroine sings to herself about love in her garden; another in which a group of picnicking girls sing about the beautiful weather!). During a nightclub musical interlude, the patrons even *join in* at one point. These are things one doesn't necessarily associate with an atmospheric vampire movie. Also unusual is the way in which the main vampire *becomes* a vampire — by fooling around with the "elixir of life." You see, he was a famous scientist trying to find a cure for death, and ... well, let's just say he found it. Now *that* is novel. (Of course, John Beal played a science-spawned bloodsucker a decade earlier in *The Vampire*, but *he* didn't acquire the penguin suit and cape, nor the mesmeric powers that this *Living Corpse* did.) Considered almost too shocking for Pakistani Cinema at the time due to its "horror" and "erotic" content (it became the only Pakistani movie in history to earn an "X" rating in its country of origin — despite a total lack of nudity), *The Living Corpse* only surfaced in America in subtitled form on home video in 2003. For those whose taste in horror runs to the offbeat, *The Living Corpse* is well worth digging up.

The Lost World of Sinbad (1963/65; Toho/AIP-TV; Japan) Original Language Title: *Daitozoku.* Toshiro Mifune stars as the fabled Sinbad in this disappointing adventure yarn. Produced by Toho, *Lost World* naturally lacks the Ray Harryhausen stop-motion animation sequences that serve as the primary attraction for the best Sinbad pictures. Alas, *Lost World* also lacks the giant monsters and other creatures that usually populate Toho genre films. In fact, aside from a meddlesome witch, it features very few fantasy elements of any sort. The story, which has no origin in the Tales of the Arabian Nights, chronicles Sinbad's struggle to overthrow an unscrupulous nobleman who leads a double life as The Black Pirate. The visual effects are few and surprisingly slipshod, and the production values chintzy. About all this film can hang its turbin on is Mifune, who makes a superb Sinbad — a larger-than-life star for a larger-than-life character. As long as he is on screen, which is most of the time, there's something diverting to watch.

Love After Death see ***Unsatisfied Love***

The Loves of Hercules see ***Hercules vs. the Hydra***

Macabre Serenade (1968; Azteca/Columbia; Mexico/U.S.) Alternate Titles: *House of Evil, Dance of the Damned.* One of the four films Boris Karloff made for Mexican producer Luis Enrique Vergara in 1968 (with all of Karloff's scenes shot back-to-back in Hollywood before the production moved to Mexico for completion), *Macabre Serenade* never saw theatrical release in the U.S. (due both to Columbia's disappointment with the finished product, and to Vergara's untimely death and the subsequent legal entanglements). American audiences didn't really miss much. Arguably the worst of the quartet (and that's saying

Boris Karloff in *Macabre Serenade* (aka *House of Evil*), a 1968 Mexican film that didn't make it north of the border until the video boom of the 1980s.

something), *Macabre Serenade* stars Karloff as Mathias Morteval, wealthy patriarch of Morhenge Manor, who calls all his relatives together ostensibly to decide upon an heir (but actually to ferret out the madman, tainted by the family insanity, who's responsible for a rash of eyeless corpses turning up). Soon the heirs themselves begin dying, killed by the sinister life-sized mechanical toys (built by Mathias' late brother) that populate the manor house. While it's fun to watch Karloff dressing down his greedy potential heirs (a bit of the old magic shines through as he alternates between surface civility and scathing contempt, obviously enjoying his own pointed barbs), there's absolutely nothing else to recommend in this awful time-waster. A slow, meandering, haphazard script (with careless dubbing to match — typified by one cousin referring to Mathias as "uncle"); murky day-for-night photography; interior lighting so poor it often obscures the (non)action; and the cheesy killer dolls (actors doing their best "Mr. Roboto" impressions), whose clicking and squeaking noises make them sound like whiny mice, mark this *Serenade* as a toneless mess.

Maciste vs. the Cyclops see *Atlas Against the Cyclops*

Maciste in the Land of the Cyclops see *Atlas Against the Cyclops*

The Magic Serpent (1966; Toei/AIP-TV; Japan) Original Language Title: *Kairyu Daikessen*. Breathlessly paced and bursting with zany ideas, this unheralded sword-and-sorcery yarn stands as one of the most entertaining, and most under-appreciated, Japanese fantasy films of the 1960s. The basic plot could come from any of the lowbrow, low-budget *chambara* (sword-fighting) epics that were Toei's usual specialty: An evil samurai betrays his master and takes over his lands, but the lord's loyal retainers steal away with his infant son. Years later, the son, Ikazuchimaru (Hiroki Matsukata), returns in search of revenge. The twist here is that Ikazuchimaru has been studying magic, and must vanquish Orochimaru (Ryutaro Otomo), an evil wizard who helped overthrow his father. *The Magic Serpent* takes place in a Never-Never Land full of ghosts, monsters and magic, where anything can happen at any moment. In one unforgettable scene, our hero is decapitated — but his head simply laughs at his opponent, then floats back onto his neck! Orochimaru is a shape-shifter, capable of changing forms into the titular dragon-like beastie. The finale pits Orochimaru in serpent form against a giant horned toad under the command of Ikazuchimaru. Along the way, there are giant birds, a colossal spider, magic duels and nearly nonstop sword fights— plus a romantic subplot involving Ikazuchimaru and a beautiful young woman named Tsunate (Tomoko Ogawa), who turns out to be the daughter of Orochimaru. *The Magic Serpent* crams all this and more into 85 action-packed minutes, but never seems frantic. (Viewers may also note several plot points echoed in George Lucas' *Star Wars* trilogy.) The film's leads perform capably — Otomo is particularly impressive as the dastardly Orochimaru — and director Tetsuya Yamauchi makes dramatic use of extreme low camera angles in key sequences. Like all Toei films, *The Magic Serpent* was made on the cheap, and it shows— the visual effects remain crude, even by *kaiju eiga* standards. But the movie is so charming and energetic, such deficiencies are easy to forgive. AIP purchased *The Magic Serpent* for American television, denying it a U.S. theatrical release, and it has remained relatively obscure ever since. It deserves a wider audience.

The Magic Sword (1962; United Artists) In this Medieval fairy tale with mild horror overtones, Gary Lockwood plays the young George who, after receiving a lightning-fast steed and magic sword from his bumbling witch mother (comically played by Estelle Winwood), heads for an evil sorcerer's castle to free an imprisoned princess. Along the way he and his companions (six brave knights called up from stone) must face each of the wizard's seven curses sent to stop him, including a 20-foot-ogre, a vampire hag (played by Maila Nurmi, Vampira herself!) and a two-headed dragon. While this may be producer-director Bert I. Gordon's most ambitious project up to this time, it still bears the decidedly cheap stamp of a Mr. B.I.G. production, with the effects consisting of still photographs, simple insertions and transparent superimpositions (not to mention his signature giant creature, a seeming obsession of the man who brought us *The Amazing Colossal Man*, *The Cyclops*, *Village of the Giants*, and several other oversized critter movies). "[Bert I. Gordon] was a special effects wizard for his time," stated *Magic Sword* star Gary Lockwood, "and you could clearly tell that he was most interested in getting to the movie's [postproduction] phase. Shooting the film was something that he *had* to do, but his skills lay in postproduction.... He was someone who thought, 'Let's get this done fast so the money doesn't dry up and I can get to postproduction where I can really show my wizardry.'" Given the spotty onscreen results, however, Gordon appears to be more fumbling acolyte than accomplished conjurer. With its simplistic story line, cardboard characters and unconvincing special effects (the dragon looks like it escaped from a Chinese New Year parade), the only reason to take up this *Magic Sword* is Basil Rathbone's wonderful sneering villainy as the evil sorcerer; his forceful presence injects some much-needed life into the pale proceedings. Shot in only 13 days, *The Magic Sword* received a big push by United Artists, who gave it a major saturation booking in 350 theaters across the U.S.

With quotes from: "A Sworded Past," by Tom Weaver, in *Fangoria* no. 288, 2009.

The Magic Voyage of Sinbad (1953/61; Moss-Film/Filmgroup; U.S.S.R./Finland) Original Language Title: *Sadko*. In 1961 Roger Corman's Filmgroup company acquired the rights to a lavish yet dull-as-dirt 1953 Russo-Finnish fantasy and turned it into a Sinbad movie via the magic of dubbing (spending $9,600 on dubbing and rescoring). That's why this blonde(!) Sinbad the Sailor sails in an oddly Viking-styled craft and wears Nordic clothing rather than the expected

Arabian Nights dress. The story has Sinbad searching for "the Bird of Happiness" in order to restore prosperity to his now-impoverished home city of Kopisan. Along the way he plays his ever-present harp(!!) at Neptune's undersea palace, and then escapes on a giant seahorse(!!!). In the end, he basically discovers that There's No Place Like Home ... Tediously paced and broadly acted (with the gestures obviously intended to match the massive sets and dress extras), *The Magic Voyage of Sinbad* is strictly kiddie fare.

Majin Strikes Again (1966, Daiei; Japan) Original Language Title: *Diamajin gyakushu* (Giant Majin's Counterattack), Alternate Title: *Revenge of Giant Majin* (DVD). This is the last and least of Daiei's trilogy of period dramas about a giant stone samurai who comes to life to rescue the downtrodden villagers who worship him. This time around, the protagonists are four young boys who journey across the Mountain of Majin to try to rescue their fathers, kidnapped by an evil lord and pressed into forced labor. Although the special effects finale proves as impressive as ever — especially the snowy mountaintop sequences— the *jidaigeki* (period drama) story elements falter, with the boys' interminable trek consuming most of the running time. *Majin Strikes Again* never received an American theatrical or television release, but finally reached the States on DVD in 2005.

Man from Tomorrow see ***Cyborg 2087***

Mantis in Lace (1968; Boxoffice International). Alternate Title: *Lila*. About the only thing on offer in this boring roughie produced by Harry Novak's Box Office International are a trapped-in-amber peek at a swinging sixties strip club, a ridiculously over-the-top and off-the-mark gander at the "drug scene," and a few unintentional laughs. The story has topless dancer Lila drop acid at her "love nest" (a disused warehouse furnished with candles and a mattress), go on a bad trip (consisting of colored lights and hallucinations of *squishy bananas*), and hack her various lovers to death with screwdriver, meat cleaver, and garden hoe! Not the brightest bulb in the makeup mirror, Lila continues to take LSD whenever she brings a new lothario to her pad (with the same bloody results) until someone finally stumbles across the gruesome mess and calls in the fuzz. Filled with lines like "Groovy pad you've got here — a little kinky, but out of sight" and "Acid, baby, the stuff dreams are made of ... you'll groove it," and padded with far too many repetitive and pointless scenes of the various strippers (including perennial sixties favorite Pat Barrington) both on and off the stage, *Mantis* quickly wears out its welcome. It only truly comes alive during the brief and brutal murder moments (in which Lila hallucinates that she's hacking up various hated fruits and vegetables, even as the blood spatters and runs). Amazingly, considering how pedestrian it looks, *Mantis in Lace* was shot by respected cinematographer Lazlo (nee Leslie) Kovacs, whose other sixties work includes *Easy Rider*, *Targets* (both 1968), and *Blood of Dracula's Castle* (1969). Kovacs went on to carve out an impressive career in mainstream Hollywood, photographing such films as *Ghost Busters* (1984), *Copycat* (1995) and *Miss Congeniality* (2000).

Mark of the Wolfman see ***Frankenstein's Bloody Terror***

Mars Needs Women (1966; AIP-TV) This direct-to-TV cheapie possesses a seminal exploitation title but little else to recommend it. Larry Buchanan, who usually settled for filming uncredited remakes of 1950s AIP scripts (*The Eye Creatures*; *In the Year 2889*; *Zontar, the Thing from Venus*), here wrote an original screenplay. "I had reached my pain threshold in the remaking of bad scripts," recounts Buchanan (without the least bit of irony) in his book *It Came from Hunger! Tales of a Cinema Schlockmeister*, "and I told the heads of AIP that, as a breather, I wanted to do my own script, *Mars Needs Women*." Larry, however, should have stuck to plagiarizing the oldies, since those "bad scripts" were infinitely more entertaining than this one. The title says it all, as Tommy Kirk plays the leader of a small Martian band sent to Earth to secure women to repopulate his dying planet. 50 million miles is a long way to go just to get a date, but when Yvonne Craig (Batgirl from TV's *Batman*) is one of the intended, you can't fault Tommy for his efforts. An incoherent screenplay, Buchanan's usual static direction and poor photography ("the finished production looks like it was lit with a flashlight," admitted Yvonne Craig to interviewer Ted Okuda), long stretches of boring filler, high school-level acting (Craig excepted, who does as well with the unwieldy and tedious dialogue as anybody could), and a total lack of monsters (Tommy Kirk and company dressed in one-piece jump suits with earphones just doesn't cut it) make this movie mess nearly unwatchable. While *Mars Needs Women*, Buchanan Needs Talent.

Master of the World (1961; AIP) In 1868, U.S. special agent John Strock (Charles Bronson), arms magnate Mr. Prudent (Henry Hull), his daughter Dorothy (Mary Webster) and her balloon enthusiast fiancé (David Frankham) are taken captive by Robur (Vincent Price), a radical pacifist who commands a futuristic, zeppelin-like airship named the Albatross. Robur plans to use the Albratross and its cache of bombs and other advanced weapons to destroy the armies and navies of every nation that refuses to voluntarily disarm. Based on two Jules Verne novels (*Robur the Conqueror* and *Master of the World*), this is one of Richard Matheson's weaker screenplays—full of simplistic caricatures, with a dearth of action but a surplus of unfunny comedy relief, mostly involving the Albatross' put-upon cook (Vitto Scotti). The source material isn't Verne's best work, either. *Master of the World* plays like what it is—a knock-off of the better-known (and just plain better) *20,000 Leagues Under the Sea*, with Robur and the Albatross standing in for Captain Nemo and the Nautilus (and without benefit of a giant squid to liven up the story). On the positive side, *Master of the World*'s visual effects are imaginative, and Price seems committed to the story's anti-war message, which (alas) remains timeless. He and Bronson enjoy some effective moments together playing mutually respectful antagonists. Hull's grating histrionics as Prudent, however, are nearly insufferable, while Webster and Frankham simply occupy space. Although diverting, *Master of the World* is no world-beater.

Colorful (and juvenile) Belgian poster for the colorful (and juvenile) *Master of the World* (1961).

Matango see *Attack of the Mushroom People*

The Medusa Against the Son of Hercules (1963; Embassy Pictures; Italy/Spain) Original Language Title: *Perseo l'Invincibile.* Alternate Title: *Perseus Against the Monsters* (UK). In the early 1960s, everybody was doing it—"it" being importing muscleman movies from Italy and Spain, and "everybody" being low-rent film distributors. Embassy Pictures picked up this tale of Perseus and the Medusa and slotted it into their "Sons of Hercules" series (consisting of a handful of other pepla, including two Maciste efforts) that they released directly to American television. The name "Perseus" held little cache with the American viewing public, but "Hercules," thanks to the successful Steve Reeves films, was a bankable moniker. Consequently, Embassy tacked on a spoken narration to each of their films' beginnings: "Through the centuries in olden times there lived the sons of Hercules. Heroes supreme, they roamed the earth righting wrongs, helping the weak and oppressed, and seeking adventure." And apparently one of those few ("descended from ordinary mortals, who have been chosen by Hercules as sons in name") was Perseus. A superior peplum in every way—acting, photography, plotting and, most importantly, monsters—it's a pity *Medusa Against the Son of Hercules* never made it to the big screen in the U.S. Perseus (played by Richard Harrison, who made a slew of gladiator movies, spaghetti westerns and ninja[!] films) appears more approachable—and likable—than most he-man heroes, as he's simply a skilled and courageous *ordinary* man rather than the usual steroid-fed slab o' beef in leather loincloth. With its expansive outdoor photography (a refreshing change from the usual cramped, phony cave sets), impressive temples, misty atmosphere (particularly surrounding the titular terror—a unique creation resembling an uprooted mobile tree with writhing tendrils and a huge glowing eye), and the most realistic-looking dragon ever to menace ancient Greece (courtesy of monster maestro Carlo Rambaldi), *Medusa Against the Son of Hercules* resides at the right hand of Mario Bava's impressive *Hercules in the Haunted World* in the peplum pantheon.

One-sheet poster for *The Mermaids of Tiburon* (1962).

The Mermaids of Tiburon (1962; Filmgroup) Alternate Title: *The Aqua Sex* (nudie version). Filmed in Mexico and off California's Catalina Island, *The Mermaids of Tiburon* was underwater photographer John Lamb's (TV's *Sea Hunt* and *Voyage to the Bottom of the Sea*) first foray into feature films. The tale has a marine biologist investigating reports of unusual sea life (and spectacular pearls) off the isolated island of Tiburon in Mexico's Gulf of California. There he encounters a bevy of mermaids who aid him in vanquishing a murderous gangster after the sea's treasures. The original version featured half a dozen gorgeous mermaids, complete with the expected fishtails, led by *Playboy* playmate Diane Webber as the Mermaid Queen. But when the movie failed to generate much business, Lamb reshot many of the mermaid sequences with topless models (sans tails) to create one of the most unusual — and beautifully photographed — nudie cuties ever filmed. (This led Lamb to a career in sexploitation, as he produced, directed, and/or wrote another half-dozen sex films over the next decade.) Lamb's stunning underwater photography here is matched only by his subject matter — whether it be dazzling marine life or gorgeous female pulchritude. Aided and abetted by Richard LaSalle's haunting musical score and the sometimes-amusing voiceover narration by Our Hero ("I was being drawn to this creature by something more than just scientific interest"), the film generates an otherworldly rhythm that transports the viewer into an aquatic fantasy world. It also offers a few startling moments, such as when the Mermaid Queen rides a large shark(!), and a shocking spray of blood when the villain shoots one of the mermaids with a spear gun (nude version only). Visually-oriented to the end, Lamb even closes his film with an artful and meaningfully poignant scene involving a pet bird and a floating guitar. Unique and oddly haunting, *The Mermaids of Tiburon* is a fish-tale worth catching (in either version).

Mighty Jack (1968/1988; Tsuburaya Productions/ King Features; Japan) Original Language Title: *Maitei Jyaku*. This is another in the seemingly endless series of bogus feature films produced by stringing together episodes of a Japanese TV show. This time the show was a Japanese variation on the theme of *Voyage to the Bottom of the Sea* (crossed with *Mission: Impossible*) originally produced in 1968. *Mighty Jack* reached America 20 years later, thanks to enterprising home video producer Sandy Frank. Three years after that, it was featured in an episode of *Mystery Science Theater 3000*.

The Minotaur: The Wild Beast of Crete (1961; Agliani-Mordini Liria Film/United Artists; Italy; b&w) Original Language Title: *Teseo Contro il Minotauro*. Filmed in Italy and Yugoslavia, this story of Greek politics, assassination attempts and foiled romance in ancient Athens and Crete turns to horror in literally its last five minutes when Theseus (Bob Mathias) enters the fabled Labyrinth of Crete to battle the monstrous Minotaur. A passable peplum, *The Minotaur* offers likable leads (6'4" two-time Olympic Decathlon winner Mathias, and the impressive Rosanna Schiaffino in a dual role) and above-average sword-and-sandal action. Unfortunately, the titular titan looks more like a clumsy, flat-faced mutant bear than the half-man, half-bull of legend, provoking peals of laughter rather than shrieks of terror.

Mission Mars (1968; Allied Artists) Three astronauts (Darren McGavin, Nick Adams and George Devries) travel to Mars, where they find a frozen cosmonaut (apparently the Soviets beat us to the red planet) and a dangerous alien intelligence (in the form of what looks like a giant ball covered with tin foil) in this tedious, cut-rate science fiction dud. Mike St. Clair's thin, sluggish screenplay is padded — no, make that overstuffed — with romantic subplots and stock footage of NASA rocket launches. The first 20 (*twenty*!) of the film's 90 minutes are devoted to astronauts Mike Blaiswick (McGavin) and Nick Grant (Adams) reassuring their worried wives about the upcoming mission and to preparations (mostly stock shots) for the launch. Once in space, the astronauts eat, exercise, play chess, give each other haircuts, etc., until they finally reach Mars (a grinding 46 minutes of screen time along). Even then, the picture continues to cut away from the action to scenes where the mission commander (Michael DeBeausset) comforts the astronauts' spouses (Heather Hewitt and Shirley Parker) back on Earth. The brief, late-arriving action sequences, which by now seem almost beside the point, play out on bargain basement space ship and Martian landscape sets (Mars isn't even red), which must have looked even more appalling since *Mission Mars* arrived the same year as *2001: A Space Odyssey* and *Planet of the Apes*. In the end, *Mission Mars* has only two things going for it — McGavin and Adams, who remain fun to watch, even in drivel like this.

Mole Men Against the Son of Hercules (1961/64; Bengala Film/Embassy Television; Italy) Original Language Title: *Maciste, l'Uomo Più Forte del Mondo*. Alternate Title: *The Strongest Man in the World* (UK). This "story of Maciste and his struggle with the Mole Men" (as the beginning narration labels it) opens with Maciste (Mark Forest) fishing on the beach and hauling in his morning catch — a full-sized whale! When the dreaded Mole Men (a race of underground dwellers who look outwardly normal but die when exposed to the rays of the sun) attack Maciste's clan, the "strongest man in the world" must invade the villains' underground domain and free his people who are being used as slaves to power a primitive diamond-making factory(!). Apart from various tussles with the Mole Men, Maciste also battles a vicious troglodyte-like monster in a cage. This about-average entry was yet another peplum purchased by Embassy Television and released directly to American TV in their "Sons of Hercules" package.

Monster from a Prehistoric Planet (1967/68; Nikkatsu/AIP-TV; Japan) Alternate Title: *Gappa, The Triphibian Monsters* (home video). This unimaginative, paint-by-numbers giant monster flick remains notable for two reasons: first, it was the only *kaiju eiga* to emanate from the Nikkatsu studio; second, its plot plays like a Japanese rewrite of *Gorgo*. Developers planning to convert a pacific atoll into an amusement park ("Playmate Land") discover and capture a baby giant monster, believing it to be the sole survivor of its species. They take the creature back to Tokyo to put it on display, but Daddy and Mommy Monster emerge to reclaim their offspring — stomping toy tanks and batting down model airplanes along the way, of course. In addition to its unoriginal scenario, the monsters look like poor imitations of Rodan (except for the baby, which looks like a cousin of Big Bird from *Sesame Street*), and the film's trite subplots (including the inevitable romantic triangle) seem overly familiar

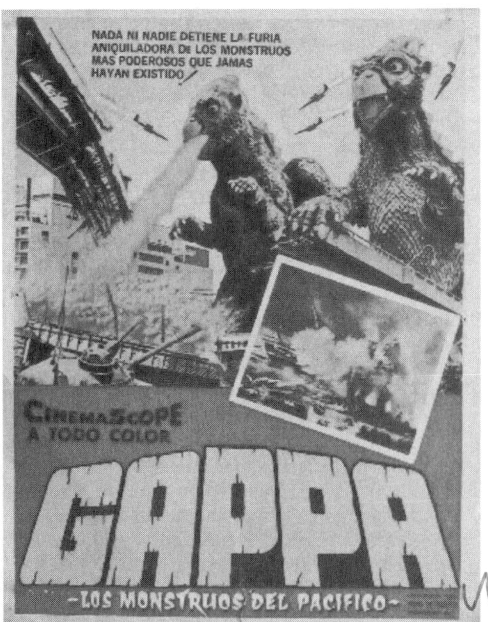

Japan's *Daikyoju Gappa* became *Monster from a Prehistoric Planet* when released in America by AIP (Mexican lobby card).

as well. Since this movie provides a surprisingly meager ration of monster action, viewers are advised to feed their *kaiju eiga* cravings elsewhere. Like several other late-60s *kaiju* flicks, *Monster from a Prehistoric Planet* did not receive a theatrical release in the U.S., but was purchased for TV by AIP.

Monster from the Unknown World see ***Atlas Against the Cyclops***

The Monster of Camp Sunshine (1965; b&w) "The motion picture that follows is a fable. In it there are many nudists but only one monster. In life, it is generally the other way around." So states the opening title card for *The Monster of Camp Sunshine*, a New York-lensed combo of nudist flick and art-trash cinema. A pair of New York City denizens, a nudist nurse and her fashion model roommate (who finally takes the plunge and agrees to model a *topless* bathing suit—on the roof of a city tenement building!) end up at an Upstate nudist camp where the local simpleton gardener, Hugo, has been turned into an axe-wielding maniac by drinking some chemically-contaminated river water. In between the slice-of-Big-City-life scenes of the two roommates smoking, listening to records and blathering on about, well, nothing at all really, are scenes of nature-loving-nudists smoking, listening to records and, well, blathering on. But the prosaic proceedings are enlivened by periodic moments of cinematic craziness, including opening credits that offer up some amusing, low-rent Terry Gilliam-esque animation, a lab-rat attack (ending with the heroine hanging outside a skyscraper window by her fingers!), and the hulking Hugo (who is so incompetent a maniac that his murderous rampage results in him killing exactly *no one*) chased down and reduced to a literal lump of cinders by an amazingly diverse collection of military stock footage (not to mention inserts of everything from Napoleonic to Civil War soldiers!). Filmed in gritty black-and-white hand-held verite "style," *The Monster of Camp Sunshine*, while still periodically dragged down to its dreary nudist roots, at least offers lovers of the outré a bit more than the usual mid-sixties nudie-cutie ennui.

The Monster of London City (1964/67; Producers Releasing Organization; West Germany; b&w) Original Language Title: *Das Ungeheuer von London City*. Based on a Bryan Edgar Wallace novel, this West German mystery/horror has "a new Jack the Ripper" emulating the murders in a popular current play based on Saucy Jack, with the stageplay's star (Hansjorg Felmy) soon becoming the prime suspect. Likable leads; shadowy, fog-shrouded ambiance; some suspenseful set pieces; and the always-intriguing Jack the Ripper angle (not to mention some fleeting female nudity) make this an above-average krimi.

Monster Zero (1965/1970; Toho; Japan) Alternate (home video) Titles: *Godzilla vs. Monster Zero*, *Invasion of Astro-Monster*. Original Language Title: *Kaiju Daisenso*. This film, a strong candidate for best Godzilla entry of the 1960s, inexplicably languished unreleased in America until 1970—two years after the death of its star, Nick Adams. Whether producers realized it or not, however, *Monster Zero* remains an excellent example of its form, with its beautiful cine-

Godzilla meets Ghidorah, the Three-Headed Monster, in *Monster Zero* (1965/70) (Italian photobusta).

matography, with first-rate production design (especially its eerie alien landscapes) and visual effects, fine score, strong cast and unusually compelling, character-driven story. It also remains notable as the first Toho movie to combine giant monsters with an alien invasion plot. Astronauts Glen (Adams) and Fuiji (Akira Takarada) travel to the newly discovered Planet X, beyond Jupiter, and encounter a race of aliens driven underground by Monster Zero (Ghidrah). The aliens offer to provide humans with a cure for cancer in exchange for the assistance of Godzilla and Rodan in the fight against Monster Zero. Earth's leaders agree to the deal, but are double-crossed by the "X-people." The picture devotes considerable time to subplots involving Fuji's sister Haruno (Keiko Sawai) and her inventor boyfriend Tetsuo (Akira Kubo), and to Glen's romance with the beautiful Miss Namikawa (Kumi Mizuno)— entertaining stories in themselves, which ultimately dovetail with the main narrative. The plot also includes a couple of well-sprung surprises. Adams and Mizuno, who sparkled together in *Frankenstein Conquers the World* (1965), click once again. The rest of the cast performs admirably, as well, particularly the amusing Kubo. Unfortunately, their performances suffer badly in the U.S. version, which features some of the worst dubbing of the series. *Monster Zero* offers intrigue, suspense, engaging characters and spectacular visuals, but runs a little short on monster-versus-monster action. The first triple-monster tussle arrives fully 53 minutes into this 94-minute picture, and runs a scant two minutes. Godzilla and company return for the finale, but remain either off-screen or inactive for most of the rest of the film. Luckily, director Ishiro Honda keeps the pace brisk and never allows the tension to flag.

Moon Zero Two (1969/70; Hammer/Warner Bros.; U.K.) Surprisingly, *Moon Zero Two*, one of the most notorious bombs ever released by Hammer Films, isn't all bad. Writer-producer Michael Carreras' script contains two forward-thinking concepts that would better serve later films: first, incorporating shoot-outs, bar fights and other elements from the Western genre into a science fiction yarn (not unlike *Star Wars* [1977]); and second, eschewing the archetypal sci-fi scientist-hero in favor of workaday everymen in outer space (a la *Dark Star* [1974] and *Alien* [1979]). *Moon Zero Two* boasts a likable leading man in James Olson (*The Andromeda Strain* [1971]). Its dialogue is sharply written, and its basic plot — about a gang of outer space outlaws trying to smuggle an ore-rich asteroid to the moon — isn't bad either. Unfortunately, everything else about this movie is *quite* bad. The overriding issue is that Hammer simply wasn't willing or able to put the money into *Moon Zero Two* that the project demanded. The picture is sunk by its abominably cut-rate production values: sub–*Dr. Who* special effects (tiny models and sloppy matte paintings); ridiculous costumes (and even worse hair styling); chintzy "futuristic" production design (lots of blank white walls, and even an inflatable chair); and a grating saxophone-and-flute-happy score. Coming on the heels of *2001: A Space Odyssey* (1968), these flaws seem all the more laughable — and less excusable. No wonder the *Mystery Science Theater 3000* crew selected *Moon Zero Two* for ridicule in 1990. Also, while Carreras' script has its merits, it runs short on action. *Moon Zero Two* drags on for 100 often lethargic, talky minutes, which is about a half-hour too long. On second thought, it's probably 100 minutes too long.

The Mummy and the Curse of the Jackals (1969/86; Vega International Pictures/Academy Home Entertainment) Shot in 1969 but unreleased (for reasons obvious to anyone who's ever seen it) until the I'll-stock-anything-on-tape video store boom of the mid–80s, the derivative, nonsensical, amateurish *Mummy and the Curse of the Jackals* stars low-rent leading man Anthony Eisley as a Las Vegas archeologist who discovers two Egyptian mummies— one a still-beautiful princess and the other a '40s Universal knockoff. Eisley succumbs to the titular "curse" and transforms into a jackal-man during the full moon. The princess revives, as does the mummy, who goes on a brief rampage before the jackal-man and the bandaged one face off in a laughable showdown. Featured in a couple of scenes is John Carradine collecting yet another I've-gotta-support-my-ex-wives paycheck. Lon Chaney, Jr., reportedly turned down the role of the mummy. Watching the Kharis clone shambling down a crowded Vegas street (with bemused bystanders gawking, laughing and following the silly-suited actor), it's little wonder why. Though *Jackals* offers the occasional unintentional chuckle ("We can't just stand by and let a 4000-year-old mummy and a jackal-man take over the city," deadpans Carradine), its dull pacing and incoherence makes it tough going even for the so-bad-it's-good crowd. Worst of all, the were-jackal appears more like a poodle in need of a groomer than a demonic denizen of the Egyptian underworld. Veteran B-Western director Oliver Drake "was quite senile at the time," related Eisley. "The director was sort of losing his faculties, and I realized after a few days that he really didn't know what the hell was going on at all times." And neither will the viewer.

With quotes from: *Interviews with B Science Fiction and Horror Movie Makers*, by Tom Weaver.

Mumsy, Nanny, Sonny & Girly (1969/70; Cinerama Releasing Corporation; U.K.) Alternate Title: *Girly*. Completed in 1969 but not released in America until February 1970, *Mumsy, Nanny, Sonny & Girly* is a twisted tale of a British family who imprison bums and partygoers as "playmates" for their childish "games" before "sending them to the angels." When their latest "new friend" turns out to be a rather clever lothario, jealousy arises between the middle-aged Mumsy and Nanny, as well as the coming-of-age Girly, disrupting their murderous ways. Though based on the play "Happy Family," *Mumsy* is anything but stagey, as director (and frequent Hammer helmer) Freddie Francis keeps his camera moving through the house and grounds of the seen-better-days country estate setting. Aiding him is Brian Comport's witty and disturbing script (adapted from his own play), and a fine cadre of principle and supporting players, the latter including Hammer stalwart Michael Ripper and

British beauty Imogen Hassell (dubbed "the Countess of Cleavage" by the press). Particularly arresting is the disturbing yet alluring performance of Vanessa Howard (*Corruption, The Vampire Beast Craves Blood*) as Girly. Though 21 in real life, she looks more like 16 and acts more like 12—albeit a psychotic, coquettish and dangerous 12. "I looked upon it as a black comedy," stated Francis, adding, "slightly more black than comedy.... Maybe I've got a peculiar sense of humor." Indeed. While a bit overlong, *Mumsy, Nanny, Sonny & Girly* remains an engrossing and disturbing portrayal of familial madness, and deserved better than its quick disappearance into obscurity.

With quotes from: *The Men Who Made the Monsters*, by Paul M. Jensen.

Murder a la Mod (1968; Aries Documentaries; b&w) Though the Something Weird Video DVD box proclaims *Murder a la Mod* "A LOST HORROR FILM FROM BRIAN DE PALMA!" this New York-lensed, low-budget, film-schoolesque experiment from the future maker of *Carrie, Dressed to Kill* and *The Untouchables* is more comedy than horror, complete with slapstick pies, speeded-up camerawork, and a clownish jokester with a trick ice pick. (Of course, this being a DePalma film, said ice pick is replaced with a real one for a nasty murder sequence—the only moment in the film approaching "horror.") The sketchy story has a young woman fall for a photographer trying to break into the movie biz by shooting a nudie, with things going horribly awry. It becomes both repetitive and silly when DePalma chooses to relate the events leading up to and just after the murder via alternate-perspective flashbacks and some stream-of-consciousness babbling from the main (goofy) suspect. *Murder a la Mod* is a tedious misfire that shows little of the stylish promise to come from the soon-to-be-successful filmmaker. (Note: According to the fine folks at Something Weird, this picture played in a *single* New York theater back in 1968 before it dropped from sight.)

My Blood Runs Cold (1965; MGM; b&w) In a California coastal town, local heiress Julie Merriday (Joey Heatherton) literally runs into a young man, Ben (Troy Donahue), who recognizes her as the reincarnation of her great-great-grandmother, Barbara Merriday. Is Ben Barbara's 100-year-gone lost love reincarnated; is he a scam artist (as Julie's manipulative father believes); or is there yet another answer? More romantic fantasy than anything else, *My Blood Runs Cold* only turns dark (or at least a slightly dimmer shade of schmaltz) at film's end when The Truth Comes Out. In fact, the movie lacks even a simple murder sequence, much less any horrific moments. The film's often weepy musical score, coupled with the Wuthering Heights-style photography, sets the melodramatic tone. In the acting department (absolutely critical for these types of Peyton Place shenanigans), bland as dry toast Donahue proves a poor match for the fiery Heatherton; what she sees in him is the *real* mystery here. And a final protracted chase after the Big Reveal adds nothing but running time as it winds down to its foregone conclusion. Given all this, the viewer's blood will most likely run tepid at best.

The Mysterious Satellite see ***Warning from Space***

Neutron and the Black Mask (1961; Clasa-Mohme, Inc.; Mexico; b&w) Original Language Title: *Neutron el Enmascarado Negro*. Santo, Blue Demon, Mil Mascaras, Neutron ... to quote from *Sesame Street*: "One of these things is not like the others." The first three are real-life masked Mexican wrestlers who starred in their own film series, while Neutron is a completely fictional character (though played by real wrestler Wolf Ruvinskis) who, in 1961, appeared in *his* own cinematic subset (lasting five films, though only four found their way north of the border). Another difference: Though Neutron dresses like a lucha libre icon (wrestling tights, bare chest, and black lucha-styled mask), he's merely a buffed-up crime-fighter (or "atomic super-man," according to the film's on-screen title). Consequently, missing from these entries are the usual two or three (or four) wrestling bouts—which may be a blessing or a curse, depending upon one's proclivities for full nelsons and horse locks. In this inaugural episode, a *white*-masked villain named Dr. Caronte conspires with a turncoat scientist to steal the formula for a "neutron bomb" (no relation to Our Hero). A trio of friends, led by a murdered scientist's son, involve themselves in the case, and aid a masked crime-fighter calling himself Neutron in tracking down Caronte and putting a stop to his nefarious scheme. Logical? Well, as Caronte (who appears to be more alchemist than scientist) himself scoffs, "Do you see any logic to all this?" A fair-to-middlin' production, *Neutron* features an impressive dungeon-like lab set in Caronte's mansion and a pit full of overalls-wearing, shaggy-haired zombie creatures (who, oddly, have no fingers—or at least never open their clenched

Ad for the lukewarm *My Blood Runs Cold* (1965).

fists). On the downside, the no-frills cinematography is as static as the dialogue, several time- (and interest-) killing nightclub musical numbers stop the story dead in its tracks, and the action set-pieces consist of disappointingly lackluster fisticuffs between Neutron and the police (before the world at large realizes our masked hero is a Good Guy), and Neutron and the zombies. Though off to a rather slow start with this opening salvo, the Neutron series would take a decidedly outré upturn with the next entry, *Neutron vs. the Death Robots*. (Note: Since the first three *Neutron* movies were shot at America Studios, which was only allowed to make shorts, they were filmed in roughly half-hour segments, ostensibly as television episodes, and then combined into feature format. Reportedly released to Spanish-speaking theaters in the U.S., the *Neutrons* didn't make their English debut until dubbed and sold directly to television.)

Neutron vs. the Amazing Dr. Caronte (1961; Clasa-Mohme, Inc.; Mexico; b&w) Original Language Title: *Neutron Contra el Dr. Caronte.* This third entry in the Neutron series can't sustain the giddy outrageousness of the second (*Neutron vs. the Death Robots*). Rather than disembodied brains and zombies ripping off their own heads, *Caronte* offers a "gang war" scenario in which the agent of an unnamed foreign power and his band of hoods face off against Caronte and his zombies for control of the neutron-bomb formula (yes, despite all indications to the contrary, the evil Doc survived being buried under tons of rubble at the close of *Death Robots*). Granted, things do take an amusingly cockeyed turn when, halfway through the feature, the identity of Caronte is finally revealed — and the evil madman promptly shoots himself! Then, through a few throwaway lines about "the transmigration of the soul," Caronte is back (inhabiting another body) at his nefarious task of trying to rule the world. Unfortunately, after this over-too-quickly bit of silly surrealism, the remainder of the film focuses on the same ol' same ol' Neutron action — threats, kidnappings, fisticuffs, etc., making *Neutron vs. the Amazing Dr. Caronte* a disappointingly anticlimactic conclusion for our Masked Hero and Diabolical Villain. (Note: Neutron returned for two more features, but with unrelated storylines; and only one was dubbed into English.)

Neutron vs. the Death Robots (1961; Clasa-Mohme, Inc.; Mexico; b&w) Original Language Title: *Los Automatas de la Muerte.* With the plot groundwork having been laid in *Neutron and the Black Mask*, this first sequel jumps right into boffo action, with megalomaniacal wannabe-world-ruler Dr. Caronte whipping up a new batch of zombies, then stealing and reanimating the disembodied brains of three murdered scientists (kept alive with the blood of murder victims) to gain the secret neutron-bomb formula. Subsequently, the zombies, led by Caronte's dwarf henchman Nick, raid warehouses to procure bomb-constructing materials, while Neutron and the three protagonists from the first film, along with a cadre of police, try to protect the one surviving professor (played by soon-to-be Jess Franco regular Jack Taylor) and stop Caronte. Whew! In between the expected fisticuffs, and a moderately suspenseful scene in which Caronte turns terrorist and plants a bomb at the airport, *Death Robots* offers such bizarre turns as having one of the zombies disguise itself as Neutron to kidnap the professor and throw suspicion onto our masked hero(!), and another zombie, ordered by Caronte to destroy itself, pulling off its own head(!!). And *Death Robots* concludes with a rambunctious, exhausting and brutally violent climactic fight between Neutron and Caronte that proves far more satisfying than the ending of the first feature. For those enamored of Mexi-monster thrills and lucha libra-style wacky action, this middle section of the Neutron trilogy offers the most bang for your pesos.

In this Mexican lobby card for *Neutron vs. the Amazing Dr. Caronte* (1961), Jack Taylor (using the stage name Grek Martin) stoically attempts to comfort Rosa Arenas.

Neutron vs. the Maniac (1961; Clasa-Mohme, Inc., Mexico; b&w) Original Language Title: *Neutron contra el Criminal Sadico.* One of two stand-alone Neutron features (the other being *Neutron Contra los Asesinos del Karate* [Neutron vs. the Karate Assassins], which was not dubbed into English), *Neutron vs. the Maniac* has masked crime-fighter Neutron tracking a murderous cloaked phantom by infiltrating a sanitarium (as his everyday alter-ego, Charles). The rather mundane plot is a disappointment after the bombastic rule-the-world shenanigans of the first three Neutrons, and a floppy-hat-wearing killer sneaking about is no replacement for the crazed Dr. Caronte and his cadre of zombie-creatures. The picture starts off on a dull note with a tepid nightclub number by a blowsy chanteuse (the film's heroine, as it turns out) and never recovers its feet, spending far too much time on interactions between the various eccentric "guests" of the sanitarium, two *more* nightclub outings, and a mundane wrestling match (*sans* Neutron), making *Neutron vs. the Maniac* a poor capper to the series.

Night Creatures (1962; Hammer/Universal; U.K.) Original Title: *Captain Clegg*. Despite its lurid American title, this is a landlocked pirate adventure with a few minor horrific flourishes, not a true horror film. But don't let that deter you—this one's a gem, one of Hammer Films' best efforts of the early 1960s. Built on one of Anthony Hinds' cleverest scripts, under the crisp direction of Peter Graham Scott, and fueled by a high-octane lead performance from Peter Cushing, *Night Creatures* features a satisfying balance of action, romance and character moments. A squad of British sailors arrives in a small seaside village to investigate reported smuggling. Locals—including the innkeeper (Martin Benson), the coffinmaker (Michael Ripper) and even the village parson (Cushing)—warn the King's men to avoid the marshes at night, due to the fearsome "Marsh Phantoms." Nothing is quite as it seems, however, and it becomes increasingly difficult to tell the Good Guys from the Bad Guys in this mildly subversive and surprisingly poetic yarn. Aside from

Italian four-sheet poster for *Night Creatures* (1962; aka *Captain Clegg*).

Cushing's fabulous work, the film also benefits from a delightful supporting turn by Michael Ripper, in one of the more substantial roles of his career, and strong showings from Oliver Reed and Yvonne Romain as the junior romantic leads. Hammer's team of behind-the-scenes artisans were working at their peak during this era and it shows, particularly in Arthur Grant's sumptuous cinematography and Don Banks' thrilling score. This is not a film to be missed by fans of either Hammer or Cushing.

Night Must Fall (1964; MGM; U.K.; b&w) *Night Must Fall* (1964) is not, strictly speaking, a remake of the 1937 thriller of the same title but rather a new adaptation of the same Emlyn Williams play, about a wheelchair-bound elderly woman who hires as a household servant a fawning young man who may or may not be a serial killer (and who carries with him a hat box that may contain the severed head of a previous victim). Still, comparisons between the two films are inescapable and uniformly unflattering to the 1964 version, which lacks the suspense and subtlety of the 1937 movie. Designed as a showcase for actor Albert Finney, who co-produced, the 1964 picture shows its cards from the beginning, with Danny dumping an elderly woman's body into the lake and tossing a bloody hatchet high into the air. So much for mystery! Worse yet, Finney's work lacks the likeability and nuance that Robert Montgomery brought to the same role. Finney's Danny vacillates between charmless clod (the kind of guy who eats with his mouth open and slaps women on the ass) and wild-eyed loony (scratching his fingernails along the walls as he paces in his room and staring bug-eyed into the camera). Although he's quite bad here, the failure of *Night Must Fall* isn't entirely Finney's fault. Clive Exton's heavy-handed screenplay bungles every opportunity for suspense, particularly overplaying the business with the hat box (Danny removes the lid from the box and stares at its contents in a mirror, grinning maniacally). The scenario limps to a conclusion with a dull anti-climax. Mona Washbourne is acceptable as the elderly Mrs. Bramson but nowhere near as effective as Dame May Whitty, who originated the role on stage and also appeared in the 1937 film. Director Karel Reisz, whose kitchen sink drama *Saturday Night and Sunday Morning* catapulted Finney to stardom in 1960, seems at sea with this sort of material. Cinematographer Freddie Francis contributes some beautifully lit shots, especially when the police drag the lake in search of Danny's earlier victim, but given the pedigree of the material and the level of talent involved, *Night Must Fall* remains a major disappointment.

Night of the Bloody Apes (1968/72; Cinematografica Calderon/Jerand Films; Mexico) Original Language Title: *La Horripilante Bestia Humana*. Alternate Titles: *Gomar: The Human Gorilla*; *Horror and Sex*. A scientist (Armando Silvestre) places the heart of a gorilla into the body of his dying son Julio (Augustin Martinez Solares), resulting in Julio's transformation into an ape-man (though he looks more Neanderthal than simian). While the father searches for a cure, Julio escapes and goes on a sex-murder ram-

page ("the lust of a man in the body of a beast!" as the film's trailer so delicately puts it). One of the most unusual Latino immigrants to slip past the border guards of 1960s cinema (though released in Mexico in 1968, the film didn't reach American theaters until 1972), *Night of the Bloody Apes* possessed all the peculiar proclivities of Mexi-movies of the time (the heroine, for instance, is a mask-wearing professional *wrestler*) while also offering a shockingly sleazy sex-and-gore quotient unheard of in the more innocent black-and-white south-of-the-border efforts made earlier in the decade. The heroine, for instance, displays her charms in not one but *two* gratuitous stepping-out-of-the-shower scenes. Then there's the gore. The angry ape-man gruesomely rips out a victim's throat; gouges out a man's eyeball with this thumb; repeatedly stabs a man in the chest with the victim's own knife; literally rips the head off another — in extreme close-up; and tears off a person's scalp. (The cheeky promotional department suggested theaters give fans the opportunity to pick out their own free miniature rubber organs in the lobby. Now *that's* entertainment!) It all serves to make this Ed-Wood-Meets-Herschell-Gordon-Lewis-in-Tijuana travesty a risible yet oddly compelling bit of Mexi-trash (though the production values here — meager as they are — appear miles above anything enjoyed by Wood or Lewis). And, like so much of the output of those two no-budget "auteurs," *Night of the Bloody Apes* offers enough eccentricities, shocks and bizarre ineptitude to hold one's interest. Though far from a good movie, *Night of the Bloody Apes* remains a bloody entertaining one.

Nights of the Werewolf (1968; Spain/France; Unreleased) Original Language Title: *Las Noches del Hombre Lobo.* Frustratingly for fans of Spain's Paul Naschy, this second entry in his unofficial, long-running Waldemar Daninsky/Wolfman series was never released (doubts remain as to whether it was even finished). Naschy himself is unsure if a complete print of the film (co-written by and starring Naschy) even exists. "That picture was shot in Paris with a fairly good budget for its time," he said. "I remember including some scenes of the Wolf Man on the Parisian rooftops surrounded by the fog. The film ran into serious economic problems which resulted in lawsuits; but the most unfortunate thing was that the director, Rene Govar, was killed in a car accident shortly after filming was completed.... It really is a 'damned' film." Naschy's description of this "damned" movie is tantalizing: "The film told the story of a professor who discovers that one of his pupils suffers from the curse of lycanthropy. Under the guise of helping him, the professor instead uses him as an instrument of revenge. He dominates the pupil during his transformations by means of sound waves, and in this manner causes him to act against the people he wants to get rid of."

With quotes from: "Interview: Paul Naschy," and "Filmography: Paul Naschy," by Michael Secula, *Videooze* 6/7, 1994.

The pajama-clad "Horrible Human Beast" from 1968's *La horripilante bestia humana*, released in the U.S. in 1972 as *Night of the Bloody Apes* (Photofest).

No Place Like Homicide (1961/62; Regal/Embassy; U.K.; b&w) Original Title (U.K.): *What a Carve Up!* Timid Ernie (Kenneth Connor), who makes his living proofreading horror novels with titles like *Blood on the Cauliflower*, travels to with his streetwise pal Sid (Sidney James) to a spooky old mansion for the reading of his uncle's will. Naturally, Ernie and a houseful of crazy relatives are trapped in the house by a thunderstorm; and inevitably his uncles and cousins begin turning up murdered. Although James and Connor are best remembered for their work in the long-running *Carry On* series (James appeared in 19 *Carry On* comedies, Connor in 17), *No Place Like Homicide* plays less like a *Carry On* film (it's much funnier than most of those) and more like an Abbott & Costello picture (specifically, *Hold That Ghost*), with James as the Bud Abbott-style wise guy and Connor taking over the Lou Costello 'fraidy cat role. Although ostensibly a remake of *The Ghoul* (1933), the horror elements in *No Place Like Homicide* remain slight. "James & Connor" are ably supported by a fine cast including standouts Donald Pleasence as an intimidating solicitor and Michael Gough as a dotty butler, along with Dennis Price (star of Ealing Films' *Kind Hearts and Coronets* [1946]) and the lovely Shirley Eaton, who had previous appeared in *Carry on Sergeant* (1958), *Carry on Nurse* (1959) and *Carry on Constable* (1960). While it contains some physical shtick (Connor takes some impressive pratfalls), most of the humor arises from the picture's razor sharp dialogue. For instance, after suspicion falls on Ernie, Pleasence remarks to James, "I'm not entirely convinced your friend is the fool he makes himself out to be." To which Connor indignantly replies, "Oh, yes I am!" While it's no lost classic, *No Place Like*

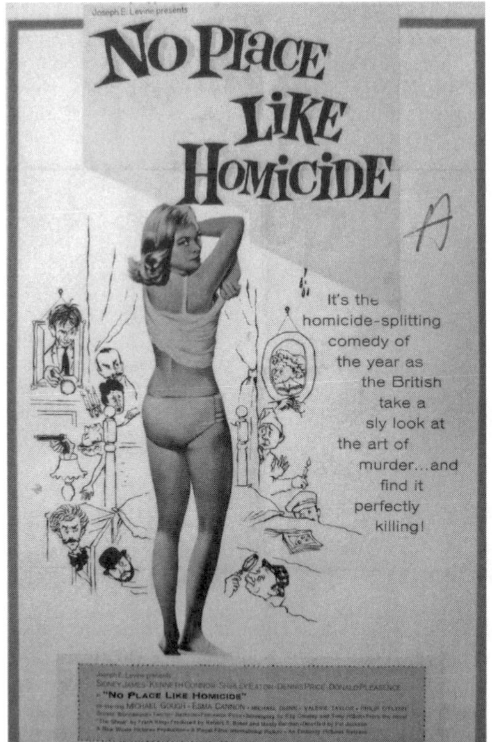

Cheeky one-sheet poster for the British horror-comedy *What a Carve-Up!* (1961/62), with the film's American title literally pasted over it.

Homicide is an endearing and at times laugh-out-loud funny spoof that should delight anyone with a taste for Old Dark House-style horror-comedies.

No Survivors Please (1964; UCC; West Germany; b&w) Original Language Title: *Der Chef Wünscht Keine Zeugen.* "We are an expeditionary force sent to Earth to annihilate mankind," explains the alien "Chief" in *No Survivors Please.* "The human bodies of great and important men we temporarily occupy are now nothing but empty shells ruled by our superior intelligence instead of primitive emotions." Said aliens possessing the bodies of "great and important men" intend to use their position to begin World War III and so destroy humanity. A reporter on the verge of discovering this plot becomes involved with the secretary (Austrian Eurostarlet Maria Perschy) of an alien-inhabited politician, and their "love" awakens dormant emotions in — and sows conflict among — the invaders. Focusing more on the antagonists' plotting and political machinations than the aliens themselves or the terror of possession, the movie resembles more of a low-rent espionage entry than a horror (or even science fiction) film. Saddled with too many characters, too much stock footage (of rocket launches, plane crashes, riots, racetrack wrecks, and even Carnival parades), and a dearth of action (little happens apart from the characters tonelessly talking among themselves— either plotting or discussing that pesky emotion "love"), *No Survivors Please* has little of the immediacy — and none of the horror — of such similarly-themed movies as *I Married a Monster from Outer Space* (1958), *The Day Mars Invaded Earth* (1963), or even the lowly *Cape Canaveral Monsters* (1960). Released theatrically in Europe and the U.K., *No Survivors Please* only invaded America via the television airwaves.

The Omegans (1968; Paramount; U.S./Philippines) A famous painter (Lucien Pan) is cuckolded by his younger wife (Ingrid Pitt) and their strapping jungle guide (Keith Larsen), then takes revenge by luring them into a "cursed" river poisoned with radiation (causing their skin to slowly deteriorate) in this sci-fi-tinged jungle melodrama, the final film directed by Billy Wilder's brother W. (Willy) Lee. "Unfortunately, the one I got wasn't the talented one," laughed Ingrid Pitt about her *Omegans* director. Indeed, Willy brought the same "talent" he showed on movies like *Killers from Space* and *The Snow Creature* to bear fully on *The Omegans*: i.e., a leaden pace, stilted performances, overlong medium shots, and a locked-down camera that literally *never* moves (even making the gorgeous Filipino jungle setting look dull). "It's a terrible film," admitted Pitt. "I was bad. I don't want to blame other people, it was me, just me." Well, on *The Omegans* it was *everybody*.

With quotes from: "Pitting Wits," by Howard Maxford, *Shivers* no. 31, July 1996.

100 Monsters (1968; Daiei; Japan) Original Language Title: *Yokai Hyaku Monogatori* (The Hundred Ghost Stories). Alternate Title: *Yokai Monsters 2: 100 Monsters* (DVD). This is the second installment in the Yokai Monsters trilogy (preceded by *Spook Warfare* and followed by *Along with Ghosts*), eccentric Japanese ghost stories featuring a host of strikingly weird-looking monsters. In this installment, the most engrossing of the series, the "apparitions" join forces with a master-less samurai to overthrow a crooked magistrate (in addition to committing murder, the magistrate turns a Buddhist shrine into a brothel!). These movies (and their monsters) truly must be seen to be believed. None of the Yokai Monsters films received a general theatrical release in the U.S., but all three reached American shores on DVD in 2003.

One Million AC/DC (1969; Canyon Films) With a screenplay by none other than Ed Wood, Jr. (using the alias "Akdon Telmig"— which is one letter shy of a reversed "vodka gimlet"), one might expect to glean some small amusement from this late-sixties sexploitationer. Unfortunately, *One Million AC/DC* offers none of the expected "Woodisms" (amusingly non-sequitor dialogue, out-of-left-field pseudo-philosophical bon mots, inappropriate references to angora), as most of the (still-excruciatingly-overlong) 65-minute running time is taken up with desperately un-erotic simulated sex scenes in which emaciated women rub and writhe against unattractive bearded men who keep their animal-fur loin cloths on at all times. The "story" follows a group of cave-people who hole up inside their cavern when a plastic dinosaur (the same pathetic puppet seen in the same year's *The Mighty Gorga*) lays siege to their rock quarry dwelling (the ubiquitous Bronson Canyon in Hollywood's Griffith Park). The occasional comedic interlude between the interminable dry-humpings (including a running gag about a cave-babe kidnapped by a gorilla for prurient purposes, and the players occasionally staring directly into the camera to make an "astute" observation) falls flatter than a stone-aged pancake, leaving nothing here but subpar simulations for the raincoat crowd.

Onibaba (1964; Toho/Continental; Japan; b&w) Alternate Title: *Demon Woman*. Director Kaneto Shindo's dark parable, freely adapted from a Buddhist fable, takes place in war-torn medieval Japan. A young woman (Jitsuko Yoshimura) and her mother-in-law (Nabuko Otowa) survive by hiding in the tall susuki grass and waylaying passing samurai, killing them and trading their weapons and armor for millet. But the bonds between the two women begin to fray when Hachi (Kei Sato), a young deserter, returns from the war with news that their husband/son has been killed. Hachi soon forms a wedge between the younger and older women, forcing the mother-in-law to desperate measures since she cannot kill without her daughter-in-law's assistance. She dons a Noh demon mask and tries to eliminate Hachi, with ironic results. Shindo, in a 2004 interview, said he wanted *Onibaba* to show human beings reduced by war to a primitive, almost feral existence, struggling to satisfy their most basic desires (nourishment and sex). The result is an intense, harrowing, sexually charged viewing experience — superbly acted, especially by Otowa, and beautifully photographed, particularly its eerily evocative shots of swaying fields of seven-foot-high susuki grass. *Onibaba* falls silent for long stretches, except for sound effects and Hikaru Hiyashi's propulsive, drum-heavy score, which enriches the film immeasurably. Although certainly horrific, the movie's horror/fantasy elements remain minor. Shindo's unnerving follow-up, *Kuroneko* (aka *The Black Cat*, 1968), was a full-tilt supernatural chiller about two women who are gang raped and murdered by a band of marauding samurai, then return as shape-shifting cat-spirits who take vengeance on their killers. Unfortunately, *Kuroneko* does not appear to have been released theatrically in America, nor yet has it reached the U.S. in an authorized home video release.

Orgy of the Dead (1965; F.O.G. Distributors) Alternate Title: *Orgy of the Vampires*. A horror writer and his girlfriend visit a cemetery where they're taken captive by the "Master of the Dead" (Criswell) and the "Princess of Darkness" (Fawn Silver), who force them to watch various zombie women called up from the dead to dance topless. The most famous of the horror-themed "nudie-cuties" of the era, *Orgy of the Dead* has very little plot to get in the way of the various strippers performing their acts on the cheap graveyard soundstage. Penned by the notorious Ed Wood, Jr. (*Plan Nine from Outer Space*), this atrocious "adult" film offers little more than a few moments of unin-

During a time of war, two women (Jitsuko Yoshimura, left, and Nobuko Otowa) kill stragglers and sell their armor for food in the mesmerizing Japanese morality tale *Onibaba* (1964).

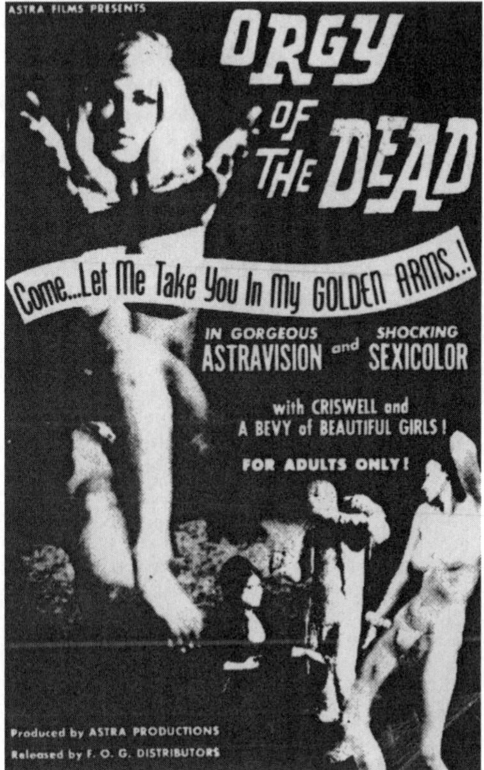

Ad for the Ed Wood--scripted *Orgy of the Bored* ... er, *Dead*.

tentional amusement via Wood's risible dialogue: "I am Criswell! For years I have told the almost unbelievable, related the unreal and showed it to be more than a fact. Now I tell the tale of the threshold people, so astounding that some of you may faint!" (an introductory quote cribbed nearly word for word from Wood's earlier opus, 1959's *Night of the Ghouls*). Despite the plethora of pulchritude on display, *Orgy of the Dead* only manages to make eyelids droop rather than temperatures rise.

Orgy of the Vampires see *Orgy of the Dead*

Panic in Year Zero! (1962; AIP; b&w) This cozy little apocalypse makes World War III seem like a weekend at 4-H camp. Harry Baldwin (Ray Milland) and family are leaving L.A. on a fishing trip when Los Angeles vanishes behind them in a giant mushroom cloud. The Baldwins' vacation is suddenly transformed into a fight for survival, and Harry is determined that his family will endure, even if it means stealing firearms from a hardware store or, later, gunning down two young, unarmed hoodlums after they try to rape his daughter. The Baldwins survive because they stick to their old-fashioned (patriarchal) American values and can rely on Harry and teenage son Rick (Frankie Avalon), both gifted in the manly arts of hunting, fishing, chopping firewood, tying knots and other merit badge-worthy skills. The upheaval envisioned by *Panic in Year Zero!* seems mild compared to the doomsday scenarios of later films like *Night of the Living Dead* (1968)—despite rampant looting and vandalism, basic societal structures, and even the federal government, remain intact; nobody shows any signs of radiation sickness. Yet, *Panic* is packed with exciting interludes, especially during the first half of the picture, as the Baldwins cope with panicked fellow survivors and potentially violent profiteers. Although it contains some howlingly bad dialogue ("Nothing like eating under an open sky, even if it is radioactive," Rick opines), John Morton and Jay Simms' script, for the most part, is very good—characters are well-defined and their actions reasonably motivated. Milland's sober, no-nonsense performance brings badly needed gravitas to the picture. Avalon delivers one of his best performances (faint praise though that may be) as Rick, who clearly enjoys the fact that the crisis has suddenly catapulted him into full manhood. Jean Hagen and Mary Mitchell find themselves stuck in thankless roles as Harry's simpering wife and sulking daughter, respectively. Milland also directs, bringing a clean, punchy style of visual storytelling that suits the material. Despite some eye-rolling interludes, *Panic in Year Zero!* remains one of the most enjoyable end-of-the-world epics of its era.

Ad for *Panic in Year Zero!* (1962).

Perseus Against the Monsters see *The Medusa Against the Son of Hercules*

The Phantom in the Red House (1954/64; Filmadora Chapultepec/Trans-International Films; Mexico; b&w) Original Language Title: *El Fantasma de la Casa Roja*. Filmed and released in Mexico in 1954, this unfunny Old Dark House spoof crossed the border when K. Gordon Murray dubbed and released it as part of his Mexican monster movie package in the 1960s. A group of potential heirs must spend three consecutive nights locked in a spooky old house to find and claim a fortune. Filled with ridiculous characters (the bubble-headed heroine's name is Mercedes Benz Raddington!), silly antics (the bumbling detective holds the cloaked phantom at gunpoint, but then absentmindedly hands the gun over to his captive while he searches for his handcuffs) and every Old House mystery cliché committed to celluloid (reaching hands, moving eyes on a portrait, etc.), the movie pads its running time via a number of superfluous cut-rate Latino musical numbers (the hero is a nightclub singer). Though most chuckles generated by this pathetic "comedy" are of the unintentional ilk, *Phantom* does contain the occasional choice bit of dialogue (e.g., "God is going to reward you, even though you are a lawyer!").

The Phantom Planet (1961; AIP; b&w) In the near future an astronaut (Dean Fredericks) crash-lands on a mysterious asteroid and inexplicably shrinks to only six inches tall (the same size as the inhabitants) when he breathes the atmosphere (never mind that something the size of an asteroid has no atmosphere or gravity to speak of since its mass is too small). The tiny asteroid people, who look just like humans, are constantly under attack by the evil Solanites (a race of ugly, dog-faced humanoids). This gives the viewer the chance to witness a space battle between what looks like a large piece of coral (the planetoid) and a flock of flaming charcoal briquettes (the Solanite ships). The effects are cheap and frequently ridiculous, the script ignores the intriguing *Gulliver's Travels* potential, the thrills are minimal and the pacing slow. Seven-foot-tall Richard Kiel plays the awkward, goofy-looking Solanite prisoner (with huge dog-like head, motley fur, cartoon eyes, and pointy shoulders) who escapes and battles the hero.

Pinocchio in Outer Space (1965; Universal) Pinocchio goes into orbit to defeat Astro the space-whale in this cheaply made sequel to (and blatant rip-off of) Disney's *Pinocchio* (1939). Even though most of the characters (including Pinocchio, Gepetto and the Blue Fairy) are drawn to closely resemble their Disney counterparts, this cheaply made U.S.–Belgian cartoon co-production is in no way comparable to the original animated classic (the songs are especially weak), but young viewers will find it passable.

Planet of the Apes (1968; Twentieth Century–Fox) Revered by legions of fans and widely regarded as one of the greatest of all science fiction movies, *Planet of the Apes* lives up to its lofty reputation. One of the most durable genre films of the 1960s, it remains fascinating even if you've seen it a dozen times (or more). Screenwriters Michael Wilson and Rod Serling retain the basic premise of Pierre Boulle's novel (astronaut George Taylor crash-lands on an unidentified planet where humans live like animals, lorded over by intelligent gorillas, chimpanzee and orangutans) but jettison nearly everything else. Luckily, what they come up with instead proves succinct, witty and powerful. Serling's influence is felt strongly, both in good ways (the film's brutally ironic ending) and sometimes in bad ones (Taylor's sometimes bombastic sermonizing). But the movie's flaws (including groan-inducing laugh lines like "human see, human do") are minor at worst. Its opening half-hour, in which Taylor and his companions fight for survival in a strange, desolate world, remains one of the greatest "pure sci-fi" sequences ever filmed. Director Franklin J. Schaffner frequently employs unorthodox (ultra-high, ultra-low or tilted) camera angles to heighten the tension. But the real keys to the film's success were John Chambers' groundbreaking ape makeup designs, Jerry Goldsmith's eerie, dissonant score and Charlton Heston's commanding performance as Taylor. Schaffner, who had worked primarily in television, went on to helm prestige projects including *Patton* (1970), *Papillon* (1973) and *The Boys from Brazil* (1979). *Planet of the Apes* spawned four sequels, a prime time television show, a Saturday morning cartoon and, in 2001, an unfortunate remake.

Earth astronaut Taylor (Charlton Heston) and his mute mate Nova (Linda Harrison) are captured by a society of intelligent simians ruling over the *Planet of the Apes* (1968).

Planet of the Dead see ***First Spaceship on Venus***

Planet on the Prowl see ***War Between the Planets***

Prehistoric Women (1967/68; Hammer/Seven Arts; U.K.) Original Title: *Slave Girls. Prehistoric Women* is an awful movie. It would be an awful movie regardless. But it seems even worse coming in the wake of *One Million Years B.C.*, which is still generally regarded as the preeminent expression of its peculiar idiom. *One Million Years B.C.* was prehistoric melodrama *par excellence*, featuring stop-motion dinosaurs animated by the great Ray Harryhausen, as well as the spectacle of Raquel Welch in a fur bikini. In their stead, *Prehistoric Women* offers a stuffed white rhino and two tribes full of bikini-clad ingénues. Set entirely in the jungles of Elstree Studios, the asinine scenario (which closely resembles that of *Queen of Outer Space* [1958]) follows a Great White Hunter (Michael Latimer) on safari in Africa who is magically transported back to the dawn of man. He discovers a kingdom ruled by women, where a tribe of rhino-worshiping brunettes (including their merciless queen, played by Martine Beswick) have

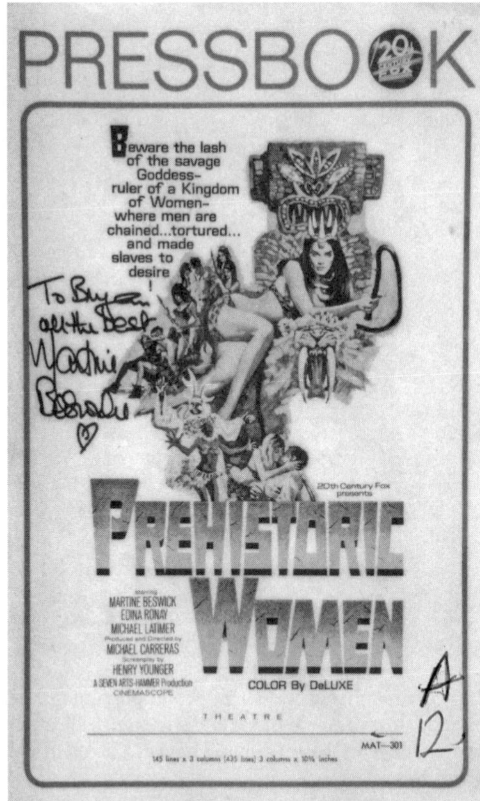

Pressbook cover for Hammer's *Prehistoric Women* (1967).

enslaved a tribe of blondes, along with all the local men. The hunter falls in love with a young blonde slave girl (Edina Ronay) and decides to help overthrow the evil queen. Producer-director-screenwriter Michael Carreras fails this project in all capacities, first by egregiously under-funding it, second with his lackluster direction and finally with a lifeless, cliché-filled script. *Prehistoric Women* features no dinosaurs or other monsters and runs extremely light on horror elements—or entertaining elements of any sort. Instead, *Prehistoric Women* piles up no fewer than five ludicrous "ritual" dances (which look like something out of bad Andrew Lloyd Weber) designed to showcase its bevy of blonde beauties (which, even added together, don't total one Raquel Welch). Serving suggestion: Fast forward through these musical numbers and the film's cheeky framing sequence, and you can shorten the 90-minute *Prehistoric Women* to about 40 minutes. Better yet, skip it altogether.

Prince of Space (1959/64; Toei/AIP-TV; Japan) Original Language Title: *Yusei Oji*. This was Toei's attempt to create a rival superhero franchise to compete with Starman for the hearts and minds of Japanese youngsters. It's just as puerile and nonsensical as the Starman films, but with bland Tatsuya Umemiya instead of the endearing Ken (Starman) Utsui. Later immortalized, after a fashion, in an episode of *Mystery Science Theater 3000*.

Project X (1968; Paramount) In the 22nd century, leading geneticist/secret agent Hagan Arnold (Christopher George) returns from a secret mission in "Sinoasia." But his memory has been "blanked"—along with information that may save the Western world from destruction. In order to "reach down deep in his subconscious mind" and retrieve the vital intelligence, the powers-that-be set up an elaborate new environment to convince the amnesiac that he's really a 20th century bank robber (an amateur historian, Arnold was an expert on the 1950s and '60s). Of course, there's an enemy agent on the loose to throw a (laser-beamed) spanner in the works. Master showman William Castle took a sharp left from his usual gimmicky horror route to produce *Project Tediu* ... er *X*. Given the limp result, he should have stuck to his main road. With its "futuristic" blue-grey jumpsuits, pink lights, *Star Trek*-level sets, cheesy psychedelic optical effects, goofy *Jetson*-esque matte paintings, and ill-conceived Hanna-Barbara animation sequences straight out of *Johnny Quest* standing in as Arnold's memories, *Project X* comes off as little more than a tepid, overlong sci-fi television drama.

Psycho Circus (1967; Warner-Pathe/A.I.P.; U.K.) Alternate Titles: *Circus of Fear* (U.K.), *Circus of Terror*. Despite its title(s), there's little horror to be found in this crime-caper picture (based on an Edgar Wallace novel) about stolen money stashed at a circus. Its police procedural tone, and the (always-welcome) presence of Klaus Kinski lurking about the fringes, conjures up images of an Edgar Wallace "krimi" (a series of West German crime films based on the prolific Wallace's books). And given its involving plot, seedy circus milieu, brutal knife-throwing murders, Christopher Lee playing a sinister hooded lion tamer, and Lee Genn as a likable, soft-spoken, put-upon inspector, one could do worse than buy a ticket to see this *Circus*.

Psychomania see *Violent Midnight*

Pyro (1964; Esamer S.A./AIP; Spain/U.S.) Original Language Title: *Fuego*. Alternate Title: *Wheel of Fire* (U.K.). The first half of this shot-in-Spain thriller comes off as a *Peyton Place*-style adult drama, with Barry Sullivan playing an American engineer working in Spain who cheats on his wife with vixen Martha Hyer. Things turn ugly when the unbalanced Hyer determines to do away with Mrs. Sullivan and their little girl by setting fire to the Sullivan home. With his family dead and himself horribly burned (while trying to rescue them), Sullivan vows vengeance from his hospital bed, chillingly hissing at Hyer through blackened lips, "I'll survive to be your death. The only reason I stay alive is to pay you back.... I won't rest until you and all of your family are dead." The film's second half focuses on Sullivan pursuing his vengeance while hiding out from the police as a carnival ferris wheel operator. (Amusingly, he hides his hideous visage behind a lifelike mask that looks like ... Barry Sullivan, with

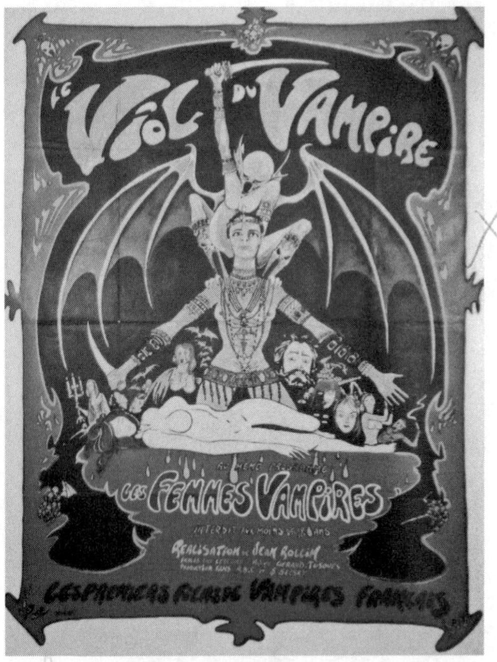

Left: **Atmospheric one-sheet poster playing up the pseudo-horrors of *Pyro* (1964). *Right:* French poster for Jean Rollin's erotic horror *Queen of the Vampires* (1967).**

the police and even his close friend failing to recognize him at one point!) High on predictability and low on chills, *Pyro* fails to ignite for much of its overlong 99 minutes, abandoning its horror potential in favor of focusing on a new love interest for the disguised Sullivan and the (admittedly beautiful) Spanish scenery. Though Sullivan makes for a likable protagonist/antagonist combo (a part originally announced for Vincent Price as early as 1961), the sexy but wholesome Hyer fails to bring any element of menace to her role of murderous firebug. Not all the production's flames occurred onscreen. Several weeks into filming, Spanish director Julio Coll (paid a mere $7,500 for his efforts) "became rude and opinionated," according to producer Sid Pink in his autobiography *So You Want to Make Movies — My Life as an Independent Film Producer*. "In fact, he was downright abusive to Martha Hyer and constantly belittled her on the set. One day he went too far and she burst into tears.... Although Julio Coll turned out to be a bastard, I must admit he did a good job on what he shot." Coll departed the unfinished project, and Coll's assistant, Luis Garcia, completed the film.

The Queen of the Vampires (1967; France; b&w) Original Language Title: *Le Viol du Vampire: Melodrame en Deux Parties*. Alternate Titles: *The Rape of the Vampire*; *Vampire Women*. This bizarre, only partially-coherent vampire "art" film by the love-him-or-hate-him French filmmaker Jean Rollin never played American theaters. "Act 1" of this "Two-Part Melodrama" (the film's subtitle) consists of a self-contained half-hour short involving four "vampire" sisters — or perhaps merely crazy girls who only *think* they're bloodsuckers — and the three "normal" people who come to cure them of their "delusions." Rollin subsequently filmed "Act 2" in order to bring his movie up to feature length. In order to do so, he had to resurrect many of his characters from the short (as well as adding new ones), thus transforming the more ambiguous premise of the admittedly haunting and visually arresting short into a more mundane "real" vampire story (albeit with plenty of outré ideas and images — including a "Vampire Queen" with a penchant for lounging topless on a tiger-skin rug). Like most of Rollin's loose-narrative horror movies, *The Queen of the Vampires* is an exercise in style over substance, with plenty of hand-held camerawork and tilted angles, and odd erotic imagery (like girls fencing half-nude by flare-light) to offset the slow pacing and narrative deficiencies. It's definitely an acquired taste.

The Rape of the Vampire see ***The Queen of the Vampires***

Ravaged see ***The Blood Rose***

Reincarnator see ***Assignment Terror***

The Return of Giant Majin (1966/68; Daiei/AIP-TV; Japan) Original Language Title: *Diamajin ikaru* (Giant Majin Grows Angry). This second entry in Daiei's underrated *Majin* trilogy — about a giant stone samurai who comes to life to rescue woebegone villagers in feudal Japan — is not so much a sequel as a remake of *Majin* (1966/68). The key difference is that the eponymous stone god resides on a sacred island instead of a mountaintop. Despite the familiarity of the basic scenario, however, *Return of Giant Majin* emerges as the most engaging of the three films, and features the series' most compelling *jidai-geki* (period drama) story line and most inventive and eye-catching special effects sequences— including a parting-of-the-waters sequence worthy of Cecil B. DeMille. While *Majin* received a limited U.S. theatrical release, *Return* went directly to TV in America.

Return of the Giant Monsters (1967; Daiei/AIP-TV; Japan) Alternate (home video) Title: *Gamera vs. Gaos*. Original Language Title: *Daikaiju Kuchusen: Gamera tai Gaos*. This third installment in Daiei's series of *kaiju eiga* epics starring the flying, snaggle-toothed turtle-hero Gamera marks a dramatic improvement over the first two entries. Although it doesn't rival Toho's better productions of the period — the plot is simple formula, the human characters forgettable, the monster costumes cut-rate and the action sequences derivative —*Return of the Giant Monsters* remains the best Gamera movie of the 1960s. It's quickly paced and action-packed, and features a fearsome adversary for Gamera in Gaos, a giant vampire bat (actually, he looks more like a poor man's Rodan) that feeds on human blood and emits a "super-sonic sound beam" that works like a laser. A series of volcanic eruptions awakens Gaos from his subterranean slumber, and the monster immediately begins gobbling up local villagers. Japanese military and scientific leaders try three elaborate plans aimed at stopping Gaos, but, ultimately, the fate of Japan rests in the flippers of Gamera. Like all of Daiei's Gamera sequels, *Return of the Giant Monsters* first reached America as part of an AIP television package. In the 1980s, producer Sandy Frank re-edited and re-dubbed the film for home video as *Gamera vs. Gaos*. Stick with the AIP version.

Revenge of Giant Majin see ***Majin Strikes Again***

Robinson Crusoe on Mars (1964; Paramount) Director Byron Haskins' straight-faced, low-key approach to space adventure, and the literary bent of Ib Mechior's screenplay (which cleverly mirrors the Daniel Dafoe novel that lends the film its title) set this film apart from most other pre-*2001* sci-fi pictures of the 1960s, which tended toward the juvenile — including Melchior's prior movies, such as *Journey to the Seventh Planet* and *Reptilicus* (both 1962). Paul Mantee stars as Commander Chris Draper, whose spaceship crashes on Mars. Mantee, onscreen virtually every second of the picture's 109 minutes, carries the film with his credible and surprisingly vulnerable portrayal of a man struggling to find the basic elements necessary for survival on an alien world — oxygen, water, food. The yarn loses some of its distinctiveness, and a bit of steam, once its Man Friday character (Vic Lundin) — an alien escaped from interplanetary slave-masters— shows up, and *Robinson Crusoe on Mars* inches closer to conventional space opera territory. But Al Nozaki's production design and Winton Hoch's widescreen cinematography are major assets throughout — imaginative, eerie and evocative, yet as scientifically accurate as possible, based on 1964 scientific knowledge. (Unfortunately, most of that knowledge was rendered obsolete when the first low-altitude photographs were sent back from Mars not long after the film's release.) Viewers will note the presence of TV's Batman, Adam West, in a cameo as Draper's captain, who is killed on impact, as well as the manta ray-like space ships from the 1953 *War of the Worlds*, re-outfitted to stand in as the space-slavers' vessels. Coincidentally, Haskin also directed the '53 *War of the Worlds*. While far outclassed by that genre landmark, *Robinson Crusoe on Mars* remains a minor classic in its own right.

The Sadist (1963; Fairway International; B&W) Although it owes more to noir thrillers such as Ida Lupino's *The Hitch Hiker* (1953) than to *Psycho* (1960), *The Sadist* remains a minor marvel, packing more thrills than most full-tilt horror pictures of its era and delivering entertainment value far beyond anything that could reasonably be expected given its minuscule budget ($33,000). Three schoolteachers on their way to a baseball game stumble into the clutches of a pair of homicidal maniacs— Charlie Tibbs (Arch Hall, Jr.)

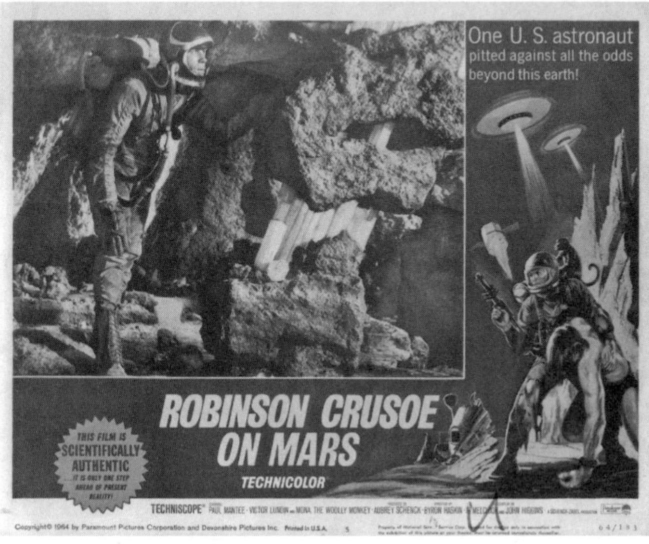

Paul Mantee as the futuristic *Robinson Crusoe on Mars* (1964) (American lobby card).

Left: "NOT FOR THE FAINT OF HEART!": *The Sadist* (1963) (ad mat, courtesy Ted Okuda). Right: This bizarre Mexican import detailing Santa's battle with a devil from Hell(!) gives even *Santa Claus Conquers the Martians* a run for its money in the Strangest Christmas Movie Ever sweepstakes (U.S. lobby card).

and his girlfriend Judy (Marilyn Manning)—when their car breaks down in a tiny California desert town. Charlie and Judy delight not only in killing, but in psychologically torturing their victims. The tension remains high throughout, but ratchets up even more during a bravura sequence in the middle of the film which concludes with the murder of one of the teachers, and again for the film's unpredictable and surprisingly vicious finale. Hall excels in the title role, affecting a babyish mush-mouthed delivery that seems jarringly creepy, especially as he coolly shoots a victim in the face. With a well-constructed, cunningly efficient script (by writer/director James Landis), uniformly convincing performances, and solid craftsmanship behind the camera, *The Sadist* is simply spellbinding. It's hard to believe that this gem emerged from Fairway International, the tiny Mom and Pop operation which also made world class stink bombs *Eegah* (1962) and *Wild Guitar* (1963). Don't be deterred by its brethren; *The Sadist* is sensational.

The Sadistic Baron Von Klaus (1962; Hispamex; Spain; b&w) Original Language Title: *La Mano de un Hombre Muerto* (Hand of a Dead Man). Never released State-side until finally making its way on DVD, *The Sadistic Baron Von Klaus* is one of Jess Franco's earliest (and best) horror films, one deserving a place alongside the better known *The Awful Dr. Orlof* (1962) and *The Diabolical Dr. Z* (1965). The beautifully photographed picture begins as a rather intriguing and atmospheric police procedural in which an inspector and a reporter track a sadistic sex murderer. But it's soon awash in melancholy tortured-soul musings, castle settings, an eerie cemetery (with backlit tombstones), and torture sequences (shot, surprisingly, with suggestive restraint by Senor Franco, who later in his career tended to wallow in sex and gore). In one standout sequence Franco generates some genuine frisson by using sound, camera movement, quick edits and a mounting sense of panic in the frightened heroine as she lay in her bed, anticipating Robert Wise's later *The Haunting* (1963). The subtly effective *Sadistic Baron Von Klaus* suggests that Jess Franco had a real knack for atmospheric horror before his obsession with crotch-shots and manic zooms overtook him.

Santa Claus (1959/60; Cinematografica Calderon S.A./K. Gordon Murray Productions; Mexico) This bizarre, surreal, subtly unsettling take on Ol' St. Nick (*and* Ol' Scratch) was K. Gordon Murray's first import, launching his Kiddie Matinee empire and paving the way for all those entertaining Mexi-horrors to come. But why is a movie titled *Santa Claus* included in a book on *horror* films? Because it's a movie about good (Santa) vs. evil ("Pitch," the chief demon of hell, who's ordered by Satan to "make all the children of the Earth do evil" and so land on Santa's "bad" list). Sporting red long johns, a goatee, plastic horns and oversized elf ears, Pitch sets about corrupting the youth of Mexico (inducing little boys to throw rocks through windows, or tempting the movie's four-year-old heroine, Lupita, to steal a dolly). Pitch also tries to foil Santa's deliveries by pushing chimneys out of alignment, lighting gigantic fires in the fire places, turning doorknobs red hot with his brimstone breath, and treeing Santa with a demented dog named Dante. Complete with wild and expansive sets (Santa's castle is not on the North Pole, as we've all been led to believe, but somewhere in outer space!), wind-up white reindeer, one especially surreal dream sequence involving creepy dancing dolls, and such outré devices as the "Master Eye," "Tele-talker," and "Earscope" (with which Santa spies on all the children of the Earth), *Santa Claus* comes across as a disturbing yet strangely affecting children's film from Bizarro Land. Murray took a real hands-on approach to this one — not only producing the English language version, but directing and narrating it himself using the pseudonym Ken Smith.

Santa Claus Conquers the Martians (1964; Embassy) Alternate Title: *Santa Claus Defeats the Aliens* (video). Sixties Cinema was nothing if not innovative. Not to be outdone by their South-of-the-Border brethren, some American moviemakers decided to produce their own twisted take on the Santa tale. Unfortunately, their efforts failed to reach the dizzyingly surreal heights of that 1960 Mexican oddity *Santa Claus*. When the children on Mars intercept an Earth television broadcast interviewing Santa (John Call) at his North Pole workshop, the Martian munchkins become disaffected with their rather sterile, joyless existence. Consequently, the Martian Leader and his cronies fly a spaceship to Earth and kidnap Santa. Will Earth have to cancel Christmas? Can Santa infuse the Martians with the Christmas spirit? Will the viewer ever be able to get that hyper theme song "Hooray for Santa Claus" out of his or her head? The ads boasted that *Santa Claus Conquers the Martians* was filmed in "Space Blazing Color," and that's about the best that can be said of this silly, puerile, sometimes-charming-but-more-often-painful potpourri of holiday hoopla and juvenile sci-fi. Released during the Christmas season of 1964 by Joseph E. (*The Producers, A Bridge Too Far*) Levine's Embassy Pictures, *SCCTM* has popped up periodically to delight — or bedevil — Christmas movie watchers ever since ("I get six dollars in residuals every year at Christmastime," laughed director Nicholas Webster).

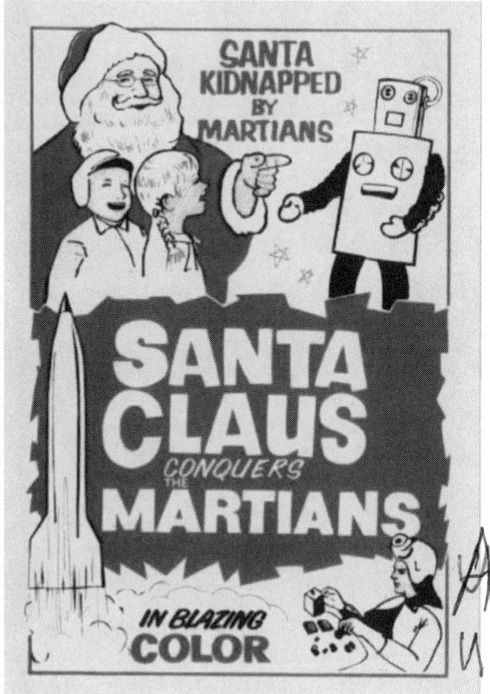

Enough said.

Santa Claus Defeats the Aliens see ***Santa Claus Conquers the Martians***

Santo and Blue Demon Against the Monsters (1969; Cinematografica Sotomayor; Mexico) Original Language Title: *Santo y Blue Demon Contra los Monstruous. Santo and Blue Demon Against the Monsters* opens, like *Abbott and Costello Meet Frankenstein*, with the two heroes and each of the featured monsters introduced during the credits. Except *Santo and Blue Demon Against the Monsters* is not a comedy — well, not intentionally anyway. The Mummy, the Cyclops, "Franquestain," the Wolf Man, the Vampire, and the Vampire Woman all receive their 15-seconds-of-fame introductory billing. But that's forgetting a diabolical bald hunchbacked dwarf named Waldo(!); a cadre of buff, green-faced zombie henchmen; a big-domed alien-like creature with exposed brain (who merely stands around as background decoration); and the evil, cackling mad scientist who creates/revives all these monsters in his laboratory cave located beneath an abandoned castle! Masked wrestlers-crimefighters El Santo and his pal Blue Demon must find a way to stop this monstrous army before it is too late. Things move at a *rapido* pace (with monster attacks coming at frequent intervals), and there's little time for the frequent filler found in many a Santo feature (one exception being a nightclub sequence in which the principals watch a silly South-of-the-Border Gene Kelly-style number that's obviously lifted from a completely different — and much older — movie). Plenty of day-for-night photography adds to the cheapo 1960s kitsch quotient (and contrasts comically with the occasional real nighttime shot). The monsters prove more amusing (unintentionally so) than terrifying. For instance, the Vampire (nobody uses the "D" word, but it's pretty obvious on what famous Count he is patterned) sports not only the expected evening dress, top hat and cape, but a set of oversized fangs and gigantic pointed ears! ("He has elf ears!" astutely proclaimed this author's then-eight-year-old son.) The elfin bloodsucker does impressively launch himself into the air in bat pose, however. Finally subtitled in English and released in America in the early 2000s, and chock full o' cheesy fun, *Santo and Blue Demon Against the Monsters* is not to be missed by any fan of south-of-the-border psychotronica.

Santo in the Treasure of Dracula (1968; Cinematografica Calderon; Mexico; b&w) Original Language Title: *Santo en el Tesoro de Drácula. Santo in* *the Treasure of Dracula* is basically Stoker's *Dracula* tale with a Santo subplot. Evocatively filmed in moody black and white, the story has masked professional wrestler and amateur scientist Santo invent a time machine that transports a subject back to his or her past life. Santo tests it on his girlfriend, who turns out to have been a Mina Harker substitute in her previous incarnation. Back in the present, a villainous gang of criminals discovers the whereabouts of Dracula's staked corpse and revives the Count, intent on stealing Drac's hidden treasure after the bloodsucker gets the meddlesome Santo out of the way. The involving *Dracula* scenario (which apes both the cut-finger episode and the classic mirror sequence—though this time using a full-sized looking glass rather than the less dramatic cigarette case from the 1931 Lugosi version) unfolds amidst eerie lighting and foggy graveyard settings, while Aldo Monti as Dracula wears the aristocratic Lugosi get-up but snarls like Christopher Lee. The film offers less Santo screen time than most entries, but a little Santo often goes a long way, and it comes off as a perfect balance of eerie Mexican horror and the straight-arrow absurdity that is the Santo milieu. Atmospheric and highly entertaining, *Santo in the Treasure of Dracula* is one of the more polished and engaging Santo-meets-the-monsters movies that finally made it to American shores in subtitled version after the turn of the millennium.

Masked wrestler/superhero/scientist El Santo prepares to test his *Time Tunnel*–like time machine by transporting his girlfriend back to her previous life—as Mina to Mexico's Dracula! (Mexican lobby card for 1968's *Santo in the Treasure of Dracula*).

Santo vs. the Martian Invasion (1966; Producciones Cinematograficas; Mexico; b&w) Original Language Title: *Santo Contra la Invasión de los Marcianos. Santo vs. the Martian Invasion* has the Silver Masked Man standing between the Earth and a horde (well, about ten anyway) of invading aliens. Eschewing the "little green men" model, these Martians are blonde, muscle-bound hombres (and beauteous chiquitas) sporting silver tights and cape, a squarish skullcap, and an "astral eye" stuck to their foreheads (a flashing eyeball-like device that serves as their own personal disintegrator ray—causing victims to just fade away in the cheapest of optical effects). Concerned about Earth's atomic capabilities, these Adonis-like aliens land in Mexico to demand total disarmament and insist the world "foster Earthly brotherhood" or face annihilation by the Martians' superior weaponry. *The Day the Earth Stood Still*'s Klaatu they ain't, as they demonstrate their power by

The Mexican wrestler/superhero Santo staves off the chokeholds of Martian marauders—*and* the amorous advances of Martian beauties—in *Santo vs. the Martian Invasion* (1966) (Spanish one-sheet poster).

killing thousands and kidnapping (via teleportation devices) select humans for study back on their home planet. The Martians turn their astral eyes toward Santo (as he represents the perfect physical specimen), and it's up to the Silver Masked Man to locate the invaders' ship, foil their plans and free the captives. "A picture that breaks new technical ground with constant action and excitement!" proclaimed the film's trailer. While the "new technical ground" is a hopeful overstatement at best (unless one counts Ed Wood-style effects and simple dissolves utilized by Georges Méliès himself six decades before as "new"), *Santo vs. the Martian Invasion* indeed offers plenty of (campy) "action" and (cheesy) "excitement." Among the highlights: space-age tonalities "borrowed" from the *Forbidden Planet* soundtrack; the Martian spaceship (looking like two silver bowls glued together) landing in an obvious table-top forest; the flying saucer's sparse interior sporting a huge lever whose only purpose appears to be to blow up the ship if pulled (*Bride of Frankenstein* must be a particular favorite on Mars); the aliens interrupting a television broadcast and insisting, "We are not just actors performing in a scary movie"(!); a Martian materializing at an outdoor sports complex to disintegrate a crowd of people—including a group of *children*(!!); a Martian taking the place of Santo's masked wrestling opponent in the ring (à la the classic vampire/werewolf battle in *Samson vs. the Vampire Women*); a camp-a-holic's dream of four Martian babes disguising themselves as a "ballet troupe" and proceeding to perform a hoochy-koochy dance number to a swingin' sixties instrumental beat; plenty of Santo-vs.-Martian grunting, sweating and fighting; and, of course, the Big Message closing narration: "The human race has been saved—for the moment. Will we learn our lesson? Or will we insist on carrying on crazy nuclear experiments until we disappear from the face of the Earth?" It took over 35 years for this fast-paced, fun and utterly charming *Martian Invasion* to finally reach America (via a subtitled DVD), but for the dedicated Mexi-movie fan, it was well worth the wait.

Satanic (1968; Rodiancines; Italy/Spain) Original Language Title: *Satanik.* When a scientist creates a cell rejuvenation serum (which has the unwanted side effect of arousing his test animals' "primordial instincts"), his elderly, scarred female colleague murders him and takes the concoction, which transforms her into a stunning beauty. She uses her newfound looks to seduce and murder her way to wealth. When the police finally catch on to her schemes, she eludes them (ironically) by inadvertently reverting back to her true, ugly self. This Eurotrash combination *Leech Woman* and police procedural looks cheap (typified by the crude and unconvincing old-age makeup), sounds cheap (an inappropriate, nondescript '60s pop-jazz score), and feels cheap (pointless zooms—easier than actually *moving* the camera—and time-filling, lackluster nightclub scenes). Since the woman proved evil from the outset (she kills to obtain the serum), the story carries no particular pathos and so becomes a rather pointless—and dull—exercise in futility. Magda Konopka (*When Dinosaurs Ruled the Earth*) does, however, make a fetching femme fatale (in a mod, mini-skirted way); too bad her acting can't match her looks.

Scream and Scream Again (1969/70; Amicus; U.K.) Filmed in 1969, but not released in the U.S. until 1970, *Scream and Scream Again* raised the ire of horror fans by prominently featuring stars Vincent Price, Christopher Lee and Peter Cushing in its advertisements, but relegating them to bit parts in the film itself. (Cushing is on screen for about three minutes, Lee for only 90 seconds!) Price spends most of the time off-screen as well, despite his key role as a mad scientist who has created a race of super-human flesh-and-plastic "composites." The narrative cuts back and forth between swinging London, where police investigate what they believe to be a serial killer, and an unnamed Iron Curtain country, rocked by a series of political intrigues. These disparate plot threads finally merge in the final act, but nearly half the film elapses before it becomes clear what one story has to do with the other. Director Gordon Hessler capitalizes on this jagged, disorienting structure in unorthodox but effective ways, keeping viewers off balance and milking the mystery for maximum suspense. The film's no-name cast members (Alfred Marks, Christopher Matthews and Judy Huxtable) garner most of the screen time and perform capably. David Whitaker's retro-hip, jazzy score is another plus. Penned at the height of the Viet Nam war, Christopher Wicking's script delivers a subtle thematic indictment of the way nation-states dehumanize their citizens to achieve political ends. While its misuse (or non-use) of its three legendary horror stars remains disappointing, *Scream and Scream Again* nonetheless emerges as a challenging but rewarding film when taken on its own merits.

Secret of the Telegian (1960; Toho/AIP-TV; Japan) Alternate Title: *The Telegraphed Man.* Original Language Title: *Denso Ningen.* Director Jun Fukuda is best known as the guy who took over the Godzilla series from Ishiro Honda—and wrecked it, with movies like *Son of Godzilla* (1967/68). Yet, this film displays extraordinary directorial skill and vision, far beyond anything in Fukuda's Godzilla pictures. A detective and a newspaper reporter work together to investigate a series of revenge murders being committed by ghostly super-scientific villain with the ability to, essentially, broadcast himself from location to location like a TV signal. Although the pace is languid and the conclusion is predictable, Fukuda generates some creepy moments along the way. He tells the story, which echoes elements from *The Fly* (1958) and *The Invisible Man* (1933), in an almost noir-like manner, with dramatic, high- and low-angle camera set-ups, imaginative transitions, and vivid color cinematography that sometimes recalls the work of Mario Bava. *Telegian* also features some of the most polished acting and best visual effects of any Toho genre effort. Unfortunately, the film never received a Stateside theatrical release and was mangled for American television: dubbed, cropped from widescreen to full screen, its Japanese stereo musical score dropped for a chintzy American mono soundtrack, the original title sequence removed. Worst of all, the TV prints were processed in black-and-white, so the color visuals were lost. The original version, however, is one of the more interesting Japanese sci-fi thrillers of the early 1960s.

The Seed of Man (1969/70; Polifilm; Italy) Original Language Title: *Il Seme dell'Uomo*. Following some devastating world-wide plague (intentionally kept vague), a young couple take up a mostly solitary existence and (obtusely) argue about whether they should have children and repopulate the earth. Though featuring an intriguing set-up rife with possibilities (impressively explored in '60s fare like *Panic in Year Zero!* and *The Last Man on Earth*), *The Seed of Man* remains a rather off-putting and pretentious entry in the post-holocaust subgenre. This is the type of film in which seemingly everything is a metaphor or allegory, including the characters (who all fail to interact — or react — in any recognizable or approachable manner, thus keeping the viewer at an uninvolved distance). Admittedly, it provokes some thought and raises a few questions, but its arms-length characterizations, sedate pace, and lack of dramatic — or involving — survival scenario (the protagonists simply occupy a comfortable beach house and spend their time playing in the sand or idly collecting civilization's artifacts) ultimately fails to satisfy on any level, either emotionally, intellectually or cinematically (though a huge beached whale carcass does make for some striking imagery).

7 Faces of Dr. Lao (1964; MGM) Tony Randall stars as the multi-dimensional Chinese mesmerist who brings a little magic (and understanding) to a turn-of-the-century Western town with his sideshow of mythical attractions. These include Merlin the Magician; the blind seer Apollonius; Medusa the gorgon; Pan, the god of joy; the Abominable Snowman; a talking snake with a human face; and a Loch Ness Monster lookalike. In an interview, Randall (who wore myriad make-ups and affected several accents) enthused, "I never wanted it to end, and that's the only time this has ever happened." And the viewer may very well feel the same way about this absolutely charming George Pal fantasy full of magical moments (including some impressive stop-motion sea serpent animation courtesy of Jim Danforth and company), warm characters, and healthy sentiment (reflecting the *positive* side of the *Something Wicked This Way Comes* coin). Sure it's rather obvious, and sure it's a bit saccharine; but remember what Dr. Lao tells the nine-year-old protagonist: "Mike, the whole world is a circus if you look at it the right way. Every time you pick up a handful of dust and see not the dust but a mystery, a marvel there in your hand; every time you stop and think, 'I'm alive and being alive is *fantastic*'; every time such a thing happens, Mike, you're part of the Circus of Dr. Lao." That's a sentiment *worth* remembering.

With quotes from: *The Fabulous Fantasy Films*, by Jeff Rovin.

The Sex Killer (1967; b&w) Alternate Title: *The Girl Killer*. Made by nudie-cutie specialist Barry Mahon (*The Beast That Killed Women*), this cheap roughie shot in New York City focuses on Tony, a worker at a mannequin factory who uses his binoculars to peep at topless rooftop sunbathers. After taking home a mannequin head and treating it with a little too much affection, he snaps and begins seeking out women to murder and *then* rape. The kills are few and far between, however, and most of the running time consists of Tony walking about the Big Apple, so that even at a scant 55 minutes, the poorly-shot *The Sex Killer* soon wears out its welcome.

She (1965; Hammer/Seven Arts; U.K.) Hammer Films lavished its largest-ever budget on *She*, traveling as far as Israel to shoot location scenes. Given all the special care and feeding that went into its creation, however, *She* seems disappointingly ordinary; although not a truly bad film, it's not a notably good one, either. Screenwriter David T. Chantler's adaptation hews closer to H. Rider Haggard's classic romantic fantasia than Merian C. Cooper's 1935 version, and Chantler's major change (a slightly revised, more downbeat and ironic conclusion) actually improves on the original. Leo, a former British soldier (John Richardson) in Palestine on his way home from World War I, encounters a mysterious, bewitching blonde (Ursula Andress) and, at her behest, sets out across the desert to find the lost city of Kor, despite hardships of every sort. Once in Kor, he discovers the blonde is the immortal,

The *7 Faces of Dr. Lao* (1964) (clockwise from top): Pan, Merlin, the Abominable Snowman, Dr. Lao, Appolonius, and the Medusa — all played by Tony Randall, whose real visage lies at the center (sporting a toupee borrowed from Gene Kelly, since Randall's head had been shaved for the film).

As the conniving Billali, Christopher Lee whispers into the ear of She-Who-Must-Be-Obeyed (Ursula Andress) in Hammer's *She* (1965).

cruel Queen Ayesha ("She Who Must Be Obeyed") and that Ayesha believes him to be the reincarnation of her long-dead lover, Killikrates. Despite its relatively large budget, *She*'s ambitions outstrip Hammer's production capacities: so many sets were needed that none appear as ornate or impressive as they should; some of the mattes and other visual effects look rushed; and the rousing slave revolt finale is staged with a cast of dozens. The picture's leaden pace, overstuffed with dry expository scenes and misty-eyed hand-wringing by Leo, proves equally frustrating. Director Robert Day's storytelling is clean but undistinguished. The challenging title role exposes the limitations of Andress' acting ability in ways her star-making turn in *Dr. No* (1962) did not. Richardson is fine in the lead but, predictably, Hammer stalwarts Peter Cushing and Christopher Lee steal the film in showy but subordinate roles.

Silent Star see ***First Spaceship on Venus***

Sinister Invasion see ***The Incredible Invasion***

Sinners of Hell see ***Jigoku***

Siren of Atlantis see ***Journey Beneath the Desert***

Slave Girls see ***Prehistoric Women***

The Snake People see ***Isle of the Snake People***

Snake Woman's Curse (1968; Toei; Japan) Original Language Title: *Kaidan hebi-onna.* Most of celebrated Japanese horror specialist Nabuo Nakagawa's films failed to earn U.S. theatrical releases in their day, but with interest surging in Asian horror during the mid–2000s, they began trickling into the States via belated DVD releases. Unfortunately, Nakagawa's pictures seldom proved to be worth the wait, or justified their elevated critical reputations. The tedious *Snake Woman's Curse* provides a case in point. The first 60 of the movie's 85 minutes are spent chronicling the misfortunes that befall a poor family of tenant farmers (father, mother, daughter and daughter's fiancé) due to mistreatment by their cruel landlord and his family. After the farmer is killed in a horse-drawn carriage accident, the lord takes the poor man's wife and daughter as debt-slaves. The lord beats the mother to death for trying to defend a snake, and his son rapes the farmer's daughter, who then commits suicide. The girl's fiancé tries to exact revenge but is killed fleeing police. This protracted, melodramatic setup is intended to prepare audiences for the upcoming savage vengeance the snake spirits (who take an interest after the mother's death). But the payoff falls well short of the buildup, with the landlord, his wife and son suffering from visions of snakes and stumbling into a series of fatal mishaps, none of which are especially spooky, ghastly or even well-staged. Nakagwa's direction, Yoshikazu Yamasawa's cinematography and the performances of the cast, while adequate, fail to stand out. Sunsuke Kikuchi's cheesy, overwrought score stands out in the wrong way. With its belabored scenario, disappointing third act and dirge-like pace, *Snake Woman's Curse* won't convert newcomers to the cult of Nakagawa. Reserve this one for true believers only.

Snow Devils (1965; MGM; Italy) Original Language Title: *I Diavola della Spazio.* One of four science fiction features shot back-to-back by Antonio Margheriti in 1964 (the others being *War Between the Planets*, *War of the Planets* and *Wild Wild Planet*), *Snow Devils* concerns a group of astronauts who discover abominable snowman-like humanoid beings on the planet Aytia. The film (a dog by reputation) has seemingly disappeared.

The Snow Maiden (1968; Lenfilm Studio; U.S.S.R.) Original Language Title: *Snegurochka.* In this slow-paced romantic fantasy from Soviet Russia, the beautiful Snow Maiden, daughter of Father Frost and Mother Spring, becomes entranced by shepherd Lel's singing and wants to live among human beings to experience love. Featuring an impressive setting — a tranquil medieval village on the banks of a river—and lots and lots of singing (by both the villagers and golden-throated Lel), *The Snow Maiden* becomes bogged down in scene after scene of various characters talking about, pining for, and seeking love, as summed up by the Snow Maiden herself: "Everything in the world that is of any value lies in just one word, and that word is 'love.'" A "forest genii" (made up to look like talking foliage) pops up once or twice to provide the film's only respite from the saccharine scenario, but does little to overcome the tedium.

The Snow Queen (1966/67; Lenfilm Studio; U.S.S.R.) Original Language Title: *Snezhnaya Koroleva.* This lavish Soviet children's fantasy, based on a fairy tale by Hans Christian Andersen, opens with Andersen himself (an actor *playing* Andersen, actually) stating: "I get tired of just telling [stories], so today I've decided to *show* you a story for a change." And show us he does, as an animated whirlwind brings a giant white face (the beautiful, icy visage of the dreaded Snow Queen) to the window of pre-teen siblings Kay and Gerta, living with their kindly grandmother. Along with this foreshadowing arrives a rude rich man in cahoots with the Snow Queen who demands to buy granny's beautiful winter roses. When she refuses to part with the flowers (they were a gift—from Andersen himself—and so are above price), the evil moneygrubber sends the Snow Queen to wither the roses and kidnap Kay. Gerta (followed by Andersen, who at one point timely steps in to lend a, er ... Hans) sets out for the Snow Queen's ice palace to get him back, encountering all manner of strange beings along the way (including chatty crows, a goofy king, forest[!] pirates, a talking reindeer, and several Russian folk songs), resulting in an imaginative and enjoyable (if sometimes too-leisurely paced) romp through some impressive sets and beautiful Russian countryside. That said, the real H.C. Andersen undoubtedly was set spinning in his grave by the transformation of his simple fairy tale about loyalty and the power of love into a thinly-veiled treatise on communism (symbolized by the flowers themselves: "The roses, in their own language," lectures Hans in a laugh-out-loud non sequitur, "say we are with you, you are with us, and we are all together"). When the Snow Queen, controlled by the Evil Capitalist, kisses Kay, the sweet boy's heart turns to ice and he becomes rude and insulting—embracing the evils of capitalism obviously corrupts. But the power of love and innocence ultimately overcomes the forces of greed, and the roses of communism bloom once more ... at least until the break-up of the Soviet Union two decades later.

Son of Godzilla (1967; Toho/AIP-TV; Japan) Original Language Title: *Kaijuto no Kessen: Gojira no musuko* (Monster Island's Decisive Battle: Godzilla's Son). Toho's flagship *kaiju eiga* series, which entered a skid with the preceding *Godzilla vs. the Sea Monster* (1966), careened into the ditch with the puerile *Son of Godzilla.* Godzilla seems like an afterthought to the story about a team of scientists performing secret experiments on a remote island who inadvertently cause the local insects to grow to giant size. Godzilla finally arrives on the island (30 minutes into the 86-minute film) to protect its newly hatched offspring, Minya. Instead of the usual city-smashing mayhem, viewers are "treated" to a succession of saccharine parent-child scenes, such as one cutesy sequence in which Minya uses Godzilla's tail for a jump rope. One of Toho's worst monster suit designs, Minya looks like a cross between a cherubic gecko and a deformed Pillsbury doughboy. Clearly, the character was introduced to position Godzilla to compete with Daiei's profitable, kid-oriented Gamera movies, but director Jun Fukuda and his cohorts succeed too well, producing a film as asinine and exasperating as most of Daiei's Gamera entries. That's too bad, especially since the basic scenario, with scientists battling giant mantises and an enormous spider, might have made an interesting film on its own. The fierce-looking insects (actually, oversized marionettes) are by far the best realized creatures in the picture. Instead, the misguided *Son of Godzilla* became the second consecutive G-film to be denied an American theatrical release, although AIP picked it up for TV. And Minya gained notoriety as the Scrappy Doo of Godzilla lore.

Son of Hercules in the Land of Darkness (1963/66; Metheus Films/Embassy Pictures; Italy) Original Language Title: *Ercole l'Invincibile.* Alternate Title: *Hercules the Invincible.* Yet another peplum that came to America under the straight-to-TV "Sons of Hercules" banner (see *Fire Monsters Against the Son of Hercules*), *Son of Hercules in the Land of Darkness* concerns the heroic, blonde-bearded Argolese (Dan Vadis) and his battle with the evil, usurping Demios people, who live inside a mountain and like to eat the flesh of their enemies in order to absorb their strength (something we never see, by the way). The film's sole fantastical element (apart from an underground city surrounded by boiling lava—something else we don't see much of) comes in the form of Argolese's brief battle with "the dragon of the mountains"—footage of the unwieldy man-in-a-suit dino-beast "borrowed" from the 1959 *Hercules.* Vadis' Argolese is strong as an oak (with wooden demeanor to match) and faces off against a tired-looking lion, a man in a bear costume, countless incompetent palace guards, and two cranky elephants trying to pull him apart. It all adds up to 80-plus minutes of half-baked tedium, with nothing to distinguish this from the dozens of other beefcake-and-brawn pictures migrating across the Atlantic in the 1960s.

Space Men see ***Assignment Outerspace***

Space Monster (1965; AIP-TV; b&w) An occasional chuckle from the amusingly non–P.C. dialogue is about all you can expect from this awful sci-fier, which AIP steered directly to television (perhaps realizing the injustice of expecting people to pay to watch a black-and-white film that's worse than the sci-fi TV shows they could see for free in their homes). "[Co-producer] Burt [Topper] created all of the sets," recalled *Space Monster* star Francine York. "He'd go to the studio at night, jump over the fence and steal little pieces of this, little pieces of that." The 80-minute feature was shot in mid–March 1965 at Producers Studio under the title *The First Woman in Space* (at that point it was still earmarked for theatrical distribution). But apparently AIP felt that a *Woman* wasn't quite as appealing as a *Monster* and so appended its appellation (thereby inadvertently disclosing its obviously prepubescent audience target). The movie's plot: A rocket carrying three men and one woman encounters an ugly humanoid alien with an exposed brain (a leftover mask from *The Wizard of Mars*) and then crash lands in the ocean of an unidentified planet inhabited by giant crabs (merely some you're-not-fooling-anyone macro-lensed sand crabs in a fish tank) and a single native gill-man left over from *War-Gods of the Deep* (1965). "Basically, everything on *Space Monster* was stolen from somewhere else," laughed York. If this sad vehicle and sexist crew was the best she could find, it's a dead certainty that The First Woman in Space had wished she'd stayed home. And unless you're particularly partial to tiny land crabs, we suggest you do the same.

With quotes from: "Anatomy of a Doll: A Candid Conversation with Francine York," by Anthony Petkovich, in *Shock Cinema* no. 37, 2009.

Space Monster Dogora see *Dagora, the Space Monster*

Space Pirate Ship see *Invasion of the Neptune Men*

Spaceflight IC-1: An Adventure in Space

(1965; Lippert/Twentieth Century–Fox; U.K.; b&w) In this cheaply made science fiction melodrama, junior officers on a ship full of refugees from the dying Earth mutiny against their tyrannical (and possibly insane) captain. The authors of this book were unable to secure a copy for review, but the film's low budget, no-name cast (Bill Williams, Norma West, John Cairney, etc.) and journeymen crew (led by director Bernard Knowles) do not inspire confidence.

Spaceship Venus Does Not Reply see *First Spaceship on Venus*

Spook Warfare (1968; Daiei; Japan) Original Language Title: *Yokai Daisenso* (Big Ghost War), Alternate Title: *Yokai Monsters 1: Spook Warfare* (DVD). "You won't believe your eyes!" warns this film's original Japanese trailer, in a rare example of truth in advertising. Even diehard fans of Japan's *kaiju eiga* (giant monster) movies may be thrown for a loop by the exceedingly offbeat, wildly imaginative Yokai Monsters series, a trilogy that begins here. The story involves an ancient Babylonian demon that travels to feudal Japan, then kills and impersonates the magistrate of a small village. Humans can't see through the demon's disguise, but Kappa, a duck-faced water imp that lives in the magistrate's pond, can. He rallies a dozen or so of his fellow "apparitions," including also include a snake-necked woman and something that looks like a folded umbrella with an enormous tongue, to battle the demon. The film's many bizarre creatures, drawn from Japanese folklore, look like nothing previously seen in America outside of (maybe) a Mardi Gras parade or the ouevre of Sid and Marty Krofft. Although it seems to be aimed primarily at children, *Spook Warfare* contains some remarkably bloody murders and a few genuinely unsettling sequences (especially the demon's attack on the magistrate). Although certainly an acquired taste, the Yokai Monsters films—which also include *100 Monsters* (1968) and *Along with Ghosts* (1969)—remain fascinating, in an acid-trip sort of way. None of the three films received a general theatrical release in the U.S., although some of them may have appeared briefly in Japanese language cinemas in the late Sixties. However, all three reached America on DVD in 2003.

Star Pilot (1965/77; Monarch Releasing Corp.; Italy) Original Language Title: *2+5: Missione Hydra*. Alternate Title: *2+5: Mission Hydra* (video). Finally released in America *12 years* after its completion (to cash in on the *Star Wars* craze), the almost nonsensical *Star Pilot* has an elderly scientist, his "liberated" daughter, a pair of hunky technicians, and a couple of Asian spies kidnapped off the island of Sardinia by a trio of aliens from the galaxy of Hydra who need them to help repair and pilot their crashed ship (a plastic coffee pot with wings that shoots gouts of flame). A series of disjointed and pointless scenes follow, "highlighted" by space walks *without* helmets (just a metal stick held between the teeth, representing a "space respirator," will do!) and an emergency landing on a cardboard set ... er, planet, inhabited by fur coat-wearing pig-men. The two females do look impressive in their leather and fishnet "uniforms," however.

Strange Obsession see *The Witch*

The Strange World of Coffin Joe see *The Strange World of Zé do Caixão*

The Strange World of Zé do Caixão (1968; Iberia Filmes; Brazil; b&w) Original Language Title: *Estranho Mundo de Zé do Caixão*. Alternate Title: *The Strange World of Coffin Joe*. This three-part anthology from Brazilian horror maven Jose Mojica Marins (*At Midnight I'll Take Your Soul, This Night I'll Possess Your Corpse*, etc.) is introduced by the diabolical Ze do Coaixao (Marins himself in his "Coffin Joe" persona), who asks pseudo-existential questions like "Who am I?" and "What is horror?" (without giving any answers, of course). First up is "The Dollmaker," about an elderly toymaker and his four daughters whose dolls possess the most extraordinary eyes. There's a typical E.C.-comics style twist in the tale when four would-be robbers/rapists come a-callin'. Next is "Obsession," about a hunchbacked beggar who stalks a beautiful girl from afar, and takes his obsession to the extreme after she's murdered on her wedding day. Unfortunately, Marins *forgot* the sting in this tale, and it simply winds down laboriously to its foregone conclusion. Last (and best) is "Theory," starring Marins himself as a sadistic "Professor" who intends to prove that "instinct" will ultimately win out over "reason" by staging various acts of sadism, depravity and even cannibalism. This segment delivers what one expects from a Marins movie, with some truly twisted and shocking scenes (accentuated by that surreal phoniness that permeates Marins' low-budget productions) interspersed with weird, gleeful ramblings from Marins himself. Ironically, *The Strange World of Zé do Caixão* may be Marins' most traditional — and *least* strange — horror film, making it more accessible to the average fan but less interesting overall. What makes his movies fascinating are their subversive themes and bizarre unpredictability. Here, at least for two-thirds of the film, Marins disappointingly sacrifices his usual outrageousness for more traditional horror tropes. *Strange World*, like all of Marins' movies, only surfaced in America via the video boom of the early 1990s.

The Strangler of Blackmoor Castle (1963; West Germany) Original Language Title: *Der Würger von Schloß Blackmoor*. A fog-shrouded English castle (complete with hidden passageways and dangerous dungeons), a hooded killer, and *several* decapitations figure into this Bryan Edgar Wallace (son of famed mystery writer Edgar Wallace) crime-mystery involving stolen diamonds, an innocent heroine, and a clever Scotland Yard detective. The sinister setting adds a touch of creepiness to the proceedings, and the decapitation sequences come as outright shocks, making this one of the more memorable horror-tinged krimis from the period.

The Stranglers of Bombay (1960; Hammer/Columbia; U.K.; b&w) Marginal as horror but marvelous as entertainment, *The Stranglers of Bombay* remains an unsung gem from director Terence Fisher. Perhaps because it's an historical drama with some grisly elements rather than a full-blooded chiller or maybe because this modest, black-and-white production fell between two higher profile, full-color Fisher masterworks—*The Mummy* (1959) and *Brides of Dracula* (1960)—*Stranglers* has never received its due, and likely never will. Yet there is much here to admire, beginning with a compelling, (loosely) fact-based scenario. In 1820s India, a courageous British officer (Guy Rolfe) battles heroically, despite the indifference of his superiors, to root out the bloodthirsty Thugee cult of stranglers. The director plays up the brutality of the Thugee (in addition to strangulation, the cultists slice out tongues and shove red-hot pokers into victims' eyes, then disembowel, dismember or burn the bodies) and recasts historical events as a typically Fisherian struggle between Christian good and Satanic evil. David Goodman's tight, suspense-filled script manages to play up these horrific aspects without seeming crass or exploitative. The cast contributes uniformly convincing performances, with Rolfe and George Pastell, as a high priest of the Cult of Kali, especially compelling. Cinematographer Arthur Grant's shadow-draped jungle sets and sweltering-looking interiors add badly needed ambiance to this small-budget, studio-bound production, as does composer James Bernard's evocative score. Although it lacks the scope and the emotional resonance of its director's best work, *Stranglers* compares favorably to better loved Fisher films such as *The Phantom of the Opera* (1962) and *The Gorgon* (1964).

The Strongest Man in the World see ***Mole Men against the Son of Hercules***

A Study in Terror (1965/66; Columbia; U.K.) "Sherlock Holmes versus Jack the Ripper!" shouted the ads for this cinematic collision of the Ripper and Holmes subgenres. Indeed, such a catchphrase provides a succinct synopsis, as Holmes and Watson become embroiled in the search for the infamous Whitechapel murderer. Unfortunately, the rather staid production offers very little for the *viewer* to shout about, at least in terms of horror content. While director James Hill (*Captain Nemo and the Underwater City*, 1969) and cinematographer Desmond Dickinson (*Horror Hotel*, 1960) do an admirable job of evoking the swirling fog and shrouded alleyways of 1888 London (or at least a Hammer-like facsimile thereof), the picture meanders to and fro over the same ground, the murder sequences remain fairly perfunctory, and John Neville and Donald Houston, as Holmes and Watson, make a misguided effort at channeling the tired spirits of Basil Rathbone and Nigel Bruce. Though the script offers a fairly novel (if meandering

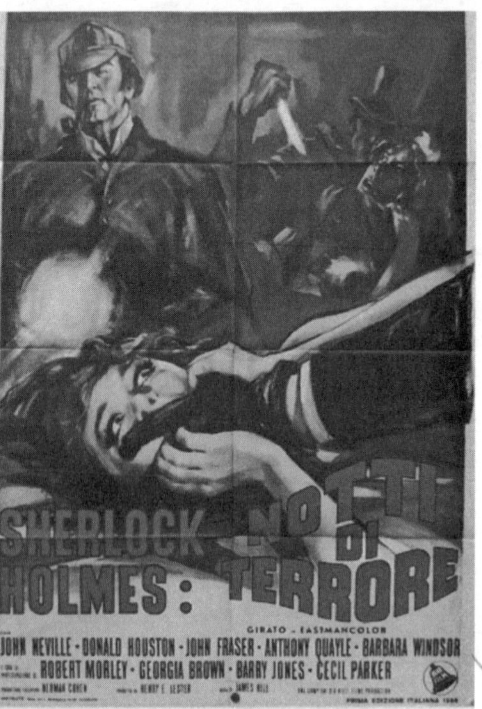

Sherlock Holmes tracks Jack the Ripper, creating *A Study in Terror* (1965/66) (Italian two-sheet poster).

and unlikely) solution to the mystery, the climax seems rushed and incomplete (particularly when a cavalier Holmes explains how he escaped the climactic fiery inferno with nothing more than a casual comment about his being "indestructible"). Failing to live up to its moniker, *A Study in Terror* is a study in disappointment, particularly given the far superior results of the next Holmes-Ripper celluloid meeting—*Murder by Decree* (1979).

The Sweet Sound of Death (1965/66; Hermic; Spain; b&w) Original Language Title: *La llamada.* This moody tale of a young Spaniard named Pablo whose French fiancée Dominique appears to die in a plane crash but then inexplicably returns, is more suited to a 30-minute *Twilight Zone* episode, or, at most, an hour-long *Thriller.* Not without interest (thanks in large part to the two likable and appealing leads, Emilio Caba [billed as Emil Cape] and Dyanik Zurakowska [trumpeted simply as "Dianik"]), and possessing a few truly eerie sequences (such as when Pablo visits Dominique's stately home in Brittany, where he encounters her odd—and obviously dead—family), the overlong feature ultimately winds down to a predictable (and perfunctory) conclusion. This low-budget Spanish film was co-produced by American Sidney Pink (*The Angry Red Planet, Reptilicus, Pyro*). Knowing there was no theatrical market, outside of the art-house circuit, in the States for a black-and-white import (the U.S. film industry had almost fully transitioned to color), Pink bundled it up with a few of his other Euro-features in a package sold directly to American television via the Westinghouse corporation in 1966.

The Sword and the Dragon (1956/60; Valiant Films; U.S.S.R./Finland) Original Language Title: *Ilya Muromets.* Alternate Title: *The Epic Hero and the Beast* (U.K.). "Cast of 106,000! 11,000 horses!" trumpeted the ads for this Russo-Finnish fantasy filmed in 1956 and released in America in 1960. While those figures may be an exaggeration, judging by the amazing production values and teeming hordes on the screen, they may not be far wrong. Big, bold and broad (just like the lead character), *The Sword and the Dragon* follows the adventures of the legendary hero Ilya Muromets as he protects his Prince and his people from "the cursed Tugars" (a Mongol-like horde) invading his homeland. He also battles a pudgy wind demon and a two-headed, fire-breathing dragon. Some impressive effects (the dragon) and unusual incidents (including the Tugar chief—dubbed by the ubiquitous voice artist Paul Frees—ordering his minions to make a mountain out of their own bodies so he can ride his horse to the top to get a good looksee) fail to compensate for a slow pace, simplistic plot, dull characters, and shout-it-to-the-winds acting (Ilya doesn't stand and converse, he poses and bellows!). This was directed by the same man, Aleksandr Ptushko, who brought us the equally epic (and equally turgid) *The Magic Voyage of Sinbad.*

The Telegraphed Man see ***Secret of the Telegian***

The Tenth Victim (1965; Embassy; Italy/France) Original Language Title: *La Decima Vittima.* In this dystopian satire (set in the near-future in which everyone wears uber-sixties "mod" fashions and lives in garishly-decorated swinging pads), the governments of the Earth sanction murder via the "Big Hunt" game to control population and ease aggressive tendencies towards war. Participants are randomly assigned as either "Hunter" or "Hunted," and must kill their opponent before he or she kills them. Those who reach ten kills without perishing receive political and financial privileges (including a million-dollar bonus). Ursula Andress plays the icy killer (who dispatched her previous victim via a bullet-barreled bra!) seeking to make her tenth and final kill in front of television cameras as a commercial for "Ming Tea" (complete with beautiful chorus girls and dancing teacups!!), while Marcello Mastroianni is the world-weary, nerve-jangled mark seeking to turn the tables on his huntress. Love blossoms like bullet hits, and various twists leads to an amusingly unexpected conclusion. *The Tenth Victim* meanders at times among various tedious subplots and superfluous characters, and the "groovy" sixties lounge music and even groovier threads and furnishings soon become tiresome. Yet, the picture's biting satire (attacking everything from

Lobby card for the opulent Russo-Finnish fantasy *Sword and the Dragon* (1956/60).

the media and politics to interpersonal relationships and organized religion) and chemistry between the two leads, as they play their deadly cat-and-mouse game, make this a hunt worth watching.

Terror Beneath the Sea (1966/71; Toei; Japan) Original Language Title: *Kaitei Daisenso.* This ultra low-budget sci-fi/action hybrid remains notable as an early starring role for future "Streetfighter" Sonny Chiba. The story is a mishmash of elements from *20,000 Leagues Under the Sea* and *The Island of Dr. Moreau*: Two intrepid journalists (Chiba and gal pal Peggy Neal) are trapped in the undersea hideout of a mad genius, who surgically transforms his victims into "cyborg" gill men. The scenario affords Chiba only limited opportunity to demonstrate the physical prowess that would soon make him a Hong Kong action hero. Director Hajime Sato would go on to helm the impressive *Body Snatcher from Hell* (1968), but this film pales in comparison with that one. *Terror Beneath the Sea* went unreleased in the U.S. until 1971, when Chiba was better known.

Terror in the Crypt (1964; Rosa/AIP-TV; b&w) Alternate Titles: *Crypt of Horror* (U.K.), *La Cripta e L'incuba* (Italy), *La Malediction de los Karnstein* (Spain), *Crypt of the Vampire* (home video). This Spanish-Italian co-production, released directly to television in the U.S., sounds good on paper: An European gothic based on Sheridan Le Fanu's frequently filmed lesbian vampire opus *Carmilla*, starring Christopher Lee. On celluloid, however, *Terror in the Crypt* ranks as a major disappointment. Count Karnstein (Lee) engages Klaus Friedrich (Jose Campos) to research the life of his ancestor, Syrah Karnstein, who was executed for witchcraft but vowed to return from the grave and exact revenge. Eventually, Klaus learns that the Count fears his daughter Laura (Adriana Ambesi) may be Syrah's reincarnation. Shortly thereafter, a beautiful young stranger, Lyuba (Pier Anna Quaglia), arrives at Castle Karnstein and quickly attaches herself to Laura, upsetting a growing romance between Laura and Klaus. Screenwriters Tonino Valeri and Ernesto Gastaldi's handling of Le Fanu's saucy, scary source material proves surprisingly tepid and chaste. The film's attempts to generate chills are few and feeble, and its eroticism is limited to a few cuddles between the nightie-clad Quaglia and Ambesi. Production values are low, and Carmillo Mastrocinque's flat, lifeless direction is sleep-inducing. And, although top-billed, Lee is wasted in a do-nothing part; Campos assumes the picture's true lead role. As a result, even Euro-horror junkies and Lee completists will find little here to hold their interest.

Terror of the Bloodhunters (1962; ADP Pictures; b&w) There's no terror and not much bloodhunting in this Z-budget jungle melodrama from schlockmeister Jerry Warren. Political prisoner Steven Duval (Robert Clarke) breaks out of Devil's Island with the help of the commandant's daughter (Dorothy Haney), but, when their original plan to fly to Brazil goes awry, the couple is forced to make their escape through untracked South American rainforest popu-

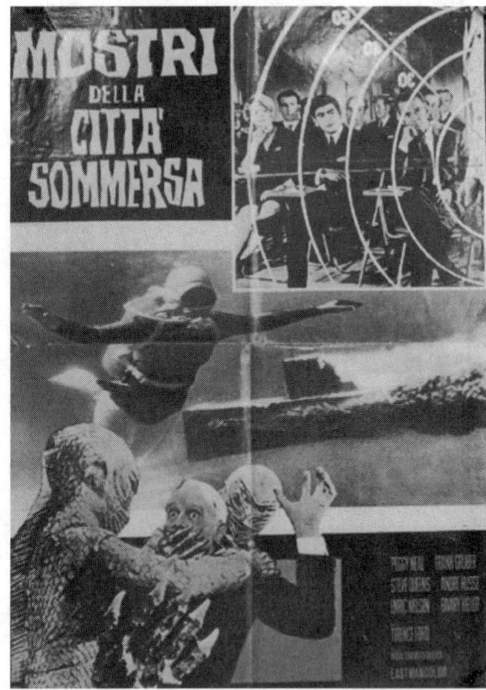

Italian one-sheet highlighting the dubious delights of *Terror Beneath the Sea* (1966).

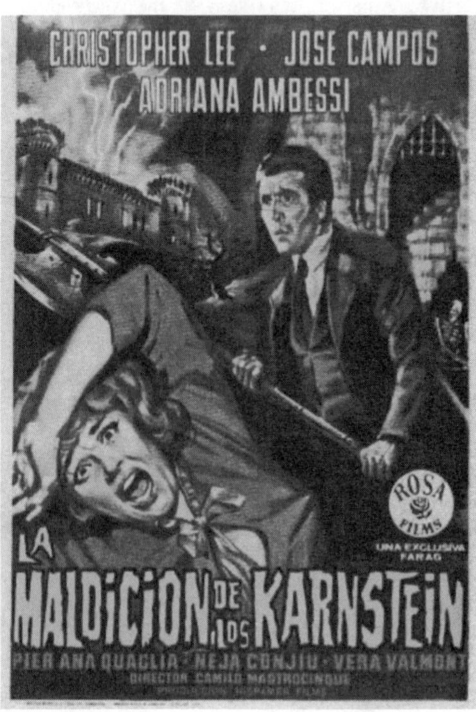

Spanish herald for the Italo-gothic *Terror in the Crypt* (1964).

lated by voodoo-practicing cannibals. Warren cobbled together *Terror of the Bloodhunters* out of reams of stock footage of snakes, alligators, panthers, etc. (even the titular "blood-hunting" natives are stock cut-ins!), intertwined with interminable scenes of Clarke and Haney tromping around the forest. To pad the film out to a semi-respectable 72 minutes, Warren (as always) loads up on static, banal dialogue scenes, and also tosses in a couple of hokey-looking native dance rituals (you guessed it — more stock footage). Aside from veteran B-movie star Clarke, who gives a game but futile effort here, the acting is wooden and listless, perfectly matching everything else in this lifeless bomb.

Terror of the Hatchet Men (1961; Hammer/Columbia; U.K.) Original Title: *The Terror of the Tongs.* The Hammer horror machine was running in top gear in the early 60s, and all the technical elements for an outstanding picture were in place for this thriller, better known under its original British title. With gorgeous, color-splashed sets designed by Bernard Robinson, beautiful lighting by cinematographer Arthur Grant and outstanding costumes and makeup by Molly Arbuthnot and Roy Ashton, respectively, *Terror of the Tongs* stands among Hammer's most visually striking products. Unfortunately, director Anthony Bushell, screenwriter Jimmy Sangster and casting supervisor Dorothy Holloway fail to hold up their end of the bargain. In 1910 Hong Kong a sea captain's daughter is killed by agents of the dreaded Red Dragon Tong, a secret society engaged in theft, white slavery, opium, gambling and murder on a massive scale. When local authorities prove ineffectual, the captain (Geoffrey Toone) sets out to topple the Tong himself. Sangster's script trades in stock characters and lacks structure. The captain's "investigation" consists of mercilessly beating one low-level Tong underling after another until he finds out What He Wants to Know. As a result, events spill out almost randomly, generating relatively little tension or suspense. Bushell, who worked primarily in television, provides competent but undistinguished direction. The film's biggest problems lie with its cast, and particularly with Toone, whose facial expression remains virtually unchanged — whether he's discovering his daughter's dead body, kissing a beautiful young woman or throwing a right cross. French sex kitten Yvonne Monlaur is also miscast as a half-Chinese slave girl. Luckily, Christopher Lee shines as the imperious Tong leader, radiating icy malevolence. Lee's fearsome performance — which serves as a blueprint for his later tenure as Dr. Fu Manchu — and the film's outstanding pictorial beauty give diehard Hammer aficionados reason to seek out *Terror of the Tongs.* Others may safely take a pass.

Terror of the Tongs see ***Terror of the Hatchet Men***

The Terrornauts (1967; Amicus/Embassy; U.K.) In this ill-advised foray into science fiction by England's Amicus Productions (best known for its long-running series of horror anthologies) a team of scientists using a radio telescope to listen for signals from intelligent life on other planets receives a distress call from an unlikely source — a tiny planetoid in the asteroid belt. After the scientists transmit a reply, a spaceship appears and whisks them away (building and all) to a robot-operated outpost on the asteroid, where they become embroiled in an interplanetary war. None of this is as exciting it sounds. Fifty of the film's 75 minutes are consumed by static, talky scenes (hand-wringing over budget cuts, interpersonal drama between the romantic leads, and comedy relief involving a weak-kneed accountant and a gabby tea service matron), filmed almost entirely in medium shot on a single cramped observatory set. Once the action finally starts, the picture's meager budget falls well short of its ambitions. Its visual effects, costumes and props are laughably cut-rate (at one point the cast walks around in shower caps with tubes sticking out of them), and the climactic space battle looks like something from the *oeuvre* of Edward D. Wood, Jr. The performances (from Simon Oates, Zena Marshall, Charles Hawtrey and the rest of the cast) and direction (by Montgomery Tully) remain perfunctory at best. After this substandard entry, and the mediocre *They Came from Beyond Space* (also 1967), Amicus wisely chose to concentrate on horror rather than sci-fi pictures.

These Are the Damned (1963/65; Hammer/Columbia; U.K.; b&w) Original Title: *The Damned.* This

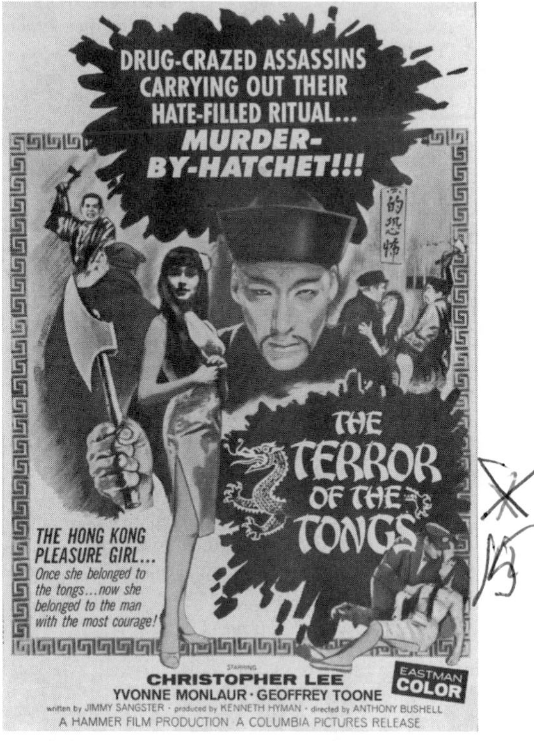

Eventful ad for *The Terror of the Tongs* (1961).

slice of high-minded atom-age paranoia from director Joseph Losey remains ambitious and artfully crafted sci-fi, even though it's not as clever as it thinks it is. Simon (Macdonald Carey), an American tourist, is mugged by a gang of British "teddy boys," lured into a trap by Joan (Shirley Ann Field), the sister of the gang leader (Oliver Reed). This sparks an unlikely romance between Simon and Joan, and also inflames her brother's incestuous jealousy. While attempting to evade Joan's brother, the lovers stumble onto a secret underground military installation where radioactive children, capable of surviving a nuclear war, are being raised. Evan Jones' script (adapted from a novel by H.L. Lawrence) seems needlessly convoluted but contains some excellent sequences and a trio of well-delineated characters. Carey, Field and especially Reed (in the film's showiest part) illuminate those characters brilliantly. Losey, a blacklisted American expatriate operating under the pronounced influence of the French *nouvelle vague*, overstuffs *The Damned* with self-consciously "edgy" cuts, compositions and camera moves. His approach lends the film a texture unique among the output of the Hammer studio, but Losey seems a bit out of his element. Unless you count the light fantasy *The Boy with Green Hair* (1948) or his misguided remake of *M* (1951), this was Losey's only sci-fi or horror project. Hammer seemed reluctant to release this atypical, politically bent thriller. Although completed in 1961, it wasn't issued to British theaters until 1963 and took nearly two years longer to reach America. Inhabiting a reality where imminent nuclear holocaust is a foregone conclusion, *The Damned* seems to spring directly from the Cold War zeitgeist. For that reason alone, it remains a fascinating cultural artifact, even if it's not entirely successful as cinema.

This Is Not a Test (1961; Allied Artists; b&w) *This Is* one of the more obscure atomic holocaust films that proliferated during the Cold War/Atomic paranoia of the 1950s and early '60s—which is a pity, since it compares favorably to such better known (and often bigger budgeted) entries as *Invasion U.S.A.* (1953) and *The Day the World Ended* (1956), and even the big studio *On the Beach* and *The World, the Flesh and the Devil* (both 1959). In telling its tale of seven disparate motorists waylaid at an isolated mountain roadblock by an overzealous deputy when the missiles start flying, *This Is Not a Test* effectively accomplishes what A-bomb films are *supposed* to do: 1) make the viewer ponder what s/he would do under such circumstances; and 2) make the viewer weigh the benefits and limitations of civilized society, and what might happen when that societal fabric starts to tear. With nary a special effect in sight (apart from one brief, enigmatically-placed blinding flash), the film accomplishes its goal via some involving characterization and surprisingly successful acting from its cast of unknowns, who embody the despair and desperation, futility and hope of such a horrifying scenario. While not on the same level as 1962's *Panic in Year Zero!* (arguably the best Atom Bomb film of the decade), *This Is Not a Test* is not just another cheap cash-in on the atomic-sized fear of the times, but an intimate, well-constructed examination of What-We-Must-Never-Let-Happen.

This Night I'll Possess Your Corpse (1967; Paranagua Cinematografica; Brazil; b&w/color) Original Language Title: *Esta Noite Encarnarei no Teu Cadaver*. "This film begins where AT MIDNIGHT I'LL TAKE YOUR SOUL ended" reads the opening scrawl of this direct sequel to the first home-grown Brazilian horror movie, *At Midnight I'll Take Your Soul*. Low-budget Brazilian producer/director/writer/actor Jose Mojica Marins returns as his signature character, the sadistic atheist undertaker named Ze do Caixao ("Coffin Joe"), who inspires fear wherever he goes. Ze is back, once again looking for a "superior woman" to bear a son for him and thus secure his "immortality." (Ze is undoubtedly the oddest champion of children in the history of cinema, as this cruel murderer believes that "a child is the most important creature in the universe"; he becomes distraught when he learns a woman he killed was pregnant, and he even turns hero to save a boy from being run over in the street!) To this end Ze kidnaps six women and subjects them to a "test"—unleashing scores of tarantulas to crawl all over their bodies (in a harrowing scene, for both viewers *and* actresses, as the huge arachnids scuttle across buttocks, bosoms and faces). Ze also has a pit full of snakes to dispose of the unwanted "failures," and a disfigured hunchback to do his bidding. *This Night* not only continues the basic plotline from the first film, it offers more of its predecessor's cramped-but-inventive settings (nearly the whole of *This Night* was shot on flimsy sets built inside an abandoned synagogue); more of Ze's anti-religious, megalomaniacal railing and ranting; and more gory and shivery set-

Brazilian horror: Jose Mojica Marins (aka "Coffin Joe") and his overgrown fingernails in *This Night I Will Possess Your Corpse* (1967).

pieces (including a startling 10-minute dream trip — in which the film turns to *color*— through Hell featuring actors and actresses literally plastered into walls being tormented by red demons with pitchforks). Nearly a third longer than its predecessor, *This Night* begins to ramble as Ze frames a rival for a murder *he* committed, actually finds a woman with compatible sensibilities (amazingly unlikely!), and fends off a group of hired assassins. But it finishes with a supernatural bang that features a bolt of lightning, a ghost's curse, and a swamp full of skeletons. Like the rest of Marins' work, *This Night I'll Possess Your Corpse* only made it to America on video in the 1990s.

A gang of cannibalistic "Morlocks" in our distant future are looking for trouble in George Pal's *The Time Machine* (1960).

The Time Machine (1960; MGM) *The Time Machine* can be counted as one of legendary producer/director George Pal's most enjoyable pictures and among the best screen adaptations of H.G. Wells. In 1899 London, inventor H. George Wells (Rod Taylor) develops a time machine and launches himself into the future, where he discovers constant World Wars and, in their aftermath, a strange world where the human race has divided into two species: the timid, sheep-like Eloi (who eat fruit and vegetables) and the brutal, ape-like Morlocks (who eat the Eloi). George falls for a young Eloi woman (Yvette Mimieux) and decides to help her people. Unlike with many Wells pictures, Pal doesn't soften the author's social criticism and even attempts to sharpen it with a sequence depicting a nuclear war (set in 1966!). At its heart, however, Pal's *Time Machine* remains a charming romantic adventure with a pair of appealing leads in Taylor and Mimieux. The supporting cast, especially Alan Young as George's loyal friend Filby, and Sebastian Cabot as the skeptical Dr. Hillyer, also contribute memorable performances. Wah Chang and Gene Warren's visual effects are, for their era, superb (particularly the time-lapse voyage through time). Russell Garcia's score — in the same sweeping romantic style later popularized by John Williams— is another major plus. For horror fans, the main attraction will be the bestial, blue-skinned, buck-fanged Morlocks, one of the most delightfully hideous movie monsters of the decade. The time machine itself, a beautifully designed Victorian contraption resembling a sled with an overstuffed velvet seat and a giant spinning dial, proved so popular it was recreated for the 1979 sci-fi adventure *Time After Time*, in which H. George Wells (Malcolm McDowell) pursues a time-traveling Jack the Ripper into the future.

Impressive one-sheet poster for the *un*impressive *The Time Travelers* (1964).

The Time Travelers (1964; AIP) A quartet of scientists accidentally opens a time portal that transports them 107 years into the future, where they encounter a nuclear-devastated Earth swarming with bald-headed, disfigured mutants. The protagonists hook up with the last surviving "normals," who now live underground and construct androids for their needs. Writer-director Ib Melchior was obviously more interested in sci-fi gadgetry and futuristic concepts than story or characterization — or thrills, for that matter — since the picture is laden with dull exposition and interminable scenes focusing on the "technical wonders" (the android factory, hydroponic gardens, matter transmitter device, etc.). Too bad the movie's low budget precludes much in the way of said gadgetry. Brightly colored, garish sets (about on the level of a low-rent *Star Trek* episode) and mod, "futuristic" clothing (high-collared jumpsuits anyone?) betray the picture's *actual* timeframe. Characterless and thrill-less, *The Time Travelers* is best avoided by sci-fi tourists of *any* time.

Tom Thumb and Little Red Riding Hood (1962/65; Mexico; K. Gordon Murray Productions, Inc.) Original Language Title: *Caperucita y Pulgarcito Contra los Monstruos.* Alternate Title: *Little Red Riding Hood and the Monsters* (video). This bizarre sequel (imported from Mexico by K. Gordon Murray) to *Little Red Riding Hood* (1960/63) has the famous fairy tale character and her friends (Tom Thumb, Stinky the Skunk, the "not so ferocious" Wolf, and a carrot-topped ogre) match wits in the Haunted Forest with the Wicked Witch and her monstrous minions, including Mr. Hurricane, a Robot (looking like it just stepped off the set of *The Robot vs. the Aztec Mummy*), "Frankensteen" (a goofy—and hairy—take on the classic Monster), a top-hatted vampire, and even a Dragon. Oh, and everybody (including the monsters) sings.

The Torture Chamber of Fu Manchu see ***The Castle of Fu Manchu***

Torture Zone see ***The Fear Chamber***

The Triumph of Hercules (1964/65; John Alexander; Italy/France) Original Language Title: *Il Trionfo di Ercole.* Alternate Titles: *Hercules vs. the Giant Warrior*; *Hercules and the Ten Avengers.* A better moniker might have been "The *Shame* of Hercules," since, when Hercules (Dan Vadis) is tricked by the duplicitous usurper Milo into wrongfully killing an innocent man, Hercules' father, Jove (the dubbers chose the Roman appellation rather than the traditional Greek "Zeus"), takes away Herc's strength as punishment, leading to a tension-filled episode involving a torture/death-trap device. Though long on action (at least of the gladiatorial sword-fighting and fisticuff variety), this one is short on monsters, with a group of seven bald, gold-skinned, supernaturally-summoned he-men being the best it can muster. Even worse, the story's novel angst angle (with the Mighty Hercules having recklessly killed an innocent) remains completely unexplored. Consequently, *The Triumph of Hercules* (released directly to television in America) is no triumph for the Peplum Pantheon.

Triumph of the Son of Hercules (1961; Embassy Pictures; France/Italy) Original Language Title: *Trionfo di Maciste.* A forgettable peplum all the way around—from the clichéd plot (evil usurping queen must be overthrown by the rightful prince with help from he-man hero) to the standard peplum "action" (boulders tossed at palace guards) to the rock-jawed muscle-bound hero (Kirk Morris as Maciste offers about as much personality as his chiseled pects)—*Triumph of the Son of Hercules* was sent directly to American television in the mid–1960s as part of Embassy's "Sons of Hercules" package. The only distinguishing feature here is an admittedly impressive giant fire-god statue whose oversized arms raise a platform from which a screaming victim falls into a pit of fire (or dry-ice "smoke," anyway). The film only enters the realm of the fantastical when Maciste braves the caverns of the cavemen-like "Yuri Men" to rescue his lady love. There he avoids what appears to be pursuing flames, battles a "giant" caveman, and tosses a few hairy Yuri Men into the pit before the stock-footage volcanic eruption wraps it all up.

12 to the Moon (1960; Columbia; b&w) An international expedition rockets to the moon to claim it for all mankind; the only problem is, the (unseen) "moon-people" already there take issue with this action. What starts out as a fairly intelligent and progressive space-travel film, complete with such important themes as international and interracial cooperation, quickly degenerates into a juvenile, simplistic space-opera. Admittedly, space operas have their place, but *Moon* fails to deliver even a single aria, much less the whole libretto. The pacing is slow, the cast uninteresting and the characters' petty squabbles, which take up much of the film's running time, are just plain embarrassing. Production-wise, the low budget shows through everywhere. One crewmember talks about the "invisible electro-magnetic ray screen which forms a protective shield over our faces" (translation: no glass in the helmets—talk about low, low, *low* budget!). But then, what can one expect from the director of *Madmen of Mandoras*?

Twisted Nerve (1968/69; British Lion/National General; U.K.) Co-written by *Peeping Tom* screenwriter Leo Marks (with director Roy Boulting), this is another story about an unusually sympathetic killer with mental problems stemming from childhood abuse. But *Twisted Nerve* is nowhere near as shocking or radical as *Peeping Tom*, and it's more a character study than a true psychological thriller. Martin Durnley (Hywell Bennett) evades a shop-lifting rap and befriends attractive young librarian Susan Harper (Hayley Mills) by pretending to be a "simple-minded" young man named Georgie. Playing on her pity, Martin schemes his way into a temporary stay at a boarding house run by Susan's mother (Billie Whitelaw). This turns out to be part of an elaborate alibi that enables Martin to sneak away and murder his severe, stiff-necked stepfather (Frank Finlay). But when Susan discovers "Georgie" is really Martin, his carefully laid plans—and teetering sanity—begins to crumble. Billie Whitelaw earned a BAFTA (British Oscar) award for her supporting turn as Susan's mother, who accepts "Georgie" like a son but later tries to seduce him. Mills displays a range untapped by her earlier roles (like in *The Parent Trap* [1961]). But the picture belongs to Hywell Bennett, whose Martin seems to be holding back ocean-like depths of rage, pain and sorrow behind the kindly face of "Georgie." His profoundly

Cleaver. Cleaver. Chop. Chop. First the mom and then the pop.
Then we'll get the pretty girl. We'll get her right between the curl.
Twisted Nerve
Hayley Mills Hywel Bennett Billie Whitelaw Phyllis Calvert

More sixties psychos (U.S. one-sheet poster for Twisted Nerve [1968/69]).

sympathetic portrayal recalls Carl Boehm's performance in *Peeping Tom*. Unfortunately, that's where the similarities end between the two pictures. *Twisted Nerve* generates none of the sustained tension or emotional impact of director Michael Powell's classic. While not without points of interest, *Twisted Nerve* is a footnote; *Peeping Tom* is a headline.

2+5: Mission Hydra see *Star Pilot*

2001: A Space Odyssey (1968; MGM) One of the greatest "pure" science fiction movies ever made — indeed, one of the best films of any type ever made — *2001* also remains one of the defining motion pictures of the 1960s (and not just because of its acid trip finale). A mysterious monolith appears from nowhere and somehow inspires a group of primitive humans to begin using tools. Thousands of years later, a similar monolith is unearthed on the moon, and sends a pulse to Jupiter. An earth-to-Jupiter mission is soon launched to investigate, led by a team of astronauts (two awake, five in "hypersleep") and assisted by a super-computer named HAL. But HAL begins to malfunction, putting the mission and the crew in deadly danger. Epic in length and scope yet reflectively paced, intellectually challenging and philosophically brooding, *2001* couldn't have been made in any prior era and probably wouldn't be green-lighted today. Its revolutionary special effects set a new standard for sci-fi cinema, and director Stanley Kubrick's brilliant melding of visuals and music (for instance, pairing Strauss' stately "Blue Danube" waltz with images of a slowly rotating space station) remains unsurpassed. But it's neither the film's technical innovations nor Kubrick's directorial genius that make it so emblematic of its era. Rather, it's the picture's underlying theme. By comparing the behavior of ape men during the early "dawn of man" sequence with that of scientists and astronauts (in both cases, people eat, care for their children, and attend to other basic tasks), *2001* suggests that, although technology has advanced spectacularly from the days of bone clubs to the era of the HAL-9000 computer, man himself hasn't changed much. Technology can carry humankind only so far (even a creation as "perfect" as HAL can break down, since he must be programmed by people); to evolve as a species, to discover our "star child" within, we must look beyond technology to contact with a higher power or toward expanded consciousness, possibly both. The picture's famously enigmatic resolution doesn't spell out everything clearly, but the general idea flows directly from the American counter-culture of the era. No wonder *2001* was so popular with hippies. It's a masterpiece of both speculative cinema and of subtle subversion.

Ulysses Against Hercules see *Ulysses Against the Son of Hercules*

Ulysses Against the Son of Hercules (1961/64; Embassy Pictures; Italy/France) Original Language Title: *Ulisse Contro Ercole*. Alternate Title: *Ulysses Against Hercules* (UK). Another of the repackaged, released-directly-to-television "Sons of Hercules" entries, *Ulysses Against the Son of Hercules* has strongman Hercules (a "son of Hercules" in name, rather than by blood) serve the will of the gods by tracking and capturing the beleaguered Ulysses. Ulysses offended the gods when he blinded the Cyclops, and he's been trying ever since to return home to his family (with the gods placing obstacles in his path at every turn). The two opponents bond when they are captured by a mysterious blonde queen and her weird feathered birdmen, and then must face down a mad king and his army of troglodyte-like cave dwellers. Meandering and dull, *Ulysses* makes the least of its opportunities (though we hear of the bird-people's sacrifices to their giant vulture god, we never *see* it). There's little here to recommend.

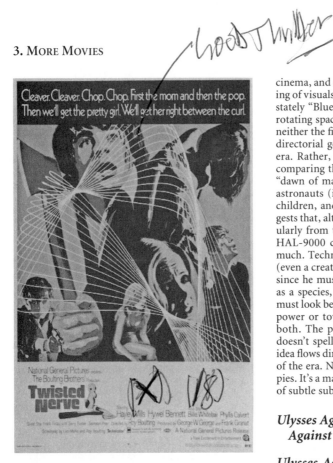

Uncle Was a Vampire (1959/64; CEI/Embassy-TV; Italy) Original Language Title: *Tempi Duri per i Vampiri* (*Hard Times for Vampires*). To pay back taxes, Baron Osvaldo (Renato Rascel) sells his castle to a hotel chain. He's left penniless, but the "kindly" hotelier agrees to hire on Osvaldo — as a bellhop. He's humiliated but thinks his troubles may be over when word arrives that a wealthy relative, Uncle Roderico (Christopher Lee), is coming to visit. Alas, Osvaldo's worries have only begun, since Uncle Roderico turns out to be — as the title indicates — a bloodthirsty vampire with his sights set on the hotel's young female guests. *Uncle Was a Vampire* is one of those dreadful horror-comedies that shortchanges viewers on both-counts— horror *and* comedy. It's difficult to discern where the six writers who collaborated on the film's screenplay thought the laughs were. The scenario features no slapstick sequences, no sight gags and very few (attempted) one-liners or other jokes. It seems the humor was supposed to simply radiate from the person of motor-mouth comedian Renato Rascel, or else arise naturally from the film's "hilarious" situations. For instance, in one scene, two would-be Lotharios attempt to get a couple of models tipsy and then seduce them, but wind up getting falling-down drunk themselves. Hardy har har. Uncle Roderico arrives about 20 minutes into this 94-minute dud and participates in only four sequences, severely curtailing Christopher Lee's screen time. As Roderico, the actor offers a slightly broader version of his familiar Hammer Dracula characterization, a low-impact approach that blurs the line between subtle and lazy. Renato Rascel's best moments (such as they are) follow Osvaldo's vampirization, when he begins aping the mannerisms (but not the speech patterns) of Bela Lugosi's Dracula. Theatrically released in Europe in 1959, *Uncle Was a Vampire* was sold directly to television in the U.S., where it debuted in 1964.

Underwater City (1962; Columbia) Not to be confused with *Captain Nemo's Underwater City* (1969/70), this 1962 science fiction yarn, directed by veteran Frank McDonald, stars William Lundigan and Julie Adams as two members of a team of scientists studying whether or not humans can live for extended periods in a shelter at the bottom of the sea. The authors were unable to secure a copy of the picture for review. However, Columbia was so discouraged by the film that, to save money, the studio printed it in black-and-white even though it was shot in color. Columbia later struck color prints of the movie when it was issued to television.

Unearthly Stranger (1963/64; Anglo-Amalgamated/AIP; U.K.; b&w) Invisible invaders from outer space take the form of human women and melt the brains of Earth scientists in this risible, sluggish and exceedingly talky British sci-fi yarn. Dr. Mark Davidson (John Neville) takes over the leadership of a secret British research program devoted to psychic teleportation — he's trying to empower humans to explore other worlds without benefit of space ships, transmitting their selves through "mental energy force" alone. But the invaders have already solved the problem, and Davidson's co-worker, Prof. Lancaster (Philip Stone), suspects that Davidson's new "Swiss" wife (Gabriella Licudi)— who does not have a pulse and never blinks—*may* be an alien. *Unearthly Stranger*'s thin plot would hardly support an *Outer Limits* episode, let alone a feature film. Its running time is padded out with endless conversations between Davidson and Lancaster, Davidson and his wife, both scientists and a numbskull intelligence officer (Patrick Newell), and on and on. Ingeniously designed to be as cheap as possible, the scenario carefully avoids any need for special effects, futuristic costumes, sets or make-ups, and requires only a small, no-name cast. The movie's only distinguishing moment is its downbeat, mildly misogynistic finale, which suggests that all Earth women are aliens— or, at the very least, that any woman you think you know secretly may be from outer space.

Unsatisfied Love (1968; Abrams & Parsi; Argentina; b&w) Alternate Title: Love After Death. Though no better than most sexploitation cheapies of the 1960s (and worse than many), this Argentinean import was something a little different for the 1960s raincoat crowd, as it turns on the macabre premise of a man being buried alive by his duplicitous wife and doctor, only to literally crawl out of his grave to take revenge. Before screwing up his courage to exact retribution, however, the resurrected schlub does a little screwing of another sort, not to mention some peeping and girl-groping as he tries to overcome being too "sick and afraid" to satisfy his libido (apparently he never consummated his six-month marriage). Apart from some awkward soft-core sex scenes and (admittedly impressive) South American pulchritude, this awful import offers only wall-to-wall, inappropriate library music; dire dubbing (the dialogue never even comes close to matching the lip movements); seedy black-and-white photography; sub-high-school-level acting; and the most pathetic Foley work in cinema history (during the film's solitary, poorly-staged gun battle, a gunshot is heard seconds before the man pulls the trigger, while another fires and drops his target in his tracks— with nary a pop on the soundtrack). A more apt title for Unsatisfied Love would be "Unsatisfied Viewer."

Vampire Women see *The Queen of the Vampires*

Vengeance see *The Brain*

The Vengeance of Fu Manchu (1968; Warner-Seven Arts; UK/West Germany/Hong Kong/Ireland) This third entry in the five-film Harry Alan Towers-produced Fu Manchu series (all starring Christopher Lee in the title role) offers better production values than most (with location filming in Hong Kong and at the Shaw Studios), some expansive outdoor photography, an impressive "palace" set, and little else. This go-round the megalomaniacal arch-villain settles on a convoluted scheme to take revenge on his old nemesis, Scotland Yard Commissioner Nayland Smith (Douglas Wilmer), by replacing him with a murderous double. Fu also receives an Organized Crime representative who wants to unite the world's criminals under Fu's banner. A general sense of dullness and lack of action pervades the film (a fistfight in a Shanghai bar is about all it offers up until the rushed climax), with far too much time spent on less-than-intriguing intrigue, and the false Smith's trial and approaching execution (about which we care nothing, since we know he's an imposter). But at least director Jeremy Summers avoids the tiresome and pointless zooms that plague the two subsequent Jess Franco–helmed efforts.

Doing the "Funky Chicken"—with a giant duck. Just one of the puerile pleasures found in the seriocomic *Village of the Giants* (1965).

The Vengeance of She (1968; Hammer/Seven Arts; U.K.) While not entirely without interest, *The Vengeance of She* remains one of the weaker Hammer Films products of the 1960s. The plot is simply a gender reversal of *She* (1965), with a reincarnated Ayesha (Olinka Berova) psychologically compelled to join her immortal lover Killikrates (John Richardson) in the legendary kingdom of Kor. Screenwriter Peter O'Donnell's scenario, set in present day and limiting the number of Kor sets, cleverly disguises the film's modest budget. And the film's first act—when "Ayesha" compulsively stows away on a millionaire's yacht, bringing tension and ultimately tragedy—is actually pretty good. Alas, it's all downhill from there, as *The Vengeance of She* simply retraces the plodding steps of Hammer's original *She* (itself not that good a film), only with lesser talents in nearly every key role, both in front of and behind the camera. Berova certainly had the figure of a reincarnated Ursula Andress (Hammer's first Ayesha), but her flat-affect performance hangs like an albatross around the movie's neck. *She* co-stars Peter Cushing and Christopher Lee are sorely missed as well, but even that dynamic duo couldn't have rescued this tired retread.

Venus in Furs (1969/70; Cinematografica Associati/AIP; Italy-West Germany-U.K.) Original Title: *Può una Morta Rivivere per Amore?* (Italy). Trumpet player Jimmy (James Darren) accidentally witnesses a bizarre sexual interlude between a young blonde, Wanda (Maria Rohm), and three strangers (played by Klaus Kinski, Dennis Price and Margaret Lee). The next day, he finds Wanda's dead body on the beach. Two years later and thousands of miles away in Brazil, Wanda mysteriously reappears. She launches an affair with Jimmy and begins meting out vengeance against her killers. This moody ghost story marked one of writer-director Jess Franco's attempts to reconcile art and exploitation filmmaking. The movie, released in 1969 in Europe but not until 1970 in the U.S., plays like a hybrid of *Carnival of Souls* and *Last Year at Marienbad* set to a jazz fusion score. Although ambitious and visually striking, *Venus in Furs* is neither fish nor fowl—too trashy to satisfy the art house crowd, too pretentious and coy to play well as exploitation fare—and is undone by a weak plot. Its narrative is willfully ambiguous—so much so that the details of the demise of the Kinski character remain incomprehensible—and often bogs down in copious location footage of Rio de Janiero and extended musical interludes. Franco lays the symbolism on thick and empties nearly his entire bag of directorial tricks, using flash forwards, slow motion, tinted and distorted images, and other devices. None of this makes up for the central weakness of the story, which resembles a dragged out *Twilight Zone* episode with a not very original or surprising twist ending. In Franco's defense, however, the filmmaker was forced to rewrite the script extensively when financial backers rejected his original idea for a movie about a black jazz musician and his affair with a ghostly white woman (this was considered too controversial for American audiences). While not a success, *Venus in Furs* remains an intriguing failure.

Village of the Giants (1965; Embassy Pictures) Bert I. Gordon goes B.I.G. once again in this teen-targeted spoof of H.G. Wells' *The Food of the Gods.* Gone are Wells' humanistic insights and social commentary, replaced by go-go-dancing teenagers and puerile comedy in a tale of juvenile delinquents growing to 35 feet tall after ingesting a mysterious substance, and taking over a small town. The fact that the film's "hero" is played by Mousekateer-turned-Beach Party regular Tommy Kirk, and that the growth "goo" is created by a prepubescent boy named "Genius" (played by a post–Opie, Ron Howard), speaks volumes on the movie's level of maturity. And a very young Beau Bridges leads the most clean-cut gang of JDs this side of a *Leave It to Beaver* episode. While Gordon seems to want to make a timely statement about young people rebelling against the older generation (a prime topic for sixties cinema), he does so from the wrong perspective; this *is*, in fact, your Dad's *Food of the Gods.* Here Wells' "power corrupts" message is delivered more along the lines of *Beach Blanket Bingo* than *Animal Farm.* That said, it's still pretty amusing to see Johnny Crawford literally hanging onto a gigantic bosom for dear life (the prime image in the film's advertising). Eleven years later Gordon left the comedy (and teens) behind to make a straight horror version of *The Food of the Gods* (1976), this one dominated by giant rats rather than rebels.

Violent Midnight (1963; Victoria Films; b&w) Alternate Title: *Psychomania* (reissue). Del Tenney's first film as producer/director (though its direction is officially credited to sexploitation veteran Richard Hilliard [*The Lonely Sex*, 1959; *Wild Is My Love*, 1963], Tenney ended up helming much of the picture due to Hilliard's "inexperience"—at least according to Tenney himself), *Violent Midnight* is more soap opera/murder mystery than outright horror. Filmed as *Black Autumn* but best known by its reissue title of *Psychomania, Violent Midnight* centers on a reclusive artist (Lee Philips) with a disturbing past who paints nudes on his inherited family estate. When his latest model is murdered by a knife-wielding killer, he becomes a suspect alongside the local town tough, played by a very young James Farentino (*Dead & Buried*, 1981). A visit from his sister, a budding romance, and a gaggle of girls at the local women's college complicates things further, leading to a second murder and a surprise revelation. Shot in and around the imposing Stamford, Connecticut, estate of Tenney's father-in-law (the former home of Mount Rushmore sculptor Gutzon Borglum), *Violent Midnight* sports the raw, often hand-held style Tenney favored on his meager budgets (this one cost a whopping $42,000), and is populated by up-and-coming New York stage actors (including a pre–TV stardom Dick Van Patton as a police detective on the case). Additionally and surprisingly (though perhaps not so much, given Hilliard's involvement), the film offers up some fleeting nudity to spice up its slow pacing, various love entanglements, and dearth of violence (with only two murders). Fortunately, Tenney would correct this genre tentitiveness by filling his subsequent productions with goofy sea monsters, gruesome decapitated heads and pasty-faced zombies: *The Horror of Party Beach*, *The Curse of the Living Corpse* (both 1964) and *I Eat Your Skin* (1964/71).

Viy (1967; Mosfilm; U.S.S.R.) It's a shame this Russian horror-fantasy never saw a theatrical release in the U.S., as it offers some unique and impressive horror imagery. The period story (based on a short novel by N. V. Gogol) sees a young, lazy (but likable) seminary student named Khoma (Leonid Kuravlyov) ordered to say prayers for three nights over the corpse of a noble's daughter, who's actually a witch. Though it takes 40 minutes for the horror to commence, it's worth the wait, as we're treated to such startling sights as the witch's coffin flying about the rustic church trying to break into the terrified Khoma's protective sacred circle (drawn in chalk on the floor), or the beautiful-but-frightening white-faced witch conjuring up a walking skeleton, gray dead hands that emerge from the gray wooden walls, a skeletal hydra-creature, and demonic wurdulaks (vampires) that crawl slowly down the walls like insects, all augmented by eerie, suspenseful music.

Voyage into Space (1968; Toei/AIP-TV; Japan) Here's yet another *faux* feature film cobbled together from a Japanese television series. In this case, the series was *Jiyaianto Robo* (*Giant Robot*), a cheap(er) knock-off of the popular *Ultraman* series. AIP picked up and dubbed *Jiyaianto Robo* for American syndication under the title *Johnny Sokko and His Flying Robot. Voyage Into Space* featured three *Johnny Sokko* episodes crudely edited together, but lacking any narrative continuity. The results are just as infantile but somewhat more entertaining than *Atomic Rulers* (1957/64) and other "movies" created by combining episodes from the *Starman* TV show.

Voyage to the Bottom of the Sea (1961; 20th Century–Fox) Even though it sired a successful TV series, *Voyage to the Bottom of the Sea* isn't terribly seaworthy as a feature film. It's sunk by a leaden pace, a talky script and tin-eared acting. During the shakedown cruise for an advanced nuclear submarine named the Seaview, Admiral Harriman Nelson (Walter Pidgeon) and Captain Lee Crane (Robert Sterling) learn that a radiation belt around the Earth has caught fire. Unless the blaze is somehow stopped, the planet will be burned to a crisp. Nelson devises a controversial plan to stop the fire by launching a nuclear missile into the atmosphere from a precise location at a specific time. When leadership dithers on whether or not to proceed with his scheme, Nelson takes off with the Seaview and her crew to save the world. Most of *Voyage to the Bottom of the Sea* is consumed by pseudo-scientific double-talk about the Van Allen radiation belt, and bickering between the hard-charging Admiral Nelson and ... well, practically everybody, but especially easy-going Captain Crane. The film's underwater special effects are reasonably good (and the Seaview is a cool-looking ship), but the screenplay, by producer-director Irwin Allen and Charles Bennett, is preposterous, slow-footed and riddled with clunky dialogue. The picture comes to life only briefly, when the Seaview tussles with a giant octopus. Usually reliable veterans such as Walter Pidgeon and Joan Fontaine play down to the level of the material with starchy performances. Robert Sterling, Barbara Eden and Frankie Avalon fare no better, and Peter Lorre looks bored throughout. Audiences will likely have the same reaction.

Voyage to the End of the Universe (1963/64; Filmove Barrandov/AIP; Czechoslovakia; b&w) Original Title: *Ikarie XB-1.* Sober in tone and epic in its aspirations, this Czech-made picture is sometimes undercut by substandard visual effects and clumsy propaganda, but remains engrossing and thought-provoking. Loosely based on Stanislaw Lem's novel *Magellan Cloud*, the narrative follows a space ship full of settlers on a 15-year interstellar journey to a new planet. Along the way they encounter a mysterious derelict space craft and an ominous nebula that emanates debilitating rays, and must overcome personal conflicts, illness, an insane crewman and other dangers. Jan Zazvorka's futuristic sets, Jindrich Polak and Pavel Juracek's heady script, and Polak's crisp direction serve the film well. For its American release (under the title *Voyage to the End of the Universe*), AIP inflicted injurious alterations on the movie, including haphazard dubbing, more than 15 minutes of cuts and (worst of all) a newly shot "surprise" ending in which the planet the crew has been seeking turns out to be (you guessed it) Earth! The Czech version (thankfully preserved on DVD) does not include this feeble finale. In its original form, *Ikarie XB-1* remains one of the more intriguing "pure" science fiction films of the pre-*2001* era.

Voyage to the Planet of the Prehistoric Women (1968; Filmgroup/AIP-TV) Producer Roger Corman purchased the Russian science fiction epic *Planeta Bur* (1962) and hired director Peter Bogdanovich (working under the pseudonym Derek Thomas) to recut it, removing the original's pro-Soviet propaganda and inserting newly shot footage of scantily clad beauties (including a past-her-prime Mamie Van Doren), then provide voiceover narration to tie together this wildly mismatched material. A team of astronauts travels to Venus and discovers dinosaurs, man-eating plants and evidence of a female-dominated civilization. However, since the astronauts and the curvaceous Venusians (decked out in bell-bottom hip huggers and sea-shell bikini tops) never actually meet, this variation on the shopworn theme of *Cat Women of the Moon* (1953) or *Queen of Outer Space* (1958) lacks even the modest degree of titillation offered by those pictures. It's tedious, predictable and poorly acted, although the miniatures and other visual effects in the Russian footage are intriguing enough to make viewers wonder what *Planeta Bur* was all about. Corman might have been better off simply dubbing and releasing the Russian film, especially since he had already used much of this same Soviet footage in *Voyage to the Prehistoric Planet* (1965). The only good to come from *Voyage to the Planet of the Prehistoric Women* is that, for his dutiful work on this misbegotten project, Bogdanovich earned a green light for his chilling and provocative *Targets* (1968).

Voyage to the Prehistoric Planet (1962/65; AIP-TV) Roger Corman bought the 1962 Russian sci-fi film *Planeta Bur* (Planet of Storms) for a reported $10,000 and then hired Curtis Harrington to dub the feature and insert poorly-matched footage of Basil Rathbone and Faith Domergue in cramped control rooms into the impressive special effects of the original movie. The result: a stilted yet visually arresting story of five astronauts and their oversized robot's adventures on Venus, including encounters with man-eating plants, huge dinosaurs, reptile-men and flowing lava. Corman sold the "new" feature directly to television via AIP.

Vulcan, God of Fire (1961/64; Embassy; Italy) Original Language Title: *Vulcano, Figlio di Giove.* Alternate Title: *Vulcan, Son of Jupiter.* Up in Olympus, in order to stop the naughty goddess Venus from catting about, Jupiter, father of the gods, decides she must marry. But which god? It comes down to a choice between Mars, god of war, and Vulcan, god of fire. The two take their tussle to Earth as "mere mortals," where Vulcan runs across a gaggle of goofy-looking Lizard men (complete with oversized fangs) and a herd of shaggy mountain goat-people before foiling the conniving Mars' plot to overthrow Jupiter (by building a gigantic tower to Olympus—which, amusingly, only rises to about 20 feet over the course of the film). Rather than the gods lurking in the background as in most pepla that feature the ancient Greco-Roman pantheon in the flesh, here the immortals take center stage—and prove even more prone to human follies and foibles than ordinary humans. Blonde beauty Annie Gorassini plays Venus as a tarty little tramp who spreads the seeds of lust wherever she goes, while Roger Browne's Mars is an egocentric rabblerouser. Then there's Gordon Mitchell's over-the-top cranky Pluto, and Rod Flash's (aka Richard Lloyd) beefy stump of a hero in the figure of the loyal (but incredibly dull) Vulcan. Though ramblingly plotted and poorly acted (even by peplum standards), there's enough brawny battles, wacky encounters (including a trip to Neptune's underwater grotto), unconvincing matte paintings, beautiful women in provocative outfits (not to mention a show-stopping, sexy dance by the pulchritudinous—and fittingly named—Bella Cortez), and just plain weirdness to keep most sword-and-sandal fans entertained. And there's a midget, too.

Vulcan, Son of Jupiter see ***Vulcan, God of Fire***

The Wacky World of Doctor Morgus (1962; Calogne-Sevin; b&w) More sci-fi spy-comedy than horror, *The Wacky World of Doctor Morgus* stars New Orleans horror host Morgus the Magnificent (Sid

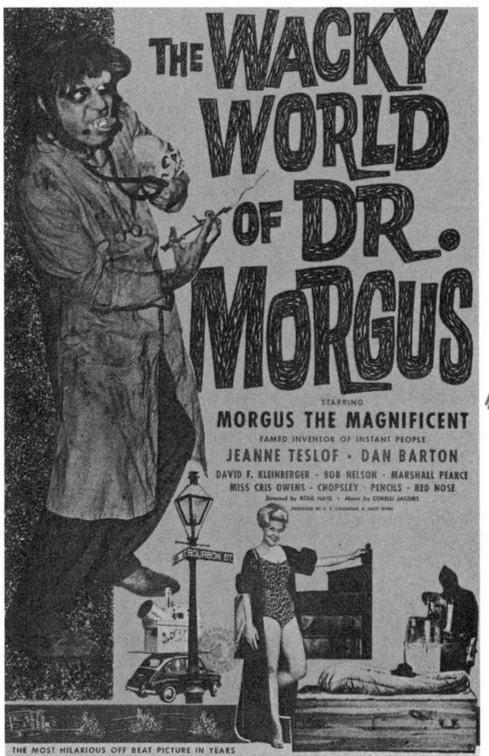

The first movie built entirely around a TV horror host: *The Wacky World of Dr. Morgus* (1962) (courtesy Ted Okuda).

Noel) as goofy scientist Dr. Morgus, who's developed an "instant people" machine which transforms humans into sand and then back again. The evil ruler of Microvania intends to use the device to infiltrate the United States with his army of spies. Released regionally in Louisiana in 1962, this hard-to-see low-budget spoof all but disappeared until given a brief afterlife by a small video company in the 1990s, only to sink into cinematic obscurity once again.

War Between the Planets (1965/71; Fanfare; Italy) Original Language Title: *Il Pianeta Errante.* Alternate Title: *Planet on the Prowl.* Yet another of the four sci-fi features shot back-to-back by Antonio Margheriti in 1964 (see *Wild Wild Planet*), this entry about a runaway planet wreaking havoc with Earth's atmospheric stability wasn't release in the U.S. until 1971.

War of the Gargantuas (1966/1970; Toho; Japan) Original Language Title: *Furankenshutain no Kaiju: Sanda tai Gaira.* Although not the finest-crafted entry in Toho's parade of giant monsters, *War of the Gargantuas,* with its frenetic tempo and surprising level of gore, remains the most intense and among the most popular. The film opens memorably, with a giant octopus attacking a ship. When all seems lost, a giant green ape-monster appears, attacking the octopus. Then, when it seems the danger is over, the ape-monster turns on the ship and sinks it anyway! The furry beastie turns out to be one of a pair of creatures, the gentle Brown Gargantua and the violent Green Gargantua. In an unusually grisly touch, the Green Gargantua not only smashes buildings and sinks boats, but also *eats* its human victims. Scientists attempt to save the Brown Gargantua, but the military wants to destroy both monsters—leading to a climactic Gargantua-versus-Gargantua free-for-all. Its visual effects remain mediocre, but the film doesn't shortchange viewers on action scenes, which are fast, furious and frequent. Unlike most of Toho's giant monsters, the Gargantua costumes weren't bulky rubber suits, which freed the stuntmen to move with extraordinary speed and agility. *War of the Gargantuas,* known in Japan as *Frankenstein Monsters: Sanda vs. Gaira,* is a direct sequel to *Frankenstein Conquers the World* (1965), although all references to the preceding film were eliminated through dubbing and re-titling. Russ Tamblyn replaces Nick Adams as the story's scientist-hero, but Kumi Mizuno returns as his assistant-girlfriend. Delayed from theatrical release in the U.S. until 1970, *War of the Gargantuas* made its belated debut as half of a very impressive *kaiju eiga* twin bill, with *Monster Zero* (1965/1970).

War of the Monsters (1966; Daiei/AIP-TV; Japan) Alternate (home video) Title: *Gamera vs. Barugon.* Original Language Title: *Daikaiju Kessen: Gamera tai Barugon.* Daiei's initial sequel to *Gammera the Invincible* (1965) was also the first Gamera movie shot in color, and the first to spell the monster's name with-

Left: **Good Gargantua vs. bad Gargantua results in the *War of the Gargantuas* (1966/70). *Right:* Large French poster for *War of the Monsters* (1966; aka *Gamera vs. Barugon*).**

one M. It's also one of the few entries not to feature a young boy as its protagonist, although *War of the Monsters* remains as childish as the rest of the series. Three greedy adventurers travel to a remote, primitive island to recover what they think is a giant opal. The artifact turns out to be a monster egg, which hatches to reveal Barugon, a giant, four-legged, iguana-like creature with a spiky back, horned nose and frog-like tongue. Naturally, the Japanese defense forces are no match for Barugon, who shoots freeze rays out of his tongue (!) and rainbow-colored heat blasts from the spines on his back. It's up to Gamera to save the day. These events unfold at a glacial pace, as *War of the Monsters* limps along for an agonizing 100 minutes. Gamera remains off-screen for most of the film, Barugon ranks among the most laughable of all the Japanese giant monsters, and none of the human characters are remotely interesting or likable. No wonder, then, that this film is generally regarded as the nadir of the franchise. AIP purchased *War of the Monsters* for release to American TV. Later, producer Sandy Frank re-edited and re-dubbed it for home video under the title *Gamera vs. Barugon*. The original AIP version represents a mild improvement over the Sandy Frank retread, but discerning viewers will steer clear of both.

War of the Planets (1965; MGM; Italy) Original Language Title: *I Diafanoidi Vengono da Morte*. This direct sequel to *Wild Wild Planet* has the same principals battling a race of beings composed of disembodied energy (represented — pathetically — by green lights and puffs of smoke) that set up house at a Martian mining base and invade the nearby space stations to possess humans. Featuring the same shiny plastic miniatures, shiny plastic sets, and shiny plastic actors (including a wasted Franco Nero just before he attained international stardom in a string of spaghetti westerns), there's not much to separate the two terrible films.

Warning from Space (1956/60; Daiei/AIP-TV; Japan) Alternate Title: *The Mysterious Satellite*. AIP picked up this slow-moving, disjointed science fiction film for American television four years after its Japanese debut. The story is an awkward attempt to meld *The Day the Earth Stood Still* with *When Worlds Collide*. Friendly aliens (who look like walking starfish with one giant eye on their bellies) travel to Earth and assume human form to issue a warning against nuclear war — and to enlist Earth's help in stopping a runaway planet that threatens to destroy both Earth and the aliens' homeworld. Except for the eye-bellied starfish aliens and the nifty, minimalist set design of the alien spaceship, *Warning from Space* remains a forgettable effort.

What a Carve-Up! see ***No Place Like Homicide***

Wheel of Fire see ***Pyro***

Wild Wild Planet (1965; MGM; Italy) Original Language Title: *I Criminali della Galassia*. This futuristic space opera (one of four sci-fi movies filmed back to back in 1964 by producer-director Antonio Margheriti for an Italian TV series called *Fantascienz*, but released theatrically instead) involves a mad sci-

A trio of spacecraft bound for the ***Wild Wild Planet*** (1965).

Spanish herald trumpeting the ***Warning from Space***.

entist who kidnaps and miniaturizes (to no great purpose, really) select individuals, with the aid of his mutant drones and female army, in a boffo plot to create the perfect human race. With its cheesy, Hot Wheels-style "futuristic city" models, unsteady rocket launchings and wobbly space station, not to mention its garish, "mod" '60s color schemes, outlandish costumes and goofy dancing, this pungent slice of Italian cheese would better be called *Wild Wild Planet Nine from Outer Space* (the hero even flits about the city in a flying saucer dangling from a string!)—except that, unlike the so-bad-it's-good Ed Wood "classic," *Wild Wild Planet*'s overall dullness places it in the so-bad-it's-*bad* camp.

The Witch (1966; Arco Film; Italy) Original Language Title: *La Strega in Amore.* Alternate Title: *Strange Obsession.* This European obscurity is, as its alternate title suggests, "strange" indeed. Richard (*The Haunting*) Johnson plays a carefree playboy in Italy who is drawn into the suffocating, insular, and twisted sphere of an aging hedonist (Sarah Feratti) in her falling-to-ruin palatial home via the charms of her odd yet beautiful daughter (Rosanna Schiafino). *The Witch* is an engrossing character study in unhealthy obsession laced with some evocative camerawork and involving acting from the four leads, including Gian Maria Volonte (*A Fistful of Dollars* and *For a Few Dollars More*) as a possibly mad member of the four-sided triangle. Though featuring a none-too-surprising supernatural-type revelation at the end, *The Witch* offers more erotically-charged drama than horror. But it does so in a thoroughly intriguing fashion, thanks to Damiano Damiani's atmospheric direction.

The Witches Attack (1965; Filmica Vergara Comisiones; Mexico; b&w) Original Language Title: *Atacan las Brujas.* After making five films for producer Alberto Lopez, masked Mexican wrestler-turned-movie star El Santo jumped ship and signed on with producer Luis Enrique Vergara (who later produced Boris Karloff's final four features). Santo made five pictures for Vergara before moving on yet again due to a contract dispute. Santo's first starring Vergara vehicles were the shot-back-to-back *The Witches Attack* and *The Diabolical Axe.* While El Santo did well for himself with the change (more than doubling his salary), this switch didn't do his films any favors, for the Vergara Santos often appear slapdash and cheap, with the more luxurious sets and professionalism of his previous surroundings at Churubusco Studios replaced with grimy location shooting and cut-rate technique. The story of *The Witches Attack* (finally subtitled and released in America via video nearly 40 years after its production) features a Satanic cult, having resurrected their Queen witch, intent on sacrificing both a beautiful girl and Santo to their Unholy Lord. The Silver Masked Man must locate the cultists and foil their evil plans. Confused, Ed Woodian day-for-night photography (this author's pre-teen son astutely asked why it was daylight on one side of the stone wall, then nighttime when Santo hops over to the other side), inappropriate stock music (climactic cues coming where there's no climax), and ridiculous effects (a "menacing" rubber spider on a string is so laugh-out-loud ludicrous that you can see its little plastic cartoon eyes; while Satan himself is some guy in a bad papier-maché horned mask wearing a cape and baggy pants) has *The Witches Attack* scraping the bottom of the Santo barrel. (The movie even steals a shot of Patricia Jessel being burned at the stake from the 1960 American film *Horror Hotel*!) But what really sinks this Santo ship is the film's tiresome repetitiveness. Santo makes *multiple* trips to the witches' "deserted" mansion (and we watch him climb the same stone wall to gain entry each time!) in which little or nothing happens. Santo is captured and chained to the same sacrificial table on *three* different occasions—and he breaks free of the chains in an identical manner every time! (One would think the witches would finally wise up and secure some better-quality manacles.) Granted, *The Witches Attack* offers a gaggle of beautiful girls in short Romanesque skirts (not to mention a seductive witch named Medusa in a spangled bikini putting the moves on El Santo), and some particularly exciting and acrobatic ringside action in front of a raucous, energized crowd. But it's not enough to gloss over the shabby production values and stultifying repetitiveness of it all.

Wizard of Mars (1965; American General) Alternate Title: *Horrors of the Red Planet* (home video). In this science fiction retelling of *The Wizard of Oz*, a manned space probe is blown off course by a space-twister and crashes on Mars. There, its four-member crew discovers a yellow brick road leading to an ancient city ruled by a wizard-like alien (John Carradine) who agrees to help them only if they perform a vital mission. This Z-budget production features a no-star cast (Roger Gentry, Eve Burkhardt, Vic McGee, Jerry Rannow), amateurish visual effects, chintzy sets and starchy, technobabble-filled dialogue. While the space-Oz concept has some novelty value, producer-director David L. Hewitt's execution of the idea is laughably inept in every department. The red planet isn't even red, since apparently Hewitt couldn't afford tinting! The story's Oz parallels don't become entirely apparent until the viewer has suffered through nearly an hour of boring survivalist melodrama (will their oxygen supply hold out?), including plenty of time-filling footage of the astronauts plodding through the "Martian" desert. All things considered, *Wizard of Mars* could have used a Wicked Witch and some flying monkeys.

The Woman Who Wouldn't Die (1965; Warner Bros.; U.K.; b&w) Original Title: *Catacombs.* The first film directed by future horror specialist Gordon Hessler, *The Woman Who Wouldn't Die* is a British-made Hitchcockian thriller with the suggestion of supernatural elements. Raymond (Gary Merrill), unhappily married to wealthy Ellen (Georgina Cookson), begins an affair with his college-age niece (Jane Merrow). When his wife discovers the lovers together, Raymond drowns Ellen in a sink full of water and buries her in the back yard. But soon he begins to believe that Ellen's vengeful spirit is haunting him. The authors of this book were unable to secure a copy of this film for review but would love to see it, given its status as an early Hessler film, and particularly because its producer, Jack Parsons, also oversaw such minor gems as *Witchcraft* (1964) and *Curse of the Fly* (1965). However, the horror content of *The Woman Who Wouldn't Die* seems to be marginal.

The cheesy sets seen in *Women of the Prehistoric Planet* (1966) are matched only by the film's cheesy action (here one of our intrepid astronauts rescues a prehistoric planet native).

Women of the Prehistoric Planet (1966; Realart) Shot in 11 days and released by the same outfit (Realart) who brought us *Bela Lugosi Meets a Brooklyn Gorilla* (1952), this shoddy no-budget sci-fi clunker has the crew of a "Centarian" spaceship, captained by Wendell Corey and John Agar, searching for survivors from another ship that crashed on a primitive planet. The closest this picture comes to any prehistoric menace is a six-foot photographically enlarged lizard and an ordinary boa constrictor.

The X from Outer Space (1967; Shockiku/AIP-TV; Japan) Original Language Title: *Uchu Daikaiju Girara*. *The X from Outer Space*, the lone *kaiju eiga* movie made by Japan's Shockiku studio, is a competently crafted but utterly generic product that mimics earlier, better films from rival Toho. The formulaic story line sends a crew of astronauts into space to investigate the mysterious disappearances of spacecraft near Mars. The Earth ship encounters a UFO (which looks like a flying apple pie) and brings back a sample of space-goo left on the side of their ship by the aliens. This goo contains a "spore," which hatches the unstoppable giant monster Guilala, and mayhem ensues. The film's visual effects are on par with Toho's work of the late 1960s, although the monster suit leaves something to be desired. With its bulbous legs, beaklike face and bobbing, crest-like antennae, the "fearsome" Guilala resembles an outsized version of Foghorn Leghorn. The cast, like almost everything else in this picture, proves adequate but undistinguished. Taku Izumi's jazzy score (at least in the original Japanese version) provides the one break from the usual Toho template, contrasting with the familiar monster marches of Akira Ifukube. However, even this difference was negated when AIP re-dubbed and re-scored the film for release to American TV. Feeding a *kaiju eiga* craving with *The X from Outer Space* is like filling up on steamed white rice — serviceable but bland.

The Yesterday Machine (1965; b&w) This no-budget, all-but-forgotten amateurish independent from the Lone Star state about a time machine run by a crazed Nazi scientist attempting to raise up Hitler and the Third Reich is one time-travel film that deserves to remain lost in the past. Poor Tim Holt (a long way from 1957's *The Monster That Challenged the World*— and even farther from the 1948 classic *The Treasure of the Sierra Madre*) is top billed and the only name actor in the cast, but he puts in only a brief cameo appearance. Holt, who'd left Hollywood for a behind-the-scenes career in Oklahoma radio, reportedly appeared in this grade-Z stinker only as a personal favor to his friend Russ Marker, the film's writer-producer-director. Marker must have been *some* friend.

Yokai Monsters 1: Spook Warfare see ***Spook Warfare***

Yokai Monsters 2: 100 Monsters see ***100 Monsters***

Yokai Monsters 3: Along with Ghosts see ***Along with Ghosts***

Yongary, Monster from the Deep (1967/70; Kuk Dong/Toei Co.; South Korea/Japan) Original Language Title: *Dai Koesu Yongkari*. The only 1960s monster movie from Korea (though it didn't land on American shores until 1970, courtesy of AIP), *Yongary* is a poor man's Godzilla — a *very* poor man. Atomic testing in China awakens a gigantic burrowing beast, dubbed "Yongari," who stomps across South Korea and smashes Seoul. With its Godzilla-like body, fiery breath, and Gamera-like head and tusks, Yongary consumes energy sources and fuel (draining oil storage containers like a dog drinking from his water bowl) until the scientist hero and his little boy helper devise a plan to neutralize the behemoth with chemical ammonia (Rachel Carson must be spinning in her grave). Sparse, unconvincing model work; poor process shots; and an ersatz monster that at one point inexplicably begins dancing consign *Yongary* to mere footnote status in the Giant Monsters Handbook.

Zontar, the Thing from Venus (1966; AIP-TV) Aaaaargh!!! Schlockmeister Larry Buchanan unleashed yet another cinematic monstrosity on unsuspecting TV viewers of the 1960s with this uncredited remake of Roger Corman's 1956 cult favorite *It Conquered the World* (no great cinematic treat itself, if truth be told). The cheap sets are of the Motel 6 variety, the acting amateurish, and what new dialogue was written is contemptible. Add to this Buchanan's standard unimaginative direction, inept camerawork, muddy lighting and a sad, dimestore monster, and the total comes to a big fat cinematic zero. John Agar (the only real professional in the cast) is given so little direction that his already flat acting style reaches new heights in banality. A few bits of dialogue provoke a snort or two of derisive laughter ("I hate your living guts for what you've done to my husband and my world!"), but it's not enough to justify 80 minutes of tedium. When one character exclaims, "Zontar, you're slimy, horrible," she could just as well be describing the movie itself.

Zotz! (1962, Columbia, b&w) In this zany comedy from producer-director William Castle, eccentric college professor Jonathan Jones (Tom Poston) comes into possession of a ancient coin that bestows supernatural powers— the ability to induce belly aches, to make objects (or people) move in slow motion, and to kill instantly by simply pointing a finger and uttering the magic word "Zotz!" Prof. Jones offers his services to the U.S. military but is turned away. Russian spies take note, however, and soon Jones becomes entangled in a web of international espionage. Poston's likeably goofy performance, complemented by amusing turns from veteran funnyfolk Jim Backus, Cecil Kellaway and Margaret Dumont, go a long way toward making this by far Castle's best comedy. But the main attraction is a series of slapstick set pieces— two calamitous dinner parties, a futile trip to the Pentagon and Jones' climactic battle with a pair of KGB thugs, all of which are laugh-out-loud funny. Castle, best remembered for his wildly imaginative promotional gimmicks for films like *House on Haunted Hill* and *The Tingler* (both 1959), for this picture gave away free replica "Zotz" coins as souvenirs. The filmmaker was so pleased with the results of this movie that he hired Poston to star in a remake of James Whale's black comedy *The Old Dark House*, co-produced with England's Hammer Films. In that case, however, the results proved far less satisfactory.

Bibliography

Books

Adamson, Joe. *A Directors Guild of America Oral History: Byron Haskin*. Metuchen, NJ: Scarecrow Press, 1984.

Aldrich, Robert, and Peter Bogdanovich. *Who the Devil Made It: Conversations with Legendary Film Directors*. New York: Alfred A. Knopf, 1997.

Anderson, Joseph L., and Donald Richie. *The Japanese Film: Art and Industry*. Expanded ed. Princeton, NJ: Princeton University Press, 1982.

Arkoff, Sam, with Richard Trubo. *Flying Through Hollywood by the Seat of My Pants*. New York: Birch Lane Press, 1992.

Biskind, Peter. *Easy Riders, Raging Bulls: How the Sex-Drugs-and-Rock-'n'-Roll Generation Saved Hollywood*. New York: Simon & Schuster, 1999.

Block, Alex Ben, ed. *George Lucas's Blockbusting: A Decade-by-Decade Survey of Timeless Movies Including Untold Secrets of Their Financial and Cultural Success*. New York: HarperCollins, 2010.

Bordwell, David. *On the History of Film Style*. Cambridge, MA: Harvard University Press, 1997.

Brosnon, John. *The Horror People*. New York: St. Martin's Press, 1976.

Buchanan, Larry. *It Came from Hunger! Tales of a Cinema Schlockmeister*. Jefferson, NC: McFarland, 1996.

Castle, William. *Step Right Up! I'm Gonna Scare the Pants Off America*. New York: Pharos Books, 1992.

Clark, Mark. *Smirk, Sneer and Scream: Great Acting in Horror Cinema*. Jefferson, NC: McFarland, 2004.

Corman, Roger, with Jim Jerome. *How I Made a Hundred Movies in Hollywood and Never Lost a Dime*. New York: Random House, 1990.

Court, Hazel. *Hazel Court: Horror Queen — An Autobiography*. Sheffield, UK: Tomahawk Press, 2008.

Cowie, Peter. *Revolution! The Explosion of World Cinema in the Sixties*. New York: Faber & Faber, 2004.

Curry, Christopher Wayne. *A Taste of Blood: The Films of Herschell Gordon Lewis*. London: Creation Books International, 1999.

Dyson, Jeremy. *Bright Darkness: The Lost Art of the Supernatural Horror Film*. London: Cassell, 1997.

Galbraith, Stuart, IV. *Japanese, Science Fiction, Fantasy and Horror Films: A Critical Analysis and Chronology of 103 Features Released in the United States, 1950–1992*. Jefferson, NC: McFarland, 1994.

_____. *Monsters Are Attacking Tokyo! The Incredible World of Japanese Fantasy Films*. Venice, CA: Feral House, 1998.

Glut, Donald F. *The Dracula Book*. Metuchen, NJ: Scarecrow Press, 1975.

Gottlieb, Sidney, ed. *Hitchcock on Hitchcock: Selected Interviews and Writings*. Berkeley: University of California Press, 1995.

Hamilton, John. *Beasts in the Cellar: The Exploitation Film Career of Tony Tenser*. Godalming, England: FAB Press, 2005.

Hardy, Phil, ed. *The Overlook Film Encyclopedia: Horror*. Woodstock, NY: Overlook Press, 1994.

_____. *The Overlook Film Encyclopedia: Science Fiction*. Woodstock, NY: Overlook Press, 1994.

Harryhausen, Ray. *Film Fantasy Scrapbook*. Cranbury, NJ: A.S. Barnes, 1972.

Hearn, Marcus, and Alan Barnes. *The Hammer Story*. London: Titan Books, 1997.

Hirano, Kyoko. *Mr. Smith Goes to Tokyo: Japanese Cinema Under the American Occupation*. Washington, DC: Smithsonian Institution, 1992.

Hoberman, J. *The Dream Life: Movies, Media and the Mythology of the Sixties*. New York: The New Press, 2005.

Jensen, Paul M. *The Men Who Made the Monsters*. New York: Twayne, 1996.

Johnson, Tom, and Mark Miller. *The Christopher Lee Filmography*. Jefferson, NC: McFarland, 2004.

Johnson, Tom, and Deborah Del Vecchio. *Hammer Films: An Exhaustive Filmography*. Jefferson, NC: McFarland, 1996.

Kinsey, Wayne. *Hammer Films: The Bray Studios Years*. London: Reynolds & Hearn, 2002.

Lee, Christopher. *Tall, Dark and Gruesome: An Autobiography*. London: Granada, 1977.

Leigh, Janet. *Psycho: Behind the Scenes of the Classic Thriller*. New York: Harmony Books, 1995.

Lentz, Harris M., III. *Feature Films, 1960–1969: A Filmography of English-Language and Major Foreign-*

Language United States Releases. Jefferson, NC: McFarland, 2001.

Lindsay, Cynthia. *Dear Boris: The Life of William Henry Pratt a.k.a. Boris Karloff*. New York: Alfred A. Knopf, 1975.

Lucas, Tim. *Mario Bava: All the Colors of the Dark*. Cincinnati: Video Watchdog, 2007.

Marcus, Greil. *Psychotic Reactions and Carburetor Dung*. New York: Anchor Books, 1987.

McCarty, John. *The Sleaze Merchants: Adventures in Exploitation Filmmaking*. New York: St. Martins Griffin, 1995.

McDonough, Jimmy. *The Ghastly One: The Sex-Gore Netherworld of Filmmaker Andy Milligan*. Chicago: A Cappella Books, 2001.

McGee, Mark Thomas. *Faster and Furiouser: The Revised and Fattened Fable of American International Pictures*. Jefferson, NC: McFarland, 1995.

Miller, David. *The Peter Cushing Companion*. Surrey, UK: Reynolds & Hearn, 2000.

Miller, Mark. *Christopher Lee and Peter Cushing and Horror Cinema: A Filmography of Their 22 Collaborations*. Jefferson, NC: McFarland, 1995.

Pink, Sidney. *So You Want to Make Movies: My Life as an Independent Film Producer*. Sarasota, FL: Pineapple Press, 1989.

Pirie, David. *A Heritage of Horror: The English Gothic Cinema, 1946–1972*. New York: Avon Books, 1973.

Pohle, Robert W., Jr., and Douglas C. Hart. *The Films of Christopher Lee*. Metuchen, NJ: Scarecrow Press, 1983.

Richie, Donald. *A Hundred Years of Japanese Film*. New York: Kondansha, 2001.

Rigby, Jonathan. *Christopher Lee: The Authorised Screen History*. London: Reynolds & Hearn, 2003.

_____. *English Gothic: A Century of Horror Cinema*. London: Reynolds & Hearn, 2000.

Rovin, Jeff. *The Fabulous Fantasy Films*. South Brunswick, NJ: A.S. Barnes, 1977.

Russo, John. *The Complete* Night of the Living Dead *Filmbook*. Pittsburgh: Imagine, 1985.

Senn, Bryan. *Drums of Terror: Voodoo in the Cinema*. Baltimore: Midnight Marquee Press, 1998.

_____. *A Year of Fear: A Day-by-Day Guide to 366 Horror Films*. Jefferson, NC: McFarland, 2007.

Spoto, Donald. *The Art of Alfred Hitchcock: Fifty Years of His Motion Pictures*. 2d ed. New York: Doubleday, 1992.

Svehla, Gary J., and Susan Svehla, eds. *Cinematic Hauntings*. Baltimore: Midnight Marquee Press, 1996.

_____. *Midnight Marquee Actors Series: Lon Chaney, Jr*. Baltimore: Midnight Marquee Press, 1997.

_____. *Midnight Marquee Actors Series: Vincent Price*. Baltimore: Midnight Marquee Press, 1998.

_____. *Son of Guilty Pleasures of the Horror Film*. Baltimore: Midnight Marquee Press, 1998.

Thompson, Kristin, and David Bordwell. *Film History: An Introduction*. 3d ed. New York: McGraw-Hill, 2010.

Truffaut, François. *Hitchcock/Truffaut*. Rev. ed. New York: Simon & Schuster, 1984.

Vatnsdal, Caelum. *They Came from Within: A History of Canadian Horror Cinema*. Winnipeg: Arbeiter Ring, 2004.

Weaver, Tom. *Attack of the Monster Movie Makers: Interviews with 20 Genre Giants*. Jefferson, NC: McFarland, 1994.

_____. *I Was a Monster Movie Maker: Conversations with 22 SF and Horror Filmmakers*. Jefferson, NC: McFarland, 2001.

_____. *Interviews with B Science Fiction and Horror Movie Makers: Writers, Producers, Directors, Actors Moguls and Makeup*. Jefferson, NC: McFarland, 1988.

_____. *John Carradine: The Films*. Jefferson, NC: McFarland, 1999.

_____. *Science Fiction and Fantasy Film Flashbacks: Conversations with 24 Actors, Writers, Producers and Directors from the Golden Age*. Jefferson, NC: McFarland, 1998.

_____. *Science Fiction Stars and Horror Heroes: Interviews with Actors, Directors, Producers and Writers of the 1940s through 1960s*. Jefferson, NC: McFarland, 1991.

Periodicals

Castle of Frankenstein
Cinefantastique
Cinema Retro
Cult Movies
Daily Cinema
Deep Red
The Economist
Fangoria
Film Bulletin
Film Comment
Filmfax
Hollywood Citizen News
The Hollywood Reporter
Little Shoppe of Horrors
London Sunday Times
Magick Theatre
Monsters from the Vault
Psychotronic Video
Scarlet Street
Scary Monsters
Shivers
Shock Cinema
Sunday Telegraph (London)
Time
Variety
Video Watchdog

Index